CALIFORNIA

Where to Stay and Eat
for All Budgets

Must-See Sights
and Local Secrets

Ratings You Can Trust

Fodor's Travel Publications   New York, Toronto, London, Sydney, Auckland
www.fodors.com

FODOR'S CALIFORNIA 2005

Editors: Sarah Gold, project editor; Paul Eisenberg, Andrea Lehman, Chris Swiac

Editorial Production: David Downing

Editorial Contributors: Rob Aikins, Collin Campbell, Cheryl Crabtree, Matthew Flynn, Lenore Greiner, Roger Grody, Lisa Hamilton, Veronica Hill, Satu Hummasti, Michael Knight, Trisa Knight, Lina Lecaro, Denise M. Leto, Kathy McDonald, Maribeth Mellin, Andy Moore, David Nelson, Reed Parsell, Anneliese Paull, Nina Rubin, Sharon Silva, Holly Smith, Sarah Sper, Lisa Trottier, John A. Vlahides, Christine Vovakes, Sharron S. Wood, Bobbi Zane

Maps: David Lindroth, *cartographer;* Bob Blake and Rebecca Baer, *map editors*

Design: Fabrizio La Rocca, *creative director;* Guido Caroti, *art director;* Moon Sun Kim, *cover designer;* Melanie Marin, *senior picture editor*

Production/Manufacturing: Colleen Ziemba

Cover Photo (Yosemite National Park): Darrell Gulin/Corbis

SPECIAL SALES

This book is available for special discounts for bulk purchases for sales promotions or premiums. Special editions, including personalized covers, excerpts of existing books, and corporate imprints, can be created in large quantities for special needs. For more information, write to Special Markets/Premium Sales, 1745 Broadway, MD 6-2, New York, New York 10019, or e-mail specialmarkets@randomhouse.com.

AN IMPORTANT TIP & AN INVITATION

Although all prices, opening times, and other details in this book are based on information supplied to us at press time, changes occur all the time in the travel world, and Fodor's cannot accept responsibility for facts that become outdated or for inadvertent errors or omissions. So **always confirm information when it matters,** especially if you're making a detour to visit a specific place. Your experiences—positive and negative—matter to us. If we have missed or misstated something, **please write to us.** We follow up on all suggestions. Contact the California editor at editors@fodors.com or c/o Fodor's at 1745 Broadway, New York, New York 10019.

PRINTED IN THE UNITED STATES OF AMERICA

10 9 8 7 6 5 4 3 2 1

DESTINATION CALIFORNIA

California is a source of endless wonder, natural and man-made. "Wow!" is a word you hear often here—at Half Dome in Yosemite, during the simulated earthquake at Universal Studios, or driving through Death Valley. If Texas is big and New York is stylish, California is dramatic. Here, the sun shines, and all is beautiful; then the earth shakes, and all is shattered. But the state always bounces back, and its restless people continue to build their nirvana. The drama of constant change and the diversity of its landscape make California too vast, too full of charming surprises to be a single state. You do not visit just one California. You choose a particular California. If you are looking for natural beauty, the Big Sur coastline isn't a bad place to start, but it's only one gem on a long, long list. If you favor worldly pleasures, San Francisco and the Wine Country beckon. Sybarites needing a fix are well advised to head to Palm Springs. Aficionados of the edgy love L.A. Wherever you go in the Golden State, there's plenty to fall in love with: very few visitors go home unsmitten. Have a great trip!

Tim Jarrell, Publisher

CONTENTS

CloseUps

ABOUT THIS BOOK

There's no doubt that the best source for travel advice is a like-minded friend who's just been where you're headed. But with or without that friend, you'll have a better trip with a Fodor's guide in hand. Once you've learned to find your way around its pages, you'll be in great shape to find your way around your destination.

SELECTION

Our goal is to cover the best properties, sights, and activities in their category, as well as the most interesting communities to visit. We make a point of including local food-lovers' hot spots as well as neighborhood options, and we avoid all that's touristy unless it's really worth your time. You can go on the assumption that everything you read about in this book is recommended wholeheartedly by our writers and editors. Flip to On the Road with Fodor's to learn more about who they are.

RATINGS

Orange stars ★ denote sights and properties that our editors and writers consider the very best in the area covered by the entire book. These, the best of the best, are listed in the Fodor's Choice section in the front of the book. Black stars ★ highlight the sights and properties we deem Highly Recommended, the don't-miss sights within any region. Fodor's Choice and Highly Recommended options in each region are usually listed on the title page of the chapter covering that region. Use the index to find complete descriptions. In cities, sights pinpointed with numbered map bullets ❶ in the margins tend to be more important than those without bullets.

SPECIAL SPOTS

Pleasures & Pastimes focuses on types of experiences that reveal the spirit of the destination. Watch for Off the Beaten Path sights. Some are out of the way, some are quirky, and all are worth your while. If the munchies hit while you're exploring, look for Need a Break? suggestions.

TIME IT RIGHT

Wondering when to go? Check On the Calendar up front and chapters' Timing sections for weather and crowd overviews and best days and times to visit.

SEE IT ALL

Use Fodor's exclusive Great Itineraries as a model for your trip. (For a good overview of the entire destination, follow those that begin the book, or mix regional itineraries from several chapters.) In cities, Good Walks guide you to important sights in each neighborhood.

BUDGET WELL

Hotel and restaurant price categories from ¢ to $$$$ are defined in the opening pages of each chapter—expect to find a balanced selection for every budget. For attractions, we always give standard adult admission fees; reductions are usually available for children, students, and senior citizens. Look in Discounts & Deals in Smart Travel Tips for information on destination-wide ticket schemes. Want to pay with plastic? AE, D, DC, MC, V following restaurant and hotel listings indicate whether American Express, Discover, Diner's Club, MasterCard, or Visa are accepted.

BASIC INFO	**Smart Travel Tips** lists travel essentials for the entire area covered by the book; city- and region-specific basics end each chapter. To find the best way to get around, see the transportation section; see individual modes of travel ("By Car," "By Train") for details.
ON THE MAPS	**Maps** throughout the book show you what's where and help you find your way around. Black and orange numbered bullets ❶ ❶ in the text correlate to bullets on maps.
FIND IT FAST	Within the book, chapters are arranged in a roughly south-to-north direction starting with San Diego. Chapters are divided into small regions, within which towns are covered in logical geographical order; attractive routes and interesting places between towns are flagged as **En Route.** Heads at the top of each page help you find what you need within a chapter.
DON'T FORGET	**Restaurants** are open for lunch and dinner daily unless we state otherwise; we mention dress only when there's a specific requirement and reservations only when they're essential or not accepted— it's always best to book ahead. Unless we state otherwise, **hotels** have private baths, phone, TVs, and air-conditioning and operate on the European Plan (a.k.a. EP, meaning without meals). We always list facilities but not whether you'll be charged extra to use them, so when pricing accommodations, find out what's included.
SYMBOLS	

Many Listings

★ Fodor's Choice
★ Highly recommended
⊠ Physical address
✛ Directions
⌖ Mailing address
☎ Telephone
🖷 Fax
⊕ On the Web
✉ E-mail
💶 Admission fee
🕓 Open/closed times
▶ Start of walk/itinerary
Ⓜ Metro stations
▭ Credit cards

Outdoors

⅃ Golf
⚠ Camping

Hotels & Restaurants

🏨 Hotel
↩ Number of rooms
♨ Facilities
†⊙† Meal plans
✗ Restaurant
✍ Reservations
👗 Dress code
⊾ Smoking
🍺 BYOB
✗🏨 Hotel with restaurant that warrants a visit

Other

🖑 Family-friendly
🛈 Contact information
⇨ See also
⊠ Branch address
☞ Take note

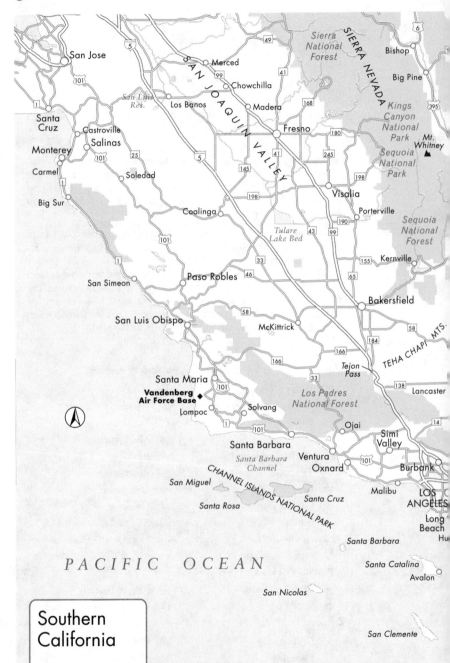

Southern California

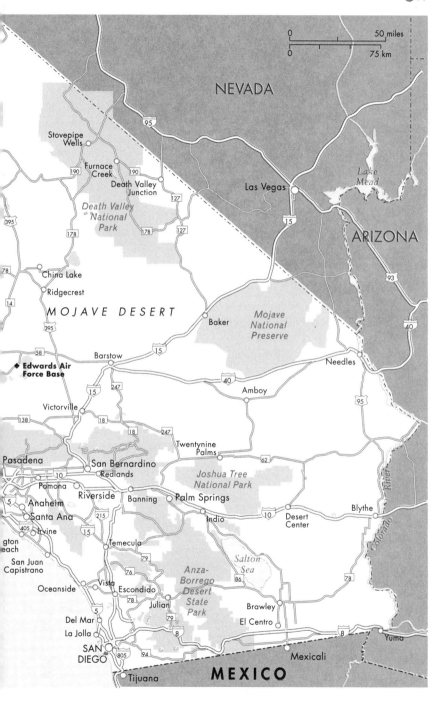

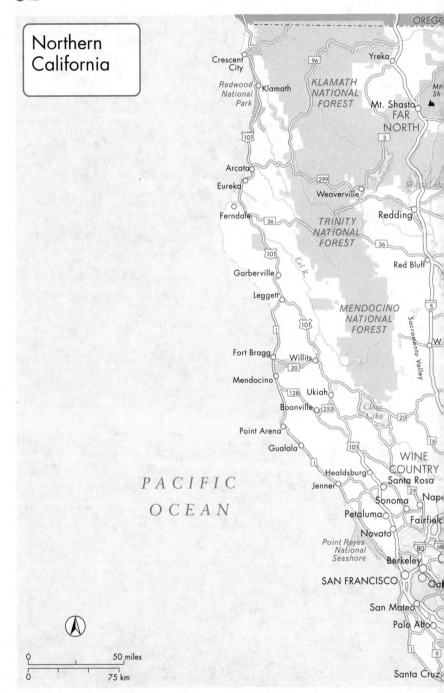

Northern California

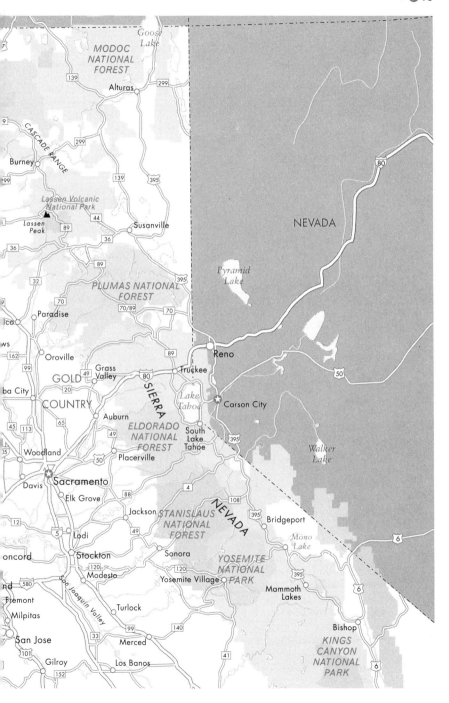

ON THE ROAD WITH FODOR'S

Our success in showing you every corner of the Golden State is a credit to our extraordinary writers. Although there's no substitute for travel advice from a good friend who knows your style, our contributors are the next best thing—the kind of people you would poll for travel advice if you knew them.

Native Californian **Cheryl Crabtree**, who updated the Central Coast chapter, has worked as a freelance writer since 1987. She has contributed to *Resorts & Great Hotels* and *Touring and Tasting: Great American Wineries.*

When he's not traveling, screenwriter, television producer, and native Angeleno **Matthew Flynn** scours L.A. for the ultimate chocolate cake and iced tea (they haven't been found). His favorite city view is from the roof of The Grove parking structure.

For the past decade, dining writer **Roger Grody,** who updated the Los Angeles dining section, has been searching out the best things to eat in Southern California. He's recorded his discoveries in such publications as *Westways, Where–Los Angeles, Sunset,* the *Gault-Millau* guides, and the *Los Angeles Times* Web site.

When not writing about California travel and outdoors, North Coast and Peninsula/South Bay updater **Lisa M. Hamilton** can be found at the beach. Accounts of her food-related journeys have appeared in *National Geographic Traveler, Gastronomica,* and *Z Magazine.*

Orange County native **Veronica Hill,** who updated the Mojave Desert and Inland Empire chapters, discovered California at a young age during "Sunday drives" with her family. Now features editor at the *Daily Press* in Victorville, her articles have also appeared in *US, Rolling Stone, Food & Wine,* and *Seventeen.*

Natives of California, **Michael and Trisa Knight** enjoy traveling with their four children. They are the authors of *Fodor's Disneyland* and *Southern California with Kids.*

Music and nightlife expert **Lina Lecaro** uncovers L.A.'s best after-dark destinations, as well as the city's plethora of multifaceted arts offerings and shopping meccas. Her work is seen regularly in the *LA Weekly, Los Angeles Times,* and on *Rollingstone.com* and *LA.com.*

When not covering the film business for the film trades, **Kathy A. McDonald** enjoys L.A.'s great weather, movies, art and design, and ever-changing restaurant scene. She is also a longtime volunteer docent at Frank Lloyd Wright's Hollyhock House in Barnsdall Art Park.

Reed Parsell, who updated the Gold Country chapter, is a features copy editor and travel writer for the *Sacramento Bee.*

Lisa Trottier, who updated the North Coast chapter, is Managing Editor and Travel Editor of *San Francisco* magazine. When not working on articles about the Wine Country and the coast, she hops into her Vanagon camper and heads for the desert.

Southern Sierra, Lake Tahoe, and Smart Travel Tips updater **John A. Vlahides** lives in San Francisco, spending his free time skiing the Sierra and touring California by motorcycle. A columnist, essayist, and former *Clefs d'Or* concierge, he also sings tenor with the San Francisco Symphony Chorus.

A freelance correspondent for the *Sacramento Bee,* Far North updater **Christine Vovakes** regularly covers area news and writes newspaper features about the region. She considers her home turf of 24 years the undiscovered gem of California.

Bobbi Zane, who updated the San Diego and Southern Desert chapters, has been living in and visiting the region since her childhood. Her articles on Palm Springs have appeared in the *Orange County Register* and *Westways* magazine. She recently contributed to *Fodor's San Diego* and *Escape to Nature Without Roughing It.*

Though most people mentally divide California into a southern and a northern region, the state might just as easily be conceived of as three long strips of land: coastal, central, and eastern. The state is divided south to north by the mighty Sierra Nevada, and the Coast ranges separate the shore towns and cities from the interior of the state. Few roads cross the mountains, and those that do can be narrow and twisting, so travel across the state often involves long, circuitous drives. The fastest north-south route through the state is I–5.

California's biggest cities—San Diego, Los Angeles, and San Francisco—are on the coast. San Diego is 136 mi south of Los Angeles on I–5, and San Francisco is 380 mi north of Los Angeles. I–5 is the quickest route between Los Angeles and the San Francisco Bay Area, but many tourists travel the gorgeous but winding coastal route—a combination of U.S. 101 and Highway 1 (the Pacific Coast Highway) instead. For planning purposes, travel time between Los Angeles and San Francisco is 6 hours via I–5, 9 hours via U.S. 101, and 12 hours via Highway 1.

① San Diego

California's beautiful, mellow southernmost city enjoys near-perfect weather. The sun shines perpetually on lush Balboa Park, on Shamu's SeaWorld home, on Pacific-pounded strands like Mission Beach and pretty La Jolla's Black's Beach. Residents of the San Diego Zoo, one of the world's greats, are at home in the warm climate. But it's not all fun in the sun here—there's history, too. The first of California's 21 Spanish missions was established in San Diego in 1769, and the city's links to its Spanish past remain strong.

② Orange County

Orange County is a prime destination for fun in the sun. The biggest draw for most nonresidents is Disneyland. Another vintage theme park nearby, Knott's Berry Farm, also offers thrill rides and attractions. Meanwhile, the Pacific exerts an irresistible pull. Between Laguna Beach and Huntington Beach are dozens of spots where you can work on your tan or learn to surf among masters.

③ Los Angeles

It's hard to be indifferent to Los Angeles. Love it or hate it, it is a city unlike any other. Sunset Boulevard takes you all the way from Hollywood to the sea, and passes through the city's multiple layers, including wealthy Bel-Air and Beverly Hills. At the ocean, you can experience beach culture as a way of life—especially at Venice Boardwalk, where Angelenos surf, skate, body-build, and stage some of the wackiest street theater in the galaxy. Also pure L.A. are Universal Studios Hollywood, where you can live the movies, and Grauman's Chinese Theatre, where celebrities press their hands and other body parts into cement for posterity. Amid the freeways and smog, the city's numerous beauty spots—the Getty Center, Griffith Park—sometimes come as a surprise.

4 The Inland Empire

Long before the suburbs and freeways moved in, the area east of Los Angeles was known for its rugged mountains and desert—and its natural wonders are still a big draw. Skiers, hikers, anglers, and bikers all head to the hills of this Inland Empire from surrounding cities. In the San Bernardino Mountains are Arrowhead and Big Bear lakes and several ski resorts; the San Jacinto Mountains have the alpine village of Idyllwild, long a Hollywood hideaway. A newcomer among the area's attractions, the Temecula Valley produces wines that are gaining respect with each passing year.

5 Palm Springs & the Southern Desert

Striking scenery and a therapeutically warm, arid climate have been luring people to the southern desert for decades. Palm Springs and its neighbors—Palm Desert, Rancho Mirage, and Indian Wells—are bastions of wealth and celebrity, where Jaguars and Bentleys are as common as driveways. Golf courses are everywhere; the area has close to 100, many of them scenic stunners. The many luxury resorts let you abandon yourself to total pampering; nature-lovers can connect with the desert's wild beauty at Joshua Tree National Park, Anza-Borrego Desert State Park, and the Salton Sea.

6 The Mojave Desert & Death Valley

A trip through the great empty spaces and striking landscapes of the Mojave Desert and Death Valley is a journey through the past. You can see the remnants of the area's mining culture at the Mojave Desert's Calico Ghost Town, and at the Harmony Borax Works in Death Valley. But the natural beauty of Trona Pinnacles and Red Rock Canyon State Park in the Mojave Desert, the sand dunes near Stovepipe Wells Village, and the brilliantly colored Artists Palette in Death Valley, are historical relics, too. All of them are striking evidence of the way wind and water shape the land.

7 The Southern Sierra

The highlight for many California travelers is a visit to one of the national parks in the southern portion of the Sierra Nevada. At Sequoia, Kings Canyon, and Yosemite national parks, nature has outdone itself, carving magnificent glacial valleys out of a titan-size landscape. In summer and early fall (or whenever snows aren't blocking the Tioga Pass), you can drive east from Yosemite National Park to see Mono Lake's tufa towers, resembling a giant's fingers. The Mammoth Lakes area, with California's best skiing in winter and many outdoor sports in summer, lies south of Mono Lake.

8 The Central Valley

The Central Valley, one of the world's most fertile agricultural zones, is California's heartland. This sunbaked region—whose anchors are Bakersfield in the south and Lodi 260 mi to the north—contains many natural waterways, which nurture vineyards, dairy farms, orchards, fields, and pastures. Markets and festivals celebrating their bounty are numerous. Munch on fresh strawberries and other fruit sold up and down the valley at roadside stands, and when you're fortified, take in attractions ranging from Victorian houses to Fresno's Forestiere Underground Gardens.

9 The Central Coast

The spectacular Central Coast stretches from northern Ventura County to Big Sur, with Highway 1 threading through a staggeringly scenic landscape between friendly small towns. Santa Barbara—which manages to feel both sophisticated and tranquil—is where the velvety Coastal Range starts to rise and the land drops precipitously into the sweeping Pacific. At San Simeon, newspaper baron William Randolph Hearst's Hearst Castle sprawls above the sea. The curving road demands an unhurried pace, but even if it didn't, you'd find yourself stopping often to take in the scenery, especially as you make your way through wild Big Sur.

10 Monterey Bay

Monterey Bay forms a crescent that begins near Carmel in the south and ends near Santa Cruz in the north. For many, the coast here is California at its best, and the Monterey Bay National Marine Sanctuary means that the waters here teem with sealife. The things that make the state so wonderful to visit converge here—from history, on view at the Carmel Mission, to natural splendor, unforgettable on 17-Mile Drive, to Pebble Beach, a golfing mecca that draws devotees from all over the world. The coastal towns will charm you with pretty streets, great food, and occasional quirkiness.

11 The Peninsula & South Bay

San Francisco lies at the tip of an approximately 35-mi-long peninsula bounded by San Francisco Bay on the east and the Pacific Ocean on the west. Highway 1 runs up the rugged coast past Año Nuevo State Reserve and Half Moon Bay, while I–280 or U.S. 101 runs down the interior Peninsula through congested Silicon Valley to San Jose and the South Bay. In the prosperous interior, Peninsula and South Bay cultural institutions glitter—from Stanford University's Iris and B. Gerald Cantor Center for Visual Arts to San Jose's Tech Museum of Innovation—and fine dining is abundant in cities like Palo Alto.

12 San Francisco

Arguably the most beautiful city in the United States, San Francisco is where you can still take cable-car rides past stunning Victorians, and stroll along thoroughfares like Lombard Street—the "crookedest street" in the country. But sightseeing is only part of the San Francisco experience; what really makes it special is its diversity. This city's wide arms embrace all kinds of ethnicities and neighborhoods, from Italian-influenced North Beach to bustling Chinatown; prosperous Pacific Heights to the Hispanic mural-painted Mission district; the gay-populated Castro to the bohemian Haight. Everyone is welcome here.

(13) The Wine Country

America's answer to Tuscany, the Wine Country looks and feels like its Italian counterpart, complete with gentle green hills and a soft coastal climate. The wine-centered life in Napa and Sonoma counties makes them a vibrant destination for gourmands and oenophiles. If you're lucky enough to visit in autumn, you can see the grape harvest—but no matter when you arrive, you'll be greeted by acres of vineyards and restaurants serving decadent cuisine. Between wine tastings remember to do some sightseeing—the towns and countryside are gorgeous.

(14) The North Coast

Migrating whales swim past the dramatic bluffs of this 400 mi of shoreline, which stretches between San Francisco and the Oregon state line. North coast pleasures are low-key, but they are hardly unrefined. Elegant country inns, and cozy Victorian B&Bs, await in Mendocino and other towns whose architecture reflects the New England origins of their founders. And then there is the beauty of the land. The North Coast's majestic redwoods inspire awe, even reverence. If no gold rush had built San Francisco, if Los Angeles were still a bunch of orange groves in search of a freeway, the glory of the North Coast would be reason enough to visit California.

(15) The Gold Country

This is where modern-day California began, along the American River on a winter's day in 1848, when James Marshall first glimpsed something shiny in the bottom of a ditch. Besides making California, gold made Sacramento, paying for the construction of the state capitol. Many museums and historic sites commemorate the gold rush—reenactors make it come alive at Coloma's Marshall Gold Discovery State Historic Park, and mining towns have been dusted off and gussied up. Sacramento's California State Railroad Museum is a must-see for train buffs.

(16) Lake Tahoe

Deep, clear, intensely blue-green, the largest alpine lake in North America straddles the California–Nevada border. Considering the area's popularity, it's no small feat that strict environmental controls have kept it and the surrounding forests pristine. If you're staying on the California side, you can golf, hike, or ski at Squaw Valley USA. Pop in to see Vikingsholm, an authentic replica of a 1,200-year-old Viking castle, built in 1929 on the shore of jewel-like Emerald Bay. On the Nevada side gambling is king and casinos abound, but once you leave the bright lights of the gaming tables you're surrounded by the beauty of the mountains and nearby desert.

(17) The Far North

California's far northeast corner is a region of soaring mountain peaks, wild rivers brimming with fish, and almost infinite recreational possibilities. Mt. Shasta, a dormant volcano that tops 14,000 feet, is the subject of eerie folklore, but its size and beauty are fantastic enough. Tramping up it in summer and schussing down it in winter are two of the main pastimes here. Anglers and boaters flock to Lake Shasta for its many watery diversions, including houseboating. Lassen Volcanic National Park, with its hot springs, steam vents, and boiling mud pots, is a geological marvel.

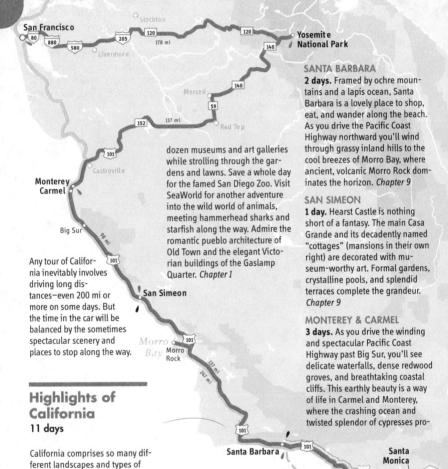

SANTA BARBARA

2 days. Framed by ochre mountains and a lapis ocean, Santa Barbara is a lovely place to shop, eat, and wander along the beach. As you drive the Pacific Coast Highway northward you'll wind through grassy inland hills to the cool breezes of Morro Bay, where ancient, volcanic Morro Rock dominates the horizon. *Chapter 9*

SAN SIMEON

1 day. Hearst Castle is nothing short of a fantasy. The main Casa Grande and its decadently named "cottages" (mansions in their own right) are decorated with museum-worthy art. Formal gardens, crystalline pools, and splendid terraces complete the grandeur. *Chapter 9*

MONTEREY & CARMEL

3 days. As you drive the winding and spectacular Pacific Coast Highway past Big Sur, you'll see delicate waterfalls, dense redwood groves, and breathtaking coastal cliffs. This earthly beauty is a way of life in Carmel and Monterey, where the crashing ocean and twisted splendor of cypresses pro-

dozen museums and art galleries while strolling through the gardens and lawns. Save a whole day for the famed San Diego Zoo. Visit SeaWorld for another adventure into the wild world of animals, meeting hammerhead sharks and starfish along the way. Admire the romantic pueblo architecture of Old Town and the elegant Victorian buildings of the Gaslamp Quarter. *Chapter 1*

Any tour of California inevitably involves driving long distances—even 200 mi or more on some days. But the time in the car will be balanced by the sometimes spectacular scenery and places to stop along the way.

Highlights of California
11 days

California comprises so many different landscapes and types of people that to visit only one area would be like seeing only a single color in a rainbow. Life here has as much to do with the silence of Yosemite as with the glitz of Hollywood. But if you tour a few of California's treasures, you soon understand why it's called the Golden State.

SAN DIEGO

2 days. Start in Balboa Park, where you can visit more than a

ORANGE COUNTY

1 day. There is no place in the world quite like Disneyland. Step into Walt's kingdom for a day and experience pure fun. As you continue to drive to Santa Barbara, you'll pass through Los Angeles. *Chapter 2*

vide a backdrop for shops and restaurants. The 17-Mile Drive gives you a glimpse of the late 20th-century mansions and golf courses of Pebble Beach. Rest up for the long drive from the coast to Yosemite. *Chapter 10*

YOSEMITE

2 days. The incomparable majesty of marvels like Half Dome and the smell of sweet meadow air make Yosemite a world unto itself. Yosemite Valley is home to the park's most photogenic wonders: gushing Yosemite Falls, proud and mighty El Capitan, and windblown and wispy Bridalveil Falls. The Mariposa Grove of Big Trees is both inspiring and humbling in its grandeur. From here, drive to San Francisco to end your trip. *Chapter 7*

Beaches & Deserts
6 to 10 days

Southern California's beaches and deserts are awash in color and life. Black hills are striped with rainbows of eroded earth; white sand is speckled with neon bikinis; and every spring, muted slopes of sage and shale give birth to a flurry of fuchsia and yellow flowers. Amid the kaleidoscope swirls a vibrant blend of surfers and screenwriters, jackrabbits and Joshua trees, and a nightly spectacle of city lights and starry skies. The horizon provides the most spectacular vision of all: Technicolor sunsets not even a postcard can capture. You may want to begin this tour in San Diego and end in Los Angeles.

PALM SPRINGS

2 or 3 days. Once a hideaway for Tinseltown stars, this oasis of green golf courses and extravagant homes stands in the midst of a stark and rugged landscape. The view from the Tramway's 8,516-foot peak illuminates the startling contrast between Palm Springs and the slopes of the San Jacinto Mountains. Named after the biblical character for their prayerlike stances, the trees of Joshua Tree National Park are strikingly silhouetted against the open skies of this vast area. *Chapter 5*

BARSTOW

2 or 3 days. The Mojave Desert can look bleak from the road, but its subtle charms are entrancing. Go for a hike along one of the many trails to experience the musky smell of sage and mesquite and the tenacity of wildflowers rooted in crumbling soil. Death Valley National Park is the final frontier in unconventional beauty, best enjoyed in the soft light of dawn or late afternoon. Consider spending a night at one of the campgrounds or hotels within the park; otherwise it's a fairly long drive back to Barstow. *Chapter 6*

SANTA MONICA

1 or 2 days. The drive to Santa Monica Bay propels you out of the desert toward the bright blue water, where you can swim and sunbathe on the white sands of Malibu. The boardwalk along Venice Beach is known for its daily parade of chain-saw jugglers and

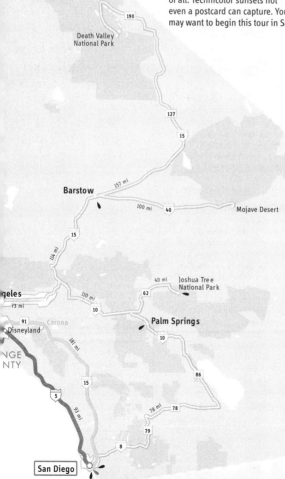

190

Death Valley
National Park

127

15

Barstow

157 mi

100 mi   40   Mojave Desert

15

114 mi

40 mi   Joshua Tree
National Park
110 mi   62

geles
73 mi

91   Corona
Disneyland

10

NGE
NTY

181 mi

10

Palm Springs

15

86

5

78 mi   78

93 mi

79

8

San Diego

MAP KEY
Highlights of California
Beaches & Deserts
The Great Outdoors
California with Kids

tattooed sun worshipers. Well-oiled bodybuilders pump iron at Venice's Muscle Beach, an open-air gym with Plexiglas walls that provide passersby a full view. *Chapter 3*

SANTA BARBARA

1 or 2 days. Santa Barbara County is bounded on one side by a ribbon of hilly coast, and right in downtown Santa Barbara is the popular and accessible East Beach. The region's most captivating shorelines are within Channel Islands National Park and Marine Sanctuary, an expansive and undeveloped offshore home to creatures including blue whales and endangered brown pelicans. For a day trip, take a cruise to Anacapa Island to admire lava tubes and sea caves and to watch seals basking at the base of 100-foot cliffs. *Chapter 9*

The Great Outdoors
9 to 12 days

If you've come to California looking for sun, sand, and surf, Northern California may come as a surprise. Towns here are remote and woodsy, colors are deep and intense rather than sun-washed. Residents of the northern coast and mountains have never disputed the image of California as a string of sunny beaches; they're happy to keep their emerald trees and sapphire seas a secret. San Francisco is the best city in which to begin and end this tour.

POINT REYES STATION

2 days. Throughout Marin County, the California coast shows one of its most dramatic incarnations. Cliffs drop into secret coves. Waves spill over the horizon. Pelicans migrate from one volcanic sea stack to another. Stinson Beach is a placid stretch of white sand amid the geological chaos. Inland, the

towering redwoods at Muir Woods National Monument cast a cool shade. Point Reyes National Seashore is a dazzling jewel in the crown that is the Pacific Coast; don't miss the black-, white-, and red-sand beaches and sentinel lighthouse. *Chapter 14*

MENDOCINO

1 or 2 days. North into Mendocino County, the craggy coast becomes increasingly striking. Victorian buildings filled with shops, restaurants, and bed-and-breakfasts make the town of Mendocino feel uniquely refined. Whether it's sunny and warm or foggy and breezy, be sure to take advantage of the local state parks' rugged and uncrowded shorelines. *Chapter 14*

NAPA

2 days. The hills of Napa and Sonoma counties offer wineries as varied and colorful as the vintages they produce. French castles and farmhouses mingle with long rows of grapevines. Vineyards offer distinctive wines in beautiful and sometimes bustling settings. Fine dining is a way of life. *Chapter 13*

SOUTH LAKE TAHOE

2 or 3 days. Although deep snow is the Lake Tahoe area's most famous commodity, outdoor adventure abounds year-round. From Tahoe City you can bicycle, rock climb, and water-ski, or spend the day golfing. On the lake's southern shore, hike the steep trail down to Vikingsholm for a tour of this elaborately decorated neo-Nordic mansion, then picnic beside gorgeous Emerald Bay. In South Lake Tahoe, be sure to ride the Heavenly Gondola: the panoramic view of the area is, well, heavenly. *Chapter 16*

YOSEMITE

2 or 3 days. Yosemite Valley offers the classic views immortalized by

photographer Ansel Adams: Half Dome's glossy face, the stately grandeur of El Capitan, and Bridalveil and Yosemite Falls, whose only rivals for perfection are each other. *Chapter 7*

MAP KEY
Highlights of California
Beaches & Deserts
The Great Outdoors
California with Kids

at Marshall Gold Discovery State Historic Park. Along historic Highway 49, towns such as Murphys and Nevada City maintain the charm of the area's colorful past. Save an afternoon to wander the streets of Old Sacramento, where

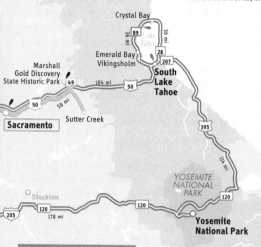

you can ride a tugboat taxi and marvel at old locomotives in the California State Railroad Museum. *Chapter 15*

California with Kids
12 to 15 days

As a real-world land of make-believe, California seems to have been created just for children. Fantasy comes to life in castles, museums, and exotic animals. New fairy tales are created daily in the studios and streets of Hollywood. Check local newspapers for seasonal children's events.

SACRAMENTO

2 days. You won't strike it rich in the Gold Country, but you can catch the spirit of the Mother Lode

SAN FRANCISCO

2 or 3 days. Seeing the city from a cable car is sure to thrill, and you can take in another panorama from Coit Tower. But high above the bay, the Golden Gate Bridge wins for best photo opportunity. Along the water, you can sample the chocolates that gave Ghirardelli Square its name, bark back at sea lions lounging on Pier 39, and ride a ferry to Alcatraz. Golden Gate Park's green pastures, woods, and water can provide a whole day of entertainment. If the weather doesn't cooperate, head inside to the Exploratorium or California Academy of Sciences for awesome hands-on exhibits. *Chapter 12*

SAN SIMEON

2 or 3 days. Allow plenty of time to enjoy the Pacific Coast Highway's curves through temperate rain forests and salty seascapes as you drive south from San Francisco. While picnicking atop the craggy cliffs of Big Sur, keep your eyes peeled for otters, seals, and sea lions surfing the waves below. Spend an afternoon daydreaming at Hearst Castle, a hilltop estate of unrivaled luxury. The drive to Los Angeles is long–about six hours– so allow ample time or plan a stopover en route. *Chapter 9*

LOS ANGELES

2 or 3 days. No visit is complete without a trip to Universal Studios for a behind-the-scenes look at the glamorous world of the movies. Night or day, stargaze for famous names along the Hollywood Walk of Fame. Haven't had your fill of celebrities yet? Seek out the rich and famous in Beverly Hills. Then head to the Page Museum at La Brea Tar Pits to visit LA's original stars–the woolly mammoths. *Chapter 3*

ORANGE COUNTY

2 days. Disneyland fulfills almost every kid's dreams. Knott's Berry Farm also offers diversion for the imagination, complete with international cuisine and lively shows re-creating California history. *Chapter 2*

SAN DIEGO

2 days. Your first stop here should be the San Diego Zoo. Wander the landscaped grounds and you're sure to find something you've never seen before, perhaps a two-headed corn snake or an East African bongo. Spend the next day at SeaWorld to see Shamu the killer whale and the world's largest collection of sharks. *Chapter 1*

WHEN TO GO

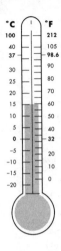

The climate varies amazingly in California, sometimes within an hour's drive. A foggy, cool August day in San Francisco makes you grateful for a sweater, but head north 50 mi to the Napa Valley, and you'll probably need no more than short sleeves. Similarly, nighttime temperatures may differ greatly from daytime temperatures.

Because the weather is so varied throughout the state, it's hard to generalize much about it. Rain comes in the winter, with snow at higher elevations. Summers are dry everywhere, except for the rare summer thunderstorm in the mountains. As a rule, compared to the coastal areas, which are cool year-round, inland regions are warmer in summer and cooler in winter. As you climb into the mountains, the climate changes more distinctly with the seasons: winter brings snow, autumn is crisp, spring is variable, and summer is clear and warm, with only an occasional thundershower.

Forecasts **National Weather Service** ⊕ www.wrh.noaa.gov. **Weather Channel** ⊕ www.weather.com.

LOS ANGELES

Jan.	64F	18C	May	72F	22C	Sept.	81F	27C
	44	7		53	12		60	16
Feb.	64F	18C	June	76F	24C	Oct.	76F	24C
	46	8		57	14		55	13
Mar.	66F	19C	July	81F	27C	Nov.	71F	22C
	48	9		60	16		48	9
Apr.	70F	21C	Aug.	82F	28C	Dec.	66F	19C
	51	11		62	17		46	8

SAN DIEGO

Jan.	62F	17C	May	66F	19C	Sept.	73F	23C
	46	8		55	13		62	17
Feb.	62F	17C	June	69F	21C	Oct.	71F	22C
	48	9		59	15		57	14
Mar.	64F	18C	July	73F	23C	Nov.	69F	21C
	50	10		62	17		51	11
Apr.	66F	19C	Aug.	73F	23C	Dec.	64F	18C
	53	12		64	18		48	9

SAN FRANCISCO

Jan.	55F	13C	May	66F	19C	Sept.	73F	23C
	41	5		48	9		51	11
Feb.	59F	15C	June	69F	21C	Oct.	69F	21C
	42	6		51	11		50	10
Mar.	60F	16C	July	69F	21C	Nov.	64F	18C
	44	7		51	11		44	7
Apr.	62F	17C	Aug.	69F	21C	Dec.	57F	14C
	46	8		53	12		42	6

Hundreds of festivals and events are held annually in California. Here are a few of the favorites. If you plan to visit during a big festival, book your accommodations and event tickets well in advance.

WINTER

December

For the Newport Harbor Christmas Boat Parade, in Newport Beach, more than 200 festooned boats glide through the harbor nightly the week before Christmas (call for exact dates).

Over the first two weekends in December the Miners' Christmas Celebration in Columbia is an extravaganza of costumed carolers and children's piñatas. Related events include a Victorian Christmas feast at the City Hotel, lamplight tours, an equestrian parade, and Las Posados Nativity Procession.

The internationally acclaimed El Teatro Campesino annually stages one of two nativity plays, *La Virgen del Tepeyac* or *La Pastorela,* in the Mission San Juan Bautista.

January

Palm Springs's annual Palm Springs International Film Festival showcases the best of international cinema, with more than 100 screenings, lectures, and workshops.

In Pasadena the annual Tournament of Roses Parade takes place on New Year's Day, with lavish flower-decked floats, marching bands, and equestrian teams, followed by the Rose Bowl game.

February

The legendary AT&T Pebble Beach National Pro-Am golf tournament begins in late January and ends in early February.

San Francisco's Chinatown is the scene of parades and noisy fireworks, all part of a several-day Chinese New Year celebration. Los Angeles also has a Chinese New Year Parade.

From early February through March, the Napa Valley Mustard Festival highlights the art, culture, cooking, and—of course—the wines of Napa.

Indio's Riverside County Fair and National Date Festival is an exotic event with an *Arabian Nights* theme; camel and ostrich races, date exhibits, and tastings are among the draws.

SPRING

March

The finest female golfers in the world compete for the richest purse on the LPGA circuit at the Nabisco Championship, in Rancho Mirage.

The North Tahoe Snow Festival celebrates the region's winter sports, with everything from slope-side parties to kids' events at venues all around North Tahoe.

	The **Mendocino/Fort Bragg Whale Festival** includes whale-watching excursions, marine art exhibits, wine and beer tastings, crafts displays, and a chowder contest.
April	The **Cherry Blossom Festival**, an elaborate presentation of Japanese culture and customs, winds up with a colorful parade through San Francisco's Japantown.
	The **Toyota Grand Prix**, in Long Beach, the largest street race in North America, draws top competitors from all over the world.
May	Oxnard celebrates its big cash crop at the **California Strawberry Festival**, with exhibitors preparing the fruit in every imaginable form—shortcake, jam, tarts, and pizza.
	Inspired by Mark Twain's story "The Notorious Jumping Frog of Calaveras County," the **Jumping Frog Jubilee**, in Angels Camp, is for frogs and trainers who take their competition seriously.
	Sacramento hosts the four-day **Sacramento Jazz Jubilee**; the late-May event is the world's largest Dixieland festival, with 125 bands from around the world.
	Thousands sign up to run the **San Francisco Bay to Breakers Race**, a 7½-mi route from the Bay side to the ocean side that's a hallowed San Francisco tradition.
	The **Santa Ysabel Art Festival** is a mountain art celebration with works by 50 San Diego area painters, sculptors, and fiber artists, plus a poetry fair and jazz and classical music.
SUMMER	
June	The **Christopher Street West Gay & Lesbian Pride Festival** celebrates the diversity of the gay and lesbian community in West Hollywood with a parade, music, dancing, food, and merchandise.
	The last week in June, the **San Francisco Lesbian, Gay, Bisexual, and Transgender Pride Celebration** culminates on Sunday, with a giant parade and festival, one of the largest of its kind in the world.
	The **Napa Valley Wine Auction**, in St. Helena, is accompanied by open houses and a wine tasting.
	During the latter part of June, Ojai hosts the **Ojai Music Festival**, a noted outdoor classical music celebration.
	During the last weekend of June or the first weekend of July Pasadena City Hall Plaza hosts the **Absolut Chalk Festival**, the world's largest chalk painting festival. Artists use the pavement as their canvas to create masterpieces that wash away once festivities have come to a close.
July	During the three weeks of the **Carmel Bach Festival**, the works of Johann Sebastian Bach and 18th-century contemporaries are performed; events include concerts, recitals, and seminars.

During the last full weekend in July, Gilroy, self-styled "garlic capital of the world," celebrates its smelly but delicious product with the Gilroy Garlic Festival, featuring such unusual concoctions as garlic ice cream.

Late July through early August the California Mid-State Fair takes place in Paso Robles. Nearly a quarter-million people show up to see wine competitions, musical performances, carnival fun, and agricultural exhibits.

| August | The late-August Cabrillo Festival of Contemporary Music, in Santa Cruz, is one of the longest-running contemporary orchestral festivals. |

The California State Fair showcases the state's agricultural side, with a rodeo, horse racing, a carnival, and big-name entertainment. It runs 18 days from August to early September in Sacramento.

Santa Barbara's Old Spanish Days Fiesta is held the first Wednesday through Sunday in August, sometimes beginning in the last days of July. There are two Mexican marketplaces, a carnival, a rodeo, and the nation's largest all-equestrian parade.

FALL

| September | On Catalina Island the Pottery & Tile Extravaganza showcases unique tile and pottery from private collections. There are displays, walking tours, demonstrations, and lectures. |

The San Francisco Blues Festival is held at Fort Mason in late September.

The Los Angeles County Fair, in Pomona, is the largest county fair in the world. It hosts entertainment, exhibits, livestock, horse racing, food, and more.

| October | The Grand National Rodeo, Horse, and Stock Show, at San Francisco's Cow Palace, is a 10-day world-class competition straddling the end of October and the beginning of November. |

Near San Luis Obispo, speakers and poets gather for readings on the beach, seminars, a banquet, a book signing, and a clam chowder contest at the Pismo Beach Clam Festival, on the Central Coast.

The Tor House Fall Festival honors the late poet Robinson Jeffers, an area resident for many years.

| November | The Death Valley '49er Encampment, at Furnace Creek, commemorates the historic crossing of Death Valley in 1849, with a fiddlers' contest, trail rides, and an art show. |

On the Sunday before Thanksgiving, Pasadena's Doo Dah Parade, a spoof of the annual Rose Parade, brings out partiers such as the Lounge Lizards, who dress as reptiles and lip-synch to Frank Sinatra favorites.

PLEASURES & PASTIMES

California Cuisine California's name has come to signify a certain type of healthful, sophisticated cuisine, often made from organically grown local ingredients, creatively combined and beautifully presented. Because the state lies along the North American edge of the Pacific Rim, and also has a large Hispanic population, Asian and Latin flavors have a large influence here. In coastal areas most menus include seafood that's fresh off the boat. The Wine Country north of San Francisco is known for superb French and Italian restaurants. San Francisco and Los Angeles have dozens of top-notch restaurants—and an expensive meal at one of these culinary shrines is often the high point of a trip to California.

Downhill Skiing Skiing in California is generally limited to the period between Thanksgiving and late April, though in years of heavy snowfall skiers have been known to hit the trails as late as July. The state's best skiing is to be had in the Sierra Nevada. Six major ski resorts and several minor ones surround Lake Tahoe, most notable among them Squaw Valley USA, site of the 1960 winter Olympics, and giant Heavenly Mountain, in South Lake Tahoe. Farther south in the Sierra, Mammoth Mountain is one of the biggest and best ski resorts in the West. Smaller-scale California ski options include Mt. Shasta, in the far north; the San Bernardino Mountains, in Southern California; and Badger Pass, in Yosemite National Park.

Golf Heaven Temperate weather throughout most of the state makes golf a year-round sport in California. Many courses have spectacular settings alongside the ocean, in mountain forests, or in wide-open deserts. The most famous course in California, and one of the most famous in the world, is Pebble Beach Golf Links, set on the stunning coastline along 17-Mile Drive. For service, it's hard to beat the courses at La Costa Resort & Spa in Carlsbad and at La Quinta Resort & Club in the southern desert. There are especially high concentrations of stellar courses in Orange, San Diego, and Monterey counties and in the Desert Resorts region around Palm Springs.

National & State Parks There are eight national parks in California, and some are among the country's most awe-inspiring: Channel Islands, Death Valley, Joshua Tree, Kings Canyon, Lassen Volcanic, Redwood, Sequoia, and Yosemite. National monuments include Cabrillo, in San Diego, and Muir Woods, north of San Francisco. California has three national recreation areas: Golden Gate, with 87,000 acres both north and south of the Golden Gate Bridge in San Francisco; the Santa Monica Mountains, with 150,000 acres from Griffith Park in Los Angeles to Point Mugu in Ventura County; and Whiskeytown-Shasta-Trinity, with 240,000 acres, including four major lakes, in the far north. The Point Reyes National Seashore is on a peninsula north of San Francisco.

California's state park system includes more than 200 sites; many are recreational and scenic, others historic or scientific. Among the most popular are Angel Island, in San Francisco Bay, reached by ferry from San Francisco or Tiburon; Anza-Borrego Desert, 600,000 acres northeast of San Diego; Humboldt Redwoods, with its tall trees; Empire Mine, one of the richest mines in the Mother Lode, in Grass Valley; Hearst Castle, at San Simeon; and Leo Carrillo Beach, north of Malibu, with lively tidal pools and numerous secret coves. Most state parks are open year-round.

On the Beach

With 1,264 mi of coastline, California has no shortage of beautiful beaches. You can walk, sun, and snooze on them, watch seabirds and hunt for shells, dig clams, or spot seals and sea otters at play. From December through March you can watch the migrations of gray whales. Beach access in California is generally excellent; both the state park system and many ocean-side communities maintain public beaches. Through the work of the California Coastal Commission, many stretches of private property that would otherwise seal off a beach from outsiders have public-access paths. Not all California beaches are good for swimming, however. From San Francisco northward the water is too cold for all but the hardiest (and wet-suited) souls, and even along the southern half of the coast some beaches have dangerous undertow. Look for signs and postings and take them seriously.

Take a Hike

The deserts, dunes, and mountains of California beg to be explored on foot. Whatever your level of ability, there are ample opportunities for you to get up close and personal with nature and to surround yourself with redwood forest, lava beds, estuaries, and just about any other kind of ecological community. Especially rewarding are hikes along the Pacific Coast bluffs at Montaña de Oro State Park, amid the granite peaks and glacial valleys of Desolation Wilderness near Lake Tahoe, and past the Joshua trees and cinder cones of Mojave National Preserve. If you're a serious backpacker, consider the Pacific Crest Trail and the John Muir Trail.

Wine Tasting

You can visit wineries in many parts of the state—not just in the Sonoma and Napa valleys. Mendocino County, in the north, and the Monterey Bay and Central Coast regions, farther south, have become major players in the world of high-quality wine. Respected appellations now include the Anderson Valley, Arroyo Seco, Edna Valley, the Santa Cruz Mountains, Santa Ynez Valley, Temecula Valley, and many more—even the Gold Country is producing wine. Most winegrowing areas publish brochures with lists of local wineries that have tours or tastings. Wineries and good wine stores throughout the state will package your purchases for safe travel or shipping.

FODOR'S CHOICE

The sights, restaurants, hotels, and other travel experiences on these pages are our editors' top picks—our Fodor's Choices. They're the best of their type in California—not to be missed and always worth your time. In the regional chapters that follow, you will find all the details.

LODGING

$$$$	**Ahwahnee Hotel & Dining Room**, Yosemite National Park. Dating back to the 1920s, this mountain lodge constructed of rocks and sugar-pine logs is a National Historical Landmark.
$$$$	**Auberge du Soleil**, Rutherford. One of the Wine Country's best-known inns stands amid olive orchards that you can gaze upon from your private terrace.
$$$$	**Carneros Inn**, Napa. The infinity pool invites impromptu dips day and night, and the hilltop dining room overlooks stunning vineyards.
$$$$	**Château du Sureau**, Oakhurst. Like a storybook castle transported to the forest—but with down comforters and superior service.
$$$$	**Claremont Resort and Spa**, Berkeley. Like a gleaming white castle in the hills, this property draws both business travelers (with in-room T1 lines) and hooneymooners (with its glorious spa).
$$$$	**Four Seasons Hotel Beverly Hills**. The lush gardens here provide seclusion; the incredible staff makes you feel like you're the center of the universe.
$$$$	**Four Seasons Hotel San Francisco**. Elegant decor, cityscape views, and free access to the magnificent Sports Club/LA facilities.
$$$$	**Four Seasons Resort Aviara**, Carlsbad. Atop a serene hill overlooking Batiquitos Lagoon and the Pacific beyond, this resort provides every luxury.
$$$$	**Gaige House Inn**, Glen Ellen. This classic country house is accented with Asian details. Try for a poolside cottage, or a room with a fireplace or whirlpool tub.
$$$$	**Hilton La Jolla Torrey Pines**, La Jolla. The Parterre Gardens are the perfect place to watch the sun set—or get married.
$$$$	**Hotel Bel-Air**, Los Angeles. In a secluded wooded canyon, this ultra-luxurious hotel feels like a grand, silk-upholstered country mansion.
$$$$	**Hotel Del Coronado**, Coronado. Red-roofed turrets and balconied walkways are the signature of this rambling Victorian confection.
$$$$	**Hotel Monaco**, San Francisco. The decor here is a riot of color and pattern; the staff is devoted to pampering.

$$$$ | **Inn on Mt. Ada**, Catalina Island. William Wrigley, Jr.'s former house has all the comforts of a millionaire's home, plus a sweeping bay view.

$$$$ | **La Quinta Resort and Club**, La Quinta. Since 1926, this desert resort has sheltered Hollywood celebrities, and others who demand "little extras" like five golf courses, 23 tennis courts, and private pools and hot tubs.

$$$$ | **La Valencia**, La Jolla. An art deco landmark near La Jolla village shops and restaurants.

$$$$ | **Lodge at Torrey Pines**, La Jolla. On a bluff overlooking miles of coastline, this lodge of gigantic pine timbers is known for its fantastic Craftsman details.

$$$$ | **Manchester Grand Hyatt San Diego**, San Diego. The 40th-floor lounge is the city's most romantic spot to watch the sun set.

$$$$ | **Mandarin Oriental**, San Francisco. The posh hotel occupies the top floors of one of the city's tallest buildings. The views are great even if you don't use the binoculars in your room.

$$$$ | **Peninsula Beverly Hills.** This palace combines French Renaissance–style and service fit for royalty. You'll have a 360-degree city view from the fifth-floor pool.

$$$$ | **Post Ranch Inn**, Big Sur. The cliff-top lodgings at this ultraluxurious retreat blend seamlessly into the landscape—and all have their own private decks, fireplaces, and massage tables.

$$$$ | **Rancho Valencia Resort**, Rancho Santa Fe. This resort has a world-class tennis school, elegantly decorated individual casitas, a gracious restaurant, and impeccable service.

$$$$ | **Ritz-Carlton, Laguna Niguel.** An especially stunning oceanfront setting and outstanding restaurant give the Ritz an edge.

$$$$ | **Ritz-Carlton Huntington**, Pasadena. The azalea-filled Japanese garden and the outstanding spa are a recipe for serenity.

$$$$ | **Ritz-Carlton, San Francisco.** The opulent lobby and elegant rooms result in the Ritz's ranking among the world's best hotels.

$$$$ | **Sherman House**, San Francisco. A historic mansion in Pacific Heights is San Francisco's most luxurious small hotel.

$$$$ | **Shutters on the Beach**, Santa Monica. The gray-shingled exterior may evoke Martha's Vineyard, but the Pacific view and plush amenities remind you you're in Tinseltown.

$$$$ | **St. Regis**, Los Angeles. An exceptional staff—including trained temporary personal assistants—keeps this handsome property running impeccably.

$$$$	**Stonepine Estate Resort**, Carmel Valley. Hike, bike, or ride on this 330-acre resort property before retiring to your suite or cottage for a massage or afternoon tea.
$$$$	**Ventana Inn & Spa**, Big Sur. Luxurious relaxation is the name of the game here: bask at the clothing-optional pool, horseback ride along the cliffs, or pamper yourself at the decadent Allegria spa.
$$$$	**Westgate Hotel**, San Diego. In a lobby decorated with Louis XIV gilded furnishings and crystal chandeliers, you can savor the best high tea in the city.
$$$–$$$$	**Black Bear Inn B&B**, South Lake Tahoe. Removed from the bustle of Tahoe's main drag, this log lodge provides quiet luxury in the style of grand old Adirondack retreats.
$$$–$$$$	**Catamaran Resort Hotel**, Mission Beach. This resort evokes Hawaii with the lobby's huge waterfall, plus tropical birds, exotic flowers, koi carp river, and palms everywhere.
$$$–$$$$	**Disney's Grand Californian**, Anaheim. This posh Craftsman-style property has plenty of kid-oriented amenities and a direct entrance into the California Adventure park.
$$$–$$$$	**Furnace Creek Inn**, Death Valley National Park. All the comforts of home, from a sauna to the tennis courts, await you at this desert adobe-and-stone oasis built in 1927.
$$$–$$$$	**Grande Colonial**, La Jolla. Exquisitely turned out with marble and French doors, this historic boutique hotel has had a prime spot in La Jolla village for more than 90 years.
$$$–$$$$	**Hotel Rex**, San Francisco. Richly decorated rooms and literary soirées evoke the spirit of salon society in the 1920s.
$$$–$$$$	**Old Monterey Inn**, Monterey. In a Tudor-style inn surrounded by grand old trees, indulge yourself with featherbeds, down comforters, and truffle-and-champagne delivery.
$$$–$$$$	**PlumpJack Squaw Valley Inn**, Olympic Valley. This small hotel at the base of Squaw Valley brings city-style luxury hip to the mountains.
$$–$$$$	**Argonaut Hotel**. The natty nautical style is apropos for this waterfront hotel, part of the Maritime National Historical Park.
$$–$$$$	**Thistle Dew Inn**, Sonoma. Borrow the inn's bicycles, then soak away your sore spots in the hot tub.
$–$$$$	**Tamarack Lodge Resort**, Mammoth Lakes. A cluster of private woodland cabins puts you smack in the middle of the wilderness. You hardly have to leave the grounds to hike, bike, fish, or canoe.

$$–$$$	**MacCallum House,** Mendocino. The rooms here—whether in the main mansion, the cottages, or the converted barn and water tower—look out over rose gardens.
$–$$$	**Gaslamp Plaza Suites,** San Diego. Enjoy European-style accommodations and a complimentary continental breakfast on the rooftop terrace.
$–$$$	**Heritage Park Inn,** San Diego. A beautiful restored Victorian home with a wraparound porch, a French toast breakfast, and old movies in the evening.
$–$$	**The Downtown L.A. Standard,** Los Angeles. Hotelier André Balazs has done it again; his signature tongue-in-cheek style extends from the rooms to the superchic rooftop lounge.

BUDGET LODGING

¢	**San Remo Hotel.** Lace curtains and brass beds are some of the charming touches in this Italianate Victorian near Fisherman's Wharf.

RESTAURANTS

$$$$	**Aubergine,** Newport Beach. An enticing, deftly executed prix-fixe menu that's worth both the drive and the cost.
$$$$	**Bastide,** West Hollywood. Provençal warmth, a beautiful patio, gracious, unfussy service, and *fantastique* cooking.
$$$$	**Chez Panisse Café & Restaurant,** Berkeley. The legendary eatery is noted for its formality and personal service. The café is informal, with lower prices and a livelier crowd.
$$$$	**Erna's Elderberry House,** Oakhurst. The cute name belies the formal elegance of this eatery, where the staff serves the six-course prix-fixe dinner with perfect choreography.
$$$$	**French Laundry,** Yountville. If you manage to get a reservation for a table at this contemporary American restaurant, you'll spend lots of time and money on your meal—and it'll be worth it.
$$$$	**Gary Danko,** San Francisco. Foodies flock to this eatery, so make sure you call ahead; tables are solidly booked six weeks in advance.
$$$$	**Masa's,** San Francisco. Chef Ron Siegel, famous for besting Japan's Iron Chef, is at the helm of this celebrated temple to food.
$$$$	**Mélisse,** Santa Monica. One of L.A.'s dressiest restaurants serves up rich French dishes made with seasonal local produce.
$$$$	**Patina,** Los Angeles. The setting—Frank Gehry's Walt Disney Concert Hall—provides a dramatic backdrop to show-stopping contemporary French cuisine.
$$$–$$$$	**Farallon,** San Francisco. Lamps take the shape of jellyfish and columns are covered in kelp at this stylish, fun seafood restaurant.

$$$–$$$$	**George's at the Cove**, La Jolla. It's hard to say what's better here: the stunning view overlooking La Jolla Cove or the superb cooking.
$$$–$$$$	**Jardinière**, San Francisco. One of the city's most talked-about restaurants is a serious pretheater event, thanks in large part to the incredible cooking of chef-owner Traci Des Jardins.
$$$–$$$$	**Prince of Wales**, Coronado. Ocean views and inventive cooking drive this Hotel Del Cornado staple.
$$$–$$$$	**Star of the Sea**, San Diego. One of San Diego's top seafood restaurants has a terrace perfect for taking in the waterfront.
$$$–$$$$	**Tapenade**, La Jolla. This superb Provençal restaurant on a quiet side street serves brisk, earthy flavors in an intimate, bistrolike dining room.
$$$–$$$$	**Wine Cask**, Santa Barbara. Sip selections from Santa Barbara's most extensive wine list on the romantic outdoor patio.
$$–$$$$	**Brother's Restaurant at Mattei's Tavern**, Los Olivos. In the stagecoach days, travelers used to fuel at this cheery way station. It's still welcoming—but these days, there's foie gras on the menu.
$$$	**Furnace Creek Inn Dining Room**, Death Valley National Park. As the sun sets outside the huge windows, taste desert delicacies like rattlesnake empanadas and crispy cactus.
$$–$$$	**Cafe Beaujolais**, Mendocino. At this charming cottage, the exquisite cross-cultural menu highlights the freshest organic and local ingredients.
$$–$$$	**Mimosa**, West Hollywood. Sunny Provençal flavors and a cheerful, laid-back atmosphere to match.
$$–$$$	**Montrio Bistro**, Monterey. If you like organic, European-inspired cuisine in a unique setting, try dinner in this quirky, converted historic firehouse.
$$–$$$	**Mustard's Grill**, Yountville. Although it's usually booked solid, there's not an ounce of pretension here—just hearty, creatively prepared fare.
$$–$$$	**PlumpJack**, Olympic Valley. The deceptively simple contemporary cuisine here maximizes the ingredients' natural flavors.
$$–$$$	**Yujean Kang's**, Pasadena. Check your preconceptions of Chinese food at the door here: this is nouvelle Chinese cooking—imaginative and unexpected.
$$–$$$	**Zuni Café**, San Francisco. Chef Judy Rodgers' Italian-Mediterranean fare is refined, not fussy, and attracts an eclectic crowd late into the night.
$–$$$	**Angelini Osteria**, Los Angeles. If you can't get to Italy, get here: the food is beautifully authentic, the staff cheerful and warm.

$-$$	**A.O.C.,** near West Hollywood. Enjoy a thoughtful selection of wines by the glass, a series of small plates, and a rich (and rare) assortment of charcuterie.
$-$$	**Delfina,** San Francisco. The simple but exquisite Italian fare at this casual, lively spot makes diners return again and again.
$-$$	**Region,** San Diego. Near-perfect entrées and fine sweets at reasonable prices.

BUDGET RESTAURANTS

¢-$$	**Sushi Ota,** San Diego. The best sushi in town. You name it, it comes right off the boat.
$	**L'Osteria del Forno,** San Francisco. This modest North Beach favorite will make you feel transported to Italy.
¢-$	**Swan Oyster Depot,** San Francisco. Grab a stool at the counter of this fish market–diner lunchtime favorite and order some chowder.
¢-$	**Taco Mesa,** near Newport Beach. An always-packed taqueria with no frills except the friendliness of the staff and the freshness of the ingredients.
¢	**Philippe The Original,** Los Angeles. L.A.'s oldest restaurant hasn't changed much since the early 1900s, and the price for a cup of coffee is stuck back in the 1940s.

DRIVES

	17-Mile Drive, Pebble Beach. Robert Louis Stevenson described the gnarled and twisted Monterey cypresses on this route between Pacific Grove and Carmel, as "ghosts fleeing before the wind."
	Highway 1, from San Simeon to Big Sur. Rocky beaches pounded by the surf, rugged cliffs dropping into the sea, trees tortured by the wind into twisted shapes, and gentle mists make this the quintessential coastal drive.
	Laguna Beach. Make your grand entrance to the fabled beach town along Laguna Canyon Road from I–405, cruising through a gorgeous coastal canyon. A glistening wedge of ocean lies at the end of the road.

HISTORY

| | **Bodie Ghost Town,** Bodie State Historic Park. Preserved in a state of "arrested decay," this once wild mining town is now a great place to come for a glimpse of prospecting life. A museum tells all about the buildings outside. |
| | **California State Railroad Museum,** Sacramento. Railroad buffs will be captivated by this museum's 21 antique locomotives and railroad cars. |

Columbia State Historic Park, Columbia. Ride a stagecoach and pan for gold, then visit this restored gold-rush town and its blast-from-the-past merchants, blacksmiths, barkeeps, and newspapermen.

Mission San Juan Capistrano, San Juan Capistrano. The adobe buildings give an evocative picture of early mission life.

Mission San Luis Rey, San Diego. Once a location for filming Disney's *Zorro* TV series, this well-preserved 1798 mission is still owned by Franciscan friars.

Mission Santa Barbara, Santa Barbara. This strikingly grand "Queen of Missions" is one of the most photographed buildings in coastal California.

Petroglyph Canyons, Ridgecrest. Two canyons hold the largest concentration of ancient rock art—well-preserved images of animals and humans—in the northern hemisphere.

MUSEUMS

The Huntington, San Marino. Extensive gardens, a fantastic British art collection, rare ancient manuscripts—all in one extraordinary estate.

Los Angeles County Museum of Art, Los Angeles. An awkward layout is more than made up for by strong collections of art from all over the world.

Maritime Museum, San Diego. A collection of five restored sail- and steam-powered ships dating from the late 19th and early 20th centuries is a must for nautical history buffs.

Museum of Contemporary Art, Los Angeles. A permanent collection of now-celebrated modern artists shares space with rotating exhibits of up-and-comers.

Norton Simon Museum, Pasadena. View rich collections of Impressionist painters, works by Rembrandt, Goya, Picasso, and dozens of Degas bronzes.

San Francisco Museum of Modern Art, San Francisco. Crossing the sky bridge in the atrium, you'll appreciate the cutting-edge designs of architect Mario Botta.

Tech Museum of Innovation, San Jose. At this hands-on museum in the capital of Silicon Valley, you can learn about everything technology-related, from virtual reality to robotics to criminal forensics.

NATURE

Channel Islands National Park, Santa Barbara. Referred to as "North America's Galapagos," this cluster of five islands is home to a plethora of wildlife, including some 30,000 seals and sea lions.

Death Valley National Park, Death Valley. The hottest spot in the western hemisphere is one of its most awe-inspiring: canyons, colorful volcanic formations, and a lonely Moorish-style mansion are among the wonders you can see here.

Havasu National Wildlife Refuge, Needles. Best seen by boat, this beautiful waterway is punctuated by sandy coves, water bird nesting areas, and cliffside petroglyphs.

Joshua Tree National Park, Twentynine Palms. Under the bluest of skies, the cartoonishly gigantic boulders and anthropomorphically contorted Joshua trees of this arid preserve can make you forget there is anyplace else on earth.

La Jolla Cove, La Jolla. At low tide the tide pools and cliff caves are perfect for explorers, while divers and snorkelers can explore the underwater delights of the San Diego–La Jolla Underwater Park and Ecological Reserve.

Lassen Volcanic National Park, Mineral. Thermal features like boiling springs, steam vents, and mud pots, and volcanic domes and flows provide an eerie glimpse of California's origins.

Monterey Bay Aquarium, Monterey. The exhibits here all give you a sense of what it's like to be in the water with sea creatures. Sardines swim around your head in a circular tank; jellyfish drift and otters backstroke at eye level.

Point Reyes National Seashore, Marin County. Elephant seals, 225 bird species, starfish, sea anemones and purple urchins thrive in the waters and grasslands along this raggedly magnificent stretch of coastline.

Yosemite Falls, Yosemite National Park. The highest waterfall in North America and the fifth-largest in the world, this thundering falls will leave you awestruck—especially after the thaw in spring and early summer.

SIGHTS

Cathedral of Our Lady of the Angels, Los Angeles. This spare, striking cathedral contains creamy panels of translucent alabaster, which take the place of stained glass.

Coit Tower, San Francisco. Glowing at night atop Telegraph Hill, this beacon of western individualism was inspired by Lily Coit, one of early San Francisco's great originals.

Farmers Market and The Grove, Los Angeles. Taste the fabulous diversity of Los Angeles with a stroll through these market stalls, cafés, and shops.

Grauman's Chinese Theatre, Los Angeles. See the footprints of Marilyn Monroe and John Wayne—and the nose print of Jimmy Durante–in the legendary cement walkway.

Lombard Street, San Francisco. The "crookedest street in the world," with its winding brick paths and its well-tended flowerbeds, is worth the queue.

Palace of Fine Arts, San Francisco. This rosy rococo palace, a San Francisco landmark, was built for the 1915 Panama-Pacific International Exposition.

Rodeo Drive, Beverly Hills. Whether or not you plan on splurging, this stretch of glittering boutiques makes for incomparable window shopping.

Venice Boardwalk, Los Angeles. Check out the streams of magicians, jugglers, bodybuilders, and other characters, either on a walk or while zipping along on a bike or 'blades.

Walt Disney Concert Hall, Los Angeles. While the nearby cathedral is all stark angles, this building's shimmering curves are courtesy of architect Frank Gehry.

PARKS & GARDENS

Balboa Park, San Diego. Amid cultivated and wild gardens overlooking the Pacific, ornate Spanish colonial revival buildings house most of the city's museums. The San Diego Zoo is here, too.

The Getty Center, Los Angeles. The combination of stunning architecture, gardens, and views make this a must-see even before you get to the art collections.

Lotusland, Santa Barbara. The guided tour of this sweeping property shows you a whimsical topiary garden, a lotus pond, and a huge collection of rare, ancient cycad plants.

Silver Strand State Beach, Coronado. Calm surf, plenty of lifeguards, and a generally quiet mood make this beach ideal for families.

TASTES OF CALIFORNIA

Clos Pegase, Calistoga. Even the tunnels of the wine cave are bedecked with artworks at this winery in a radically post-modern building.

Copia: The American Center for Wine, Food & the Arts, Napa. After visiting this temple of American food and wine, your taste buds will never be the same again.

Frog's Leap, Rutherford. The perfect place to begin your education in wine—and taste world-class zinfandel and sauvignon blanc.

Hess Collection Winery and Vineyards, Napa. Check out work by contemporary artists like Robert Motherwell, Francis Bacon, and Frank Stella while indulging in fabulous cabernet.

Mount Palomar Winery, Temecula. Considered the leading winery in the Temecula Valley, Mount Palomar stands out for such Mediterranean varietals as sangiovese and cortese.

Niebaum-Coppola Estate, Rutherford. At Francis Ford Coppola's winery you can combine your wine tasting with a look at Coppola's Hollywood movie memorabilia.

THEME PARKS & ATTRACTIONS

Disneyland, Anaheim. The original and still the best.

Legoland California, Carlsbad. Let the little ones loose at this fantasyland here everything—including mini–roller coasters and water rides—is made out of Lego.

San Diego Wild Animal Park, Escondido. Endangered species from Africa, Asia, and Australia populate this preserve operated by the San Diego Zoo.

San Diego Zoo, San Diego. By foot or by tram, visit Malayan tapirs, Siberian reindeer, and giant pandas in re-creations of their native habitats.

SeaWorld of California, San Diego. Watch sharks and walruses in walk-through marine environments, or watch killer whales, sea lions, and otters perform in one of four arenas.

VIEWS

Emerald Bay State Park, Lake Tahoe. Massive glaciers carved this fjordlike bay millions of years ago. Famed for its jewel-like shape and colors, it surrounds Fannette, Tahoe's only island.

Glacier Point, Yosemite National Park. This scenic overlook provides stunning vistas of Yosemite Valley and the High Sierra—as well as neighboring Nevada. Don't miss it at sunset.

Heavenly Gondola, South Lake Tahoe. Whether you ski or not, you can be whisked right from town up Heavenly Mountain for stunning views of cobalt-blue Lake Tahoe.

Mammoth Mountain Ski Area, Mammoth. Even if you're not a skier, you'll appreciate the stunning views from atop this dormant volcano: to the west, you can see across the state to the Coastal Range; to the east are the highest peaks of Nevada and the Great Basin beyond.

The Top of the Hyatt, San Diego. The lounge here crowns the tallest waterfront building in California.

SMART TRAVEL TIPS

Finding out about your destination before you leave home means you won't squander time organizing everyday minutiae once you've arrived. You'll be more streetwise when you hit the ground as well, better prepared to explore the things about California that drew you here in the first place. The organizations in this section can provide information to supplement this guide; contact them for up-to-the-minute details, and consult the A to Z sections that end each chapter. Happy landings!

AIR TRAVEL

BOOKING

When you book, look for nonstop flights and remember that "direct" flights stop at least once. Try to avoid connecting flights, which require a change of plane. Two airlines may operate a connecting flight jointly, so ask whether your airline operates every segment of the trip; you may find that the carrier you prefer flies you only part of the way. To find more booking tips and to check prices and make online flight reservations, log on to www.fodors.com.

CARRIERS

United, with hubs in San Francisco and Los Angeles, has the greatest number of flights into and within California. But most national and many international airlines fly here.

🛪 Major Airlines **Air Canada** ☎ 888/247-2262 ⊕ www.aircanada.com. **Alaska** ☎ 800/426-0333 ⊕ www.alaskaair.com. **America West** ☎ 800/235-9292 ⊕ www.americawest.com. **American** ☎ 800/433-7300 ⊕ www.aa.com. **British Airways** ☎ 800/247-9297 ⊕ www.britishairways.com. **Cathay Pacific** ☎ 800/233-2742 ⊕ www.cathaypacific.com. **Continental** ☎ 800/525-0280 ⊕ www.continental.com. **Delta** ☎ 800/221-1212 ⊕ www.delta.com. **Japan Air Lines** ☎ 800/525-3663 ⊕ www.japanair.com. **Northwest/KLM** ☎ 800/225-2525 ⊕ www.nwa.com. **Qantas** ☎ 800/227-4500 ⊕ www.qantas.com. **Southwest** ☎ 800/435-9792 ⊕ www.southwest.com. **United** ☎ 800/241-6522 ⊕ www.united.com. **US Airways** ☎ 800/428-4322 ⊕ www.usairways.com.

🛪 Smaller Airlines **American Trans Air** ☎ 800/435-9282 ⊕ www.ata.com. **Horizon** ☎ 800/547-

9308 ⊕ www.horizonair.com. **Midwest Airlines**
☎ 800/452-2022 ⊕ www.midwestairlines.com.
🔽 **From the U.K. American** ☎ 8457/789-789.
British Airways ☎ 0870/850-9850. **Delta**
☎ 0800/414-767. **United** ☎ 0845/8444-777. **Virgin
Atlantic** ☎ 0870/380-2007.

CHECK-IN & BOARDING

Always find out your carrier's check-in
policy. Plan to arrive at the airport about
two hours before your scheduled departure time for domestic flights and 2½ to 3
hours before international flights. You
may need to arrive earlier if you're flying
from one of the busier airports or during
peak air-traffic times. To avoid delays at
airport-security checkpoints, try not to
wear any metal. Jewelry, belt and other
buckles, steel-toe shoes, barrettes, and un-
derwire bras are among the items that can
set off detectors.

Assuming that not everyone with a ticket
will show up, airlines routinely overbook
planes. When everyone does, airlines ask
for volunteers to give up their seats. In return, these volunteers usually get a several-
hundred-dollar flight voucher, which can
be used toward the purchase of another
ticket, and are rebooked on the next flight
out. If there are not enough volunteers, the
airline must choose who will be denied
boarding. The first to get bumped are passengers who checked in late and those flying on discounted tickets, so get to the
gate and check in as early as possible, especially during peak periods.

Always bring a government-issued photo
ID to the airport; even when it's not required, a passport is best.

CUTTING COSTS

The least expensive airfares to California
are priced for round-trip travel and must
usually be purchased in advance. Airlines
generally allow you to change your return
date for a fee; most low-fare tickets, however, are nonrefundable. It's smart to call a
number of airlines and check the Internet;
when you are quoted a good price, book it
on the spot—the same fare may not be
available the next day, or even the next
hour. Always check different routings and
look into using alternate airports. Also,

price off-peak flights, which may be significantly less expensive than others. Travel
agents, especially low-fare specialists
(⇨ Discounts & Deals), are helpful.

Consolidators are another good source.
They buy tickets for scheduled flights at
reduced rates from the airlines, then sell
them at prices that beat the best fare
available directly from the airlines. (Many
also offer reduced car-rental and hotel
rates.) Sometimes you can even get your
money back if you need to return the
ticket. Carefully read the fine print detailing penalties for changes and cancella-
tions, purchase the ticket with a credit
card, and confirm your consolidator reservation with the airline.

When you fly as a courier, you trade your
checked-luggage space for a ticket deeply
subsidized by a courier service. There are
restrictions on when you can book and
how long you can stay. Some courier
companies list with membership organizations, such as the Air Courier Association and the International Association of
Air Travel Couriers; these require you to
become a member before you can book
a flight.

Many airlines, singly or in collaboration,
offer discount air passes that allow for-
eigners to travel economically in a particular country or region. These visitor passes
usually must be purchased before you
leave home. Information about passes can
be found on most airlines' international
Web pages.

Many airlines, singly or in collaboration,
offer discount air passes that allow foreign-
ers to travel economically in a particular
country or region. These visitor passes usually must be reserved and purchased before
you leave home. Information about passes
often can be found on most airlines' international Web pages, which tend to be
aimed at travelers from outside the carrier's
home country. Also, try typing the name of
the pass into a search engine, or search for
"pass" within the carrier's Web site.

🔽 **Consolidators AirlineConsolidator.com** ☎ 888/
468-5385 ⊕ www.airlineconsolidator.com, for international tickets. **Best Fares** ☎ 800/880-1234 or
800/576-8255 ⊕ www.bestfares.com; $59.90 annual

membership. **Cheap Tickets** ☎ 800/377–1000 or 800/652–4327 ⊕ www.cheaptickets.com. **Expedia** ☎ 800/397–3342 or 404/728–8787 ⊕ www.expedia.com. **Hotwire** ☎ 866/468–9473 or 920/330–9418 ⊕ www.hotwire.com. **Now Voyager Travel** ⊠ 45 W. 21st St., Suite 5A, New York, NY 10010 ☎ 212/459–1616 🖶 212/243–2711 ⊕ www.nowvoyagertravel.com. **Onetravel.com** ⊕ www.onetravel.com. **Orbitz** ☎ 888/656–4546 ⊕ www.orbitz.com. **Priceline.com** ⊕ www.priceline.com. **Travelocity** ☎ 888/709–5983, 877/282–2925 in Canada, 0870/876–3876 in the U.K. ⊕ www.travelocity.com.

🛪 **Courier Resources Air Courier Association/Cheaptrips.com** ☎ 800/280–5973 or 800/282–1202 ⊕ www.aircourier.org or www.cheaptrips.com; $34 annual membership. **International Association of Air Travel Couriers** ☎ 308/632–3273 ⊕ www.courier.org; $45 annual membership. **Now Voyager Travel** ⊠ 45 W. 21st St., Suite 5A, New York, NY 10010 ☎ 212/459–1616 🖶 212/243–2711 ⊕ www.nowvoyagertravel.com.

ENJOYING THE FLIGHT

State your seat preference when purchasing your ticket, and then repeat it when you confirm and when you check in. For more legroom, you can request one of the few emergency-aisle seats at check-in, if you're capable of moving obstacles comparable in weight to an airplane exit door (usually between 35 pounds and 60 pounds)—a Federal Aviation Administration requirement of passengers in these seats. Seats behind a bulkhead also offer more legroom, but they don't have underseat storage. Don't sit in the row in front of the emergency aisle or in front of a bulkhead, where seats may not recline.

On long flights, try to maintain a normal routine, to help fight jet lag. At night, get some sleep. By day, eat light meals, drink water (not alcohol), and move around the cabin to stretch your legs. For additional jet-lag tips consult *Fodor's FYI: Travel Fit & Healthy* (available at bookstores everywhere).

Smoking policies vary from carrier to carrier. Many airlines prohibit smoking on all of their flights; others allow smoking only on certain routes or certain departures. Ask your carrier about its policy.

FLYING TIMES

Flying time to California is roughly six hours from New York and four hours from Chicago. Travel from London to Los Angeles or San Francisco takes about 10 hours and from Sydney approximately 14. Flying between San Francisco and Los Angeles takes one hour.

HOW TO COMPLAIN

If your baggage goes astray or your flight goes awry, complain right away. Most carriers require that you **file a claim immediately.** The Aviation Consumer Protection Division of the Department of Transportation publishes *Fly-Rights*, which discusses airlines and consumer issues and is available online. You can also find articles and information on mytravelrights.com, the Web site of the nonprofit Consumer Travel Rights Center.

🛪 **Airline Complaints Aviation Consumer Protection Division** ⊠ U.S. Department of Transportation, Office of Aviation Enforcement and Proceedings, C-75, Room 4107, 400 7th St. SW, Washington, DC 20590 ☎ 202/366–2220 ⊕ airconsumer.ost.dot.gov. **Federal Aviation Administration Consumer Hotline** ⊠ For inquiries: FAA, 800 Independence Ave. SW, Washington, DC 20591 ☎ 800/322–7873 ⊕ www.faa.gov.

RECONFIRMING

Check the status of your flight before you leave for the airport. You can do this on your carrier's Web site, by linking to a flight-status checker (many Web booking services offer these), or by calling your carrier or travel agent. Always confirm international flights at least 72 hours ahead of the scheduled departure time.

AIRPORTS

The major gateways to California are Los Angeles International Airport (LAX), San Francisco International Airport (SFO), San Diego International Airport (SAN), and San Jose International Airport (SJC).

🛪 **Airport Information Los Angeles International Airport** ☎ 310/646–5252 ⊕ www.lawa.org. **San Diego International Airport** ☎ 619/231–2100 ⊕ www.san.org. **San Francisco International Airport** ☎ 650/761–0800 ⊕ www.flysfo.com. **San Jose International Airport** (SJC) ☎ 408/277–4759 ⊕ www.sjc.org.

BIKE TRAVEL

There are beautiful places to bike throughout California. For each part of the state, please see the specific chapter on that area for biking ideas.

BIKES IN FLIGHT

Most airlines accommodate bikes as luggage, provided they are dismantled and boxed; check with individual airlines about packing requirements. Some airlines sell bike boxes, which are often free at bike shops, for about $20 (bike bags can be considerably more expensive). International travelers often can substitute a bike for a piece of checked luggage at no charge; otherwise, the cost is about $100. Most U.S. and Canadian airlines charge $40–$80 each way.

BUSINESS HOURS

Banks in California are typically open from 9 to 4 and are closed most holidays (⇨ Holidays). Smaller shops usually operate from 10 to 6, with larger stores remaining open until 8 or later. Hours vary for museums and historical sites, and many are closed one or more days a week. It's a good idea to check before you visit a tourist site. Many gas stations are open 24 hours, especially on interstate highways. In rural areas many close early, so fill up before nightfall.

BUS TRAVEL

Because of the state's size, traveling by bus in California can be slow. But if you don't want to rent a car and wish to go where the train does not, a bus may be your only option. Greyhound is the major carrier for intermediate and long distances, though smaller, regional bus service is available in metropolitan areas. Check the specific chapters for the regions you plan to visit. Smoking is prohibited on all buses in California.

⛷ Bus Information **Greyhound** ☎ 800/231-2222 ⊕ www.greyhound.com.

CAMERAS & PHOTOGRAPHY

The pounding surf, majestic mountains, sprawling deserts, towering trees, and sparkling beaches—not to mention the cities and towns in between—make California a photographer's dream destination.

Bring lots of film (or plenty of digital memory) to capture the special moments of your trip.

The *Kodak Guide to Shooting Great Travel Pictures* (available at bookstores everywhere) is loaded with tips.

⛷ Photo Help **Kodak Information Center** ☎ 800/242-2424 ⊕ www.kodak.com.

EQUIPMENT PRECAUTIONS

Don't pack film or equipment in checked luggage, where it is much more susceptible to damage. X-ray machines used to view checked luggage are extremely powerful and therefore are likely to ruin your film. Try to ask for hand inspection of film, which becomes clouded after repeated exposure to airport X-ray machines, and keep videotapes and computer disks away from metal detectors. Always keep film, tape, and computer disks out of the sun. Carry an extra supply of batteries, and be prepared to turn on your camera, camcorder, or laptop to prove to airport security personnel that the device is real.

CAR RENTAL

A car is essential in most parts of California. In compact San Francisco it's better to use public transportation to avoid parking headaches. In sprawling cities such as Los Angeles and San Diego, however, getting just about anywhere requires making use of the freeways.

Rates in Los Angeles and San Francisco begin at around $35 a day and $175 a week. This does not include tax on car rentals, which is 8¼% in Los Angeles, and 8½% in Los Angeles. In San Diego, rates for an economy car with unlimited mileage begin around $30 a day and $150 a week. The tax is an additional 7¾%. If you pick up at an airport, there may also be a facility charge of as much as $12 per rental. Vehicle license fees are no longer legal in California.

⛷ Major Agencies **Alamo** ☎ 800/327-9633 ⊕ www.alamo.com. **Avis** ☎ 800/331-1212, 800/879-2847 or 800/272-5871 in Canada, 0870/606-0100 in the U.K., 02/9353-9000 in Australia, 09/526-2847 in New Zealand ⊕ www.avis.com. **Budget** ☎ 800/527-0700, 0870/156-5656 in the U.K. ⊕ www.budget.com. **Dollar** ☎ 800/800-4000,

0800/085-4578 in the U.K. ⊕ www.dollar.com.
Hertz ☎ 800/654-3131, 800/263-0600 in Canada,
0870/844-8844 in the U.K., 02/9669-2444 in Australia, 09/256-8690 in New Zealand ⊕ www.hertz.
com. **National Car Rental** ☎ 800/227-7368, 0870/
600-6666 in the U.K. ⊕ www.nationalcar.com.

CONVERTIBLES & SUVS

If you dream of driving down the coast
with the top down, or you want to explore
the desert landscape not visible from the
road, consider renting a specialty vehicle.
Agencies that specialize in convertibles and
sport-utility vehicles will often arrange airport delivery in larger cities.

▸ **Specialty Car Agencies** In San Francisco,
SpecialtyRentals.com ☎ 800/400-8412
⊕ www.specialtyrentals.com; in Los Angeles,
Budget of Beverly Hills ☎ 800/729-7350
⊕ www.budgetbeverlyhills.com; in San
Diego, **Rent-a-Vette** ☎ 800/627-0808
⊕ http://sandiegosportscarrental.com.

CUTTING COSTS

For a good deal, book through a travel
agent who will shop around. Also, price
local car-rental companies—whose prices
may be lower still, although their service
and maintenance may not be as good as
those of major rental agencies—and research rates on the Internet. Consolidators
that specialize in air travel can offer good
rates on cars as well (⇨ Air Travel). Remember to ask about required deposits,
cancellation penalties, and drop-off
charges if you're planning to pick up the
car in one city and leave it in another. If
you're traveling during a holiday period,
also make sure that a confirmed reservation guarantees you a car.

INSURANCE

When driving a rented car you are generally responsible for any damage to or loss
of the vehicle. You also may be liable for
any property damage or personal injury
that you may cause while driving. Before
you rent, see what coverage you already
have under the terms of your personal
auto-insurance policy and credit cards.

For about $9 to $25 a day, rental companies sell protection, known as a collision-
or loss-damage waiver (CDW or LDW),
that eliminates your liability for damage

to the car; it's always optional and should
never be automatically added to your bill.
In most states you don't need a CDW if
you have personal auto insurance or other
liability insurance. Some states, including
California, have capped the price of the
CDW and LDW but the cap has a floating
value, depending on the cost of the vehicle; for those valued at over $35,000,
there is no maximum. Verify the cost of
the CDW/LDW at the time you book.
Make sure you have enough coverage to
pay for the car. If you do not have auto
insurance or an umbrella policy that covers damage to third parties, purchasing liability insurance and a CDW or LDW is
highly recommended.

Some credit-card companies cover the cost
of CDW/LDW if you pay using that card.
Check with the credit-card company to determine if you are eligible for these coverages. Credit cards do not provide liability
insurance, only CDW/LDW.

Rental agencies in California aren't required to include liability insurance in the
price of the rental. If you cause an accident, you may expose your assets to litigation. When in doubt about your own
policy's coverage, take the liability coverage that the agency offers. If you plan to
take the car out of California, ask if the
policy is valid in other states or countries.
Most car-rental companies won't insure a
loss or damage that occurs outside of their
coverage area—particularly in Mexico.

REQUIREMENTS & RESTRICTIONS

In California you must be 21 to rent a car,
and rates may be higher if you're under
25. Some agencies will not rent to those
under 25; check when you book. You'll
pay extra for child seats (about $5 per
day), which are compulsory for children
under five. Children up to age six or 60
pounds must be placed in booster seats.
There is no extra charge for an additional
driver. Non–U.S. residents must have a license whose text is in the Roman alphabet. Though it need not be entirely written
in English, it must have English letters that
clearly identify it as a driver's license. An
international license is recommended but
not required.

SURCHARGES

Before you pick up a car in one city and leave it in another, ask about drop-off charges or one-way service fees, which can be substantial. Also inquire about early-return policies; some rental agencies charge extra if you return the car before the time specified in your contract while others give you a refund for the days not used. To avoid a hefty refueling fee, fill the tank just before you turn in the car, but be aware that gas stations near the rental outlet may overcharge. It's almost never a deal to buy the tank of gas that's in the car when you rent it; the understanding is that you'll return it empty, but some fuel usually remains. Surcharges may apply if you're under 25 or if you take the car outside the area approved by the rental agency. You'll pay extra for child seats (about $8 a day), which are compulsory for children under five, and usually for additional drivers (up to $25 a day, depending on location).

CAR TRAVEL

Three major highways—Interstate 5 (I–5), U.S. 101, and Highway 1—run north–south through California. The main routes into the state from the east are I–15 and I–10 in southern California and I–80 in northern California.

EMERGENCY SERVICES

Dial 911 to report accidents on the road and to reach police, the California Highway Patrol, or the fire department. On some rural highways and on most interstates, look for emergency phones on the side of the road.

GASOLINE

Gasoline prices in California vary widely depending on location, oil company, and whether you buy it at a full-serve or self-serve pump. At this writing regular unleaded gasoline cost about $2 a gallon. It is less expensive to buy fuel in the southern part of the state than in the north. If you are planning to travel near Nevada, you can save a lot by purchasing gas over the border.

Gas stations are plentiful throughout the state. Most stay open late (24 hours along major highways and in big cities), except in rural areas, where Sunday hours are limited and where you may drive long stretches without a chance to refuel.

ROAD CONDITIONS

Rainy weather can make driving along the coast or in the mountains treacherous. Some of the smaller routes over the mountain ranges are prone to flash flooding. When the rains are severe, coastal Highway 1 can quickly become a slippery nightmare, buffeted by strong winds and obstructed by falling debris from the cliffs above. When the weather is particularly bad, Highway 1 may be closed. Drivers should check road and weather conditions before heading out.

Many smaller roads over the Sierra Nevada are closed in winter, and if it is snowing, tire chains may be required on routes that are open, most notably those to Yosemite and Lake Tahoe. From October through April, if it is raining along the coast, it is usually snowing at higher elevations. Do not wait until the highway patrol's chain-control checkpoint to look for chains; you'll be unable to turn around, and you will get stuck and have to wait out the storm. Rent a four-wheel-drive vehicle or purchase chains before you get to the mountains. If you delay and purchase them in the vicinity of the chain-control area, the cost may double. Be aware that most rental-car companies prohibit chain installation on their vehicles. If you choose to risk it and do not tighten them properly, they may snap; insurance will not cover the damage that could result. Uniformed chain installers on I–80 and U.S. 50 will apply them at the checkpoint for $20 or take them off for $10. On smaller roads you are on your own. Always carry extra clothing, blankets, and food when driving to the mountains in the winter, and keep your gas tank full to prevent the fuel line from freezing.

In larger cities the biggest driving hazards are traffic jams. Avoid major urban highways, especially at rush hour.

Road Conditions Statewide hotline 800/GAS-ROAD or 916/445-1534 www.dot.ca.gov/hq/roadinfo.

Weather Conditions National Weather Service 707/443-6484 (northernmost California), 831/656-

1725 (San Francisco Bay Area and Central California), 775/673-8100 (Reno, Lake Tahoe, and the northern Sierra), 805/988-6610 (Los Angeles area), 858/675-8700 (San Diego area) ⊕ www.weather.gov.

ROAD MAPS

You can buy detailed maps in bookstores and gas stations and at some grocery stores and drugstores.

RULES OF THE ROAD

Always strap children under age six or weighing 60 pounds or less into approved child-safety seats; also children up to age six and weighing up to 60 pounds must be placed in booster seats designed to reduce seat belt injuries. Seat belts are required at all times; tickets can be given for failing to comply. Children must wear seat belts regardless of where they're seated (studies show that children are safest in the rear seats).

Unless otherwise indicated, right turns are allowed at red lights after you've come to a full stop. Left turns between two one-way streets are allowed at red lights after you've come to a full stop. Drivers with a blood-alcohol level higher than 0.08 who are stopped by police are subject to arrest, and police officers can detain those with a level of 0.05 if they appear impaired. California's drunk-driving laws are extremely tough. The licenses of violators may immediately be suspended, and offenders may have to spend the night in jail and pay hefty fines.

The speed limit on many rural highways is 70 mph. In the cities, freeway speed limits are between 55 mph and 65 mph. Many city routes have commuter lanes during rush hour, but the rules vary from city to city: in San Francisco, for example, you need three people in a car to use these lanes; in Los Angeles only two. Read the signs. Failure to comply with the rules could cost you nearly $300 in fines.

CHILDREN IN CALIFORNIA

California is made to order for traveling with children: youngsters love Disneyland; Legoland, in Carlsbad; the San Diego Zoo; the Monterey Aquarium; San Francisco cable cars; the gold mine in Placerville; Forestiere Underground Gardens in

Fresno; and the caverns near Lake Shasta. *Fodor's Around Los Angeles with Kids* and *Fodor's Around San Francisco with Kids* (available in bookstores everywhere) can help you plan your days together.

If you are renting a car, don't forget to arrange for a car seat when you reserve. For general advice about traveling with children, consult *Fodor's FYI: Travel with Your Baby* (available in bookstores everywhere).

FLYING

If your children are two or older, ask about children's airfares. As a general rule, infants under two not occupying a seat fly at greatly reduced fares or even for free. But if you want to guarantee a seat for an infant, you have to pay full fare. Consider flying during off-peak days and times; most airlines will grant an infant a seat without a ticket if there are available seats.

Experts agree that it's a good idea to use safety seats aloft for children weighing less than 40 pounds. Airlines set their own policies: if you use a safety seat, U.S. carriers usually require that the child be ticketed, even if he or she is young enough to ride free, because the seats must be strapped into regular seats. And even if you pay the full adult fare for the seat, it may be worth it, especially on longer trips. Do check your airline's policy about using safety seats during takeoff and landing. Safety seats are not allowed everywhere in the plane, so get your seat assignments as early as possible.

When reserving, request children's meals or a freestanding bassinet (not available at all airlines) if you need them. But note that bulkhead seats, where you must sit to use the bassinet, may lack an overhead bin or storage space on the floor.

LODGING

Most hotels in California allow children under a certain age to stay in their parents' room at no extra charge, but others charge for them as extra adults; be sure to find out the cutoff age for children's discounts.

SIGHTS & ATTRACTIONS

Places that are especially appealing to children are indicated by a rubber-duckie icon (🐤) in the margin.

CONSUMER PROTECTION

Whether you're shopping for gifts or purchasing travel services, pay with a major credit card whenever possible, so you can cancel payment or get reimbursed if there's a problem (and you can provide documentation). If you're doing business with a particular company for the first time, contact your local Better Business Bureau and the attorney general's offices in your state and (for U.S. businesses) the company's home state as well. Have any complaints been filed? Finally, if you're buying a package or tour, always consider travel insurance that includes default coverage (⟹ Insurance).

7 BBBs **Council of Better Business Bureaus** ✉ 4200 Wilson Blvd., Suite 800, Arlington, VA 22203 ☎ 703/276-0100 ➗ 703/525-8277 ⊕ www. bbb.org.

CUSTOMS & DUTIES

When shopping abroad, keep receipts for all purchases. Upon reentering the country, be ready to show customs officials what you've bought. Pack purchases together in an easily accessible place. If you think a duty is incorrect, appeal the assessment. If you object to the way your clearance was handled, note the inspector's badge number. In either case, first ask to see a supervisor. If the problem isn't resolved, write to the appropriate authorities, beginning with the port director at your point of entry.

IN AUSTRALIA

Australian residents who are 18 or older may bring home A$400 worth of souvenirs and gifts (including jewelry), 250 cigarettes or 250 grams of cigars or other tobacco products, and 1,125 ml of alcohol (including wine, beer, and spirits). Residents under 18 may bring back A$200 worth of goods. Members of the same family traveling together may pool their allowances. Prohibited items include meat products. Seeds, plants, and fruits need to be declared upon arrival.

7 **Australian Customs Service** ⟳ Regional Director, Box 8, Sydney, NSW 2001 ☎ 02/9213-2000 or 1300/363263, 02/9364-7222 or 1800/020-504 quarantine-inquiry line ➗ 02/9213-4043 ⊕ www. customs.gov.au.

IN CANADA

Canadian residents who have been out of Canada for at least seven days may bring in C$750 worth of goods duty-free. If you've been away fewer than seven days but more than 48 hours, the duty-free allowance drops to C$200. If your trip lasts 24 to 48 hours, the allowance is C$50. You may not pool allowances with family members. Goods claimed under the C$750 exemption may follow you by mail; those claimed under the lesser exemptions must accompany you. Alcohol and tobacco products may be included in the seven-day and 48-hour exemptions but not in the 24-hour exemption. If you meet the age requirements of the province or territory through which you reenter Canada, you may bring in, duty-free, 1.5 liters of wine *or* 1.14 liters (40 imperial ounces) of liquor *or* 24 12-ounce cans or bottles of beer or ale. Also, if you meet the local age requirement for tobacco products, you may bring in, duty-free, 200 cigarettes and 50 cigars. Check ahead of time with the Canada Customs and Revenue Agency or the Department of Agriculture for policies regarding meat products, seeds, plants, and fruits.

You may send an unlimited number of gifts (only one gift per recipient, however) worth up to C$60 each duty-free to Canada. Label the package UNSOLICITED GIFT—VALUE UNDER $60. Alcohol and tobacco are excluded.

7 **Canada Customs and Revenue Agency** ✉ 2265 St. Laurent Blvd., Ottawa, Ontario K1G 4K3 ☎ 800/ 461-9999 in Canada, 204/983-3500, 506/636-5064 ⊕ www.ccra.gc.ca.

IN NEW ZEALAND

All homeward-bound residents may bring back NZ$700 worth of souvenirs and gifts; passengers may not pool their allowances, and children can claim only the concession on goods intended for their own use. For those 17 or older, the duty-free allowance also includes 4.5 liters of wine or beer; one 1,125-ml bottle of spirits; and either 200 cigarettes, 250 grams of tobacco, 50 cigars, *or* a combination of the three up to 250 grams. Meat products, seeds, plants, and fruits must be declared upon arrival to the Agricultural Services Department.

New Zealand Customs ⊠ Head office: The Customhouse, 17-21 Whitmore St., Box 2218, Wellington ☎ 09/300-5399 or 0800/428-786 ⊕ www.customs.govt.nz.

IN THE U.K.

From countries outside the European Union, including United States, you may bring home, duty-free, 200 cigarettes, 50 cigars, 100 cigarillos, or 250 grams of tobacco; 1 liter of spirits or 2 liters of fortified or sparkling wine or liqueurs; 2 liters of still table wine; 60 ml of perfume; 250 ml of toilet water; plus £145 worth of other goods, including gifts and souvenirs. Prohibited items include meat and dairy products, seeds, plants, and fruits.

HM Customs and Excise ⊠ Portcullis House, 21 Cowbridge Rd. E, Cardiff CF11 9SS ☎ 0845/010-9000 or 0208/929-0152 advice service, 0208/929-6731 or 0208/910-3602 complaints ⊕ www.hmce.gov.uk.

IN THE U.S.

If you decide to cross the border into Mexico, bear in mind that U.S. residents who have been out of the country for at least 48 hours may bring home, for personal use, $800 worth of foreign goods duty-free, as long as they haven't used the $800 allowance or any part of it in the past 30 days. This exemption may include 1 liter of alcohol (for travelers 21 and older), 200 cigarettes, and 100 non-Cuban cigars. Family members from the same household who are traveling together may pool their $800 personal exemptions. For fewer than 48 hours, the duty-free allowance drops to $200, which may include 50 cigarettes, 10 non-Cuban cigars, and 150 ml of alcohol (or 150 ml of perfume containing alcohol). The $200 allowance cannot be combined with other individuals' exemptions, and if you exceed it, the full value of all the goods will be taxed. Antiques, which U.S. Customs and Border Protection defines as objects more than 100 years old, enter duty-free, as do original works of art done entirely by hand, including paintings, drawings, and sculptures. This doesn't apply to folk art or handicrafts, which are in general dutiable.

You may also send packages home duty-free, with a limit of one parcel per addressee per day (except alcohol or tobacco products or perfume worth more than $5). You can mail up to $200 worth of goods for personal use; label the package PERSONAL USE and attach a list of its contents and their retail value. If the package contains your used personal belongings, mark it AMERICAN GOODS RETURNED to avoid paying duties. You may send up to $100 worth of goods as a gift; mark the package UNSOLICITED GIFT. Mailed items do not affect your duty-free allowance on your return.

To avoid paying duty on foreign-made high-ticket items you already own and will take on your trip, register them with Customs before you leave the country. Consider filing a Certificate of Registration for laptops, cameras, watches, and other digital devices identified with serial numbers or other permanent markings; you can keep the certificate for other trips. Otherwise, bring a sales receipt or insurance form to show that you owned the item before you left the United States.

For more about duties, restricted items, and other information about international travel, check out U.S. Customs and Border Protection's online brochure, *Know Before You Go.*

U.S. Customs and Border Protection ⊠ For inquiries and equipment registration, 1300 Pennsylvania Ave. NW, Washington, DC 20229 ⊕ www.cbp.gov ☎ 877/287-8667, 202/354-1000 ⊠ For complaints, Customer Satisfaction Unit, 1300 Pennsylvania Ave. NW, Room 5.2C, Washington, DC 20229.

DISABILITIES & ACCESSIBILITY

California is a national leader in making attractions and facilities accessible to people with disabilities.

LODGING

Despite the Americans with Disabilities Act, the definition of accessibility seems to differ from hotel to hotel. Some properties may be accessible by ADA standards for people with mobility problems but not for people with hearing or vision impairments, for example.

If you have mobility problems, ask for the lowest floor on which accessible services are offered. If you have a hearing impairment, check whether the hotel has devices to alert you visually to the ring of the telephone, a knock at the door, and a fire/emergency alarm. Some hotels provide these devices without charge. Discuss your needs with hotel personnel if this equipment isn't available, so that a staff member can personally alert you in the event of an emergency.

If you're bringing a guide dog, get authorization ahead of time and write down the name of the person with whom you spoke.

PARKS

The National Park Service provides a Golden Access Passport for all national parks free of charge to those who are medically blind or have a permanent disability; the passport covers the entry fee for the holder and anyone accompanying the holder in the same private vehicle as well as a 50% discount on camping and various other user fees. Apply for the passport in person at a national recreation facility that charges an entrance fee; proof of disability is required.

RESERVATIONS

When discussing accessibility with an operator or reservations agent, ask hard questions. Are there any stairs, inside *or* out? Are there grab bars next to the toilet *and* in the shower/tub? How wide is the doorway to the room? To the bathroom? For the most extensive facilities meeting the latest legal specifications, opt for newer accommodations. If you reserve through a toll-free number, consider also calling the hotel's local number to confirm the information from the central reservations office. Get confirmation in writing when you can.

TRANSPORTATION

Hertz and Avis (⇨ Car Rental) are able to supply cars modified for those with disabilities, but they require one to two days' advance notice. Discounts are available for travelers with disabilities on Amtrak (⇨ Train Travel). On Greyhound (⇨ Bus Travel), your companion can ride free.

🛂 Complaints **Aviation Consumer Protection Division** (⇨ Air Travel) for airline-related problems.

Departmental Office of Civil Rights ✉ For general inquiries, U.S. Department of Transportation, S-30, 400 7th St. SW, Room 10215, Washington, DC 20590 ☎ 202/366-4648 🖷 202/366-9371 ⊕ www.dot.gov/ost/docr/index.htm. **Disability Rights Section** ✉ NYAV, U.S. Department of Justice, Civil Rights Division, 950 Pennsylvania Ave. NW, Washington, DC 20530 ☎ ADA information line 202/514-0301, 800/514-0301, 202/514-0383 TTY, 800/514-0383 TTY ⊕ www.ada.gov. **U.S. Department of Transportation Hotline** ☎ For disability-related air-travel problems, 800/778-4838 or 800/455-9880 TTY.

TRAVEL AGENCIES

In the United States, the Americans with Disabilities Act requires that travel firms serve the needs of all travelers. Some agencies specialize in working with people with disabilities.

🛂 Travelers with Mobility Problems **Access Adventures/B. Roberts Travel** ☎ 206 Chestnut Ridge Rd., Scottsville, NY 14624 ☎ 585/889-9096 ⊕ www.brobertstravel.com ✍ dltravel@prodigy.net, run by a former physical-rehabilitation counselor. **Accessible Vans of America** ✉ 9 Spielman Rd., Fairfield, NJ 07004 ☎ 877/282-8267 or 888/282-8267, 973/808-9709 reservations 🖷 973/808-9713 ⊕ www.accessiblevans.com. **CareVacations** ✉ No. 5, 5110-50 Ave., Leduc, Alberta, Canada, T9E 6V4 ☎ 780/986-6404 or 877/478-7827 🖷 780/986-8332 ⊕ www.carevacations.com, for group tours and cruise vacations. **Flying Wheels Travel** ✉ 143 W. Bridge St., Box 382, Owatonna, MN 55060 ☎ 507/451-5005 🖷 507/451-1685 ⊕ www.flyingwheelstravel.com.

🛂 Travelers with Developmental Disabilities **New Directions** ✉ 5276 Hollister Ave., Suite 207, Santa Barbara, CA 93111 ☎ 805/967-2841 or 888/967-2841 🖷 805/964-7344 ⊕ www.newdirectionstravel.com. **Sprout** ✉ 893 Amsterdam Ave., New York, NY 10025 ☎ 212/222-9575 or 888/222-9575 🖷 212/222-9768 ⊕ www.gosprout.org.

DISCOUNTS & DEALS

Be a smart shopper and compare all your options before making decisions. A plane ticket bought with a promotional coupon from travel clubs, coupon books, and direct-mail offers or purchased on the Internet may not be cheaper than the least expensive fare from a discount ticket agency. And always keep in mind that what you get is just as important as what you save.

DISCOUNT RESERVATIONS

To save money, look into discount reservations services with Web sites and toll-free numbers, which use their buying power to get a better price on hotels, airline tickets (⇨ Air Travel), even car rentals. When booking a room, always call the hotel's local toll-free number (if one is available) rather than the central reservations number—you'll often get a better price. Always ask about special packages or corporate rates.

Airline Tickets Air 4 Less ☎ 800/AIR4LESS; low-fare specialist.

Hotel Rooms Accommodations Express ☎ 800/444-7666 or 800/277-1064 ⊕ www.acex. net. **Central Reservation Service (CRS)** ☎ 800/ 555-7555 or 800/548-3311 ⊕ www.crshotels.com. **Hotels.com** ☎ 800/246-8357 ⊕ www.hotels.com. **Quikbook** ☎ 800/789-9887 ⊕ www.quikbook.com. **Steigenberger Reservation Service** ☎ 800/223-5652 ⊕ www.srs-worldhotels.com. **Turbotrip.com** ☎ 800/473-7829 ⊕ www.turbotrip.com.

PACKAGE DEALS

Don't confuse packages and guided tours. When you buy a package, you travel on your own, just as though you had planned the trip yourself. Fly–drive packages, which combine airfare and car rental, are often a good deal. In cities, ask the local visitor's bureau about hotel and local transportation packages that include tickets to major museum exhibits or other special events.

DIVERS ALERT

Do not fly within 24 hours of scuba diving.

EATING & DRINKING

California has led the pack in bringing natural and organic foods to the forefront of American cooking. Though rooted in European cuisine, California cooking has incorporated strong Asian and Latin influences. Wherever you go, you're likely to find that dishes are made with fresh produce and other local ingredients.

The restaurants we list are the cream of the crop in each price category. Properties indicated by an ✕⊡ are lodging establishments whose restaurant warrants a special trip. Lunch is typically served 11:30–2:30, and dinner service in most restaurants begins at 5:30 and ends at 10. Some restaurants in larger cities stay open until midnight or later, but in smaller towns evening service may end as early as 8.

CATEGORY	COST
$$$$	over $30
$$$	$23–$30
$$	$16–$22
$	$10–$15
¢	under $10

Prices are for a main course at dinner, excluding tip and tax.

MEALTIMES

Unless otherwise noted, the restaurants listed in this guide are open daily for lunch and dinner.

RESERVATIONS & DRESS

Reservations are always a good idea; we mention them only when they're essential or not accepted. Book as far ahead as you can, and reconfirm as soon as you arrive. (Large parties should always call ahead to check the reservations policy.) We mention dress only when men are required to wear a jacket or a jacket and tie.

WINE, BEER & SPIRITS

If you like wine, your trip to California won't be complete unless you try a few of the local vintages. Throughout the state, most famously in the Napa and Sonoma valleys, you can visit wineries, most of which have tasting rooms and many of which offer tours. The legal drinking age is 21.

ECOTOURISM

When traveling in wilderness areas and parks, remember to tread lightly. Do not drive an SUV through sensitive habitats, and pack out what you pack in. Many remote camping areas do not provide waste disposal. It's a good idea to bring plastic bags to store refuse until you can dispose of it properly. Recycling programs are abundant in California, and trash at many state and national parks is sorted. Look for appropriately labeled garbage contain-crs. Numerous ecotours are available in California (⇨ Tours & Packages).

GAY & LESBIAN TRAVEL

San Francisco, Los Angeles, West Hollywood, San Diego, and Palm Springs are among the California cities with the most visible lesbian and gay communities. Though it is usually safe to be visibly "out" in many areas, you should always use common sense when in unfamiliar places. Gay bashings still occur in both urban and rural areas. For details about the gay and lesbian scene, consult *Fodor's Gay Guide to the USA* (available in bookstores everywhere).

LOCAL INFORMATION

Many California cities large and small have lesbian and gay publications available in sidewalk racks and at bars, bookstores, and other social spaces; most have extensive events and information listings.
🗐 Community Centers **Billy DeFrank Lesbian & Gay Community Center** ✉ 938 The Alameda, San Jose 95126 ☎ 408/293-2429 ⊕ www.defrank.org. **L.A. Gay and Lesbian Center** ✉ 1625 N. Schrader Blvd., Los Angeles 90028 ☎ 323/993-7400 ⊕ www.laglc.org. **Lambda Community Center** ✉ 1927 L St., Sacramento 95814 ☎ 916/442-0185 ⊕ www.lambda-sacramento.com. **Lavender Youth Recreation & Information Center** ✉ 127 Collingwood St., San Francisco 94114 ☎ 415/703-6150, 415/863-3636 for hotline ⊕ www.lyric.org. **Lesbian and Gay Men's Community Center** ✉ 3909 Centre St., San Diego 92103 ☎ 619/692-2077 ⊕ www.thecentersd.org. **Pacific Center Lesbian, Gay and Bisexual Switchboard** ✉ 2712 Telegraph Ave., Berkeley 94705 ☎ 510/548-8283 ⊕ www.pacificcenter.org.

The Center (San Francisco Lesbian, Gay, Bisexual, Transgender Community Center) ✉ 1800 Market St. ☎ 415/865-5555 ⊕ www.sfgaycenter.org.
🗐 Local Publications **Bay Area Reporter** ☎ 415/861-5019. **Bottom Line** ☎ 760/323-0552. **Frontiers** ☎ 323/848-2222. **Update** ☎ 619/299-0500.
🗐 Gay- & Lesbian-Friendly Travel Agencies **Different Roads Travel** ✉ 8383 Wilshire Blvd., Suite 520, Beverly Hills, CA 90211 ☎ 323/651-5557 or 800/429-8747 (Ext. 14 for both) 🖨 323/651-5454 ✒ lgernert@tzell.com. **Kennedy Travel** ✉ 130 W. 42nd St., Suite 401, New York, NY 10036 ☎ 212/840-8659, 800/237-7433 🖨 212/730-2269 ⊕ www.kennedytravel.com. **Now, Voyager** ✉ 4406 18th St.,

San Francisco, CA 94114 ☎ 415/626-1169 or 800/255-6951 🖨 415/626-8626 ⊕ www.nowvoyager.com. **Skylink Travel and Tour/Flying Dutchmen Travel** ✉ 1455 N. Dutton Ave., Suite A, Santa Rosa, CA 95401 ☎ 707/546-9888 or 800/225-5759 🖨 707/636-0951; serving lesbian travelers.

HOLIDAYS

Many traditional businesses are closed the following days, but tourist attractions, as well as some shops and restaurants, are usually open except on Thanksgiving, Christmas, and New Year's Day.

Major national holidays are New Year's Day (Jan. 1); Martin Luther King Day (3rd Mon. in Jan.); Presidents' Day (3rd Mon. in Feb.); Memorial Day (last Mon. in May); Independence Day (July 4); Labor Day (1st Mon. in Sept.); Columbus Day (2nd Mon. in Oct.); Thanksgiving Day (4th Thurs. in Nov.); Christmas Eve and Christmas Day (Dec. 24 and 25); and New Year's Eve (Dec. 31).

INSURANCE

The most useful travel-insurance plan is a comprehensive policy that includes coverage for trip cancellation and interruption, default, trip delay, and medical expenses (with a waiver for preexisting conditions).

Without insurance you'll lose all or most of your money if you cancel your trip, regardless of the reason. Default insurance covers you if your tour operator, airline, or cruise line goes out of business—the chances of which have been increasing. Trip-delay covers expenses that arise because of bad weather or mechanical delays. Study the fine print when comparing policies.

U.K. residents can buy a travel-insurance policy valid for most vacations taken during the year in which it's purchased (but check preexisting-condition coverage).

Always buy travel policies directly from the insurance company; if you buy them from a cruise line, airline, or tour operator that goes out of business you probably won't be covered for the agency or operator's default, a major risk. Before making any purchase, review your existing health and home-owner's policies to find what they cover away from home.

Travel Insurers In the U.S.: **Access America** ✉ 2805 N. Parham Rd., Richmond, VA 23294 ☎ 800/284–8300 📠 804/673–1491 or 800/346–9265 🌐 www.accessamerica.com. **Travel Guard International** ✉ 1145 Clark St., Stevens Point, WI 54481 ☎ 715/345–0505 or 800/826–1300 📠 800/955–8785 🌐 www.travelguard.com.

FOR INTERNATIONAL TRAVELERS

For information on customs restrictions, *see* Customs & Duties.

CAR RENTAL

When picking up a rental car, non-U.S. residents need a reservation voucher for any prepaid reservations that were made in the traveler's home country, a passport, a driver's license, and a travel policy that covers each driver.

CAR TRAVEL

Highways are well paved. Interstate highways—limited-access, multilane highways whose numbers are prefixed by "I–"—are the fastest routes. Interstates with three-digit numbers encircle urban areas, which may have other limited-access expressways, freeways, and parkways as well. Tolls may be levied at bridge crossings. So-called U.S. highways and state highways are not necessarily limited-access but may have several lanes.

Along larger highways, roadside stops with restrooms, fast-food restaurants, and sundries stores are well spaced. State police and tow trucks patrol major highways and lend assistance. If your car breaks down on an interstate, pull onto the shoulder and wait for help, or have your passengers wait while you walk to an emergency phone. If you carry a cell phone, dial 911, noting your location on the small green roadside mileage markers.

Motorists drive on the right side of the road in the United States. Do obey speed limits posted along roads and highways. Watch for lower limits in small towns and on back roads. California requires front-seat passengers to wear seat belts. On weekdays between 6 and 10 AM and again between 3 and 7 PM expect heavy traffic in urban and suburban areas. To encourage carpooling, some freeways have special lanes for so-called high-occupancy vehicles (HOV)—cars carrying more than one or two passengers, depending on where you are. The pavement is marked with a white diamond. If you do not meet the criteria for travel in these lanes and you get stopped by the police, you can get fined upwards of $300 and receive a point on your license.

In California you may turn right at a red light after stopping if there is no oncoming traffic unless a sign forbids you to do so. You may also turn left on red between two one-way streets. But when in doubt, wait for the green. Be alert for one-way streets, "no left turn" intersections, and blocks closed to car traffic. Bookstores, gas stations, convenience stores, and rest stops sell maps (about $3) and multiregion road atlases (about $10). For more information on driving in California, *see* Car Travel, *above*.

CONSULATES & EMBASSIES

Australia ✉ Century Plaza Towers, 2049 Century Park E, 19th fl., Los Angeles 90067, ☎ 310/229–4800 📠 310/277–5620 ✉ 625 Market St., Suite 200, San Francisco 94105 ☎ 415/536–1970.

Canada ✉ 550 S. Hope St., 9th fl., Los Angeles 90071–2627 ☎ 213/346–2700 ✉ 555 Montgomery St., Suite 1288 ☎ 415/834–3180.

New Zealand ✉ 12400 Wilshire Blvd., Suite 1150, Los Angeles 90025 ☎ 310/207–1605 ✉ 1 Maritime Plaza, Suite 400, San Francisco 94111.

United Kingdom ✉ 11766 Wilshire Blvd., Suite 1200, Los Angeles 90025 ☎ 310/481–0031 ✉ 1 Sansome St., Suite 850, San Francisco 94104 ☎ 415/617–1300.

CURRENCY

The dollar is the basic unit of U.S. currency. It has 100 cents. Coins are the copper penny (1¢); the silvery nickel (5¢), dime (10¢), quarter (25¢), and half-dollar (50¢); and the golden $1 coin, replacing a now-rare silver dollar. Bills are denominated $1, $5, $10, $20, $50, and $100, all mostly green and identical in size; designs and background tints vary. In addition, you may come across a $2 bill, but the chances are slim. The exchange rate at this writing is US$1.83 per British pound, $.73

per Canadian dollar, $.69 per Australian dollar, and $.63 per New Zealand dollar.

ELECTRICITY

The U.S. standard is AC, 110 volts/60 cycles. Plugs have two flat pins set parallel to each other.

EMERGENCIES

For police, fire, or ambulance, **dial 911** (0 in rural areas).

INSURANCE

Britons and Australians need extra medical coverage when traveling overseas.

🔢 Insurance Information In the U.K.: **Association of British Insurers** ✉ 51 Gresham St., London EC2V 7HQ ☎ 020/7600-3333 🖷 020/7696-8999 ⊕ www.abi.org.uk. In Australia: **Insurance Council of Australia** ✉ Insurance Enquiries and Complaints, Level 12, Box 561, Collins St. W, Melbourne, VIC 8007 ☎ 1300/780808 or 03/9629-4109 🖷 03/9621-2060 ⊕ www.iecltd.com.au. In Canada: **RBC Insurance** ✉ 6880 Financial Dr., Mississauga, Ontario L5N 7Y5 ☎ 800/668-4342 or 905/816-2400 🖷 905/813-4704 ⊕ www.rbcinsurance.com. In New Zealand: **Insurance Council of New Zealand** ✉ Level 7, 111-115 Customhouse Quay, Box 474, Wellington ☎ 04/472-5230 🖷 04/473-3011 ⊕ www.icnz.org.nz.

MAIL & SHIPPING

You can buy stamps and aerograms and send letters and parcels in post offices. Stamp-dispensing machines can occasionally be found in airports, bus and train stations, office buildings, drugstores, and the like. You can also deposit mail in the stout, dark blue, steel bins at strategic locations everywhere and in the mail chutes of large buildings; pickup schedules are posted. You can deposit packages at public collection boxes as long as the parcels are affixed with proper postage and weigh less than one pound. Packages weighing one or more pounds must be taken to a post office or handed to a postal carrier.

For mail sent within the United States, you need a 37¢ stamp for first-class letters weighing up to 1 ounce (23¢ for each additional ounce) and 23¢ for postcards. You pay 80¢ for 1-ounce airmail letters and 70¢ for airmail postcards to most other countries; to Canada and Mexico, you need a 60¢ stamp for a 1-ounce letter

and 50¢ for a postcard. An aerogram—a single sheet of lightweight blue paper that folds into its own envelope, stamped for overseas airmail—costs 70¢.

To receive mail on the road, have it sent c/o General Delivery at your destination's main post office (use the correct five-digit ZIP code). You must pick up mail in person within 30 days and show a driver's license or passport.

PASSPORTS & VISAS

When traveling internationally, carry your passport even if you don't need one (it's always the best form of ID) and make two photocopies of the data page (one for someone at home and another for you, carried separately from your passport). If you lose your passport, promptly call the nearest embassy or consulate and the local police.

Visitor visas aren't necessary for Canadian or European Union citizens, or for citizens of Australia who are staying fewer than 90 days.

🔢 Australian Citizens **Passports Australia** ☎ 131-232 ⊕ www.passports.gov.au. **United States Consulate General** ✉ MLC Centre, Level 59, 19-29 Martin Pl., Sydney, NSW 2000 ☎ 02/9373-9200, 1902/941-641 fee-based visa-inquiry line ⊕ usembassy-australia.state.gov/sydney.

🔢 Canadian Citizens **Passport Office** ✉ To mail in applications: 200 Promenade du Portage, Hull, Québec J8X 4B7 ☎ 819/994-3500 or 800/567-6868, 866/255-7655 TTY ⊕ www.ppt.gc.ca.

🔢 New Zealand Citizens **New Zealand Passports Office** ✉ For applications and information, Level 3, Boulcott House, 47 Boulcott St., Wellington ☎ 0800/22-5050 or 04/474-8100 ⊕ www.passports.govt.nz. **Embassy of the United States** ✉ 29 Fitzherbert Terr., Thorndon, Wellington ☎ 04/462-6000 ⊕ usembassy.org.nz. **U.S. Consulate General** ✉ Citibank Bldg., 3rd fl., 23 Customs St. E, Auckland ☎ 09/303-2724 ⊕ usembassy.org.nz.

🔢 U.K. Citizens **U.K. Passport Service** ☎ 0870/521-0410 ⊕ www.passport.gov.uk. **American Consulate General** ✉ Danesfort House, 223 Stranmillis Rd., Belfast, Northern Ireland BT9 5GR ☎ 028/9032-8239 🖷 028/9024-8482 ⊕ usembassy.org.uk. **American Embassy** ✉ For visa and immigration information or to submit a visa application via mail (enclose an SASE), Consular Information Unit, 24 Grosvenor Sq., London W1 1AE ☎ 09055/444-546

for visa information (per-minute charges), 0207/
499–9000 main switchboard ⊕ www.usembassy.
org.uk.

TELEPHONES

All U.S. telephone numbers consist of a
three-digit area code and a seven-digit
local number. Within many local calling
areas, you dial only the seven-digit number. Within some area codes, you must dial
"1" first for calls outside the local area. To
call between area-code regions, dial "1"
then all 10 digits; the same goes for calls
to numbers prefixed by "800," "888,"
"866," and "877"—all toll free. For calls
to numbers preceded by "900" you must
pay—usually dearly.

For international calls, dial "011" followed by the country code and the local
number. For help, dial "0" and ask for an
overseas operator. The country code is 61
for Australia, 64 for New Zealand, 44 for
the United Kingdom. Calling Canada is
the same as calling within the United
States. Most local phone books list country codes and U.S. area codes. The country
code for the United States is 1.

For operator assistance, dial "0." To obtain someone's phone number, call directory assistance at 555–1212 or
occasionally 411 (free at many public
phones). To have the person you're calling
foot the bill, phone collect; dial "0" instead of "1" before the 10-digit number.

At pay phones, instructions often are
posted. Usually you insert coins in a slot
(usually 25¢–50¢ for local calls) and wait
for a steady tone before dialing. When
you call long-distance, the operator tells
you how much to insert; prepaid phone
cards, widely available in various denominations, are easier. Call the number on the
back, punch in the card's personal identification number when prompted, then dial
your number.

🔢 Long-Distance Carriers **AT&T** ☎ 800/225–5288.
MCI ☎ 800/888–8000. **Sprint** ☎ 800/366–2255.

LODGING

The lodgings we list are the cream of the
crop in each price category. We always list
the facilities that are available, but we
don't specify whether they cost extra;
when pricing accommodations, always ask
what's included and what costs extra.

Properties are assigned price categories
based on the range between their least and
most expensive standard double room at
high season (excluding holidays) to the
most expensive.

Properties marked ✕▣ are lodging establishments whose restaurants warrant a
special trip.

Assume that hotels operate on the European Plan (EP, with no meals) unless we
specify that they use the Continental Plan
(CP, with a continental breakfast), Breakfast Plan (BP, with a full breakfast), Modified American Plan (MAP, with breakfast
and dinner), or the Full American Plan
(FAP, with all meals).

PRICES

Properties are assigned price categories
based on the range from their least-expen-
sive standard double room at high season
(excluding holidays) to the most expensive.

CATEGORY	COST
$$$$	over $250
$$$	$176–$250
$$	$121–$175
$	$90–$120
¢	under $90

*Prices are for two people in a standard double
room in high season, excluding service charges
and tax. Hotel taxes vary from city to city, but
the average is around 10%, with higher rates in
major urban areas.*

APARTMENT & HOUSE RENTALS

If you want a home base that's roomy
enough for a family and comes with cooking facilities, consider a furnished rental.
These can save you money, especially if
you're traveling with a group. Home-exchange directories sometimes list rentals as
well as exchanges.

🔢 International Agents **Hideaways International**
✉ 767 Islington St., Portsmouth, NH 03801 ☎ 603/
430–4433 or 800/843–4433 🖷 603/430–4444
⊕ www.hideaways.com, annual membership $145.
Vacation Home Rentals Worldwide ✉ 235 Kensington Ave., Norwood, NJ 07648 ☎ 201/767–9393 or
800/633–3284 🖷 201/767–5510 ⊕ www.vhrww.com.

CAMPING

California offers numerous camping options, from family campgrounds with all the amenities to secluded hike-in campsites with no facilities. Some are operated by the state, others are on federal land, and still others are private. Rules vary for each. You can camp anywhere in a national forest, but in a national park, you must use only specific sites. Whenever possible, book well in advance, especially if your trip will be in summer or on a weekend. Contact the National Parks Reservation Service to reserve a campsite in a national park. ReserveUSA handles reservations for campgrounds administered by the U.S. Forest Service and the Army Corps of Engineers; ReserveAmerica handles reservations for many of the campgrounds in California state parks. On their Web sites you can search for locations, view campground maps, check availability, learn rules and regulations, and find driving directions.

🔳 Reservations **National Parks Reservation Service** ☎ 800/436-7275 or 800/365-2267 ⊕ reservations.nps.gov. **ReserveAmerica** ☎ 877/444-6777 ⊕ www.reserveamerica.com. **ReserveUSA** ☎ 800/444-7275 ⊕ www.reserveusa.com.

HOME EXCHANGES

If you would like to exchange your home for someone else's, join a home-exchange organization, which will send you its updated listings of available exchanges for a year and will include your own listing in at least one of them. It's up to you to make specific arrangements.

🔳 Exchange Clubs **HomeLink International** ⊕ Box 47747, Tampa, FL 33647 ☎ 813/975-9825 or 800/638-3841 🖷 813/910-8144 ⊕ www.homelink. org; $110 yearly for a listing, online access, and catalog; $70 without catalog. **Intervac U.S.** ⊠ 30 Corte San Fernando, Tiburon, CA 94920 ☎ 800/756-4663 🖷 415/435-7440 ⊕ www.intervacus.com; $125 yearly for a listing, online access, and a catalog; $65 without catalog.

HOSTELS

No matter what your age, you can save on lodging costs by staying at hostels. In some 4,500 locations in more than 70 countries around the world, Hostelling International (HI), the umbrella group for a number of national youth-hostel associations, offers single-sex, dorm-style beds and, at many hostels, rooms for couples and family accommodations. Membership in any HI national hostel association, open to travelers of all ages, allows you to stay in HI-affiliated hostels at member rates; one-year membership is about $28 for adults (C$35 for a two-year minimum membership in Canada, £14 in the U.K., A$52 in Australia, and NZ$40 in New Zealand); hostels charge about $10–$30 per night. Members have priority if the hostel is full; they're also eligible for discounts around the world, even on rail and bus travel in some countries.

🔳 Organizations **Hostelling International–USA** ⊠ 8401 Colesville Rd., Suite 600, Silver Spring, MD 20910 ☎ 301/495-1240 🖷 301/495-6697 ⊕ www. hiusa.org. **Hostelling International–Canada** ⊠ 205 Catherine St., Suite 400, Ottawa, Ontario K2P 1C3 ☎ 613/237-7884 or 800/663-5777 🖷 613/237-7868 ⊕ www.hihostels.ca. **YHA England and Wales** ⊠ Trevelyan House, Dimple Rd., Matlock, Derbyshire DE4 3YH, U.K. ☎ 0870/870-8808, 0870/770-8868, 0162/959-2600 🖷 0870/770-6127 ⊕ www.yha.org.uk. **YHA Australia** ⊠ 422 Kent St., Sydney, NSW 2001 ☎ 02/9261-1111 🖷 02/9261-1969 ⊕ www.yha.com.au. **YHA New Zealand** ⊠ Level 1, Moorhouse City, 166 Moorhouse Ave., Box 436, Christchurch ☎ 03/379-9970 or 0800/278-299 🖷 03/365-4476 ⊕ www.yha.org.nz.

HOTELS

All hotels listed have private bath unless otherwise noted.

Most major hotel chains are represented in California. All hotels listed have private bath unless otherwise noted. Make any special needs known when you book your reservation. Guarantee your room with a credit card, or many hotels will automatically cancel your reservations if you don't show up by 4 PM. Many hotels, like airlines, overbook. It is best to **reconfirm your reservation directly with the hotel on the morning of your arrival date.**

🔳 Toll-Free Numbers **Best Western** ☎ 800/528-1234 ⊕ www.bestwestern.com. **Choice** ☎ 800/424-6423 ⊕ www.choicehotels.com. **Clarion** ☎ 800/424-6423 ⊕ www.choicehotels.com. **Comfort Inn** ☎ 800/424-6423 ⊕ www.choicehotels.com. **Days Inn** ☎ 800/325-2525 ⊕ www.daysinn.com. **Dou-**

bletree Hotels ☎ 800/222-8733 ⊕ www. doubletree.com. **Embassy Suites** ☎ 800/362-2779 ⊕ www.embassysuites.com. **Fairfield Inn** ☎ 800/228-2800 ⊕ www.marriott.com. **Four Seasons** ☎ 800/332-3442 ⊕ www.fourseasons.com. **Hilton** ☎ 800/445-8667 ⊕ www.hilton.com. **Holiday Inn** ☎ 800/465-4329 ⊕ www.ichotelsgroup.com. **Howard Johnson** ☎ 800/446-4656 ⊕ www.hojo.com. **Hyatt Hotels & Resorts** ☎ 800/233-1234 ⊕ www.hyatt.com. **Inter-Continental** ☎ 800/327-0200 ⊕ www.ichotelsgroup.com. **La Quinta** ☎ 800/531-5900 ⊕ www.lq.com. **Marriott** ☎ 800/228-9290 ⊕ www.marriott.com. **Nikko Hotels International** ☎ 800/645-5687 ⊕ www.nikkohotels.com. **Omni** ☎ 800/843-6664 ⊕ www.omnihotels.com. **Quality Inn** ☎ 800/424-6423 ⊕ www.choicehotels.com. **Radisson** ☎ 800/333-3333 ⊕ www.radisson.com. **Ramada** ☎ 800/228-2828, 800/854-7854 international reservations ⊕ www.ramada.com or www.ramadahotels.com. **Red Lion and WestCoast Hotels and Inns** ☎ 800/733-5466 ⊕ www.redlion.com. **Renaissance Hotels & Resorts** ☎ 800/468-3571 ⊕ www.renaissancehotels.com/. **Ritz-Carlton** ☎ 800/241-3333 ⊕ www.ritzcarlton.com. **Sheraton** ☎ 800/325-3535 ⊕ www.starwood.com/sheraton. **Sleep Inn** ☎ 800/424-6423 ⊕ www.choicehotels.com. **Westin Hotels & Resorts** ☎ 800/228-3000 ⊕ www.starwood.com/westin. **Wyndham Hotels & Resorts** ☎ 800/822-4200 ⊕ www.wyndham.com.

MEDIA

NEWSPAPERS & MAGAZINES

California's major daily newspapers, the *Los Angeles Times,* the *San Diego Union-Tribune,* and the *San Francisco Chronicle,* maintain up-to-the-minute Web sites. The state's weekly newspapers are usually the best source of arts and entertainment information, from what shows are on the boards to who's playing the clubs. Visit the Web sites of the *L.A. Weekly,* the *San Diego Reader,* the *San Francisco Bay Guardian,* the *San Jose Metro* (MetroActive), and *SF Weekly* for the latest information on events in your destination.

🗗 **Web Sites** *L.A. Weekly* ⊕ www.laweekly.com. *Los Angeles Times* ⊕ www.latimes.com. **MetroActive** ⊕ www.metroactive.com. *San Diego Reader* ⊕ www.sdreader.com. *San Diego Union-Tribune* ⊕ www.signonsandiego.com. *San Francisco Bay Guardian* ⊕ www.sfbayguardian.com. *San Fran-* *cisco Chronicle* ⊕ www.sfgate.com. *SF Weekly* ⊕ www.sfweekly.com.

MONEY MATTERS

Los Angeles and San Francisco tend to be expensive cities to visit, and rates at coastal and desert resorts are almost as high. A day's admission to a major theme park can run upward of $45 a head, hotel rates average $150–$250 a night (though you can find cheaper places), and dinners at even moderately priced restaurants often cost $20–$40 per person. Costs in the Gold Country, the Far North, and the Death Valley/Mojave Desert region are considerably less—many fine Gold Country B&Bs charge around $100 a night, and some motels in the Far North and the Mojave charge $50–$70.

Prices throughout this guide are given for adults. Substantially reduced fees are almost always available for children, students, and senior citizens. For information on taxes, *see* Taxes.

ATMS

ATMs are readily available throughout California. If you withdraw cash from a bank other than your own, expect to pay a fee of up to $2.50. If you're going to very remote areas of the mountains or deserts, take some extra cash with you or find out ahead of time if you can pay with credit cards.

CREDIT CARDS

Throughout this guide, the following abbreviations are used: **AE,** American Express; **D,** Discover; **DC,** Diners Club; **MC,** MasterCard; and **V,** Visa.

🗗 **Reporting Lost Cards** **American Express** ☎ 800/992-3404. **Diners Club** ☎ 800/234-6377. **Discover** ☎ 800/347-2683. **MasterCard** ☎ 800/622-7747. **Visa** ☎ 800/847-2911.

NATIONAL PARKS

Look into discount passes to save money on park entrance fees. For $50, the National Parks Pass admits you (and any passengers in your private vehicle) to all national parks, monuments, and recreation areas, as well as other sites run by the National Park Service, for a year. (In parks that charge per person, the pass admits you, your spouse and children, and your parents, when you arrive together.) Camping and parking are extra. The $15 Golden Eagle Pass, a hologram you affix to your National Parks Pass, functions as an upgrade, granting entry to all sites run by the NPS, the U.S. Fish and Wildlife Service, the U.S. Forest Service, and the Bureau of Land Management. The upgrade, which expires with the parks pass, is sold by most national-park, Fish-and-Wildlife, and BLM fee stations. A major percentage of the proceeds from pass sales funds National Parks projects.

Both the Golden Age Passport ($10), for U.S. citizens or permanent residents who are 62 and older, and the Golden Access Passport (free), for persons with disabilities, entitle holders (and any passengers in their private vehicles) to lifetime free entry to all national parks, plus 50% off fees for the use of many park facilities and services. (The discount doesn't always apply to companions.) To obtain them, you must show proof of age and of U.S. citizenship or permanent residency—such as a U.S. passport, driver's license, or birth certificate—and, if requesting Golden Access, proof of disability. The Golden Age and Golden Access passes are available only at NPS-run sites that charge an entrance fee. The National Parks Pass is also available by mail and via the Internet.

🗺 **National Park Foundation** ✉ 11 Dupont Circle NW, 6th fl., Washington, DC 20036 ☎ 202/238-4200 ⊕ www.nationalparks.org. **National Park Service** ✉ National Park Service/Department of Interior, 1849 C St. NW, Washington, DC 20240 ☎ 202/208-6843 ⊕ www.nps.gov. **National Parks Conservation Association** ✉ 1300 19th St. NW, Suite 300, Washington, DC 20036 ☎ 202/223-6722 ⊕ www.npca.org. 🗺 **Passes by Mail & Online National Park Foundation** ⊕ www.nationalparks.org. **National Parks Pass** National Park Foundation ✆ Box 34108, Washington, DC 20043 ☎ 888/467-2757 ⊕ www.nationalparks.org; include a check or money order payable to the National Park Service, plus $3.95 for shipping and handling (allow 8 to 13 business days from date of receipt for pass delivery), or call for passes.

PACKING

When packing for a California vacation, prepare for changes in temperature. Take along sweaters, jackets, and clothes for layering as your best insurance for coping with variations in temperature. Know that San Francisco and other coastal towns can be chilly at any time of the year, especially in summer, when the fog descends in the afternoon. Even when it's chilly, though, it's smart to bring a bathing suit; many lodgings have heated pools, spas, and saunas. Casual dressing is a hallmark of the California lifestyle, but in the evening men will need a jacket and tie at more formal restaurants, and women will be most comfortable in something dressier than sightseeing garb. Check *Fodor's How to Pack* (available in bookstores everywhere) for more tips.

In your carry-on luggage, pack an extra pair of eyeglasses or contact lenses and enough of any medication you take to last a few days longer than the entire trip. You may also ask your doctor to write a spare prescription using the drug's generic name, as brand names may vary from country to country. In luggage to be checked, **never pack prescription drugs, valuables, or undeveloped film.** And don't forget to carry with you the addresses of offices that handle refunds of lost traveler's checks. Check *Fodor's How to Pack* (available at online retailers and bookstores everywhere) for more tips.

To avoid customs and security delays, carry medications in their original packaging. Don't pack any sharp objects in your carry-on luggage, including knives of any size or material, scissors, nail clippers, and corkscrews, or anything else that might arouse suspicion.

To avoid having your checked luggage chosen for hand inspection, don't cram bags full. The U.S. Transportation Security Administration suggests packing shoes on top and placing personal items you don't want touched in clear plastic bags.

CHECKING LUGGAGE

You're allowed to carry aboard one bag and one personal article, such as a purse or a laptop computer. Make sure what you carry on fits under your seat or in the overhead bin. Get to the gate early, so you can board as soon as possible, before the overhead bins fill up.

Baggage allowances vary by carrier, destination, and ticket class. On international flights, you're usually allowed to check two bags weighing up to 70 pounds (32 kilograms) each, although a few airlines allow checked bags of up to 88 pounds (40 kilograms) in first class. Some international carriers don't allow more than 66 pounds (30 kilograms) per bag in business class and 44 pounds (20 kilograms) in economy. On domestic flights, the limit is usually 50 to 70 pounds (23 to 32 kilograms) per bag. In general, carry-on bags shouldn't exceed 40 pounds (18 kilograms). Most airlines won't accept bags that weigh more than 100 pounds (45 kilograms) on domestic or international flights. Expect to pay a fee for baggage that exceeds weight limits. Check baggage restrictions with your carrier before you pack.

Airline liability for baggage is limited to $2,500 per person on flights within the United States. On international flights it amounts to $9.07 per pound or $20 per kilogram for checked baggage (roughly $640 per 70-pound bag), with a maximum of $634.90 per piece, and $400 per passenger for unchecked baggage. You can buy additional coverage at check-in for about $10 per $1,000 of coverage, but it often excludes a rather extensive list of items, shown on your airline ticket.

Before departure, itemize your bags' contents and their worth, and label the bags with your name, address, and phone number. (If you use your home address, cover it so potential thieves can't see it readily.) Include a label inside each bag and **pack a copy of your itinerary.** At check-in, make sure each bag is correctly tagged with the destination airport's three-letter code. Because some checked bags will be opened for hand inspection, the U.S. Transportation Security Administration recommends that you leave luggage unlocked or use the plastic locks offered at check-in. TSA screeners place an inspection notice inside searched bags, which are resealed with a special lock.

If your bag has been searched and contents are missing or damaged, file a claim with the TSA Consumer Response Center as soon as possible. If your bags arrive damaged or fail to arrive at all, file a written report with the airline before leaving the airport.

🖪 **Complaints** U.S. **Transportation Security Administration Contact Center** ☎ 866/289-9673 ⊕ www.tsa.gov.

PASSPORTS & VISAS

If you're planning to make a jaunt down to Mexico, be sure to bring along your passport. The best time to apply for a passport or to renew is in fall and winter. Before any trip, check your passport's expiration date, and, if necessary, renew it as soon as possible.

When traveling internationally, carry your passport even if you don't need one (it's always the best form of ID) and make two photocopies of the data page (one for someone at home and another for you, carried separately from your passport). If you lose your passport, promptly call the nearest embassy or consulate and the local police.

U.S. passport applications for children under age 14 require consent from both parents or legal guardians; both parents must appear together to sign the application. If only one parent appears, he or she must submit a written statement from the other parent authorizing passport issuance for the child. A parent with sole authority must present evidence of it when applying; acceptable documentation includes the child's certified birth certificate listing only the applying parent, a court order specifically permitting this parent's travel with the child, or a death certificate for the nonapplying parent. Application forms and instructions are available on the Web site of the U.S. State Department's Bureau of Consular Affairs (⊕ travel.state.gov).

🖪 U.S. Citizens **National Passport Information Center** ☎ 877/487-2778, 888/874-7793 TDD/TTY ⊕ travel.state.gov.

SENIOR-CITIZEN TRAVEL

To qualify for age-related discounts, mention your senior-citizen status up front when booking hotel reservations (not when checking out) and before you're seated in restaurants (not when paying the bill). Be sure to have identification on hand. When renting a car, ask about promotional car-rental discounts, which can be cheaper than senior-citizen rates.

⚐ Educational Programs **Elderhostel** ✉ 11 Ave. de Lafayette, Boston, MA 02111-1746 ☎ 877/426-8056, 978/323-4141 international callers, 877/426-2167 TTY 🖷 877/426-2166 ⊕ www.elderhostel.org. **Interhostel** ✉ University of New Hampshire, 6 Garrison Ave., Durham, NH 03824 ☎ 603/862-1147 or 800/733-9753 🖷 603/862-1113 ⊕ www.learn.unh.edu.

SMOKING

Smoking is illegal in all California bars and restaurants, except on outdoor patios or in smoking rooms. This law is typically not well enforced and some restaurants and bars do not comply, so take your cues from the locals. Hotels and motels are also decreasing their inventory of smoking rooms; inquire at the time you book your reservation if any are available. In addition, there is a selective tax on cigarettes sold in California, and prices can be as high as $6 per pack. You might want to bring a carton from home.

SPORTS & OUTDOORS

In California you can scale high peaks, hike through sequoia groves, climb boulders in the desert, fish, bike, sail, dive, ski, or golf. Whatever sport you love, you can do it in California.

FISHING

You'll need a license to fish in California. State residents pay $32.80, but nonresidents are charged $88.20 for a one-year license or $32.80 for a 10-day license. Both residents and nonresidents can purchase a two-day license for $16.55. You can purchase them at outlets, such as sporting good stores and bait-and-tackle shops, throughout the state, or from DFG field offices (call for locations). The Web site of the California Department of Fish and Game provides information on fishing zones, licenses, and schedules.

⚐ **Department of Fish and Game; Licensing Dept.** ✉ 3211 S St., Sacramento 95816 ☎ 916/227-2245 ⊕ www.dfg.ca.gov/licensing/fishing/sportfishing.html.

STATE PARKS

California's state parks range from lush coastside recreation areas to ghost towns in the high-mountain deserts of the eastern Sierra Nevada. The extremely useful State Park Web site has a comprehensive list of all them, including facilities lists and campground information.

⚐ **California State Park System** ⌖ Dept. of Parks and Recreation, Box 942896, Sacramento 94296 ☎ 916/653-6995 or 800/777-0369 ✉ info@parks.ca.gov ⊕ www.parks.ca.gov.

STUDENTS IN CALIFORNIA

⚐ IDs & Services **STA Travel** ✉ 10 Downing St., New York, NY 10014 ☎ 212/627-3111, 800/777-0112 24-hr service center 🖷 212/627-3387 ⊕ www.sta.com. **Travel Cuts** ✉ 187 College St., Toronto, Ontario M5T 1P7, Canada ☎ 800/592-2887 in the U.S., 416/979-2406 or 866/246-9762 in Canada 🖷 416/979-8167 ⊕ www.travelcuts.com.

TAXES

Sales tax in California varies from about 7¼% to 8½% and applies to all purchases except for prepackaged food; restaurant food is taxed. Airlines include departure taxes and surcharges in the price of the ticket.

TELEPHONES

Pay phones cost 25¢–50¢ in California.

TIME

California is in the Pacific time zone. Pacific daylight time (PDT) is in effect from early April through late October; the rest of the year the clock is set to Pacific standard time (PST). Clocks are set ahead one hour when daylight saving time begins, back one hour when it ends.

TIPPING

At restaurants, a 15% tip is standard for waiters; up to 20% may be expected at more expensive establishments. The same goes for taxi drivers, bartenders, and hairdressers. Coat-check operators usually expect $1; bellhops and porters should get $1–$2 per bag; hotel maids in upscale hotels should get about $2 per day of your stay. A concierge typically receives a tip of $5–$10, with an additional gratuity for special services or favors.

On package tours, conductors and drivers usually get $1 per person from the group as a whole; check whether this has already been figured into your cost. For local sightseeing tours, you may individually tip the driver-guide 10%–15% if he or she has been helpful or informative. Ushers in theaters do not expect tips.

TOURS & PACKAGES

Because everything is prearranged on a prepackaged tour or independent vacation, you spend less time planning—and often get it all at a good price.

BOOKING WITH AN AGENT

Travel agents are excellent resources. But it's a good idea to collect brochures from several agencies, as some agents' suggestions may be influenced by relationships with tour and package firms that reward them for volume sales. If you have a special interest, find an agent with expertise in that area; the American Society of Travel Agents (ASTA; ⇨ Travel Agencies) has a database of specialists worldwide. You can log on to the group's Web site to find an ASTA travel agent in your neighborhood.

Make sure your travel agent knows the accommodations and other services of the place being recommended. Ask about the hotel's location, room size, beds, and whether it has a pool, room service, or programs for children, if you care about these. Has your agent been there in person or sent others whom you can contact?

Do some homework on your own, too: local tourism boards can provide information about lesser-known and small-niche operators, some of which may sell only direct.

BUYER BEWARE

Each year consumers are stranded or lose their money when tour operators—even large ones with excellent reputations—go out of business. So check out the operator. Ask several travel agents about its reputation, and try to book with a company that has a consumer-protection program. (Look for information in the company's brochure.) In the United States, members of the United States Tour Operators Association are required to set aside funds ($1

million) to help eligible customers cover payments and travel arrangements in the event that the company defaults. It's also a good idea to choose a company that participates in the American Society of Travel Agents' Tour Operator Program; ASTA will act as mediator in any disputes between you and your tour operator.

Remember that the more your package or tour includes, the better you can predict the ultimate cost of your vacation. Make sure you know exactly what is covered, and beware of hidden costs. Are taxes, tips, and transfers included? Entertainment and excursions? These can add up.

🚩 **Tour-Operator Recommendations American Society of Travel Agents** (⇨ Travel Agencies). **National Tour Association** (NTA) ⊠ 546 E. Main St., Lexington, KY 40508 ☏ 859/226-4444 or 800/682-8886 🖷 859/226-4404 ⊕ www.ntaonline.com. **United States Tour Operators Association** (USTOA) ⊠ 275 Madison Ave., Suite 2014, New York, NY 10016 ☏ 212/599-6599 🖷 212/599-6744 ⊕ www.ustoa.com.

TRAIN TRAVEL

Amtrak's *California Zephyr* train from Chicago via Denver terminates in Oakland. The *Pacific Surfliner* connects San Diego and Paso Robles. The *Coast Starlight* train travels between Los Angeles and the state of Washington. The *Sunset Limited* heads west from Florida through New Orleans and Texas to Los Angeles.

🚩 **Train Information Amtrak** ☏ 800/872-7245 ⊕ www.amtrak.com.

TRAVEL AGENCIES

A good travel agent puts your needs first. Look for an agency that has been in business at least five years, emphasizes customer service, and has someone on staff who specializes in your destination. In addition, make sure the agency belongs to a professional trade organization. The American Society of Travel Agents (ASTA)—the largest and most influential in the field with more than 20,000 members in some 140 countries—maintains and enforces a strict code of ethics and will step in to help mediate any agent-client disputes involving ASTA members if necessary. ASTA (whose motto is "Without a travel agent, you're on your own") also maintains a Web site that includes a directory of agents. (If a travel agency is also acting as your tour operator, *see* Buyer Beware *in* Tours & Packages.)

F Local Agent Referrals **American Society of Travel Agents** (ASTA) ✉ 1101 King St., Suite 200, Alexandria, VA 22314 ☎ 703/739-2782 or 800/965-2782 24-hr hotline 🖷 703/684-8319 ⊕ www. astanet.com. **Association of British Travel Agents** ✉ 68-71 Newman St., London W1T 3AH ☎ 020/7637-2444 🖷 020/7637-0713 ⊕ www.abta.com. **Association of Canadian Travel Agencies** ✉ 130 Albert St., Suite 1705, Ottawa, Ontario K1P 5G4 ☎ 613/237-3657 🖷 613/237-7052 ⊕ www.acta.ca. **Australian Federation of Travel Agents** ✉ Level 3, 309 Pitt St., Sydney, NSW 2000 ☎ 02/9264-3299 or 1300/363-416 🖷 02/9264-1085 ⊕ www.afta.com.au. **Travel Agents' Association of New Zealand** ✉ Level 5, Tourism and Travel House, 79 Boulcott St., Box 1888, Wellington 6001 ☎ 04/499-0104 🖷 04/499-0786 ⊕ www.taanz.org.nz.

VISITOR INFORMATION

Learn more about foreign destinations by checking government-issued travel advisories and country information. For a broader picture, consider information from more than one country.

For general information about California, contact the California Division of Tourism. The California Division of Tourism Web site has travel tips, events calendars, and other resources, and the site will link you—via the Regions icon—to the Web sites of city and regional tourism offices and attractions. For the numbers of regional and city visitors bureaus and chambers of commerce *see* the A to Z section at the end of each chapter.

If you are coming to California from overseas, you can check with your home government for official travel advisories and destination information. For a broader picture, consider information from more than one country.

F Tourist Information **California Division of Tourism** ✉ 1102 Q St., Sacramento, CA 95814 ☎ 916/444-4429 or 800/862-2543 🖷 916/444-0410 ⊕ www.gocalif.ca.gov.

F Government Advisories **Consular Affairs Bureau of Canada** ☎ 800/267-6788 or 613/944-6788 ⊕ www.voyage.gc.ca. **U.K. Foreign and Commonwealth Office** ✉ Travel Advice Unit, Consular Division, Old Admiralty Bldg., London SW1A 2PA ☎ 0870/606-0290 or 020/7008-1500 ⊕ www.fco.gov.uk/travel. **Australian Department of Foreign Affairs and Trade** ☎ 300/139-281 travel advice, 02/6261-1299 Consular Travel Advice Faxback Service ⊕ www.dfat.gov.au. **New Zealand Ministry of Foreign Affairs and Trade** ☎ 04/439-8000 ⊕ www.mft.govt.nz.

WEB SITES

Do check out the World Wide Web when planning your trip. You'll find everything from weather forecasts to virtual tours of famous cities. Be sure to visit Fodors.com (⊕ www.fodors.com), a complete travel-planning site. You can research prices and book plane tickets, hotel rooms, rental cars, vacation packages, and more. In addition, you can post your pressing questions in the Travel Talk section. Other planning tools include a currency converter and weather reports, and there are loads of links to travel resources.

The California Parks Department site has the lowdown on state-run parks and other recreational areas. A must-visit for outdoors and adventure travel enthusiasts, the Great Outdoor Recreation Page is arranged into easily navigated categories. The site of the Wine Institute, which is based in San Francisco, provides events listings and detailed information about the California wine industry and has links to the home pages of regional wine associations.

F Web Sites **California Parks Department** ⊕ www. parks.ca.gov. **Great Outdoor Recreation Page** ⊕ www.gorp.com. **Wine Institute** ⊕ www.wineinstitute.org.

SAN DIEGO
WITH NORTH COUNTY

1

Updated by
Rob Aikins

SAN DIEGO IS A BIG CITY,where locals take pride in its small-town feel. With more than 1 million people, San Diego is second only to Los Angeles in population among California cities. It also covers a lot of territory, roughly 400 square mi of land and sea. To the north and south of the city are 70 mi of beaches. Inland, a succession of chaparral-covered mesas are punctuated with deep-cut canyons that step up to savannalike hills, separating the verdant coast from the arid Anza-Borrego Desert. Unusually clear skies make the inland countryside ideal for stargazing.

The San Diego area, the birthplace of California, was claimed for Spain by explorer Juan Rodríguez Cabrillo in 1542 and eventually came under Mexican rule. You'll find reminders of San Diego's Spanish and Mexican heritage throughout the region—in architecture and place-names, in distinctive Mexican cuisine, and in the historic buildings of Old Town.

In 1867 developer Alonzo Horton, who called the town's bay-front "the prettiest place for a city I ever saw," began building a hotel, a plaza, and prefab homes on 960 downtown acres. The city's fate was sealed in 1908, when President Theodore Roosevelt's Great White Fleet sailed into the bay. The U.S. Navy, impressed by the city's excellent harbor and temperate climate, decided to build a destroyer base on San Diego Bay in the 1920s. The newly developed aircraft industry soon followed (Charles Lindbergh's plane *Spirit of St. Louis* was built here). The military, which operates many bases and installations throughout the county, continues to contribute to the local economy.

EXPLORING SAN DIEGO

Although many attractions in San Diego are separated by some distance, the downtown area is delightfully urban and accessible. You can walk around the Gaslamp Quarter and the harbor, then catch a trolley or bus to the Balboa Park museums and zoo, the funky neighborhood of Hillcrest, the Old Town historic sites, and Mission Bay marine park and SeaWorld. After that, a car is the quickest way to get to the Coronado, Point Loma, and the beachside communities, though public transportation is available and reliable.

Numbers in the text correspond to numbers in the margin and on the neighborhood maps.

Balboa Park

Fodor'sChoice
★

Overlooking downtown and the Pacific Ocean, 1,200-acre Balboa Park is the cultural heart of San Diego, where you'll find most of the city's museums, the San Diego Zoo, restaurants, performance venues, and picnic areas. Cultivated and wild gardens are an integral part of Balboa Park, thanks to the "Mother of Balboa Park," Kate Sessions, who made sure the park was planted with thousands of palms, purple-blossoming jacarandas, and other trees.

If you have 3 days

Start your first day early with a morning visit to the San Diego Zoo in Balboa Park. In the afternoon stroll along El Prado, and stop into the museum of your choice. On your second day, head downtown to Seaport Village. After browsing the shops, catch a ferry from the Broadway Pier to Coronado, and board a bus going down Orange Avenue to see the Hotel Del Coronado. Back in San Diego after lunch, walk north on the Embarcadero to Ash Street; if you have time, you can explore the Maritime Museum. Spend the morning of your third day shopping in the Gaslamp Quarter, and in the afternoon head to La Jolla for a walk on the beach, dinner, and a sunset.

If you have 5 days

Follow the three-day itinerary above, then begin your fourth day with a morning visit to Cabrillo National Monument on Point Loma. Have lunch at one of the seafood restaurants on Scott Street, then drive to Old Town (Rosecrans Street north to San Diego Avenue). If low tide is in the afternoon, reverse the order to catch the tide pools at Cabrillo. Spend your fifth day at Legoland California in Carlsbad if you have children. En route to North County, stop off for a picnic at Torrey Pines State Park. If you're not going to Legoland, take Interstate 5 north to Del Mar for lunch, shopping, and sea views. A visit to Mission San Luis Rey, slightly inland from Oceanside on Highway 76, will infuse some history and culture into the tour.

Many of the park's Spanish-colonial revival buildings were meant to be temporary exhibit halls for the Panama–California International Exposition of 1915, which celebrated the opening of the Panama Canal. Fortunately, city leaders realized the value of the buildings and incorporated them into their plans for Balboa Park's acreage, which had been set aside by the city founders in 1868.

Parking near Balboa Park's museums is no small accomplishment. If you end up parking a bit far from your destination, consider the stroll back through the greenery part of the day's recreational activities. Alternatively, you can park at Inspiration Point on the east side of the park, off Presidents Way. Free trams run from there to the museums every 8 to 10 minutes, 9:30–5:30 daily.

It's impossible to cover all the park's museums in one day, so choose your focus before you head out. Enter via Cabrillo Bridge through the West Gate, which depicts the Panama Canal's linkage of the Atlantic and Pacific oceans. Park south of the ► **Alcazar Garden ❶**. It's a short stretch north across El Prado to the landmark California Building, home to the San Diego Museum of Man. Next door are the Globe Theatres, which adjoin the sculpture garden of the **San Diego Museum of Art ❷**, an ornate Plateresque-style structure built to resemble the 17th-century University of Salamanca in Spain.

Continuing east you'll come to the Botanical Building, the Timken Museum of Art, and the Spanish colonial revival–style Casa del Prado. At the end of the row is the San Diego Natural History Museum. If you were to continue north, you would come to the carousel, the miniature railroad, and, finally, the entrance to the **San Diego Zoo** ❸.

Return to the Natural History Museum and cross the Plaza de Balboa—its large central fountain is a popular meeting spot—to reach the **Reuben H. Fleet Science Center** ❹. On the south side of the Prado heading west, you'll next pass Casa de Balboa; inside are the model-railroad and photography museums and the historical society. Next door in the House of Hospitality is the Balboa Park Visitors Center, where you can buy a reduced-price pass to the museums, and the Prado restaurant. Across the Plaza de Panama, the Franciscan mission–style House of Charm holds the Mingei International Museum and a gallery for San Diego artists. Your starting point, the Alcazar Garden, is west of the House of Charm.

For another good walk, head south from the Plaza de Panama to the ornate Spreckels Organ Pavilion, the San Diego Aerospace Museum, and the San Diego Halls of Champions.

TIMING Unless you're pressed for time, you'll want to devote an entire day to the perpetually expanding zoo, and return another day to see the museums and gardens. The zoo is free for kids the entire month of October.

Most of the park's museums are open from Tuesday to Sunday, 10 to 4, though many have extended hours in summer. On Tuesday the museums have free admission to their permanent exhibits on a rotating basis; call the Balboa Park Visitors Center for a schedule. Free architectural, historical, or nature tours depart from the visitor center every Saturday at 10, while park ranger–led tours start out from the visitor center at 1 PM every Tuesday and Sunday.

What to See

▶ ❶ **Alcazar Garden.** The colorful gardens surrounding the Alcazar Castle in Seville, Spain, inspired the landscaping here; you'll feel like royalty resting on the benches by the tiled fountains. It's next to the House of Charm and across from the Museum of Man. ⊠ *Off El Prado, Balboa Park.*

off the beaten path

HILLCREST – Northwest of Balboa Park, Hillcrest is San Diego's center for the gay community and artists of all types. University, 4th, and 5th avenues are filled with cafés, interesting boutiques, and indie bookstores, selling new and used books. The self-contained residential–commercial Uptown District, on University Avenue at 8th Avenue, was built to resemble an inner-city neighborhood, with shops and restaurants within easy walking distance of high-priced town houses. To the northeast, Adams Avenue, reached via Park Boulevard heading north off Washington Street, has many antiques stores. Adams Avenue leads east into Kensington, a handsome old neighborhood that overlooks Mission Valley.

❹ **Reuben H. Fleet Science Center.** Children and adults alike enjoy the Fleet Center's clever interactive exhibits that are sneakily educational.

Beaches

San Diego's coastline shimmers with crystalline Pacific waters rolling up to some of the prettiest beaches on the West Coast. Some, like the Silver Strand on Coronado, are wide and sandy; others, like Sunset Cliffs on Point Loma, are narrow and rocky. You can join the athletes and sun-worshipers on the beaches of Mission Bay, or wander the tiny, little-known coves of Point Loma and the North County community of Encinitas. Families with children love to explore the tidal pools at La Jolla Cove. Check the weather page of a local newspaper for information about tides and pollution before you head out.

Eating Well

Striving to become one of the nation's premier "food cities" of the 21st century, sun-drenched San Diego has abandoned its former laissez-faire attitude toward serious cooking and adopted the point of view that a region this blessed with gorgeous vegetables, fruits, herbs, and seafood should make a culinary statement. The result is a generation of chefs more eager to spend time in the kitchen than at the beach—a largely youthful group that likes to surprise, dazzle, and delight diners with inventive, California-colorful creations. A stroll down the 5th Avenue restaurant row reveals San Diego's preference for Italian cuisine above all others, but the selection nonetheless is cosmopolitan and extends to casual and *haute* French fare, Spanish tapas and paellas, traditional and contemporary Mexican cuisine, and all-American thick-cut steaks. Seafood, of course, abounds, and there's a whole lot of "fusion" going on, which is to say that many chefs borrow idiosyncratically from a mixture of culinary traditions.

History

As the site of California's earliest European settlement, San Diego occupies a special place in U.S. history. Well-preserved and reconstructed historic sites, such as Cabrillo National Monument, Old Town State Historic Park, and Mission San Luis Rey in Oceanside help you to imagine what the San Diego area was like when Spanish and Portuguese explorers and missionaries arrived, usually by sea, in the 16th and 17th centuries. You can see evidence of *Star of India,* and strolling along the Prado in Balboa Park.

Shopping

Horton Plaza, in the heart of downtown, is the place to go for department stores, mall shops, and one-of-a-kind boutiques; the adjoining Gaslamp Quarter is chock-full of art galleries, antiques shops, and specialty stores. Seaport Village on the waterfront is thick with theme shops and arts-and-crafts galleries. Coronado has a few blocks of fancy boutiques and galleries as well as Ferry Landing Marketplace, a waterfront shopping and dining center. Bazaar del Mundo in the historic Old Town district resembles a colorful Mexican marketplace, where you can browse in shops selling international goods, toys, souvenirs, and arts and crafts. Hillcrest is the place to go for vintage clothing, furnishings, and accessories. La Jolla has a collection of trendy designer boutiques and galleries along Prospect Street and Girard Avenue. Discounted designer fashions can also be found at the popular Carlsbad Company Stores.

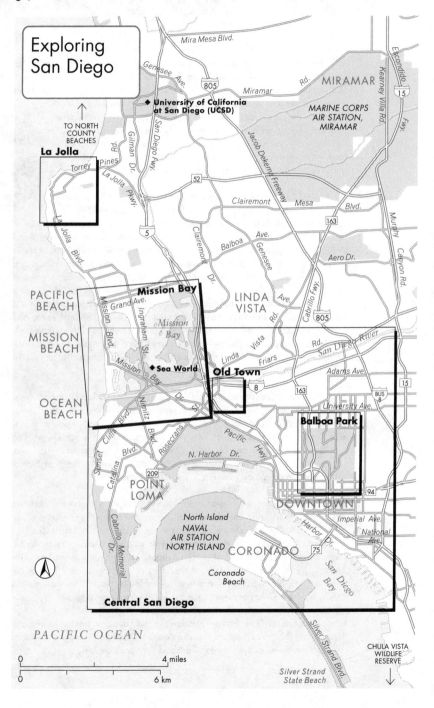

Exploring San Diego

Mira Mesa Blvd.

Genesee Ave.

805

Miramar Rd.

MIRAMAR

MARINE CORPS
AIR STATION,
MIRAMAR

Kearney Villa Rd.

Escondido Fwy.

15

◆ University of California
at San Diego (UCSD)

↑
TO NORTH
COUNTY
BEACHES

La Jolla

Torrey Pines Rd.

Gilman Dr.

San Diego Fwy.

La Jolla Pkwy.

52

Clairemont Mesa Blvd.

163

Aero Dr.

Murphy Canyon Rd.

La Jolla Blvd.

5

Clairemont Dr.

Balboa Ave.

Genesee Ave.

Cabrillo Fwy.

805

PACIFIC
BEACH

Mission Bay

Grand Ave.

Mission Blvd.

Ingraham St.

LINDA
VISTA

Rd.

MISSION
BEACH

*Mission
Bay*

Linda Vista Rd.

San Diego River

Mission Bay Dr.

Friars Rd.

Adams Ave.

BUS
8

15

◆ Sea World

Old Town

8

163

OCEAN
BEACH

Nimitz Blvd.

University Ave.

Balboa Park

Sunset Cliffs Blvd.

Catalina Blvd.

Rosecrans Blvd.

Pacific Hwy.

N. Harbor Dr.

94

209

**POINT
LOMA**

DOWNTOWN

Imperial Ave.

National Ave.

Cabrillo Memorial Dr.

North Island
NAVAL
AIR STATION
NORTH ISLAND

Harbor Dr.

CORONADO

75

San Diego Bay

Coronado
Beach

Central San Diego

Silver Strand Blvd.

PACIFIC OCEAN

CHULA VISTA
WILDLIFE
RESERVE
↓

0 ——————— 4 miles
0 ——————— 6 km

*Silver Strand
State Beach*

You can reconfigure your face on video to have two left sides, or, by replaying an instant video clip, watch yourself coming and going at different speeds. The IMAX Dome Theater screens exhilarating nature and science films. The SciTours simulator is designed to take you on virtual voyages—stomach lurches and all. The Meteor Storm lets up to six players at a time have an interactive virtual-reality experience, this one sans motion sickness potential. ☒ *1875 El Prado, Balboa Park* ☎ *619/238–1233* ⊕ *www.rhfleet.org* ☒ *Gallery exhibits $6.75; gallery exhibits and one IMAX film $11.75* ☉ *Mon.–Thurs. 9:30–5, Fri. and Sat. 9:30–8, Sun. 9:30–6; hrs vary seasonally, call to check.*

need a break?

You'll find a tranquil oasis at the **Japanese Friendship Garden** (☒ In front of Spreckels Organ Pavilion ☎ 619/232–2721 ⊕ www. niwa.org ☉ Tues.–Sun. 10–4), where you can meander under a wisteria arbor, sip green tea, and watch koi cruising in a pond.

★ ❷ **San Diego Museum of Art.** Known primarily for its Spanish Baroque and Renaissance paintings, including works by El Greco, Goya, Rubens, and van Ruisdael, San Diego's most comprehensive art museum also has strong holdings of South Asian art, Indian miniatures, and contemporary California paintings. The Baldwin M. Baldwin collection includes more than 100 pieces by Toulouse-Lautrec. An outdoor sculpture garden exhibits both traditional and modern pieces. Free docent-led tours are offered throughout the day. ☒ *Casa de Balboa, 1450 El Prado, Balboa Park* ☎ *619/232–7931* ⊕ *www.sdmart.org* ☒ *$8, $10–$12 for special exhibits* ☉ *Tues.–Sun. 10–6, 'til 9 on Thurs.*

☺ ❸ **San Diego Zoo.** Balboa Park's—and perhaps the city's—most famous attraction is its 100-acre zoo, and it deserves all the press it gets. Nearly 4,000 animals of some 800 diverse species roam in hospitable, expertly crafted habitats that replicate natural environments as closely as possible. Walkways wind over bridges and past waterfalls ringed with tropical ferns; elephants in a sandy plateau roam so close you're tempted to pet them.

Fodor's Choice
★

Construction on a new entrance and on central areas in the zoo is underway through 2005. The **New Heart of the Zoo** is slated to include a flamingo lagoon and African and Asian tropical forests with homes for many more mammals, reptiles, and birds.

Open-air trams can whisk you around 85% of the exhibits, but the zoo is at its best when you wander the paths, such as the one that climbs through the huge, enclosed **Scripps Aviary,** where brightly colored tropical birds swoop between branches just inches from your face, and into the neighboring **Gorilla Tropics,** among the zoo's latest ventures into bioclimatic zone exhibits. Here animals live in enclosed environments modeled on their native habitats. These zones may look natural, but they're helped a lot by modern technology: the sounds of the tropical rain forest emerge from a 144-speaker sound system that plays CDs recorded in Africa.

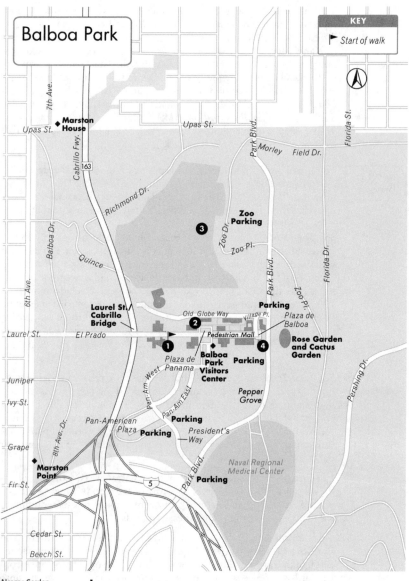

Balboa Park

7th Ave.

Marston House

Upas St.

Cabrillo Fwy.

163

Richmond Dr.

Balboa Dr.

Quince

6th Ave.

Laurel St.

El Prado

Juniper

Ivy St.

Grape

Marston Point

Fir St.

Upas St.

Park Blvd.

Morley Field Dr.

Florida St.

Zoo Parking

Zoo Dr.

Zoo Pl.

Park Blvd.

Florida Dr.

Zoo Pl.

Laurel St./ Cabrillo Bridge

Old Globe Way

Village Pl.

Parking

Plaza de Balboa

Rose Garden and Cactus Garden

Pedestrian Mall

Balboa Park Visitors Center

Parking

Plaza de Panama

Pan-Am West

Pan-Am East

Pepper Grove

Pershing Dr.

Pan-American Plaza

Parking

Parking

President's Way

Naval Regional Medical Center

Park Blvd.

Parking

5

Cedar St.

Beech St.

The zoo's simulated Asian rain forest, **Tiger River,** has 10 exhibits with more than 35 species of animals; tigers, Malayan tapirs, and Argus pheasants wander among the collection of exotic trees and plants. At the popular **Polar Bear Plunge,** where you can watch the featured animals take a chilly dive, Siberian reindeer, white foxes, and other Arctic creatures are separated from their predatory neighbors by a series of camouflaged moats. **Ituri Forest**—a 4-acre African rain forest at the base of Tiger River—lets you glimpse huge but surprisingly graceful hippos frolicking underwater, and buffalo cavorting with monkeys.

The zoo's most famous residents are a pair of giant pandas, Bai Yun and her companion Gao Gao, whom you can visit at the **SBC Giant Panda Research Station.** Bai Yun is the mother of Hua Mei, the first surviving panda cub to be born in the United States. Gao Gao, a high-spirited male, came to the exhibit in spring 2003. The rambunctious pandas are on loan to the zoo from the People's Republic of China as part of a captive-breeding program. ⊠ *2920 Zoo Dr., Balboa Park* ☎ *619/234-3153, 888/697-2632 Giant panda hotline* ⊕ *www.sandiegozoo.org* ✉ *$21 includes zoo, Children's Zoo, and animal shows; $32 includes above, plus 40-min guided bus tour and round-trip Skyfari ride; Kangaroo bus tour $12 additional, only $3 additional for purchasers of $32 ticket; zoo free for children under 12 in Oct. and for all 1st Mon. in Oct.; $52.65 pass good for admission to zoo and San Diego Wild Animal Park within 5 days* ⊟ *AE, D, MC, V* ☺ *July–Sept., daily 9–9; Sept.–May, daily 9–4; Children's Zoo and Skyfari ride generally close 1 hr earlier.*

Downtown

Downtown is San Diego's Lazarus. Written off as moribund by the 1970s, when few people willingly stayed in the area after dark, downtown is now one of the city's prime draws for tourists and real estate agents. Massive redevelopment started in the late 1970s, giving rise to the Gaslamp Quarter Historic District, Horton Plaza shopping center, and San Diego Convention Center, which have spurred an upsurge of elegant hotels, upscale condominium complexes, and swank, trendy cafés and restaurants that have people lingering downtown well into the night—if not also waking up there the next morning.

Of the newest downtown projects—there are more than 100 in the works—the most ambitious is the 26-block Ballpark District, slated to occupy the East Village area that extends between the railroad tracks up to J Street, and from 6th Avenue east to around 10th Street. It will include the 42,000-seat Petco Park baseball stadium for the San Diego Padres; a distinctively San Diego–style, 8-acre "Park at the Park" containing gardens, an amphitheater, and a kids entertainment area; a sports-related retail complex; at least 850 hotel rooms; and several apartment and condominium complexes.

There are reasonably priced ($4–$7 per day) parking lots along Harbor Drive, Pacific Highway, and lower Broadway and Market Street. The price of many downtown parking meters is $1 per hour (quarters only), with a maximum stay of two hours (meters are in effect Mon-

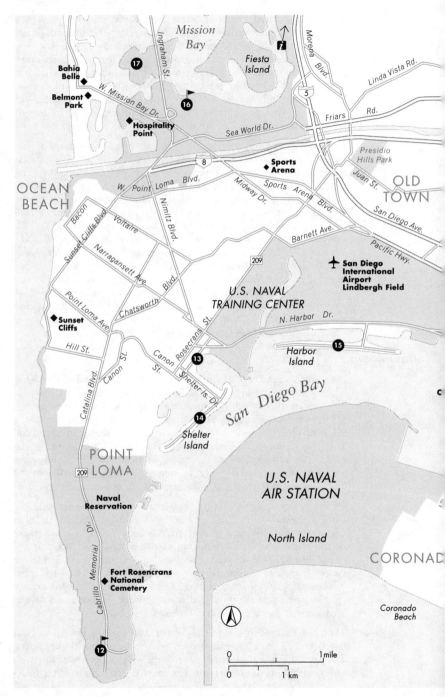

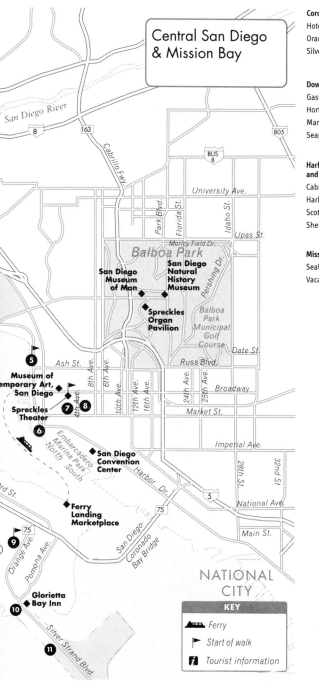

Central San Diego
& Mission Bay

San Diego River

University Ave.

Balboa Park

San Diego
Museum
of Man

San Diego
Natural
History
Museum

Spreckles
Organ
Pavilion

Balboa
Park
Municipal
Golf
Course

Date St.

Ash St.

Russ Blvd.

Museum of
emporary Art,
San Diego

Broadway

Spreckles
Theater

Market St.

Imperial Ave.

San Diego
Convention
Center

Ferry
Landing
Marketplace

National Ave.

Main St.

NATIONAL
CITY

Glorietta
Bay Inn

Silver Strand Blvd.

KEY

🚂 *Ferry*

▶ *Start of walk*

ℹ️ *Tourist information*

day–Saturday [except holidays], 8–6); unless you know for sure that your stay in the area will be short, you're better off in a lot.

Two Good Walks

Most people do a lot of parking-lot hopping when visiting downtown, but for the energetic, two distinct areas may be explored on foot.

To stay near the water, start a walk of the **Embarcadero** at the foot of Ash Street on Harbor Drive, where the *Star of India,* flagship of the ▶ **Maritime Museum ❺**, is moored. At Harbor Drive and Broadway, you can catch harbor excursion boats and the little ferry to Coronado; or walk inland two long blocks to Kettner Boulevard to see the mosaic-domed Santa Fe Depot and the tracks for the trolley to Tijuana. Next to the depot is the downtown branch of the Museum of Contemporary Art, San Diego. Return to Harbor Drive and continue south past Tuna Harbor to **Seaport Village ❻**.

A tour of the working heart of downtown can begin near the corner of 1st Avenue and Broadway, at ▶ **Spreckels Theater,** a grand old stage that presents pop concerts and touring plays. Two blocks east and across the street sits the historic U. S. Grant Hotel, built in 1910. If you cross Broadway, you'll be able to enter **Horton Plaza ❼**, San Diego's fanciful retail playland. Fourth Avenue, the eastern boundary of Horton Plaza, doubles as the western boundary of the 16-block **Gaslamp Quarter ❽**. Head south to Island Avenue and 4th Avenue to the William Heath Davis House, where you can get a touring map of the district.

TIMING   The above walks take about an hour each, though there's enough to do in downtown San Diego to keep you busy for at least two days. For a guided tour of the Gaslamp Quarter, plan to visit on Saturday. A boat trip on the harbor, or at least a hop over to Coronado on the ferry, is a must at any time of year, but during the gray whales' migration, from December through March, you should definitely consider booking a half-day whale-watching excursion from the Broadway Pier.

What to See

Embarcadero (☎ 619/525–5000). The bustle along Harbor Drive's waterfront walkway comes less these days from the activities of fishing folk than from the throngs of tourists, but it remains the nautical soul of San Diego. People here still make a living from the sea. Seafood restaurants line the piers, as do sea vessels of every variety—cruise ships, ferries, tour boats, houseboats, and naval destroyers.

On the north end of the Embarcadero, at Ash Street, you'll find the Maritime Museum. South of it, the **B Street Pier Cruise Ship Terminal** is used by ships from major cruise lines as both a port of call and a departure point. Day-trippers getting ready to set sail gather at the **Broadway Pier,** also known as the excursion pier. Tickets for the harbor tours and whale-watching trips are sold here. The terminal for the Coronado Ferry lies just beyond the Broadway pier.

The USS *Midway* is scheduled to open to the public in spring 2004. It will house the much-anticipated **San Diego Aircraft Carrier Museum** (☎ 619/702–7700 ⊕ www.midway.org), which will include five aircraft, a flight simulator, and interactive exhibits focusing on naval aviation. The U.S. Navy has control of the next few waterfront blocks to the south—**destroyers, submarines, and carriers** cruise in and out, some staying for weeks at a time. A pleasant park offers a great view across the bay of North Island, where aircraft carriers often dock.

The next bit of seafront greenery is a few blocks south along the paved promenade at **Embarcadero Marina Park North,** an 8-acre extension into the harbor from the center of Seaport Village. It's usually full of kite fliers, in-line skaters, and picnickers. Seasonal celebrations are held here and at the similar **Embarcadero Marina Park South.** The **San Diego Convention Center,** on Harbor Drive between 1st and 5th avenues, was designed by Arthur Erickson. The center often holds trade shows that are open to the public, and tours of the building are available.

8 **Gaslamp Quarter.** The 16-block national historic district between 4th and 5th avenues from Broadway to Market Street contains most of San Diego's Victorian-style commercial buildings. Businesses thrived in this area in the latter part of the 19th century, but at the turn of the century downtown's commercial district moved west toward Broadway, and many of San Diego's first buildings fell into disrepair. During the early 1900s the quarter became known as the Stingaree district. Prostitutes picked up sailors in lively area taverns, and dance halls and crime flourished.

History buffs, developers, architects, and artists formed the Gaslamp Quarter Council in 1974. Bent on preserving the district, they gathered funds from the government and private benefactors and began cleaning up the quarter, restoring the finest old buildings, and attracting businesses and the public back to the heart of New Town. Their efforts have paid off. Former flophouses have become choice office buildings, and the area is now filled with shops, restaurants, and entertainment venues.

The **William Heath Davis House** (✉ 410 Island Ave., at 4th Ave., Downtown ☎ 619/233–4692 ☉ Tues.–Sun. 11–3), one of the first residences in town, now serves as the information center for the historic district. Davis was a San Franciscan whose ill-fated attempt to develop the waterfront area preceded the more successful one of Alonzo Horton. Two-hour walking tours ($8) of the historic district leave from the house on Saturday at 11. The museum also sells detailed self-guided-tour maps ($2).

The Victorian **Horton Grand Hotel** (✉ 311 Island Ave., Gaslamp Quarter ☎ 619/544–1886) was created in the mid-1980s by joining together two historic hotels, the Kahle Saddlery and the Grand Hotel, built in the boom days of the 1880s; Wyatt Earp stayed at the Kahle Saddlery—then called the Brooklyn Hotel—while he was in town speculating on real estate ventures and opening gambling halls. The two hotels were dismantled and reconstructed about four blocks from their original locations. A small Chinese Museum serves as a tribute to the surrounding Chinatown district, a collection of modest structures that once housed Chinese laborers and their families.

The majority of the quarter's landmark buildings are on 4th and 5th avenues, between Island Avenue and Broadway. Highlights on 5th Avenue include the Backesto Building (No. 614), the Mercantile Building

(No. 822), the Louis Bank of Commerce (No. 835), and the Watts-Robinson Building (No. 903). The Tudor-style **Keating Building** (⊠ 432 F St., at 5th Ave., Downtown) was designed by the same firm that created the famous Hotel Del Coronado. The section of G Street between 6th and 9th avenues has become a haven for galleries; stop in one of them to pick up a map of the downtown arts district. For additional information about the historic area, call the **Gaslamp Quarter Association** (☎ 619/233–5227 ⊕ www.gaslamp.org) or log on to their Web site.

★ ❼ **Horton Plaza.** Downtown's centerpiece is the shopping, dining, and entertainment mall that fronts Broadway and G Street from 1st to 4th avenues, covering more than six city blocks. A collage of pastels with elaborate, colorful tile work on benches and stairways, banners waving in the air, and modern sculptures marking the entrances, Horton Plaza rises in uneven, staggered levels to six floors; great views of downtown from the harbor to Balboa Park and beyond can be had here. The complex's architecture has strongly affected the rest of downtown's development—new apartment and condominium complexes along G and Market streets mimic its brightly colored towers and cupolas.

Inside you'll find more than 150 stores, a movie complex, and restaurants and food shops. The respected San Diego Repertory Theatre has two stages below ground level. Most stores are open weekdays from 10 to 9, Saturday from 10 to 6, and Sunday from 11 to 7, but in summer and during the winter holidays many retailers stay open later. The **International Visitor Information Center** (⊠ 11 Horton Plaza ☎ 619/236–1212 ⊕ www.sandiego.org), at street level on the corner of 1st Avenue and F Street, is the best resource for information on San Diego. It's open Monday through Saturday from 8:30 to 5. From June to August, it's also open on Sunday from 11 to 5.

Horton Plaza has a multilevel parking garage, although lines to find a space can be long. The first three hours of parking are free; after that it's $1 for every 20 minutes. If you use this notoriously confusing fruit-and-vegetable–theme garage, be sure to remember at which produce level you've left your car. If you're staying downtown, inquire at your hotel about the complimentary Horton Plaza shopping shuttle, which stops at the cruise ship terminal and the convention center in addition to several downtown hotels.

🕲 ▶ ❺ **Maritime Museum.** A must for anyone with an interest in nautical history—or who has ever read a Patrick O'Brian novel—this collection of six restored ships affords a fascinating glimpse of San Diego during its heyday as a commercial seaport. The museum's headquarters are the *Berkeley,* an 1898 ferryboat moored at the foot of Ash Street. The steam-driven ship, which served the Southern Pacific Railroad at San Francisco Bay until 1958, played its most important role during the great earthquake of 1906, when it carried thousands of passengers across San Francisco Bay to Oakland. Its ornate carved-wood paneling, stained-glass windows, and plate-glass mirrors have been restored, and its main deck serves as a floating museum, with permanent exhibits on West Coast maritime history and complementary rotating exhibits. Anchored next to the *Berkeley,* the small Scottish steam yacht *Medea,* launched in 1904, may be

FodorsChoice
★

boarded but has no interpretive displays. The state's official tall ship ambassador, the *Californian,* joined the collection in 2003.

The most historically significant of the six ships is the *Star of India,* an iron windjammer built in 1863, when iron ships were still a novelty. The ship's high wooden masts and white sails flapping in the wind have been a harbor landmark since 1927. The *Star of India* made 21 trips around the world in the late 1800s, when it traveled the East Indian trade route, shuttled immigrants from England to New Zealand, and served the Alaskan salmon trade. The oldest active iron sailing ship in the world, it makes rare short excursions but for the most part stays moored at the pier and open to visitors. In summer, old movies are projected on the sails. ✉ *1492 N. Harbor Dr., Embarcadero* ☎ *619/234–9153* ⊕ *www. sdmaritime.org* ✉ *$8, includes entry to all ships* ☉ *Daily 9–8, until 9 in summer.*

Museum of Contemporary Art, San Diego. The downtown branch of the city's modern art museum has cutting-edge exhibitions that are perfectly complemented by the steel-and-glass transportation complex of which it's a part. Four small galleries in the two-story building host rotating shows, some from the permanent collection in the La Jolla branch, others loaned from far-flung international museums. Look for Wendy Jacob's "breathing" wall on the second floor's far gallery, an artful lesson in paying attention to your surroundings. ✉ *1001 Kettner Blvd., Downtown* ☎ *619/ 234–1001* ⊕ *www.mcasd.org* ✉ *Free* ☉ *Daily 11–5* ☉ *Closed Wed.*

☺ ❻ **Seaport Village.** On a prime stretch of waterfront that spreads across 14 acres, the village's three bustling shopping plazas reflect the architectural styles of early California, especially New England clapboard and Spanish mission. A ¼-mi wooden boardwalk that runs along the bay and 4 mi of paths lead to specialty shops, snack bars, and restaurants. Seaport Village's shops are open daily 10 to 9 (10 to 10 in summer). Charles I. D. Looff crafted the hand-carved, hand-painted steeds on the **Broadway Flying Horses Carousel.** Strolling clowns, balloon sculptors, mimes, musicians, and magicians are also on hand throughout the village to entertain kids; those not impressed by such pretechnological displays can duck into the Time Out entertainment center near the carousel and play video games. ✉ *Embarcadero* ☎ *619/235–4014, 619/234–6133 for carousel information, 619/ 235–4013 for events hotline* ⊕ *www.seaportvillage.com.*

Coronado

Although it's actually an isthmus, easily reached from the mainland if you head north from Imperial Beach, Coronado has always seemed like an island—and is often referred to as such. The streets of Coronado are wide, quiet, and friendly, with lots of neighborhood parks and grand Victorian homes. North Island Naval Air Station, established in 1911, was the site of Charles Lindbergh's departure on the transcontinental flight that preceded his famous transatlantic voyage.

Coronado is visible from downtown and Point Loma and accessible via the toll-free San Diego–Coronado Bridge. Until the bridge was completed in 1969, visitors and residents relied on the Coronado Ferry. San Diego's

Metropolitan Transit System runs a shuttle bus, No. 901, around the island; you can pick it up where you disembark the ferry and ride it out as far as the Silver Strand State Beach. Buses start leaving from the ferry landing at 10:30 AM and run once an hour on the half hour until 6:30 PM.

You can board the ferry, operated by **San Diego Harbor Excursion** (☏ 619/ 234–4111 or 800/442–7847), at downtown San Diego's Embarcadero from the excursion dock at Harbor Drive and Broadway; you arrive at the Ferry Landing Marketplace in Coronado. Boats depart on the hour from the Embarcadero and on the half hour from Coronado, Sunday through Thursday from 9 to 9, Friday and Saturday until 10; the fare is $2, 50¢ extra for bicycles. San Diego Harbor Excursion also offers **water taxi service** (☏ 619/235–8294) Sunday–Friday 2–10, and Friday and Saturday 11–11, between any two points in San Diego Bay. The fare is $6 per person.

a good tour

Coronado is easy to navigate without a car. When you depart the ferry, you can explore the shops at the Ferry Landing Marketplace and from there rent a bicycle or catch the shuttle bus that runs down ▶ **Orange Avenue** ❾, Coronado's main tourist drag. Disembark the bus near the Coronado Museum of History and Art, which houses a visitor center, to pick up a map, then stroll along the boutiques-filled promenade until you reach the **Hotel Del Coronado** ❿ at the end of Orange Avenue. Right across the street from the Del is the Glorietta Bay Inn, another of the island's outstanding early structures. On Tuesday, Thursday, and Saturday mornings at 11, the Glorietta is the departure point for a fun and informative 1½-hour walking tour of a few of the area's 86 officially designated historical homes. If you've brought your swimsuit, you might continue on to **Silver Strand State Beach** ⓫—just past the Hotel Del, Orange Avenue turns into Silver Strand Boulevard, which soon resumes its original across-the-bridge role as Route 75.

TIMING   A leisurely stroll through Coronado takes an hour or so, more if you shop or walk along the beach. The last shuttle to the Ferry Landing Marketplace leaves from the Loews Coronado Bay Resort at 6:57.

What to See

Coronado Museum of History and Art. The neoclassical Historic First Bank building, constructed in 1910, was restored and reopened as the headquarters of the Coronado Historical Society, the Museum of History and Art, and the Coronado Visitors Center. The collection celebrates Coronado's history with photographs and displays of its major sights. To check out the town's historic houses, pick up a copy of the inexpensive *Coronado California Centennial History & Tour Guide* at the gift shop. There's also a café and lecture hall. ✉ *1100 Orange Ave., Coronado* ☏ *619/435–7242* ⊕ *www.coronadohistory.org* ✎ *Donations accepted* ☽ *Weekdays 9–5, Sat 10–5, Sun. 11–4.*

Coronado Walking Tours. Leisurely guided 90-minute walking tours take in some of Coronado's most historic sites: the mansion built by John Spreckels, the Victorian home of *Wizard of Oz* author L. Frank Baum, and the public areas of the Del Coronado Hotel. ✉ *Departs from Glorietta Bay Inn* ☏ *619/435–5993* ✎ *$6* ☽ *Tues, Thurs., and Sat. at 11.*

Ferry Landing Marketplace. This collection of shops at the point of disembarkation for the ferry is on a smaller—and generally less interesting—scale than Seaport Village, but you do get a great view of downtown's skyline from here. If you want to rent a bike or in-line skates, stop at Bikes and Beyond ⊠ *1201 1st St., at B Ave., Coronado* ☎ *619/435–7180.*

★ ❿ **Hotel Del Coronado.** The "Del" has a colorful history, integrally connected with that of Coronado itself. The hotel opened in 1888 as the brainchild of financiers Elisha Spurr Babcock Jr. and H. L. Story, who saw the potential of Coronado's virgin beaches and its view of San Diego. When built, the Del perched right on the ocean's edge, but over the years the watery front yard filled in. A $55 million restoration completed in 2001 included construction of the oceanfront Windsor Lawn, reconnecting the hotel to the beach. Also restored was the Otis #61 lobby elevator, still hand-operated and one of the first elevators manufactured in America. The Del's distinctive red-tile peaks and Victorian gingerbread architecture has served as a set for many movies, political meetings, and extravagant social happenings. Fourteen presidents have been guests of the Del, and the film *Some Like It Hot*— starring Marilyn Monroe, Jack Lemmon, and Tony Curtis—was filmed here. The gift shop sells books that elaborate on the hotel's history and resident ghost; several restaurants offer breakfast, lunch, dinner, and drinks. ⊠ *1500 Orange Ave., Coronado* ☎ *619/435–6611* ⊕ *www.hoteldel.com.*

▶ ❾ **Orange Avenue.** It's easy to imagine you're on a street in Cape Cod when you stroll along this thoroughfare, Coronado's version of a downtown: the clapboard houses, small restaurants, and boutiques are in some ways more characteristic of New England than they are of California.

☾ ⓫ **Silver Strand State Beach.** The stretch of sand that runs along Silver Strand Boulevard from the Hotel Del Coronado to Imperial Beach is a perfect family gathering spot, with restrooms and lifeguards. Don't be surprised if you see groups exercising in military style along the beach; this is a training area for the U.S. Navy's SEAL teams. ⊠ *Coronado.*

Harbor Island, Point Loma & Shelter Island

Point Loma protects the center city from the Pacific's tides and waves. It's shared by military installations, funky motels and fast-food shacks, stately family homes, and private marinas packed with sailboats and yachts. Adjacent Harbor and Shelter islands were created out of sand dredged from the San Diego Bay in the second half of the past century. They've become tourist hubs supporting high-rise hotels, seafood restaurants, and boat-rental centers.

a good tour

Take Catalina Boulevard all the way south to the tip of Point Loma to reach ▶ **Cabrillo National Monument** ⓬; you'll be retracing the steps of the earliest European explorers if you use this as a jumping-off point for a tour. North of the monument, as you head back into the neighborhoods of Point Loma, you'll see the white headstones of Fort Rosecrans National Cemetery, with its rows upon rows of white markers. Continue north on Catalina Boulevard to Hill Street and turn left to reach the dramatic Sunset Cliffs, at the western side of Point Loma near

Ocean Beach. There are many lovely viewpoints from which to watch the sunset on these 60-foot-high bluffs. Return to Catalina Boulevard and backtrack south for a few blocks to find Canon Street, which leads to the peninsula's eastern (bay) side. Almost at the shore you'll see **Scott Street** ⑬, Point Loma's main commercial drag. Scott Street is bisected by Shelter Island Drive, which leads to **Shelter Island** ⑭. For another example of what can be done with tons of material dredged from a bay, go back up Shelter Island Drive, turn right on Rosecrans Street, and make another right on North Harbor Drive to reach **Harbor Island** ⑮.

TIMING   If you're interested in seeing the tide pools at Cabrillo National Monument, call the visitor desk at the monument or check the weather page of the *Union-Tribune* to find out when low tide will occur. Scott Street is a good place to find yourself at lunchtime. This drive takes about an hour if you stop briefly at each sight, but you'll want to devote at least an hour to Cabrillo National Monument.

What to See

★ ☺ ► ⑫ **Cabrillo National Monument.** This 144-acre preserve marks the site of the first European visit to the San Diego area, made by 16th-century explorer Juan Rodríguez Cabrillo—historians have never conclusively determined whether he was Spanish or Portuguese. Cabrillo came to this spot, which he called San Miguel, in 1542. In 1913 public land was set aside to commemorate his discovery, and today the site, with its rugged cliffs and shores and outstanding overlooks, is one of the most frequently visited of all the national monuments.

The **visitor center** presents an interactive exhibit, "Juan Rodríguez Cabillo and the Age of Exploration," focusing on the life of the explorer and other 16th-century conquistadors. **Interpretive stations** with recorded information have been installed along the walkways that edge the cliffs. The moderately steep 2-mi **Bayside Trail** (☺ 9–4) winds through coastal sage scrub, curving under the cliff-top lookouts and bringing you ever closer to the bay-front scenery. You cannot reach the beach from this trail and must stick to the path to protect the cliffs from erosion and yourself from thorny plants and snakes—including rattlers. The climb back is long but gradual, leading up to the **Old Point Loma Lighthouse** (☺ 9–5).

You can see sea creatures in the **tide pools** (☺ 9–4:30) at the foot of the monument's western cliffs. Drive north from the visitor center to the first road on the left, which winds down to the coast guard station and the shore. The western and southern cliffs are prime whale-watching territory in January and February. A sheltered viewing station has a tape-recorded lecture describing the great gray whales' migration from the Bering and Chukchi seas near Alaska to Baja California, and high-powered telescopes help you focus on the whales' water spouts. ⊠ *1800 Cabrillo Memorial Dr., Point Loma* ☎ *619/222–8211 for visitor information line, 619/557–5450 for park headquarters* ⊕ *www.nps.gov/cabr* ☒ *$5 per car, $3 per person entering on foot or by bicycle* ☺ *Daily 9–5:15; hrs vary in summer.*

⑮ **Harbor Island.** Following the success of nearby Shelter Island, the U.S. Navy decided to use the residue that resulted from digging berths deep enough to accommodate aircraft carriers to build another recreational island. In 1961 a 1½-mi-long peninsula was created adjacent to San Diego International Airport out of 12 million cubic yards of sand and mud dredged from San Diego Bay. Restaurants and high-rise hotels now line the inner shores of Harbor Island. The bay shore has pathways, gardens, and picnic spots for sightseeing or working off the calories from the various indoor or outdoor food fests. On the west point, Tom Ham's Lighthouse restaurant has a Coast Guard–approved beacon shining from its tower. ⊠ *Off N. Harbor Dr., in San Diego Bay.*

⓮ Scott Street. Running along Point Loma's waterfront from Shelter Island to the former Naval Training Center on Harbor Drive, this thoroughfare is lined with deep-sea fishing charters and whale-watching boats. It's a good spot from which to watch fishermen (and women) haul marlin, tuna, and puny mackerel off their boats. ⊠ *Point Loma.*

⓯ Shelter Island. In 1950 San Diego's port director thought there should be some use for the sand and mud dredged by the Works Project Administration to deepen the ship channel in the 1930s and '40s. He decided it might be a good idea to raise the shoal that lay off the eastern shore of Point Loma above sea level, landscape it, and add a 2,000-ft causeway to make it accessible. His hunch paid off. Shelter Island—actually a peninsula—now supports a cluster of resorts, restaurants, and marinas. It is also the center of San Diego's yacht-building industry, and boats in every stage of construction are visible in the yacht yards. On the bay side, fishermen launch their boats or simply stand on shore and cast. Families relax at picnic tables along the grass, where there are fire rings and permanent barbecue grills. ⊠ *Off Rosecrans St., in San Diego Bay.*

Mission Bay & the Beaches

The 4,600-acre Mission Bay aquatic park is San Diego's monument to sports and fitness. Admission to its 27 mi of bay-shore beaches and 17 mi of ocean frontage is free. Playgrounds and picnic areas abound on the beach and the low, grassy hills of the park. In the daytime, swimmers, water-skiers, and boaters—some in single-person kayaks, others in crowded powerboats—vie for space in the water. On weekday evenings, joggers, bikers, and skaters take over.

Mission Boulevard runs along a narrow strip flanked by the Pacific Ocean on the west (Mission Beach), and the bay on the east. The pathways in this area are lined with vacation homes, many of which can be rented by the week or month.

One Mission Bay caveat: swimmers should note signs warning about water pollution; certain areas of the bay are chronically polluted, and bathing is strongly discouraged.

a good tour

If you're coming from I–5, stop to pick up maps and information at the San Diego Visitor Information Center just about at the end of the Clairemont Drive–East Mission Bay Drive exit (you'll see the prominent sign). At the point where East Mission Bay Drive turns into Sea World Drive, you can detour left to Fiesta Island, popular with jet skiers and speedboat racers. Continue around the curve to the west to reach ☛ **SeaWorld of California ⓰**, the area's best-known attraction.

You'll next come to Ingraham Street, the central north–south drag through the bay. If you take it north, you'll shortly spot Vacation Road, which leads into the focal point of this part of the bay, the waterskiing hub of **Vacation Isle** 🔟. At Ingraham, Sea World Drive turns into Sunset Cliffs Boulevard and intersects with West Mission Bay Drive. Past this intersection, Quivira Way leads west toward Hospitality Point, where there are nice, quiet places to have a picnic.

If you continue west on West Mission Bay Drive, just before it meets Mission Boulevard, you'll come to the Bahia Resort Hotel, where you can catch the *Bahia Belle* for a cruise around the bay. Ventura Cove, opposite the Bahia Hotel, is another good spot to unpack your cooler. Almost immediately south of where West Mission Bay Drive turns into Mission Boulevard is the resurrected Belmont Park amusement park, with its 1925 roller coaster.

TIMING It should take less than an hour to drive this tour. You may not find a visit to SeaWorld fulfilling unless you spend at least a half day; a full day is recommended. The park is open daily, but not all its attractions are open year-round.

What to See

🔵 ⤳ 🔟 **SeaWorld of California.** One of the world's largest marine-life amusement
Fodor'sChoice parks, SeaWorld is spread over 100 tropically landscaped bay-front
★ acres—and it seems to be expanding into every square inch of available space with new exhibits, shows, and activities. The newest adventure, **R. L. Stine's Haunted Lighthouse,** is an interactive 4-D film, starring Christopher Lloyd and Lea Thompson, that tells the tale of a pair of kids who track down the facts behind the legend of a haunted lighthouse.

Walk-through marine environments make up the majority of exhibits. Kids get a particular kick out of the **Shark Encounter,** where they come face-to-face with sandtiger, nurse, bonnethead, black-tipped, and white-tipped reef sharks by walking through a 57-foot clear acrylic tube that passes through the 280,000-gallon shark habitat. At **Wild Arctic,** a simulated helicopter ride takes you to a research post at the "North Pole," where you can observe beluga whales, walruses, and polar bears.

SeaWorld also has four large entertainment arenas. The stadiums are large enough for everyone to get a seat even at the busiest times, and if you arrive 10 or 15 minutes in advance, you can get front-row seats. The traditional favorite is the **Shamu Adventure,** starring Shamu, Baby Shamu, and other killer whales; if you get a front-row seat for this show expect to get wet. **Fools With Tools** stars two California sea lions, Clyde and Seamore, as comic handymen whose best-laid plans are foiled by a supporting cast of Asian sea otters. Next to the stadium, the **Shipwreck Rapids** ride takes you through raging rapids, under roaring waterfalls, past sunbathing sea turtles, and through a forbidding tunnel into a ship's engine room.

SeaWorld is open late in summer, when special Shamu, sea lion, and otter evening shows precede a fireworks display. ⊠ *1720 South Shores Rd., near the west end of I–8, Mission Bay* ☎ *619/226–3815* ⊕ *www. seaworld.com* ☑ *$49.75, 2-day package $48.95; parking $7–$9; 60-min behind-the-scenes walking tours $10 additional* ⊟ *AE, D, MC, V* ⊙ *Daily 10–dusk; extended hrs in summer.*

Old Town
San Diego

⑰ Vacation Isle. Ingraham Street bisects the island, providing two distinct experiences for visitors. The west side is taken up by the San Diego Paradise Point Resort, but you don't have to be a guest to enjoy the hotel's lushly landscaped grounds and bay-front restaurants. The water-ski clubs congregate at **Ski Beach** on the east side of the island, where there's a parking lot as well as picnic areas and rest rooms. At a pond on the south side of the island, children and young-at-heart adults take part year-round in motorized miniature boat races. ⌧ *Mission Bay.*

Old Town

San Diego's Spanish and Mexican history and heritage are most evident in Old Town, north of downtown at Juan Street, near the intersection of Interstates 5 and 8. Old Town is the first European settlement in southern California, but the pueblo's true beginnings took place on a hill (Presidio Park) overlooking Old Town. It was on this hill that Father Junípero Serra established the first of California's missions, San Diego de Alcalá, in 1769. On San Diego Avenue, the district's main drag, art galleries and expensive gift shops are interspersed with tacky curio shops, restaurants, and open-air stands selling inexpensive Mexican pottery, jewelry, and blankets. The Old Town Esplanade on San Diego Avenue between Harney and Conde streets is the best of several mall-like affairs constructed in mock Mexican-plaza style. Shops and restaurants also line Juan and Congress streets.

Ten bus lines stop in Old Town, as do the San Diego Trolley and the Coaster commuter rail lines. Driving here, you'll find signage leading from I–8 to the Transit Center easy to follow. If you're not familiar with the area, however, avoid the "Old Town" exit from I–5, which leaves you floundering near Mission Bay without further directions. Parking on the street around Old Town can be a challenge, so head for one of the two large parking lots; one is at the Transit Center, the other is on Juan Street east of the park.

a good tour

It's possible to trek around Old Town and see all its sights in one long day, but a walking-driving combination is more efficient.

Visit the information center at Seeley Stable, just off Old Town Plaza, to orient yourself to the various sights in ▶ **Old Town San Diego State Historic Park** ⑱. When you've had enough history, cross north on the west side of the plaza to Bazaar del Mundo, where you can shop or enjoy some nachos on the terrace of a Mexican restaurant. Walk down San Diego Avenue, which flanks the south side of Old Town's historic plaza. If you have the time, detour on Harney Street to the Thomas Whaley Museum, or continue east 2½ blocks on San Diego Avenue to the El Campo Santo cemetery. Heritage Park, with a number of restored Victorian buildings, is perched on a hill above Juan Street, north of the museum and cemetery. Drive west on Juan Street and north on Taylor Street to Presidio Drive, which will lead you up the hill to **Presidio Park** ⑲ and the Junípero Serra Museum.

TIMING Try to time your visit to coincide with the free tours of Old Town led daily at 11 AM and 2 PM by costumed park service employees at Seeley Stable. It takes about two hours to walk through Old Town. If you drive to Presidio Park, allot another hour to explore the grounds and museum.

What to See

★ ▶ ⑱ **Old Town San Diego State Historic Park.** The six square blocks on the site of San Diego's original pueblo are the heart of Old Town. Most of the 20 historic or re-created buildings cluster around **Old Town Plaza** and along San Diego Avenue, which is closed to vehicles here. Worth exploring in the plaza area are the Casa de Bandini (now a restaurant), Seeley Stable, Casa de Estudillo, Dental Museum, Mason Street School, Wells Fargo Museum, San Diego Courthouse, Commercial Kitchen Museum, and the Machade Stewart Adobe Museum. The **Robinson-Rose House** (☎ 619/220–5422) was old San Diego's first commercial center, housing railroad offices, law offices, and a newspaper press in the late 19th century. Now it serves as the park's visitor and administrative center, and has on display a model of Old Town as it looked in 1872.

On San Diego Avenue at Arista Street, you'll find **El Campo Santo,** the cemetery that served San Diego between 1849 and 1880. The adobe-walled cemetery was the burial place for many members of Old Town's founding families, as well as gamblers and bandits. Antonio Garra, a chief who led an uprising of the San Luis Rey Indians, was executed at El Campo Santo in front of the open grave he was forced to dig for himself. These days the small cemetery is a peaceful stop for visitors to Old Town. Most of the markers only approximate the grave sites; some of the early settlers laid to rest at El Campo Santo actually reside under San Diego Avenue.

The **Thomas Whaley Museum** (⌧ 2482 San Diego Ave., Old Town ☎ 619/297–7511 ✐ $5) commemorates a New York entrepreneur who came to California during the gold rush. Whaley wanted to provide his East Coast wife all the comforts of home, so in 1856 he built southern California's first two-story brick structure. The house stands in strong contrast to the Spanish-style adobe residences in the nearby plaza and marks an early stage of San Diego's "Americanization." During the 1870s, the house served as the county courthouse and government seat. A reconstructed courtroom houses historical artifacts, including one of the six original life masks of Abraham Lincoln. The museum is open from Wednesday to Monday, 10 to 4:30.

⑲ Presidio Park. The hillsides of the 40-acre green space overlooking Old Town from the north end of Taylor Street are popular with picnickers. It's a nice walk to the summit from Old Town if you're in good shape and wearing the right shoes—it should take about a half hour. You can also drive to the top of the park via Presidio Drive, off Taylor Street. Presidio Park has a canyon surrounded by palms at the bottom of the hill, off Taylor Street before it intersects with I–8.

If you do decide to walk, look in at the Presidio Hills Golf Course on Mason Street, which has an unusual clubhouse: it incorporates the ruins of Casa de Carrillo, the town's oldest adobe, constructed in 1820. At the end of Mason Street, veer left on Jackson Street to reach the **Presidio Ruins,** where adobe walls and a bastion have been built above the foundations of the original fortress and chapel. Also on the site are the 28-foot-high Serra Cross, built in 1913 out of brick tiles found in the ruins, and a bronze statue of Father Serra. Before you do much poking around here, however, it's a good idea to get some historical perspective at the **Junípero Serra Museum** (⌧ 2727 Presidio Dr., Old Town ☎ 619/297–3258 ✐ $5) just to the east. It's open Friday through Sunday from 10 to 4; Tuesday through Sunday in summer. Take Presidio Drive southeast of the museum and you'll come to the site of Fort Stockton, built to protect Old Town and abandoned by the United States in 1848. ⌧ *1 block north of Old Town, Old Town.*

La Jolla

La Jollans have long considered their village to be the Monte Carlo of California, and with good cause. Its coastline curves into natural coves backed by verdant hillsides covered with homes worth millions. Although La Jolla is within the city of San Diego, it has its own postal zone and a coveted sense of class; it's gotten far more plebeian these days, but old-monied residents still mingle here with visiting celebrities.

The Native Americans called the site La Hoya, meaning "the cave," referring to the grottoes that dot the shoreline. The Spaniards changed the name to La Jolla (same pronunciation as La Hoya), "the jewel," and its residents have cherished the name and its allusions ever since.

To reach La Jolla from I–5, if you're traveling north, take the Ardath Road exit, which veers into Torrey Pines Road, and turn right onto Prospect Street. If you're heading south, get off at the La Jolla Village Drive exit, head west to Torrey Pines Road, and turn left. Traffic is always congested in this busy intersection, so pay close attention to highway signs. For those who enjoy meandering, the best way to approach La Jolla from the south is to drive through Mission and Pacific beaches on Mission Boulevard, which becomes La Jolla Boulevard. You'll pass homes designed by such respected architects as Frank Lloyd Wright and Irving Gill. As you approach the village, La Jolla Boulevard turns into Prospect Street. Prospect Street and Girard Avenue, the village's main drags, are lined with expensive shops and office buildings. La Jolla nightlife scene is an active one, with jazz clubs, piano bars, and watering holes for the well-heeled younger set.

a good tour

At the intersection of La Jolla Boulevard and Nautilus Street, turn toward the sea to reach Windansea Beach, one of the best surfing spots in town. Mount Soledad, about 1½-mi east on Nautilus Street, is La Jolla's highest spot and a good place to see a view of San Diego on a clear day. Down in the village you'll find the town's cultural center, the ▶ **Museum of Contemporary Art, San Diego ❶**, on the less trafficked southern end of Prospect. A bit farther north, at the intersection of Prospect Street and Girard Avenue, sits the pretty-in-pink La Valencia hotel. The hotel looks out onto the village's great natural attraction, **La Jolla Cove ❷**, which can be accessed from Coast Boulevard, one block to the west. Past the far northern point of the cove, a trail leads down to **La Jolla Caves ❸**. The beaches along La Jolla Shores Drive north of the caves are some of the finest in the San Diego area, with long stretches allotted to surfers or swimmers. Nearby is the campus of the Scripps Institution of Oceanography. The Birch Aquarium at Scripps is inland a bit, off Torrey Pines Road, across from the campus of the University of California at San Diego.

La Jolla Shores Drive eventually curves onto Torrey Pines Road, off which you'll soon glimpse the world-famous **Salk Institute,** designed by Louis I. Kahn. The same road that leads to the institute ends at the cliffs used as the Torrey Pines Glider Port. The hard-to-reach stretch of sand at the foot of the cliffs is officially named Torrey Pines City Park Beach, but locals call it Black's Beach. At the intersection of Torrey Pines Road and Genesee Avenue you'll come to the northern entrance of the huge campus of the University of California at San Diego and, a bit farther north, to the stretch of wilderness that marks the end of what most locals consider San Diego proper, **Torrey Pines State Beach and Reserve ❹**.

TIMING   This tour makes for a leisurely day, although it can be driven in a couple of hours, including stops to take in the views and explore the village of La Jolla (though not to hit any of the beaches—or even a fraction of the pricey boutiques). The Museum of Contemporary Art is closed Monday, and guided tours of the Salk Institute are given on weekdays only.

What to See

Birch Aquarium at Scripps. The Scripps Institution of Oceanography hosts the largest oceanographic exhibit in the United States at this aquarium just north of La Jolla Village Drive. More than 30 tanks are filled with colorful saltwater fish, and a 70,000-gallon tank simulates a La Jolla kelp forest. Besides the fish themselves, attractions include a gallery with sea-theme exhibits, a simulated submarine ride, supermarket shelves stocked with products derived from the sea (including some surprisingly common ones), and other educational exhibits. A concession sells food, and there are outdoor picnic tables. The museum also conducts seasonal whale-watching tours. ✉ *2300 Expedition Way, off N. Torrey Pines Rd., La Jolla* ☎ *858/534–3474* ⊕ *www.aquarium. ucsd.edu* ✉ *$10, parking free for 3 hrs* ⊙ *Daily 9–5.*

Golden Triangle. The La Jolla area's newest enclave, spreading through the Sorrento Valley east of I–5, is a far cry from the beach communities with which the name La Jolla has long been associated. High-tech research-and-development companies, attracted to the Golden Triangle area in part by the facilities of the University of California at San Diego, the Scripps Institution of Oceanography, and the Salk Institute, have developed huge state-of-the-art compounds in areas that were populated solely by coyotes and jays not so long ago. The area along La Jolla Village Drive and Genesee Avenue has become an architectural proving ground for futuristic buildings. The most striking are those in the Michael Graves–designed Aventine complex, visible from I–5 at the La Jolla Village Drive exit. A bit south, near the Nobel exit, and eye-catching in another way, the huge, white Mormon Temple looks like a psychedelic medieval castle; completed in 1993, it still startles drivers heading up the freeway. ✉ *La Jolla.*

🕑 ❸ **La Jolla Caves.** It's a walk down 145 sometimes slippery steps to Sunny Jim Cave, the largest of the seven grottoes in La Jolla Cove. The cave entrance is through the Cave Store, a throwback to the 1902 shop that served as the underground portal. Some of the other caves can be visited on foot when there's a minus low tide or by kayakers at other times. ✉ *1325 Cave St., La Jolla* ☎ *858/459–0746* ✉ *$3* ⊙ *Daily 9–5.*

★ ❷ **La Jolla Cove.** The wooded spread that looks out over a shimmering blue inlet is what first attracted everyone to La Jolla, from Native Americans to the glitterati; it is the village's enduring cachet. You'll find the cove beyond where Girard Avenue dead-ends into Coast Boulevard, marked by towering palms that line a promenade. An underwater preserve at the north end of La Jolla Cove makes the adjoining beach the most popular one in the area. On summer days, the beach and water seem to disappear under the mass of bodies swimming, snorkeling, or sunbathing. The **Children's Pool**, at the south end of the park, has a curving beach protected by a seawall from strong currents and waves. Due to an ever-growing population of sea lions, it's not open to swimmers, but it's the best place on the coast to view these engaging creatures. Walk through **Ellen Browning Scripps Park,** past the groves of twisted junipers to the cliff's edge. You can spread your picnic out on a table at one of the open-air shelters and enjoy the scenery.

Mount Soledad. La Jolla's highest spot can be reached by taking Nautilus Street all the way east. The top of the mountain is an excellent vantage point from which to get a sense of San Diego's geography: looking down from here you can see the coast from the county's northern bor-

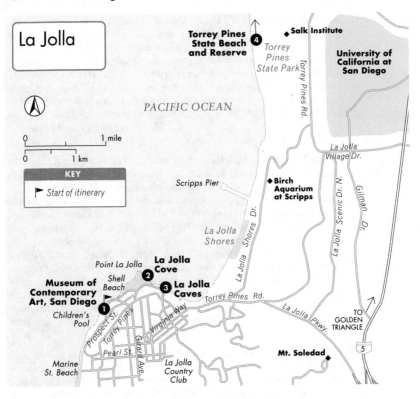

der to the south far beyond downtown—barring smog and haze. A half-acre on the summit is used to honor those killed in wars. The steel-and-concrete cross memorializes veterans, and services are held here on Memorial Day. ✉ *La Jolla.*

★ ▶ ❶ **Museum of Contemporary Art, San Diego.** The oldest section of San Diego's modern art museum was a residence designed by Irving Gill for philanthropist Ellen Browning Scripps in 1916. Robert Venturi and his colleagues at Venturi, Scott Brown and Associates updated and expanded the compound in the mid-1990s. A patterned terrazzo floor leads to galleries where the museum's permanent collection of post-1950s art and rotating exhibits are on display. Works by Andy Warhol, Robert Rauschenberg, Frank Stella, Joseph Cornell, and Jenny Holzer, to name a few, get major competition from the setting: you can look out from the top of a grand stairway onto a landscaped garden that contains permanent and temporary sculpture exhibits as well as rare 100-year-old California plant specimens and, beyond that, to the Pacific Ocean. ✉ *700 Prospect St., La Jolla* ☎ *858/454-3541* ⊕ *www.mcasd.org* 🌐 *$6; free 1st Sun. and 3rd Tues. of month* ☉ *Thurs. 11–7, Fri.–Tues 11–5.*

Salk Institute. The world-famous biological-research facility founded by polio vaccine inventor Jonas Salk sits on 26 cliff-top acres. For the original 1965 twin structures designed in consultation with Dr. Salk, modernist architect Louis I. Kahn used poured concrete and other low-maintenance materials to clever effect. The thrust of the laboratory–office complex is outward toward the Pacific Ocean, an orientation that is accentuated by a foot-wide "Stream of Life" that flows through the center of a travertine marble courtyard between the buildings. The courtyard and stream of water were inspired by architect Louis Barragán. Architects-to-be and building buffs enjoy the free tours of the property; call to book, because the tours take place only when enough people express interest. ✉ *10010 N. Torrey Pines Rd., La Jolla* ☎ *858/453–4100 Ext. 1200* 🖥 *Free* ☉ *Grounds weekdays 9–5; guided architectural tours Mon., Wed., and Fri. at noon, Thurs. at 12:30 and every other Tues. at 11. Reservations required.*

❹ **Torrey Pines State Beach and Reserve.** *Pinus torreyana*, the rarest native pine tree in the United States, enjoys a 1,750-acre sanctuary at the northern edge of La Jolla. Hiking trails lead to the cliffs, 300 foot above the ocean; trail maps are available at the park station. Wildflowers grow profusely in the spring, and the ocean panoramas are always spectacular. When the tide is out, it's possible to walk south all the way past the lifeguard towers to Black's Beach over rocky promontories. **Los Peñasquitos Lagoon** at the north end of the reserve is a good place to watch shorebirds. Volunteers lead guided nature walks at 11:30 and 1:30 on most weekends. There are two large parking lots on both sides of Los Peñasquitos Lagoon, and another up the hill by the visitor center. ✉ *N. Torrey Pines Rd. (Old Hwy. 101), La Jolla, Exit I–5 onto Carmel Valley Rd. going west, then turn left (south) on Old Hwy. 101* ☎ *858/ 755–2063* 🖥 *Parking $6* ☉ *Daily 8–sunset.*

WHERE TO EAT

Updated by
David Nelson

Freshness and diversity define San Diego's culinary scene. Area farmers produce more than 200 edible crops, samples of which quickly find their way onto local restaurant tables, and seafood is plucked from the Pacific Ocean and the Gulf of California. Downtown's Little Italy district, especially 5th Avenue, has become a center for excellent, affordable Italian dining. A bit farther south, the dramatically restored Gaslamp Quarter offers some 50 more restaurants and a vigorous nightlife. Asian and North African cuisines have taken a stronghold in several of San Diego's outlying neighborhoods, such as Hillcrest, Kearny Mesa, and the beach communities. And Mexican cuisine from a variety of regions can be found throughout the city. Up north, rich, elegant La Jolla has many of San Diego's most exquisite and expensive restaurants. Casual attire is the norm at most area restaurants.

WHAT IT COSTS				
$$$$	**$$$**	**$$**	**$**	**¢**
AT DINNER over $30	$23–$30	$16–$22	$10–$15	under $10

Prices are for a main course, excluding 7.75% tax.

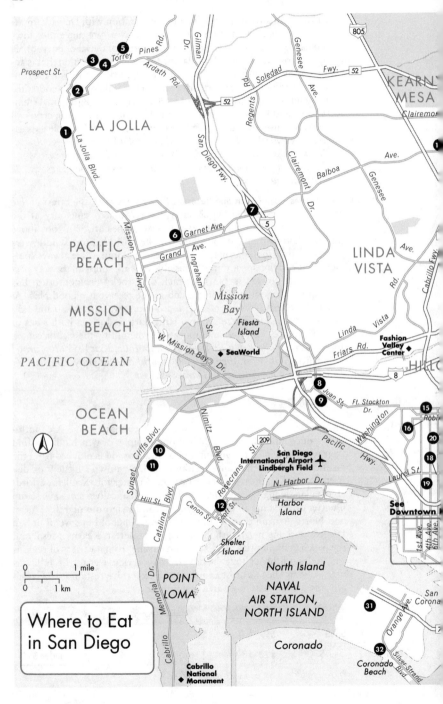

Where to Eat
in San Diego

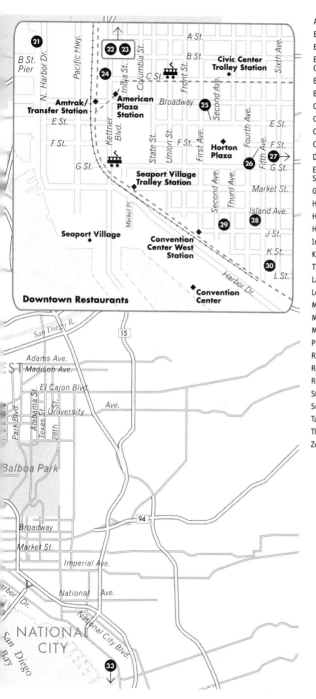

Downtown Restaurants

Downtown

American

¢–$$ ✕ **Hob Nob Hill.** That Hob Nob never seems to change suits San Diego just fine. This is the type of place where regulars arrive on the same day of the week at the same time and order the same meal they've been ordering for 20 years. With its dark-wood booths and patterned carpets, Hob Nob Hill seems suspended in the 1950s, but you don't need to be a nostalgia buff to appreciate the bargain-price American home cooking—dishes such as oat-raisin French toast, fried chicken, and corned beef like your mother never really made. The crowds line up morning, noon, and night. Reservations are suggested for Sunday breakfast. ⊠ *2271 1st Ave., Middletown* ☎ *619/239–8176* ⊟ *AE, D, MC, V.*

¢ ✕ **Bread on Market.** The baguettes at this artisan bakery near the Petco Park baseball stadium are every bit as good as in Paris. Baguettes, focaccia, and other superior loaves are the building blocks for solid, sometimes creative sandwiches, which range from the simple goodness of Genoa salami and sweet butter, to a vegan sandwich that includes locally grown avocado. The menu extends to a daily soup, a fruit-garnished cheese plate, and an appetizing Mediterranean salad. Snackers gravitate here for fudge-textured brownies, orange-almond biscotti, and other irresistible sweets. ⊠ *730 Market St., Downtown* ☎ *619/795–2730* ⊟ *MC, V* ⊘ *Closed Sun. No dinner.*

Contemporary

$$–$$$$ ✕ **Laurel.** Laurel is a premier dinner address, especially among those attending a performance at the Old Globe Theatre in Balboa Park. Polished service, a smart, contemporary design, and a notable wine list set the stage for an imaginative, expertly prepared seasonal menu that takes its inspiration from Mediterranean cuisine. Look for appetizers such as Pacific oysters on the half-shell with red wine "mignonette" sauce, and warm tart of Roquefort cheese and caramelized onions. Among the main courses, reliable choices include the chicken roasted in a clay pot, crisp duck confit, and pan-seared sea scallops. Leave time for a superb artisan cheese before curtain call. ⊠ *505 Laurel St., Middletown* ☎ *619/ 239–2222* ⊟ *AE, D, DC, MC, V* ⊘ *No lunch.*

$–$$
Fodor'sChoice
★
✕ **Region.** Only the finest local produce is used to create traditional recipes at Region, one of the most intriguing recent culinary additions to San Diego. Specialties include osso buco, roast pork with sweet potatoes, and pan-gilded skate (a fish rarely encountered on local menus) that flakes at the touch of a fork. The menu changes daily, but count on fine sweets like cooked-to-order doughnuts with olive oil gelato. The dining room is somewhat spare, but the food and prices make this less important than it would be at other top establishments. Reservations are strongly advised. ⊠ *3671 5th Ave., Hillcrest* ☎ *619/299–6499* ⊟ *AE, D, DC, MC, V* ⊘ *No lunch. No dinner Sun. and Mon.*

French

$$$–$$$$ ✕ **Le Fontainebleau.** On the second floor of the Westgate Hotel, Le Fontainebleau is worthy of the famous chateau for which it is named. Normandy-born chef Fabrice Hardel writes seasonal menus, but usually offers classics like French pepper steak (dramatically flambeed at table) and lobster Thermidor. The multicourse tasting menu paired with specially selected wines costs more than $100 per person, a price that seems not unreasonable when read to the accompaniment of the harp or piano music that is a restaurant staple. ⊠ *1055 2nd Ave., Downtown* ☎ *619/557–3655* 🏛 *Jacket required* ⊟ *AE, D, DC, MC, V.*

★ **$$–$$$$** ✕ **Bertrand at Mister A's.** Restaurateur Bertrand Hug's sumptuous 12th-floor dining room has vanilla walls, contemporary paintings, and a view that stretches from the mountains to Mexico and San Diego Bay. You can watch the aerial ballet of jets descending upon nearby Lindbergh Field. Ideal for a special occasion, Bertrand at Mister A's serves luxurious seasonal dishes such as sautéed foie gras with caramelized fruit and Dover sole in lemon butter. The dessert list encompasses a galaxy of sweets every bit as memorable as the view. ⊠ *2550 5th Ave., Middletown* ☎ *619/239–1377* ⚓ *Reservations essential* 🏛 *Jacket required* ⊟ *AE, DC, MC, V* ⊗ *No lunch weekends.*

Indian

★ **$–$$** ✕ **Bombay Exotic Cuisine of India.** Notable for its elegant dining room, Bombay employs a chef whose generous hand with raw and cooked vegetables gives each course a colorful freshness reminiscent of California cuisine, though the flavors definitely hail from India. Try the tandoori lettuce wrap appetizer and any of the stuffed *nan* (a delectably chewy tandoori bread). The unusually large selection of curries may be ordered with meat, chicken, fish, or tofu. The curious should try the *dizzy noo shakk*, a sweet and spicy banana curry. Try a "thali," a plate that includes an entrée, traditional sides, nan, dessert, and tea. ⊠ *Hillcrest Center, 3975 5th Ave., Suite 100, Hillcrest* ☎ *619/298–3155* ⊟ *AE, D, DC, MC, V.*

$–$$ ✕ **Monsoon.** The attractive dining room here has a waterfall that splashes like a cloudburst from a bower of hanging plants. Folding doors allow some tables to share the outdoor atmosphere of the terrace, but at a distance from the sidewalk. The menu offers many unusual dishes, including a sweetly spiced mango soup, and "balti"-style pan-sautéed lamb. The dozens of curries and similar dishes are spiced to taste. ⊠ *729–733 4th Ave., Gaslamp Quarter* ☎ *619/234–5555* ⊟ *AE, MC, V.*

Italian

$–$$$ ✕ **Buon Appetito.** Old-world–style cooking is offered here in a cheerful but decidedly sophisticated environment. Choose a table on the sidewalk, where the breeze blows in from San Diego Bay, or in an indoor room jammed with art and fellow diners. Baked eggplant all' Amalfitana is a dream of a dish, and in San Diego, tomato sauce doesn't get better than this. Other great choices are veal with tuna sauce, a hot chicken liver salad, fusilli pasta in savory duck ragu, and hearty seafood *cioppino*. ⊠ *1609 India St., Little Italy* ☎ *619/238–9880* ⊟ *MC, V.*

Mexican

$$$–$$$$ ✕ **Candelas.** The scents and flavors of imaginative Mexican cuisine permeate this handsome, romantic hideaway in the shadow of San Diego's tallest residential towers. Candles glow everywhere around the small, comfortable dining room and the bar. Fine openers such as cream of black bean and beer soup, and salad of watercress with bacon and pistachios warm diners up for local lobster stuffed with mushrooms, jalapeño peppers, and aged tequila; or tequila-flamed jumbo prawns over creamy, seasoned goat cheese. The new, adjacent bar pours many elegant tequilas. ⊠ *416 3rd Ave., Gaslamp Quarter* ☎ *619/702–4455* ▭ *MC, V* ⊙ *Closed Sun. No lunch weekends.*

$$–$$$ ✕ **The Latin Room.** This stylish restaurant brings a hip salsa beat to the Gaslamp Quarter. Before 9 PM you can count on a fairly quiet environment in which to enjoy expertly prepared appetizers like quesadillas *de cuitlacoche,* which wrap fragrant "corn fungus" mushrooms inside tender corn tortillas, and such entrées such as giant prawns in a tart, puckery tamarind sauce. As the night wears on, however, guests take to the dance floor and concentrate more on cocktails than dinner. ⊠ *560 4th Ave., Gaslamp Quarter* ☎ *619/237–7800* ▭ *AE, D, MC, V* ⊙ *No lunch.*

Seafood

$$$–$$$$ ✕ **Star of the Sea.** The formal dining room here epitomizes elegance (although dress is quite casual). The menu changes seasonally, but you may find listings for exceptional oysters on the half shell, white-corn agnolotti pasta with shaved truffles, whole roasted snapper with Manila clams and marinated squid, and grilled escolar with a racy "tapenade" of sun-dried tomatoes. The baked-to-order soufflés are puffy, fragrant, and lovely on the palate. The outdoor patio takes full advantage of the choice waterfront location. ⊠ *1360 N. Harbor Dr., Downtown* ☎ *619/232–7408* ▭ *AE, D, DC, MC, V* ⊙ *No lunch.*

Fodor'sChoice
★

¢–$ ✕ **The Tin Fish.** Rainy days are the only times when this eatery next to the Petco Park baseball stadium isn't packed (its 100-odd seats are all outdoors). Musicians entertain some evenings, providing accompaniment for dinners of grilled and fried fish and shellfish, as well as Mexican-style seafood burritos and tacos. The bread used for sandwiches stuffed with fried oysters and the like is baked fresh at the restaurant. For kids (or unadventurous grown-ups) there's an inexpensive peanut butter and jelly sandwich. ⊠ *170 6th Ave., Gaslamp Quarter* ☎ *619/238–8100* ⌲ *Reservations not accepted* ▭ *MC, V.*

Southwestern

$$–$$$ ✕ **Indigo Grill.** Chef–partner Deborah Scott uses inspirations from Mexico to Alaska to infuse her contemporary Southwestern cuisine. The breezes out on the terrace may cool you as you enjoy the chile pepper–infused stacked beet salad, pecan-crusted trout, plank-roasted salmon, and venison chops. Creative desserts are often so generous in size that they can easily satisfy two. ⊠ *1536 India St., Little Italy* ☎ *619/234–6802* ▭ *AE, D, DC, MC, V* ⊙ *No lunch weekends.*

Steak Houses

★ **$$$–$$$$** ✕ **Rainwater's on Kettner.** San Diego's premier homegrown steak house has the luxurious look and mood of an old-fashioned Eastern men's club. You can settle back into the exceptionally deep banquettes and start with Rainwater's signature black bean soup with Madeira, then continue with the tender, expertly roasted prime rib. The menu also includes superb calves' liver with onions and bacon, broiled free-range chicken, fresh seafood, and amazingly succulent pork chops, all served in vast portions with plenty of hot-from-the-oven cornsticks on the side. The well-chosen wine list has pricey but superior selections. ⊠ *1202 Kettner Blvd., Downtown* ☎ *619/233–5757* ⊟ *AE, D, MC, V* ⊗ *No lunch weekends.*

Thai

¢–$$ ✕ **Celadon Fine Thai Cuisine.** Talk to young proprietor Alex Thao if you want to try some of the specialties not listed on the menu, like the spicy, stir-fried cashew appetizer, or the tart, invigorating stir-fry of shredded dried beef and citrus sauce. These dishes are superb, but the everyday menu is good enough to keep the small, well-furnished dining room jumping, even on Monday nights. Start with "Celadon squares," small toasts covered with a paste of shrimp and pork, and move along to refreshing, if spicy, papaya salad, the excellent *tom kha* soup, and such entrées as deep-fried whole striped bass with green mangoes. ⊠ *540 University Ave., Hillcrest* ☎ *619/297–8424* ⊟ *MC, V.*

Coronado

Seafood

$$$–$$$$ ✕ **Azzura Point.** This restaurant offers unbeatable views of San Diego Bay, the Coronado Bridge, and the downtown skyline. Expect thoroughly contemporary preparations of first-class seasonal produce, such as sautéed foie gras with braised pineapple, pan-roasted ahi tuna with ginger-infused rice, and herb-crusted veal chop with polenta fritters. The herbs often come from the restaurant's extensive garden. Several choice, artisan cheeses are an alternative to the deftly executed desserts. ⊠ *Loews Coronado Bay Resort, 4000 Coronado Bay Rd., Coronado* ☎ *619/424–4477* ⊟ *AE, DC, MC, V* ⊗ *Closed Mon. No lunch.*

$$$–$$$$ ✕ **Prince of Wales.** The 1930s live on in the Hotel Del Coronado's re-
Fodor's Choice stored Prince of Wales, which affords sweeping ocean views from an el-
★ egant indoor room and a breezy terrace. The inventive cooking includes such creations as a "Napoleon" of Hudson Valley foie gras with Port wine-fig mousse, a pan-crisped filet of Hawaiian red snapper with cauliflower mousse, and roasted duck breast with Port-braised short ribs and a toothsome "hash" of root vegetables. After all this, the "trilogy" of a molten-centered cake, a mousse, and a soup of white chocolate and walnuts concludes the affair convincingly. ⊠ *Hotel Del Coronado, 1500 Orange Ave., Coronado* ☎ *619/435–6611* ⊟ *AE, D, DC, MC, V* ⊗ *No lunch.*

★ ¢–$$$$ ✕ **Baja Lobster.** The closest thing to dining in Puerto Nuevo, Baja California—the famed lobstering village 20 mi south of the border—is Baja Lobster. Here, locally caught lobsters are split and lightly fried served with family-style portions of fresh flour tortillas, creamy beans crammed with flavor, and well-seasoned rice. While lobsters are the big catch, steak and chicken options are on the menu, too. A pair of high-quality shrimp tacos costs just $5.95. Note that a similarly named chain, Rockin' Baja Lobster, is not related to Baja Lobster. ⊠ *1060 Broadway, Chula Vista* ☎ *619/425–2512* ⊟ *MC, V.*

Kearny Mesa

Chinese

★ **$–$$$$** ✕ **Emerald Chinese Seafood Restaurant.** The first Hong Kong–style restaurant to open in San Diego, Emerald holds pride of place among fanciers of elaborate, carefully prepared, and sometimes costly seafood dishes. The shrimp, prawns, lobsters, clams, and fish reside in tanks until the moment of cooking. Simple preparations flavored with scallions, black beans, and ginger are among the best. Other highlights are beef with Singapore-style satay sauce, honey-walnut shrimp, baked chicken in five spices, Peking duck served in two savory courses, and, at lunch, the dim sum. ✉ *3709 Convoy St., Kearny Mesa* ☎ *858/565–6888* ▭ *AE, MC, V.*

★ **¢–$** ✕ **Dumpling Inn.** Modest, family-style, and absolutely wonderful, this tiny establishment loads its tables with bottles of aromatic and spicy condiments for the boiled, steamed, and fried dumplings that are the house specialty. These delicately flavored, hefty mouthfuls preface a meal that may continue simply, with hearty pork and pickled cabbage soup, or elaborately, with Shanghai-style braised pork shank. Ask about daily specials, such as shredded pork in plum sauce served on a sea of crispy noodles. You may bring your own wine or beer; the house serves only tea and soft drinks. ✉ *4619 Convoy St., #F, Kearny Mesa* ☎ *858/268–9638* ⌦ *Reservations not accepted* ▭ *MC, V* ◷ *Closed Mon.*

Mission Bay & the Beaches

American

¢–$ ✕ **Hodad's.** Get ready for a 1960s flashback at this fabulously funky burger joint. Walls here are covered with license plates, and the amiable tattooed servers tend to a crowd of unrepentant hippies. Burgers are the thing, loaded with onions, pickles, tomatoes, lettuce, and condiments, and so gloriously messy that you might wear a swimsuit so you can stroll to the beach for a bath afterward. The mini-hamburger is good, the double bacon cheeseburger absolutely awesome. ✉ *5010 Newport Ave., Ocean Beach* ☎ *619/224–4623* ▭ *AE, MC, V.*

German

$$–$$$ ✕ **Kaiserhof.** Without question this is the best German restaurant in San Diego County, and the lively bar and beer garden work to inspire a sense of *Gemutlichkeit* (happy well-being). Tourist board-style posters of Germany's romantic destinations hang on the wall, Warsteiner and St. Pauli Girl flow from the tap. Since the gigantic portions are accompanied by side dishes like potato pancakes, bread dumplings, red cabbage, and spaetzle noodles, only the truly famished should attempt starters. Entrées include sauerbraten, Wiener schnitzel, goulash, and smoked pork chops, plus excellent daily specials such as venison medallions in green peppercorn sauce. Reservations are a good idea. ✉ *2253 Sunset Cliffs Blvd., Ocean Beach* ☎ *619/224–0606* ▭ *MC, V* ◷ *Closed Mon. No lunch Tues.–Thurs.*

Italian

¢–$$$ ✕ **Caffe Bella Italia.** Contemporary Italian cooking as prepared in Italy—an important point in fusion-mad San Diego—is the rule at this simple restaurant near one of the main intersections in Pacific Beach. The menu presents Neapolitan-style macaroni with sausage and artichoke hearts in spicy tomato sauce, *pappardelle* (wide ribbons of pasta) with a creamy Gorgonzola and walnut sauce, plus formal entrées like chicken breast sautéed with balsamic vinegar, and slices of rare filet mignon tossed with herbs and topped with arugula and Parmesan shavings. Impressive daily specials include beet-stuffed ravioli in creamy saffron sauce. ⊠ *1525 Garnet Ave., Pacific Beach* ☎ *858/273–1224* ▭ *MC, V* ⊘ *Closed Mon.*

Japanese

¢–$$ ✕ **Sushi Ota.** Wedged into a minimall between a convenience store and
Fodor'sChoice a looming medical building, Sushi Ota initially seems less than impres-
★ sive. But don't be fooled—this is San Diego's best sushi place. Besides the usual California roll and tuna and shrimp sushi, sample the sea urchin or surf clam sushi, and the soft-shell crab roll. Sushi Ota offers the cooked as well as the raw. There's additional parking behind the mall. ⊠ *4529 Mission Bay Dr., Pacific Beach* ☎ *619/270–5670* ⌕ *Reservations essential* ▭ *AE, D, MC, V* ⊘ *No lunch Sat.–Mon.*

Seafood

¢–$ ✕ **Hudson Bay Seafood.** Part of the pleasure in this small, friendly, waterside fish house is watching the day-charter boats arrive at the adjacent dock and discharge their passengers. More than a few march right up the wooden walkway to this eatery, where fresh-baked sourdough rolls enclose fried fish fillets or shellfish. The french fries are scrumptious, the fish tacos taste of Mexico, and even the tartar sauce is homemade. There are salads and excellent breakfasts, too; even the burgers are exceptional. ⊠ *1403 Scott St., Shelter Island* ☎ *619/222–8787* ▭ *MC, V.*

Old Town

Mexican

$–$$ ✕ **Zocalo Grill.** The best tables here are on the firelit covered terrace, but the contemporary Mexican food tastes just as good inside. Instead of traditionally simmering the *carnitas* (pork chunks) in well-seasoned lard, Zocalo braises them in a mixture of honey and Porter beer and serves the dish with mango salsa and avocado salad. Recommended starters include artichoke fritters and crisp shrimp skewers with pineapple-mango relish. The Seattle surf and turf roasts wild salmon and forest mushrooms on a cedar plank. ⊠ *2444 San Diego Ave., Old Town* ☎ *619/298–9840* ▭ *AE, D, DC, MC, V.*

Seafood

$$–$$$ ✕ **Cafe Pacifica.** The airy Cafe Pacifica serves eclectic contemporary cuisine with an emphasis on seafood. Fresh fish is grilled with your choice of savory sauces. Other good bets include the griddle-fried mustard catfish, sole stuffed with rock shrimp and Dungeness crab, and grilled, line-caught salmon. The crème brûlée is worth blowing any diet for. The wine list has received kudos from *Wine Spectator* magazine, but also consider the pomegranate-flavored margarita. ⊠ *2414 San Diego Ave., Old Town* ☎ *619/291–6666* ▭ *AE, D, DC, MC, V* ⊘ *No lunch.*

La Jolla

Contemporary

$$$–$$$$
Fodor'sChoice
★

✕ **George's at the Cove.** Hollywood types are often spotted in the elegant main dining room, where a wall-length window overlooks La Jolla Cove. Chef Trey Foshee works wonders here with fresh seafood, beef and lamb, and with seasonal produce from local specialty growers. Give special consideration to imaginatively garnished, wild California salmon, or choice cuts of beef and pork from the state's celebrated Niman Ranch. For more informal dining and a sweeping view of the coast try the rooftop Ocean Terrace ($–$$). ⊠ *1250 Prospect St., La Jolla* ☎ *858/454-4244* ⌕ *Reservations essential* ☱ *AE, D, DC, MC, V.*

$$$–$$$$

✕ **Marine Room.** You can ocean-gaze at this venerable La Jolla Shores mainstay and, if you're lucky, watch the grunion run or the waves race across the sand and beat against the glass. Creative seasonal menus score with "trilogy" plates that combine three meats, sometimes including game, in distinct preparations. Disparate elements like candied chestnuts, apple curry sauce, and green beans enhance such entrées as gooseberry-glazed chicken breast. Watercress salad and a limoncello liqueur–chervil emulsion add sparkle to the taste of butter-basted lobster tail. Sunday brunch is lavish; in winter call for information about the high-tide breakfasts. ⊠ *2000 Spindrift Dr., La Jolla* ☎ *858/459-7222* ☱ *AE, D, DC, MC, V.*

★ $$–$$$$

✕ **Roppongi.** A hit from the moment it opened, Roppongi serves global cuisine with strong Asian notes. The contemporary dining room done in wood tones and accented with Asian statuary has a row of comfortable booths along one wall. It can get noisy when crowded; tables near the bar are generally quieter. Order the imaginative Euro-Asian tapas as appetizers or combine them for a full meal. Try the barbecued mini lamb chops, seafood pot stickers with caviar sauce, and the high-rising Polynesian crab stack. Good entrées are boneless beef shortribs with honey-mustard glaze, and fresh seafood. ⊠ *875 Prospect St., La Jolla* ☎ *858/551-5252* ☱ *AE, D, DC, MC, V.*

French

$$$–$$$$
Fodor'sChoice
★

✕ **Tapenade.** Inspired by the south of France, celebrated Tapenade (named after the delicious Provençal black olive–and–anchovy paste that accompanies the bread) has shed some of the cuisine's weight in the cross-Atlantic delivery. In an unpretentious, light, and airy room lined with 1960s French movie posters, it serves cuisine to match. Very fresh ingredients, a delicate touch with sauces, and an emphasis on seafood characterize the menu. It changes frequently, but with good fortune may include pan-gilded sea scallops in fragrant curry sauce, veal with morel mushrooms, and desserts like crisp, pear-stuffed spring rolls with caramel sauce. ⊠ *7612 Fay Ave., La Jolla* ☎ *858/551-7500* ☱ *AE, D, DC, MC, V.*

¢–$$$

✕ **Michele Coulon Dessertier.** A "dessertier" is one who creates desserts—and Michele Coulon does so exceedingly well in the back of this small, charming shop in the heart of La Jolla's "village." Colorful raspberry pinwheel *bombe* (a molded dessert of cake, jam, and creamy filling), Amareno cherry torte, and a tri-color mousse of chocolate and coffee creams are a few treats. Weekday lunches and Thursday-through-Saturday dinners are prepared by son Nathan Coulon, whose evening specialties include chicken breast in Normandy-style cream sauce, halibut in an artichoke-enriched butter sauce, and a meltingly tender pepper steak. Make reservations for dinner, which is served at oak tables set with roses fresh from a family member's garden. ✉ *7556 Fay Ave., La Jolla* ☎ *858/ 456–5098* ⚖ *Reservations essential* ▤ *AE, D, MC, V* ⊘ *Closed Sun. No dinner Mon.–Wed.*

WHERE TO STAY

Updated by
Lenore Grenier

San Diego is spread out, so the first thing to consider when selecting lodging is location. If you choose a hotel with a waterfront location and extensive outdoor sports facilities, you may decide never to leave. But if you plan to sightsee, take into account a hotel's proximity to attractions. Lodging in San Diego is mostly in hotels and motels, though there are a few well-maintained bed-and-breakfasts.

Prices

Even the most expensive areas, like Coronado, have some reasonably priced rooms, and specials are frequent. High season is summer, and rates are lowest in the fall. An ocean-view room will cost significantly more than a non–ocean-view room.

WHAT IT COSTS				
$$$$	**$$$**	**$$**	**$**	**¢**
FOR 2 PEOPLE	over $250	$176–$250	$121–$175	$90–$120	under $90

Prices are for a standard double room in high (summer) season, excluding 10.5% tax.

Downtown

$$$$

FodorsChoice

★

🏨 **Manchester Grand Hyatt San Diego.** Two high-rise towers—one of them completed in 2003—make up the largest hotel in San Diego, right next to Seaport Village. Inside, old-world opulence combines with California airiness. Palm trees pose next to ornate tapestry couches in the light-filled lobby, and all of the British Regency–style guest rooms have views of the water. A trolley station is one block away. The 40th-floor Top of the Hyatt lounge in the first tower is one of the city's most romantic spots to watch the sun set. ✉ *1 Market Pl., Embarcadero 92101* ☎ *619/232–1234 or 800/233–1234* 🖷 *619/233–6464* ⊕ *www. manchestergrand.hyatt.com* ⇨ *1,625 rooms, 95 suites* ⚖ *3 restaurants, room service, in-room data ports, minibars, cable TV, 4 tennis courts, pool, health club, outdoor hot tub, sauna, steam room, boating, bicycles, 2 bars, shops, dry cleaning, laundry service, concierge, concierge floor, business services, meeting rooms, airport shuttle, car rental, parking (fee); no smoking* ▤ *AE, D, DC, MC, V.*

$$$$

🏨 **San Diego Marriott Hotel and Marina.** This 25-story twin tower next to the San Diego Convention Center has everything a businessperson—or leisure traveler—could want. Lagoon-style pools nestled between cascading waterfalls are among the appealing on-site features. Seaport Village and a trolley station are nearby. The standard rooms are smallish, but pay a

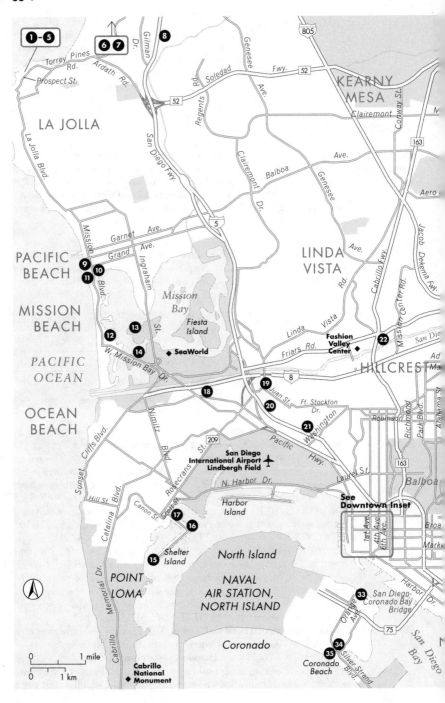

1-5
6 7
8

Torrey Pines Rd.
Prospect St.
Ardath Rd.
Gilman Dr.
Regents Rd.
Soledad
Fwy.
52
805

KEARNY MESA

LA JOLLA

52

Clairemont
163

La Jolla Blvd.
San Diego Fwy.
Ave.
Balboa
Ave.
Aero

5

Garnet Ave.
Grand Ave.
Mission Blvd.
Ingraham St.

PACIFIC BEACH
9
10
11

LINDA VISTA

Ave.

Genesee

MISSION BEACH

Mission Bay
Fiesta Island

12
13
14

PACIFIC OCEAN

W. Mission Bay Dr.
◆ SeaWorld

Linda
Vista
Rd.

Friars Rd.

Fashion Valley Center ◆
22

Mission Center Rd.
San Die

HILLCREST

Ad
Ma

OCEAN BEACH

18
19
20
Juan St.
Ft. Stockton Dr.
21
Washington
Robinson
Richmond
Park Blvd.
Alabama St.

Nimitz Blvd.
Sunset Cliffs Blvd.
Hill St.
Catalina Blvd.
Canon St.
Scott St.
Rosecrans St.
209

8

Pacific Hwy.

San Diego International Airport Lindbergh Field ✈

N. Harbor Dr.

Harbor Island

Laurel St.
163
Balboa

See Downtown Inset

1st Ave
4th Ave
6th Ave
Broa
Mark

17
16
15
Shelter Island

North Island

POINT LOMA

Memorial Dr.
Cabrillo

NAVAL AIR STATION, NORTH ISLAND

Orange Ave
Silver Strand Blvd.

33 San Diego–Coronado Bay Bridge
75

Harbor

San Diego Bay

N

Coronado

34
35
Coronado Beach

◉ (compass)

0   1 mile
0   1 km

◆ **Cabrillo National Monument**

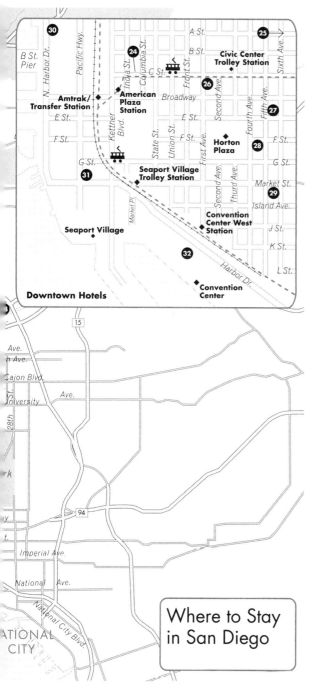

Downtown Hotels

Where to Stay in San Diego

bit extra for a room with a balcony overlooking the bay and you'll have a serene, sparkling world spread out before you. ☒ *333 W. Harbor Dr., Embarcadero 92101* ☎ *619/234–1500 or 800/228–9290* 🖷 *619/234–8678* ⊕ *www.marriotthotels.com/sandt* ➥ *1,300 rooms, 54 suites* ♨ *3 restaurants, room service, in-room data ports, cable TV with movies, 6 tennis courts, 2 pools, aerobics, health club, hair salon, outdoor hot tub, massage, sauna, boating, bicycles, basketball, 3 bars, recreation room, video game room, shops, laundry facilities, concierge, concierge floor, business services, convention center, meeting rooms, airport shuttle, car rental, parking (fee); no smoking* ⊟ *AE, D, DC, MC, V.*

$$$$
Fodor'sChoice
★
🏨 **Westgate Hotel.** A nondescript, modern high-rise across from Horton Plaza hides what must be the most opulent hotel in San Diego. The lobby, modeled after the anteroom at Versailles, has hand-cut Baccarat chandeliers. Rooms are individually furnished with antiques, Italian marble counters, and bath fixtures with 24-karat-gold overlays. From the ninth floor up the views of the harbor and city are breathtaking. Afternoon high tea is served in the lobby to the accompaniment of piano and harp music. The San Diego Trolley stops right outside the door. ☒ *1055 2nd Ave., Gaslamp Quarter 92101* ☎ *619/238–1818 or 800/221–3802, 800/522–1564 in CA* 🖷 *619/557–3737* ⊕ *www.westgatehotel. com* ➥ *223 rooms* ♨ *2 restaurants, room service, in-room data ports, cable TV with movies, health club, hair salon, spa, bicycles, bar, concierge, business services, meeting rooms, airport shuttle, parking (fee); no smoking* ⊟ *AE, D, DC, MC, V.*

$$$–$$$$
🏨 **Holiday Inn San Diego on the Bay.** On the Embarcadero and overlooking San Diego Bay, this twin high-rise hotel has unsurprising but spacious rooms and views from the balconies are hard to beat. Although the hotel grounds are nice if fairly sterile, the bay is just across the street and offers boat rides, restaurants, and picturesque walking areas. The hotel is very close to the airport and Amtrak station. The English-style Elephant and Castle Pub is a great place for food, drink, and meeting people. ☒ *1355 N. Harbor Dr., Embarcadero 92101* ☎ *619/232–3861 or 800/877–8920* 🖷 *619/232–4924* ⊕ *www.holiday-inn.com* ➥ *600 rooms, 17 suites* ♨ *3 restaurants, in-room data ports, cable TV, 2 pools, gym, outdoor hot tub, sauna, bar, shops, laundry facilities, concierge, business services, meeting rooms, airport shuttle, car rental, parking (fee); no smoking* ⊟ *AE, D, DC, MC, V.*

★ **$$$–$$$$**
🏨 **W Hotel.** The W chain's urban finesse adapts to San Diego with nautical blue-and-white rooms with beach-ball pillows and goose-down comforters atop the beds. The Beach bar has a heated sand floor and fire pit, but the pool is tiny by San Diego standards. The lobby doubles as the futuristic Living Room lounge, a local hipster nightspot where non-hotel guests have to wait behind a velvet rope. Be sure to get a room on an upper floor—the leather- and black-clad crowd parties into the night. The hotel restaurant, Rice, serves stylish Asian and Latin cuisine. The spa, Away, opened in 2004. ☒ *421 West B St., Downtown 92101* ☎ *619/231–8220 or 877/946–8357* 🖷 *619/232–3626* ⊕ *www.whotels. com/sandiego* ➥ *277 rooms, 16 suites* ♨ *Restaurant, room service, in-room data ports, cable TV with video games, in-room VCRs, gym,*

bars, spa, concierge, business services, meeting rooms, airport shuttle, parking (fee); no smoking ⊟ AE, D, MC, V.

$–$$$ 🏨 **Gaslamp Plaza Suites.** On the National Registry of Historic Places,
Fodor's Choice   this 11-story structure a block from Horton Plaza was built in 1913 as
★   one of San Diego's first "skyscrapers." Appealing public areas have old marble, brass, and mosaics. Although most rooms are rather small, they are well decorated with dark-wood furnishings that give the hotel an elegant flair. You can enjoy the view and a complimentary continental breakfast on the rooftop terrace. Book ahead if you're visiting in summer. *⊠ 520 E St., Gaslamp Quarter 92101 ☎ 619/232–9500 or 800/ 874–8770 ⊟ 619/238–9945 ⊕ www.gaslampplaza.com ⇨ 52 suites ⚲ Cable TV with VCR, restaurant, microwaves, refrigerators, hot tub, bar, nightclub, parking (fee); no a/c ⊟ AE, D, DC, MC, V ⧖ CP.*

★ ¢–$$ 🏨 **Comfort Inn Downtown.** This three-story, stucco property surrounds a parking lot and courtyard. There's nothing fancy about the accommodations, but some rooms on the south side of the hotel have good views of the city skyline. It's close to downtown hot spots as well as the attractions of Balboa Park. *⊠ 719 Ash St., Downtown 92101 ☎ 619/ 232–2525 or 800/404–6835 ⊟ 619/687–3024 ⊕ www.comfortinn. com ⇨ 45 rooms ⚲ In-room data ports, microwave, cable TV with movies, hot tub, business services, airport shuttle, car rental, free parking; no smoking ⊟ AE, D, DC, MC, V.*

¢   🏨 **HI–San Diego Downtown.** This two-story hostel has basic, modern furnishings and facilities. A special event—from pizza and movie parties to discussions on traveling in Mexico—is scheduled every evening. There are 150 beds, a large common kitchen, and a TV room. Most rooms are dorm style with four bunks each. There are a few doubles, coed dorms, and group rooms (with 10 beds). *⊠ 521 Market St., Gaslamp Quarter 92101 ☎ 619/525–1531 or 800/909–4776 ⊟ 619/338–0129 ⚲ Bicycles, billiards, laundry facilities; no room phones, no room TVs, no smoking, no a/c ⊟ MC, V.*

¢   🏨 **USA Hostels.** This bright, clean hostel is friendly and communal, but strictly for the independent backpacker (any nationality, any age) with a valid passport showing international travel. It makes its home in an 1887 Victorian hotel in the heart of the Gaslamp Quarter. There are 60 beds and five private rooms (two doubles and a triple). A variety of tours and parties are hosted weekly including beach and Tijuana trips. Continental breakfast is complimentary and there's a kitchen for guest use, but you are asked to clean up after yourself. *⊠ 726 5th Ave., Gaslamp Quarter 92101 ☎ 619/232–3100 or 800/438–8622 ⊟ 619/232–3106 ⊕ www.usahostels.com ⚲ Recreation room, laundry facilities, airport shuttle, travel services; no room phones, no room TVs, no smoking, no a/c ⊟ MC, V ⧖ CP.*

Coronado

$$$$ 🏨 **Coronado Island Marriott Resort.** Near San Diego Bay, this snazzy hotel has many rooms with great views of downtown's skyline. Large rooms and suites in low-slung buildings are done in a cheerful California–country French fashion, with colorful Impressionist prints; all rooms have separate showers and tubs and come with plush robes. *⊠ 2000*

2nd St., Coronado 92118 ☎ *619/435–3000 or 800/543–4300* 🖷 *619/ 435–3032* ⊕ *www.marriotthotels.com/sanci* ➶ *273 rooms, 27 suites* ♨ *4 restaurants, room service, in-room data ports, cable TV with movies, 6 tennis courts, 3 pools, aerobics, health club, hair salon, 2 outdoor hot tubs, massage, sauna, spa, beach, snorkeling, windsurfing, boating, jet skiing, waterskiing, bicycles, bar, shops, laundry service, concierge, business services, convention center, meeting rooms, parking (fee); no smoking* ▤ *AE, D, DC, MC, V.*

$$$$
Fodor'sChoice
★

🏨 **Hotel Del Coronado.** "The Del" stands as a social and historic landmark, its whimsical red turrets and balconied walkways taking you as far back as 1888, the year it was built. U.S. presidents, European royalty, and movie stars have stayed in the Victorian rooms and suites, all renovated with the necessities of modern-day life. Public areas always bustle with activity; for quieter quarters, consider staying in the contemporary, seven-story Ocean Towers building or in one of the eight beachfront cottages. Rates are defined largely by room views. ✉ *1500 Orange Ave., Coronado 92118* ☎ *619/435–6611 or 800/468–3533* 🖷 *619/ 522–8262* ⊕ *www.hoteldel.com* ➶ *676 rooms* ♨ *2 restaurants, coffee shop, room service, in-room data ports, cable TV with movies, 3 tennis courts, 2 pools, gym, hair salon, outdoor hot tub, massage, sauna, spa, steam room, beach, bicycles, 4 bars, piano bar, shops, children's programs (ages 3–17), laundry service, concierge, business services, convention center, meeting rooms, parking (fee); no smoking* ▤ *AE, D, DC, MC, V.*

$$–$$$$
🏨 **Glorietta Bay Inn.** The main building of this property—adjacent to the Coronado harbor, and near many restaurants and shops—was built in 1908 for sugar baron John D. Spreckels, who once owned much of downtown San Diego. The Edwardian-style mansion is much smaller than the Hotel Del across the street, but more rooms are available in the adjacent, newer motel-style buildings. Some rooms have patios or balconies. Ginger snaps and lemonade are served daily from 3 to 5. ✉ *1630 Glorietta Blvd., Coronado 92118* ☎ *619/435–3101 or 800/ 283–9383* 🖷 *619/435–6182* ⊕ *www.gloriettabayinn.com* ➶ *100 rooms* ♨ *Dining room, in-room data ports, some kitchenettes, refrigerators, cable TV with movies, pool, outdoor hot tub, bicycles, library, laundry service, concierge, business services, free parking; no smoking* ▤ *AE, MC, V.*

Harbor Island, Point Loma & Shelter Island

$$–$$$$
🏨 **Humphrey's Half Moon Inn & Suites.** This sprawling South Seas–style resort has grassy open areas with palms and tiki torches. Rooms, some with kitchens and some with harbor or marine views, have modern furnishings. Locals throng to Humphrey's, the hotel's seafood restaurant, and to the jazz lounge; the hotel also hosts outdoor jazz and pop concerts from June through October. ✉ *2303 Shelter Island Dr., Shelter Island 92106* ☎ *619/224–3411 or 800/542–7400* 🖷 *619/224–3478* ⊕ *www.halfmooninn.com* ➶ *128 rooms, 54 suites* ♨ *Restaurant, room service, in-room data ports, kitchenettes, minibars, refrigerators, cable TV with movies and video games, putting green, pool, pond, health club, hot tub, boating, bicycles, croquet, Ping-Pong, bar, concert*

hall, laundry facilities, business services, meeting rooms, airport shuttle, free parking; no smoking ⊟ *AE, D, DC, MC, V.*

$$–$$$ 🏨 **Shelter Pointe Hotel & Marina.** This 11-acre property blends Mexican and Mediterranean styles. The spacious and light-filled lobby, with its Mayan sculptures and terra-cotta tiles, opens onto a lush esplanade that overlooks the hotel's marina. The rooms are well appointed, if a bit small, and most look out onto either the marina or San Diego Bay. The attractive hotel is popular for business meetings. ⊠ *1551 Shelter Island Dr., Shelter Island 92106* ☎ *619/221–8000 or 800/566–2524* 🖷 *619/221–5953* ⊕ *www.shelterpointe.com* 🛏 *206 rooms, 31 suites* ♨ *Restaurant, room service, kitchenettes, cable TV with movies and video games, 2 tennis courts, 2 pools, health club, 2 hot tubs, 2 saunas, beach, boating, marina, bicycles, volleyball, bar, meeting rooms, airport shuttle, free parking; no smoking* ⊟ *AE, D, DC, MC, V.*

★ $$ 🏨 **Holiday Inn Express.** In Point Loma near the West Mission Bay exit off I–8, this Holiday Inn Express is a surprisingly quiet lodging despite proximity to bustling traffic. The three-story building is only about a half mile from both SeaWorld and Mission Bay. Continental breakfast is included. ⊠ *3950 Jupiter St., Sports Arena 92110* ☎ *619/226–8000 or 800/320–0208* 🖷 *619/226–1409* ⊕ *www.basshotels.com/holiday-inn* 🛏 *70 rooms, 2 suites* ♨ *In-room data ports, refrigerator, cable TV with movies, pool, hot tub, laundry service, concierge, business services, free parking; no smoking* ⊟ *AE, D, DC, MC, V* ⦿ *CP.*

$–$$ 🏨 **Vagabond Inn–Point Loma.** This two-story budget motel is safe, clean, and comfortable, close to the airport, yacht clubs, and Cabrillo National Monument—and the popular and excellent Point Loma Seafoods restaurant is next door. A daily newspaper and continental breakfast are included. ⊠ *1325 Scott St., Point Loma 92106* ☎ *619/224–3371* 🖷 *619/223–0646* ⊕ *www.vagabondinn.com* 🛏 *40 rooms* ♨ *Restaurant, in-room safes, some kitchens, some refrigerators, cable TV with movies, pool, bar, airport shuttle, free parking; no smoking* ⊟ *AE, D, DC, MC, V.*

Mission Bay & the Beaches

$$$$ 🏨 **San Diego Paradise Point Resort &Spa.** The beautiful landscape at this 44-acre resort on Vacation Isle has been the setting for a number of movies. The botanical gardens have ponds, waterfalls, footbridges, waterfowl, and more than 600 varieties of tropical plants. It makes a convincing backdrop for the Balinese spa. Many recreation activities are offered and there's access to a marina. The room's bright fabrics and plush carpets are cheery; unfortunately, the walls here are motel-thin. ⊠ *1404 W. Vacation Rd., Mission Bay 92109* ☎ *858/274–4630 or 800/344–2626* 🖷 *858/581–5929* ⊕ *www.paradisepoint.com* 🛏 *462 cottages* ♨ *3 restaurants, room service, in-room data ports, refrigerators, cable TV with movies, putting green, 6 tennis courts, 6 pools, pond, fitness classes, gym, outdoor hot tub, massage, sauna, spa, beach, boating, jet skiing, bicycles, croquet, shuffleboard, volleyball, 2 bars, concierge, business services, meeting rooms, airport shuttle, free parking; no smoking* ⊟ *AE, D, DC, MC, V.*

$$$–$$$$ 🏨 **Bahia Resort Hotel.** This huge complex on a 14-acre peninsula in Mission Bay Park has studios and suites with kitchens; many have wood-

beam ceilings and a tropical theme. The hotel's *Bahia Belle* offers complimentary cruises on the bay at sunset and also has a Blues Cruise on Saturday night and live entertainment on Friday night. Rates are reasonable for a place so well located—within walking distance of the ocean—and with so many amenities, including use of the facilities at its sister hotel, the nearby Catamaran. ⊠ *998 W. Mission Bay Dr., Mission Bay 92109* 🕾 *858/488–0551 or 800/576–4229* 🖷 *858/488–1387* ⊕ *www. bahiahotel.com* ↝ *321 rooms* ⚭ *Restaurant, room service, in-room data ports, kitchenettes, cable TV with movies, 2 tennis courts, pool, gym, outdoor hot tub, boating, bicycles, 2 bars, shops, business services, meeting rooms, free parking; no smoking* ⊟ *AE, D, DC, MC, V.*

$$$-$$$$ 🏨 **Catamaran Resort Hotel.** Exotic birds perch in the lush lobby of this
Fodor$Choice appealing hotel on Mission Bay. Tiki torches light the way through
★ grounds thick with tropical foliage to the six two-story buildings and the 14-story high-rise. The room design continues the Hawaiian theme. The popular Cannibal Bar hosts rock bands; a classical or jazz pianist tickles the ivories nightly at the Moray Bar. The resort's many water-oriented activities include free cruises on Mission Bay aboard a stern-wheeler. ⊠ *3999 Mission Blvd., Mission Beach 92109* 🕾 *858/488–1081 or 800/422–8386* 🖷 *858/488–1387* ⊕ *www.catamaranresort.com* ↝ *313 rooms* ⚭ *Restaurant, room service, in-room data ports, kitchenettes, refrigerators, cable TV with movies, pool, gym, outdoor hot tub, beach, boating, jet skiing, bicycles, volleyball, 2 bars, nightclub, shops, business services, meeting rooms, parking (fee); no smoking* ⊟*AE, D, DC, MC, V.*

$$-$$$ 🏨 **Dana Inn & Marina.** This lovely inn is one of Mission Bay's hidden jewels. It's an expansive waterfront property with lovely marina and water views from rooms and garden areas. Simply furnished rooms are large and some have high ceilings. SeaWorld and the beach are within walking distance. ⊠ *1710 W. Mission Bay Dr., Mission Bay 92109* 🕾 *619/ 222–6440 or 800/326–2466* 🖷 *619/222–5916* ⊕ *www.danainn.com* ↝ *196 rooms* ⚭ *Restaurant, room service, cable TV with movies, 2 tennis courts, pool, outdoor hot tub, boating, waterskiing, fishing, bicycles, Ping-Pong, shuffleboard, bar, laundry service, business services, meeting rooms, airport shuttle, car rental, free parking; no smoking* ⊟*AE, D, DC, MC, V.*

★ **$-$$** 🏨 **Surfer Motor Lodge.** This four-story building is right on the beach and directly behind a shopping center with restaurants and boutiques. Rooms are plain, but those on the upper floors have good views. ⊠ *711 Pacific Beach Dr., Pacific Beach 92109* 🕾 *858/483–7070 or 800/787–3373* 🖷 *858/274–1670* ⊕*www.surfermotorlodge.com* ↝*52 rooms* ⚭ *Restaurant, kitchenettes, pool, beach, bicycles, laundry service, free parking; no smoking, no a/c* ⊟ *AE, DC, MC, V.*

¢ 🏨 **Banana Bungalow San Diego.** Literally a few feet from the beach, and near to many restaurants, this hostel's location is its greatest asset. Rooms surround a patio with tropical landscaping, and another beachfront patio has a barbecue. All dorm rooms are coed and there are a total of 70 beds. There are lockers and a small TV room. ⊠ *707 Reed Ave., Pacific Beach 92109* 🕾 *858/273–3060 or 800/546–7835* 🖷 *858/ 273–1440* ⊕ *www.bananabungalow.com* ⚭ *Beach, bicycles, volley-*

ball, airport shuttle, travel services; no room phones, no room TVs, no smoking, no a/c ▭ *MC, V.*

Old Town & Mission Valley

$$$ ⊞ **Doubletree Hotel San Diego Mission Valley.** Near Fashion Valley Center and adjacent to the Hazard Center—which has a seven-screen movie theater, four major restaurants, a food pavilion, and more than 20 shops—the Doubletree is also convenient to Route 163 and I–8. A San Diego Trolley station is within walking distance. Public areas are bright and comfortable, well suited to this hotel's large business clientele. Spacious rooms decorated in pastels have ample desk space. ⊠ *7450 Hazard Center Dr., Mission Valley 92108* ☎ *619/297–5466 or 800/222–8733* 🖷 *619/297–5499* ⊕ *www.doubletree.com* ☞ *294 rooms, 6 suites* ♢ *Restaurant, room service, in-room data ports, minibars, cable TV with movies, 2 tennis courts, 2 pools, gym, outdoor hot tub, sauna, 2 bars, shops, laundry facilities, laundry service, concierge, business services, meeting rooms, airport shuttle, free parking; no smoking* ▭ *AE, D, DC, MC, V.*

★ **$$–$$$**   ⊞ **San Diego Marriott Mission Valley.** This 17-floor high-rise sits in the middle of the San Diego River valley near Qualcomm Stadium and the Rio Vista Plaza shopping center, minutes from several malls. The San Diego Trolley stops across the street. The hotel is well equipped for business travelers—the front desk provides 24-hour fax and photocopy services, and rooms come with desks and private voice mail—but the Marriott also caters to vacationers by providing comfortable rooms (with balconies), a friendly staff, and free transportation to the malls. ⊠ *8757 Rio San Diego Dr., Mission Valley 92108* ☎ *619/692–3800 or 800/228–9290* 🖷 *619/692–0769* ⊕ *www.marriott.com* ☞ *350 rooms, 5 suites* ♢ *Restaurant, room service, in-room data ports, minibars, cable TV with movies, tennis court, pool, gym, health club, outdoor hot tub, sauna, sports bar, nightclub, shops, laundry service, concierge, concierge floor, Internet, business services, meeting rooms, airport shuttle, parking (fee); no smoking* ▭ *AE, D, DC, MC, V.*

$$–$$$ ⊞ **Holiday Inn Express–Old Town.** Already an excellent value for Old Town, this cheerful property throws in such perks as garage parking, continental breakfast, and afternoon snacks. Rooms have a European look. If you've had enough of the heated pool off the shaded courtyard, the historic park's attractions and restaurants are nearby. ⊠ *3900 Old Town Ave., Old Town 92110* ☎ *619/299–7400 or 800/272–6232* 🖷 *619/299–1619* ⊕ *www.basshotels.com/holiday-inn* ☞ *125 rooms, 4 suites* ♢ *Restaurant, room service, in-room data ports, microwaves, refrigerators, cable TV, pool, outdoor hot tub, shops, laundry service, concierge, business services, meeting rooms, airport shuttle, free parking; no smoking* ▭ *AE, D, DC, MC, V* ⦿ *CP.*

$–$$$ ⊞ **Heritage Park Inn.** The beautifully restored mansions in Heritage
Fodor'sChoice   Park include this romantic 1889 Queen Anne–style B&B. Rooms
★   range from smallish to ample, and most are bright and cheery. A two-bedroom suite is decorated with period antiques, and there's also a minisuite. A full breakfast and afternoon tea are included. There is a two-night minimum stay on weekends, and weekly and monthly rates

THE SAN DIEGO SPA CRAZE

THE FIRST SPAS TO TAKE *advantage of San Diego's temperate year-round climate opened their doors to a discriminating clientele nearly a quarter of a century ago. Today the area has one of the largest concentrations of European-style spa resorts in the country.*

*The Hollywood crowd hides out and gets refreshed at **Cal-a-Vie** (✉ 2249 Somerset Rd., Vista ☎ 760/945-2055 ⊕ www.cal-a-vie.com), in the hills near Escondido. Sharon Stone, Russell Crowe, and Oprah Winfrey have come to this French country–style estate to hike, work out, attend health and nutrition lectures, be massaged and wrapped, and devour delicious healthy meals. A fitness facility with weight room, Olympic pool, exercise classrooms, and tennis courts were scheduled for completion in late 2004. A new chef prepares delicious nutritionally balanced meals and even teaches guests how to cook that way at home.*

*The spa and fitness center at **Four Seasons Resort Aviara** (✉ 7100 Four Seasons Point, Carlsbad ☎ 760/603–6800 ⊕ www.fourseasons.com/aviara), has 25 treatment rooms, including five outdoor massage cabanas in a zen garden and a couple's suite. After a hydrating avocado body wrap or an invigorating citrus sugar scrub, you can relax before a fireplace in the solarium.*

*The venerable spa at **La Costa Resort & Spa** (✉ 2100 Costa Del Mar Rd., Carlsbad ☎ 760/931–7570 or 800/*

729–4772 ⊕ www.lacosta.com) got a major makeover in 2003 and joined forces with the Chopra Center to add therapies for the body and mind, including medical consultation, philosophy, psychology, and ayurvedic oils, herb, and aroma treatments. La Costa's new spa facilities are available à la carte and individuals and couples can select from a menu of one-day themed Spa Journeys. Facilities now include 42 treatment rooms, a Roman waterfall shoulder-pounding massage, sunbathing areas, outdoor pool and Jacuzzi, and an outdoor aromatic–herbal steam gazebo. There's also a full-service Athletic Club, which is home to the United States Golf Fitness Association; a Yamaguchi Salon; a spa café, and boutique.

***The Spa at Torrey Pines** (✉ 11480 N. Torrey Pines Rd., La Jolla ☎ 858/453–4420 ⊕ www.spatorreypines.com) is an intimate, full-service facility with 14 treatment rooms, herbal-infused steam rooms, and aromatherapy-inhalation rooms. Programs may include beach walks, fitness classes, yoga, meditation, and tai chi, plus skin and body treatments, such as mud or champagne facials, Swedish or shiatsu massage, and seaweed or honey body wraps.*

are available. Some rooms share a bath. Classic vintage films are shown nightly in the parlor on a small film screen. ✉ *2470 Heritage Park Row, Old Town 92110* ☎ *619/299–6832 or 800/995–2470* 🖷 *619/299–9465* ⊕ *www.heritageparkinn.com* 🛏 *10 rooms, 2 suites* ⚹ *In-room data ports, cable TV, library, meeting rooms; no smoking* ▭ *AE, MC, V* ⦿ *BP.*

★ ¢–$ 🏨 **Western Inn–Old Town.** The three-story Western Inn is decorated in a Spanish motif and is close to shops and restaurants, but far enough away from the main tourist drag that you don't have to worry about noise and congestion. There's a free continental breakfast, and a barbecue area where you can cook for yourself. A bus, trolley, and Coaster station is a few blocks away. ✉ *3889 Arista St., Old Town 92110* 🕾 *619/298–6888 or 888/475–2353* 🖷 *619/692–4497* ⊕ *www. westerninn.com* ⇨ *29 rooms, 6 suites* ♿ *In-room data ports, refrigerators, cable TV, airport shuttle, free parking; no smoking* ▤ *AE, D, DC, MC, V* ⦿| *CP.*

La Jolla

$$$$ 🏨 **Hilton La Jolla Torrey Pines.** The hotel blends discreetly into the Torrey Pines cliff top, overlooking the Pacific Ocean and the 18th hole of the Torrey Pines Municipal Golf Course, site of the 2008 U.S. Open. Oversize accommodations are simple but elegant; most have balconies or terraces. Torreyana Grille's menu changes with the seasons. Caesar salad and filet mignon are menu stalwarts, but you're likely to find lobster pot stickers and coffee-lacquered duck breast as well. ✉ *10950 N. Torrey Pines Rd., La Jolla 92037* 🕾 *858/558–1500 or 800/774–1500* 🖷 *858/450–4584* ⊕ *www.hilton.com* ⇨ *377 rooms, 17 suites* ♿ *3 restaurants, room service, in-room data ports, in-room safes, minibars, cable TV with movies, putting green, 3 tennis courts, pool, gym, outdoor hot tub, sauna, bicycles, 3 bars, babysitting, laundry service, concierge, business services, meeting rooms, airport shuttle, car rental, parking (fee); no smoking* ▤ *AE, D, DC, MC, V.*

FodorsChoice ★

$$$$ 🏨 **Hotel Parisi.** A Zen-like peace welcomes you in the lobby with its skylit waterfall and Asian art. The suites are decorated using the principles of Feng-shui; you can order a massage, a yoga session, or the on-staff psychologist from room service. Favored by celebrities, each hushed, earthtone suite has granite bathrooms, fluffy robes, and ergonomic tubs. The rooms are set back enough from the street noise, but in the ocean-view suites you have to look over buildings across the street to view the Pacific. Continental breakfast is served daily in a breakfast room off the lobby. ✉ *1111 Prospect St., La Jolla 92037* 🕾 *858/454–1511* 🖷 *858/ 454–1531* ⊕ *www.hotelparisi.com* ⇨ *20 suites* ♿ *Room service, in-room data ports, in-room safes, minibar, cable TV with movies, in-room VCR, massage, business services, meeting rooms, free parking; no smoking* ⦿| *CP* ▤ *AE, D, MC, V.*

★ $$$$ 🏨 **La Valencia.** This pink Spanish-Mediterranean confection drew Hollywood film stars in the 1930s and '40s with its setting and views of La Jolla Cove. Many rooms have a genteel European look, with antique pieces and richly colored rugs. The personal attention provided by the staff, as well as the plush robes and grand bathrooms, make the stay even more pleasurable. The hotel is near the shops and restaurants of La Jolla Village. Rates are lower if you're willing to look out on the village. Be sure to stroll the tiered gardens in back. ✉ *1132 Prospect St., La Jolla 92037* 🕾 *858/454–0771 or 800/451–0772* 🖷 *858/456–3921* ⊕ *www.lavalencia.com* ⇨ *117 rooms, 15 villas* ♿ *3 restaurants, room* *service, in-room safes, minibars, cable TV with movies and video games, in-room VCRs, pool, health club, outdoor hot tub, massage, sauna, beach, bicycles, Ping-Pong, shuffleboard, bar, lounge, laundry facilities, concierge, business services, meeting rooms, airport shuttle, parking (fee); no smoking* ▭ *AE, D, MC, V.*

$$$$ 🏨 **Lodge at Torrey Pines.** Many believe this Craftsman-style lodge is the
Fodor'sChoice most beautiful hotel in San Diego. The lodge, made of gigantic pine tim-
★ bers, reflects the designs of architects Greene and Greene, and stands harmoniously on a bluff overlooking Torrey Pines Golf Course and miles of coastline. The soaring lobby is appointed with Stickley leather and oak chairs, Oriental rugs, and stained glass. Luxurious rooms are furnished similarly, and many have balconies and fireplaces. The service is excellent and the restaurant, A. R. Valentin, serves fine California cuisine. ⊠ *11480 N. Torrey Pines Rd., La Jolla 92037* 🕾 *858/453–4420 or 800/995–4507* 🖷 *858/453–7464* ⊕ *www.lodgetorreypines.com* ⇌ *175 rooms* ⟂ *2 restaurants, in-room data ports, in-room safes, kitchenettes, cable TV, 18-hole golf course, pool, gym, hot tub, massage, spa, 2 bars, Internet, meeting rooms, free parking; no smoking* ▭ *AE, D, DC, MC, V.*

$$$–$$$$ 🏨 **The Grande Colonial.** This white wedding-cake–style hotel has ocean
Fodor'sChoice views and is in central La Jolla village. Built in 1913 and expanded and
★ redesigned in 1925–26, the Colonial is graced with charming European details: chandeliers, a marble hearth, mahogany railings, oak furnishings, and French doors. The hotel's restaurant, NINE-TEN, is run by chef Michael Stebner and is well liked by locals for its fresh, seasonal California cuisine. ⊠ *910 Prospect St., La Jolla 92037* 🕾 *858/454–2181 or 800/826–1278* 🖷 *858/454–5679* ⊕ *www.thegrandecolonial.com* ⇌ *58 rooms, 17 suites* ⟂ *Restaurant, room service, in-room data ports, cable TV with movies and video games, pool, bar, meeting rooms, parking (fee); no smoking* ▭ *AE, D, DC, MC, V.*

$$$–$$$$ 🏨 **Scripps Inn.** You'd be wise to make reservations well in advance for this small, quiet inn tucked away on Coast Boulevard; its popularity with repeat visitors ensures that it's booked year-round. Lower weekly and monthly rates (not available in summer) make it attractive to long-term guests. Rooms are done with Mexican and Spanish decor, with wood floors, and all have ocean views; some have fireplaces. Continental breakfast is served in the lobby each morning. ⊠ *555 S. Coast Blvd., La Jolla 92037* 🕾 *858/454–3391 or 800/439–7529* 🖷 *858/456–0389* ⊕ *www.jcresorts.com* ⇌ *14 rooms* ⟂ *In-room safes, cable TV, some kitchens, free parking; no smoking* ▭ *AE, D, MC, V* ⁅◉⁆ *CP.*

★ **$$–$$$$** 🏨 **Hyatt Regency La Jolla.** The Hyatt is in the Golden Triangle area, about 10 minutes from the beach and the village of La Jolla. The postmodern design of architect Michael Graves' striking lobby continues in the spacious rooms, where warm cherry-wood furnishings contrast with austere gray closets. Fluffy down comforters and cushy chairs and couches make you feel right at home, though, and business travelers will appreciate the endless array of office and in-room services. The hotel's four trendy restaurants include Cafe Japengo. Rates are lowest on weekends. ⊠ *Aventine Center, 3777 La Jolla Village Dr., La Jolla 92122* 🕾 *858/552–1234 or 800/233–1234* 🖷 *858/552–6066* ⊕ *www.*

hyatt.com ⤴ *419 rooms, 20 suites* ♨ *4 restaurants, room service, minibar, cable TV with movies, 2 tennis courts, pool, health club, hair salon, outdoor hot tub, massage, basketball, bar, dry cleaning, laundry service, concierge, business services, meeting rooms, parking (fee); no smoking* ☰ *AE, D, DC, MC, V.*

$$–$$$ ▦ **La Jolla Inn.** One block from the beach and near some of the best shops and restaurants, this European-style inn with a delightful staff sits in a prime spot in La Jolla Village. Many rooms have sweeping ocean views from their balconies; one spectacular penthouse suite faces the ocean, another the village. Enjoy the delicious complimentary continental breakfast on the upstairs sundeck. ✉ *1110 Prospect St., La Jolla 92037* ☎ *858/454–0133 or 800/433–1609* 🖷 *858/454–2056* ⊕ *www.lajollainn. com* ⤴ *21 rooms, 2 suites* ♨ *Room service, in-room data ports, some kitchenettes, some refrigerators, cable TV with movies, library, shop, dry cleaning, laundry facilities, concierge, business services, free parking; no smoking* ☰ *AE, D, DC, MC, V* ⭗ *CP.*

NIGHTLIFE & THE ARTS

Updated by
Rob Aikins

San Diego supports vibrant and varied nightlife and arts scenes. Music at local clubs ranges from easy-on-the-ears rock to edgy alternative fare from San Diego's hottest up-and-coming bands. Dance clubs and bars in the Gaslamp Quarter, La Jolla, and at Pacific and Mission beaches tend to be the most crowded spots in the county on weekends, but don't let that discourage you from heading out to these venues. Authentic country-western music is also an option. Should your tastes run toward softer music, there are plenty of piano bars in which to unwind. Smooth and classic jazz also fill the air at waterside venues and in downtown clubs. Trendy Hillcrest pulses with the majority of San Diego's lesbian and gay bars. And coffeehouse culture thrives in San Diego, especially downtown, in Hillcrest, and in the beach communities.

Check the *Reader,* San Diego's free alternative newsweekly; *San Diego* magazine's "Restaurant & Nightlife Guide"; or the *San Diego Union-Tribune* Thursday "Night and Day" insert for the full slate of after-dark possibilities.

The Arts

Book tickets well in advance, preferably at the same time you make hotel reservations. You can buy half-price tickets to most theater, music, and dance events on the day of performance at **Times Arts Tix** (✉ Horton Plaza, Gaslamp Quarter ☎ 619/497–5000). Advance full-price tickets are also sold here. **Ticketmaster** (☎ 619/220–8497) sells tickets to many performances. Service charges vary according to the event, and most tickets are nonrefundable.

Dance

California Ballet Company (☎ 858/560–6741) performs high-quality contemporary and traditional works, from story ballets to Balanchine, from September through May.

Film

Hillcrest Cinemas (✉ 3965 5th Ave., Hillcrest ☎ 619/299–2100) is a posh multiplex right in the middle of uptown's action. **Ken Cinema** (✉4061 Adams Ave., Kensington ☎ 619/283–5909), playing art and revival films, is considered by many to be the last bastion of true avant-garde film in San Diego. It publishes its listings in the *Ken*, a small newspaper distributed in nearly every coffeehouse and music store in the county. The **Museum of Photographic Arts** (✉ 1649 El Prado, Balboa Park ☎619/238–7559) runs a regular film program that includes classic American and international cinema from prominent filmmakers, as well as the occasional cult film.

Part of the Museum of Contemporary Art, the **Sherwood Auditorium** (✉ 700 Prospect St., La Jolla ☎ 858/454–2594) hosts foreign and classic film series and special cinema events, including the wildly popular Festival of Animation, from January through March.

Science, space-documentary, observation-of-motion, and sometimes psychedelic films are shown on the IMAX screen at the **Reuben H. Fleet Science Center** (✉ 1875 El Prado, Balboa Park ☎ 619/238–1233).

Music

Coors Amphitheatre (✉ 2050 Otay Valley Rd., Chula Vista ☎ 619/ 671–3500), the largest concert venue in town, can accommodate 20,000 concertgoers with reserved seats and lawn seating. It presents top-selling national and international acts during its late spring to late summer season.

East County Performing Arts Center (✉ 210 E. Main St., El Cajon ☎619/ 440–2277) hosts a variety of performing arts events, but mostly music. Internationally touring jazz, classical, blues, and world-beat musicians have ensured its popularity among locals. **La Jolla Chamber Music Society** (☎858/ 459–3728) presents internationally acclaimed chamber ensembles, orchestras, and soloists at Sherwood Auditorium and the Civic Theatre.

San Diego Opera (✉ Civic Theatre, 3rd Ave. and B St., Downtown ☎ 619/232–7636) draws international artists. Its season runs from January through May. Past performances have included *The Magic Flute, Faust, Idomeneo,* and *Aida.*

San Diego Symphony Orchestra (✉ 750 B St., Downtown ☎ 619/235– 0804) presents special events year-round, including classic concerts and summer and winter pops. Performances are at Copley Symphony Hall, except the Summer Pops series at the Navy Pier downtown.

Spreckels Organ Pavilion (✉ Balboa Park ☎ 619/702–8138) holds a giant outdoor pipe organ dedicated in 1915 by sugar magnates John and Adolph Spreckels. The beautiful Spanish Baroque structure hosts concerts by civic organist Carol Williams on most Sunday afternoons and on most Monday evenings in summer. Local military bands, gospel groups, and barbershop quartets also perform here. All shows are free.

Spreckels Theatre (✉ 121 Broadway, Downtown ☎ 619/235–0494), a designated-landmark theater erected in 1912, hosts musical events—everything from mostly Mozart to small rock concerts. Ballets and theatrical productions are also held here. Its acoustics and historical status make this a special venue.

Theater

California Center for the Arts, Escondido (✉ 340 N. Escondido Blvd., Escondido ☎ 800/988–4253) presents mainstream theatrical productions such as *Grease* and *The Odd Couple.*

Diversionary Theatre (✉ 4545 Park Blvd., North Park ☎ 619/220–0097) is San Diego's premier gay and lesbian company.

★ **La Jolla Playhouse** (✉ Mandell Weiss Center for the Performing Arts, University of California at San Diego, 2910 La Jolla Village Dr., La Jolla ☎ 858/550–1010) crafts exciting productions from May through November. Many Broadway shows, such as *Tommy* and *How to Succeed in Business Without Really Trying,* have previewed here before heading for the East Coast.

Lamb's Players Theatre (✉ 1142 Orange Ave., Coronado ☎ 619/437–0600) offers five productions from February through November and stages a musical, *Festival of Christmas,* in December. **Lyceum Theatre** (✉ 79 Horton Plaza, Gaslamp Quarter ☎ 619/544–1000) is home to the San Diego Repertory Theatre and also presents productions from visiting theater companies.

Old Globe Theatre (✉ Simon Edison Centre for the Performing Arts, 1363 Old Globe Way, Balboa Park ☎ 619/239–2255) is the oldest professional theater in California, performing classics, contemporary dramas, and experimental works. It produces the famous summer Shakespeare Festival at the Old Globe and its sister theaters, the Cassius Carter Centre Stage and the Lowell Davies Festival Theatre.

Starlight Musical Theatre (✉ Starlight Bowl, 2005 Pan American Plaza, Balboa Park ☎ 619/544–7827 in season), a summertime favorite, is a series of musicals performed in an outdoor amphitheater from mid-June through early September. Because of the theater's proximity to the airport, actors often freeze mid-scene while a plane flies over. **Theatre in Old Town** (✉ 4040 Twiggs St., Old Town ☎ 619/688–2494) presents punchy revues and occasional classics. Shows like *Forbidden Broadway, Ruthless, Gilligan's Island,* and *Beehive* have made this a popular place.

Horton Grand Theatre (✉ Hahn Cosmopolitan Theatre, 444 4th Ave., Gaslamp Quarter ☎ 619/234–9583) stages comedies, dramas, mysteries, and musicals at a 250-seat venue.

Welk Resort Theatre (✉ 8860 Lawrence Welk Dr., Escondido ☎ 760/749–3448 or 800/932–9355), a famed dinner theater about a 45-minute drive northeast of downtown on I–15, puts on polished Broadway-style productions.

Nightlife

The Gaslamp Quarter abounds in nightclubs, dance clubs, and coffee houses. Some stay open after hours (though no alcohol is served after 2 AM) for dancing and entertainment. Special events, such as Mardi Gras and St. Patrick's Day celebrations, draw hordes of locals and visitors.

CloseUp

CASINO COUNTRY

SINCE THE STATE GRANTED 12 Native American tribes permission to operate casinos in greater San Diego, the county has become the undisputed casino capital of California. The casinos range from sprawling Las Vegas–style resorts, with big-name entertainment and golf courses, to small card rooms tucked away on rural crossroads. Most of the tribes are investing heavily in expansion: two resort hotels opened on casino properties in 2003, and more are on the way. Many casinos offer bus transport, so call before visiting and save on gas. You must be at least 18 years old to gamble legally in California.

Viejas Casino (✉ 5000 Willows Rd., off I-8, Alpine ☎ 619/445–5400 ⊕ www.viejas.com) is a sprawling entertainment complex with 2,000 Nevada-style slot machines, plus blackjack, poker, bingo, Pai Gow, and off-track betting. If you can tear yourself away from the casino you can enjoy dinner at one of five restaurants, cocktails in a lounge, and entertainment in the Dream Catcher Showroom. A Native American–theme factory-outlet mall and entertainment center across from the casino has 57 shops, restaurants, and a landscaped amphitheater where evening shows are presented.

Barona Valley Ranch Resort and Casino (✉ 1000 Wildcat Canyon Rd., Lakeside ☎ 619/443–2300 ⊕ www.barona.com) is an all-in-one gaming destination. More than 2,000 slot machines, including progressives like Wheel of Fortune; 31 gaming tables, including California's highest-limit blackjack; a bingo hall; off-track betting; and mini-baccarat await you. In 2003 the resort opened a 400-room lakeside hotel overlooking the 18-hole Barona Creek Golf Club. A food court, Las Vegas–style buffet, and formal restaurant give you the choice to eat in a hurry and get back to the tables or linger

a while and count your winnings (or rue your losses). No alcohol is served here, though the resort is pending approval of a liquor license in 2004.

Sycuan Casino (✉ 5469 Dehesa Rd., El Cajon ☎ 619/445–6002 ⊕ www.sycuan.com) has a 102-room hotel, three restaurants, two 18-hole golf courses, 11 tennis courts, and a theater, in addition to slot machines, gaming tables, off-track betting, and a bingo hall.

Pala Casino (✉ 11154 Rte. 76, Pala 92059 ☎ 877/946–7252 ⊕ www.palacasino.com) secured its place in the resort casino scene with the opening of a 507-room luxury hotel and spa in 2003. In addition to eight restaurants, a bar with entertainment, and plenty of event and meeting space, there are 2,000 Las Vegas–style slot machines in denominations starting at 2¢ and increasing to $100; and 50 table games, such as blackjack, mini-baccarat, Pai Gow, and Caribbean stud poker.

Valley View Casino (✉ 16300 Nyemii Pass Rd., Valley Center ☎ 866/726–7277 ⊕ www.valleyviewcasino.com), a small facility on a backroad just east of Escondido, has more than 750 slots, a dozen blackjack tables, and a 24-hour buffet.

Tropically themed **Casino Pauma** (✉ 777 Pauma Reservation Rd., Pauma Valley ☎ 760/742–2177), a huge tent surrounded by orange orchards in the Pauma Valley, has 850 slot machines, 24 gaming tables, a café, and two bar-lounges. In 2003 the casino announced plans to enlarge the facility, adding restaurants and lounges.

Bars

The **Bitter End** (✉ 770 5th Ave., Gaslamp Quarter ☎ 619/338–9300) is a sophisticated martini bar and a hip dance club where you can kick up your feet. **Blind Melons** (✉ 710 Garnet Ave., Pacific Beach ☎ 858/483–7844), not named after the band, draws well-known local and national bands to play rock and blues tunes that will keep you groovin'. At **'Canes Bar and Grill** (✉ 3105 Ocean Front Walk, Mission Beach ☎ 858/488–1780) rock, reggae, and hip-hop music blends with the sound of crashing waves outside.

Dave & Buster's (✉ 2931 Camino Del Rio N, Mission Valley ☎ 619/275–1515) comprises a restaurant, two bars, billiards, shuffleboard, and a midway packed with arcade games. It's a place to let your inner wild child loose.

Karl Strauss' Old Columbia Brewery & Grill (✉ 1157 Columbia St., Downtown ☎ 619/234–2739 ✉ 1044 Wall St., La Jolla ☎ 858/551–2739), San Diego's first microbrewery, draws an after-work downtown crowd and later fills with beer connoisseurs from all walks of life; the newer La Jolla version draws a mix of locals and tourists. **Martini Ranch** (✉ 528 F St., Gaslamp Quarter ☎ 619/235–6100) mixes more than 30 varieties of its namesake. Actually two clubs in one, the original Martini Ranch hosts jazz groups on weekdays and a DJ spining an eclectic mix on Friday and Saturday. Next door in the larger Shaker Room, local and traveling DJs spin dance beats.

Onyx Room (✉ 852 5th Ave., Gaslamp Quarter ☎ 619/235–6699) is the hippest split-level in town. Onyx is downstairs and feels like two bars in one. In front there's a mood-lit cocktail lounge, and in the next room acid jazz bands and DJs keep the crowds dancing on the tiny dance floor. **Pacific Beach Bar & Grill** (✉ 860 Garnet Ave., Pacific Beach ☎ 858/272–4745) is a stumbling block away from the beach. The popular nightspot has a huge outdoor patio so you can enjoy star-filled skies as you party. The lines here on the weekends are generally the longest of any club in Pacific Beach. The three bars at the **W Hotel** (✉ 421 W. B St., Downtown ☎ 619/231–8220) are among the trendiest places to be for the young bar-hopping set. On the ground floor, Living Room's cozy chairs and couches in alcoves give a true lounge feel. Grab a bite to eat at Magnet, the restaurant bar, before heading up to Beach, an open-air rooftop bar with private cabanas, firepits, and heated sand covering the floor. Get here before 9 PM on weekends to avoid a line.

Coffeehouses

★ **Brockton Villa Restaurant** (✉ 1235 Coast Blvd., La Jolla ☎ 858/454–7393), a palatial café overlooking La Jolla Cove, has indoor and outdoor seating, as well as scrumptious desserts and coffee drinks. It closes at 9 most nights, earlier on Sunday and Monday.

Claire de Lune (✉ 2906 University Ave., North Park ☎ 619/688–9845) won an award for its redesign of the historic Oddfellows building. The wood-floor hangout has sofas and armchairs for lounging as well as tables for studying. Local musicians and poets take the stage on various nights, and San Diego's most popular and longest running open-mic

★ poetry night takes place every Tuesday. **Extraordinary Desserts** (✉ 2929 5th Ave., Hillcrest ☎ 619/294–7001) has award-winning cakes, tortes, and pastries of exceptional beauty (many are decorated with fresh flowers). Offerings change daily so it's worth stopping in more than once.

Javanican (✉ 4338 Cass St., Pacific Beach ☎ 858/483–8035) serves the young beach-community set. Aside from a good cup of joe, live acoustic entertainment is a draw. Adventurous musicians can sign up to play at the open mike Monday night. Other local musicians headline throughout the week.

Comedy & Cabaret

Comedy Store La Jolla (✉ 916 Pearl St., La Jolla ☎ 858/454–9176), like its sister establishment in Hollywood, hosts some of the best touring and local talent. **Lips** (✉ 2770 5th Ave., Hillcrest ☎ 619/295–7900) serves you dinner while female impersonators entertain. Their motto, "where the men are men and so are the girls," says it all.

Country-Western

In Cahoots (✉ 5373 Mission Center Rd., Mission Valley ☎ 619/291–1184), with its great sound system, large dance floor, dance lessons, and DJ, is the destination of choice for cowgirls, cowboys, and city slickers alike. **Tio Leo's** (✉ 5302 Napa St., Bay Park ☎ 619/542–1462) is a throwback to the days when nightclubs were dark and vinyl-filled. The lounge is within a Mexican restaurant, and an incredible variety of country, rockabilly, and swing acts grace the small stage.

Dance Clubs

★ **Deco's** (✉ 721 5th Ave., Gaslamp Quarter ☎ 619/696–3326) is a popular high-end martini–dance bar in the Gaslamp Quarter. The indoor room plays house while the packed open-air area in the back plays hip-hop mixes. **E Street Alley** (✉ 919 4th Ave., Gaslamp Quarter ☎ 619/231–9200) is a spacious hotspot where DJs spin Top 40 and club tunes
★ Thursday through Sunday. **On Broadway** (✉ 615 Broadway, Gaslamp Quarter ☎ 619/231–0011) is a huge, trendy dance club in a former bank building. Open only Friday and Saturday, the $20 cover charge does not discourage San Diego's best-dressed young professionals from waiting hours on long lines to spend their hard-earned money inside. **Plan B** (✉ 945 Garnet Ave., Pacific Beach ☎ 858/483–9921) has a stainless-steel dance floor and numerous places from which to view it, as well as the only permanent laser show in San Diego. **Sevilla** (✉ 555 4th Ave., Gaslamp Quarter ☎ 619/233–5979) brings a Latin flavor to the Gaslamp. Get fueled up at the tapas bar before venturing downstairs for dancing. This is the best place in San Diego to take lessons in salsa and lambada.

Gay & Lesbian Nightlife

MEN'S BARS **Bourbon Street** (✉ 4612 Park Blvd., University Heights ☎ 619/291–0173) has karaoke in the front and a large-screen TV in the back courtyard. Weekends, a back area known as the Stable Bar has DJs who turn the small room into a dance floor. **Brass Rail** (✉ 3796 5th Ave., Hillcrest ☎ 619/298–2233), a fixture since the early 1960s, is the oldest gay bar in San Diego. There's dancing nightly, or you can just pass time playing pool on one of the three tables. **Flicks** (✉ 1017 University Ave., Hillcrest ☎ 619/297–2056), a hip video bar that's popular with the see-and-be-seen crowd, plays music and comedy videos on four big screens. Drink specials vary each night.

WOMEN'S BARS **The Flame** (✉ 3780 Park Blvd., Hillcrest ☎ 619/295–4163), fronted by a red neon sign resembling a torch, is a San Diego institution. The friendly dance club caters to lesbians most of the week. (Tuesday is Boys' Night.)

MIXED BARS **Club Montage** (✉ 2028 Hancock St., Middletown ☎ 619/294–9590) is one of the largest and best clubs in town. The three-level club was originally oriented to the gay crowd, but now all types come for the high-tech lighting system and nationally known DJs. For a breath of fresh air, step out to view the skyline and enjoy a drink from the rooftop bar.

Jazz

Croce's (✉ 802 5th Ave., Gaslamp Quarter ☎ 619/233–4355), the intimate jazz cave of restaurateur Ingrid Croce (singer-songwriter Jim Croce's widow), books superb acoustic-jazz musicians. Next door, Croce's Top Hat has R&B bands nightly from 9 to 2. **Dizzy's** (✉ 344 7th Ave., Gaslamp Quarter ☎ 858/270–7467) late-night jazz jam is Friday after midnight. During the week are jazz, art, and spoken-word events.

★ No alcohol. Perched on the top floor of the Hotel La Jolla, **Elario's Bistro & Sky Lounge** (✉ 7955 La Jolla Shores Dr., La Jolla ☎ 858/551–3620) delivers a lineup of locally acclaimed jazz musicians Tuesday through Saturday. **Humphrey's by the Bay** (✉ 2241 Shelter Island Dr., Shelter Island ☎ 619/523–1010 for concert information), surrounded by water, is the summer stomping grounds for musicians such as Harry Belafonte and Chris Isaak. From May through September this dining and drinking oasis hosts the city's best outdoor jazz, folk, and light-rock concert series. The rest of the year the music moves indoors for some first-rate jazz most Sunday, Monday, and Tuesday nights, with piano-bar music on other nights.

Night Bay Cruises

Bahia Belle (✉ 998 W. Mission Bay Dr., Mission Bay ☎ 619/539–7779) is a paddlewheeler that offers relaxing evening cruises along Mission Bay that include cocktails, dancing, and live music. The $6 fare is less than most nightclub covers. Reservations are required. **Hornblower Cruises** (✉ 1066 N. Harbor Dr., Downtown ☎ 619/686–8700) makes nightly dinner-dance cruises aboard the *Lord Hornblower*—passengers are treated to fabulous views of the San Diego skyline. **San Diego Harbor Excursion** (✉ 1050 N. Harbor Dr., Downtown ☎ 619/234–4111 or 800/442–7847) welcomes guests aboard with a glass of champagne as a prelude to nightly dinner-dance cruises.

Piano Bars

Hotel Del Coronado (✉ 1500 Orange Ave., Coronado ☎ 619/435–6611), the famous fairy-tale hostelry, has piano music in the Palm Court. **Palace Bar** (✉ 311 Island Ave., Gaslamp Quarter ☎ 619/544–1886), in the historical Horton Grand Hotel, is one of the most mellow lounges in the Gaslamp. **Top of the Hyatt** (✉ 1 Market Pl., Embarcadero ☎ 619/232–

1234) crowns the tallest waterfront building in California. The fantastic views and mood lighting make this one of the most romantic spots in town. **Top o' the Cove** (⊠ 1216 Prospect St., La Jolla ☎ 858/454–7779), also a magnificent Continental restaurant, has pianists playing show tunes and standards from the 1940s to the '80s.

Rock, Pop, Folk, World & Blues

Belly Up Tavern (⊠ 143 S. Cedros Ave., Solana Beach ☎ 858/481–9022), a regular fixture on local papers' "best of" lists, has been hosting quality live entertainment, from reggae to folk to rock, since it opened in the mid-'70s. **Casbah** (⊠ 2501 Kettner Blvd., Middletown ☎ 619/232–4355), near the airport, is a small club with a national reputation for showcasing up-and-coming acts. Nirvana, Smashing Pumpkins, and Alanis Morissette all played the Casbah on their way to stardom. **Dream Street** (⊠ 2228 Bacon St., Ocean Beach ☎ 619/222–8131) is the place to see local rock bands playing music that's on the heavy side. **Patrick's II** (⊠ 428 F St., Gaslamp Quarter ☎ 619/233–3077) serves up live New Orleans–style jazz, blues, and rock in an Irish setting.

SPORTS & THE OUTDOORS

Updated by
Rob Aikins

At least one stereotype of San Diego is true—it is an active, outdoors-oriented community, thanks to the constant sunshine. People recreate more than spectate. It's hard not to, with the number of choices available, from boccie and ballooning to golf, surfing, sailing, and volleyball. The northern coastal part of the county has lured many resident professional triathletes, surfers, and bicyclists, who all take advantage of the climate, both meteorological and social.

Ballooning

You can enjoy views of the Pacific, the mountains, and the coastline from Mexico to San Clemente from a hot-air balloon. The conditions are perfect: high winds and wide-open spaces.

A Balloon Adventure by California Dreamin' (⊠ 162 S. Rancho Santa Fe Rd., Suite F35, Encinitas ☎ 800/373–3359) offers sunset and sunrise flights from several North County spots. Temecula wine country flights are also available. **Skysurfer Balloon Company** (⊠ 1221 Camino del Mar, Del Mar ☎ 858/481–6800 or 800/660–6809) takes off from several locations—depending on wind and weather conditions—and will take you on one-hour flights in North County or Temecula. Hors d'oeuvres and beverages are included.

Baseball

The **San Diego Padres** finally have a park designed specifically for baseball. Opening day 2004 also opened **Petco Park** (⊠ 100 Park Blvd., Downtown ☎ 888/697–2373), which harkens back to the great ballparks of yesteryear. The park's design incorporates existing antique buildings to give it a classic ambience that preserves some of the area's heritage. Fans hope the new digs will energize the team. Tickets are usually available on game day.

Beaches

San Diego's beaches are among its greatest natural attractions. In some places the shorefront is wide and sandy; in others it's narrow and rocky or backed by impressive sandstone cliffs. You'll find beaches awhirl with activity and deserted coves for romantic sunset walks. Water temperatures range from 65°F to 75°F from July through September, and 55°F to 65°F from October through June. For a surf and weather report, call ☎ 619/221–8824. For a general beach and weather report, call ☎ 619/289–1212. Pollution has long been a problem at some beaches, particularly following rain storms. The weather page of the *San Diego Union-Tribune* includes pollution reports along with tide tables and listings of surfing and diving conditions.

Overnight camping is not allowed on any San Diego city beaches, but there are campgrounds at some state beaches in the county. Lifeguards are stationed at city beaches in summer, but coverage in winter is provided by roving patrols only. Leashed dogs are permitted on most San Diego beaches and adjacent parks from 6 PM to 9 AM; they can run unleashed anytime at Dog Beach at the north end of Ocean Beach and at Rivermouth in Del Mar.

Pay attention to signs listing illegal activities; undercover police often patrol the beaches, carrying their ticket books in coolers. Glass is prohibited on all beaches, and fires are allowed only in fire rings or elevated barbecue grills. Alcoholic beverages—including beer—are completely banned on some city beaches; on others, you are allowed to drink from 8 AM to 8 PM. Imbibing in beach parking lots, on boardwalks, and in landscaped areas is always illegal. While it may be tempting to take a starfish or some other sea creature as a souvenir from a tide pool, it upsets the delicate ecological balance and is illegal to do, too.

Parking near the ocean can be hard to find in the summer but is unmetered at all San Diego city beaches. The beaches below are listed from south to north.

CORONADO **Silver Strand State Beach.** This quiet Coronado beach is ideal for families. The water is relatively calm, lifeguards and rangers are on duty year-round, and there are places to rollerblade or ride bikes. Four parking lots provide room for more than 1,500 cars. RV campsites ($18) are available on a first-come, first-served basis; stays are limited to seven nights. ⊠ *From San Diego–Coronado Bay Bridge, turn left onto Orange Ave., which becomes Rte. 75, and follow signs* ☎ 619/435–5184.

★ ♻ **Coronado Beach.** With the Hotel Del Coronado as a backdrop, this stretch of sandy beach is one of San Diego County's largest and most picturesque. It's perfect for sunbathing, people-watching, or Frisbee. Navy SEAL teams are known to exercise here. ⊠ *From the Coronado–San Diego Bay Bridge, turn left on Orange Ave. and follow signs.*

POINT LOMA **Sunset Cliffs.** Beneath the jagged cliffs on the west side of the Point Loma peninsula is a secluded beach popular with surfers and locals. Near Cabrillo Point, tide pools teeming with small sea creatures are revealed at low tide. ⊠ *Take I–8 west to Sunset Cliffs Blvd. and head west.*

Ocean Beach. This mile-long beach is a haven for volleyball players, sun-bathers, and swimmers. The area around the municipal pier at the south end is a hangout for surfers and transients; the pier itself is open for fishing and has a restaurant at the middle. The beach is south of the Mission Bay channel. Limited parking is available. Swimmers should beware of unusually vicious rip currents. ⊠ *Take I–8 west to Sunset Cliffs Blvd. and head west. Turn right on Santa Monica Ave.*

Mission Beach. San Diego's most popular beach draws huge crowds on hot summer days. The 2-mi-long stretch extends from the north entrance of Mission Bay to Pacific Beach. The boardwalk is popular with walkers, runners, skaters, and bicyclists. Surfers, swimmers, and volleyball players congregate at the south end. Toward the north end, near the Belmont Park roller coaster, the beach narrows and the water becomes rougher. The crowds grow thicker and somewhat rougher as well. ⊠ *Exit I–5 at Garnet Ave. and head west to Mission Blvd. Turn south and look for parking.*

Pacific Beach/North Pacific Beach. The boardwalk turns into a sidewalk here, but there are still bike paths and picnic tables along the beachfront. Pacific Beach runs from the north end of Mission Beach to Crystal Pier. North Pacific Beach extends from the pier north. The scene here is particularly lively on weekends. There are designated surfing areas, and fire rings are available. Parking can be a challenge, but there are plenty of restrooms and restaurants in the area. ⊠ *Exit I–5 at Garnet Ave. and head west to Mission Blvd. Turn north and look for parking.*

Tourmaline Surfing Park. This is one of the area's most popular beaches for surfing and sailboarding year-round. The parking lot is usually full by midday. ⊠ *Take Mission Blvd. north (it turns into La Jolla Blvd.) and turn west on Tourmaline St.*

Windansea Beach. The beach's sometimes towering waves (caused by an underwater reef) are truly world-class. With its incredible views and secluded sunbathing spots set among sandstone rocks, Windansea is also one of the most romantic of West Coast beaches, especially at sunset. ⊠ *Take Mission Blvd. north (it turns into La Jolla Blvd.) and turn west on Nautilus St.*

Marine Street Beach. Wide and sandy, this strand of beach often teems with sunbathers, swimmers, walkers, and joggers. The water is good for surfing and bodysurfing, though you'll need to watch out for riptides. ⊠ *Accessible from Marine St., off La Jolla Blvd.*

Children's Pool/Shell Beach. Though you can't swim here, these two coves offer panoramic views and the chance to observe resident sea lions sunning themselves and frolicking in the water. ⊠ *Follow La Jolla Blvd. north. When it forks, stay to the left, then turn right onto Coast Blvd. Shell Beach is north of the Children's Pool along Coast Blvd.*

Fodor'sChoice
★ **La Jolla Cove.** This is one of the prettiest spots on the California coast. Palm-lined Scripps Park sits on top of cliffs formed by the incessant pounding of the waves. At low tide the tide pools and cliff caves provide a destination for explorers. Divers and snorkelers can explore the under-

water delights of the San Diego–La Jolla Underwater Park and Ecological Reserve. The cove is also a favorite of rough-water swimmers. ⊠ *Follow Coast Blvd. north to signs, or take the La Jolla Village Dr. exit from I–5, head west to Torrey Pines Rd., turn left, and drive downhill to Girard Ave. Turn right and follow signs.*

★ ☾ **La Jolla Shores.** On summer holidays all access routes are usually closed to one of San Diego's most popular beaches. The lures here are a wide sandy beach and the most gentle waves in San Diego. A concrete boardwalk parallels the beach. Arrive early to get a parking spot in the lot at the foot of Calle Frescota. ⊠ *From I–5 take La Jolla Village Dr. west and turn left onto La Jolla Shores Dr. Head west to Camino del Oro or Vallecitos St. Turn right.*

Torrey Pines City Park Beach. The powerful waves at this beach, known as Black's Beach, attract surfers, and its relative isolation appeals to nudists (although by law nudity is prohibited). Access to parts of the shore coincides with low tide. There are no lifeguards on duty, and strong ebb tides are common—only experienced swimmers should take the plunge. The cliffs are dangerous to climb. ⊠ *Take Genesee Ave. west from I–5 and follow signs to Glider Port; easier access, via a paved path, available on La Jolla Farms Rd., but parking is limited to 2 hrs.*

DEL MAR **Torrey Pines State Beach/Reserve.** One of San Diego's best beaches con-
★ tains 1,700 acres of bluffs, bird-filled marshes, and sandy shoreline. A network of trails leads through rare pine trees to the coast below. The large parking lot is rarely full. Lifeguards are on duty daily (weather permitting) from late May to early September, and on weekends in May and September. ⊠ *Take the Carmel Valley Rd. exit west from I–5, turn left on Rte. S21* ☎ *858/755–2063* ⊠ *Parking $3.*

Del Mar Beach. The numbered streets of Del Mar, from 15th to 29th, end at a wide beach popular with volleyball players, surfers, and sunbathers. Parking can be a problem on nice summer days. The portions of Del Mar south of 15th Street are lined with cliffs and are rarely crowded. ⊠ *Take the Via de la Valle exit from I–5, and head west to Rte. S21 (also known as Camino del Mar in Del Mar) and turn left.*

ENCINITAS **Swami's.** Extreme low tides expose tidepools that harbor anemones, starfish, and other sea creatures. Remember to look but don't touch; all sea life here is protected. The beach is also a top surfing spot. The only access is by a long stairway leading down from the cliff-top park. ⊠ *Follow Rte. S21 north from Cardiff, or take exit I–5 at Encinitas Blvd., go west to Rte. S21, and turn left.*

Moonlight Beach. Large parking areas and lots of facilities make this beach, tucked into a break in the cliffs, a pleasant stop. To combat erosion, sand is trucked in every year. Volleyball courts on the north end attract competent players, including a few professionals. ⊠ *Take the Encinitas Blvd. exit from I–5 and head west to the Moonlight parking lot.*

CARLSBAD **Carlsbad State Beach.** Erosion from winter storms has made the southern Carlsbad beaches rockier than most beaches in southern California. This is particularly true of **South Carlsbad State Beach,** a stretch of which is named in honor of Robert C. Frazee, a local politician and civic booster. Still, it's a good swimming spot, there are fine street- and beach-level promenades outside of downtown Carlsbad, and there is overnight camping for self-contained RVs. ⊠ *Exit I–5 at La Costa Ave. and head west to Rte. S21. Turn north and follow coastline* ☎ *760/438–3143, 800/444–7275 for camping reservations* 🎟 *Free.*

Bicycling

On any summer day **Route S21**, which stretches from La Jolla to Oceanside for about 15 mi, looks like a freeway for cyclists. Never straying more than a quarter-mile from the beach, it is easily the most popular and scenic bike route in the area. For those who want to take their biking experience to the extreme, the **Magdalena Ecke YMCA Skate/BMX park** (⊠ 200 Saxony Rd., Encinitas ☎ 760/942–9622) has set times when BMXers can rip it up on the same wood vert ramp and street courses that skateboarders use. Local bookstores and camping stores sell guides to some challenging mountain-bike trails in outer San Diego County. A free map of all county bike paths is available from the local office of the **California Department of Transportation** (⊠ 2829 Juan St., Old Town 92110 ☎ 619/688–6699). **Bicycle Barn** (⊠ 746 Emerald St., Pacific Beach ☎ 858/581–3665) rents mountain bikes to beach cruisers. **Mission Beach Surf and Skate** (⊠ 704 Ventura Pl., Mission Beach ☎ 858/488–5050) is right on the boardwalk and rents bikes, skates, and boards of all types.

Boating, Jet Skiing & Waterskiing

Most bay-side resorts rent equipment for on-the-water adventures. Other sources can be found in marinas.

Coronado Boat Rentals (⊠ 1715 Strand Way, Coronado ☎ 619/437–1514) has kayaks, Jet Skis, fishing skiffs, and power boats from 15 foot to 19 foot in length as well as sailboats from 18 foot to 36 foot long. The **Mission Bay Sports Center** (⊠ 1010 Santa Clara Pl., Mission Bay ☎ 858/488–1004) rents kayaks, catamarans, single-hull sailboats, power boats, Jet Skis, and boards. **Seaforth Boat Rentals** (⊠ 1641 Quivira Rd., Mission Bay ☎ 619/223–1681) rents Jet Skis, paddleboats, sailboats, and skiffs. **Snug Harbor Marina** (⊠ 4215 Harrison St., Carlsbad ☎ 760/434–3089) rents power boats, kayaks, canoes, waverunners, tubes, Jet Skis, and boards. **Carlsbad Paddle Sports** (⊠ 2002 S. Coast Hwy., Oceanside ☎ 760/434–8686) handles kayak sales, rentals, and instruction for coastal North County.

Diving

Enthusiasts the world over come to San Diego to snorkel and scuba-dive off La Jolla and Point Loma. At La Jolla Cove you'll find the **San Diego–La Jolla Underwater Park and Ecological Reserve.** Because all sea life here is protected, it's the best place to see large lobster, sea bass, and sculpin, as well as numerous golden Garibaldi, the state saltwater fish. It's not uncommon to see hundreds of beautiful leopard sharks schooling on the north end of the cove, near La Jolla shores, especially in summer.

Off the south end of Black's Beach, the rim of **Scripps Canyon** lies in about 60 foot of water. The canyon plummets to more than 900 foot in some sections. The HMCS *Yukon,* a decommissioned Canadian warship, was intentionally sunk off **Mission Beach** to create a diving spot. Beware and exercise caution: even experienced divers have become disoriented inside the wreck. **Sunset Cliffs** in Point Loma is best enjoyed by experienced divers, who mostly prefer to make their dives from boats. The *San Diego Union–Tribune* includes diving conditions on its weather page. For recorded diving information, call the **San Diego City Lifeguard Service** (☎ 619/221–8824).

San Diego Divers Supply (✉ 4004 Sports Arena Blvd., Sports Arena ☎ 619/224–3439) provides equipment, instruction, and maps of local wrecks and attractions. **Diving Locker** (✉ 1020 Grand Ave., Pacific Beach ☎ 858/272–1120) has been a fixture in San Diego since 1959.

Fishing

No license is required to fish from a public pier, such as the Ocean Beach and Oceanside piers. A fishing license from the state **Department of Fish and Game** (✉ 4949 Viewridge Ave., Kearny Mesa, San Diego 92123 ☎ 858/467–4201), available at most bait-and-tackle and sporting-goods stores, is required for fishing from the shoreline. **Fisherman's Landing** (✉ 2838 Garrison St., Point Loma ☎ 619/221–8500) has a fleet of luxury vessels from 57 foot to 124 foot long, offering long-range multiday trips in search of yellowfin tuna, yellowtail, and other deep-water fish. **H&M Landing** (✉ 2803 Emerson St., Point Loma ☎ 619/222–1144) schedules fishing trips year-round. **Helgren's Sportfishing** (✉ 315 Harbor Dr. S, Oceanside ☎ 760/722–2133) is your best bet in North County, with trips departing from Oceanside Harbor.

Fitness

Frog's Athletic & Racquet Club (✉ 901 Hotel Circle S, Mission Valley ☎ 619/291–3500) has a weight room, tennis and racquetball courts, and saunas. The **24 Hour Fitness Centers** (✉ 5885 Rancho Mission Rd., Mission Valley ☎ 619/281–5543 ✉ 3675 Midway Dr., Sports Arena ☎ 619/224–2902 ✉ 4405 La Jolla Village Dr., La Jolla ☎ 858/457–3930) welcome nonmembers for a small fee. **Gold's Gym** (✉ 2949 Garnet Ave., Pacific Beach ☎ 858/272–3400) allows drop-ins. **Bodyworks Health & Fitness** (✉ 1130 7th Ave., Downtown ☎ 619/232–5500) allows nonmembers to use the facilities for a small fee.

Football

The **San Diego Chargers** (✉ 9449 Friars Rd., Mission Valley ☎ 619/280–2121) of the National Football League fill Qualcomm Stadium from August through December.

Top college teams from the PAC 10 and Big 12 square off each December in the **Holiday Bowl** (☎ 619/283–5850), played at Qualcomm Stadium.

Golf

It's hard to find a better place to play golf year-round than San Diego. The climate—generally sunny, without a lot of wind—is perfect for the sport, and there are courses in the area to suit every level of expertise.

Experienced golfers can play the same greens as PGA tournament participants, and beginners or rusty players can book a week at a golf resort and benefit from expert instruction.

For information about public and private courses all over the county, request a golf map from the **San Diego Convention and Visitors Bureau** (☎ 800/472–6343). The **Southern California Golf Association** (☎ 818/980–3630) publishes an annual directory ($15) with detailed and valuable information on all clubs. The **Southern California Public Links Golf Association** (☎ 714/994–4747) will answer questions over the phone or, for $5, will provide you with a roster of member courses.

The **Balboa Park Municipal Golf Course** (✉ 2600 Golf Course Dr., Balboa Park ☎ 858/570–1234) is in the heart of Balboa Park, making it convenient for downtown visitors. Greens fees are $34 to $39. **Coronado Municipal Golf Course** (✉ 2000 Visalia Row, Coronado ☎ 619/435–3121) has 18 holes and views of San Diego Bay and the Coronado Bridge from the back nine holes. Greens fees are $20 to $35. **Mission Bay Golf Resort** (✉ 2702 N. Mission Bay Dr., Mission Bay ☎ 858/490–3370) is an 18-hole, not-very-challenging course lighted for night play. Greens fees are $19 to $23.

Torrey Pines Municipal Golf Course (✉ 11480 N. Torrey Pines Rd., La Jolla ☎ 800/985–4653) is one of the best public golf courses in the United States, with views of the Pacific from every hole. It has 36 holes, a driving range, and equipment rentals. The par-72 South Course was designed by Rees Jones. It's not easy to get a good tee time here as professional brokers buy up the best ones. Out-of-towners are better off booking the instructional Golf Playing Package, which includes cart, greens fees, and a golf-pro escort for the first three holes. Greens fees are $65 to $125.

★ **Aviara Golf Club** (✉ 7447 Batiquitos Dr., Carlsbad ☎ 760/603–6900) has 18 holes designed by Arnold Palmer and views of the Batiquitos Lagoon and the Pacific Ocean. Greens fees are $175 to $195. **La Costa Resort and Spa** (✉ 2100 Costa del Mar Rd., Carlsbad ☎ 760/438–9111 or 800/854–5000) has two 18-hole PGA-rated courses. One of the premier golf resorts in southern California, it hosts the Accenture World Match Play Championships each February. Greens fees are $185 to $195. **Rancho Bernardo Inn and Country Club** (✉ 17550 Bernardo Oaks Dr., Rancho Bernardo ☎ 858/675–8470 Ext. 1) has 45 holes. Greens fees are $85 to $110.

For information about public and private courses all over the county, request a golf map from the **San Diego Convention and Visitors Bureau** (☎ 800/472–6343). The **Southern California Golf Association** (☎ 818/980–3630) publishes an annual directory ($15) with detailed and valuable information on all clubs. The **Southern California Public Links Golf Association** (☎ 714/994–4747) will answer questions over the phone or, for $5, will provide you with a roster of member courses.

Hiking & Nature Trails
The **San Dieguito River Park** (✉ 21 mi north of San Diego on I–5 to Lomas Santa Fe Dr., east 1 mi to Sun Valley Rd., north into park; Solana

Beach ☎ 858/664–2270) is a 55-mi corridor that begins at the mouth of the San Dieguito River in Del Mar, heading from the riparian lagoon area through coastal sage scrub and mountain terrain to end in the desert just east of Volcan Mountain near Julian. **Mission Trails Regional Parks** (✉ 1 Father Junípero Serra Tr., Mission Valley ☎ 619/668–3275 ⊕ www.mtrp. org) encompasses nearly 6,000 acres of mountains, wooded hillsides, lakes, and riparian streams beginning only 8 mi northeast of downtown. Trails range from easy to difficult; they include one with a superb city view from Cowles Mountain and another along a historic missionary path.

Surfing

If you're a beginner, consider paddling in the waves off Mission Beach, Pacific Beach, Tourmaline, La Jolla Shores, Del Mar, or Oceanside. More experienced surfers usually head for Sunset Cliffs, the La Jolla reef breaks, Black's Beach, or Swami's in Encinitas. **Surf Diva Surf School** (✉ 2160-A Avenida de la Playa, La Jolla ☎ 858/454–8273) offers clinics, surf camps, surf trips, and private lessons catered to women. Many local surf shops rent both surf and bodyboards. **Mission Beach Surf & Skate** (✉ 704 Ventura Pl., Mission Beach ☎ 858/488–5050) is right on the boardwalk, just steps from the waves. **Star Surfing Company** (✉ 4652 Mission Blvd., Pacific Beach ☎ 858/273–7827) can get you out surfing around the Crystal Pier. **La Jolla Surf Systems** (✉ 2132 Avenida de la Playa, La Jolla ☎ 858/456–2777) takes care of your needs if you want to surf the reefs or beachbreaks of La Jolla. **Hansen's** (✉ 1105 S. Coast Hwy. 101, Encinitas ☎ 760/753-6595) is just a short walk from Swami's beach.

Tennis

Most of the more than 1,300 courts around the county are at private clubs, but a few are public. The **Balboa Tennis Club at Morley Field** (✉ 2221 Morley Field Dr., Balboa Park ☎ 619/295–9278) has 12 lighted courts. Courts are available on a first-come, first-served basis for a $5-per-person fee. Heaviest usage is 9AM–11AM and after 5PM. Several San Diego resorts have top-notch, professionally staffed tennis programs. **La Costa Resort and Spa** (✉ Costa Del Mar Rd., Carlsbad ☎ 760/438–9111), home of the annual Accura Tennis Classic, has 21 courts, including two Wimbledon-quality grass courts and two clay courts, and offers clinics and workouts. **Rancho Bernardo Inn** (✉ 17550 Bernardo Oaks Dr., Rancho Bernardo ☎ 858/675–8500) has 12 tennis courts and packages that include instruction, accommodations, and meals. **Rancho Valencia Tennis Resort** (✉ 5921 Valencia Circle, Rancho Santa Fe ☎ 858/756–1123), among the finest tennis resorts in the nation, has 18 hard courts, top facilities, and several instruction programs.

Windsurfing

Windsurfing is a sport best practiced on smooth waters, such as those in Mission Bay and near the Snug Harbor Marina at the intersection of I–5 and Tamarack Avenue in Carlsbad. If you are an experienced windsurfer, you may enjoy taking a board out on the ocean. Wave-jumping is especially popular at the Tourmaline Surfing Park in La Jolla and in the Del Mar area. Sailboarding rentals and instruction are available at the **Bahia Resort Hotel** (✉ 998 W. Mission Bay Dr., Mission Bay ☎ 858/

488–0551), and the affiliated Catamaran Resort Hotel. The **Snug Harbor Marina** (✉ 4215 Harrison St., Carlsbad ☎ 760/434–3089) has rentals and instruction and can advise those looking to windsurf on Agua Hedionda lagoon.

SHOPPING

Updated by
Lenore Grenier

Downtown

Art galleries, antiques stores, and boutiques fill the Victorian buildings and renovated warehouses of the lively **Gaslamp Quarter**, especially along 4th and 5th avenues. ✉ *Downtown*.

Westfield Shoppingtown Horton Plaza (✉ Gaslamp Quarter ☎ 619/238–1596) is a multilevel, open-air shopping, dining, and entertainment complex with a lively terra-cotta color scheme and flag-draped facades. There are nearly 200 stores and kiosks, several fast-food counters, and a couple of upscale restaurants, plus the Lyceum Theater and cinemas, at the mall.

Seaport Village (✉ W. Harbor Dr. at Kettner Blvd., Embarcadero ☎ 619/235–4014) is a waterfront complex of 74 shops and restaurants within walking distance of hotels. You may also find horse and carriage rides, an 1890 Looff carousel, and some form of public entertainment.

Coronado

The **Ferry Landing Marketplace** (✉ 1201 1st St., at B Ave., Coronado) has 30 shops plus a Tuesday-afternoon **Farmers Market. Orange Avenue** has six blocks lined with classy boutiques and galleries. ✉ *Coronado*.

Hillcrest, North Park & Uptown

Although their boundaries blur, each of the neighborhoods of Hillcrest, North Park, and Uptown (north and northeast of downtown) contains a distinct urban village. You'll find funky, one-of-a-kind shops, and many ethnic restaurants and entertainment venues. Hillcrest is San Diego's most prominent gay neighborhood. Most of the activity is on **University Avenue,** which runs through all three neighborhoods. On any given Saturday the sidewalks are crowded with shoppers popping in and out of the many gift, book, and music stores. Retro rules in North Park. Nostalgia shops along Park Boulevard and University Avenue at 30th Street carry clothing, accessories, furnishings, wigs, and bric-a-brac of the 1920s to the 1960s. The Uptown District, an open-air shopping center on University Avenue, has several furniture, gift, and specialty stores. Washington Street and side streets branching off University and Washington are also lively shopping areas.

Old Town

The colorful Old Town historic district recalls a Mexican marketplace. Adobe architecture, flower-filled plazas, fountains, and courtyards decorate the shopping areas of Bazaar del Mundo and Old Town Esplanade, where you'll find international goods, toys, souvenirs, and arts and crafts. **Bazaar del Mundo** (✉ 2754 Calhoun St., Old Town ☎ 619/296–3161) has boutiques selling designer items, crafts, fine arts, and fashions from around the world. The best time to visit is during the annual Santa Fe Market in March, when you can browse collections of jewelry, replica artifacts, wearable-art clothing and accessories, pottery, and blankets—all crafted by Southwestern artists.

Mission Valley

The Mission Valley/Hotel Circle area, northeast of downtown near I–8 and Route 163, has a few major shopping centers. **Fashion Valley Center** (⌧ 7007 Friars Rd., Mission Valley ☎ 619/297–3381), with lush landscaping, a contemporary Mission theme, and more than 200 shops and restaurants, is San Diego's upscale shopping mall. There's a San Diego Trolley station in the parking lot. The major department stores are Macy's, Nordstrom, Saks Fifth Avenue, Neiman Marcus, and Robinsons-May. **Park Valley Center** (⌧ 1750 Camino de la Reina, Mission Valley), across the street from Westfield Shoppingtown Mission Valley, is a U-shape strip mall, anchored by **OFF 5th** (☎ 619/296–4896), which offers last-season's fashions by Ralph Lauren, Armani, and Burberry at Costco prices. **Westfield Shoppingtown Mission Valley** (⌧ 1640 Camino del Rio N, Mission Valley ☎ 619/296–6375), is an outdoor shopping mall with department stores and discount stores carrying merchandise that might be found at higher prices in the mall up the road.

La Jolla

This seaside village has chic boutiques, art galleries, and gift shops lining narrow twisty streets. On the east side of I–5, office buildings surround **Westfield Shoppingtown UTC** (⌧ La Jolla Village Dr., between I–5 and I–805, La Jolla ☎ 858/546–8858) has 155 shops, several department stores, a cinema, 25 eateries, and an ice-skating rink.

SIDE TRIPS TO NORTH COUNTY

Updated by
Bobbi Zane

San Diego North County sprawls from the Pacific Ocean to Anza-Borrego Desert State Park on the eastern boundary. The beach communities of Del Mar, Encinitas, Carlsbad, and Oceanside draw multitudes of San Diego residents and visitors to its accessible beaches, surfable waves, and star attractions (like the Legoland theme park). Inland North County attracts animal and nature lovers to the San Diego Wild Animal Park and, in spring, a desert in full bloom.

Numbers in the margin correspond to points of interest on the San Diego North County map.

Del Mar

23 mi north of downtown San Diego on I–5; 9 mi north of La Jolla on Rte. S21.

Del Mar is best known for its racetrack, chic shopping strip, celebrity visitors, and wide beaches. Along with its collection of shops, **Del Mar Plaza** also contains outstanding restaurants and landscaped plazas and gardens with Pacific views.

➊ **Del Mar Fairgrounds** hosts the **Del Mar Thoroughbred Club** (⌧ 2260 Jimmy Durante Blvd. ☎ 858/755–1141 ⊕ www.delmarracing.com).

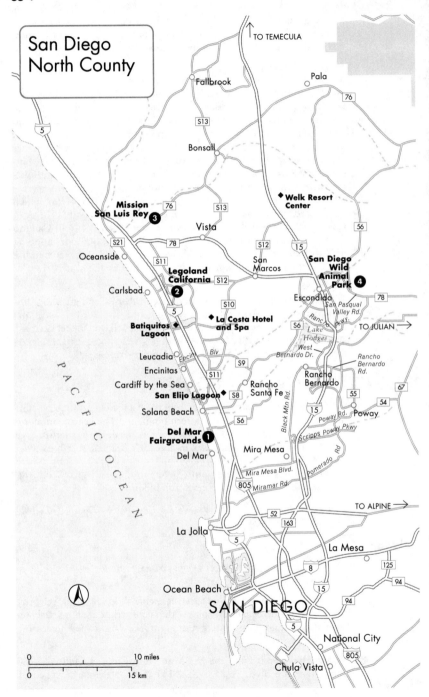

San Diego North County

TO TEMECULA

Fallbrook

Pala

76

S13

Bonsall

Welk Resort Center

Mission San Luis Rey ❸

76

S13

Vista

S12

15

56

5

S21

Oceanside ○

78

San Marcos

San Diego Wild Animal Park ❹

S11

Legoland California ❷

S12

78

Carlsbad ○

5

S10

Escondido

San Pasqual Valley Rd.

Ranc...

TO JULIAN →

La Costa Hotel and Spa

S6

Lake Hodges

Batiquitos Lagoon ◆

West Bernardo Dr.

Rancho Bernardo Rd.

Leucadia ○ Encin... Blv

S9

Encinitas ○

S11

Rancho Bernardo

Cardiff by the Sea ○

San Elijo Lagoon ◆

S8

Rancho Santa Fe

55

67

Black Mtn Rd.

15

54

Solana Beach ○

S6

Poway Rd. Poway

Del Mar Fairgrounds ❶

Scripps Poway Pkwy

Del Mar ○

Mira Mesa

Pomerado Rd.

PACIFIC OCEAN

Mira Mesa Blvd.

805 Miramar Rd.

TO ALPINE →

52

163

La Jolla ○

5

La Mesa

8

125

15

94

Ocean Beach ○

SAN DIEGO

94

5

National City

805

0 _____ 10 miles

0 _____ 15 km

Chula Vista ○

Crooner Bing Crosby and his Hollywood buddies—Pat O'Brien, Gary Cooper, and Oliver Hardy, among others—organized the club in the 1930s, and Del Mar soon developed into a popular destination for the stars of stage and screen. Even now the racing season here is one of the most fashionable in California. Del Mar Fairgrounds hosts more than 100 different events each year, including the San Diego County Fair and a number of horse shows. ⊠ *Head west at I–5's Via de la Valle Rd. exit* ☎ *858/793–5555* ۞ *July–Sept., Wed.–Mon. post time 2 PM.*

Where to Stay & Eat

$–$$$$ ✕ **Jake's Del Mar.** This enormously popular oceanfront restaurant has a close-up view of the water and a menu of simple but well-prepared fare that ranges from a dressy halibut sandwich to crab-crowned swordfish Del Mar to mustard-crusted rack of lamb with port-flavored garlic sauce. A menu note reminds that the legendary ice-cream-stuffed hula pie is "what the sailors swam ashore for in Lahaina." ⊠ *1660 Coast Blvd., Del Mar* ☎ *858/755–2002* ⌂ *Reservations essential* ▤ *AE, D, MC, V* ۞ *No lunch Mon.*

$$–$$$ ✕ **Pacifica Del Mar.** This lovely restaurant overlooks the sea from the plush precincts of Del Mar Plaza. Highly innovative, the restaurant frequently rewrites the menu to show off such show-stoppers as a barbecued sugar-spiced salmon with mustard sauce and filet mignon with potato–white cheddar gratin. ⊠ *Del Mar Plaza, 1515 Camino del Mar, Del Mar* ☎ *858/792–0476* ▤ *AE, D, MC, V.*

★ $–$$$ ✕ **Fish Market.** There's no ocean view at the North County branch of downtown's waterfront restaurant, but this eatery remains popular with residents and tourists for its simple preparations of very fresh fish and shellfish. The scene is lively, crowded, and noisy. Singles flock here, but it's also a great place to bring the kids. ⊠ *640 Via de la Valle, Del Mar* ☎ *858/755–2277* ▤ *AE, D, DC, MC, V.*

$$$$ ▦ **L'Auberge Del Mar Resort and Spa.** Although it looks rather like an upscale condominium complex, L'Auberge is modeled on the Tudor-style hotel that once stood here, a playground for the early Hollywood elite. The beach is a three-minute walk downhill. Rooms are decorated in pink and green pastels and have marble bathrooms. Most rooms have sitting areas, balconies, and gas fireplaces. Across the street are boutiques and restaurants at Del Mar Plaza. ⊠ *1540 Camino del Mar, Del Mar 92014* ☎ *858/259–1515 or 800/901–9514* ⎙ *858/ 755–4940* ⊕ *www.laubergedelmar.com* ⤷ *112 rooms, 8 suites* ⌂ *Restaurant, room service, in-room data ports, minibars, cable TV with movies, 2 tennis courts, 2 pools, gym, outdoor hot tub, massage, sauna, spa, steam room, bar, meeting room, parking (fee); no smoking* ▤ *AE, D, DC, MC, V.*

Rancho Santa Fe

4 mi east of Solana Beach on Rte. S8 (Lomas Santa Fe Dr.); 29 mi north of downtown San Diego on I–5 to Rte. S8 east.

Groves of huge, drooping eucalyptus trees cover the hills of exclusive Rancho Santa Fe. East of I–5 on Via de la Valle Road, Rancho Santa Fe is horse country. It's common to see entire families riding the many trails that crisscross the hillsides. Lillian Rice, one of the first women to graduate with a degree in architecture from the University of California, designed the town, modeling it after villages in Spain. The challenging Rancho Santa Fe Golf Course, the original site of the Bing Crosby Pro-Am and considered one of the best courses in southern California, is open only to members of the Rancho Santa Fe community and guests of the inn.

Where to Stay & Eat

★ $$$–$$$$ ✕ **Mille Fleurs.** Mille Fleurs has a winning combination, from its location in the heart of wealthy, horsey Rancho Santa Fe to the warm Gallic welcome extended by proprietor Bertrand Hug, and the talents of chef Martin Woesle. The quiet dining rooms are decorated like a French villa. Menus are written daily to reflect the market and Woesle's mood, but sometimes feature a soup of *musque de Provence* (pumpkin with cinnamon croutons), sautéed *lotte* (monkfish) with okra and curry sauce, stuffed quail with peaches, and oven-roasted baby lamb with summer vegetable ratatouille. ✉ *Country Squire Courtyard, 6009 Paseo Delicias, Rancho Santa Fe* ☎ *858/756–3085* ⊕ *www. millefleurs.com* ⌂ *Reservations essential* ⊟ *AE, DC, MC, V* ⊘ *No lunch weekends.*

$$$$ ✕▦ **Rancho Valencia Resort.** One of southern California's hidden trea-
Fodor'sChoice sures has luxurious accommodations in Spanish-style casitas scattered
★ on 40 acres of landscaped grounds. Suites have corner fireplaces, luxurious Berber carpeting, and shuttered French doors leading to private patios. Six suites also have private outdoor hot tubs and wall-mounted plasma flat screen TVs. Rancho Valencia is one of the top tennis resorts in the nation and is adjacent to three well-designed golf courses. The inn's first-rate restaurant ($$$$) has a seasonal menu that might include a foie gras Napoleon; pasilla-chili crab cakes; farm-raised abalone steaks with a miso shiro butter sauce; and prime rib-eye steak in a Calvados-scented brown sauce. ✉ *5921 Valencia Circle, Rancho Santa Fe 92067* ☎ *858/756–1123 or 800/548–3664* ☒ *858/756–0165* ⊕ *www.ranchovalencia.com* ⇨ *49 suites* ⌂ *Restaurant, room service, in-room safes, some in-room hot tubs, minibars, refrigerators, cable TV with movies, 18 tennis courts, 2 pools, health club, 3 outdoor hot tubs, spa, bicycles, croquet, hiking, bar, shops, meeting rooms, business services, free parking, no-smoking rooms* ⊟ *AE, DC, MC, V.*

★ $$$ ▦ **Inn at Rancho Santa Fe.** Understated elegance is the theme of this genteel old resort in the heart of the Spanish Colonial village of Rancho Santa Fe. Guest rooms are in red-tiled cottages spread around the property's 20 lushly landscaped acres. Many have private patios and woodburning fireplaces. The inn also has membership at the exclusive Rancho Santa Fe Golf Club and privileges at five other nearby, exclusive courses. ✉ *5951 Linea del Cielo, Rancho Santa Fe 92067* ☎ *858/756–1131 or 800/843–4661* ☒ *858/759–1604* ⊕ *www. theinnatrsf.com* ⇨ *73 rooms, 5 suites, 8 private 1-, 2- and 3-bedroom cottages* ⌂ *Dining room, room service, in-room data ports, in-room safes, some in-room hot tubs, some kitchens, minibars, microwaves,* *cable TV with movies, 3 tennis courts, pool, exercise equipment, croquet, bar, library, meeting room, free parking, some pets allowed; no smoking* ▭ *AE, DC, MC, V.*

Carlsbad

15 mi north of Rancho Santa Fe via Hwy. S9 to Hwy. S21; 36 mi north of downtown San Diego on I–5.

Since the Legoland California theme park moved in east of Carlsbad, this once laid-back Bavarian-inspired coastal community has enjoyed a thriving economy. The theme park is at the center of a tourist complex that includes resort hotels, a shopping mall, colorful flower fields, and golf courses. Carlsbad owes its name and Bavarian look to John Frazier, who lured people to the area a century ago with talk of the healing powers of mineral water bubbling from a coastal well. The water was found to have the same properties as water from the German mineral wells of Karlsbad—hence the name of the community. Remnants from this era, including the original well and a monument to Frazier, are found at the **Alt Karlsbad Haus** (✉ 2802 Carlsbad Blvd. ☎ 760/434–1887), a stone building that houses a small day spa and the Carlsbad Famous Water Co., a 21st-century version of Frazier's waterworks.

☾ ❷ **Legoland California** offers a full day of entertainment for pint-size fun-
Fodor'sChoice seekers and their parents. Popular attractions include Miniland, an an-
★ imated collection of cities constructed entirely of Lego blocks; the Driving School, where kids can ride in electric Lego cars; the Kid-Power Tower, a giant jungle gym; the pint-size Dragon and Spellbound roller coasters; and Aquazone Wave Racers, the first power-ski water ride in North America. Kids can climb on, operate, manipulate, and explore dozens of displays and attractions constructed out of plastic blocks. Legoland is best appreciated by kids ages 2 to 10. ✉ *1 Lego Dr., exit I–5 at Cannon Rd. and follow signs east ¼ mi, Carlsbad* ☎ *760/918–5346* ⊕ *www.legolandca.com* 🎟 *$41.95* ☉ *Mid-Sept.–mid-June, daily 10–5; mid-June–early Sept., daily 9–9.*

In spring the hillsides are abloom at **Flower Fields at Carlsbad Ranch,** the largest bulb production farm in southern California, where you can walk through fields planted with thousands of giant ranunculus displayed in rows of every rainbow color against a backdrop of the blue Pacific Ocean. The rose garden displays All-American Rose selections of the last half century. You can shop for plants, garden accessories, and bulbs at the unusually large and well-stocked Armstrong Garden Center at the exit. ✉ *5704 Paseo del Norte, east of I–5, Carlsbad* ☎ *760/431–0352* ⊕ *www.theflowerfields.com* 🎟 *$7* ☉ *Mar.–May, daily 9–6.*

☾ Take an interactive journey through 100 years of popular music at the **Museum of Making Music,** which displays more than 450 vintage instruments and samples of memorable tunes from the past century. Hands-on activities include playing a digital piano, drums, guitar, and electric violin. ✉ *5790 Armada Dr., east of I–5, Carlsbad* ☎ *760/438–5996* ⊕ *www.museumofmakingmusic.org* 🎟 *$5* ☉ *Tues.–Sun. 10–5.*

California Surf Museum displays a large collection of surfing memorabilia, photos, vintage boards, apparel, and accessories. ⊠ *223 N. Coast Hwy., Oceanside* 🕾 *760/721–6876* ⊕ *www.surfmuseum.org* 🖾 *Free* ⊙ *Daily 10–4.*

③ **Mission San Luis Rey** was built by Franciscan friars in 1798 under the direction of Father Fermin Lasuen, the successor to Father Junípero Serra, to help educate and convert Native Americans. Once a location for filming Disney's *Zorro* TV series, the well-preserved mission is still owned by Franciscan friars. San Luis Rey was the 18th and largest of California's missions. The *sala* (parlor), a friar's bedroom, a weaving room, the kitchen, and a collection of religious art convey much about early mission life. From the ocean, go east of I–5 on Route 76, then north on Rancho Del Oro Drive. ⊠ *4050 Mission Ave., Oceanside* 🕾 *760/757–3651* ⊕ *www.sanluisrey.org* 🖾 *$5* ⊙ *Daily 10–4:30.*

FodorśChoice
★

Where to Stay & Eat

$$$$ 🏨 **Four Seasons Resort Aviara.** This hilltop resort sitting on 30 acres overlooking Batiquitos Lagoon is one of the most luxurious in the San Diego area, with gleaming marble corridors, original artwork, crystal chandeliers, and enormous flower arrangements. Rooms have every possible amenity: oversize closets, private balconies or garden patios, and marble bathrooms with double vanities and deep soaking tubs. The resort is exceptionally family friendly, providing a wide selection of in-room amenities designed for the younger set. The kids also have their own pool, nature walks with wildlife demonstrations, video and board games. ⊠ *7100 Four Seasons Point, Carlsbad 92009* 🕾 *760/603–6800 or 800/332–3442* 🖶 *760/603–6878* ⊕ *www. fourseasons.com/aviara* 🛏 *285 rooms, 44 suites* ♂ *4 restaurants, room service, in-room data ports, in-room safes, minibars, cable TV with movies and games, 18-hole golf course, 6 tennis courts, 3 pools, 2 whirlpools, health club, massage, sauna, spa, steam room, bicycles, hiking, volleyball, shops, babysitting, children's programs (ages 5–12), laundry service, concierge, business services, meeting room, airport shuttle, car rental, some pets allowed (fee), parking (fee); no smoking* 🚭 *AE, D, DC, MC, V.*

FodorśChoice
★

$$$$ 🏨 **La Costa Resort and Spa.** This famous resort is surprisingly low-keys. Its unusually large guest rooms, renovated in 2003–2004, have a traditional look with lots of dark wood and opulent marble bathrooms. Also revamped is the legendary spa, now home to the Deepak Chopra Center, which provides integrated medical consultations to complement spa services. The resort also has two PGA championship golf courses and the Jim McLean golf school, plus a large tennis center. ⊠ *2100 Costa del Mar Rd., Carlsbad 92009* 🕾 *760/438–9111 or 800/854–5000* 🖶 *760/931–7569* ⊕ *www.lacosta.com* 🛏 *474 rooms, 77 suites* ♂ *Restaurant, room service, in-room data ports, in-room safes, minibars, some refrigerators, cable TV with movies, driving range, 2 18-hole golf courses, putting green, 21 tennis courts, pro shop, 4 pools, health club, hair salon, 3 outdoor hot tubs, sauna, spa, steam room, bicycles, croquet, hiking, lounge, shops, babysitting, children's programs (ages 5–12), dry cleaning, laundry service, concierge, business services, meet-*

ing rooms, car rental, pets allowed (fee), no-smoking rooms ☰ *AE, D, DC, MC, V.*

★ **$$–$$$$** ⊡ **Oceanside Marina Suites.** Of all the oceanfront lodgings in North County towns, this motel occupies the best location—a spit of land surrounded by water and cool ocean breezes on all sides. All rooms have either ocean or harbor views. The rooms are unusually large and have fireplaces and expansive balconies. There are barbecues for guest use. A free boat shuttles you to the beach in summer. Continental breakfast is included in the price. ⊠ *2008 Harbor Dr. N, Oceanside 92054* ☎ *760/722–1561 or 800/252–2033* 🖷 *760/439–9758* ⊕ *www.omihotel. com* ⤳ *64 suites* ⚐ *In-room data ports, kitchens, cable TV with movies, pool, hot tub, sauna, Ping-Pong, volleyball, laundry facilities, free parking; no a/c, no smoking* ☰ *AE, MC, V* ⭇ *CP.*

Escondido

8 mi north of Rancho Bernardo on I–15; 31 mi northeast of downtown San Diego on I–15.

Escondido is a thriving, rapidly expanding residential and commercial city of more than 120,000 people.

🌀 ❹ **San Diego Wild Animal Park,** an extension of the San Diego Zoo, is a 35-

Fodor'sChoice minute drive south of downtown San Diego. The 1,800-acre preserve

★ in the San Pasqual Valley is designed to protect endangered species from around the world. Exhibit areas have been carved out of the dry, dusty canyons and mesas to represent the animals' natural habitats—North Africa, South Africa, East Africa, Heart of Africa, Australian Rain Forest, Asian Swamps, and Asian Plains.

The best way to see these preserves is on the 60-minute, 5-mi Wgasa Bushline Railway (included in the price of admission). The 1¼-mi-long **Kilimanjaro Safari Walk,** in the East Africa section, winds through some of the park's hilliest terrain, with observation decks overlooking the elephants and lions. A 70-foot suspension bridge spans a steep ravine, leading to the final observation point and a panorama of the entire park and the San Pasqual Valley. Along the trails of 32-acre **Heart of Africa** you can follow the paths of early explorers through forests and lowlands, across a floating bridge to a research station where an expert is on hand to answer questions. Finally you arrive at Panorama Point, where you get an up-close-and-personal view of cheetahs, a chance to feed the giraffes, and a distant glimpse of the expansive savanna where rhinos, impalas, wildebeest, oryx, and beautiful migrating birds reside. The Wild Animal Park, which conducts captive breeding programs to save rare and endangered species, shows off one of its most successful efforts, the California Condor, at the **Condor Ridge** exhibit. The exhibit occupies nearly the highest point in the park. You can camp overnight in the park in summer on a Roar and Snore Campover ($139.50), take a Sunrise Safari in August, and celebrate the holidays during the annual Festival of Lights. ⊠ *15500 San Pasqual Valley Rd., Escondido, take I–15 north to Via Rancho Pkwy. and follow signs (6 mi)* ☎ *760/747–8702* ⊕ *www.wildanimalpark.org* 🎟 *$29.50 includes* *all shows and monorail tour; a $52.65 combination pass grants entry, within 5 days of purchase, to San Diego Zoo and San Diego Wild Animal Park; parking $6* ☉ *Mid-June–early Sept., daily 9–8; Mid-Sept.–mid-June, daily 9–4* ☱ *D, MC, V.*

Where to Stay & Eat

★ $$–$$$$ ✕ **150 Grand Cafe.** Popular with patrons of nearby California Center for the Arts, this store-front café showcases contemporary cuisine with flair. The seasonal menu might feature miso-braised salmon on barley risotto, hoisin-crusted pork tenderloin with couscous, or open-faced seafood ravioli with broccoli rabe. ⊠ *150 W. Grand Ave., Escondido* ☎ *760/738–6868* ☱ *AE, DC, MC, V* ☉ *Closed Sun.*

$$–$$$ ✕ **Vincent's Sirino's.** Try the grilled salmon with roasted garlic, the duck breast confit, or the rack of lamb; good homemade bread accompanies them. The wine list is serious, as are the desserts. ⊠ *113 W. Grand Ave., Escondido* ☎ *760/745–3835* ⊕ *www.vincentsirinos.com* ☱ *AE, D, MC, V* ☉ *Closed Mon. No lunch weekends.*

$–$$ ⬚ **Welk Resort Center.** This resort sprawls over 600 acres of rugged, oak-studded hillside. Built by band leader Lawrence Welk in the 1960s, the resort includes a hotel, time-share condominiums, and a recreation and entertainment complex. A museum displays Welk memorabilia, a theater presents Broadway-style musicals year-round, and there are many shops on the premises. Hotel rooms, decorated with a Southwestern flair, have golf-course views. ⊠ *8860 Lawrence Welk Dr., Escondido 92026* ☎ *760/749–3000 or 800/932–9355* 🖷 *760/749–6182* ⊕ *www.welkresort. com* ⮡ *137 rooms, 10 suites* ♿ *3 restaurants, grocery, in-room data ports, cable TV, 2 18-hole golf courses, 5 tennis courts, 6 pools, health club, 7 hot tubs, bar, theater, shops, meeting room, travel services, free parking, no-smoking rooms* ☱ *AE, D, DC, MC, V.*

SAN DIEGO A TO Z

To research prices, get advice from other travelers, and book travel arrangements, visit ⊕ *www.fodors.com*

AIRPORTS & TRANSFERS

All major and some regional U.S. carriers serve San Diego International Airport. British Airways, Aero Mexico, and Air Canada are the only international carriers that fly to San Diego. All others will require a connecting flight, usually in Los Angeles. Other connection points are Chicago, Dallas, and San Francisco. San Diego International Airport (SAN) is a five-minute drive from downtown. McClellan Palomar Airport serves North County. America West Express and United Express operate flights between McClellan and Los Angeles International Airport. *See* Air Travel *in* Smart Travel Tips A to Z for airline phone numbers.

🛈 **McClellan Palomar Airport** ⊠ 2198 Palomar Airport Rd., Carlsbad ☎ 760/431–4646. **San Diego International Airport** ⊠ Off I-5 at the San Diego Airport exit ☎ 619/400–2400 ⊕ www.san.org.

🛈 **Shuttles & Buses Cloud 9 Shuttle** ☎ 800/974–8885 San Diego County, 858/974–8885 elsewhere ⊕ www.cloud9shuttle.com. **San Diego Transit** ☎ 619/233–3004 ⊕ www.sdcommute.com.

BUS TRAVEL TO & FROM SAN DIEGO

Greyhound operates 16 buses a day between San Diego and Los Angeles, connecting with buses to all major U.S. cities.

📋 **Greyhound** ✉ 120 W. Broadway, Downtown ☎ 619/239-8082 or 800/231-2222 ⊕ www.greyhound.com.

BUS & TROLLEY TRAVEL WITHIN SAN DIEGO COUNTY

San Diego Transit buses connect with the San Diego Trolley light rail system and serve the city, East County, and North County from the Mexico border to Del Mar. The North County Transit District covers San Diego County from Del Mar north. Buses and trolleys run at about 15-minute intervals. Bus and trolley connections are posted at each station.

📋 **North County Transit District** ☎ 800/266-6883. **San Diego Transit** ☎ 619/233-3004, 619/234-5005 TTY/TDD ⊕ www.sdcommute.com.

CAR RENTAL

All of the major car-rental companies have offices at San Diego International Airport. *See* Car Rental *in* Smart Travel Tips A to Z for national rental agency phone numbers.

CAR TRAVEL

Interstate 5 stretches from Canada to the Mexican border and bisects San Diego. Interstate 8 provides access from Yuma, Arizona, and points east. Drivers coming from Nevada and the mountain regions beyond can reach San Diego on I–15. Running parallel west of I–5 is Route S21, also known and sometimes indicated as Highway 101, Old Highway 101, or Coast Highway 101, which never strays too far from the ocean.

EMERGENCIES

In case of emergency dial 911.

📋 Hospitals **UCSD Medical Center–Hillcrest** ✉ 200 West Arbor Dr., Hillcrest ☎ 619/543-6222.

LODGING

San Diego Hotel Reservations is a free service that can help you find a hotel anywhere in the county. San Diego Hotels specializes in discount rates at hotels in the city. If you are planning an extended stay or need lodgings for four or more people, consider an apartment rental. Oakwood Apartments rents comfortable furnished apartments in the Mission Valley, La Jolla Colony, and Coronado areas, with maid service and linens. The Bed and Breakfast Guild of San Diego lists high-quality member inns.

📋 **Bed and Breakfast Guild of San Diego** ☎ 619/523-1300 ⊕ www.bandbguildsandiego. org. **Oakwood Apartments** ☎ 800/888-0808 ⊕ www.oakwood.com. **San Diego Hotel Reservations** ☎ 800/728-3227 ⊕ www.sandiegohotelres.com. **San Diego Hotels** ☎ 800/311-5045 ⊕ www.san-diego-ca-hotels.com.

TAXIS

You can generally hail a cab downtown, but in most cases you'll need to telephone for taxi service, and you might have to wait as much as an hour for your car to show up, depending on where you are. The companies listed below do not serve all areas of San Diego County. If you're going someplace other than downtown, **ask if the company serves that area.**

🚖 **Crown City Cab** ☎ 619/437-8885 ⊕ www.driveu.com. **Orange Cab** ☎ 619/291-3333 ⊕ www.home.pacbell.net/orangesd. **Silver Cabs** ☎ 619/280-5555. **Yellow Cab** ☎ 619/234-6161 ⊕ www.driveu.com.

TOURS

BOAT TOURS Three companies operate one- and two-hour harbor cruises as well as seasonal whale-watching excursions. San Diego Harbor Excursion and Hornblower Invader Cruises boats depart from the Broadway Pier. No reservations are necessary for the $13 to $18 voyages. Classic Sailing Adventures has morning, afternoon, and evening tours of the harbor and San Diego Bay for $65 per person.

🚖 **Classic Sailing Adventures** ⊠ 1220 Rosecrans St., No. 137 ☎ 800/659-0141 ⊕ www.classicsailingadventures.com. **Hornblower Invader Cruises** ⊠ 1066 N. Harbor Dr. ☎ 619/234-8687 ⊕ www.hornblower.com. **San Diego Harbor Excursion** ⊠ 1050 N. Harbor Dr. ☎ 619/234-4111 or 800/442-7847 ⊕ www.harborexcursion.com.

BUS & TROLLEY TOURS Old Town Trolley Historic Tours take you on narrated tours, and you can get on and off as you please at any stop, for $25. Contactours offers half-day city sightseeing tours and full-day tours with harbor excursions or visits to Mexico. Rates start at $27.

🚖 **Contactours** ⊠ 1726 Wilson Ave., National City ☎ 619/477-8687 or 800/235-5393 ⊕ www.contactours.com. **Old Town Trolley Historic Tours** ⊠ 2115 Kurtz St. ☎ 619/298-8687 or 800/808-7482 ⊕ www.historictours.com.

TRAIN TRAVEL

Amtrak serves downtown San Diego's Santa Fe Depot with daily trains to and from Los Angeles, Santa Barbara, and San Luis Obispo. Amtrak trains stop in San Diego North County at Solana Beach and Oceanside. The last train leaves San Diego at about 7 each night (9 on Friday; the last arrival is at about midnight).

Coaster commuter trains, which run between Oceanside and San Diego Monday–Saturday, stop at Del Mar, Solana Beach, Encinitas, Carlsbad, and Oceanside.

🚖 **Amtrak** ☎ 800/872-7837 ⊕ www.amtrakcalifornia.com. **Coaster** ☎ 800/262-6883 ⊕ www.sdcommute.com. **Santa Fe Depot** ⊠ 1050 Kettner Blvd., Downtown ☎ 619/239-9021.

VISITOR INFORMATION

🚖 **Balboa Park Visitors Center** ⊠ 1549 El Prado ☎ 619/239-0512 ⊕ www.balboapark.org, open daily 9–4. **California Welcome Center Oceanside** ⊠ 928 N. Coast Hwy., 92054 ☎ 760/721-1011 or 800/350-7873 ⊕ www.oceansidechamber.com. **Carlsbad Convention & Visitors Bureau** ⊠ 400 Carlsbad Village Dr., 92008 ☎ 800/227-5722 ⊕ www.visitcarlsbad.com. **Coronado Visitor Center** ⊠ 1100 Orange Ave., 92118 ☎ 619/437-8788 ⊕ www.coronadovisitorcenter.org. **Del Mar Regional Chamber of Commerce** ⊠ 1104 Camino del Mar, 92014 ☎ 858/793-5292 ⊕ www.delmarchamber.org. **Encinitas Chamber of Commerce** ⊠ 138 Encinitas Blvd., 92024 ☎ 760/753-6041 ⊕ www.encinitaschamber.com. **San Diego Convention & International Visitor Information Cen-**

ter ✉ 1040 1/3 W. Broadway at the Cruise Ship terminal, San Diego ☎ 619/232-3101 ⊕ www.sandiego.org ✉ Herschel Ave. at Prospect St. ☎ 619/236-1212 ⊕ www. sandiego.org ✉ 401 B St., Suite 1400, San Diego 92101. **San Diego North Convention & Visitors Bureau** ✉ 360 N. Escondido Blvd., Escondido 92025 ☎ 760/745-4741 or 800/848-3336 ⊕ www.sandiegonorth.com.

San Diego Visitor Information Center ✉ 2688 E. Mission Bay Dr., off I-5 at the Clairemont Dr. exit, Mission Bay ☎ 619/275-8259 ⊕ www.infosandiego.com/visitor, open daily 9-dusk.

ORANGE COUNTY
WITH CATALINA ISLAND

2

Updated by
Michael &
Trisa Knight

FEW OF THE CITRUS GROVES that gave Orange County its name remain. This region south and east of Los Angeles is now a high-tech business hub where tourism is the number-one industry. Angelenos may make cracks about theme parks being the extent of culture here, but in fact the county has all kinds of interesting sights and communities. With its tropical flowers and palm trees, the stretch of coast between Seal Beach and San Clemente is often called the "California Riviera." Exclusive Newport Beach, artsy Laguna, and the up-and-coming surf town of Huntington Beach are the stars, but lesser-known gems on the glistening coast—such as Corona del Mar—are also worth visiting. Offshore, there's also gorgeous Catalina Island, a terrific spot for diving, snorkeling, and hiking.

Exploring Orange County

Like Los Angeles, Orange County stretches over a large area, lacks a singular focal point, and has limited public transportation. You'll need a car and a sensible game plan to make the most of your visit. If you're headed to Disneyland, you'll probably want to stay in or near Anaheim, organize your activities around the inland-county attractions, and take excursions to the coast. If the mouse's kingdom is not part of your itinerary, try staying at a midpoint location such as Irvine or Costa Mesa, both equidistant from inland tourist attractions and the coast. These towns are less crowded than Anaheim and less expensive than the beach cities. Of course, if you can afford it, staying at the beach is always recommended.

Numbers in the text correspond to numbers in the margin and on the Orange County map.

About the Restaurants

Restaurants in Orange County are often more casual than in L.A. While diners may forgo jeans in the more upscale places, you'll rarely see men in jackets and ties. Of course, there's also a swath of supercasual places along the beachfronts—fish taco take-out, taquerias, burger joints—where they don't mind if you wear flip-flops. Reservations are recommended for the nicest restaurants. Many places don't serve past 11 PM. Remember that according to California law, smoking is prohibited in all enclosed areas. Unless otherwise noted, the restaurants listed here are open daily for lunch and dinner.

WHAT IT COSTS				
	$$$$	**$$$**	**$$**	**$**	**¢**
RESTAURANTS	over $30	$23–$30	$16–$22	$10–$15	under $10

Prices are for a main course at dinner, excluding 8.25% sales tax.

About the Hotels

Orange County has lodging available in all price ranges. Many of the luxury hotels are located on the coast and can be a vacation in themselves. There are also plenty of low-key hotels in the area, and those around the theme parks are very family-friendly. The prices listed in this chapter are based on summer rates. Prices are often lower in winter, especially near Disneyland, unless there's a convention in Anaheim, and weekend rates are often rock-bottom at business hotels. It's worth calling around to search for bargains.

WHAT IT COSTS				
$$$$	$$$	$$	$	¢
HOTELS	over $250	$176–$250	$121–$175	$90–$120	under $90

Prices are for two people in a standard double room in high season, excluding service charges and taxes of 9%–14%.

Timing

The sun shines year-round in Orange County, though in early summer there are the occasional "June gloom" days with overcast skies. Beat the crowds and the heat by visiting in winter, spring, or fall. Smart parents give kids their Disney fix on weekdays or during the winter months.

THE COAST

Running along the Orange County coastline is the scenic Pacific Coast Highway (Highway 1, known locally as PCH). Older beachfront settlements here, with their modest bungalow-style homes, are now increasingly outnumbered by posh gated communities. Though the coastline is rapidly being filled in, there are still a few stretches of beautiful, protected open land. And at many places along the way you can catch an idealized glimpse of surfers hitting the beach, boards under their arms.

San Juan Capistrano

5 mi north of Dana Point, Hwy. 74; 60 mi north of San Diego, I–5.

San Juan Capistrano, one of the few noteworthy historical districts in Southern California, is best known for its mission. Traditionally, this building has been a place where swallows return after migrating for the winter—although these days the birds are just as likely to choose other local sites for nesting. St. Joseph's Day, March 19, launches a week of festivities celebrating the return of the swallows.

If you arrive by train, you'll be dropped off across from the mission at the San Juan Capistrano depot. With its appealing brick café and preserved Santa Fe cars, the depot retains much of the magic of early American railroads. If driving, park near Ortega and Camino Capistrano, the city's main streets.

❶ **Mission San Juan Capistrano,** founded in 1776 by Father Junípero Serra, was the major Roman Catholic outpost between Los Angeles and San Diego. Though the original Great Stone Church is permanently supported by scaffolding, many of the mission's adobe buildings have been preserved to illustrate mission life, with exhibits of an olive millstone, tallow ovens, tanning vats, metalworking furnaces, and padres' living quarters. The bougainvillea-covered Serra Chapel is believed to be the

Fodor'sChoice ★

Numbers in the margin correspond to numbers in the text and on the Orange County map.

If you have
1 day

Who are we kidding? You're going to **Disneyland** ⑳ ▶.

If you have
3 days

You're still going to **Disneyland** ⑳ ▶ (stay overnight in ▦ **Anaheim**), and if it's up to the kids you could add **Disney's California Adventure** ⑳ to the mix and easily devote all three days (not to mention a considerable amount of money) to the Disneyland Resort. If you'd prefer to escape the Magic Kingdom or avoid it altogether, get an early start and head to ▦ **Laguna Beach**, before the crowds arrive. Breakfast alfresco, then take a walk on the sand. Afterward, stroll around the local streets lined with boutiques and art galleries. On Day 3, visit **Newport Beach** or **Huntington Beach,** then head inland to **Costa Mesa,** where you can browse through **South Coast Plaza** ⑭ one of the world's largest retail, entertainment, and dining complexes, or visit the smaller nearby shopping centers. Alternatively, catch an early boat out to **Catalina Island** for the day.

2

---

oldest building standing in California. Mass takes place Monday–Saturday at 7 AM in the chapel and 8:30 in the new church. ⊠ *Camino Capistrano and Ortega Hwy.* ☎ *949/234–1300* ⊕ *www.missionsjc.com* ✉ *$6* ☉ *Daily 8:30–5.*

❷ Near Mission San Juan Capistrano is the **San Juan Capistrano Library,** a postmodern building erected in 1983. Architect Michael Graves combined classical and mission styles to striking effect here. The courtyard is a wonderful place for secluded reading. ⊠ *31495 El Camino Real* ☎ *949/493–1752* ⊕ *www.oc.ca.gov/ocpl/sanjuan/sanjuan.htm* ☉ *Mon.–Wed. 10–8, Thurs. 10–6, Sat. 10–5, Sun. noon–5.*

Where to Eat

$–$$$ ✕ **L'Hirondelle.** Roast duck, rabbit, and Belgian dishes are the standouts at this restaurant across the street from the mission (its name means "the swallow" in French). The extensive wine list is matched by an impressive selection of Belgian beers. You can dine inside or out on the patio. Sunday brunch is superb. ⊠ *31631 Camino Capistrano, San Juan Capistrano* ☎ *949/661–0425* ▤ *AE, DC, MC, V* ☉ *Closed Mon. No lunch Tues.*

¢–$$$ ✕ **Cedar Creek Inn.** Equally suitable for family meals and romantic dinners, this inn has a children's menu as well as a secluded outdoor patio. The contemporary American menu features crowd-pleasers like ahi burgers, rack of lamb, and herb-crusted halibut. ⊠ *26860 Ortega Hwy., San Juan Capistrano* ☎ *949/240–2229* ▤ *AE, MC, V.*

¢–$ ✕ **The Ramos House Cafe.** This historic, 19th-century building sits practically right on the railroad tracks. If you nab a table on the patio for a hearty breakfast or light lunch, you may be saluted by the roar of a passing Amtrak. ⊠ *31752 Los Rios St., San Juan Capistrano* ☎ *949/443–1342* ▤ *AE, D, DC, MC, V* ☉ *Closed Mon.*

Nightlife

Coach House (⊠ 33157 Camino Capistrano, San Juan Capistrano ☎ 949/496–8930), a roomy, casual club with long tables and a dark-wood bar, draws crowds of varying ages for entertainment from hip new bands to Dick Dale, the take-no-prisoners king of the surf guitar.

If you're looking for a cowboy saloon with western ambience, then stop by **The Swallows Inn** (⊠ 31786 Camino Capistrano, San Juan Capistrano ☎ 949/493–3188). Despite a somewhat tough look, it pulls in all kinds—bikers, college kids, marines from San Diego, grandparents—all of whom come for drinks, a casual bite, and rowdy live music. There's no cover charge.

Dana Point

5 mi south of San Juan Capistrano, Hwy. 74.

Dana Point's claim to fame is its small-boat marina, which is tucked into a dramatic natural harbor and surrounded by high bluffs. In late February, a whale festival features concerts, films, sports competitions, and a weekend street fair. **Dana Point Harbor** (☎ 949/496–1094 ⊕ www.danapointharbor.com) was first described more than 100 years ago by its namesake Richard Henry Dana in his book *Two Years Before the Mast.* At the marina are docks for small boats, marine-oriented shops, and some restaurants.

Inside Dana Point Harbor, **Swim Beach** has a fishing pier, barbecues, food stands, parking, restrooms, and showers. At the south end of Dana Point, **Doheny State Park** (☎ 949/496–6171) is one of Southern California's top surfing destinations, but there's a lot more to do within this 63-acre area. Divers and anglers hang out at the beach's western end, and during low tide there are tidal pools to poke around in. There are also indoor tanks and an interpretive center devoted to the wildlife of the Doheny Marine Refuge, as well as food stands and shops, picnic facilities, volleyball courts, and a pier for fishing. Camping is permitted, though there are no RV hookups.

☙ ❸ Two indoor tanks at the **Ocean Institute** contain touchable sea creatures, as well as the complete skeleton of a gray whale. Anchored near the institute is *The Pilgrim,* a full-size replica of the square-rigged vessel on which Richard Henry Dana sailed. You can tour the boat daily 10–3. Weekend cruises are also available. You can arrange to go on marine-mammal exploration cruises from January through March, or to explore regional tide pools year-round. ⊠ *24200 Dana Point Harbor Dr., Dana Point* ☎ *949/496–2274* ⊕ *www.ocean-institute.org* ▤ *Donation requested for ship and tide pool tours; cruise prices vary* ☉ *Weekends 10–4:30.*

Monarch Beach Golf Links (⊠ 22 Monarch Beach Resort Dr., Dana Point ☎ 949/240–8247) is an 18-hole, par 70 course located right along the

The Beach

Wave action along the coastline ranges from beginner to expert. Beginners can get a feel for the waves by riding a Boogie board at Seal Beach or at the Newport River Jetties. Surfing is permitted at most beaches year-round (check local newspapers or talk to lifeguards for conditions), and surfboard-rental stands line the coast. The best waves are usually at San Clemente, Newport Beach, and Huntington Beach.

2

From June through September the ocean temperature can reach 70°, and lifeguards patrol almost every beach. Keep a lookout for signs warning of dangerous conditions: undertow, strong currents, and big waves can all be hazardous. Avoid swimming near surfers. When yellow flags with a black circle are flying (known to locals as "black balling") no hard boards are allowed, so swimming and bodyboarding are permitted in that area. Many beaches close just after sunset. Local newspapers print beach reports with wave information and notice of any closures. You can also check local news on surf and water quality through the **Surfrider Foundation** (⊕ www.surfrider.org).

Great Golf

There are some noteworthy golfing opportunities in Orange County, thanks to the area's great weather and dozens of facilities. For more information contact the **Southern California Golf Association** (☎ 818/980–3630 ⊕ www.scga.org). Another resource is the **Southern California Public Links Golf Association** (☎ 714/994–4747 ⊕ www.plga.org).

Jogging, Walking & Biking

For those who wish to enjoy the coastline by bike or on foot, the Santa Ana Riverbed Trail hugs the Santa Ana River for 20½ mi between PCH at Huntington State Beach and Imperial Highway in Yorba Linda. Joggers enjoy an uninterrupted path the entire way and don't have to run alongside cars. There are entrances, rest rooms, and drinking fountains at all crossings. A bike path winds south from Marina del Rey all the way to San Diego with only minor breaks. Most beaches have bike rental stands.

Pacific Ocean. Greens fees range from $150 to $185 with cart fees included. This course also has one of the top 100 golf shops in the country, making this a great place to play and then shop for a memento of your game.

off the beaten path

SAN CLEMENTE – Bikers looking for a low-key ride can drive 10 mi south of Dana Point on PCH to San Clemente. There, 20 square mi of prime bicycling terrain await. Camp Pendleton, the country's largest Marine Corps base, welcomes cyclists to use some of its roads—just don't be surprised to see a troop helicopter taking off right beside you. Surfers favor **San Clemente State Beach** (☎ 949/492–3156), which has camping facilities, RV hookups, and fire rings. San Onofre State Beach, just south of San Clemente, is another popular surfing destination.

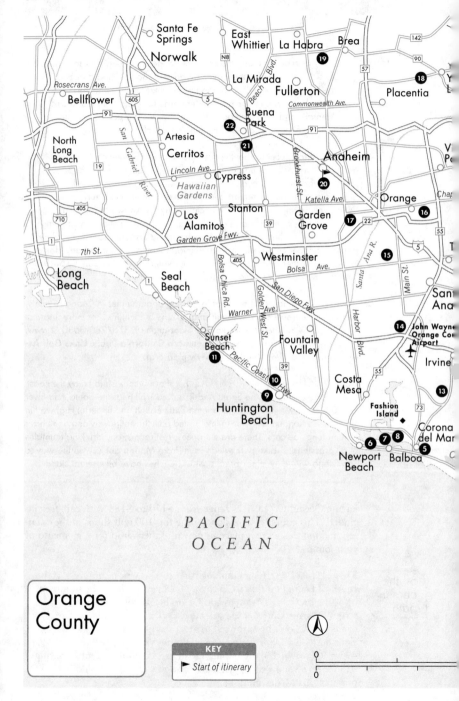

Orange County

KEY

▶ Start of itinerary

PACIFIC
OCEAN

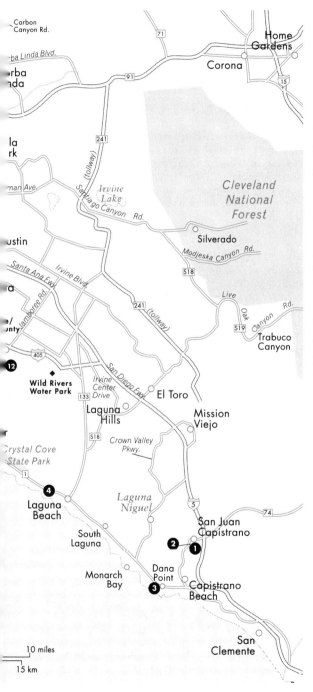

Where to Stay & Eat

$–$$$ ✕ **Luciana's.** This intimate restaurant can be relied on for straightforward Italian meals. Dining rooms are small, warmed by two fireplaces inside and yet another fireplace on the patio. Don't miss the linguine with clams, shrimp, calamari, and mussels in a light tomato sauce. ✉ *24312 Del Prado Ave., Dana Point* ☎ *949/661–6500* ▤ *AE, DC, MC, V* ☺ *No lunch.*

¢ ✕ **Proud Mary's.** On a terrace overlooking the harbor, this friendly, welcoming eatery serves burgers, gourmet sandwiches, and a South of the Border menu. You can also order breakfast all day. ✉ *34689 Golden Lantern St., Dana Point* ☎ *949/493–5853* ▤ *AE, D, MC, V* ☺ *No dinner.*

$$$$ ✕▣ **Ritz-Carlton, Laguna Niguel.** An unrivaled setting on the edge of the
Fodor'sChoice   Pacific combined with hallmark Ritz-Carlton service have made this re-
★   sort justly famous. Rooms have marble bathrooms and private balconies with ocean or pool views. Tea is served afternoons in the library. In the formal Dining Room ($$$–$$$$, no lunch; reservations essential) chef Yvon Goetz's French Continental prix-fixe menu includes items such as veal tournedos with cipollini (wild onions), walnut emulsion, port wine, and thyme cream. ✉ *1 Ritz-Carlton Dr., Laguna Niguel 92629* ☎ *949/ 240–2000 or 800/241–3333* 🖷 *949/240–0829* ⊕ *www.ritzcarlton.com* ⇨ *362 rooms, 31 suites* ⚬ *3 restaurants, in-room data ports, in-room safes, minibars, cable TV with movies and video games, 2 tennis courts, 2 pools, health club, hair salon, massage, lobby lounge, concierge, Internet, business services, meeting rooms* ▤ *AE, D, DC, MC, V.*

$$$$ ✕▣ **St. Regis Monarch Beach Resort and Spa.** Indulgence is the name of the game here; you can even have someone unpack your suitcase for you. The 172-acre grounds include a private beach, a Robert Trent Jones Jr.–designed golf course, and tennis courts across the street. Rooms have CD and DVD players, and views of either the coast or the lush landscaping. Michael Mina's Aqua ($$$$) restaurant serves sumptuous seafood dishes, such as ahi medallions in Pinot Noir sauce, and miso-glazed sea bass. The signature dessert is an old-fashioned root beer float with warm chocolate-chip cookies. ✉ *1 Monarch Beach Resort, off Niguel Rd., Monarch Bay 92629* ☎ *949/234–3200 or 800/722–1543* 🖷 *949/ 234–3201* ⊕ *www.stregismonarchbeach.com* ⇨ *326 rooms, 74 suites* ⚬ *3 restaurants, in-room data ports, in-room safes, minibars, cable TV with movies and video games, 18-hole golf course, 3 pools, health club, hair salon, massage, spa, beach, bar, lobby lounge, dry cleaning, laundry facilities, concierge, Internet, business services, some pets allowed (free)* ▤ *AE, D, DC, MC, V.*

★ **$$–$$$$** ▣ **Blue Lantern Inn.** Combining New England–style architecture with a Southern California setting, this white clapboard B&B rests on a bluff overlooking the harbor and ocean. A fire warms the intimate, inviting living area, where you can enjoy complimentary snacks and play backgammon every afternoon. The Nantucket-style guest rooms also have fireplaces and whirlpool tubs. The top-floor tower suite has a 180-degree ocean view. ✉ *34343 St. of the Blue Lantern, Dana Point 92629* ☎ *949/ 661–1304 or 800/950–1236* 🖷 *949/496–1483* ⊕ *www.foursisters.com* ⇨ *29 rooms* ⚬ *In-room data ports, cable TV with in-room VCRs, gym, concierge, meeting rooms; no smoking* ▤ *AE, DC, MC, V* ⑩ *BP.*

Sports & the Outdoors

Rental stands for surfboards, Windsurfers, small powerboats, and sailboats can be found near most of the piers. **Dana Wharf Sportfishing** (⊠ 34675 Golden Lantern St., Dana Point ☎ 949/496–5794 ⊕ www.danawharfsportfishing.com) runs charters and whale-watching excursions from early December to late March. **Embarcadero Marina** (⊠ 34512 Embarcadero Pl., Dana Point ☎ 949/496–6177 ⊕ www.danaharbor.com) has small powerboats and sailboats for rent near the launching ramp at Dana Point Harbor. **Hobie Sports** (⊠ 24825 Del Prado, Dana Point ☎ 949/496–2366) rents boogie and surfboards.

Laguna Beach

Fodor'sChoice
★

10 mi north of Dana Point, via PCH; 10 mi south of Newport Beach via PCH

Even the approach tells you that this town is exceptional. Driving in along Laguna Canyon Road from the I–405 freeway gives you the chance to cruise through a gorgeous coastal canyon, large stretches of which are undeveloped and pristine. After winding through the canyon you'll arrive at a glistening wedge of ocean, at the intersection with PCH.

Laguna's welcome mat is legendary. For decades in the mid-20th century a local booster, Eiler Larsen, greeted everyone downtown. (There's now a statue of him on the main drag.) On the corner of Forest and Park avenues you can see a 1930s gate proclaiming "This gate hangs well and hinders none, refresh and rest, then travel on."

There's a definite arty feel to this tight-knit community. The California Plein Air movement coalesced here in the early 1900s; by the middle of that century an annual arts festival was established, and art galleries now dot the village streets. The town's main street, PCH, is referred to as either South Coast or North Coast Highway, depending on the address. From this waterfront, the streets slope up steeply to the residential areas. All along the highway and side streets, you'll find dozens of eclectic fine-art and crafts galleries, clothing boutiques, and jewelry shops.

The **Laguna Coast Wilderness Park** (☎ 949/923–2235 ⊕ www.lagunacanyon.org) spreads over 19 acres of fragile coastal territory, including the canyon. The trails are great for hiking and mountain biking, but some areas are restricted for weekend use only. Docent-led hikes are given regularly; call for information.

An outdoor amphitheater near the mouth of the canyon hosts the annual **Pageant of the Masters** (☎ 949/494–1145 or 800/487–3378 ⊕ www.foapom.com), Laguna's most impressive—and truly unique—event. Local participants arrange tableaux vivants, in which live models and carefully orchestrated backgrounds merge in striking mimicry of classical and contemporary paintings. The Pageant is part of the **Festival of Arts,** held in July and August; tickets are much in demand, so plan ahead.

❹ The **Laguna Art Museum** displays American art, with an emphasis on California artists and works. Special exhibits change quarterly. Galleries throughout the area stay open late in coordination with the museum on the first Thursday of each month (www.firstthursdaysartwalk.com). Free shuttle service runs from the museum to galleries and studios along Laguna Canyon Road and PCH's Gallery Row. ⊠ *307 Cliff Dr., Laguna Beach* ☎ *949/494–6531* ⊕ *www.lagunaartmuseum.org* ▨ *$7* ☉ *Daily 11–5.*

Laguna Beach's **Main Beach Park,** at the end of Broadway at South Coast Highway, has a stocky 1920s lifeguard tower, sand volleyball, two half-basketball courts, children's play equipment, picnic areas, restrooms, showers, and street parking. A boardwalk separates the sand from a strip of lawn before the highway, and there's always plenty of people-watching. **Aliso Beach County Park** (☎ 949/661–7013), in south Laguna, is a recreation area with a playground, fire pits, parking, food stands, and restrooms. **Woods Cove,** off South Coast Highway at Diamond Street, is especially quiet during the week. Big rock formations hide lurking crabs. As you climb the steps to leave, you can see an English-style mansion that was once the home of Bette Davis.

Where to Stay & Eat

★ **$$–$$$$** ✕ **Five Feet.** Others have attempted to mimic this restaurant's innovative blend of Chinese and French cooking styles, but Five Feet remains the leader of the pack. Among the standout dishes is the whole, braised catfish, which is prepared in a mildly spicy tomato-ginger-citrus sauce. The setting is pure Laguna: exposed ceiling, open kitchen, high noise level, and brick walls hung with works by local artists. ⊠ *328 Glenneyre St., Laguna Beach* ☎ *949/497–4955* ▭ *AE, D, DC, MC, V* ☉ *No lunch.*

$$–$$$$ ✕ **French 75.** This bistro and champagne bar, which evokes a 1940s-style Paris supper club, offers intimate dining in an opulent setting. Daring entrées include duck in caramelized honey and tangerine sauce. ⊠ *1464 S. Coast Hwy., Laguna Beach* ☎ *949/494–8444* ▭ *AE, D, DC, MC, V* ☉ *No lunch.*

$–$$$ ✕ **Javier's Cantina and Grill.** "Homemade, but not necessarily traditional," is how owner Javier Sosa describes his restaurant's brand of Mexican cuisine. Fresh lobster enchiladas, mole poblano, and *lomo* Azteca (pork loin medallions in chipotle cream sauce), are all popular choices. The two patios offer plenty of outdoor seating. ⊠ *480 S. Coast Hwy., Laguna Beach* ☎ *949/494–1239* ▭ *AE, D, DC, MC, V.*

¢–$$$ ✕ **Mosun Sushi and Sake Bar.** Fans of this restaurant-nightclub come for the Pacific Rim cuisine, fresh sushi, and large selection of sake. Standout entrées are the teriyaki steak and pan-seared, five-spice duck breast. ⊠ *680 S. Coast Hwy., Laguna Beach* ☎ *949/497–5646* ⌕ *Reservations essential* ▭ *AE, D, DC, MC, V* ☉ *No lunch.*

$$ ✕ **Ti Amo Ristorante.** A romantic setting and creative Mediterranean cuisine (try the seared ahi with a sesame-seed crust) have earned acclaim for this Tuscan villa–themed restaurant. All the nooks and crannies are charming, candlelit, and private, but for maximum intimacy, request a table in the enclosed garden in back. ⊠ *31727 S. Coast Hwy., Laguna Beach* ☎ *949/499–5350* ▭ *AE, D, DC, MC, V* ☉ *No lunch.*

¢–$ ✕ **Zinc Café and Market.** Laguna Beach cognoscenti gather at the tiny counter and plant-filled patio of this vegetarian breakfast-and-lunch café.

Oatmeal is sprinkled with berries in season, poached eggs are dusted with herbs, and the orange juice is fresh-squeezed. For lunch, try the spicy Thai pasta, asparagus salad with orange peel and capers, or one of the gourmet pizzettes. ⊠ *350 Ocean Ave., Laguna Beach* ☎ *949/494–6302* ☒ *No credit cards.*

$$$$ ✕⌂ **Montage Resort & Spa.** This Craftsman-style resort, one of the
Fodor's Choice newest in the area, celebrates art, nature, and luxury in equal measure.
★ Works by contemporary and early-20th-century artists fill the interior; outside, an oceanfront bluff eases down to a pristine white beach, where you can meet with an on-staff marine biologist to learn about the local marine life. Guest rooms are plush, with ocean views, CD/DVD players, and extra-deep tubs. At the oceanfront spa and fitness center, you can indulge in a sea-salt scrub, take a yoga class, or hit the lap pool. The restaurant, Studio ($$$$; no lunch except on Sunday), has gained national recognition for chef James Boyce's contemporary French cuisine. ⊠ *30801 S. Coast Hwy., Laguna Beach 92651* ☎ *866/271–6953* ☐ *949/715–6100* ⊕ *www.montagelagunabeach.com* ⤷ *211 rooms, 51 suites* ⌂ *3 restaurants, room service, in-room data ports, in-room safes, minibars, 3 pools, health club, outdoor hot tub, spa, 2 bars, children's programs (ages 5–12), dry cleaning, laundry service, concierge, business services, meeting rooms, parking (fee)* ☒ *AE, MC, V.*

★ **$$$$** ⌂ **Surf & Sand Resort.** Right on the beach, this hotel has guest rooms with private balconies that look out over the ocean. Rooms also have CD players, and plush robes; the in-house fitness center offers everything from free weights to yoga classes. After a tough workout, you can relax at the Aquaterra Spa with a massage, body scrub, or a Mediterranean-mud body mask. ⊠ *1555 S. Coast Hwy., Laguna Beach 92651* ☎ *949/497–4477 or 800/524–8621* ☐ *949/497–1092* ⊕ *www.surfandsandresort.com* ⤷ *154 rooms, 10 suites* ⌂ *Restaurant, minibars, cable TV with movies, pool, health club, spa, beach, bar, concierge, meeting rooms* ☒ *AE, D, DC, MC, V.*

$$–$$$$ ⌂ **Inn at Laguna Beach.** On a bluff overlooking the ocean, this inn's terracotta tiles and exotic flower gardens evoke a Mediterranean villa. Most guest rooms have views; the best look out over the oceanfront cliffs. The property is close to Main Beach, a popular destination, but still far enough away to feel secluded. ⊠ *211 N. Coast Hwy., Laguna Beach 92651* ☎ *949/497–9722 or 800/544–4479* ☐ *949/497–9972* ⊕ *www.innatlagunabeach.com* ⤷ *70 rooms* ⌂ *In-room data ports, minibars, some microwaves, refrigerators, cable TV, in-room VCRs, pool, meeting rooms* ☒ *AE, D, DC, MC, V.*

$–$$$$ ⌂ **Hotel Laguna.** The oldest hotel in Laguna (it was opened in 1890) has manicured gardens, beach views, and an ideal location downtown. Among the perks is access to the hotel's private beach, where guests are provided with lounges, umbrellas, and towels, and can order lunch or cocktails from the Beach Club menu. Complimentary wine and cheese are served in the afternoon. ⊠ *425 S. Coast Hwy., Laguna Beach 92651* ☎ *949/494–1151 or 800/524–2927* ☐ *949/497–2163* ⊕ *www.hotellaguna.com* ⤷ *65 rooms* ⌂ *2 restaurants, cable TV, some in-room VCRs, beach, bar, meeting rooms, parking (fee); no a/c* ☒ *AE, DC, MC, V* ⏀ *CP.*

★ **$$–$$$** ⌂ **Eiler's Inn.** Named for Laguna's late official greeter, this B&B centers on a bright courtyard with a fountain. Every room is different, but all are full of antiques and travelers' journals for you to read and write in. Afternoon wine and cheese is served in the courtyard or in the cozy reading room, where you'll find the inn's only TV and phone. A sundeck in back has an ocean view. ⊠ *741 S. Coast Hwy., Laguna Beach 92651* ☎ *949/494–3004* ⎙ *949/497–2215* ⇝ *12 rooms* ⌂ *No room phones, no room TVs* ⊟ *AE, D, DC, MC, V* ❏❘ *BP.*

★ **$–$$$** ⌂ **La Casa del Camino.** This Spanish-style hotel was built in 1927 as a retreat for artists and movie stars. Its ace in the hole is its large rooftop terrace, with clear ocean views—an ideal spot for watching the sun set. Rooms have warm color schemes; beds have feather duvets to ward off any seaside chill. ⊠ *1289 S. Coast Hwy., Laguna Beach 92651* ☎ *949/ 497–2446 or 888/367–5232* ⎙ *949/494–5581* ⊕ *www.casacamino. com* ⇝ *34 rooms, 7 suites* ⌂ *Restaurant, cable TV, bar, Internet, free parking, some pets allowed* ⊟ *AE, D, DC, MC, V.*

Nightlife & the Arts

The **Laguna Playhouse** (⊠ 606 Laguna Canyon Rd., Laguna Beach ☎ 949/497–2787 ⊕ www.lagunaplayhouse.com), dating back to the 1920s, mounts a variety of productions, from classics to youth-oriented plays. The **Sawdust Arts Festival** (☎ 949/494–3030 ⊕ www. sawdustartfestival.org), held in July and August opposite the Festival of the Arts amphitheater, always includes musicians and entertainers as part of its lineup.

The **Boom Boom Room** (⊠ Coast Inn, 1401 S. Coast Hwy., Laguna Beach ☎ 949/494–7588) is the town's most popular gay club. The **Sandpiper** (⊠ 1183 S. Coast Hwy., Laguna Beach ☎ 949/494–4694), a hole-in-the-wall dancing joint, attracts an eclectic crowd. **White House** (⊠ 340 S. Coast Hwy., Laguna Beach ☎ 949/494–8088), a chic club on the main strip, has nightly entertainment and dancing.

Sports & the Outdoors

BICYCLING   Mountain bikes and helmets can be rented at **Rainbow Bicycles** (⊠ 485 N. Coast Hwy., Laguna Beach ☎ 949/494–5806 ⊕ www.teamrain.com).

GOLF   **Aliso Creek Golf Course** (⊠ 31106 S. Coast Hwy., Laguna Beach ☎ 949/ 499–1919 ⊕ www.alisocreekinn.com) is a scenic 9-hole facility with a putting green. Greens fees are $19–$28; carts (optional) cost $2 for pull carts and $9 for motorized. Reservations are accepted up to a week in advance.

TENNIS   Six metered courts can be found at **Laguna Beach High School.** Two courts are available at the **Irvine Bowl.** Six courts are available at **Alta Laguna Park** on a first-come, first-served basis. For more information, call the **City of Laguna Beach Recreation Department** (☎ 949/497–0716).

WATER SPORTS   Because its entire beach area is a marine preserve, Laguna Beach is ideal for snorkelers. Scuba divers should head to the Marine Life Refuge area, which runs from Seal Rock to Diver's Cove. During the winter months, wetsuits are advised and can be rented locally. Also bodyboards are available for rent at **Hobie Sports** (⊠ 294 Forest Ave., Laguna Beach ☎ 949/497–6011).

Shopping

Forest and Ocean avenues and Glenneyre Street are full of art galleries and fine jewelry and clothing boutiques. Get your sugar fix at the time-warped **Candy Baron** (⊠ 231 Forest Ave. ☎ 949/497–7508), filled with old-fashioned goodies like gumdrops, bull's-eyes, and more than a dozen barrels of saltwater taffy. Browse **Georgeo's Art Glass and Jewelry** (⊠ 269 Forest Ave., Laguna Beach ☎ 949/497–0907) for a large selection of etched-glass bowls, vases, and fine jewelry. The **Tung & Groov** (⊠ 950 Glenneyre St., Laguna Beach ☎ 949/494–0768) has an eclectic mix of handcrafted and decorator items like traditional umbrellas from Bali, brass elephant bells from India, and papier-mâché boxes.

Corona del Mar

8 mi north of Laguna Beach, via PCH; 2 mi south of Newport Beach, via PCH.

A small jewel on the Pacific Coast, Corona del Mar (known by locals as "CDM") has exceptional beaches that some say resemble their majestic northern California counterparts. **Corona del Mar Beach** (☎ 949/644–3151) is actually made up of two beaches, Little Corona and Big Corona, which are separated by a cliff. Facilities include fire pits, volleyball courts, food stands, restrooms, and parking. Two colorful reefs (and the fact that it's off-limits to boats) make Corona del Mar great for snorkeling and for beachcombers who prefer privacy.

Midway between Corona del Mar and Laguna, stretching along both sides of PCH, **Crystal Cove State Park** (☎ 949/494–3539 ⊕ www.crystalcovestatepark.com) is a favorite of local beachgoers and wilderness trekkers. It encompasses a 3½-mi stretch of unspoiled beach and has some of the best tide-pooling in Southern California; you can see starfish, crabs, and other sea creatures among the rocks. The park's 2,400 acres of backcountry are ideal for hiking, horseback riding, and mountain biking, but it's best to stay on trails to preserve the landscape. Docents lead nature walks on most weekend mornings. Parking costs $3.

❺ **Sherman Library and Gardens,** a botanical garden and library specializing in the history of the Pacific Southwest, provides a diversion from sun and sand. You can wander among cactus gardens, rose gardens, a wheelchair-height touch-and-smell garden, and a tropical conservatory. ⊠ 2647 PCH, Corona del Mar ☎ 949/673–2264 ⊕ *www.slgardens. org* ☞ *$3, free on Mon. and for children under 12* ☉ *Daily 10:30–4.*

Where to Eat

★ **$$–$$$** ✕ **Oysters.** This hip yet convivial seafood restaurant, complete with a bustling bar and live music, caters to a late-night crowd. The eclectic menu runs the gamut, from fire-roasted artichokes to terrific ahi tuna dishes. There's also a substantial list of outstanding desserts, cognacs, and dessert wines. ⊠ *2515 E. Coast Hwy., Corona del Mar* ☎ *949/675–7411* ▤ *AE, D, DC, MC, V* ☉ *No lunch.*

Newport Beach

2 mi north of Corona del Mar via PCH; 6 mi south of Huntington Beach via PCH.

Newport Beach has two distinct personalities. First, there's the island-dotted yacht harbor, where the idle wealthy play. (Newport is said to have the highest per-capita number of Mercedes-Benz cars in the world.) Just southwest of John Wayne airport, however, inland Newport Beach—lined with high-rise office buildings, shopping centers, and hotels—is all business.

★ ❻ **Newport Harbor,** which shelters nearly 10,000 small boats, may seduce even those who don't own a yacht. Exploring the charming avenues and surrounding alleys can be great fun. To see Newport Harbor from the water, take a one-hour gondola cruise operated by the **Gondola Company of Newport** (✉ 3400 Via Oporto, Suite 102B, Newport Beach ☎ 949/675–1212). It costs $75 for two and includes salami, cheese, bread, ice, glasses, blankets, music, and a Polaroid picture. Bottles of wine, however, cost extra.

Within Newport Harbor are eight small islands, including Balboa and Lido. The houses lining the shore may seem modest, but this is some of the most expensive real estate in the world. Several grassy areas on Lido Isle have views of Newport Harbor, but, unfortunately, each of these is marked PRIVATE COMMUNITY PARK.

Newport Pier, which juts out into the ocean near 20th Street, is the heart of Newport's beach community and a popular fishing spot. Street parking is difficult at the pier, so grab the first space you find and be prepared to walk. A stroll along West Ocean Front reveals much of the town's character. On weekday mornings, if you head for the beach near the pier, you'll likely encounter the dory fishermen hawking their predawn catches, as they've done for generations. On weekends the walk is alive with rollerbladers, skateboarders, and bikers, who dodge pedestrians and whiz past the fast-food joints, swimsuit shops, and bars.

Newport's best beaches are on **Balboa Peninsula,** where the many jetties surround ideal swimming areas. At the south end of the peninsula is the best body-surfing place in Orange County (and arguably on the West Coast), known as **The Wedge.** Created by accident in the 1930s when the Federal Works Progress Administration built a jetty to protect Newport Harbor, the break is pure euphoria for highly skilled body surfers. Since the waves generally break very close to shore and rip currents are strong, lifeguards strongly discourage visitors from attempting it.

❼ The **Balboa Pavilion,** on the bay side of the peninsula, was built in 1905 as a bath- and boathouse. Today it houses a restaurant and shops and is a departure point for harbor and whale-watching cruises. Look for it on Main Street, off Balboa Boulevard. Adjacent to the pavilion is the three-car ferry that connects the peninsula to Balboa Island. Several blocks surrounding the pavilion contain restaurants, beachside shops, and the small **Fun Zone**—a local kiddie hangout with a Ferris wheel, video games, rides, and arcades. On the other side of the narrow peninsula is the **Balboa Pier,** with the original branch of Ruby's (a 1940s-esque burgers-and-shakes joint) on the end.

Shake the sand out of your shoes to head inland to the ritzy **Fashion Island** outdoor mall, a cluster of arcades and courtyards marooned in a sea of parking spaces. While it doesn't have the international-designer clout of South Coast Plaza, it has plenty of department stores, including Neiman Marcus, as well as upscale chains like L'Occitane and Design Within Reach. There are are also restaurants, and the requisite movie theater. ⊠ *410 Newport Center Dr., between Jamboree and MacArthur Blvds., off PCH, Newport Beach* ☎ *949/721–2000* ⊕ *www.shopfashionisland.com.*

❽ The **Orange County Museum of Art** has gathered an esteemed collection of Abstract Expressionist paintings and cutting-edge contemporary works by California artists. The museum also displays some of its collection at a gallery at South Coast Plaza, free of charge; it's open the same hours as the mall. ⊠ *850 San Clemente Dr., Newport Beach* ☎ *949/759–1122* ⊕ *www.ocma.net* ⊠ *$5* ☉ *Tues.–Sun. 11–5.*

Where to Stay & Eat

$$$–$$$$ ✕ **Restaurant Pascal.** Chef and owner Pascal Olhats' establishment has
Fodor's Choice been rated by *Zagat's* as the number-one restaurant in Orange County
★ for several years in a row. Although it's humbly tucked into a shopping center, the restaurant's interior and menu are elegant; dishes change frequently, but might include roasted duck breast; fresh-caught day boat scallops; shrimp scampi *magali* with tomato, basil, and heavy cream; and chicken breast Provençal with wine and herbs. There's also a popular, five-course prix-fixe dinner menu. ⊠ *1000 N. Bristol St., Newport Beach* ☎ *949/752–0107* ⌨ *Reservations essential* ▤ *AE, D, MC, V* ☉ *Closed Sunday. No dinner Mon. No lunch Sat.*

$$–$$$$ ✕ **The Ritz.** This posh eatery—complete with black-leather booths, etched-glass mirrors, polished-brass trim, and the requisite attitude—lives up to its name. Don't pass up the "carousel" appetizer—a lavish spread of cured gravlax, shrimp, Dungeness crab legs, Maine lobster tails, filet mignon tartare, and other surf-and-turf treats served on a lazy Susan. Dessert soufflés are also a specialty. ⊠ *880 Newport Center Dr., Newport Beach* ☎ *949/720–1800* ⌨ *Reservations essential* ▤ *AE, D, DC, MC, V* ☉ *No lunch weekends.*

★ $–$$$$ ✕ **The Cannery.** This 1920s cannery building still teems with fish, although you'll only find them now on the Asian-style menu. You can settle in at the sushi bar, dining room, or patio to debate between sashimi or mahimahi with a coconut curry sauce. ⊠ *3010 Lafayette Rd., Newport Beach* ☎ *949/566–0060* ▤ *AE, D, DC, MC.*

¢–$$ ✕ **Thaifoon.** Bamboo walls, a waterfall, and gentle amber lighting set the mood at this low-key Thai restaurant. The menu has many of the usual Southeast Asian specialties, including curries and satays, but an especially good (and well-named) choice is the Evil Jungle Princess—chicken stir-fried with long beans in a peanut-chile sauce. The bar serves a refreshing, unfiltered sake. ⊠ *Fashion Island, 857 Newport Center Dr., Newport Beach* ☎ *949/644–0133* ▤ *AE, D, DC, MC, V.*

¢ ✕ **Big Belly Deli.** Just steps from the sand, this casual spot is perfect for grabbing a sandwich, a buffalo chicken pizza, or a microbrew. ⊠ *6310 W. Coast Hwy., Newport Beach* ☎ *949/645–2888* 🖃 *AE, D, MC, V.*

¢ ✕ **Taco Mesa.** There's a good reason why the golden-arched fast-food

Fodor'sChoice chain next door to this taqueria is always empty. This extremely pop-

★ ular and cheerful spot serves up fantastic *carne asada* (steak) tacos, giant burritos, and superfresh salsa, all at bargain prices. It's close to the end of the Highway 55 freeway, technically in Costa Mesa. ⊠ *647 W. 19th St., Costa Mesa* ☎ *949/642–0629* 🖃 *No credit cards.*

★ **$$$$** ✕🖾 **Four Seasons Hotel.** A suitably stylish hotel in an ultrachic neighborhood (it's across the street from the tony Fashion Island mall), the 20-story Four Seasons caters to luxury seekers with weekend golf packages through the nearby Pelican Hill golf course. Guest rooms have outstanding views, private bars, and original art. Kids are given special treatment: balloons, cookies and milk, game books, video games, and more. Overlooking the hotel gardens, the Pavilion restaurant ($$–$$$$) features Mediterranean cuisine and is considered one of the best restaurants in Newport Beach. The prix-fixe dinner menu, which offers a four-course meal, is a great value. ⊠ *690 Newport Center Dr., Newport Beach 92660* ☎ *949/759–0808 or 800/332–3442* 🖨 *949/759–0568* ⊕ *www.fourseasons.com* ➳ *295 rooms, 92 suites* ⚭ *2 restaurants, room service, cable TV with movies and video games, 2 tennis courts, pool, health club, hair salon, massage, sauna, mountain bikes, bar, concierge, Internet, business services, some pets allowed (fee)* 🖃 *AE, D, DC, MC, V.*

★ **$$$–$$$$** 🖾 **The Balboa Bay Club and Resort.** This plush property, which resembles a waterfront Italian piazza, offers panoramic views of the bay. The guest rooms, which look out over the water or the tropical gardens, have plantation shutters, rattan furniture, and marble baths; many have private patios with deck chairs. There's a spa with Jacuzzis, a sauna, and steam room, and a fire-lighted relaxation lounge; the $35 daily guest fee is waived when you book any spa service. ⊠ *1221 W. Coast Highway, Newport Beach 92663* ☎ *949/645–5000 or 888/445–7153* 🖨 *949/630–4215* ⊕ *www.balboabayclub.com* ➳ *150 rooms, 10 suites* ⚭ *2 restaurants, lounge, cable TV, refrigerators, pool, health club, spa, concierge, Internet, business services* 🖃 *AE, D, DC, MC, V.*

$$–$$$ 🖾 **Newport Beach Marriott Hotel and Tennis Club.** The location of this hotel couldn't be more opulent: it's across from Fashion Island, next to a country club, and with a view toward Newport Harbor. Rooms are in one of two towers; all have balconies or patios that look out onto lush gardens or toward the Pacific. ⊠ *900 Newport Center Dr., Newport Beach 92660* ☎ *949/640–4000 or 800/228–9290* 🖨 *949/640–5055* ⊕ *www.marriott.com* ➳ *577 rooms, 6 suites* ⚭ *Restaurant, cable TV with movies, 8 tennis courts, 2 pools, health club, sauna, bar, concierge, Internet, business services, meeting rooms, some pets allowed (fee)* 🖃 *AE, D, DC, MC, V.*

$$ 🖾 **Sutton Place Hotel.** An eye-catching ziggurat design is the trademark of this ultramodern hotel in Koll Center. Despite its futuristic exterior, the inside is decorated with traditional furniture in beige and burgundy. ⊠ *4500 MacArthur Blvd., Newport Beach 92660* ☎ *949/476–2001 or 800/243–4141* 🖨 *949/476–0153* ⊕ *www.suttonplace.com* ➳ *435 rooms, 24 suites* ⚭ *2 restaurants, in-room data ports, minibars, cable TV with* *movies, 2 tennis courts, pool, health club, bicycles, 2 bars, concierge, Internet, business services, airport shuttle* ☰ *AE, D, DC, MC, V.*

Sports & the Outdoors

BOAT RENTAL You can tour Lido and Balboa isles by renting kayaks ($12 an hour), sailboats ($35 an hour), small motorboats ($50 an hour), cocktail boats ($65 an hour), and ocean boats ($75–$85 an hour) at **Balboa Boat Rentals** (✉ 510 E. Edgewater Ave., Newport Beach ☎ 949/673–7200 ⊕ www.boats4rent. com). You must have a driver's license, and some knowledge of boating is helpful; rented boats are not allowed out of the bay.

BOAT TOURS **Catalina Passenger Service** (✉ 400 Main St., Newport Beach ☎ 949/673–5245 ⊕ www.catalinainfo.com) at the Balboa Pavilion operates 90-minute sightseeing tours for $13.50 and daily round-trip passage to Catalina Island for $42. **Hornblower Cruises & Events** (✉ 2431 W. Coast Hwy., Newport Beach ☎ 949/646–0155 or 800/668–4322 ⊕ www. hornblower.com) books three-hour weekend dinner cruises with dancing for $60 on Friday, $66 on Saturday; two-hour Sunday brunch cruises are $59. Reservations are required.

FISHING In addition to a complete tackle shop, **Davey's Locker** (✉ Balboa Pavilion, 400 Main St., Newport Beach ☎ 949/673–1434 ⊕ www. daveyslocker.com) operates sportfishing trips as well as private charters and, in winter, whale-watching trips.

GOLF **Newport Beach Golf Course** (✉ 3100 Irvine Ave., Newport Beach ☎ 949/852–8681), an 18-hole, par-59 course, is lighted for nighttime play. Greens fees range from $12 to $22 for 18-holes; hand carts are $3. Reservations are accepted up to one week in advance, but walk-ups are accommodated when possible. **Pelican Hill Golf Club** (✉ 22651 Pelican Hill Rd. S, Newport Beach ☎ 949/960–0707) has two 18-hole courses (par 70 and 71) with canyon and ocean views. Greens fees range from $175 to $270 and include the mandatory cart.

RUNNING The **Beach Trail** runs along the coast from Huntington Beach to Newport. Paths throughout **Newport Back Bay** (☎ 949/640–6746 ⊕ www. newportbay.org) wrap around a marshy area inhabited by lizards, rabbits, and waterfowl. For information on free walking tours in this ecological reserve, call the **Newport Bay Naturalists.**

TENNIS Call the **recreation department** (☎ 949/644–3151) for information about use of the courts in locations throughout Orange County where play is free and first-come, first-served. Reservations are required at the **Newport Beach Marriott Hotel and Tennis Club** (✉ 900 Newport Center Dr., Newport Beach ☎ 949/640–4000). The cost is $15 per person per hour for nonguests.

Huntington Beach

6 mi north of Newport Beach via PCH; 25 mi west of Anaheim, Hwy. 57 south to Hwy. 22 west to I-405.

Once a sleepy residential town with little more than a string of rugged surf shops, Huntington Beach is slowly transforming itself into a resort destination. The town's appeal is its broad white-sand beaches with often-towering waves, complemented by a lively pier, a large shopping center on Main Street, and the luxurious Hilton Waterfront Beach Resort. A draw for sports fans: the U.S. Open professional surf competition takes place here every August. There's even a Surfing Walk of Fame, with plaques set in the sidewalk around the intersection of PCH and Main Street.

9 Huntington Pier stretches 1,800 feet out to sea, well past the powerful waves that make Huntington Beach America's "Surf City." A farmers' market is held on Friday; an informal arts fair sets up most weekends. At the end of the pier sits **Ruby's** (☎ 714/969–7829), part of a California chain of 1940s-style burger joints. The **Pierside Pavilion** (⊠ PCH across from Huntington Pier) contains shops, restaurants, bars with live music, and a theater complex. The best surf gear source is **Huntington Surf and Sport Pierside** (☎ 714/841–4000), where employees are true surf enthusiasts.

10 Just up Main Street from the pier, the **International Surfing Museum** contains the Surfing Hall of Fame, which has an impressive collection of surfboards and surf memorabilia. They've even got the Bolex camera with which *The Endless Summer* was shot. ⊠ *411 Olive Ave., Huntington Beach* ☎ *714/960–3483* ⊕ *www.surfingmuseum.org* ☜ *$2* ☉ *June–Sept., daily noon–5; Oct.–May, Thurs.–Mon. noon–5.*

Huntington City Beach (☎ 714/536–5281) stretches for 3 mi from the pier area. The beach is most crowded around the pier; amateur and professional surfers brave the waves daily on its north side. Continuing north, **Huntington State Beach** (☎ 714/536–1454) parallels PCH. On the state and city beaches there are changing rooms, concessions, lifeguards, and ample parking; the state beach also has barbecue pits. At the northern section of the city, **Bolsa Chica State Beach** (☎ 714/846–3460) has barbecue pits and RV campsites and is usually less crowded than its southern neighbors.

★ 11 Bolsa Chica Ecological Reserve beckons wildlife-lovers and bird-watchers with an 1,180-acre salt marsh that is home to 315 species of birds, including great blue herons, snowy and great egrets, and common loons. Throughout the reserve are trails for bird-watching, including a comfortable 1½-mi loop. Free guided tours depart from the walking bridge the first Saturday of each month at 9 AM. ⊠ *Entrance at Warner Ave. and PCH, opposite Bolsa Chica State Beach* ☎ *714/840–1575* ☜ *Free* ☉ *Daily dawn–sunset.*

Where to Stay & Eat

$–$$$ ✕ **Baci.** With a rustic decor reminiscent of an Italian villa, Baci serves dependable Italian food. The menu lists every kind of pasta-and-sauce combination imaginable and almost as many meat dishes (which include a side of pasta or vegetable). ⊠ *18748 Beach Blvd., Huntington Beach* ☎ *714/965–1194* ⊕ *www.bacirestaurant.com* ▤ *AE, D, DC, MC, V* ☉ *No lunch weekends.*

★ $–$$$ ✕ **Inka Grill.** Founded by a Peruvian family, this local chain provides a fresh alternative to the usual beachfront eateries. There are dozens of South American–style dishes, including ceviche, spicy lamb stew, and seafood paella. The bar attracts a lively crowd on weekend nights. ⊠ *301 E. Main St., Huntington Beach* ☎ *714/374–3399* ⊕ *www. inkagrill.com* ⊟ *AE, D, MC, V.*

★ ¢–$$ ✕ **Red Pearl Kitchen.** This hip, lacquer-red space near Main Street may put its bar front and center, but the Pan-Asian food deserves a following of its own. The menu, divided into small and large servings, might include lemongrass coconut soup, spicy spare ribs, or Szechuan pepper steak with sweet-and-sour eggplant. Desserts are also excellent. DJs spin several nights a week, upping the energy but making it difficult to talk. Keep the no-reservations policy in mind—if you come on a weekend, you'll likely need to wait awhile. ⊠ *412 Walnut Ave., Huntington Beach* ☎ *714/969–0224* ⌑ *Reservations not accepted* ⊟ *AE, MC, V.*

¢ ✕ **Wahoo's Fish Taco.** Proximity to the ocean makes the mahimahi- and wahoo-filled tacos at this surf sticker–covered spot taste even better. This healthful fast-food chain brought Baja's fish tacos north of the border to quick success, and one bite will tell you why. ⊠ *120 Main St., Huntington Beach* ☎ *714/536–2050* ⊟ *MC, V.*

★ $$$–$$$$ ✕⌂ **Hyatt Regency Huntington Beach Resort and Spa.** Reflecting the architecture and style of Andalusia in southern Spain—each room is outfitted with Andalusian wood furnishings and art—this hotel is connected to 8 mi of beach by a pedestrian walkway. Camp Hyatt offers activities for kids throughout the day (evening sessions are also available). Grownups can have fun in the sun, too; the hotel has teamed up with a local surf shop that gives surfing and bodyboarding lessons, and the posh Pacific Waters Spa offers a menu of facial and body treatments, including the luscious-sounding Pure Fiji Sugar Scrub. One of the hotel restaurants, the Californian ($$–$$$$), has some of the best California cuisine in the area (don't miss the lobster Napoleon). ⊠ *21500 PCH, Huntington Beach 92648* ☎ *714/698–1234 or 888/ 591–1234* ⌨ *714/ 845–4636* ⊕ *http://huntingtonbeach.hyatt.com* ⇨ *517 rooms, 57 suites* ⌑ *3 Restaurants, cable TV, 2 tennis courts, pool, health club, 4 hot tubs, spa, 2 lounges, Internet, business services* ⊟ *AE, D, DC, MC, V.*

$$$–$$$$ ⌂ **Hilton Waterfront Beach Resort.** Rising 12 stories above the surf, this waterfront hotel caters to all kinds of travelers: couples, families, business types. All guest rooms have private balconies, many with panoramic ocean views. The grounds are extensive, and include a sand volleyball court and a free-form pool; the staff can even arrange the fixings for a cookout on the beach. ⊠ *21100 PCH, Huntington Beach 92648* ☎ *714/ 960–7873 or 800/822–7873* ⌨ *714/845–8425* ⊕ *www. waterfrontbeachresort.hilton.com* ⇨ *266 rooms, 24 suites* ⌑ *Restaurant, some microwaves, cable TV with movies, tennis court, pool, gym, hot tub, 2 bars, concierge floor, Internet, business services, meeting rooms, airport shuttle, some pets allowed (fee)* ⊟ *AE, D, DC, MC, V.*

¢–$ ⌂ **Best Western Regency Inn.** Forgo an ocean view and you can save a lot of money. This moderately priced, tidy hotel is near PCH and close to the main drag of restaurants and shops. Rooms are cookie-cutter, but some have private whirlpools. ⊠ *19360 Beach Blvd., Huntington Beach 92648* ☎ *714/962–4244 or 800/780–7234* ⌨ *714/963–4724* ⊕ *www.bestwestern. com* ⇨ *64 rooms* ⌑ *In-room data ports, refrigerators, cable TV, pool, hot tub, laundry facilities, meeting room* ⊟ *AE, D, DC, MC, V.*

Sports & the Outdoors

SURFING **Corky Carroll's Surf School** (☎ 714/969–3959 ⊕ www.surfschool.net) organizes lessons, weeklong workshops, and surfing trips. You can rent surf or boogie boards at **Dwight's** (☎ 714/536–8083), one block south of the pier. **Huntington Beach Surfing Instruction** (☎ 714/962–3515), a group of off-duty lifeguards, offers private and group lessons by appointment only.

INLAND ORANGE COUNTY

If you head south from downtown Los Angles on I–5 (also known as the Santa Ana Freeway), after about 40 minutes of driving—assuming normal traffic—you will come to Anaheim, the tourist center of Orange County and the home of the Disneyland Resort. There is more to this area, however, than theme parks, hotels, and shopping centers. In the Old Towne section of Orange, for instance, hundreds of antiques and collectibles dealers fill early-20th-century buildings. Little Saigon, a large Vietnamese community, is between Westminster and Garden Grove. Farther south and inland, the Santiago, Silverado, and Modjeska canyons meander toward the marvelous Cleveland National Forest, which stretches from Orange County to San Diego.

Irvine

6 mi south of Santa Ana, via Hwy. 55 to I–405; 12 mi south of Anaheim, via I–5.

Irvine—characterized by its rows of large, cream-color tract homes, tree-lined streets, uniformly manicured lawns, and pristine parks—may feel surreal to urban visitors. The master-planned community has top-notch schools, a university and a community college, plus dozens of shopping centers, and a network of well-lit walking and biking paths.

⓬ Some of the Californian impressionist paintings on display at the small yet intriguing **Irvine Museum** depict the state's rural landscape in the years before massive freeways and sprawling housing developments. The paintings, which are displayed on the 12th floor of the marble-and-glass Tower 17 building, were assembled by Joan Irvine Smith, granddaughter of James Irvine, a rancher who once owned one-quarter of what is now Orange County. ⊠ *18881 Von Karman Ave., at Martin St. north of the UC Irvine campus, Irvine* ☎ *949/476–2565* ⊕ *www.irvinemuseum. org* ⊒ *Free* ☉ *Tues.–Sat. 11–5.*

⓭ The **University of California at Irvine** was established on 1,000 acres of rolling ranch land donated by the Irvine family in the mid-1950s. The campus contains more than 11,000 trees from around the world and features a stellar biological science department and creative writing program. The school's anteater mascot—in case you're wondering—was chosen during the 1960s; it's a character from the syndicated cartoon *B.C.* The **Irvine Barclay Theater** (☎ 949/854–4646) presents an impressive roster of music, dance, and dramatic events, and there's not a bad seat in the house. The **Art Gallery at UC Irvine** (☎ 949/824–6610) sponsors exhibitions of student and professional art. It's free and open mid-

September–mid-June, Tuesday–Sunday noon–5, until 8 Thursday. ⊠ *I–405 to Jamboree Rd., west to Campus Dr. S, Irvine* ☎ *949/824–5011* ⊕ *www.uci.edu.*

☙ **Wild Rivers Water Park** has more than 40 rides and attractions, including a wave pool, daring slides, and an inner-tube river ride. ⊠ *8770 Irvine Center Dr., off I–405, Irvine* ☎ *949/788–0808* ⊕ *www.wildrivers.com* ☜ *$27, $18 for children under 48" tall* ☉ *Late-May–Sept., call for hrs.*

Where to Stay & Eat

$–$$$ ✕ **Il Fornaio.** Two weeks a month, regional dishes from Tuscany or Puglia supplement the regular fare—house-made pastas, pizza, veal scallopini, succulent grilled eggplant with goat cheese—at this elegant Italian chain restaurant. A pair of boccie courts sets this branch apart; borrow a boccie set and play a game before your meal. ⊠ *18051 Von Karman Ave., Irvine* ☎ *949/261–1444* ☰ *AE, D, DC, MC, V* ☉ *No lunch Sun.*

$–$$$ ✕ **Bistango.** This sleek, art-filled bistro serves first-rate American cuisine—salads, steak, seafood, pasta, and pizzas—with a European flair. The tuna grilled rare is especially good. Be sure to book a table in advance, especially on weekends; this place is very popular with locals. ⊠ *19100 Von Karman Ave., near the John Wayne Airport, Irvine* ☎ *949/752–5222* ☰ *AE, D, DC, MC, V* ☉ *No lunch weekends.*

★ **$–$$$**   ✕ **Prego.** Reminiscent of a Tuscan villa, this much-larger sister to the Beverly Hills Prego has soft lighting, golden walls, and an outdoor patio. The spit-roasted meats and chicken, the charcoal-grilled fresh fish, and the pizzas from the oak-burning oven are all top-notch. California and Italian wines are reasonably priced. ⊠ *18420 Von Karman Ave., Irvine* ☎ *949/553–1333* ☰ *AE, D, DC, MC, V* ☉ *No lunch weekends.*

¢–$ ✕ **Kitima Thai Cuisine.** Tucked away on the ground floor of an office building, Orange County's best Thai restaurant is a favorite with the business-lunch crowd. The names may be gimmicky—one choice is called rock-and-roll shrimp salad—but fresh ingredients are used in every dish. ⊠ *2010 Main St., Suite 170, Irvine* ☎ *949/261–2929* ☰ *AE, MC, V* ☉ *Closed Sun.*

$$–$$$$ ⊞ **Hyatt Regency Irvine.** The sleek, ultramodern rooms here offer practical amenities such as coffeemakers, irons, and hair dryers. Special golf packages at nearby Oak Creek and Pelican Hills are available. ⊠ *17900 Jamboree Rd., near the John Wayne Airport, Irvine 92614* ☎ *949/975–1234 or 800/233–1234* 🖷 *949/852–1574* ⊕ *www.hyatt.com* ☞ *536 rooms, 20 suites* ♨ *2 restaurants, cable TV with movies, 4 tennis courts, pool, health club, bicycles, 2 bars, concierge, Internet, business services, airport shuttle* ☰ *AE, D, DC, MC, V.*

$$$ ⊞ **Irvine Marriott John Wayne Airport.** Towering over Koll Business Center, the Marriott offers a convenient location and amenities that appeal to business travelers. Despite its size, the hotel has an intimate feel, due in part to the convivial lobby with love seats and evening entertainment. Weekend discounts and packages are available, and there's a courtesy van to South Coast Plaza and the airport. ⊠ *18000 Von Karman Ave., Irvine 92612* ☎ *949/553–0100 or 800/228–9290* 🖷 *949/261–7059* ⊕ *www.marriott.com* ☞ *485 rooms, 10 suites* ♨ *2 restaurants, cable TV with movies, 4 tennis courts, pool, health club, hot tub, Internet,* *business services, meeting rooms, airport shuttle, some pets allowed (fee)* ▭ *AE, D, DC, MC, V.*

Nightlife

The **Improv Comedy Nite Club** (⊠ Irvine Spectrum, 71 Fortune Dr., Irvine ☎ 949/854–5455) is open nightly. The **Verizon Wireless Amphitheater** (⊠ 8808 Irvine Center Dr., Irvine ☎ 949/855–8095 or 949/855–6111 ⊕ www.improv.com), a 16,300-seat open-air venue, presents musical events April through October. Tickets are available online.

Costa Mesa

6 mi northeast of Irvine, via I–405 to Bristol St.

Though it's probably best known for its shopping malls, Costa Mesa is also the performing-arts hub of Orange County, and a formidable local business center. Patrons of the domestic and international theater, opera, and dance productions fill area restaurants and nightspots. Movie buffs have several theaters to choose from, too.

★ ⑭ Costa Mesa's most famous landmark, **South Coast Plaza,** is an immense complex that's gotten ritzier by the year as designer boutiques jostle for platinum-card space. The original section has the densest concentration of luxe: Gucci, Armani, Burberry, La Perla, Hermès, Versace, and Prada are just a few of the shops here. The usual moderately priced mall chains are here, too, from Sunglass Hut to Banana Republic. One standout is the excellent Book Soup bookstore. Major department stores, including Saks and Nordstrom, flank the exterior. A pedestrian bridge crosses Bear Street to the second wing, a smaller offshoot with a huge Crate & Barrel. ⊠ *3333 S. Bristol St., off I–405 north, Costa Mesa* ☎ *714/435–2000* ⊕ *www.southcoastplaza.com* ☉ *Weekdays 10–9, Sat. 10–7, Sun. 11–6:30.*

South Coast Plaza has gradually become surrounded by other shopping complexes with different twists. Across Sunflower Avenue is an outdoor shopping area called South Coast Plaza Village (technically in Santa Ana), while on the other side of Bear Street is Metro Pointe, a conglomerate mass of supersized, often bargain-oriented stores. Farther down Bristol on the other side of the I–405 you'll find the **Lab** (⊠ 2930 Bristol St., Costa Mesa ⊕ www.thelab.com), also known as the "anti-mall." Can this courtyard-centered cluster of shops truly break from mall culture or is that just wishful thinking? Mull it over with a coffee in the kitschy Gypsy Den or while browsing through the alterna-clothes at Electric Chair. The **Camp** (⊠ 2937 Bristol St. ⊕ www.thecampsite.net), another outdoor "retail community," takes a mellower, ecofriendly approach, devoting itself to sports-related stores like Adventure 16 and Cycle Werks. Liburdi's Scuba Center even has a small pool for instruction. Grab a snack from the bakery and hang out in the grassy bowl.

Costa Mesa's role in consumer consumption is happily matched by its arts venues. The **Orange County Performing Arts Center** (⊠ 600 Town Center Dr., east of Bristol St. ☎ 714/556–2787 ⊕ www.ocpac.org) houses Segerstrom Hall for opera, ballet, symphony, and musicals and the more intimate Founders Hall for chamber music. Richard Lippold's enormous *Firebird,* an angular sculpture of polished metal that resembles a bird taking flight, extends outward from the glass-enclosed lobby. Across the way is the highly regarded South Coast Repertory Theater. *See* Nightlife & the Arts, *below,* for more info.

★ Tucked between mirrored-glass office towers near the Performing Arts Center is the **California Scenario** (✉ 611 Anton Blvd.), a 1½-acre sculpture garden designed by Isamu Noguchi, who carved this compact space into distinct areas with his abstract designs. Each represents an aspect of the state's terrain. Smooth granite boulders punctuate the sweep of flat stone paving. A pine tree–trimmed grassy slope faces a circular area planted with cacti, while a sunken stream curls towards a low stone pyramid. The garden can be hard to find; it's a block from the South Coast Repertory Theater, by the El Torito restaurant.

Where to Stay & Eat

$$$–$$$$ ✕ **Troquet.** On the third floor of the South Coast Plaza, this bistro attracts locals as well as visitors for its French cosmopolitan cuisine. While its menu changes frequently, standout dishes include the honey-and-coriander-crusted Long Island duck breast and the foie gras terrine. Be sure to save room for sinful desserts like the warm Valrhona chocolate soufflé. ✉ *3333 Bristol St., Costa Mesa* ☎ *714/708–6865* ▤ *AE, DC, MC, V.*

$$–$$$$ ✕ **La Cave.** This underground steak house doesn't offer a menu; instead, a cart with various cuts of beef and varieties of seafood is wheeled to your table so you can choose. The prime rib and filet mignon are perennially popular choices; the carrot cake is excellent for dessert. There's a speakeasy-type back room where live music is played most evenings. ✉ *1695 Irvine Ave. Costa Mesa* ☎ *949/646–7944* ▤ *AE, D, MC, V.*

$$–$$$ ✕ **Marrakesh.** It's easy to pretend you're in Morocco when dining at this restaurant. Sumptuous, multicourse meals of North African–style spiced meats and vegetables are served to you at ground level, where you sit on comfy cushions rather than chairs. Eating with your hands is encouraged— although joining in with the performing belly dancers is not. ✉ *1976 Newport Blvd., Costa Mesa* ☎ *949/645–8384* ▤ *AE, D, DC, MC, V.*

★ $$–$$$ ✕ **Pinot Provence.** Chef Joachim Splichal (of L.A.'s Patina) fuses fresh California ingredients with traditional Provençal dishes at this elegant eatery in the Westin South Coast Plaza. The milk-fed lamb ragout is a standout entrée; the seafood platters (which include generous portions of lobster, shellfish, and caviar) are listed as appetizers but are big enough for a meal. Brunch is served on the weekends; try for a table out on the pretty patio. ✉ *Westin South Coast Plaza, 686 Anton Blvd., Costa Mesa* ☎ *714/444–5900* ▤ *AE, D, DC, MC, V.*

$–$$ ✕ **Habana Restaurant and Bar.** In this formerly industrial space, now warmed with wall murals and rustic candelabras, the Cuban and Caribbean specialties are as flavorful as the setting is cool. Chocolate lovers shouldn't miss the Café Cubano—chocolate mousse topped with chocolate whipped cream and rum sauce. With entertainment two nights a week (including flamenco on Wednesday) this restaurant is a popular nightspot. ✉ *The Lab, 2930 Bristol St., Costa Mesa* ☎ *714/556–0176* ▤ *AE, D, MC, V.*

$$–$$$$ ☒ **Westin South Coast Plaza.** This downtown high-rise adjoins the South Coast Plaza complex—you can roll out of bed and hit the stores. The beds in these comfortably sized rooms come with feather duvets. Tennis courts are nearby. ⊠ *686 Anton Blvd., Costa Mesa 92626* ☎ *714/ 540–2500 or 800/937–8461* ⊟ *714/662–6695* ⊕ *www.westin.com* ⇱ *393 rooms, 3 suites ♿ Restaurant, in-room data ports, cable TV with movies, pool, Internet, business services, meeting rooms, some pets allowed* ▤ *AE, D, DC, MC, V.*

$–$$$$ ☒ **Country Inn and Suites.** The Queen Anne–style decor, with warm colors, floral upholstery, and mahogany furniture, gives this hotel a less corporate feel than other hotel chains; plus you can mingle with other guests when evening cocktails and hors d'oeuvres are served. ⊠ *325 Bristol St., Costa Mesa 92626* ☎ *714/549–0300 or 800/322–9992* ⊟ *714/ 662–0828* ⊕ *www.ayreshotels.com* ⇱ *149 rooms, 132 suites ♿ Restaurant, some microwaves, refrigerators, cable TV with movies and video games, 2 pools, gym, 2 hot tubs, bar, laundry facilities, meeting rooms* ▤ *AE, D, DC, MC, V.*

$$–$$$ ☒ **Hilton Costa Mesa.** At this modern, spacious hotel you can stay near John Wayne Airport without the air traffic sounding too close. In-room desks and business services make it a good stop if you're bound for the nearby office parks. ⊠ *3050 Bristol St., Costa Mesa 92626* ☎ *714/540– 7000 or 800/445–8667* ⊟ *714/540–9176* ⊕ *www.hilton.com* ⇱ *486 rooms, 12 suites ♿ Restaurant, some microwaves, cable TV with movies, pool, health club, hair salon, hot tub, lobby lounge, laundry facilities, business services, meeting rooms* ▤ *AE, D, DC, MC, V.*

Nightlife & the Arts

★ The **Orange County Performing Arts Center** (⊠ 600 Town Center Dr., Costa Mesa ☎ 714/556–2787 ⊕ www.ocpac.org) consistently presents impressive internationally renowned arts performances. Companies such as the American Ballet Theater make annual appearances, as do the touring groups of major Broadway hits. Other highlights range from the Kirov Ballet to the Count Basie Orchestra to Tony Bennett. Free guided backstage tours are conducted Monday, Wednesday, and Saturday at 10:30 AM. The **South Coast Repertory Theater** (⊠ 655 Town Center Dr., Costa Mesa ☎ 714/708–5555 ⊕ www.scr.org) is a Tony award–winning theater presenting new and traditional works on three stages.

Santa Ana

6 mi north of Irvine, via I-405 to Hwy. 55; 12 mi south of Anaheim, via I-5 to Hwy. 55.

☾ ⑮ The main attraction in the county seat is the **Bowers Museum of Cultural Art.** Permanent exhibits include Pacific Northwest wood carvings; beadwork of the Plains cultures; California basketry; and still-life paintings. Special exhibits such as a show on Tibetan treasures rotate through on

☾ a regular basis. The **Bowers Kidseum** (⊠ 1802 N. Main St.) has interactive exhibits geared toward kids ages 6–12, in addition to classes, storytelling, and arts and crafts workshops. Admission is included in the general museum ticket. ⊠ *2002 N. Main St., off I–5, Santa Ana* ☎ *714/ 567–3600* ⊕ *www.bowers.org* ☒ *$14* ☉ *Tues.–Sun. 11–4.*

Where to Eat

$ ✕ **Tangata.** Inside the Bowers Museum, this eatery has a menu overseen by owner/executive chef Joachim Splichal. Choose among salads, pastas, soups, French-style roasted chicken, lamb shank over polenta, and tasty desserts. Dine on the patio or, in the main dining room, watch the "chef theater." ✉ *2002 N. Main St., Santa Ana* ☎ *714/550–0906* ▭ *AE, D, DC, MC, V* ☉ *Closed Mon. No dinner.*

★ **¢–$** ✕ **Zov's Bistro.** There's a well-worn path to both entrances of Zov's. The out-front restaurant prepares bistro favorites with a Middle Eastern spin, such as rack of lamb with pomegranate sauce, or chicken *geras* (stuffed with wild rice and almonds and accompanied by a sour-cherry sauce). Go around back and you'll find a separate café and bakery filled with locals picking up fresh-baked pastries or deciding between the sirloin burger or *mezes* (shared appetizers) for lunch. Both sides have patio tables. It's just on the other side of the Highway 55 freeway from Santa Ana; take the 17th Street exit. ✉ *Enderle Center, 17440 E. 17th St., Tustin* ☎ *714/838–8855* ▭ *AE, D, DC, MC, V.*

Toward Cleveland National Forest

East of Orange; 4 mi east of Santa Ana.

If you're craving a breath of nonurban air, the eastern part of Orange County is where sprawl gives way to beautiful open country, a mix of parkland and privately held areas. A few two-lane, gently winding roads reach into these toast-color hills, heading toward the Cleveland National Forest. The main roads are named for the canyons they follow: Santiago, Modjeska, and Silverado. It's chaparral country, with dry grasses, wheeling hawks overhead, and stands of live oaks. While development is creeping in, especially along Santiago Canyon Road, the canyons are known for their small, fiercely independent communities of longtime residents. Santiago is also a favorite for cyclists, so watch for them on the shoulder.

Driving along Santiago Canyon Road from the border of Orange, you'll pass Irvine Lake, a reservoir, on your left. The road dips and curves for a few miles before you'll reach an intersection with Silverado Canyon Road branching off to the left. Silverado Canyon Road is the usual entry point to **Cleveland National Forest** (☎ 858/673–6180 ⊕ www.fs.fed.us/ r5/cleveland). However, the road is sometimes closed due to fire risk or for environmental reasons; always call ahead.

The next offshoot, another few miles ahead, is Modjeska Canyon Road, to the left. The canyon is named for Helena Modjeska, a famed Polish actress who emigrated to what was an extremely remote area in the late 1800s. After a failed attempt at communal farm living with a group of fellow Polish emigrés—none of whom had any agricultural experience—she went back to the stage and became one of the most acclaimed actresses in America in the 1880s and '90s. **Arden** (☎ 949/855–2028), the Stanford White–designed home Helena Modjeska occupied at the end of her life, still stands; you can see it on tours given by the Heritage

Hill Historical Park with an advance reservation. Modjeska's exceptional life was fictionalized by Susan Sontag in her novel *In America* (2001).

Continue on Santiago and you may see a gleam of chrome where Live Oak Canyon Road forks off to the left—the shine from rows of motorcycles parked in front of **Cook's Corner** (✉ 19122 Live Oak Canyon Rd. ☎ 949/858–0266), a gritty, decades-old roadhouse. Kick back with a beer or a burger in the dark bar or out on the patio—it's a friendly, no-fuss place, a favorite with "weekend warrior" bikers. Soak it up while you can; encroaching development is threatening this classic canyon spot.

Garden Grove & Orange

South of Anaheim, via I–5 to Hwy. 22.

The city of Orange started as a legal fee; back in 1871, the parcel of land that became the town center was given to a pair of lawyers as payment for services. Orange Plaza (or Orange Circle, as locals call it), is

⑯ the heart of **Old Towne Orange,** around the intersection of Glassell Street and Chapman Avenue. The area is listed on the National Register of Historic Places and is a must-stop for antiques browsers and architecture aficionados. You can scout out everything here from antique armoires to flapper-era accessories to 1950s toys. Locals take great pride in their many California Craftsman–style cottages; Christmas is a particularly lovely time to visit, when many of the area's homes are festooned with tasteful yet elaborate decorations. If the town looks familiar to you, it may be because several films have been shot here in recent years, including Tom Hanks's *That Thing You Do!*

The Block at Orange (☎ 714/769–3800), a major mall complex near I–5 and Highway 22, is home to the popular **Vans skateboarding park,** where skaters swoop through specially designed bowls and courses. You can rent boards, pads, and helmets to hit the ramps—there's a special area for kids and beginners—or just watch.

⑰ In Garden Grove the main attraction is the **Crystal Cathedral,** the domain of television evangelist Robert "Hour of Power" Schuller. Designed by architect Philip Johnson, the sparkling glass structure resembles a four-pointed star, with more than 10,000 panes of glass covering a weblike steel truss to form transparent walls. Two annual pageants, "The Glory of Christmas" and "The Glory of Easter," feature live animals, flying angels, and other special effects. ✉ *12141 Lewis St., take I–5 to Chapman Ave. W, Garden Grove* ☎ *714/971–4000 or 714/971–4013* ⊕ *www.crystalcathedral.org* 🎟 *Tickets for the pageants $18–$48* ☉ *Guided tours Mon.–Sat. 9–3:30; call for schedule. Sun. services at 9:30, 11, and 6.*

> off the beaten path

LITTLE SAIGON – Little Saigon, the largest Vietnamese community outside of Vietnam, encompasses much of the city of Westminster. But the heart of the action is around Brookhurst and Bolsa streets, where colorful Little Saigon Plaza tempts shoppers with jewelry and gift shops, Asian herbalists, and informal family restaurants. ✉ *Bolsa St. between Bushard and Magnolia Sts., Westminster.*

Where to Stay & Eat

$$–$$$$
Fodor'sChoice
★
✕ **La Brasserie.** This restaurant is so traditionally French that you may feel transported back to Toulouse-Lautrec–era Paris. Dining among the chandeliers and oil paintings here is a formal affair; waiters wear white jackets, dishes are served on doilies, and the place settings each have a half-dozen pieces of cutlery. The cuisine is also quintessentially, deliciously French; the lobster Newburg, duck à l'orange, escargot, and veal cordon bleu are all sublime. While you wait for your order, you can sip a glass of wine and admire some of the wonderful oil paintings that cover the walls. ⊠ *202 S. Main St., Orange* 🕾 *714/978–6161* ⌔ *Reservations essential* ▤ *AE, D, DC, MC, V* ⊘ *Closed Sun.*

$–$$$
✕ **Citrus City Grill.** The surroundings may be Old Towne, but the menu certainly isn't. Choices range from vegetable spring rolls to pot roast, but the roast duck and Chilean sea bass are particular standouts. The inviting half-moon bar is a lively and popular gathering place. ⊠ *122 N. Glassell St., Orange* 🕾 *714/639–9600* ▤ *AE, DC, MC, V* ⊘ *Closed Sun.*

$$
✕ **P. J.'s Abbey.** Formerly an abbey of a Victorian Baptist Church, this restaurant serves American favorites like pork chops with garlic-mashed potatoes, rack of lamb, and fresh-baked desserts beneath original stained-glass windows. ⊠ *182 S. Orange St., Old Towne Orange* 🕾 *714/771–8556* ▤ *AE, D, DC, MC, V* ⊘ *No lunch Sat–Mon.*

¢–$
✕ **Felix Continental Cafe.** Facing Orange Circle's park, Felix draws crowds with its Cuban and Spanish dishes. You may have to wait for a table during the lunch and early dinner rushes, but try for an outdoor table, and order the chicken with garlicky *mojo* sauce. ⊠ *36 Plaza Sq., Orange* 🕾 *714/633–5842* ▤ *AE, DC, MC, V.*

¢–$$
🏨 **Doubletree Hotel Anaheim/Orange.** This contemporary 20-story hotel has a dramatic lobby of marble and granite, with waterfalls cascading down the walls. Rooms are comfortable, and have specious work areas. The hotel is near the Block, Anaheim Stadium, and the Anaheim Convention Center. ⊠ *100 The City Dr., Downtown Orange 92868* 🕾 *714/634–4500 or 800/528–0444* 🖷 *714/978–3839* ⊕ *www.doubletreehotels.com* ⇄ *454 rooms, 11 suites* ⚒ *Restaurant, in-room data ports, cable TV with movies, pool, health club, bar, concierge floor, Internet, meeting rooms, parking (fee), no-smoking rooms* ▤ *AE, D, DC, MC, V.*

Yorba Linda, La Habra & Brea

7–12 mi north of Anaheim, via Hwy. 57.

Clustered together just north of Anaheim, Yorba Linda, La Habra, and Brea are quiet suburban towns characterized by lush parks and family-oriented shopping centers complete with megacinemas. The redevelopment of downtown Brea has brought shopping, dining, and entertainment to the Birch Street Promenade.

⑱ Yorba Linda's main claim to fame is the **Richard Nixon Presidential Library and Birthplace,** final resting place of the 37th president and his wife, Pat. Exhibits illustrate the checkered career of Nixon, from heralded leader of the free world to beleaguered resigner. You can listen to the so-called smoking-gun tape from the Watergate days, among other recorded material. Life-size sculptures of foreign world leaders, gifts Nixon received from international heads of state, and a large graffiti-covered section of the Berlin Wall are on display. You can also visit Pat Nixon's tranquil rose garden and the small farmhouse where Richard Nixon was born in 1913. Don't miss the bookstore, selling everything from birdhouses to photos of Nixon with Elvis. ✉ *18001 Yorba Linda Blvd., at Imperial Hwy., Yorba Linda* ☎ *714/993–3393* ⊕ *www.nixonlibrary.org* 🎫 *$5.95* ⊙ *Mon.–Sat. 10–5, Sun. 11–5.*

ⓒ ❶❾ The **Children's Museum at La Habra** is in a 1923-vintage Union Pacific railroad depot, with old railroad cars resting nearby. Children can climb behind the wheel of Buster the Bus, a retired transit bus, or "dig up" bones in the huge Dinosaur Dig sandbox. There's also an informative railroad safety exhibit. ✉ *301 S. Euclid St., La Habra* ☎ *562/905–9793* ⊕ *www.lhcm.org* 🎫 *$5* ⊙ *Mon. 10–1, Tues.–Sat. 10–5, Sun. 1–5.*

Where to Eat

★ **$$$$** ✕ **La Vie en Rose.** It's worth the detour to Brea to sample the traditional French cuisine served in this faux Norman farmhouse. You can choose from several prix-fixe meals that include appetizers, entrées, and desserts such as silky crème brûlée or Grand Marnier soufflé. ✉ *240 S. State College Blvd., across from Brea mall, Brea* ☎ *714/529–8333* ▭ *AE, MC, V* ⊙ *Closed Sun.*

Anaheim

26 mi southeast of Los Angeles, via I–5.

Once upon a time, the snowcapped Matterhorn—then the centerpiece for Disney's Magic Kingdom—was the main landmark seen by motorists as they approached Anaheim on I–5. In recent years, however, the mountain has been joined by other recently built and equally towering Disney attractions, including Grizzly Peak, a large Ferris wheel, and the newly opened Tower of Terror.

Since Walt Disney chose this once-quiet farming community for the site of his first amusement park in 1955, Disneyland has attracted nearly 500 million visitors and thousands of workers, and Anaheim has been their host. To understand the symbiotic relationship between Disneyland and Anaheim, one need only look at the $4.2 billion spent in a combined effort by the Walt Disney Company and Anaheim, the latter to revitalize the city's tourist center and run-down areas, the former to expand and renovate the Disney properties into what is known now as the Disneyland Resort. The resort is a sprawling complex that includes Disney's two amusement parks, three hotels, and Downtown Disney, a shopping, dining, and entertainment promenade. Anaheim's tourist center also includes Edison International Field, home of the Anaheim Angels baseball team; Arrowhead Pond, where the Mighty Ducks hockey team plays; and the enormous Anaheim Convention Center.

★ ⓒ ⌐ ❷⓪ In the past, trips to **Disneyland** were often day trips—and ones that many families took "just for the kids." Things have changed since then. Today's Disneyland includes tons of attractions geared to adults as well as children, and it's so expansive that you may need two or three full days to see it all. (You may even want to stay for four or five days, to take advantage of the many amenities at Disneyland Resort.)

Disneyland is divided into eight themed areas that comprise more than 60 major attractions, 50 shops, and 30 restaurants. At the entrance, you walk through one of two tunnels, past a re-created 19th-century railroad station, and exit onto **Main Street, U.S.A.** Walt's hometown of Marceline, Missouri was the inspiration behind this romanticized image of small-town America, circa 1900. Trolleys, double-decker buses, and horse-drawn wagons travel up and down the scaled-down thoroughfare, and the sidewalks are lined with rows of shops selling everything from crystalware to sports memorabilia to photo supplies. At the railroad station, you can board a steam train for a ride around the park, making three other stops before returning to Main Street station.

As you walk to the end of Main Street, you will reach a central plaza, which serves as a hub for the rest of the park. Directly ahead is Sleeping Beauty's Castle, which marks the entrance to **Fantasyland.** Built with a medieval European village theme, this is where you'll find many of the kiddie rides (including such favorites as the spinning tea cups of the Mad Tea Party and the King Arthur Carrousel). You can ride on the Casey Jr. Circus Train, go soaring on Dumbo the Flying Elephant, or race down the Matterhorn in a bobsled. There are also attractions where you can ride in small cars through various scenes from several Disney animated movies, including *Peter Pan, Alice in Wonderland,* and *Snow White.* Finally, "It's a Small World" takes you for a boat ride through many different countries as the cloying tune plays in the background. Be sure to see "Snow White: An Enchanting New Musical," a live action show retelling the classic fairy tale.

As you walk through Fantasyland, you will come to a tunnel leading under the railroad tracks and find yourself in **Mickey's Toontown.** This entire area makes you feel as if you are in a cartoon. The homes of Mickey, Donald, Goofy, and many other Disney characters can be explored here. After a tour of Mickey's House, you have a chance to meet Mickey and have your photo taken with him. At Goofy's Bounce House, children can jump on the furniture and everything else inside. Gadget's Go Coaster is a small roller coaster designed to give children their first taste of this kind of ride.

Tomorrowland is located in the eastern part of the park. Here you can ride on the Astro Orbitor and pilot small rockets around in a circle, or drive miniature cars at the Tomorrowland Autopia. No driver's license is required. If you're a *Star Wars* fan, you can try Star Tours, a flight simulator that allows you to experience space travel and even re-enact one of the battle scenes. Space Mountain (reopening in 2005) lets you take a thrilling roller-coaster ride in complete darkness. There are also shows at Tomorrowland, which include the 3-D *Honey, I Shrunk the Audience,* and a Buzz Lightyear stage show for fans of the *Toy Story* space ranger.

Moving to the western side of the park, you come to **Frontierland.** The Big Thunder Mountain Railroad roller coaster, themed after a runaway mine train, is popular here; so are cruises around the Rivers of America on the *Mark Twain* riverboat or the sailing ship *Columbia.* If you want to explore Tom Sawyer's island, you can hop aboard a raft and sail over to kids area, complete with places to explore (such as Injun Joe's cave), treehouses to climb, and jungle gyms to play on. The Golden Horseshoe Stage runs two different Western-themed shows on different days.

Next to Frontierland is the jungle-themed **Adventureland.** Here, the Indiana Jones Adventure lets you take a hair-raising jeep ride through the Temple of the Forbidden Eye, and the Jungle Cruise takes you down a tropical river where lions, tigers, elephants, and even headhunters can be seen on shore. If you don't mind lots of stairs, you can climb up into Tarzan's treehouse for a bit of relaxation; you can also stop and watch birds and flowers sing in the Enchanted Tiki Room.

Just up the river and outside the jungle is **New Orleans Square.** In addition to quaint shops, restaurants, and live Dixieland music, two of Disneyland's most popular attractions are here. Pirates of the Caribbean lets you take a cruise past cursed treasure and participate in a pirate raid on a coastal town. For a spookier thrill, you can pay your respects at the Haunted Mansion. Though few adults find this attraction scary, some small children may be frightened by the dark areas in the ride. In November and December, the Haunted Mansion has special holiday decorations based on the movie *The Nightmare Before Christmas.*

Critter Country is past New Orleans Square. This rather small area has just two attractions. Splash Mountain is a flume where you ride in logs through scenes from Disney's *Song of the South,* before racing down a five-story drop into the briar patch below. (Plan on getting a little wet if you take this ride.) The Many Adventures of Winnie the Pooh is a movie-themed ride similar to those in Fantasyland. This time you ride in "hunny" pots through the story of Pooh Bear and his friends.

Disneyland puts on some excellent shows. In addition to the daily parade, be sure to check out the fireworks show that runs nightly during the summer, weekends, and holidays. In summer be sure to see **Fantasmic.** This musical, fireworks, and laser show features Mickey and friends waging a spellbinding battle against Disney's villains. The battle takes place on the Rivers of America, so be sure to pick out a good spot along the river in Frontierland or New Orleans Square early.

In May of 2005, Disneyland plans to begin its 18-month celebration of its 50th anniversary. As a part of the festivities, Disneyland will feature a new parade and fireworks show. Space Mountain is slated to reopen with even more thrills than before, and a new attraction, Buzz Lightyear's Astro Blaster, is expected to open, allowing you to board a space cruiser and fire personal laser cannons to hit targets and earn points.

In summer Disneyland usually fills with visitors. If possible, visit on a midweek day, and buy your tickets in advance either online or from one of the area hotels. If you're planning on purchasing tickets at the park, arrive early; the box office opens a half hour before the park does. It's a good idea to hit the most popular rides either just after the park opens or in the evening, when crowds are thinner. You can best avoid long lines by using a FASTPASS, which allows you to schedule times when you want to go on rides, and wait in shorter lines—usually only 10 to 15 minutes. FASTPASS machines are located near the entrances of the top attractions. Simply feed in your park admission ticket, and you receive a pass with a printed one-hour time frame (generally 1–2 hours later) during which you can return.

Disney characters appear for autographs and photos throughout the day; check the printed program, which you can pick up at the entrance for information about designated character greetings as well as showtimes.

Plan meals to avoid peak mealtime crowds and more long lines. If you want to eat at the **Blue Bayou** in New Orleans Square, make reservations in person as soon as you get to the park—or better yet phone ahead (reservations are taken up to a month in advance).

You can store belongings in lockers just off Main Street; purchases can also be sent to the Package Pickup desk at the front of the park. Main Street stays open an hour after the attractions close, so you may want to save your shopping for the end of your visit. If you plan to visit for more than a day, you can save money by buying two-, three- and five-day Park Hopper tickets, which grant same-day "hopping" privileges between Disneyland and Disney's California Adventure. ⊠ *1313 Harbor Blvd., Anaheim* ☎ *714/781–4565, 714/781–3463 for dinner reservations at all resort restaurants* ⊕ *www.disneyland.com* ✉ *$50 (1-day pass), $98 (2-day), $124 (3-day), $184 (5-day)* ☉ *Daily, year-round, with longer hrs on weekends, holidays, and in summer. Call for hrs.*

★ ☾ ⑳ The 55-acre **Disney's California Adventure,** which sprawls out right next to Disneyland (their entrances face each other) pays tribute to the Golden State with four theme areas. **Paradise Pier** re-creates the glory days of California's seaside piers. If you're looking for thrills, the California Screamin' roller coaster takes its riders from 0 to 55 mph in about four seconds and proceeds through scream tunnels, steeply angled drops, and a 360-degree loop. The Sun Wheel, a giant Ferris wheel, provides a good view of the grounds at a more leisurely pace.

At the **Hollywood Pictures Backlot** you can indulge in an "I want to be in pictures" moment. *Who Wants to Be a Millionaire—Play It!* is a replica of the set where the popular game show is filmed, and where you can play for prizes. The Disney Animation attraction gives an insider's look demonstrating how many of Disney's animated movies and characters were created. The Hyperion theater hosts *Aladdin—A Musical Spectacular,* a 45-minute live performance with terrific visual effects, which is well worth the usual hour-long wait. The park's newest attraction, the Tower of Terror, is themed after a 1930s hotel that appeared in *The Twilight Zone.* The scariest part of this attraction is the service elevator ride, which carries you from the basement of the Hollywood Tower Hotel to the 13th floor—and then back down again at scream-inducing speed.

A bug's land, inspired by the film *A Bug's Life,* has attractions that give you an insect's point of view. At Princess Dot Puddle Park, you can cool off—or get soaked—by a giant-size garden hose; you can also ride in pill bug–shaped bumper cars. The short show *It's Tough to be a Bug!* gives you a 3-D look at insect life.

Golden State celebrates California's history and natural beauty with several regions, including the Bay Area, Pacific Wharf, and Condor Flats, where you can enjoy Soarin' Over California, a spectacular simulated hang-glider ride over California terrain. Grizzly River Run is a white-water raft ride, which culminates in a drop down a 22-foot waterfall. (Plan on getting wet or purchasing a poncho from the nearby kiosk.) The film *Golden Dreams* is a sentimental dash through California history, hosted by Whoopi Goldberg. There's also a working 1-acre farm and winery, a nature trail, and a tortilla factory. At night, be sure to catch Disney's Electrical Parade—a procession where all the floats and characters are festooned with thousands of little lights. ⊠ *1313 Harbor Blvd., Anaheim* ☎ *714/781–4565* ⊕ *www.disneyland.com* ⊠ *$50 (1-day pass), $98 (2-day), $124 (3-day), $184 (5-day)* ⊘ *Daily, year-round, with longer hrs on weekends, holidays, and in summer. Call for hrs.*

Downtown Disney is a 20-acre, nongated promenade of dining, shopping, and entertainment that connects the Disneyland Resort hotels and theme parks. Restaurant-nightclubs here include the **House of Blues,** which spices up its Delta-inspired ribs and seafood with various live music acts on an intimate two-story stage. At **Ralph Brennan's Jazz Kitchen** you can dig into New Orleans–style food and music. Sports fans can gravitate to **ESPN Zone,** a sports bar–restaurant–entertainment center with American grill food, interactive video games, and 175 video screens telecasting worldwide sports events. There's also an **AMC** megaplex movie theater with stadium-style seating, which plays the latest blockbusters and, naturally, kids' flicks. Promenade shops sell everything from Disney goods to fine art. ⊠ *Disneyland Dr. between Ball Rd. and Katella Ave., Anaheim* ☎ *714/300–7800, 714/781–3463 for dinner reservations at all resort restaurants* ⊕ *www.disneyland.com* ⊠ *Free* ⊘ *Daily 7 AM–2 AM; hrs at shops and restaurants vary.*

Where to Stay & Eat

Most Anaheim hotels have complimentary shuttle service to a designated drop-off/pick-up area within the Disneyland Resort, though many hotels are within walking distance.

$$$–$$$$ ✕ **Anaheim White House.** Several small dining rooms are set with crisp linens and candles in this flower-filled 1909 mansion. The northern Italian menu includes pasta, rack of lamb, and a large selection of fresh seafood. A three-course fixed-price express lunch, served weekdays only, costs $19. ⊠ *887 S. Anaheim Blvd., Anaheim* ☎ *714/772–1381* ⊕ *www.anaheimwhitehouse.com* ⊟ *AE, MC, V* ⊘ *No lunch weekends.*

★ **$$–$$$$**   ✕ **Napa Rose.** One of the best new restaurants in the area, the Napa Rose offers a changing menu that highlights California cuisine. If you're lucky, the menu might include oysters "Napa Rose-a-Feller," grilled sturgeon, pheasant, and even venison. There is also a children's menu. The focus is on Napa Valley Wine Country, so there's an extensive list of California wines that you can enjoy with dinner or take home with you. ⊠ *1600 S. Disneyland Dr., Disney's Grand Californian Hotel* ☎ *714/781–3463* ⊟ *AE, D, DC, MC, V.*

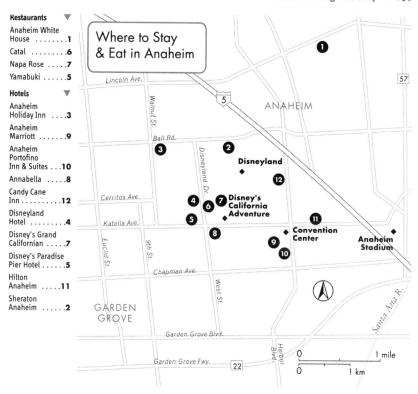

Where to Stay & Eat in Anaheim

$–$$$$ ✕ **Catal Restaurant & Uva Bar.** Famed chef Joachim Splichal takes a casual approach at this bi-level Mediterranean spot. At the ground-level Uva bar (the name is Spanish for "grape"), you can peruse a menu of tapas that borders on finger food—including olives and Spanish ham—and choose from 40 wines by the glass. Upstairs, Catal serves wonderful paella, rotisserie chicken, and salads. ☒ *1580 Disneyland Dr., Suite 103, Downtown Disney* ☎ *714/774–4442* ▤ *AE, D, DC, MC, V.*

$–$$$ ✕ **Yamabuki.** Part of Disney's Paradise Pier Hotel complex, this stylish Japanese restaurant serves traditional dishes and has a full sushi bar. The plum-wine ice cream is a treat. ☒ *1717 S. Disneyland Dr., Disneyland Resort* ☎ *714/956–6755* ▤ *AE, D, DC, MC, V* ⊙ *No lunch weekends.*

$$$$ ▦ **Disney's Grand Californian.** The newest of Disney's Anaheim hotels,
Fodor's Choice this Craftsman–style luxury property has guest rooms with views of the
★ California Adventure park and Downtown Disney. Restaurants include the Napa Rose dining room, Hearthstone Lounge, and Storytellers Cafe, where Disney characters entertain children at breakfast. Of the three pools, one just for kids is in the shape of Mickey Mouse, and there's an evening child-activity center. Room-and-ticket packages are available, and the hotel has its own entry gate to California Adventure. ☒ *1600 S. Disneyland Dr., Disneyland Resort 92803* ☎ *714/635–2300* ▤ *714/300–7701* ⊕ *www.disneyland.com* ▧ *713 rooms, 38 suites* ⚭ *2 restaurants, room*

service, in-room data ports, in-room safes, minibars, cable TV, pool, health club, hot tub, 2 lounges, video game room, shop, children's programs (ages 5–12), dry cleaning, laundry service, concierge, Internet, business services, parking (fee); no smoking ⊟ *AE, D, DC, MC, V.*

★ **$$$–$$$$** 🏨 **Disneyland Hotel.** Not surprisingly, Disney's first hotel is the most Disney-themed of the resort's three properties. It's filled with Disney memorabilia and attractions, including a Peter Pan–themed pool with a wooden bridge, 110-foot water slide, and relaxing whirlpool. South-facing rooms in the Sierra Tower have the best views of Downtown Disney, while north-facing rooms in the Bonita Tower overlook the koi ponds and waterfalls. At Goofy's Kitchen, kids can dine with Disney characters. Room-and-ticket packages are available. ⊠ *1150 Magic Way, Disneyland Resort 92802* ☎ *714/778–6600* 🖷 *714/956–6582* ⊕ *www. disneyland.com* 🛏 *990 rooms, 62 suites* ♨ *5 restaurants, café, room service, in-room data ports, in-room safes, minibars, cable TV, 3 pools, health club, hot tub, massage, sauna, spa, beach, 2 bars, video game room, laundry service, concierge, business services, airport shuttle, car rental, parking (fee)* ⊟ *AE, D, DC, MC, V.*

★ **$$$–$$$$** 🏨 **Disney's Paradise Pier Hotel.** The Paradise Pier has many of the same Disney touches as the Disneyland Hotel, but it's a bit quieter and tamer. You can walk to Disneyland from here, or take the monorail from the Downtown Disney station. The hotel has its own entrance into Disney's California Adventure. Kids can start the day with a Minnie and Friends character breakfast. Room-and-ticket packages are available. ⊠ *1717 S. Disneyland Dr., Disneyland Resort 92802* ☎ *714/999–0990* 🖷 *714/776–5763* ⊕ *www.disneyland.com* 🛏 *502 rooms, 38 suites* ♨ *2 restaurants, room service, in-room data ports, in-room safes, minibars, cable TV, pool, health club, 2 lounges, video game room, dry cleaning, laundry service, concierge, business services, parking (fee)* ⊟ *AE, D, DC, MC, V.*

★ **$$–$$$$** 🏨 **Sheraton Anaheim Hotel.** In this sprawling replica of a Tudor castle, you can escape the commercial atmosphere of many of the hotels near Disneyland. The flower-and-plant-filled lobby is serene, and has a grand fireplace where you can sit and relax. "Smart Rooms" come equipped for business with copier-printer-fax machines, and include a daily continental breakfast and evening hors d'oeuvres. Rooms are sizable; some first-floor rooms open onto interior gardens and a pool area. A shuttle to Disneyland is available. ⊠ *1015 W. Ball Rd., Downtown Anaheim 92802* ☎ *714/778–1700 or 800/325–3535* 🖷 *714/535–3889* ⊕ *www. sheraton.com/anaheim* 🛏 *447 rooms, 42 suites* ♨ *Restaurant, café, room service, in-room data ports, in-room safes, cable TV with movies and video games, pool, health club, outdoor hot tub, bar, video game room, laundry facilities, laundry service, concierge, meeting rooms, parking (fee), no-smoking rooms* ⊟ *AE, D, DC, MC, V.*

$$–$$$ 🏨 **Anaheim Marriott.** Rooms at this convention hotel are well equipped for business travelers, with desks, two phones, and data ports. Some rooms have balconies, and accommodations on the north side have good views of Disneyland's summer fireworks shows. Discounted weekend and Disneyland packages are available. ⊠ *700 W. Convention Way, Downtown Anaheim 92802* ☎ *714/750–8000 or 800/228–9290* 🖷 *714/750–9100* ⊕ *www.marriott.com* 🛏 *1,031 rooms, 52 suites* ♨ *2 restau-*

rants, room service, in-room data ports, in-room safes, cable TV with movies, 2 pools, health club, 2 hot tubs, lounge, piano, video game room, laundry facilities, laundry service, concierge, Internet, meeting rooms, car rental, parking (fee), some pets allowed (fee), no-smoking floors ⊟AE, D, DC, MC, V.

★ ¢–$$$ 🏨 **Anaheim Portofino Inn and Suites.** What really makes this hotel stand out are the family-friendly Kids' Suites. Each of these two-room suites has a parents' room and a kids' room complete with bunk beds, a sofa sleeper, and an activity table. Each room has its own TV, and the two are divided by French doors. This arrangement allows both parents and children to relax in their own way. A shuttle to Disneyland stops nearby at regular intervals or you can walk the 1½ blocks to the park. ✉ *1831 S. Harbor Blvd., 92802* ☎ *714/782–7600 or 800/511–6907* 🖷 *714/635–2262* ⊕ *www.portofinoinnanaheim.com* ⇗ *144 rooms, 46 suites* ⌂ *In-room data ports, cable TV with movies, pool, hot tub, health club, laundry services, laundry facilities, video game room, no smoking rooms* ⊟ *AE, D, DC, MC, V.*

¢–$$$ 🏨 **Hilton Anaheim.** Next to the Anaheim Convention Center, this busy Hilton is the largest hotel in Southern California: it even has its own post office, as well as shops, restaurants, and cocktail lounges. Rooms are pleasingly bright, and there's a shuttle that runs to Disneyland (if you'd rather not walk the few blocks). Special summer children's programs include a "Vacation Station Lending Desk" with games, toys, and books, as well as children's menus. There's a $12 fee to use the health club. ✉ *777 Convention Way, Downtown Anaheim 92802* ☎ *714/750–4321 or 800/445–8667* 🖷 *714/740–4460* ⊕ *www.hilton.com* ⇗ *1,576 rooms, 95 suites* ⌂ *4 restaurants, room service, cable TV with movies, pool, health club, hair salon, hot tub, massage, sauna, 2 lounges, piano, laundry service, concierge, Internet, business services, meeting rooms, airport shuttle, car rental, travel services, parking (fee), no-smoking floor* ⊟ *AE, D, DC, MC, V.*

$–$$ 🏨 **The Annabella.** This mission-style hotel is across from Disneyland Resort on the convention center campus. The hotel's "Oasis," with its hot tub and two pools (one for adults only), is perfect for soaking and sunning. The Tangerine Grill and Patio serves a fantastic tangerine cheesecake. ✉ *1030 W. Katella Ave., Downtown Anaheim 92802* ☎ *714/905–1050 or 800/863–4888* 🖷 *714/905–1054* ⊕ *www.anabellahotel.com* ⇗ *359 rooms, 12 suites* ⌂ *Restaurant, room service, in-room data ports, in-room safes, microwaves, refrigerators, cable TV with movies, 2 pools, health club, outdoor hot tub, lounge, laundry facilities, laundry service, business services, free parking* ⊟ *AE, D, DC, MC, V.*

★ $–$$ 🏨 **Candy Cane Inn.** One of Anaheim's most beautiful boutique hotels, the Candy Cane has gorgeously landscaped gardens with cascading fountains (be sure to ask for a room with a garden view). Rooms here are spacious but simple, with tiled floors and plantation shutters; the heated pool is a great place to relax. The hotel is just steps from the Disneyland parking lot, and a free Disneyland shuttle runs every half hour. ✉ *1747 S. Harbor Blvd., Downtown Anaheim 92802* ☎ *714/774–5284 or 800/345–7057* 🖷 *714/772–5462* ⊕ *www.candycaneinn.net* ⇗ *172 rooms* ⌂ *Refrigerators, cable TV, pool, wading pool, outdoor* *hot tub, laundry facilities, laundry service, free parking, no-smoking rooms* ⊟ *AE, D, DC, MC, V* ⦿ *CP.*

¢–$ 🏨 **Anaheim Holiday Inn.** This hotel's Old West theme includes swinging saloon doors and a *Bonanza*-style lobby. A shuttle heads to Disneyland, one long block away, every 15 minutes. Kids 12 and under eat free at the hotel restaurant. ⊠ *1240 S. Walnut Ave., Downtown Anaheim 92802* ☎ *714/535–0300 or 800/824–5459* 🖷 *714/491–8953* ⊕ *www. holidayinn-anaheim.com* ⇥ *229 rooms, 26 suites* ⚭ *Restaurant, room service, some microwaves, cable TV, pool, exercise equipment, outdoor hot tub, bar, video game room, laundry service, business services, meeting rooms, free parking, no-smoking rooms* ⊟ *AE, D, DC, MC, V.*

Nightlife

★ The little red roadhouse known as **The Doll Hut** (⊠ 107 S. Adams St., Anaheim ☎ 714/533–1286) was once a truck stop between L.A. and San Diego. Famed Southern California music booster Linda Jemison then turned it into a great place to hear about-to-break bands. In 2001 she turned it over to new owners, who are maintaining its rep for supporting up-and-comers and those below the music-industry radar. Rockabilly, big-band, punk—whatever your pleasure, there will be a low cover.

The Grove of Anaheim (⊠ 2200 E. Katella Ave. ☎ 714/712–2700 ⊕ www. thegroveofanaheim.com) is a mid-size concert venue, which means nearly every seat is a good one. It books all kinds of bands and the occasional comedy act; the Gipsy Kings, India.Irie, Willie Nelson, and Blondie have all hit the stage here.

At the **House of Blues** (☎ 714/778–2583 ⊕ www.hob.com), in the Downtown Disney promenade, you can catch some of the best bands from the 1980s and '90s for a relatively low cover. Shows often sell out, so call ahead.

Sports

Pro baseball's **Anaheim Angels** play at **Edison International Field** (⊠ 2000 Gene Autry Way, East Anaheim ☎ 714/634–2000 ⊕ www.angelsbaseball. com). The National Hockey League's **Mighty Ducks of Anaheim** play at **Arrowhead Pond** (⊠ 2695 E. Katella Ave., East Anaheim ☎ 714/704–2700 ⊕ www.mightyducks.com).

Buena Park

25 mi south of Los Angeles, via I–5.

The land where the boysenberry was invented (by crossing red raspberry, blackberry, and loganberry bushes) is now occupied by Knott's Berry Farm. You can see Buena Park in a day, but plan to start early and finish fairly late; heavy traffic can sometimes cause delays.

★ ☻ ㉑ **Knott's Berry Farm** got its start in 1934, when Cordelia Knott began serving chicken dinners on her wedding china to supplement her family's income. The dinners and her boysenberry pies proved more profitable than husband Walter's berry farm, so the two moved first into the restaurant business and then into the entertainment business. The park is now a 150-acre complex with 100-plus rides and dozens of restaurants and shops. While it's got some good attractions for small children, the park is also known for its roster of awesome thrill rides.

Ghost Town is made up of authentic old buildings relocated from their original mining-town sites. You can stroll down the street, stop and chat with the blacksmith, pan for gold, crack open a geode, ride in an authentic 1880s passenger train, or take the Gold Mine ride and descend into a replica of a working gold mine. A real treasure here is the antique Dentzel carousel. **GhostRider** towers over it all; it's Orange County's first wooden roller coaster. Traveling 56 mph at its fastest and reaching 118 foot at its highest, the coaster is riddled with sudden dips and curves, subjecting riders to G-forces comparable to three times the force of the Earth's gravitational pull.

Smaller fry may want to head straight for **Camp Snoopy,** a miniature High Sierra wonderland where the *Peanuts* gang hangs out. At nearby **Big Foot Rapids** you can ride white-swater in rafts. At **The Boardwalk,** you'll find the Boomerang roller coaster and the **Perilous Plunge,** billed as the world's tallest, steepest and—thanks to its big splash—wettest thrill ride. The 1950s hot rod–themed **Xcelerator** opened in 2002; it launches you hydraulically into a super-steep U-turn, topping out at 205 feet. Over in **Fiesta Village** are two more musts for adrenaline junkies: **Montezooma's Revenge,** a roller coaster that goes from 0 to 55 mph in less than five seconds, and **Jaguar!,** which simulates the motions of a cat stalking its prey, twisting, spiraling, and speeding up and slowing down as it takes you on its stomach-dropping course. It's a good idea to confirm the park's opening hours, which are subject to change. Each October, the park celebrates Halloween by shifting into Knott's Scary Farm mode at night. The attractions take on scary new guises, and costumed cast members prowl around to spook you. The Scary Farm is not open for kids under 13. ⊠ *8039 Beach Blvd., between La Palma Ave. and Crescent St., 2 blocks south of Hwy. 91, Buena Park* ☎ *714/220–5200* ⊕ *www.knotts. com* ☞ *$40* ⊘ *June–mid-Sept., daily 9 AM–midnight; mid-Sept.–May, weekdays 10–6, Sat. 10–10, Sun. 10–7. Closed during inclement weather.*

㉒ More than 75 years of movie magic are immortalized at the **Movieland Wax Museum.** The hundreds of wax-sculpted Hollywood stars and American political figures include Julia Roberts, John Wayne, Marilyn Monroe, a *Matrix*-era Keanu Reeves, and George W. Bush. Likenesses ranging from the haunting to the comical are displayed in a maze of realistic sets from movies such as *Gone With the Wind, Star Trek, The Wizard of Oz,* and *Titanic.* A combination ticket for $16.90 includes admission to the so-so **Ripley's Believe It or Not!,** across the street. ⊠ *7711 Beach Blvd., between La Palma and Orangethorpe Aves., Buena Park* ☎ *714/522–1155* ⊕ *www.movielandwaxmuseum.com* ☞ *$12.95* ⊘ *Weekdays 10–7:30, weekends 9–8:30.*

Where to Stay & Eat

★ ¢–$ ✕**Mrs. Knott's Chicken Dinner Restaurant.** Cornelia Knott's fried chicken and boysenberry pies drew crowds so big that Knott's Berry Farm was built to keep the hungry customers occupied while they waited. The restaurant's current incarnation at the park's entrance still serves crispy fried chicken, along with tangy coleslaw and Mrs. Knott's signature chilled cherry-rhubarb compote. You can get breakfast here, too. There can be long lines on weekends, so get there early. Park admission is not necessary and there is a store nearby where you can purchase Knott's Berry Farm jam and other products. ⊠ *Knott's Berry Farm, 8039 Beach Blvd., Buena Park* ☎ *714/220–5080* ▤ *AE, D, DC, MC, V.*

$ 🏨 **The Radisson Resort Knott's Berry Farm.** The only hotel on Knott's Berry Farm grounds has family-oriented "camp rooms" that are decorated in a Camp Snoopy motif. Shuttle service to Disneyland and nearby golf courses is available. Ask about packages that include entry to Knott's Berry Farm. ⊠ *7675 Crescent Ave., Buena Park 90620* ☎ *714/995–1111 or 800/333–3333* 🖷 *714/828–8590* ⊕ *www.radisson.com/buenapark* ➾*304 rooms, 16 suites* ◌ *Restaurant, room service, cable TV with movies and video games, tennis court, pool, health club, hot tub, bar, video game room, laundry facilities, concierge, Internet* ▤ *AE, D, DC, MC, V.*

Nightlife

For $46 a person ($32 for children under 12), the **Medieval Times Dinner and Tournament** (⊠ 7662 Beach Blvd., Buena Park ☎ 714/521–4740 or 800/899–6600 ⊕ www.medievaltimes.com) brings back the days of yore, with medieval games, fighting, and jousting. Standard chicken-and-ribs dinners with plenty of sides are served as if you were in the Middle Ages: no utensils.

ORANGE COUNTY A TO Z

To research prices, get advice from other travelers, and book travel arrangements, visit www.fodors.com.

AIRPORTS

The county's main facility is John Wayne Airport (SNA), conveniently near the intersection of the I–405 and Highway 55 freeways. It is served by 10 major domestic airlines and 4 commuter lines. It's a glossy facility and its relatively small size makes it easy to negotiate. Still, you should leave plenty of time for security checks and parking. Long Beach Airport (LGB), near the south end of Los Angeles County by I–405, serves four airlines, including its major player, JetBlue. It's smaller and more low-key than John Wayne; it may not have many airport amenities, but parking is generally a snap. It's roughly 20–30 minutes by car from Anaheim. Los Angeles International Airport (LAX) is only 35 mi west of Anaheim. Ontario International Airport (ONT) is just northwest of Riverside, 30 mi north of Anaheim. *See* Air Travel *in* Smart Travel Tips A to Z for airline phone numbers.

🛈 John Wayne Airport ⊠ MacArthur Blvd. at I–405, Santa Ana ☎ 949/252-5252 ⊕ www. ocair.com. **Long Beach Airport** ⊠ 4100 Donald Douglas Dr., Long Beach ☎ 562/570- 2600 ⊕ www.lgb.org. **Los Angeles International Airport (LAX)** ☎ 310/646-5252 ⊕ www.lawa.org. **Ontario International Airport** ⊠ Airport Dr. and Vineyard Ave. ☎ 909/937-2700 ⊕ www.lawa.org.

AIRPORT 🛈 **Airport Bus** ☎ 800/772-5299 ⊕ www.airportbus.com. **Prime Time Airport Shut-**
TRANSFERS **tle** ☎ 800/262-7433 ⊕ www.primetimeshuttle.com. **SuperShuttle** ☎ 714/517-6600 ⊕ www.supershuttle.com.

BUS TRAVEL

The Los Angeles MTA has limited service to Orange County. From downtown L.A., Bus 460 goes to Knott's Berry Farm and Disneyland Resort. Greyhound serves Anaheim and Santa Ana. The Orange County Transportation Authority will take you virtually anywhere in the county, but it will take time; OCTA buses go from Knott's Berry Farm and Disneyland to Huntington Beach and Newport Beach. Bus 1 travels along the coast; the 701 and 721 buses go express to Los Angeles.

🖪 **Greyhound** ☎ 714/999-1256 or 800/231-2222 ⊕ www.greyhound.com. **Los Angeles MTA** ☎ 213/626-4455 ⊕ www.mta.net. **The Orange County Transportation Authority (OCTA)** ☎ 714/636-7433 ⊕ www.octa.net.

CAR RENTAL

All of the national car-rental agencies are represented at Los Angeles International Airport, and many have bureaus at John Wayne Airport. The Ontario and Long Beach airports each have a limited number of car-rental agencies. *See* Car Rental *in* Smart Travel Tips for national rental agency phone numbers.

CAR TRAVEL

The San Diego Freeway (I–405) and the Santa Ana Freeway (I–5) run north–south through Orange County. South of Laguna I–405 merges into I–5 (called the San Diego Freeway south from this point). Do your best to avoid freeways during rush hours (6–9 AM and 3:30–6:30 PM).

Highways 55 and 91 head west to the ocean and east into the mountains. Highway 91, which goes to Garden Grove and inland points (Buena Park, Anaheim), has some Express lanes for which drivers pay a toll to ostensibly avoid the worst of rush-hour traffic. If you have three or more people in your car, though, you can use the Highway 91 Express lanes during most of the day for free (the exception being 4–6 PM on weekdays, when you pay half-fare). Highway 55 leads to Newport Beach. PCH (Highway 1) allows easy access to beach communities and is the most scenic route.

Laguna Canyon Road, the beautiful route that winds through a coastal canyon, is undergoing a widening project. The work is expected to be completed by the winter of 2006–2007, but the road will remain open throughout. The old road is quite narrow and used by cyclists as well as drivers, so be especially cautious and turn on your headlights even in daytime.

TRAIN TRAVEL

When planning train travel, consider where the train stations are in relation to your ultimate destination. You may need to make extra transportation arrangements once you've arrived in town. From the station in San Juan Capistrano, for instance, you can walk through the historic part of town; the station in Anaheim, on the other hand, is not within walking distance of Disneyland. Amtrak makes daily stops in Orange County at Anaheim, Santa Ana, Irvine, San Juan Capistrano, and San Clemente.

🖪 **Amtrak** ☎ 800/872-7245 ⊕ www.amtrakcalifornia.com.

VISITOR INFORMATION
🔢 **Anaheim-Orange County Visitor and Convention Bureau** ⊠ Anaheim Convention Center, 800 W. Katella Ave., Anaheim 92802 ☎ 714/765-8888 ⊕ www.anaheimoc. org. **Buena Park Convention and Visitors Office** ⊠ 6601 Beach Blvd., Buena Park 90621 ☎ 800/541-3953 ⊕ www.buenapark.com. **Costa Mesa Conference and Visitors Bureau** 🔳 Box 5071, Costa Mesa 92628 ☎ 714/384-0493 or 800/399-5499 ⊕ www. costamesa-ca.com. **Huntington Beach Conference and Visitors Bureau** ⊠ 310 Main St., Huntington Beach 92648 ☎ 714/969-3492 ⊕ www.hbvisit.com. **Laguna Beach Visitors Bureau** ⊠ 252 Broadway, Laguna Beach 92651 ☎ 949/376-0511 or 800/877-1115 ⊕ www.lagunabeachinfo.org. **Newport Beach Conference and Visitors Bureau** ⊠ 3300 W. Coast Hwy., Newport Beach 92663 ☎ 800/942-6278 ⊕ www.newportbeach-cvb.com. **San Juan Capistrano Chamber of Commerce and Visitors Center** ⊠ 31781 Camino Capistrano, Suite 306, San Juan Capistrano 92693 ☎ 949/493-4700 ⊕ www. sanjuanchamber.com.

CATALINA ISLAND

Just 22 mi out from the L.A. coastline, across from Newport Beach and Long Beach, Catalina has virtually unspoiled mountains, canyons, coves, and beaches; best of all, it gives you a glimpse of what undeveloped Southern California once looked like.

In summer, and on weekends and holidays, Catalina crawls with thousands of L.A.-area boaters, who moor their vessels in protected Avalon Bay and other coves. Although Catalina is not known for wide, sandy beaches, sunbathing and water sports are big draws; divers and snorkelers come for the exceptionally clear water surrounding the island. The main town of Avalon is a charming, old-fashioned beach community that looks over the crescent-shape bay. Wander beyond the main drag and you'll find brightly painted little bungalows fronting the sidewalks, with the occasional golf cart purring down the street.

Cruise ships sail into Avalon twice a week and smaller boats shuttle between Avalon and Two Harbors, a small isthmus cove on the island's western end. You can also take bus excursions beyond Avalon. Roads are limited and nonresident vehicles prohibited, so hiking (by permit only) and cycling are the only other means of exploring.

Perhaps it's no surprise that Catalina's rugged beauty has long attracted filmmakers and movie stars. In the more distant past, however, the island also sheltered Russian fur trappers seeking sea-otter skins, pirates, gold miners, and bootleggers (who communicated with the mainland via carrier pigeons). In 1919 William Wrigley Jr., the chewing-gum magnate, purchased a controlling interest in the company developing Catalina Island; its most famous landmark, the Casino, was subsequently built in 1929 under his orders. Wrigley was also responsible for making Catalina the site of spring training for the Chicago Cubs baseball team (until 1951).

Zane Grey—the writer who put the Western novel on the map—spent a lot of time on Catalina, and his influence is still evident in a peculiar way. When the movie version of Grey's book *The Vanishing American* was filmed here in 1924, American bison were ferried across from the mainland to simulate the look of the Western plains. When the moviemakers packed up and left, the buffalo stayed, and a small herd still remains and grazes the interior.

In 1975 the Santa Catalina Island Conservancy, a nonprofit foundation, acquired about 86% of the island to help preserve the area's natural resources. These days the conservancy is restoring the land with plantings of native grasses and trees. Along the coast you might spot protected marine creatures like electric perch, saltwater goldfish, and flying fish.

Although Catalina can be seen in a day, several inviting hotels make it worth extending your stay for one or more nights. A short itinerary might include breakfast along the boardwalk, a tour of the interior, a snorkeling excursion at Casino Point, and dinner in Avalon.

Avalon

1- to 2-hr ferry ride from Long Beach, Newport Beach, Dana Point, or San Pedro; 15-min helicopter ride from Long Beach or San Pedro.

Avalon, Catalina's only real town, extends from the shore of its natural harbor to the surrounding hillsides. Most of the city's activity, however, is centered along the pedestrian mall of Crescent Avenue, and most sights are easily reached on foot. Private cars are restricted and rental cars aren't allowed, but taxis, trams, and shuttles can take you anywhere you need to go. Bicycles and golf carts can be rented from shops along Crescent Avenue.

A walk along **Crescent Avenue** is a nice way to begin a tour of the town. You'll notice that vivid art deco tiles adorn the avenue's fountains and planters. Fired on the island by the now defunct Catalina Tile Company, the tiles are a coveted commodity. Head to the **Green Pleasure Pier**, at the center of Crescent Avenue, for a good vantage point of Avalon. At the top of the hill on your left you'll spot the Inn at Mt. Ada, now a top-of-the-line B&B originally built by William Wrigley Jr., for his wife. On the pier you'll find the Catalina Island Visitor's Bureau, snack stands, the Harbor Patrol, and scads of squawking seagulls.

★ On the northwest point of Avalon Bay (looking to your right from Green Pleasure Pier) is the majestic landmark **Casino**. This circular white structure is considered one of the finest examples of art deco architecture anywhere. Its Spanish-inspired floors and murals gleam with brilliant blue and green Catalina tiles. "Casino" is the Italian word for "gathering place" and in this case has nothing to do with gambling. Rather, Casino life revolves around the magnificent ballroom: the same big-band dances that made the Casino famous in the 1930s and '40s still take place on holiday weekends. The **New Year's Eve dance** (☎ 310/510–1520) is hugely popular and sells out well in advance. Santa Catalina Island Company leads tours of the Casino, lasting about 55 minutes, for $9. You can also visit the **Catalina Island Museum,** in the lower level of the Casino, which investigates 7,000 years of island history; or stop at the **Casino Art Gallery** to see works by local artists. First-run movies are screened on weekends at the **Avalon Theatre,** noteworthy for its classic 1929 theater

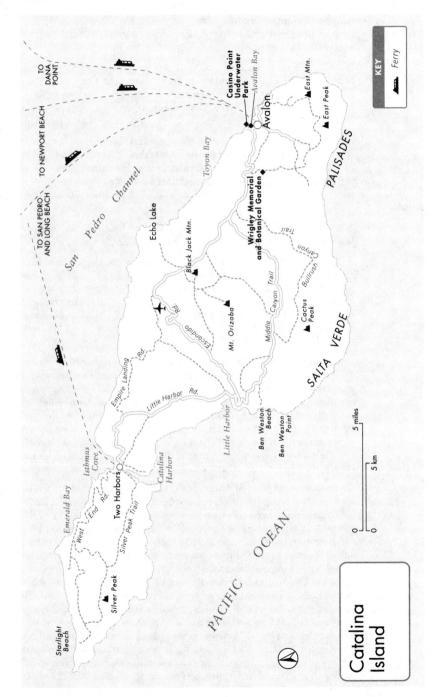

Catalina Island

pipe organ. ⊠ *1 Casino Way, Avalon* ☎ *310/510–2414 for museum, 310/510–0808 for art gallery, 310/510–0179 for Avalon Theatre* 🖾 *Museum $2.50, art gallery free* ⊙ *Museum: daily 10–4; closed Thurs., Jan.–Mar. Art gallery: daily 10:30–4; closed Mon. and Wed., Jan.–Mar. 15.*

In front of the Casino are the crystal-clear waters of the **Casino Point Underwater Park,** a marine preserve protected from watercraft where moray eels, bat rays, spiny lobsters, halibut, and other sea animals cruise around kelp forests and along the sandy bottom. It's a terrific site for scuba diving, with some shallow areas suitable for snorkeling. Scuba and snorkeling equipment can be rented on and near the pier. The shallow waters of **Lover's Cove,** east of the boat landing, are also good for snorkeling.

Two miles south of the bay via Avalon Canyon Road is the **Wrigley Memorial and Botanical Garden.** Here you'll find plants native to Southern California, including several that grow only on Catalina Island: Catalina ironwood, wild tomato, and rare Catalina mahogany. The Wrigley family commissioned the garden as well as the monument, which has a grand staircase and a Spanish mausoleum inlaid with colorful Catalina tile. (The mausoleum was never used by the Wrigleys, who are buried in Los Angeles.) Taxi service from Avalon is available, or you can take a tour bus from the downtown Tour Plaza or ferry landing. ⊠ *Avalon Canyon Rd., Avalon* ☎ *310/510–2288* 🖾 *$3* ⊙ *Daily 8–5.*

Santa Catalina Island Interpretive Center has exhibits and displays that offer information about Catalina Island's flora and fauna, marine life, history, ecology, and early inhabitants. ⊠ *1202 Avalon Canyon Rd., Avalon* ☎ *310/510–2514* 🖾 *Free* ⊙ *Daily 9–5.*

Walk through the residential hills of Avalon and you'll see such interesting architecture as the modern **Wolfe House,** on Chimes Tower Road, built in 1928 by noted architect Rudolf Schindler. Its terraced frame is carefully set into a steep site, affording extraordinary views. The house is a private residence, but you can get a good view of it from the path below and from the street. Across the street the **Zane Grey Pueblo** (⊠ 199 Chimes Tower Rd., Avalon ☎ 310/510–0966 or 800/378–3256) has been transformed into a rustic hotel.

Where to Stay & Eat

$–$$$$ ✕ **Cafe Prego.** This cozy Italian waterfront restaurant specializes in pasta, seafood, and steak. Try the excellent calamari; the house Chianti goes well with the spicy minestrone. Reserve ahead, or be prepared for a wait. ⊠ *603 Crescent Ave., Avalon* ☎ *310/510–1218* 🖃 *MC, V.*

$$ $$$ ✕ **Catalina Country Club.** The spring training clubhouse built for the Chicago Cubs now does duty as a restaurant for surf -and-turf standbys. The adjacent bar is great for an after-dinner drink; it connects to the old Cubs locker room. ⊠ *1 Country Club Dr., Avalon* ☎ *310/510–7404* 🖎 *Reservations essential* 🖃 *AE, D, MC, V.*

★ $$–$$$ ✕ **Channel House.** A longtime Avalon family owns this restaurant, serving dishes such as Catalina swordfish, coq au vin, and pepper steak. There's a patio facing the harbor, as well as an Irish-style bar. ⊠ *205 Crescent Ave., Avalon* ☎ *310/510–1617* 🖃 *AE, D, MC, V* ⊙ *Closed Mon. mid-Oct.–Easter.*

¢ ✕ **Eric's.** Stroll out on the pier to this laid-back counter spot for a buffalo burger to go (consider it population control), or snag a patio table and an order of fish-and-chips or nachos. ⊠ *Green Pier #2, Avalon* ☎ *310/510–0894* ☰ *AE, MC, V.*

$$$$ 🏨 **Inn on Mt. Ada.** In the mansion where William Wrigley Jr. once lived,
Fodor'sChoice the island's most exclusive hotel has all the comforts of a millionaire's
★ home—at millionaires' prices. However, breakfast, lunch, beverages, snacks, and use of a golf cart are included. The guest rooms are traditional and elegant; some have fireplaces and all have water views. The hilltop tableau overlooking the curving bay is especially spectacular. ⊠ *398 Wrigley Rd., Avalon 90704* ☎ *310/510–2030 or 800/608–7669* 🖷 *310/510–2237* ⊕ *www.catalina.com/mtada* ☙ *6 rooms* ⚘ *Dining room, meeting rooms, no-smoking rooms; no room phones* ☰ *MC, V* ⦿⊙⦿ *BP.*

$$–$$$$ 🏨 **Hotel Metropole and Market Place.** This romantic hotel could easily be in the heart of New Orleans' French Quarter. Some guest rooms have balconies overlooking a flower-filled courtyard of restaurants and shops; others have ocean views. Many have fireplaces. For a stunning panorama, head for the rooftop deck. ⊠ *205 Crescent Ave., Avalon 90704* ☎ *310/510–1884 or 800/541–8528* 🖷 *310/510–2534* ⊕ *www.hotel-metropole. com* ☙ *44 rooms, 4 suites* ⚘ *Some in-room hot tubs, some minibars, cable TV, no-smoking rooms* ☰ *AE, MC, V* ⦿⊙⦿ *CP.*

$–$$$$ 🏨 **Hotel Vista del Mar.** Contemporary rooms full of rattan furniture and greenery open onto a skylighted atrium. Some rooms have fireplaces, whirlpool tubs, and wet bars. Two larger rooms have ocean views. ⊠ *417 Crescent Ave., Avalon 90704* ☎ *310/510–1452 or 800/601–3836* 🖷 *310/510–2917* ⊕ *www.hotel-vistadelmar.com* ☙ *15 rooms* ⚘ *Some in-room hot tubs, minibars, refrigerators, cable TV, in-room VCRs, no-smoking rooms* ☰ *AE, D, MC, V* ⦿⊙⦿ *CP.*

$–$$$ 🏨 **Hotel Villa Portofino.** Steps from the Pleasure Pier, this hotel has a distinctly European flair. Rooms are named after Italian cities and most are decorated in deep jewel tones. Some ocean-facing rooms have open balconies, fireplaces, and marble baths. You can sunbathe on the private deck, or ask for beach towels and chairs to take to the cove. ⊠ *111 Crescent Ave., Avalon 90704* ☎ *310/510–0555* 🖷 *310/510–0839* ⊕ *www.hotelvillaportofino.com* ☙ *34 rooms* ⚘ *Restaurant, minibars, cable TV* ☰ *AE, D, DC, MC, V* ⦿⊙⦿ *CP.*

Nightlife

El Galleon (⊠ 411 Crescent Ave., Avalon ☎ 310/510–1188) has microbrews and karaoke. **Luau Larry's** (⊠ 509 Crescent Ave., Avalon ☎ 310/510–1919), famous for the potent blue Whicky Whacker cocktail, comes alive with boisterous tourists and locals on summer weekends.

Sports & the Outdoors

BICYCLING Bike rentals are widely available in Avalon for about $6 per hour. Look for rental shops on Crescent Avenue and Pebbly Beach Road, such as **Brown's Bikes** (⊠ 107 Pebbly Beach Rd., next to Island Rentals, Avalon ☎ 310/510–0986 🖷 310/510–0747 ⊕ www.catalinabiking.com).

DIVING & The Casino Point Underwater Park, with its handful of wrecks, is best
SNORKELING suited for diving. Lover's Cove is better for snorkeling (no scuba diving allowed, but you will share the area with glass-bottom boats). Both

are protected marine preserves. **Catalina Divers Supply** (⊠ Green Pleasure Pier ☎ 310/510–0330 or 800/353–0330 ⊕ www.catalinadiverssupply.com) rents equipment, runs guided scuba and snorkel tours, gives certification classes, and more. It has an outpost at Casino Point.

HIKING   Permits from the Conservancy are required for hiking into Catalina Island's interior. The permits are free and can be picked up at the main house of the **Santa Catalina Island Conservancy** (⊠ 3rd and Claressa Sts., Avalon ☎ 310/510–2595), at the **Santa Catalina Interpretive Center** (⊠ 1202 Avalon Canyon Rd. ☎ 310/510–2514), or at the airport. You don't need a permit for shorter hikes, such as the one from Avalon to the Botanical Garden. The Conservancy has maps of the island's east-end hikes, such as Hermit's Gulch trail. It's possible to hike between Avalon and Two Harbors, starting at the Hogsback gate above Avalon, though the 28-mi journey has an elevation gain of 3,000 feet and is not for the weak. For a pleasant 4-mi hike out of Avalon, take Avalon Canyon Road to Wrigley Gardens and follow the trail to Lone Pine. At the top, you'll have an amazing view of the Palisades cliffs and beyond them, the sea. If you plan to backpack overnight, you'll need a camping reservation. The interior is dry and desertlike; bring plenty of water and sunblock.

HORSEBACK RIDING   Horseback riders can wrangle four-legged transportation for scenic trail rides. Guided rides start at $30 at **Catalina Stables** (⊠ 600 Avalon Canyon Rd., Avalon ☎ 310/510–0478).

Two Harbors

45- to 60-min ferry ride (summer only) or 90-min bus ride from Avalon; 3-hr ferry ride (summer only) from Los Angeles.

This fairly primitive community toward the western end of the island has long been a summer boating destination. The area is named for its two harbors, which are separated by a ½-mi-wide isthmus. Once inhabited by pirates and smugglers, Two Harbors recalls the days before tourism became the island's major industry. This side of the island is less tame, with abundant wildlife, including the herd of buffalo imported to Catalina as extras in the 1925 film *The Vanishing American*. The Santa Catalina Island Company has activity information and services.

Where to Stay

Tiny Two Harbors has limited overnight accommodations. All reservations are made through the **visitor services office** (⌂ Box 2530, Two Harbors 90704 ☎ 310/510–0303 🖷 310/510–0224 ⊕ www.scico.com/twoharbors), which you'll see when you arrive.

$$–$$$ 🏠 **Banning House Lodge.** This pretty white 1910 lodge is as close as you'll find to luxury on this end of the island. Rooms have oak furniture and lace curtains. A free shuttle transports you to and from the village. ⊠ *Check-in at visitor services, Two Harbors* ☎ *310/510–0303 or 800/ 322–3434* ⤴ *11 rooms* ⌂ *No room phones, no room TVs, no a/c, no smoking* ⊟ *AE, D, MC, V* ⦿ *CP.*

⚜ **Two Harbors Cabins.** These simple, two-person camping cabins have full or bunk beds and refrigerators. An outdoor community cooking facility with gas burners and grills, and common restrooms with pay showers, are nearby. It takes three minutes to reach the cabins by foot from the pier. Check-in at visitor services. ☎ 310/510–4205 or 800/ 322-3434 ⇌ 21 cabins ▧ $25–$40 ➡ AE, D, MC, V ⊘ Closed June–Oct.

⚜ **Two Harbors Campground.** A quarter-mile outside the village, this campground on the beach has great swimming and snorkeling. Spaces have fire pits and picnic tables. There are showers and restrooms. Check-in at visitor services. ☎ 310/510–4205 or 800/322-3434 ⇌ 54 sites ▧ $12 ➡ AE, D, MC, V.

CATALINA ISLAND A TO Z

To research prices, get advice from other travelers, and book travel arrangements, visit www.fodors.com.

AIR TRAVEL

Island Express helicopters depart hourly from San Pedro and Long Beach (8 AM–sunset). The trip takes about 15 minutes and costs $78 one-way, $148 round-trip. Reservations are recommended a week in advance. 🚹 **Island Express** ☎ 310/510-2525 or 800/228-2566 ⊕ www.islandexpress.com.

BOAT & FERRY TRAVEL

Two companies offer ferry service to Catalina Island. Boats have both indoor and outdoor seating and snack bars. Excessive baggage is not allowed, and there are extra fees for bicycles and surfboards. The waters around Santa Catalina can get rough, so if you're prone to seasickness, come prepared.

Catalina Express makes an hour-long run from Long Beach or San Pedro to Avalon, and 90-minute runs from Dana Point to Avalon and from San Pedro to Two Harbors; round-trip fare from Long Beach or San Pedro to Avalon or Two Harbors is $45; from Dana Point to Avalon it's $47. Service from Newport Beach to Avalon is available through Catalina Passenger Service. Boats leave from Balboa Pavilion at 9 AM (in season), take 75 minutes to reach the island, and cost $42 round-trip. Return boats leave Catalina at 4:30 PM. Reservations are advised in summer and on weekends for all trips. Keep an eye out for dolphins, which sometimes swim alongside the ferries.

FARES & SCHEDULES 🚹 **Catalina Express** ☎ 310/519-1212 or 800/995-4386 🖷 800/410-9159 ⊕ www. catalinaexpress.com. **Catalina Passenger Service** ☎ 949/673-5245 or 800/830-7744 🖷 949/673-8340 ⊕ www.catalinainfo.com.

BUS TRAVEL

The Two Harbors Safari Bus has regular bus service (in season) between Avalon, Two Harbors, and several campgrounds. The trip between Avalon and Two Harbors takes two hours and costs $20 one-way. 🚹 **Two Harbors Safari Bus** ☎ 310/510-0303 or 800/322-3434.

GOLF CARTS

Golf carts constitute the island's main form of transportation. You can rent them along Avalon's Crescent Avenue and Pebbly Beach Road for about $30 per hour.

Island Rentals ⊠ 125 Pebbly Beach Rd., Avalon ☎ 310/510-1456.

LODGING

Between late May and early September, be sure to make reservations *before* heading here. After early September, rooms are much easier to find on shorter notice, rates drop dramatically, and many hotels offer packages that include transportation from the mainland and/or sightseeing tours. If you're interested in camping, Santa Catalina Island Company can offer you a place to pitch your tent almost anywhere on the island.

TOURS

Santa Catalina Island Company runs the following Discovery Tours: a summer-only coastal cruise to Seal Rocks; the *Flying Fish* boat trip (summer evenings only); the comprehensive inland motor tour (which includes an Arabian horse performance); the Skyline Drive; the Casino tour; the Avalon scenic tour; a glass-bottom-boat tour; an undersea tour on a semi-submersible vessel; and the Botanical Garden tour. Reservations are highly recommended for the inland tours. Tours cost $10 to $50. There are ticket booths on the Green Pleasure Pier, at the Casino, in the plaza, and at the boat landing. Catalina Adventure Tours, which has booths at the boat landing and on the pier, arranges similar excursions at comparable prices.

The Santa Catalina Island Conservancy organizes ecotours of the interior; naturalist guides drive open Jeeps through some gorgeously untrammeled parts of island. Each tour can accommodate up to six people and costs $495 for a four-hour trip. You can also book full-day tours. The tours run year-round.

Catalina Adventure Tours ☎ 310/510-2888 🖷 310/510-2797 ⊕ www.catalinaadventuretours.com. **Santa Catalina Island Company** ☎ 310/510-8687 or 800/322-3434 ⊕ www.catalina.com/scico. **Santa Catalina Island Conservancy** ⊠ 3rd and Claressa Sts., Avalon 90704 ☎ 310/510-2595 ⊕ www.catalinaconservancy.org.

VISITOR INFORMATION

Catalina Island Visitor's Bureau ⊠ Green Pleasure Pier, Box 217, Avalon 90704 ☎ 310/510-1520 🖷 310/510-7606 ⊕ www.catalina.com.

LOS ANGELES

EXPLORING LOS ANGELES

Updated by
Matthew Flynn

Looking at a map of sprawling Los Angeles, first-time visitors are sometimes overwhelmed. Where to begin? What to see first? And what about all those freeways? Here's some advice: relax, do your best to accept the traffic, and set your priorities. Movie and television fans should first head to Hollywood, Universal Studios, and a taping of a television show. Beach lovers and outdoorsy types might start out in Santa Monica or Venice or Malibu, or spend an afternoon in Griffith Park, one of the largest city parks in the country. Those with a cultural bent should probably make a beeline for the Getty Center, the Huntington, or the Norton Simon Museum. And architecture buffs should begin with a visit to downtown Los Angeles.

Numbers in the text correspond to numbers in the margin and on the neighborhood maps.

Downtown Los Angeles

For the past few decades, Los Angeles has continually tried to reinvent its downtown area, cultivating new businesses, attractions, and cultural landmarks in an effort to create a core for a city that is in many ways decentralized. Valiant efforts to bring the suburban-bound masses back to the city center have yielded mixed results, including the stunning Walt Disney Concert Hall, the Cathedral of Our Lady of the Angels, and the world's most expensive, but still limited, subway. The changes may not happen as quickly as the city's movers and shakers might like, but downtown L.A. is keeping its place as the cultural and historic heart of the city, and its pulse is slowly getting stronger.

a good tour

Begin a downtown tour by heading north on Broadway from 8th or 9th streets. At the southeast corner of Broadway and 3rd is the **Bradbury Building** ❷ ▶, with its fascinating interior court. (You can park behind the Bradbury Building on Spring Street for about $6.) Across the street is the Grand Central Market—once you've made your way through its tantalizing stalls you'll come out the opposite side onto Hill Street.

Cross Hill Street and climb steps up a steep hill to Watercourt, a friendly plaza with cafés and cascading fountains. (Unfortunately, the Angels Flight Railway won't be able to save you the hike since it's out of service.) Next, walk toward the glass pyramidal skylight topping the **Museum of Contemporary Art (MOCA)** ❶, half a block north on Grand Avenue.

Across from MOCA glimmers the swooping stainless-steel skin of the Walt Disney Concert Hall, one of the performance venues along Grand that comprises the Music Center. Heading north, you'll spot the stark concrete bell tower of the love-it-or-hate-it **Cathedral of Our Lady of the Angels** ❼.

Now walk south on Grand to 5th Street, where you'll find two of downtown's historical and architectural treasures: the Millennium Biltmore Hotel and the Central Library. Take a breather behind the library in the tranquil Maguire Gardens. Across 5th Street are the Bunker Hill Steps, L.A.'s version of Rome's Spanish Steps.

Back in your car, continue north on Broadway to 1st Street. Make a right turn here and drive a few blocks to Little Tokyo and the expanded **Japanese American National Museum** ❹. **The Geffen Contemporary** ❸ art museum, an arm of MOCA, is one block north on Central.

From Little Tokyo, turn left (north) from 1st onto Alameda Street. As you pass over the freeway, you'll come to the next stop, **Union Station** ❺, on the right. Street parking is limited, so your best bet is to park in the pay lot at Union Station (about $5). After a look inside this grand railway terminal, cross Alameda to **Olvera Street** ❻.

From Union Station, turn right on Alameda and then immediately left on Cesar Chavez Avenue for three blocks. At Broadway, turn right to Chinatown. If you have kids in tow, reverse your route on Broadway from Chinatown; cross back over the freeway, and at Temple Street make a left. Look to the right as you drive down Temple to see the back of City Hall of Los Angeles. Head out of downtown Los Angeles (take Los Angeles Street south to 11th Street, turn west onto 11th toward Figueroa, then turn south onto Figueroa Street) past Staples Center with its flying saucer–esque roof to Exposition Park, site of three fascinating museums: the **California Science Center** ❽, the **Natural History Museum of Los Angeles County** ❾, and the **California African-American Museum** ❿. Adjacent to Exposition Park is the University of Southern California.

Return to downtown at night for a performance at the Music Center, and after the show take in the bright lights of the big city at BonaVista, the revolving rooftop lounge atop the Westin Bonaventure Hotel & Suites, or take your chances of getting a rooftop seat at the ultrahip Downtown L.A. Standard hotel.

A convenient and inexpensive minibus service—DASH, or Downtown Area Short Hop—has several routes that travel past most of the sights on this tour, stopping every two blocks or so. Each ride costs 25¢, so you can hop on and off without spending a fortune. Special (limited) routes operate on weekends. Call **DASH** (☎ 808–2273 from all Los Angeles area codes) for routes and hours of operation.

TIMING Weekdays are the best time to experience downtown, when the area is bustling with activity and cafés are open for lunch. On weekends you may be able to find street parking, but you might keep asking yourself, "where did everyone go?" Seeing everything included on this tour in one day will require running shoes, stamina, and careful timing. Spread it over two days if possible, especially if you plan on spending time in the museums. Keep in mind that some museums are closed Monday. The **Los Angeles Conservancy** (☎ 213/623–2489 ⊕ www.laconservancy.org) regularly conducts Saturday morning walking tours of downtown architectural landmarks and districts. Most tours begin at 10 AM, last about 2½ hours, and are offered rain or shine. Reservations are required. Call for schedule and fees.

What to See

❷ **Bradbury Building.** Designed in 1893 by a novice architect who drew his inspiration from a science-fiction story and a conversation with his

3

If you have
3 days

Fortify yourself for your first whirlwind day with pancakes and coffee at the Farmers Market on Fairfax Avenue. Then drive north on Fairfax to Sunset Boulevard. Turn left onto the fabled Sunset Strip and stay on Sunset as it snakes past the lush estates of Beverly Hills and Bel Air. As you approach the San Diego freeway (I–405), follow signs to the Getty Center, or if you prefer sand with your sun, skip the Getty and keep heading west on Sunset through Brentwood until the winding road gives way to breathtaking views of the Pacific Ocean. Spend the afternoon lolling on Will Rogers State Beach or farther up the coast on Malibu's Zuma Beach. As the sun sets, head south on the PCH to Santa Monica for dinner.

Start Day 2 on Hollywood Boulevard, following the pink terrazzo stars of the Walk of Fame to Grauman's Chinese Theatre. Hop on the Red Line Metro for the 20-minute ride downtown to Union Station and head over to Olvera Street and El Pueblo de Los Angeles Historical Monument. If you're an architecture buff, the Bradbury Building on Broadway (across from the market) and the Central Library's eight-story atrium a few blocks away on 5th Street are worth a look. Then head up Grand Avenue to see the swooping new Walt Disney Concert Hall and the stark Cathedral of Our Lady of the Angels. Before dark, drive or catch the Red Line Metro back to Hollywood.

On your third day get an early start and head to Universal Studios Hollywood. After the tour there, visit to the adjacent CityWalk, and finish with dinner at one of the many restaurants that line nearby Ventura Boulevard.

If you have
5 days

Follow the three-day itinerary above, and on Day 4 hop onto the Ventura Freeway (Hwy. 134) and go east to Old Town Pasadena. Browse your way down Colorado Boulevard or duck into the small-but-exceptional Norton Simon Museum. Swing by the cluster of Greene and Greene Craftsman houses on Arroyo Terrace, then drive to San Marino's Huntington Library, Art Collections, and Botanical Gardens. On your last day, cater to your cravings. Curious about the entertainment studios? Head to Burbank and take a studio tour of either NBC or Warner Bros. If you prefer urban wilderness over show business, go for a hike in Griffith Park or around the Hollywood Reservoir (with a backdrop of the HOLLYWOOD sign). If you'd rather exercise your credit cards, choose the neighborhoods that seem most up your alley—Beverly Hills, Santa Monica, and West Hollywood for luxe, Los Feliz, Silver Lake, and Echo Park for funky—and put in a few hours of shopping. Or explore the southern part of L.A. County by taking the Pacific Coast Highway to Long Beach.

dead brother via a Ouija board, this office building is a marvelous specimen of Victorian-era commercial architecture. Originally the site of turn-of-the-20th-century sweatshops, it now houses somewhat more genteel firms beyond its pink marble staircases. The interior atrium courtyard, with its glass skylight, wrought-iron balconies, and caged elevators, is frequently used as a movie locale (*Blade Runner* was filmed here). The building is open daily from 9 to 5 if you want a peek; just don't wander beyond the first-floor landing. The building makes the perfect venue for the intimate **A+D Architecture and Design Museum,** whose exposed-beam gallery shows exhibits on all aspects of architecture and design. ✉ *304 S. Broadway (southeast corner Broadway and 3rd St.), Downtown* ☎ *213/626–1893.*

⑩ California African-American Museum. Works by 20th-century African-American artists and contemporary works of the African diaspora are the backbone of this museum's permanent collection. Its exhibits document the African-American experience from Emancipation and Reconstruction through the 20th century, especially as expressed by artists in the West and California. ✉ *600 State Dr., Exposition Park* ☎ *213/744–7432* ⊕ *www.caam.ca.gov* ✎ *Free, parking $6* ⊘ *Wed.–Sat. 10–4.*

⑧ California Science Center. Clusters of interactive exhibits here illustrate the relevance of science to everyday life, from bacteria to airplanes. Tess, the 50-foot animatronic star of the exhibit "Body Works," dramatically demonstrates how the body's organs work together to maintain balance. Other hands-on exhibits challenge you to construct earthquake-resistant structures and match actual brains with their animal owners. A cavernous Air and Space Gallery includes the Gemini 11 space capsule that gave us our first view of earth as a sphere. An IMAX theater shows large-format releases. ✉ *700 State Dr., Exposition Park* ☎ *323/724–3623* ⊕ *www.casciencectr.org* ✎ *Free, except for IMAX (prices vary); parking $6* ⊘ *Daily 10–5.*

⑦ Cathedral of Our Lady of the Angels. Controversy surrounded Spanish architect José Rafael Moneo's unconventional, costly, austere design for the seat of the Archdiocese of Los Angeles. But judging from the swarms of visitors and the standing-room-only holiday masses, the church has carved a niche in downtown's daily life. Opened in 2002, the ocher concrete cathedral looms up by the Hollywood Freeway. Its 5½-acre complex includes two gardens and a plaza dotted with café tables. The bronze entry doors, designed by local artist Robert Graham, are decorated with multicultural icons and New World images of the Virgin Mary. The canyonlike interior of the church is spare, polished, and airy—unique for a Catholic cathedral. By day, sunlight illuminates the sanctuary through translucent curtain walls of thin Spanish alabaster, a departure from the usual stained glass. Free guided tours start at the entrance fountain at 1 on weekdays. There's plenty of underground visitor parking; the vehicle entrance is on Hill Street. ✉ *555 W. Temple St., Downtown* ☎ *213/680–5200* ⊕ *www.olacathedral.org* ✎ *Free; parking $3 every 20 min, $14 maximum* ⊘ *Weekdays 6:30 AM–7 PM, Sat. 9–7, Sun. 7–7.*

Fodor'sChoice ★

★ ③ The Geffen Contemporary. Back in 1982, Disney Concert Hall architect Frank Gehry transformed a warehouse in Little Tokyo into a temporary space while the permanent home for the **Museum of Contemporary Art (MOCA)** was being built a mile away. The Temporary Contemporary—with its large, flexible space, anti-establishment character, and lively exhibits—was such a hit that it remains part of the museum facility. Now called the Geffen, it houses a concise sample of MOCA's permanent collection, which spans the years from the 1940s

Art & Architecture

Topping this art-loving city's museum list are the Getty Center; the Los Angeles County Museum of Art (LACMA) in the mid-Wilshire district; the two sites of the Museum of Contemporary Art (MOCA); the Huntington Library, Art Collections, and Botanical Gardens, in San Marino; and the Norton Simon Museum in Pasadena. More than 50 other area museums house everything from medieval illuminated manuscripts to contemporary artworks. The city's art galleries have also been picking up steam, especially at Santa Monica's 5-acre Bergamot Station Art Center.

3

Beaches

L.A.'s combination of sun, sand, and 72 mi of gorgeous coastline is hard to beat. It's all here: more than 30 mi of wide beaches, beach towns from the laid-back to the superchic, and plenty of sunny days to enjoy it all. Zuma Beach, north of Malibu, has always been popular with Angelenos for its pristine water and excellent facilities. Easily accessible Santa Monica beaches are always a scene, though the bay could be cleaner. Regardless of whether you like your beach rugged or serene, crowded or private, getting some sand on the floor of your car is practically a requirement here.

Nightlife

It's hip, it's hot, and it's one of the world's best: the club scene, that is, from hard-hitting rock, heart-thumping techno, sophisticated jazz, and wailing blues joints to comedy clubs, dance clubs, and discos. The Sunset Strip and its environs in West Hollywood are famous for club- and bar-hopping. Though clubs on the Strip play to a young crowd, there are plenty of venues for grown-ups throughout the area, from the Troubadour to Bar Marmont. The bars of any hotels touched by hotelier André Balazs are virtually guaranteed buzz. West Hollywood's Santa Monica Boulevard is the core of the gay-and-lesbian club and coffeehouse scene. And from Echo Park to Malibu, small clubs and bars hum with local up-and-coming bands.

The Restaurant Scene

L.A.'s fantastic mix of cultures makes for a brilliant blend of cuisines. French or French-influenced cooking has been the focus at many high-profile new restaurants, but not surprisingly, Asian and Latin American elements have been sparking up menus, too. Chefs who make their mark in L.A. achieve near-celebrity status; new chefs who have struck out on their own become the next big thing, and there are also established favorites that have attracted a devoted following for years. The list includes Joachim Splichal, of Patina and the Pinot restaurants; Piero Selvaggio, of Valentino; and the king of sushi, Nobu Matsuhisa.

Shopping

Of course L.A. has malls, from the upscale designer-boutique variety to the mega-discount outlet type. But what Angelenos appreciate most are the city's unique shopping streets and outdoor markets. These are the places where you can not only see the sky, but also find great shops with merchandise the malls don't carry, and pop into terrific restaurants, bakeries, bookstores, and galleries. Among these places are trendy Robertson Boulevard, the Third Street Promenade in Santa Monica, elegant Rodeo Drive in Beverly Hills, and trendy Melrose Avenue.

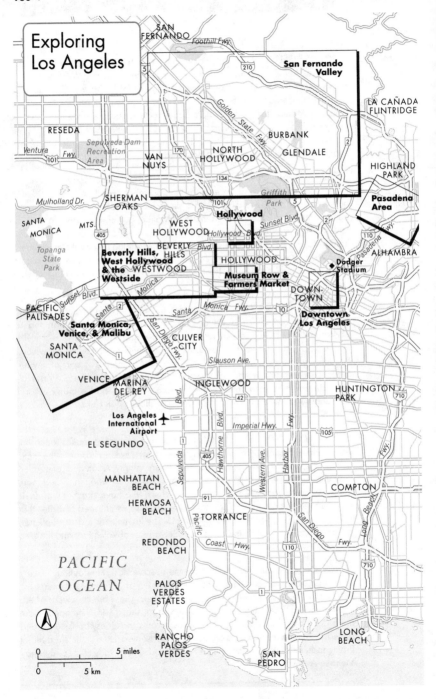

Exploring Los Angeles

SAN FERNANDO

Foothill Fwy.

San Fernando Valley

LA CAÑADA FLINTRIDGE

Golden State Fwy.

RESEDA

Sepulveda Dam Recreation Area

BURBANK

Ventura Fwy.

VAN NUYS

NORTH HOLLYWOOD

GLENDALE

HIGHLAND PARK

Mulholland Dr.

SHERMAN OAKS

Pasadena Area

SANTA MONICA MTS.

WEST HOLLYWOOD

Hollywood

Hollywood Blvd.

Sunset Blvd.

Pasadena Fwy.

ALHAMBRA

Topanga State Park

Beverly Hills, West Hollywood & the Westside

BEVERLY HILLS

Beverly Blvd.

HOLLYWOOD

WESTWOOD

Museum Row & Farmers Market

Monica

Dodger Stadium

DOWN-TOWN

PACIFIC PALISADES

Sunset Blvd.

Santa Monica Fwy.

10

Downtown Los Angeles

Santa Monica, Venice, & Malibu

Santa

San Diego Fwy.

Santa Monica Fwy.

CULVER CITY

SANTA MONICA

1

Slauson Ave.

VENICE

MARINA DEL REY

INGLEWOOD

42

HUNTINGTON PARK

710

Los Angeles International Airport

Blvd.

Imperial Hwy.

Fwy.

105

EL SEGUNDO

1

405

Hawthorne Blvd.

Western Ave.

Harbor

MANHATTAN BEACH

91

COMPTON

HERMOSA BEACH

Pacific

TORRANCE

San Diego Fwy.

Long Beach Fwy.

PACIFIC OCEAN

REDONDO BEACH

Coast Hwy.

110

710

PALOS VERDES ESTATES

1

LONG BEACH

RANCHO PALOS VERDES

SAN PEDRO

0   5 miles
0   5 km

to the present, and usually one or two temporary exhibits that merit a visit. ✉ *152 N. Central Ave., Downtown* ☎ *213/626–6222* ⊕ *www.moca-la.org* ✉ *$8; free with MOCA admission on same day, free Thurs. 5–8* ☉ *Mon. and Fri. 11–5, Thurs. 11–8, weekends 11–6.*

❹ Japanese American National Museum. What was it like to grow up on a coffee plantation in Hawaii? How difficult was life for Japanese Americans interned in concentration camps during World War II? These questions are addressed by changing exhibits at this museum. Insightful volunteer docents are on hand to share their own stories and experiences. The museum occupies an 85,000-square-foot adjacent pavilion as well as its original site in a renovated 1925 Buddhist temple. ✉ *369 E. 1st St., at Central Ave., (next to the Geffen Contemporary) Downtown* ☎ *213/625–0414* ⊕ *www.janm.org* ✉ *$6; free Thurs. 5–8, 10–8 3rd Thurs. of the month* ☉ *Tues., Wed., and Fri.–Sun. 10–5, Thurs. 10–8.*

★ ❶ The Museum of Contemporary Art (MOCA). The MOCA's permanent collection of American and European art from 1940 to the present divides itself between two spaces: the linear, red sandstone building at California Plaza and the **Geffen Contemporary** in nearby Little Tokyo. Likewise, its exhibitions are split between the established and the cutting-edge. Heavy hitters such as Mark Rothko, Franz Kline, Susan Rothenberg, Diane Arbus, and Robert Frank are fixtures, while at least 20 themed shows rotate through annually. It's a good idea to check the schedule in advance since some shows sell out, especially on weekends. ✉ *250 S. Grand Ave., Downtown* ☎ *213/626–6222* ⊕ *www.moca.org* ✉ *$8; free on same day with Geffen Contemporary admission, and also Thurs. 5–8* ☉ *Mon. and Fri. 11–5, Thurs. 11–8, weekdays 11–6.*

☾ ❾ Natural History Museum of Los Angeles County. With more than 3½ million specimens in its halls and galleries, this is the third-largest museum of its type in the United States after the Field Museum in Chicago and the American Museum of Natural History in New York. It has a rich collection of prehistoric fossils and extensive bird, insect, and marine-life exhibits. Brilliant stones shimmer in the Gem and Mineral Hall. An elaborate taxidermy exhibit shows North American and African mammals in detailed replicas of their natural habitats. Exhibits typifying various cultural groups include pre-Columbian artifacts and a display of crafts from the South Pacific. The Times-Mirror Hall of Native American Cultures delves into the history of Los Angeles's earliest inhabitants. The Ralph M. Parsons Discovery Center for children has hands-on exhibits. ✉ *900 Exposition Blvd., Exposition Park* ☎ *213/763–3466* ⊕ *www.nhm.org* ✉ *$9; free 1st Tues. of the month* ☉ *Weekdays 9:30–5, weekends 10–5.*

★ ☾ ❻ Olvera Street. This busy pedestrian block tantalizes with ceramic tiles, piñatas, mariachis, and fragrant Mexican food. As the major draw of the oldest section of the city, known as **El Pueblo de Los Angeles,** Olvera Street has come to represent the rich Mexican heritage of L.A. It had a close shave with disintegration in the early 20th century, until Christine Sterling walked through in 1926. Jolted by the historic area's decay, Sterling fought to preserve key buildings and led the transformation of the street into a Mexican-American marketplace. Today this character remains;

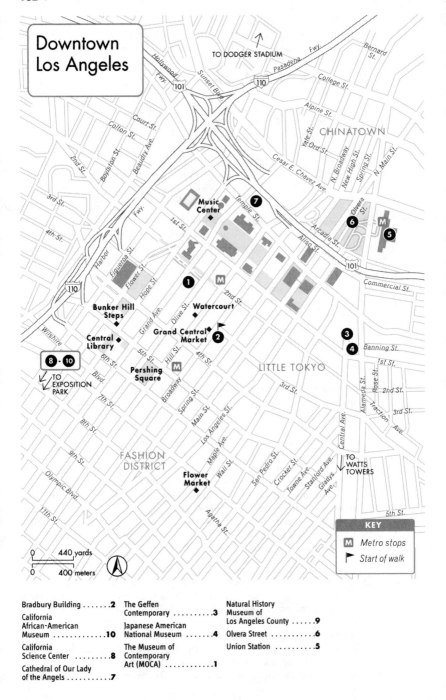

Downtown Los Angeles

TO DODGER STADIUM

Pasadena Fwy.

Bernard St.

College St.

Alpine St.

CHINATOWN

Hollywood Fwy.

Sunset Blvd.

101

110

Court St.

Colton St.

Boylston St.

Beaudry Ave.

3rd St.

4th St.

Harbor Fwy.

Figueroa St.

Flower St.

Hope St.

Grand Ave.

Olive St.

1st St.

Temple St.

Cesar E. Chavez Ave.

Yate St.

Ord St.

N. Broadway

New High St.

Spring St.

N. Main St.

Olvera St.

Arcadia St.

Aliso St.

Commercial St.

Music Center

7

6

M

5

101

Wiltshire

110

1

M

2nd St.

Bunker Hill Steps

Watercourt

Grand Central Market

2

3

4

Banning St.

Central Library

5th St.

Hill St.

4th St.

LITTLE TOKYO

1st St.

Rose St.

Alameda St.

2nd St.

8 · 10

TO EXPOSITION PARK

Blvd.

6th St.

Pershing Square

M

Broadway

3rd St.

Central Ave.

Traction Ave.

3rd St.

7th St.

Spring St.

Main St.

Los Angeles St.

8th St.

9th St.

FASHION DISTRICT

Maple Ave.

Wall St.

San Pedro St.

Crocker St.

Towne Ave.

Stanford Ave.

Gladys Ave.

TO WATTS TOWERS

Olympic Blvd.

11th St.

Flower Market

Agatha St.

5th St.

0   440 yards
0   400 meters

vendors sell puppets, leather goods, sandals, serapes and handcrafts from stalls that line the center of the narrow street. On weekends, the restaurants are packed as musicians play in the central plaza. The weekends that fall around two Mexican holidays, Cinco de Mayo (May 5) and Independence Day (September 16), also draw huge crowds. To see Olvera Street at its quietest and perhaps loveliest, visit late on a weekday afternoon, when long shadows heighten the romantic feeling of the passageway. For information, stop by the **Olvera Street Visitors Center** (⊠ 622 N. Main St., Downtown ☎213/628–1274 ⊕ www.olvera-street.com), in the Sepulveda House, a Victorian built in 1887 as a hotel and boardinghouse. The center is open Monday through Saturday 10–3. Free 50-minute walking tours leave here at 10, 11, and noon Wednesday–Saturday.

❺ Union Station. Built in 1939 as one of the country's last great rail stations, Union Station was the key entry point into Los Angeles prior to the opening of LAX. Designed by City Hall architects John and Donald Parkinson, it combines Spanish Colonial Revival and art deco styles. The waiting hall's commanding scale and enormous chandeliers have provided the setting for so many films and TV shows that you may feel you've been here before. The station's restaurant, **Traxx,** is a great place for lunch, evoking a time where travel and style went hand in hand. ⊠ *800 N. Alameda St., Downtown.*

Hollywood

You'll need a director's eye to find the glitter within this legendary, now largely grim locale. Still, there is some magic left, and much of it can be found on foot around the recently relocated home of the Academy Awards at the Kodak Theatre, part of the Hollywood & Highland entertainment complex. The adjacent Grauman's Chinese Theatre delivers silver-screen magic with its cinematic facade and ornate interiors from a bygone era. A shining example of a successful Hollywood revival can be seen and experienced at the 1926 El Capitan Theatre just across Hollywood Boulevard. which offers live stage shows and Wurlitzer organ music before selected movie engagements. If you walk the renowned Hollywood Walk of Stars to find your favorite celebrities, you'll encounter derelict diversions literally screaming for your attention (and dollar), as well as numerous panhandlers and an occasional costumed superhero not sanctified by Marvel comics. A developer-interpreted vision of Schwab's Pharmacy at Sunset and Vine, across the street from the once-futuristic Cinerama Dome movie theater, draws crowds. At sundown, you can admire Hollywood's crowning jewel: the Hollywood Bowl, summer home to the Los Angeles Philharmonic.

a good tour

Start off by driving up into the Hollywood Hills on Beachwood Drive (off Franklin Avenue, just east of Gower Street) for an up-close look at one of the world's most familiar icons: the **HOLLYWOOD sign ❶ ▶**. Follow the small sign pointing the way to the LAFD Helispot. Turn left onto Rodgerton Drive, which twists and turns higher into the hills. At Deronda Drive, turn right and drive to the end. The HOLLYWOOD sign looms off to the left. Turn around and retrace your route down the hill, back to Beachwood for the drive into Hollywood.

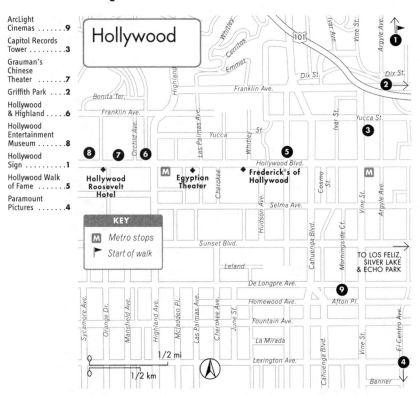

Make a right (west) at Franklin Avenue, and prepare to turn left at the next light at Gower Street. Stay on Gower, driving through the section of Sunset Boulevard known as Gower Gulch. At Gower and Santa Monica Boulevard, look for the entrance to Hollywood Forever Cemetery, half a block east on Santa Monica, where you can pay your respects to Rudolph Valentino and Mel "That's all folks!" Blanc. From the cemetery, retrace your route back to Gower Street and turn left to drive along the western edge of the cemetery flanking Gower. Abutting the cemetery's southern edge is **Paramount Pictures** ❹. The famous gate Norma Desmond (Gloria Swanson in *Sunset Boulevard*) was driven through is no longer accessible to the public, but a replica marks the entrance on Melrose Avenue: turn left from Gower Street to reach the gate.

Next, drive west (right off Gower) on Melrose for three blocks to Vine Street, turn right, and continue to Hollywood and Vine—an intersection whose fame is worldwide. Across the street, the so-called "record stack" **Capitol Records Tower** ❸ resembles—to those who remember vinyl—a stack of 45s. A few steps east of the intersection on Hollywood Boulevard is the restored, ornate Pantages Theater. A block west on Ivar Street are the former homes of literary giants William Faulkner and Nathanael West.

Drive west along Hollywood Boulevard. Stop along the way for a look at the bronze stars that make up the **Hollywood Walk of Fame** ❺, or to visit the Lingerie Museum at the purple Frederick's of Hollywood or the Hollywood Wax Museum, Guinness World of Records, and Ripley's Believe It or Not Museum triangle—all shrines to Hollywood camp. Metered parking is fairly easy to find. If not, small lots just north and south of the boulevard have reasonable hourly rates.

At Hollywood Boulevard and Las Palmas Avenue is the Egyptian Theatre, Hollywood's first movie palace. Continue west on Hollywood Boulevard two blocks until you see the giant, Babylonian-themed, hotel-retail-entertainment complex **Hollywood & Highland** ❻, which includes the 3,300-seat Kodak Theatre, the new permanent home to the Academy Awards.

Adjacent to Hollywood & Highland is **Grauman's Chinese Theatre** ❼, a genuine monument to Hollywood history. The elaborate pagoda-style movie palace is still the biggest draw along Hollywood Boulevard. Also on the north side of the boulevard and west of the Chinese Theatre is the **Hollywood Entertainment Museum** ❽. From the museum, cross Hollywood Boulevard and loop back east past the historic Hollywood Roosevelt Hotel. In the next block, you can see the impeccably restored and elaborate facade of the El Capitan Theatre.

Several blocks north of the boulevard on Highland Avenue is the Hollywood Bowl, where you can visit its interesting museum in the daytime or enjoy the outdoor concerts on summer evenings.

For a spectacular Cinemascope view of the glittering city lights, from Hollywood to the ocean, head up to the Griffith Observatory, perched on a promontory in **Griffith Park** ❷. From Hollywood Boulevard, go north on Western Avenue, which becomes Los Feliz Boulevard. Take a left on Vermont Avenue and follow the signs that lead you into the park and up the hill to the observatory.

TIMING Plan to spend the better part of a morning or afternoon taking in Hollywood. Hollywood Boulevard still has some less-than-salubrious characters; if you've got children in tow, stick to a daytime walk. Later in the evening, you can return to Hollywood for a cabaret performance at the Roosevelt Hotel's Cinegrill, a movie at the Chinese or the Egyptian, or a summertime concert at the Hollywood Bowl.

What to See

❾ **ArcLight Cinemas and Cinerama Dome.** A new star was born in Hollywood when this cinema complex opened in 2002 and reinvented the art of upscale moviegoing. The enormous complex, which encompasses 14 plush theaters including the legendary 1963 Cinerama Dome, offers first-class reserved seats, a full-service bar, trendy café, snappy customer service, and steep ticket prices to match (up to $14). ArcLight Weekend nights take on an especially hip buzz as film enthusiasts and entertainment industry power couples mingle outside theaters in the soaring lobby. Buy your tickets in advance, and arrive early for the show before the show. ✉ *6360 Sunset Blvd., Hollywood* ☎ *323/464-4226* ⊕ *www. arclightcinemas.com.*

❸ Capitol Records Tower. The romantic story about the origin of this symbol of '50s chic is that singer Nat King Cole and songwriter Johnny Mercer suggested that the record company's headquarters be shaped to look like a stack of 45s. Architect Welton Becket claimed he just wanted to design a structure that economized space and in so doing, he created the world's first cylindrical office building. On its south wall, L.A. artist Richard Wyatt's mural *Hollywood Jazz, 1945–1972* immortalizes musical greats Duke Ellington, Billie Holiday, Ella Fitzgerald, and Miles Davis. At the top of the tower, a blinking light spells out "Hollywood" in Morse code. ⊠ *1750 N. Vine St., Hollywood.*

★ ❼ Grauman's Chinese Theatre. This exaggeratedly ornate, Chinese pagoda–style movie palace is an icon of Hollywood fantasy. Although you have to buy a movie ticket to appreciate the massive interior, the courtyard is open to the public. Here you'll find those oh-so-famous cement hand- and footprints. This tradition is said to have begun at the theater's opening in 1927, with the premiere of Cecil B. DeMille's *King of Kings,* when actress Norma Talmadge accidentally stepped into the wet cement. Now more than 160 celebrities have contributed imprints of their appendages for posterity, along with a few other oddball imprints, like the one of Jimmy Durante's nose. ⊠ *6925 Hollywood Blvd., Hollywood* ☎ *323/461–3331.*

❷ Griffith Park. L.A.'s communal backyard is the largest municipal park and urban wilderness area in the United States; its 4,100 acres sprawl over the northwest corner of the city. The park was named after Griffith J. Griffith, a mining tycoon who donated much of the land to the city in 1896. It has been used as a filming location since the early days of motion pictures. One of the most famous filming sites is the **Griffith Observatory** (⊠ 2800 E. Observatory Rd. ☎ 323/664–1191 ⊕ www.griffithobservatory.org), an art deco landmark that has been immortalized in such movies as *Rebel Without a Cause* and *The Terminator.* The building itself is closed until early 2006 for major renovations, but you can still take in an incredible city view from its hillside perch. The park also includes a zoo, hiking paths, tennis and golf facilities, the Autry Museum of Western Heritage, a theater, and more. Griffith Park is accessible in several places: off Los Feliz Boulevard at Western Canyon Avenue, Vermont Avenue, Crystal Springs Drive, and Riverside Drive; from the Ventura/134 Freeway at Victory Boulevard, Zoo Drive, or Forest Lawn Drive; from the Golden State Freeway (I–5) at Los Feliz Boulevard and Zoo Drive. The park is open from 5 AM to 10 PM. The **ranger station** (☎ 323/913–7390) is on Crystal Springs Drive, near the merry-go-round.

★ ❻ Hollywood & Highland. This megamillion-dollar hotel-retail-entertainment complex makes a swaggering attempt to recapture the glitz of old Hollywood—with mixed results. Heavy on stucco and low on color and character, this glorified shopping center is presided over by a pair of 33-foot-high elephants and a towering gray arch inspired by the 1916 movie *Intolerance.* On clear days the HOLLYWOOD sign can be seen perfectly centered in the archway opening. High-style bowling, chain retail stores, a good selection of restaurants, movie theaters, and and a live-broadcast studio complete the picture. In the northeast section of the complex stands the 22-story, 640-room **Renaissance Hollywood Hotel.** Academy Awards attendees enter the plush **Kodak Theatre** through a red-carpeted portal lined with various boutiques and candy stores that are closed and covered with drapery come Oscar day. There's plenty of underground parking accessible from Highland Avenue. ⊠ *Hollywood Blvd. and Highland Ave., Hollywood* ⊕ *www.hollywoodandhighland. com* ⊠ *Parking $2 with validation.*

★ ❶ HOLLYWOOD Sign. With letters 50 feet tall, Hollywood's trademark sign can be spotted from miles away. The sign, which originally spelled out "Hollywoodland," was erected on Mt. Lee in the Hollywood Hills in 1923 to promote a real-estate development. In 1949 the "land" portion of the sign was taken down. Over the years pranksters have altered it, albeit temporarily, to spell out "Hollyweed" (in the 1970s, to commemorate lenient marijuana laws), "Go Navy" (before a Rose Bowl game), and "Perotwood" (during the 1992 presidential election). In 1994, however, a fence and surveillance equipment were installed surrounding the sign to deter intruders. If you want to see the sign up close and are game for a hike, there are several trails in Griffith Park that can take you near the iconic letters.

★ ❺ Hollywood Walk of Fame. Along Hollywood Boulevard runs a trail of affirmations for entertainment-industry overachievers. On this mile-long stretch of sidewalk, names are embossed in brass, each at the center of a pink star embedded in dark-gray terrazzo. The first eight stars were unveiled in 1960. Since then, more than 1,600 others have been immortalized. Here's a miniguide to a few of the more famous celebs' stars: Marlon Brando at 1765 Vine, Charlie Chaplin at 6751 Hollywood, W. C. Fields at 7004 Hollywood, George and Ira Gershwin at 7083 Hollywood, Clark Gable at 1608 Vine, Greta Garbo at 6901 Hollywood, Marilyn Monroe at 6774 Hollywood, Rudolph Valentino at 6164 Hollywood, and John Wayne at 1541 Vine. Recent arrivals include Drew Barrymore at 6925 Hollywood and Dr. Seuss at 6600 Hollywood. You can contact the **Hollywood Chamber of Commerce** (⊠ 7018 Hollywood Blvd. ☎ 323/469–8311 ⊕ www.hollywoodcoc.org) for celebrity-star locations and information on future star installations.

❹ Paramount Pictures. The last major studio still in Hollywood dates from the early 1920s. Some of Hollywood's most luminous stars called this studio home: Rudolph Valentino, Mae West, Mary Pickford, and Lucille Ball, who filmed episodes of *I Love Lucy* here. Movies and TV shows are still filmed at the studio, and while tours of the facilities are no longer offered, you can be part of the audience for live TV tapings. Tickets are free; call for listings and times. ⊠ *5555 Melrose Ave., Hollywood* ☎ *323/956–1777* ⊕ *www.paramount.com/studio.*

off the beaten path

LOS FELIZ, SILVER LAKE, AND ECHO PARK – Over the past few years, these neighborhoods east of Hollywood have become an intriguing mix of subcultures. Low rents drew artists and musicians to Los Feliz, then farther southeast to Silver Lake and lately, Echo Park. Funky, independent boutiques, galleries, and cafés have followed in their wake; now Los Feliz is the most gentrified, Echo

Park the least. Silver Lake has a lovely oasis in its namesake reservoir, plus a cluster of modernist homes designed by Richard Neutra and R. M. Schindler. Echo Park's Echo Lake has a sprawling lotus bed; its slender Sunset Art Park at 1478 Sunset Boulevard gives a glimpse of "drive-by art." The easiest way to reach these neighborhoods is to drive east on Sunset Boulevard, then head north up Hillhurst or Vermont avenues to Los Feliz, or continue southeast on Sunset to Silver Lake and Echo Park.

Wilshire Boulevard, Museum Row & Farmers Market

Just east of Fairfax Avenue in the Miracle Mile district is the three-block stretch of Wilshire Boulevard known as Museum Row, with five museums of widely varying themes and a prehistoric tar pit to boot. Only a few blocks away are the lively Farmers Market and The Grove shopping center, a great place to people-watch. You can glimpse the former city center along Wilshire from Fairfax Avenue to downtown, where celebs once partied at the Coconut Grove and dined at Perino's. Finding parking along Wilshire Boulevard can present a challenge anytime of the day; you'll find advice on the information phone lines of most attractions.

a good tour

Start the day with pumpkin pancakes at **Kokomo Cafe**, at the **Farmers Market ❶ ▶**, a few blocks north of Wilshire Boulevard at 3rd Street and Fairfax Avenue. Drive south on Fairfax Avenue to the Miracle Mile district of Wilshire Boulevard. The black-and-gold art deco building on the northeast corner is a former May Company department store that's now called LACMA West and houses satellite exhibition galleries of the Los Angeles County Museum of Art (LACMA). Turn left onto Wilshire and proceed to Ogden Drive or a block farther to Spaulding Avenue, where you can park the car and set out on foot to explore the museums.

The large complex of contemporary buildings surrounded by a park on the corner of Wilshire and Ogden Drive is the **Los Angeles County Museum of Art (LACMA) ❷**, the largest art museum west of Chicago. Also in the park are the prehistoric **La Brea Tar Pits ❸**, where many of the fossils displayed at the adjacent Page Museum at the La Brea Tar Pits were found. Across Wilshire is the Craft and Folk Art Museum (CAFAM) and, back at the corner of Wilshire and Fairfax, the **Petersen Automotive Museum ❹**, which surveys the history of the car in Los Angeles.

From Museum Row and Miracle Mile, a drive east along Wilshire Boulevard to downtown gives you a minitour of a historical and cultural cross section of Los Angeles. At Highland Avenue you enter the old-money enclave of the Hancock Park neighborhood. At Western Avenue the Wiltern Theater, an outstanding example of art deco architecture, stands across the street from the intersection's Metro station. The frequency of Korean-language signs in this area is a clue that you're now driving along the edge of Koreatown. Just past Normandie Avenue is the now-closed Ambassador Hotel, where presidential nominee Robert F. Kennedy was assassinated in 1968. Farther on, as Wilshire crosses Vermont Avenue toward downtown Los Angeles, you'll pass the magnificent art deco Bullock's Wilshire building.

TIMING The museums open between 10 and noon, so plan your tour around the opening time of the museum you wish to visit first. LACMA is open Monday but closed Wednesday, and has extended hours into the evening, closing at 8 (9 on Friday). The other museums are closed on Monday (except the Page). If you're on a tight budget, keep tabs on museum free days; for instance, on the second Tuesday of the month LACMA admission to all but ticketed exhibits is free. Set aside a day to do this entire tour: two to three hours for the Farmers Market and The Grove, about three hours for the museums, and an hour for the Wilshire Boulevard sights.

What to See

❶ ▶ **Farmers Market and The Grove.** In 1934 two entrepreneurs convinced oil
Fodor'sChoice magnate E. B. Gilmore to open a vacant field for a bare-bones market;
★ a group of farmers simply pulled up their trucks and sold fresh produce off the back. From this seat-of-the-pants situation grew a European-style open-air market and local institution at the corner of 3rd Street and Fairfax Avenue. This is the place where you can truly experience L.A.'s diversity: old and young, natives and transplants all eating, shopping and singing karaoke together on warm summer evenings. There are 33 dining options, ranging from candlelit French cuisine at **Monsieur Marcel** to authentic Mexican at **Loteria Grill.** Adjacent to Farmers Market is The Grove, a shopping center inspired by Disneyland's Main Street, complete with a free double-decker trolley. While the setting is over the top, the stores are not; standbys like Nordstrom, Banana Republic, Crate & Barrel, and the Gap fill the ornate buildings. The 14 stadium-style movie theaters sell out on weekends, so plan ahead. ⊠ *6333 W. 3rd St., Fairfax District* ☎ *323/933–9211 Farmers Market, 888/315–8883 The Grove* ⊕ *www.farmersmarketla.com, www.thegrovela.com* ☉ *Farmers Market weekdays 9–9, Sat. 9–8, Sun. 10–9; The Grove Mon.–Thurs. 10–9, Fri. and Sat. 10–10, Sun. 11–7.*

❸ **La Brea Tar Pits.** About 40,000 years ago, deposits of oil rose to the Earth's surface, collected in shallow pools, and coagulated into sticky asphalt. In the early 20th century, geologists discovered that the sticky goo contained the largest collection of Pleistocene, or Ice Age, fossils ever found at one location: more than 600 species of birds, mammals, plants, reptiles, and insects. More than 100 tons of fossil bones have been removed in excavations over the last seven decades, making this one of the world's most famous fossil sites. You can see most of the pits through chain-link fences. Pit 91 is the site of ongoing excavation; tours are available and you can volunteer to help with the excavations in summer. Statues of a family of mammoths in the big pit near the corner of Wilshire and Curson suggest how many of them were entombed: edging down to a pond of water to drink, animals were caught in the tar and unable to extricate themselves. There are several pits scattered around Hancock Park and the surrounding neighborhood; construction in the area has often had to accommodate them and, in nearby streets and along sidewalks, little bits of tar occasionally and unstoppably ooze up. The **Page Museum at the La Brea Tar Pits** (☎ 323/934–7243) displays fossils from the tar pits. ⊠ *Hancock Park, Miracle Mile* ⊕ *www.tarpits.org* ✉ *Free.*

❷ Los Angeles County Museum of Art (LACMA). Since it opened in 1966,
FodorśChoice LACMA has assembled an encyclopedic collection of more than 150,000
★ works from around the world; its collection is widely considered the most comprehensive in the western United States. American, Latin American, Far Eastern, Islamic, and South and Southeast Asian works are especially well represented. Other standout areas include costumes and textiles, decorative arts, European paintings and sculpture, photography, drawings, and prints. Architectural cohesiveness, on the other hand, is not LACMA's strong suit: the collections are spread through five buildings on the main campus, plus another building two blocks away. Most of LACMA's buildings cluster around a courtyard. The Ahmanson building is the equivalent of Art History 101, with everything from Mesoamerican artifacts to 19th-century European masters. Hit the Robert O. Anderson building for 20th-century and contemporary art. A special pavilion showcases Japanese art. LACMA West, a Streamline Moderne building a short walk from the main campus, is heavy on Mexican modern masters (Rivera, Tamayo, Orozco, Siquieros). It also contains the Experimental Gallery that, with its interactive technologies, reading room, and video stations, is geared primarily to schoolchildren and families. ⊠ *5905 Wilshire Blvd., Miracle Mile* ☎ *323/857–6000, 323/857–0098 TDD* ⊕ *www.lacma.org* ✉ *$7, free 2nd Tues. of the month* ☉ *Mon., Tues., Thurs. noon–8, Fri. noon–9, weekends 11–8.*

☾ ❹ Petersen Automotive Museum. More than just a building full of antique or unusual cars, the Petersen is highly entertaining and informative, thanks to the lifelike dioramas and street scenes that help establish a context for the history of the automobile. Rotating exhibits on the second floor may include Hollywood-celebrity and movie cars, "muscle" cars (like a 1969 Dodge Daytona 440 Magnum), or motorcycles. You'll also learn about the history of L.A.'s formidable freeway network. A children's interactive Discovery Center illustrates the mechanics of the automobile. ⊠ *6060 Wilshire Blvd., Miracle Mile* ☎ *323/930–2277* ⊕ *www. petersen.org* ✉ *$10* ☉ *Tues.–Sun. 10–6.*

Beverly Hills & West Hollywood

While much of L.A. is fragmented and occasionally disappointing, Beverly Hills delivers big-time. In this foot-friendly district of extreme makeovers and opulent wealth, the fable of the Los Angeles lifestyle is on daily parade. World-famous Rodeo Drive—with its tony boutiques, swaying palms, and sunny skies—will make you feel you're on a movie set. Stars (along with their kids, nannies, and agents) dine, shop, and stroll here for all to see—so remember to bring your camera.

Just east of Beverly Hills is West Hollywood, which isn't so much a place to "see" things (like museums or movie studios) as it is a place to "do" things—like go nightclubbing, eat at top-notch restaurants, and attend gallery openings. Since the end of Prohibition, West Hollywood's Sunset Strip has been the city's nighttime playground, and today it's still going strong.

But hedonism isn't all that drives West Hollywood. The area attracted a particularly dedicated community and in the 1980s, a coalition of seniors, gays, and lesbians spearheaded a grassroots effort to make it an independent city. The coalition succeeded in 1984, and today West Hollywood has emerged as one of the most progressive cities in Southern California. It's also one of the most gay-friendly cities anywhere, with one third of its population estimated to be either gay or lesbian. The annual Gay Pride Parade is one of the largest in the nation, drawing tens of thousands of participants each June.

a good drive

Begin a tour of Beverly Hills on **Sunset Boulevard** ❺ ▶, at the landmark Beverly Hills Hotel, a.k.a. the Pink Palace. If you'd like to see some of the luxe estates that give the 90210 zip code its cachet, loop along a few of the streets north of Sunset. Otherwise, turn south onto **Rodeo Drive** ❶ ▶ (pronounced ro-*day*-o). You'll pass through a residential neighborhood before hitting the shopping stretch of Rodeo south of Santa Monica Boulevard. Find a parking space and flex your credit card. Across Wilshire, the Regent Beverly Wilshire Hotel serves as a temporary residence for the rich and famous. The **Museum of Television & Radio** ❷ stands a block east of Rodeo, on Beverly Drive at Santa Monica Boulevard. A few blocks west of Beverly Hills is the high-rise office-tower and shopping-center area known as Century City.

Head north on Beverly Drive for a few blocks to get back to Sunset Boulevard, turning right (east) toward West Hollywood. Once you pass Doheny Drive, you'll have technically left Beverly Hills and be cruising the **Sunset Strip** ❻, known for nightclubs such as the Whisky A Go-Go, the Roxy, and the Viper Room. Sunset Plaza is a good place to get out of the car and take a stroll, do some high-end window-shopping, or pass the time people-watching from a sidewalk café. Look for parking in the lot behind the shops, off Sunset Plaza Drive. A bit further east, past La Cienega Boulevard, is the all-white ultrahip Mondrian Hotel. Back in your car, you can continue east toward Crescent Heights Boulevard if you'd like a glimpse of the famous hotel Chateau Marmont. Turning south on La Cienega will take you to Santa Monica Boulevard; from

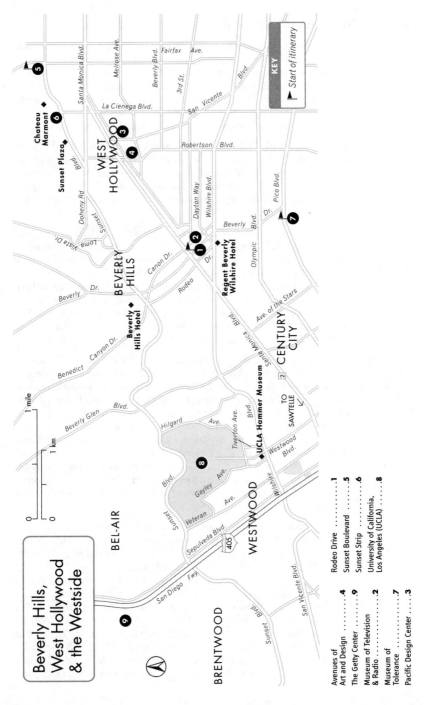

Beverly Hills,
West Hollywood
& the Westside

KEY

▲ Start of itinerary

BRENTWOOD

BEL-AIR

WESTWOOD

CENTURY
CITY

BEVERLY
HILLS

WEST
HOLLYWOOD

Chateau
Marmont ◆ ⑥

Sunset Plaza ◆

Beverly
Hills Hotel ◆

Regent Beverly
Wilshire Hotel ◆

UCLA Hammer Museum ◆

Santa Monica Blvd.
Fairfax Ave.
Melrose Ave.
Beverly Blvd.
3rd St.
San Vicente
La Cienega Blvd.
Robertson Blvd.
Dayton Way
Wilshire Blvd.
Beverly Blvd.
Pico Blvd.
Olympic
Ave. of the Stars
Santa Monica Blvd.
Canon Dr.
Rodeo
Beverly Dr.
Doheny Rd.
Sunset
Loma Vista Dr.
Canyon Dr.
Benedict
Beverly Glen Blvd.
Hilgard Ave.
Tiverton Ave.
Westwood Blvd.
Gayley Ave.
Veteran Ave.
Sepulveda Blvd.
San Diego Fwy.
San Vicente Blvd.
Sunset
Wilshire
405
TO SAWTELLE

1 mile
1 km
0
0

⑤ ⑥ ③ ④ ① ② ⑦ ⑧ ⑨

roughly La Cienega to Robertson Boulevard, Santa Monica Boulevard is the commercial core of West Hollywood's large gay and lesbian community. (It's also part of historic Route 66.) A left turn at San Vicente Boulevard will bring you to West Hollywood's most visible landmark, the **Pacific Design Center** ❸. There's public parking available at the PDC, and you can get out and walk back a block to Santa Monica Boulevard or head west on Melrose Avenue. This walkable section of town is known as the **Avenues of Art and Design** ❹, so designated because of the proliferation of design studios and art galleries.

TIMING   Plan to arrive in Beverly Hills mid-morning. Most stores open by 10 or 11 AM, with limited hours on Sunday. (Some are closed on Sunday or Monday.) Park your car in one of several municipal lots (the first one or two hours are free; after that it's then $6 per hour), and spend as long as you like strolling along Rodeo Drive. There are plenty of reasonably priced cafés and restaurants for lunch. The major routes in and out of Beverly Hills—Wilshire and Santa Monica boulevards—get very congested during rush hours.

Traffic on Sunset and Santa Monica boulevards is heavy most of the day, especially at night and on weekends. Special "no-cruising" regulations are in effect at certain times on certain streets. Weekday afternoons are generally the easiest driving times. For street parking, bring plenty of quarters; parking on residential streets is by permit only.

What to See

❹ **Avenues of Art and Design.** A concentration of design studios and art and antique galleries along Melrose Avenue, San Vicente Boulevard, Robertson Boulevard, North Almont, and other streets around the Pacific Design Center has given rise to this catch-all designation. The galleries are very high-end, but it doesn't cost anything to look (sometimes the window is as far as you can get; many of these studios are "to the trade only"). Periodically, usually on the first Saturday evening of the month, several of the galleries host group-opening receptions, or "Gallery Walks," to premiere new exhibits and artists. Contact the **West Hollywood Convention and Visitors Bureau** for information. ☎ *310/289–2525 or 800/368–6020 ⊕ www.visitwesthollywood.com.*

❷ **Museum of Television & Radio.** You can revisit your favorite *Mary Tyler Moore* episodes at this sister to the Museum of Television & Radio in New York; its collection of 100,000 programs spans eight decades. Search for your favorite commercials and television and radio shows on easy-to-use computers, and then watch or listen to them in an adjacent room. There are special exhibits of television- and radio-related art and costumes, as well as frequent seminars with television and radio cast members. ⊠ *465 N. Beverly Dr., Beverly Hills* ☎ *310/786–1000 ⊕ www.mtr.org* 🗌 *$10 suggested donation* ⊙ *Wed.–Sun. noon–5.*

❸ **Pacific Design Center.** Cesar Pelli designed these two architecturally intriguing buildings, one sheathed in blue glass (the "Blue Whale"), the other in green (the "Green Whale"). Together, they house 150 design showrooms, making this the largest interior design complex in the western United States. But the showrooms are open only to the trade; unless you've got your interior decorator in tow, your browsing options are limited. You can, however, take advantage of the stylish adjacent plaza with its reflecting pool and fountain. The downtown Museum of Contemporary Art has a satellite **MOCA Gallery** (☎ 213/626–6222 ⊕ www.moca.org) here, though, which opens intermittently for shows on architecture and design. ⊠ *8687 Melrose Ave., West Hollywood* ☎ *310/657–0800* ⊕ *www.pacificdesigncenter.com* ☉ *Weekdays 9–5.*

▶ ★ ❶ **Rodeo Drive.** No longer an exclusive shopping street where well-heeled clients shop for $200 pairs of socks, Rodeo Drive is one of Southern California's bona fide tourist attractions. Just as if they were at Disneyland or in Hollywood, T-shirt-and-shorts-clad tourists wander along this tony stretch of avenue, window shopping at Tiffany & Co., Gucci, Armani, Hermès, Harry Winston, and Lladro. Several nearby restaurants have patios where you can sip a drink while watching fashionable shoppers saunter by. At the southern end of Rodeo Drive (at Wilshire Boulevard) is **Via Rodeo,** a curvy cobblestone street that makes for a pretty picture-taking spot. ⊠ *Beverly Hills.*

▶ ❺ **Sunset Boulevard.** One of the most fabled avenues in the world, Sunset Boulevard began humbly enough in the 18th century as a route from El Pueblo de Los Angeles (today's downtown L.A.) to the ranches in the west and then to the Pacific Ocean. Now as it winds its way across the L.A. Basin to the ocean, it cuts through gritty urban neighborhoods and what used to be the working center of Hollywood's movie industry. In West Hollywood, it becomes the sexy and seductive Sunset Strip, then slips quietly into the tony environs of Beverly Hills and Bel Air, twisting and winding past gated estates. Continuing on past UCLA in Westwood, through Brentwood and Pacific Palisades, Sunset finally descends to the beach, the edge of the continent, and the setting sun.

★ ❻ **Sunset Strip.** For decades the Hollywood nighttime crowd has headed for the 1¾-mi stretch of Sunset Boulevard between Crescent Heights Boulevard and Doheny Drive, known as the Sunset Strip. In the 1930s and '40s, stars like Tyrone Power, Errol Flynn, Norma Shearer, and Rita Hayworth came for wild evenings of dancing and drinking at nightclubs like Trocadero, Ciro's, and Mocambo. By the '60s and '70s, the Strip had become the center of rock 'n' roll: Johnny Rivers, the Byrds, the Doors, Elton John, and Bruce Springsteen gave legendary performances on stages at clubs like the Whisky A Go-Go and Roxy. Nowadays it's the Viper Room and the House of Blues, where you'll find on-the-cusp actors, rock stars, and out-of-towners all mingling over drinks and live music. Parking is tough, especially on weekends, but the time and money may be worth it if you plan on making the rounds—most clubs are within walking distance of each other.

The Westside

For some privileged Los Angelenos, the city begins west of La Cienega Boulevard, where "keeping up with the Joneses" takes place on an epic scale. Chic, attractive neighborhoods with coveted zip codes—Bel Air, Brentwood, Westwood, West Los Angeles, and Pacific Palisades—are home to power couples pushing power kids in power strollers. But the Westside is also rich in culture—and not just entertainment-industry culture. It's home to UCLA, the monumental Getty Center, and the compelling Museum of Tolerance.

a good tour

The major sights on the Westside are spread out, so choosing a starting point is arbitrary; the best strategy is to select one of the major attractions as a destination and plan your visit accordingly. A visit to the **Museum of Tolerance** ❼ ☞ in the morning, for example, can be easily followed with lunch and shopping in Beverly Hills or Century City. Afterward, you might drive through the Westwood Village district, home of the **University of California, Los Angeles** ❽ campus and the Fowler Museum of Cultural History, then stop at the UCLA Hammer Museum. The vast **Getty Center** ❾ offers the trifecta of art, architecture, and sweeping views at its hilltop perch in Brentwood.

TIMING   Advance reservations are not essential, but well-advised, for visits to the Museum of Tolerance (closed Saturday), and the Getty Center (closed Monday), so plan accordingly. Each museum merits at least a half day. In the evening and on weekends, Westwood Village and Brentwood's commercial district on San Vicente Boulevard come alive with a busy restaurant, café, and street scene. The afternoon rush hour is predictably congested along Wilshire and Sunset boulevards.

What to See

😊 ❾ **The Getty Center.** With its curving walls and isolated hilltop perch, the
Fodor'sChoice Getty Center resembles a pristine fortified city of its own. You may be
★ lured up by the beautiful views of L.A. (on a clear day stretching all the way to the Pacific Ocean), but the architecture, the uncommon gardens, and the fascinating art collections are more than enough to hold your attention. When the sun's out, the complex's rough-cut travertine marble skin seems to soak up the light.

J. Paul Getty, the billionaire oil magnate and art collector, began collecting Greek and Roman antiquities and French decorative arts in the 1930s. He opened the J. Paul Getty Museum at his Malibu estate in 1954, and in the 1970s, he built a re-creation of an ancient Roman village to house his initial collection. The Malibu villa, closed in 1997, is under renovation until further notice; when it reopens as Getty Villa in 2006, it will be devoted to the antiquities. The Getty Center, designed by Richard Meier, opened in 1998. It pulls together the rest of the continually expanding collections, and the museum's affiliated research, conservation, and philanthropic institutes.

The Getty's five pavilions surround a central courtyard and are bridged by walkways. Artist Robert Irwin created the Central Garden, whose focal point is an azalea maze in a pool. At almost every turn you'll spot terrific views of the city. The permanent collections include European paintings, drawings, sculpture, illuminated manuscripts, and decorative arts, as well as American and European photographs. Notable among the paintings are Rembrandt's *The Abduction of Europa,* van Gogh's *Irises,* Monet's *Wheatstack, Snow Effects, Morning,* and James Ensor's

Christ's Entry Into Brussels. Don't miss the exceptional collection of French furniture and decorative arts.

Parking is free and based on availability; reservations are no longer required. ⊠ *1200 Getty Center Dr., Brentwood* ☎ *310/440-7300* ⊕ *www.getty.edu* ▣ *Free; $5 parking* ⊙ *Tues.–Thurs., Sun. 10–6, Fri. and Sat. 10–9.*

▶ ★ **❼** **Museum of Tolerance.** Using interactive technology, this important museum (part of the Simon Weisenthal Center) challenges visitors to confront bigotry and racism. One of the most affecting sections covers the Holocaust, with film footage of deportation scenes and simulated sets of concentration camps. Anne Frank artifacts are part of the museum's permanent collection. Interactive exhibits include the "Millennium Machine," which engages visitors in finding solutions to human rights abuses around the world, and the "Point of View Diner," a recreation of a 1950s diner, red booths and all, that "serves" a menu of controversial topics on video jukeboxes. To ensure a visit to this popular museum, make reservations in advance (especially for Friday, Sunday, and holidays), and plan to spend at least three hours there. In-person testimony from Holocaust survivors is offered periodically. Museum entry stops at least two hours before the actual closing time. A photo ID is required for admission. ⊠ *9786 W. Pico Blvd., just south of Beverly Hills* ☎ *310/553-8403* ⊕ *www.museumoftolerance.com* ▣ *$10* ⊙ *Nov.–Mar., Mon.–Thurs. 11:30–6:30, Fri. 11:30–3, Sun. 11–7:30; Apr.–Oct., Mon.–Thurs. 11:30–6:30, Fri. 11:30–5, Sun. 11–7:30.*

❽ **University of California, Los Angeles (UCLA).** With spectacular buildings such as a Romanesque library, the parklike UCLA campus is a wonderful place to stroll. In the heart of the north campus, the Franklin Murphy Sculpture Garden contains more than 70 works by such artists as Henry Moore and Gaston Lachaise. The Mildred Mathias Botanic Garden, which contains some 5,000 species of plants from all over the world in a 7-acre outdoor garden, is in the southeast section of the campus. West of the main campus bookstore, the Morgan Center Hall of Fame displays the sports memorabilia and trophies of the university's athletic departments.

Many visitors head straight to the **UCLA Fowler Museum of Cultural History** (☎ 310/825–4361 ⊕ www.fmch.ucla.edu), which presents changing exhibits on the world's diverse cultures and visual arts, especially those of Africa, Asia, Oceania, and Native and Latin America. Just south of the main campus area is the **UCLA Hammer Museum** (⊠ 10899 Wilshire Blvd. ☎ 310/443–7000 ⊕ www.hammer.ucla.edu), with its trove of works by Old Masters, French Impressionists, and graphic artists.

Campus maps and information are available at drive-by kiosks at major entrances. The main entrance gate is on Westwood Boulevard. Campus parking costs $7. ⊠ *Bordered by Le Conte, Hilgard, and Gayley Aves. and Sunset Blvd., Westwood* ⊕ *www.ucla.edu.*

Santa Monica, Venice & Malibu

The desirable, varied communities of Santa Monica, Venice, and Malibu curve along L.A.'s coastline. These high-rent areas hug Santa Mon-

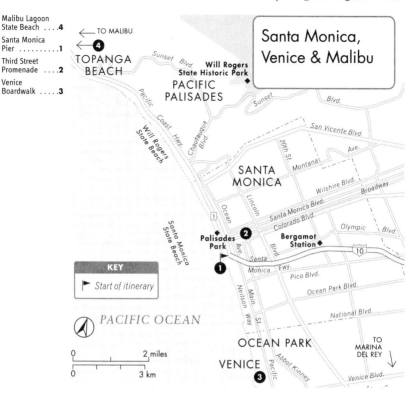

← TO MALIBU

←**4**

**Santa Monica,
Venice & Malibu**

TOPANGA
BEACH

Sunset *Blvd.*

**Will Rogers
State Historic Park** ◆

PACIFIC
PALISADES

Sunset *Blvd.*

Pacific *Coast* *Hwy.*

Chautauqua *Blvd.*

*Will Rogers
State Beach*

San Vicente Blvd.

20th St.

Montana *Ave.*

SANTA
MONICA

Lincoln

Wilshire Blvd.

Broadway

Santa Monica Blvd.

Ocean *Ave.*

Colorado Blvd.

Olympic *Blvd.*

1

*Santa Monica
State Beach*

**Palisades
Park** ◆

2

**Bergamot
Station** ◆

10

KEY

▶ *Start of itinerary*

1

*Santa
Monica* *Fwy.*

Pico Blvd.

Neilson *Way*

Main *St.*

Ocean Park Blvd.

National Blvd.

◈ *PACIFIC OCEAN*

OCEAN PARK

TO
MARINA
DEL REY
↓

0 ——— 2 miles
0 ——— 3 km

VENICE

3

Abbot Kinney

Pacific

Venice Blvd.

ica Bay in an arc of diversity, from the ultracasual, ultrarich Malibu to the bohemian-seedy mix of Venice. What they have in common, however, is cleaner air, mild temperatures, often horrific traffic, and an emphasis on the beach-focused lifestyle that many people consider the hallmark of Southern California.

a good drive

Look for the arched neon sign at the foot of Colorado Avenue marking the entrance to the **Santa Monica Pier ❶ ▶**, the city's number-one landmark, built in 1906. Park on the pier and take a turn through Pacific Park, a 2-acre amusement park. The wide swath of sand on the north side of the pier is Santa Monica Beach, on hot summer weekends one of the most crowded beaches in Southern California. From the pier, walk to Ocean Avenue, where Palisades Park, a strip of lawn and palms above the cliffs, provides panoramic ocean views. Three blocks inland is **Third Street Promenade ❷**, a popular outdoor mall.

Next stop: **Venice Boardwalk ❸**. Retrieve your car and drive two blocks inland on Colorado to Main Street. Turn right and continue until you reach Rose Avenue. You'll spot an enormous pair of binoculars, the front of the Frank Gehry–designed Chiat-Day Mojo building. Find a parking place, then head toward the sea and the boardwalk, where California beach culture is on colorful display.

For the drive to Malibu, retrace your route along Main Street. At Pico Boulevard, turn west, toward the ocean, and then right on Ocean Avenue. When you pass the pier, prepare to turn left down the California Incline (the incline is at the end of Palisades Park at Wilshire Boulevard) to the Pacific Coast Highway (Highway 1), also known as PCH. Drive roughly 11 mi north into Malibu, park in the lot adjacent to the Malibu Pier, and take a stroll out to the end for a view of the coast. Back on land, take a walk on **Malibu Lagoon State Beach** ❹, also known as Surfrider Beach. On the highway side of the beach is the Moorish-Spanish Adamson House and Malibu Lagoon Museum, a tiled beauty with a great Pacific view. From here, you can walk along the strand of beach that fronts the famed Malibu Colony, the exclusive residential enclave of film, television, and recording stars.

TIMING   If you've got the time, break your coastal visit into two excursions: Santa Monica and Venice in one, and Malibu in another. The best way to "do" L.A.'s coastal communities is to park the car, rent a bike or a pair of in-line skates in Santa Monica or Venice, and walk, cycle, or skate along the 3-mi beachside bike path. For this, of course, a sunny day is best; on all but the hottest days, when literally millions of Angelenos flock to the beaches, try to get started in the late morning. Places like Santa Monica Pier, Main Street, and the Venice Boardwalk are more interesting to observe as the day progresses. Try to avoid the boardwalk, beach, and back streets of Santa Monica and Venice at night, when the crowds dissipate. Main Street is a good place for lunch, shopping, and great people-watching; Third Street Promenade comes to life at night when the restaurants and movie theaters fill up. Avoid driving to Malibu during rush hour, when traffic along the PCH moves at a snail's pace. It's best to hit Malibu before seasonal costal fog rolls in, so that you can catch the sunset.

What to See

❹ **Malibu Lagoon State Beach.** Visitors are asked to stay on the boardwalks at this 5-acre haven for native and migratory birds so that the egrets, blue herons, avocets, and gulls can enjoy the marshy area. The signs listing opening and closing hours refer only to the parking lot; the lagoon itself is open 24 hours and is particularly enjoyable in the early morning and at sunset. Street-side parking is available at those times, but not at midday. ✉ *23200 Pacific Coast Hwy., Malibu.*

▶ ⊙ ❶ **Santa Monica Pier.** Eateries, souvenir shops, a psychic adviser, arcades, and the **Pacific Park** amusement area are all part of this truncated pier at the foot of Colorado Boulevard below Palisades Park. The pier's trademark 46-horse Looff carousel, built in 1922, has appeared in many films, including *The Sting*. Free concerts are held on the pier in summer. A small, interactive aquarium is tucked under the eastern end of the pier. ✉ *Colorado Blvd. and the ocean, Santa Monica* ☎ *310/458–8900* ⊕ *www. santamonicapier.org* ⊟ *Rides 50¢–$1* ⊗ *Carousel 11–7; hrs for rest of park vary.*

★ ❷ **Third Street Promenade.** This pedestrian-only three-block stretch of 3rd Street, just a whiff away from the Pacific and lined with jacaranda trees, ivy-topiary dinosaur fountains, and strings of lights, is a great place to stretch your legs. Outdoor cafés, street vendors, movie theaters, and a rich nightlife make this a main gathering spot for locals, visitors . . . and the homeless. It's fun to watch the mix of people here, from elderly couples out for a bite to skateboarders and street musicians. ⊠ *3rd St. between Wilshire Blvd. and Broadway, Santa Monica* ⊕ *www.downtownsm.com.*

❸ **Venice Boardwalk.** "Boardwalk" may be something of a misnomer—it's really a five-block section of paved walkway—but this L.A. mainstay delivers year-round action. Bicyclists zip along and bikini-clad rollerbladers attract crowds as they put on impromptu demonstrations, vying for attention with magicians, fortune tellers, a chain-saw juggler, and sand mermaids. At the adjacent **Muscle Beach,** bulging bodybuilders with an exhibitionist streak pump iron at an outdoor gym. Pick up some cheap sunglasses, grab a hot dog, and enjoy the boardwalk's show. You can rent in-line skates, roller skates, and bicycles (some with baby seats) at the south end of the boardwalk (officially known as Ocean Front Walk), along Washington Street near the Venice Pier.

FodorsChoice
★

The San Fernando Valley

There are other valleys in the Los Angeles area, but this is the one that people refer to simply as the Valley. Sometimes, there's a note of derision in their tone; to some Angelenos, the Valley just isn't cool. True, most of the Valley is blanketed with suburban tract homes and strip malls, but that doesn't mean you should write off the area entirely. The name Burbank may not have the same cachet as Hollywood, but it's home to most of the major film and television studios, such as Warner Bros., Disney, ABC, and NBC. There's also Universal City—a one-industry town dominated by Universal Studios, which has been here since 1915. Now the hilly area includes Universal Studios Hollywood theme park, the Universal Amphitheater, CityWalk (a pedestrian zone filled with shops and restaurants), and hotels.

a good drive

On a clear day or evening, a trip along Mulholland Drive ▶ gives you a spectacular view of the sprawling San Fernando Valley below. Just over the hill from Hollywood via the Hollywood Freeway (U.S. 101, north) is Universal City, which has its own freeway off-ramp (Universal Center Drive). **Universal Studios Hollywood** ❶ is on a large hill overlooking the San Fernando Valley, a city-within-a-city. As you exit Universal, follow signs to Barham Boulevard. At Barham, turn left toward Burbank. After driving about a mile, the street curves around **Warner Bros. Studios** ❷, whose outside wall is covered with billboards of current films and television shows. After the curve, you will be on West Olive Avenue. Keep to the right and look for the entrance to Gate No. 4 at Hollywood Way.

Just a minute away, at the second big intersection of West Olive and Alameda avenues, is the main entrance to **NBC Television Studios** ❸. Continue east on Alameda; on the next block to your right is Disney Studios, with its animation building topped with a giant "Sorcerer's Apprentice" hat. Drive south on Buena Vista and then turn left on Riverside to get a good look at Michael Graves's Team Disney building with the Seven Dwarfs supporting the roof.

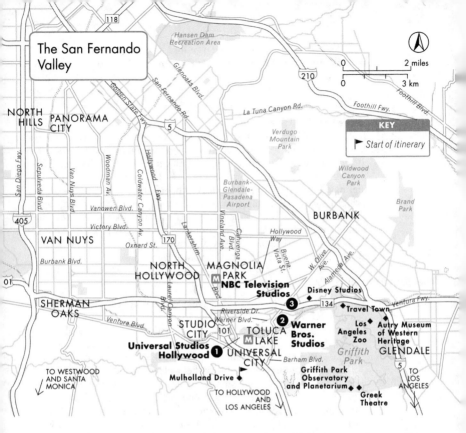

The San Fernando Valley

NORTH HILLS
PANORAMA CITY
VAN NUYS
SHERMAN OAKS
STUDIO CITY
NORTH HOLLYWOOD
MAGNOLIA PARK
TOLUCA LAKE
UNIVERSAL CITY
BURBANK
GLENDALE

KEY
▶ Start of itinerary

Universal Studios Hollywood ❶
NBC Television Studios ❸
Warner Bros. Studios ❷
Disney Studios
Travel Town
Los Angeles Zoo
Autry Museum of Western Heritage
Griffith Park
Griffith Park Observatory and Planetarium
Greek Theatre
Mulholland Drive

TO WESTWOOD AND SANTA MONICA
TO HOLLYWOOD AND LOS ANGELES
TO LOS ANGELES

Hansen Dam Recreation Area
Verdugo Mountain Park
Wildwood Canyon Park
Brand Park
Burbank-Glendale-Pasadena Airport

TIMING The Valley is surrounded by mountains and the major routes to and from it go through mountain passes. During rush hour, traffic jams on the Hollywood Freeway (U.S. 101/Highway 170), San Diego Freeway (I–405), and Ventura Freeway (U.S. 101/Highway 134) can be brutal, so avoid trips to or from the Valley at those times. Expect to spend a full day at Universal Studios Hollywood and CityWalk; studio tours at NBC and Warner Bros. last up to two hours.

What to See

▶ **Santa Monica Mountains National Recreation Area.** The boundary of the San Fernando Valley is one of the most famous thoroughfares in this vast metropolis. **Mulholland Drive** cuts through the Santa Monica Mountains National Recreation Area, a vast parkland that stretches along the top and west slopes of the Santa Monica Mountains from Hollywood to the Ventura County line. Driving the length of the hilltop road is slow and can be treacherous, but the rewards are sensational views of the valley and city—and some amazing homes—along the way. From Hollywood you can reach Mulholland Drive via Outpost Drive off Franklin Avenue, or via Cahuenga Boulevard west off Highland Avenue north. ⊠ *401 W. Hillcrest Dr., Thousand Oaks* ☎ *310/589–3200* ☑ *Free* ☉ *Daily 9–5.*

❸ NBC Television Studios. This major network's headquarters is in Burbank, as any regular viewer of *The Tonight Show* will know. If you want to be part of a live studio audience, free tickets are made available for tapings of the various NBC shows. Call for ticket information, or look for distribution at the Chinese Theatre in Hollywood and CityWalk at Universal Studios. ✉ *3000 W. Alameda Ave., Burbank* ☎ *818/840–3537.*

★ ☾ ❶ **Universal Studios Hollywood.** Though you probably won't see anything that actually has to do with making a real film, visiting this theme park is an entertaining introduction to the principles of special effects. From a seat on a comfortable tour tram, you can experience the parting of the Red Sea, an avalanche, a snowstorm, rain forest fog, and a flood; meet a 30-foot-tall version of King Kong; be attacked by the ravenous killer shark of *Jaws* fame; survive an all-too-real simulation of an earthquake that measures 8.3 on the Richter scale. The trams have state-of-the-art sound and LCD systems, and the guided 45-minute trips circle the 415-acre complex all day long.

Many attractions are based on Universal films and television shows; you can check out the 3-D effects in *Terminator 2: 3D* and *Shrek 4D* or ride an indoor roller coaster inspired by the films *The Mummy* and *The Mummy Returns.* Aside from the park, **CityWalk** is a separate venue, where you'll find a slew of shops, restaurants, nightclubs, and movie theaters, including IMAX 3D. ✉ *100 Universal City Plaza, Universal City* ☎ *818/622–3801* ⊕ *www.universalstudios.com* 💲 *$49.75, parking $8* ☉ *Hrs change daily but are typically mid-June–early Sept., daily 9–9; early Sept.–mid-June, daily 10–6.*

❷ **Warner Bros. Studios.** Two-hour tours at this major studio center in Burbank involve a lot of walking, so dress comfortably and casually. The tours are somewhat technically oriented and center more on the actual filmmaking process than the Universal tours do. You start with a short film on Warner Bros. movies and TV shows, then hop into a tour cart for a ride to the studio museum. The archives here include costumes, props, and scripts from the studio's productions. Finally you visit the sets and sound stages, where you might spot a celeb or see a shoot in action—tours change from day to day to depending on the productions taking place. Reservations are required. Call at least one week in advance and ask about provisions for people with disabilities; children under 8 are not admitted. Tours are given at least every hour, and more frequently from May to September. ✉ *4301 W. Olive Ave., Burbank* ☎ *818/846–1403* ⊕ *www.wbsf.com* 💲 *$32* ☉ *Tours Oct.–Apr., weekdays 9–3; May–Sept., weekdays 9–4.*

off the beaten path

Six Flags Magic Mountain – If you're a true thrill-seeker and roller-coaster fanatic, this anti-Disney amusement park, less than an hour north of L.A., is where you'll find several of the biggest, fastest, and scariest rides in the entire world. Their latest, the "floorless" Scream, drops you 150 feet and tears through a 128-foot vertical loop. On X, you start with a climb of 200 feet before dropping head-first at an 89-degree angle. Superman: The Escape is a 41-story coaster that hurtles you from 0 to 100 mph in under seven seconds. On Riddler's Revenge, the world's tallest and fastest stand-up roller coaster, you stand for a mile-long 65 mph total panic attack. As at other theme parks, there are shows and parades, along with rides for younger kids, to fill out a long day. Weekends are peak times here, so be prepared to stand in line for the more popular rides. (In warm weather, be sure you've got sunscreen and water.) You can beat the crowds by going on a weekday, or before or after the busy summer season. ⊠ *Magic Mountain Parkway, off I–5, 25 mi northwest of Universal Studios, Valencia* ☎ *661/255–4100* ⊕ *www.sixflags.com* ⊡ *$46.99* ⊙ *Mid-Mar.–mid-Sept., daily; mid-Sept.–early Mar., weekends and holidays; call for hrs.*

Pasadena Area

Although seemingly absorbed into the general Los Angeles sprawl, Pasadena is an altogether distinct city. It's full of noteworthy sights, from its significant residential architecture to its exceptional museums, particularly the Norton Simon and the Huntington Library, Art Collections, and Botanical Gardens. Where else can you see a Chaucer manuscript and rare cacti in one place?

To reach Pasadena from downtown Los Angeles, drive north on the Pasadena Freeway (I–110). From Hollywood and the San Fernando Valley use the Ventura Freeway (Highway 134, east), which cuts through Glendale, skirting the foothills, before arriving in Pasadena.

a good tour

A good place to start a short driving tour of Pasadena is on Orange Grove Boulevard ▶, a.k.a. Millionaire's Row, where wealthy Easterners built grand mansions. One example is the Wrigley Mansion at 391 South Orange Grove, an Italian Renaissance wedding cake of a house. To get there, take the Orange Grove exit off the Ventura Freeway (Highway 134); turn right at Orange Grove and travel five blocks. From the Pasadena Freeway (Highway 110), stay on the freeway until it ends at Arroyo Parkway. From Arroyo Parkway turn left at California Boulevard and then right at Orange Grove.

From the Wrigley Mansion, travel north on Orange Grove to Arroyo Terrace, where a left turn will take you into an architectural wonderland. Greene and Greene, the renowned Pasadena architects, designed all of the houses on Arroyo Terrace, as well as others in the area. To view their Craftsman masterpiece, the three-story, shingled **Gamble House ❶**, turn right on Westmoreland Place. Also in this section is the Frank Lloyd Wright–designed Millard House ("La Miniatura") on Prospect Crescent (from Westmoreland, turn left onto Rosemont Avenue, right on Prospect Terrace, and right onto Prospect Crescent to No. 645). The famous **Rose Bowl ❷** is nestled in a gully just to the west off Arroyo Boulevard. Leave this area via Rosemont Avenue, driving away from the hills to the south. From Rosemont, turn right onto Orange Grove Boulevard. Then, at Colorado Boulevard, turn left. Immediately on the left is the contemporary, austere **Norton Simon Museum ❸**, a familiar backdrop to so many viewers of the annual New Year's Day Tournament of Roses Parade. West of the museum, paralleling the modern freeway bridge,

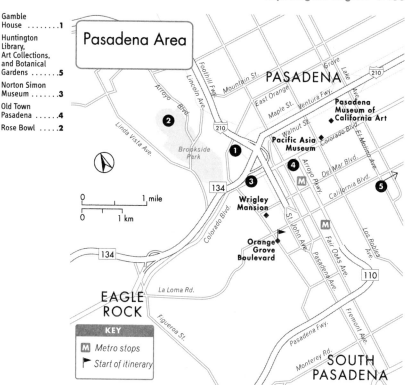

Pasadena Area

KEY

Ⓜ *Metro stops*

☛ *Start of itinerary*

Colorado crosses the historic concrete-arched Colorado Street Bridge, built in 1913, rising 160 feet above the Arroyo Seco gorge.

East of the Norton Simon Museum, you'll enter **Old Town Pasadena ④**. Walk around this section of Pasadena, heading east on Colorado. Just north of Colorado you'll find a couple of museums, the Pacific Asia Museum and the stark Pasadena Museum of California Art, on Los Robles Avenue and East Union Street, respectively. But you should save some museum energy for the phenomenal **Huntington Library, Art Collections, and Botanical Gardens ⑤**. The Huntington is in San Marino; to get there, drive south on El Molino to California Boulevard, where a left turn will take you into San Marino (signs point the way).

TIMING Get a late-morning or early afternoon start to see the important architectural sights on this tour; save Old Pasadena for last since it offers an outstanding evening street scene. Shops and restaurants stay open late in this relatively safe neighborhood and it's easy to find parking in nearby garages.

A stop at the Gamble House shouldn't take more than an hour, leaving plenty of time for an afternoon visit to the Norton Simon Museum. Unless you're planning on seeing a game or hitting the flea market, you may want to skip the Rose Bowl. Set aside most of a day for the Huntington—in summer, visit the gardens in the morning to avoid the midday heat. Keep in mind that many museums are closed Monday, though the Norton Simon is closed Tuesday.

What to See

★ ❶ **Gamble House.** Built by Charles and Henry Greene in 1908, this is a spectacular example of Craftsman-style bungalow architecture. The term "bungalow" can be misleading, since the Gamble House is a huge three-story home. To wealthy Easterners such as the Gambles (as in Procter & Gamble), this type of vacation home seemed informal compared with their larger mansions. The house showcases an incredible amount of hand craftsmanship, including a teak staircase and cabinetry, Greene-designed furniture, and an Emil Lange glass door. The dark exterior has broad eaves, with sleeping porches on the second floor. If you want to see more Greene and Greene homes in the neighborhood, buy a self-guided tour map in the Gamble House's bookstore. ⊠ *4 Westmoreland Pl., Pasadena* ☎ *626/793-3334* ⊕ *www.gamblehouse.org* ⊡ *$8* ☾ *Thurs.–Sun. noon–3, tickets go on sale at 10, 1-hr tour every 20 min.*

❺ **Huntington Library, Art Collections, and Botanical Gardens.** If you have time

Fodor'sChoice for only one stop in the Pasadena area, it should be the Huntington, built
★ in the early 1900s as the home of railroad tycoon Henry E. Huntington. Henry and his wife Arabella (previously his aunt by marriage) voraciously collected rare books and manuscripts, botanical specimens, and 18th-century British art. The institution they established became one of the most extraordinary cultural complexes in the world.

The Huntington Gallery, housed in the original 1911 Georgian mansion, holds a world-famous collection of British paintings, including the monumental *Sarah Siddons as the Tragic Muse,* by Joshua Reynolds, and John Constable's intimate *View on the Stour near Dedham.* In a too-cute pairing, Gainsborough's *Blue Boy* faces *Pinkie,* by Thomas Lawrence. American paintings and decorative arts are housed in the Virginia Steele Scott Gallery of American Art. The library contains more than 600,000 books and some 300 manuscripts, including such treasures as a Gutenberg Bible, the Ellesmere manuscript of Chaucer's *Canterbury Tales,* George Washington's genealogy in his own handwriting, scores of works by William Blake, and an unrivaled collection of early editions of Shakespeare. The estate grounds, now the Huntington Botanical Gardens, include a 12-acre Desert Garden, a Japanese Garden, a 3-acre rose garden, a Shakespeare garden, and more. ⊠ *1151 Oxford Rd., San Marino* ☎ *626/405-2100* ⊕ *www.huntington.org* ⊡ *$12.50, free 1st Thurs. of the month* ☾ *Tues.–Fri. noon–4:30, weekends 10:30–4:30.*

❸ **Norton Simon Museum.** Long familiar to television viewers of the New

Fodor'sChoice Year's Day Rose Parade, this brown, low-profile building is more than
★ just a background for the passing floats. It's one of the finest small museums anywhere, with an excellent collection that spans more than 2,000 years of Western and Asian art. It all began in the 1950s when Norton Simon (Hunt-Wesson Foods, McCalls Corporation, and Canada Dry) started collecting the works of Degas, Renoir, Gauguin, and Cézanne. His collection grew to include Old Masters, impressionists

and modern work from Europe, and Indian and Southeast Asian art. After he retired, Simon reorganized the failing Pasadena Art Institute and continued to assemble one of the world's finest collections. Today the Norton Simon Museum is richest in works by Rembrandt, Goya, Picasso, and most of all, Degas—this is one of the only two U.S. institutions to hold the complete set of the artist's model bronzes (the other is the Metropolitan Museum of Art, in New York). Renaissance, baroque, and rococo masterpieces include Raphael's profoundly spiritual *Madonna with Child with Book* (1503); Rembrandt's *Portrait of a Bearded Man in a Wide-Brimmed Hat* (1633); and a magical Tiepolo ceiling, *The Triumph of Virtue and Nobility Over Ignorance* (1740–50). The museum's collections of impressionist (van Gogh, Matisse, Cézanne, Monet, Renoir) and cubist (Braque, Gris) work are extensive. Several Rodin sculptures are placed throughout the museum. Head down to the bottom floor to see the phenomenal Southeast Asian and Indian sculptures and artifacts, where graceful pieces like a Ban Chiang blackware vessel date to earlier than 1,000 BC. Don't miss the living artwork outdoors: the garden, conceived by noted Southern California landscape designer Nancy Goslee Power. The tranquil pond was inspired by Monet's gardens at Giverny. ⊠ *411 W. Colorado Blvd., Pasadena* ☎ *626/449–6840* ⊕ *www.nortonsimon.org* ✎ *$6* ⊘ *Wed.–Thurs. and Sat.–Mon. noon–6, Fri. noon–9.*

❹ **Old Town Pasadena.** This area was revitalized in the 1990s as a blend of restored 19th-century brick and contemporary buildings. A phalanx of chain stores has moved in, but there are still some less-familiar shops and plenty of tempting cafés and restaurants. In the evenings and on weekends, streets are packed with people and Old Town crackles with energy. The 12-block historic district is anchored along Colorado Boulevard, between Pasadena Avenue and Arroyo Parkway.

❷ **Rose Bowl.** With an enormous rose, the city of Pasadena's logo, adorned on its exterior, it's hard to miss this 100,000-seat stadium, host of many Super Bowls and home to the UCLA Bruins and the L.A. Galaxy soccer team. Set in Brookside Park at the wide bottom of an arroyo, the facility is closed except during games and special events such as the monthly Rose Bowl Swap Meet, which is considered the granddaddy of West Coast flea markets. ⊠ *Rose Bowl Dr. at Rosemont Ave., Pasadena* ☎ *626/577–3100* ⊕ *www.rosebowlstadium.com* ✎ *$7–$20* ⊘ *Flea market, 2nd Sun. of the month 7–3.*

Long Beach

Long Beach, down at the tail end of Los Angeles County, was long stuck in limbo between Los Angeles and Orange County in the minds of visitors, but it's now rebuilding its place in the Southern California scheme. Founded as a seaside resort in the 19th century, Long Beach boomed in the early 20th century as oil discoveries drew in Midwesterners and Dust Bowlers. Bust followed boom, and for many years the city took on a somewhat raw, industrial, neglected feel. These days, however, a long-term redevelopment plan begun in the 1970s has finally come to fruition, and the city has turned back into a seaside destination.

Begin a tour of Long Beach at what is still the city's most famous attraction, the art deco ship the **Queen Mary** ▶. Then take the Queens Way Bridge back across the bay to the **Aquarium of the Pacific** and the Pike shopping area. From here, stops along Shoreline Drive at Rainbow Harbor or the colorfully painted waterfront shopping center, Shoreline Village, give the best views of the harbor and the Long Beach skyline. In the evening, head east along Ocean Boulevard to Alamitos Bay for a stroll through Naples, a picturesque enclave of canals and marinas.

TIMING   Guided tours of the *Queen Mary* last about an hour. If you've planned in advance, you could end the day with a sunset gondola cruise on the canals in Naples.

What to See

🐤 **Aquarium of the Pacific.** Sea lions, nurse sharks, octopuses, and . . . parrots. This aquarium focuses primarily on ocean life from the Pacific Ocean, with a detour into antipodean birds. The main exhibits include lively sea lions, a crowded tank of various sharks, and ethereal sea-dragons, which the aquarium has successfully bred in captivity. For a nonaquatic experience, head over to Lorikeet Forest, a walk-in aviary full of the friendliest parrots from Down Under. Purchase a cup of nectar and smile as you become a human bird perch. Since these birds spend most of their day feeding, you're guaranteed a noisy Lorikeet encounter—with all the trimmings. (A sink, soap, and towels are strategically placed at the exhibit exit.) ⊠ *100 Aquarium Way, Long Beach* ☎ *562/590–3100* ⊕ *www.aquariumofpacific.org* ⊠ *$18.95* ⊗ *Daily 9–6.*

▶ 🐤 **Queen Mary.** Very few places are able to make you feel as lost in time as this gracious passenger ship. Its teak decks, elegant parlors, and fading staterooms strongly evoke its art deco past. Built in Scotland and launched in 1934, it made 1,001 transatlantic crossings before finally berthing in Long Beach in 1967. The most substantial, informative tour is the one-hour Behind the Scenes visit, an extensive trek through the public and private areas of the ocean liner led by friendly, knowledgeable guides. The ship's neighbor, a geodesic dome originally built to house Howard Hughes's *Spruce Goose* aircraft, is now part of a terminal for Carnival Cruise Lines. ⊠ *Pier J, Long Beach* ☎ *562/435–3511* ⊕ *www.queenmary.com* ⊠ *$23 for self-guided tours; $28 for guided tours* ⊗ *Call for times and frequency of guided tours.*

WHERE TO EAT

Updated by Roger J. Grody

Celebrity is big business in Los Angeles, so it's no accident that the concept of the celebrity chef—emerging from an exhibition kitchen to schmooze with an equally illustrious clientele—is a key part of the city's dining scene. Wolfgang Puck, whose culinary empire of restaurants, food products, and cooking shows has made him a household name from Peoria to Portland, epitomizes this phenomenon. And L.A. keeps coming up with fresh stars to fill its ever-expanding universe of kitchens.

While Los Angeles doesn't pretend to rival New York in terms of high-end dining rooms, its strategic location contributes to a varied and innovative local cuisine. Local produce is a linchpin; fresh, seasonal ingredients are the bedrock of California cuisine. As one of the capitals of the Pacific Rim, L.A. also absorbs the culinary influences of its Asian communities. And the city's proximity to Latin America adds further depth, as local chefs incorporate ingredients indigenous to El Salvador, Colombia, and the rich culinary regions of Mexico.

	WHAT IT COSTS				
	$$$$	$$$	$$	$	¢
AT DINNER	over $30	$23–$30	$16–$22	$10–$15	under $10

Prices are for a main course at dinner, excluding 8.25% sales tax.

Downtown

AMERICAN/ CASUAL
¢
Fodor'sChoice
★
✕ **Philippe The Original.** Not only is this L.A.'s oldest restaurant (it opened in 1908), but it's reputedly where the French Dip sandwich originated. Here you can get one made with beef, pork, ham, lamb, or turkey on a freshly baked roll; the house hot mustard is as famous as the sandwiches. Philippe earns its reputation by maintaining its traditions, from sawdust on the floor to long, wooden tables where customers can sit and socialize. The home cooking includes hearty breakfasts, chili, pickled eggs, and an enormous pie selection. The best bargain: a cup of java for only 9¢. ✉ *1001 N. Alameda St., Downtown* ☎ *213/628–3781* ✍ *Reservations not accepted* ▭ *No credit cards.*

FRENCH
$$$$
Fodor'sChoice
★
✕ **Patina.** In a bold move, chef-restaurateur Joachim Splichal moved his flagship restaurant from Hollywood into downtown's striking Frank Gehry–designed Walt Disney Concert Hall. The contemporary space, surrounded by a rippled "curtain" of rich walnut, is an elegant, dramatic stage for the restaurant's acclaimed contemporary French cuisine. Specialties include seared foie gras with quince, champagne-vanilla bean risotto with lobster, braised veal cheeks with parsnip puree, and a *côte du boeuf* for two, carved tableside. In addition to gorgeous desserts, Patina offers a truly impressive cheese cart. ✉ *Walt Disney Concert Hall, 141 S. Grand Ave.* ☎ *213/972–3331* ✍ *Reservations essential* ▭ *AE, D, DC, MC, V* ◷ *No lunch weekends.*

$$–$$$ ✕ **Café Pinot.** One of Patina's more moderately priced siblings, this warm, convivial restaurant is housed in a contemporary pavilion adjacent to the garden of the historic Los Angeles Central Library. If the weather's cooperative, you can dine outside on the terrace, surrounded by old olive trees and skyscrapers; it offers one of downtown's most spectacular street-level views. The menu is sprinkled with traditional French bistro standards—classic onion soup, mustard-crusted rotisserie chicken—but also offers fresh fish, worthy pastas and contemporary Asian-inspired dishes. ✉ *700 W. 5th St., Downtown* ☎ *213/239–6500* ✍ *Reservations essential* ▭ *AE, D, DC, MC, V* ◷ *No lunch weekends.*

ITALIAN
★ $$–$$$$
✕ **Cicada.** Cicada, certainly one of the most romantic and architecturally remarkable dining venues in L.A., occupies the ground floor of the 1928 art deco Oviatt Building. The glass doors are Lalique, carved

Where to Stay &
Eat in Downtown
Los Angeles

maple columns soar two stories to a gold leaf ceiling, and from the balcony, a glamorous bar overlooks the spacious dining room. "Modern Italian" best describes the menu: as well as osso buco, there's ahi tuna carpaccio with wasabi caviar, shiitake gnocchi with mushroom ragout and port wine, and shrimp ravioli with asparagus in curry sauce. ⊠ *617 S. Olive St., Downtown* ☎ *213/488–9488* ⌂ *Reservations essential* 🖃 *AE, DC, MC, V* ☉ *Closed Sun. No lunch Sat.*

Hollywood

AMERICAN   ✕ **Musso & Frank Grill.** Liver and onions, lamb chops, goulash, shrimp Louis
$$–$$$$ salad—you'll find all the old favorites here in Hollywood's oldest restaurant. A film industry hangout since it opened in 1919, Musso & Frank still welcomes the working studio set to its maroon, faux-leather booths. Great breakfasts are served all day, but the kitchen's famous "flannel cakes" (pancakes) are served only 'til 3 PM. ⊠ *6667 Hollywood Blvd., Hollywood* ☎ *323/467–7788* 🖃 *AE, DC, MC, V* ☉ *Closed Sun. and Mon.*

CONTEMPORARY   ✕ **Vert.** Here Wolfgang Puck mixes traditional brasserie fare and con-
$–$$$ temporary California dishes in a fun, lively setting. Casual French classics like a *pissaladière* (a pizza-like tart) and *moules marinières* (mussels cooked with shallots and white wine) are served, along with grilled ahi

tuna and a hefty Gorgonzola-topped burger. Hidden in the monster Hollywood & Highland center, the restaurant has dining room walls covered with whimsical abstract art, and a bar that's backlit in the signature color (green). ⊠ *6801 Hollywood Blvd., Hollywood* ☎ *323/491–1300* ⚑ *Reservations essential* ▤ *AE, D,DC, MC,V.*

MIDDLE EASTERN ✕ **Zankou Chicken.** Zankou's aromatic, Armenian-style rotisserie chicken
¢   with perfectly crisp, golden skin—served with pita bread, veggies, hummus, and an unforgettable garlic sauce—is one of L.A.'s truly great budget meals. Zankou also serves kebabs, falafel, and sensational *shawarma* (spit-roasted lamb or chicken) plates. This fast-food oasis was even mentioned in a Beck song—and it should make you forget you ever met the Colonel. ⊠ *5065 W. Sunset Blvd., Hollywood* ☎ *323/665–7845* ⚑ *Reservations not accepted* ▤ *No credit cards.*

Los Feliz

ECLECTIC ✕ **Fred 62.** Fred Eric created this tongue-in-cheek take on the Ameri-
¢–$ can diner, where toasters sit on every table and the usual burgers and shakes are joined by choices like oxtail or tofu scrambles. Nobody's out of place here; everybody from buttoned-up businesspeople to tattooed musicians show up at some point during the 24/7 cycle. ⊠ *1850 N. Vermont Ave., Los Feliz* ☎ *323/667–0062* ⚑ *Reservations not accepted* ▤ *AE, DC, MC, V.*

INDIAN ✕ **Tantra.** As the name suggests, this is a very sexy place, accented with
$–$$ bold colors, dramatic silk lighting fixtures, and a hanging curtain of oxidized metal. But it's not just aesthetics that draw people here; the regional Indian cuisine is first-rate. The menu includes mango-and-cheese samosas, *kerela uttapam* (pancakes made with rice, lentils, and mint), shrimp masala, and a drink called *nimboo-paani* (sweetened lime juice with saffron); for dessert, don't miss the chocolate-filled samosas. The adjoining bar-lounge has become a popular local haunt. ⊠ *3705 Sunset Blvd., Silver Lake* ☎ *323/663–8268* ⚑ *Reservations essential* ▤ *AE, MC, V* ☉ *Closed Mon.*

MEXICAN ✕ **Yuca's Hut.** Blink and you might miss this place; its reputation far ex-
¢   ceeds its size. It's known for carne asada, carnitas, and *cochinita pibil* (Yucatán-style roasted pork) tacos and burritos. There's no chance of satisfying a late-night craving, though; it closes at 6 PM. ⊠ *2056 N. Hillhurst Ave., Los Feliz* ☎ *323/662–1214* ⚑ *Reservations not accepted* ▤ *No credit cards* ☉ *No dinner; closed Sun.*

Beverly Hills

CONTEMPORARY ✕ **Spago Beverly Hills.** Wolfgang Puck, the chef who helped define Cal-
★ $$$–$$$$ ifornia cuisine, closed his original Sunset Strip location in 2001 to open this more cosmopolitan venue. The casually elegant restaurant centers around an outdoor courtyard shaded by hundred-year-old olive trees, from which you can glimpse the exhibition kitchen and, on occasion, the affable chef–owner greeting his famous friends. (The people-watching at this quintessentially L.A. spot is worth the price of admission.) The daily-changing menu is likely to offer several renditions of foie gras,

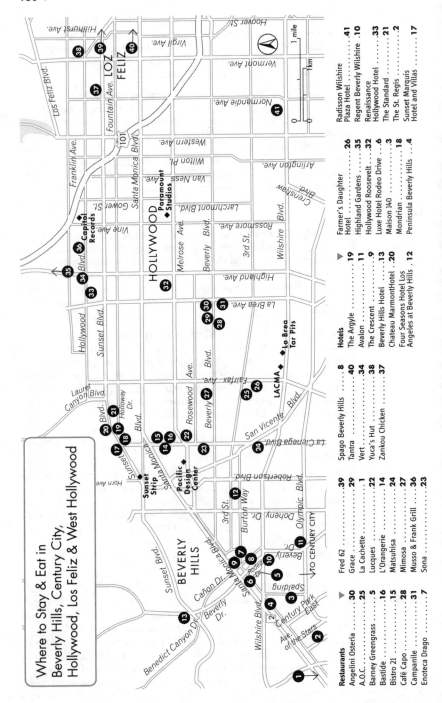

Where to Stay & Eat in Beverly Hills, Century City, Hollywood, Los Feliz & West Hollywood

Restaurants

Angelini Osteria	**30**
A.O.C.	**25**
Barney Greengrass	**5**
Bastide	**16**
Bistro 21	**15**
Café Capo	**28**
Campanile	**31**
Enoteca Drago	**7**
Fred 62	**39**
Grace	**29**
La Cachette	**22**
Lucques	**14**
L'Orangerie	**24**
Matsuhisa	**27**
Mimosa	**36**
Musso & Frank Grill	**23**
Sona	
Spago Beverly Hills	**8**
Tantra	**40**
Vert	**34**
Yuca's Hut	**38**
Zankou Chicken	**37**

Hotels

▶ The Argyle	**19**
Avalon	**11**
The Crescent	**9**
Beverly Hills Hotel	**13**
Chateau Marmont Hotel	**20**
Four Seasons Hotel Los Angeles at Beverly Hills	**12**
Farmer's Daughter Hotel	**26**
Highland Gardens	**35**
Hollywood Roosevelt	**32**
Luxe Hotel Rodeo Drive	**6**
Maison 140	**3**
Mondrian	**18**
Peninsula Beverly Hills	**4**
Radisson Wilshire Plaza Hotel	**41**
Regent Beverly Wilshire	**10**
Renaissance Hollywood Hotel	**33**
The Standard	**21**
The St. Regis	**2**
Sunset Marquis Hotel and Villas	**17**

pan-roasted halibut in a saffron-champagne sauce, Cantonese-style roasted duck with wild huckleberries, and some traditional Austrian specialties—plus incredible finales from acclaimed pastry chef Sherry Yard. ⊠ *176 N. Cañon Dr., Beverly Hills* ☎ *310/385–0880* ⌕ *Reservations essential* ⊟ *AE, D, DC, MC, V* ☺ *No lunch Sun.*

DELICATESSENS ✕ **Barney Greengrass.** This *haute* deli on the fifth floor of Barneys has
¢–$$ an appropriately high-class aesthetic: limestone floors, mahogany furniture, and a wall of windows. At tables shaded by large umbrellas on the outdoor terrace, you can savor flawless smoked salmon, sturgeon, and whitefish flown in fresh from New York. This deli keeps store hours, closing Thursday at 8, Sunday at 6, and every other day at 7. ⊠ *Barneys, 9570 Wilshire Blvd., Beverly Hills* ☎ *310/777–5877* ⊟ *AE, DC, MC, V.*

ITALIAN ✕ **Enoteca Drago.** Prominent chef–restaurateur Celestino Drago and his
★ ¢–$$ brothers have introduced a stylish but casual eatery—an *enoteca* is essentially a wine bar serving small tapas-like plates—that's a surefire recipe for fun. In addition to 50 Italian wines by the glass, the menu offers a plethora of shareable dishes, such as addictive deep-fried olives, beef carpaccio with mustard dressing, chicken liver mousse with crostini, miniature wild mushroom ravioli with foie gras–truffle sauce, and even some fine thin-crust pizzas. It's open for breakfast, too. ⊠ *410 N. Cañon Dr.* ☎ *310/786–8236* ⌕ *Reservations essential* ⊟ *AE, D, DC, MC, V.*

JAPANESE ✕ **Matsuhisa.** Freshness and innovation are the hallmarks at this flag-
★ $$$–$$$$ ship restaurant of superchef Nobu Matsuhisa's growing empire. It's surprisingly inelegant for such a famous venue (it lacks table linens, fashionable lighting, and art, and it looks like any suburban sushi bar), but the cuisine is opulent and artistic. Here you'll encounter such dishes as caviar-capped tuna stuffed with black truffles, foie gras sushi, and monkfish liver pâté wrapped in gold leaf. Reflecting his experience working as a sushi chef in Peru and Argentina, Matsuhisa often incorporates exotic Latin ingredients into traditional Japanese cuisine. ⊠ *129 N. La Cienega Blvd., Beverly Hills* ☎ *310/659–9639* ⌕ *Reservations essential* ⊟ *AE, DC, MC, V* ☺ *No lunch weekends.*

Century City

FRENCH ✕ **La Cachette.** A *cachette* is a little, secret hiding place, or in this case,
$$–$$$ a sumptuous, flower-laden setting in which to enjoy both classic and modern French fare. Among chef–owner Jean-François Meteigner's deftly prepared and smartly presented dishes are a buttery foie gras terrine seasoned with black pepper and Muscat wine, blackened swordfish with wasabi-mustard emulsion, and venison in blueberry sauce. The traditional cassoulet and bouillabaisse are also excellent. ⊠ *10506 Santa Monica Blvd., Century City* ☎ *310/470–4992* ⌕ *Reservations essential* ⊟ *AE, D, DC, MC, V* ☺ *No lunch weekends.*

West Hollywood

CONTEMPORARY ✕ **Campanile.** In what was once Charlie Chaplin's office complex,
★ $$$–$$$$ chef–owner Mark Peel and wife Nancy Silverton blend robust Mediter-

ranean flavors with those of down-home American cooking. Appetizers may include brandade-filled agnolotti in saffron broth, or spicy octopus salad; among the entrées are braised veal short ribs, grilled prime rib with black-olive tepenade, and roasted pork loin with braised fennel, roasted cherries, and bitter-almond pesto. The desserts here are some of the best anywhere (Silverton is the founder of adjacent La Brea Bakery)—try the light-as-a-feather *panna cotta* (an Italian variation on caramel custard) or the all-American cobbler. For an ultimate-L.A. experience, have weekend brunch on the enclosed patio. ⊠ *624 S. La Brea Ave., Miracle Mile* ☎ *323/938–1447* ⌂ *Reservations essential* ▱ *AE, D, DC, MC, V* ⊙ *No dinner Sun.*

★ **$$$–$$$$** ✕ **Sona.** Intense, innovative chef David Myers and wife Michelle (former pastry chef at Patina) deliver memorable gastronomic experiences here. The prix-fixe tasting menus are especially popular, since they allow you to try several of Myers's unique dishes. An occasional item may strike you as fussy or contrived, but most of the choices are top-notch. If you're lucky, they may include *hamachi* (yellowtail) sashimi, foie gras with Asian pear, or cod and Spanish cuttlefish with white-bean puree. ⊠ *401 N. La Cienega Blvd., West Hollywood* ☎ *310/659–7708* ⌂ *Reservations essential* ▱ *AE, D, DC, MC, V* ⊙ *Closed Sun. and Mon. No lunch.*

$$–$$$$ ✕ **Grace.** After years of moving through the city's top kitchens, chef Neal Fraser is doing his best cooking yet in a place of his own. He mixes contrasting flavors and textures in dishes like risotto with pumpkin, sea urchin, and sweet shrimp; wild boar with Savoy cabbage, Yukon potato spaetzle, and violet mustard sauce; and duck with baby bok choy, rosemary risotto cake, and carrot-ginger emulsion. ⊠ *7360 Beverly Blvd., south of West Hollywood* ☎ *323/934–4400* ⌂ *Reservations essential* ▱ *AE, MC, V* ⊙ *Closed Mon. No lunch.*

★ **$$–$$$$** ✕ **Lucques.** This historic brick building, once silent-film star Harold Lloyd's carriage house, has morphed into a chic restaurant that's a big hit with the younger, well-heeled set. Chef Suzanne Goin works magic here using an intriguing variety of vegetables; among the choices are a wild mushroom salad with dandelion, hazelnuts, and pecorino; lamb carpaccio with artichoke fritters and olive aioli; pancetta-wrapped trout with sorrel, fennel gratin, *verjus,* and crushed grapes; and braised beef short ribs with horseradish cream. ⊠ *8474 Melrose Ave., West Hollywood* ☎ *323/655–6277* ⌂ *Reservations essential* ▱ *AE, D, DC, MC, V* ⊙ *Closed Mon. No lunch.*

$$–$$$ ✕ **Bistro 21.** In L.A. it's not unusual to strike gold in a minimall; this restaurant is proof of that. The refined decor has subtle Japanese inflections; likewise, chef Koichiro Kikuchi infuses his classical-French dishes with Asian elements. For instance, you might find seared foie gras with braised daikon or salmon with curried yogurt. ⊠ *846 N. La Cienega Blvd., West Hollywood* ☎ *310/967–0021* ⌂ *Reservations essential* ▱ *AE, MC, V* ⊙ *Closed Mon. No lunch.*

FRENCH   ✕ **Bastide.** *Bastide* may be the word for farmhouse in southern France, **$$$$**   but there's nothing rustic about this intimate, graceful restaurant. New FodorśChoice   chef Ludovic Lefebvre, formerly of L'Orangerie, introduces a more con- ★   temporary menu that is seriously French but boldly original . . . and fun. You'll find plenty of foie gras and silky sauces here, but the dynamic young "Ludo" incorporates exotic spices (e.g., lemongrass, tamarind, green tea) into some of his memorable creations. Try for a table on the olive tree–shaded patio. ⊠ *8475 Melrose Pl., West Hollywood* ☎ *323/ 651–5950* ⚲ *Reservations essential* ▤ *AE, DC, MC, V* ⊘ *Closed Sun. and Mon. No lunch.*

★ **$$$$** ✕ **L'Orangerie.** This extravagantly formal restaurant is the closest L.A. gets to a Michelin–three-star dining room. The regal setting, with is soaring French doors and dramatic flower arrangements, taps into the spirit of Versailles—and is the perfect place to celebrate a special occasion. Specialties include foie gras terrine with spiced pear and apple chutney, salt-crusted chicken perfumed with tarragon and chervil, and roasted squab with quince, wild mushrooms, and roasted chestnuts. ⊠ *903 N. La Cienega Blvd., West Hollywood* ☎ *310/652–9770* ⚲ *Reservations essential* ▤ *AE, D, DC, MC, V* ⊘ *Closed Mon. No lunch.*

★ **$–$$$** ✕ **Mimosa.** If you're craving a classic Provençal meal, chef Jean-Pierre Bosc's menu satisfies. You can choose from *salade Lyonnaise*, served with its poached egg; a wonderful tomato tarte tatin; a generous charcuterie plate, bouillabaisse, and fillet of sole *au pistou* (with basil-garlic paste). The bistro-style dining room has mustard walls, cozy banquettes, and jars of olives and cornichons delivered to every table upon arrival. ⊠ *8009 Beverly Blvd., West Hollywood* ☎ *323/655–8895* ▤ *AE, DC, MC, V* ⊘ *Closed Sun. and Mon. No lunch.*

ITALIAN ✕ **Angelini Osteria.** You might not guess it from the modest, somewhat
$$–$$$$ congested dining room, but this is one of L.A.'s most celebrated Italian
Fodor'sChoice restaurants. The key is in owner–chef Gino Angelini's thoughtful use of
★ superb ingredients, evident in dishes such as fresh anchovies with artichokes and beets; pumpkin tortellini with butter, sage, and asparagus; and an awesome lasagna. Whole branzino (a type of sea bass) crusted in sea salt, and unusual specials like veal kidneys with white wine and onions, are consistently impressive. An intelligent selection of mostly Italian wines compliments the menu. ⊠ *7313 Beverly Blvd., Beverly-La Brea* ☎ *323/297–0070* ▤ *AE, MC, V* ⊘ *Closed Mon. No lunch weekends.*

$$–$$$$ ✕ **Café Capo.** With generously-spaced tables topped with crisp white linen and tall candles, Café Capo is a stylish, seductive venue. The room's vibrant contemporary art is rivaled by artistic presentations of sophisticated dishes such as foie gras terrine or Maine lobster risotto, but rustic Italian specialties (e.g. gnocchi in Gorgonzola cream, lamb osso buco) and American comfort foods like butter-tender short ribs and hearty steaks—all served with marvelous produce direct from the farmers market—dominate the menu. An eclectic, globetrotting wine list complements the diverse fare. ⊠ *7450 Beverly Blvd., south of West Hollywood* ☎ *323/857–0660* ⚲ *Reservations essential* ▤ *AE, DC, MC, V* ⊘ *Closed Sun. No lunch.*

MEDITERRANEAN ✕ **A.O.C.** This trendy, versatile spot has practically changed the way An-
¢–$$ gelenos dine. It's dominated by a long, candle-laden wine bar serving
Fodor'sChoice more than 50 vintages by the glass. There's also an L.A. rarity, a char-
★ cuterie bar. The small-plates menu is perfectly calibrated for the wine list; you could pick a salt cod–potato gratin or an indulgent slab of pork *rillettes*, or just plunge into one of the city's best cheese selections.

⊠ *8022 W. 3rd St., south of West Hollywood* ☎ *323/653–6359* ⌕ *Reservations essential* ▤ *AE, MC, V* ☉ *No lunch.*

West Los Angeles

AMERICAN/
CASUAL

✕ **The Apple Pan.** Since 1947, this unassuming joint with its horseshoe-shaped counter—no tables here—has been a mecca for burger-lovers.

★ ¢ The cheeseburger topped with Tillamook cheddar is mouthwatering, as is the hickory burger with barbecue sauce. You'll also find fab fries and, of course, an apple pie good enough to name a restaurant after (although many regulars would argue the banana cream deserves the honor). Be prepared to wait. ⊠ *10801 W. Pico Blvd., West L.A.* ☎ *310/475–3585* ⌕ *Reservations not accepted* ▤ *No credit cards* ☉ *Closed Mon.*

INDIAN
¢–$$

✕ **Bombay Cafe.** Some of the dishes here are strictly authentic, others have been lightened up a bit to suit Southern California sensibilities, and a few are truly innovative. Regulars (and there are many) swear by the chile-laden lamb frankies (burritolike snacks sold by vendors on the beaches of Bombay) and *sev puri* (wafers topped with onions, potatoes, and chutneys). ⊠ *12021 Pico Blvd., West L.A.* ☎ *310/473–3388* ▤ *MC, V* ☉ *No lunch weekends.*

MEXICAN
¢–$$

✕ **La Serenata Gourmet.** Crowding into this Westside branch of the East L.A. original can be a bit claustrophobic, but the restaurant scores points for its flavorful Mexican cuisine. Moles and pork dishes are delicious, but seafood is the real star—there are chubby *gorditas* (cornmeal pockets stuffed with shrimp), juicy fish enchiladas, and a soupy ceviche that sings with flavor. If your experience with Mexican food has been on the Tex-Mex end of the spectrum, come here to broaden your horizons. ⊠ *10924 W. Pico Blvd., West L.A.* ☎ *310/441–9667* ⌕ *Reservations not accepted* ▤ *AE, D, MC, V.*

Santa Monica

CONTEMPORARY
$$$–$$$$

✕ **Chinois on Main.** A once-revolutionary outpost in Wolfgang Puck's repertoire, this is still one of L.A.'s most crowded restaurants—and one of the noisiest. The jazzy interior is just as loud as the clientele. The happy marriage of Asian and French cuisines yields seasonal dishes such as grilled Mongolian lamb chops with wok-fried vegetables, Shanghai lobster with spicy ginger-curry sauce, and Cantonese duck with fresh plum sauce. ⊠ *2709 Main St., Santa Monica* ☎ *310/392–9025* ⌕ *Reservations essential* ▤ *AE, D, DC, MC, V* ☉ *No lunch Sat.–Tues.*

★ $$–$$$

✕ **Röckenwagner.** Local celebrity chef Hans Röckenwagner has been around since the mid-1980s, but he hasn't missed a step. In 2003 the restaurant's Frank Gehry–designed building was revamped to hold two dining areas: a casual brasserie and a smaller, more formal space. Hit the brasserie for hearty dishes such as veal goulash with spaetzle and braised pork belly with red cabbage. The other dining room's prix-fixe menus highlight the sharp, contemporary California-French cooking that made Röckenwagner's reputation. ⊠ *2435 Main St., Santa Monica* ☎ *310/399–6504* ⌕ *Reservations essential* ▤ *AE, DC, MC, V* ☉ *No lunch.*

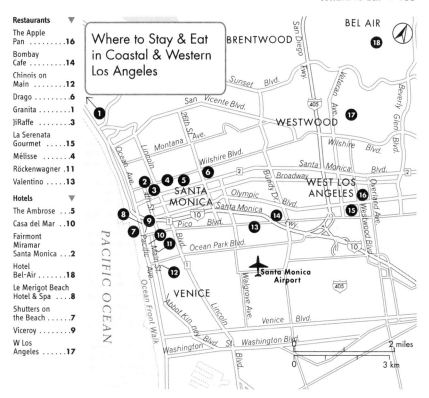

Where to Stay & Eat
in Coastal & Western
Los Angeles

★ **$$–$$$** ✕ **JiRaffe.** The gleaming, wood-paneled, two-story dining room with ceiling-high windows is as handsome here as the menu is tasteful. Seasonal appetizers include goat cheese, leek, and roasted-tomato ravioli, and a roasted-beet salad with caramelized walnuts and dried Bing cherries. Main dishes, like crispy-skinned salmon with parsnip puree, braised fennel, and a sweet balsamic reduction, are also memorable. ✉ *502 Santa Monica Blvd., Santa Monica* ☎ *310/917–6671* ⌖ *Reservations essential* ▤ *AE, DC, MC, V* ⊗ *No lunch Sat.–Mon.*

FRENCH ✕ **Mélisse.** In a city where informality reigns, this place offers a dressy—
$$$$ but never stuffy—dining experience. A crystal chandelier hangs in the main
Fodor'sChoice dining room; the garden room has a stone fountain and a retractable roof.
★ Chef–owner Josiah Citrin enriches his modern French menu with seasonal California produce; choices include salsify soup with black truffle mousse, Maine lobster with a carrot emulsion, and duck with blood-orange glaze. There's also tableside cheese service. Although jackets aren't required, they are definitely preferred. ✉ *1104 Wilshire Blvd., Santa Monica* ☎ *310/ 395–0881* ⌖ *Reservations essential* ▤ *AE, D, DC, MC, V* ⊗ *No lunch.*

ITALIAN ✕ **Valentino.** Among the nation's best Italian restaurants, Valentino also
★ **$$–$$$$** has one of the top wine lists; its cellar contains more than 200,000 bottles. In the 1980s, suave owner Piero Selvaggio introduced L.A. to his

exquisite modern Italian cuisine, including risotto with white truffles, spaghetti with garlic and *bottarga* (tuna roe), and grilled squab in honey–fig–red wine sauce—and he's been pulling in crowds ever since. ⊠ *3115 Pico Blvd., Santa Monica* ☎ *310/829–4313* ⌁ *Reservations essential* ▤ *AE, DC, MC, V* ⊗ *Closed Sun. No lunch Sat. and Mon.–Thurs.*

$–$$$ ✕ **Drago.** Native Sicilian Celestino Drago's home-style fare is carefully prepared and attentively served here in stark designer surroundings. The menu adds sophisticated finesse to rustic dishes like pappardelle with pheasant-morel mushroom sauce, squid-ink risotto, and lamb loin with garlic sauce. ⊠ *2628 Wilshire Blvd., Santa Monica* ☎ *310/828–1585* ▤ *AE, DC, MC, V* ⊗ *No lunch weekends.*

Malibu

CONTEMPORARY
$$–$$$$

✕ **Granita.** Wolfgang Puck's famed Granita is a glamorous—some call it garish—fantasy world of handmade tiles embedded with seashells, blown-glass lighting fixtures, and an exotic koi pond. The beachside location underscores the marine motif, as does chef Jennifer Naylor's seafood-focused menu. Bouillabaisse, grouper with sweet lemon–garlic nage, and bigeye tuna with shiitake-plum wine glaze are among the choices. Nonoceanic options might include Cantonese duck and rib-eye steak. ⊠ *23725 W. Malibu Rd., Malibu* ☎ *310/456–0488* ⌁ *Reservations essential* ▤ *D, DC, MC, V* ⊗ *Closed Mon. No lunch weekdays.*

Pasadena

CHINESE
$–$$$
Fodor's Choice
★

✕ **Yujean Kang's Gourmet Chinese Cuisine.** Forget any and all preconceived notions of what Chinese food should look and taste like—Kang's cuisine is nouvelle Chinese. Tender slices of veal are served on a bed of enoki mushrooms, and topped with a tangle of quick-fried shoestring yams; sea bass is paired with kumquats and passion-fruit sauce. Even traditional dishes, such as the crispy sesame beef, are a revelation here. The sweet bean curd crepes or delicate Mandarin orange cheesecake are the perfect way to end your meal. ⊠ *67 N. Raymond Ave., Pasadena* ☎ *626/585–0855* ▤ *AE, D, DC, MC, V* ⊗ *No lunch weekends.*

CONTEMPORARY
★ **$$$–$$$$**

✕ **The Dining Room.** Until the arrival of charismatic young chef Craig Strong, there wasn't much to say about this high-priced hotel restaurant. But Strong, a perfectionist whose bosses indulge him with the finest ingredients, put it on the map. His five-course tasting menus are filled with surprises, like seared foie gras with foie gras–pineapple ravioli, strawberry (yes, strawberry) gazpacho with langoustines, and poached Maine lobster with orange-curry sauce. ⊠ *Ritz-Carlton Huntington Hotel & Spa, 1401 S. Oak Knoll Ave., Pasadena* ☎ *626/577–2867* ▤ *AE, D, DC, MC, V* ⊗ *No lunch. Closed Sun. and Mon.*

INDIAN
¢–$

✕ **All India Cafe.** Old Pasadena may be the last place you'd expect to find an authentic Indian restaurant, but authentic this is. Ingredients are fresh and flavors bold without relying on overpowering spiciness. Start with the *bhel puri,* a savory puffed rice-and-potatoes dish. In addition to meat curries and *tikkas,* there are many vegetarian selections and some hard-to-find items such as the burritolike frankies, a favorite Bombay street food. The prices are as palatable as the meals. ⊠ *39 S. Fair Oaks Ave., Pasadena* ☎ *626/440–0309* ⊟ *AE, MC, V.*

ITALIAN ✕ **Trattoria Tre Venezie.** To get noticed in this town, an Italian restaurant
$$–$$$$ has to be special. This one does it by excelling in specialties from a trio of Italy's northernmost regions along the Austrian border, collectively referred to as *Tre Venezie.* Appetizers include *fegato grasso* (foie gras), swordfish carpaccio and poppy-seed ravioli filled with red beets; a great entrée choice is the house-smoked, pan-roasted pork chop served with sauerkraut and Gorgonzola sauce. ⊠ *119 W. Green St., Pasadena* ☎ *626/795–4455* ⊟ *AE, DC, MC, V* ☉ *Closed Mon. No lunch Tues. and weekends.*

WHERE TO STAY

Updated by Kathy A. McDonald

Los Angeles is a town of excess, and there's no shortage of decadent palaces where you can rest your head. But whether you're going high-style or budget, make sure to consider location when selecting your hotel. Planning to hit the beach? Give some thought to Santa Monica. Want to stay out late and enjoy L.A.'s legendary nightlife? Stay in West Hollywood or the Hollywood Boulevard area. For upscale and posh, you can't do better than Beverly Hills. In Pasadena you can enjoy the charm of Old Town and some of the best public gardens in the area. If you are seeking high culture, downtown is the place to stay.

WHAT IT COSTS					
	$$$$	$$$	$$	$	¢
FOR 2 PEOPLE	over $250	$176–$250	$121–$175	$90–$120	under $90

Prices are for a standard double room in high season, excluding 9%–14% tax.

Downtown

$$$$ ▦ **New Otani Hotel and Garden.** "Japanese Experience" rooms at the New Otani have tatami mats, futon beds, extra-deep bathtubs, and shoji screens on the windows. The American-style rooms are somewhat plain, but you can liven them up with a tea service and shiatsu massage. Two of the restaurants serve authentic Japanese cuisine; a third has continental fare. The hotel is on the edge of Little Tokyo. If you're looking for a sanctuary or just a Kodak moment, visit the ½-acre Japanese garden on the roof. ⊠ *120 S. Los Angeles St., Little Tokyo 90012* ☎ *213/629–1200 or 800/639–6826* 🖷 *213/622–0980* ⊕ *www.newotani.com* ⬎ *416 rooms, 20 suites ⌂ 3 restaurants, room service, in-room data ports, in-room safes, minibars, cable TV with movies, gym, hot tub, massage, sauna, 2 bars, shops, dry cleaning, laundry service, concierge, Internet, business services, meeting rooms, car rental, parking (fee), no-smoking rooms* ⊟ *AE, D, DC, MC, V.*

★ $$$ ▦ **Hilton Checkers Los Angeles.** Opened as the Mayflower Hotel in 1927, Checkers retains much of its original character; its various size rooms all have charming period details, although they also have modern luxuries like pillow-top mattresses, coffeemakers, 24-hour room service, and cordless phones. The rooftop pool deck overlooks the L.A. library and nearby office towers. The plush lobby bar and lounge look like they belong in a private club, with comfy leather chairs and a large plasma-screen TV. In the mornings, a complimentary car service can drive you anywhere within a 2-mi radius. ⊠ *535 S. Grand Ave., Downtown 90071* ☎ *213/624–0000 or 800/445–8667* 🖷 *213/626–9906* ⊕ *www. hiltoncheckers.com* ⌨ *188 rooms, 9 suites* ♨ *Restaurant, room service, in-room data ports, minibars, cable TV with movies and video games, pool, gym, outdoor hot tub, massage, sauna, spa, steam room, bar, library, baby-sitting, dry cleaning, laundry service, concierge, Internet, business services, meeting room, parking (fee), some pets allowed (fee), no-smoking rooms* ▤ *AE, D, DC, MC, V.*

$$$ 🏨 **Millennium Biltmore Hotel.** This elegant, gilded beaux arts masterpiece has a storied past. The lobby (formerly the Music Room) was the head-quarters of J.F.K.'s presidential campaign, and the ballroom hosted some of the earliest Academy Awards. These days, the Biltmore draws business types with its central downtown location and ample meeting spaces. Guest rooms are classically styled with upholstered headboards, shuttered windows, and marble bathrooms, plus up-to-date amenities like CD players and cordless phones. Stay on the Club Level for excellent views and complimentary breakfast and evening cocktails. And bring your bathing suit for the vintage tiled indoor pool and adjacent steam room. ⊠ *506 S. Grand Ave., Downtown 90071* ☎ *213/624–1011 or 800/245–8673* 🖷 *213/612–1545* ⊕ *www.millenniumhotels.com* ⌨ *683 rooms, 56 suites* ♨ *3 restaurants, 2 cafés, room service, in-room data ports, in-room safes, minibars, cable TV with movies and video games, indoor pool, health club, hair salon, hot tub, massage, sauna, steam room, 3 bars, lobby lounge, sports bar, piano, shops, babysitting, laundry service, concierge, concierge floor, Internet, business services, convention center, car rental, parking (fee), no-smoking floors* ▤ *AE, D, DC, MC, V.*

$$ 🏨 **Inn at 657.** Proprietor Patsy Carter provides a homey, welcoming atmosphere at her intimate bed-and-breakfast–style inn near the University of Southern California. Rooms in this 1904 Craftsman have down comforters, Oriental silks on the walls, and needlepoint rugs. The vintage dining room table seats 12; conversation is encouraged. You are welcome to hang out with the hummingbirds in the private garden. All rooms includes a hearty breakfast, homemade cookies, and free local phone calls. ⊠ *657 W. 23rd St., Downtown 90007* ☎ *213/741–2200 or 800/ 347–7512* ⊕ *www.patsysinn657.com* ⌨ *11 rooms* ♨ *Dining room, in-room data ports, some microwaves, refrigerators, cable TV, in-room VCRs, outdoor hot tub, laundry service, business services, free parking; no smoking* ▤ *MC, V* ⋈| *BP.*

$–$$ 🏨 **The Standard Downtown L.A.** Originally constructed in 1955 as an oil company's headquarters, the Standard Downtown's modernist building was completely revamped under the sharp eye of owner André Balazs. The large guest rooms are practical and funky: all have orange built-in couches; windows that actually open; and platform beds. (Some also have large plush toys in the shape of human feet—not particularly practical, but definitely funky). Bathrooms have extra-large tubs, which you can

Fodor's Choice
★

fill with Mr. Bubble from the minibar. The rooftop lounge, surrounded by skyscrapers, is *the* most happening downtown bar. Daytime traffic and the nightly bar scene make some rooms noisy. ⊠ *550 S. Flower St., Downtown 90071* ☎ *213/892–8080* 🖷 *213/892–8686* ⊕ *www. standardhotel.com* ⟳ *205 rooms, 2 suites* ⌂ *Restaurant, room service, in-room data ports, in-room safes, minibars, cable TV with movies and video games, pool, gym, massage, 2 bars, lobby lounge, dry cleaning, laundry service, concierge, Internet, business services, meeting rooms, parking (fee), some pets allowed, no-smoking rooms* ⊟ *AE, D, DC, MC, V.*

Hollywood

$$$ 🖫 **Hollywood Roosevelt Hotel.** The Spanish tiles, painted ceilings, arches, and other historic details in this hotel's Spanish Colonial Revival main building recall early Hollywood glamour. The hotel was the site of the first Academy Awards ceremony in 1929; photos of Tinseltown luminaries throughout honor that golden age. Sophisticated rooms have contemporary platform beds and fine linens; poolside facing rooms have dark-wood furnishings and comfy, curtain-draped beds. All overlook the David Hockney–painted pool, with its playful, curvy design. The Hollywood & Highland entertainment complex is across Hollywood Boulevard. On the lower level, Feinstein's at the Cinegrill presents cabaret and jazz most nights in a acoustically ideal setting. ⊠ *7000 Hollywood Blvd., Hollywood 90028* ☎ *323/466–7000 or 800/950–7667* 🖷 *323/462–8056* ⊕ *www.hollywoodroosevelt.com* ⟳ *305 rooms, 48 suites* ⌂ *2 restaurants, room service, in-room data-ports, in-room safes, minibars, cable TV with movies and video games, pool, gym, outdoor hot tub, massage, 3 bars, lobby lounge, cabaret, shops, dry cleaning, laundry service, concierge, Internet, business services, meeting rooms, parking (fee), no-smoking rooms* ⊟ *AE, D, DC, MC, V.*

$$$ 🖫 **Radisson Wilshire Plaza Hotel.** The ordinary, no-frills rooms here have all the necessary amenities: there are oak desks and armoires, and floor-to-ceiling windows with views of Hollywood. Rooms on the business floor are virtual offices with fax/copier/printers and two-line phones. L.A.'s best Korean restaurants and spas are nearby. Across the street is a Red Line station, with convenient service to downtown and Hollywood. A limo rental service is available on-site. ⊠ *3515 Wilshire Blvd., Mid-Wilshire 90010* ☎ *213/381–7411 or 800/333–3333* 🖷 *213/386–7379* ⊕ *www.radwilshire.com* ⟳ *380 rooms, 13 suites* ⌂ *3 restaurants, café, room service, in-room data ports, some in-room faxes, minibars, cable TV, pool, gym, hair salon, lobby lounge, shop, laundry service, concierge, Internet, business services, meeting room, car rental, parking (fee), no-smoking rooms* ⊟ *AE, D, DC, MC, V.*

$$–$$$ 🖫 **Renaissance Hollywood Hotel.** Part of the massive Hollywood & Highland entertainment complex, this 20-story hotel is at the center of the action. Contemporary art (notably by L.A. favorites Charles and Ray Eames), retro '60s furniture, terrazzo floors, and a Zen rock garden greet you in the lobby. Rooms are vibrant, with bright-red chairs and molded blue plastic lamps. Blackout shades keep the fierce sun at bay. For the ultimate party pad, book the Panorama Suite, with angled floor-to-ceiling windows, vintage Eames furniture, a grand piano, and a sunken Jacuzzi tub with a view. ⊠ *1755 N. Highland Ave., Hollywood 90028* ☎ *323/ 856–1200 or 800/468–3571* 🖷 *323/856–1205* ⊕ *www. renaissancehollywood.com* 🗗 *604 rooms, 33 suites* ⚘ *Restaurant, room service, in-room data ports, in-room safes, minibars, cable TV with movies and video games, pool, gym, 2 bars, shop, babysitting, dry cleaning, laundry service, concierge, concierge floor, Internet, business services, convention center, parking (fee), no-smoking rooms* ☰ *AE, D, DC, MC, V.*

$ 🏨 **Farmer's Daughter Hotel.** Country style is the name of the game at this smartly updated motor hotel: rooms are upholstered in blue gingham with denim beaspreads, and staff members all wear overalls. A curving blue wall secludes the interior courtyard, complete with teak patio furniture and open-air lobby. Rooms are snug but outfitted with whimsical original art and high-tech amenities such as CD and DVD players. It's a favorite of TV's *Price is Right* hopefuls; the show tapes at CBS's nearby studios. The Grove, L.A.'s outdoor shopping-and-entertainment megamall, and the cheap eats of the Farmers Market are directly across Fairfax Avenue. ⊠ *115 S. Fairfax Ave., between Hollywood and West Hollywood, 90036* ☎ *323/937–3930 or 800/334–1658* 🖷 *323/932–1608* ⊕ *www.farmersdaughterhotel.com* 🗗 *63 rooms, 2 suites* ⚘ *In-room data ports, in-room safes, refrigerators, cable TV, in-room VCRs, pool, babysitting, dry cleaning, laundry service, concierge, Internet, meeting room, car rental, free parking, some pets allowed (fee); no smoking rooms.* ☰ *AE, D, DC, MC, V.*

¢ 🏨 **Highland Gardens Hotel.** A large, sparkling pool and a lush, if somewhat overgrown, tropical garden sets this hotel apart from other budget lodgings. Basic but spacious units have either two queen-size beds, or a king bed with a queen-size sleeper sofa, plus a desk and sitting area with Formica tables. Rooms facing busy Franklin Avenue are noisy; ask for one facing the courtyard. The hotel is just blocks from the Walk of Fame and a few minutes' drive off the Sunset Strip. ⊠ *7047 Franklin Ave., Hollywood 90028* ☎ *323/850–0536 or 800/404–5472* 🖷 *323/ 850–1712* ⊕ *www.highlandgardenshotel.com* 🗗 *70 rooms, 48 suites* ⚘ *Some kitchenettes, refrigerators, pool, laundry facilities, free parking; no smoking* ☰ *AE, MC, V* ⦿⧆ *CP.*

Beverly Hills

★ $$$$ 🏨 **Beverly Hills Hotel.** Ever since its opening in 1912, the "Pink Palace" has attracted Hollywood's elite. Celebrity guests favor the private bungalows complete with *all* of life's little necessities (Bungalow 5, for example, has its own lap pool). Standard rooms are also decadent, with original artwork, butler service, Frette linens, and duvets, walk-in closets, and huge marble bathrooms. Famed Swiss skincare company La Prairie partnered with the hotel in 2004 to open an ultraluxe day spa that specializes in de-aging treatments. The Polo Lounge, with its banana-leaf wallpaper, remains a fabled Hollywood meeting place. Canine guests are equally pampered here; 24-hour dog-walking service is available. ⊠ *9641 Sunset Blvd., Beverly Hills 90210* ☎ *310/276–2251 or 800/ 283–8885* 🖷 *310/887–2887* ⊕ *www.beverlyhillshotel.com* 🗗 *203 rooms, 21 bungalows* ⚘ *4 restaurants, room service, in-room data* *ports, in-room fax, in-room safes, some kitchenettes, minibars, cable TV with movies and video games, in-room VCRs, 2 tennis courts, pool, gym, hair salon, hot tub, spa, bar, piano, shops, babysitting, dry cleaning, laundry service, concierge, Internet, convention center, parking (fee), some pets allowed (fee), no-smoking rooms ⊟ AE, DC, MC, V.*

$$$$ ⊞ **Four Seasons Hotel Los Angeles at Beverly Hills.** High hedges and patio
Fodor's Choice gardens make this hotel a secluded retreat that even the hum of traffic
★ can't permeate. The staff here will make you feel pampered, as will the lavish guest rooms with their Frette-dressed beds, soft robes and slippers, and French doors leading to balconies. Extras include 24-hour business services, choice of pillow style, overnight shoe shine, and morning newspaper. At the opulent spa, treatments incorporate seasonal scents like jasmine and orange. For the ultimate luxury, book a massage outside in a poolside cabana. ⊠ *300 S. Doheny Dr., Beverly Hills 90048* ☎ *310/273–2222 or 800/332–3442* 🖷 *310/859–3824* ⊕ *www. fourseasons.com/losangeles* ⤴ *187 rooms, 98 suites* ♿ *2 restaurants, café, room service, in-room data ports, minibars, cable TV with movies and video games, in-room VCRs, pool, gym, hot tub, sauna, spa, steam room, bar, dry cleaning, laundry service, concierge, Internet, business services, meeting rooms, car rental, parking (fee), some pets allowed; no-smoking rooms* ⊟ *AE, DC, MC, V.*

$$$$ ⊞ **Luxe Hotel Rodeo Drive.** Refined design rules at this boutique hotel discreetly tucked away between twin Valentino boutiques. Dark mahogany and brushed metals fill the lobby, and the compact rooms are outfitted with black-and-white photography, 8-foot-high mirrors, Frette linens, robes, and slippers. Café Rodeo, Luxe's intimate sky-lit restaurant, draws a well-heeled local lunch crowd with upscale comfort food and potent martinis. ⊠ *360 N. Rodeo Dr., Beverly Hills 90210* ☎ *310/273–0300 or 866/ 589–3411* 🖷 *310/859–8730* ⊕ *www.luxehotels.com* ⤴ *84 rooms, 4 suites* ♿ *Restaurant, room service, in-room data ports, in-room safes, refrigerators, cable TV with movies, gym, bar, babysitting, laundry service, concierge, Internet, business services, meeting room, car rental, parking (fee), some pets allowed (fee), no-smoking rooms* ⊟ *AE, D, DC, MC, V.*

$$$$ ⊞ **Peninsula Beverly Hills.** At this French Renaissance–style palace rooms
Fodor's Choice overflow with antiques, artwork, and marble; high-tech room ameni-
★ ties are controlled by a bedside panel. Whatever luxuries aren't on the standard bill of fare can be requested (individually monogrammed pillowcases, anyone?). For the full treatment, reserve one of the residential-style villas, which have private entrances, terraces, fireplaces, and Bose entertainment systems; some have kitchens and hot tubs. Soak up the sun by the fifth-floor pool, or sip afternoon tea in the living room. A chauffeured courtesy Rolls-Royce will drive you three blocks to prime Beverly Hills shopping. ⊠ *9882 S. Santa Monica Blvd., Beverly Hills 90212* ☎ *310/551–2888 or 800/462–7899* 🖷 *310/788–2319* ⊕ *www. peninsula.com* ⤴ *196 rooms, 43 suites, 16 villas* ♿ *2 restaurants, room service, in-room data ports, in-room fax, in-room safes, minibars, cable TV with movies and video games, in-room VCRs, pool, gym, outdoor hot tub, sauna, spa, steam room, bar, shops, babysitting, dry cleaning, laundry service, concierge, business services, meeting rooms, parking (fee), some pets allowed (fee); no smoking* ⊟ *AE, D, DC, MC, V.*

★ $$$$ 🏨 **Regent Beverly Wilshire.** The moniker "grande dame" fits the landmark Regent Beverly Wilshire like a white kid glove. Extravagant—there's an in-house florist who looks after stunning seasonal arrangements—and completely devoted to the whims of its guests, the hotel has long been a home-away-from-home for visiting royalty, presidents, and heads of state. Built in 1928, the Italian Renaissance–style Wilshire wing is replete with elegant details: crystal chandeliers, oak paneling, walnut doors, crown moldings, and pink marble. Added in 1971, the Beverly wing is more contemporary and equally luxurious. Rodeo Drive beckons outside; a complimentary limo can drive you anywhere within 3 mi of the hotel. ✉ *9500 Wilshire Blvd., Beverly Hills 90212* ☎ *310/275–5200, 800/421–4354 in CA, 800/427–4354 elsewhere* 🖷 *310/274–2851* ⊕ *www.fourseasons.com* 🛏 *280 rooms, 115 suites* ⚒ *2 restaurants, room service, in-room data ports, in-room safes, minibars, cable TV with movies and video games, pool, health club, hair salon, outdoor hot tub, sauna, spa, bar, lobby lounge, piano, babysitting, dry cleaning, laundry service, concierge, Internet, business services, meeting rooms, travel services, parking (fee), some pets allowed, no-smoking floors* ▭ *AE, DC, MC, V.*

$$$ 🏨 **Avalon.** This relaxed but cosmopolitan boutique hotel combines Googie-era style with tech-savvy substance. Rooms at the three-building property incorporate '50s retro design, with classic pieces from George Nelson, Eames, and Thonet; there are also Frette linens and chenille throws, and a menu of spa treatments that can be ordered in-room. For extended stays, the Avalon offers stylish apartments with all hotel services, including twice-daily housekeeping. At cocktail hour, look for the martini crowd poolside or lounging in private cabanas. ✉ *9400 W. Olympic Blvd., Beverly Hills 90212* ☎ *310/277–5221 or 800/535–4715* 🖷 *310/277–4928* ⊕ *www.avalonbeverlyhills.com* 🛏 *78 rooms, 10 suites* ⚒ *Restaurant, room service, in-room data ports, in-room fax, in-room safes, minibars, cable TV with movies and video games, in-room VCRs, pool, gym, massage, bar, dry cleaning, laundry facilities, laundry service, concierge, Internet, business services, meeting room, parking (fee), some pets allowed (fee), no-smoking rooms* ▭ *AE, DC, MC, V.*

$$–$$$ 🏨 **Maison 140.** Though the rooms are compact at this 1930s boutique hotel, they are grandly designed: antiques from France and the Far East, textured wallpaper, and colorfully painted rooms are a feast for the eyes. Extras include down comforters, Frette linens, and bathrobes. Beverly Hills' golden triangle of shopping is within blocks. You can take advantage of the pool and restaurant at sister property the Avalon Hotel, 1 mi away. ✉ *140 S. Lasky Dr., Beverly Hills 90212* ☎ *310/281–4000 or 800/432–5444* 🖷 *310/281–4001* ⊕ *www.maison140beverlyhills.com* 🛏 *43 rooms* ⚒ *Room service, in-room data ports, in-room safes, minibars, cable TV with movies, some in-room VCRs, gym, massage, lobby lounge, dry cleaning, laundry service, concierge, Internet, free parking, no-smoking rooms* ▭ *AE, DC, MC, V.*

$$ 🏨 **The Crescent.** Built in 1926 as a dorm for silent-film actors, the Crescent received a super-stylish makeover in 2003. Low couches and tables, French doors that open to a streetside patio, and plenty of candlelight (at night) give the lobby and bar a sophisticated look. Rooms are small,

but platform beds and built-in furniture maximize the space and create a loftlike feel. Bathrooms are finished in concrete—utilitarian but coolly cozy. There are lots of high-tech amenities, including flat-screen TVs, in-room iPods, and a library of the latest CDs and DVDs. Within walking distance are most of Beverly Hills' restaurants, shops, salons, spas, and entertainment-related businesses. ✉ *403 N. Crescent Dr., Beverly Hills 90210* ☎ *310/247–0505 or 800/451–1566* 🖷 *310/247–9053* 🌐 *www.crescentbh.com* 🖙 *40 rooms* 🖒 *Restaurant, room service, in-room data ports, in-room safes, minibars, cable TV, massage, lobby lounge, dry cleaning, laundry service, concierge, Internet, parking (fee), some pets allowed; no smoking* ▭ *AE, CB, D, MC, V.*

Century City

$$$$ 🏨 **The St. Regis, Los Angeles.** Luxury, privacy, attention to detail, exemplary service, and panoramic views define the St. Regis. The multilingual staff (including trained temporary personal assistants) exudes professionalism. Rooms are formal, beds are big and plush, and high-tech extras abound (there are DVD players, cordless phones, and bedside digital-control panels). The marble bathrooms, with glass-enclosed showers, are large by any standard. The luxe lobby bar has deep leather banquettes; Provençal cuisine is served at Encore, the hotel's airy and quiet restaurant. Pets get pampered with their own amenities. ✉ *2055 Ave. of the Stars, Century City 90067* ☎ *310/277–6111 or 877/787–3452* 🖷 *310/277–6311* 🌐 *www.stregis.com* 🖙 *260 rooms, 36 suites* 🖒 *Restaurant, room service, in-room data ports, in-room fax, in-room safes, minibars, cable TV with movies and video games, in-room VCRs, pool, gym, hair salon, outdoor hot tub, sauna, spa, steam room, bar, shop, dry cleaning, laundry service, concierge, convention center, parking (fee), some pets allowed, no-smoking rooms* ▭ *AE, D, DC, MC, V.*

FodorsChoice
★

West Hollywood

★ **$$$$** 🏨 **Chateau Marmont Hotel.** The Chateau's swank exterior reflects its lurid place in Hollywood history—locals remember it as the scene of John Belushi's fatal overdose in 1982. Actors like Johnny Depp and Keanu Reeves appreciate the hotel for its secluded cottages, bungalows, and understated suites and penthouses. The interior is 1920s-style, although some of the decor looks dated rather than chicly vintage. Trendy Bar Marmont serves food until 1:30 AM—unusual in L.A. ✉ *8221 Sunset Blvd., West Hollywood 90046* ☎ *323/656–1010 or 800/242–8328* 🖷 *323/655–5311* 🌐 *www.chateaumarmont.com* 🖙 *11 rooms, 63 suites* 🖒 *Restaurant, room service, in-room data ports, in-room fax, in-room safes, minibars, cable TV with movies, in-room VCRs, pool, gym, massage, bar, dry cleaning, laundry service, concierge, Internet, business services, parking (fee), some pets allowed (fee), no-smoking rooms* ▭ *AE, DC, MC, V.*

★ **$$$$** 🏨 **Mondrian.** Ian Schrager, famed for his hipper-than-hip hotels, is the mastermind behind this all-white, high-rise, urban resort. Mod, apartment-size accommodations have floor-to-ceiling windows, slip-covered sofas, and marble coffee tables; all have kitchens. Desks and multiline phones aid business travelers, but the happening social scene in the lobby will certainly distract. The dining experience at Asia de Cuba provides amazing views and a fusion of Asian and Latin flavors. Sip sake and sample sushi at the alabaster topped Seabar for a lighter repast. The indoor-outdoor lobby and Skybar overflow with party people weekend nights. Rooms on the lower floors facing Sunset are unbearably noisy; insist on a room that faces west. ⊠ *8440 Sunset Blvd., West Hollywood 90069* ☎ *323/650–8999 or 800/525–8029* 📠 *323/650–9241* ⊕ *www.mondrianhotel.com* ⤳ *53 rooms, 185 suites* ⚭ *Restaurant, café, room service, in-room data ports, in-room safes, kitchens, refrigerators, cable TV with movies, pool, gym, sauna, spa, steam room, 2 bars, shop, laundry service, concierge, Internet, business services, meeting room, parking (fee), no-smoking rooms* ⊟ *AE, D, DC, MC, V.*

★ **$$$$** 🏨 **Sunset Marquis Hotel and Villas.** If you're in town to cut your new hit single, you'll appreciate the two on-site recording studios here. But even the musically challenged will appreciate this property. Suites and ultra-private villas, which are set amid lush gardens, are roomy and plush, with soundproof windows and black-out curtains for total serenity. All have surround-sound systems; some have grand pianos (virtuosos, after all, need accompaniment). Guests may visit the hotel's ultraexclusive nightspot, the Whiskey Bar. ⊠ *1200 N. Alta Loma Rd., West Hollywood 90069* ☎ *310/657–1333 or 800/858–9758* 📠 *310/652–5300* ⊕ *www.sunsetmarquishotel.com* ⤳ *102 suites, 12 villas* ⚭ *2 restaurants, room service, in-room data ports, in-room safes, minibars, cable TV with movies and video games, 2 pools, gym, outdoor hot tub, massage, sauna, steam room, bar, babysitting, dry cleaning, laundry service, concierge, Internet, business services, meeting rooms, car rental, parking (fee), some pets allowed, no-smoking rooms* ⊟ *AE, D, DC, MC, V.*

$$$–$$$$ 🏨 **The Argyle.** You can't miss this hotel's gunmetal-gray, pink, and neon-lit art deco facade. Inside, reproduction objets d'art and paintings fill the public spaces. Rooms are also deco. Though small, each has a separate living room with fantastic views over greater L.A. Bathrooms are done in black-and-white marble. The poolside city views are impressive. Most of the Sunset Strip's hot spots are within walking distance. ⊠ *8358 Sunset Blvd., West Hollywood 90069* ☎ *323/654–7100 or 800/225–2637* 📠 *323/654–9287* ⊕ *www.argylehotel.com* ⤳ *20 rooms, 44 suites* ⚭ *Restaurant, room service, in-room data ports, in-room fax, in-room safes, minibars, cable TV, in-room VCRs, pool, gym, sauna, bar, laundry service, concierge, business services, meeting rooms, parking (fee); no smoking* ⊟ *AE, D, DC, MC, V.*

★ **$$** 🏨 **The Standard.** Hotelier André Balazs created this affordable, hip Sunset Strip hotel from a former retirement home. Now it's a buzzing, trendy hotspot, with a pop-arty, '70s-kitsch design aesthetic: shag carpets and ultrasuede sectionals fill the lobby; the rooms have inflatable sofas, beanbag chairs, surfboard tables, and Warhol poppy-print curtains. Nightly, the aquarium behind the front desk holds comely humans instead of fish, and out on the pool deck a DJ provides sonic entertainment. Hollywood's beautiful people populate the space-age lounge and the 24-hour coffee shop. ⊠ *8300 Sunset Blvd., West Hollywood 90069* ☎ *323/650–9090* 📠 *323/650–2820* ⊕ *www.standardhotel.com* ⤳ *138* *rooms, 8 suites ⑤ Coffee shop, room service, in-room data ports, mini-bars, cable TV with movies, in-room VCRs, pool, hair salon, spa, bar, lobby lounge, shop, laundry service, concierge, Internet, meeting rooms, parking (fee), no-smoking rooms ☰ AE, D, DC, MC, V.*

Westwood

$$$$ 🔲 **W Los Angeles.** You'll walk on water when you enter the W—frosted-glass stairs over a fiber-optic-lit waterfall lead to the lobby. Sophisticated, luxurious surroundings are enhanced by the latest in cutting-edge technology. A beautiful garden terrace overlooks the pool. Cabanas wired for Internet access are perfect for lounging day or night. Business travelers will appreciate the "Cyber suites," complete with combination printer-fax-scanners, VCRs, and three phone lines each. ⊠ *930 Hilgard Ave., Westwood 90024* ☎ *310/208–8765 or 877/946–8357* 📠 *310/824–0355* ⊕ *www.whotels.com* 🛏 *258 suites ⑤ 2 restaurants, café, room service, in-room data ports, in-room safes, minibars, refrigerators, cable TV with movies and video games, in-room VCRs, 2 pools, exercise equipment, spa, bar, lobby lounge, laundry service, concierge, Internet, business services, meeting rooms, car rental, parking (fee), some pets allowed (fee), no-smoking rooms ☰ AE, D, DC, MC, V.*

Bel Air

$$$$ 🔲 **Hotel Bel-Air.** In a wooded canyon with verdant gardens and a swan-**Fodor's**Choice filled lake, the Hotel Bel-Air's distinctive luxury and seclusion have made ★ it a favorite of discreet celebs (and royalty) for decades. Bungalow-style, country French–inspired rooms feel like fine homes with expensively upholstered furniture in silk or chenille; many have hardwood floors. Most rooms have wood-burning fireplaces (the bell captain will build a fire for you). Eight suites have private outdoor hot tubs. Complimentary tea service greets you upon arrival; enjoy it on the terrace warmed by heated tiles. A pianist plays nightly in the bar. The hotel's excellent restaurant spills into the garden and a heated, vine-draped terrace. ⊠ *701 Stone Canyon Rd., Bel Air 90077* ☎ *310/472–1211 or 800/648–4097* 📠 *310/476–5890* ⊕ *www.hotelbelair.com* 🛏 *52 rooms, 39 suites ⑤ Restaurant, room service, in-room data ports, in-room safes, minibars, cable TV with movies and video games, in-room VCRs, pool, gym, massage, piano bar, shop, babysitting, dry cleaning, laundry service, concierge, Internet, business services, meeting rooms, free parking, no-smoking rooms ☰ AE, DC, MC, V.*

Santa Monica

★ **$$$$** 🔲 **Casa del Mar.** In the 1920s it was a posh beach club catering to the city's elite; now the Casa del Mar is one of SoCal's most luxurious beachfront hotels, with three extravagant, two-story penthouses, a raised deck and pool, and an elegant ballroom facing the sand. Guest rooms are designed to evoke the French Riviera, with modern amenities like CD players and direct-dial phones. Bathrooms are gorgeous, with sunken whirlpool tubs and glass-enclosed showers. Spa services are top-notch. The clubby, living room–like Lobby Lounge, with its sunset views and fireplace, is a pricey, but cozily elegant sanctuary. ✉ *1910 Ocean Front Way, Santa Monica 90405* ☎ *310/581–5533 or 800/898–6999* 🖷 *310/ 581–5503* ⊕ *www.hotelcasadelmar.com* ➥ *125 rooms, 4 suites ⚅ 2 restaurants, room service, in-room data ports, in-room safes, minibars, cable TV with movies and video games, in-room VCRs, pool, gym, spa, lobby lounge, dry cleaning, laundry service, concierge, business services, meeting rooms, parking (fee), some pets allowed; no smoking* ▤ *AE, D, DC, MC, V.*

$$$$ 🏨 **Le Merigot Beach Hotel & Spa.** Mere steps from Santa Monica's expansive beach, Le Merigot caters to a corporate upmarket clientele (it's a JW Marriott property). Upper floors have panoramic views of the Santa Monica Pier and the Pacific; many rooms have terraces. Contemporary rooms have feather beds and Frette linens, and bathrooms come with playful bath toys and votive candles. A checkerboard slate courtyard—including a pool, cabanas, fountains, and outdoor living room—is the center of activity. You can book a massage at the spa for a true attitude adjustment and dine in French country style at the comfortable Cézanne restaurant. ✉ *1740 Ocean Ave., Santa Monica 90405* ☎ *310/395–9700 or 888/539–7899* 🖷 *310/395–9200* ⊕ *www.lemerigothotel.com* ➥ *162 rooms, 13 suites ⚅ Restaurant, room service, in-room data ports, in-room safes, minibars, cable TV with movies and video games, pool, fitness classes, gym, hair salon, sauna, spa, steam room, beach, bicycles, 2 bars, shop, babysitting, dry cleaning, laundry service, concierge, Internet, business services, meeting rooms, parking (fee), some pets allowed (fee), no-smoking rooms* ▤ *AE, D, DC, MC, V.*

$$$$ 🏨 **Shutters on the Beach.** Set right on the sand, the gray-shingled inn (think
Fodor'sChoice Martha's Vineyard) has become synonymous with in-town escapism. A
★ whirlpool tub, candles and dimmer switches, plush mattresses with Frette linens, a minibar stocked with splits of boutique California wines, and shutter doors (hence the hotel's name) all await you in your room. Shutters is a favorite of corporate executives who come for the personalized service, homelike touches (books and scenic framed photographs bedside), and high-tech extras such as wireless high-speed Internet access throughout the property. ✉ *1 Pico Blvd., Santa Monica 90405* ☎ *310/458–0030 or 800/334–9000* 🖷 *310/458–4589* ⊕ *www.shuttersonthebeach.com* ➥ *186 rooms, 12 suites ⚅ Restaurant, café, room service, in-room data ports, in-room safes, in-room hot tubs, minibars, cable TV, in-room VCRs, pool, gym, outdoor hot tub, sauna, spa, steam room, beach, mountain bikes, bar, lobby lounge, piano, shop, baby-sitting, dry cleaning, laundry service, concierge, Internet, business services, meeting rooms, parking (fee), no-smoking rooms* ▤ *AE, D, DC, MC, V.*

$$$–$$$$ 🏨 **Fairmont Miramar Hotel Santa Monica.** Close to Santa Monica's popular 3rd Street Promenade, the Fairmont Miramar presents a quiet enclave and professional service at land's end. Spread out over five landscaped acres are an 1889 mansion and newly refurnished residential-style bungalows, originally constructed between 1920 and 1946. There are also rooms in a 10-story tower with beautiful ocean views, marble entries, alabaster light fixtures, carved-wood armoires, Bose stereo systems, and down duvets. Extensive business services are available (leach room comes with a wicker basket of office supplies), and a personal trainer is on-site. ✉ *101 Wilshire Blvd., Santa Monica 90401* ☎ *310/576–7777 or 800/441–1414* 🖨 *310/458–7912* ⊕ *www.fairmont.com* ⬎ *302 rooms, 55 suites, 32 bungalows* ⚘ *Restaurant, room service, in-room data ports, in-room safes, minibars, cable TV with movies and video games, pool, gym, hair salon, outdoor hot tub, sauna, spa, steam room, bar, piano, babysitting, laundry service, concierge, Internet, business services, convention center, car rental, travel services, parking (fee), some pets allowed, no-smoking rooms* ☰ *AE, D, DC, MC, V.*

$$$ 🏨 **Viceroy.** Euro-chic whimsy abounds at this stylized seaside escape—there are porcelain dogs as lamp bases and Spode china plates mounted on the walls. The compact rooms all have French balconies, and the mostly marble bathrooms have seated vanities. Glamazons socialize in the pool and cabana area amid all-white armchairs and divans. Whist, the hotel's restaurant, serves cutting-edge contemporary cuisine. ✉ *1819 Ocean Ave., Santa Monica 90401* ☎ *310/451–8711 or 800/622–8711* 🖨 *310/ 394–6657* ⊕ *www.viceroysantamonica.com* ⬎ *165 rooms, 5 suites* ⚘ *Restaurant, room service, in-room data ports, in-room safe, minibars, cable TV with movies and video games, 2 pools, gym, massage, bar, lobby lounge, library, dry cleaning, laundry service, concierge, Internet, business services, meeting rooms, parking (fee), some pets allowed, no-smoking rooms* ☰ *AE, DC, MC, V.*

$$ 🏨 **The Ambrose.** An air of tranquillity pervades the four-story Ambrose, which blends right into its mostly residential Santa Monica neighborhood. The decor incorporates many Asian accents, and follows the principles of feng shui. There's a Zen garden and koi pond at the entrance and Japanese wood-block prints throughout. Rooms have deluxe extras like chenille throws, Italian linens, Frette towels and robes, and a minibar with healthful elixirs. Windows are double-paned for quiet; upper floors have partial ocean views. Room service and the breakfast buffet include organic specialties. A vintage London taxi is on call for free short jaunts in the area. ✉ *1255 20th St., Santa Monica 90404* ☎ *310/ 315–1555 or 877/262–7673* 🖨 *310/315–1556* ⊕ *www.ambrosehotel. com* ⬎ *77 rooms* ⚘ *Room service, some fans, in-room data ports, in-room safes, minibars, cable TV, in-room VCRs, fitness classes, gym, massage, bicycles, library, babysitting, dry cleaning, laundry service, concierge, Internet, meeting room, car rental, free parking, some pets allowed, no-smoking rooms* ☰ *AE, D, DC, MC, V* ⦿ *CP.*

Burbank

★ $$$ 🏨 **The Graciela Burbank.** Close to Burbank's TV and movie studios, the smartly designed Graciela feels like a Beverly Hills boutique hotel. Over the years, it's become a favorite of women business travelers who like its understated look (muted beiges and greens) and residential vibe. Feather beds are covered in comfy duvets and chenille throws; thoughtful touches include hooks for hanging garment bags. Generous work spaces have state-of-the-art lighting. Bathrooms have granite vanities, bathrobes, and shelves for storage. The rooftop sundeck has a brightly striped cabana and view of the nearby hills. ✉ *322 N. Pass Ave., Burbank 91505* ☎ *818/842–8887 or 888/956–1900* 🖨 *818/260–8999* ⊕ *www. thegraciela.com* ⬎ *91 rooms, 10 suites* ⚘ *Dining room, room service,* *in-room data ports, in-room safes, some kitchenettes, refrigerators, cable TV with movies, in-room VCRs, gym, outdoor hot tub, massage, sauna, lobby lounge, library, dry cleaning, concierge, Internet, business services, meeting rooms, airport shuttle, parking (fee), some pets allowed (fee), no-smoking rooms* ⊟ *AE, D, DC, MC, V* ⵏ❍⵱ *BP.*

Pasadena

$$$$ ▦ **Ritz-Carlton Huntington Hotel & Spa.** An azalea-filled Japanese garden
Fodor'sChoice   and an unusual Picture Bridge whose murals celebrate California's his-
  ★   tory make this an especially scenic place to stay. The Mediterranean-
style main building is surrounded by 23 acres of green lawns. Traditional
guest rooms are handsome if a bit small. Suites and cottages, however,
are as lavish as they come; Frette bed linens, feather beds, and thick
bathrobes are standard. The hotel's restaurant, the Dining Room, serves
contemporary cuisine in a formal setting. ⊠ *1401 S. Oak Knoll Ave.,
Pasadena 91106* ☎ *626/568–3900 or 800/241–3333* 🖷 *626/585–1842*
⊕ *www.ritzcarlton.com* ⵏ *361 rooms, 31 suites* ⵖ *2 restaurants, room
service, in-room data ports, in-room safes, minibars, cable TV with movies,
3 tennis courts, pool, fitness classes, health club, hair salon, outdoor hot
tub, sauna, spa, steam room, bar, shops, babysitting, children's programs
(ages 7–12, summertime only), dry cleaning, laundry service, concierge,
concierge floor, business services, meeting rooms, car rental, travel services, parking (fee), some pets allowed (fee), no-smoking rooms* ⊟ *AE,
D, DC, MC, V.*

$ ▦ **Artists' Inn & Cottage.** In a quiet residential neighborhood of Crafts-
man bungalows, not far from the distractions of downtown L.A. or the
antique shops of South Pasadena, is this charming 1895 B&B. Once a
chicken farm, the Artists' Inn still retains a country air with more than
100 rose bushes in the garden, wicker furniture on the front porch, and
home-cooked breakfasts and afternoon tea. Some rooms have fireplaces; all have themes relating to a particular period of art (like Im-
pressionism) or famous artist (Degas, van Gogh, O'Keeffe). Close by is
a Gold Line Metro stop for easy access to downtown L.A. ⊠ *1038 Magnolia St., Pasadena 91030* ☎ *626/799–5668 or 888/799–5668* 🖷 *626/
799–3678* ⊕ *www.artistsinns.com* ⵏ *10 rooms* ⵖ *In-room data ports,
free parking; no TV in some rooms, no smoking* ⊟ *AE, MC, V* ⵏ❍⵱ *BP.*

Los Angeles International Airport

$$ ▦ **Summerfield Suites by Wyndham.** There's room to spread out in these
extra-large one- and two-bedroom suites; there are even living-room
sleeper sofas. You can cook in the fully outfitted kitchens or on the gas
grills outside; the staff will stock your refrigerator with groceries (the
service is free but you'll have to pay for the groceries). Weeknights, you
can attend a happy hour with complimentary drinks and snacks. ⊠ *810
S. Douglas Ave., El Segundo 90245* ☎ *310/725–0100 or 800/996–
3426* 🖷 *310/725–0900* ⊕ *www.wyndham.com* ⵏ *122 suites* ⵖ *Din-
ing room, BBQs, in-room data ports, kitchens, refrigerators, cable TV,
in-room VCRs, pool, gym, hot tub, basketball, dry cleaning, laundry
facilities, laundry service, concierge, Internet, business services, meet-*

ing rooms, free parking, some pets allowed (fee), no-smoking rooms ➯ *AE, D, DC, MC, V* ❧❘ *BP.*

$$ 🖭 **Westin Los Angeles Airport.** This is a great place to stay if you want both the convenience of airport proximity and the luxury of Beverly Hills accommodations. Rooms are spacious with Heavenly-brand beds for supreme sleeping comfort; many suites have private outdoor hot tubs. The on-site Charisma Café serves American cuisine and specializes in seafood. ✉ *5400 W. Century Blvd., LAX 90045* ☎ *310/216–5858 or 800/937–8461* 📠 *310/417–4545* ⊕ *www.westin.com* ☚ *723 rooms, 42 suites* ⚱ *Restaurant, room service, in-room data ports, some in-room faxes, in-room safes, minibars, refrigerators, cable TV with movies, pool, gym, hot tub, sauna, billiards, bar, children's programs (ages 6–12), laundry service, concierge, Internet, business services, meeting room, airport shuttle, car rental, parking (fee), some pets allowed (fee), no-smoking rooms* ➯ *AE, D, DC, MC, V.*

NIGHTLIFE & THE ARTS

Updated by
Lina Lecaro

Hollywood and West Hollywood are the chief focus of L.A. nightlife, where hip and happening nightspots liberally dot Sunset and Hollywood boulevards. L.A. is one of the best places in the world for seeing soon-to-be-famous rockers as well as top jazz, blues, and classical performers. Film emporia are naturally well represented here, but so are dance events, performance art, and an underrated theater community that might just be L.A.'s best-kept secret.

For a thorough listing of local events, consult *Los Angeles Magazine.* The Calendar section of the *Los Angeles Times* also lists a wide survey of Los Angeles arts events, especially on Thursday and Sunday, as do the more alternative publications, the *LA Weekly* and the *LA Citybeat* (both free, and issued every Thursday). Call ahead to confirm that what you want to see is ongoing. Most tickets can be purchased by phone with a credit card. **Good Time Tickets** (☎ 323/464–7383) tries to compete with Ticketmaster by acquiring harder-to-get tickets. For events at museums and small theaters, call **Murray's Tickets** (☎ 323/234–0123). Try **TeleCharge** (☎ 800/762–7666) for theater events. **Ticketmaster** (☎ 213/ 480–3232, 213/365–3500 fine arts) is still the top dog. **Tickets L.A** (☎ 323/655–8587) brokers shows and cultural events, primarily at museums and smaller theaters.

The Arts

Concert Halls

☾ A brand- (and grand) new addition to L.A.'s Music Center, the **Walt Dis-**
Fodor'sChoice **ney Concert Hall** (✉ 151 S. Grand Ave., Downtown ☎ 323/850–2000)
★ is now the home of the Los Angeles Philharmonic and the Los Angeles Master Chorale, plus an array of eclectic, multicultural musical performers. A sculptural monument of gleaming, curved steel, the 2,265-seat theater also boasts a public park, gardens, and shops as well as two outdoor amphitheaters for children's and preconcert events. Also part of the Music Center complex, the 3,200-seat **Dorothy Chandler Pavilion**

(✉ 135 N. Grand Ave., Downtown ☎ 213/972–7211) presents an array of music programs and the L.A. Opera's classics from September through June. In Griffith Park, the open-air auditorium known as the **Greek Theater** (✉ 2700 N. Vermont Ave., Los Feliz ☎ 323/665–1927), complete with Doric columns, presents big-name performers in its mainly pop-rock-jazz schedule from June through October.

★ Ever since it opened in 1920, in a park surrounded by mountains, trees, and gardens, the **Hollywood Bowl** (✉ 2301 Highland Ave., Hollywood ☎ 323/850–2000 ⊕ www.hollywoodbowl.com) has been one of the world's largest and most atmospheric outdoor amphitheaters. Its season runs from early July through mid-September; the L.A. Philharmonic spends its summer season here. There are performances daily except Monday (and some Sundays); the program ranges from jazz to pop to classical. Concertgoers usually arrive early, bringing picnic suppers; there are plenty of picnic tables. Additionally, a moderately priced outdoor grill and a more upscale restaurant are among the dining options operated by the **Patina Group** (☎ 323/850–1885). Avoid the hassle of parking by taking one of the Park-and-Ride buses, which leave from various locations around town; call the Bowl for information.

★ The jewel in the crown of Hollywood & Highland is the **Kodak Theatre** (✉ 6801 Hollywood Blvd., Hollywood ☎ 323/308–6363 ⊕ www.kodaktheatre.com). It was created to be the permanent host of the Academy Awards, but the lavish 3,500-seat theater also presents music concerts and ballets. Seeing a show here is worthwhile just to glimpse the gorgeous, sparkling interior. The one-of-a-kind, 6,300-seat ersatz-Arabic **Shrine Auditorium** (✉ 665 W. Jefferson Blvd., Downtown ☎ 213/749–5123), built in 1926 as Al Malaikah Temple, hosts touring companies from all over the world, assorted gospel and choral groups, and other musical acts as well as high-profile televised awards shows, such as the Grammys. It's used mainly for sporting events, but the **Staples Center** (✉ 1111 S. Figueroa St. ☎ 213/742–7300 ⊕ www.staplescenter.com) also offers blockbuster concerts. Madonna and Britney Spears both took their megabudget extravaganzas to this huge, state-of-the-art arena. Adjacent to Universal Studios, the 6,250-seat **Universal Amphitheater** (✉ 100 Universal City Plaza, Universal City ☎ 818/622–4440) holds more than 100 performances a year, including the Radio City Christmas Spectacular and star-studded benefit concerts. The **Wiltern Theater** (✉ 3790 Wilshire Blvd., Mid-Wilshire ☎ 213/380–5005), a green terracotta, art deco masterpiece constructed in 1930 and listed in the National Register of Historic Places, is a fine place to see pop, rock, jazz, and dance performances. In 2001 the seats were ripped out and the space remodeled as standing-room-only venue (there are still a few seats on the balcony, however).

Film

ART & REVIVAL HOUSES The **American Cinemathèque Independent Film Series** (✉ 6712 Hollywood Blvd., Hollywood ☎ 323/466–3456) screens classics plus recent independent films, sometimes with question-and-answer sessions with the filmmakers. The main venue is the Lloyd E. Rigler Theater, within the 1922 Egyptian Theater, a stylized contrast of vintage exterior (pharaoh sculptures, columns) and modern, high-tech interior. At this writing, a second location was underway at the 64-year-old **Aero Theater** (✉ 1328 Montana Ave., Santa Monica).

★ Taking the concept of dinner and a movie to a whole new level, **Cinespace** (✉ 6356 Hollywood Blvd., Hollywood ☎ 323/817–3456) screens classics and edgy indie flicks in its digital theater–restaurant. Finally, good food (gourmet comfort grub) and good film (everything from documentaries to old school faves like *Grease*) can be enjoyed at the same time, in the same place. Those looking to do more than stare at the screen can sip cocktails in the industrial-looking front bar, where hip young celluloid buffs enjoy a more clubby atmosphere with DJ-provided music and a smoking patio that hovers over bustling Hollywood Boulevard. The best of Hollywood classics and kitsch, foreign films and, occasionally, documentaries, are on tap at the **New Beverly Cinema** (✉ 7165 Beverly Blvd., Hollywood ☎ 323/938–4038), where there's always a double bill. **Nuart** (✉ 11272 Santa Monica Blvd., West L.A. ☎ 310/281–8223) is the best-kept of L.A.'s revival houses, with good, relatively new seats,
★ an excellent screen, and special midnight shows. The **Silent Movie Theater** (✉ 611 N. Fairfax Ave., Fairfax District ☎ 323/655–2520 ⊕ www.silentmovietheater.com) is a treasure. Thursday through Sunday it screens exclusively the cream of the pretalkies era with live musical accompaniment, plus shorts before the films. Each show is made to seem like an event in itself, and it's the only such theater of its kind on five continents (there *is* a teensy silents-only theater in Australia). **UCLA** has two fine film series. The program of the **Film and Television Archives at the James Bridges Theater** (✉ Hilgard Ave. near Sunset Blvd., Westwood ☎ 310/206–3456 or 310/206–8013 ⊕ www.cinema.ucla.edu) runs the gamut from documentaries to children's films. The **School of Film & Television** (⊕ www.tft.ucla.edu) also uses the Bridges Theater, but it has its own program of newer, avant-garde films.

MOVIE PALACES **The Arclight** (✉ 6360 Sunset Blvd., Hollywood ☎ 323/464–4226), which includes the futuristic, geodesic Cinerama Dome (the first theater in the United States designed specifically for the enormous screen and magnificent sound system of Cinerama) as its centerpiece, has 14 additional screens, a full restaurant, a bar, and a mall. It's the only theater in L.A. to offer greetings and background commentary about the film by theater staff before screenings.

You almost don't mind paying the extra bucks to see a flick at **The Bridge Cinema De Lux** (✉ 6081 Center Dr., in the Promenade at Howard Hughes Center, West L.A. ☎ 310/568–3375), with its super-wide screens (including one that shows IMAX films), comfy leather recliners, and top-notch food and drink offerings. Sip a cocktail at the bar or order a meal to take into the theater.

Fodor'sChoice **Grauman's Chinese Theatre** (✉ 6925 Hollywood Blvd., Hollywood
★ ☎ 323/464–8111), open since 1927, is perhaps the world's best-known theater, with its cement walkway marked by movie stars' hand- and footprints and its traditional gala premieres. After some years with the Mann's moniker it has gone back to its old name, and added more—

albeit smaller—screens at the Mann Chinese Six, in the adjoining Hollywood & Highland Complex.

☺ Across the street from the Chinese Theatre is the **Pacific's El Capitan** (✉ 6838 Hollywood Blvd., Hollywood ☎ 323/467–7674), a classic art deco masterpiece meticulously renovated by Disney. First-run movies alternate with Disney revivals, and the theater often presents live stage shows in conjunction with Disney animation pictures.

Television

Audiences Unlimited (✉ 100 Universal City Plaza, Bldg. 153, Universal City 91608 ☎ 818/506–0043 ⊕ www.tvtickets.com) helps fill seats for television programs (and sometimes for televised award shows). There's no charge, but tickets are distributed on a first-come, first-served basis. Shows that may be taping or filming include *Will & Grace* and *Everybody Loves Raymond*. Tickets are received by mail or reserved over the Internet only. Note: you must be 16 or older to attend a television taping. For a schedule, send a self-addressed, stamped envelope to Audiences Unlimited a few weeks prior to your visit. Note that most network comedies are on hiatus from April through July.

Theater

Los Angeles isn't quite the "Broadway of the West," as some have claimed—the scope of theater here doesn't compare to that in New York. Still, the theater scene's growth has been impressive. Small theaters are blossoming all over town, and the larger houses, despite price hikes to as much as $70 for a single ticket, are usually full. Even small productions might boast big names from the entertainment industry.

Now Playing (⊕ www.reviewplays.com) lists what's currently in L.A. theaters and what's coming up in the next few months. **LA Stage Alliance** (⊕ www.lastagealliance.org) also gives information on what's playing in Los Angeles (although the synopses are usually either noncommittal or positively biased). Its LAStageTIX service allows you to buy tickets online the day of the performance at half-price or less (plus a small service charge).

MAJOR THEATERS Jason Robards and Nick Nolte got their starts at **Geffen Playhouse** (✉ 10886 Le Conte Ave., Westwood ☎ 310/208–5454 ⊕ www. geffenplayhouse.com), an acoustically superior, 498-seat theater that showcases new plays in the summer—primarily musicals and comedies. Many of the productions here are on their way to or from Broadway. In addition to theater performances, lectures, and children's programs, free summer jazz, dance, cabaret, and occasionally Latin and rock concerts ☺ take place at the **John Anson Ford Amphitheater** (✉ 2580 Cahuenga Blvd. E, Hollywood ☎ 323/461–3673 ⊕ www.fordamphitheater.org), a 1,300-seat outdoor venue in the Hollywood Hills. Winter shows typically are staged at the smaller indoor theater, **Inside the Ford.**

There are three theaters in the big downtown complex known as the ★ **Music Center** (✉ 135 N. Grand Ave., Downtown ☎ 213/972–7211 ⊕ www.musiccenter.org) : the 2,140-seat **Ahmanson Theatre** (☎ 213/ 628–2772 ⊕ www.taperahmanson.com) presents both classics and new plays; the 3,200-seat **Dorothy Chandler Pavilion** shows a smattering of plays between the more prevalent musical performances; and the 760-seat **Mark Taper Forum** (☎ 213/628–2772 ⊕ www.taperahmanson.com) presents new works that often go on to Broadway, such as *Angels in America* and *Master Class.*

The home of the Academy Awards telecast from 1949 to 1959, the **Pantages Theatre** presents large-scale Broadway musicals such as *The Lion King.* The 1,900-seat, art deco **Wilshire Theatre** (⊠ 8440 Wilshire Blvd., Beverly Hills ☎ 323/468–1716 ⊕ www.nederlander.com) presents Broadway musicals like *Annie Get Your Gun* and occasional concerts.

SMALLER THEATERS ★ The founders of **Actors' Gang Theater** (⊠ 6209 Santa Monica Blvd., Hollywood ☎ 323/465–0566 ⊕ www.theactorsgang.com) include film star Tim Robbins; the fare runs from Molière to Eric Bogosian to international works by traveling companies. **The Coronet Theatre** (⊠ 366 N. La Cienega Blvd., between Beverly Blvd. and Melrose Ave., West Hollywood ☎ 310/657–7377 ⊕ www.coronet-theatre.com) proves good things come in small packages. It's actually three small theaters in one, with consistently funny comedy or one-person performance pieces (sometimes audience-interactive) running on all stages simultaneously. The **Edgemar Theatre** (⊠ 2437 Main St., Santa Monica ☎☎ 310/399–3666) is a nonprofit performance and rehearsal space offering dramatic performances, dance, music, and film. Its notable supporters include Neil Simon, Jason Alexander, and Kate Capshaw. **The Evidence Room** (⊠ 2220 Beverly Blvd., Downtown ☎ 213/381–7118 ⊕ www.evidenceroom. com) is a group of actors, directors, and designers who've earned high honors for their individual work, and who have collaborated to host works of other theatrical organizations and of the city's best performance artists. **The Knightsbridge Theatre** (⊠ 1944 Riverside Dr., Silver Lake ☎ 626/440–0821 ⊕ www.knightsbridgetheatre.com) has a reputation as one of the city's chief recyclers of classic theater, both famous (Shakespeare's *All's Well That Ends Well*) and less-so (Gilbert & Sullivan's *Ruddygore*), with results that range from so-so to sensational. Founded in 1962, the nonprofit theater co-op **Theatre West** (⊠ 3333 Cahuenga Blvd. W, near Universal Center Dr., North Hollywood ☎ 323/851–7977 or 818/761–2203 ⊕ www.theatrewest.org) has produced an acclaimed body of work both in Los Angeles and on tour across America and even the British Isles. Its plays have gone on to Broadway (*Spoon River Anthology*) and been made into films (*A Bronx Tale*), and stars like the late Carroll O'Connor and Richard Dreyfuss have acted with the company. Its interactive **Storybook Theatre** (for 3–9-year-olds) is a long-running favorite.

THEATER ENSEMBLES ★ Some of Los Angeles's best theater is put on by ensembles that do not have permanent home theaters. **Circle X** (☎ 323/461–6069 ⊕ www. circlextheatre.org) is one of the most acclaimed local ensembles; since 1996, its members have been heavily represented in annual awards lists. Whether finding exciting new plays (or generating them) or devising novel means of presenting classics, Circle X's well-trained and inspired troupe finds ways to dazzle audiences on a shoestring budget.

Nightlife

Despite the high energy level of the L.A. nightlife crowd, don't expect to be partying until dawn—this is still an early-to-bed city. Liquor laws require that bars stop serving alcohol at 2 AM, and by this time, with the exception of a few after-hours venues and coffeehouses, most music and dance clubs have also closed for the night. Due to the smoking ban, most bars and clubs with a cover charge allow "in and outs," which permit you to leave the premises and return (usually with a hand stamp or paper bracelet).

One thing to keep in mind when going out—especially in West Hollywood's Sunset Strip area—is that "attitude" is the name of the game. Be prepared to endure highly developed snobbishness, even from the door guys. Another thing to remember is that parking, especially after 7 PM, is at a premium in West Hollywood, and in fact is restricted on virtually every side street along the "hot zone" (Sunset Boulevard from Fairfax to Doheny). There are small pockets of metered street parking (don't count on finding one of those spaces), which is fine as long as you feed the meter every half hour or hour until 10 PM. Signage indicating the restrictions is usually clear but is naturally harder to pick up at night. Paying $5–$10, and at some venues even $15, for valet parking is often the easiest way to go.

Bars

Like so many nightspots in this neck of the woods, the popularity and clientele of **Bar Marmont** (✉ 8171 Sunset Blvd., near Crescent Heights Ave., West Hollywood ☎ 323/650–0575) ballooned—and changed—after word got out it was a favorite of celebrities. The bar is adjacent to the inimitable hotel, Chateau Marmont. The **Beauty Bar** (✉ 1638 Cahuenga Blvd., Hollywood ☎ 323/464–7676) offers manicures and makeovers along with perfect martinis, but the hotties who flock to this retro salon-bar (the little sister of the Beauty Bars in N.Y.C. and San Fran) don't really need the cosmetic care—this is where the edgier "beautiful people" hang.

Fodor'sChoice ★ Hotel-and-nightlife impresario Andre Balazs (Chateau Marmont, N.Y.C.'s Mercer Hotel) has done it again with **The Downtown L.A. Standard** (✉ 550 S. Flower St., Downtown ☎ 213/892–8080), the sister venue to his other L.A. hipster haven, the Standard on Sunset. The neo-retro space-age hotel has a groovy lounge with pink sofas and chill-beat DJs, as well as an all-white restaurant that looks like something out of *2001: A Space Odyssey*. The rooftop bar (with an amazing view of the city's illuminated skyscrapers, a heated swimming pool, and private, podlike waterbed tents) has become almost impossible to get into, especially on weekends.

★ **The Echo** (✉ 1822 Sunset Blvd., Echo Park ☎ 213/413–8200) sprang from the people behind the Silver Lake rock joint Spaceland. Most evenings it's a chill spot for artsy locals, but things rev up when the DJs spin hip-hop, electroclash, and funk a few nights a week. The **Rainbow Bar & Grill** (✉ 9015 Sunset Blvd., West Hollywood ☎ 310/278–4232), in the heart of the Strip and next door to the legendary Roxy, is a landmark in its own right as *the* drinking spot of the '80s hair-metal scene—and it still attracts a music-industry crowd.

It's hard to believe, but the smart, brash-looking **Standard** hotel (⊠ 8300 Sunset Blvd., at Sweetzer Ave., West Hollywood ☎ 323/650–9090), used to be a Sunset Strip nursing home. Nowadays, its clientele is young, hip, and connected in "The Biz." A decidedly shaggier crowd flocks to **Star**
★ **Shoes** (⊠ 6364 Hollywood Blvd. ☎ 323/462-7827) where rock, electro, and soul is on the turntables and vintage footwear (all of it for sale) embellishes the walls.

★ **Tiki Ti** (⊠ 4427 W. Sunset Blvd., Silver Lake ☎ 323/669–9381 ☉ Wed.–Sat.), is one of the most charming drinking huts in the city. You can spend hours just looking at the Polynesian artifacts strewn around the place, but be careful—time flies in this tiny tropical bar, and the colorful drinks can be so potent that you may have to stay marooned for a while. The casually hip **Three Clubs** (⊠ 1123 N. Vine St., just north of Santa Monica Blvd., Hollywood ☎ 323/462–6441) is furtively located in a strip mall, beneath the fantastic Bargain Clown Mart. The DJs here spin an eclectic mix of rock-and-roll and dance music. With dark-wood paneling, lamp-lit tables, and even some sofas, you could be in a giant basement rec room from decades past. No cover charge, but it's often so packed you might have to wait for people to leave to get in.

A lovely L.A. tradition is to meet at **Yamashiro** (⊠ 1999 N. Sycamore Ave., Hollywood ☎ 323/466–5125) for cocktails at sunset. In the elegant restaurant, waitresses glide by in kimonos, and entrée prices can zoom up to $39; on the terrace, a spectacular hilltop view spreads out before you. Mandatory valet parking is $3.50, but happy hour drinks are just a bit more than that.

Blues

Babe & Ricky's Inn (⊠ 4339 Leimert Blvd., Leimert Park ☎ 323/295–9112) is an old blues favorite. The great jukebox, the photo and poster gallery, and the barbecue and brew (or wine) will help get you in the mood. Covers range from $5 to $10, and for Monday night's jam, admission will also get you a fried-chicken dinner, served at 10 PM. It's closed Tuesday and Wednesday. **B. B. King's Blues Bar** (⊠ 1000 Universal Center Dr., Universal City ☎ 818/622–5464) is a spacious, three-story venue at Universal CityWalk, with music nightly (at 8) and Southern cooking. Cover runs from $5 to $15.

Cabaret, Performance & Variety

The Cinegrill (⊠ Hollywood Roosevelt Hotel, 7000 Hollywood Blvd., Hollywood ☎ 323/466–7000) was remodeled in 2002 but it still has an intimate, old-time feel. It's worth a visit not only for the top-tier cabaret and jazz vocalists, but also for the Hollywood artifacts in the lobby of the adjoining landmark hotel. Helping bring old-fashioned burlesque
★ to contemporary nightlife is **Forty Deuce** (⊠ 5574 Melrose Ave., Hollywood ☎ 323/465–4242), where sultry yet relatively demure strip shows recall another era. The eye candy here is nonstop, but not just on stage—the lounge-bar is one of the most celeb-studded hangouts in town. With seating for 120, **Highways Performance Space** (⊠ 1651 18th St., Santa

Monica ☎ 310/453–1755 or 310/315–1459) is one of the primary venues for avant-garde, offbeat, and alternative performance art, theater, dance, and comedy programs—plus, it has two art galleries.

Coffeehouses

Espresso Mi Cultura (✉ 5625 Hollywood Blvd., Hollywood ☎ 323/461–0808) is a coffeehouse and bookstore celebrating Latino culture with readings and musical performances. It's a friendly, highly creative place.

★ **Highland Grounds** (✉ 742 N. Highland Ave., near Melrose Ave., Hollywood ☎ 323/466–1507) is one of L.A.'s oldest coffeehouses. It serves meals, plus it has a balcony, a patio, and a wide selection of beers as well as coffee drinks. Nightly entertainment is usually of the unplugged variety. A good place to take a break from the nonstop party of L.A. is the **Un-urban Coffee House** (✉ 3301 Pico Blvd., at Urban Ave., Santa Monica ☎ 310/315–0056). It serves up luscious chai tea, good but inexpensive breakfasts and sandwiches, and live music or spoken word performances on Sunday and weekend evenings.

Comedy & Magic

The zany performances at the **Acme Comedy Theater** (✉ 135 N. La Brea Ave., Hollywood ☎ 323/525–0202) include improv, sketch comedy, an improvised game show and an improvised 1940s-style radio drama. A nightly premier comedy showcase, **Comedy Store** (✉ 8433 Sunset Blvd., West Hollywood ☎ 323/656–6225) has been going strong for more than two decades. Famous comedians occasionally make unannounced appearances here. Cover is sometimes free, but can go up to $20. Look for top stand-ups—and frequent celeb residents, like Bob Saget, or

★ unannounced drop-ins, like Rodney Dangerfield—at **Laugh Factory** (✉ 8001 Sunset Blvd., West Hollywood ☎ 323/656–1336). The club has shows nightly at 8 PM, plus added shows at 10 and midnight on Friday; the cover is $10–$12.

Dance Clubs

Though the establishments listed below are predominantly dance clubs as opposed to live music venues, there is often some overlap. Also, a given club can vary wildly in genre from night to night, or even on the same night. Gay-lesbian and promoter-driven theme nights tend to "float" from venue to venue. Call ahead to make sure you don't end up looking for retro '60s music at an industrial bondage celebration (or vice versa). Covers vary according to the night and the DJs.

Formerly the Palace, **Avalon** (✉ 1735 N. Vine St. ☎ 323/462–3000) has retained its art deco splendor despite a major recent makeover. The rooftop patio has been reincarnated as the now-very-VIP **Spider Club,** and on most nights only admits celebs or "members." Downstairs the big room hosts two of L.A.'s biggest dance parties: the Brent Bolthouse–hosted hip-hop fest on Friday, and the electronica party known as "Giant" on Saturday. There are occasional live concerts held in the earlier evenings. Club covers range from $15 to $25. As a bar, **Boardner's** (✉ 1652 N. Cherokee Ave., Hollywood ☎ 323/462–9621) has a history that spans decades (in the '20s it was a speakeasy), but the adjoining ballroom added a couple of years ago, helped make it a state-of-the-art dance club. Depending on the night, DJs spin music ranging from electronica to funk to goth—the latter at the popular Saturday promotion "Bar Sinister," where the dress code is simply "black." The cover is anywhere from free to $10.

With private party rooms, a scantily clad crowd, and some see-through walls, **Deep** (✉ 1707 N. Vine St., Hollywood ☎ 323/462–1144) is one of the sexiest clubs in Tinseltown. The exclusive dance club has DJs spinning everything from techno to old school to current dance hits, plus grindingly good go-go dancers. **Gabah** (✉ 4658 Melrose Ave., Hollywood ☎ 323/664–8913) means "jungle" in Arabic, and it's a fitting moniker for a place offering such exotic and diverse music. DJs spin everything from hip-hop to dub and reggae to obscure rarities at weekly club promotions like the long-running Saturday Chocolate Bar.

Ivar (✉ 6356 Hollywood Blvd., Hollywood ☎ 310/829–1933) always attracts the model-actor "discover me" set with weekly hip-hop, electronic, and old-school music promotions, but the futuristic-looking spot has also been the site for some big Hollywood parties, where real celebs escape in its multiple VIP rooms. (These include a two-level, neon-lit, cylindrical-platformed area that looks like something out of *Star Trek*.) **The Lounge** (✉ 9077 Santa Monica Blvd., West Hollywood ☎ 310/888–8811) was a Latin music venue when it first opened, but these days, the upscale restaurant-nightclub is all about American music and American idols; stars such as Justin Timberlake often hang here when in town.

Gay & Lesbian Clubs

Some of the most popular gay and lesbian "clubs" are weekly theme nights at various venues, so read the preceding list of clubs, *LA Weekly* listings, and gay publications such as *Odyssey* in addition to the following recommendations.

The Factory (✉ 652 La Peer Dr., near Santa Monica Blvd., West Hollywood ☎ 310/659–4551) churns out the dance music: Wednesday is the mixed flashback "That '80s Night"; Friday, the lesbian night "Girl Bar." In the adjoining **Ultra Suede** (✉ 661 N. Robertson Blvd., West Hollywood), there's '80s and '90s pop on Wednesday and Friday. Saturday, the two houses combine for an event called "The Factory"—except on the first Saturday of the month, when Ultra Suede hosts a gay Asian night. Covers range from $5 to $15. A long-running gay-gal fave, **The Palms** (✉ 8572 Santa Monica Blvd., West Hollywood ☎ 310/652–6188) continues to thrive thanks to great DJs spinning dance tunes Wednesday–Sunday, plus an outdoor patio, pool tables, and occasional live performances.

The Parlour Club (✉ 7702 Santa Monica Blvd., West Hollywood ☎ 310/650–7968) hosts unique music-themed nights, featuring so-bad-they're-good AM radio hits, campy punk rock, Roaring '20s music, and retro pop from Japan, Spain, and France. Most nights are free; live performances usually command a $5–$10 cover. **Peanuts** (✉ 7969 Santa Monica Blvd., West Hollywood ☎ 323/654–0280) hosts mixed–gay theme nights, including the drag diva party called "Illusions" and the straight rock-and-roll strip–style romp (there are poles on the stage, after all) of "Pink Pussycat."

Jazz

Big-name acts take the stage at the new location of **Catalina Bar and Grill** (✉ 6725 Sunset Blvd., Hollywood ☎ 323/466–2210), which still ties with rival Jazz Bakery for the title of top jazz club in town. Shows start at 8:30 and 10:30 Tuesday–Saturday; Sunday shows are at 7:15 and 9:15. There are occasional Monday-night and Sunday brunch shows, too. The cover ranges from $16 to $20. L.A.'s most dapper swingsters put on the ritz at **The Derby** (✉ 4500 Los Feliz Blvd., Los Feliz ☎ 323/663–8979), a spacious, elegant club with a 360-degree brass-railed bar and plush-velvet curtained booths. There's live music most nights with the emphasis on swing and jazz. There are free dance lessons at 8 PM, the music begins at 9:30 or 10, and the cover is $7–$10. Come to **Jazz Bakery** (✉ 3233 Helms Ave., Culver City ☎ 310/271–9039) for world-class jazz nightly at 8 and 9:30, in a quiet, respectful concertlike setting. The adjoining Cafe Cantata serves coffee, beer, wine, snacks, and desserts. The cover is $10–$30; parking is free.

Latin

★ The **Conga Room** (✉ 5364 Wilshire Blvd., Mid-Wilshire ☎ 323/938–1696), which is co-owned by local celebs, including Jimmy Smits, presents Latin music (primarily salsa) and the odd rock or soul show. The tropical interiors and hot music may not soften the blow to your wallet; regular admission is $10–$20, but VIP treatment costs $30–$40. There are dance lessons Thursday through Saturday, 8–9 PM for $10. The Cuban food at **El Floridita** (✉ 1253 N. Vine St., Hollywood ☎ 323/871–8612) is anywhere from good to great—and the music (Monday, Friday, and Saturday) is anywhere from very good to through the roof. A frequent guest is ex-New Yorker Johnny Polanco, backed by the sizzling Conjunto Amistad. Even watching some of the paying customers who get up to dance is worth the price of admission (usually $10, or free with dinner).

Rock & Other Live Music

★ It may be on the Sunset Strip, but the **Key Club** (✉ 9039 Sunset Blvd. ☎ 310/274–5800) is nothing like the other 100% rock-driven joints on the boulevard. It's extremely eclectic, with everything from glittering burlesque spectacles to noisy punk-rock bashes to mellow jazz nights.

The Knitting Factory (✉ 7021 Hollywood Blvd., Hollywood ☎ 323/463–0204) is the L.A. offshoot of the eponymous downtown N.Y.C. club. The modern, medium-size room seems all the more spacious for its balcony-level seating and sizable stage. Despite its dubious location on Hollywood Boulevard's tourist strip—in the building housing the Galaxy movie theater—it's a great set-up for the arty, big-name performers it presents. There's live music almost every night in the main room and in the smaller Alter-Knit Lounge; there's also a restaurant, a full bar, and Web stations for surfing music sites. Covers are free to $40.

Musician and producer Jon Brion (Fiona Apple, Aimee Mann, et al.) shows off his ability to play virtually any instrument or song in the rock lexicon—and beyond—as host of a popular evening of music every Friday at **Largo** (✉ 432 N. Fairfax Ave., Hollywood ☎ 323/852–1073). Other nights, low-key rock and singer-songwriter fare is offered at this cozy supper club–bar. And when comedy acts come in, about one night a week, they're usually some of the hippest around (Margaret Cho, for example, has been known to appear). Reservations are required for tables, but bar stools are open. **McCabe's Guitar Shop** (⊠ 3101 Pico Blvd., Santa Monica ☎ 310/828–4497, 310/828–4403 concert information) is rootsy-retro-central, where all things earnest and (preferably) acoustic are welcome—chiefly folk, blues, bluegrass, and rock; usually electrified performers will go unplugged (or semi, anyway) to play here. It *is* a guitar shop (so no liquor license), with a room full of folding chairs for concert-style presentations. Make reservations well in advance.

Neighborhoody and relaxed **Silver Lake Lounge** (⊠ 2906 Sunset Blvd., Silver Lake ☎ 323/666–2407) is patronized by both collegiate and boho crowds. The club is very unmainstream "cool," the booking policy an adventurous mix of local and touring alt-rockers. Bands play three to five nights a week; covers vary but are inexpensive. The hottest bands of tomorrow, surprises from yesteryear, and unclassifiable bands of

★ today perform at **Spaceland** (⊠ 1717 Silver Lake Blvd., Silver Lake ☎ 323/661–4380), which has a bar, jukebox, and pool table. Monday is usually free. Spaceland has a nice selection of beers, some food if you're hungry, and a hip but relaxed interior.

★ **The Troubadour** (⊠ 9081 Santa Monica Blvd., near Doheny Dr., West Hollywood ☎ 310/276–6168), one of the best and most comfortable clubs in town, has weathered the test of time since its '60s debut as a folk club. After surviving the '80s heavy-metal scene, this all-ages, wood-paneled venue has caught a second (third? fourth?) wind by booking hot alternative rock acts. There's valet parking, but if you don't mind walking up Doheny a block or three, there's usually ample street parking (check the signs carefully). At the **Viper Room** (⊠ 8852 Sunset Blvd., West Hollywood ☎ 310/358–1880), formerly owned by actor Johnny Depp, the live music is purely contemporary and decidedly eclectic, occasionally featuring names normally too big to play such a small venue. **Whisky-A-Go-Go** (⊠ 8901 Sunset Blvd., West Hollywood ☎ 310/652–4202) is the most famous rock-and-roll club on the Strip, where back in the '60s, Johnny Rivers cut hit singles and the Doors, Love, and the Byrds cut their musical eyeteeth. It's still going strong, with up-and-coming alternative, hard rock, and punk bands. Mondays showcase L.A.'s cutting-edge acts.

SPORTS & THE OUTDOORS

Updated by Matthew Flynn

From surfing to whale-watching, L.A. has an enviable scope of activities. Given the right weather conditions, it's possible to choose between skiing and a trip to the beach. A word to the wise, though: the air is dry, so no matter where your adventures take you, bring bottled water and lip balm. Also, don't forget sunscreen; even on overcast days the sunburn index can be high.

Beaches

From downtown, the easiest way to hit the coast is by taking the Santa Monica Freeway (I–10) due west. Once you reach the end of the freeway, I–10 runs into Highway 1 (better known as the Pacific Coast Highway, or PCH). Highway 1 continues north to Sonoma County and south to San Diego. MTA buses run from downtown along Pico, Olympic, Santa Monica, Sunset, and Wilshire boulevards.

Los Angeles County beaches (and state beaches operated by the county) have lifeguards on duty year-round, with expanded forces in summer. Public parking is usually available, though fees can be as much as $8; in some areas, it's possible to find free street and highway parking. Several beaches have improved their parking facilities, and both rest rooms and beach access have been brought up to Americans with Disabilities Act standards. Generally, the northernmost beaches are best for surfing, hiking, and fishing, and the wider and sandier southern beaches are better for tanning and relaxing. Almost all are great for swimming, but beware: pollution in Santa Monica Bay sometimes approaches dangerous levels, particularly after storms. Call ahead or check online for **beach conditions** (☎ 310/457–9701 Malibu, 310/578–0478 Santa Monica, 310/379–8471 South Bay area ⊕ www.healthebay.org).

Leo Carrillo State Beach. On the very edge of Ventura County, this narrow beach is better for exploring than for swimming or sunning. On your own or with a ranger, you can venture down at low tide to examine the tide pools among the rocks. Sequit Point, a promontory dividing the northwest and southeast halves of the beach, creates secret coves, sea tunnels, and boulders on which you can perch and fish. Generally, anglers stick to the northwest end of the beach; experienced surfers brave the rocks to the southeast. Campgrounds are set back from the beach; call ahead to reserve campsites. ⊠ *35000 PCH, Malibu* ☎ *818/880–0350, 800/444–7275 camping reservations* ☞ *Parking, lifeguard (year-round, except only as needed in winter), restrooms, showers, fire pits.*

Robert H. Meyer Memorial State Beach. Part of Malibu's most beautiful coastal area, this beach is made up of three minibeaches: El Pescador, La Piedra, and El Matador. "El Mat" has a series of caves, Piedra some nifty rock formations, and Pescador a secluded feel, but they all have spectacular views and a fair amount of privacy. You may see the occasional nude sunbather—although in recent years, police have been cracking down. ⊠ *32350, 32700, and 32900 PCH, Malibu* ☎ *818/880–0350* ☞ *Parking, 1 roving lifeguard unit, restrooms.*

Zuma Beach Park. This 2-mi stretch of white sand has it all: from fishing and diving to swings for the kids to volleyball courts; there are even decent restrooms. This is the perfect beach for clean water, swimming, boogie boarding, dolphin sightings, sand castles, and powerful surf. ⊠ *30050 PCH, Malibu* ☎ *310/457–9891* ☞ *Parking, lifeguard (year-round, except only as needed in winter), restrooms, food concessions, playground, volleyball.*

Malibu Lagoon State Beach/Surfrider Beach. Steady 3- to 5-foot waves make this beach, just west of Malibu Pier, a popular surfing location. The International Surfing Contest is held here in September, and the surf is best around that time. Water runoff from Malibu Canyon forms a natural lagoon 75 yards inland that's a sanctuary for 250 species of birds. Unfortunately, the lagoon is often polluted and algae-filled. If you're leery of going into the water, you can bird-watch, play volleyball, or take a sunset stroll on one of the nature trails. ⊠ *23200 PCH, Malibu* ☎ *818/ 880–0350* ☞ *Parking, lifeguard (year-round), restrooms, picnicking, visitor center.*

Will Rogers State Beach. This clean, sandy, 3-mi beach, with a dozen volleyball nets, gymnastics equipment, and playground equipment for kids, is an all-around favorite. The surf is gentle, perfect for swimmers and beginning surfers. Fortunately, with improved sewage treatment, the water quality at this once polluted beach has continued to improve. However, it is always a good idea to check water quality immediately following a rain storm due to increased bacterial levels. ⊠ *15100 PCH, 2 mi north of Santa Monica pier, Pacific Palisades* ☎ *310/577–5700* ☞ *Parking, lifeguard (year-round, except only as needed in winter), restrooms.*

Santa Monica State Beach. It's the first beach you'll hit after the Santa Monica Freeway (I–10) runs into the PCH, and it's one of L.A.'s best-known and most crowded. Wide and sandy, it's *the* place for sunning and socializing: be prepared for a mob scene on summer weekends, when parking becomes an expensive ordeal. Swimming is fine (with the usual post-storm pollution caveat); surfers will want to go elsewhere. For a memorable view, climb up the stairway over the PCH to Palisades Park, a grassy strip at the top of the bluffs. Summer evening concerts are often held here. ⊠ *1642 Promenade (PCH at California Incline), Santa Monica* ☎ *310/ 577–5700* ☞ *Parking, lifeguard (year-round), restrooms, showers.*

Venice City Beach. The surf and sand of Venice are fine, but the main attraction here is the boardwalk scene. There's also swimming, fishing, surfing, and basketball courts (it's the site of some of L.A.'s most hotly contested pickup games), racquetball, handball, and shuffleboard. You can rent a bike or some in-line skates and hit the bike path (the Strand). ⊠ *West of Pacific Ave., Venice* ☎ *310/577–5700* ☞ *Parking, playground, restrooms, showers, food concessions.*

Sports

The **City of Los Angeles Department of Recreation and Parks** (⊠ 200 N. Main St., Suite 1350, 90012 ☎ 888/527–2757 ⊕ www.cityofla.org/rap) has information on city parks. For information on county parks, such as Eaton Canyon and Vasquez Rocks, contact the **Los Angeles County Department of Parks and Recreation** (⊠ 433 S. Vermont Ave., 90020 ☎ 213/ 738–2961 ⊕ http://parks.co.la.ca.us).

Los Angeles is home to some of the greatest franchises in pro basketball and baseball, and the greater L.A. area has two teams in each of those pro sports, as well as hockey, too. For tickets to most sporting events, call **Ticketmaster** (☎ 213/480–3232 ⊕ www.ticketmaster.com), or the venue box office.

Baseball

You can watch the **Dodgers** take on their National League rivals while you munch on a foot-long "Dodger dog" at **Dodger Stadium** (⊠ 1000 Elysian

Park Ave., exit off I–110, Pasadena Freeway ☎ 323/224–1448 for ticket information ⊕ www.dodgers.com). The **Anaheim Angels** won the World Series in 2002, the first time since the team formed in 1961. For Angels ticket information, contact **Edison International Field** (✉ 2000 Gene Autry Way, Anaheim ☎ 714/663–9000 ⊕ www.angelsbaseball.com). Several colleges in the area also have baseball teams worth watching, especially USC's, which has been a perennial source of major league talent.

Basketball

L.A.'s pro basketball teams play at the plush **Staples Center** (☎ 213/742–7340 ⊕ www.staplescenter.com). The **Los Angeles Lakers** (☎ 310/426–6000 ⊕ www.nba.com/lakers) have captured the heart of the city with star players and personalities like Shaquille O'Neal and the now-retired Magic Johnson. Celebrity fans like Jack Nicholson often show up at Laker games. Tickets to see L.A.'s "other" team, the much-maligned but newly revitalized **Clippers** (☎ 213/742–7500 ⊕ www.nba.com/clippers), are generally cheaper and easier to get than those for Lakers' games. The **Los Angeles Sparks** (☎ 877/447–7275 ⊕ www.lasparks.com) have built a WNBA dynasty around former USC star Lisa Leslie.

Bicycling

For an overview of L.A. area bike routes, including maps and useful links, check online at **Los Angeles Bike Paths** (⊕ www.labikepaths.com).

★ The most famous bike path in the city, which runs for 22 mi along the ocean from Will Rogers State Beach down to Torrance Beach, is known as the **Strand.** Two-wheelers share the path with joggers, skateboarders, in-line skaters, walkers, and other nonvehicular traffic (although for some stretches, bikes have their own parallel path). The sunny beach scenery is uninterrupted, save for a couple of short city-street detours around the Marina del Rey Harbor and the Redondo Beach Pier. The ride can be done in a long leisurely afternoon. You can rent a bike at one of many shops along the Strand's middle section. Cyclists often refer to the 18$\frac{4}{10}$-mi section south of the Santa Monica Pier as the South Bay Bicycle Trail.

The flat, 3-mi paved path around **Lake Hollywood** is a great place to take in views of the HOLLYWOOD sign. Griffith Park, Malibu Creek State Park, and Topanga State Park are all part of the **Santa Monica Mountains,** which have good mountain-biking paths.

Perry's has two bike-rental locations along the Strand: **Perry's Bike & Skate** (✉ 2600 Ocean Front Walk, Venice ☎ 310/584–9306), and **Perry's Beach Rentals** (✉ 2400 Ocean Front Walk, Venice ☎ 310/452–7609). **Spokes 'N Stuff** (✉ Griffith Park, 4400 Crystal Springs Dr., Los Feliz ☎ 323/653–4099 ✉ Strand, 1700 Ocean Ave., Santa Monica ☎ 310/395–4748 ✉ Strand, 4175 Admiralty Way, Marina Del Rey ☎ 310/306–3332) has a rental shop behind the ranger station in Griffith Park and two rental places on the Strand.

Fishing

Shore fishing and surf casting are excellent on many of the beaches, and pier fishing is popular because no license is necessary to fish off public piers. The **Fish and Game Department** (☎ 562/342–7100, 562/590–5020 for lake-stocking information) can answer questions about licenses and give advice. The **Santa Monica, Redondo Beach,** and **Malibu** piers have bait-and-tackle shops with everything you'll need.

If you want to break away from the piers, sign up for a boat excursion with one of the local charters, most of which will sell you a fishing license and rent tackle. Most also offer whale-watching excursions. **Del Rey Sport Fishing** (⊠ 13759 Fiji Way, dock 52, Marina Del Rey ☎ 310/ 822–3625) runs excursions for $28 per half day and $40 for three-quarters of a day, with tackle rental another $8. **Redondo Sport Fishing Company** (⊠ 233 N. Harbor Dr., Redondo Beach ☎ 310/372–2111) has half-day charters starting at $27 and three-quarter-day cruises for $39 per person. Sea bass, halibut, bonita, yellowtail, and barracuda are the usual catch.

Golf

The City Parks and Recreation Department lists seven public 18-hole courses in Los Angeles, and L.A. County runs some good ones, too. **Rancho Park Golf Course** (⊠ 10460 W. Pico Blvd., West L.A. ☎ 310/838–7373 ⊕ www. laparks.org) is one of the most heavily played links in the country. It's a beautifully designed course, but the towering pines present an obstacle for those who slice or hook. There's a two-level driving range, a 9-hole pitch 'n' putt, a snack bar, and a pro shop where you can rent clubs.

★ If you want a scenic course, head for the county-run, par-71 **Los Verdes Golf Course** (⊠ 7000 W. Los Verdes Dr., Rancho Palos Verdes ☎ 310/ 377–7370 ⊕ http://parks.co.la.ca.us/golfcourses.html). You get a cliff-top view of the ocean—time it right and you can watch the sun set behind Catalina Island—and it's one of California's best-run courses to boot.

Griffith Park has two splendid 18-hole courses along with a challenging 9-hole course. **Harding Municipal Golf Course** and **Wilson Municipal Golf Course** (⊠ 4730 Crystal Springs Dr., Los Feliz ☎ 323/663–2555 ⊕ www.laparks.org) are about 1½ mi inside the park entrance at Riverside Drive and Los Feliz Boulevard. Bridle paths surround the outer fairways, and the San Gabriel Mountains make a scenic background. The 9-hole **Roosevelt Municipal Golf Course** (⊠ 2650 N. Vermont Ave., Los Feliz ☎ 323/665–2011 ⊕ www.laparks.org) can be reached through the park's Vermont Avenue entrance.

Hiking

"Nobody Walks in L.A." sang the music group Missing Persons back in the '80s, and it's as true as ever—but Los Angelenos do like to hike. The coast, the Hollywood Hills, and the greater Santa Monica Mountains are all convenient getaways. Remember not to venture deep into the national parks and forests alone—and be sure to bring water and sunblock with you. For information on hiking locations and scheduled outings in Los Angeles, contact the **Sierra Club** (⊠ 3435 Wilshire Blvd., Suite 320, Los Angeles 90010 ☎ 213/387–4287 ⊕ www.sierraclub.org).

★ One of the best places to begin is **Griffith Park** (⊠ Ranger Station, 4730 Crystal Springs Dr., Los Feliz ☎ 323/913–4688); pick up a map from the ranger station. Many of the paths in the park are not shaded and can be quite steep. A nice short hike from Canyon Drive, at the south-west end of the park, takes you to **Bronson Caves,** where the *Batman* television show was filmed. Begin at the Observatory for a 3-mi round-trip hike to the top of **Mt. Hollywood.**

As a walk, run, or bike ride, the **Hollywood Reservoir (a.k.a. Lake Hollywood) trail** (☎ 323/463–0830) is probably one of the best places to work up a sweat in all of L.A. The 4-mi flat walk around the reservoir provides great views of hillside mansions, the HOLLYWOOD Sign, and the reservoir itself. The park is open dawn to dusk. To get there, exit U.S. 101 at Barham Boulevard (near Universal City). Look for Lake Holly-wood Drive on your right and take it, making sure you stay the course through its tricky turns. Park when you see the gate and enter to begin your power walk or stroll.

★ It's possible that many of Will Rogers's famed witticisms came to him while he and his wife hiked or rode horses along the **Inspiration Point Trail** from their Pacific Palisades ranch, now **Will Rogers State Historic Park** (✉ 1501 Will Rogers State Park Rd., at Sunset Blvd., Pacific Palisades ☎ 310/454–8212 ⊕ www.parks.ca.gov). The point is on a de-tour off the lovely 2-mi loop, which you pick up right by the riding stables beyond the parking lot ($5 per car). On a clear (or even just semi-clear) day, the panorama is one of L.A.'s widest and most "wow"-inducing, from the peaks of the San Gabriel Mountains in the distant east, to the Oz-like cluster of Downtown L.A. skyscrapers rising out of the clouds, to Catalina Island looming off the coast to the southwest. If you're look-ing for a longer trip, the top of the loop meets up with the 65-mi Back-bone Trail, which connects to Topanga State Park.

Surfing

Surfing is the sport that truly symbolizes L.A. and Southern California in general; it has a long cultural history here. If you're not a strong swim-mer, though, don't even consider it; fighting the surf to where the waves break is a strenuous, sometimes even dangerous, proposition. The best and safest way to learn is by taking a lesson. Always give other surfers plenty of space—do *not* cut them off—and avoid swimmers.

A lesson from **Malibu Ocean Sports** (✉ 22935 PCH, across from the pier at Malibu Point ☎ 310/456–6302) will keep you on the sand for at least 45 minutes while you learn the basics. **The Surf Academy** (✉ 302 19th St., Hermosa Beach ☎ 310/372–2790 ⊕ www.surfacademy.org) teaches at El Segundo (Dockweiler) and Manhattan Beach, with lessons start-ing at $35. You'll find plenty of surf shops with rentals at all the surf-ing hot spots. Competition keeps prices comparable; most rent long, short, and miniboards (kid-size surfboards) from $18 per day, and wet suits from $8 per day (some give discounts for additional days).

Call the **L.A. County Lifeguards** (☎ 310/457–9701 Malibu, 310/578–0478 Santa Monica, 310/379–8471 Manhattan, Redondo, and Hermosa beaches) for prerecorded surf conditions hotlines.

Tennis

L.A. Department of Recreation and Parks (✉ 200 N. Main St., Downtown ☎ 213/473–7070 ⊕ www.cityofla.org/rap/dos/tennis/tennis.htm) has a complete list of the city's more than 75 public tennis courts. Some are always free, others only weekdays, and still others charge $5–$8 an hour per court, depending on time of day. Reservations are a must during peak hours at the most popular pay courts; to make them, apply for a reservation card (click on "Permits") at the Web site or call 213/625–1010.

Whale-Watching

From December to March or April, California gray whales migrate from northern waters to their breeding and birthing grounds off the coast of Mexico. To get an up-close look at these magnificent animals as they make their journey, hop aboard one of the **whale-watching tour boats** that depart from Long Beach and San Pedro; prices are $8–$20 per person, and reservations are recommended. Bring binoculars, dress warmly, and remember that winter seas can be rough. Contact the following tour operators for specific schedules: **Spirit Cruises** (☎ 310/548–8080 ⊕ www. spiritdinnercruises.com) or **Long Beach Sportfishing** (☎ 562/432–8993 ⊕ www.longbeachsportfishing.com). You can also contact any of the expedition companies listed under Fishing, *above*; they run whale-watching outings, too.

Yoga

Classes for beginner, intermediate, and advanced yogis and yoginis—and even those with injuries—are held at **Yoga Inside Out**. The teachers here empahsize the principles of Anusara alignment. Classes are held throughout the day every day, and are $15 each (a 5-class series is $65). ✉ *8741 Santa Monica Blvd., West Hollywood* ☎ *310/855–YOGA* ⊕ *www.yogainsideout.com*. Kundalini yoga, meditation, prenatal yoga, and yoga for kids are all offered at **Golden Bridge**. Single classes are $15; a set of 5 costs $60. ✉ *5901 West 3rd Street (4 Blocks West of La Brea), Los Angeles* ☎ *323/ 936-4172* ⊕ *www.goldenbridgeyoga.com.*

SHOPPING

Updated by
Lina Lecaro

As neighborhoods wax and wane, new shopping districts pop up seemingly overnight—there's always a freshly minted hot destination to explore. Sometimes, though, you just need a mall fix. Rest assured: California has more mall space, by far, than any other state. Since distances between shopping districts can be vast in this notoriously car-dependent city, don't try to hit too many shopping areas in one day or you'll spend more time driving than spending.

Shopping Neighborhoods

Shopping in **Beverly Hills** centers mainly around the three-block stretch of **Rodeo Drive** between Santa Monica and Wilshire boulevards. Also known also as Via Rodeo, this super-swanky street is where you'll find boutiques for all the highest-end designers—Gucci, Armani, Chanel—as well as famed jewelers Tiffany, Cartier and Harry Winston. Wilshire is home to bigger, but no less exclusive, department stores such as Saks Fifth Avenue and Barneys. While you may feel cowed by some of the astronomical prices or chicer-than-thou attitudes among salespeople at these stores, most shops present a friendly sales front to the public. Around this tourist hot spot, many celebrities sneak into their favorite shops before or after hours or through back entrances. Be advised: some stores are by-appointment only. There are several free (for two hours) parking lots in the vicinity.

Century City is L.A.'s errand central, where entertainment executives and industry types do their serious shopping. In general, it's more affordable than Beverly Hills. Although the Century City Shopping Center has changed names (to Westfield Shoppingtown Century City), it's the same mall in quality and substance: everything from large retail favorites like Macy's and Bloomingdale's to small outdoor carts hawking jewelry and candles are still here.

Dotted with ethnic enclaves (Olvera Street, Chinatown, Koreatown) and several large, open-air shopping venues (the Fashion District, the Flower Mart, Grand Central Market and the Jewelry District), **downtown L.A.** offers an urban shopping experience to counterbalance the precious atmosphere cultivated by the boutiques of the Westside. Check out Santee Alley, where street vendors hawk trendy clothing—and plenty of knock-off designer sunglasses and purses. You can also buy materials to make your own fashions in the area's numerous fabric stores; the most popular of these, Michael Levine, offers free parking with purchase.

★ The retail-hotel-dining-entertainment complex Hollywood & Highland bills itself as the "epicenter of pop culture." A tall claim perhaps, but it did help upgrade the image of **Hollywood** when TV personality Ryan Seacrest began broadcasting his live show here. Along the boulevard, it's one souvenir store after the next, but a few shops—like Frederick's of Hollywood for lingerie, and Hollywood Toy and Costume for kitschy toys, get-ups, and games—are worth the stroll. Outside of Hollywood, especially along La Brea Avenue and Cahuenga Boulevard near Sunset (the home of the city's biggest and best music store, Amoeba Music), you'll find plenty of trendy, quirky, and hip merchandise to splurge on.

As **Los Feliz and Silver Lake** gentrify, distinct shopping areas are rapidly gelling. Many boutiques are clustered along Vermont Avenue and Hollywood Boulevard in Los Feliz, and Sunset Boulevard in Silver Lake; two of the best are Vermont Avenue's Y-Que (which sells the popular "Free Winona" T-shirts) and Soap Plant/Wacko on Sunset, which sells cool art books and hipster housewares. Eastward down Sunset, you'll find plenty of galleries, vintage shops, and local designers offering one of a kind items.

Melrose Avenue has something of a split personality. From North Highland to Sweetzer, it's a bohemian-punk shopping district, where vintage–resale oasis Wasteland, rock-star clothiers Serious, and even a shop selling bones (called Necromance) attract the alternative set. On upper Melrose Avenue and Melrose Place, the shopping scene is more upscale and design-y; shops include such pricey boutiques as Agent Provocateur, Betsy Johnson, Miss Sixty, and the mecca for celebrity stylists, Fred Segal.

Less frenetic and status-conscious than Beverly Hills, **Santa Monica** is ideal for leisurely shopping. Most shopping activity takes place on and around the 3rd Street Promenade, the strip of 3rd Street between Broadway and

Wilshire Boulevard, where hip houses of style like Urban Outfitters are always bustling. Montana Avenue has lots of unique boutiques, especially between 7th and 17th streets; one is Patrick Reid, a saucy little frock shop run by the brother of actress Tara Reid, and another is Imagine That!, a creative book and toy store for kids. Parking in Santa Monica is next to impossible on Wednesday, when some streets are blocked for the city's fabulous **Farmers Market.**

West Hollywood is a diverse, terrific shopping destination. You'll find every kind of Angeleno browsing the record stores along Sunset Boulevard, while the well-heeled haunt upscale boutiques like MAC Cosmetics, Cynthia Rowley, Kate Spade, and Lisa Kline on Robertson Boulevard and between Beverly Boulevard and 3rd Street. The big blue Pacific Design Center, on Melrose at San Vicente Boulevard, is the focal point for the neighborhood's art and interior design–related stores, including many on nearby Beverly Boulevard. At Fairfax and 3rd Street you'll find the historic Farmers Market and the adjacent shopping mecca The Grove.

Malls & Markets

Beverly Center. An extensive collection of upscale shops draws a high-end and international clientele here. There's a terrific view of the city from the eighth-floor terrace and rooftop food court. The **California Welcome Center** (☎ 310/854–7616), on the first floor, provides shopping discounts plus information and tickets for most of L.A.'s attractions. ☒ *8500 Beverly Blvd., bounded by Beverly, La Cienega, and San Vicente blvds. and 3rd St., between Beverly Hills and West Hollywood* ☎ *310/854–0070.*

★ ♻ **Farmers Market and The Grove.** The granddaddy of L.A. markets dates back to 1935, and the huddle of clapboard stalls, eccentric regulars, and, oh yes, produce and wares must be experienced to be appreciated. The Grove, extending from the old marketplace, has an ersatz European feel, with an outdoor café, fountain, tiled walkways and a small trolley that gives rides around the property. ☒ *6333 W. 3rd St., at Fairfax Ave., Fairfax District* ☎ *Farmers Market, 323/933–9211, The Grove, 323/900–8080 or 888/315–8883.*

★ ♻ **Hollywood & Highland.** Dozens of stores, the Kodak Theatre, and a slew of eateries fill this outdoor complex, which is meant to embody cinematic glamour. Sweeping steps lead between floors of designer shops and chain stores. From the upper levels, there's a camera-perfect view of the famous HOLLYWOOD sign. ☒ *Hollywood Blvd. and Highland Ave., Hollywood* ☎ *323/960–2331.*

Rose Bowl Flea Market. The vendors come out on the second Sunday of every month, rain or shine. If you expect bargains, you're in for a shock unless you're an expert haggler. This massive, extremely popular market attracts more than 2,200 vendors looking for top dollar for their antiques, crafts, and new furniture. ☒ *1001 Rosebowl Dr., Pasadena* ☎ *323/560–7469.*

Third Street Promenade. The pedestrian-only street is lined mainly with chain stores, movie theaters, bookstores, pubs, and restaurants. Day or night, wacky street performers, missionaries, and protesters work the crowds.

Westfield Shoppingtown Century City. Set among office buildings on what used to be Twentieth Century Fox film studios' back lot, this open-air mall pulls has an array of upscale shops. ⊠ *10250 Santa Monica Blvd., Century City* ☎ *310/277–3898.*

LOS ANGELES A TO Z

AIR TRAVEL

The major gateway to L.A. is Los Angeles International Airport (LAX); it's serviced by more than 85 major airlines. Flights in and out of LAX are seldom delayed because of weather and generally run on time. Because of heavy traffic around the airport and difficult parking, however, you should allow plenty of time to arrive at the airport prior to scheduled departure or arrival times. There are three other nearby airports that serve L.A. County; they're smaller and have more limited services, but are worth investigating when booking flights.

🚇 **Bob Hope Airport (a.k.a. Burbank/Glendale/Pasadena Airport)** ⊠ 2627 N. Hollywood Way, Burbank ☎ 818/840–8830 or 818/840–8847 ⊕ www.burbankairport.com. **Long Beach Airport** ⊠ 4100 Donald Douglas Dr. ☎ 562/570–2600 ⊕ www.lgb.org. **Los Angeles International Airport (LAX)** ☎ 310/646–5252 ⊕ www.lawa.org. **Ontario International Airport** ⊠ Airport Dr. and Vineyard Ave. ☎ 909/937–2700 ⊕ www.lawa.org. 🚇 Shuttles **Xpress Shuttle** ☎ 800/427–7483 ⊕ www.expressshuttle.com. **Prime Time** ☎ 800/733–8267 ⊕ www.primetimeshuttle.com. **SuperShuttle** ☎ 213/688–0444, 323/775–6600, 310/782–6600, or 800/258–3826 ⊕ www.supershuttle.com.

BUS TRAVEL TO AND FROM L.A.

🚇 **Greyhound** ⊠ 1716 E. 7th St., Downtown ☎ 213/629–8405 or 800/231–2222 ⊕ www.greyhound.com.

BUS TRAVEL WITHIN L.A.

Inadequate public-transportation systems have been an L.A. problem for decades. That said, many local trips can be made, with time and patience, by bus. In certain cases, it may be your best option; for example, if you're visiting the Getty Center with no prior parking reservation. The Metropolitan Transit Authority DASH (Downtown Area Short Hop) minibuses cover six different circular routes in Hollywood, Mid-Wilshire, and the downtown area. The Santa Monica Municipal Bus Line, also known as the Big Blue Bus, is a pleasant and inexpensive way to move around the Westside, where the MTA lines leave off.

🚇 **Smart Traveler** ☎ 800/266–6883 ⊕ www.smart-traveler.com. **DASH** ☎ 213/626–4455 or 310/808–2273 ⊕ www.ladottransit.com/dash. **Metropolitan Transit Authority (MTA)** ☎ 213/626–4455 or 800/266–6883 ⊕ www.mta.net. **Santa Monica Municipal Bus Line** ☎ 310/451–5444 ⊕ www.bigbluebus.com.

CAR RENTAL

In Los Angeles, it's not a question of whether wheels are a hindrance or a convenience: they're a necessity. Major-chain rates in L.A. begin at about $25 a day and $125 a week, plus 8.25% sales tax. Luxury and sport utility vehicles start at approximately $49 a day. Some local rental agencies offer specialty vehicles, from classic cars to Ferraris to the latest Hummer. *See* Car Rental *in* Smart Travel Tips for national rental agency contact information.

🚗 Local Agencies **Beverly Hills Budget Car Rental** ✉ 9815 Wilshire Blvd. ☎ 310/274-9173 or 800/227-7117 ⊕ www.budgetbeverlyhills.com. **Beverly Hills Rent-A-Car** ✉ 9220 S. Sepulveda Blvd., near LAX ☎ 310/337-1400 or 800/479-5996 ⊕ www.bhrentacar.com.

CAR TRAVEL

Finding your way by car in Los Angeles can be a piece of cake or a nightmare. The city may be sprawling and traffic-clogged, but at least it has evolved with the automobile in mind. Streets are wide and parking garages abound, but rush hours (7 AM to 10 AM and 3 PM to 7 PM) can be horribly slow. Keep a good map, such as the *Thomas Guide*, on hand at all times, get clear directions and stick to them. Both KFWB 980 AM and KNX 1070 AM have frequent traffic reports. Los Angeles area gas prices tend to be among the highest in the nation. For assistance in finding competitively priced stations, consult ⊕ www.losangelesgasprices.com.

EMERGENCIES

In case of emergency, dial 911 for police, fire, or ambulance services. In addition to dozens of smaller community hospitals, L.A. is home to several world-renowned medical centers. Many branches of the Rite Aid and Savon drug store chains maintain 24-hour pharmacies.

🏥 **UCLA Medical Center** ✉ 10833 Le Conte Ave., Westwood ☎ 310/825-9111 ⊕ www.healthcare.ucla.edu. **Los Angeles County-U.S.C. Medical Center** ✉ 1200 N. State St., Downtown ☎ 323/226-2622 ⊕ www.dhs.co.la.ca.us. **Rite Aid** ☎ 800/748-3243 ⊕ www.riteaid.com. **Savon** ☎ 888/746-7252 ⊕ www.savon.com.

METRO RAIL TRAVEL

Metro Rail covers a limited area of L.A.'s vast expanse, but what there is, is helpful and frequent. The most useful line for visitors is the underground Red Line, which runs from Union Station downtown through Mid-Wilshire, Hollywood, and Universal City on its way to North Hollywood, stopping at the most popular tourist destinations along the way. The Blue Line runs from Union Station to Long Beach, and the Gold Line, which debuted in 2003, begins at Union Station and heads northeast to Pasadena.

🚈 **Metropolitan Transit Authority (MTA)** ☎ 800/266-6883 or 213/626-4455 ⊕ www.mta.net.

TAXIS

Don't even try to hail a cab on the street in Los Angeles. Instead, phone one of the many taxi companies. The metered rate is $2 per mile, plus a $2 per-fare charge. Taxi rides from LAX have an additional $2.50 surcharge. Be aware that distances between sights in L.A. are vast, so cab fares add up quickly.

🚕 **Beverly Hills Cab** ☎ 800/273-6611. **Checker Cab** ☎ 800/300-5007. **Yellow Cab** ☎ 800/200-1085 or 800/200-0011.

TOURS

BUS & VAN
TOURS
Casablanca Tours gives sightseeing tours all around L.A., but their specialty is an insider's look at Hollywood and Beverly Hills; it's available

in two- and four-hour versions ($29–$88). L.A. Tours and Sightseeing has several tours ($29–$89), by van and bus, covering various parts of the city, including downtown, Hollywood, and Beverly Hills. The company also operates tours to Disneyland, Universal Studios, Magic Mountain, beaches, and stars' homes. Starline Tours of Hollywood ($16–$95) picks up passengers from area hotels and from Grauman's Chinese Theatre. Sights such as Universal Studios, Knott's Berry Farm, stars' homes, and Disneyland are on this popular tour company's agenda.

Casablanca Tours ☎ 323/461-0156 ⊕ www.casablancahollywoodtours.com. **L.A. Tours and Sightseeing** ☎ 323/460-6490 or 800/881-7715 ⊕ www.latours.net. **Starline Tours of Hollywood** ☎ 323/463-3333 or 800/959-3131 ⊕ www.starlinetours.com.

WALKING TOURS   The Los Angeles Conservancy offers walking tours (each about 2½ hours long), chiefly of the architectural history of the downtown area. Cost is $8 per person (except for the Angelino Heights tour, which is $10).

Los Angeles Conservancy ☎ 213/623-2489 ⊕ www.laconservancy.org.

TRAIN TRAVEL TO AND FROM L.A.

Union Station in downtown Los Angeles is one of the grande dames of railroad stations, and its meticulous restoration has made it truly shine. As the city's rail hub, it's the place to catch an Amtrak train. Amtrak's luxury *Coast Starlight* travels along the spectacular coastline from Seattle to Los Angeles in just a day and a half (though it's often not quite on time). You can make reservations in advance by phone or at the station.

Amtrak ☎ 800/872-7245 ⊕ www.amtrakcalifornia.com. **Union Station** ⊠ 800 N. Alameda St. ☎ 213/683-6979.

VISITOR INFORMATION

Beverly Hills Conference and Visitors Bureau ⊠ 239 S. Beverly Dr., 90212 ☎ 310/248-1000 or 800/345-2210 ⊕ www.beverlyhillsbehere.com. **Hollywood Chamber of Commerce** ⊠ 7018 Hollywood Blvd., 90028 ☎ 323/469-8311 ⊕ www.hollywoodcoc.org. **L.A. Inc./The Convention and Visitors Bureau** ⊠ 333 S. Hope St., 18th fl., 90071 ☎ 213/624-7300 or 800/228-2452 ⊕ www.lacvb.com. **Pasadena Convention & Visitors Bureau** ⊠ 171 S. Los Robles Ave., 91101 ☎ 626/795-9311 or 800/307-7977 ⊕ www.pasadenacal.com. **Santa Monica Convention & Visitors Bureau** ⊠ 520 Broadway, Suite 250, 90401 ☎ 310/319-6263 or 800/544-5319 ⊕ www.santamonica.com. **Santa Monica Visitors Centers** ⊠ 1400 Ocean Ave., 90401 ☎ 310/393-7593 ⊠ Santa Monica Place (shopping center), Suite 203, 90401 ☎ 310/393-7593. **West Hollywood Convention and Visitors Bureau** ⊠ 8687 Melrose Ave., Suite M-38, 90069 ☎ 310/289-2525 or 800/368-6020 ⊕ www.visitwesthollywood.com.

THE INLAND EMPIRE

EAST OF LOS ANGELES TO THE SAN JACINTO MOUNTAINS

4

By Veronica
Hill

FEW PEOPLE THINK OF THE REGION east of Los Angeles as a worthwhile travel destination. But the Inland Empire, an area often overlooked by vacationers because of its tangled freeways and suburban sprawl, does have its charms. It may sound like a cliché, but no more than a couple of hours' drive from metropolitan Los Angeles, you really can go skiing on a 7,000-foot mountain overlooking a crystal blue lake and wine tasting at a vineyard swept by ocean breezes. At the heart of this desert and mountain region is Riverside, the birthplace of California's multi-million-dollar navel orange industry, established in 1875. The tree that started it all still flourishes on Magnolia Avenue. Today the streets of downtown buzz with people on their way to shop for antiques, eat in exciting restaurants, and listen to live jazz. The scene is completely different northeast of Riverside, in the San Bernardino Mountains. There, Wrightwood, Big Bear Lake, and Lake Arrowhead lie amid prime ski country. To the south, in the San Jacinto Mountains just west of Palm Springs, Idyllwild is a popular year-round getaway with romantic bed-and-breakfasts, fashionable boutiques, and cozy restaurants. In the southernmost reaches of the Inland Empire, on the way from Riverside to San Diego, is the wine-growing region around Temecula. The rapidly growing community and its maturing wine industry are gaining attention from wine-lovers seeking an alternative to the slickness of Napa and Sonoma.

Exploring the Inland Empire

Several major freeways provide access to the Inland Empire. Ontario, Corona and Temecula line up along I–15, while I–215 and State Route 91 lead to Riverside and San Bernardino. The area's popularity as a bedroom community for Los Angeles has created some nasty freeway congestion, so try to avoid driving during rush hour, usually 4–7 PM.

About the Restaurants

Inland Empire residents no longer have to travel to their big-sister communities of L.A. or Orange County for a good meal. Downtown Riverside is home to some ambitious restaurants, along with the chains you'll find in most areas. The college towns of Claremont and Redlands are great showcases for creative vegetarian cuisine. In Temecula, the choices expand to wine country cooking, with many vintners showcasing their products alongside California-French dishes. Your options are limited in the smaller mountain communities; typically each town supports a single upscale restaurant, along with fast-food outlets, steak-and-potatoes family spots, and perhaps an Italian or Mexican eatery. Universally, dining out is casual. Reservations are a good idea at the most popular spots.

About the Hotels

In the San Gabriel and San Bernardino mountains most accommodations are B&Bs or rustic cabins, though Lake Arrowhead offers more luxurious resort lodging. Rates for Big Bear lodgings fluctuate widely, depending on the season. When winter snow brings droves of Angelenos to the mountains for skiing, expect to pay sky-high prices for any

Numbers in the margin correspond to numbers on the Inland Empire map.

If you have 3 days

If you only have three days to visit the Inland Empire, start your visit in the vineyards surrounding 🖼 **Temecula** ⑪ ⌐, being sure to sample the champagne flight at Thornton Winery and the highly recommended Castelletto at Mount Palomar. Splurge for the evening at Churon Vineyards, a French château-style bed-and-breakfast that also makes a fine syrah. Next morning, hitch a ride on a hot air balloon for a bird's-eye view of the valley followed by a brunch, and then head to **Corona** ⑤ for a soak in the mud bath at Glen Ivy Hot Springs. That evening, book into the magnificent Mission Inn in 🖼 **Riverside** ⑥ and head for dinner. On Day 3, spend the morning taking in the beautiful historic homes of Riverside and **Redlands** ⑦, followed by a leisurely drive into the San Bernardino Mountains for an afternoon of shopping and exploring in the village of 🖼 **Lake Arrowhead** ⑧.

If you have 5 days

Follow the three-day itinerary, and on Day 4 continue your exploration of the San Bernardino Mountains by moving on to 🖼 **Big Bear Lake** ⑨, a mountain town with a host of fine restaurants, ski resorts, and fishing and hiking opportunities. On your last day, slow down the pace with a drive to **Wrightwood** ④, a laid-back mountain community bordering the Mojave Desert—it lies at the highest point on the San Andreas Fault.

kind of room. Most establishments require a two-night stay on weekends. In Riverside, you might enjoy a stay at the landmark Mission Inn, a rambling Spanish-style hotel with elaborate courtyards, fountains, and ornate Mission Revivalist architecture. Down in wine country, lodging choices range from chain hotels and motels to golf resorts.

WHAT IT COSTS				
	$$$$	**$$$**	**$$**	**$**	**¢**
RESTAURANTS	over $30	$23–$30	$16–$22	$10–$15	under $10
HOTELS	over $250	$176–$250	$121–$175	$90–$120	under $90

Restaurant prices are for a main course at dinner, excluding sales tax of 7¾%. Hotel prices are for two people in a standard double room in high season, excluding service charges and 7¾% tax.

Timing

The climate varies greatly depending on what part of the Inland Empire you're visiting. Summer temperatures in the mountains and in Temecula, just 20 mi from the coast, usually hover around 80°, while it's not uncommon for Riverside to reach temperatures over 100°. In winter, temperatures in the mountains and in Temecula usually range from 30° to 55°, and in the Riverside area 40°–60°. Most of the ski resorts open when the first natural snow falls (usually in November) and close in mid-March, when even the best snowmaking equipment can't compete with rising spring temperatures.

THE WESTERN EMPIRE
POMONA, CLAREMONT &
THE SAN GABRIEL MOUNTAINS

Set at the foot of the San Gabriel Mountains, the tree-lined communities of Pomona and Claremont are known for their prestigious colleges: California State Polytechnic University–Pomona and the Claremont Colleges (Claremont Graduate School, Claremont McKenna College, Harvey Mudd College, Pitzer College, Pomona College, and Scripps College). Turn north into the hills and you'll find Wrightwood, an old-fashioned small town that makes a great base for outdoor adventure.

Pomona

❶ *23 mi north of Anaheim on Hwy. 57; 27 mi east of Pasadena on I–210.*

The green hills of Pomona, dotted with horses and houses, are perhaps best known as the site of the Los Angeles County Fair and of California State Polytechnic University–Pomona. Named for the Roman goddess of fruit, the city was established in 1938 and has a rich citrus-growing heritage. Today, Pomona is known for its art galleries and antique stores.

Site of the Los Angeles County Fair (ninth largest in the U.S.), the **Fairplex** exposition center has a 9,500-seat grandstand, an outdoor exhibit area, and nine exhibit buildings. The venue hosts open air markets, antique shows, and the annual Wines of the World competition. Fairplex houses the **NHRA Motorsports Museum** (☎ 909/622–2133 ⊕ www.nhra.com/museum ✆ $5 ☉ Wed.–Sun. 10–5), dedicated to the history of American motor sports. ✉ *1101 W. McKinley Ave.* ☎ *909/623–3111* ⊕ *www.fairplex.com* ☉ *Call for current show listings and admission prices.*

Where to Stay & Eat

$$–$$$$ ✕ **Pomona Valley Mining Company.** Perched on a hilltop near an old mining site, this rustic steak-and-seafood restaurant offers a glittering view of the city at night. The decor reflects the local mining heritage, with many authentic gold rush pieces displayed on the walls. The food is well prepared, with a special nod to prime rib, and service is friendly. During June, book early—this is a favorite spot on prom nights. ✉ *1777 Gillette Rd.* ☎ *909/623–3515* ⊕ *www.pomonavalleyminingco.com* ☐ *AE, D, DC, MC, V.*

$$$ ▥ **Sheraton Suites Fairplex.** County fair murals and whimsical carousel animals welcome you to this all-suite hotel at the entrance to Pomona's Fairplex. Contemporary in style, rooms are done in neutral tans and blues and have coffeemakers and wet bars. The Brass Ring restaurant serves California cuisine. Mountain Meadows Golf Course is 1 mi away. ✉ *601 W. McKinley Ave., 91768* ☎ *888/627–8074* ⊕ *www.sheraton.*

Sports & the Outdoors

Those in search of the great outdoors in Southern California invariably make their way to the Inland Empire's mountain ranges. In winter, ski resorts in Wrightwood and Big Bear offer great snow and challenging terrain, along with often crowded conditions. Summer brings opportunities for hiking the Pacific Crest Trail, fishing in streams or lakes such as Silverwood and Big Bear, and camping at thousands of sites peppered through the mountains. If you're going to do any hiking, camping, or fishing, you need a National Forest Adventure Pass (909/382–2622, www.fsadventurepass.org), which costs $5 per vehicle, per day. Anglers must have a valid license from the California Department of Fish and Game (916/227–2245, www.dfg.ca.gov/licensing/index.html), which you can purchase at Kmart, Longs Drugs, Wal-Mart, Big 5 Sporting Goods, and many other stores throughout Riverside County.

Wine Tasting

It may not be Napa or Sonoma, but the Temecula Valley is quickly gaining a reputation as an outstanding wine region. At the area's 20-odd vineyards, most of them along Rancho California Road, you can taste wines made from a wide range of varietals using diverse winemaking styles. Wilson Creek's almond champagne is a crowd-pleaser, as is the sauvignon blanc at Maurice Car'rie. Stuart Cellars' 1998 port has received high accolades from international experts. For tried-and-true quality head for Mount Palomar, which has received dozens of medals for its Castelletto line.

---

com ⇆ 247 suites ⚬ *Restaurant, in-room data ports, microwaves, refrigerators, pool, gym, outdoor hot tub, sauna, shop, business services, airport shuttle, some pets allowed* ⊟ *AE, D, DC, MC, V.*

Claremont

❷ *4 mi north of Pomona along Gary Ave., then 2 mi east on Foothill Blvd.*

Founded in 1887 as one of 30 towns along the Santa Fe Railroad between San Bernardino and Los Angeles, Claremont is today a college town. Nicknamed "Oxford in the Orange Belt," the six Claremont Colleges are among the most prestigious in California. Pomona College was chartered in 1888. In its heyday, Claremont was the home of the Sunkist cooperative movement. Today, Claremont Village harks back to the 1950s with its main street and hot-rod shows. The downtown district is a beautiful place to visit, with citrus and oak-lined streets and Victorian, Craftsman, and Spanish colonial buildings. College walking tours, a downtown tour, and historic home tours are offered throughout the year by **Claremont Heritage** (☎ 909/621–0848). On the first Saturday of each month the organization offers walking tours of the village.

★ Founded in 1927 by Susanna Bixby Bryant, a wealthy landowner and conservationist, **Rancho Santa Ana Botanical Gardens** is a living museum

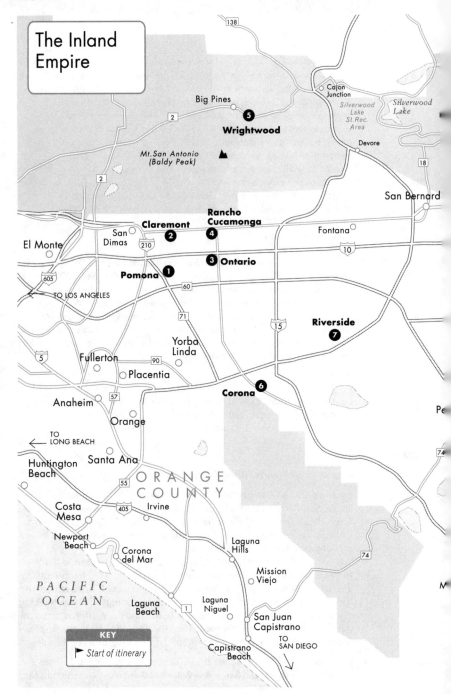

The Inland Empire

138

Big Pines

2

5

Wrightwood

Cajon Junction

Silverwood Lake St. Rec. Area

Silverwood Lake

Devore

Mt. San Antonio
(Baldy Peak) ▲

2

18

San Bernard

Claremont

Rancho Cucamonga

San Dimas

210

2

4

Fontana

10

El Monte

3 **Ontario**

605

Pomona **1**

60

← TO LOS ANGELES

71

Riverside

7

15

Yorba Linda

Fullerton

90

Placentia

Corona **6**

Anaheim

57

Orange

Pe

74

TO
← LONG BEACH

Santa Ana

ORANGE
COUNTY

55

Huntington Beach

Costa Mesa

405

Irvine

Newport Beach

Corona del Mar

Laguna Hills

74

Mission Viejo

*PACIFIC
OCEAN*

Laguna Beach

1

Laguna Niguel

San Juan Capistrano

M

TO
SAN DIEGO
↓

Capistrano Beach

KEY
▶ *Start of itinerary*

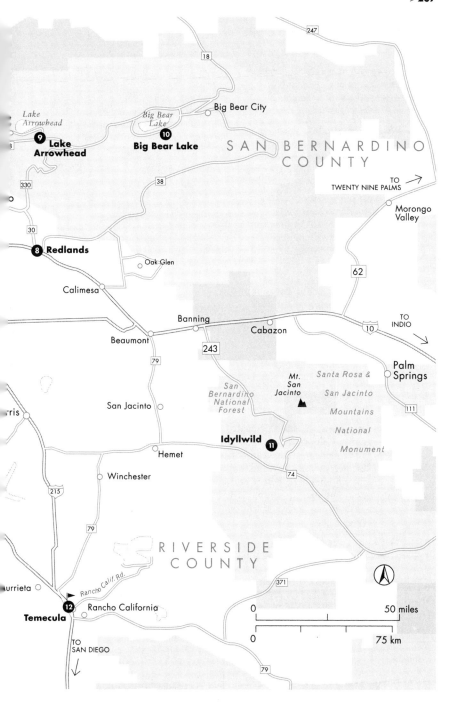

CloseUp

GOOD AS GOLD

In 1873, a woman named Eliza Tibbets changed the course of California history when she planted two Brazilian navel orange trees in her Riverside garden.

The trees (which were called "Washington Navels" in honor of America's first president), flourished in the area's warm climate and rich soil—and before long, Tibbets' garden was producing the sweetest seedless oranges anyone had ever tasted. After winning awards at several major exhibitions, Tibbets realized she could make a profit from her trees. She sold buds to the increasing droves of citrus farmers flocking to the Inland Empire, and by 1882, almost 250,000 citrus trees had been planted in Riverside alone. California's citrus industry had been born.

Today, Riverside still celebrates its citrus-growing heritage. The downtown Marketplace district contains several restored packing houses, and the Riverside Municipal Museum is home to a permanent exhibit of historic tools and machinery once used in the industry. The University of California at Riverside still remains at the forefront of citrus research; its Citrus Variety Collection includes 900 different fruit trees from around the world.

and research center dedicated to the conservation of more than 2,800 native-California plant species. Meandering trails, set on 86 acres of ponds and greenery, guide visitors past such fragrant specimens as wild lilacs, big berry manzanita, and four-needled piñon. Countless birds also make their homes here. Before you start your tour, pick up a native-bird field guide at the gift shop. ⊠ *1500 N. College Ave.* ☎ *909/625–8767* ⊕ *www.rsabg.org* ✉ *$4 donation requested* ☉ *Daily 8–5.*

Where to Eat

★ **$$** ✕ **Caffe Allegro.** This romantic spot in downtown Upland resembles an Italian country villa, complete with low-lit candles, worn-looking walls, and an ornate wood bar. Locals rave about the chicken marsala, served on a bed of spinach fettucine. ⊠ *186 N. 2nd Ave., Upland* ☎ *909/949–0805.* ⊟ *AE, D, MC, V.*

$–$$ ✕ **Cafe Provencal.** If you're in the mood for something fancy, this is the place. Decorated in the style of a French country kitchen, complete with ceramic plates from Provence and hand-made dolls from Marseille, the restaurant is cozy and inviting. The menu is heavy on classic dishes from the French Mediterranean and Italy. ⊠ *967 W. Foothill Blvd., Upland* ☎ *909/608–7100* ⊟ *AE, D, DC, V.*

¢–$$ ⨯ **Viva Madrid!** More than 40 different tapas are offered at this festive old-world restaurant in Claremont Village. Start out with a cool glass of sangria, followed by the signature paella, which comes to your table sizzling in a cast-iron pan. On Wednesday nights, you can enjoy live Spanish guitar. ⊠ *225 Yale Ave.* ☎ *909/624–5500* ▭ *D, MC, V* ⊘ *Closed Monday. No lunch.*

Nightlife

As a college town, Claremont has lots of bars and cafés, some of which showcase bands. Karaoke and live jazz is popular at the **British Bulldog Pub and Restaurant** (⊠ 1667 N. Mountain Ave., Upland ☎ 909/946–6614). Karaoke is popular at the **Claremont Inn** (⊠ 455 W. Foothill Blvd. ☎ 909/626–1254). Both college kids and old-timers appreciate the **Buffalo Inn** (⊠ 1814 W. Foothill Blvd., Upland ☎ 909/981–5515), a rustic bar and hamburger joint along historic Route 66. On summer nights, acoustic musicians sing Jim Croce covers on the firelit patio.

Sports & the Outdoors

SKIING The 10,064-foot mountain's real name is Mount San Antonio, but **Mount Baldy Ski Resort**—the oldest ski area in Southern California—takes its name from the treeless slopes. It's known for its steep triple-diamond runs, though the facilities could use some updating. The Mount Baldy base lies at 6,500 feet, and four chair lifts ascend to 8,600 feet. There are 26 runs; the longest is 2,100 vertical feet. Whenever there's abundant fresh snow, there is a danger of avalanche in out-of-bounds areas. Backcountry skiing is offered via shuttle in the spring, and there's a kiddie school ($75, including lift ticket and lunch) on weekends for children ages 5–11. Winter or summer, you can take a scenic chairlift ride ($10) to the Top of the Notch restaurant, and hiking and mountain biking trails. ✛ *From E. Foothill Blvd. about ½-mi north on N. Claremont Blvd., then 3 mi north on Monte Vista Ave. and 7 mi east on Mount Baldy Rd.* ☎ *909/981–3344* ⊕ *www.mtbaldy.com* 🎫 *Full day $40; half day (1–4) $25* ⊘ *Snow season Nov.–Mar. and Apr., weekdays 8–4:30, weekends 7:30–4:30; summer season May–Oct., weekends 9–4:30.*

WATER PARK **Raging Waters,** a tropical-theme water park in San Dimas (10 mi west from Claremont), has 17 chutes and slides with names like Neptune's Fury, Thunder Rapids, and Dragon's Den. When you're ready for a break, head over to the sandy beach lagoon and relax, or go to the Tropical Bar for a fruit drink or funnel cake. The Tropical Trading Post sells swimsuits, tanning lotion, and sunglasses. Lockers rent for $4–$6, inner tubes for $4. Check the Web site for online coupons. ⊠ *111 Raging Waters Dr., San Dimas* ☎ *909/802–2200* ⊕ *www.ragingwaters.com.* 🎫 *$28* ⊘ *Late June–Aug., daily 10–8; 1st 3 wks of June, daily 10–6; May, weekends 10–6; Sept.–mid-Oct., call for hrs.*

Ontario

❸ *Junction of I–10 and I–15, 6 mi east of Pomona.*

Ontario, in the Cucamonga Valley, has a rich agricultural and industrial heritage. The valley's warm climate once supported vineyards that produced Mediterranean grape varietals such as grenache, mourvedre, and zinfandel. Today, almost all of the vineyards have been replaced by housing tracts and shopping malls. But the Inland Empire's major airport is here, so you may well find yourself passing through Ontario.

Ontario's oldest existing business, **Graber Olive House,** opened in 1894. At the urging of family and friends, C. C. Graber bottled his meaty, tree-ripened olives and started selling them; they are still sold throughout the United States. Stop by the gourmet shop for a jar, then have a picnic on the shaded grounds. Free tours are offered year-round; in fall you can watch workers grade, cure, and can the olives. ⊠ *315 E. 4th St.* ☏ *909/983–1761 or 800/996–5483* ⊕ *www.graberolives.com* ✉ *Free* ☾ *Mon.–Sat. 9–5:30, Sun. 9:30–6.*

Where to Stay

★ **$$–$$$** 🏨 **Doubletree Hotel Ontario Airport.** A beautifully landscaped courtyard greets you at this exceptional chain, which is the only full-service hotel in Ontario. Rooms here are spacious, and decorated in jewel tones and dark wood; the business center has printers, a copier, and laptop hookups as well as a computer with Internet access. There's also a fitness center and pool, and golfing and vineyards are only a few miles away. ⊠ *222 N. Vineyard Ave.* ☏ *909/937–0900 or 800-222-8733* ⊕ *www.doubletree. com* ⇆ *484 rooms, 22 suites* ♨ *2 restaurants, refrigerators, cable TV with movies, pool, gym, hot tub, 2 lounges, shop, laundry service, concierge, business services, Internet, meeting rooms, car rental, room service, some pets allowed, no-smoking rooms* ⊟ *AE, D, MC, V.*

$$–$$$ 🏨 **Ontario Airport Marriott.** The central location and airport proximity of this chain hotel make it a convenient base for exploring the Inland Empire. Rooms are modern and colorful, and the on-site Pacific Grille Restaurant serves traditional American favorites. Newspapers are delivered to your room, and cribs are available. ⊠ *2200 E. Holt Blvd., 91761* ☏ *909/975–5000 or 800/228–9290* ⊕ *www. marriotthotels.com* ⇆ *299 rooms* ♨ *In-room data ports, some microwaves, cable TV, tennis court, 2 pools, health club, steam room, basketball, racquetball, meeting rooms, some pets allowed, no-smoking rooms* ⊟ *AE, D, DC, MC, V.*

$ 🏨 **Baymont Inn & Suites.** Known for its "Ovations" rooms with pillow-top mattresses, ergonomic chairs, and and oversize desks, this chain offers great value. It's steps away from Ontario Mills Mall and dozens of restaurants. ⊠ *4395 E. Ontario Mills Pkwy.* ☏ *909/987–5940 or 866/999–1111* ⊕ *www.baymontinns.com* ⇆ *86 rooms, 19 suites* ♨ *Internet, cable TV with movies, pool, gym, airport shuttle, no-smoking rooms* ⊟ *AE, D, MC, V* ℣◉❙ *CP.*

Shopping

☾ The gargantuan **Ontario Mills Mall** is California's largest, packing in more than 200 outlet stores, a 30-screen movie theater, and the Improv comedy theater. Also in the mall are three entertainment complexes: Dave&Buster's pool hall-restaurant-arcade, Vans Skate Park, and GameWorks video game center. Dining options include the kid-friendly jungle-themed Rainforest Cafe (complete with animatronic elephants and simulated thunderstorms), the chic Wolfgang Puck Cafe, and a 1,000-seat food court. Tourist services include currency ex-

change and complimentary discount coupon books. ⊠ *1 Mills Circle
(4th St. and I–15)* ☎ *909/484–8300* ⊕ *www.ontariomills.com*
⊗ *Mon.–Sat. 10–9:30, Sun. 10–8.*

Rancho Cucamonga

❹ *5 mi north of Ontario on I–15.*

Once a thriving winemaking area with more than 50,000 acres of wine
grapes, Rancho Cucamonga lost most of its pastoral charm after real
estate developers bought up the land for a megamall and affordable housing. It's now a squeaky-clean planned community, but you can still get
a taste of the grape here. At the **Joseph Filippi Winery,** J. P. and Gino Filippi continue the family tradition that was started in 1922. They produce handcrafted wines from cabernet, sangiovese, and zinfandel grapes,
among other varieties. You can taste up to four wines for $5, and take
the free guided tour that's given at noon, Wednesday–Sunday. ⊠ *12467
Base Line Rd.* ☎ *909/899–5755* ⊕ *www.josephfilippiwinery.com*
🎟 *Free* ⊗ *Mon.–Sat. 10–6, Sun. 11–5.*

Where to Stay & Eat

★ **$$–$$$** ✕ **The Sycamore Inn.** Flickering gas lamps and a glowing fireplace greet
you at this rustic, tree-shaded inn. Built in 1921, the restaurant stands
on the site of a pre-statehood stagecoach stop; it is one of the oldest buildings in town. The specialty of the house is the rack of Colorado lamb,
pan-seared and roasted with a mustard-breadcrumb crust and a red wine
reduction. The wine list is impressive; by the glass, you can choose from
more than 20 vintages from the Central Coast, Napa Valley, and nearby
wineries like Joseph Filippi and Temecula. ⊠ *8318 Foothill Blvd.* ☎ *909/
982–1104* ⊕ *www.thesycamoreinn.com* ☰ AE, D, MC, V.

★ **¢** ✕ **Vince's Spaghetti House.** This boisterous family eatery, open since
1945, claims to serve more than 15,000 mi of spaghetti every year. The
menu is limited, but reliably good. The *mostaccioli* with meat sauce and
the meatball sandwiches are excellent choices. ⊠ *8241 Foothill Blvd.*
☎ *909/981–1003.*

$–$$ 🏨 **Best Western Heritage Inn.** Along with gorgeous views of the San
Gabriel mountains, this hotel offers contemporary-style rooms, and
wine-and-cheese tasting at dusk. In the morning you can pick up the
newspaper that's been delivered to your door and brew some java in
the in-room coffeemaker, or head across the parking lot to Mimi's Cafe,
a cheerful eatery known for its breakfast. ⊠ *8179 Spruce Ave., 91730*
☎ *909/466–1111 or 800/780–7234* 🖷 *909/466–3876* ⊕ *www.
bestwestern.com* 🛏 *116 rooms* ⅋ *In-room data ports, some in-room
minibars, some in-room microwaves, some in-room refrigerators, cable
TV with movies, pool, gym, outdoor hot tub, dry cleaning, laundry service, business services, meeting room* ❡⧉ CP.

Wrightwood

❺ *39 mi north of Ontario, via I–15, Hwy. 138, and Hwy. 2.*

With about 3,500 full-time residents, Wrightwood prides itself on having no stoplights, fast-food restaurants, or chain stores. What you will

find are old-fashioned candy purveyors, antiques shops, and crafts boutiques. The **Four Seasons Gallery** shows local art ranging from landscape paintings to Native American sculptures and crafts. ⊠ *6013 Park Dr.* ☎ *760/249–3712* 🖃 *Free* ⊘ *Wed.–Sun. 11–5.*

At the **Old Firehouse Museum** you can see exhibits on the area's mining heritage and natural history. Upstairs, step back in time into the village's first firefighters' quarters. ⊠ *6000 Cedar St.* ☎ *760/249–4650* 🖃 *Free* ⊘ *Sat. 10–2 or by appointment.*

♻ An old stone tower at **Big Pines Visitors Center,** part of Angeles National Forest, marks the highest spot (6,862 foot) along the San Andreas Fault, the unstable crack in the earth's crust that has caused so many California earthquakes. At the visitor center you can get information on camping, fishing, and hiking in the forest, buy souvenirs, and get the National Forest Adventure passes ($5 per vehicle day) that allow you access to the forest. ⊠ *Hwy. 2, 3 mi west of Wrightwood* ☎ *760/249–3504* ⊘ *Fri.–Sun. 8:30–4:30, Tues.–Thurs. 7:30–3:30.*

Where to Stay & Eat

$–$$$ ✕ **Blue Ridge Inn.** This rustic 1948 lodge has a woodsy theme, from the bar with its huge fireplace to the cozy paneled dining room with flickering lanterns, 19th-century clocks, and friendly waitstaff. The food—surf-and-turf specialties such as grilled Malaysian shrimp and prime rib—is probably the best you'll find in Wrightwood. ⊠ *6060 Park Dr.* ☎ *760/ 249–3440* 🖃 *AE, MC, V* ⊘ *Closed Mon. No lunch.*

¢ ✕ **Mountain Top Cafe.** Homesteaders John and Doris Lovett started this diner in 1940, serving up fried chicken and lemon cream pie to hungry soldiers on their way to Edwards Air Force Base. Today this down-home restaurant still delivers good old-fashioned food and is famous for its country breakfasts. Don't miss the Lumberjack Breakfast, a hot mound of eggs, bacon, sausage, ham, and country fries. ⊠ *Hwys. 138 and 2* ☎ *760/249–4811* 🖃 *AE, D, MC, V.*

$$ 🏨 **The Golden Acorn.** With a lush English garden and bubbling fountain, this large estate wraps you in splendor. Each room is furnished with a four-poster bed and oval soaking tub.; the Honeymoon Suite has a floor-to-ceiling canopy bed and a fireplace that opens onto the bath as well as the bedroom. ⊠ *5487 Morningstar Ct.* ☎ *760/249–6252* ⊕ *www.thegoldenacorn.com* ➥ *2 rooms* ♿ *Cable TV; no smoking* 🖃 *MC, V* ⦾ *BP.*

¢–$$ 🏨 **Pines Motel and Cabins.** If you don't mind rusticity, this property has plenty of simple charm. The motel is steps from Wrightwood's village, which has a park, restaurants, shops, and bars. Rooms have knotty-pine walls and lodge-style beds with country quilts. Cabins have living rooms with fireplaces, kitchens, and separate bedrooms; studio suites have dining areas and entertainment centers. ⊠ *6045 Pine St., 92397* ☎ *760/ 249–9974* ➥ *10 rooms, 2 cabins, 2 suites* ♿ *Picnic area, BBQs, fans, some kitchenettes, some microwaves, some refrigerators, some in-room fireplaces, cable TV, playground* 🖃 *AE, D, MC, V.*

⚠ **Table Mountain.** Scenic views of the desert from 7,000 feet make this park a popular spot for weddings. The campground stands next to Big

Pines Visitor Center. You can buy firewood at the campground, and there is a restaurant nearby. Reservations must be made at least four days in advance, and no refunds are given in case of bad weather. ⟐ *Grills, pit toilets, portable toilets, drinking water, bear boxes, fire pits, picnic tables, public telephone, ranger station* ⤴ *118 sites* ✉ *22223 Big Pines Hwy.* ☎ *805/944-2187 or 877/444-6777* ⊕ *www.reserveusa.com* ⛏ *Reservations essential* ✉ *$13–$26* ⊟ *AE, D, MC, V* ☉ *May–Nov.*

Sports & the Outdoors

HIKING Wrightwood is a major stopping point for hikers traveling the **Pacific Crest Trail** (✉ Big Pines Visitors Center, Rte. 2, 3 mi west of Wrightwood ☎ 760/249-3504), which runs 2,600 mi from Mexico to Canada. There is a trailhead near Inspiration Point on Highway 2, 5 mi west of Wrightwood.

SKIING In addition to two mountains, a vertical drop of 8,200 foot, and 220 skiable acres, **Mountain High** (✉ 24510 Hwy. 2 ☎ 760/249-5808 ⊕ www. mthigh.com ✉ $44 day pass; $26 night skiing 5–10) has 46 trails for skiing and snowboarding. The Flex ticket allows you to ski in 4- or 8-hour blocks, while the Point Ticket lets you choose the number of runs you want to take. Snowboarders flock to Mountain High to test their skills at Faultline Terrain Park. There is regular bus service between the mountains.

RIVERSIDE AREA

In the late 1700s, Mexican rancheros called this now-suburban region Valle de Pariaso. Citrus-growing here began in 1873, when homesteader Eliza Tibbets planted two navel orange trees in her yard.

Corona

❻ *13 mi south of Ontario on I-15.*

Corona's Temescal Canyon is named for the dome-shape mud saunas that the Luiseno Indians built around the artesian hot springs in the early 19th century. Starting in 1860, weary Overland Stage Company passengers stopped to relax in the soothing mineral springs. In 1890 Mr. and Mrs. W. G. Steers turned the springs into a resort whose popularity has never faded.

FodorsChoice Presidents Herbert Hoover and Ronald Reagan are among the thousands
★ of guests who have soaked their toes at **Glen Ivy Hot Springs.** Colorful bougainvillea and birds of paradise surround the secluded canyon spa, which offers a full range of facials, manicures, pedicures, body wraps, and massages; some treatments are performed in underground granite spa chambers known collectively as the Grotto. Don't bring your best bikini if you plan to dive into the red clay (brought in daily from a local mine) of Club Mud. Children under 16 are not permitted at the spa except on three family days: Memorial Day, July 4, and Labor Day. ✉ *25000 Glen Ivy Rd., Glen Ivy* ☎ *909/277-3529* ⊕ *www.glenivy.com* ✉ *Mon.–Thurs. $30; Fri.–Sun. $42* ☉ *Apr.–Oct., daily 9:30–6; Nov.–Mar., daily 9:30–5.*

Paying homage to the rock-and-roll, jazz, country, and blues greats who've used Fender guitars, the **Fender Museum of Music and the Arts** features a 48-track digital recording studio, outdoor amphitheater, gift shop, and art gallery. The permanent exhibit includes two guitars once owned by Kurt Cobain and Courtney Love, Dick Dale's reverb unit, and a portrait of Stevie Ray Vaughn painted on a piece of the Berlin Wall. ⊠ *365 N. Main St.* ☎ *909/735–2440* ⊕ *www.fendermuseum.com* ⊠ *$5* ☉ *Wed. and Fri.–Sun. 11–4, Thurs. 11–8.*

★ ☯ Opened as a produce stand in 1974, **Tom's Farms** has grown to include a hamburger stand, furniture showroom, and health food store. You can still buy produce here, but the big draw is the duck pond, and the zoo with llamas, goats, and deer. The wine-and-cheese shop showcases more than 600 varieties of wine, including many from nearby Temecula Valley; wine tasting ($1 for three samples) takes place daily 11–6. On weekends there is a country fair with children's crafts, face painting, and snacks. ⊠ *23900 Temescal Canyon Rd.* ☎ *909/277–4422* ⊕ *www. tomsfarms.com* ⊠ *Free* ☉ *Daily 8–8.*

Where to Stay & Eat

★ **$$–$$$$** ✕ **Napa 29.** A cellar with more than 220 wines from California's Napa Valley and Central Coast is the main draw at this stylish restaurant and specialty foods shop. Dark wood and white tablecloths are the backdrop for stellar California cuisine, such as cold smoked buffalo and macadamia-crusted sea bass with chardonnay sauce. Live jazz is performed on Thursday, Friday, and Saturday nights. ⊠ *280 Teller St., Suite 130* ☎ *909/273–0529* ⊕ *www.napa29.com* ⊟ *AE, MC, V* ☉ *Closed Mon.*

$ ▥ **Country Suites By Ayres at Corona West.** This ranch-style hotel, with its leather couches, wrought-iron light fixtures, and courtyard adobe fireplace, harkens back to the days of Spanish California. All rooms have ceiling fans, hair dryers, irons and ironing boards, and coffeemakers; some have fireplaces. If you feel inclined, you can mingle with fellow guests over beer, cheese and crackers during the 5–7 PM "social hour." ⊠ *1900 W. Frontage Rd., 92882* ☎ *909/738–9113 or 800/676–1363* ⊕ *www.countrysuites.com/coronawest.htm* ⊰ *114 rooms* ⚷ *In-room data ports, microwaves, refrigerators, cable TV, pool, gym, hot tub, meeting rooms* ⊟ *AE, D, MC, V* ⎮◉⎮ *BP.*

Riverside

❼ *14 mi north of Corona on Route 91; 34 mi from Anaheim on Route 91.*

By 1882 Riverside was home to more than half of California's citrus groves, making it the state's wealthiest city per capita in 1895. The prosperity produced a downtown area of magnificent architecture, which is well preserved today. Main Street's pedestrian strip is lined with antique and gift stores, art galleries, salons, and the UCR / California Museum of Photography.

Fodor'sChoice The crown jewel of Riverside is the **Mission Inn,** a remarkable Spanish
★ Revival hotel whose elaborate turrets, clock tower, mission bells, and flying buttresses rise above downtown. The inn was designed in 1902

by Arthur B. Benton and Myron Hunt, who took cues from the Spanish missions in San Gabriel and Carmel. You can climb to the top of the Rotunda Wing's five-story spiral stairway, or linger a while in the Courtyard of the Birds, where a tinkling fountain and shady trees invite meditation. You can also peek inside the St. Francis Chapel, where folks like Bette Davis, Humphrey Bogart and Richard and Pat Nixon tied the knot before the Mexican cedar altar. The Presidential Lounge, a dark, wood-panel bar, has been patronized by eight U.S. presidents. ⊠ *3649 Mission Inn Ave.* ☎ *909/784–0300 or 800/843–7755* 🖷 *909/683–1342* ⊕ *www.missioninn.com.*

Fodor'sChoice
★ While you're in Riverside, pamper yourself at the Mission Inn's luxurious **Kelly's Spa,** a 6,000-square-foot poolside retreat opened in May 2004. Warm-tone woods, hand-painted frescos, Venetian chandeliers, and barrel-vaulted ceilings set the scene for this tranquil Tuscan-style escape, which has six treatments rooms and two private villas. The villas, which run $249 for a half-day and $399 for a full day, have outdoor teak rain showers and marble-encased aromatherapy baths, as well as flat-screen TVs. After a round in the eucalyptus-infused steam room, you can grab your white cashmere robe and indulge in your choice of facials, massages, and body polishes. Guests ages 14–18 must be accompanied by a parent, and must wear swimsuits during treatment. ⊠ *3649 Mission Inn Ave.* ☎ *909/341–6725 or 800/440–5910.* ⊕ *www. kellysspa.com* 🖅 *Complimentary for guests receiving services; $25 without treatment* ⊙ *Daily 7:30 PM–8:30 PM.*

When Catherine Bettner's homegrown variety of oranges won awards at the 1885 New Orleans Exposition, she poured much of the prize money into her Queen Anne Victorian. **Heritage House,** built in 1891 on a scenic drive shadowed by magnolia, palm, and citrus trees, soon earned praise as the most beautiful in the city. Today it has been completely restored and furnished with 19th-century furniture. To see the interior of the house you must take a 45-minute guided tour. ⊠ *8193 Magnolia Ave.* ☎ *909/689–1333 or 909/826–5273* ⊕ *www.riversideca.gov/ museum/rmm/hh.htm* 🖅 *Donations accepted* ⊙ *Tours Sept.–June, Thurs.–Fri. noon–3, weekends noon–3:30.*

California Citrus State Historic Park. A celebration of California's citrus-growing history, this Victorian-style park occupies 377 well-kept acres of working citrus groves. The grounds, developed in 1880, are perfect for a leisurely afternoon picnic. Work off your lunch on the 2-mi interpretive trail, or check out the park's Craftsman-style bungalows, Victorian banister house, or museum and gift shop. Guided tours are offered Saturday at 10 AM and by request. On Friday from June through August, free concerts present the bluegrass and jazz of 1900–1930. ⊠ *1879 Jackson St.* ☎ *909/780–6222* ⊕ *www.co.riverside.ca.us/activity/ parks/citrus.htm* 🖅 *Free* ⊙ *Apr.–Sept., daily 8–7; Oct.–Mar., daily 8–5.*

Riverside celebrates its juicy raison d'être each April at the **Orange Blossom Festival** (☎ 800/382–8202). The **National Orange Show** (☎ 909/ 888–6788), held in May, includes orange-crate label exhibits, orange-packing demonstrations, and other citrus-related fun.

> **off the beaten path**

OAK GLEN – More than 60 varieties of apples are grown in Oak Glen, a rustic village of farms, produce stands, and homey cafés. Don't miss **Oak Tree Village** (☎ 909/797–4020 ⌁ $3 ⊙ Daily 10–5), a children's park with miniature train rides, trout fishing, gold panning, and a petting zoo. Oak Glen holds an apple blossom festival in April, but the town really comes alive during the fall harvest, which is celebrated with piggyback races, live entertainment, and other events. ⊠ *I–10 east through Redlands, exit on Cherry Valley Blvd.* ☎ *909/797–6833* ⊕ *www.oakglen.net.*

Where to Stay & Eat

$–$$$
Fodor's Choice
★

✕ **Mario's Place.** The clientele is as beautiful as the food at this intimate jazz and supper club. The northern Italian cuisine is first-rate, as are the bands that perform Friday and Saturday at 10 PM. Try the pear and Gorgonzola wood-fired pizza followed by the caramelized banana napoleon (made with hazelnut phyllo, vanilla mascarpone, and coffee sauce). ⊠ *3646 Mission Inn Ave.* ☎ *909/684–7755* ⊕ *www.mariosplace.com* ▭ *AE, D, MC, V* ⊙ *No lunch Sat.–Thurs.*

¢

✕ **Simple Simon's.** Expect to wait in line at this little sandwich shop located on the pedestrian-only shopping strip outside the Mission Inn. Traditional salads, soups, and sandwiches on house-baked breads are served; standout specialties include the chicken-apple sausage sandwich and the roast lamb sandwich topped with grilled eggplant, red peppers, and tomato-fennel-olive sauce. ⊠ *3636 Main St.* ☎ *909/369–6030* ▭ *No credit cards* ⊙ *Closed Sun.*

$$–$$$$
Fodor's Choice
★

✕🏠 **Mission Inn.** This grand Spanish colonial-era hotel was designated a National Historic Landmark in 1977. Most standard rooms have an early Spanish California look, with Mission-style artwork and dark wooden headboards. Dining at the Mission Inn is a rewarding experience, whether you choose the grand Duane's Steakhouse ($$–$$$$), famed for its maple-leaf duck breast and osso buco; Las Campanas ($–$$), where Mexican-style *carnitas* (shredded pork) are served in a pool of *mole negro* (a savory chili-and-chocolate-based sauce); or the Mission Inn Restaurant ($–$$), where you can enjoy Sunday brunch next to a bubbling fountain on the Spanish patio. For true decadence, head to Kelly's Spa after your meal for a "Tuscan Bliss" body treatment, which includes a green tea-and-ginger body wrap. ⊠ *3649 Mission Inn Ave.* ☎ *909/784–0300 or 800/843–7755.* 🖷 *909/683–1342* ⊕ *www.missioninn.com* 🛏 *211 rooms, 28 suites ⚃ 3 restaurants, café, room service, in-room data ports, minibars, cable TV with movies and video games, pool, gym, massage, spa, steam room, 2 lounges, shop, dry cleaning, laundry service, business services, meeting rooms, airport shuttle, no-smoking rooms* ▭ *AE, D, DC, MC, V.*

Nightlife & the Arts

NIGHTLIFE

Savor tapas and sangria at **Cafe Sevilla** (⊠ 3252 Mission Inn Ave. ☎ 909/778–0611) while enjoying live flamenco, salsa, and rumba music on weeknights. Dance lessons are offered Tuesday and Thursday nights. On weekend nights, the restaurant hosts a Latin–Euro Top 40 dance club.

THE ARTS

Sol De Mexico Ballet Folklorico, Ballet Folklorico de Riverside, and the Riverside County Philharmonic often perform at the **Riverside Munici-**

pal **Auditorium** (✉ 3485 Mission Ave. ☎ 909/788–3944). The **Riverside Community Players** (✉ 4026 14th St. ☎ 909/686–4030 ⊕ www.riversidecommunityplayers.org), has been performing regularly since 1925.

Shopping

Some fine boutiques, antique stores, and specialty shops line pedestrian-only Main Street between 6th and 10th streets. British-theme **Farthings** (✉ 3653 Main St. ☎ 909/784–3111), which specializes in seasonal gifts and garden art, also has a nice line of upscale stationery and wrapping paper. You can buy Mission Inn souvenirs at **Inn-credible Gift Corner** (✉ 3668 Main St. ☎ 909/788–8090). The three-story **Mission Galleria** (✉ 3700 Main St. ☎ 909/276–8000) is an antique mall specializing in vintage furniture, with a café downstairs. **Tiggy-Winkles Gift Shoppe** (✉ Main and 7th Sts. ☎ 909/683–0221) carries all things Curious George and Beatrix Potter, as well as designer jewelry, porcelain knick-knacks, potpourri, and soap. The incense-scented **Dragonmarsh** (✉ 3744 Main St. ☎ 909/276–1116) has Renaissance-style jewelry, candles, crystal balls, and swords.

Sports & the Outdoors

Golfing enthusiasts have eight courses to choose from around Riverside. **Riverside Golf Club** (✉ 1011 N. Orange St. ☎ 909/682–3748 ▱ $25–$37) is an 18-hole, par-72 public course with a full-service restaurant and bar. The Harold Heers and Jimmy Powell course at **Indian Hills Golf Club** (✉ 5700 Club House Dr. ☎ 909/360–2090 ⊕ www.indianhillsgolf.com ▱ 18 holes $48; 9 holes $24) is a scenic 18-hole, par-70 championship course.

Redlands

❽ *15 mi northeast of Riverside via I–215 north and I–10 east.*

This well-maintained city lies at the center of what once was the largest navel-orange producing region in the world. The town's main artery, Orange Street, is lined with fancy boutiques, trendy restaurants, and antiques shops. Orange groves are still plentiful throughout the area. You can glimpse Redlands' origins in several fine examples of California Victorian residential architecture. In 1897 Cornelia A. Hill built **Kimberly Crest House and Gardens** to mimic the châteaux of France's Loire Valley. Surrounded by orange groves, lily ponds, and terraced Italian gardens, the mansion has a French Revival parlor, a mahogany staircase, a glass mosaic fireplace, and a bubbling fountain in the form of Venus rising from the sea. In 1905 the property was purchased by Kimberly-Clark Paper Company founders Alfred and Helen Kimberly. Their daughter, Mary, lived in the house until 1979. Almost all of the home's 22 rooms are in original condition. Guided tours begin at 1 and run every 30 minutes; the last tour is at 3:30. ✉ *1325 Prospect Dr.* ☎ *909/792–2111* ⊕ *www.kimberlycrest.org* ▱ *$7* ☉ *Sept.–July, Thurs.–Sun. 1–4.*

To learn more about Southern California's shaky history, head to the ☾ **San Bernardino County Museum,** where you can watch a working seismometer or check out a display about the San Andreas Fault. Specializing in the natural and regional history of Southern California, the museum is big on birds, eggs, dinosaurs, and mammals. ⊠ *2024 Orange Tree La.* ☎ *909/307–2669* ⊕ *www.sbcounty.gov/museum* 🎫 *$6* ☉ *Tues.–Sun. 9–5.*

The only museum of its kind west of the Mississippi, the **Historical Glass Museum** shimmers with more than 3,000 pieces of American-made glass. Many items in the 1903 Victorian house date back to the early 1800s. ⊠ *1157 Orange St.* ☎ *909/798–0868* ⊕ *www.rth.org/lookingglass* 🎫 *Free* ☉ *Weekends noon–4.*

The **Lincoln Memorial Shrine** houses the largest collection of Abraham Lincoln artifacts on the West coast. You can view a marble bust of Lincoln by sculptor George Grey Barnard, along with more than a dozen letters and rare pamphlets. The gift shop sells many books, toys, and reproductions pertaining to the Civil War. ⊠ *125 W. Vine St.* ☎ *909/ 798–7636 or 909/798–7632* ⊕ *www.lincolnshrine.org* 🎫 *Free* ☉ *Tues.–Sun. 1–5.*

After the Franciscan Fathers of Mission San Gabriel built it in 1830, the **Asistencia Mission de San Gabriel** only functioned as a mission for a few years. After Indian attacks in 1834 it became part of a Spanish colonial rancho; it later served as a school and a factory and was finally purchased by the county, which restored it in 1937. The landscaped courtyard contains an old Spanish mission bell; one building holds a small museum. ⊠ *26930 Barton Rd.* ☎ *909/793–5402* 🎫 *$1* ☉ *Tues.–Sat. 10–3.*

Where to Eat

$$–$$$$ ✕ **Joe Greensleeves.** Housed in the 19th-century brick Board of Trade building, this classic American restaurant is homey and inviting. Steaks, chicken, and fish take up most of the menu, but adventurous eaters may enjoy the mallard duck or the elk chops. ⊠ *220 N. Orange St.* ☎ *909/ 792–6969* ▭ *AE, D, DC, MC, V* ☉ *Closed Mon. No lunch weekends.*

$–$$$ ✕ **Citrone.** This hip and casual downtown bistro has won Wine Spectator awards continually since 1998. More than 600 wines are offered here, which complement such light California fare as the Citrone Stack (layered roasted red peppers, red onion, grilled tomato, potato, mushrooms and buffalo mozzarella), or the signature pizza, topped with feta cheese, onions and sliced apples. Don't miss the Citrone martini, made with premium vodka and fresh-squeezed lemons. ⊠ *328 Orange St.* ☎ *909/793– 6635* ▭ *AE, MC, V.*

FodorśChoice
★

¢–$ ✕ **Royal Falconer.** This stately British-themed pub is a great spot to enjoy a pint and a traditional English meal of shepherd's pie, fish-and-chips, or bangers-and-mash. There are 20 beers on tap and 30 by the bottle. The upstairs game room has pool tables and dart boards. ⊠ *106 Orange St.* ☎ *909/307–8913* ▭ *AE, MC, V.*

The Arts

Redlands Bowl, a 6,000-seat outdoor amphitheater in the juniper-shaded Smiley Park, is the scene of ballet, opera, and symphony performances as well as jazz and folk concerts. On Tuesday and Friday nights, June through August, there are free performances at 8:15. ⊠ *Eureka St. at Redlands Blvd.* ☎ *909/793–7316* ⊕ *www.redlandsbowl.org* 🎫 *Free.*

SAN BERNARDINO MOUNTAINS

The twin resorts of Lake Arrowhead and Big Bear are the recreational center of this area; though the two are geographically close, they're distinct in appeal. Lake Arrowhead, with its cool mountain air, trail-threaded woods, and brilliant lake, draws a summertime crowd—a well-heeled one, if the prices in its shops and restaurants are any indication. Big Bear's ski and snowboarding slopes, cross-country trails, and cheerful lodges come alive in winter. Even if you're not interested in the resorts themselves, the Rim of the World Scenic Byway (Highway 18), which connects the two at an elevation of 8,000 feet, is a magnificent drive with spectacular views.

Lake Arrowhead

❾ *37 mi northeast of Riverside via I–215 north to Hwy. 330 north to Hwy. 18 west.*

Lake Arrowhead Village is an alpine community with offices, shops, outlet stores, and eateries that descend the hill to the lake. Outside the village, access to the lake and its beaches is limited to area residents and their guests. You can take a 45-minute cruise on the *Arrowhead Queen,* operated daily by **LeRoy Sports** (☎ 909/336–6992) from the waterfront marina in Lake Arrowhead Village. Tickets are first-come, first-served and cost $12. Call for departure times.

★ ☼ If you're in the mood to skate, head over to **Ice Castle** where you may catch a glimpse of Olympic gold-medalist Michelle Kwan, who regularly trains on its International-sized rink. Skate rentals cost $1.50 per person. ⊠ *410 Burnt Mill Rd.* ☎ *909/337–5283* ⊕ *www.icecastle.us* 🖼 *$7* ☼ *Tues. and Fri. 7:30 PM–9 PM, Sat. 2:30–4:30 and 5–7, Sun. 11–1.*

Where to Stay & Eat

★ $$–$$$ ✕ **Casual Elegance.** This intimate house with a fireplace is just a couple of miles outside Arrowhead Village. Featured menu items change weekly, but the steaks and seafood are first-rate. ⊠ *26848 Hwy. 189, Blue Jay* ☎ *909/337–8932* ▭ *AE, D, DC, MC, V.*

★ $–$$ ✕ **The Chef's Inn & Tavern.** This romantic lakefront restaurant, which survived Cedar Glen's devastating 2003 wildfires, is a favorite of locals. Once a mountain bordello, the historic building is decorated in the Victorian style with antiques and has a lower-level saloon. Standout dishes such as the chateaubriand and German sausage platter are accompanied by soup, salad, and dessert. ⊠ *29020 Oak Terrace, Cedar Glen* ☎ *909/336–4488* ▭ *AE, MC, V.*

★ $$–$$$ ✕▦ **Lake Arrowhead Resort.** This lakeside lodge has an Alpine look and an old-world feeling. Most rooms have water or forest views. The on-premises Village Bay Spa offers facials, massages, and other body treatments; the Barkley restaurant ($–$$) serves casual American food such as mango-papaya chicken salad and home-style meat loaf. ⊠ *27984 Hwy. 189, Lake Arrowhead Village 92352* ☎ *909/336–1511 or 800/800–6792* 🖨 *909/336–1378* ⊕ *www.lakearrowheadresort.com* ☞ *177 rooms, 4 suites, 3 condos* �? *Restaurant, cable TV, pool, health club, spa, beach,* *bar, children's programs (ages 4–12), meeting rooms, no-smoking rooms* ⊟ *AE, D, DC, MC, V.*

$$–$$$ ▢ **Fleur de Lac European Inn.** This elegant 1915 home, decorated like a French château, offers style, comfort, and a great location just steps from the village. Each room has an antique carved-wood bed with luxury linens, whirlpool bath, and private balcony. In the Great Room you can sit by the massive granite fireplace and enjoy a glass of Fleur de Lac's signature red wine. If you're lucky, the breakfast menu may include crème brûlée French toast. Children are politely discouraged. ⊠ *285 Hwy. 173, just outside Lake Arrowhead Village 92352-2688* ☎ *909/ 336–4612* ⊕ *www.fleurdelac.com* ⤵ *5 rooms* ♨ *In-room hot tubs, cable TV, in-room VCR, health club, meeting room; no kids, no smoking* ⊟ *MC, V* ⊙ *BP.*

Sports & the Outdoors

Waterskiing and wakeboarding lessons are available on Lake Arrowhead in summer at **McKenzie Waterski School** (☎☎ 909/337–3814 ⊕ www. mckenzieskischool.com).

Lovely **Lake Gregory** was formed by a dam constructed in 1938. Because the summer water temperature is often quite warm (rare for lakes at this altitude), this is the best swimming lake in the area. It's open in summer only, and there's a nominal charge to swim. Fishing is permitted, there are water slides, and you can rent rowboats at Lake Gregory Village. ⊠ *Lake Dr. off Rim of the World Hwy.*

en route   When driving east from Lake Arrowhead on Highway 18, you'll reach **Snow Valley** (☎ 909/867–5151 ⊕ www.snow-valley.com ▩ $43) before Big Bear's other ski resorts; it's 5 mi east of Running Springs. Snow Valley has snowmaking capabilities (although the snow isn't always as good here as it is at Big Bear) and 11 lifts. In summer you can use the trails for hiking, horseback riding, and mountain biking.

Big Bear Lake

❿ *24 mi east of Lake Arrowhead on Hwy. 18 (Rim of the World Hwy.).*

The town of Big Bear Lake, on the lake's south shore, has a classic Western-Alpine style; you'll spot the occasional chaletlike building here. Big Bear City, at the east end of Big Bear Lake, has restaurants, motels, and a small airport. From May through October, the paddle wheeler *Big Bear Queen* departs daily at noon, 2, and 4 from **Big Bear Marina** (⊠ 500 Paine Rd., Big Bear Lake ☎ 909/866–3218 ⊕ www.bigbearmarina.com) for 90-minute tours of the lake; the cost is $11; $16.50 for dinner cruises.

⟳ **Moonridge Animal Park,** a rescue and rehabilitation center, specializes in animals native to the San Bernardino Mountains. Among its residents are black bears, bald eagles, coyote, beavers, and bobcats. You can catch an educational presentation at noon and feeding tour at 3. ⊠ *43285 Goldmine Dr.* ☎ *909/584–1171* ⊕ *www.moonridgezoo.org* ▩ *$4* ⊙ *May–Sept., daily 10–5; Oct.–Apr., daily 10–4.*

Take a ride down a twisting bobsled course in winter, or beat the summer heat on a dual waterslide at **Alpine Slide at Magic Mountain.** Miniature golf and go-karts add to the fun. ☒ *800 Wildrose La., ¼ mi west of Big Bear Village* ☎*909/866–4626* ⊕*www.alpineslideatmagicmountain. com* ☒ *$20* ☉ *Daily 10–6.*

Fodor'sChoice
Big Bear Discovery Center. Operated by the forest service, this nature center is the place to sign up for a canoe ride through Grout Bay, or naturalist-led Discovery Tours, including visits to bald eagle nesting grounds, wildflower fields, and historic gold mines. The Flowers and Flames Tour takes you to the 90,000-acre burn area of 2003's Old Fire, where plant life has begun to sprout from the blackened remains. The center also has rotating flora and fauna exhibits, and a nature-oriented gift shop. ☒ *North Shore Drive (Hwy. 38) between Fawnskin and Stanfield Cutoff* ☎ *909/866–3437* ⊕ *www.bigbear.info* ☒ *Free* ☉ *June–Aug., daily 8–6; Sept.–May, daily 8–4:30.*

Where to Stay & Eat

$$–$$$ ✕ **The Iron Squirrel.** Dark-wood paneling, colorful oil paintings, and black booths with crisp white tablecloths set the scene at this cozy French country eatery, known for its Veal Normandie (veal scallopini sautéed with apples, calvados, and cream) and duck à l'orange. Fresh fish, grilled meats, pastas, and salads round out the menu. ☒ *646 Pine Knot Blvd.* ☎ *909/ 866–9121* ⊟ *AE, MC, V.*

$$–$$$ ✕ **Madlon's.** The menu at this gingerbread-style cottage includes sophisticated dishes such as lamb chops with Gorgonzola butter, cream of jalapeño soup, and Asian black peppercorn filet mignon. Reservations are essential on weekends. ☒ *829 W. Big Bear Blvd., Big Bear City* ☎ *909/585–3762* ⊟ *D, DC, MC, V* ☉ *Closed Mon.*

$–$$$$ ⛺ **Robinhood Inn.** Across the street from the Pine Knot Marina, this family-oriented motel has affordable rooms, most with fireplaces and some with whirlpool tubs or kitchenettes. Also available are several condos just feet from Snow Summit ski resort. ☒ *40797 Lakeview Dr., 92315* ☎ *909/866–4643 or 800/990–9956* ⛁ *909/866–4645* ⊕ *www. robinhoodinn.com* ⇗ *50 rooms, 8 condos* ⌂ *Restaurant, bar, some kitchenettes, some in-room hot tubs, cable TV with movies, in-room VCRs, outdoor hot tub, no-smoking rooms; no a/c in some rooms* ⊟ *AE, D, MC, V.*

★ $$–$$$ ⛺ **Apples Bed & Breakfast Inn.** Despite its location on a busy road to the ski lifts, the Apples Inn feels remote and peaceful, thanks to the surrounding pine trees. The colorful rooms have names like Golden Delicious, Royal Gala, and Sweet Bough; all have gas fireplaces, and four have Jacuzzis. A common room has a wood-burning stove, baby grand piano, game table, and library loft. A full breakfast, afternoon refreshments, and evening dessert are included. ☒ *42430 Moonridge Rd., 92315* ☎ *909/866–0903* ⊕ *www.applesbedandbreakfast.com* ⇗ *13 rooms* ⌂ *Some in-room hot tubs, cable TV, in-room VCRs, outdoor hot tub, paddle tennis, volleyball, meeting room; no a/c, no room phones, no smoking* ⊟ *AE, D, MC, V* ⏻ *BP.*

$$–$$$ ⛺ **Gold Mountain Manor.** This restored log mansion, originally built in 1928, has a wide porch under wooden eaves and an Adirondack style swing set on the lawn. Each room has its own theme; the Clark Gable room, for example, contains the old Franklin stove that once graced Gable's and Carole Lombard's honeymoon suite. All rooms have fireplaces and log beds original to the house. The common area has a TV, a VCR, and a collection of videos. Afternoon hors d'oeuvres and wine are included. ✉ *1117 Anita Ave., off North Shore Dr., Big Bear City 92314* ☎ *909/585–6997 or 800/509–2604* 🖷 *909/585–0327* ⊕ *www.goldmountainmanor.com* ⇦ *4 rooms, 3 suites* ঌ *Some in-room hot tubs, no-smoking rooms; no room phones, no room TVs, no a/c* ▤ *AE, D, MC, V* ⧦ *BP.*

$$$ ▦ **Northwoods Resort.** A giant log cabin with the amenities of a resort, Northwoods has a lobby that resembles a 1930s hunting lodge: canoes, antlers, fishing poles, and a grand stone fireplace all decorate the walls. Rooms are large but cozy; some have fireplaces and whirlpool tubs. Stillwells Restaurant, next to the lobby, serves hearty American fare. Ski packages are available. ✉ *40650 Village Dr., 92315* ☎ *909/866–3121 or 800/866–3121* 🖷 *909/878–2122* ⊕ *www.northwoodsresort.com* ⇦ *138 rooms, 9 suites* ঌ *2 restaurants, some in-room hot tubs, cable TV with movies and video games, pool, gym, outdoor hot tub, sauna, bar, no-smoking rooms* ▤ *AE, D, DC, MC, V.*

Sports & the Outdoors

★ You don't have to be a mountain biker to enjoy Bear Mountain's **Scenic Sky Chair.** The lift takes you to the mountain's 8,400-foot peak, where you can lunch at View Haus (¢), a casual outdoor restaurant with breathtaking views of the lake and San Gorgonio mountain. Fare includes barbecued chicken sandwiches, hot dogs, and burgers, along with cold beer and wine. ✉ *43101 Goldmine Dr.* ☎ *909/866–5766* ⊕ *www.bigbearmountainresorts.com* ✉ *$10 round-trip* ⊙ *Mid-June–early Sept., daily 9–4; early Sept.–mid-June, weekends, call for hrs.*

If you're looking for adventure, ride a horse through the snow-covered forest at **Baldwin Lake Stables**(✉ ☎ 909/585–6482) or hit the lake for a day of waterskiing, tubing or parasailing at **Big Bear Parasail and Water Sports.** ✉ *439 Pine Knot Ave., Big Bear Lake* ☎ *909/866–4359.*

Jet Ski, water ski, fishing boat, and equipment rentals are available from **Big Bear Marina** (✉ Paine Rd. ☎ 909/866–3218). **Pine Knot Landing** (✉ 439 Pine Knot ☎ 909/866–2628) rents fishing boats and sells bait, ice, and snacks.

SKIING   Snow Summit and Bear Mountain merged in October 2002, creating
★ **Big Bear Mountain Resorts,** Southern California's largest winter resort. Here you can board more than 200 freestyle terrain features at Bear Mountain's massive snowboard terrain park, then shuttle 1 mi down the road to Snow Summit for its open skiing terrain and special area designed for kids. The megaresort offers 430 skiable acres, 55 runs, and 23 chairlifts, including four high-speed quads. An all-day lift ticket includes admission and shuttle rides at both resorts. On busy winter weekends and holidays it's best to reserve tickets before heading to either mountain. ✉ *Big Bear, 43101 Goldmine Dr., off Moonridge Rd.* ✉ *Snow Summit, 880 Summit Blvd., off Big Bear Blvd.* ☎ *909/866–5766* ⊕ *www. bigbearmountainresorts.com* ✉ *$48; $55 on holidays.*

THE SOUTHERN EMPIRE
THE SAN JACINTO MOUNTAINS & TEMECULA VALLEY

Life is quieter in the southern portion of the Inland Empire than it is to the north. In this corner of Riverside County, small towns like Idyllwild and Temecula are oases of the good life for locals and visitors alike.

Idyllwild

⑪ *85 mi south of Big Bear Lake via Hwys. 18, 330 and 30, then I–10 east to Hwy. 243 south; 51 mi southeast of Rte. 60 east and Hwy. 243 south.*

Famous as a serene hideaway and artists' colony, Idyllwild also has great rock-climbing, hiking, and shopping. On weekends and by appointment May through November, **Idyllwild Tours** (☎ 909/659–4335 ☎ $10) operates narrated shuttle rides through the town's most scenic locations. On summer weekends, hitch a ride with **The Hay Dude Ranch** (☎ 909/ 659–0383 or 909/763–2473), which runs $20 horse-drawn carriage tours of downtown Idyllwild as well as personalized trail rides.

At the **Idyllwild Nature Center,** you can learn about the area's Native American history, try your hand at astronomy, and listen to traditional storytellers. Outside there are 3 mi of hiking trails, plus picnic areas. Native-plant lectures and wildflower walks are offered every Memorial Day weekend during the center's Wildflower Show. ⊠ *25225 Hwy. 243* ☎ *909/659–3850* ⊕ *www.idyllwildnaturecenter.net* ☎ *$2* ☉ *May–Sept., Thurs.–Sun. 9–4:30; Oct.–Apr., Fri.–Sun. 9–4.*

Where to Stay & Eat

★ **$–$$$** ✕ **Restaurant Gastrognome.** Elegant and dimly lit, with wood paneling and an often-glowing fireplace, "The Gnome" is where locals go for refined American fare. The French onion soup is a standout appetizer; the calamari amandine, and Southwest grilled pork are excellent entrées. The crème brûlée makes for a sweet finale. ⊠ *54381 Ridgeview Dr.* ☎ *909/659–5055* ▤ *MC, V.*

¢ ✕ **Oma's European Bakery and Restaurant.** Three generations of the Solleveld family run this breakfast and lunch spot, tempting early birds with hot *roerei* (a scramble of eggs, onions, and tomatoes) and cinnamon rolls. For lunch, don't miss the Black Forest ham on black bread with German *butterkase* (jack) cheese, or Oma's wurst platter, stacked high with three European links, red cabbage, or sauerkraut, and German potatoes. ⊠ *54241 Ridgeview Dr.* ☎ *909/659–2979* ▤ *MC, V* ☉ *Closed Tues. and Wed. No dinner.*

$–$$$ ▦ **Cedar Street Inn.** This Victorian-style inn, made from two converted 1930s homes, offers suites within walking distance of the village and hiking trails. Most rooms have knotty-pine walls and are decorated with antiques and quilts. If you're on a budget, the cozy Attic Room, accessed by a spiral staircase, is a good choice for its views of the trees. The inn also rents out cabins; the Hobbit House comes with its own Jacuzzi, wet bar, and sauna. ⊠ *25880 Cedar St., 92549* ☎ *909/659–4789* 🖨 *909/ 659–1049* ⊕ *www.cedarstreetinn.com* ⌇ *9 suites, 3 cabins* ♿ *Refrigerators, cable TV, meeting rooms; no a/c* ⊟ *D, MC, V.*

¢–$$ 🖭 **Atipahato Lodge.** Perfect for nature-lovers, this woodsy retreat is set on 5 acres of hilltop that overlook the San Jacinto Wilderness. Each room has pine-paneled walls, a vaulted ceiling, and a balcony. Each of two luxury cabins includes a fireplace, Jacuzzi, full kitchen, private deck, CD stereo, cable TV, and VCR. While you're here, check out the nature trail, which passes a springtime stream and waterfall and a Native American Nature Center. ⊠ *25525 Hwy. 243, 92549* ☎ *888/400–0071* 🖨 *909/ 966–9822* ⊕ *www.atipahato.com* ⌇ *18 rooms, 2 cabins* ♿ *Kitchenettes, some microwaves, refrigerators, some in-room hot tubs, some in-room VCRs, meeting rooms; no a/c in suites* ⊟ *AE, D, MC, V.* $85–$180

★ 🖭 **Strawberry Creek Inn.** This charming bed-and-breakfast nestled among the pines consistently draws raves from visitors. Many rooms have wood-burning fireplaces. In the morning don't miss the Inn's famous German-style French toast, topped with sliced Granny Smith apples, cinnamon sugar, and smoked bratwurst. The cottage is a nice honeymoon spot, equipped with a full kitchen, microwave, fireplace, and deck. ⊠ *26370 Hwy. 243* ☎ *909/659–3202 or 800/262–8969* ⊕ *www. strawberrycreekinn.com* ⌇ *9 rooms, 1 cottage* ♿ *Some fireplaces, some refrigerators, some in-room VCRs* ⊟ *D, MC, V* ⏀ *BP.*

Sports & the Outdoors

FISHING **Lake Fulmor** (⊠ Hwy. 243, 10 mi north of Idyllwild ☎ 909/659–2117) is stocked with rainbow trout. To fish here you'll need a California fishing license and a National Forest Adventure Pass ($5 per vehicle per day). Adventure Passes are available at the **Idyllwild Ranger Station** (⊠ Pine Crest Ave. off Hwy. 243 ☎ 909/659–2117).

HIKING Hike the 2.6-mi Ernie Maxwell Scenic Trail at **Humber Park** (⊠ At the top of Fern Valley Rd. ☎ 909/659–2117). Along the way you'll have views of Little Tahquitz Creek, Marion Mountain, and Suicide Rock. A permit is not required to hike this trail. The **Pacific Crest Trail** is accessible at Highway 74 1 mi east of Highway 371, or via the Fuller Ridge Trail at Black Mountain Road 15 mi north of Idyllwild. Permits ($5 per day), are required for camping and day hikes in San Jacinto Wilderness. They are available through the **Idyllwild Ranger Station** (⊠ Pine Crest Ave., off Hwy. 243 ☎ 909/659–2117).

Temecula

▶ ⑫ *43 mi south of Riverside on I–15; 60 mi north of San Diego in I–15; 90 mi southeast of Los Angeles via I–10 and I–15.*

In the mood for wine but can't make it to Northern California? Temecula, with its rolling green vineyards, comfy country inns, and first-rate restaurants, makes a fine alternative to Napa Valley. There are 20 wineries in the Temecula Valley, with still more being built. The name Temecula comes from a Luiseno Indian word meaning "where the sun shines through the mist"—ideal conditions for wine growing. Intense afternoon sun and cool nighttime temperatures, complemented by ocean breezes that flow through the Rainbow and Santa Margarita gaps in the coastal range, help grapevines flourish in the area's granitic soil. The Temecula Valley is known for chardonnay, merlot and sauvignon blanc, but in recent years there has been a trend toward viognier, syrah and pinot gris varietals. Most wineries charge a small fee ($2–$6) for a tasting of several wines.

Temecula is more than just vineyards and tasting rooms. For a bit of old-fashioned fun, head to historic **Old Town Temecula** (⊠ Front St. between Rancho California Rd. and Hwy. 79 ☎ 909/694–6412), a turn-of-the-20th-century cluster of storefronts and boardwalks that holds more than 640 antiques stores, boutiques, and art galleries. This is where special events such as the Rod Run, Frontier Days Rodeo, and Fall Car Cruise take place. A farmers market is held here every Saturday from 8 to noon.

In September check out the annual **Temecula Valley International Film Festival** (☎ 909/699–6267 ⊕ www.tviff.com), which has honored celebs including the late Ray Charles, Carl Reiner, and Michael York. The event also hosts film industry workshops, panel discussions, and seminars, all open to the public. Temecula hosts its annual **Balloon and Wine Festival** (☎ 909/676–6713) each June. The spectacular event includes 50 hot air balloons, a gourmet food court, a wine-tasting garden, and live music.

Most of the Temecula wineries are located close to each other on Rancho California Road. If you plan to visit a lot of wineries (and taste a lot of wine), catch the **Grapeline Wine Country Shuttle** (⊠ 29909 Corte Castille ☎ 909/693–5463 or 888/894–6379 ⊕ www.gogrape.com ⊠ $38), which operates weekends and some holidays. Private shuttles are available daily.

Baily Vineyard & Winery has grown to include an 8,000-square-foot winemaking facility with 50,000 gallons of wine tanks. Most folks come here for their two noteworthy restaurants, Carol's and Baily's. In the tasting room, browse the gourmet gift shop before sampling the cabernet, reisling, and muscat blanc. ⊠ *33440 La Serena Way* ☎ *909/676–9463* ⊕ *www.baily.com* ⊠ *Free* ⊙ *Daily 11–5, Sat. 10–5.*

Established in 1969, **Callaway Coastal Vineyards** is well-known for chardonnays and merlots by winemaker Art Villarreal. Complimentary tours are offered weekdays at 11, 1 and 3, and on weekends, 11–4 on the hour. You are welcome to picnic in the arbor or dine alfresco at the vineyard-view **Allie's** (☎ 909/694–0560), which serves California-Mediterranean fare. ⊠ *32720 Rancho California Rd.* ☎ *909/676–4001* ⊕ *www.callawaycoastal.com* ⊠ *Free* ⊙ *Daily 10:30–5.*

Bringing a bit of French country elegance to Temecula, **Churon Winery** welcomes you to its tasting room via a winding stone staircase. Try winemaker Don Frangipani's cabernet sauvignon, viognier, chenin blanc and syrah at the large, dark-wood bar with ample seating and a fine art gallery. A deli offers gourmet items that you can take outside to the gorgeous patio. ⊠ *33233 Rancho California Rd.* ☎ *909/694–9070* ⊕ *www.innatchuronwinery.com* ⊠ *Free* ⊙ *Daily 10–5.*

Falkner Winery's big, Western-style barn with a wraparound deck overlooking the vineyards is a great spot to enjoy Temecula's cool ocean breezes. Falkner has garnered great word-of-mouth, especially for their red Tuscan Amante. Winemaker Steve Hagata is also known for his viognier, chardonnay, and riesling. Packaged snacks, along with a huge variety of gourmet gifts, are available in the shop. Free tours are given at 11 AM on weekends. ✉ *40620 Calle Contento Rd.* ☏ *909/676–8231* ⊕ *www.falknerwinery.com* 📧 *Free; $5 tastings* ◷ *10–5 daily.*

Maurice Car'rie Vineyard & Winery, housed in an 1800s-style farmhouse, is one of the few Temecula wineries that offers complimentary tastings. Winemaker Mike Tingley works with 16 different varietals, producing wines such as a light and fruity pineapple-flavored sparkling wine. On your way out, stop by the gourmet shop for a chunk of homemade sourdough-and-brie bread. ✉ *34225 Rancho California Rd.* ☏ *909/676–1711* ⊕ *www.mauricecarriewinery.com* 📧 *Free* ◷ *Daily 10–5.*

★ Perched on a hilltop, **Miramonte Winery** is Temecula's hippest, thanks to the vision of owner Cane Vanderhoof, who replanted the vineyard to almost 100 percent syrah grapes. Listen to Spanish guitar recordings while sampling the Opulente meritage, a supple sauvignon blanc, or the smooth Cinsault rosé. On Friday nights from 5 to 7, the winery turns into a hot spot with tastings ($5), tapas ($5), live flamenco music, and dancing that spills out into the vineyards. You can take a wine-tasting class or view film classics like *Casablanca* or *Blazing Saddles* on monthly movie nights ($15). ✉ *33410 Rancho California Rd.* ☏ *909/506–5500* ⊕ *www.miramontewinery.com* 📧 *Free; $7 tastings* ◷ *Tastings daily 10–5.*

★ **Mount Palomar Winery** is generally considered to produce the best wines in Temecula. Winemaker Etienne Cowper trained under Jed Steele of Kendall-Jackson and Villa Mt. Eden fame, and with Andre Tchelistcheff, a mentor of Robert Mondavi and creator (at Beaulieu Vineyards in the 1930s) of California's first world-class cabernets. Mount Palomar was the first winery to introduce sangiovese grapes to Temecula, and the variety has proven perfectly suited to the region's soil and climate. In a Spanish colonial-style building, the tasting room offers must-tries like red meritage, white cortese, and a cream sherry to die for. If you want to picnic on the grounds, stop by the deli for top-notch potato salad and Italian-style sandwiches. ✉ *33820 Rancho California Rd.* ☏ *909/676–5047* ⊕ *www.mountpalomar.com* 📧 *Free; $5 tastings* ◷ *Daily 10–4.*

★ A rambling French-Mediterranean-style stone building houses **Thornton Winery,** a producer best known for its sparkling wine. You can taste winemaker Jon McPherson's outstanding brut reserve and cuveé rouge at a table in the lounge, or along with some food at Café Champagne. On the weekend, take a free tour of the grounds and the wine cave. Longer hours, summer smooth jazz concerts (admission is charged) and elaborate winemaker dinners ($80–$90) make this a fun place to spend an evening. Tastings here—$9 for 4 tastes; $12 for all 4 champagnes; $15 for reserve wines plus 2 champagnes and 2 reds—are pricier than at other area wineries. ⊠ *32575 Rancho California Rd.* ☎ *909/699–0099* ⊕ *www.thorntonwine.com* 🖳 *Free* ☉ *Daily 11–9.*

A small stream winds through flower gardens and vineyards at peaceful, park-like **Wilson Creek Winery & Vineyard.** In the huge tasting room you'll find a little bit of heaven in the "Decadencia" chocolate port and the almond Oh-My-Gosh sparkling wine, named for taster's reactions. ⊠ *35960 Rancho California Rd.* ☎ *909/699–9463* ⊕ *www. wilsoncreekwinery.com* 🖳 *Free; $6 tastings* ☉ *Daily 10–5.*

Where to Stay & Eat

$$$–$$$$
Fodor'sChoice
★ ✕ **Café Champagne.** The spacious patio, with its bubbling fountain, flowering trellises, and views of Thornton Winery's vineyards, is the perfect place to lunch on a sunny day. Inside, the dining room is decked out in French country style, and the kitchen turns out warm Brie en croute, and crispy roast duck breast drizzled with ginger-lavender honey sauce. The eclectic menu is complemented by a reasonably priced wine list featuring Italian, French, and California wines—including, of course, Thornton sparklers. Sunday brunch is accompanied by live accordion and violin music. ⊠ *32575 Rancho California Rd.* ☎ *909/699–0088* ⊕ *www.thorntonwine.com/cafe.html* 🖃 *AE, D, MC, V* ☉ *No dinner Mon.–Sat.*

★ ¢ ✕ **Carol's.** Gray stone walls and a shining suit of armor welcome you to this genteel lunch spot beside the tasting room at Baily Vineyard & Winery. Wine-friendly dishes such as chicken and smoked gouda on a croissant, and a vineyard salad with cabernet-citrus vinaigrette, often include produce from the garden outside. ⊠ *33440 La Serena Way* ☎ *909/676–9243* 🖃 *AE, MC, V* ☉ *Closed Mon. No dinner.*

★ **$$$** ✕🖾 **Temecula Creek Inn.** If you want the relaxation of the wine country and the challenge of hitting the links on a championship golf course, this is the place for you. Each room has a private patio or balcony overlooking the course and is decorated in soothing earth tones with a Southwestern theme. The on-site restaurant, Temet Grill ($$–$$$) serves regional fare and local wines. ⊠ *44501 Rainbow Canyon Rd., 92592* ☎ *909/694–1000 or 800/962–7335* ⊕ *www. temeculacreekinn.com* ⤺ *130 rooms* ⚬ *Restaurant, minibars, refrigerators, cable TV, 27-hole golf course, pool, gym, hot tub, lounge, meeting rooms* 🖃 *AE, D, MC, V.*

★ **$$–$$$$** 🖾 **Inn at Churon Winery.** You'll feel like royalty when you stay at this château-style winery perched on a hill overlooking manicured gardens and vineyards. Butter-yellow hallways lead to a library nook, where you can relax over a cup of coffee by the fire. Rooms are decorated with French antiques and outfitted with gas-burning fireplaces and marble hot tubs. Each evening a private wine reception is held in the tasting room, with crusty homemade pizza for nibbling. ⊠ *33233 Rancho California Rd., 92591* ☎ *909/694–9070* ⊕ *www.innatchuronwinery. com* ⤺ *16 rooms, 6 suites* ⚬ *In-room hot tubs, cable TV, meeting rooms; no smoking* 🖃 *AE, D, DC, MC, V* ⓣⓞⓘ *BP.*

$–$$ 🖾 **Comfort Inn.** The best value in Temecula, this hotel has large rooms appointed with faux-cherrywood furniture, coffeemakers, hair dryers, irons, and ironing boards. The business center provides free DSL Internet access, and your room rate includes a daily newspaper and a deluxe Continental breakfast. ⊠ *27338 Jefferson Ave., 92590* ☎ *909/296–3788 or 877/424–6423* 🖨 *909/296–5188* ⊕ *www.comfortinn.com* ⥳ *72 rooms, 2 suites ⚭ Some kitchenettes, some microwaves, some refrigerators, cable TV, pool, gym, hot tub, Internet, business services, meeting rooms* ⊟ *AE, D, DC, MC, V* ⧌ *BP.*

Shopping

While you're shopping in Old Town, stop by the **Temecula Olive Oil Company** tasting room for a sample of its extra-virgin olive oils, bath products, and Mission, Ascalano, and Italian olives. ⊠ *42030 Main St., Suite H* ☎ *866/654–8396* ⊘ *Daily 9–5.*

Sports & the Outdoors

GOLF Temecula has seven championship golf courses cooled by the valley's ocean breezes. **Redhawk Golf Club** (⊠ 45100 Redhawk Pkwy. ☎ 909/302–3850 ⊕ www.redhawkgolfcourse.com) has an 18-hole championship course designed by Ron Fream. For a special treat, head to the **Temecula Creek Inn Golf Resort** (⊠ 44501 Rainbow Canyon Rd. ☎ 909/676–2405 ⊕ www.temeculacreekinn.com), whose 27-hole course was designed by Ted Robinson and Dick Rossen.

HOT-AIR BALLOONING If you're in the mood to swoop or float above Temecula's green vineyards and country estates, sign up for a trip with **California Dreamin' Balloon & Biplane Rides** (☎ 800/373–3359 ⊕ www.californiadreamin.com). Balloon trips depart from Thornton Winery at 5:30 AM; the $118 per-person fee includes champagne and coffee.

INLAND EMPIRE A TO Z

To research prices, get advice from other travelers, and book travel arrangements, visit www.fodors.com.

AIR TRAVEL

Aero Mexico, Alaska, America West, American, Continental, Delta, Frontier, Hawaiian, JetBlue, Lineas Aereas Azteca, Northwest, Southwest, United, and United Express serve Ontario International Airport. *See* Air Travel *in* Smart Travel Tips A to Z for airline phone numbers.

🖪 **Ontario International Airport** ⊠ Airport Dr., Archibald Ave. exit off I-10, Ontario ⊕ www.lawa.org/ont/ontframe.html ☎ 866/456–3900 or 909/937–2700.

BUS TRAVEL

Greyhound serves Claremont, Corona, Fontana, Moreno Valley, Perris, Riverside, San Bernardino, and Temecula. Most stations are open daily during business hours; some are open 24 hours.

The Foothill Transit Bus Line serves Pomona, Claremont, and Montclair, with stops at Cal Poly and the Fairplex. Riverside Transit Authority (RTA) serves Riverside and some outlying communities, as does OmniTrans.

🖪 **Foothill Transit** ☎ 800/743–3463 ⊕ www.foothilltransit.org. **Greyhound** ☎ 800/231–2222 ⊕ www.greyhound.com. **OmniTrans** ☎ 800/966–6428 ⊕ www.omnitrans.org. **Riverside Transit Authority** ☎ 800/800–7821 ⊕ www.rrta.com.

CAR RENTAL
Alamo, Avis, Budget, Dollar, Hertz, and National have offices at Ontario International Airport. You can rent from Avis, Budget, or Hertz in Riverside. *See* Car Rental *in* Smart Travel Tips A to Z for national rental agency phone numbers.

CAR TRAVEL
Most destinations in the Inland Empire are easily accessible from the I–15 and I–10 freeways. Avoid Highway 91 if possible; it's almost always backed up from Corona through Orange County.

🚗 **California Highway Patrol 24-hr road info** ☎ 800/427-7623 ⊕ www.dot.ca.gov/hq/roadinfo.

EMERGENCIES
In an emergency dial 911.

🚗 **Parkview Community Hospital** ⊠ 3865 Jackson St., Riverside ☎ 909/688-2211. **Rancho Springs Medical Center** ⊠ 25500 Medical Center Dr., Murrieta ☎ 909/696-6000. **Riverside Community Hospital** ⊠ 4445 Magnolia Ave., Riverside ☎ 909/788-3000. **St. Bernardine Medical Center** ⊠ 2101 N. Waterman Ave., San Bernardino ☎ 909/883-8711. **San Bernardino County Sheriff** ☎ 909/955-2444.

TRAIN TRAVEL
Metrolink has several Inland Empire stations on its Inter-County, San Bernardino, and Riverside rail lines. The Riverside Line connects downtown Riverside, Pedley, East Ontario, and downtown Pomona with City of Industry and with Union Station in Los Angeles. The Inter-County Rail Line connects San Bernardino, downtown Riverside, Riverside La Sierra, and West Corona with San Juan Capistrano and Orange County. Metrolink's busiest train, the San Bernardino Line, connects Pomona, Claremont, Montclair, and San Bernardino with the San Gabriel Valley and downtown Los Angeles. Bus service extends the reach of train service, to spots including Ontario Airport, the Claremont Colleges, and the Fairplex at Pomona. You can buy tickets and passes at the ticket vending machine at each station, or by telephone. A recorded message announces Metrolink schedules 24 hours a day.

🚗 **Metrolink** ☎ 800/371-5465 ⊕ www.metrolinktrains.com.

VISITOR INFORMATION
🚗 **Big Bear Lake Resort Association** ⊠ 630 Bartlett Rd., Big Bear Lake 92315 ☎ 909/866-7000 or 800/424-4232 🖷 909/866-5671 ⊕ www.bigbearinfo.com. **Claremont Chamber of Commerce** ⊠ 205 Yale Ave., Claremont 91711 ☎ 909/624-1681 ⊕ www.claremontchamber.org. **Corona Chamber of Commerce** ⊠ 904 E. 6th St., Corona 92879 ☎ 909/737-3350 ⊕ www.coronachamber.org. **Idyllwild Chamber of Commerce** ⊠ 54295 Village Center Dr., Box 304, Idyllwild 92549 ☎ 909/659-3259 or 888/659-3259 ⊕ www.idyllwild.com. **Lake Arrowhead Communities Chamber of Commerce** ⊠ 28200 Hwy. 189, Bldg. F, Suite 290 (Box 219), Lake Arrowhead 92352 ☎ 909/337-3715 🖷 909/336-1548 ⊕ www.lakearrowhead.com. **Ontario Convention & Visitors Authority** ⊠ 2000 Convention Center Way, Ontario 91764 ☎ 909/937-3000 ⊕ wwww.ontariocvb.com. **Pomona Chamber of Commerce** ⊠ 401 S. Main St., #210, Pomona 91769 ☎ 909/622-1256 ⊕ www.pomonachamber.org. **Redlands Chamber of Commerce** ⊠ 1 East Redlands Blvd., Redlands 92373 ☎ 909/793-2546 ⊕ www.redlandschamber.

org. **Riverside Convention and Visitors Bureau** ✉ 3750 University Ave., #175, Riverside 92501 ☎ 888/748-7733 or 909/222-4700 ⊕ www.riversidecb.com. **Temecula Valley Chamber of Commerce** ✉ 26790 Ynez Court, Temecula 92591 ☎ 909/676-5090 ⊕ www.temecula.org. **Wrightwood Chamber of Commerce** 🕭 Box 416, Wrightwood 92397 ☎ 760/249-4320, 760/249-6822 for recorded information ⊕ www.wrightwoodcalifornia.com.

PALM SPRINGS & THE SOUTHERN DESERT

WITH JOSHUA TREE NATIONAL PARK

5

Updated by
Bobbi Zane

IMAGINE THE DESERT HERE AS THE BOTTOM OF A VAST SEA. Many millions of years ago, that's what it was. By 10 million years ago, the waters had receded and the climate was hospitable to prehistoric mastodons, zebras, and camels. As recently as 10,000 years ago, the Colorado River still spilled into this basin intermittently, and around AD 700 Lake Cahuilla formed. The first human inhabitants of record were the Agua Caliente, part of the Cahuilla people, who settled in and around the Coachella Valley (the northwestern portion of the Colorado Desert, between the San Jacinto and Little San Bernardino mountain ranges) about 1,000 years ago. Lake Cahuilla dried up about 300 years ago, but by then the Agua Caliente had discovered the area's hot springs and were making use of their healing properties during winter visits to the desert. The springs became a tourist attraction in 1871, when the tribe built a bathhouse (on a site near the current Spa Resort Casino in Palm Springs) to serve passengers on a pioneer stage highway. The Agua Caliente still own about 32,000 acres of desert, 6,700 of which lie within the city limits of Palm Springs.

In the last half of the 19th century, farmers established a date-growing industry at the southern end of the Coachella Valley. By 1900 word had spread about the manifold health benefits of the area's dry climate, inspiring the gentry of the northern United States to winter under the warm desert sun. In the mid-1900s, farmers southeast of the Coachella began turning the barren Imperial Valley—home of the broad, brackish Salton Sea—into rich fields of tomatoes, corn, and grain. The Anza-Borrego Desert, which stretches from the southern end of the Coachella Valley nearly to the Mexican border, was then a mostly unpopulated desert outpost occupied by a few hardy homesteaders and visited in winter by a few adventurous campers. Growth hit the Coachella Valley in the 1970s, when developers began to construct the fabulous golf courses, country clubs, and residential communities that would draw celebrities, tycoons, and politicians. Communities sprang up south and east of what is now Palm Springs, creating a sprawl of tract houses and strip malls and forcing nature lovers to push farther south into the sparsely settled Anza-Borrego Desert and the Imperial Valley.

Exploring the Southern Desert

The desert resort cities of the Coachella Valley—Palm Springs, Cathedral City, Rancho Mirage, Palm Desert, Indian Wells, La Quinta, and Indio—are strung out along Highway 111, with Palm Springs at the northwestern end of this strip and Indio at the southeastern end. North of Palm Springs, between I–10 and Highway 62, is Desert Hot Springs. Northeast of Palm Springs, the towns of the Morongo Valley lie along Twentynine Palms Highway (Highway 62), which leads to Joshua Tree National Park. Head south on Highway 86 from Indio to reach Anza -Borrego State Park and the Salton Sea. All of the area's attractions are easy day trips from Palm Springs.

About the Restaurants

Long a culinary wasteland, the desert now supports many trendy if not overly ambitious restaurants. Italian cuisine remains popular, but

Numbers in the text correspond to numbers in the margin and on the Palm Springs and Southern Desert maps.

If you have
1 day

If you've just slipped into the desert for a day, focus your activities around ▶ **Palm Springs ❶–❿**. Get an early-morning scenic overview by taking the **Palm Springs Aerial Tramway ❶** to the top of Mt. San Jacinto. In the afternoon head for Palm Canyon Drive, where you can have lunch and pick up tickets for an evening performance of the Fabulous Palm Springs Follies (better still, make reservations before your visit). In the afternoon visit **Palm Desert ⓭**, the trendiest of the desert cities, for a walk through the canyons and hillsides of the Living Desert Zoo and Gardens and a preshow dinner at a restaurant on El Paseo.

If you have
3 days
▶

Palm Springs ❶–❿ makes a good base for exploring the area. On your first day head to the **Palm Springs Aerial Tramway ❶** in the morning and have lunch on Palm Canyon Drive. Spend the afternoon browsing through the Palm Canyon shops or (unless it's the height of summer) hiking through the **Indian Canyons ❿**. On Day 2 take an early morning drive to **Twentynine Palms ⓲** and Joshua Tree National Park, where you can explore the terrain, crawl through the entrance to Hidden Valley, and stop by the Oasis Visitor Center. Have a picnic lunch in the park or head back to El Paseo, in **Palm Desert ⓭**, for a mid-afternoon bite before exploring the chic shopping area. On the third morning take in the **Palm Springs Desert Museum ❹**, where you can learn about the natural history of the desert and see some great art. In the afternoon pamper yourself at one of the spas for which Palm Springs is famous. Then have dinner and take in a performance of the Fabulous Palm Springs Follies.

If you have
5 days

If you have five days to spend in the desert, you'll have time to explore beyond the immediate ▶ **Palm Springs ❶–❿** area. On your first day take in a sweeping view of the Coachella Valley from the top of the **Palm Springs Aerial Tramway ❶** in the morning, and stroll along Palm Canyon Drive in the afternoon. On the second morning visit the **Palm Springs Desert Museum ❹**. Then grab a picnic lunch and head out to **Indian Canyons ❿**, where you can eat by a waterfall. By evening you'll be ready to live it up at one of the desert's nightspots. Spend Days 3 and 4 at Joshua Tree National Park. You can camp in the park or stay at a B&B in **Twentynine Palms ⓲**, just outside the park. In the evening take an hour to gaze at the stars. On Day 5 get an early start and complete your drive through the park so you can arrive back in the Palm Springs area for lunch. Check into a spa for the afternoon, and catch the Fabulous Palm Springs Follies on your last night.

Alternatively, you can spend Days 3 and 4 in quiet **Borrego Springs ⓳**, exploring the wonders of Anza-Borrego Desert State Park and the **Salton Sea ⓴**. On the fifth morning drive to **Palm Desert ⓭** to visit the Living Desert Zoo and Gardens, have lunch on El Paseo, do some shopping, and head back to your hotel for one last dip in the pool.

5

you can now dine at restaurants that serve fare from Thai to Indian, from seafood to vegetarian, and from classic French to contemporary Californian. You can find Mexican food everywhere; in the smaller communities it may be your best choice. Dining throughout the region is casual. Many restaurants that were traditionally closed in summer (the off season) are now opening on a limited basis: hours vary, so call to check.

About the Hotels

You can stay in the desert for as little as $40 or spend more than $1,000 a night. Rates vary widely by season: from low in summer to high in winter. Hotel prices are frequently 50% less in summer than in winter and early spring. January through April, prices soar, and accommodations can be difficult to secure, so reserve as far ahead as you can. In any season it pays to inquire about hotel and resort packages that include extras such as golf or spa services. Many desert hotels add a resort fee of about $10 to the daily rate. Discounts are sometimes given for extended stays. Year-round, budget lodgings are most easily found in Palm Springs and in the less glamorous towns of Cathedral City, Indio, Borrego Springs, El Centro, and in the Morongo Valley towns along Twentynine Palms Highway.

WHAT IT COSTS					
	$$$$	$$$	$$	$	¢
RESTAURANTS	over $30	$23–$30	$16–$22	$10–$15	under $10
HOTELS	over $250	$176–$250	$121–$175	$90–$120	under $90

Restaurant prices are for a main course at dinner, excluding sales tax of 7¼%. Hotel prices are for two people in a standard double room in high season, excluding service charges and 9%–11% tax.

Timing

Because Palm Springs and the surrounding desert average 350 sunny days a year, you are almost assured a chance to get in a round or two of golf or some lounging by the pool whenever you visit. During the season (January–April), as everybody calls it, the desert weather is at its best, with daytime temperatures ranging between 70°F and 90°F. This is the time when you're most likely to see colorful displays of wildflowers and when most of the golf and tennis tournaments take place. The fall months are nearly as lovely, with the added bonus of being less crowded and less expensive. In summer, daytime temperatures may rise above 110°F, though evenings cool to the mid-70s. Some attractions and restaurants, particularly those in the Borrego Springs area, close during this period.

THE DESERT RESORTS

INCLUDING PALM SPRINGS

Around the desert resorts, privacy is the watchword. Celebrities flock to the desert from Los Angeles, and many communities are walled and guarded. Still, you might spot Hollywood stars, sports personalities, politi-

Desert Wildlife

The southern desert is a land of fascinating geology and wildlife. Explore the terrain at ground level at the Living Desert Zoo and Gardens. Other great places to learn about the natural history of the desert are the Palm Springs Desert Museum, Indian Canyons, Joshua Tree National Park, Anza-Borrego Desert, and along the shores of the Salton Sea.

Nightlife & the Arts

Nightlife is concentrated—and abundant—in the resort communities near Palm Springs. Options include a good jazz bar, a clutch of retro shows and glamorous clubs, several dance clubs, and hotel entertainment. The *Fabulous Palm Springs Follies*—a vaudeville-style revue starring retired professional performers—is a must-see for most visitors. Arts festivals occur on a regular basis, especially in winter and spring. The "Desert Guide" section of *Palm Springs Life* magazine (available at most hotels and visitor information centers) has nightlife listings, as does the "Weekender" pullout in the Friday edition of the *Desert Sun* newspaper. The gay scene is covered in the *Bottom Line* and in the *Gay Guide to Palm Springs,* published by the Desert Gay Tourism Guild.

Sports & the Outdoors

The Palm Springs area has some 100 golf courses, many of which are familiar to fans of the sport as the sites of championship and celebrity tournaments seen on television. You can tee off where the pros play at PGA West, Mission Hills North, and La Quinta, all of which have instructors ready to help you finesse your swing. Even Borrego Springs and El Centro have golf courses.

The desert holds a world of athletic opportunities for nongolfers, too. With almost 30,000 public and private pools in the region, swimming and sunning are a daily ritual. More than 35 mi of bike trails crisscross the mostly flat Palm Springs area alone. Indian Canyons, Mount San Jacinto State Park, Living Desert Zoo and Gardens, Joshua Tree National Park, Anza-Borrego Desert, and Big Morongo Canyon Preserve have scenic hiking trails. The Salton Sea attracts many migratory birds, especially in winter. Some of the best rock-climbing highways in the world are in Joshua Tree National Park.

Whatever your sport, avoid outdoor activities midday during the hot season (roughly May through October). Any time of the year, take precautions against the sun, such as wearing a hat and using sunscreen. Always drink plenty of water—at least a gallon of water per day (more if you are exercising)—to prevent dehydration.

Shopping

Designer boutiques, antiques shops, art galleries, vintage resale palaces, and a huge upmarket discount mall lure dedicated shoppers to the desert. Popular shopping venues include the Thursday-night Palm Springs Village Fest; El Paseo, in Palm Desert; Desert Hills Factory Stores, in Cabazon; and the consignment and resale shops in many desert communities.

cians, and other high-profile types in restaurants, out on the town, or on a golf course. For the most part the desert's social, sports, shopping, and entertainment scenes center on Palm Springs and Palm Desert.

Palm Springs

90 mi southeast of Los Angeles on I–10.

▶ A tourist destination since the late 19th century, Palm Springs had already caught Hollywood's eye by the time of the Great Depression. It was an ideal hideaway: celebrities could slip into town, play a few sets of tennis, lounge around the pool, attend a party or two, and, unless things got out of hand, remain safely beyond the reach of gossip columnists. But it took a pair of tennis-playing celebrities to put Palm Springs on the map. In the 1930s actors Charlie Farrell and Ralph Bellamy bought 200 acres of land for $30 an acre and opened the Palm Springs Racquet Club, which soon listed Ginger Rogers, Humphrey Bogart, and Clark Gable among its members.

During its slow, steady growth period from the 1930s to 1970s, the Palm Springs area drew some of the world's most famous architects to design homes for the rich and famous. The collected works, inspired by the mountains and desert sands and notable for the use of glass and indoor/outdoor space, became known as Palm Springs Modernism. The city lost some of its luster in the 1970s as the wealthy moved to newer down-valley communities. But Palm Springs reinvented itself, restoring the lovely old houses and hotels, and cultivating a welcoming atmosphere for well-heeled gay visitors. You'll find reminders of the city's glamorous past in its unique architecture and renovated hotels, while change and progress are evidenced by trendy restaurants and upscale shops. Formerly exclusive Palm Canyon Drive is now a lively avenue with coffeehouses, outdoor cafés and bars, and frequent special events.

Note: Tahquitz Canyon Way marks the division between north and south on major streets (e.g., North and South Palm Canyon Drive).

★ ⟲ ❶ A trip on the **Palm Springs Aerial Tramway** provides a 360-degree view of the desert through the picture windows of Rotair rotating tram cars. The 2½-mi ascent through Chino Canyon, the steepest vertical cable ride in the United States, brings you to an elevation of 8,516 feet in less than 20 minutes. On clear days, which are common, the view stretches 75 mi—from the peak of Mount San Gorgonio in the north, to the Salton Sea in the southeast. At the top, a bit below the summit of Mt. San Jacinto are several diversions. Mountain Station has an observation deck, a restaurant, a cocktail lounge, apparel and gift shops, picnic facilities, and a theater that screens a worthwhile 22-minute film on the history of the tramway. Take advantage of free guided and self-guided nature walks, or if there's snow on the ground, rent skis, snowshoes, or snow tubes (inner tubes or similar contraptions for sliding down hills). Ride-and-dine packages are available in late afternoon. The tram is a popular attraction; to avoid a two-hour or longer wait, arrive before the first car leaves. ✉ *1 Tramway Rd.* ☎ *760/325–1391 or 888/515–8726* ⊕ *www.pstramway.com* 💲 *$20.80; ride-and-dine package $30* ☉ *Tram*

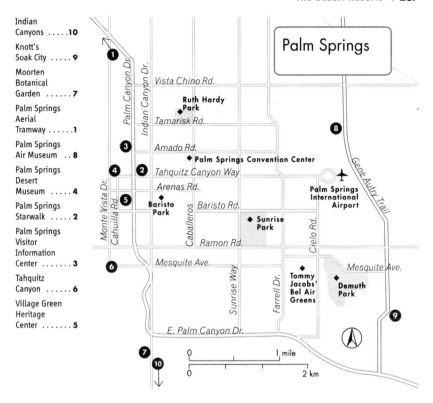

cars depart at least every 30 min from 10 AM weekdays and 8 AM weekends; last car up leaves at 8 PM, last car down leaves Mountain Station at 9:45 PM.

off the beaten path

MOUNT SAN JACINTO STATE PARK – The park, accessible by hiking or via the Palm Springs Aerial Tramway, has primitive camping and picnic areas and 54 mi of hiking trails. You can take guided mule rides through the wilderness during snow-free months. The Nordic Ski Center rents cross-country ski equipment. You must get a free permit before coming for day or overnight wilderness hiking. ⊠ *Mountain Station* ☎ *909/659–2607* ⊕ *www.sanjac.statepark.org* 🔌 *Free.*

② A stroll down shop-lined Palm Canyon Drive will take you past the **Palm Springs Starwalk** (⊠ Palm Canyon Dr. around Tahquitz Canyon Way, and Tahquitz Canyon Way between Palm Canyon and Indian Canyon Drs.), whose nearly 200 bronze stars are embedded in the sidewalk (à la the Hollywood Walk of Fame). Most of the names, all with a Palm Springs connection, are ones you'll recognize (such as Elvis Presley, Marilyn Monroe, Lauren Bacall, and Liberace). Others are local celebrities.

❸ Stop at the **Palm Springs Visitor Information Center** for information on sights to see and things to do in the area. ✉ *777 N. Palm Canyon Dr.* ☎ *760/327–2828 or 800/927–7256* ⊕ *www.palm-springs.org* ⊙ *Mon. and Wed.–Sat. 10–5:30.*

★ ☽ ❹ The exhibits at the **Palm Springs Desert Museum** span natural science, the visual arts, and the performing arts. For example, the museum and grounds include a display on the natural history of the desert, which draws school children on a regular basis; several striking sculpture courts; and a modern-art gallery, with works by such artists as Alberto Giacometti, Henry Moore, and Helen Frankenthaler. Movie fans might be interested in the exhibits of the late actor William Holden's art collection, and furniture designed and crafted by actor George Montgomery. Nature hikes offered by the museum provide an opportunity to explore little-known desert sites, both historic and natural. The Annenberg Theater presents plays, concerts, lectures, operas, and other cultural events. ✉ *101 Museum Dr.* ☎ *760/325–7186* ⊕ *www.psmuseum. org* ✍ *$7.50; free 1st Fri. of month* ⊙ *Tues.–Sat. 10–5, Sun. noon–5.*

❺ Three small museums at the **Village Green Heritage Center** illustrate pioneer life in Palm Springs. The **Agua Caliente Cultural Museum** (free) is devoted to the culture and history of the Cahuilla tribe. The **McCallum Adobe** ($2) holds the collection of the Palm Springs Historical Society. **Rudy's General Store Museum** (95¢) is a re-creation of a 1930s general store. ✉ *221 S. Palm Canyon Dr.* ☎ *760/327–2156* ⊙ *Call for hrs.*

❻ Ranger-led tours of **Tahquitz Canyon** take you into a secluded, long-closed, and culturally sensitive canyon on the Agua Caliente Reservation. Within the canyon are a spectacular 60-foot waterfall, rock art, ancient irrigation systems, and native wildlife and plants. Tours are conducted several times daily; participants must be able to navigate 100 steep steps. A visitor center at the canyon entrance shows a video tour, displays artifacts, and sells maps. ✉ *500 W. Mesquite Ave.* ☎ *760/416–7044* ⊕ *www.tahquitzcanyon.com* ✍ *$12.50* ⊙ *Daily 7:30–5.*

❼ Four-acre **Moorten Botanical Garden** nurtures more than 3,000 plant varieties in settings that simulate their original environments. Native American artifacts, rock, and crystal are exhibited. ✉ *1701 S. Palm Canyon Dr.* ☎ *760/327–6555* ✍ *$2.50* ⊙ *Mon. and Tues., Thurs.–Sat. 9–4:30, Sun. 10–4.*

☽ ❽ The **Palm Springs Air Museum** showcases 26 World War II aircraft, including a B-17 Flying Fortress bomber, a P-51 Mustang, a Lockheed P-38, and a Grumman TBF Avenger. Cool exhibits include a Grumman Goose into which kids can crawl, model warships, a Pearl Harbor diorama, and a map of the European theater. ✉ *745 N. Gene Autry Trail* ☎ *760/778–6262* ⊕ *www.air-museum.org* ✍ *$8* ⊙ *Daily 10–5.*

☽ ❾ For a break from the desert heat, head for **Knott's Soak City.** You'll find 13 water slides, a huge wave pool, an arcade, and other fun family attractions. ✉ *1500 Gene Autry Trail* ☎ *760/327–0499* ⊕ *www.knotts. com* ✍ *$24.95* ⊙ *Mid-Mar.–early Sept., daily; early Sept.–Oct., weekends; hrs 10–varying closing times.*

🐚 🔟 The **Indian Canyons** are the ancestral home of the Agua Caliente, part of the Cahuilla people. You can see remnants of their ancient life including rock art, house pits and foundations, irrigation ditches, bedrock mortars, pictographs, and stone houses and shelters built atop high cliff walls. The attraction includes three canyons open for touring: Palm Canyon, noted for its stand of Washingtonia palms; Murray Canyon, home of Peninsula bighorn sheep and a herd of wild ponies; and Andreas Canyon, where a stand of fan palms contrasts with sharp rock formations. Ranger-led hikes to Palm and Andreas canyons are offered daily for an additional charge. The trading post in Palm Canyon has hiking maps and refreshments, as well as Native American art, jewelry, and weavings. ✉ *38–500 S. Palm Canyon Dr.* ☎ *800/790–3398* ⊕ *www. indian-canyons.com* ✂ *$6* ☽ *Daily 8–6.*

Where to Stay & Eat

★ **$$$–$$$$** ✕ **Le Vallauris.** Housed in the historic Roberson home and graced by a colorful, tree-shaded garden, Le Vallauris serves California-accented French cuisine—dishes such as grilled veal chop with apples and Calvados, as well as grilled halibut with sun-dried-tomato crust and lemon sauce. A pianist plays nightly, and Sunday brunch is a hit. ✉ *385 W. Tahquitz Canyon Way* ☎ *760/325–5059* ✍ *Reservations essential* ▭ *AE, D, DC, MC, V* ☽ *No lunch Wed.–Sat. in July and Aug.*

$$–$$$$ ✕ **St. James at the Vineyard.** A multihue interior, an outdoor terrace with street views, and a bubbling modern fountain set a playful mood at this hot spot for dining and sipping cocktails. The eclectic menu roams the world, from bouillabaisse Burmese (fish soup) to a selection of curries. Delicate eaters can order half portions of most entrées, and some vegetarian items are available. The service can be chaotic on weekend nights in high season. ✉ *265 S. Palm Canyon Dr.* ☎ *760/320–8041* ✍ *Reservations essential* ▭ *AE, D, DC, MC, V* ☽ *No lunch.*

$–$$$$ ✕ **Otani Garden Restaurant.** You can dine on sushi, tempura, or grilled chicken or seafood in a serene garden or eat at the popular sushi bar. A Sunday brunch buffet includes tempura, stir-fried entrées, salads, and desserts. ✉ *266 Avenida Caballeros* ☎ *760/327–6700* ▭ *AE, D, DC, MC, V* ☽ *Closed Mon. No lunch Sat.*

$–$$$ ✕ **Blue Coyote Grill.** Diners munch on burritos, tacos, and fajitas—or more unusual items, such as Yucatán-style mahimahi or orange chicken—at this casual restaurant. Choose between several flower-decked patios and indoor dining rooms. Two busy cantinas serve tasty margaritas to a youngish crowd. ✉ *445 N. Palm Canyon Dr.* ☎ *760/327–1196* ▭ *AE, DC, MC, V.*

$–$$$ ✕ **Deck Restaurant and Sky Bar.** On a balmy spring evening, the second-floor deck provides one of the best seats in town. Here you can savor goodies while either watching the action on the street below or sitting around a big stone fire pit. Small plates (appetizers) include crisp and crusty ahi sushi rolls and Louisiana lump crab cakes. Topping the large-plate list are several prime steaks, succulent Hawaiian barbecued ribs, and jerk-seasoned fish tacos. ✉ *262 S. Palm Canyon Dr.* ☎ *760/325–5200* ▭ *AE, D, DC, MC, V.*

$–$$$ ✕ **Edgardo's Cafe Veracruz.** For a sampling of Maya and Aztec flavors, try some of the unusual items on Edgardo's menu, such as soup made with *nopales* (cactus) and roast pork wrapped in banana leaves. The menu also has more familiar items, such as tamales and enchiladas. ⊠ *494 N. Palm Canyon Dr.* ☎ *760/320–3558* ⌕ *Reservations essential* ▤ *AE, D, MC, V.*

$–$$ ✕ **Wang's in the Desert.** Locals flock to Wang's for its lovely Asian setting, complete with koi pond, indoor garden, and original art on the walls. The menu's well-chosen selection of Chinese and Asian-influenced entrées ranges from Kung Pao chicken to beef Stroganoff Chinoise. ⊠ *424 S. Indian Canyon Dr.* ☎ *760/325–9264* ▤ *AE, D, DC, MC, V* ☽ *No lunch.*

¢–$$ ✕ **Thai Kitchen II.** With attentive service, this tidy corner storefront restaurant serves up large portions of popular Thai items, including *pad thai* (a traditional noodle dish made with chilies, finely chopped nuts, bean sprouts, and tofu or meat, among other ingredients), fish cake, tamarind duck, and many curries. ⊠ *787 N. Palm Canyon Dr.* ☎ *760/ 323–4527* ▤ *AE, D, MC, V.*

¢ ✕ **Peabody's Café Bar & Coffee.** The place to go for a cup of joe and early-morning people-watching, Peabody's has been a Palm Canyon Drive institution for years. By day Peabody's serves breakfast and lunch, including four French toast preparations and nine omelets for the former and salads and hot and cold sandwiches for the latter. By night the place becomes a popular bar (open to 1:30 Thursday–Saturday). ⊠ *134 S. Palm Canyon Dr.* ☎ *760/322–1877* ▤ *AE, D, DC, MC, V* ☽ *No dinner Mon.–Wed.*

$–$$$$ ✕▥ **Ingleside Inn.** This hacienda-style inn attracts its share of Hollywood personalities, who appreciate the attentive service and relative seclusion. Many rooms have antiques, fireplaces, whirlpool tubs, stocked refrigerators, and private patios. Accommodations in the main building are dark and cool, even in summer. Melvyn's Restaurant at the Ingleside ($$–$$$$), one of the desert's best-known celebrity haunts, is also one of the few remaining places where you can experience the old Palm Springs lifestyle. ⊠ *200 W. Ramon Rd., 92264* ☎ *760/325– 0046 or 800/772–6655* ⊜ *760/325–0710* ⊕ *www.inglesideinn.com* ↩ *30 rooms* ⌕ *Restaurant, room service, some refrigerators, cable TV, in-room VCRs, pool, outdoor hot tub, bicycles, bar, library, piano, laundry service, concierge, no-smoking rooms* ▤ *AE, D, DC, MC, V* ⑩ *CP, FAP.*

$$$$ ▥ **Le Parker Meridien.** A major renovation in 2004 transformed the familiar white wedding-cake Givenchy (which had previously been owned by Merv Griffin and Gene Autry, among others) into an exotic and eclectic mid-century estate. Rooms have textured sisal floor coverings, exotic woven fabrics in bright reds and browns, and leather seating. All have private balconies or patios. A date palm grove replaces the hotel's massive rose garden, and hidden paths meander through secret gardens. The emphasis here is on personal service. ⊠ *4200 E. Palm Canyon Dr., 92264* ☎ *760/770–5000 or 800/543–4300* ⊜ *760/324–2188* ⊕ *www. parkermeridien.com* ↩ *145 rooms* ⌕ *2 restaurants, room service, in-room data ports, in-room safes, minibars, refrigerators, cable TV with movies and video games, 4 tennis courts, 4 pools, health club, hair salon, spa, boccie, croquet, bar, shops, dry cleaning, laundry service, con-*

cierge, business services, meeting room, car rental, free parking, some pets allowed, no-smoking rooms ☰ AE, D, DC, MC, V.

★ $$$$ 🏨 **Willows Historic Palm Springs Inn.** This luxurious hillside B&B is within walking distance of many village attractions. An opulent Mediterranean-style mansion built in the 1920s, it has gleaming hardwood and slate floors, stone fireplaces, fresco ceilings, hand-painted tiles, iron balconies, antiques throughout, and a 50-foot waterfall that splashes into a pool outside the dining room. There's even a private hillside garden planted with native flora, which affords one of the best views in the area. Guest rooms are decorated to recall the movies of Hollywood's golden era. ⊠ *412 W. Tahquitz Canyon Way, 92262* ☎ *760/320–0771 or 800/966–9597* 🖷 *760/320–0780* ⊕ *www.thewillowspalmsprings.com* ⇨ *8 rooms* ⚲ *In-room data ports, pool, outdoor hot tub; no smoking* ☰ *AE, D, DC, MC, V* ⏐◯⏐ *BP.*

★ $$$–$$$$ 🏨 **Orbit Oasis.** Step back to 1957 at this hip inn. Rooms, appointed with mid-century furnishings by such designers as Eames, Noguchi, and Breuer, surround a pool with expansive deck. Some rooms have private patios; all have a few melmac dishes tucked here and there. There's an outside shower, cruiser bikes are available, and there's a small collection of books, games, and videos available for guest use. The Oasis is paired with the Hideaway to form the Orbit In resort. ⊠ *562 W. Arenas Rd., 92262* ☎ *760/323–3585 or 877/996–7248* 🖷 *760/323–3599* ⊕ *www.orbitin.com* ⇨ *10 rooms* ⚲ *In-room data ports, some kitchenettes, cable TV with movies, saltwater pool, outdoor hot tub, massage, spa, bicycles, library, free parking, no-smoking rooms* ☰ *AE, DC, MC, V* ⏐◯⏐ *CP.*

$$–$$$$ 🏨 **Ballantine's Hotel.** Once known as the Mira Loma Hotel, this small property hosted Marilyn Monroe and Gloria Swanson in the late 1940s, when Monroe was still undiscovered and Swanson was a big star. By the 1960s the glamour had disappeared and the hotel faded, but renovation has recaptured the essence of the 1940s and 1950s, with furnishings by Eames, Biller, Bertoia, and Knoll. It's all quite retro—and a bit synthetic—with rotary phones, lava lamps, louvered windows, period appliances in kitchenettes, a collection of classic films for your VCR, and private sunbathing patios. ⊠ *1420 N. Indian Canyon Dr., 92262* ☎ *760/320–1178 or 800/485–5808* 🖷 *760/320–5308* ⊕ *www.ballantineshotels.com* ⇨ *14 rooms* ⚲ *In-room data ports, some kitchens, refrigerators, in-room VCRs, pool, bar, dry cleaning, laundry service, concierge, Internet, business services, some pets allowed (fee), no-smoking rooms* ☰ *AE, MC, V* ⏐◯⏐ *CP.*

$$–$$$$ 🏨 **Harlow Club Hotel.** This resort that caters to gay men is ideal for those seeking secluded accommodations in lush garden surroundings, including a clothing-optional sunbathing area. Many rooms have fireplaces, private patios, and unusually large bathrooms. Crimson bougainvillea cascades from the rooftops, and date palms and orange, tangerine, and grapefruit trees grow on the property. Room rates include breakfast and lunch. ⊠ *175 E. El Alameda, 92262* ☎ *760/323–3977 or 888/547–7881* 🖷 *760/323–4033* ⊕ *www.theharlow.com* ⇨ *15 rooms, 1 suite* ⚲ *In-room data ports, cable TV, in-room VCRs, pool, gym, outdoor hot tub, no-smoking rooms* ☰ *AE, D, DC, MC, V* ⏐◯⏐ *BP.*

CloseUp

PALM SPRINGS MODERNISM

W ITH ONE OF THE LARGEST concentrations of modern architecture in the world, Palm Springs displays a distinctive style, known as Desert or Palm Springs Modernism. Its signature is simple, single-story buildings inspired by vast expanses of desert sand, surrounded by towering mountains, and set against a clear blue sky.

Some of the world's most forward-looking architects designed and constructed buildings around Palm Springs between 1940 and 1970, and modernism, also popular elsewhere in California in the years following World War II, became an ideal fit for desert living, because it minimizes the separation between indoors and outdoors. See-through houses with glass exterior walls are common. Oversize flat roofs provide shade from the sun, while many buildings' sculptural forms reflect nearby landforms. The style is notable for elegant informality, clean lines, and simple landscaping. Emblematic structures in Palm Springs include public buildings, hotels, stores, banks, and private residences.

Most obvious to visitors are three buildings that are part of the Palm Springs Aerial Tramway complex, all built in the 1960s. Albert Frey, a Swiss-born architect whose name is associated with a clutch of historic buildings, designed the soaring A-frame Tramway Gas Station, visually echoing the pointed peaks behind it. Frey also created the glass-walled Valley Station, from which you get your initial view of the Coachella Valley before you board the tram to the Mountain Station, designed by E. Stewart Williams.

Frey, a Palm Springs resident for more than 60 years, also designed the indoor–outdoor City Hall, Fire Station #1, and numerous houses. You can see his

second home, perched atop stilts on the hillside above the Desert Museum; it affords a sweeping view of the Coachella Valley through glass walls. Ballantine's Hotel, one of the first buildings Frey designed in the desert, may seem like a typical 1950s motel with rooms surrounding a swimming pool now, but when it was built as the San Jacinto Hotel in 1935, it was years ahead of its time.

Donald Wexler, who honed his vision with Los Angeles architect Richard Neutra, brought new ideas about the use of materials to the desert, where he teamed up with William Cody on a number of projects, including the terminal at the Palm Springs airport. Many of Wexler's buildings have soaring overhanging roofs, designed to provide shade under the blazing desert sun. Wexler also experimented with steel framing back in 1961, but the metal proved too expensive. Seven of his steel-frame houses can be seen in a neighborhood off Indian Canyon and Frances drives.

The Palm Springs Modern Committee is protecting these period structures, occasionally protesting projected demolition projects. The committee also publishes a map and driving guide to 52 historic buildings, which is available for $5 at either of the Palm Springs Visitor Information Centers or at www.psmodcom.com.

$$$ ☷ **Hyatt Regency Suites.** An enormous metal sculpture suspended from the ceiling dominates this hotel's six-story asymmetrical atrium lobby. One- and two-bedroom suites have private balconies and two TVs. Suites in the back have views of the pool and mountains. There's free underground parking, and you have golf privileges at Rancho Mirage Country Club and four other area courses. ⊠ *285 N. Palm Canyon Dr., 92262* ☏ *760/322–9000 or 800/633–7313* 🖷 *760/325–4027* ⊕ *www. palmsprings.hyatt.com* ⤵ *192 suites* ♿ *3 restaurants, room service, minibars, cable TV with movies, golf privileges, pool, gym, hair salon, outdoor hot tub, bar, babysitting, dry cleaning, laundry service, concierge, Internet, business services, meeting room, airport shuttle, no-smoking rooms* ⊟ *AE, D, DC, MC, V.*

$$–$$$ ☷ **Calla Lily Inn.** A tranquil palm-shaded oasis located a block from Palm Canyon Drive, this inn has spacious rooms decorated in a vaguely tropical style. Furnishings are contemporary wicker, and an image of a calla lily adorns every room. Rooms surrounding the pool encourage a convivial atmosphere. ⊠ *350 S. Belardo Rd., 92262* ☏ *760/323–3654 or 888/888–5787* 🖷 *760/323–4964* ⊕ *www.callalilypalmsprings.com* ⤵ *9 rooms* ♿ *In-room data ports, refrigerators, cable TV, in-room VCRs, pool, outdoor hot tub, massage, free parking, no-smoking rooms* ⊟ *AE, D, MC, V.*

$$–$$$ ☷ **Casitas Laquita.** A collection of Spanish-style bungalows occupying more than an acre, this small lodging caters mainly to lesbians. Rooms, decorated with a Southwestern theme, have handcrafted furnishings; many have fireplaces. The innkeepers regularly host informal social activities. ⊠ *450 E. Palm Canyon Dr., 92264* ☏ *760/416–9999 or 877/203–3410* 🖷 *760/416–5415* ⊕ *www.casitaslaquita.com* ⤵ *15 rooms* ♿ *In-room data ports, kitchenettes, cable TV, pool, massage, no-smoking rooms* ⊟ *MC, V.*

$$–$$$ ☷ **Spa Resort Casino.** Part of a complex that includes a spa and a casino across the street, this hotel, owned and operated by the Agua Caliente, is adjacent to a mineral-water spring used by generations of Native Americans. (The spa uses the healing mineral waters in treatments that draw locals on a regular basis.) Until 2003 the hotel was a bit dowdy, but a renovation brought rooms and public areas up-to-date with soothing desert colors and added amenities. ⊠ *100 N. Indian Canyon Dr., 92262* ☏ *760/325–1461 or 800/854–1279* 🖷 *760/325–3344* ⊕ *www. sparesortcasino.com* ⤵ *220 rooms, 10 suites* ♿ *2 restaurants, room service, in-room data ports, refrigerators, cable TV with movies, 2 pools, fitness classes, gym, hair salon, 2 outdoor hot tubs, sauna, spa, steam room, 2 bars, casino, laundry service, concierge, meeting room, no-smoking rooms* ⊟ *AE, D, MC, V.*

$$–$$$ ☷ **Villa Royale Inn.** This refurbished Mediterranean-style inn has lavish gardens, secluded patios with gentle fountains, and courtyards filled with citrus trees, jasmine, and lavender. Rooms have private entrances, and many of the suites have fireplaces, private outdoor patios, and fully equipped kitchens. One- and two-room suites are large enough for an extended stay. ⊠ *1620 Indian Trail, 92264* ☏ *760/327–2314 or 800/ 245–2314* 🖷 *760/322–3794* ⊕ *www.villaroyale.com* ⤵ *24 rooms, 7 suites* ♿ *Restaurant, some kitchens, cable TV, 2 pools, outdoor hot tub,* *massage, bar, dry cleaning, laundry service, no-smoking rooms* ▤ *AE, D, DC, MC, V* ⦿ *BP.*

$–$$ ▦ **Casa Cody.** The service is personal and gracious at this large, Western-style B&B a few steps from the Palm Springs Desert Museum. Spacious studios and one- and two-bedroom suites are furnished simply. Some have fireplaces, and most have kitchens. The homey rooms are situated in four buildings surrounding courtyards lushly landscaped with bougainvillea and citrus. There are also two historic adobe cottages, one of which was the desert home of opera singer Lawrence Tibbett. ⊠ *175 S. Cahuilla Rd., 92262* ☎ *760/320–9346 or 800/231–2639* ₰ *760/325–8610* ⊕ *www.casacody.com* ⤳ *17 rooms, 7 suites, 2 cottages* ⅄ *In-room data ports, some kitchens, refrigerators, 2 pools, outdoor hot tub, some pets allowed (fee), no-smoking rooms* ▤ *AE, D, MC, V* ⦿ *CP.*

¢ ▦ **Vagabond Inn.** Rooms are smallish at this centrally located motel, but they're clean, comfortable, and a good value. ⊠ *1699 S. Palm Canyon Dr., 92264* ☎ *760/325–7211 or 800/522–1555* ₰ *760/322–9269* ⊕ *www.vagabondinn.com* ⤳ *117 rooms, 3 suites* ⅄ *Coffee shop, in-room data ports, pool, outdoor hot tub, 2 saunas, no-smoking rooms* ▤ *AE, D, DC, MC, V.*

Nightlife & the Arts

NIGHTLIFE Next to the Plaza Theatre, **Blue Guitar** (⊠ 120 S. Palm Canyon Dr. ☎ 760/327–1549), owned by jazz artists Kal David and Lauri Bono, presents jazz and blues. Call for a current schedule. **Hair of the Dog English Pub** (⊠ 238 N. Palm Canyon Dr. ☎ 760/323–9890) is a friendly bar popular with a young crowd that likes to tip back English ales and ciders. **Heaven** (⊠ 611 S. Palm Canyon Dr. ☎ 760/416–0950), is a multitiered dance club catering to a mixed gay clientele; it has state-of-the-art sound and lighting systems. **Zelda's** (⊠ 169 N. Indian Canyon Dr. ☎ 760/325–2375) has two rooms, one featuring Latin sounds and another with Top 40 dance music and a male dance revue. It's closed Sunday through Tuesday.

Casino Morongo (⊠ Cabazon off-ramp, I–10 ☎ 909/849–3080) is about 20 minutes west of Palm Springs. The classy **Spa Resort Casino** (⊠ 401 E. Amado Rd. ☎ 800/258–2946), which opened in late 2003, holds 1,000 slot machines, blackjack tables, a high-limit room, four restaurants including Rappongi, two bars, and a lounge with entertainment.

In late March, when the world's finest female golfers hit the links for the Annual LPGA Kraft Nabisco Championship in Rancho Mirage, thousands of lesbians converge on Palm Springs for a four-day party popularly known as **Dinah Shore Weekend–Palm Springs** (☎ 888/575–4787 ⊕ www.clubskirts.com). The **White Party** (☎ 310/860–0101 for tickets), held on Easter weekend, draws tens of thousands of gay men from around the country to the Palm Springs area for a round of parties and gala events.

THE ARTS At the Palm Springs Desert Museum, the **Annenberg Theater** (⊠ 101 Museum Dr. ☎ 760/325–4490 ⊕ www.psmuseum.org) hosts Broadway shows, opera, lectures, Sunday-afternoon chamber concerts, and other events. The Spanish-style **Historic Plaza Theatre** (⊠ 128 S. Palm Canyon Dr. ☎ 760/327–0225) opened in 1936 with a glittering premiere of the

MGM film *Camille*. In the '40s and '50s, it presented some of Hollywood's biggest stars, including Bob Hope, Bing Crosby, and Frank Sinatra. Today it plays host to the hottest ticket in the desert, the **Fabulous Palm Springs Follies** (⊕ www.palmspringsfollies.com), which mounts 10 sellout performances each week, November through May. The vaudeville-style revue, about half of which focuses on World War II nostalgia, stars extravagantly costumed, retired (but very fit) showgirls, singers, and dancers. Tickets are $39 to $85. In addition to the follies, the theater is home to a January film festival and is favored by fans of old-time radio even in the off-season.

Sports & Leisure

BICYCLING **Big Horn Bicycles** (⊠ 302 N. Palm Canyon Dr. ☎ 760/325–3367) operates two-wheel tours to celebrity homes and Indian Canyons and also rents bikes. **Palm Springs Recreation Department** (⊠ 401 S. Pavilion Way ☎ 760/323–8272 ⊘ Weekdays 7:30–6) can provide you with maps of city bike trails.

GOLF Palm Springs hosts more than 100 golf tournaments annually. The Palm Springs Desert Resorts Convention and Visitors Bureau **Events Hotline** (☎ 760/770–1992) lists dates and locations. **Class A PGA** (☎ 760/324–5012) can match golfers with courses and arrange tee times. If you know which course you want to play, you can book tee times online (⊕ www.palmspringsteetimes.com).

Tahquitz Creek Palm Springs Golf Resort (⊠ 1885 Golf Club Dr. ☎ 760/328–1005 ⊕ www.tahquitzcreek.com) has two 18-hole, par-72 courses and a 50-space driving range. Greens fees, including cart, run $70–$90, depending on the course and day of the week. **Tommy Jacobs' Bel Air Greens Country Club** (⊠ 1001 S. El Cielo Rd. ☎ 760/322–6062) has a 9-hole executive course. Greens fees are $17 ($10 for replay).

SPAS The **Palms at Palm Springs** (⊠ 572 N. Indian Canyon Dr. ☎ 760/325–1111 or 800/753–7256 ⊕ www.palmsspa.com) has a full-day spa program that begins with an early-morning walk. The package includes a choice of 14 classes, the use of exercise equipment, admission to lectures, and individually designed low-calorie meals and snacks. Massage, facials, and wraps are among the options. Taking the waters at the **Spa Resort Casino** (⊠ 100 N. Indian Canyon Dr. ☎ 760/778–1772 ⊕ www.sparesortcasino.com) is an indulgent pleasure. You can spend a full day enjoying a five-step wet-and-dry treatment program that includes a mineral bath, steam, sauna, and eucalyptus inhalation. The program allows you to take fitness classes and use the gym and, for an extra charge, add massage or body treatments. The rate is $35 for a full day, less if you combine it with a treatment.

TENNIS **Demuth Park** (⊠ 4375 Mesquite Ave. ☎ No phone) has four lighted courts. **Ruth Hardy Park** (⊠ Tamarisk Rd. and Avenida Caballeros ☎ No phone) has eight lighted courts.

Shopping

The main **North Palm Canyon Drive shopping district** (⊠ Between Alejo and Ramon Rds.) is the commercial core of Palm Springs. Anchoring the center of the drive is the Palm Springs Mall, with about 35 boutiques.

★ Every Thursday night, the **Village Fest** (⊠ Palm Canyon Dr. between Tahquitz Canyon Way and Baristo Rd. ☎ 760/778–8415 ⊕ www. palm-springs.org) fills the drive with street musicians, a farmers' market, and stalls with food, crafts, art, and antiques. It's a great place for celebrity spotting.

Extending north of the main shopping area, the **Uptown Heritage District** (⊠ N. Palm Canyon Dr. between Amado Rd. and Tachevah Dr. ☎ 760/778–8415 ⊕ www.palm-springs.org) is a collection of consignment and secondhand shops, galleries, and restaurants whose theme is decidedly retro. Many shops and galleries offer mid-century modern furniture and decorator items, while others carry consignment clothing and estate jewelry. The area assumes a festive mood on the first Friday of each month, when most of the shops remain open until 9. Trendy shops include **Jade** (⊠ 787 N. Palm Canyon Dr.) and **Galaxy 500** (⊠ 1007 N. Palm Canyon Dr.).

East Palm Canyon Drive can be a source of great bargains. **Estate Sale Co.** (⊠ 4185 E. Palm Canyon Dr. ☎ 760/321–7628) is the biggest consignment store in the desert, with a warehouse of furniture, fine art, china and crystal, accessories, jewelry, movie memorabilia, and exercise equipment. Prices are set to keep merchandise moving, but it's closed Monday and Tuesday.

Not far from Palm Springs proper, **Hadley's Fruit Orchards** (⊠ 48–980 Seminole Dr., Cabazon ☎ 909/849–5255 ⊕ www.hadleyfruitorchards. com) sells dried fruit, nuts, date shakes, and wines.

Cathedral City

⑪ *2 mi southeast of Palm Springs on Hwy. 111.*

One of the fastest-growing communities in the desert, Cathedral City is more residential than tourist oriented. However, the city has a number of good restaurants and entertainment venues with moderate prices.

Pickford Salon, a small museum inside the Mary Pickford Theater, showcases the life of the famed actress. On display is a selection of personal items contributed by family members, including her 1976 Oscar for contributions to the film industry, a gown she wore in the 1927 film *Dorothy Vernon of Haddon Hall,* and dinnerware from Pickfair. One of the two biographical video presentations was produced by Mary herself. ⊠ 36–850 Pickfair St. ☎ 760/328–7100 ☞ Free ☉ Daily 10:30 AM–*midnight.*

☺ At **Boomers Camelot Park** you can play miniature golf, drive bumper boats, swing in the batting cages, test your skill in an arcade, and play video games. ⊠ 67–700 E. Palm Canyon Dr. ☎ 760/770–7522 ☞ $5–$7 per activity ☉ Mon.–Thurs. 11–10, Fri.–Sun. 11–11.

Where to Stay & Eat

★ **$–$$$**   ✕ **Oceans.** This bistro tucked into the back corner of a shopping center serves a surprising selection of beautifully prepared seafood. Start with

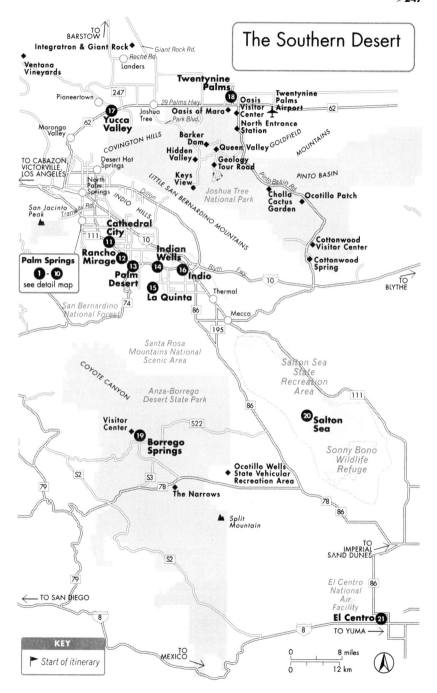

The Southern Desert

Mussels Oceans, a bowl of tender bivalves in a creamy anisette broth. Entrées include perfectly grilled ahi tuna, blackened catfish with Cajun seasonings, and lobster ravioli with saffron cream sauce. ✉ *Canyon Plaza S, 67–555 E. Palm Canyon Dr.* ☎ *760/324–1554* ⚄ *Reservations essential* ▭ *AE, D, DC, MC, V* ☉ *No lunch Sun.*

$–$$$ ⊞ **Comfort Suites.** This chain motel is about as close as you can get to Rancho Mirage without paying sky-high prices. Public areas are spacious, modern, and attractively appointed. Some accommodations here are cramped, even though most are one- or two-bedroom suites. Noise can be a problem, because the motel is on busy Highway 111. ✉ *69–151 E. Palm Canyon Dr., 92234* ☎ *760/324–5939 or 800/862–5085* 🖷 *760/324–3034* ⊕ *www.comfortsuites.com* ↩ *21 rooms, 77 suites* ⚄ *In-room data ports, some kitchens, microwaves, refrigerators, cable TV, pool, outdoor hot tub, laundry facilities, meeting room, free parking, some pets allowed (fee)* ▭ *AE, D, DC, MC, V* ⚅ *CP.*

$–$$ ⊞ **Doral Desert Princess Resort.** Rooms at this business hotel have expansive views of surrounding golf courses and mountains. It's a well-kept older hotel with spacious rooms, many opening onto the pool area. Bathrooms are large, and rooms have separate vanity areas, capacious closets, and a soft desert-beige color scheme. The quiet property is close to I-10. ✉ *67–967 Vista Chino, 92234* ☎ *760/322–7000* 🖷 *760/322–6853* ⊕ *www.doralpalmsprings.com* ↩ *285 rooms* ⚄ *Restaurant, room service, in-room data ports, refrigerators, cable TV with movies, 3 9-hole golf courses, putting green, 10 tennis courts, pool, 2 outdoor hot tubs, massage, spa, racquetball, meeting rooms, free parking* ▭ *AE, D, DC, MC, V.*

Nightlife

The **Desert IMAX Theater** (✉ Hwy. 111 at Cathedral Canyon Dr. ☎ 760/324–7333), the only IMAX theater in the region, screens such BIG-screen films as *Alaska: Spirit of the Wild* and *Lewis & Clark: Great Journey West* for about the cost of a regular big-screen movie.

Rancho Mirage

⑫ *4 mi southeast of Cathedral City on Hwy. 111.*

Much of the scenery in exclusive Rancho Mirage is concealed behind the walls of gated communities and country clubs. The rich and famous live in estates and patronize elegant resorts and expensive restaurants. The city's golf courses are the site of world-class tournaments. The Betty Ford Center, for those recovering from alcohol and drug addiction, is also here.

☾ The **Children's Discovery Museum of the Desert** contains instructive hands-on exhibits—a miniature rock-climbing area, a magnetic sculpture wall, make-it-and-take-it-apart projects, a rope maze—and an area for toddlers. ✉ *71–701 Gerald Ford Dr.* ☎ *760/321–0602* ⊕ *www.cdmod.org* ▱ *$6* ☉ *Tues.–Sat. 10–5, Sun. noon–5.*

Where to Stay & Eat

$–$$$ ✗ **Las Casuelas Nuevas.** Hundreds of artifacts from Guadalajara, Mexico, lend festive charm to this casual restaurant with a garden patio.

Tamales and shellfish dishes are among the specialties. The margaritas will make you wish you'd brought your cha-cha heels. ⊠ *70–050 Hwy. 111* ☎ *760/328-8844* ⊟ *AE, D, DC, MC, V.*

$–$$$ ✕ **Shame on the Moon.** Old-fashioned ambience complete with big booths, friendly service, an eclectic menu, and modest prices make this one of the most popular restaurants in the desert. Entrées include salmon Napoleon stacked with portobellos, sautéed chicken coated with hazelnuts, veal short ribs, and Long Island duck with black figs. Portions leave you plenty to take home. ⊠ *69–950 Frank Sinatra Dr.* ☎ *760/324-5515* ◬ *Reservations essential* ⊟ *AE, MC, V* ⊗ *No lunch.*

$$$$ ▦ **Westin Mission Hills Resort.** A sprawling Moroccan-style resort on 360 acres, the Westin is surrounded by fairways and putting greens. Rooms, in two-story buildings amid patios and fountains, are decorated with soft desert colors; most have balconies or private patios. Paths and creeks meander through the complex, and a lagoon-style swimming pool is encircled with a waterslide several stories high. ⊠ *71–333 Dinah Shore Dr., 92270* ☎ *760/328-5955 or 800/335-3545* 🖷 *760/770-2199* ⊕ *www.westin.com* ➥ *472 rooms, 40 suites* ◬ *2 restaurants, 3 snack bars, room service, in-room data ports, minibars, some refrigerators, cable TV with movies and video games, 2 18-hole golf courses, 7 tennis courts, 3 pools, health club, hair salon, 4 outdoor hot tubs, spa, steam room, croquet, shuffleboard, volleyball, bar, recreation room, children's programs (ages 4–12), playground, convention center, some pets allowed (fee), no-smoking rooms* ⊟ *AE, D, DC, MC, V.*

$$$–$$$$ ▦ **Lodge at Rancho Mirage.** Tucked into a hillside in the Santa Rosa Mountains, this hotel has sweeping views of the valley below. Gleaming marble and brass, original artwork, and plush carpeting create remarkable comfort. All rooms are spacious and meticulously appointed with antiques, Frette linens, and fabric wall coverings, and have private balconies or patios with pool or mountain views. Multilingual staff and 24-hour secretarial service are available. The luxurious spa offers 30 treatments. ⊠ *68–900 Frank Sinatra Dr., 92270* ☎ *760/321-8282 or 866/518-6870* 🖷 *760/770-7605* ⊕ *www.rockresorts.com* ➥ *219 rooms, 21 suites* ◬ *3 restaurants, room service, in-room data ports, minibars, cable TV, golf privileges, putting green, 8 tennis courts, pool, health club, hair salon, outdoor hot tub, spa, basketball, croquet, hiking, volleyball, 2 bars, shops, children's programs (ages 5–12), laundry service, concierge, concierge floor, business services, meeting room, airport shuttle, car rental; no smoking* ⊟ *AE, D, DC, MC, V.*

$$$ ▦ **Marriott Rancho Las Palmas Resort & Spa.** The mood is luxuriously laid back at this family-oriented resort on 240 landscaped acres. A Spanish theme prevails throughout the public areas and guest accommodations. Rooms in the two-story buildings are unusually large; all have sitting areas, private balconies or patios, and views of colorful gardens or well-manicured fairways and greens. One of the swimming pools has a 100-foot water slide. ⊠ *41–000 Bob Hope Dr., 92270* ☎ *760/568-2727 or 800/458-8786* 🖷 *760/862-4565* ⊕ *www.marriotthotels.com* ➥ *422 rooms, 22 suites* ◬ *5 restaurants, room service, in-room data ports, in-room safes, some minibars, some refrigerators, cable TV with movies, 27-hole golf course, putting green, 25 tennis courts, pro shop, 3 pools,* *health club, hair salon, 3 outdoor hot tubs, massage, spa, bicycles, bar, children's programs (ages 5–12), playground, laundry facilities, laundry service, concierge, Internet, business services, convention center, car rental, free parking, no-smoking rooms* ⊟ *AE, D, DC, MC, V.*

¢　▣ **Motel 6.** This motel may be bare-bones, but it puts you in tony Rancho Mirage, right in the shadow of the Lodge at Rancho Mirage up the hill. Kids stay free, and you can help yourself to free morning coffee. ⊠ *69–570 Hwy. 111, 92270* ☎ *760/324–8475 or 800/466–8356* 🖷 *760/328–0864* ⊕ *www.motel6.com* ⇨ *103 rooms* ♺ *In-room data ports, cable TV, pool, outdoor hot tub, no-smoking rooms* ⊟ *AE, D, DC, MC, V.*

Nightlife

The elegant and surprisingly quiet **Agua Caliente Casino** (⊠ 32–250 Bob Hope Dr. ☎760/321–2000) contains 1,000 slot machines, 48 table games, a 1,000-seat bingo room, a high-limit room, and even a no-smoking area. The Cahuilla Showroom presents such headliners as the Smothers Brothers and Carrot Top as well as live boxing, and there are three restaurants and a food court.

Sports & the Outdoors

The best female golfers in the world compete in the LPGA **Kraft Nabisco Championship** (⊠ Mission Hills Country Club ☎ 760/324–4546 ⊕ www. kraftnabiscochampionship.com) held in late March.

★　Of the two golf courses at the **Westin Mission Hills Resort Golf Club** (⊠ 71–501 Dinah Shore Dr. ☎ 760/328–3198 ⊕ www.troongolf.com), the 18-hole, par-70 Pete Dye course is especially noteworthy. The club hosts a number of major tournaments, is a member of the Troon Golf Institute, and has several teaching facilities, including the Westin Mission Hills Resort Golf Academy and the Golf Digest Golf School. Greens fees are $145 during peak season, including a mandatory cart; off-season promotional packages sometimes run as low as $60.

Shopping

The **River at Rancho Mirage** (⊠ 71–800 Hwy. 111 ☎ 760/341–2711) is a shopping/dining/entertainment complex with a collection of 20 high-end shops. Bang & Olufsen, Bath and Body Works, Borders Books & Music, Tulip Hill Winery tasting room, and other shops front a faux river with cascading waterfalls. The complex includes a 12-screen cinema, an outdoor amphitheater, and seven restaurants.

Palm Desert

⑬　*2 mi southeast of Rancho Mirage on Hwy. 111.*

Palm Desert is a thriving retail and business community, with some of the desert's most popular restaurants, private and public golf courses, and premium shopping.

★　West of and parallel to Highway 111, **El Paseo** (⊠ Between Monterey and Portola Aves. ☎ 877/735–7273 ⊕ www.elpaseo.com) is a mile-long Mediterranean-style avenue with fountains and courtyards, French and Italian fashion boutiques, shoe salons, jewelry stores, children's shops, restaurants, and nearly 30 art galleries. The pretty strip is a pleasant place to stroll, window-shop, people-watch, and exercise your credit cards. Each November, the **Palm Desert Golf Cart Parade** (☎ 760/346–6111 ⊕ www.golfcartparade.com) celebrates golf with a procession of 100 carts disguised as floats buzzing up and down El Paseo.

Come eyeball to eyeball with wolves, coyotes, mountain lions, cheetahs, bighorn sheep, golden eagles, warthogs, and owls at the **Living Desert Zoo and Gardens.** Easy to challenging scenic trails traverse 1,200 acres of desert preserve populated with plants of the Mojave, Colorado, and Sonoran deserts in 11 habitats. A family of reticulated giraffes moved into the park in 2002, and 2003 brought Gecko Gulch Children's Play Land and its crawl-through underground tunnels and climb-on snake sculptures. At the 3-acre African Wa TuTu village, there's a traditional marketplace as well as camels, leopards, hyenas, and other African animals. Children can pet African domestic animals, including goats and guinea fowl, in a petting kraal. Yet another exhibit demonstrates the path of the San Andreas Fault across the Coachella Valley. The Tennity Amphitheater stages daily wildlife shows, and "Wildlights," an evening light show, takes place during the winter holidays. A garden center sells native desert flora, much of which is unavailable elsewhere. ⊠ 47–900 Portola Ave. ☎ 760/346–5694 ⊕ www.livingdesert.org ⊠ $7.95 mid-June–Aug.; $10.50 Sept.–mid-June ☉ Mid-June–Aug., daily 8–1:30; Sept.–mid-June, daily 9–5.

The **Santa Rosa Mountains/San Jacinto National Monument,** administered by the Bureau of Land Management, protects Peninsula bighorn sheep and other wildlife on 272,000 acres of desert habitat. For an introduction to the site, stop by the visitor center—staffed by knowledgeable volunteers—for a look at exhibits illustrating the natural history of the desert. A landscaped garden displays native plants and frames a sweeping view. ⊠ 51–500 Hwy. 74 ☎ 760/862–9984 ⊕ www.ca.blm.gov/palmsprings ⊠ Free ☉ Daily 9–4.

Where to Stay & Eat

★ **$$$–$$$$** ✕ **Cuistot.** Once hidden in an El Paseo courtyard, Cuistot is now easy to find. In late 2003 chef-owner Bernard Dervieux opened his new restaurant in a big, bright, airy replica of a French farmhouse on El Paseo's west end. An enlarged menu lists rabbit in Dijon sauce along with such signature dishes as skillet-roasted veal chop with mushrooms and roasted garlic, Maine lobster (swimming live in a tank until prepared by the chef) with baby asparagus, and handmade vegetable ravioli with white truffle oil. ⊠ 72–595 El Paseo ☎ 760/340–1000 ⌂ Reservations essential ⊟ AE, DC, MC, V ☉ Closed Mon. No lunch Sun.

★ **$$–$$$$** ✕ **Augusta.** Despite its size—a large dining room and even larger outdoor area under a palapa—Augusta is a well-kept secret. Pity. Stained-glass art is a feast for the eyes, while menu items are a feast for the palate. Try mussels in coconut red Thai curry broth, a huge portion for an appetizer. Entrées include flavorful wild Oregon salmon with roasted pear coulis and grilled Colorado lamb chops with garlic ratatouille. ⊠ 73–951 El Paseo ☎ 760/779–9200 ⊟ AE, DC, MC, V ☉ Closed July–mid-Sept. No lunch Sun.

$$-$$$$ ✕ **Jillian's.** Husband-and-wife team Jay and June Trubee are the stars behind this trendy restaurant. Antiques and art fill the space, and the nighttime sky sets the mood in the center courtyard. Try the monumental appetizer called Tower of Crab (layers of crab, tomatoes, avocados, and brioche) and main dishes such as salmon baked in parchment and fettuccine with lobster. Save room for the Hawaiian cheesecake with macadamia-nut crust. Men will feel more comfortable wearing jackets, and shorts are not allowed. ⌧ *74–155 El Paseo* ☎ *760/776–8242* ⌂ *Reservations essential* ▭ *AE, D, DC, MC, V* ☯ *Closed Sun. and mid-June–Oct. No lunch.*

$-$$$$ ✕ **Palomino.** The emphasis here is on grilled and roasted entrées: spit-roasted garlic chicken, oak-fired thin-crust pizza, paella, and oven-roasted prawns. Huge reproductions of famous French impressionist paintings cover the walls of the busy room. ⌧ *73–101 Hwy. 111* ☎ *760/773–9091* ▭ *AE, D, DC, MC, V* ☯ *No lunch.*

$-$$$ ✕ **Café des Beaux Arts.** This café brings a little bit of Paris to the desert, with sidewalk dining, colorful flower boxes, and a bistro menu of French and Californian favorites, such as a broiled portobello mushroom with duck confit served with a sherry sauce, and ravioli stuffed with lobster. Leisurely dining is encouraged, which allows more time to savor the well-chosen French and domestic wines. ⌧ *73–640 El Paseo* ☎ *760/346–0669* ▭ *AE, D, DC, MC, V* ☯ *Closed July and Aug.*

★ **$-$$$** ✕ **Palmie.** Its humble location in the back of a shopping center gives nary a hint of the subtle creations prepared at this gem of a French restaurant. The two-cheese soufflé is one of several mouthwatering appetizers. Equally impressive are the duck cassoulet, duck fillets served with pear slices in red wine, and Palmie's signature dish: a perfectly crafted fish stew in a thin yet rich butter-cream broth. ⌧ *44–491 Town Center Way* ☎ *760/341–3200* ▭ *AE, DC, MC, V* ☯ *Closed Sun. and Aug.–mid-Sept. No lunch.*

¢-$$$ ✕ **Daily Grill.** This combination upscale coffee shop and bar serves good salads (the Niçoise is particularly scrumptious), a fine gazpacho, zesty pasta dishes, and various blue-plate specials. The sidewalk terrace invites people-watching, and the weekend brunches are very festive. ⌧ *73–061 El Paseo* ☎ *760/779–9911* ▭ *AE, D, DC, MC, V.*

¢-$ ✕ **Native Foods.** Despite what the menu implies, you'll find no meat at this brightly lit, contemporary, totally vegan restaurant. The Bali surf burger contains tempeh, lettuce, tomato, plus other fixings, but no meat. Same story with Spikes BBQ, made with soy "chicken," barbecue sauce, and carmelized onions. ⌧ *73–890 El Paseo* ☎ *760/836–9396* ▭ *AE, MC, V* ☯ *Closed Sun.*

$$$$ ⊡ **J. W. Marriott's Desert Springs Resort and Spa.** This sprawling convention-oriented hotel set on 450 landscaped acres has a dramatic U-shape design. The building wraps around the desert's largest private lake, into which an indoor, stair-stepped waterfall flows. Rooms have lake or mountain views, balconies, and oversize bathrooms. It's a long walk from the lobby to the rooms; if you are driving, you might want to request a room close to the parking lot. Costa's nightclub here has dancing nightly and live entertainment on weekends. ⌧ *74–855*

Country Club Dr., 92260 ☎ 760/341–2211 or 800/331–3112 🖷 760/ 341–1872 ⊕ www.desertspringsresort.com ⇔ 833 rooms, 51 suites ♨ 11 restaurants, snack bar, in-room data ports, in-room safes, minibars, cable TV with movies, driving range, 2 18-hole golf courses, putting green, 20 tennis courts, 5 pools, health club, hair salon, 4 outdoor hot tubs, spa, basketball, croquet, volleyball, 2 bars, nightclub, shop, children's programs (ages 5–12), laundry service, Internet, business services, convention center, car rental, no-smoking rooms ▤ AE, D, DC, MC, V.

$$–$$$ ⊡ **Tres Palmas Bed & Breakfast.** Enormous windows, high open-beam ceilings, light wood, and textured peach tile floors lend this contemporary inn near El Paseo a bright and spacious feel. The Southwestern accents in common areas and guest rooms (which are more functional than luxurious) include old Navajo rugs. ⊠ *73–135 Tumbleweed La., 92260 ☎ 760/773–9858 or 800/770–9858 🖷 760/776–9159 ⇔ 4 rooms ♨ Cable TV, pool, outdoor hot tub; no room phones, no smoking ▤ AE, MC, V ⦿ CP.*

$$ ⊡ **Mojave.** This tranquil inn, just steps from busy El Paseo, is a 1940s motel that's been transformed into a retro urban oasis. Rooms surround a landscaped courtyard, where a small stream and pond are shaded by mature trees bearing oranges and grapefruit. Large rooms are furnished with reproductions of 1940s chairs, armoires, and tables. Minibars come stocked with bottles of Nehi sodas, and there is a video library of vintage films. All rooms have outdoor sitting areas appointed with director's chairs. In-room spa services are available. ⊠ *73–721 Shadow Mountain Dr., 92260 ☎ 760/346–6121 or 800/391–1104 🖷 760/674– 9072 ⊕ www.hotelmojave.com ⇔ 22 rooms, 2 suites ♨ In-room data ports, some kitchens, minibars, cable TV, in-room VCRs, pool, outdoor hot tub, massage, meeting room, no-smoking rooms ▤AE, MC, V ⦿ CP.*

The Arts

McCallum Theatre (⊠ 73–000 Fred Waring Dr. ☎ 760/340–2787 ⊕ www. mccallumtheatre.com), the principal cultural venue in the desert, presents film, classical and popular music, opera, ballet, and theater. In mid-January the **Palm Springs International Film Festival** (☎ 760/322–2930 ⊕ www.psfilmfest.org) brings stars and more than 150 feature films from 25 countries, plus panel discussions, short films, and documentaries, to the McCallum and other venues.

Sports & the Outdoors

BALLOONING **Fantasy Balloon Flights** (⊠74–181 Parosella St. ☎760/568–0997 ⊕www. fantasyballoonflights.com) operates sunrise excursions over the southern end of the Coachella Valley. Flights ($160) run from an hour to an hour and a half, followed by a traditional champagne toast.

BICYCLING **Big Wheel Bike Tours** (☎ 760/779–1837) delivers rental mountain, three-speed, and tandem bikes to area hotels.

GOLF **Desert Willow Golf Resort** (⊠ 38–500 Portola Ave. ☎ 760/346–7060 ⊕ www.desertwillow.com) is one of the newest golf resorts in the desert. A public course managed by the City of Palm Desert, it has two challenging 18-hole links. Greens fees are $167 including cart.

Shopping

In addition to El Paseo's other shopping treasures, check out **Gardens on El Paseo** (⊠ El Paseo at San Pablo Ave. ☎ 760/862–1990 ⊕ www. thegardensonelpaseo.com), a shopping center anchored by Saks Fifth Avenue and populated by such mainstream retailers as Brooks Brothers, Ann Taylor, Williams-Sonoma, Baccarat, and Le Gourmandise French Bakery & Restaurant.

Indian Wells

⑭ *5 mi east of Palm Desert on Hwy. 111.*

For the most part a quiet residential community, Indian Wells hosts golf and tennis tournaments throughout the year, including the Pacific Life Open tennis tournament. Most dining and shopping venues are inside the two huge hotels that dominate the resort scene.

Where to Stay

★ **$$$$** 🏨 **Hyatt Grand Champions Resort.** This stark white resort on 34 acres completed a major renovation and expansion in 2003, adding suites and a spa to the already lavish accommodations. Even standard rooms are suites and large by local standards, with balconies and sunken sitting areas. Private villas each have a secluded garden courtyard with outdoor whirlpool tub, a living room with fireplace, a dining room, and a bedroom. In addition to the rest of the multilingual staff, who specialize in pampering, a private butler attends to your every whim. The pool area is a kind of garden water park, surrounded by palms and private cabanas. ⊠ *44–600 Indian Wells La., 92210* ☎ *760/341–1000 or 800/552–4386* 🖨 *760/568–2236* ⊕ *www.grandchampions.hyatt.com* 🛏 *460 suites, 19 villas ⚖ 3 restaurants, room service, in-room safes, minibars, cable TV with movies, driving range, 2 18-hole golf courses, putting green, 3 tennis courts, pro shop, 6 pools, health club, hair salon, 3 outdoor hot tubs, massage, sauna, spa, steam room, bicycles, 2 bars, shop, children's programs (ages 3–12), dry cleaning, laundry service, business services, convention center, meeting rooms, car rental, no-smoking rooms* ⊟ *AE, D, DC, MC, V.*

$$$–$$$$ 🏨 **Renaissance Esmeralda Resort and Spa.** The centerpiece of this luxurious Mediterranean-style resort is an eight-story atrium lobby with a fountain whose water flows through a rivulet in the floor into cascading pools and outside to lakes surrounding the property. Given its size, the hotel is surprisingly intimate. Spacious guest rooms are equipped with sitting areas, balconies, refreshment centers, two TV sets, and travertine vanities in the bathrooms; some rooms have fireplaces. One pool has a sandy beach. ⊠ *44–400 Indian Wells La., 92210* ☎ *760/ 773–4444 or 800/468–3571* 🖨 *760/773–9250* ⊕ *www.marriotthotels. com* 🛏 *560 rooms, 22 suites ⚖ 5 restaurants, room service, in-room data ports, minibars, cable TV with movies, 2 18-hole golf courses, putting green, 4 tennis courts, pro shop, 3 pools, wading pool, gym, hair salon, 2 outdoor hot tubs, massage, sauna, spa, steam room, bicycles, basketball, volleyball, bar, shop, babysitting, children's programs (ages 5–12), laundry facilities, laundry service, concierge, Internet, business services,* *meeting rooms, car rental, free parking, no-smoking rooms* ⊟ *AE, D, DC, MC, V.*

Sports & the Outdoors

GOLF Next door to the Hyatt Grand Champions Resort, the **Golf Resort at Indian Wells** (⊠ 44–500 Indian Wells La. ☎ 760/346–4653) has two 18-hole Ted Robinson–designed championship courses: the 6,500-yard West Course and the 6,700-yard East Course. A public course, it has been named one of the country's top 10 resorts by *Golf Magazine*. Monday through Thursday greens fees are $120; Friday through Sunday they're $130 (fees may be deeply discounted in summer). The resort also offers instruction through the Indian Wells Golf School.

TENNIS The **Pacific Life Open** (☎ 760/360–3346, 800/999–1585 for tickets ⊕ www.pacificlifeopen.com) tennis tournament draws 200 of the world's top players to the Indian Wells Tennis Garden for two weeks in March. With more than 16,000 seats, the stadium is the second largest in the nation.

La Quinta

🕔 *4 mi south of Indian Wells via Washington St.*

The desert became a Hollywood hideout in the 1920s, when La Quinta Hotel (now La Quinta Resort) opened, introducing the Coachella Valley's first golf course. Although there are a number of restaurants and strip malls in La Quinta, life here really revolves around the resort and its associated PGA West golf complex.

Where to Stay & Eat

$$$–$$$$ ✕ **Omri and Boni.** Chef Omri Siklai showed the same flair decorating this establishment that he displays nightly in the kitchen cooking up contemporary Mediterranean dishes. Caesar salads, chicken and veal dishes—even ostrich and venison—are prepared with skill and imagination. Pastas and breads made on the premises are egg-free. ⊠ 47–474 *Washington St.* ☎ 760/773–1735 ⌖ *Reservations essential* ⊟ *AE, MC, V* ☉ *Closed Tues. and Aug. and Sept. No lunch.*

$–$$ ✕ **La Quinta Cliffhouse.** Sweeping mountain views at sunset and the early California look of a western movie set draw patrons to this restaurant perched halfway up a hillside. The eclectic menu roams the globe: ahi carpaccio, New Zealand rack of lamb, and, for dessert, Kimo's Hula Pie with house-made macadamia-nut ice cream. ⊠ 78–250 *Hwy. 111* ☎ 760/360–5991 ⌖ *Reservations essential* ⊟ *AE, MC, V* ☉ *No lunch.*

$$$$ 🛏 **La Quinta Resort and Club.** Opened in 1926, the desert's oldest resort
Fodor's Choice is a lush green oasis. Broad expanses of lawn separate the adobe casitas
★ that house some rooms; other rooms are in newer two-story units surrounding individual swimming pools and hot tubs amid brilliant gardens. Fireplaces, stocked refrigerators, and fruit-laden orange trees contribute to a discreet and sparely luxurious air. A premium is placed on privacy, which accounts for La Quinta's continuing popularity with Hollywood celebrities. Guests can play on the championship golf courses either at La Quinta or at the adjacent PGA West. ⊠ 49–499 *Eisenhower Dr., 92253* ☎ 760/564–4111 *or* 800/598–3828 ⊟ 760/564–5768

⊕ *www.laquintaresort.com* ⇆ *640 rooms, 244 suites ♨ 7 restaurants, room service, in-room data ports, some in-room safes, refrigerators, cable TV with movies and video games, 2 18-hole golf courses, golf privileges, putting green, 23 tennis courts, 42 pools, gym, hair salon, 52 outdoor hot tubs, spa, croquet, volleyball, children's programs (ages 4–16), concierge, business services, meeting room, no-smoking rooms* ⊟ *AE, D, DC, MC, V.*

The Arts

La Quinta Arts Festival (☎ 760/564–1244 ⊕ www.lqaf.com), normally held the third weekend in March, showcases painting, sculpture, photography, drawing, and printmaking. The show is accompanied by entertainment and food.

Sports & the Outdoors

★ **PGA West** (⊠ 49–499 Eisenhower Dr. ☎ 760/564–7170, 760/564–5729 for tee times ⊕ www.pgawest.com) operates three 18-hole, par-72 championship courses and provides instruction and golf clinics. Greens fees (which include a mandatory cart) range from $70 on weekdays in summer to $235 on weekends in February and March. Bookings are accepted 30 days in advance, but prices are lower when you book close to the date you need.

Indio

🔟 *5 mi east of Indian Wells on Hwy. 111.*

More a farming community than a resort, Indio is the home of the date shake, which is exactly what it sounds like: a delicious, extremely thick milk shake made with dates. The city and surrounding countryside generate 95% of the dates grown and harvested in the United States. If you take a hot-air balloon ride, you will likely drift over the tops of date palm trees.

Displays at the **Coachella Valley Museum and Cultural Center,** in a former farmhouse, explain how dates are harvested and how the desert is irrigated for date farming. On the grounds you'll find a smithy and an old sawmill. ⊠ *82–616 Miles Ave.* ☎ *760/342–6651* 🎟 *Free* ☉ *Sept.–June, Wed.–Sat. 10–4, Sun. 1–4.*

You can buy a date shake and take a walking tour of the 175-acre palm arboretum and orchard at **Oasis Date Gardens.** On the tour you learn how dates are pollinated, grown, sorted, stored, and packed for shipping. **Camel Safari** (☎ 760/399–5665 ⊕ www.movielandanimals.com) offers one-hour guided camelback rides ($75) through Oasis Date Gardens in spring and fall. ⊠ *59–111 Hwy. 111, Thermal* ☎ *800/827–8017* ⊕ *www.oasisdategardens.com* 🎟 *Free* ☉ *Walking tours daily 10:30 and 2:30.*

☾ Indio celebrates its raison d'être each February at the **National Date Festival and Riverside County Fair.** The mid-month festivities include an Arabian Nights pageant, camel and ostrich races, and exhibits of local dates. ⊠ *Riverside County Fairgrounds, 46–350 Arabia St.* ☎ *760/863–8247 or 800/811–3247* ⊕ *www.datefest.org* 🎟 *$7.*

Where to Stay & Eat

$–$$ ✕ **Ciro's Ristorante and Pizzeria.** This popular casual restaurant has been serving up pizza and pasta since the 1970s. The menu lists some unusual pizzas, such as western-style (loaded with sausage, pepperoni, Canadian bacon, and vegetables) and cashew with three cheeses. Daily pasta specials vary but might include red- or white-clam sauce or scallops with parsley and red wine. ⊠ *81–963 Hwy. 111* ☎ *760/347–6503* ⊕ *www.cirospasta.com* ☲ *AE, DC, MC, V* ⊘ *No lunch Sun.*

¢–$$ ▦ **Best Western Date Tree Inn.** Landscaped citrus and cactus gardens surround this hotel. Nicely appointed rooms are spacious enough for families, as are the pool-side barbecues. ⊠ *81–909 Indio Blvd., 92201* ☎ *760/347–3421 or 800/292–5599* 🖷 *760/347–3421* ⊕ *www.datetree. com* ⇗ *114 rooms, 5 suites* ⚬ *In-room data ports, some in-room hot tubs, some kitchens, microwaves, refrigerators, cable TV with movies, pool, gym, laundry facilities, no-smoking rooms* ☲ *AE, D, DC, MC, V* ❄⊙ *CP.*

Nightlife

Fantasy Springs Casino (⊠ 84–245 Indio Springs Pkwy. ☎ 760/342–5000 ⊕ www.fantasyspringsresort.com) has 850 Las Vegas–style gaming machines, off-track wagering, gaming tables, and a high-limit area, plus two restaurants, a cocktail lounge, and a showroom featuring big-name entertainers.

Sports & the Outdoors

The **Eldorado Polo Club** (⊠ 50–950 Madison St. ☎ 760/342–2223), known as the winter polo capital of the West, hosts world-class polo events. You can pack a picnic and watch practice matches for free during the week.

en route — For a glimpse of how the desert appeared before development, head northeast from Palm Springs to **Coachella Valley Preserve** (⊠ From the Ramon Rd. exit off I–10, drive east to Thousand Palm Canyon Dr., turn north and continue for 2 mi). The preserve has a system of sand dunes and several palm oases that were formed because the San Andreas fault lines here allow water flowing underground to rise to the surface. A mile-long walk along Thousand Palms Oasis reveals pools supporting the tiny endangered desert pupfish and more than 183 bird species. Managed by the Nature Conservancy, the preserve has a visitor center, nature and equestrian trails, restrooms, and picnic facilities; it is exceptionally hot in summer. **Covered Wagon Tours** (⊠ East end of Ramon Rd. ☎ 760/347–2161 or 800/367–2161 ⊕ www.coveredwagontours.com) can take you on a two- or four-hour tour of the Coachella Valley Preserve via mule-drawn covered wagon. Schedule your visit with or without a cookout and entertainment at the end of the journey.

If you are headed for Joshua Tree National Park from the desert resorts area, you will pass **Desert Hot Springs,** 9 mi north of Palm Springs on Gene Autry Trail. The town's famous hot mineral waters, thought by some to have curative powers, bubble up from underground at temperatures of 90°F–148°F and flow into the wells of more than 40 hotel spas.

Once a Native American village and later a cattle ranch, **Big Morongo Canyon Preserve** is a serene oasis around a natural spring generated by snowmelt from the surrounding mountains. About 11 mi north of I–10 via Highway 62, the preserve attracts all manner of birds and animals to a riparian woodland filled with cottonwoods and willows. You're likely to spot great horned owls and many songbirds here any time of the year. A shaded meadow is a fine place for a picnic, and you can hike on several choice trails. No pets are permitted. ⊠ *East Dr., Morongo Valley* ☎ *760/363–7190* ⊕ *www. bigmorongo.org* 🖾 *Free* ⊙ *Daily 7:30–sunset.*

ALONG TWENTYNINE PALMS HIGHWAY
INCLUDING JOSHUA TREE NATIONAL PARK

The towns of Yucca Valley and Twentynine Palms punctuate Twentynine Palms Highway (Highway 62), the northern highway from the desert resorts to Joshua Tree National Park, and provide lodging and other visitor services to park goers. Flanked by Twentynine Palms Highway on the north and I–10 on the south, the park protects some of the southern desert's most interesting and beautiful scenery. A visit to the park provides a glimpse of the rigors of desert life in the Little San Bernardino Mountains. You can see the park highlights in a half day or take a daylong expedition into the backcountry.

Yucca Valley

⑰ *30 mi northeast of Palm Springs on Hwy. 62 (Twentynine Palms Hwy.).*

One of the fastest-growing cities in the high desert, Yucca Valley is emerging as a bedroom community for people who work as far away as Ontario, 85 mi to the west. In this sprawling suburb you can shop for necessities, get your car serviced, and chow down at the fast-food outlets. For some fun, head a few miles north to Pioneertown.

☾ The **Hi-Desert Nature Museum** has a small zoo containing creatures that make their homes in Joshua Tree, including scorpions, snakes, ground squirrels, and chuckawallas, a type of lizard. There's also a collection of rocks, minerals, and fossils from the Paleozoic era. ⊠ *57–116 Twentynine Palms Hwy.* ☎ *760/369–7212* ⊕ *www.yucca-valley.org* 🖾 *Free* ⊙ *Tues.–Sun. 10–5.*

In 1946 Roy Rogers, Gene Autry, and Russ Hayden built **Pioneertown** (⊠ 4 mi north of Yucca Valley on Pioneertown Rd. ⊕ www.pioneertown. com), an 1880s-style Wild West movie set complete with hitching posts, saloon, and an OK Corral. Today 250 people call the place home, even as film crews continue shooting. You can stroll past wooden and adobe storefronts and feel like you're back in the Old West. The new owners of Pappy & Harriet's have started building an outdoor concert venue for about 500 people and have started booking popular bands and singers. Gunfights are staged April through November, Saturday at 1 and 2 and Sunday at 2:30.

<table>
<tr><td>

off the
beaten
path

</td><td>

INTEGRATRON AND GIANT ROCK – UFO fanatic George Van Tassel spent 18 years building the 38-foot-tall dome that is the Integratron, completed in the early 1960s. Intended as a sort of combination cosmic fountain of youth and time machine, the structure contains a private "sound bath," where (by reservation) you can experience the dome's multiple-wave, surround-sound, sound chamber in a floating sky chair. Don't miss the UFO landing strip nearby. Between the 1950s and 1970s Van Tassel drew thousands of believers to his UFO conventions and held weekly alien séances in the cave below Giant

</td></tr>
</table>

Rock, about 3 mi from the Integratron. The 23,000-ton freestanding boulder, one of the largest such rocks in the world, stands about 70 feet tall. The cave beneath the boulder was once the home of a prospector. To get to the Integratron, take Highway 62 8 mi east of Yucca Valley to Sunburst Avenue (in Joshua Tree). Head north. When the pavement ends (at Golden), turn right and drive to Border, where you'll take a left. Drive about 6 mi to where the pavement ends and turn left onto Reche Road. Follow Reche Road about 6 mi into the town of Landers, and turn right onto Belfield Boulevard, which ends at Linn Road after about a mile. The Integratron entrance is on the right. ⊠ *Linn Rd. at Belfield Blvd., Landers* ☎ *760/364–3126* ⊕ *www.integratron.com* ✉ *$5 tour; $35 sound bath* ☼ *1st 3 wks of month, Fri.–Sun. noon–4.*

Where to Stay & Eat

$–$$ ✕ **Pappy & Harriet's Pioneertown Palace.** Smack in the middle of a western-movie-set town is this western-movie-set saloon where you can have dinner, dance to live country-and-western music, or just relax with a drink at the bar. The food ranges from Tex-Mex to Santa Maria barbecue to steak and burgers—no surprises but plenty of fun. Pappy & Harriet's may be in the middle of nowhere, but you'll need reservations for dinner on weekends. ⊠ *Pioneertown Rd., Pioneertown* ☎ *760/ 365–5956* ⊕ *www.pappyandharriets.com* ☐ *AE, D, MC, V* ☼ *No lunch Mon.–Wed.*

¢–$ ✕ **Edchada's.** Rock climbers who spend their days in Joshua Tree National Park swear by the margaritas at this Mexican restaurant, which also has a location in Twentynine Palms. Specialties include fajitas, carnitas, seafood enchiladas, and fish tacos. ⊠ *56–805 Twentynine Palms Hwy.* ☎ *760/365–7655* ☐ *AE, D, MC, V* ✉ *73–502 Twentynine Palms Hwy., Twentynine Palms* ☎ *760/367–2131* ☐ *AE, D, MC, V.*

$–$$ ▦ **Rimrock Ranch Cabins.** The quiet beauty of the surrounding desert attracts Hollywood writers, artists, and musicians to these four circa-1940s housekeeping cabins. Owners Szu and Dusty Wakeman have restored the cabins to their original condition, complete with knotty-pine paneling, vintage Wedgwood stoves, artisan tiles, and antique furnishings. Special touches include outdoor fireplaces and espresso machines in the fully equipped kitchens. The grounds include a stargazing deck, campfire pit, and a deep-pit barbecue. ⊠ *Pioneertown Rd., Pioneertown 92268* 🕾 *760/228–1297* 🖷 *818/557–6383* ⊕ *www.rimrockranchcabins. com* ⇌ *4 cabins* ⚬ *Kitchens, in-room VCRs, pool, massage, some pets allowed; no room phones, no room TVs, no smoking* ⊟ *MC, V.*

¢ ⊞ **Pioneertown Motel.** Built in 1946 as a bunkhouse for Western film and stars shooting in Pioneertown, this motel sticks close to its roots. Each room, from the Cowboy Room to the Twilight Zone Room, has a theme that matches its name. For example, the Flower Room is all about buds and blooms. Hiking trails outside the motel lead into the desert. Bring your horse—there are corrals for visiting animals. ⊠ *Pioneertown Rd., Pioneertown 92268* 🕾 *760/365–4879* 🖷 *760/365– 3127* ⊕ *www.pioneertown.com* ⇌ *15 rooms* ⚬ *Some kitchenettes, microwaves, refrigerators, some in-room VCRs, some pets allowed; no a/c in some rooms, no room phones, no TV in some rooms* ⊟ *AE, D, MC, V.*

Twentynine Palms

⑱ *24 mi east of Yucca Valley on Hwy. 62 (Twentynine Palms Hwy.).*

The main gateway town to Joshua Tree National Park, Twentynine Palms is also the location of the U.S. Marine Air Ground Task Force Training Center. You can find services, supplies, and lodgings in town. The history and current life of Twentynine Palms is depicted in **Oasis of Murals,** a collection of 17 murals painted on the sides of buildings. If you drive around town you can't miss them, but you can also pick up a free map from the **Action Council for 29 Palms** (⊠ 6455B Mesquite Ave. 🕾 760/ 361–2286 ⊕ www.oasisofmurals.com).

☾ The area's big draw, however, is **Joshua Tree National Park,** whose main
FodorśChoice entrance is 2 mi south of Twentynine Palms. In part because it is so close
★ to Los Angeles and San Diego, this 794,000-acre expanse of complex, ruggedly beautiful desert scenery receives more than a million visitors each year. Its boulder-strewn mountains, natural cactus gardens, and lush oases shaded by tall fan palms mark the meeting place of the Mojave (high) and Colorado (low) deserts. This is prime hiking, rock-climbing, and exploring country, where coyotes, desert pack rats, and exotic plants like the white yucca, red-tipped ocotillo, and cholla cactus reside. Extensive stands of Joshua trees (they're actually shrubs, not trees) give the park its name. The plants reminded early white settlers of the biblical Joshua, with their thick, stubby branches representing his arms raised toward heaven. You can see portions of the park in a half-day excursion from Palm Springs or the other desert resort cities. A full-day driving tour allows time for a nature walk or two and stops at many of the 50 wayside exhibits, which provide insight into Joshua Tree's geology and rich vegetation.

The elevation in some areas of the park exceeds 4,000 feet, and light snowfalls and cold, strong north winds are common in winter. There are no services within the park and little water, so you should carry a gallon of water per person per day. Use sunscreen liberally any time of the year.

To get oriented, head to the **Oasis Visitor Center** (✉ Utah Trail, ½ mi south of Hwy. 62 ☎ 760/367–5500), about 3 mi north of the north entrance to the park. It has many free and inexpensive brochures, books, posters, and maps as well as several educational exhibits. Rangers are on hand to answer questions. Walk ½ mi from the visitor center to the **Oasis of Mara.** Inhabited by Native Americans and later by prospectors and homesteaders, the oasis provides a home for birds, small mammals, and other wildlife.

Driving south from the visitor center, you can drive west on Park Boulevard to take in several scenic valleys, a dam, and an old ranch, or you can head southwest on Pinto Basin Road for a stunning desert drive through Pinto Basin.

On the Park Boulevard side, you can hike the ¼-mi **Skull Rock Trail** (✉ Jumbo Rocks Campground, just beyond loop E), which passes through boulder piles, desert washes, and a rocky alley. About 10 mi from the North Entrance Station, **Geology Tour Road** (✉ South of Queen Valley) is an 18-mi dirt road with 18 stops, recommended only for four-wheel-drive vehicles. The road winds through some of the park's most fascinating landscapes. Alternatively, you can drive east to west through **Queen Valley** (✉ Barker Dam Rd.) to see stands of Joshua trees that are particularly alluring in spring. **Hidden Valley,** a boulder-strewn area, was once a cattle rustlers' hideout. You'll understand why the bandits chose this spot when you crawl between the big rocks. A 1¹⁄₁₀-mi loop trail leads from Hidden Valley to **Barker Dam.** Built around 1900 by ranchers and miners to hold water for cattle and mining operations, the dam now serves the same purpose for wildlife.

Near Hidden Valley you can take the 90-minute guided **Desert Queen Ranch walking tour.** This ranger-led tour explores the homestead created by Joshua Tree pioneers William and Frances Keys and provides a glimpse of the 60 years the couple spent raising a family and working the land under extreme desert conditions. Bill Keys dug wells by hand and installed an irrigation system to water his vegetable gardens, fruit orchards, and wheat and alfalfa fields. The ranch has been restored to look much as it did when he died in 1969—the missus succumbed years earlier. The house, schoolhouse, store, and workshop still stand; the orchard has been replanted; and the grounds are full of old trucks, cars, and mining equipment. ✉ *Off Park Blvd., 2 mi north of intersection with western end of Barker Dam Rd.* ☎ *760/367–5555* ✇ *$5* ✲ *June–Sept., Wed. and Fri. 5:30; Oct.–May, daily 10 and 1.*

Survey all of Hidden Valley from **Keys View** (✉ Keys View Rd., 21 mi south of west entrance), the most dramatic overlook in Joshua Tree National Park. At 5,185 feet, the spot has a view across the desert to Mt. San Jacinto near Palm Springs, and, on clear days, as far south as the Salton Sea. Sunrise and sunset are magical times, when the light throws rocks and trees into high relief before (or after) bathing the hills in brilliant shades of red, orange, and gold. A fairly strenuous 4-mi round-trip hike on **Lost Horse Mine Trail** (✉ Parking area 1¼ mi east of Keys View Rd.) takes you along a former mining road to a well-preserved stamp mill, which was used to crush rock mined from the nearby mountain in search of gold. The operation was one of the most successful around, and the mine's cyanide settling tanks and stone buildings are the area's best preserved. Allow about four hours for the hike. From the mill area, a short but steep 10-minute climb takes you to the top of a 5,278-foot mountain.

If, on the other hand, you head east on Pinto Basin Road, you'll get to **Cholla Cactus Gardens** (⊠ Pinto Basin Rd., 10 mi southeast of junction with Park Blvd.). Here you can see a stand of Bigelow cholla, sometimes called the jumping cholla because its hooked spines seem to jump at you as you walk past. The chollas are best seen and photographed in late afternoon, when their backlighted, spiky stalks stand out against a colorful sky. The **Ocotillo Patch** (⊠ Pinto Basin Rd., about 3 mi east of Cholla Cactus Gardens) has a roadside exhibit on the dramatic display made by the red-tipped succulent following even the shortest rain shower.

Follow Pinto Basin Road south toward **Cottonwood Visitor Center** (⊠ Pinto Basin Rd., 32 mi southeast of North Entrance Station ☎ No phone), which has a small museum, picnic tables, drinking water, and restrooms. (Those coming on I–10 enter at this end of the park.) A 1-mi trail leads from the visitor center to the **Cottonwood Spring Oasis**. Noted for its abundant birdlife, the palm-shaded oasis was an important water stop for prospectors, miners, and teamsters traveling between the small town of Mecca (to the southwest) and mines to the north. You can see the remains of an *arrastra,* a primitive type of gold mill, near the oasis, as well as the concrete ruins of two gold mines. Bighorn sheep frequent this area in winter.

⊠ 74–485 *National Park Dr., Twentynine Palms* ☎ 760/367–5500 ⊕ *www.nps.gov/jotr* ⊠ *$10 per vehicle, $5 per person on foot or bike* ⊙ *Daily 24 hrs.; visitor centers daily 8–5.*

need a break? There are no restaurants inside Joshua Tree, so you have to bring your own lunch. **Picnic areas** within the park are equipped with just the basics—picnic tables, fire pits, and primitive restrooms. Only those near the entrances have water. There are picnic areas at the Cottonwood Spring Visitor Center and in Hidden Valley, as well as at Live Oak Springs, on Park Boulevard east of Jumbo Rocks.

Where to Stay & Eat

¢ ✕ **Park Rock Café.** If you're on your way to the national park on Highway 62, stop in the town of Joshua Tree (not to be confused with the park) to stoke up on a hearty breakfast bagel sandwich and order a box lunch to take with you. The café creates some unusual sandwiches, such as nutty chicken salad pita or roast beef Philly cheese. Outside dining is pleasant here. ⊠ *6554 Park Blvd., Joshua Tree* ☎ *760/366–3622* ▭ *AE, D, MC, V* ⊙ *Closed Mon. No dinner.*

¢–$$ ✕▢ **29 Palms Inn.** The funky 29 Palms, on the Oasis of Mara, is the lodging closest to the entrance to Joshua Tree National Park. The collection of adobe and wood-frame cottages is scattered over 70 acres of grounds that are popular with birds and bird-watchers year-round. Innkeeper Jane Smith's warm, personal service more than makes up for the cottages' rustic qualities. Ranging from pasta to seafood, the contemporary fare at the inn's restaurant ($–$$) is more sophisticated than its Old West appearance might suggest. ⊠ *73–950 Inn Ave., 92277* ☎ *760/367–3505* 🖨 *760/367–4425* ⊕ *www.29palmsinn.com* ↪ *15 rooms, 4 suites* ⚖ *Restaurant, pool, hot tub, some pets allowed (fee); no a/c, no room phones, no TV in some rooms, no smoking* ⊟ *AE, D, DC, MC, V* ¶⊙¶ *CP.*

★ $$ 🖭 **Roughley Manor.** To the wealthy pioneer who erected the stone mansion now occupied by this B&B, expense was no object. A 50-foot-long planked maple floor is the pride of the great room, the carpentry on the walls throughout is intricate, and huge stone fireplaces warm the house on the rare cold night. Original fixtures still gleam in the bathrooms, and bedrooms hold pencil and canopy beds and some fireplaces. The innkeepers serve afternoon tea and evening dessert. An acre of gardens shaded by Washingtonia palms surrounds the house. ⊠ *74–744 Joe Davis Rd., 92277* ☎ *760/367–3238* 🖨 *760/367–4483* ⊕ *www.roughleymanor.com* ↪ *2 suites, 7 cottages* ⚖ *Some kitchens, microwaves, refrigerators, outdoor hot tub; no TV in some rooms, no smoking* ⊟ *DC, MC, V* ¶⊙¶ *BP.*

¢ 🖭 **Best Western Garden Inn &Suites.** This bright complex has smartly furnished rooms, some of which have coffeemakers and hot tubs. ⊠ *71–487 Twentynine Palms Hwy., 92277* ☎ *760/367–9141* 🖨 *760/367–2584* ⊕ *www.bestwestern.com* ↪ *72 rooms, 12 suites* ⚖ *In-room data ports, some kitchenettes, some microwaves, some refrigerators, cable TV with movies, pool, outdoor hot tub, laundry facilities, free parking, no-smoking rooms* ⊟ *AE, D, DC, MC, V* ¶⊙¶ *CP.*

¢ △ **Cottonwood Campground.** In spring this campground is surrounded by some of the desert's finest wildflowers. Joshua Tree National Park's southernmost campground, Cottonwood is often the last to fill up. Reservations are not accepted. ⊠ *Pinto Basin Rd., 32 mi south of North Entrance Station* ☎ *760/367–5500* ⊕ *www.nps.gov.jotr* ↪ *62 sites, 3 group sites* ⚖ *Flush toilets, dump station, fire pits, picnic tables, ranger station.*

¢ △ **Hidden Valley Campground.** This campground is most popular with rock climbers, who make their way up valley rock formations that have names like the Blob, Old Woman, and Chimney Rock. RVs are permitted, but there are no hookups. Reservations are not accepted. ⊠ *Off Park Blvd., 20 mi southwest of Oasis of Mara* ☎ *760/367–5500* ⊕ *www. nps.gov.jotr* ↪ *39 sites* ⚖ *Pit toilets, fire pits, picnic tables.*

Sports & the Outdoors

Joshua Tree Rock Climbing School offers several programs, from one-day introductory classes to multiday programs for experienced climbers. The school provides all needed equipment. Beginning classes are limited to six people age 13 or older. 🖉 *HCR Box 3034, Joshua Tree 92252* ☎ *800/ 890–4745* ⊕ *www.joshuatreerockclimbing.com* 🖾 *$110 for beginner class* ⊙ *Closed July.*

Vertical Adventures Climbing School trains about 1,000 climbers each year in Joshua Tree National Park. Classes meet at a designated location in the park. All equipment is provided. ☎ *800/514–8785* ⊕ *www. verticaladventures.com* ✉ *$90–$95 per person for one-day classes* ⊘ *Closed July and Aug.*

ANZA-BORREGO DESERT

Largely uninhabited, the Anza-Borrego Desert is popular with those who love solitude, silence, space, starry nights, light, and sweeping vistas. The desert lies south of the Palm Springs area, stretching along the western shore of the Salton Sea down to I–8 along the Mexican border. Isolated from the rest of California by mile-high mountains to the north and west, most of this desert falls within the borders of Anza-Borrego Desert State Park, which at more than 600,000 acres is the largest state park in the contiguous United States. This is a place where you can escape the cares of the human world.

For thousands of years Native Americans of the Cahuilla and Kumeyaay people inhabited this area, spending their winters on the warm desert floor and their summers in the mountains. The first Europeans—a party led by Spanish explorer Juan Baptiste de Anza—crossed this desert in 1776. Anza, for whom the desert is named, made the trip through here twice. Roadside signs along Highways 86, 78, and S2 mark the route of the Anza expedition, which spent Christmas Eve 1776 in what is now Anza-Borrego Desert State Park. Seventy-five years later thousands of immigrants on their way to the goldfields up north crossed the desert on the Southern Immigrant Trail, remnants of which remain along Highway S2. Permanent settlers arrived early in the 20th century, and by the 1930s the first adobe resort cottage had been built.

Borrego Springs

❶⑨ *59 mi south of Indio via Hwys. 86 and S22.*

The permanent population of Borrego Springs, set squarely in the middle of Anza-Borrego Desert State Park, hovers around 2,500. Long a quiet town, it is emerging as a laid-back destination for desert lovers. September through June, when temperatures stay in the 80s and 90s, you can engage in outdoor activities such as hiking, nature study, golf, tennis, horseback riding, and mountain biking. If winter rains cooperate, Borrego Springs puts on some of the best wildflower displays in the low desert. In some years the desert floor is carpeted with color: yellow dandelions and sunflowers, pink primrose, purple sand verbena, and blue phacelia. The bloom generally runs from late February through April. For current information on wildflowers around Borrego Springs, call 760/767–4684 or visit ⊕ www.borregosprings.com.

★ One of the richest living natural-history museums in the nation, **Anza-Borrego Desert State Park** is a vast, nearly uninhabited wilderness where you can step through a field of wildflowers, cool off in a palm-shaded oasis, count zillions of stars in the black night sky, and listen to coyotes howl at dusk. The landscape, largely undisturbed by humans, reveals a rich natural history. There's evidence of a vast inland sea in the piles of oyster beds near Split Mountain and of the power of natural forces such as earthquakes and flash floods. In addition, scientists have discovered the fossilized remains of mammoths and sites that were inhabited by early humans. Today its most treasured inhabitants are the herds of elusive and endangered native bighorn sheep, or *borego,* for which the park is named. Among the strange desert plants you may observe are the gnarly elephant trees. As these are endangered, rangers don't encourage visitors to seek out the secluded grove at Fish Creek, but there are a few examples at the visitor center garden. Following a wet winter you can see a short-lived but stunning display of cacti, succulents, and desert wildflowers in bloom.

Anza-Borrego Desert State Park is unusually accessible to visitors. Admission to the park is free, and few areas are off-limits. Unlike most parks in the country, Anza-Borrego lets you camp anywhere; just follow the trails and pitch a tent wherever you like. There are more than 500 mi of dirt roads, two huge wilderness areas, and 110 mi of riding and hiking trails. Many of the park's sites can be seen from paved roads, but some require driving on dirt roads, for which rangers recommend you use a four-wheel-drive vehicle. When you do leave the pavement, carry the appropriate supplies: a shovel and other tools, flares, blankets, and plenty of water. The canyons are susceptible to flash flooding, so inquire about weather conditions (even on sunny days) before entering.

To get oriented and obtain information on weather and wildlife conditions, stop by the **Visitors Information Center.** Designed to keep cool during the desert's blazing hot summers, the center is built underground, beneath a demonstration desert garden. A nature trail here takes you through a garden containing examples of most of the native flora and a little pupfish pond. ⊠ *200 Palm Canyon Dr. (Hwy. S22)* ☎ *760/767– 5311, 760/767–4684 wildflower hotline* ⊕ *www.anzaborrego.statepark. org* ☉ *June–Sept., weekends and holidays 9–5; Oct.–May, daily 9–5.*

At **Borrego Palm Canyon** (⊠ Palm Canyon Dr. [Hwy. S22], about 1 mi west of the Visitors Information Center), a 1½-mi trail leads to one of the few native palm groves in North America. There are more than 1,000 native fan palms in the grove, and a stream and waterfall greet you at trail's end. The moderate hike is the most popular in the park.

Yaqui Well Nature Trail (⊠ Hwy. 78, across from Tamarisk Campground) takes you along a path to a desert water hole where birds and wildlife are abundant. It's also a good place to look for wildflowers in spring.

Coyote Canyon (⊠ Off DiGiorgio Rd., 4½ mi north of Borrego Springs) has a year-round stream and lush plant life. Portions of the canyon road follow a section of the old Anza Trail. The canyon is closed between June 15 and September 15 to allow native bighorn sheep undisturbed use of the water. The dirt road that gives access to the canyon may be sandy enough to require a four-wheel-drive vehicle.

The late-afternoon view of the Borrego badlands from **Font's Point** (⊠ Off Borrego Salton Seaway [Hwy. S22], 13 mi east of Borrego Springs) is one of the most breathtaking views seen in the desert, especially when the setting sun casts a golden glow on the eroded mountain slopes. The road from the Font's Point turnoff can be rough; inquire about its condition at the visitor center before starting out. Even if you can't make it out on the paved road, you can see some of the view from the highway.

Narrows Earth Trail (⊠ Off Hwy. 78, 13 mi west of Borrego Springs) is a short walk off the road east of Tamarisk Grove campground. Along the way you can see evidence of the many geologic processes involved in forming the canyons of the desert, such as a contact zone between two earthquake faults, and sedimentary layers of metamorphic and igneous rock.

Geology students from all over the world visit the Fish Creek area of Anza-Borrego to explore a canyon known as **Split Mountain** (⊠ Split Mountain Rd., 9 mi south of Hwy. 78 at Ocotillo Wells). The narrow gorge with 600-foot walls was formed by an ancient stream. Fossils in this area indicate that a sea once covered the desert floor.

The easy, mostly flat **Pictograph/Smuggler's Canyon Trail** (⊠ Blair Valley, Hwy. S2, 6 mi southeast of Hwy. 78 at Scissors Crossing intersection) traverses a boulder-strewn trail. At the end is a collection of rocks covered with muted red and yellow pictographs painted within the last hundred years or so by Native Americans. Walk about ½ mi beyond the pictures to reach Smuggler's Canyon, where an overlook provides views of the Vallecito Valley. The hike is 2–3 mi round-trip.

Just a few steps off the paved road, **Carrizo Badlands Overlook** (⊠ Off Hwy. S2, 40 mi south of Scissors Crossing [intersection of Hwys. S2 and 78]) offers a view of eroded and twisted sedimentary rock that obscures the fossils of the mastodons, saber-tooths, zebras, and camels that roamed this region a million years ago. The route to the overlook through Earthquake Valley and Blair Valley parallels the Southern Emigrant Stage Route.

off the beaten path

OCOTILLO WELLS STATE VEHICULAR RECREATION AREA – The sand dunes and rock formations here are a challenge for off-road enthusiasts, with more than 40,000 acres of open desert to explore. You can get maps and information from the ranger station. RV camping is permitted here. There are about 125 sites, with ramadas, tables, and fire pits, scattered around the area. There are showers with hot water and pit toilets, but the water may not be safe to drink—so bring your own. ⊠ 5172 Hwy. 78, Ocotillo Wells ☎ 760/ 767–5391 ⊕ www.ohv.parks.ca.gov ⌑ Free ⊙ Ranger station hrs vary.

Where to Stay & Eat

$–$$ ✕ **Bernard's.** In a single large room with a wall of windows, chef-owner Bernard offers casual dining with an Alsatian flavor. Try sauerkraut Alsatian style, daily regional Alsatian preparations of duck, and roast leg of lamb. ⊠ 501 Palm Canyon Dr. ☎ 760/767–5666 ⊟ AE, D, MC, V ⊙ Closed Sun.

¢–$$ ✕**Krazy Coyote.** Dine inside in the cozy bar or outside by the pool at this restaurant at the Palms at Indianhead. Either way you'll hear Bing Crosby and Peggy Lee softly crooning '50s songs in the background as you enjoy a surprisingly well prepared seared ahi salad, spicy Santa Fe crab cakes, or sesame-garlic grilled pork tenderloin. Be warned that summer hours vary. ✉ *2220 Hoberg Rd.* ☎ *760/767–7788* ▭ *AE, D, DC, MC, V.*

★ **$$$–$$$$** ✕▦ **La Casa del Zorro.** This serene resort owned by San Diego's prominent Copley family pampers guests with spectacular desert scenery, luxurious accommodations, and gracious and superb service. You need walk only a few hundred yards from your room to find yourself in a quiet desert garden surrounded by ocotillo and cholla or at night alone under the stars. Accommodations range from ample standard rooms to private casitas with their own pools or private garden outdoor hot tubs. The elegant Dining Room ($$$–$$$$) has excellent service, fireside dining, and a good Sunday brunch. Entrées include gulf prawns with saffron risotto, Nebraska prime grade beef tenderloin, and rack of Colorado lamb. La Casa schedules a number of wine, music, and astronomy weekends throughout the year. During summer, prices are deeply discounted. ✉ *3845 Yaqui Pass Rd., 92004* ☎ *760/767–5323 or 800/824– 1884* ▤ *760/767–5963* ⊕ *www.lacasadelzorro.com* ⤳ *48 rooms, 12 suites, 19 1- to 4-bedroom casitas* ⌂ *Restaurant, room service, BBQs, fans, in-room data ports, some in-room hot tubs, minibars, microwaves, cable TV with movies, putting green, 6 tennis courts, 5 pools, fitness classes, health club, hair salon, 3 outdoor hot tubs, massage, bicycles, archery, boccie, croquet, hiking, horseback riding, horseshoes, Ping-Pong, shuffleboard, volleyball, lounge, children's programs (ages 7–12), business services, meeting room, airport shuttle, free parking, no-smoking rooms* ▭ *AE, D, MC, V.*

$$–$$$ ▦ **Borrego Valley Inn.** Desert gardens of mesquite, ocotillo, and creosote surround adobe southwestern-style buildings. Spacious rooms with plenty of light are decorated in Indian-design fabrics and hold original art. Furnishings include lodgepole beds with down comforters and serape-stripe bedspreads, walk-in showers with garden views, and double futons facing corner fireplaces. Every room opens out to its own enclosed garden with chaises, chairs, and table. Friendly innkeepers serve a tasty Continental breakfast and you can enjoy the courtyard desert garden while dining. The inn is very pet friendly; the innkeepers even have bowls of water in the lobby. ✉ *405 Palm Canyon Dr., 92004* ☎ *760/ 767–0311 or 800/333–5810* ▤ *760/767–0900* ⊕ *www.borregovalleyinn. com* ⤳ *14 rooms, 1 suite* ⌂ *In-room data ports, some kitchenettes, microwaves, refrigerators, cable TV, 2 pools, 2 outdoor hot tubs, some pets allowed (fee); no smoking* ▭ *D, MC, V* ⦿| *CP.*

¢–$$ ▦ **Borrego Springs Resort.** This quiet resort offers good value when compared to other Borrego Springs lodgings. Large rooms in a collection of two-story buildings surrounding the swimming pool are nicely kept and appointed with simple oak furnishings. All have shaded balconies or patios. In spring desert gardens surrounding the property show a colorful bloom. The Borrego Springs Country Club restaurant on site is open daily except Monday for lunch and dinner. ✉ *1112 Tilting T Dr., 92004* ☎ *760/767–5700 or 888/826–7734* ▤ *760/767–5710* ⊕ *www.*

borregospringsresort.com ⇨ *68 rooms, 32 suites* ⚐ *Restaurant, in-room data ports, microwaves, refrigerators, cable TV, 3 9-hole golf courses, putting green, 6 tennis courts, 2 pools, gym, outdoor hot tub, lounge, meeting room, some pets allowed (fee), no-smoking rooms* ▭ *AE, D, MC, V.*

$–$$ **Palm Canyon Resort.** One of the largest properties around, Palm Canyon Resort includes a hotel a quarter mile from the park visitor center and an RV park with 130 spaces. Rooms are western-style and some have balconies. ✉ *221 Palm Canyon Dr., 92004* ☎ *760/767–5341 or 800/242–0044* 📠 *760/767–4073* 🌐 *www.pcresort.com* ⇨ *60 rooms, 1 suite* ⚐ *Restaurant, in-room data ports, refrigerators, cable TV with movies, pool, gym, outdoor hot tub, lounge, shop, laundry facilities, meeting room, no-smoking rooms* ▭ *AE, D, DC, MC, V.*

¢ **Borrego Palm Canyon.** This pleasant campground is near the Borrego Palm Canyon trailhead. There are two sections: one for recreational vehicles with hookups and another without hookups, designed for tent campers. Tent sites have ramadas (rock walls with thatched roofs) for shade. ✉ *Palm Canyon Dr. (Hwy. S22), about 1 mi west of Visitors Information Center* ☎ *760/767–5311, 800/444–7275 for reservations* 🌐 *www.anzaborrego.statepark.org* ⇨ *52 RV sites, 65 tent sites* ⚐ *Flush toilets, full hookups, drinking water, showers, fire pits, picnic tables, public telephone.*

¢ **Tamarisk Grove.** Campsites are tucked under the shade of sprawling tamarisk trees at this campground across the road from the 1½-mi Yaqui Well Nature Trail. There are no hookups, but the sites can hold RVs up to 21 feet. ✉ *Yaqui Pass Rd., 13 mi west of Borrego Springs* ☎ *760/767–5311, 800/444–7275 for reservations* 🌐 *www.anzaborrego.statepark.org* ⇨ *27 sites* ⚐ *Flush toilets, drinking water, showers, fire pits, picnic tables.*

Sports & the Outdoors

The 27 holes of golf at **Borrego Springs Resort and Country Club** (✉ 1112 Tilting T Dr. ☎ 760/767–3330 🌐 www.borregospringsresort.com) are open to the public. Three 9-hole courses, with natural desert landscaping and mature date palms, can be played individually or in any combination. Greens fees are $54–$64, depending on the course and the day of the week, and include a cart. Another worthwhile public course is the 18-hole **Rams Hill Country Club** (✉ 1881 Rams Hill Dr. ☎ 760/767–5124 🌐 www.ramshillgolf.com). Greens fees are $85–$95, depending on the day of the week and season, and include a mandatory cart. **Roadrunner Club** (✉ 1010 Palm Canyon Dr. ☎ 760/767–5374 🌐 www.roadrunnerclub.com) has an 18-hole, par-3 golf course. Greens fees are $25.

IMPERIAL VALLEY

FROM THE SALTON SEA TO THE MEXICAN BORDER

Imperial County lies between the Colorado River, to the east, and the Anza-Borrego Desert, to the west. The area is both a great desert and one of the richest agricultural regions in the world, producing primarily winter vegetables, grains, and cattle. The briny Salton Sea, California's largest lake, occupies a large portion of Imperial County. The sea is a vast inland water recreation area, while El Centro is the commercial and business heart of the valley. This is stereotypical desert, complete with miles and miles of sand dunes, an average annual rainfall of less than 1 inch, and summer temperatures soaring above 100°F.

Salton Sea

★ *30 mi southeast of Indio via Hwy. 86 on the western shore and via Hwy. 111 on the eastern shore; 29 mi east of Borrego Springs via Hwy. S22.*

The Salton Sea, barely 100 years old, is the product of both natural and artificial forces. The sea occupies the Salton Basin, a remnant of prehistoric Lake Cahuilla. Over the centuries the Colorado River flooded the basin and the water drained into the Gulf of California. In 1905 a flood once again filled the Salton Basin. Because the exit to the gulf was now blocked by sediment, the flood waters remained in the basin. The resulting body of water was trapped 228 feet below sea level, creating a saline lake about 35 mi long and 15 mi wide, with a surface area of nearly 380 square mi. The lake has no real inflow, so over the years evaporation has made it 25% saltier than the ocean, creating a rare and splendid habitat for birds and fish. Lying along the Pacific Flyway, the sea supports 400 species of birds. Four sport fish inhabit the Salton Sea: corvina, sargo, Gulf croaker, and tilapia. Fishing, boating, camping, and birdwatching are popular activities year-round. However, efforts to develop expensive waterfront communities and resorts along the western shore have failed because the lake sometimes has a pungent odor. The remnants of the developments now resemble other desert ghost towns. In fact, the future of the sea remains uncertain.

On the north shore of the sea, the huge **Salton Sea State Recreation Area** draws thousands each year to its playgrounds, hiking trails, fishing spots, boat launches, and swimming areas. The Headquarters Visitor Center contains exhibits and shows a short film on the history of the Salton Sea. Summer is the best time for fishing here. ✉ *100–225 State Park Rd., North Shore* ☎ *760/393–3052* ⊕ *www.parks.ca.gov* ✂ *$4* ☉ *Park daily 8–sunset, visitor center Oct.–Mar., daily 8–sunset.*

The 1,785-acre **Sonny Bono National Wildlife Refuge,** on the Pacific Flyway, is a wonderful spot for viewing migratory birds. You might see eared grebes, burrowing owls, great blue herons, ospreys, yellow-footed gulls, white and brown pelicans, and snow geese heading south from Canada. Facilities include a visitor center with bird displays, self-guided trails, observation platforms, and interpretive exhibits. Fishing and waterfowl hunting are permitted in season in designated areas. ✉ *906 W. Sinclair Rd., Calipatria* ☎ *760/348–5278* ⊕ *pacific.fws.gov/salton/* ✂ *Free* ☉ *Daily sunrise–sunset. Visitor center Apr.–Sept., weekdays 7–3:30; Oct.–Mar., daily 7–3:30.*

Sports & the Outdoors

At the Salton Sea all sorts of water sports are popular. You can waterski, kayak, and canoe, or fish from the shore, from a boat, and from the jetty at Varner Harbor. Swimming is permitted at beaches anywhere along the shoreline, but be warned that the water is brackish. You can launch your boat at **Varner Harbor** (⊠ 100–225 State Park Rd., North Shore ☎ 760/393–3052, 800/444–7275 for reservations), where a ramp and five docks are available. The fee is $4.

Camping

¢ ⚠ **New Camp.** Near park headquarters, New Camp is designed for tent campers. Sites have shaded ramadas and paved parking stalls. It's a short walk from here to the Varner Harbor boat-launching area and the park's prime fishing spots. ⊠ *100–225 State Park Rd., North Shore* ☎ *760/ 393–3052, 800/444–7275 for reservations* ⊕ *www.parks.ca.gov* ⇨ *25 sites* ⚬ *Flush toilets, drinking water, showers, fire pits, picnic tables.*

¢ ⚠ **Salton Sea State Recreation Area Headquarters.** This tree-shaded parking area for RVs is right on the sand, just steps from the beach. It is adjacent to New Camp. ⊠ *100–225 State Park Rd., North Shore* ☎ *760/ 393–3052, 800/444–7275 for reservations* ⊕ *www.parks.ca.gov* ⇨ *15 sites* ⚬ *Flush toilets, full hookups, dump station, drinking water, showers, fire pits, picnic tables, playground.*

El Centro

㉑ *28 mi south of Salton Sea on Hwy. 86.*

Bisected by I–8, El Centro lies close to the Mexican border at the southern end of the Imperial Valley. Primarily a commercial and business community, it occupies some of the richest farmland in California, with more than a half million acres in cultivation. Year-round the region produces bumper crops of lettuce, carrots, sugar beets, seed, and grain.

Naval Air Facility El Centro, the winter home of the Blue Angels aerobatic team, opens each March for a huge air show with stunt flying, displays of antique and experimental aircraft, and a food fest ($5). ⊠ *Bennett Rd.* ☎ *760/339–2519* ⊕ *www.nafec.navy.mil* 🎫 *Free.*

off the
beaten
path

IMPERIAL SAND DUNES – This 40-mi-long dune system east of El Centro is one of the largest in the United States. Formed from the windblown beach sands of the prehistoric Blake Sea, which once occupied this portion of the desert, some dune crests reach heights of more than 300 feet. The impressive vistas make the dunes a popular filming location. You can maneuver your four-wheel-drive vehicle or dune buggy up, down, and around the mountains of sand. Although there are no real facilities, this is a popular weekend camping destination, one where crowds swell to 100,000 people on holiday weekends. To reach the dunes from El Centro, drive 15 mi north on Highway 86 to Brawley, then 23 mi east on Highway 78. ⊠ *Gecko Rd., ½ mi south of Hwy. 78, Glamis* ☎ *760/344–3919* ⊕ *www.ca. blm.gov/elcentro* 🎫 *$25 per week* ⊙ *Park open daily; Cahuilla ranger station Oct.–May, Fri.–Sun. 7–5:30.*

Where to Stay & Eat

¢–$ ✕ **Celia's.** The quesadillas and *carne asada* (strips of marinated grilled beef) are standouts at this classic south-of-the-border–style, family-oriented restaurant. ⊠ *1530 W. Adams Ave.* ☎ *760/352–4570* ▭ *MC, V* ⊘ *Closed July and Aug.*

¢–$ ✕⬚ **Barbara Worth Golf Resort and Convention Center.** Taking its name from the 1911 Harold Bell Wright book *The Winning of Barbara Worth*, about turning the desert into farmland by irrigation, this resort is a green spot in the desert. Low-lying buildings overlooking the golf course house pleasant rooms with exterior entrances. The dining room ($–$$$) has a Polynesian look, but the kitchen is American. Evenings at the karaoke bar can be lively. ⊠ *2050 Country Club Dr., Holtville 92250* ☎ *760/ 356–2806 or 800/356–3806* 🖷 *760/356–4653* ⊕ *www.bwresort.com* ↵ *104 rooms* ⚴ *Restaurant, room service, in-room data ports, some in-room safes, microwaves, refrigerators, cable TV, driving range, 18-hole golf course, putting green, 2 pools, gym, hot tub, lounge, meeting rooms, no-smoking rooms* ▭ *AE, D, DC, MC, V.*

¢–$ ⬚ **Best Western John Jay Inn.** The federalist architecture of this three-story motel stands out in the desert environment, and the traditional theme is carried into the well-appointed rooms. Suites have coffeemakers, microwaves, and minibars, and a complimentary continental breakfast is available each morning. ⊠ *2352 S. 4th St., 92243* ☎ *760/337–8677* 🖷 *760/337–8693* ⊕ *www.bestwestern.com* ↵ *50 rooms, 8 suites* ⚴ *In-room data ports, some minibars, some microwaves, some refrigerators, cable TV, pool, gym, hot tub, sauna, laundry facilities, no-smoking rooms* ▭ *AE, D, DC, MC, V* ⫿⊙⫿ *CP.*

¢ ⬚ **Vacation Inn and Suites.** The largest lodging in El Centro is this Spanish-style, two-story motel with spacious rooms and suites. Rooms have coffeemakers, and local phone calls are free. The motel also has an RV park with showers and restrooms. ⊠ *2015 Cottonwood Dr., 92243* ☎ *760/352–9523 or 800/328–6289* 🖷 *760/352–7620* ↵ *160 rooms, 11 suites* ⚴ *Restaurant, in-room data ports, kitchenettes, microwaves, refrigerators, cable TV, 2 pools, outdoor hot tub, bar, business services, meeting rooms, airport shuttle, some pets allowed, no-smoking rooms* ▭ *AE, D, DC, MC, V* ⫿⊙⫿ *CP.*

PALM SPRINGS & THE SOUTHERN DESERT A TO Z

To research prices, get advice from other travelers, and book travel arrangements, visit ⊕ *www.fodors.com.*

AIRPORTS & TRANSFERS

Palm Springs International Airport is the major airport serving California's southern desert. Airlines that fly to Palm Springs include Alaska, American, America West, Continental, Delta, Northwest, and United. The airport is about 2 mi from downtown Palm Springs. SkyWest/Delta Connection serves Imperial County Airport. A Valley Cabousine has taxis serving the Palm Springs airport. *See* Air Travel *in* Smart Travel Tips for airline phone numbers.

🛈 **Imperial County Airport** ☎760/355–7944. **Palm Springs International Airport** ☎760/ 318–3800 ⊕ www.palmspringsairport.com. **A Valley Cabousine** ☎ 760/340–5845.

BUS TRAVEL

Greyhound provides service to the El Centro and Palm Springs depots. Imperial County Transit provides bus service for the El Centro and Salton Sea communities. SunBus, operated by the SunLine Transit Agency, serves the entire Coachella Valley, from Desert Hot Springs to Mecca. **Greyhound** 🕾 800/231-2222 ⊕ www.greyhound.com. **El Centro Depot** ⊠ 460 State St. 🕾 760/352-6363. **Palm Springs Depot** ⊠ 311 N. Indian Canyon Dr. 🕾 760/325-9557. **Imperial County Transit** 🕾 800/804-3050. **SunLine Transit** 🕾 760/343-3456 or 800/347-8628 ⊕ www.sunline.org.

CAR RENTAL

Most major car-rental companies are represented in the Palm Springs area; Budget and Enterprise have outlets in El Centro. *See* Car Rental *in* Smart Travel Tips A to Z *for national car-rental agency phone numbers.*

CAR TRAVEL

The desert resort communities occupy a 20-mi stretch between I–10, to the east, and Palm Canyon Drive (Highway 111), to the west. The area is about a two-hour drive east of Los Angeles and a three-hour drive northeast of San Diego. From Los Angeles take the San Bernardino Freeway (I–10) east to Highway 111. From San Diego I–15 heading north connects with the Pomona Freeway (Highway 60), leading to the San Bernardino Freeway (I–10) east. If you're coming from the Riverside area, you can also take Highway 74 east.

To reach Borrego Springs from Los Angeles, take I–10 east past the desert resorts area to Highway 86 south, and follow it to the Borrego Salton Seaway (Highway S22). Drive west on S22 to Borrego Springs. You can reach the Borrego area from San Diego via I–8 to Highway 79 through Cuyamaca State Park. This will take you to Highway 78 in Julian, which you follow east to Yaqui Pass Road (S3) into Borrego Springs.

The Imperial Valley lies south of S22 on Highway 86. Salton Sea attractions are on the south and east sides of the sea. El Centro is about a two-hour drive east of San Diego via I–8.

EMERGENCIES

In the event of an emergency, dial 911.

In the desert you should play it safe by being prepared and taking a few simple safety precautions. Always travel with a companion, especially if you are not familiar with the area. Let someone know about your trip, destination, and estimated time and date of return. Carry a cell phone as a precaution, but know that reception in the desert can be spotty at best. Before setting out, make sure that your vehicle is in good condition. Carry a jack, tools, and tow rope or chain. Fill up your tank whenever you see a gas pump—it can be miles between service stations. Stay on main roads: if you drive even a few feet off the pavement, you could get stuck in sand. Plus, venturing off-road is illegal in many areas. When driving, watch out for wild burros, horses, and range cattle. They roam free throughout much of the desert and have the right-of-way.

Drink at least one gallon of water per day, preferably more (three gallons if you plan on hiking or engaging in other strenuous activity), even if you don't feel thirsty. Dress in layered clothing and wear comfortable, sturdy shoes and a hat. Keep snacks, sunscreen, and a first-aid kit on hand. If you suddenly have a headache or feel dizzy or nauseous, you could be suffering from dehydration. Get out of the sun immediately and drink plenty of water. Dampen your clothing to lower your body temperature.

Avoid canyons during rainstorms. Floodwaters can quickly fill up dry riverbeds and cover or wash away roads. Never place your hands or feet where you can't see them. Rattlesnakes, scorpions, and black widow spiders may be hiding there.

⁊ Hospitals **Borrego Medical Center** ⊠ 4343 Yaqui Pass Rd., Borrego Springs ☎ 760/767-5051. **Desert Regional Medical Center** ⊠ 1150 N. Indian Canyon Dr., Palm Springs ☎ 760/323-6511. **El Centro Regional Medical Center** ⊠ 1415 Ross Ave., El Centro ☎ 760/339-7100.

LODGING

The Palm Springs Visitor Information Center represents 85 properties in the desert resorts area and can help you arrange for lodgings there. Palm Springs Desert Resorts Authority can make accommodation reservations throughout the area (⇨ Visitor Information, *below* for both). McLean Company Rentals, Rental Connection, and ResortQuest arrange vacation rentals by the day, week, or month.

⁊ **McLean Company Rentals** ☎ 760/322-2500 ⊕ www.ps4rent.com. **Rental Connection** ☎ 760/320-7336 or 800/462-7256 ⊕ www.therentalconnection.com. **ResortQuest** ☎ 800/869-1130 ⊕ www.resortquest.com.

TAXIS

A Valley Cabousine serves Palm Desert and goes to the Palm Springs airport. Mirage Taxi serves the Coachella Valley and the Los Angeles and Ontario International airports. Fares in the Coachella Valley run about $2.25 per mile and up to $240 one-way to LAX. Yellow Cab of El Centro serves the Imperial Valley. Service within the El Centro city limits is $3.50 per trip.

⁊ Taxi Companies **A Valley Cabousine** ☎ 760/340-5845. **Mirage Taxi** ☎ 760/322-2008. **Yellow Cab of El Centro** ☎ 760/352-3100.

TOURS

Desert Adventures takes to the wilds with two- to four-hour Jeep tours ($59–$99) on private land along the canyons of the San Andreas earthquake fault. Departures are from Palm Springs and La Quinta; hotel pickups are available. Three thousand windmills churn mightily on the slopes surrounding Palm Springs, generating electricity used by southern California residents. Each windmill stands more than 150 feet high. EV Adventures conducts 1½-hour tours among the giant rotors, towers, and blades in what NASA declares is one of the most consistently windy places on earth. Palm Springs Celebrity Tours conducts 2½-hour tours that cover Palm Springs–area history, points of interest, and celebrity homes. Trail Discovery–Desert Safari Guides conducts tours of various lengths through the Indian Canyons, moonlight hiking in the

Palm Springs area, and daytime excursions to Joshua Tree National Park. Transportation from most area hotels is included. Adventures in Good Company conducts a one-week rock climbing trip to Joshua Tree for women only in mid-March. Fees ($995–$1095) include guides, gear, most meals, and miscellaneous fees.

🎒**Adventures in Good Company** ✉5913 Brackenridge Ave., Baltimore, MD 21212 ☎877/ 439-4042 ⊕ www.goodadventure.com. **Desert Adventures** ✉ 67-555 E. Palm Canyon Dr., Cathedral City ☎ 760/324-5337 ⊕ www.red-jeep.com. **EV Adventures** ✉ 62-950 20th Ave., North Palm Springs ☎ 760/251-1997 ⊕ www.windmilltours.com. **Palm Springs Celebrity Tours** ✉ 4751 E. Palm Canyon Dr., Palm Springs ☎ 760/770-2700 ⊕ www.celebrity-tours.com. **Trail Discovery–Desert Safari Guides** ☎ 760/325-4453 or 888/324-4453 ⊕ www.palmspringshiking.com.

TRAIN TRAVEL

The Amtrak *Sunset Limited,* which runs between Florida and Los Angeles, stops in Palm Springs and Indio.

🎒 **Amtrak** ☎ 800/872-7245 ⊕ www.amtrakcalifornia.com.

VISITOR INFORMATION

🎒**Borrego Springs Chamber of Commerce** ✉786 Palm Canyon Dr., 92004-0420 ☎760/ 767-5555 or 800/559-5524 ⊕ www.borregosprings.org. **El Centro Chamber of Commerce & Visitors Bureau** ✉ 1095 S. 4th St., 92243 ☎ 760/352-3681 ⊕ www. elcentrochamber.com. **Joshua Tree National Park** ✉ 74-485 National Park Dr., Twentynine Palms 92277 ☎ 760/367-5500 ⊕ www.nps.gov/jotr. **Palm Springs Desert Resorts Authority** ✉ 69-930 Hwy. 111, Suite 201, Rancho Mirage 92270 ☎ 760/770-9000 or 800/417-3529, 760/770-1992 for activities hotline ⊕ www.palmspringsusa. com. **Palm Springs Visitor Information Centers** ✉ 2901 N. Palm Canyon Dr., 92262 ☎ 800/347-7746 ✉ 777 N. Palm Canyon Dr., Suite 101, 92262 ☎ 800/927-7256 ⊕ www.palm-springs.org.

THE MOJAVE DESERT
& DEATH VALLEY
WITH THE OWENS VALLEY

6

Updated by
Veronica Hill

DUST AND DESOLATION, tumbleweeds and rattlesnakes, barren land-scapes—these are the bleak images that come to mind when most people hear the word *desert*. But east of the Sierra Nevada, where the land quickly flattens and the rain seldom falls, the desert is anything but a wasteland. The topography here is extreme; while Death Valley drops to almost 300 feet below sea level and contains the lowest (and hottest) spot in the western hemisphere, the Mojave Desert, which lies to the south, has elevations ranging from 3,000 to 5,000 feet. These remote regions (which are known, respectively, as low desert and high desert) possess a singular beauty found nowhere else in California: there are vast open spaces populated with spiky Joshua trees, undulating sand dunes, faulted mountains, and dramatic rock formations. Owens Valley is where the desert meets the mountains; its 80-mi width separates the depths of Death Valley from Mt. Whitney, the highest mountain in the continental United States. Exploring the wonders of Death Valley in the morning and then heading to the Sierra to cool off in the afternoon is an amazing study in contrasts.

Believe everything you've ever heard about desert heat: it can be brutal. To avoid dehydration and sunburn, you need sunglasses, sunblock, a hat, and clothing that blocks the sun's rays and the wind. Because this region is vast—about as big as Ohio—and the weather is unpredictable, you'll also need to make careful driving plans. Facilities like gas stations and supermarkets are few, so be sure to fill your gas tank whenever you can and check your vehicle's fluids and tire pressure frequently. Shut off your car's air-conditioning on steep grades to avoid engine overheating. At the start of each day load the car with three gallons of water per person, plus additional radiator water, and a cooler stocked with extra food. Be sure to bring reliable maps; signage can be limited and, in some places, nonexistent. It's a good idea to have a compass and a cellular phone (though the signal may fade in remote areas). A pair of binoculars can also come in handy, and don't forget your camera—you're likely to see things you've never seen before.

Exploring the Mojave Desert & Death Valley

Be sure to stop in Death Valley National Park, with its miles of dunes, crusted salt flats, and jagged canyons. A drive east takes you to the Mojave National Preserve, 1.4 million acres of sand, scrub, volcanic cinder cones, and rock-strewn mountains. The eastern Mojave stretches to the Arizona border at the Colorado River—a popular place for swimming and water sports. You may spot fossils at some of the archaeological sites in the desert. If you do, leave them where they are; it's against the law to remove them.

About the Restaurants

Throughout the desert and the eastern Sierra, dining is a fairly simple affair. Owens Valley is home to many mom-and-pop eateries, as well as a few fast-food chains. The restaurants in Death Valley range from coffee shops to upscale cafés. In the Mojave there are chain establishments in Ridgecrest, Victorville, and Barstow, as well as some ethnic eateries.

Numbers in the text correspond to numbers in the margin and on the Owens Valley and Death Valley map and the Mojave Desert map.

6

If you have
3 days

Start in ▶ **Death Valley National Park** ⑭–㉗. Stop for lunch at **Stovepipe Wells Village** ㉖; then spend the rest of the afternoon at **Scotty's Castle** ㉒ and **Ubehebe Crater** ㉓. Stay the night in ⊞ **Furnace Creek Village** ⑮ and explore the southern half of the park on Day 3. Be sure not to miss the vivid desert colors of **Artists Palette** ⑯, the western hemisphere's lowest spot, at **Badwater** ⑱, or the stunning panorama from **Dante's View** ⑲.

If you have
7 days

Spend two days exploring the many wonders of ▶ ⊞ **Death Valley National Park** ⑭–㉗. On your third day head out of the park to ⊞ **Ridgecrest** ❹ for a hike through Red Rock Canyon, Fossil Falls, or Trona Pinnacles Natural National Landmark. If you're visiting on a spring or fall weekend, make advance arrangements at the Maturango Museum to tour Petroglyph Canyons. The next morning continue south to **Lancaster** ❷ to see Antelope Valley Poppy Reserve, where poppies cover the hillsides as far as the eye can see. Move on to **Palmdale** ❶ and its Antelope Valley Indian Museum, then drive to Pearblossom to pick up some ceramic tiles at St. Andrew's Abbey. Return to Palmdale for dinner and a night's rest. On the morning of Day 5, after a stop at Big Pines Visitor Center, at the highest point on the San Andreas Fault, venture north on I-15 into Route 66 country. In **Victorville** ❺, the California Route 66 Museum tells the story of one of America's most famous roads. Heading for ⊞ **Barstow** ❻, get another hit of Route 66 nostalgia at Casa del Desierto Harvey House, site of the Route 66 Mother Road Museum and Gift Shop. Explore the Barstow area, including Desert Discovery Center, Calico Ghost Town, and Rainbow Basin National Natural Landmark, on Day 6. The next morning drive to **Mojave National Preserve** ❾ to see Kelso Dunes and to tour Mitchell Caverns, in Providence Mountains State Recreation Area. If time and road conditions permit, drive through Afton Canyon on your way back to Barstow.

About the Hotels

Hotel chains and roadside motels make up most of the lodging options in the desert. The tourist season runs through the summer months, from late May through September, when many travelers are heading out of California on the I-15. Reservations are never a problem: you're almost always guaranteed a room. But if your plans take you to the most luxurious resort in the entire desert—the Furnace Creek Inn, in Death Valley—be sure to book in advance for the winter season. This hottest of spots is busiest during the cooler months. For a true American experience, visit one of the many historic Route 66 motels along the "Mother Road," which travels through the heart of the Mojave Desert along I-40 and I-15.

WHAT IT COSTS					
	$$$$	**$$$**	**$$**	**$**	**¢**
RESTAURANTS	over $30	$23–$30	$16–$22	$10–$15	under $10
HOTELS	over $250	$176–$250	$121–$175	$90–$120	under $90

Restaurant prices are for a main course at dinner, excluding sales tax of 7¾%. Hotel prices are for two people in a standard double room in high season, excluding service charges and 7¼% tax.

Timing

Spring and fall are the best seasons to tour the desert and Owens Valley. Winters are generally mild, but summers can be cruel. If you're on a budget, keep in mind that room rates drop as the temperatures rise. Early morning is the best time to visit sights and avoid crowds, but some museums and visitor centers don't open until 10. If you schedule your town arrivals for late afternoon, you can drop by the visitor centers just before closing hours to line up an itinerary for the next day. Plan indoor activities for midday during hotter months. Because relatively few people visit the desert, many attractions have limited hours of access: for instance, Petroglyph Canyon tours are given only on weekends in fall and spring, and the Calico Early Man Archeological Site does not offer tours Monday and Tuesday. Summer is the best time to visit the Ancient Bristlecone Pine Forest, near Big Pine; in winter, snowpack may prohibit vehicles from entering the area.

THE WESTERN MOJAVE

Stretching from the town of Ridgecrest to the base of the San Gabriel Mountains, the western Mojave is a varied landscape of ancient Native American petroglyphs, tufa towers, and hillsides covered in bright-orange poppies.

Palmdale

❶ *60 mi north of Los Angeles on Hwy. 14.*

Before calling itself the aerospace capital of the world, the desert town of Palmdale was an agricultural community. Swiss and German descendants, moving west from Nebraska, first settled here in 1886. Most residents made their living as farmers, growing alfalfa, pears, and apples. After World War II, with the creation of Edwards Air Force Base and U.S. Air Force Plant 42, the area turned into a center for aerospace and defense, with such big companies as McDonnell Douglas, Rockwell, Northrop, and Lockheed establishing factories here. Today, it is one of the fastest-growing cities in Southern California.

Notable for its one-of-a-kind Native American artifacts, **Antelope Valley Indian Museum** has more than 2,500 items on display, including pieces from California, Southwestern, and Great Basin tribes. The unusual Swiss chalet–style building, built in 1928 by homesteader Howard Arden Edwards, clings to the rocky hillside of Piute Butte and is listed

Camping

There's nothing like sleeping under a starry desert sky or amid a Sierra forest. There are many campgrounds in the area that allow you to do this, including the ones at Hole-in-the-Wall and Red Rock Canyon State Park. Wherever you choose to pitch your tent, be prepared for weather extremes. Make sure your equipment can handle (and protect you from) the Mojave's hot sun, as well as the sometimes freezing temperatures and sudden storms of the eastern Sierra. Campgrounds throughout the region are inexpensive or free, and sites tend to be primitive.

6

Hiking

Hiking trails are abundant throughout the desert and along the eastern base of the Sierra, meandering toward sights that you can't see from the road. Some of the best trails are unmarked; ask locals for directions. Among the prime hiking spots are Death Valley National Park and the John Muir Trail, which starts near Mt. Whitney. Whether you're exploring the high or low desert, wear sunblock, protective clothing, and a hat. Plan your desert walks for before or after midday, when the sun is hottest, and be wary of tarantulas, black widows, scorpions, snakes, and other potentially hazardous creatures (if you wear closed shoes and watch where you're walking, these shouldn't be a problem). Paths through canyons are sometimes partially shielded from the sun and not as hot, so if your time is limited, save these for midday.

---

on the National Register of Historic Places. ⊠ *Ave. M between 150th and 170th Sts. E, 17 mi east of Antelope Valley Freeway (Hwy. 14)* ☎ *661/ 942–0662* ⊕ *www.avim.av.org* ⊠ *$1* ☉ *Mid-Sept.–mid-June, weekends 11–4; tours available Tues.–Thurs. by appointment.*

Just a mile from the San Andreas Fault, the namesake of the **Devil's Punchbowl Natural Area** is a natural bowl-shape depression in the earth, framed by 300-foot rock walls. At the bottom is a stream, which you can reach via a 1-mi hike; at the top an interpretive center has displays of native flora and fauna, including live animals such as snakes, lizards, and birds of prey. ⊠ *28000 Devil's Punchbowl Rd., south of Hwy. 138, Pearblossom* ☎ *661/944–2743* ⊠ *Free* ☉ *Daily 8–4.*

The Benedictine monastery **St. Andrew's Abbey** stands on 760 acres of lush greenery and natural springs. A big draw here is the property's ceramics studio, established in 1969; St. Andrew's Ceramics sells handmade tile saints, angels, and plaques designed by Father Maur van Doorslaer, a monk from Sint Andries in Brugges, Belgium, whose work is collected across the United States and Canada. Don't miss the abbey's fall festival, where you can sample tasty dishes and enjoy entertainment that includes singing nuns. ⊠ *31101 N. Valyermo Rd., south of Hwy. 138, Valyermo* ☎ *661/944–2178, 661/944–1047 for ceramic studio* ⊕ *www.saintsandangels.org* ⊠ *Free* ☉ *Weekdays 9–11:30 and 1:30–4, weekends 9:30–11:45 and 1:30–4:30.*

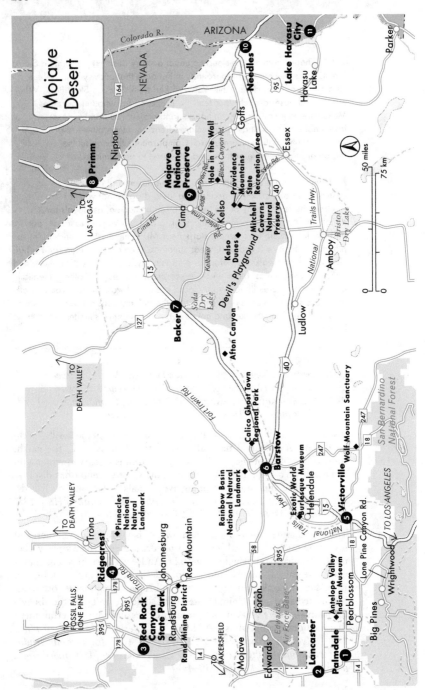

Where to Stay

$–$$$ ▢ **Residence Inn Palmdale.** Accommodations here range from studios to one-bedroom suites, all with full kitchens, sitting areas, and sleeper sofas. Some suites have fireplaces, and each has an iron and ironing board, a hair dryer, and a two-line phone with voice mail. Sip your complimentary in-room coffee while reading the free newspaper that's delivered to your room weekdays. There's complimentary hot breakfast daily, and you can have dinner delivered from several local restaurants. The staff will even do your grocery shopping for you. ✉ *514 W. Ave. P, 93551* ☎ *661/947–4204 or 800/331–3131* ⊕ *www.residenceinn.com.* ↩ *90 suites* � *In-room data ports, kitchens, refrigerators, cable TV, tennis court, indoor pool, gym, hot tub, dry cleaning, laundry facilities, laundry service, concierge, business services, meeting room, car rental* ▤ *AE, D, DC, MC, V* ⤅ *BP.*

$–$$ ▢ **Best Western John Jay Inn & Suites.** Antique furnishings decorate the rooms and suites at this full-service hotel. Each room has a coffeemaker, a hair dryer, an iron and ironing board, a two-line speakerphone, and a large desk with ergonomic chair. Suites have balconies, fireplaces, wet bars, and Jacuzzis. Buffet breakfast and a *USA Today* newspaper is included in your room rate. ✉ *600 W. Palmdale Blvd., 93551* ☎ *661/ 575–9322* 🖷 *661/575–9495* ⊕ *www.bwjohnjaypalmdale.com* ↩ *45 rooms, 18 suites* ⅆ *In-room data ports, microwaves, refrigerators, some in-room hot tubs, cable TV with movies, pool, gym, sauna, laundry service, business services, meeting room, no-smoking rooms* ▤ *AE, D, DC, MC, V* ⤅ *CP.*

Lancaster

❷ *8 mi north of Palmdale via Hwy. 14.*

Lancaster was founded in 1876, when the Southern Pacific Railroad arrived. Before that it was inhabited by Native American tribes: Kawarisu, Kitanemuk, Serrano, Tataviam, and Chemehuevi. Descendants of some of these tribes still live in the surrounding mountains. Points of interest around Lancaster are far from the downtown area, some in neighboring communities.

★ California's state flower, the California poppy, can be spotted just about anywhere in the state, but the densest concentration is in the **Antelope Valley Poppy Reserve.** Seven miles of trails lead you through 1,745 acres of hills carpeted with poppies and other wildflowers as far as the eye can see. Peak blooming time is usually March through May. The visitor center has books and information about the reserve and other desert areas. Many trails are wheelchair- and stroller-accessible. ✉ *Ave. I between 110th and 170th Sts. W* ☎ *661/724–1180 or 661/942–0662* ⊕ *www.calparksmojave.com* 🎟 *$2 per vehicle* ⊙ *Visitor center mid-Mar.–mid-May, weekdays 9–4, weekends 9–5.*

⟳ Thirteen species of wild cats, from the weasel-size jaguarundi to leopards, tigers, and jaguars, inhabit the **Exotic Feline Breeding Compound & Feline Conservation Center.** You can see the cats (behind barrier fences) in the parklike public zoo and research center. The center's biggest achievement has been the successful breeding of the rare Amur leopard, whose native habitat is remote border areas between Russia and China. ✉ *Off Mojave-Tropico Rd., Rosamond, 4½ mi west of Hwy. 14 via Rosamond Blvd., 10 mi north of Lancaster* ☎ *661/256–3793, 661/256–3332 for recorded information* ⊕ *www.cathouse-fcc.org* 🎫 *$3* ☉ *Thurs.–Tues. 10–4.*

Where to Stay & Eat

¢–$ ✕🛏 **Desert Inn.** Year after year this 1950s hotel remains a popular dining and lodging spot. The rooms are basic, decorated in dusty-purple tones. On the premises are the D. I. Cafe (¢–$) and the fancier Granada Room ($–$$), where you can dine on American-French dishes like breaded, baked chicken breast stuffed with cream cheese and walnuts, or beef tenderloin stuffed with a medley of shrimp, mushrooms, and Swiss cheese. The well-kept, parklike grounds are a half mile from downtown Lancaster. ✉ *44219 N. Sierra Hwy., 93534,* ☎ *661/942–8401 or 800/942–8401* 🖶 *661/942–8950* ⊕ *www.desert-inn.com* 🛌 *144 rooms* ⚭ *2 restaurants, room service, in-room data ports, refrigerator, some microwaves, cable TV, 3 pools, gym, massage, business services* 🖃 *AE, D, DC, MC, V.*

Red Rock Canyon State Park

➌ *48 mi north of Lancaster via Hwy. 14; 17 mi west of U.S. 395 via Red Rock–Randsburg Rd.*

A geological feast for the eyes with its layers of pink, white, red, and brown rock, Red Rock Canyon State Park is also a region of fascinating biological diversity—the ecosystems of the Sierra Nevada, the Mojave Desert, and the Basin Range all converge here. Entering the park from the south on Red Rock–Randsburg Road, you pass through a steep-walled gorge to a wide bowl tinted pink by volcanic ash. Native Americans known as the Old People lived here some 20,000 years ago; later, Mojave Indians roamed the land for centuries. Gold-rush fever hit the region in the mid-1800s, and you can still see remains of mining operations in the park. In the 20th century Hollywood invaded the canyon, shooting westerns, TV shows, commercials, music videos, and movies such as *Jurassic Park* here. Be sure to check out the Red Cliffs Preserve on Highway 14, across from the entrance to the Red Rock campground. ✉ *Ranger station: Abbott Dr. off Hwy. 14* ☎ *661/942–0662* ⊕ *www.calparksmojave.com/redrocks* 🎫 *$3* ☉ *Visitor center, weekends and occasional weekdays.*

Camping

⚠ **Red Rock Canyon State Park.** Open year-round, the park's campground is in the colorful cliff region of the southern El Paso Mountains, where there are lots of hiking trails. Spring and fall book quickly, so be sure to arrive early to get a spot. ⚭ *Pit toilets, drinking water, fire pits, picnic tables* 🛌 *50 sites* ✉ *Off Hwy. 14, 30 mi southwest of Ridgecrest* ☎ *661/942–0662* ⚭ *Reservations not accepted* 🎫 *$8.*

Ridgecrest

❹ *28 mi northeast of Red Rock Canyon State Park via Hwy. 14; 77 mi south of Lone Pine via U.S. 395.*

A military town that serves the U.S. Naval Weapons Center, to its north, Ridgecrest has dozens of stores, restaurants, and hotels. It is a good base for exploring the northwestern Mojave, as it's the last big city you'll hit along U.S. 395 before you enter the desert.

The **Maturango Museum,** which also serves as a visitor information center, has pamphlets and books about the region. Small but informative exhibits detail the natural and cultural history of the northern Mojave. The museum runs wildflower tours in March and April. ✉ *100 E. Las Flores Ave.* ☏ *760/375–6900* 🖷 *760/375–0479* ⊕ *www.maturango.org* 🖃 *$2* ☉ *Daily 10–5.*

Fodor'sChoice
★
Guided tours conducted by the Maturango Museum are the only way to see **Petroglyph Canyons,** among the desert's most amazing spectacles. The two canyons, commonly called Big Petroglyph and Little Petroglyph, are in the Coso Mountain range on the million-acre U.S. Naval Weapons Center at China Lake. Each of the canyons holds a superlative concentration of ancient rock art, the largest of its kind in the northern hemisphere. Thousands of well-preserved images of animals and humans—some more than 16,000 years old—are scratched or pecked into dark basaltic rocks. The tour takes you through 3 mi of sandy washes and boulders, so wear comfortable walking shoes. At an elevation of 5,000 feet weather conditions can be quite extreme, so dress in layers and bring plenty of drinking water (none is available at the site) and snacks. Children under 10 are not allowed on the tour. The military requires everyone to produce a valid driver's license, social security number, passport, and vehicle registration prior to the trip (nondrivers must provide a birth certificate). ✉ *Tours depart from Maturango Museum* ☏ *760/375–6900* ⊕ *www.maturango.org* 🖃 *$35* ☉ *Tours Mar.–June and Sept. or Oct.–early Dec.; call for tour times.*

☺
Rounded up by the Bureau of Land Management on public lands throughout the Southwest, the animals at the **Wild Horse and Burro Corrals** are available for adoption. You can bring along an apple or carrot to feed the horses, but the burros are usually too wild to approach. ✉ *Off Hwy. 178, 3 mi east of Ridgecrest* ☏ *760/384–5765 or 866/468–7826* ⊕ *www.adoptahorse.blm.gov* 🖃 *Free* ☉ *Weekdays 7–4.*

It's worth the effort (especially for sci-fi buffs, who will recognize the landscape from the film *Star Trek V*) to seek out **Trona Pinnacles National Natural Landmark.** These fantastic-looking formations of calcium carbonate, known as tufa, were formed underwater along fault lines in the bed of what is now Searles Dry Lake. A ½-mi trail winds around this surreal landscape of more than 500 spires, some of which stand as tall as 140 feet. Wear sturdy shoes—tufa cuts like coral. The best road to the area can be impassable after a rainstorm. ✉ *5 mi south of Hwy. 178, 18 mi east of Ridgecrest* ☏ *760/384–5400 Ridgecrest BLM office* ⊕ *www.ca.blm.gov/ridgecrest/trona.*

off the beaten path

FOSSIL FALLS – About 30 mi northwest of Ridgecrest via U.S. 395, a stark area of dark basalt rocks is evidence of volcanic eruptions 20,000 years ago. You'll find neither fossils nor waterfalls here, but the name given to this tumble of solidified lava is apt. A short hike to the bottom of the formation leads to a spot where Native Americans once camped. South of the falls, the Owens River cut the huge valley between the Sierra Nevada range, to the west, and the Coso range, to the east. There's a primitive campsite amid the boulders. ⊠ *Cinder Cone Rd., ½ mi east of U.S. 395.*

Where to Stay & Eat

★ $–$$ ✕ **Santa Fe Grill.** Locals say this is the best of Ridgecrest's numerous restaurants. The health-conscious menu includes New Mexico–style dishes. Hot tortillas, made on the premises, come to the table with a wonderful smoky salsa made from fire-grilled chiles. Beans (not refried) and sweet-corn cake accompany most entrées. ⊠ *901 N. Heritage Dr.* ☎ *760/446–5404* ⊟ *AE, D, MC, V.*

$$ ✕▥ **Carriage Inn.** Large and well-kept, this hotel has large and tastefully decorated rooms. You can also stay in poolside cabanas that are a bit homier. A mister cools off sunbathers during the hot summer months. Café Potpourri serves a mix of American, Italian, and Southwestern specials. Charlie's Pub & Grill serves up burgers and sandwiches, which go nicely with the custom home-brewed ale from Indian Wells Valley Brewery. ⊠ *901 N. China Lake Blvd.* ☎ *760/446–7910 or 800/ 772–8527* 🖷 *760/446–6408* ⊕ *www.carriageinn.biz* ⟿ *152 rooms, 8 suites, 2 cabanas* ♻ *2 restaurants, café, pool, gym, hot tub, sauna, bar, meeting room, in-room data ports, cable TV with video games* ⊟ *AE, D, DC, MC, V* ꜟ⊙ꜞ *MAP.*

$ ✕▥ **Heritage Inn.** This well-appointed though somewhat bland establishment is geared toward business travelers, but the staff is equally attentive to tourists' concerns. The Farris Restaurant ($–$$), with an American-casual menu, is a favorite fine-dining spot for locals. ⊠ *1050 N. Norma St.* ☎ *760/446–6543 or 800/843–0693* 🖷 *760/446–2884* ⊕ *www.greatwesternhotels.com* ⟿ *125 rooms, microwaves, refrigerators, cable TV, pool, gym, hot tub, bar, laundry facilities, business services, meeting room* ⊟ *AE, D, DC, MC, V* ꜟ⊙ꜞ *BP.*

en route

The towns of Randsburg, Red Mountain, and Johannesburg make up the **Rand Mining District** (⊠ U.S. 395, 20 mi south of Ridgecrest), which first boomed with the discovery of gold in the Rand Mountains in 1895. Rich tungsten ore, used in World War I to make steel alloy, was discovered in 1907, and silver was found in 1919. The boom has gone bust, but the area still has a few residents, a dozen antiques shops, and plenty of character. Johannesburg is overlooked by an archetypal Old West cemetery in the hills above town. Randsburg's tiny city jail is among the original buildings still standing; its White House Saloon is one of the Wild West's few surviving saloons, swinging wooden doors and all. The small **Desert Museum** (⊠ 161 Butte Ave., Randsburg ☎ No phone) exhibits mining paraphernalia and historic photos.

THE EASTERN MOJAVE

Like the western Mojave, the east has plenty of flat, open land dotted with Joshua trees and rock-strewn mountains. It also has more greenery and regular stretches of cool weather. Much of this area is uninhabited, so be cautious when driving the back roads, where towns and services are few and far between.

Victorville

❺ *87 mi south of Ridgecrest on U.S. 395. Turn east onto Bear Valley road and travel 2 mi to town center.*

At the southwest corner of the Mojave is the sprawling town of Victorville, a town rich in Route 66 heritage. Victorville was named for Santa Fe Railroad pioneer Jacob Nash Victor, who drove the first locomotive through the Cajon Pass here in 1885. Once home to Native Americans, the town later became a rest stop for Mormons and missionaries. In 1941 George Air Force Base (which now serves as an airport and storage area), brought scores of military families to the area, many of whom have stayed on to raise families of their own.

Fans of the Mother Road can visit the **California Route 66 Museum**, whose exhibits chronicle the history of America's most famous highway. At the museum you can pick up a book that details a self-guided tour of the old Sagebrush Route from Oro Grande to Helendale. The road passes Route 66 icons such as Potapov's Gas and Service Station (where the words BILL'S SERVICE are still legible) and the once-rowdy Sagebrush Inn, now a private residence. ⊠ *16825 D St. (Rte. 66)* ☎ *760/951–0436* ⊕ *www.califrt66museum.org* ☜ *Free* ☉ *Thurs.–Mon. 10–4.*

☾ The California high desert's only zoo, the small-scale **Cinema Safari** houses animals that have retired from or are still working in the entertainment industry. Among the residents are a lion, a tiger, and a baboon; performing-animal shows are sometimes held. You can visit Cinema Safari on a regularly scheduled tour or by appointment. ⊠ *19038 Willow St., Hesperia* ☎ *760/948–9430* ☜ *$6* ☉ *Tours weekends 11 and 2.*

> **off the beaten path**

WOLF MOUNTAIN SANCTUARY – Apache Indian Tonya "Littlewolf" Carloni founded this desert sanctuary in 1980. Today it is a refuge for a dozen injured or abused wolves, including the rare buffalo wolf, the white arctic tundra wolf, and the Alaskan timber wolf. The most ☾ famous resident is Apache Moon, a McKenzie timber wolf "ambassador" who visits local schools. ⊠ *7520 Fairlane St., Lucerne Valley* ☎ *760/248–7818* ⊕ *www.wolfmountain.com* ☜ *$10* ☉ *By appointment.*

Where to Stay & Eat

★ **$-$$** ✕ **Pagano's Restaurant.** Don't let the strip mall location and minimal decor at this family-owned eatery fool you; chef and owner Claudio Pagano is known throughout the desert for his fine Italian cuisine, including osso buco, cioppino, and Gamberoni champagne shrimp. ⊠ *14747 Bear*

Valley Rd. ☎ *760/948–4880* ⊗ *Closed Mon. and Tues. No lunch Wed. and Thurs. and weekends* ⊟ *AE, D, DC, MC, V.*

¢–$ ✕ **Emma Jean's Hollandburger Cafe.** This circa-1940s diner sits right on U.S. Historic Route 66 and is favored by locals for its generous portions and old-fashioned home cooking. Try the biscuits and gravy, chicken-fried steak, or the famous Trucker's Sandwich, chock-full of roast beef, bacon, chiles, and cheese. ⊠ *17143 D St.* ☎ *760/243–9938* ⊟ *AE, MC, V* ⊗ *Closed Sun. No dinner.*

$ ▦ **La Quinta Inn and Suites Victorville.** If you're looking for a clean and comfortable hotel with reasonable prices, this is a good choice. Rooms are modern, decorated in rich earth tones with floral bedspreads and cherry-color furniture. ⊠ *12000 Mariposa Rd., Hesperia 92345* ☎ *760/949–9900* ⊕ *www.lq.com* ⇄ *53 rooms, 22 suites* ⚷ *In-room data ports, microwaves, refrigerators, cable TV, pool, hot tub, gym, sauna, laundry service, business services.* ⊟ *AE, D, DC, MC, V* ⏀ *CP.*

⚠ **Mojave Narrows Regional Park.** In one of the few spots where the Mojave River flows above ground, this park has two lakes surrounded by cottonwoods and cattails. You'll find fishing, rowboat rentals, a bait shop, equestrian paths, and a wheelchair-accessible trail. The campsites cluster by the lake amid grass and trees. ⚷ *Grills, snack bar, playground, flush toilets, full hookups, dump station, drinking water, showers, fire pits, picnic tables, electricity, public telephone* ⇄ *87 sites, 37 with hookups* ⊠ *18000 Yates Rd.* ☎ *760/245–2226* ⊕ *www.co.san-bernardino.ca.us/parks/mojave.htm* ▤ *$10–$17 camping, $3 day use.*

---

en route   Along National Trails Highway in Helendale, about halfway between Victorville and Barstow, 1950s burlesque beauty Dixie Evans runs the entertaining and bawdy **Exotic World Burlesque Museum** (⊠ 29053 Wild Rd. ☎ 760/243–5261 ⊕ www.exoticworldusa.org ▤ Donation ⊗ Tues.–Sun. 10–4). The place is filled with naughty burlesque costumes, jewelry, and photos dating from the 19th century. In June the museum hosts the annual Exotic World Contest, which draws bodacious women from around the globe.

Barstow

❻   *32 mi northeast of Victorville on I–15.*

In 1886, when a subsidiary of the Atchison, Topeka, and Santa Fe Railway began construction of a depot and hotel here, Barstow was born. Today outlet stores, chain restaurants, and motels define the landscape, though old-time neon signs light up the town's main street.

The **California Welcome Center** has exhibits about desert ecology, wildflowers, and wildlife, as well as general visitor information for the state of California. ⊠ *2796 Tanger Way* ☎ *760/253–4782* ⊕ *www. visitmojavedesert.com/welcomecenter* ⊗ *Daily 9–6.*

The earliest-known Americans fashioned the artifacts buried in the walls and floors of the pits at **Calico Early Man Archaeological Site.** Nearly 12,000 stone tools—used for scraping, cutting, and gouging—have been excavated here. The apparent age of some of these items (said to be as much as 200,000 years old) contradicts the dominant archaeological theory that humans populated North America only 13,000 years ago. Noted archaeologist Louis Leakey was so impressed with the Calico site that he became its director in 1963 and served in that capacity until his death in 1972. His old camp is now a visitor center and museum. The only way into the site itself is by guided tour (call ahead, as scheduled tours sometimes don't take place). ⊠ *Off I-15, Minneola Rd. exit, 15 mi northeast of Barstow* ☎ *760/254-2248* 🖃 *Donation requested* ⊙ *Visitor center Wed. 12:30–4:30, Thurs.–Sun. 9–4:30; tours Wed. 1:30 and 3:30, Thurs.–Sun. 9:30, 11:30, 1:30, and 3:30.*

Ⓒ **Calico Ghost Town** was once a wild and wealthy mining town. In 1881

Fodor's Choice prospectors found a rich deposit of silver in the area, and by 1886 more

★ than $85 million worth of silver, gold, and other precious metals had been harvested from the surrounding hills. Once the price of silver fell, though, the town slipped into decline. Many buildings here are authentic, but the restoration has created a theme-park version of the 1880s. You can stroll the wooden sidewalks of Main Street, browse shops filled with western goods, roam the tunnels of Maggie's Mine, and take a ride on the Calico-Odessa Railroad. Festivals in March, May, October, and November celebrate Calico's Wild West theme. ⊠ *Ghost Town Rd., 3 mi north of I-15, 5 mi east of Barstow* ☎ *760/254-2122* ⊕ *www. calicotown.com* 🖃 *$6* ⊙ *Daily 9–5.*

A Spanish-named spot meaning "house of the desert," the **Casa Del Desierto Harvey House** was one of many hotel and restaurant depots opened by Santa Fe railroad guru Fred Harvey in the early 20th century. The location where Judy Garland's film *The Harvey Girls* was shot, the building is now completely restored. Inside Casa Del Desierto is the Route 66 Mother Road Museum and Gift Shop. ⊠ *681 N. 1st Ave.* ☎ *760/ 255-1890* ⊕ *barstow66museum.itgo.com* 🖃 *Free* ⊙ *Fri.–Sun. 11–4. Guided tours by appointment.*

Ⓒ Stop by the **Desert Discovery Center** to see exhibits of fossils, plants, and local animals. The main attraction here is Old Woman, the second-largest iron meteorite ever found in the United States. It was discovered in 1976 about 50 mi from Barstow in the Old Woman Mountains. The center also has visitor information for the Mojave Desert. ⊠ *831 Barstow Rd.* ☎ *760/ 252-6060* ⊕ *www.discoverytrails.org* 🖃 *Free* ⊙ *Tues.–Sat. 11–4.*

One of the world's largest natural Native American art galleries, **Inscription Canyon,** north of Barstow in the Black Mountains, has nearly 10,000 petroglyphs and pictographs of bighorn sheep and other Mojave wildlife. ⊠ *EF373, off Copper City Rd., 10 mi west of Fort Irwin Rd.* ☎ *760/ 252-6000.*

★ So many science-fiction movies set on Mars have been filmed at **Rainbow Basin National Natural Landmark,** 8 mi north of Barstow, that you may feel like you're visiting the red planet. Huge slabs of red, orange, white, and green stone tilt at crazy angles like ships about to capsize; hike the washes, and you'll likely see the fossilized remains of creatures (like mastodons and dog-bears) that roamed the basin up to 16 million years ago. You can camp here, at Owl Canyon Campground, on the east side of Rainbow Basin. Part of the drive to the basin is on dirt roads. ⊠ *Fossil Bed Rd., 3 mi west of Fort Irwin Rd.* ☎ *760/252–6000* ⊕ *www.ca.blm.gov/barstow/basin.html.*

🔄 If you're a railroad buff, then you'll love the **Western American Rail Museum.** It houses memorabilia from Barstow's early railroad days, as well as interactive and historical displays on railroad history. Be sure to check out the old locomotives and cabooses for a truly nostalgic experience. ⊠ *685 N. 1st St.* ☎ *760/256–9276* ⊕ *www.barstowrailmuseum. org* ☉ *Fri.–Sun. 11–4.*

Where to Stay & Eat

★ **$–$$$** ✕ **Idle Spurs Steakhouse.** Since the 1950s this roadside ranch has been a Barstow dining staple. Covered in cacti outside and Christmas lights inside, it's a colorful, cheerful place with a big wooden bar. The menu features prime cuts of meat, ribs, and lobster, and there's a great microbrew list. ⊠ *690 Hwy. 58* ☎ *760/256–8888* 🖃 *AE, D, MC, V.*

★ **¢–$** ✕ **Bagdad Café.** Tourists from all over the world flock to the site where the 1988 film of the same name was shot. Built in the 1940s, this Route 66 eatery serves up a home-style menu of burgers, chicken-fried steak, and seafood. An old Airstream trailer from the movie sits outside the café. ⊠ *46548 National Trails Hwy., Newberry Springs* ☎ *760/257–3101* 🖃 *AE, MC, V.*

¢ 🏨 **Ramada Inn.** Though this large property is slightly more expensive than others lining Main Street, it also has more amenities (which is why it tends to attract comfort-loving business travelers). The modern rooms have a desert theme and are decorated in browns and pinks that evoke the surrounding landscape. ⊠ *1511 E. Main St.* ☎ *760/256–5673* 🖨 *760/256–5917* ⊕ *www.ramada.com* 📑 *148 rooms* ⚭ *Restaurant, room service, in-room data ports, cable TV with movies, pool, hot tub, laundry service, meeting room, some pets allowed (fee), no-smoking rooms* 🖃 *AE, D, DC, MC, V.*

🏕 **Calico Ghost Town Regional Park.** This dusty, flat campsite with views of the ghost town provides an authentic Wild West atmosphere. In addition to the campsites, you have six cabins ($28) and bunkhouse accommodations ($5 per person, with a 12-person minimum) to choose from. There is a two-night minimum during Calico Ghost Town festival weekends. ⚭ *Restaurant, grills, flush toilets, full hookups, partial hookups, dump station, drinking water, showers, fire pits, picnic tables, electricity, public telephone, general store* 📑 *250 sites, 104 with hookups* ⊠ *Ghost Town Rd., 3 mi north of I–15, 5 mi east of Barstow* ☎ *760/254–2122 or 800/862–2542* ⊕ *www.calicotown.com* 💲 *$18–$22* 🖃 *D, MC, V.*

en route Because of its colorful, steep walls, **Afton Canyon** (⊠ Off Afton Canyon Rd., 36 mi northeast of Barstow via I–15) is often called the Grand Canyon of the Mojave. It was carved over thousands of years by the rushing waters of the Mojave River, which makes one of its few aboveground appearances here. Where you find water in the desert you'll also find trees, grasses, and wildlife, so the canyon has attracted people for a long time: Native Americans and, later, settlers following the Mojave Trail from the Colorado River to the Pacific Ocean set up camp here. Now you can, too, at a 22-site campground amid high-desert cliffs and a mesquite thicket. The dirt road that leads to the canyon is ungraded in spots, so you are best off driving it in an all-terrain vehicle. Check with the **Mojave Desert Information Center** (☎ 760/733–4040 ⊕ www.nps.gov/moja), in Baker, regarding road conditions before you head in.

Baker

❼ *63 mi northeast of Barstow on I–15; 84 mi south of Death Valley Junction via Hwy. 127.*

The small town of Baker is Death Valley's gateway to the western Mojave. There are several gas stations and restaurants (most of them fast-food outlets), a few motels, and one general store, which has the distinction of selling the most winning Lotto tickets in California.

You can't help but notice Baker's 134-foot-tall **thermometer** (✉ 72157 Baker Blvd.), whose height in feet pays homage to the record-high U.S. temperature: 134°F, recorded in Death Valley on July 10, 1913. The Baker thermometer marks the location of the National Park Service's **Mojave Desert Information Center** (☎ 760/733–4040 ⊕ www.nps.gov/moja ⊙ 9–5 daily), where you can browse the bookstore, pick up maps, and buy souvenir posters and postcards. The center also has visitor information for Mojave National Preserve, Death Valley, and other Mojave attractions.

Where to Stay & Eat

¢–$ ✕ **The Mad Greek.** This whimsical, over-the-top place somehow manages to fuse the cultures of ancient Athens, Los Angeles, and the Mojave Desert. Deep-blue ceramic tiles adorn the walls, and neoclassical statues pose amid the tables. The food ranges from traditional Greek (gyros, kebabs, strong coffee) to classic American (hot dogs and ice cream sundaes). ✉ *72112 Baker Blvd., at I–15* ☎ *760/733–4354* ▤ *AE, D, DC, MC, V.*

¢ ▦ **Wills Fargo Motel.** Two of Baker's three motels have the same owner and are just down the road from each other, so there's little difference in their rates or amenities. This one, however, has rooms with marginally more character, as well as a pool and a small lawn out front. ✉ *72252 Baker Blvd., 92309* ☎ *760/733–4477* 🖷 *760/733–4680* 🛏 *30 rooms* ⌂ *Cable TV, pool* ▤ *AE, D, DC, MC, V.*

Primm, NV

❽ *52 mi northeast of Baker, via I–15; 118 mi east of Death Valley, via Hwy. 160 and I–15; 114 mi north of Barstow, via I–15.*

Amid the rugged beauty of the Mojave's landscapes, this bustling mecca for gamblers and theme-park lovers has sprung up on the border between California and southern Nevada. The casino resorts here are the first to greet you on the lonely stretch of road connecting Los Angeles with Las Vegas—and increasingly, visitors are simply stopping and spending their gambling vacations here.

One of Primm's greatest claims to fame is its 24-hour **Bonnie and Clyde Gangster Exhibit.** Here, you'll find the bullet-riddled Ford car in which the 1930s duo perished in a hailstorm of gunfire in Louisiana on May

3, 1934. There's also other Bonnie and Clyde memorabilia, such as newspaper clippings and items owned by the couple, and a restored 1931 armored Lincoln belonging to gangsters Al Capone and Dutch Schultz. The exhibits are free to view in the rotunda connecting Primm Valley Resort and Casino with the Fashion Outlet Mall. ⊠ *32100 Las Vegas Blvd. S* ☎ *702/874–1400 Ext. 7073, 888/424–6898 for Fashion Outlet Mall* ⊕ *www.fashionoutletlasvegas.com.*

Though there are plenty of family-friendly activities in Primm (like shopping at the mall, hitting the water slide at Whiskey Pete's or the amusement park at Buffalo Bill's), guests under 21 are not allowed on the casino floors, and children under 13 may not be left unattended. Each of the casinos has a video arcade, which may provide some solace for the teenage set.

Where to Stay & Eat

¢–$$ ✗▥ **Buffalo Bill's Resort and Casino.** Decorated in the style of a Western frontier town, this hotel is the biggest and most popular in Primm. Its buffalo-shape swimming pool and a large amusement park—which features several roller coasters and other rides—makes the property a hit with families. The casino itself is enormous (46,000 square feet), and rooms here are bright and cheery and decorated with lodge-style furniture. Among the resort's several restaurants, Batelli's Italiano Restaurante and Oyster Bar ($–$$$) is a favorite; chef Fernando Batelli serves up his signature cioppino (a hearty seafood stew) and other Italian favorites with brio. ⊠ *31700 Las Vegas Blvd. S, 89019* ☎ *702/386–7867 or 800/386–7867* ⊕ *www.primmvalleyresorts.com* ⊅ *1,193 rooms, 49 suites* ⚫ *8 restaurants, coffee shop, food court, ice-cream parlor, pizzeria, some in-room hot tubs, some kitchenettes, some minibars, some refrigerators, cable TV with movie, pool, outdoor hot tub, 2 bars, lounge, casino, showroom, video game room, shop, concierge, no-smoking rooms* ▭ *AE, D, DC, MC, V.*

¢–$$ ✗▥ **Primm Valley Resort and Casino.** This elegant resort, which evokes a 1930s country club, is conveniently located near the Primm Valley Conference Center. Rooms are decorated in warm tones, with dark-wood furniture. If you feel like splurging, check into one of the 640-square-foot Jacuzzi suites. GP's ($–$$$), one of the on-site restaurants is the fanciest in town, and popular for its aged prime rib and veal cordon bleu. ⊠ *31900 Las Vegas Blvd. S, 89019* ☎ *702/386–7867 or 800/386–7867* ⊕ *www.primmvalleyresorts.com* ⊅ *592 rooms, 31 suites* ⚫ *3 restaurants, café, food court, ice-cream parlor, pizzeria, snack bar, room service, some in-room hot tubs, some kitchenettes, some minibars, some refrigerators, cable TV with movies, pool, outdoor hot tub, 2 bars, piano bar, casino, video game room, shops, Internet, convention center, meeting rooms, no-smoking rooms.* ▭ *AE, D, DC, MC, V.*

¢–$$ ✗▥ **Whiskey Pete's Hotel and Casino.** Opened in 1977, this castle-inspired property is the oldest of the three casinos in Primm. Rooms are decorated in mahogany and have Spanish tile floors; each of the 725-square-foot Jacuzzi suites has a four-person hot tub in the living room and a full bar. If you're visiting in summer, the tropical-theme pool with its shade trees and waterslide, is a cool retreat. The Silver Spur

Steakhouse ($–$$) serves excellent prime rib and chateaubriand. ⊠ *100 W. Primm Blvd., 89019* ☎ *702/386–7867 or 800/386–7867* ⊕ *www.primmvalleyresorts.com* ⤳ *765 rooms, 12 suites* ⌂ *4 restaurants, coffee shop, room service, some in-room hot tubs, some kitchenettes, some minibars, some microwaves, some refrigerators, cable TV with movies, pool, gym, outdoor hot tub, 2 bars, casino, comedy club, showroom, video game room, shops, no-smoking rooms* ⊟ *AE, D, DC, MC, V.*

Mojave National Preserve

❾ *Between I–15 and I–40, roughly east of Baker and Ludlow to the California/Nevada border.*

The 1.4 million acres of the Mojave National Preserve hold a surprising abundance of plant and animal life—especially considering their elevation (nearly 8,000 feet in some areas). There are traces of human history here as well, including abandoned army posts and vestiges of mining and ranching towns. The town of Cima still has a small functioning store.

Created millions of years ago by volcanic activity, **Hole in the Wall** formed when gases were trapped between layers of deposited ash, rock, and lava; the gas bubbles left holes in the solidified material. The area was named by Bob Hollimon, a member of the Butch Cassidy gang, because it reminded him of his former hideout in Wyoming. To hike the canyon, you first must make your way down Rings Trail, a narrow 200-foot vertical chute. To make the rather strenuous descent you must grasp a series of metal rings embedded in the rock. The trail drops you into Banshee Canyon, where you are surrounded by steep, pock-marked walls and small caverns. You can explore the length of the canyon, but climbing the walls is not recommended, as the rock is soft and crumbles easily. Keep your eyes open for native lizards such as the chuckwalla. The Hole in the Wall ranger station has docents that can answer questions about the area. ⊠ *Black Canyon Rd., 9 mi north of Mitchell Caverns* ☎ *760/255–8801, 769/928–2572, or 760/733–4040* ⊕ *www.nps.gov/ moja* ☉ *Weekends 10–2.*

As you enter the preserve from the south, you'll pass miles of open scrub brush, Joshua trees, and beautiful red-black cinder cones before encountering the **Kelso Dunes** (⊠ Kelbaker Rd., 90 mi east of I–15 and 14 mi north of I–40 ☎ 760/255–8801 or 760/733–4040 ⊕ www.nps.gov/moja). These perfect, pristine slopes of gold-white sand cover 70 square mi, often reaching heights of 500–600 feet. You can reach them via a ½-mi walk from the main parking area. When you reach the top of a dune, kick a little bit of sand down the lee side and listen to the sand "sing." North of the dunes in the town of Kelso, a Mission Revival–style train depot dating from 1925 is one of the few of its kind still standing. Primitive campsites are available at no charge near the dunes' main parking area.

The National Park Service administers most of the Mojave preserve, but **Providence Mountains State Recreation Area** is under the jurisdiction of the California Department of Parks. The visitor center has views of mountain peaks, dunes, buttes, crags, and desert valleys. At **Mitchell**

Caverns Natural Preserve (✉ $4) you have a rare opportunity to see all three types of cave formations—dripstone, flowstone, and erratics—in one place. The year-round 65°F temperature provides a break from the desert heat. Tours are given weekdays at 1:30 and weekends at 10, 1:30, and 3. Arrive a half- hour before tour time to secure a spot. Between late May and early September, tours are given only on weekends and holidays, at 1:30. ⊠ *Essex Rd., 16 mi north of I–40* ☎ *760/928–2586* ⊕ *www.calparksmojave.com* ⊙ *Visitor center May–Sept., Fri. and Sat. 9–4.*

off the beaten path

AMBOY – South of Mojave National Preserve, about midway between Barstow and Needles, lies tiny Amboy, a privately owned desert town. Here 250-foot-high Amboy Crater, an 8,000-year-old volcanic cinder cone, is surrounded by a lava field. In winter experienced hikers can take the marked trail to the top and back, a round-trip trek of about three hours. While you're in Amboy, don't miss **Roy's Cafe, Gas and Motel** (⊠ 6666 Old National Trails Hwy. ☎ 760/733–4263 ⊕ www.rt66roys.com), which founder Buster Burris called "the crustiest, dustiest gas stop in all of Route 66." Built in 1938, the joint is preserved in its original condition. The restaurant serves greasy-spoon grub such as burgers, homemade chili, and tart home-style lemonade. ⊠ *Old National Trails Hwy., 28 mi east of Ludlow and 47 mi west of Fenner.*

Camping

⚠ **Hole-in-the-Wall Campground.** At a cool 4,500 feet above sea level, backed by volcanic rock formations, this is a fine place to spend a quiet night and use as a base for hiking. The campground is near the Hole in the Wall ranger station. ⌂ *Pit toilets, dump station, drinking water, fire pits, picnic tables* ↪ *35 RV/trailer sites, 2 walk-in tent sites* ⊠ *Black Canyon Rd. north of Essex* ☎ *760/255–8801 or 760/733–4040* ⊕ *www.nps.gov/moja* ⊟ *No credit cards* ⌂ *Reservations not accepted* ✉ *$12.*

Needles

❿ *I–40, 150 mi east of Barstow.*

On Route 66 and the Colorado River, Needles is a good base for exploring many desert attractions, including Mojave National Preserve. Founded in 1883, the town of Needles, named for the jagged mountain peaks that overlook the city, served as a stop along Santa Fe Railroad. One of its crown jewels was the elegant El Garces Harvey House Train Depot, which is currently being restored. Today, Needles is a thriving community and a popular getaway for California residents who want to enjoy the river a little closer to home.

Don't miss the historic 1908 **El Garces Harvey House Train Depot** (⊠ 900 Front St. ☎ 760/326–5678), one of the many restaurant–boarding houses built by the Fred Harvey company. Renovations on the property will keep it closed to tours until mid-2005, but the exterior architecture is still worth a look. **Mystic Maze** (⊠ Park Moabi Rd., off I–40

11 mi southeast of Needles ☎ 760/326–5678) is an unexplained geological site of spiritual significance to Pipa Aha Macav (Fort Mojave) Indians. The maze consists of several rows of rocks and mounds of dirt in different patterns.

In 1941, after the construction of Parker Dam, President Franklin D. Roosevelt set aside **Havasu National Wildlife Refuge,** a 24-mi stretch of land along the Colorado River between Needles and Lake Havasu City. Best seen by boat, this beautiful waterway is punctuated with isolated coves, sandy beaches, and Topock Marsh, a favorite nesting site of herons, egrets, and other water birds. You can see wonderful petroglyphs on the rocky red canyon cliffs of Topock Gorge. The park has 11 access points, including boat launches at Catfish Paradise, Five Mile Landing, and Pintail Slough. There is camping below Castle Rock. ⊠ *3 mi southeast of Needles off I–40* ☎ *760/326–3853* ⊕ *http://southwest.fws. gov/refuges/arizona/havasu.*

Moabi Regional Park, on the banks of the Colorado River, is a good place for swimming, boating, picnicking, horseback riding, and fishing. Bass, bluegill, and trout are plentiful in the river. There are 600 campsites with full amenities, including RV hookups, laundry and showers, and grills. ⊠ *11 mi southeast of Needles on Park Moabi Rd.* ☎ *760/326–3831* ⊕ *www.moabi.com* ☞ *$6 day use, $12–$20 camping.*

Where to Stay & Eat

¢–$$ ✕ **Hungry Bear Restaurant.** If you've got a big appetite, head to this family diner for chicken-fried steak or top sirloin. You can also get breakfast. ⊠ *1906 Needles Hwy.* ☎ *760/326–2988* ⊟ *AE, DC, MC, V.*

¢–$$ ▦ **Best Western Colorado River Inn.** Each room at this property off I–40 has a hair dryer; deluxe rooms also have coffeemakers. Local phone calls are free, and there is complimentary coffee in the lobby every morning. The country-Western style rooms are spartan, but decorated in rich colors. ⊠ *2371 Needles Hwy., 92363* ☎ *760/326–4552 or 800/780–7234* ┗ *760/326–4562* ⊕ *www.bestwestern.com* ☞ *63 rooms* ♂ *In-room data ports, some microwaves, some refrigerators, cable TV with movies, indoor pool, hot tub, sauna, laundry facilities, some pets allowed, no-smoking rooms* ⊟ *AE, DC, MC, V.*

△ **Needles Marina Park.** This luxury campground sits along the glassy waters of the Colorado River and is just a 30-minute boat ride from Topock Gorge or a 1½-hour ride from London Bridge on Lake Havasu. A recreation room, Jacuzzi, and 18-hole golf course are at your disposal. The resort has its own boat ramp and slips. ♂ *Grills, pool, playground, laundry facilities, flush toilets, full hookups, drinking water, showers, picnic tables, electricity, public telephone, general store* ☞ *194 sites with hookups* ⊠ *River Rd. off Broadway* ☎ *760/326–2197* ⊕ *www. needlesmarina.com* ⊟ *MC, V* ☞ *$28–$30.*

Lake Havasu City, AZ

⓫ *Hwy. 95, 43 mi southeast of Needles in Arizona.*

In summer Los Angelenos throng Lake Havasu for wet-and-wild fun. This wide spot in the Colorado River, which has backed up behind Parker

Dam, is accessed from its eastern shore in Arizona. Here you can swim; zip around on a Jet Ski; paddle a kayak; fish for trout, bass, or bluegill; or boat beneath the London Bridge, one of the desert's oddest sights. During sunset the views are breathtaking.

★ ☾ Once home to the Mohave Indians, this riverfront community (which means blue water) was settled in the 1930s with the construction of Parker Dam. But what really put this town on the map was the piece-by-piece reconstruction in 1971 of **London Bridge.** by town founder Robert P. Mc-Culloch. Today the circa-1831 bridge, designed by John Rennie, connects the city to a small island, and is the center of a town including numerous restaurants, hotels, RV parks, and a reconstructed English village. ☎ *928/855–4115* ⊕ *www.havasuchamber.com* ✉ *Free* ☉ *Daily 24 hrs.*

Where to Stay & Eat

★ **$-$$$** ╳ **Shugrue's.** This lakefront restaurant, a favorite of locals and tourists, serves up beautiful views of London Bridge and the English Village. Heavy on fresh seafood, steak, and lobster, the restaurant is also known for such specials as Bombay chicken and shrimp, served with spicy yogurt sauce and mango chutney. ✉ *1425 McCulloch Blvd.* ☎ *928/453–1400* ⊕ *www.shugrueslhc.com* ☰ *AE, D, DC, V.*

★ **$-$$$$** ╳▣ **Nautical Inn Resort and Conference Center.** This riverfront property, completely remodeled in 2002, has views of Lake Havasu and the nearby mountain ranges. The modern water-view rooms all have oversized patios or balconies. You can rent water-sports equipment, and dock your boat outside the hotel. There's an 18-hole golf course next door, and the hotel arranges golf packages with three other local courses. You can dine on the waterfront at Captain's Table ($-$$), which serves up such American fare as London broil and grilled halibut, or enjoy a drink at sunset at the Naked Turtle Beach Bar. ✉ *1000 McCullough Blvd.,* *86403* ☎ *928/855–2141 or 800/892–2141* ⊕ *www.nauticalinn.com* ⇗ *76 rooms, 63 suites* ⌂ *Restaurant, some kitchenettes, refrigerators, microwaves, cable TV, pool, lake, hot tub, beach, dock, boating, jet skiing, marina, parasailing, fishing, hiking, bar, shop, laundry services, meeting rooms* ☰ *AE, D, MC, V.*

Nightlife

One of the hottest dance clubs on Lake Havasu is **Kokomo's on the Channel** (✉ 1477 Queen's Bay ☎ 928/855–0888 ☉ Mar.–Oct., daily 11–1), an island-theme watering hole with a full selection of drinks and a killer view of the river.

Sports & the Outdoors

☾ Docked at the London Bridge, **The Dixie Bell** (☎ 928/453–6776 ✉ $13) offers a leisurely way to spend an afternoon. The two-story, old-fashioned paddle-wheel boat, with air-conditioning and a cocktail lounge, takes guests on a one-hour narrated tour around the island. Tours are given daily at 11:30, 1, and 2:30. **London Bridge Watercraft Tours & Rentals** (✉ 141 Swanson Ave. ☎ 928/453–8883 ⊕ www.havasuwatercraftrentals. com) is the place to rent a personal watercraft such as Jet Skis and Sea Doos for a day or to join a 50-mi personal-watercraft adventure through Topock Gorge.

DEATH VALLEY

Anglo-Americans first learned of the existence of Death Valley in 1849, when wayward travelers looking for a shortcut to the California goldfields stumbled into the area and were temporarily stranded. By 1873 borax, the so-called white gold of the desert, was found in the valley, and 20-mule teams hauled borax out from 1883 to 1889.

The topography of Death Valley is a geology lesson in itself. Some 200 million years ago, seas covered the area, depositing layers of sediment and fossils. Between 35 million and 5 million years ago, faults in the earth's crust and volcanic activity pushed and folded the ground, causing mountain ranges to rise and the valley floor to drop. The valley was then filled periodically by lakes, which eroded the surrounding rocks into fantastic formations and deposited the salts that now cover the floor of the basin. The area has 14 square mi of sand dunes, 200 square mi of crusty salt flats, and hills, mountains, and canyons of many colors. If you have a four-wheel-drive vehicle, bring it—many of Death Valley's most spectacular canyons are only reachable in a 4x4.

The desert appears quite barren most of the year, but if you visit in April or May expect a wonderful treat. More than 1,000 species of plants and trees thrive here, 21 of which (including the yellow Panamint daisy and the blue-flowered Death Valley sage) are unique to the valley. Many annual plants lie dormant as seeds for all but a few months of the year, when spring rains trigger a bloom. At higher elevations you will find piñon, juniper, and bristlecone pine. Wildlife such as bighorn sheep spend most of their time in rugged, secluded canyons and upper ridges. You may see coyotes lazing in the shade at lower elevations, and the smaller desert fox is a regular sight among the sand dunes.

Shoshone

⑫ *Hwy. 127, 202 mi north of Ridgecrest, via U.S. 395, Rte. 58, and I–15.*

Unincorporated Shoshone started as a mining town where prospectors lived in small caves dynamited out of the rock. Today, Shoshone is a popular stop on the way in to Death Valley National Park. The area, dotted with tamarisk trees and date palms, is home to a natural warm springs pool fed by an underwater river. It is named for the Shoshone Indians who once lived here.

Visit the **Shoshone Museum** to see a complete woolly mammoth skeleton that was excavated nearby. The museum also houses antiques, minerals, and other items related to the history of Death Valley. ✉ *Hwy. 127* ☎ *760/852–4524* ⊕ *www.shoshonevillage.com* ✆ *Free* ☉ *Daily 8–4.*

Where to Stay & Eat

$–$$ ✕ **Crowbar Café & Saloon.** Housed in an old wooden building where antique photos adorn the walls and mining equipment stands in the corners, the Crowbar serves enormous helpings of regional dishes like steak and taco salads. Home-baked fruit pies make fine desserts, and

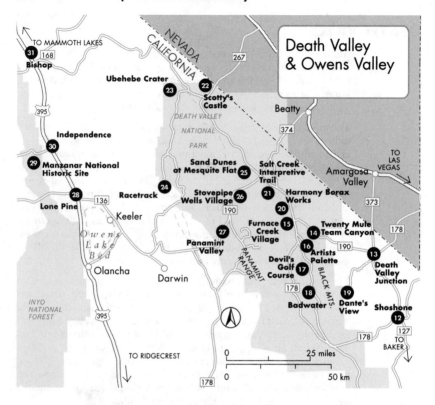

frosty beers are surefire thirst quenchers. ⊠ *Hwy. 127* ☎ *760/852–4180* ⊟ *AE, D, MC, V.*

¢–$ 🏨 **Shoshone Inn.** Built in 1956, the rustic Shoshone Inn is the only motel in town. Rooms are simple and bright with Southwest accents, but the big draw here is the warm spring-fed swimming pool built into the foothills. A market, café, gas station, and museum are all within walking distance. ⊠ *Hwy. 127* ✆ *Box 67, 92384* ☎ *760/852–4335* 🖷 *760/852–4250* ⊕ *www.shoshonevillage.com* ⇆ *16 rooms* ⌂ *Some kitchenettes, cable TV, laundry facilities, some pets allowed; no a/c, no smoking* ⊟ *AE, D, MC, V.*

Death Valley Junction

⑬ *30 mi north of Shosone on Hwy. 127.*

With the exception of the opera house and hotel, Death Valley Junction has little to offer, but it is a fine place to stop and stretch your legs. There are no services here.

Marta Becket's Amargosa Opera House is an unexpected novelty in the desert. An artist and dancer from New York, Becket first visited the former railway town of Amargosa while on tour in 1964. Three years later she returned to town and bought a boarded-up theater that sat amid a group of run-down mock–Spanish colonial buildings. To compensate for the sparse audiences in the early days, Becket painted a Renaissance-era Spanish crowd on the walls and ceiling, turning the theater into a trompe l'oeil masterpiece. Now in her late 70s, Becket performs her blend of ballet, mime, and 19th-century melodrama to sellout crowds. After the show you can meet her in the adjacent gallery, where she sells her paintings and autographs her books. There are no performances May through September. ⊠ *Hwy. 127* ☎ *760/852–4441* 🖷 *760/852–4138* ⊕ *www.amargosa-opera-house.com* 🎟 *$15* ⊗ *Oct.–mid-May, Sat. 8:15.*

Where to Stay

¢ 🏨 **Opera House Hotel.** The Pacific Coast Borax Company built this hotel in 1923 to serve railroad passengers. Listed on the National Register of Historic Places, it has rooms with one or two double beds, furnished with antiques and adorned with murals. It's nothing fancy, but if you are planning a winter visit, make your reservations at least two months in advance. ⊠ *Hwy. 127* ☎ *760/852–4441* 🖷 *760/852–4138* ⊕ *www.amargosa-opera-house.com* 🛏 *14 rooms* ⚄ *No room phones, no room TVs* 🖃 *AE, MC, V.*

Death Valley National Park

⚑ *105 mi west of Lone Pine on Hwys. 136 and 190 (to Furnace Creek).*

Fodor's Choice
★
With more than 3.3 million acres (5,200 square mi), Death Valley National Park is America's largest national park outside Alaska. The Panamint Range parallels Death Valley to the west; the Amargosa Range, to the east. Minerals and ores in the rock here have tinted the mountains and canyons all shades of green, yellow, brown, white, and black. Of course, Death Valley is hot: the park's record high temperature (and the record high for the entire United States), recorded in 1913, was 134°F. Seeing nature at its most extreme is precisely what attracts many people; there are more visitors to Death Valley in July and August than in December and January. Despite its popularity, Death Valley is still an empty and lonely place. Although some sights appear in clusters, others require extensive travel. The 54-mi trip from Furnace Creek to Scotty's Castle, for example, can take two hours or more.

The park entrance fee is $10 per vehicle and $5 for those entering on foot, bus, bike, or motorcycle. Admission, valid for seven consecutive days, is collected at the park's entrance stations and at the visitor center at Furnace Creek. 🗐 *Box 579, Death Valley 92328* ☎ *760/786–3200* 🖷 *760/786–3283* ⊕ *www.nps.gov/deva.*

⓮ A drive in colorful **Twenty Mule Team Canyon** delivers quite a few thrills. The canyon was named for the 20-mule teams, who between 1883 and 1889 carried 10-ton loads of borax through the burning desert. At places along the loop road off Highway 190 the soft rock walls reach high on both sides, making it seem like you're on an amusement-park ride. Remains of prospectors' tunnels are visible here, along with some brilliant rock formations. You can park and walk in places. ⊠ *20 Mule Team Rd. off Hwy. 190, 4 mi south of Furnace Creek, 20 mi west of Death Valley Junction* ⚒ *Trailers not permitted.*

⑮ Furnace Creek Village is a center of activity amid the sprawling quiet of Death Valley. Covered with tropical landscaping, it has jogging and bicycle paths, golf, tennis, a general store, and—rare for these parts—a few different dining options. The exhibits and artifacts at **Death Valley Visitors Center** (☎ 760/786–2331 ⊕ www.nps.gov/deva) provide a broad overview of how Death Valley formed; you can pick up maps at the bookstore run by the Death Valley Natural History Association. Furnace Creek Ranch conducts guided horseback, carriage, and hayrides that traverse trails with views of the surrounding mountains, where multicolor volcanic rock and alluvial fans make a dramatic backdrop for date palms and other vegetation. ⊠ *4 mi north of 20 Mule Team Canyon on Hwy. 190, 54 mi south of Scotty's Castle, 25 mi southeast of Stovepipe Wells Village on Hwy. 190.*

★ **⑯ Artists Palette,** so called for the brilliant colors of its volcanic deposits, is one of the most magnificent sights in Death Valley. Artists Drive, the approach to the area, is one-way heading north off Badwater Road, so if you're visiting Badwater, it saves time to come here on the way back. The drive winds through foothills of sedimentary and volcanic rocks. Within the palette, the huge expanses of Death Valley are replaced by intimate, small-scale natural beauty. It's a quiet, lonely drive. ⊠ *11 mi south of Furnace Creek off Badwater Rd.*

⑰ At **Devil's Golf Course** thousands of miniature salt pinnacles carved into surreal shapes by the desert wind dot the landscape. The salt was pushed up to the earth's surface by pressure created as underground salt- and water-bearing gravel crystallized. In some spots, perfectly round holes descend into the ground (hence the name of this site). Nothing grows in this barren landscape. ⊠ *Badwater Rd., 13 mi south of Furnace Creek. Turn right onto dirt road and drive 1 mi.*

⑱ Reaching **Badwater,** you'll see a shallow pool containing mostly sodium chloride—the pool is saltier than the sea—in an expanse of desolate salt flats. It's a sharp contrast to the expansive canyons and elevations nearby. At 282 feet below sea level, Badwater is the lowest spot on land in the western hemisphere—and also one of the hottest. The legend of its name is that an early surveyor noticed his mule wouldn't drink from the pool and wrote "badwater" on his map. ⊠ *Badwater Rd., 19 mi south of Furnace Creek.*

★ **⑲ Dante's View** is more than 5,000 feet up in the Black Mountains. In the dry desert air you can see across most of 110-mi-wide Death Valley. The view is astounding: you can see the highest and lowest spots in the contiguous United States from the same vantage point. The tiny blackish patch far below is Badwater, at 282 feet below sea level; on the western horizon is Mt. Whitney, which rises to 14,496 feet. It's one of the most extraordinary sights anywhere in California. ⊠ *Dante's View Rd. off Hwy. 190, 35 mi from Badwater, 20 mi south of 20 Mule Team Canyon.*

⑳ From the **Harmony Borax Works,** Death Valley's mule teams hauled borax to the railroad town of Mojave, 165 mi away. The teams plied the route until 1889, when the railroad finally arrived in Zabriskie. Constructed in 1883, one of the oldest buildings in Death Valley houses the **Borax Museum** (⊠ Hwy. 190, 2 mi south of the borax works 🖭 Free). Originally a miners' bunkhouse, the building once stood in Twenty Mule Team Canyon. Now it displays mining machinery and historical exhibits. The adjacent structure is the original mule-team barn. *⊠ Harmony Borax Works Rd., west of Hwy. 190, 2 mi north of Furnace Creek ☉ Daily 9–4:30.*

On Highway 190, south of its junction with Scotty's Castle Road and 14 mi north of the town of Furnace Creek, is a 1-mi gravel road that leads to the **Salt Creek Interpretive Trail.** The trail, a ½-mi boardwalk circuit, loops through a spring-fed wash. The nearby hills are brown and gray, but the floor of the wash is alive with aquatic plants like pickerelweed and salt grass. The stream and ponds here are among the few places in the park to see the rare pupfish, the only native fish species in Death Valley. The tiny fish are shy and hard to see, so you'll have to be a little sneaky or stand quietly and wait for them to appear. Animals such as bobcats, fox, coyotes, and snakes visit the spring, and you may also see ravens, common snipes, killdeer, and great blue herons. *⊠ Off Hwy. 190, 14 mi north of Furnace Creek.*

★ ☾ ㉒ **Scotty's Castle** is an odd apparition rising out of a canyon. This Moorish-style mansion, begun in 1924 and never completed, takes its name from Walter Scott, better known as Death Valley Scotty. An ex-cowboy, prospector, and performer in Buffalo Bill's Wild West Show, Scotty always told people the castle was his, financed by gold from a secret mine. In reality, there was no mine, and the house belonged to a Chicago millionaire named Albert Johnson (advised by doctors to spend time in a warm, dry climate), whom Scott had finagled into investing in the fictitious mine. The house functioned for a while as a hotel—guests included Bette Davis and Norman Rockwell—and still contains works of art, imported carpets, handmade European furniture, and a tremendous pipe organ. Costumed rangers re-create life at the castle circa 1939. Try to arrive for the first tour of the day to avoid a wait. *⊠ Scotty's Castle Rd., 53 mi north of Salt Creek Interpretive Trail on Hwy. 267 ☎ 760/786– 2392 ⊕ www.nationalparks.com 🖭 $9 ☉ Daily 7–6; tours daily 9–5.*

need a break? At **Xanterra Concessions** (☎ 760/786–2325), outside the castle, you can refuel on a steak, roast beef, or turkey sandwich for around $5. The snack bar is open 8:30–5:30, and there are picnic areas on the castle grounds where you can kick back with your refreshments.

㉓ The impressive **Ubehebe Crater,** 500 feet deep and ½ mi across, is the result of underground steam and gas explosions about 3,000 years ago. Its volcanic ash spreads out over most of the area, and the cinders lie as deep as 150 feet, near the crater's rim. You'll get superb views of the valley from here, and you can take a fairly easy hike around the west side of the rim to Little Hebe Crater, one of a smaller cluster of craters to the south and west. It's always windy here, so hold on to your hat. *⊠ 8 mi northwest of Scotty's Castle on N. Death Valley Hwy.*

★ ㉔ Although reaching the **Racetrack** involves a 27-mi journey over rough and almost nonexistent dirt road, the trip is well worth the reward. Where else in the world do rocks move on their own? This phenomenon has baffled scientists for years. Is it some sort of magnetic field? No one has actually seen the rocks in motion, but theory has it that when it rains, the hard-packed lake bed becomes slippery enough that gusty winds push the rocks along—sometimes for several hundred yards. When the mud dries, a telltale trail remains. The trek to the Racetrack can be made in a passenger vehicle, but high-clearance is suggested. ⊠ *From Ubehebe Crater, west 27 mi on the dirt road.*

㉕ Made up of minute pieces of quartz and other rock, the **Sand Dunes at Mesquite Flat** are ever-changing products of the wind—rippled hills with curving crests and a sun-bleached hue. The dunes are the most photographed destination in the park, and you can see them at their best at sunrise and sunset. There are no trails; you can roam where you please. Keep your eyes open for animal tracks—you may even spot a fox or coyote roaming the dunes. Bring plenty of water, and remember where you parked your car: it's easy to become disoriented in this ocean of sand. If you lose your bearings, simply climb to the top of a dune and scan the horizon for the parking lot. ⊠ *19 mi north of Hwy. 190, northeast of Stovepipe Wells Village.*

㉖ **Stovepipe Wells Village** was the first resort in Death Valley. The tiny town, which dates to 1926, takes its name from the stovepipe that an early prospector left to indicate where he found water. The area contains a motel, a restaurant, a grocery store, campgrounds, and a landing strip. The multicolor walls of **Mosaic Canyon** (⊠ Off Hwy. 190, on a 3-mi gravel road immediately southwest of Stovepipe Wells Village) are extremely close together in spots. A ¾-mi hike will give you a good sense of the area. If weather permits, it's rewarding to continue into the canyon for a few more miles. Be prepared to clamber over larger boulders. ⊠ *2 mi from Sand Dunes; 77 mi east of Lone Pine on Hwy. 190.*

㉗ The **Panamint Valley,** west of the forbidding Panamint Range, is a great place to stop if you're arriving late in the day and don't want to drive over the winding mountain roads into Death Valley after dark. The views here are spectacular. From Highway 178 south of Highway 190, turn north on Wildrose Canyon Road and east onto the dirt track leading to the **Charcoal Kilns** (⊠ 9 mi east of Hwy. 178). The drive will take about a half hour, but it's worth it. Ten stone kilns, each 30 feet high and 25 feet wide, stand as if on parade in a line up a mountain. The kilns, built by Chinese laborers in 1879, were used to burn wood from piñon pines to turn it into charcoal. The charcoal was then transported over the mountains into Death Valley, where it was used to extract lead and silver from the ore mined there. If you hike nearby Wildrose Peak, you will be rewarded with terrific views of the kilns, with Death Valley's phenomenal colors as a backdrop. ⊠ *31 mi southwest of Stovepipe; 51 mi southeast of Lone Pine on Hwy. 190.*

Where to Stay & Eat

$$$$ ✕▦ **Furnace Creek Inn.** Built in 1927, this adobe-brick-and-stone lodge
Fodor'sChoice   is nestled in one of the park's greenest oases. A warm mineral stream
★   gurgles across the property, and its 85°F waters feed into a swimming

pool. All the rooms here have views, and some have balconies. The rooms are decorated in earth tones, and furnished in a style reminiscent of the inn's early days. Certain amenities, such as room service and massage, are only available from October through May. The top-notch Furnace Creek Inn Dining Room ($$$) serves up desert-theme dishes like rattlesnake empanadas and crispy cactus, as well as less exotic fare like cumin-lime shrimp, lamb, and New York strip steak. Afternoon tea has been a tradition there since 1927. The Inn is closed mid-May through mid-October. ⊠ *Furnace Creek Village, Hwy. 190, 92328* ☎ *760/786–2361* 🖷 *760/786–2514* ⊕ *www.furnacecreekresort.com* 🛏 *66 rooms* ⚘ *Restaurant, room service, in-room data ports, some refrigerators, cable TV with video games, 4 tennis courts, pool, hot tubs, massage, sauna, bar, shop, meeting rooms* ☱ *AE, D, DC, MC, V.*

$$–$$$ ✕🏨 **Furnace Creek Ranch.** Originally crew headquarters for the Pacific Coast Borax Company, the four buildings here have motel-type rooms that are good for families. The best ones overlook the green lawns of the resort and the surrounding mountains. All rooms were renovated in 2004. The property is adjacent to a golf course with its own team of pros, and also has a general store and a campground. The family-style Wrangler Steak House ($$$) and 49er Café ($) serve American fare in simple surroundings. ⊠ *Furnace Creek Village, 92328* ☎ *760/786–2345* 🖷 *760/786–9945* ⊕ *www.furnacecreekresort.com* 🛏 *224 rooms* ⚘ *Restaurant, coffee shop, grocery, in-room data ports, some refrigerators, cable TV with movies, golf course, pro shop, 4 tennis courts, pool, horseback riding, bar, shop, playground, laundry facilities; no smoking* ☱ *AE, D, DC, MC, V.*

$ ✕🏨 **Stovepipe Wells Village.** If you prefer quiet nights and an unfettered view of the night sky and nearby sand dunes, this property is for you. No telephones break the silence here, and only the deluxe rooms have televisions. Rooms are simple yet comfortable and provide wide-open desert vistas. The Toll Road Restaurant ($–$$$) serves American breakfast, lunch, and dinner favorites, from omelets and sandwiches to burgers and steaks. RV campsites with full hookups ($22) are available on a first-come, first-served basis. ⊠ *Stovepipe Wells Village, Hwy. 190, 92328* ☎ *760/786–2387* 🖷 *760/786–2389* ⊕ *www.stovepipewells. com* 🛏 *83 rooms* ⚘ *Restaurant, some refrigerators, pool, bar, shop, airstrip; no TV in some rooms, no room phones* ☱ *AE, D, MC, V.*

△ **Sunset Campground.** This campground is a gravel-and-asphalt RV city. Hookups are not available, but you can walk across the street to the showers, laundry facilities, and swimming pool at Furnace Creek Ranch. Many of Sunset's denizens are senior citizens who migrate to Death Valley each winter to play golf and tennis or just to enjoy the mild, dry climate. ⚘ *Playground, flush toilets, dump station, drinking water, ranger station* 🛏 *1,000 sites* ⊠ *1 mi north of Furnace Creek Village* ☎ *760/786–2331* ⊕ *www.nps.gov/deva* ⚑ *Reservations not accepted* ☱ *No credit cards* ☼ *Mid-Oct.–mid-Apr.* 🖭 *$10.*

Sports & the Outdoors

BIRD-WATCHING Approximately 250 bird species have been identified in Death Valley. The best place to see the park's birds is along the Salt Creek Interpretive Trail, where you can spot ravens, common snipes, killdeer, spotted sandpipers, and great blue herons. Along the fairways at Furnace Creek Golf Club, you can see kingfishers, peregrine falcons, hawks, Canada geese, yellow warblers, and the occasional golden eagle—just remember to stay off the greens.

GOLF At **Furnace Creek Golf Club,** the lowest golf course in the world, you can opt to play 9 or 18 holes. The club rents clubs and carts, and greens fees are reduced if you're a guest of Furnace Creek Ranch or Furnace Creek Inn. In winter, reservations are essential. ⊠ *Furnace Creek Village* ☎ *760/786–2301* ✑ *$55* ⊘ *Tee times daily sunrise–sundown; pro shop daily 7–5.*

HIKING Hiking trails and routes abound throughout Death Valley National Park, though few are maintained by the Park Service. Try the 2-mi round-trip Keane Wonder Mine Trail, with spectacular views of the valley; the winding 4-mi round-trip Mosaic Canyon Trail, between smoothly polished walls of a narrow canyon; or Natural Bridge Canyon Trail, an easy half-mile round-trip to a bridge formation. Plan to take your walks before or after midday, when the sun is hottest. Be sure to carry plenty of water, wear protective clothing, and be wary of tarantulas, black widows, scorpions, snakes, and other potentially dangerous creatures. Some of the best trails are unmarked; ask locals for directions.

en route Leaving Death Valley via the west entrance and heading northwest on Hwy. 136/190, you will pass **Keeler** about 35 mi northwest of Panamint Springs. Now something of a ghost town, Keeler had a population of 300 in the 1880s and was the dumping site for silver, lead, and zinc gathered from the mine at Cerro Gordo, one of the greatest silver mines in California. A handful of people still live here, and many of the town's early structures still stand, including the old train station and remnants of the mill site that once processed the ore.

OWENS VALLEY
ALONG U.S. 395 EAST OF THE SIERRA NEVADA

Lying in the shadow of the eastern Sierra Nevada, the Owens Valley stretches along U.S. 395 from the Mono–Inyo county line, in the north, to the town of Olancha, in the south. This stretch of highway is dotted with tiny towns, some containing only a minimart and a gas station. If you're traveling from Yosemite National Park to Death Valley National Park or are headed from Lake Tahoe or Mammoth to the desert, U.S. 395 is your corridor.

Lone Pine

28 *30 mi west of Panamint Valley via Hwy. 190*

Mt. Whitney towers majestically over this tiny community, which supplied nearby gold- and silver-mining outposts in the 1860s. In more recent decades–especially the 1950s and '60s—the town has been touched by Hollywood glamour: more than 300 movies, TV shows, and com-

CELEBRITY DUDE RANCHES

DURING THE EARLY 1900S, California's high desert was a popular destination for stressed-out Angelenos and screen stars looking for a little rest and relaxation.

Apple Valley's Rancho Yucca Loma was a favorite of French and Canadian poet laureates, while Murray's Overall-Wearing Dude Ranch was the first to cater to black visitors. Owned by Pearl Bailey, its famous guests included Bill "Bojangles" Robinson, Lena Horne and boxer Joe Louis, who set up his training camp there in 1937.

North Verde Ranch, run by Kemper and Litta Belle Campbell, was a favorite among stars like Groucho Marx, Greta Garbo, Henry Fonda and Gene Autry. For $25 a week, guests could enjoy swimming, tennis, and horseback riding followed by ranch meals over a desert sunset. Clark Gable often hunted and fished along the Mojave River, while John Wayne honed his horseback riding skills on the trails.

In 1940, director Orson Welles sent screenwriter Herman Mankiewicz to Verde Ranch for 12 weeks to secretly work on one of the greatest films ever made—"Citizen Kane"—based on the life of newspaper magnate William Randolph Hearst. Since drinking was strictly forbidden at Verde Ranch, many stars—including Wayne and Mankiewicz—would sneak off to the Green Spot Cafe and Bar in Victorville for a scotch. It was here that Welles met with Mankiewicz and cowriter John Houseman to review the script over lunch.

Verde Ranch—later renamed Kemper Campbell ranch—was the last of the celebrity ranches to close in September of 1975. "We met many fascinating and famous people," said the Campbell's granddaughter Jean DeBlasis. "We still get calls asking for reservations."

---

mercials have been filmed here. The Lone Pine Film Festival now takes place here every October.

Drop by the Lone Pine Visitor Center for a map of the **Alabama Hills** and take a drive up Whitney Portal Road (turn west at the light) to this wonderland of granite boulders. Erosion has worn the rocks smooth; some have been chiseled to leave arches and other formations. The hills have become a popular location for rock climbing. There are three campgrounds among the rocks, each with a stream for fishing. ⊠ *Whitney Portal Rd., 4½ mi west of Lone Pine.*

Straddling the border of Sequoia National Park and Inyo National Forest–John Muir Wilderness, **Mt. Whitney** (14,496 feet) is the highest mountain in the continental United States. A favorite game for travelers passing through Lone Pine is trying to guess which peak is Mt. Whitney. Almost no one gets it right because Mt. Whitney is hidden behind other mountains. There is no road that ascends the peak, but you can catch a glimpse of the mountain by driving curvy Whitney Portal Road west from Lone Pine into the mountains. The pavement ends at the trailhead to the top of the mountain, which is also the start of the 211-mi John Muir Trail from Mt. Whitney to Yosemite National Park.

At the portal there are a restaurant (known for its pancakes) and a small store that mostly cater to hikers and campers staying at Whitney Portal Campground. You can see a waterfall from the parking lot and go fishing in a small trout pond. The portal area is closed from mid-October to early May; the road closes when snow conditions require.

Climbers from around the world come to Mt. Whitney to tackle its slopes. The hike of 6,000 vertical feet and 11 mi is for experienced backcountry hikers only, and trailhead reservations are difficult to obtain. Permits ($15) are available through the **U.S. Forest Service** (⊠ 873 N. Main St., Bishop 93514 ☎ 760/873–2400 ⊕ www.r5.fs.fed.us/inyo) by a lottery held each February. In May a few permits usually become available if other hikers have canceled. ⊠ *Whitney Portal Rd., 13 mi west of Lone Pine* ☎ *909/734–7726 or 760/876–6200* ⊕ *www.r5.fs.fed.us/inyo/vvc/mtwhtny/wtportal.*

Where to Stay & Eat

¢–$$ ✕ **Seasons Restaurant.** This inviting, country-style diner serves up all kinds of traditional American fare. For a special treat, try the medallions of Cervena venison, smothered in port wine, dried cranberries, and toasted walnuts; finish with the Baily's Irish Cream cheesecake or the lemon crème brûlée for dessert. Children's items include a mini sirloin steak. ⊠ *206 S. Main St.* ☎ *760/876–8927* ⊟ *AE, D, MC, V* ☉ *Closed Sun. No lunch.*

¢–$ ✕ **Mt. Whitney Restaurant.** A boisterous family-family restaurant with a game room and 50-inch television, this place is especially popular during Monday Night Football. The best burgers in town are here—but as well as the usual beef variety, you can also choose from ostrich, venison, and buffalo burgers. There's a gift shop on the premises. ⊠ *227 S. Main St.* ☎ *760/876–5751* ⊟ *D, MC, V.*

$–$$ ▥ **Dow Villa Motel and Hotel.** John Wayne slept here, and you can, too. Built in 1923 to cater to the film industry, Dow Villa is in the center of Lone Pine. Some rooms have views of the mountains; both buildings are within walking distance of just about everything in town. There are in-room coffeemakers and whirlpool tubs, though some of the guest rooms share bathrooms. Pets are allowed only in smoking rooms. Many units have an Old West feel, and are decorated with antique furniture and pictures of John Wayne or Mt. Whitney. ⊠ *310 S. Main St.* ☎ *760/876–5521 or 800/824–9317* ⊟ *760/876–5643* ⊕ *www.dowvillamotel.com* ➴ *91 rooms* ⚷ *In-room data ports, refrigerators, cable TV, in-room VCRs, pool, hot tub, no-smoking rooms* ⊟ *AE, D, DC, MC, V.*

¢–$ ▥ **Best Western Frontier.** Just minutes from the base of Mt. Whitney, this single-level property has rooms decorated in a Western motif, with photos of old cowboy movies, rustic lampshades and Southwest-style bedding. Some have views of the nearby Sierra Nevada. ⊠ *1008 S. Main St.* ☎ *760/876–5571 or 800/780–7234* ⊟ *760/876–5357* ⊕ *www.bestwesterncalifornia.com* ➴ *73 rooms* ⚷ *In-room data ports, refrigerators, cable TV, pool, some pets allowed, no-smoking rooms* ⊟ *AE, D, DC, MC, V* ⏸⊙ *CP.*

⚠ **Whitney Portal.** The campsites here are spread beneath towering pines and adjacent to a small pond. The campground can accommodate tents or RVs up to 16 feet. The camp is popular with hikers, so it's best to reserve a spot in advance. The property has a store and café that are open in summer. ♿ *Flush toilets, drinking water, showers, fire grates, picnic tables, public telephone* ⊷ *43 sites* ⊠ *Whitney Portal Rd., 13 mi west of Lone Pine* ☎ *760/867–6200 or 877/444–6777* 🖷 *760/876–6202* ⊕ *www.reserveusa.com* ⚓ *Reservations essential* ⊟ *AE, D, MC, V* ☼ *Early May–mid-Oct.* ☒ *$14.*

Manzanar National Historic Site

㉙ *U.S. 395, 11 mi north of Lone Pine.*

A reminder of an ugly episode in U.S. history, the remnants of the Manzanar War Relocation Center have been designated the Manzanar National Historic Site. This is where some 10,000 Japanese-Americans were confined behind barbed-wire fences between 1942 and 1945. Manzanar was the first of 10 such internment camps erected by the federal government following Japan's attack on Pearl Harbor in 1941. In the name of national security, American citizens of Japanese descent were forcibly relocated to these camps, many of them losing their homes, businesses, and most of their possessions in the process. Today not much remains of Manzanar but a guard post, the auditorium, and some concrete foundations. But you can stop at the entrance station, pick up a brochure, and drive the one-way dirt road past the ruins to a small cemetery, where a monument stands as a reminder of what took place here. Signs mark where structures such as the barracks, a hospital, school, and fire station once stood. An 8,000-square-foot interpretive center also opened in April 2004, with exhibits and a 15-minute film. ⏏ *Manzanar Information, c/o Superintendent: Death Valley National Park, Death Valley 92398* ☎ *760/878–2932* ⊕ *www.nps.gov/manz* ☒ *Free.*

Independence

㉚ *U.S. 395, 5 mi north of Manzanar National Historic Site.*

Named for a military outpost that was established near here in 1862, Independence is small and sleepy. But the town has some wonderful historic buildings and is certainly worth a stop on your way from the Sierra Nevada to Death Valley.

☺ As you approach Independence from the north, you'll pass the **Mt. Whitney Fish Hatchery,** a delightful place for a family picnic. Bring some dimes for the machines filled with fish food; the hatchery's lakes are full of hefty, always-hungry breeder trout. Built in 1915, the hatchery was one of the first trout farms in California, and today it produces fish that stock lakes throughout the state. ⊠ *Fish Hatchery Rd., 1 mi north of Independence* ☎ *760/878–2272* ⊕ *www.independence-ca.com/hatchery* ☒ *Free* ☼ *Daily 8–5.*

The **Eastern California Museum** provides a glimpse of Inyo County's history. Highlights include a fine collection of Paiute and Shoshone Indian basketry and a yard full of agricultural implements used by early area miners and farmers. ⊠ *155 N. Grant St.* ☎ *760/878–0364* ⊕ *www. independence-ca.com* ☒ *Donations suggested* ☼ *Wed.–Mon. 10–4.*

<table>
<tr><td>

off the
beaten
path

</td><td>

ONION VALLEY – Thirteen miles west of Independence on Onion
Valley Road, Onion Valley (so called because wild onions grow here) is
one of the main access points to the eastern slope of the Sierra Nevada.
At 9,600 feet, where the valley enters the John Muir Wilderness, a
trailhead leads to popular Kearsarge Pass. The trail takes you through
mountain valleys where glacial lakes teem with trout, eventually
reaching Kings Canyon National Park. If you make reservations, you
can camp in Onion Valley. ⊠ *Off U.S. 395* ☎ *760/ 876–6200.*

</td></tr>
</table>

Where to Stay

¢–$ 🏨 **Winnedumah Hotel Bed & Breakfast.** This 1927 B&B has the best—
and most famous—digs in town: celebrities like Roy Rogers, John
Wayne, and Bing Crosby all stayed here while filming nearby. Outfitted in an eclectic mix of Wild West chic and modern bric-a-brac, the
rooms are simple yet comfortable. There are also hostel rooms. Breakfast is usually a hearty affair of bacon, eggs, waffles, and fresh fruit. ⊠ *211
N. Edwards St.* ☎ *760/878–2040* 🖷 *760/878–2833* 🛏 *24 rooms, 14
with bath* ⚬ *Some pets allowed (fee); no phones in some rooms, no room
TVs, no smoking* ▤ *AE, D, DC, MC, V* ⭕️ *BP.*

<table>
<tr><td>

en route

</td><td>

Traveling north from Independence on U.S. 395, turn onto Highway
168 and follow the signs 31 mi to the **Ancient Bristlecone Pine
Forest.** Here you can see some of the oldest living trees on earth,
some of which date back more than 40 centuries. These rare, gnarled
pines in the White Mountains can only grow in harsh, frigid
conditions above 9,000 feet. At the **Schulman Grove Visitor Center**
(☎ 760/873–2500 ⊕ www.r5.fs.fed.us/inyo/vvc/bcp), open from 8
to 4:30 weekdays, late May through October, you can learn about
the bristlecone and take a walk to the 4,700-year-old Methuselah
tree. Admission to the forest is $2.

</td></tr>
</table>

★ ⓒ

Bishop

🟤 *U.S. 395, 43 mi north of Independence.*

One of the biggest towns along U.S. 395, Bishop has views of the Sierra
Nevada and the White and Inyo mountains. First settled by the Northern Paiute Indians, the area was named in 1861 for cattle rancher
Samuel Bishop, who established a camp here. Paiute and Shoshone people reside on four reservations in the area.

One of Bishop's biggest draws is its **Mule Days Celebration** each Memorial Day weekend. More than 40,000 tourists and RVers pack into this
lazy town for the longest nonmotorized parade in the world, mule races,
a rodeo, and good old-fashioned country-and-western concerts. ☎ *760/
872–4263* ⊕ *www.muledays.org.*

ⓒ The **Laws Railroad Museum** is a complex of historic buildings and train
cars from the Carson and Colorado Railroad Company, which set up
a narrow-gauge railroad yard here in 1883. Among the exhibits are a
self-propelled car from the Death Valley Railroad and a full village of
rescued buildings, including a post office, an 1883 train depot, the 1909

North Inyo Schoolhouse, and a restored 1900 ranch house. ⊠ *U.S. 6, 3 mi north of U.S. 395* ☎ *760/873–5950* ⊕ *www.thesierraweb.com/ bishop/laws* ⊠ *$3 donation requested* ☉ *Daily 10–4.*

To learn about life in the Bishop region before white settlers arrived, visit the **Paiute-Shoshone Indian Cultural Center,** a museum on the Bishop Paiute Indian Reservation. Here you can see exhibits of early clothing, shelters, tools and basketry used by these tribes. ⊠ *2300 W. Line Rd.* ☎ *760/873–4478* ⊕ *www.paiute.com* ⊠ *$4* ☉ *Daily 9–4.*

Where to Stay & Eat

★ ¢–$$$ ✕ **Whiskey Creek.** Since 1924, this Wild West–style saloon, restaurant, and gift shop has been serving crisp salads, warm soups, and juicy bar-becued steaks to locals and tourists. Warm days are perfect for sitting on the shaded deck and enjoying one of the many available micro-brews. ⊠ *524 N. Main St.* ☎ *760/873–7174* ⊟ *AE, MC, V.*

¢–$ ✕ **Erick Schat's Bakery.** A popular stop for motorists traveling to and from Mammoth Lakes, this shop is chock-full of delicious pastries, cookies, rolls, and other baked goods. But the biggest draw here is the sheep-herder bread, a hand-shaped and stone hearth–baked sourdough that was introduced during the gold rush by immigrant Basque sheepherders in 1907. In addition to the bakery, Schat's has a gift shop and a sand-wich bar. ⊠ *763 N. Main St.* ☎ *760/873–7156* ⊟ *AE, MC, V.*

$–$$$ ▥ **Best Western Creekside Inn.** One of the nicest spots to stay in Bishop, this clean and comfortable mountain-style hotel is a good base from which to explore the town or go skiing and trout fishing nearby. Rooms are elegantly furnished with cherrywood armoires and beds; the ranch-style lobby has a wonderfully large brick hearth. In summer you can sit on the patio near a trickling creek. ⊠ *725 N. Main St.* ☎ *760/872–3044 or 800/273–3550* ⊕ *www.thesierraweb.com/lodging/creeksideinn* ↘ *89 rooms* ⅏ *Some kitchenettes, cable TV, pool, hot tub* ⊟ *AE, MC, V* ⑂ *CP.*

Sports & the Outdoors

Sierra Mountain Center (⊠ 174 W. Line St. ☎ 760/873–8526 ⊕ www. sierramountaincenter.com) provides instruction and guided hiking, ski-ing, snowshoe, rock-climbing, and mountain-biking trips for all levels of expertise.

FISHING   The Owens Valley is trout country; its glistening alpine lakes and streams are brimming with feisty rainbow, brown, brook, and golden trout. Pop-ular spots include Owens River, the Owens River gorge, and Pleasant Val-ley Reservoir. Although you can fish year-round here, some fishing is catch-and-release. Bishop hosts fishing derbies throughout the year, in-cluding the popular Blake Jones Blind Bogey Trout Derby, in March. Whether you want to take a fly-fishing class or a guided wade trip, **Brock's Flyfishing Specialists and Tackle Experts** (⊠ 100 N. Main St. ☎ 760/ 872–3581 or 888/619–3581 ⊕ www.brocksflyfish.com) is a valuable re-source. **Osprey Lure** (⊠ 287 Academy Ave., #C ☎ 760/873–0014 ⊕ www. ospreylure.com) will craft flies that will help you catch the really big ones.

HORSE PACKING   The **Rock Creek Pack Station** (⊕ Box 248, 93516 ☎ 760/935–4493 in summer, 760/872–8331 in winter ⊕ www.rockcreekpackstation.com) outfit runs 3- to 24-day horse-packing trips in the High Sierra, including Mt. Whitney, Yosemite National Park, and other parts of the John Muir Wilderness. One expedition tracks wild mustangs through Inyo National Forest; another is an old-fashioned horse drive between the Owens Valley and the High Sierra.

THE MOJAVE A TO Z

To research prices, get advice from other travelers, and book travel arrangements, visit ⊕ www.fodors.com

AIRPORTS & TRANSFERS

Inyokern Airport, near Ridgecrest, is served by United Express from Los Angeles. McCarran International Airport, in Las Vegas, Nevada, served by dozens of major airlines, is about as close to Furnace Creek, in Death Valley National Park, as is Inyokern Airport. Needles Airport serves small, private planes. *See* Air Travel *in* Smart Travel Tips A to Z for airline phone numbers.

🚩 **Inyokern Airport** ⊠ Inyokern Rd. (Hwy. 178), 9 mi west of Ridgecrest, Inyokern ☎ 760/ 377-5844 ⊕ www.inyokernairport.com. **McCarran International Airport** ⊠ 5757 Wayne Newton Blvd., Las Vegas, Nevada ☎ 702/261-5733 ⊕ www.mccarran.com. **Needles Airport** ⊠ 711 Airport Rd., Needles ☎ 760/326-5263.

BUS TRAVEL

Greyhound serves Baker, Barstow, Ridgecrest, and Victorville, but traveling by bus to the Mojave Desert is neither convenient nor cheap. There is no scheduled bus service to Death Valley National Park or within Owens Valley. Victor Valley Transit serves Victorville, Hesperia, Phelan, Adelanto, and other nearby areas.

🚩 **Greyhound** ☎ 800/231-2222 ⊕ www.greyhound.com. **Victor Valley Transit** ☎ 760/ 948-3030 ⊕ www.vvta.org.

CAR RENTAL

In the Owens Valley, reliable regional car-rental agencies include Eastern Sierra Motors and U-Save Auto Rentals. The major national agencies serve the larger cities of the Mojave Desert: Barstow has Hertz and Avis offices and Victorville has Avis, Budget, and Enterprise offices. *See* Car Rental *in* Smart Travel Tips A to Z for national rental agency phone numbers.

🚩 **Local Agencies Eastern Sierra Motors** ⊠ 1440 N. U.S. 6, Bishop ☎ 760/873-4291 or 877/503-6257. **U-Save Auto Rentals** ⊠ 1075 Main St., Bishop ☎ 800/207-2681 ⊕ www. usavemammothbishop.com.

CAR TRAVEL

Much of the desert can be seen from the comfort of an air-conditioned car, though you need not despair if you're without air-conditioning— just avoid driving in the middle of the day and in the middle of summer. You can approach Death Valley from the west or the southeast. Whether you've come south from Bishop or north from Ridgecrest, head east from U.S. 395 on Highways 190 or 178. To enter Death Valley from the southeast, take Highway 127 north from I–15 in Baker and link up with Highway 178, which travels west into the valley and then cuts north toward Highway 190 at Furnace Creek.

The Mojave is shaped like a giant L, with one leg jutting north toward the Owens Valley and the other extending east toward California's borders with Nevada and Arizona. The major north–south route through the western Mojave is U.S. 395, which intersects with I–15 between Cajon Pass and Victorville. U.S. 395 travels north into the Owens Valley, passing such dusty little stops as Lone Pine, Independence, Big Pine, and Bishop. Farther west, Highway 14 runs north–south between Inyokern (near Ridgecrest) and Palmdale. Two major east–west routes travel through the Mojave: to the north, I–15 between Barstow and Las Vegas, Nevada; to the south, I–40 between Barstow and Needles. At the intersection of the two interstates, in Barstow, I–15 veers south toward Victorville and Los Angeles, and I–40 gives way to Highway 58 toward Bakersfield.

🚗 **California Highway Patrol 24-hour road info** ☎ 800/427-7623 ⊕ www.dot.ca.gov/hq/roadinfo.

EMERGENCIES

In an emergency dial 911.

Emergencies can arise easily in the desert, but you can go a long way toward avoiding them if you take a few simple safety precautions. Never travel alone. Always take a companion, especially if you are not familiar with the area. Let someone know your trip route, destination, and estimated time and date of return. Before setting out, make sure your vehicle is in good condition. Carry a jack, tools, and tow rope or chain. Fill up your tank whenever you see a gas pump—it might be many miles before you see another service station. Stay on main roads: if you drive even a few feet off the pavement, you can get stuck in sand (and besides, venturing off-road is illegal in many areas). When driving, watch out for wild burros, horses, and range cattle. They roam free throughout much of the desert and have the right-of-way.

Drink at least a gallon of water a day (three gallons if you are hiking or otherwise exerting yourself), even if you don't feel thirsty. Dress in layered clothing and wear comfortable, sturdy shoes and a hat. Keep snacks, sunscreen, and a first-aid kit on hand. If you suddenly have a headache or feel dizzy or nauseous, you could be suffering from dehydration. Get out of the sun immediately and drink plenty of water. Dampen your clothing to lower your body temperature.

Do not enter mine tunnels or shafts. The structures may be unstable, and there may be hidden dangers such as pockets of bad air. Avoid canyons during rainstorms. Floodwaters can quickly fill up dry riverbeds and cover or wash away roads. Never place your hands or feet where you can't see them. Rattlesnakes, scorpions, and black widow spiders may be hiding there.

🚗 **BLM Rangers** ☎ 760/255-8700. **Community Hospital** ✉ Barstow ☎ 760/256-1761. **Northern Inyo Hospital** ✉ 150 Pioneer La., Bishop ☎ 760/873-5811. **San Bernardino County Sheriff** ☎ 760/256-1796 in Barstow, 760/733-4448 in Baker.

TOURS

Old West Tours operates luxury bus tours of some of the most breathtaking Mojave Desert and eastern Sierra sights, from majestic Red Rock

Canyon and Mt. Whitney to the dusty ghost towns of Bodie and Cerro Gordo. Lodging, snacks, and most meals are included. Tours depart from locations in Lancaster, Palmdale, and Rosamond. The Mojave Group of the Sierra Club regularly organizes field trips to interesting spots such as Red Mountain, Silverwood Lake, and the San Gabriel Mountains. The San Gorgonio Sierra Club chapter also conducts desert excursions. ⁊ **Old West Tours** ⊕ Box 2240, Rosamond 93560 ☎ 800/868-7777 ⊕ www. oldwesttours.com. **Sierra Club** ✉ 3345 Wilshire Blvd., Suite 508, Los Angeles 90010 ☎ 213/387-4287, 909/686-6112 for San Gorgonio chapter ⊕ www.sierraclub.com.

TRAIN TRAVEL

Amtrak makes stops in Victorville, Barstow, and Needles, but the stations are not staffed and do not have phone numbers, so you have to purchase your tickets in advance and handle your own baggage. You can travel west to connect with the *Coast Starlight* in Los Angeles or the *San Diegan* in Fullerton. The *Southwest Chief* stops twice a day at the above cities on its route from Los Angeles to Chicago and back. The Barstow station is served daily by Amtrak California motor coaches that travel between San Joaquin, Bakersfield, and Las Vegas. ⁊ **Amtrak** ☎ 800/872-7245 ⊕ www.amtrakcalifornia.com.

VISITOR INFORMATION

⁊ **Big Pine Chamber of Commerce** ✉ 128 S. Main St., Big Pine 93513 ☎ 760/938-2114. **Bishop Chamber of Commerce** ✉ 690 N. Main St., Bishop 93514 ☎ 760/873-8405 ⊕ www.bishopvisitor.com. **Bureau of Land Management** ✉ California Desert District Office, 6221 Box Springs Blvd., Riverside 92507 ☎ 909/697-5200 ⊕ www.ca. blm.gov. **California Welcome Center** ✉ 2796 Tanger Way, Barstow 92311 ☎ 760/253-4782 ⊕ www.barstowchamber.com. **Death Valley Chamber of Commerce** ✉ 118 Hwy. 127, Shoshone 92384 ☎ 760/852-4524 ⊕ www.deathvalleychamber.org. **Death Valley National Park** ✉ Visitor Center at Furnace Creek, Death Valley 92328 ☎ 760/786-2331 ⊕ www.nps.gov/deva. **Death Valley Natural History Association** ⊕ Box 188, Death Valley 92328 ☎ 800/478-8564. **Desert Discovery Center** ✉ 831 Barstow Rd., Barstow 92311 ☎ 760/252-6060. **Independence Chamber of Commerce** ✉ 139 N. Edwards, Independence 93526 ☎ 760/878-0084 ⊕ www.independence-ca.com. **Lone Pine Chamber of Commerce** ✉ 126 S. Main St., Lone Pine 93545 ☎ 760/876-4444 or 877/253-8981 ⊕ www.lonepinechamber.org. **Needles Chamber of Commerce** ✉ 100 G St., Needles 92363 ☎ 760/326-2050 ⊕ www.needleschamber.com. **Ridgecrest Area Convention and Visitors Bureau** ✉ 100 W. California Ave., Ridgecrest 93555 ☎ 760/375-8202 or 800/847-4830 ⊕ www.visitdeserts.com. **San Bernardino County Regional Parks Department** ✉ 777 E. Rialto Ave., San Bernardino 92415 ☎ 909/387-2594 ⊕ www. co.san-bernardino.ca.us/parks. **Wrightwood Chamber of Commerce** ✉ 1270 Irene St., Box 416, Wrightwood 92397 ☎ 760/249-4320, 760/249-6822 for recorded information ⊕ www.wrightwoodcalifornia.com. **Victorville Chamber of Commerce** ✉ 14174 Green Tree Blvd., Victorville 92393 ☎ 760/245-6506 ⊕ www.vvchamber.com.

THE SOUTHERN SIERRA

WITH SEQUOIA, KINGS CANYON & YOSEMITE NATIONAL PARKS

7

PLAY KING OF THE MOUNTAIN
from high atop Moro Rock ⇨*p.319*

HUG A GIANT TREE
at Redwood Mountain Grove ⇨*p.321*

FALL IN LOVE
with Yosemite's stunning waterfalls ⇨*p.328*

SEE FOR MILES
Yosemite's Glacier Point overlook ⇨*p.330*

BE A HAPPY CAMPER
at Tuolumne Meadows ⇨*p.330*

SCHUSS LIKE A SUPERSTAR
at Mammoth Mountain Ski Area ⇨*p.342*

PRACTICE YOUR MUSHING
with Mammoth Dog Teams ⇨*p.341*

Updated by
John A.
Vlahides

VAST GRANITE PEAKS AND GIANT SEQUOIAS are among the mind-boggling natural wonders of the southern Sierra, many of which are protected in three national parks. Endowed with glacially carved valleys, deep canyons, and towering peaks and trees, Kings Canyon and Sequoia national parks abut each other and are easy to visit together. Yosemite, the state's most famous national park, is renowned for its staggering U-shape valleys and mile-high walls of granite formed during the Ice Age. Outside the parks, pristine lakes, superb ski resorts, and small towns complete the picture of the southern Sierra.

Exploring the Southern Sierra

For the full Sierra experience, explore the national forests as well as the national parks. Stop at any of the ranger stations near the forests' borders and pick up information on lesser-known sights and attractions. Spend a few nights in the small towns outside the parks. If, however, you're tight on time and want to focus on the attractions that make the region famous, then stay in the parks themselves instead of the "gateway cities" in the foothills or the Central Valley; you won't want to lose time shuttling back and forth.

Yosemite Valley is the primary destination for many visitors. Because the valley is only 7 mi long and averages less than 1 mi wide, you can visit its attractions in whatever order you choose and return to your favorites at different times of the day. Famous for hiking trails and giant sequoias, Kings Canyon and Sequoia provide a truer wilderness experience, less tainted by civilization and crowds.

About the Restaurants

Towns in the Sierra Nevada are small, but they usually have at least one diner or restaurant. In the national parks, snack bars, coffee shops, and cafeterias are not expensive. The three fanciest lodgings within Yosemite National Park are prime dining spots, with hefty price tags to match. With few exceptions, which are noted, dress is casual at the restaurants listed in this chapter.

When you're traveling in the area, you can expect to spend a lot of time in the car, so pick up snacks and drinks to keep with you, and keep the gas tank full—especially in winter, when roads sometimes close due to heavy snow (having tire chains or four-wheel drive in winter is also strongly recommended). Stopping at a grocery store and filling the ice chest before you set out will also allow you to explore the national parks without having to search for food. With picnic supplies on hand you can enjoy a meal under giant trees; just be certain to clean up after yourself and leave no food or trash behind.

About the Hotels

Towns are few and far between in the southern Sierra. Whenever possible, book lodging reservations in advance—especially in summer—or plan to camp out. If you don't, you may find yourself driving long distances to find a place to sleep.

Most accommodations inside Sequoia, Kings Canyon, and Yosemite national parks can best be described as "no frills"—many have no elec-

7

Numbers in the text correspond to numbers in the margin and on the Sequoia & Kings Canyon National Parks, Yosemite National Park, and Southern Sierra maps.

If you have
3 days

If your time is limited, explore Yosemite National Park. Use the Big Oak Flat Entrance on Highway 120, and head east toward ➤ 🔲 **Yosemite Valley** ⑬–㉓. Once you reach the valley floor, traffic is diverted onto a one-way loop road. Continue east, following the signs to **Yosemite Village** ⑬ and the Valley Visitor Center. Loop back west for a short hike near **Yosemite Falls** ⑭, the highest waterfall in North America. Continue west for a valley view of the famous **El Capitan** ⑮ monolith. This area is a good place for a picnic. Backtrack onto Southside Drive, stopping at misty **Bridalveil Fall** ⑰; then follow Highway 41/Wawona Road south 14 mi to the Chinquapin junction and make a left turn onto Glacier Point Road. From **Glacier Point** ㉒ (road closed in winter) you'll get a phenomenal bird's-eye view of the entire valley, including **Half Dome** ㉑, **Vernal Fall** ⑲, and **Nevada Fall** ⑳. If you want to avoid the busloads of tourists at Glacier Point, stop at **Sentinel Dome** ㉓ instead.

On Day 2, head south again on Highway 41/Wawona Road and visit the **Mariposa Grove of Big Trees** ㉕ at the southern end of the park. Afterward, head north to the Wawona Hotel (closed weekdays much of the winter), where you can have lunch or a relaxing drink on the veranda or in the charming lobby bar. Afterward tour the Pioneer Yosemite History Center. Head back to Yosemite Valley on Wawona Road, and stop at the mouth of the tunnel on Highway 41, just before you drop into the valley, for one of the park's most famous and spectacular views. On the third day, have breakfast near the Valley Visitor Center before hiking to Vernal Fall or Nevada Fall. If you are up for a strenuous hike, you can climb to the top of Yosemite Falls.

If you have
5 days

On your first day, stop briefly at the ➤ **Foothills Visitor Center** ❸ in Sequoia National Park to pick up park information and tickets to **Crystal Cave** ❺. After visiting the cave, stop to explore the museum at **Giant Forest** ❹ and the park's other sights; if you're fit, be sure to climb Moro Rock. Spend the night in 🔲 **Grant Grove** ⑩ or 🔲 **Wuksachi Village** ❼. On Day 2, explore the sights in Grant Grove, then drive east along Kings Canyon Highway (Highway 180) to **Cedar Grove** ⑪. After lunch, double back on Highway 180, continuing west out of the park to Fresno, where you'll turn north onto Highway 41 toward Yosemite National Park. (It will take you three to four hours to reach the park.) Spend the night just south of the park in 🔲 Oakhurst or just inside the south entrance gate at 🔲 **Wawona** ㉔.

On your third morning, visit the Pioneer Yosemite History Center, and wander beneath the giant sequoias at the nearby **Mariposa Grove of Big Trees** ㉕. From here, head to 🔲 **Yosemite Valley** ⑬–㉓, where you should stay the next two nights. Stop just past the tunnel on Highway 41 to take in the dramatic view of **Half Dome** ㉑. Dedicate Day 4 to exploring the valley. On your last day, pack a picnic and drive 55 mi east on Tioga Road to Tuolumne Meadows, the largest subalpine meadow in the Sierra.

tricity or indoor plumbing. In Sequoia and Kings Canyon, lodging rates remain the same throughout the year. In winter, only some lodgings in Grant Grove remain open. Other than the Ahwahnee and Wawona hotels in Yosemite, lodgings tend to be basic motels or rustic cabins. Except during the off-peak season, from November through March, rates in Yosemite are pricey.

	WHAT IT COSTS				
	$$$$	$$$	$$	$	¢
RESTAURANTS	over $30	$23–$30	$16–$22	$10–$15	under $10
HOTELS	over $250	$176–$250	$121–$175	$90–$120	under $90

Restaurant prices are for a main course at dinner, excluding sales tax of 7¼%. Hotel prices are for two people in a standard double room in high season, excluding service charges and 9–10% tax.

Timing

Summer is by far the busiest season for all the parks, though things never get as hectic at Sequoia and Kings Canyon as they do at Yosemite. During extremely busy periods, like the Fourth of July, you may experience delays at the entrance gates. If you can only make it here in the warmest months, try to visit midweek. In winter, heavy snows occasionally cause road closures, and tire chains or four-wheel drive may be required on roads that remain open; trails in the backcountry and in wilderness areas aren't accessible. To avoid these problems, visit between mid-April and late May, or early September to mid-October, when the parks are less busy and the weather is usually hospitable.

The falls at Yosemite are at their most spectacular in May and June. By the end of summer some will have dried up. They begin flowing again in late fall with the first storms, and during winter they may be hung with ice, a dramatic sight. "Spring" wildflowers can bloom late into the summer as you rise in elevation. Snow on the floor of Yosemite Valley is rarely deep, so you can often camp there even in winter (January highs are in the mid-40s, lows in the mid-20s). Tioga Road is usually closed from late October through May; unless you ski or snowshoe in, you can't get to Tuolumne Meadows then. The road from the turnoff for Badger Pass to Glacier Point is not cleared in winter, but it is groomed for cross-country skiing, a 10-mi trek one-way.

SEQUOIA & KINGS CANYON

Naturalist John Muir declared in the early 20th century that the beauty of Sequoia and Kings Canyon national parks easily rivaled that of Yosemite; he described the sequoia trees here as "the most beautiful and majestic on Earth." The largest living things on the planet, *Sequoiadendron giganteum* trees are not as tall as the coast redwoods (*Sequoia sempervirens*), but on average they are older and more massive. Exhibits at the visitor centers explain why they can live so long and grow so big, as well as the special relationship between these trees and fire (their thick,

Camping

Camping in the Sierra Nevada means awakening to the sights of nearby meadows and streams and the unforgettable landscape of giant granite. Camping here also means gazing up at an awe-inspiring collection of constellations and spying a shooting star in the night sky. Dozens of campgrounds, from remote, tents-only areas to sprawling full-service facilities close to the main attractions, operate in the southern Sierra's three national parks. Of the numerous campgrounds in Yosemite National Park, Tuolumne Meadows campground may be the prettiest of the easily accessible spots, so it's also among the most popular. Spectacular camping abounds outside the national parks, as well, at sites such as Lake Mary Campground in the Mammoth Lakes area.

Hiking & Walking

Hiking is the primary outdoor activity in the Sierra Nevada. Whether you walk the paved loops that pass by major attractions in the national parks or head off the beaten path into the backcountry, a hike through groves and meadows or alongside streams and waterfalls will allow you to see, smell, and feel nature up close. Some of the most popular trails are described briefly in this chapter; stop by the visitor centers for maps and advice from park rangers. No matter which trail you decide to take, always carry lots of water and a pocket-size emergency rain poncho for unexpected summer thunderstorms.

Winter Sports

Famous for its incredible snowpack—some of the deepest anywhere on the North American continent—the Sierra Nevada has something for every winter sports fan. Sequoia and Kings Canyon national parks are great places for snowshoeing and cross-country skiing. At Yosemite Mountaineering School you can learn how to snowshoe, cross-country ski, telemark ski, and skate-ski, and at Yosemite's Badger Pass Ski Area you can schuss down the slopes alpine-style. But Mammoth Mountain Ski Area is the star of the southern Sierra winter sports scene. One of the biggest and best ski resorts in the western United States, Mammoth offers terrain to suit downhill skiers' every taste and ability level, plus great facilities for snowboarders.

---

fibrous bark helps protect them from flames and insects, and their seeds can't germinate until they first explode out of a burning pinecone).

A little more than 1.5 million people visit Sequoia and Kings Canyon annually, wandering trails through groves and meadows or tackling the rugged backcountry. The topography of the two parks runs the gamut from chaparral, at an elevation of 1,500 feet, to the giant sequoia belt, at 5,000–7,000 feet, to the towering peaks of the Great Western Divide and the Sierra crest. Mt. Whitney, the highest point in the contiguous United States, at 14,494 feet, is the crown jewel of the parks' less-crowded eastern side (the border between Sequoia National Park and John Muir Wilderness runs right through the summit of Mt. Whitney). You cannot access Mt. Whitney from Sequoia's western side; you must circumnavigate the Sierra range via a 10-hour, nearly 400-mi drive outside the park (*see* Chapter 6, The Mojave Desert and Death Valley, *for* Mt. Whitney).

Sequoia and Kings Canyon national parks share their administration and are connected by the Generals Highway (Highway 198). Kings Canyon Highway (Highway 180) runs east from Grant Grove to Cedar Grove. The entrance fee to Sequoia and Kings Canyon (good for admission to both on seven consecutive days) is $20 per vehicle, or $10 per person for those who don't arrive by car. An information-packed quarterly newspaper and a map are handed out at the parks' entrances.

Three Rivers

❶ *200 mi north of Los Angeles via I–5 to Hwy. 99 to Hwy. 198; 8 mi south of Ash Mountain/Foothills entrance to Sequoia National Park on Hwy. 198.*

In the foothills of the Sierra along the Kaweah River, this sparsely populated hamlet serves as the parks' main gateway town. Its livelihood depends largely on tourism from the national parks, courtesy of two markets, several service stations, banks, a post office, and several lodgings, which are good spots to find a room when park accommodations are full.

Where to Stay & Eat

$–$$$ ✕ **Gateway Restaurant and Lodge.** The patio of this raucous roadhouse overlooks the Kaweah River, and though the food is nothing special, the location makes it worth a visit. Standout dishes include baby-back ribs and eggplant parmigiana; there is also a cocktail lounge and guest rooms for overnight visitors. Breakfast isn't served on weekdays, and reservations are essential on weekends. ⊠ *45978 Sierra Dr.* ☎ *559/561–4133* ⊟ *AE, D, MC, V.*

$–$$ ✕ **Main Fork Bistro.** The Kaweah River flows within view of the many windows at Three Rivers's best restaurant. The menu offers a good selection of eggs and pancakes for breakfast; salads, open-face sandwiches, and meat loaf for lunch; and steak and seafood for dinner. There's also a good vegetarian menu. ⊠ *41775 Sierra Dr.* ☎ *559/561–4917* ⊟ *AE, D, MC, V.*

$$–$$$ ▣ **Cinnamon Creek Ranch.** Rooms have mountain views at this 10-acre country-casual ranch on a creek that feeds the Kaweah River. One room has a private terrace overlooking the river, but everyone can enjoy the resident donkeys. ⌂ *Box 54, 93271* ☎ *559/561–1107* ⊞ *559/561–3407* ⊕ *www.cinnamoncreek.com* ⋗ *2 rooms, 2 cabins* ⌂ *BBQs, some kitchens, in-room VCRs, hot tub, hiking, some pets allowed (fee); no smoking* ⊟ *AE, MC, V.*

¢–$$ ▣ **Lazy J Ranch Motel.** Surrounded by green lawns and a split-rail fence, the Lazy J is a modest, well-kept, single-story motel on the banks of the Kaweah River. Some rooms have gas fireplaces; all have coffeemakers. ⊠ *39625 Sierra Dr., 93271* ☎ *559/561–4449 or 888/315–2378* ⊞ *559/561–4889* ⊕ *www.bvilazyj.com* ⋗ *11 rooms, 7 cottages* ⌂ *Picnic area, BBQs, some kitchens, refrigerators, cable TV, in-room VCRs, pool, fish-*

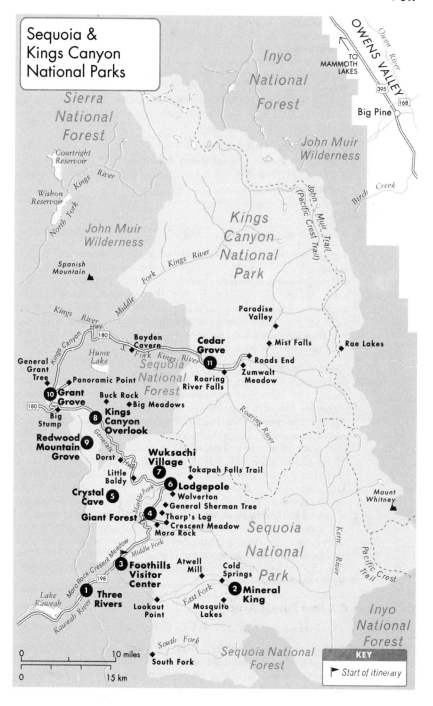

Sequoia &
Kings Canyon
National Parks

ing, playground, laundry facilities, some pets allowed (fee), no-smoking rooms ☐ *AE, D, DC, MC, V* ⦿ *CP.*

¢ 🏠 **Sierra Lodge.** Hundred-year-old oak trees surround this property, which is near the entrance to Sequoia National Park and Lake Kaweah. The 1960s cinder-block, motel-style lodge has mountain views. Some rooms have wood-burning fireplaces. ⊠ *43175 Sierra Dr., 93271* 🕾 *559/561–3681 or 800/ 367–8879* 🖷*559/561–3264* ⊕*www.sierra-lodge.com* ↩*22 rooms, 5 suites* ᇰ *Picnic area, BBQs, some kitchenettes, refrigerators, pool, some pets allowed (fee), no-smoking rooms* ☐ *AE, D, DC, MC, V* ⦿ *CP.*

Sports & the Outdoors

Contact the **Sequoia Natural History Association** (📇 HCR 89, Box 10, 93271 🕾 559/565–3759 ⊕ www.sequoiahistory.org) for information on bird-watching in the southern Sierra.

Mineral King

② *25 mi east of Three Rivers via Hwy. 198 and Mineral King Rd.*

Incorporated into Sequoia National Park in 1978, the Mineral King area is accessible from late May through October (weather permitting) by a narrow, twisting, steep road (trailers and RVs are prohibited) off High-way 198, several miles outside the park entrance. This tough but ex-citing drive (budget 90 minutes each way) leads to an alpine valley, where there are two campgrounds and a ranger station. Facilities are limited, but some supplies are available. Many backpackers use this as a trail-head, and fine day-hiking trails lead from here as well.

Where to Stay

¢–$$$ 🏠 **Silver City Resort.** High on the Mineral King Road, this resort offers an excellent alternative to the crowded properties at the parks' lower elevations. Lodgings range from modern Swiss-style chalets to traditional rustic alpine cabins. There is a small general store and modestly priced restaurant on-site, though the latter serves Thursday through Monday only. Some cabins share a central shower and bath. ⊠ *Mineral King Rd., 20 mi east of Hwy. 198, 93271* 🕾 *559/561–3223 or 805/528–2730* 🖷 *805/528–8039* ⊕ *www.silvercityresort.com* ↩ *13 cabins* ᇰ *Restaurant, some in-room data ports, some kitchens, beach, hiking; no a/c, no phones in some rooms, no room TVs* ☐ *MC, V* ⊗ *Closed Nov.–May.*

¢ 🏕 **Atwell Mill Campground.** Set at 6,650 feet, this tents-only campground is just south of the Western Divide. There are telephones and a general store ½ mi away at the Silver City Resort. Reservations are not accepted. ⊠ *Mineral King Rd., 20 mi east of Hwy. 198* 🕾 *559/565–3341* ↩ *23 sites* ᇰ *Pit toilets, drinking water, showers, bear boxes, fire grates, picnic tables* ⊗ *Closed Nov.–Apr.*

Lodgepole & Giant Forest Area

16–27 mi northeast of the Foothills Visitor Center on Generals Hwy.

To see Sequoia National Park from the south, you drive on Generals Highway, which begins at the park's Ash Mountain/Foothills entrance. ▶ **③** Before you venture into the park, it's helpful to stop at the **Foothills Visitor Center** for information and tickets to Crystal Cave. ⊠ *Generals*

Hwy. ☎ *559/565–3135* 🎫 *Free* ⊙ *Mid-May–Oct., daily 8–5; closed Oct.–mid-May.*

★ ❹ A 50-minute drive from Foothills, **Giant Forest** is known for its trails through a series of sequoia groves. You can get the best views of the big trees from the park's meadows, where flowers are in full bloom by June or July. The outstanding exhibits at the **Giant Forest Museum** trace the ecology of the giant sequoia. The **Big Trees Trail**, a ¾-mi paved trail, is easy to reach from the museum. ⊠ *Generals Hwy., 16 mi northeast of Foothills Visitor Center* ☎ *559/565–4480 museum* ⊙ *Museum: late May–mid-June, daily 8–5; mid-June–early Sept., daily 8–6; early Sept.–late May, daily 9–4:30.*

The **Moro Rock–Crescent Meadow Road** is a 3-mi spur road (closed in winter) that begins just south of the Giant Forest Museum and leads to Crescent Meadow, passing several landmarks along the way. The **Auto Log** is a wide fallen tree that visitors used to be able to drive their cars on; it's a great place to pose for photographs. The road also passes through the **Tunnel Log,** which is exactly that: a tunnel through a fallen sequoia tree. If your vehicle is too tall—7 foot 9 inches or more—a bypass is provided. (There is no standing drive-through Sequoia tree in the park. There used to be one in Yosemite, but it fell in 1969.) John Muir called **Crescent Meadow** the "gem of the Sierra"—brilliant wildflowers bloom here by midsummer; and a nearly 2-mi trail loops around the meadow. A 1½-mi round-trip trail that begins at Crescent Meadow leads to **Tharp's Log,** named for Hale Tharp, who built a pioneer cabin (still standing) out of a fire-hollowed sequoia.

★ **Moro Rock,** an immense granite monolith, stands along Moro Rock–Crescent Meadow Road, rising 6,725 feet from the edge of the Giant Forest. Four hundred steps lead to the top; the trail often climbs along narrow ledges over steep drops. The view from the top is stunning. To the southwest you look down the Kaweah River to Three Rivers, Lake Kaweah, and—on clear days—the Central Valley and the Coast Range. To the east stand the jagged peaks of the High Sierra.

The most famous sequoia in the Giant Forest area is the **General Sherman Tree** (⊠ 1 mi north of the Giant Forest, off Generals Hwy.). Benches allow you to sit and contemplate the tree's immensity: weighing in at 2.7 million pounds, it has the greatest volume of any living thing in the world. The first major branch is 130 feet above the ground. The paved **Congress Trail,** a popular 2-mi hike, starts at the General Sherman Tree and loops through the heart of the Giant Forest. In the one to two hours it takes to complete the loop you will pass groups of trees known as the House and Senate and individual trees called the President and McKinley.

★ ☾ ❺ Discovered in 1918 by two park employees, **Crystal Cave** is the best known of Sequoia's many caverns. Its interior, which was formed from limestone that metamorphosed into marble, is decorated with stalactites and stalagmites of various shapes, sizes, and colors. To visit the cave, you must first stop at the Foothills or Lodgepole Visitor Center to buy tickets; they are not sold at the cave. A narrow, twisting 7-mi road off the

Generals Highway leads you 2.2 mi south of the old Giant Forest Village. From the parking area it's a 15-minute hike down a steep path to the cave's entrance. It's cool inside—48°F—so bring a sweater. ⊠ *Crystal Cave Rd., off Generals Hwy.* ☎ *559/565–3759* ⊕ *www.sequoiahistory. org* ⊠ *$9* ⊙ *May–mid-Nov.; call for tour times.*

❻ Lodgepole sits in a canyon on the Marble Fork of the Kaweah River. Lodgepole pines, rather than sequoias, grow here because the U-shape canyon funnels in air from the high country that is too cold for the big trees. This area has a campground and a post office open year-round. A snack bar, market and deli, public laundry, and showers are open in the summer only. The **Lodgepole Visitor Center** has extensive exhibits, a small theater where you can watch an orientation slide show, and a first-aid center. You can buy tickets for the Crystal Cave, get advice from park rangers, purchase maps and books, and pick up wilderness permits. The **Tokopah Falls Trail** is an easy and rewarding 3½-mi round-trip hike from the Lodgepole Campground up the Marble Fork of the Kaweah River. The walk to the 1,200-foot falls, which flow down granite cliffs, is the closest you can get to the high country without substantial wear and tear on your hiking boots. Trail maps are available at the Lodgepole Visitor Center. Bring insect repellent during the summer; the mosquitoes can be ferocious. ⊠ *Generals Hwy., 5 mi north of Giant Forest Museum* ☎ *559/ 565–3782* ⊠ *Free* ⊙ *Visitor center mid-Apr.–mid-June, daily 8–5; mid-June–early Sept., daily 8–6; early Sept.–mid-Apr., weekends 9–4:30.*

❼ The dining and lodging facilities at **Wuksachi Village** (⊠ Generals Hwy., 6 mi north of Lodgepole) have replaced the antiquated facilities of the old Giant Forest Village, most of which has been demolished. These are the nicest facilities in the area. There's also a gift shop.

Where to Stay & Eat

★ **$–$$** ✕ **Wuksachi Village Dining Room.** In the high-ceiling dining room at Sequoia's only upscale restaurant, huge windows run the length of the room, providing a view of the surrounding trees. The dinner menu lists everything from sandwiches and burgers to steaks and pasta. Breakfast and lunch are also served. ⊠ *Wuksachi Village* ☎ *559/565–4070* ⟁ *Reservations essential* ⊟ *AE, D, DC, MC, V.*

★ **$$–$$$** ▥ **Wuksachi Village Lodge.** These cedar-and-stone lodge buildings, which blend with the landscape, house comfortable rooms with modern amenities. The village is 7,200 feet above sea level; many of the rooms have spectacular views of the surrounding mountains. ⊠ *Wuksachi Village* ☎ *559/565–4070 front desk, 559/253–2199, 888/252–5757 reservations* ⊟ *559/456–0542* ⊕ *www.visitsequoia.com* ⟲ *102 rooms* ⟁ *Restaurant, fans, in-room data ports, refrigerators, cable TV, hiking, cross-country skiing, ski storage, bar, meeting room, no-smoking rooms; no a/c* ⊟ *AE, D, DC, MC, V.*

¢ ⛺ **Lodgepole Campground.** The largest Lodgepole area campground is also the noisiest, though things do quiet down at night. Restrooms are nearby. Lodgepole and Dorst (a mile or so to the west) are the two campgrounds within Sequoia that accept reservations (essential up to five months in advance for stays between mid-May and mid-October). ⊠ *Off Generals Hwy. beyond Lodgepole Village* ☎ *559/565–3341 Ext. 2 informa-*

tion, 800/365–2267 reservations ⊕ *http://reservations.nps.gov* ⤳ *214 sites (tent and RV)* ♿ *Flush toilets, dump station (summer only), drinking water, showers (summer only), guest laundry (summer only), bear boxes, fire grates, picnic tables, public telephone, general store.*

Sports & the Outdoors

Hiking and backpacking are the top outdoor activities in Sequoia National Park (*see* Camping *in* the Southern Sierra A to Z). In winter you can cross-country ski, snowshoe, and sled, and in summer mule rides are available. The visitor centers have information on trail conditions. Conditions permitting, you can rent winter sports equipment at **Wuksachi Village Lodge** (☎ 559/565–4070).

Sequoia National Forest

15–20 mi northwest of Lodgepole on Generals Hwy.

Though you may not even notice the change, on your way to Grant Grove, the Generals Highway leaves Sequoia National Park and passes through a section of Sequoia National Forest.

❽ **Kings Canyon Overlook,** a large turnout on the north side of the Generals Highway, has views across the canyon of mountain peaks and the backcountry. If you drive to Cedar Grove (about 1 hour east of Grant Grove on Highway 180, open summer only) along the south fork, you will see these spectacular canyons at much closer range.

★ ❾ The **Redwood Mountain Grove** is the largest grove of sequoias in the world. As you enter Kings Canyon on the Generals Highway, several paved turnouts allow you to look out over the grove (and into the smog of the Central Valley). The grove itself is accessible only on foot or horseback.

Where to Stay

$$ 🏨 **Stony Creek.** Sitting at 6,800 feet among the peaceful pines, Stony Creek is on national forest land between Giant Forest and Grant Grove. Rooms are plain but are carpeted and have private showers. A restaurant is adjacent to the lodge. ⊠ *Generals Hwy.* ⊕ *Sequoia Kings Canyon Park Services Co., 5755 E. Kings Canyon Rd., Suite 101, Fresno 93727* ☎ *559/565–3909 or 866/522–6966* 🖷 *559/565–3913* ⊕ *www.sequoia-kingscanyon.com* ⤳ *11 rooms* ♿ *Restaurant, in-room data ports, cable TV, Internet; no a/c, no smoking* ⊟ *AE, D, MC, V* ☉ *Closed Sept.–May* ⊘ *CP.*

¢–$ 🏨 **Montecito-Sequoia Lodge.** A summer-camp atmosphere prevails all year long at this family-oriented resort just south of Kings Canyon National Park. Specializing in all-inclusive vacations, it offers everything from skiing and snowboarding in winter to sailing and horseback riding in summer. From mid-June to early September there's normally a six-night minimum, but you can book a one-night stay on Saturdays. ⊠ *Generals Hwy., 11 mi south of Grant Grove* ☎ *559/565–3388 or 800/227–9900* 🖷 *650/967–0540* ⊕ *www.montecitosequoia.com* ⤳ *32 rooms, 13 cabins* ♿ *Dining room, snack bar, BBQs, tennis court, pool, lake, boating, waterskiing, fishing, bicycles, archery, hiking, horseback riding, volleyball, cross-country skiing, ice-skating, children's programs (ages 2–18); no a/c, no room phones, no room TVs* ⊟ *AE, D, MC, V* ⊘ *FAP.*

Grant Grove

❿   *27 mi north of Lodgepole via Generals Hwy. to Kings Canyon Hwy.*

Kings Canyon's most developed area was designated General Grant National Park (the forerunner of Kings Canyon National Park) in 1890. This is another entry point to the national parks, and the **Grant Grove Visitor Center** is a good place to get information and to see exhibits on the sequoias and the area. ⊠ *Kings Canyon Hwy., Grant Grove Village* ☎ *559/565–4307* 🎟 *Free* ☯ *May–mid-June and early Sept.–Oct., daily 8–5; mid-June–early Sept., daily 8–6; Nov.–Apr., daily 9–4:30.*

The visitor center is part of compact and often crowded **Grant Grove Village,** which also contains a grocery store, gift shop, campgrounds, a restaurant that has family dining, overnight lodging, and a post office. A walk along 1-mi **Big Stump Trail,** which starts near the park entrance, graphically demonstrates the toll heavy logging takes on wilderness. The **General Grant Tree Trail,** a paved ⅓-mi path, winds past the General Grant, an enormous, 2,000-year-old sequoia, the world's third-largest, which has been designated "the nation's Christmas tree." The **Gamlin Cabin,** an 1867 pioneer cabin, is listed on the National Register of Historic Places. Also within Grant Grove is the **Centennial Stump,** the remains of a huge sequoia cut for display at the 1876 Philadelphia Centennial Exhibition.

> **off the beaten path**

HUME LAKE. – This reservoir, built by loggers in the early 1900s, is now the site of several church-affiliated camps, a gas station, and a public campground. Outside Kings Canyon's borders, the small lake has views of the mountains in the distance. ⊠ *Hume Lake Rd., off Kings Canyon Hwy., 8 mi northeast of Grant Grove.*

Where to Stay

$$ 🏨 **John Muir Lodge.** This modern, timber-sided lodge is nestled in a wooded area near Grant Grove Village. The 24 rooms and six suites all have queen beds and private baths, and there's a comfortable lobby with a stone fireplace where you can play cards and board games. The inexpensive, family-style Grant Grove Restaurant is a three-minute walk away. Though it's little more than a good motel, this is the best place to stay in Grant Grove. ⊠ *Kings Canyon Hwy., ¼ mi north of Grant Grove Village* ⊕ *Sequoia Kings Canyon Park Services Co., 5755 E. Kings Canyon Rd., Suite 101, Fresno 93727* ☎ *559/335–5500 or 866/522–6966* 🖷 *559/335–5507* ⊕ *www.sequoia-kingscanyon.com* 🛏 *24 rooms, 6 suites* ♿ *Meeting room; no a/c, no room TVs* ▤ *AE, D, MC, V.*

¢ 🏕 **Azalea Campground.** One of three campgrounds in the Grant Grove area (the others are Sunset and Crystal Springs, both open May through September only), Azalea is open year-round. It sits at 6,500 feet amid giant sequoias, yet is close to restaurants, stores, and other facilities. Some sites at Azalea are wheelchair accessible. The campground can accommodate RVs up to 30 feet. Though it costs $18 May to mid-October—and reservations are not accepted—it's free the rest of the year. ⊠ *Kings Canyon Hwy., ¼ mi north of Grant Grove Village* ☎ *559/565–3341*

🔌 *113 sites (tent or RV)* ♿ *Flush toilets, drinking water, showers, bear boxes, fire grates, picnic tables, public telephone, general store.*

Sports & the Outdoors

The primary activities in Kings Canyon are hiking and backpacking (*see* Camping *in* The Southern Sierra A to Z). Bicycling is discouraged, because the only paved roads outside village areas are the Kings Canyon and Generals highways, both winding mountain roads with heavy traffic. Horseback riding is an enjoyable alternative in summer. Winter snows turn the park into a playground for cross-country skiers and snowshoers, and there are dedicated areas for sledding. Check with the visitor center for conditions and trail maps.

HORSEBACK RIDING **Grant Grove Stables** (✉ Grant Grove Village ☎ 559/335–9292 mid-June–Sept., 559/594–9307 Oct.–mid-June) organizes rides of various lengths.

WINTER SPORTS Pick up ski and snowshoe rentals (sleds are for sale only) at **Grant Grove Village Market** (☎ 559/335–5500).

en route A spectacular 30-mi descent along **Kings Canyon Highway** takes about an hour from Grant Grove to Roads End, where you can hike or camp. Built by convict labor in the 1930s, the road (usually closed from mid-October through April) clings to some dramatic cliffs along the way: watch out for falling rocks. The highway passes the scars where large groves of sequoias were felled at the beginning of the 20th century. It runs along the south fork of the Kings River and through dry hills covered with yuccas that bloom in the summer. There are amazing views into the deepest gorge in the United States (deeper even than the Grand Canyon) and up the canyons to the High Sierra.

Cedar Grove

⑪ *31 mi east of Grant Grove on Kings Canyon Hwy.*

Named for the incense cedars that grow in the area, Cedar Grove is nestled in a valley that snakes along the south fork of the Kings River. **Cedar Grove Village** (✉ East end of Kings Canyon Hwy. ☎ 559/565–3793 visitor center) has campgrounds, lodgings, a small visitor center, a snack bar, a cafeteria, a convenience market, and a gift shop, but it's only open April to November, depending on snowfall.

About 4½ mi southeast of Cedar Grove Village, short trails circle grassy **Zumwalt Meadow,** which is surrounded by towering granite walls. Trails from Zumwalt Meadow lead to the base of **Roaring River Falls,** which run hardest in spring and early summer.

Where to Stay & Eat

$ ✕🛏 **Cedar Grove Lodge.** Although accommodations are close to the road, this lodge manages to deliver peace and quiet. Book far in advance—the lodge has only 21 rooms. Each room has two queen-size beds, and three have kitchenettes. You can order trout, hamburgers, hot dogs, and sandwiches at the snack bar (¢–$) and take them to one of the picnic tables along the river's edge. ⊠ *Kings Canyon Hwy.* ⚙ *Sequoia Kings Canyon Park Services Co., 5755 E. Kings Canyon Rd., Suite 101, Fresno 93727* ☎ *559/335–5500 or 866/522–6966* 🖷 *559/335–5507* ⊕ *www.sequoia-kingscanyon.com* ⇆ *21 rooms* ⌂ *Snack bar, some kitchenettes, hiking, laundry facilities; no room phones, no room TVs, no smoking* ⊟ *AE, D, MC, V* ⊘ *Closed mid-Oct.–mid-May.*

Sports & the Outdoors

For horseback rides in the wilderness, head to **Cedar Grove Pack Station** (⊠ Cedar Grove Village ☎ 559/565–3464 mid-June–Sept., 559/337–2314 Oct.–mid-June).

SOUTH OF YOSEMITE

FROM BASS LAKE TO EL PORTAL

Several gateway towns to the south and west of Yosemite National Park, most within an hour's drive of Yosemite Valley, have food, lodging, and other services. Highway 140 heads east from the San Joaquin Valley to El Portal. Highway 41 heads north from Fresno to Oakhurst and Fish Camp; Bass Lake is off Highway 41.

Bass Lake

50 mi north of Fresno via Hwy. 41 to Bass Valley Rd.

For the most part surrounded by the Sierra National Forest, Bass Lake is a warm-water reservoir whose waters can reach 80° in summer. Created by a dam on a tributary of the San Joaquin River, the lake is owned by Pacific Gas and Electric Company and is used to generate electricity as well as for recreation.

Where to Eat

¢–$$$ ✕ **Ducey's on the Lake/Ducey's Bar & Grill.** With elaborate chandeliers sculpted from deer antlers, the lodge-style restaurant at Ducey's (part of the larger Pines Resort complex) attracts boaters, locals, and tourists with its lake views and standard lamb, beef, seafood, and pasta dishes. For cheap eats, head upstairs to Ducey's Bar & Grill for burgers, salads, tacos, and sandwiches. ⊠ *54432 Rd. 432* ☎ *559/642–3121* ⊟ *AE, D, DC, MC, V.*

Sports & the Outdoors

Bass Lake Water Sports and Marina (⊠ Bass Lake Reservoir ☎ 559/642–3565) rents ski boats, patio boats, and fishing boats.

Oakhurst

40 mi north of Fresno and 23 mi south of Yosemite National Park's South Entrance on Hwy. 41.

Motels and restaurants line both sides of Highway 41 as it cuts through the town of Oakhurst. You can stock up on provisions at the grocery and general stores.

Where to Stay & Eat

$$$$ ✕ **Erna's Elderberry House.** Operated by Erna Kubin, owner of Château
FodorsChoice du Sureau, this restaurant has a beautiful setting and impeccable service.
★ Red walls and dark beams accent the dining room's high ceilings, and
arched windows reflect the glow of candles. A seasonal six-course prix-
fixe dinner is accompanied by superb wines. When the waitstaff places
all the plates on the table in perfect synchronicity, you know this will be
a meal to remember. A small bistro menu is also served in the former
wine cellar. ✉ *48688 Victoria La.* ☎ *559/683–6800* ⚓ *Reservations essential* ▤ *AE, D, MC, V* ⊘ *Closed 1st 3 wks in Jan. No lunch Mon.–Sat.*

$$$$ ⌂ **Château du Sureau.** This romantic inn, adjacent to Erna's Elderberry
FodorsChoice House, is out of a children's book. From the moment you drive through
★ the wrought-iron gates and up to the fairy-tale castle, you feel pampered.
After falling asleep by the glow of a crackling fire amid goose-down pillows, you can enjoy a hearty European breakfast in the dining room,
or relax in the piano room, which has an exquisite ceiling mural. Cable
TV is available by request only. ✉ *48688 Victoria La.* ✉ *Box 577, 93644*
☎ *559/683–6860* 📠 *559/683–0800* ⊕ *www.elderberryhouse.com* ⇨ *10
rooms, 1 villa* ⚭ *Restaurant, in-room data ports, golf privileges, pool,
pond, boccie, bar, shop, laundry service, Internet; no kids under 12, no
smoking* ▤ *AE, MC, V* †⊙† *BP.*

$$–$$$$ ⌂ **Homestead Cottages.** Serenity is the order of the day at this secluded
getaway in Ahwahnee, 6 mi west of Oakhurst. On 160 acres that once
held a Miwok village, these cottages have fireplaces, living rooms,
fully equipped kitchens, and queen-size beds; the largest sleeps six. The
cottages, hand-built by the owners, are stocked with soft robes, over-
size towels, and a good supply of paperbacks. ✉ *41110 Rd. 600, 2½
mi off Hwy. 49, Ahwahnee 93601* ☎ *559/683–0495 or 800/483–0495*
📠 *559/683–8165* ⊕ *www.homesteadcottages.com* ⇨ *5 cottages, 1
loft* ⚭ *BBQs, kitchens, cable TV, hiking; no room phones, no smok-
ing* ▤ *AE, D, MC, V.*

$–$$ ⌂ **Shilo Inn.** Rooms at this four-story motel are spacious and sunny and
offer extra amenities such as in-room coffeemakers, irons, and hair
dryers. ✉ *40644 Hwy. 41, 93644* ☎ *559/683–3555 or 800/222–2244*
📠 *559/683–3386* ⊕ *www.shiloinns.com* ⇨ *80 rooms, 1 suite* ⚭ *Microwaves, refrigerators, cable TV with movies, pool, gym, hot tub,
sauna, steam room, laundry facilities, no-smoking rooms* ▤ *AE, D, DC,
MC, V* †⊙† *CP.*

Fish Camp

⑰ *57 mi north of Fresno and 4 mi south of Yosemite National Park's South
Entrance on Hwy. 41.*

In this small town there is a post office and a general store. The **Yosemite
♻ Mountain Sugar Pine Railroad** has a narrow-gauge steam engine that
chugs through the forest. It follows 4 mi of the route the Madera Sugar
Pine Lumber Company cut through the forest in 1899 in order to har-
vest timber. On Saturday (and Wednesday in summer), the Moonlight
Special dinner excursion (reservations essential) includes music by the
Sugar Pine Singers. ✉ *56001 Hwy. 41* ☎ *559/683–7273* ⊕ *www.
ymsprr.com* ✉ *$14; Moonlight Special $38* ⊘ *Mar.–Oct., daily.*

Where to Stay & Eat

★ **$$$$** ✕⌧ **Tenaya Lodge.** One of the region's largest hotels, the Tenaya Lodge is ideal for people who enjoy wilderness treks by day but prefer luxury at night. The ample regular rooms are decorated in pleasant earth tones, deluxe rooms have minibars and other extras, and the suites have balconies. The cozy Sierra Restaurant ($$–$$$$), with its high ceilings and giant fireplace, serves continental cuisine. The more casual Jackalopes Bar and Grill ($–$$) has burgers, salads, and sandwiches. ✉ *1122 Hwy. 41 ⌂ Box 159, 93623* ☎ *559/683–6555 or 888/514–2167* ⌸ *559/683–0249* ⊕ *www.tenayalodge.com* ⇨ *244 rooms, 6 suites ⌂ 2 restaurants, snack bar, room service, in-room data ports, some minibars, cable TV with movies and video games, indoor pool, health club, hot tub, mountain bikes, hiking, cross-country skiing, bar, recreation room, babysitting, children's programs (ages 5–12), playground, laundry service, concierge, business services, meeting room; no smoking* ⊟ *AE, D, DC, MC, V.*

$–$$ ✕⌧ **Narrow Gauge Inn.** All of the rooms at this well-tended property have great views of the surrounding woods and are comfortably furnished with old-fashioned accents and railroad memorabilia. The restaurant ($–$$$), which specializes in steaks and American fare, is festooned with moose, bison, and other wildlife trophies. It's open April–October, Wednesday–Sunday. ✉ *48571 Hwy. 41, 93623* ☎ *559/683–7720 or 888/644–9050* ⌸ *559/683–2139* ⊕ *www.narrowgaugeinn.com* ⇨ *25 rooms, 1 suite ⌂ Restaurant, in-room data ports, cable TV, some in-room VCRs, pool, hot tub, bar, some pets allowed (fee); no a/c in some rooms, no smoking* ⊟ *D, MC, V* ⦿ *CP.*

El Portal

14 mi west of Yosemite Valley on Hwy. 140.

The market in town is a good place to pick up provisions before you get to Yosemite. There is also a post office and a gas station.

Where to Stay

$$–$$$ ⌧ **Yosemite View Lodge.** Many rooms here have whirlpool baths, fireplaces, kitchenettes, and balconies overlooking the boulder-strewn Merced River and majestic pines. Also in view is a picnic patio with hot tubs and heated pools. The pleasant facility is on the public bus route to Yosemite National Park and near fishing and river rafting. ✉ *11136 Hwy. 140, 95318* ☎ *209/379–2681 or 888/742–4371* ⌸ *209/379–2704* ⊕ *www.yosemite-motels.com* ⇨ *276 rooms ⌂ Restaurant, pizzeria, some kitchenettes, cable TV, 2 pools (1 indoor), some in-room hot tubs, bar, laundry facilities, meeting room, some pets allowed (fee), no-smoking rooms* ⊟ *AE, MC, V.*

$–$$ ⌧ **Cedar Lodge.** The lobby of this motel-style lodge in the pines is filled with teddy bears. Rooms range from suites with kitchenettes to family units to romantic accommodations with whirlpool tubs for two. ✉ *9966 Hwy. 140, 95318* ☎ *209/379–2612 or 888/742–4371* ⌸ *209/379–2712* ⊕ *www.yosemite-motels.com* ⇨ *188 rooms, 22 suites, 2 apartments, 1 house ⌂ Restaurant, BBQs, some kitchenettes, cable TV, 2 pools, hot tub, no-smoking rooms* ⊟ *AE, MC, V.*

YOSEMITE NATIONAL PARK

➤ Yosemite, with 1,189 square mi of parkland, is 94.5% undeveloped wilderness, most of it accessible only on foot or horseback. The western boundary dips as low as 2,000 feet in the chaparral-covered foothills; the eastern boundary rises to 13,000 feet at points along the Sierra crest.

Yosemite is so large you can think of it as five different parks. Yosemite Valley, famous for waterfalls and cliffs, and Wawona, where the giant sequoias stand, are open all year. Hetch Hetchy, home of less-used backcountry trails, closes after the first big snow and reopens in May or June. The subalpine high country, Tuolumne Meadows, is open for summer hiking and camping; in winter it's accessible only by cross-country skis or snowshoes. Badger Pass Ski Area is open in winter only. The fee to visit Yosemite National Park (good for seven days) is $20 per car, $10 per person if you don't arrive in a car.

On entering the park, you'll receive two free newspapers, which you really should read. *Yosemite Today* lists locations and times for ranger-hosted nature walks. The *Yosemite Guide* lists useful, but more general, information.

Yosemite Valley

214 mi east of San Francisco via I–80 to I–580 to I–205 to Hwy. 120; 330 mi northeast of Los Angeles via I–5 to Hwy. 99 to Hwy. 41.

Yosemite Valley has been so extravagantly praised (John Muir described it as "a revelation in landscape") and so beautifully photographed (by Ansel Adams, who said, "I knew my destiny when I first experienced Yosemite") that you may wonder if the reality can possibly measure up. For almost everyone it does. It's a true reminder of what "breathtaking" really means. The Miwok, the last of several Native American people to inhabit the Yosemite area (they were forced out by gold miners in 1851), named the valley "Ahwahnee," which is thought to mean "the place of the gaping mouth."

It's important to remember a few things when visiting the valley. The roads at the eastern end of the valley are closed to private cars, but a free shuttle bus runs frequently from the village (7 AM–10 PM May–September, 9 AM–10 PM the rest of the year). Directions to the day-use parking lot, near the intersection of Sentinel and Northside drives, can be found on the back of the *Yosemite Guide*. Bears are a huge problem in Yosemite; be sure to read pamphlets on the subject or speak with a ranger, and take proper precautions while in the park.

⑬ The center of activity in Yosemite Valley is **Yosemite Village,** which contains restaurants, stores, a post office, and a clinic; the Ahwahnee Hotel and Yosemite Lodge are nearby. You can get your bearings, pick up maps, and obtain information from park rangers at the village's **Valley Visitor Center.** A 1-mi paved loop from the visitor center, called **A Changing Yosemite,** traces the park's natural evolution and includes a couple of interesting stops. At the **Wilderness Center** you can find out everything you need to know about backcountry activities like hiking and camping. The **Yosemite Museum** has an Indian cultural exhibit, with displays about the Miwok and Paiute people who lived in the region; there's a re-created Ahwahneechee village behind it. The **Ansel Adams Gallery** shows works of the master photographer and sells prints and camera equipment. ⊠ *Off Northside Dr.* ☎ *209/372–0200 visitor center, 209/372–4413 gallery* ⊙ *Visitor center fall–spring, daily 9–5; summer, daily 8–6.*

⓮ **FodorśChoice** **★** Yosemite Valley is famed for its waterfalls, and the mightiest of them all is **Yosemite Falls,** the highest waterfall in North America and the fifth-highest in the world. The upper fall (1,430 feet), the middle cascades (675 feet), and the lower fall (320 feet) combine for a total drop of 2,425 feet. In spring and early summer, when the falls run their hardest, you can hear them thunder all across the valley. (Be warned, though, that the falls slow to a trickle in winter.) When viewed from the valley, the three sections appear as a single waterfall. A ¼-mi trail leads from the parking lot to the base of the falls. The Upper Yosemite Fall Trail, a strenuous 3½-mi climb rising 2,700 feet, takes you above the top of the falls. It starts at Camp 4, formerly known as Sunnyside Campground.

★ ⓯ Yosemite Valley's waterfalls tumble past magnificent geological scenery. **El Capitan,** rising 3,593 feet above the valley, is the largest exposed granite monolith in the world, almost twice the height of the Rock of Gibraltar.

⓰ At 1,612 feet, **Ribbon Fall** is the highest single fall in North America. It is also the first waterfall in the valley to dry up; the rainwater and melted snow that create the slender fall evaporate quickly at this height.

★ ⓱ **Bridalveil Fall,** a filmy fall of 620 feet that is often diverted as much as 20 feet one way or the other by the breeze, is the first view of Yosemite Valley for those who arrive via Wawona Road. Native Americans called the fall Pohono ("spirit of the puffing wind"). A ¼-mi trail leads to the base of the fall from the parking lot off the intersection of Southside Drive and Wawona Road.

⏣ ⓲ As you venture through the valley amid Yosemite's natural wonders, stop at the **Happy Isles Nature Center** to see ecology exhibits and find books for children. ⊠ *½ mi east of Curry Village* ☎ *209/372–0299* ⊙ *May–Oct., daily 9–5 but may vary.*

⓳ Fern-covered black rocks frame **Vernal Fall** (317 feet), and rainbows play in the spray at its base. The hike from the Happy Isles Nature Center to the bridge at the base of Vernal Fall is less than 1 mi long, on a paved trail, and only moderately strenuous. It's another steep (and often wet) ¾ mi up the Mist Trail—which is open only from late spring to early fall—to the top of Vernal Fall. Allow two to four hours for the 3-mi round-trip hike.

⓴ **Nevada Fall** (594 feet) is the first major fall as the Merced River plunges out of the high country toward the eastern end of Yosemite Valley. A strenuous 2-mi section of the Mist Trail leads from Vernal Fall to the top of Nevada Fall. Allow six–eight hours for the full 7-mi round-trip hike.

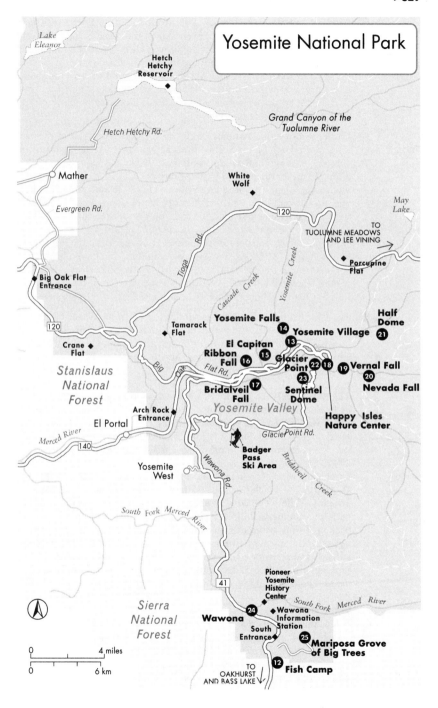

Yosemite National Park

★ ㉑ Astounding **Half Dome** rises 4,733 feet from the valley floor to a height 8,842 feet above sea level. The west side of the dome is fractured vertically and cut away to form a 2,000-foot cliff. The highly strenuous **John Muir Trail,** which incorporates the Mist Trail, leads from Yosemite Valley to the top of Half Dome. Allow 10–12 hours for the 16¾-mi round-trip; start early in the morning and beware of afternoon thunderstorms. If you plan to take this hike, inquire about necessary preparations at one of the ranger stations.

㉒ **Glacier Point** yields what may be the most spectacular vista of the val-
Fodor'sChoice ley and the High Sierra that you can get without hiking, especially at
★ sunset. Glacier Point Road splits off from Wawona Road (Highway 41) about 23 mi southwest of the valley; then it's a 16-mi drive through the woods into higher country. From the parking area walk a few hundred yards, and you'll be able to see Nevada, Vernal, and Yosemite Falls as well as Half Dome and other peaks. You can hike to the valley floor (3,214 feet below) via the Panorama or Four-Mile trails. To avoid a grueling round-trip, catch a ride to Glacier Point on one of the three daily **hikers' buses** (☎ 209/372–1240 reservations), which run from late spring through October; the cost is $15 one-way, $29.50 round-trip. In winter, Glacier Point Road is closed beyond the turnoff for the Badger Pass Ski Area, making Glacier Point inaccessible.

㉓ The view from **Sentinel Dome** is similar to that from Glacier Point, except you can't see the valley floor. A 1.1-mi path begins at a parking lot on Glacier Point Road a few miles below Glacier Point. The trail is long and steep enough to keep the crowds and tour buses away, but not overly rugged.

off the beaten path

The **HETCH HETCHY RESERVOIR, –** which supplies water and hydroelectric power to San Francisco, is about 40 mi from Yosemite Valley via Big Oak Flat Road to Highway 120 to Evergreen Road to Hetch Hetchy Road. Some say John Muir died of heartbreak when this valley was dammed and flooded beneath 300 feet of water in 1913.

Spectacularly scenic Tioga Road is the only route to **TUOLUMNE MEADOWS, –** which sits at 8,575 feet in altitude about 55 mi from Yosemite Valley. The largest subalpine meadow in the Sierra, it bursts with late-summer wildflowers; it's also the trailhead for many backpack trips into the High Sierra. The area contains campgrounds, a gas station, a store (with limited and expensive provisions), stables, a lodge, and a visitor center that is open from late June until early September from 9 to 5. Tioga Road (Highway 120) stays open until the first big snow of the year, usually about mid-October.

Where to Stay & Eat

$$–$$$ ✕ **Mountain Room Restaurant.** Though very good, the food becomes secondary when you see Yosemite Falls through this dining room's wall of windows. Almost every table has a view of the falls. Grilled trout and salmon, steak, pasta, and several children's dishes are on the menu. ⊠ *Yosemite Lodge off Northside Dr.* ☎ *209/372–1281* ⌣ *Reservations*

essential ☰ *AE, D, DC, MC, V* ☻ *Closed weekdays Thanksgiving–Easter except holiday periods. No lunch.*

$$$$ ✕⌨ **Ahwahnee Hotel & Dining Room.** This grand 1920s-era mountain lodge,
Fodor'sChoice designated a National Historic Landmark, is constructed of rocks and
★ sugar-pine logs. Many of the amenities found in a luxury hotel, including turn-down service and guest bathrobes, are here. The Dining Room ($$$–$$$$), which has a 34-foot-tall beamed ceiling, full-length windows, and wrought-iron chandeliers, is by far the most impressive eating establishment in the park. Specialties include sautéed salmon, roast duckling, and prime rib. Jackets are required, and reservations are essential. ⊠ *Ahwahnee Rd. north of Northside Dr., 95389* ☏ *Yosemite Reservations, 5410 E. Home Ave., Fresno 93727* ☎ *559/252–4848 lodging reservations, 209/372–1489 restaurant* ⊕ *www.yosemitepark. com* ⇗ *99 rooms, 4 suites, 24 cottages* ⚲ *Restaurant, in-room data ports, refrigerators, cable TV, tennis court, pool, lounge, concierge, no-smoking rooms; no a/c in some rooms* ☰ *AE, D, DC, MC, V.*

$–$$ ✕⌨ **Yosemite Lodge.** This lodge near Yosemite Falls, which dates from 1915, once housed the U.S. army cavalry. Today it looks like a 1950s motel-resort complex, with several brown-and-white buildings that blend in with the landscape. Rooms have two double beds, and larger rooms also have dressing areas and balconies. A few have views of the falls. Of the lodge's eating places, the Mountain Room Restaurant ($$–$$$) is the most formal. The cafeteria-style Food Court (¢–$) serves three meals a day and offers salads, soups, sandwiches, pastas, and roasted meats. ⊠ *Off Northside Dr., 95389* ☏ *Yosemite Reservations, 5410 E. Home Ave., Fresno 93727* ☎ *559/252–4848* 🖷 *559/456–0542* ⊕ *www.yosemitepark.com* ⇗ *239 rooms* ⚲ *Restaurant, cafeteria, fans, in-room data ports, pool, bicycles, bar, no-smoking rooms; no a/c, no room TVs* ☰ *AE, D, DC, MC, V.*

¢–$ ⌨ **Curry Village.** Opened in 1899 as a place where travelers could enjoy the beauty of Yosemite for a modest price, Curry Village has plain accommodations: standard motel rooms, cabins, and tent cabins, which have rough wood frames and canvas walls and roofs. The latter are a step up from camping, with linens, blankets, and maid service provided. Most of the cabins share shower and toilet facilities. ⊠ *South side of Southside Dr., 95389* ☏ *Yosemite Reservations, 5410 E. Home Ave., Fresno 93727* ☎ *209/372–8333 front desk, 559/252–4848 reservations* 🖷 *559/456–0542* ⊕ *www.yosemitepark.com* ⇗ *19 rooms; 182 cabins, 102 with bath; 427 tent cabins* ⚲ *Cafeteria, pizzeria, pool, bicycles, ice-skating, no-smoking rooms; no a/c, no room phones, no room TVs* ☰ *AE, D, DC, MC, V.*

¢ ⌨ **Housekeeping Camp.** Set along the Merced River, these three-sided concrete units with canvas roofs may look a bit rustic, but they're good for travelers with RVs or those without a tent who want to camp. You can cook here on gas stoves rented from the front desk, or you can use the fire pits. Toilets and showers are in a central building, and there is a camp store for provisions. ⊠ *North side of Southside Dr., near Curry Village* ☏ *Yosemite Reservations, 5410 E. Home Ave., Fresno 93727* ☎ *209/ 372–8338, 559/252–4848 reservations* 🖷 *559/456–0542* ⊕ *www. yosemitepark.com* ⇗ *226 units* ⚲ *Picnic area, beach, laundry facilities;*

no a/c, no room phones, no room TVs ☰ *AE, D, DC, MC, V* ☉ *Closed early Oct.–late Apr.*

¢ ⛺ **Camp 4.** Formerly known as Sunnyside Walk-In, this is the only valley campground available on a first-come, first-served basis and the only one west of Yosemite Lodge. Open year-round, it is a favorite for rock climbers and solo campers, so it fills quickly and is typically sold out by 9 AM every day from spring through fall. ✉ *Base of Yosemite Falls Trail, near Yosemite Lodge* ☎ *209/372–0265* 🖷 *209/372–0371* 🛏 *35 sites* ⚲ *Flush toilets, drinking water, showers, bear boxes, fire grates, picnic tables, public telephone, ranger station.*

¢ ⛺ **Tuolumne Meadows.** In a wooded area at 8,600 feet, just south of its namesake meadow, this campground is one of the most spectacular and sought-after campgrounds in Yosemite. Hot showers can be used at the Tuolumne Meadows Lodge, though only at certain strictly regulated times. Half the sites are first-come, first-served, so arrive early or make reservations. The campground is open July–September. ✉ *Hwy. 120, 46 mi east of Big Oak Flat entrance station* ☎ *209/372–0265 or 800/436–7275* 🖷 *209/372–0371* ⊕ *http://reservations.nps.gov* 🛏 *314 sites (tent or RV)* ⚲ *Flush toilets, dump station, drinking water, bear boxes, fire grates, picnic tables, public telephone, general store, ranger station.*

Sports & the Outdoors

BICYCLING You can explore the 12 mi of dedicated bicycle paths in Yosemite Valley or, if you don't mind traffic, ride the park's 196 mi of paved roads. **Yosemite Lodge** (☎ 209/372–1208) rents bicycles all year for $5.50 an hour or $21 per day. Rental bikes are available at **Curry Village** (☎ 209/372–8319) from April through October. Baby jogger strollers and bikes with child trailers are also available.

HIKING Yosemite's 840 mi of hiking trails range from short strolls to rugged multiday treks. The park's visitor centers have trail maps and information, and rangers will recommend easy trails to get you acclimated to the altitude. The staff at the **Wilderness Center** (✉ Yosemite Village, near Ansel Adams Gallery ⌂ Yosemite Wilderness Reservations, Box 545, Yosemite 95389 ☎ 209/372–0740 ⊕ www.nps.gov/yose) provides free wilderness permits, which are required for overnight camping (reservations are available for $5 and are highly recommended for popular trailheads from May through September and on weekends). They also provide maps and advice to hikers heading into the backcountry.

Yosemite Mountaineering School (☎ 209/372–8344), at the Curry Village Mountain Shop and other satellite locations, has guided half- and full-day treks, conducts rock-climbing and backpacking classes, and can design customized hikes for you.

HORSEBACK RIDING **Tuolumne Meadows Stables** (☎ 209/372–8427) runs two-, four- and eight-hour trips, costing $51–$94, and High Sierra four- to six-day camping treks on mules beginning at $617. You can tour the valley and the start of the high country on two-hour, four-hour, and all-day rides at **Yosemite Valley Stables** (✉ Near Curry Village ☎ 209/372–8348).

ICE-SKATING The outdoor **ice-skating rink** (✉ South side of Southside Dr., Curry Village ☎ 209/372–8341) is open from Thanksgiving through April, afternoons and evenings, with morning sessions on the weekends. Admission is $9.75, including skate rental.

SKIING California's first ski resort, **Badger Pass Ski Area** has nine downhill runs, 90 mi of groomed cross-country trails, and two excellent ski schools. Free shuttle buses from Yosemite Valley operate in ski season (December–early April, weather permitting). Lift tickets are $31, downhill equipment rents for $22.50, and snowboard rental is $32.50. The gentle slopes of Badger Pass make **Yosemite Ski School** (☎ 209/372–8430) an ideal spot for children and beginners to learn downhill skiing or snowboarding. The highlight of Yosemite's cross-country skiing center is a 21-mi loop from Badger Pass to Glacier Point. You can rent cross-country skis for $17 per day at the **Cross-Country Ski School** (☎ 209/372–8444), which also rents snowshoes ($15 per day), telemarking equipment ($21.50), and skate-skis ($19.50). ⊠ *Badger Pass Rd., off Glacier Point Rd., 18 mi from Yosemite Valley* ☎ *209/372–8430* ☞ *9 trails on 85 acres, rated 35% beginner, 50% intermediate, 15% advanced. Longest run ³⁄₁₀ mi, base 7,200′, summit, 8,000′. Lifts: 5.*

Yosemite Mountaineering School (⊠ Badger Pass Ski Area ☎ 209/372–8344) conducts snowshoeing, cross-country skiing, telemarking, and skate-skiing classes.

Wawona

㉔ *25 mi south of Yosemite Valley and 16 mi north of Fish Camp on Hwy. 41.*

The historic buildings in **Pioneer Yosemite History Center** were moved to Wawona from their original sites in the park. You can take a self-guided tour around their exteriors at any time, day or night. Wednesday through Sunday in summer, costumed docents re-create 19th-century Yosemite life in a blacksmith's shop, a jail, and other buildings. At the nearby information center, you can ask about schedules of ranger-led walks and horse-drawn stage rides (alternatively, check *Yosemite Today*). ⊠ *Hwy. 41* ☎ *209/375–9531 or 209/379–2646* ☒ *Free* ☉ *Grounds daily 24 hrs. Buildings mid-June–early September, Wed. 2–5, Thurs.–Sun. 10–1 and 2–5. Information center late May–early September, daily 8:30–4:30.*

㉕ **Mariposa Grove of Big Trees,** Yosemite's largest grove of giant sequoias, can be visited on foot—trails all lead uphill—or, in summer, on one-hour tram rides (reservations essential). The Grizzly Giant, the oldest tree here, is estimated to be 2,700 years old. In summer, a free shuttle connects Wawona to the Mariposa Grove between 9 and 6 (the last shuttle leaves Wawona at 4:30, the grove at 6). If the road to the grove is closed, which happens when Yosemite is crowded (or when there's been heavy snow), park in Wawona and take the free shuttle, which makes pickups near the gas station. You can also walk, snowshoe, or ski in, a worthwhile effort when the woods fall silent under a mantle of white. ⊠ *Off Hwy. 41, 2 mi north of South Entrance* ☎ *209/375–1621 or 209/375–6551* ☒ *Free; tram tour $11* ☉ *Tram May–Oct., daily 9–5; shuttle Mlate May–early September, daily 9–6.*

Where to Stay & Eat

$–$$ ✕🏠 **Wawona Hotel and Dining Room.** This 1879 National Historic Landmark sits at Yosemite's southern end, near the Mariposa Grove of Big Trees. It's an old-fashioned New England–style estate, with white-washed buildings, wraparound verandas, and small, pleasant rooms decorated with period pieces (many share a bath; inquire when you book). In the romantic, candlelit dining room ($$–$$$), the smoky corn-trout soup hits the spot on cold winter nights. (The dining room is closed weekdays November–Easter except holidays, and reservations are recommended.) Afterward, you can visit the cozy Victorian parlor, which has a fireplace, board games, and a pianist who plays ragtime most evenings. ⊠ *Hwy. 41* 🕀 *Yosemite Reservations, 5410 E. Home Ave., Fresno 93727* 📞 *559/252–4848 lodging reservations, 209/375–1425 dining reservations* 🖷 *559/456–0542* ⊕ *www.yosemitepark.com* ↙ *104 rooms, 52 with bath* ♿ *Restaurant, 9-hole golf course, putting green, tennis court, pool, horseback riding, bar; no a/c, no room phones, no room TVs, no smoking* 🚫 *AE, D, DC, MC, V.*

¢ 🏕 **Wawona.** Near the Mariposa Grove, just downstream from a good fishing spot, this year-round campground (reservations essential May–September) has larger, less closely packed sites than campgrounds in the valley. The downside is that it's an hour's drive to the valley's major attractions. ⊠ *Hwy. 41, 1 mi north of Wawona* 📞 *209/372–0265 or 800/436–7275* 🖷 *209/372–0371* ⊕ *http://reservations.nps.gov* ↙ *93 sites (tent or RV)* ♿ *Flush toilets, drinking water, dump station, bear boxes, fire grates, picnic tables, ranger station, swimming (river).*

Sports & the Outdoors

Wawona Stables (📞 209/375–6502) has several rides, starting at $51.

MAMMOTH AREA

A jewel in the vast eastern Sierra Nevada, the Mammoth Lakes area lies just east of the Sierra crest, on the back side of Yosemite and the Ansel Adams Wilderness. It's a place of rugged beauty, where giant sawtooth mountains drop into the vast deserts of the Great Basin. In winter 11,053-foot-high Mammoth Mountain provides the finest skiing and snowboarding south of Lake Tahoe—sometimes as late as June or even July. Once the snows melt, Mammoth transforms itself into a warm-weather playground, with fishing, mountain biking, golfing, hiking, and horseback riding. Nine deep-blue lakes are spread through the Mammoth Lakes Basin, and another 100 lakes dot the surrounding countryside. Crater-pocked Mammoth Mountain hasn't had a major eruption for 50,000 years, but the region is alive with hot springs, mud pots, fumaroles, and steam vents.

Mammoth Lakes

㉖ *30 mi south of eastern edge of Yosemite National Park on U.S. 395.*

Much of the architecture in the hub town of Mammoth Lakes (elevation 7,800 feet) is of the faux-alpine variety. You'll find mostly basic dining and lodging options here—although international real-estate de-

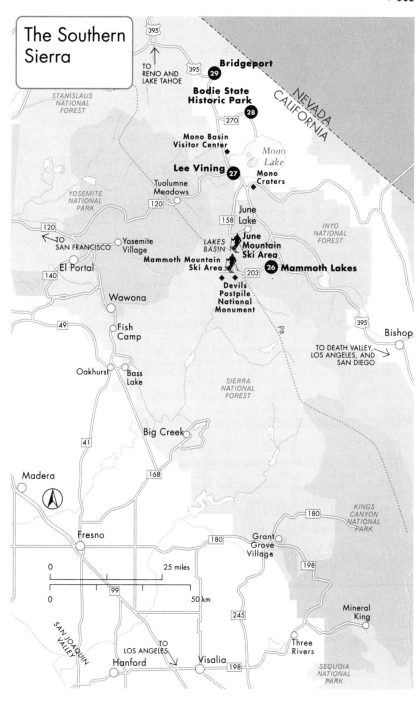

The Southern Sierra

velopers have recently joined forces with Mammoth Mountain Ski Area and are planning to develop the once sleepy town into a chic ski destination. Highway 203 heads west from U.S. 395, becoming Main Street as it passes through the town of Mammoth Lakes, and later Minaret Road (which makes a right turn) as it continues west to the Mammoth Mountain ski area and Devils Postpile National Monument.

The lakes of the **Mammoth Lakes Basin,** reached by Lake Mary Road off Highway 203 southwest of town, are popular for fishing and boating in summer. First comes Twin Lakes, at the far end of which is Twin Falls, where water cascades 300 feet over a shelf of volcanic rock. Also popular are Lake Mary, the largest lake in the basin, Lake Mamie, and Lake George. Horseshoe Lake is the only lake in which you can swim.

The glacial-carved sawtooth spires of the Minarets, the remains of an ancient lava flow, are best viewed from the **Minaret Vista,** off Highway 203 west of Mammoth Lakes.

★ ℭ Even if you don't ski, ride the **Panorama Gondola** to see Mammoth Mountain, the aptly named dormant volcano that gives Mammoth Lakes its name. Gondolas serve skiers in winter and mountain bikers and sightseers in summer. The high-speed, eight-passenger gondolas whisk you from the chalet to the summit, where you can read about the area's volcanic history. Remember, though, that the air is thin at the 11,053-foot summit; carry water, and don't overexert yourself. The boarding area is at the Main Lodge. ⊠ *Off Hwy. 203* ☎ *760/934–2571 Ext. 2400 information, Ext. 3850 gondola station* ⌑ *$16 in summer* ☉ *July 4–Oct., daily 9–4:30; Nov.–July 3, daily 8:30–4.*

The overwhelming popularity of Mammoth Mountain has generated a real-estate boom, and a huge new complex of shops, restaurants, and luxury accommodations, called the **Village at Mammoth,** has become the town's tourist center.

off the beaten path

DEVILS POSTPILE NATIONAL MONUMENT – An easy 10-minute walk from the ranger station takes you to a geologic formation of smooth, vertical basalt columns sculpted by volcanic and glacial forces. A short but steep trail winds to the top of the 60-foot-high rocky cliff, where you'll find a bird's-eye view of the columns. A 2-mi hike past the Postpile leads to the monument's second scenic wonder, **Rainbow Falls,** where a branch of the San Joaquin River plunges more than 100 feet over a lava ledge. When the water hits the pool below, sunlight turns the resulting mist into a spray of color. Walk down a bit from the top of the falls for the best view.

In summer, Devils Postpile National Monument is accessible only via a shuttle bus that begins operation as soon as the road is cleared of snow—usually in June, but sometimes as late as July. The shuttle departs from the Adventure Center at the Mammoth Mountain Main Lodge gondola building approximately every 20–30 minutes, generally from 7 AM to 7 PM, with the last ride out of the valley at 8:30. The shuttle stops running at the end of September, but you can drive to the

WHY IS THERE SO MUCH SNOW?

THE SIERRA NEVADA MOUNTAINS receive some of the deepest snow anywhere in North America. In winter, houses literally get buried, and homeowners have to build tunnels to their front doors (though many install enclosed wooden walkways). In the high country, it's not uncommon for a single big storm to bring 10 feet of snow and for 30 feet of snow to accumulate at the height of the season. In the enormous bowls of Mammoth Mountain, you might ski past a tiny pine that looks like a miniature Christmas tree—until you remember that there are 30 more feet of tree under the snow.

To understand the weather, you have to understand the terrain. The Sierra Nevada are marked by a gentle western rise from sea level to the Sierra crest, which tops out at a whopping 14,494 feet in Sequoia National Park's Mt. Whitney, the highest point in the continental United States. On the eastern side of the crest, at the escarpment, the mountains drop sharply—as much as 5,000 feet—giving way to the Great Basin and the high-mountain deserts of Nevada and Utah.

When winter storms blow in off the Pacific, carrying vast stores of water with them, they race across the relatively flat, 100-mi-wide Central Valley. As they ascend the wall of mountains, though, the decrease in temperature and the increase in pressure on the clouds force them to release their stores of water. Between October and April, that means snow—lots of it. Storms can get hung up on the peaks for days, dumping foot after foot of precipitation. By the time they finally cross over the range and into the Great Basin, there isn't much moisture left for the lower elevations on the eastern side. This is why, if you cross the Sierra eastward on your way to U.S. 395, you'll notice that brightly colored wildflowers and forest-green trees give way to pale-green sagebrush and brown sand as you drop out of the mountains.

The coastal cities and farmlands of the rest of the state depend heavily on the water from the Sierra snowpack. Most of the spring and summer runoff from the melting snows is caught in reservoirs in the foothills and routed to farmlands and cities throughout the state via a complex system of levees and aqueducts, which you'll no doubt see in the foothills and Central Valley, to the west of the range. But much of the water remains in the mountains, forming lakes, most notably giant Lake Tahoe to the north and Mammoth Lakes to the south. The lakes are an essential part of the ecosystem, providing water for birds, fish, and plant life.

falls until the snows come again, usually around the beginning of November. Scenic picnic spots dot the bank of the San Joaquin River. ⊠ *Hwy. 203, 13 mi west of Mammoth Lakes* ☎ *760/934–2289, 760/924–5502 shuttle bus information* 🎫 *$7* ⊙ *Shuttle mid-June–mid-Sept., daily; mid–late Sept., Fri.–Sun., weather permitting.*

Where to Stay & Eat

★ **$$–$$$** ✕ **Nevados.** The top choice of many locals, Nevados has a contemporary California menu that draws inspiration from Europe and Asia. Choose from imaginative preparations of seafood, duck, veal, beef, and game or the excellent three-course prix-fixe menu. The atmosphere here is convivial and welcoming—if a bit loud. ⊠ *Main St. and Minaret Rd.* ☎ *760/934–4466* ♨ *Reservations essential* ☰ *AE, D, DC, MC, V* ⊙ *No lunch.*

★ **$$–$$$** ✕ **Restaurant at Convict Lake.** Tucked in a grove of aspens, 10 minutes south of town, one of the best restaurants in the Mammoth area offers wonderful service in a rustic dining room. You can sit beside the fire under the knotty-pine cathedral ceiling and sup on such dishes as sautéed venison medallions, pan-seared local trout, and beef Wellington. This is a haven for wine aficionados, with an extensive selection of reasonably priced European and California varietals. ⊠ *2 mi off U.S. 395, 4 mi south of Mammoth Lakes* ☎ *760/934–3803* ♨ *Reservations essential* ☰ *AE, D, MC, V* ⊙ *No lunch early Sept.–July 4.*

$$ ✕ **Alpenrose** Hearty portions of classic Swiss-inspired dishes like Wiener-schnitzel, rib-eye steak au poivre, and cheese fondue are served up at cozy booths beneath alpine murals. There's also a good selection of reasonably priced wines. If you're on a budget, come before 6:30 PM for the early-bird special. ⊠ *343 Old Mammoth Rd.* ☎ *760/934–3077* ♨ *Reservations essential* ☰ *AE, D, MC, V* ⊙ *No lunch Mon.–Sat. in winter.*

¢–$$ ✕ **Berger's.** Don't even think about coming to this bustling restaurant unless you're hungry. Berger's is known, appropriately enough, for its burgers and sandwiches, and everything comes in mountainous portions. At lunch try the sourdough patty melt, at dinner the beef ribs. The seasoned french fries are delicious. ⊠ *Minaret Rd. near Canyon Blvd.* ☎ *760/934–6622* ☰ *MC, V* ⊙ *Closed 2 wks May and 4–6 wks Oct.–Nov.*

¢–$ ✕ **Giovanni's Pizza.** Children love this casual restaurant. It serves standard Italian dinners, but stick to the delicious pizza. Don't come here expecting quiet conversation, though—it's a high-decibel joint. ⊠ *Minaret Village Mall, Old Mammoth Rd. and Meridian St.* ☎ *760/934–7563* ☰ *AE, MC, V* ⊙ *No lunch Sun.*

¢–$$$$ ✕🏨 **Tamarack Lodge Resort.** Tucked away on the edge of the John Muir Wilderness Area, where cross-country ski trails loop through the woods, this original 1924 lodge has rustic and charming accommodations. Rooms in the main lodge can have fairly spartan furnishings, and some share a bathroom. If you prefer more privacy, opt for one of the cabins, which range from simple to luxurious; many have fireplaces, kitchens, or wood-burning stoves. In warm months, fishing, canoeing, hiking, and mountain biking are right outside. The small and romantic Lakefront Restaurant ($$–$$$) serves outstanding contemporary French-inspired

*Fodor's*Choice
★

dinners, with an emphasis on game. Reservations are essential. ⊠ *Lake Mary Rd. off Hwy. 203* 🕾 *Box 69, 93546* ☎ *760/934–2442 or 800/ 626–6684* 🖷 *760/934–2281* ⊕ *www.tamaracklodge.com* ➷ *11 rooms, 25 cabins* ⚘ *Restaurant, fans, some kitchens, some kitchenettes, lake, boating, fishing, hiking, cross-country skiing, ski shop, lobby lounge; no a/c, no room TVs, no smoking* ⊟ *AE, MC, V.*

$$$$ ▦ **Village at Mammoth.** This cluster of four-story timber-and-stone buildings is in the middle of the newly developed town center. The units each come with gas fireplaces, kitchens or kitchenettes, daily maid service, high-speed Internet access, DVD player, slate-tile bathroom floors, and comfortable furnishings. The buildings are connected by a ground-floor pedestrian mall, where you'll find shops, restaurants, and bars. Best of all, a gondola (winter only) whisks you right from the Village to the mountain. ⊠ *100 Canyon Blvd.* 🕾 *Box 3459, 93546* ☎ *760 /934–1982 or 800/626–6684* 🖷 *760/934–1494* ⊕ *www.mammothmountain.com* ➷ *277 units* ⚘ *In-room data ports, some kitchens, some kitchenettes, cable TV, gym, hot tub, downhill skiing, ski storage, laundry facilities, free parking; no smoking* ⊟ *AE, MC, V.*

$$$–$$$$ ▦ **Juniper Springs Lodge.** One of the area's top choices for slope-side luxury, this lodging contains condominium-style units with full kitchens and ski-in, ski-out access to the mountain. Amenities include stone fireplaces, balconies, and stereos with CD players. The heated outdoor pool—surrounded by a heated deck—is open year-round. ⊠ *4000 Meridian Blvd.* 🕾 *Box 2129, 93546* ☎ *760/924–1102 or 800/626–6684* 🖷 *760/924– 8152* ⊕ *www.mammothmountain.com* ➷ *10 studios, 99 1-bedrooms, 92 2-bedrooms, 5 3-bedrooms* ⚘ *Restaurant, café, room service, fans, in-room data ports, kitchens, microwaves, refrigerators, cable TV, in-room VCRs, 18-hole golf course, pool, exercise equipment, 2 hot tubs, mountain bikes, downhill skiing, ski shop, ski storage, bar, laundry service, concierge, meeting rooms; no a/c, no smoking* ⊟ *AE, MC, V.*

$$–$$$$ ▦ **Mammoth Mountain Inn.** If you want to be within walking distance of the Mammoth Mountain Main Lodge, this is the place. In winter, check your skis with the concierge, pick them up in the morning, and head directly to the lifts. In summer the proximity to the gondola means you can hike and mountain bike to your heart's delight. The accommodations, which vary in size, include standard hotel rooms and condo units; the latter have kitchenettes, and many have lofts. The inn has licensed on-site child care. ⊠ *Minaret Rd., 4 mi west of Mammoth Lakes* 🕾 *Box 353, 93546* ☎ *760/934–2581 or 800/626–6684* 🖷 *760/934–0701* ⊕ *www.mammothmountain.com* ➷ *124 rooms, 91 condos* ⚘ *2 restaurants, fans, some in-room data ports, some kitchenettes, some microwaves, some refrigerators, cable TV, hot tub, hiking, downhill skiing, ski storage, bar, video game room, shop, babysitting, playground, laundry facilities, meeting room, no-smoking rooms; no a/c* ⊟ *AE, MC, V.*

$–$$$ ▦ **Convict Lake Resort.** The lake on which this resort stands (about 10 minutes south of Mammoth Lakes) was named for an 1871 gunfight between local vigilantes and six escaped prisoners. Rustic cabins come with fully equipped kitchens (including coffeemakers and premium coffee), and large luxury homes can sleep up to 35 people. ⊠ *2 mi off U.S. 395* ☎ *760/934–3800 or 800/992–2260* ⊕ *www.convictlakeresort. com* ➷ *29 cabins* ⚘ *Restaurant, some in-room hot tubs, kitchens,* some microwaves, cable TV, lake, boating, fishing, bicycles, horseback riding, shop, Internet, some pets allowed (fee); no a/c, no room phones ⊟ AE, D, MC, V.

$$ ▦ **Holiday Inn Mammoth Lakes.** In a town known for vintage-1970s condo units, this stands out as being the only modern, full-service, mid-price hotel. Rooms and public areas are sparklingly clean, and extra amenities include wireless high-speed Internet, voice mail, irons, microwaves, and refrigerators. In the afternoon, cookies and coffee are served in the lobby. Families enjoy the special "kids' suites," which have bunk beds and video games. There's also a year-round indoor pool. ⊠ 3236 Main St., 93546 ☎ 760/924–1234 or 866/924–1234 🖷 760/934–3626 ⊕ www.holidayatmammoth.com ➴ 71 rooms, 3 suites ⌖ Cafeteria, in-room data ports, microwaves, refrigerators, cable TV, indoor pool, exercise equipment, hot tub, billiards, Ping-Pong, bar, laundry facilities, meeting room; no smoking ⊟ AE, MC, V.

¢–$$ ▦ **Cinnamon Bear Inn Bed and Breakfast.** Though it's located in a nothing-special business district off Main Street and though its exterior looks more like a motel than an inn, this B&B has very comfortable rooms decorated in New England–colonial style. Some have four-poster beds. Rates include a delicious homemade breakfast and wine and cheese in the afternoon. ⊠ 6209 Minaret Rd. ⌕ Box 3338, 93546 ☎ 760/934–2873 or 800/845–2873 🖷 760/934–2873 ⊕ www.cinnamonbearinn.com ➴ 22 rooms ⌖ Some kitchenettes, cable TV, some in-room VCRs, outdoor hot tub, ski storage, lounge; no a/c, no smoking ⊟ AE, D, MC, V �|O| BP.

¢ ⛺ **Convict Lake Campground.** This campground, near the Convict Lake Resort, 35 mi north of Bishop, is run by the U.S. Forest Service. It's open May to October, and sites are available on a first-come, first-served basis and are extremely popular. ⊠ 2 mi off U.S. 395 ☎ 760/924–5500 ⊕ www.fs.fed.us/r5/inyo ➴ 88 campsites ⌖ Lake, flush toilets, dump station, drinking water, showers, fire pits, general store.

¢ ⛺ **Lake Mary Campground.** There are few sites as beautiful as this lake-side campground at 8,900 feet, open June to September. Accordingly, it is extremely popular. If it's full, try the adjacent Coldwater campground. You can catch trout in Lake Mary, the biggest lake in the region. and a general store is nearby. ⊠ Lake Mary Loop Dr. off Hwy. 203 ☎ 760/924–5500 🖷 760/924–5537 ⊕ www.fs.fed.us/r5/inyo ➴ 48 sites (tent or RV) ⌖ Flush toilets, drinking water, fire grates, picnic tables.

Nightlife & the Arts

The summertime **Mammoth Lakes Jazz Jubilee** (☎ 760/934–2478 or 800/367–6572 ⊕ www.mammothjazz.org) is hosted by the local Temple of Folly Jazz Band and takes place in 10 venues, most with dance floors. For one long weekend every summer, Mammoth Lakes hosts **Bluesapalooza** (☎760/934–0606 or 800/367–6572 ⊕www.mammothconcert. com), a blues and beer festival—with emphasis on the beer tasting. Concerts occur throughout the year on Mammoth Mountain; contact **Mammoth Mountain Music** (☎ 760/934–0606 ⊕ www.mammothconcert. com) for listings.

Thursday to Saturday nights, you can dance to a DJ at **La Sierra's** (⊠ Main St. near Minaret Rd. ☎760/934–8083), which has Mammoth's largest dance floor. On Tuesday and Saturday evenings, you can sing karaoke at **Shogun** (⊠ 452 Old Mammoth Rd. ☎ 760/934–3970), Mammoth's only Japanese restaurant. The bar at **Whiskey Creek** (⊠ Main St. and Minaret Rd. ☎ 760/934–2555) hosts musicians on weekends winter through summer and on some weeknights in winter.

Sports & the Outdoors

For information on winter conditions around Mammoth, call the **Snow Report** (☎ 760/934–7669 or 888/766–9778). The **U.S. Forest Service ranger station** (☎ 760/924–5500) can provide general information year-round.

BICYCLING **Mammoth Mountain Bike Park** (⊠ Mammoth Mountain Ski Area ☎ 760/934–0706) opens when the snow melts, usually by July, with 70-plus mi of single-track trails—from mellow to super-challenging. Chairlifts and shuttles provide trail access, and rentals are available.

DOGSLEDDING **Mammoth Dog Teams** (⊠ Kennels Hwy. 203, 4 mi east of Mammoth Lakes ☎ 760/934–6270) operates rides through the forest on sleds pulled by teams of 10 dogs. Options range from 25-minute rides to overnight excursions; book three to seven days in advance. In summer you can tour the kennels (at 10, 1, and 3) and learn about the dogs.

FISHING Crowley Lake is the top trout-fishing spot in the area; Convict Lake, June Lake, and the lakes of the Mammoth Basin are other prime spots. One of the best trout rivers is the San Joaquin, near Devils Postpile. Hot Creek, a designated Wild Trout Stream, is renowned for fly-fishing (catch and release only). The fishing season runs from the last Saturday in April until the end of October. **Kittredge Sports** (⊠ Main St. and Forest Trail ☎ 760/934–7566) rents rods and reels and conducts guided trips.

GOLF Because it's nestled right up against the forest, you might see deer and bears on the fairways at the 18-hole **Sierra Star Golf Course** (⊠ 2001 Sierra Star Pkwy. ☎ 760/924–2200).

HIKING Trails wind around the Lakes Basin and through pristine alpine scenery. Stop at the **U.S. Forest Service ranger station** (⊠ Hwy. 203 ☎ 760/924–5500), on your right just before the town of Mammoth Lakes, for a Mammoth area trail map and permits for backpacking in wilderness areas.

HORSEBACK RIDING Stables around Mammoth are typically open from June through September. There are several outfitters. **Mammoth Lakes Pack Outfit** (⊠ Lake Mary Rd., between Twin Lakes and Lake Mary ☎ 760/934–2434 ⊕ www.mammothpack.com) runs day and overnight horseback trips. **McGee Creek Pack Station** (☎ 760/935–4324 or 800/854–7407 ⊕ www.mcgeecreekpackstation.com) can set you up with horses and gear. Operated by the folks at McGee Creek, **Sierra Meadows Ranch** (⊠ Sherwin Creek Rd. off Old Mammoth Rd. ☎ 760/934–6161) conduct horseback and wagon rides from one hour to all day.

HOT-AIR BALLOONING The balloons of **Mammoth Balloon Adventures** (☎ 760/937–8787) glide over the countryside in the morning from spring until fall, weather permitting.

SKIING **June Mountain Ski Area.** This low-key resort, 20 mi north of Mammoth Mountain and 20 minutes north of Mammoth Lakes, is a favorite of snowboarders, who have a half-pipe all to themselves. Three freestyle terrain areas are for both skiers and boarders, and there's rarely a line for the lifts. The area is better protected from wind and storms than Mammoth Mountain. (If it starts to storm, you can use your Mammoth ticket at June.) A rental and repair shop, a ski school, and a sport shop are all on the premises. A lift ticket costs $50. ⊠ *Off June Lake Loop (Hwy. 158) June Lake* ☎ *760/648–7733 or 888/586–3686* ☞ *35 trails on 500 acres, rated 35% beginner, 45% intermediate, 20% advanced. Longest run 2½ mi, base 7,510', summit, 10,174'. Lifts: 7.*

Fodor'sChoice **Mammoth Mountain Ski Area.** If you ski only one mountain in California, make it Mammoth. One of the West's largest and best ski resorts, ★ Mammoth has more than 3,500 acres of skiable terrain and a 3,100-foot vertical drop. Standing atop this dormant volcano, you can look west 150 mi across the state to the Coastal Range; to the east are the highest peaks of Nevada and the Great Basin beyond. Below, you'll find a 6½-mi-wide swath of groomed boulevards and canyons, as well as tree skiing and a dozen vast bowls. Snowboarders are welcome on all slopes; there are three outstanding freestyle terrain parks of varying technical difficulty, with jumps, rails, table tops, and giant superpipes. Mammoth's season begins in November and often lingers until June or beyond. Lift tickets cost $62, lessons and rental equipment are available, and there's a children's ski and snowboard school. Mammoth runs four free shuttle bus routes around town and to the ski area, and the Village Gondola runs from the Village complex to Canyon Lodge. However, since only overnight guests are allowed to park at the Village for more than a few hours, if you want to ride the gondola to the mountain, take a shuttle bus to the Village. ⊠ *Minaret Rd. west of Mammoth Lakes* ☎ *760/ 934–2571 or 800/626–6684, 760/934–0687 shuttle* ☞ *150 trails on 3,500 acres, rated 30% beginner, 40% intermediate, 30% advanced. Longest run 3 mi, base 7,953', summit 11,053'. Lifts: 27, including 9 high-speed.*

Trails at **Tamarack Cross Country Ski Center** (⊠ Lake Mary Rd. off Hwy. 203 ☎ 760/934–5293 or 760/934–2442), adjacent to Tamarack Lodge, meander around several lakes. Rentals are available.

Mammoth Sporting Goods (⊠ 1 Sierra Center Mall, Old Mammoth Rd. ☎ 760/934–3239) tunes and rents skis and sells equipment, clothing, and accessories.

SNOWMOBILING **Mammoth Snowmobile Adventures** (⊠ Mammoth Mountain Main Lodge ☎ 760/934–9645 or 800/626–6684) conducts guided tours along wooded trails.

EAST OF YOSEMITE NATIONAL PARK
FROM LEE VINING TO BRIDGEPORT

The area to the north and east of Yosemite National Park includes some ruggedly handsome, albeit desolate, terrain, most notably around Mono Lake. The area is best visited by car, as distances are great and public transportation is limited. U.S. 395 is the main north–south road on the eastern side of the Sierra Nevada, at the western edge of the Great Basin; drive with your lights on, even in daytime.

Lee Vining

❷ *20 mi east of Tuolumne Meadows via Hwy. 120 to U.S. 395; 30 mi north of Mammoth Lakes on U.S. 395.*

Lee Vining is known mostly as the eastern gateway to Yosemite National Park (summer only) and the location of Mono Lake. Pick up supplies or stop for lunch here before or after a drive through the high country. In winter the town is all but deserted, but the general store remains open.

★ Eerie tufa towers—calcium carbonate formations that often resemble castle turrets—rise from impressive **Mono Lake.** Since the 1940s, the city of Los Angeles has diverted water from streams that feed the lake, lowering its water level and exposing the tufa. Court victories by environmentalists in the 1990s forced a reduction of the diversions, and the lake has since risen about 9 feet. From April through August, millions of migratory birds nest in and around Mono Lake. The best place to view the tufa is at the south end of the lake along the mile-long **South Tufa Trail.** To reach it, drive 5 mi south from Lee Vining on U.S. 395, then 5 mi east on Highway 120. There is a $3 fee. You can swim (or float) in the salty water at Navy Beach near the South Tufa Trail or take a kayak or canoe trip for close-up views of the tufa (check with rangers for boating restrictions during bird-nesting season). The **Scenic Area Visitor Center** (⊠U.S. 395 ☎760/647–3044) is open daily from June through September, 9–4:30, and the rest of the year Friday through Monday 9–4. Rangers and naturalists lead walking tours of the tufa daily in summer and on weekends (sometimes on cross-country skis) in winter.

Where to Stay & Eat

★ **$$–$$$** ✕ **Mono Inn at Mono Lake.** It's worth the long drive to get to this updated 1922 roadhouse. Impeccably decorated with Stickley furniture and contemporary crafts, the dining room has drop-dead postcard views of Mono Lake. During a full moon, the glow on the water is magical. The delicious menu lists everything from filet mignon and duck breast to salmon and salads; on Friday and Saturday there's prime rib. ⊠ *U.S. 395, north of Lee Vining* ☎ *760/647–6581* ⚃ *Reservations essential* ▤ *AE, D, MC, V* ☉ *Closed Nov.–early May. No lunch.*

★ **$** ✕ **Tioga Gas Mart & Whoa Nelli Deli.** This culinary oasis near the eastern entrance to Yosemite has some of the best food in Mono County. The succulent mahimahi tacos are delicious, as are the gourmet pizzas, Angus roast-beef sandwiches, and herb-crusted pork tenderloin with berry glaze. Order at the counter and grab a seat inside or out. Oh, and while you're here, you might as well get fuel: it's hard to believe, but this place is in a gas station, perhaps the only one in the United States that serves cocktails. ⊠ *Hwy. 120 and U.S. 395* ☎ *760/647–1088* ▤ *AE, MC, V* ☉ *Closed mid-Nov.–mid-Apr.*

¢–$ ✕ **Nicely's.** Plants and pictures of local attractions decorate this diner, which has been around since 1965. Try the blueberry pancakes and homemade sausages at breakfast. For lunch or dinner try the chicken-fried steak or the fiesta salad. There's also a kids' menu. ⊠ *U.S. 395 and 4th St.* ☎ *760/647–6477* ☰ *MC, V* ☾ *Closed Tues. and Wed. in winter.*

¢–$ 🏠 **Tioga Lodge.** Just 2½ mi north of Yosemite's eastern gateway, this 19th-century building has been by turns a store, a saloon, a tollbooth, and a boarding house. Now restored and expanded, it's a popular lodge that's close to ski areas and fishing spots. Rooms are simply furnished and a bit close to the road, but the views of Mono Lake can't be beat. Be sure to ask about summer boat tours. ⊠ *U.S. 395* ⬧ *Box 580, 93541* ☎*760/647–6423 or 888/647–6423* 🖷*760/647–6074* ⊕*www.tiogalodge. com* ⬅*13 rooms* ♿ *Restaurant; no a/c, no room phones, no room TVs, no smoking* ☰ *AE, D, MC, V* ☾ *Closed Nov.–Mar.*

Bodie State Historic Park

28 *23 mi northeast of Lee Vining via U.S. 395 to Hwy. 270 (last 3 mi are unpaved).*

Old shacks and shops, abandoned mine shafts, a Methodist church, the mining village of Rattlesnake Gulch, and the remains of a small Chinatown are among the sights at fascinating **Bodie Ghost Town.** The town,
Fodor'sChoice at an elevation of 8,200 feet, boomed from about 1878 to 1881, as gold
★ prospectors, having worked the best of the western Sierra mines, headed to the high desert on the eastern slopes. Bodie was a mean place—the booze flowed freely, shootings were commonplace, and licentiousness reigned. Evidence of the town's wild past survives today at an excellent museum, and you can tour an old stamp mill (where ore was stamped into fine powder to extract gold and silver) and a ridge that contains many mine sites. No food, drink, or lodging is available in Bodie, and the nearest picnic area is a half-mile away. Though the park stays open in winter, snow may close Highway 270. ⊠ *Museum: Main and Green Sts.* ☎ *760/647–6445* 🎫 *Park $3; museum free* ☾ *Park: late May–early Sept., daily 8–7; early Sept.–late May, daily 8–4. Museum: late May–early Sept., daily 9–6; early Sept.–late May, hrs vary.*

Bridgeport

29 *25 mi north of Lee Vining and 55 mi north of Mammoth Lakes on U.S. 395.*

Historic Bridgeport lies within striking distance of a myriad of alpine lakes and streams and both forks of the Walker River, making it a prime spot for fishing. It is also the gateway to Bodie Ghost Town. In winter much of the town shuts for the season.

Where to Stay & Eat

$–$$$ ✗ **Bridgeport Inn.** Tables spread with white linen grace the dining room of this clapboard Victorian inn, built in 1877. The prime rib and fresh seafood are complemented by homemade soups, pastas, and a large wine list. Victorian-appointed guest rooms are available upstairs. ⊠ *205 Main St.* ☎ *760/932–7380* ☰ *MC, V* ☾ *Closed Dec.–Feb.*

$–$$ 🏠 **Cain House.** This old home has been refurbished as a B&B in elegant country style. Afternoon wine-and-cheese service is offered daily, and all beds have down comforters. ⊠ *340 Main St., 93517* ☎ *760/932–*

7040 or 800/433–2246 🖷 *760/932–7419* ⊕ *www.cainhouse.com* ➹ *7 rooms* ♨ *Some refrigerators, cable TV, tennis court; no smoking* ▤ *AE, D, MC, V* ⊘ *Closed Nov.–Mar.* ⑩ *BP.*

$–$$ 🖫 **Walker River Lodge.** Right in the center of Bridgeport, this motel has a charming antiques shop in its lobby. Many rooms overlook the East Walker River. ⊠ *100 Main St., 93517* ☎ *760/932–7021 or 800/688–3351* 🖷 *760/932–7914* ⊕ *www.walkerriverlodge.com* ➹ *36 rooms* ♨ *Microwaves, refrigerators, cable TV, some in-room VCRs, pool, hot tub, fishing, some pets allowed, no-smoking rooms* ▤ *AE, D, MC, V* ⑩ *CP.*

THE SOUTHERN SIERRA A TO Z

To research prices, get advice from other travelers, and book travel arrangements, visit ⊕ *www.fodors.com.*

AIRPORTS & TRANSFERS

Fresno Yosemite International Airport (FYI) is the nearest airport to Sequoia and Kings Canyon national parks. Alaska, American, America West, Allegiance, Continental, Delta, Hawaiian, Northwest, Horizon, United Express, and several regional carriers fly here. *See* Air Travel *in* Smart Travel Tips for airline phone numbers.

🚩 **Fresno Yosemite International Airport** ⊠ 5175 E. Clinton Ave., Fresno ☎ 559/498–4095 ⊕ www.flyfresno.org.

BUS TRAVEL

Greyhound serves Fresno, Merced, and Visalia from many California cities. VIA Adventures runs three daily buses from Merced to Yosemite Valley; buses also depart daily from Mariposa. The 2½-hour ride from Merced costs $20 round-trip, which includes admission to the park.

🚩 **Greyhound** ☎ 800/231–2222 ⊕ www.greyhound.com. **VIA Adventures** ☎ 209/384–1315 or 800/369–7275 ⊕ www.via-adventures.com.

CAMPING

In the national parks you can camp only in designated areas, but in the national forests you can pitch a tent anywhere you want, so long as there are no signs specifically prohibiting camping in that area. Always know and obey fire regulations; you can find out what they are in a specific area by checking with forest service rangers, either by telephone or at any of the ranger stations just inside park boundaries.

Except for Lodgepole and Dorst in Sequoia, all sites at the campgrounds near each of the major tourist centers in Sequoia and Kings Canyon parks are assigned on a first-come, first-served basis; on weekends in July and August they are often filled by Friday afternoon. Lodgepole, Potwisha, and Azalea campsites stay open all year, but Lodgepole is not plowed, and camping is limited to snow-tenting or recreational vehicles in plowed parking lots. Other campgrounds in Sequoia and Kings Canyon are open from whenever the snow melts until late September or early October.

If you plan to camp in the backcountry in Sequoia or Kings Canyon national parks, your group must have a backcountry camping permit, which costs $15 for hikers or $30 for stock users (horseback riders, etc.). One permit covers a group of up to 15 people. Availability of permits depends upon trailhead quotas. Advance reservations are accepted by mail or fax beginning March 1 and must be made at least three weeks in advance. Without a reservation, you may still get a permit on a first-come, first-served basis starting at 1 PM the day before you plan to hike. Whether you reserve or not, permits must be picked up in person from the permit issuing station nearest your trailhead. For more information on backcountry camping or travel with pack animals, call the Wilderness Permit Office.

Most of Yosemite's 14 campgrounds are in Yosemite Valley and along the Tioga Road. Glacier Point and Wawona have one each. Several campgrounds operate on a first-come, first-served basis year-round (some 400 of the park's sites remain open year-round), while some take reservations in high season; during summer reservations are strongly recommended. It's sometimes possible to get a campsite on arrival by stopping at the campground reservations office in Yosemite Valley, but this is a risky strategy. Yosemite Campground Reservations handles all bookings for the reservable campgrounds within the park. During the last two weeks of each month, beginning on the 15th, you can reserve a site up to five months in advance. DNC Parks & Resorts at Yosemite handles reservations for the tent-cabins at Curry Village and for the camping shelters at Housekeeping Camp. If you want to overnight in Yosemite's backcountry, you'll need a wilderness permit. They're free, but it's best to reserve one in advance for $5. You can request a reservation between 24 weeks and two days ahead, but making a request doesn't guarantee a reservation. For more information, contact the Wilderness Permit Office.

RVs and trailers are permitted in most national park campgrounds, though space is scarce at some. The length limit is 40 feet for RVs and 35 feet for trailers, but the park service recommends that trailers be no longer than 22 feet. Disposal stations are available in the main camping areas.

The Sierra Nevada is home to thousands of bears, and if you plan on camping, you should take all necessary precautions to keep yourself—and the bears—safe. Bears that acquire a taste for human food can become very aggressive and destructive and often must eventually be destroyed by rangers. The national parks' campgrounds and some campgrounds outside the parks provide food-storage boxes that can keep bears from pilfering your edibles (portable canisters for backpackers can be rented in most park stores). It is imperative that you move all food, coolers, and items with a scent (including toiletries, toothpaste, chewing gum, and air fresheners) from your car (including the trunk) to the storage box at your campsite. If you don't, a bear may break into your car by literally peeling off the door or ripping open the trunk, or it may ransack your tent. The familiar tactic of hanging your food from high tree limbs is not an effective deterrent, as bears can easily scale trees. In the southern Sierra, bear canisters are the only effective and proven method for preventing bears from getting human food. Whether hiking or camping, it's important to respect the landscape and wildlife around you. For detailed information about responsible outdoor recreation, visit the web site of the Leave No Trace Center for Outdoor Ethics.

DNC Parks & Resorts at Yosemite 559/252-4848 www.yosemitepark.com. **Inyo National Forest** 760/873-2400 760/873-2458 www.r5.fs.fed.us/inyo. **Leave No Trace Center for Outdoor Ethics** 303/442-8222 or 800/332-4100 www.lnt. org. **Lodgepole/Dorst campgrounds** 301/722-1257 or 800/365-2267 http://reservations.nps.gov. **Sequoia campgrounds** 559/565-3341 www.nps.gov/seki. **Sequoia National Forest** 559/784-1500 559/781-4744 www.r5.fs.fed.us/sequoia. **Wilderness Permit Office, Sequoia-Kings Canyon** 559/565-3766 www.nps. gov/seki. **Wilderness Permit Office, Yosemite** 209/372-0740 permit office, 209/372-0200 general inquiries www.nps/gov/yose. **Yosemite Campground Reservations** 301/722-1257 or 800/436-7275 reservations.nps.gov.

CAR RENTAL

The car-rental outlets closest to the southern Sierra are at Fresno Yosemite International Airport, where the national chains have outlets. If you're traveling to Mammoth Lakes and the eastern Sierra in winter, the closest agencies are in Reno. *See* Car Rental *in* Smart Travel Tips for national rental-agency phone numbers.

CAR TRAVEL

From San Francisco, I–80 and I–580 are the fastest routes toward the central Sierra Nevada, but avoid driving these routes during weekday rush hours. Through the Central Valley, I–5 and Highway 99 are the fastest north–south routes, but the latter is narrower and has heavy farm-truck traffic. To get to Kings Canyon, plan on a six-hour drive. Two major routes, Highways 180 and 198, intersect with Highway 99 (Highway 180 is closed east of Grant Grove in winter). To get to Yosemite, plan on driving four to five hours. Enter the park either on Highway 140, which is the best route in inclement weather, or on Highway 120, which is the fastest route when the roads are clear. To get to Mammoth Lakes in summer and early fall (or whenever snows aren't blocking Tioga Road), you can travel via Highway 120 (to U.S. 395 south) through the Yosemite high country; the quickest route in winter is I–80 to U.S. 50 to Highway 207 (Kingsbury Grade) to U.S. 395 south; either route takes six to seven hours.

Keep your tank full, especially in winter. Distances between gas stations can be long, and there is no fuel available in Yosemite Valley, Sequoia, or Kings Canyon. If you're traveling from October through April, rain on the coast can mean heavy snow in the mountains. Carry tire chains, and know how to put them on (on I–80 and U.S. 50 you can pay a chain installer $20 to do it for you, but on other routes you'll have to do it yourself). Always check road conditions before you leave. Traffic in national parks in summer can be heavy, and there are sometimes travel restrictions.

Northern California Road Conditions 800/427-7623. **Sequoia-Kings Canyon Road and Weather Information** 559/565-3341. **Yosemite Area Road and Weather Conditions** 209/372-0200.

EMERGENCIES

In an emergency dial 911.

Emergency Services Mammoth Hospital 85 Sierra Park Rd., Mammoth Lakes 760/934-3311 www.mammothhospital.com. **Yosemite Medical Clinic** Ahwahnee Rd. north of Northside Dr. 209/372-4637.

LODGING

Most lodgings in the southern Sierra are simple and basic. A number of agencies can help you find a room.

🔳 Reservation Services **DNC Parks & Resorts at Yosemite** ☎ 559/252-4848 ⊕ www. yosemitepark.com. **Kings Canyon Lodging** ☎ 559/335-5500 or 866/522-6966 ⊕ www. sequoia-kingscanyon.com. **Mammoth Lakes Visitors Bureau Lodging Referral** ☎ 760/ 934-2712 or 888/466-2666 ⊕ www.visitmammoth.com. **Mammoth Reservations** ☎ 760/934-5571 or 800/223-3032 ⊕ www.mammothreservations.com. **Sequoia Lodging** ☎ 559/253-2199 or 888/252-5757 ⊕ www.visitsequoia.com. **Three Rivers Reservation Center** ☎ 559/561-0410 ⊕ www.rescentre.com.

TOURS

San Francisco's California Parlor Car Tours serves Yosemite through one-day and overnight trips as well as some rail-bus combinations, though the latter are logistically inconvenient from San Francisco. DNC Parks & Resorts at Yosemite operates guided bus tours of the Yosemite Valley floor daily year-round, plus seasonal tours of Glacier Point and the Mariposa Grove of Big Trees. The company's Grand Tour ($55), offered between late May and early November, weather permitting, covers the park's highlights. VIA Adventures runs bus tours to Yosemite Valley from Merced, some in conjunction with Amtrak. For $50 you get transportation, lunch, park admission, and a two-hour tour.

🔳 **California Parlor Car Tours** ⊠ 1255 Post St.† #1011 San Francisco ☎ 415/474-7500 or 800/227-4250 ⊕ www.calpartours.com. **DNC Parks & Resorts at Yosemite** ⌂ Box 578, Yosemite National Park 95389 ☎ 209/372-1240 ⊕ www.yosemitepark.com. **VIA Adventures** ⊠ 300 Grogan Ave., Merced ☎ 209/384-1315 or 800/369-7275 ⊕ www. via-adventures.com.

VISITOR INFORMATION

🔳 **Bridgeport Chamber of Commerce** ⌂ Box 541, Bridgeport 93517 ☎ 760/932-7500 ⊕ www.ca-biz.com/bridgeportchamber. **DNC Parks & Resorts at Yosemite** ⌂ Box 578, Yosemite National Park 95389 ☎ 209/372-1000 ⊕ www.yosemitepark.com. **Lee Vining Chamber of Commerce** ⌂ Box 29, Lee Vining 93541 ☎ 760/647-6595 ⊕ www. monolake.org/chamber. **Mammoth Lakes Visitors Bureau** ⊠ Along Hwy. 203 [Main St.], near Sawmill Cutoff Rd., Box 48, Mammoth Lakes 93546 ☎ 760/934-2712 or 888/ 466-2666 ⊕ www.visitmammoth.com. **Mono Lake** ⌂ Box 49, Lee Vining 93541 ☎ 760/ 647-3044 ⊕ www.monolake.org. **Sequoia-Kings Canyon National Park** ⊠ Three Rivers, 93271 ☎ 559/565-3341 or 559/565-3134 ⊕ www.nps.gov/seki. **Yosemite National Park** ⌂ Information Office, Box 577, Yosemite National Park 95389 ☎ 209/372-0200 or 209/372-0264 ⊕ www.nps.gov/yose. **Yosemite Sierra Visitors Bureau** ⊠ 41969 Hwy. 41, Box 1998, Oakhurst 93644 ☎ 559/683-4636 ⊕ www.go2yosemite.net.

THE CENTRAL VALLEY

HIGHWAY 99 FROM BAKERSFIELD TO LODI

8

Updated by
Anneliese Paull

AMONG THE WORLD'S MOST FERTILE working land, the Central Valley is California's heartland and the country's breadbasket. Lush fields and orchards crisscrossed by miles of back roads define the landscape of this sunbaked region, and a wealth of rivers, lakes, and waterways provide relief from the flat farmland that carpets much of the valley. The agriculturally rich area hosts a tremendous diversity of wildlife. Nearly every telephone post is crowned by a hawk or kestrel hunting the land below. Humans, in turn, have created a profusion of vineyards, dairy farms, orchards, and pastures that stretch to the horizon. In the towns, museums and historical societies display artifacts of the valley's eccentric past, and museums, concert halls and restored theaters showcase a vibrant contemporary culture. Whether on back roads or main streets, people are not only friendly but proud to help outsiders explore the beauty of the Central Valley.

If the well-populated Central Valley appears at first glance to be a traveler's void, it's because most folks never leave the highway. Many choose to drive boring I–5 instead of Highway 99, which is framed by farms, vineyards, and dairies. The valley's history of being passed over dates back hundreds of years. Until the mid-19th century, the area was a desert. Gold discoveries, starting in the 1850s, sparked the birth of some towns; the arrival of the railroad in following decades spurred the development of others. But it was the coming of water, courtesy of private dams and, in the 1930s, the Central Valley Project, that transformed this land into the country's most vital agricultural region.

As soon as irrigation gave potential to the valley's open acres, the area became a magnet for farmers, ranchers, developers, World War II refugees, and immigrants from places as diverse as Portugal, China, Armenia, and Laos. Today refugees from the state's big cities come in search of cheaper real estate, safer neighborhoods, and more space. With development has come some unsightly sprawl, air pollution, and pressure on crucial water supplies. Nevertheless, the valley still retains many of its traditional charms. The region's cultural diversity and agricultural roots have woven a textured social fabric that has been chronicled by some of the country's finest writers, including Fresno native William Saroyan, Stockton native Maxine Hong Kingston, and *Grapes of Wrath* author John Steinbeck.

Just as these authors found inspiration in a place you cannot view while speeding down the highway, you must invest time and footwork to appreciate the Central Valley. The rewards can be surprising, relaxing, thrilling. . . even poetic.

Exploring the Central Valley

The 225-mi Central Valley cuts through Kern, Tulare, Kings, Fresno, Madera, Merced, Stanislaus, and San Joaquin counties. It is bounded on the east by the mighty Sierra Nevada and on the west by the smaller coastal ranges. I–5 runs south–north through the valley, as does Highway 99.

8

Numbers in the text correspond to numbers in the margin and on the Central Valley and Fresno Area maps.

If you have
1 day

Touring the Fresno area is a good strategy if you only have a day to spend in the valley. ► **Roeding Park** ⑥ has a striking tropical rain forest within Chaffee Zoological Gardens; the park's Playland and Storyland are great stops if you are traveling with children. Don't miss the **Forestiere Underground Gardens** ⑫, on Shaw Avenue. In springtime take the self-guided **Blossom Trail** driving tour through orchards, vineyards, and fields. Along the trail in Reedley is the Mennonite Quilt Center. Depending on your mood and the weather, you can spend part of the afternoon at Wild Water Adventures or visit the **Fresno Metropolitan Museum** ⑦, whose highlights include an exhibit about author William Saroyan.

If you have
3 days

Start your trip through the Central Valley in ► **Bakersfield** ①, with a visit to the Kern County Museum. Drive north on Highway 99 and west on Highway 122 to drive to **Colonel Allensworth State Historic Park,** ③ which is on the site of a now-deserted town founded by African-Americans in 1908. Continue north on Highway 34 to 🅷 **Hanford** ⑤ and stroll around Courthouse Square and China Alley. The next morning proceed to 🅷 **Fresno** ⑥–⑬ via Highways 43 and 99 north and spend the day there, as in the one-day itinerary above. In the evening take in a show at Roger Rocka's or the Tower Theatre, both in Fresno's Tower District. On Day 3 continue up Highway 99 and stop off at the Castle Air Museum, north of **Merced** ⑭ in Atwater. **Modesto** ⑮ is a good place to stop for lunch. In the afternoon, choose from a rafting trip on the Stanislaus River near **Oakdale** ⑯, an hour or two of art appreciation at the Haggin Museum in **Stockton** ⑰, and a tour of the wineries around **Lodi** ⑱. Lodi is a pleasant place to overnight.

About the Restaurants

Fast-food places and chain restaurants dominate valley highways, but away from the main drag, independent and family-owned eateries will awaken your taste buds. Many cutting-edge bistros and fine restaurants take advantage of the local produce and locally raised meats that are the cornerstone of California cuisine. Even simple restaurants produce hearty, tasty fare that often reflects the valley's ethnic mix. Some of the nation's best Mexican restaurants call the valley home. Chinese, Italian, Armenian, and Basque restaurants also are abundant; many serve massive, many-course meals. Although dress at most valley eateries is casual, diners at some of the finer establishments won't feel out of place in jacket and tie or cocktail dress. Such attire, however, is not required.

About the Hotels

The Central Valley has many chain motels and hotels, but independently owned hotels and bed-and-breakfasts also can be found. There's a large selection of upscale lodgings as well as ones that are simply utilitarian while clean and comfortable. The Victorian-style B&Bs in the area are a good bet because they offer a taste of local life.

	WHAT IT COSTS				
	$$$$	$$$	$$	$	¢
RESTAURANTS	over $30	$23–$30	$16–$22	$10–$15	under $10
HOTELS	over $250	$176–$250	$121–$175	$90–$120	under $90

Restaurant prices are for a main course at dinner, excluding sales tax of 7–10% (depending on location). Hotel prices are for two people in a standard double room in high season, excluding service charges and 8–13% tax.

Timing

Spring, when wildflowers are in bloom and the scent of fruit blossoms is in the air, and fall, when the air is brisk and leaves turn red and gold, are the best times to visit. Many of the valley's biggest festivals take place during these seasons. (If you're an allergy-sufferer, though, beware of spring, when stone-fruit trees blossom.) Summer, when temperatures often top 100°F, can be oppressive. June–August, though, are great months to visit area water parks and lakes or to take in the museums, where air-conditioning provides a reprieve from the heat. Many attractions close in winter, which can get cold and dreary. Thick, ground-hugging fog, called tule fog by locals, is a common driving hazard November–February.

SOUTHERN CENTRAL VALLEY
BAKERSFIELD & KERNVILLE

When gold was discovered in Kern County in the 1860s, settlers flocked to the southern end of the Central Valley. Black gold—oil—is now the area's most valuable commodity; the county provides 64% of California's oil production. Kern is also among the country's five most productive agricultural counties. From the flat plains around Bakersfield, the landscape grows gently hilly and then graduates to mountains as it nears Kernville, which lies in the Kern River valley.

Bakersfield

▶ ❶ *110 mi north of Los Angeles on I–5 and Hwy. 99; 110 mi west of Ridgecrest via Hwy. 14 south and Hwy. 58 west.*

Bakersfield's founder, Colonel Thomas Baker, arrived with the discovery of gold in the nearby Kern River valley in 1851. Now Kern County's biggest city (it has a population of 279,000, which includes the largest Basque community in the United States), Bakersfield probably is best known as Nashville West, a country-music haven and hometown of performers Buck Owens and Merle Haggard. It also has its own symphony orchestra and two good museums.

★ ☽ The **Kern County Museum and Lori Brock Children's Discovery Center** form one of the Central Valley's top museum complexes. The indoor-outdoor Kern County Museum is set up as an open-air, walk-through historic

Festivals, Tours & Tastings

The Central Valley is a great destination for anyone who likes produce fresh from the fields. As billboards announce, fruit and nut orchards as well as cheese factories offer educational tours that include tastings. Better yet, there are farmers' markets in virtually every town, and roadside stands in between. Good places to find produce stands are Highway 198 between Visalia and Hanford, Herndon Avenue in Fresno and Clovis, and Highway 12 in Lodi. Prime season for farmers' markets is May through October, though many larger ones are open year-round, including those held every Saturday in Bakersfield, Fresno, Merced, Stockton, and Visalia. Especially in fall check with chambers of commerce for festivals celebrating everything from the asparagus and raisin crops to residents' Chinese, Greek, and Swedish roots.

8

Sports & the Outdoors

Several cities and towns serve as convenient starting points for white-water rafting trips on the Stanislaus, Merced, Kings, and Kern rivers. Fishing in the rivers and lakes is another favored activity; the lakes are also prime spots for boating and swimming. Stockton is a popular rental area for houseboating on the Sacramento River delta, and Bakersfield is a center for NASCAR racing. The San Francisco Giants' Triple-A team, the Fresno Grizzlies, plays in a stadium opened in 2002 in Fresno. Wildlife refuges are world-class sites for watching birds, especially migrating waterfowl.

---

village with more than 50 restored or re-created buildings dating from the 1860s–1940s. "Black Gold: The Oil Experience," a permanent exhibit that opened in November 2002, shows how oil is created, discovered, and extracted. The Children's Discovery Center has hands-on displays and activities. ⊠ *3801 Chester Ave.* ☎ *661/852–5000* ⊕ *www.kcmuseum. org* 🖼 *$8* ⊘ *Mon.–Sat. 10–5, Sun. noon–5.*

★ ☾ At the **California Living Museum,** a combination zoo, botanical garden, and natural-history museum, the emphasis is on zoo. All animal and plant species displayed are native to the state. Within the reptile house lives every species of rattlesnake found in California. The landscaped grounds— in the hills about a 20-minute drive northeast of Bakersfield—also shelter captive bald eagles, tortoises, coyotes, mountain lions, black bears, and foxes. ⊠ *10500 Alfred Harrell Hwy., Hwy. 178 east, then 3½ mi northwest on Alfred Harrell Hwy.* ☎ *661/872–2256* ⊕ *www.calmzoo. org* 🖼 *$4.50* ⊘ *Tues.–Sun. 9–5.*

Where to Stay & Eat

$–$$$ ✕ **Uricchio's Trattoria.** This downtown restaurant draws everyone from office workers to oil barons—all attracted by the tasty food and casual atmosphere. *Panini* (Italian pressed sandwiches, served at lunch only), pasta, and Italian-style chicken dishes dominate the menu; the chicken piccata outsells all other offerings. ⊠ *1400 17th St.* ☎ *661/326–8870* ▤ *AE, D, DC, MC, V* ⊘ *Closed Sun. No lunch Sat.*

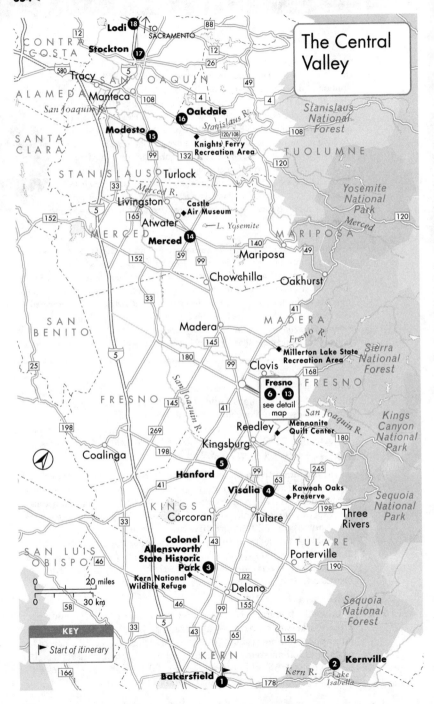

The Central Valley

$–$$ ✗ **Woolgrower's Restaurant.** Thick lamb chops, roast lamb, oxtail stew, and shrimp scampi have made this spot popular with locals. All meals are served family style, so you might share your table with diners you don't know. Meals include vegetables and a potato or rice dish. ⊠ *620 E. 19th St.* ☎ *661/327–9584* ▤ *AE, D, MC, V* ⊗ *Closed Sun.*

¢ ✗ **Jake's Tex Mex Cafe.** Don't let the cafeteria-style service fool you; this is probably the best lunch place in Bakersfield. The chicken burritos and the chili fries (with meaty chili ladled on top) are superb. For dessert, try the Texas sheet cake or the homemade chocolate chip cookies. It's open for dinner, too. ⊠ *1710 Oak St.* ☎ *661/322–6380* ⚐ *Reservations not accepted* ▤ *AE, D, MC, V* ⊗ *Closed Sun.*

$–$$$ ▦ **Four Points by Sheraton.** Fountains, lush lawns, and exotic plants provide a spectacular setting for this hotel. Occupying 7.5 acres in Bakersfield's business district, it's a mile west of Highway 99. The large rooms come equipped with coffeemakers, irons, hair dryers, and DSL connections. The pool is just shy of Olympic size. ⊠ *5101 California Ave., 93309* ☎ *661/325–9700 or 800/368–7764* 🖷 *661/323–3508* ⊕ *www. fourpoints.com* ↴ *198 rooms* ♨ *In-room data ports, cable TV, pool, gym, hot tub, meeting rooms, airport shuttle, no-smoking rooms* ▤ *AE, D, DC, MC, V.*

¢ ▦ **Quality Inn.** Near downtown in a relatively quiet location off Highway 99, this two-story motel offers good value. Most rooms have king- or queen-size beds, and all have HBO. Some have refrigerators and a patio or a balcony overlooking the heated pool. Complimentary coffee is available all day. ⊠ *1011 Oak St., 93304* ☎ *661/325–0772 or 877/ 424–6423* 🖷 *661/325–4646* ⊕ *www.qualityinn.com* ↴ *89 rooms* ♨ *Some refrigerators, cable TV, pool, gym, hot tub, laundry facilities* ▤ *AE, D, DC, MC, V* ⊠ *BP.*

Nightlife & the Arts

The **Bakersfield Symphony Orchestra** (⊠ 1328 34th St., Suite A ☎ 661/ 323–7928 ⊕ www.bakersfieldsymphony.org) performs classical music concerts at the convention center from October through May.

Buck Owens' Crystal Palace (⊠ 2800 Buck Owens Blvd. ☎ 661/328–7560 ⊕ www.buckowens.com) is a combination nightclub, restaurant, and showcase of country music memorabilia. Country-and-western singers perform here, including Buck Owens and the Buckaroos. A dance floor beckons customers who can still twirl after sampling the menu of steaks, burgers, nachos, and gooey desserts. Entertainment is free on most weeknights; on Friday and Saturday nights when Owens performs, there's a cover charge (usually $6–$12); there's also a cover for some of the more well-known entertainers.

Sports & the Outdoors

CAR RACING At **Bakersfield Speedway** (⊠ 5001 N. Chester Extension ☎ 661/393– 3373 ⊕ www.bakersfieldspeedway.com), stock and sprint cars race around a ⅓-mi clay oval track. **Mesa Marin Raceway** (⊠ 11000 Kern Canyon Rd. ☎ 661/366–5711 ⊕ www.mesamarin.com) presents high-speed stock-car, Craftsman Truck, and NASCAR racing on a ½-mi paved oval course.

SKATING The free skate park at **Beach Park** (⊠ Oak and 21st Sts. ⏲ Daily 5 AM–10 PM) has good street skating as well as a relaxing grassy area.

Shopping

Many antiques shops are on 18th and 19th streets between H and R streets, and on H Street between Brundage Lane and California Avenue. **Central Park Antique Mall** (⊠ 701 19th St. ☎ 661/633–1143) has a huge selection. The **Great American Antique Mall** (⊠ 625 19th St. ☎ 661/322–1776) is full of treasures.

Dewar's Candy Shop (⊠ 1120 Eye St. ☎ 661/322–0933) was founded in 1909 and has been owned by the Dewar family since. The hand-dipped chocolate cherries are delicious; so are the Dewar's Chews, a mouth-watering taffy concoction available in peanut butter, peppermint, caramel, and almond flavors. There's also an old-fashioned soda fountain.

Kernville

❷ *50 mi from Bakersfield, northeast on Hwy. 178 and north on Hwy. 155.*

The wild and scenic Kern River, which flows through Kernville en route from Mount Whitney to Bakersfield, delivers some of the most exciting white-water rafting in the state. Kernville (population 1,700) rests in a mountain valley on both banks of the river and also at the northern tip of Lake Isabella (a dammed portion of the river used as a reservoir and for recreation). A center for rafting outfitters, Kernville has lodgings, restaurants, and antiques shops. The main streets are lined with Old West–style buildings, reflecting Kernville's heritage as a rough-and-tumble gold-mining town once known as Whiskey Flat. (Present-day Kernville dates from the 1950s, when it was moved upriver to make room for Lake Isabella.) The road from Bakersfield winds between the rushing river on one side and sheer granite cliffs on the other.

Where to Stay & Eat

¢–$ ✕ **That's Italian.** For northern Italian cuisine in a typical trattoria, this is the spot. Try the braised lamb shanks in a Chianti wine sauce or the linguine with clams, mussels, calamari, and shrimp in a white-wine clam sauce. ⊠ *9 Big Blue Rd.* ☎ *760/376–6020* ▭ *AE, D, MC, V* ⏲ *No lunch Nov.–Apr.*

$$–$$$ 🏨 **Whispering Pines Lodge.** Perched on the banks of the Kern River, this 8-acre property gives you a variety of overnight options. All units are housed in bungalows. Some have full kitchens, fireplaces, queen-size sleepers, and whirlpool tubs; all have coffeemakers and king-size beds. ⊠ *13745 Sierra Way, 93238* ☎ *760/376–3733 or 877/241–4100* 🖷 *760/376–6513* 🌐 *www.kernvalley.com/whisperingpines* *17 rooms* *Some kitchenettes, refrigerators, cable TV, pool* ▭ *AE, D, MC, V* *BP.*

Sports & the Outdoors

BOATING & WINDSURFING The Lower Kern River, which extends from Lake Isabella to Bakersfield and beyond, is open for fishing year-round. Catches include rainbow trout, catfish, smallmouth bass, crappie, and bluegill. Lake Isabella is popular with anglers, water-skiers, sailors, and windsurfers. Its shoreline marinas have boats for rent, bait and tackle, and moorings. **North Fork Marina** (☎ 760/376–1812) is in Wofford Heights, on the lake's west shore. **French Gulch Marina** (☎ 760/379–8774) nestles in a cove on Lake Isabella's north shore.

WHITE-WATER RAFTING The three sections of the Kern River—known as the Lower Kern, Upper Kern, and the Forks—add up to nearly 50 mi of white water, ranging from Class I (easy) to Class V (expert). The Lower and Upper Kern are the most popular and accessible sections. Organized trips can last from one hour (for as little as $20) to more than two days. Rafting season usually runs from late spring until the end of summer. **Chuck Richards Whitewater** (☎ 760/379–4444 ⊕ www.chuckrichards.com) is easy on the pocketbook and has a variety of trips to choose from. **Kern River Tours** (☎ 800/844–7238 ⊕ www.kernrivertours.com) offers several tours from half-day trips to three days of navigating Class V rapids. **Mountain & River Adventures** (☎ 760/376–6553 or 800/861–6553 ⊕ www.mtnriver. com) has calm-water kayaking tours as well as white-water offerings. Half-day Class II and III white-water raft trips are emphasized at **Sierra South** (☎ 760/376–3745 or 800/457–2082 ⊕ www.sierrasouth.com).

MID-CENTRAL VALLEY
FROM VISALIA TO FRESNO

The Mid-Central Valley extends over three counties—Tulare, Kings, and Fresno. Historic Hanford and bustling Visalia are unadvertised but wonderful discoveries. From Visalia, Highway 198 winds east 35 mi to Generals Highway, which leads into Sequoia and Kings Canyon national parks. Highway 180 snakes east 55 mi to Sequoia and Kings Canyon. From Fresno, Highway 41 leads north 95 mi to Yosemite National Park.

Colonel Allensworth State Historic Park

★ ❸ *45 mi north of Bakersfield on Hwy. 43.*

A former slave who became the country's highest-ranking black military officer of his time founded Allensworth—the only California town settled, governed, and financed by African-Americans—in 1908. After enjoying early prosperity, the town was plagued by hardships and was eventually deserted. Its rebuilt or restored buildings reflect the era when it thrived. Festivities each October commemorate the town's rededication. ⊠ *4129 Palmer Ave.* ☎ *661/849–3433* ⊕ *www.cal-parks.ca.gov* ▣ *$3 per car* ⊙ *Daily sunrise–sunset, visitor center open daily 10–4, buildings open by appointment.*

off the beaten path

KERN NATIONAL WILDLIFE REFUGE – Snowy egrets, peregrine falcons, warblers, dozens of types of ducks, and other birds inhabit the marshes and wetlands here from November through April. Follow the 6½-mi loop drive (pick up maps at the entrance) to find good viewing spots, but beware that waterfowl hunting is allowed October through January. ⊠ *10811 Corcoran Rd., 18 mi west of Delano on Hwy. 155 (Garces Hwy.); from Allensworth take Hwy. 43 south to Hwy. 155 west* ☎ *661/725–2767* ⊕ *www.natureali.org/ knwrvisitors.htm* ▣ *Free* ⊙ *Daily sunrise–sunset.*

Visalia

❹ *40 mi north of Colonel Allensworth State Historic Park on Hwy. 99 and east on Hwy. 198; 75 mi north of Bakersfield via Hwy. 99 north and Hwy. 198 east.*

Visalia's combination of a reliable agricultural economy and immense civic pride has yielded perhaps the most vibrant downtown in the Central Valley. A clear day's view of the Sierra from Main Street is spectacular, and even Sunday night finds the streets busy with pedestrians, many coming from Bakersfield and Fresno for the excellent restaurants that abound here. Founded in 1852, the town contains many historic homes; ask for a free guide at the **visitor center** (⊠ 720 W. Mineral King Ave., 93921 ☎ 559/734–5876 ☉ Weekdays 8:30–5).

The **Chinese Cultural Center,** housed in a pagoda-style building, mounts exhibits about Asian art and culture. ⊠ *500 S. Akers Rd., at Hwy. 198* ☎ *559/625–4545* ☜ *Free* ☉ *Wed.–Sun. 11–4.*

☺ In oak-shaded **Mooney Grove Park** you can picnic alongside duck ponds, rent a boat for a ride around the lagoon, and view a replica of the famous *End of the Trail* statue. The original, designed by James Earl Fraser for the 1915 Panama-Pacific International Exposition, is now in the Cowboy Hall of Fame in Oklahoma. ⊠ *27000 S. Mooney Blvd., 5 mi south of downtown* ☎ *559/733–6291* ☜ *$5 per car, free in winter, dates vary* ☉ *Late May–early Sept., weekdays 8–7, weekends 8 AM–9 PM; early Sept.–Oct. and Mar.–late May, Mon., Thurs., and Fri. 8–5, weekends 8–7; Nov.–Feb., Thurs.–Mon. 8–5.*

The indoor-outdoor **Tulare County Museum** contains several re-created environments from the pioneer era. Also on display are Yokuts tribal artifacts (basketry, arrowheads, clamshell-necklace currency) as well as saddles, guns, dolls, quilts, and gowns. ⊠ *Mooney Grove Park, 27000 S. Mooney Blvd., 5 mi south of downtown* ☎ *559/733–6616* ☜ *Free* ☉ *Late May–Sept., Thurs.–Mon. 10–4; Oct.–late May; Mon.–Tues. and Fri. 10–4, weekends 1–4.*

Trails at the 300-acre **Kaweah Oaks Preserve,** a wildlife sanctuary off the main road to Sequoia National Park, lead past oak, sycamore, cottonwood, and willow trees. Among the 125 bird species you might spot are hawks, hummingbirds, and great blue herons. Lizards, coyotes, and cottontails also live here. ⊠ *Follow Hwy. 198 for 7 mi east of Visalia, turn north on Rd. 182, and proceed ½ mi to gate on left side of road* ☎ *559/738–0211* ⊕ *www.sequoiariverlands.org* ☜ *Free* ☉ *Daily sunrise–sunset.*

Where to Stay & Eat

★ **$$–$$$** ✕ **The Vintage Press.** Built in 1966, the Vintage Press is the best restaurant in the Central Valley. Cut-glass doors and bar fixtures decorate the artfully designed rooms. The California-Continental cuisine includes dishes such as crispy veal sweetbreads with a port wine sauce, and a bacon-wrapped filet mignon stuffed with mushrooms. The chocolate Grand Marnier cake is a standout among the homemade desserts and ice creams. The wine list has more than 900 selections. ⊠ *216 N. Willis St.* ☎ *559/733–3033* ▤ *AE, DC, MC, V.*

¢–$$ ✕ **Café 225.** This downtown favorite combines high ceilings and warm yellow walls with soft chatter and butcher-papered tables to create an elegance that's relaxed enough for kids. The basic menu of pastas and grilled items is highlighted with unusual treats, such as Gorgonzola amandine and the house specialty, oak-rotisserie chicken. ⊠ *225 W. Main St.* ☎ *559/733–2967* ☰ *AE, D, DC, MC, V.*

¢–$$ ✕ **Henry Salazar's.** Traditional Mexican food with a contemporary twist is served at this restaurant that uses fresh ingredients from local farms. Bring your appetite if you expect to finish the Burrito Fantastico, a large flour tortilla stuffed with your choice of meat, beans, and chile sauce, and smothered with melted Monterey Jack cheese. Another signature dish is grilled salmon with lemon-butter sauce. Colorfully painted walls, soft reflections from candles in wall niches, and color-coordinated tablecloths and napkins make the atmosphere cozy and restful. ⊠ *123 W. Main St.* ☎ *559/741–7060* ☰ *AE, D, MC, V.*

$ ▥ **Ben Maddox House.** Housed in a building dating to 1876, this homey B&B offers the best of all worlds: plush beds, a cool swimming pool, and excellent service remind you you're on vacation; private bathrooms and dining tables on the sunny porch make the surroundings homey and comfortable. The Water Tower Room has its own sitting area, and all rooms have wireless Internet. ⊠ *601 N. Encina St., 93291* ☎ *559/ 739–0721 or 800/401–9800* ☎ *559/625–0420* ⊕ *www.benmaddoxhouse. com* ▭ *5 rooms* ₺ *In-room data ports, cable TV, pool; no smoking* ☰ *AE, D, MC, V* ℺ *BP.*

$ ▥ **The Spalding House.** This restored colonial revival B&B is decked out with antiques, oriental rugs, handcrafted woodwork, and glass doors. The house, built in 1901, has suites with separate sitting rooms and private baths. The quiet neighborhood, also home to the Ben Maddox House, offers a place for one of life's simple pleasures: an evening walk on lovely, tree-lined streets. ⊠ *631 N. Encina St., 93291* ☎ *559/739–7877* ☎ *559/ 625–0902* ⊕ *www.thespaldinghouse.com* ▭ *3 suites* ₺ *No-smoking rooms; no room phones, no room TVs* ☰ *AE, MC, V* ℺ *BP.*

Hanford

★ ❺ *20 mi west of Visalia on Hwy. 198; 43 mi north of Colonel Allensworth State Historic Park on Hwy. 43.*

Founded in 1877 as a Southern Pacific Railroad stop, Hanford had one of California's largest Chinatowns—the Chinese came to help build the railroads and stayed on to farm. You can take a self-guided walking tour with the help of a free brochure, or take a driving tour in a restored 1930s Studebaker fire truck ($35 for up to 15 people) through the **Hanford Visitor Agency** (☎ 559/582–5024 ⊕ www.visithanford.com). One tour explores the restored buildings of Courthouse Square, another heads to narrow China Alley; if you have specific interests, a tour can also be designed for you.

The **Hanford Carnegie Museum** displays fashions, furnishings, toys, and military artifacts that tell the region's story. The living-history museum is inside the former Carnegie Library, a Romanesque building dating from 1905. ⊠ *109 E. 8th St.* ☎ *559/584–1367* ▱ *$2* ☉ *Wed.–Sat. 10–2.*

A first-floor museum in the 1893 **Taoist Temple** displays photos, furnishings, and kitchenware from Hanford's once-bustling Chinatown. The second-floor temple, largely unchanged for a century, contains altars, carvings, and ceremonial staves. You can visit as part of a guided tour or by calling the temple and making an appointment two weeks in advance. ⊠ *12 China Alley* ☎ *559/582–4508* ✑ *Free; donations welcome.*

Where to Stay & Eat

$$ ✕ **Imperial Dynasty.** Despite its name and elegant Chinese teak and porcelain accents, Imperial Dynasty serves primarily continental cuisine. This is one of the better restaurants in the valley and fills up quickly on weekends. For a memorable meal start with the garlicky escargots and continue with the veal sweetbreads or rack of lamb. The extensive wine list contains many prized vintages. ⊠ *China Alley, 7th and Green Sts.* ☎ *559/582–0196* ▤ *AE, D, MC, V* ⊘ *Closed Mon. No lunch.*

¢ ✕ **La Fiesta.** Mexican-American families, farmworkers, and farmers all eat here, polishing off traditional Mexican dishes such as enchiladas and tacos. The Fiesta Special—for two or more—includes nachos, garlic shrimp, shrimp in a spicy red sauce, clams, and two pieces of top sirloin. ⊠ *106 N. Green St.* ☎ *559/583–8775* ▤ *AE, D, MC, V.*

★ ¢ ▦ **Irwin Street Inn.** This inn is one of the few lodgings in the valley that warrant a detour. Four tree-shaded, restored Victorian homes have been converted into spacious accommodations with comfortable rooms and suites. Most have antique armoires, dark-wood detailing, lead-glass windows, and four-poster beds; bathrooms have old-fashioned tubs, brass fixtures, and marble basins. ⊠ *522 N. Irwin St., 93230* ☎ *559/583–8000 or 866/583–7378* ⊟ *559/583–8793* ⊕ *www.irwinstreetinn.com* ⇥ *30 rooms* ⚘ *Restaurant, pool* ▤ *AE, D, DC, MC, V* ¶◎ *CP.*

Nightlife & the Arts

The restored Moorish-Castilian–style **Hanford Fox Theatre** (⊠ 326 N. Irwin St. ☎ 559/584–7823 ⊕ www.foxhanford.com) was built as a movie palace in 1929. The 1,000-seat venue now hosts a variety of live performances, including jazz, country, pop, and comedy.

Fresno

35 mi north of Hanford via Hwys. 43 and 99 north.

Sprawling Fresno, with more than 450,000 people, is the center of the richest agricultural county in America. Cotton, grapes, and tomatoes are among the major crops; poultry and milk are other important products. The city's most famous native, Pulitzer Prize–winning playwright and novelist William Saroyan (*The Time of Your Life, The Human Comedy*), was born here in 1908. About 75 ethnic groups, including Armenians, Laotians, and Indians, call Fresno home. The city has a burgeoning arts scene, several public parks, and an abundance of low-priced restaurants serving tasty food. The Tower District, with its chic restaurants, coffeehouses, and boutiques, is the trendy spot.

☾ ▶ ➏ Tree-shaded **Roeding Park** is a place of respite on hot summer days; it has picnic areas, playgrounds, tennis courts, horseshoe pits, and a zoo. The most striking exhibit at **Chaffee Zoological Gardens** (☎ 559/498–2671

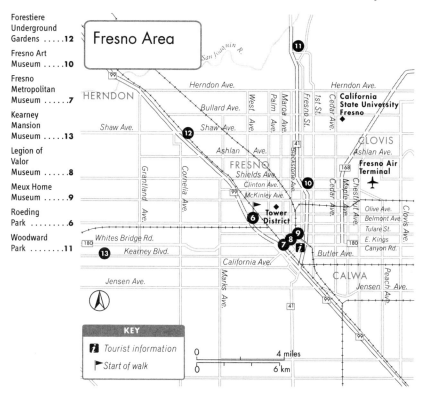

www.chaffeezoo.org $7 ☉ Feb.–Oct., daily 9–4; Nov.–Jan., daily 10–3) is the tropical rain forest, where you'll encounter exotic birds along the paths and bridges. Elsewhere you'll find tigers, grizzly bears, sea lions, tule elk, camels, elephants, and hooting siamangs. Also here are a high-tech reptile house and a petting zoo. A train, little race cars, paddleboats, and other rides for kids are among the amusements that operate March–November at **Playland** (☎ 559/486–2124 ☉ Wed.–Fri. 11–5:30, weekends 10:30–6:30). Children can explore attractions with fairy-tale themes at **Storyland** (☎ 559/264–2235 ☉ Weekdays 11–5:30), which is also open March–November. ✉ *Olive and Belmont Aves.* ☎ *559/498–1551* 🎫 *Free; $1 parking and $4 for Storyland.*

❼ The **Fresno Metropolitan Museum** mounts art, history, and hands-on science exhibits, many of them quite innovative. The William Saroyan History Gallery presents a riveting introduction in words and pictures to the author's life and times. ✉ *1515 Van Ness Ave.* ☎ *559/441–1444* ⊕ *www.fresnomet.org* 🎫 *$7, $1 Thurs. nights after 5 ☉ Tues., Wed., and Fri.–Sun. 11–5, Thurs. 11–8.*

❽ The **Legion of Valor Museum** is a real find for military history buffs of all ages. It has German bayonets and daggers, a Japanese Namby pistol, a Gatling gun, and an extensive collection of Japanese, German, and

American uniforms. The staff is extremely enthusiastic. ⊠ *2425 Fresno St.* ☎ *559/498–0510* ⊕ *www.legionofvalor.com/museum.php* ⊠ *Free* ⊙ *Mon.–Sat. 10–3.*

❾ Inside a restored 1889 Victorian, the **Meux Home Museum** displays furnishings typical of early Fresno. Guided tours proceed from the front parlor to the backyard carriage house. ⊠ *Tulare and R Sts.* ☎ *559/233–8007* ⊕ *www.meux.mus.ca.us* ⊠ *$5* ⊙ *Fri.–Sun. noon–3:30.*

❿ The **Fresno Art Museum** exhibits American, Mexican, and French art; highlights of the permanent collection include pre-Columbian works and graphic art from the Postimpressionist period. The 152-seat Bonner Auditorium hosts lectures, films, and concerts. ⊠ *Radio Park, 2233 N. 1st St.* ☎ *559/441–4221* ⊕ *www.fresnoartmuseum.org* ⊠ *$4; free Tues.* ⊙ *Tues., Wed., and Fri. 11–5, Thurs. 11–8, weekends 11–5.*

★ **⓫** **Woodward Park,** 300 acres of jogging trails, picnic areas, and playgrounds in the northern reaches of the city, is especially pretty in the spring, when plum and cherry trees, magnolias, and camellias bloom. Outdoor concerts take place in summer. The **Shinzen Friendship Garden** has a teahouse, a koi pond, arched bridges, a waterfall, and Japanese art. ⊠ *Audubon Dr. and Friant Rd.* ☎ *559/621-2900* ⊠ *$3 per car Feb.–Oct.; additional $3 for Shinzen Garden* ⊙ *Apr.–Oct., daily 7 AM–10 PM; Nov.–Mar., daily 7–7.*

★ ☾ **⓬** Sicilian immigrant Baldasare Forestiere spent four decades (1906–46) carving out the **Forestiere Underground Gardens,** a subterranean realm of rooms, tunnels, grottoes, alcoves, and arched passageways that extends for more than 10 acres beneath busy, mall-pocked Shaw Avenue. Only a fraction of Forestiere's prodigious output is on view, but you can tour his underground living quarters, including bedrooms (one with a fireplace), the kitchen, living room, and bath, as well as a fish pond and an aquarium. Skylights allow exotic full-grown fruit trees, including one that bears seven kinds of citrus as a result of grafting, to flourish more than 20 feet below ground. Reservations are recommended. ⊠ *5021 W. Shaw Ave., 2 blocks east of Hwy. 99* ☎ *559/271–0734* ⊠ *$9* ⊙ *Tours: weekends noon and 2. Call for other tour times.*

⓭ The drive along palm-lined Kearney Boulevard is one of the best reasons to visit the **Kearney Mansion Museum,** which stands in shaded 225-acre **Kearney Park.** The century-old home of M. Theo Kearney, Fresno's onetime "raisin king," is accessible only by taking a guided 45-minute tour. ⊠ *7160 W. Kearney Blvd., 6 mi west of Fresno* ☎ *559/441–0862* ⊠ *$4; park entrance $3, waived for museum visitors* ⊙ *Park hrs: 7 AM–10 PM; museum tours Fri.–Sun. at 1, 2, and 3.*

off the
beaten
path

BLOSSOM TRAIL – This 62-mi self-guided driving tour takes in Fresno-area orchards, citrus groves, and vineyards during spring blossom season. Pick up a route map at the **Fresno Convention & Visitors Bureau** (⊠ *848 M St., 3rd fl.* ☎ *559/233–0836 or 800/ 788–0836* ⊕ *www.fresnochamber.com/blossom.html*). The route passes through small towns and past rivers, lakes, and canals. The most colorful and aromatic time to go is from late February to mid-

March, when almond, plum, apple, orange, lemon, apricot, and peach blossoms shower the landscape with shades of white, pink, and red. Directional and crop identification signs mark the trail. Allow at least 2–3 hours for the tour.

Along the Blossom Trail, roughly halfway between Fresno and Visalia, the colorful handiwork of local quilters is on display at the **Mennonite Quilt Center** (⊠ 1012 G St. [take Manning Ave. exit off Hwy. 99 and head east 12 mi], Reedley ☎ 559/638–3560). The center is open weekdays 9:30–4:30 and Saturday 10–4, but try to visit on Monday (except holidays) between 8 and noon, when two dozen quilters stitch, patch, and chat over coffee. Prime viewing time—with the largest number of quilts—is in February and March, before the center's early-April auction. Ask a docent to take you to the locked upstairs room, where most of the quilts hang; she'll explain the fine points of patterns such as the Log Cabin Romance, the Dahlia, and the Snowball-Star. Admission is free.

Where to Stay & Eat

$$–$$$ ✕ **Echo.** This Tower District restaurant has a well-appointed dining room and a chic sensibility. Its tantalizing menu draws largely on locally grown food, much of it organic, with exquisite results. The grilled house-cured pork tenderloin with baby fennel sauce is excellent; so is the organic beef with red wine and yellowfoot mushrooms; and the signature dessert, apricot bread pudding with caramel. The food is tasty, but portions are small. ⊠ 609 E. Olive Ave. ☎ 559/442–3246 ⊟ AE, D, MC, V ⊙ Closed Sun. and Mon.

$–$$ ✕ **La Rocca's Ristorante Italiano.** The sauces that top these pasta and meat dishes will make your taste buds sing. The rich tomato sauce, which comes with or without meat, is fresh and tangy. The marsala sauce—served on either chicken or veal—is rich but not overpowering. Typical red-sauce dishes such as spaghetti, rigatoni, and lasagna are offered here, but you'll also be happily surprised with more adventurous offerings such as the bowtie pasta with cream, peas, bacon, tomato sauce, and olive oil. Pizzas also are served. ⊠ 6735 N. 1st St. ☎ 559/431–1278 ⊟ AE, MC, V ⊙ No lunch weekends.

$–$$ ✕ **Tahoe Joe's.** This restaurant is known for its steaks; other selections include the slow-roasted prime rib, center-cut pork chops, and chicken breast served with a whiskey peppercorn sauce. But if it's a steak you want, all cuts, including sirloin, rib eye, strip, and filet mignon, will satisfy. The baked potato that accompanies almost every dish is loaded tableside with your choice of butter, sour cream, chives, and bacon bits. Tahoe Joe's has two Fresno locations. ⊠ 7006 N. Cedar Ave. ☎ 559/299–9740 ⌦ Reservations not accepted ⊟ AE, D, MC, V ⊙ No lunch ⊠ 2700 W. Shaw Ave. ☎ 559/277–8028 ⌦ Reservations not accepted ⊟ AE, D, MC, V ⊙ No lunch.

¢–$ ✕ **El Rosal.** Authentic Mexican food served in a friendly atmosphere draws locals to this eatery. Try the Modesto Meat Combo, which includes carne asada (thin strips of marinated and grilled beef), pork chop, and grilled chicken breast. Other good choices include beef, chicken, or shrimp fajitas, and the jumbo burritos stuffed with rice, beans, and a meat of your choice. Carnitas (tender bits of pork served with condiments and hot tortillas) are served Friday and Saturday. ✉ *5730 N. 1st St.* ☎ *559/437–9614* ☱ *AE, D, MC, V* ⊘ *Closed Sun.*

¢–$ ✕**Irene's.** Downtown workers pack this Tower District restaurant at lunchtime. Handmade, half-pound burgers are the most popular, and most filling, items on the menu. Other popular dishes include the smoked ham and melted Swiss cheese sandwich served on a hard roll, and fresh salads. For breakfast, homemade granola, huge buttermilk pancakes, and the Denver omelet (with ham, onions, and green peppers) will fill up even those with the most hearty appetites. ✉ *747 E. Olive Ave.* ☎ *559/237–9919* ☱ *AE, D, MC, V.*

$$ ▦**Piccadilly Inn Shaw.** This two-story property has 7½ attractively land-scaped acres and a big swimming pool. The sizable rooms have king- and queen-size beds, robes, ironing boards, and coffeemakers; some have fire-places. ✉ *2305 W. Shaw Ave., 93711* ☎ *559/226–3850* ▤ *559/226–2448* ⊕ *www.piccadilly-inn.com/westshaw* ⚑ *194 rooms, 5 suites* ⚒ *In-room data ports, cable TV, some microwaves, some refrigerators, pool, gym, hot tub, laundry facilities, laundry service, business services, meeting rooms, shuttle service, no-smoking rooms* ☱ *AE, D, DC, MC, V.*

¢–$ ▦**La Quinta Inn.** Rooms are ample at this basic three-story motel near downtown. Most rooms have large desks that prove helpful for business travelers. ✉ *2926 Tulare St., 93721* ☎ *559/442–1110 or 866/725–1661* ▤ *559/237–0415* ⚑ *129 rooms* ⚒ *In-room data ports, cable TV, some microwaves, some refrigerators, gym, pool, no-smoking rooms* ☱ *AE, D, DC, MC, V* ⦿❘ *CP.*

Nightlife & the Arts

The **Fresno Philharmonic Orchestra** (☎ 559/261–0600 ⊕ www.fresnophil. org) performs classical concerts (sometimes pops) on weekends, usually at the **William Saroyan Theatre** (✉ 700 M St.), from September through June. **Roger Rocka's Dinner Theater** (✉ 1226 N. Wishon Ave. ☎ 559/266–9494 or 800/371–4747), in the Tower District, stages six Broadway-style musicals a year. The **Tower Theatre for the Performing Arts** (✉ 815 E. Olive Ave. ☎ 559/485–9050 ⊕ www.towertheatrefresno.org) has given its name to the trendy Tower District of theaters, clubs, restaurants, and cafés. The restored 1930s art deco movie house presents theater, ballet, concerts, and other cultural events year-round.

Sports & the Outdoors

Kings River Expeditions (✉ 211 N. Van Ness Ave. ☎ 559/233–4881 or 800/846–3674 ⊕ www.kingsriver.com) arranges one- and two-day white-water rafting trips on the Kings River. **Wild Water Adventures** (✉ 11413 E. Shaw Ave., Clovis ☎ 559/299–9453 or 800/564–9453 ⊕ www.wildwater.net ⊠ $22, $16 after 4 PM), a 52-acre water theme park about 10 mi east of Fresno, is open from late May to early September.

Shopping

Old Town Clovis (✉ Upper Clovis Ave., Clovis) is an area of restored brick buildings with numerous antiques shops and art galleries (along with restaurants and saloons). Be warned, though: not much here is open on Sunday. Head east on Fresno's Herndon Avenue about 10 mi, and then turn right onto Clovis Avenue.

NORTH CENTRAL VALLEY
FROM MERCED TO LODI

The northern section of the valley cuts through Merced, Madera, Stanislaus, and San Joaquin counties, from the flat, abundantly fertile terrain between Merced and Modesto north to the edges of the Sacramento River delta and the fringes of the Gold Country. If you're heading to Yosemite National Park from northern California, chances are you'll pass through (or very near) at least one of these gateway cities.

Merced

⑭ *50 mi north of Fresno on Hwy. 99.*

Thanks to a branch of the University of California opening in 2005 and an aggressive community redevelopment plan, the downtown of county seat Merced is coming back to life. The transformation is not yet complete, but there are promising signs: a brewpub, several boutiques, the restoration of numerous historic buildings, and foot traffic won back from outlying strip malls.

Even if you don't go inside, be sure to swing by the **Merced County Courthouse Museum.** The three-story former courthouse, built in 1875, is a striking example of Victorian Italianate style. The upper two floors are a museum of early Merced history. Highlights include ornate restored courtrooms and an 1870 Chinese temple with carved redwood altars. ⊠ *21st and N Sts.* ☎ *209/723–2401* ☒ *Free* ☉ *Wed.–Sun. 1–4.*

The **Merced Multicultural Arts Center** displays paintings, sculpture, and photography. The Big Valley Arts & Culture Festival, which celebrates the area's ethnic diversity and children's creativity, is held here on the first weekend in October. ⊠ *645 W. Main St.* ☎ *209/388–1090* ⊕ *www. artsmerced.org* ☒ *Free* ☉ *Weekdays 9–5, Sat. 10–2.*

> **off the beaten path**
>
> **MILLERTON LAKE STATE RECREATION AREA** – This lake at the top of Friant Dam is a great place for boating, fishing, camping, and summertime swimming. The lake and its surrounding hills are wintering grounds for bald eagles, and boat tours are available to view the birds between December and February. ⊠ *5290 Millerton Rd., 20 mi northeast of Fresno via Hwy. 41 and Hwy. 145, Friant* ☎ *559/822–2225* ☒ *$8 per car* ☉ *Daily Oct.–Mar., 6 AM–6 PM; Apr.–Sept., 6 AM–10 PM.*

Where to Stay & Eat

$$–$$$ ✕ **The Branding Iron.** Beef is what this restaurant is all about. The juicy cut of prime rib paired with potato and Parmesan-cheese bread will satisfy diners with even the most ravenous appetites. This restaurant is a favorite among farmers and ranchers looking for a place to refuel as they travel through cattle country. California cattle brands decorate the walls, and when the weather is nice, cooling breezes refresh diners on the outdoor patio. ✉ *640 W. 16th St.* ☎ *209/722–1822* 🍽 *AE, MC, V* ⊘ *No lunch weekends.*

★ **$–$$$** ✕ **DeAngelo's.** This restaurant isn't just the best in Merced—it's one of the best in the Central Valley. Chef Vincent DeAngelo, a graduate of the Culinary Institute of America, brings his considerable skill to everything from basic ravioli to portobello mushrooms stuffed with sausage, peppers, and cheese. Half the restaurant is occupied by a new bar–bistro with its own menu, which includes brick-oven pizza. The delicious crusty bread comes from the Golden Sheath bakery, in Watsonville. ✉ *350 W. Main St.* ☎ *209/383–3020* 🍽 *AE, D, MC, V* ⊘ *No lunch weekends.*

¢ ✕ **Main Street Café.** This bright downtown café dishes up tasty breakfast and lunch fare. Sandwiches (try the chicken breast with pesto mayonnaise on French bread) are served with tasty side salads. You can also get pastries, along with espresso or cappuccino. ✉ *460 W. Main St.* ☎ *209/ 725–1702* 🍽 *AE, MC, V* ⊘ *Closed Sun. No dinner.*

$–$$ 🏚 **Hooper House Bear Creek Inn.** This 1931 neocolonial home stands regally at the corner of M Street. The immaculately landscaped 1½-acre property has fruit trees and grapevines, while the house offers a sunroom, well-chosen antiques, and big, soft beds. Breakfast (which can be served in your room) is hearty and imaginative, featuring locally grown foods such as fried sweet potatoes and black walnuts. ✉ *575 W. N. Bear Creek Dr., at M St., 95348* ☎ *209/723–3991* 📠 *209/723–7123* 🌐 *www. hooperhouse.com* ↩ *2 rooms, 1 suite, 1 cottage* ⚒ *In-room data ports, cable TV, no-smoking rooms* 🍽 *AE, D, MC, V* ⦿ *BP.*

Sports & the Outdoors

At **Lake Yosemite Regional Park** (✉ N. Lake Rd. off Yosemite Ave., 5 mi northeast of Merced ☎ 209/385–7426 🎫 $5 per car late May–early Sept.), you can boat, swim, windsurf, water-ski, and fish on a 387-acre reservoir. Paddleboat rentals and picnic areas are available.

en route Heading north on Highway 99 from Merced, stop at the outdoor **Castle Air Museum,** adjacent to the former Castle Air Force Base (now Castle Airport). You can stroll among fighter planes and other historic military aircraft. The 46 restored vintage war birds include the B-25 Mitchell medium-range bomber (best known for the Jimmy Doolittle raid on Tokyo following the attack on Pearl Harbor) and the speedy SR-71 Blackbird, used for reconnaissance over Vietnam and Libya. ✉ *Santa Fe Ave. and Buhach Rd. (6 mi north of Merced, take the Buhach Rd. exit off Hwy. 99 in Atwater and follow signs), Atwater* ☎ *209/723–2178* 🎫 *$8* ⊘ *Apr.–Sept., daily 9–5; Oct.–Mar., Wed.–Mon. 10–4.*

Modesto

⑮ *38 mi north of Merced on Hwy. 99.*

Modesto, a gateway to Yosemite and the southern reaches of the Gold Country, was founded in 1870 to serve the Central Pacific Railroad. The frontier town was originally to be named Ralston, after a railroad baron, but as the story goes, he modestly declined—thus the name Modesto. The Stanislaus County seat, a tree-lined city of 180,000, is perhaps best known as the site of the annual Modesto Invitational Track Meet and Relays and birthplace of film producer-director George Lucas, creator of the *Star Wars* film trilogy.

The **Modesto Arch** (⊠ 9th and I Sts.) bears the city's motto: WATER, WEALTH, CONTENTMENT, HEALTH. The prosperity that water brought to Modesto has attracted people from all over the world. The city holds a well-attended **International Festival** (☎ 209/521–3852) in early October that celebrates the cultures, crafts, and cuisines of many nationalities. You can witness the everyday abundance of the Modesto area at the **Blue Diamond Growers Store** (⊠ 4800 Sisk Rd. ☎ 209/545–3222), which offers free samples, shows a film about almond-growing, and sells many roasts and flavors of almonds, as well as other nuts.

★ A rancher and banker built the 1883 **McHenry Mansion,** the city's sole surviving original Victorian home. The Italianate-style mansion has been decorated to reflect Modesto life in the late 19th century. Oaks, elms, magnolias, redwoods, and palms shade the grounds. ⊠ *15th and I Sts.* ☎ *209/577–5341* ⊕ *www.mchenrymuseum.org* ⊠ *Free* ☉ *Sun.–Thurs. 1–4, Fri. noon–3.*

The **McHenry Museum of Arts** is a jumbled repository of early Modesto and Stanislaus County memorabilia, including re-creations of an old-time doctor's office, a blacksmith's shop, and a general store stocked with period goods such as hair crimpers and corsets. ⊠ *14th and I Sts.* ☎ *209/577–5366* ⊠ *Free* ☉ *Tues.–Sun. noon–4.*

Where to Stay & Eat

$$$–$$$$ ✗ **Hazel's Elegant Dining.** Hazel's is *the* special-occasion restaurant in Modesto. The seven-course dinners include continental entrées served with appetizer, soup, salad, pasta, and dessert. Members of the Gallo family, which owns much vineyard land in the Central Valley, eat here often, perhaps because the wine cellar's offerings are so comprehensive. ⊠ *431 12th St.* ☎ *209/578–3463* ⊟ *AE, D, DC, MC, V* ☉ *Closed Sun. and Mon. No lunch Sat.*

$–$$ ✗ **Tresetti's World Café.** An intimate setting with white tablecloths and contemporary art draws diners to this eatery—part wine shop, part restaurant—with a seasonally changing menu. For a small fee, the staff will uncork any wine you select from the shop. The creole fried buttermilk chicken is outstanding, as are the Cajun-style crab cakes. ⊠ *927 11th St.* ☎ *209/572–2990* ⊟ *AE, D, DC, MC, V* ☉ *Closed Sun.*

¢–$ ✗ **St. Stan's.** Modesto's renowned microbrewery makes St. Stan's beers. The 14 on tap include the delicious Whistle Stop pale ale and Red Sky ale. The restaurant is casual and serves up good corned beef sandwiches loaded with sauerkraut as well as a tasty beer-sausage nibbler. ⊠ *821 L St.* ☎ *209/524–2337* ⊟ *AE, MC, V* ☉ *Closed Sun.*

$–$$ ▦ **Doubletree Hotel.** Modesto's largest hotel rises 15 stories over the downtown area. Each room has a coffeemaker, hair dryer, iron, and desk. The convention center is adjacent, and St. Stan's brewpub is across the street. ⊠ *1150 9th St., 95354* ☎ *209/526–6000 or 800/222–8733* ⊟ *209/526–6096* ⊕ *www.doubletree.com* ⊅ *258 rooms* ⌂ *Café, room service, pool,* *gym, beauty salon, hot tub, sauna, nightclub, laundry service, meeting rooms, airport shuttle, no-smoking rooms* ⊟ *AE, D, DC, MC, V.*

¢ 🏨 **Best Western Town House Lodge.** The downtown location is the primary draw for this hotel. The county's historical library is across the street, and the McHenry Mansion and the McHenry Museum are nearby. All rooms come equipped with a coffeemaker, hair dryer, and iron. ⊠ *909 16th St., 95354* ☎ *209/524–7261 or 800/772–7261* 🖨 *209/ 579–9546* ⊕ *www.bestwestern.com* 🛏 *59 rooms* ♨ *Refrigerators, microwaves, cable TV pool, hot tub, free parking, no-smoking rooms* ⊟ *AE, D, DC, MC, V* ⎮○⎮ *CP.*

en route ·

The top attraction in Manteca, the largest town between Modesto and Stockton, is Manteca Waterslides. Kids usually head straight for the wild Thunder Falls, which has three three-story slides, and the ☺ V-Max, which stretches six stories tall. ⊠ *874 E. Woodward Ave., between I–5 and Hwy. 99* ☎ *209/249–2500 or 877/625–9663* ⊕ *www. oakwoodlake.com* 🎟 *$25* ☉ *Daily May–Sept., call for specific hrs.*

Oakdale

🔟 *15 mi northeast of Modesto on Hwy. 108.*

Oakdale is a bit off the beaten path from Modesto. You can sample the wares at **Oakdale Cheese & Specialties** (⊠ 10040 Hwy. 120 ☎ 209/848–3139 ⊕ www.oakdalecheese.com), which has tastings (try the aged Gouda) and cheese-making tours. There's a picnic area and a petting zoo.

If you're in Oakdale—home of a Hershey's chocolate factory—the third weekend in May, check out the **Oakdale Chocolate Festival** (☎ 209/847–2244), which attracts 50,000–60,000 people each year. The event's main attraction is Chocolate Avenue, where vendors proffer cakes, cookies, ice cream, fudge, and cheesecake.

★ ☺ The featured attraction at the **Knights Ferry Recreation Area** is the 355-foot-long Knights Ferry covered bridge. The beautiful and haunting structure, built in 1863, crosses the Stanislaus River near the ruins of an old gristmill. The park has picnic and barbecue areas along the riverbanks, as well as three campgrounds accessible only by boat, bicycle, or by foot. You can hike, fish, canoe, and raft on 4 mi of rapids. ⊠ *Corps of Engineers Park, 17968 Covered Bridge Rd., Knights Ferry, 12 mi east of Oakdale via Hwy. 108* ☎ *209/881–3517* 🎟 *Free* ☉ *Daily dawn–dusk.*

Sports & the Outdoors

Rafting on the Stanislaus River is a popular activity near Oakdale. **River Journey** (⊠ 14842 Orange Blossom Rd. ☎ 209/847–4671 or 800/292–2938 ⊕ www.riverjourney.com) will take you out for a few hours of fun. To satisfy your white-water or flat-water cravings, contact **Sunshine River Adventures** (☎ 209/848–4800 or 800/829–7238 ⊕ www. raftadventure.com).

Stockton

⑰ *29 mi north of Modesto on Hwy. 99.*

California's first inland port—connected since 1933 to San Francisco via a 60-mi-long deepwater channel—is wedged between I–5 and Highway 99, on the eastern end of the Sacramento River delta. Stockton, founded during the gold rush as a way station for miners traveling from San Francisco to the Mother Lode and now a city of 261,000, is where many of the valley's agricultural products begin their journey to other parts of the world. If you're here in late April, don't miss the **Stockton Asparagus Festival** (☎ 209/644–3740 ⊕ www.asparagusfest.com), at the Downtown Stockton Waterfront. The highlight of the festival is the food; organizers try to prove that almost any dish can be made with asparagus. A car show, kids' activity area, and musical entertainment also are part of the event.

★ The **Haggin Museum,** in pretty Victory Park, has one of the Central Valley's finest art collections. Highlights include landscapes by Albert Bierstadt and Thomas Moran, a still life by Paul Gauguin, a Native American gallery, and an Egyptian mummy. ⊠ *1201 N. Pershing Ave.* ☎ *209/940–6300* ⊕ *www.hagginmuseum.org* ⊠ *$5* ⊙ *Wed.–Sun. 1:30–5.*

Where to Stay & Eat

$$–$$$ ✕**Le Bistro.** This upscale restaurant serves fairly standard continental fare—rack of lamb, fillet of sole, sautéed shrimp, soufflé Grand Marnier—but you can count on high-quality ingredients and presentation with a flourish. ⊠ *Marina Center Mall, 3121 W. Benjamin Holt Dr., off I–5, behind Lyon's* ☎ *209/951–0885* ⊟ *AE, D, DC, MC, V* ⊙ *No lunch weekends.*

¢–$ ✕**On Lock Sam.** This Stockton landmark (it's been operating since 1898) is in a modern pagoda-style building with framed Chinese prints on the walls, a garden outside one window, and a sparkling bar area. One touch of old-time Chinatown remains: a few booths have curtains that can be drawn for complete privacy. The Cantonese food is among the best in the valley's. ⊠ *333 S. Sutter St.* ☎ *209/466–4561* ⊟ *AE, D, MC, V.*

¢ 🏨 **Best Western Stockton Inn.** Four miles from downtown, this large motel has a convenient location off Highway 99. The central courtyard with a pool and lounge chairs is a big plus on hot days. Most rooms are spacious. ⊠ *4219 Waterloo Rd., 95215* ☎ *209/931–3131 or 888/829–0092* ☐ *209/931–0423* ⊕ *www.bestwesterncalifornia.com* ⇆ *136 rooms, 5 suites* ⚕ *Restaurant, in-room data ports, microwaves, refrigerators, cable TV, pool, wading pool, hot tub, bar, laundry service, meeting room, no-smoking rooms* ⊟ *AE, D, DC, MC, V.*

¢ 🏨 **La Quinta Inn.** Close to downtown and near many upscale restaurants, this is a good choice for business and pleasure travelers. The spacious and quiet rooms have large desks and televisions; if you're feeling active, you can get free passes to a nearby gym. ⊠ *2710 W. March La., 95219* ☎ *209/952–7800 or 866/725–1661* ☐ *209/472–0732* ⊕ *www. laquinta.com* ⇆ *151 rooms* ⚕ *In-room data ports, cable TV with movies, pool, laundry service, meeting rooms, no-smoking rooms* ⊟ *AE, D, DC, MC, V.*

Sports & the Outdoors

Several companies rent houseboats (of various sizes, usually for three, four, or seven days) on the Sacramento River delta waterways near Stockton. Houseboats, patio boats, fishing boats, and ski boats can be rented through the **Delta Houseboat Rental Hotline** (✉ 6333 Pacific Ave., Suite 152 ☎ 209/477–1840). **Herman & Helen's Marina** (✉ 15135 W. 8 Mile Rd. ☎ 209/951–4634) has houseboats with hot tubs and fireplaces. **Paradise Point Marina** (✉ 8095 Rio Blanco Rd. ☎ 209/952–1000) offers a variety of rentals, including patio boats and personal watercraft.

Lodi

🔞 *13 mi north of Stockton and 34 mi south of Sacramento on Hwy. 99.*

Founded on agriculture, Lodi was once the watermelon capital of the country, and today it is surrounded by fields of asparagus, pumpkins, beans, safflowers, sunflowers, kiwis, melons, squashes, peaches, and cherries. It also has become a wine grape capital of sorts, producing zinfandel, merlot, cabernet sauvignon, chardonnay, and sauvignon blanc grapes. For years California wineries have built their reputations on the juice of grapes grown around Lodi. Now the area that includes Lodi, Lockeford, and Woodbridge is a wine destination boasting about 40 wineries, many offering tours and tastings. Lodi still retains an old rural charm. You can stroll downtown or visit a wildlife refuge, all the while benefiting from a Sacramento River delta breeze that keeps this microclimate cooler in summer than anyplace else in the area. With a short, mild winter and a long, rain-free summer, Lodi is ideal for outdoor recreation.

😊 The 65-acre **Micke Grove Park and Zoo,** an oak-shaded county park off I–5, includes a Japanese garden, picnic areas, a golf course, and an agricultural museum with a collection of 94 tractors. Geckos and frogs, black-and-white ruffed lemurs, and hissing cockroaches found only on the African island of Madagascar inhabit "An Island Lost in Time," an exhibit at the **Micke Grove Zoo** (☎ 209/953–8840 ⊕ www.mgzoo.com ☉ Daily 10–5). California sea lions bask on rocks much as they do off the coast of San Francisco in the " Islands Close to Home" exhibit, another highlight of this compact facility. Most rides and diversions at Micke Grove's **Funderwoods Playland** (☎ 209/368–1092 ☉ Weekdays 11:30–6, weekends 10:30–6), a family-oriented amusement park, are geared to children. ✉ *11793 N. Micke Grove Rd.* ☎ *209/331–7400* 💲 *Zoo admission $2; parking $2 weekdays, $5 weekends and holidays.*

★ Stop by the **Lodi Wine & Visitor Center** (✉ 2545 W. Turner Rd. ☎ 209/ 365–0621) to see exhibits on Lodi's viticultural history. Here you can pick up a map of area wineries, as well as buy wine. One of the standout wineries in the area is **Jessie's Grove** (✉ 1973 W. Turner Rd. ☎ 209/ 368–0880 ⊕ www.jgwinery.com ☉ Fri.–Sun. 11–4), a wooded horse ranch and vineyard that has been in the same family since 1863. In addition to producing outstanding old-vine zinfandels, it presents blues concerts on various Saturdays May–October. At the **Woodbridge Winery** (✉ 5950 E. Woodbridge Rd., Acampo ☎ 209/369–5861 ⊕ www.

woodbridgewines.com ☉ Tues.–Sun. 10:30–4:30), you can take a free 30-minute tour of the vineyard and aging room. At its homey facility, kid-friendly **Phillips Farms** (✉ 4580 W. Hwy. 12 ☎ 209/368–7384 ⊕ www.lodivineyards.com) offers tastings from its affordable Michael-David Vineyard. You can also cut flowers from the garden, pet the animals, eat breakfast or lunch at the café, and buy Phillips' produce. **Vino Piazza** (✉ 12470 Locke Rd., Lockeford ☎ 209/727–9770) is a sort of wine co-op housed in the old Lockeford Winery building, where 13 vineyards operate tasting rooms. If you don't have time to see the vineyards themselves, this is a good way to sample the area's many wines.

Where to Stay & Eat

$–$$ ✕ **Rosewood Bar & Grill.** In downtown Lodi, Rosewood offers fine dining without formality. Operated by the folks at Wine & Roses Hotel and Restaurant, this low-key spot serves American fare with a twist, such as meat loaf wrapped in bacon, and daily seafood specials. There's a large bar with its own menu, plus live music on Thursday. ✉ *28 S. School St.* ☎ *209/369–0470* ⊟ *AE, D, DC, MC, V* ☉ *No lunch.*

¢–$ ✕ **Habanero Hots.** If your mouth can handle the heat promised by the restaurant's name, try the tamales. If you want to take it easy on your taste buds, stick with the rest of the menu. ✉ *1024 E. Victor Rd.* ☎ *209/369–3791* ⊟ *AE, MC, V.*

¢ ✕ **Angelo's.** Authentic Mexican dishes such as chile verde, steak ranchero and all-meat chimichangas draw locals to this downtown eatery. The service is friendly and quick, and the atmosphere is casual. ✉ *28 N. School St.* ☎ *209/366–2728* ⊟ *AE, DC, MC, V.*

★ $$–$$$ ✕🏨 **Wine & Roses Hotel and Restaurant.** Set on 7 acres amid a tapestry of informal gardens, this hotel has cultivated a sense of refinement typically associated with Napa or Carmel. Rooms are decorated in rich earth tones, and linens are imported from Italy. Some rooms have fireplaces; all have coffeemakers, irons, and hair dryers. Some of the bathrooms even have TVs. The restaurant ($$$) is *the* place to eat in Lodi. Lunch and dinner served in the light and airy dining room feature fresh local produce. The Sunday buffet champagne brunch includes ham, prime rib, and made-to-order crepes and omelets. If that doesn't leave you feeling pampered enough, head to the spa for a facial or herbal body scrub. ✉ *2505 W. Turner Rd., 95242* ☎ *209/334–6988* 🖷 *209/371–6049* ⊕ *www.winerose.com* ⟿ *36 rooms, 4 suites* ⌂ *Restaurant, room service, in-room data ports, refrigerators, cable TV, bar, spa, laundry service, no-smoking rooms* ⊟ *AE, D, DC, MC, V* ⏐◉⏐ *CP.*

$$ 🏨 **The Inn at Locke House.** Built in 1865, this B&B was a pioneer family's home and is on the National Register of Historic Places. Rooms are filled with antique furnishings, and all have fireplaces. The centerpiece of the Water Tower Suite is a queen canopy bed; it also has a deck and a private sitting room. In the oak-paneled parlor, you'll find books, games, historical artifacts, and an old pump organ. Refreshments are served when you arrive. ✉ *19960 N. Elliott Rd., Lockeford 95237* ☎*209/ 727–5715* 🖷 *209/727–0873* ⊕ *www.theinnatlockehouse.com* ⟿ *4 rooms, 1 suite* ⌂ *Library, no-smoking rooms; no room TVs* ⊟ *AE, D, DC, MC, V* ⏐◉⏐ *BP.*

¢ ⌨ **Lodi Comfort Inn.** This downtown motel has quiet rooms with contemporary furnishings and blow dryers in the bathrooms. It's easily accessible from Highway 99. Donuts, waffles, bagels, juice, and coffee make up the complimentary breakfast. ✉ *118 N. Cherokee La.* ☎ *209/367–4848 or 877/424–6423* 🖨 *209/367–4898* ⊕ *www.comfortinn.com* ↩ *55 rooms* ♿ *Microwaves, refrigerators, in-room data ports, cable TV, pool, hot tub, laundry facilities, laundry service* ▤ *AE, D, DC, MC, V* �ⓄⒾ *CP.*

Sports & the Outdoors

Even locals need respite from the heat of Central Valley summers, and **Lodi Lake Park** (✉ 1101 W. Turner Rd. ☎ 209/333–6742 ⊠ $5) is where they find it. The banks, shaded by grand old elms and oaks, are much cooler than other spots in town. Swimming, bird-watching, and picnicking are possibilities, as is renting a kayak, canoe, or pedal boat ($2–$4 per half hour, Tuesday–Sunday, late May–early Sept. only).

THE CENTRAL VALLEY A TO Z

To research prices, get advice from other travelers, and book travel arrangements, visit ⊕ *www.fodors.com.*

AIRPORTS & TRANSFERS

Fresno Yosemite International Airport is serviced by America West, Alaska, Allegiant, American and American Eagle, Air Canada, Continental, Delta, Hawaiian, Horizon, Northwest, Skywest, US Airways, United and United Express. Kern County Airport at Meadows Field is serviced by America West Express, Continental, and United Express. United Express flies from San Francisco to Modesto City Airport and from Los Angeles to Visalia Municipal Airport. *See Air Travel in Smart Travel Tips A to Z for airline phone numbers.*

🛈 **Fresno Yosemite International Airport** ✉ 4995 E. Clinton Way, Fresno ☎ 559/621-4500 ⊕ www.fresno.gov/flyfresno. **Kern County Airport at Meadows Field** ✉ 1401 Skyway Dr., Bakersfield ☎ 661/393-7990 ⊕ www.meadowsfield.com. **Modesto City Airport** ✉ 617 Airport Way, Modesto ☎ 209/577-5318 ⊕ www.modairport.com. **Visalia Municipal Airport** ✉ 9501 W. Airport Dr., Visalia ☎ 559/713-4201 ⊕ www.flyvisalia.com.

BUS TRAVEL

Greyhound provides service between major valley cities. Orange Belt Stages provides bus service, including Amtrak connections, to many valley locations, including Bakersfield, Hanford, Fresno, Modesto, Merced, and Stockton.

🛈 **Greyhound** ☎ 800/231-2222 ⊕ www.greyhound.com. **Orange Belt Stages** ☎ 800/266-7433 ⊕ www.orangebelt.com.

CAR RENTAL

Avis, Budget, Dollar, Enterprise, Hertz, and National rent cars at Fresno Yosemite International Airport. Avis, Budget, Hertz, and National rent cars at Kern County Airport at Meadows Field. Avis, Enterprise, and Hertz rent cars at Modesto City Airport. Avis, Budget, and Enterprise are represented at Visalia Municipal Airport. *See* Car Rental *in* Smart Travel Tips A to Z *for national rental-agency phone numbers.*

CAR TRAVEL

To reach the Central Valley from Los Angeles, follow I–5 north; Highway 99 veers north about 15 mi after entering the valley. To drive to the valley from San Francisco, take I–80 east to I–580 and then I–580 east to I–5, which leads south into the valley (several roads from I–5 head east to Highway 99); or continue east on I–580 to I–205, which leads to I–5 north to Stockton or (via Highway 120) east to Highway 99 at Manteca.

Highway 99 is the main route between the valley's major cities and towns. Interstate 5 runs roughly parallel to it to the west but misses the major population centers; its main use is for quick access from San Francisco or Los Angeles. Major roads that connect I–5 with Highway 99 are Highways 58 (to Bakersfield), 198 (to Hanford and Visalia), 152 (to Chowchilla, via Los Banos), 140 (to Merced), 132 (to Modesto), and 120 (to Manteca). For road conditions, call the California Department of Transportation hotline.

🚩 **California Department of Transportation** ☎ 800/266–6883 or 916/445–1534.

EMERGENCIES

In an emergency dial 911.

🚩 Hospitals **Bakersfield Memorial Hospital** ✉ 420 34th St., Bakersfield ☎ 661/327–4647. **St. Joseph's Medical Center** ✉ 1800 N. California St., Stockton ☎ 209/943–2000. **University Medical Center** ✉ 445 S. Cedar Ave., Fresno ☎ 559/459–4000.

TOURS

Central Valley Tours provides general and customized tours of the Fresno area and the valley, with special emphasis on the fruit harvests and blossom trail.

🚩 **Central Valley Tours** ☎ 559/276–4479 ⊕ www.angelfire.com/poetry/inc/valleytours.html.

TRAIN TRAVEL

Amtrak's daily *San Joaquin* travels between Bakersfield, San Jose, and Oakland, stopping in Hanford, Fresno, Madera, Merced, Modesto, and Stockton. Amtrak Thruway bus service connects Bakersfield with Los Angeles.

🚩 **Amtrak** ☎ 800/872–7245 ⊕ www.amtrakcalifornia.com.

VISITOR INFORMATION

🚩 **Fresno City & County Convention and Visitors Bureau** ✉ 848 M St., Fresno 93721 ☎ 559/233–0836 or 800/788–0836 ⊕ www.fresnocvb.org. **Greater Bakersfield Convention & Visitors Bureau** ✉ 515 Truxton Ave., Bakersfield 93301 ☎ 661/325–5051 or 866/425–7353 ⊕ www.bakersfieldcvb.org. **Hanford Visitor Agency** ✉ 200 Santa Fe Ave., Suite D, Hanford 93230 ☎ 559/582–5024 ⊕ www.visithanford.com. **Kern County Board of Trade** ✉ 2101 Oak St., Bakersfield 93301 ☎ 661/861–2367 or 800/500–5376 ⊕ www.co.kern.ca.us/boardoftrade. **Lodi Conference and Visitors Bureau** ✉ 2545 W. Turner Dr., Lodi 95242 ☎ 209/365–1195 or 800/798–1810 ⊕ www.visitlodi.com. **Merced**

Conference and Visitors Bureau ✉ 710 W. 16th St., Merced 95340 ☎ 209/384-2791 ⊕ www.yosemite-gateway.org. **Modesto Convention and Visitors Bureau** ✉ 1150 9th St., Suite C, Modesto 95353 ☎ 800/266-4282 ⊕ www.visitmodesto.com. **Stockton Visitors Bureau** ✉ 46 W. Fremont St., Stockton 95202 ☎ 209/937-5089 ⊕ www. visitstockton.org. **Visalia Chamber of Commerce and Visitors Bureau** ✉ 720 W. Mineral King Ave., Visalia 93291 ☎ 559/734-5876 ⊕ www.cvbvisalia.com.

THE CENTRAL COAST
FROM VENTURA TO BIG SUR

9

Updated by
Cheryl
Crabtree

THE COASTLINE BETWEEN SANTA BARBARA AND CARMEL, a distance of about 200 mi, is one of the most popular drives in California. Except for a few smallish cities—Ventura and Santa Barbara, in the south, and San Luis Obispo, in the north—the area is sparsely populated. The countryside's few inhabitants relish their isolation at the sharp edge of land and sea. Around Santa Barbara, Ventura, and Oxnard, Southern California peters out in long, sandy beaches. To the north the shoreline gradually rises into hills dotted with cattle, and by the time you reach Big Sur the Santa Lucia Mountains drop down to the Pacific with dizzying grandeur.

Sunny, well-scrubbed Santa Barbara, only 95 mi north of Los Angeles, is the link between Northern and Southern California. Santa Barbara's Spanish-Mexican heritage is reflected in the architectural style of the mission, courthouse, and many homes and public buildings. Inland from the Pacific a burgeoning Central Coast wine region stretches 100 mi from Santa Ynez north to Paso Robles; the 150-plus wineries here have earned reputations for high-quality vintages that rival those of Northern California. Visual artists create and sell their works in towns like Ojai and Cambria. The town of Solvang, where restaurants serve Danish fare and windmills line the streets, is a Scandinavian outpost in this otherwise quintessentially Californian landscape.

Exploring the Central Coast

Driving is the easiest way to experience the Central Coast, which extends from Ventura County in the south to the Big Sur coastline in the north. A car gives you the flexibility to stop at scenic vista points along Highway 1, take detours through wine country and drive to rural lakes and mountains. Traveling north through Ventura County to San Luis Obispo, you can feast your eyes on the rolling hills, peaceful valleys, and rugged mountains that stretch for miles along the shore. Especially in summer, you'll need to make reservations for a visit to Hearst San Simeon State Historical Monument well before you depart for the coast. In summer and on foggy days the traffic on windy, two-lane Highway 1 can seem to move at a snail's pace from Cambria to Big Sur. Moving slowly, though, will give you the chance to enjoy the breathtaking views.

About the Restaurants

The cuisine in Santa Barbara is every bit as eclectic as it is in California's bigger cities. Fresh seafood is a standout, whether it's prepared simply in wharf-side hangouts or incorporated into sophisticated bistro menus. If you're after good, cheap food with an international flavor, follow the locals to Milpas Street, on the eastern edge of Santa Barbara's downtown. Dining attire on the Central Coast is generally casual, though slightly dressy casual wear is the custom at pricier restaurants.

The Central Coast, from Solvang to Big Sur, is far enough off the interstate to ensure that nearly every restaurant or café has its own personality—from chic to down-home and funky. Cambria's cooks, true to the town's British-Welsh origins, craft English dishes complete with peas and Yorkshire pudding but also serve continental and contemporary fare. There aren't many restaurants between Hearst San Simeon State Historical Monument and Big Sur.

Numbers in the text correspond to numbers in the margin and on the Ventura & Santa Barbara Counties, Santa Barbara, and San Luiso Obispo County & Big Sur maps.

9

If you have
3 days

Start your trip in ► ⊞ **Santa Barbara** ⑤–㉟, where you can tour the **Santa Barbara County Courthouse** ⑫ and **Mission Santa Barbara** ⑮. In the afternoon explore **Stearns Wharf** ⑧ and other waterfront sights, and stroll State Street if you like to shop, or have some fun at the **Santa Barbara Zoo** ⑱. The next day, drive up to ⊞ **San Luis Obispo** ㉖ and visit Mission San Luis Obispo de Tolosa and the nearby County Historical Museum. Pausing north of town to poke your head into the kitschy Madonna Inn, drive to **Morro Bay** ㉗ to stroll the Embarcadero and see Morro Rock. Stop at Montaña de Oro State Park for a late-afternoon hike and spend the evening in ⊞ San Luis Obispo. In the morning, start bright and early, driving north through **Cambria** ㉙ to **San Simeon** ㉚ for a tour of Hearst San Simeon State Historical Monument. Next, head for the Big Sur coastline, where you can have a sunset dinner at Nepenthe and spend the night in or near ⊞ **Pfeiffer Big Sur State Park** ㉜.

If you have
7 days

Get your tour off to a natural start in ► ⊞ **Ventura** ②, on a morning cruise to **Channel Islands National Park** ③. In the afternoon, take Highway 33 east to see **Ojai** ④. On Day 2, drive to ⊞ **Santa Barbara** ⑤–㉟ and get a feel for the city's architecture, history, and vegetation at the **Santa Barbara County Courthouse** ⑫, **Mission Santa Barbara** ⑮, and the **Santa Barbara Botanic Garden** ⑰. Have dinner in **Montecito** ㉟ and explore the Coast Village Road shopping district. It's a short walk south from here to the shore to catch the sunset before or after you eat. The next day take it easy with a visit to **Stearns Wharf** ⑧, a walk or bike along East Beach, and a prowl through **Andree Clark Bird Refuge** ⑲. Have dinner on State Street and check out the area's shops and clubs. Day 4 starts with a drive up U.S. 101 to Highway 246 west to reach La Purisima Mission State Historic Park in **Lompoc** ㉔. Spend the afternoon in Santa Barbara wine country, stopping at wineries in Santa Ynez and Los Olivos. Another option is to browse the shops in Danish **Solvang** ㉓ where there are plenty of places to choose from for dinner. In the morning continue north through **Morro Bay** ㉗ to **Cambria** ㉙, a good place for lunch, and take an afternoon tour of Hearst San Simeon State Historical Monument. After a night in ⊞ **San Simeon** ㉚, head for the Big Sur coast on Day 6. Observe the glories of Los Padres National Forest up close by hiking one of the many trails in the Ventana Wilderness, or stay along the shore and hunt for jade at Jade Cove. Overnight at one of the spots around ⊞ **Pfeiffer Big Sur State Park** ㉜ and on your last day watch the waves break on Pfeiffer Beach, one of the few places in the area where you can actually set foot on the shore. If you're here on a weekend (or on Wed. Apr.–Oct.), tour Point Sur State Historic Park.

About the Hotels

Santa Barbara's numerous hotels and B&Bs—despite rates that range from pricey to downright shocking—attract thousands of patrons year-round. Air-conditioning is a rarity at coastal lodgings from Pismo Beach to Big Sur, because the sea breeze cools the air. Many moderately priced hotels and motels—most of them just decent places to hang your hat—can be found between San Luis Obispo and San Simeon. Big Sur has only a few lodgings, but even its budget accommodations have character.

Budget-conscious travelers will find more affordable options in Carpinteria, Ventura, and Oxnard, just a short drive south of Santa Barbara along the coast, or inland, in smaller towns such as Paso Robles. If possible, visit sometime between October and March, when many Central Coast lodgings offer reduced rates and promotional packages. Otherwise, try for midweek specials. Wherever you stay, be sure to make reservations for the summer and holiday weekends (especially Memorial Day, Labor Day, and Thanksgiving) well ahead of time. It's not unusual for all coastal accommodations (meaning every single one) to fill completely during these busy times. It's also common for hotels to double their rates during festivals and other events.

Hot Spots (☎ 805/564–1637 or 800/793–7666 ⊕ www.hotspotsusa. com) provides room reservations and tourist information for destinations in Ventura, Santa Barbara, and San Luis Obispo counties.

WHAT IT COSTS				
$$$$	$$$	$$	$	¢
RESTAURANTS over $30	$23–$30	$16–$22	$10–$15	under $10
HOTELS over $250	$176–$250	$121–$175	$90–$120	under $90

Restaurant prices are for a main course at dinner, excluding sales tax of 7¼–7¾% (depending on location). Hotel prices are for two people in a standard double room in high season, excluding service charges and 9–10% tax.

Timing

The Central Coast is hospitable most of the year. Santa Barbara and Ventura are pleasant year-round. Fog often rolls in north of Pismo Beach in summer; you'll need a jacket, especially after sunset, close to the shore. The rains usually come from December through March. Hotel rooms fill up in summer, but from April to early June and in the early fall the weather is almost as fine and the pace is less hectic. And remember that hotels offer considerable discounts during the winter.

VENTURA COUNTY
WITH CHANNEL ISLANDS NATIONAL PARK

Ventura County was first settled by the Chumash Indians, an agricultural society. Spanish missionaries were the first Europeans to arrive, followed by Americans and other Europeans, who established bustling towns, transportation networks, and highly productive farms. Since

Missions Five important California missions established by Franciscan friars are within the Central Coast region. San Miguel (closed to the public due to earthquake damage in 2004) is one of California's best-preserved missions. La Purisima is the most fully restored; Mission Santa Barbara is perhaps the most beautiful in the state; and Mission San Luis Obispo de Tolosa has a fine museum with many Chumash Indian artifacts. Mission San Buenaventura has 250-year-old paintings and historic statuary.

Wineries Hundreds of vineyards and wineries dot the hillsides from Paso Robles to San Luis Obispo, through the scenic Edna Valley and south to northern Santa Barbara County. The wineries offer much of the variety of Northern California's Napa and Sonoma valleys—without the glitz and crowds. Since the early 1980s the region has steadily increased production and developed an international reputation for quality wines, most notably pinot noir, chardonnay, and zinfandel. Today there are more than 150 wineries. They tend to be small, but most have tasting rooms (some have tours), and you'll often meet the winemakers themselves. There are maps and brochures at the visitor centers in Solvang, San Luis Obispo, and Santa Barbara, or you can contact the wine associations of Paso Robles, Edna Valley-Arroyo Grande, and Santa Barbara. Many tasting rooms, hotels, and motels also keep a supply of wine-touring maps for visitors.

9

---

the 1920s, though, agriculture has been steadily replaced as the area's main industry—first by the oil business, and more recently, by tourism.

Oxnard

❶ *54 mi north of Santa Monica off U.S. 101.*

Oxnard has a reputation as a drowsy agricultural burg (a broccoli and lettuce capital), but lately it's been promoting its charms as an undiscovered beach town and a gateway to the Channel Islands. Its 7 mi of uncrowded beaches are great for folks who want to sail, windsurf, or just feel the sand between their toes. Be sure not to confuse Channel Islands Harbor in Oxnard and Ventura Harbor, 5 mi north. While both locations offer access to the Channel Islands, the Channel Islands National Park Visitor Center is in Ventura Harbor.

Take a stroll along **Heritage Square** to see more than a dozen late-19th-century homes and other buildings, many with manicured gardens and courtyards. Docent-led tours allow you to see the gracious interiors. ⊠ *715 S. A St.* ☎ *805/483–7960* ⊕ *www.heritagesquare.com* ✉ *$2* ☉ *Guided tours Sat. 10–2.*

★ More than 2,600 boats are moored at **Channel Islands Harbor,** a classic Southern California–style harbor that's the fifth largest for small-craft recreation in the state. Concerts, boat shows, fireworks displays, art festivals, and other events take place here year-round. At the **Ventura**

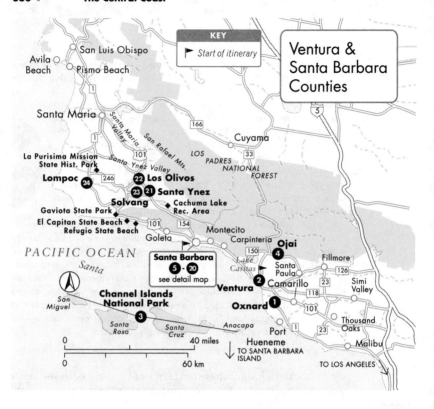

County Maritime Museum (☎ 805/984–6260), you can learn everything you ever wanted to know about the shipping, whaling history of the Channel Islands. You can rent bikes, paddleboats, and electric boats to tour the harbor. A visitor center, adjacent to the Maritime Museum, can help you get oriented. ⊠ *2741 S. Victoria Ave., Suite F* ☎ *805/985–4852* ⊕ *www.channelislandsharbor.org* ☜ *Free.*

The hands-on exhibits at the ocean-inspired ⟳ **Ventura County Gull Wings Children's Museum** include a tide-pool touch tank, a space center with a shuttle cockpit and moon room, and a "bistro" where kids can play chef. ⊠ *418 W. 4th St.* ☎ *805/483–3005* ⊕ *www. gullwingsmuseum4kids.org* ☜ *$4* ⟳ *Tues.–Sun. 10–5.*

Where to Stay & Eat

$–$$ ✕ **The Whale's Tail.** This popular seafood house in Channel Islands Harbor includes a casual upstairs shellfish bar with indoor–outdoor seating and a more formal dining room downstairs. Practically all the tables have waterfront views. Besides the fresh fish (delivered to the restaurant's dock each day), be sure to try the triple-fried "Yankee fries," the restaurant's signature twist on French fries. ⊠ *3950 Bluefin Circle* ☎ *805/985–2511* ▭ *AE, MC, V.*

¢–$ ✕ **Cabo Seafood Grill and Cantina.** Crowds of locals gather at this lively restaurant and bar for south-of-the-border seafood specialties served with fresh handmade tortillas. The rainbow-hue dining rooms and patio are casual and cheery. If you're not a seafood fan, try the *carne asada* (marinated strips of beef) or one of the filling combination plates. ⊠ *1041 S. Oxnard Blvd.* ☎ *805/487–6933* ▭ *AE, D, DC, MC, V.*

¢ ✕ **Mrs. Olson's Coffee Hut.** Mouthwatering homemade breakfasts featuring eggs Benedict, chilaquiles—sautéed corn tortilla strips scrambled with eggs, onion, cheese, and ranchero sauce—and crab cakes at this tiny, nautical-themed café have lured crowds of hungry locals for decades. You can also lunch on sandwiches, burgers, Mexican dishes, and salads. Unless you arrive early for breakfast (between 7 and 9 AM on weekdays, even earlier on weekends), expect a worthwhile wait. ⊠ *117 Los Altos St., Hollywood Beach* ☎ *805/985–9151* ⚠ *No reservations* ▭ *MC, V* ⊘ *No dinner.*

$$$–$$$$ ✕🏨 **Embassy Suites Mandalay Beach Resort.** Set on 8 acres of white-sand beach north of Channel Islands Harbor, this complex is surrounded by landscaped grounds, small waterfalls, and sprawling pool areas. The two- and three-room suites all have marble baths, and rates include complimentary cooked-to-order breakfasts. Capistrano's restaurant ($$–$$$) serves California cuisine in a garden courtyard and Polynesian-inspired dining rooms (don't miss the Sunday brunch). On Friday and Saturday nights, you can dance to live jazz, rock, and piano performances. ⊠ *2101 Mandalay Beach Rd., 93035* ☎ *805/984–2500 or 800/362–2779* 🖶 *805/ 984–8339* ⊕ *www.embassymandalay.com* ⬔ *249 suites* ⚏ *Restaurant, in-room data ports, microwaves, refrigerators, cable TV, 2 tennis courts, pool, gym, hot tub, spa, bicycles, bar, seasonal children's programs (ages 5–12), Internet, business services, airport shuttle, parking (fee), no-smoking rooms* ▭ *AE, D, DC, MC, V* ⋈ *BP.*

$$ 🏨 **Residence Inn by Marriott.** The expansive lobby of this hotel has tile floors and cherrywood furnishings; many of the spacious, comfortable rooms have their own wood-burning fireplaces. The 15-acre property is adjacent to the River Ridge Golf Course, 4 mi east of downtown. ⊠ *2101 W. Vineyard Ave., 93030* ☎ *805/278–2200 or 800/331–3131* 🖶 *805/983–4470* ⊕ *www.residenceinn.com* ⬔ *252 suites* ⚏ *In-room data ports, kitchens, cable TV, 5 tennis courts, 2 pools, exercise equipment, 3 hot tubs, laundry facilities, business services, meeting rooms, some pets allowed (fee), no-smoking rooms* ▭ *AE, D, DC, MC, V* ⋈ *BP.*

¢–$ 🏨 **Casa Sirena Resort.** Because it sits on a peninsula right in the middle of the Channel Islands Harbor Marina, this hotel has dynamite water views from many of its rooms. There are landscaped grounds with walkways surrounding the Spanish-style buildings, and a park nearby. ⊠ *3605 Peninsula Rd., 93035* ☎ *805/985–6311 or 800/447–3529* 🖶 *805/985– 4329* ⊕ *www.casasirenahotel.com* ⬔ *241 rooms, 30 suites* ⚏ *Restaurant, in-room data ports, some kitchenettes, refrigerators, cable TV, putting green, tennis courts, pool, gym, hair salon, hot tub, bar, playground, business services, meeting rooms, airport shuttle, some pets allowed, no-smoking rooms; no a/c in some rooms* ▭ *AE, D, DC, MC, V.*

Ventura

▶ ❷ *1 mi north of Oxnard on U.S. 101.*

Like Los Angeles, the city of Ventura enjoys gorgeous weather and sun-kissed beaches—but without the smog and congestion. The miles of beautiful beach attract both athletes—body-surfers and boogie-boarders, runners and bikers—and those who'd rather doze beneath a rented umbrella all day. Ventura Harbor is home to the Channel Islands National Park Visitor Center and myriad fishing boats, restaurants, and water-activity centers where you can rent boats and take harbor cruises. Foodies can get their fix here, too; dozens of upscale cafés and wine and tapas bars have opened in recent years. Ventura is also a magnet for antiques buffs, who come to browse the dozens of shops in the downtown area. You can pick up an antiques guide downtown at the **visitor center** (✉ 89 S. California St., #C ☎ 805/648–2075 ⊕ www.ventura-usa.com) run by the Ventura Visitors and Convention Bureau.

More than three millennia of human history in the Ventura region is charted in the archaeological exhibits at the small **Albinger Archaeological Museum.** Some of the relics on display date back to 1600 BC. ✉ *113 E. Main St.* ☎ *805/648–5823* 🎫 *Free* ☉ *June–Aug., Wed.–Sun. 10–4; Sept.–May, Wed.–Fri. 10–2, weekends 10–4.*

☪ Lunker largemouth bass, rainbow trout, crappie, red-ears, and channel catfish live in the waters at **Lake Casitas Recreation Area,** an impoundment of the Ventura River. The lake is one of the country's best bass-fishing areas, and anglers come from all over the United States to test their luck. The park, nestled below the Santa Ynez Mountains' Laguna Ridge, is also a beautiful spot for pitching a tent or having a picnic. The Blue Heron Water Adventure, which has a water playground and lazy river for tubing and floating, is a great place to take kids in summer ($10 for an all-day pass; $5 from 5 to 7 PM). The park is 13 mi northwest of Ventura. ✉ *Hwy. 33* ☎ *805/649–2233, 805/649–1122 for campground reservations* ⊕ *www.casitaswater.org* 🎫 *$6.50 per vehicle, $12.50 per boat* ☉ *Daily.*

The ninth of the 21 California missions, **Mission San Buenaventura** burned to the ground in the 1790s. It was rebuilt and rededicated in 1809. A self-guided tour takes you through a small museum, a quiet courtyard, and a chapel with 250-year-old paintings. ✉ *211 E. Main St.* ☎ *805/643–4318* ⊕ *www.sanbuenaventuramission.org* 🎫 *1$* ☉ *Weekdays 10–5, Sat. 9–5, Sun. 10–4.*

⎛ off the
⎜ beaten
⎝ path

SANTA PAULA – Eighteen miles northeast of Ventura on Highway 126, past the orange, lemon, and avocado orchards of Heritage Valley, lies this picturesque little town. Queen Anne and Victorian homes line the streets here, as do antiques stores and galleries. The **California Oil Museum** (✉ 1001 E. Main St. ☎ 805/933–0076 ⊕ www.oilmuseum.net), in the 1890 Union Oil Building, has exhibits about the history and impact of the oil industry in the region. It's open Wednesday–Sunday 10–4, and admission is $2.

FILLMORE – Visiting the tiny, well-preserved downtown of Fillmore, east of Santa Paula on Highway 126, is like entering turn-of-the-20th-century California. If you're here on a weekend, hop aboard the **Fillmore & Western Railway** (⊠ 351 Santa Clara Ave. ☏ 805/524–2546 or 800/773–8724 ⊕ www.fwry.com). The vintage trains travel on century-old restored track to Santa Paula and back (the ride usually takes 2½ hours).

Where to Stay & Eat

$$–$$$ ✕ **Jonathan's at Peirano's.** The main dining room here has a gazebo where you can eat surrounded by plants and local art. The menu has dishes from Spain, Portugal, France, Italy, Greece, and Morocco. Standouts are the Moroccan-inspired chicken, the *penne checca* pasta, and the halibut with almonds. The owners also run an evening tapas bar next door, which serves exotic martinis. ⊠ *204 E. Main St.* ☏ *805/648–4853* ▤ *AE, D, DC, MC, V* ☉ *Closed Mon. No lunch Sun.*

$$–$$$ ✕ **71 Palm Restaurant.** This elegant restaurant occupies a 1910 house, and it still has touches that make it feel like a home: lace curtains, wood floors, a dining patio for good weather, and a fireplace that's often crackling in winter. A standout appetizer is the homemade country pâté with cornichons; for dinner, try the grilled salmon on a potato pancake, or the New Zealand rack of lamb Provençal. ⊠ *71 N. Palm St.* ☏ *805/653–7222* ▤ *AE, D, DC, MC, V* ☉ *Closed Sun. No lunch Sat.*

¢–$ ✕ **Andria's Seafood.** At this casual, family-oriented restaurant, the specialties are fish-and-chips (made with angel shark) and homemade clam chowder. After placing your order at the counter, you can sit outside on the patio where with a view of the harbor and marina. ⊠ *1449 Spinnaker Dr., Suite A* ☏ *805/654–0546* ▤ *MC, V.*

¢   ✕ **Christy's.** You can get breakfast all day—don't miss the breakfast burrito—at this locals' hangout across the water from the Channel Islands. It also serves burgers, sandwiches, and soup. ⊠ *1559 Spinnaker Dr.* ☏ *805/642–3116* ▤ *D, MC, V.*

$–$$$ 🛏 **The Brakey House.** Built circa 1890, this three-story Victorian sits on a steep hillside near the courthouse in the heart of the historic district. All five individually themed rooms have private entrances, DVD players, pillow-top queen beds and private baths; two also have whirlpool tubs. When you rise for a traditional Bavarian breakfast in the breakfast room, you can also feast your eyes on a view of the ocean and offshore islands. ⊠ *411 Poli St., 93001* ☏ *805/643–3600* 🖷 *805/653–7329* ⊕ *www.brakeyhouse.com* ➫ *5 rooms* ♨ *Cable TV, in-room VCRs, outdoor hot tub, Internet; some pets allowed; no a/c in some rooms* ▤ *AE, D, MC, V* ❑ *BP.*

$$ 🛏 **Pierpont Inn & Racquet Club.** Back in 1910, Josephine Pierpont-Ginn built the original Pierpont Inn on a hill overlooking Ventura Beach. Today's renovated complex, which includes an Arts-and-Crafts lobby and English Tudor cottages set amid gardens and gazebos, reflects much of the hotel's original elegance. For a fee you can work out at the neighboring Pierpont Racquet Club, which has indoor and outdoor pools, 15 tennis courts, racquetball courts, spa services, aerobics, and child care. The inn's restaurant has great views of the ocean and harbor; breakfast is included on weekdays. ⊠ *550 Sanjon Rd., 93001* ☏ *805/643–6144*

or 800/285–4667 🖶 *805/643–9167* ⊕ *www.pierpontinn.com* ⛶ *65 rooms, 9 suites, 2 cottages* ⅍ *Restaurant, some refrigerators, cable TV with movies, bar, Internet, meeting rooms; no a/c in some rooms, no smoking* ⊟ *AE, D, DC, MC, V* ⅋ *CP.*

$–$$ 🖾 **Best Western Inn of Ventura.** A block off U.S. 101 in the historic district, this hotel has large rooms with oversize beds and high-speed Internet access. Some rooms have ocean views. Beaches, restaurants, and theaters are within walking distance. ⊠ *708 E. Thompson Blvd., 93001* ☎ *805/648–3101 or 800/648–1508* 🖶 *805/648–4019* ⊕ *www. bestwestern.com* ⛶ *75 rooms* ⅍ *In-room data ports, cable TV, pool, hot tub, no-smoking rooms* ⊟ *AE, D, DC, MC, V* ⅋ *CP.*

Sports & the Outdoors

The most popular outdoor activity in Ventura is whale-watching. California gray whales migrate offshore through the Santa Barbara Channel from late December through March; giant blue and humpback whales feed here from mid-June through September. In fact, the channel is teeming with marine life year-round, so tours include more than just whale sightings. A cruise through the Santa Barbara Channel with **Island Packers** (⊠ 1691 Spinnaker Dr., Ventura Harbor ☎ 805/642–1393 ⊕ www.islandpackers.com) will give you the chance to spot dolphins and seals—and sometimes even whales—throughout the year.

Channel Islands National Park

❸ *In Santa Barbara Channel southwest of Ventura and Oxnard; accessi-*
Fodor'sChoice *ble from Ventura, Santa Barbara, Camarillo, and Oxnard.*
★

Often referred to as North America's Galapagos, this park includes five of the eight Channel Islands and the nautical mile of ocean that surrounds them. The Channel Islands range in size from 1-square-mi Santa Barbara to 96-square-mi Santa Cruz. Together they form a magnificent nature preserve, home of wildlife unique to the islands, such as the island scrub-jay, the island fox, and the Anacapa deer mouse. Plant species, such as the Santa Rosa Torrey pine and the island oak, have also evolved differently from their counterparts on the mainland. It all adds up to a living laboratory not unlike the one naturalist Charles Darwin discovered off the coast of Ecuador more than 150 years ago.

The channel waters are also teeming with life, including dolphins, whales, seals, sea lions, and sea birds. If you visit East Anacapa in spring or summer, you'll walk through a nesting area of western gulls. If you're lucky enough to get to windswept San Miguel, you might have a chance to see as many as 30,000 pinnipeds (seals and sea lions) camped out on the beach. If you're a kayaker, you can paddle close to the seals (as long as you don't disturb them); if you're a diver or snorkeler, you can explore some of the world's richest kelp forests. Even traveling on an excursion boat gives you a chance to view sea lions, brown pelicans, and spouting whales.

★ Whether or not you plan to visit the islands, you should definitely stop by the **Channel Islands Visitor Center.** The center has a museum, a bookstore, a three-story observation tower with telescopes, and island exhibits. There's a tide pool where you can see a brilliant orange garibaldi, sea stars clinging to rocks, and anemones waving their colorful, spiny tentacles. There are also full-size replicas of a male northern elephant seal and the pygmy mammoth skeleton unearthed on Santa Rosa Island in 1994. On weekends and holidays at 11 and 3, rangers lead various free public programs describing park resources; they can also provide you with a detailed map and trip-planning packet, if you want to visit the actual islands. ✉ *1901 Spinnaker Dr., Ventura* ☎ *805/658–5730* 🌐 *www.nps.gov/chis* 🎫 *Free* 🕒 *Daily 8:30–5.*

You can get to the Channel Islands with **Island Packers** (✉ 1691 Spinnaker Dr., Suite 105 B, Ventura ☎ 805/642–1393 🌐 www.islandpackers.com), which sails from Ventura and Oxnard. Two 64-foot high-speed catamarans zip over to Santa Cruz Island, with stops at Anacapa Island, almost daily. Boats in the fleet travel to Anacapa daily in summer, less frequently the rest of the year. Island Packers also visits the other islands three or four times a month and provides transportation for campers. **Truth Aquatics** (✉ 301 W. Cabrillo Blvd., Santa Barbara ☎ 805/962–1127 🌐 www.truthaquatics.com) departs from the Santa Barbara Harbor for single- and multiday hiking, scuba, and camping excursions to Santa Cruz, Santa Rosa, and San Miguel islands. **Channel Islands Aviation** (✉ 305 Durley Ave., Camarillo ☎ 805/987–1301 🌐 www.flycia.com) provides charter flights from Camarillo Airport, about 10 mi east of Oxnard, to an airstrip on Santa Rosa. It will also pick up groups of six or more at Santa Barbara Airport. Day trips are usually from 9:30 to 4.

Although most people think of it as an island, **Anacapa** actually comprises three narrow islets. The tips of these volcanic formations nearly touch, but they are inaccessible from each other except by boat. All three islets have towering cliffs, isolated sea caves, and natural bridges; Arch Rock, on East Anacapa, is one of the best-known symbols of Channel Islands National Park. Wildlife viewing is the reason most people come to East Anacapa, particularly in summer when seagull chicks are newly hatched and sea lions and seals lounge on the beaches. The compact **museum** on East Anacapa tells the history of the island, and houses, among other things, the original lead-crystal Fresnel lens from the lighthouse on East Anacapa (circa 1937). If you come in summer, you can also learn about the nearby kelp forests by asking questions of underwater rangers, who communicate via microphone and camera. The sessions take place Tuesday and Thursday afternoons at 2 and are broadcast live to the visitor center. Depending on the season and the number of desirable species lurking about there, a limited number of boats travel to Frenchy's Cove, at West Anacapa, where there are pristine tide pools. The rest of West Anacapa and Middle Anacapa are closed to protect nesting brown pelicans.

Five miles west of Anacapa, 96-square-mi **Santa Cruz** is the largest of the Channel Islands. The National Park Service manages the easternmost 25% of the island; the rest is owned by the Nature Conservancy, which requires a permit to land. When your boat drops you off on the 70 mi of craggy coastline, you'll find two rugged mountain ranges with peaks soaring to 2,500 feet and deep canyons traversed by steams. This landscape is the habitat of a remarkable variety of flora and fauna—

more than 600 types of plants, 140 kinds of land birds, 11 mammal species, five varieties of reptiles, and three amphibian species. Bird-watchers may want to look for the endemic scrub-jay, found nowhere else in the world.

The largest and deepest known sea cave in the world, **Painted Cave** lies along the northwest coastline of Santa Cruz Island. Named for the colorful lichen and algae that cover its walls, Painted Cave is nearly ¼ mi long and 100 feet wide. In spring a waterfall cascades over the entrance. Kayakers may encounter seals or sea lions cruising alongside their boats inside the cave. Remnants of a dozen Chumash villages can be seen here. The largest of these villages, at the eastern end of the island, occupied the area now called **Scorpion Ranch**. The Chumash mined extensive chert deposits on the island for tools to produce shell-bead money, which they traded with people on the mainland. Remnants of the early 1900s ranching era can also be seen in the restored historic buildings, equipment, and adobe ovens that produced bread for the entire island.

Between Santa Cruz and San Miguel islands, **Santa Rosa** is the second largest of the Channel Islands. The island has a relatively low profile, broken by a central mountain range rising to 1,589 feet. The coastal areas range from broad sandy beaches to sheer cliffs. The island is the home of about 500 species of plants, including the rare Torrey pine. Three unusual mammals—the endemic island fox, spotted skunk, and deer mouse—are among those that make their home here. On Santa Rosa Island, you can visit **Vail and Vickers,** a ranch where sheep and cattle have been raised for 160 years. The westernmost of the Channel Islands, **San Miguel** is frequently battered by storms sweeping across the Pacific. The 15-square-mi island's wild, windswept landscape is lush with vegetation. Point Bennett, at the western tip of the island, offers one of the world's most spectacular wildlife displays when more than 30,000 pinnipeds hit the beach. Explorer Juan Rodríguez Cabrillo was the first European to visit this island; he claimed it for Spain in 1542. Legend holds that Cabrillo died on the island; no one knows where he's buried, but there's a memorial to him on a bluff above Cuyler Harbor.

At about 1 square mi, **Santa Barbara** is the smallest of the Channel Islands. It's also the southernmost island in the chain, separated from the others by nearly 35 mi. Roughly triangular in shape, its steep cliffs are topped by twin peaks. The island was visited in 1602 by explorer Sebastian Vizcaino, who named it in honor of St. Barbara. Come in spring to see a brilliant display of yellow coreopsis. The cliffs here offer a perfect nesting spot for the Xantus' murrelet, a rare seabird. With exhibits on the region's natural history, the small Santa Barbara Island **museum** is a great place to learn about the wildlife on and around the Channel Islands.

Camping

Camping is the best way to experience the natural beauty and isolation of Channel Islands National Park. Unrestricted by tour schedules, you'll have plenty of time to explore mountain trails, snorkel in the kelp forests, or kayak into sea caves. There are five campgrounds, located on East Anacapa, Santa Cruz (near Scorpion Ranch), Santa Rosa, San

THE CHUMASH

I N 1542, when Portuguese explorer Juan Rodriguez Cabrillo sailed into the Santa Barbara Channel, he and his party encountered a huge surprise: friendly natives in unusual canoes paddling out to greet them, bearing gifts of beads, animals skins, and food. The welcome party were Chumash Indians, whose homeland stretched from Malibu in the south to what is now San Luis Obispo County in the north, plus the four northern Channel Islands. It would be another 230 years before European settlers came to stay. Still, this was their first encounter with one of North America's most fascinating native cultures.

Ancestors of the Chumash first occupied the Central Coast region some 13,000 years ago. By the time of Cabrillo's visit, the tribe had evolved into a complex culture with an elaborate trading system stretching across much of California. The Channel Island Chumash, in particular, were known for crafting currency out of shell beads, which were exchanged for food, tools, and services. The name Chumash roughly translates as "those who make shell bead money."

Chumash land was abundant in wild game, fish, nuts, seeds, and other natural resources. Tribe members were so successful at hunting, gathering, and storing food that they didn't need to farm or raise domestic animals. This left much time to pursue a rich religious life, and create remarkable crafts. As well as being some of the finest basket makers in the world, the Chumash also built swift, light canoes, called tomols, that were engineering wonders.

Life changed dramatically for the Chumash in 1769, when Gaspar de Portolá and his land expedition arrived in the area. The Spanish established five missions in Chumash territory, and induced many natives to move to the

mission and learn to farm. At the time of initial Spanish contact there were about 20,000 Chumash people, but in the missions many died from European diseases. By the end of the mission system in 1834, fewer than 3,000 Chumash people remained.

In 1901 the United States government recognized the Santa Ynez band of Chumash as an official tribal nation and established the Santa Ynez Reservation, which occupies about 75 acres next to the town of Santa Ynez. Today, the Reservation has about 150 registered tribal members. About 3,000 other people of Chumash descent live elsewhere in the Central Coast region.

You can learn more about Chumash culture and history at a number of Central Coast museums, including Santa Barbara's Museum of Natural History. For information about modern Chumash life, pop into the Chumash Casino in Santa Ynez, or log onto www.chumashcasino.com or www.SantaYnezChumash.org.

Miguel, and Santa Barbara islands. Campsites are primitive, with no water (except on Santa Rosa and Santa Cruz) or electricity; enclosed camp stoves must be used. Campfires are not allowed on the island except in a ring at Scorpion Beach, and then only between December and mid-May. You must carry all your gear and pack out all trash. Campers must arrange transportation to the islands prior to reserving a campsite (and yes, this information is checked by park personnel). You can get specifics on each campground and reserve a campsite ($10 per night) by contacting the **National Park Service Reservation System** (☎ 800/365–2267 ⊕ http://reservations.nps.gov) up to five months in advance.

Sports & the Outdoors

Because private vehicles are not allowed on the islands, hiking is the only way to explore them. Terrain on most islands ranges from flat to moderately hilly. Santa Cruz has the most options, from a ½-mi stroll to the historic Vail and Vickers ranch to a strenuous 8-mi off-trail climb up an 1,808-foot peak. Naturalist-led day trips and overnight camping trips are available year-round through the two official park concessionaires: Island Packers and Truth Aquatics. Several other outfits also arrange sailing, diving, hiking, and kayak excursions around but not on the islands; contact the Channel Islands Visitor Center for more information. There are no services (including public phones, and cell phone reception is dicey) on the islands—you have to bring all your own food, water (except on Santa Cruz and Santa Rosa), and supplies.

Ojai

❹ *15 mi north of Ventura, U.S. 101 to Hwy. 33.*

The Ojai Valley, which director Frank Capra used as a backdrop for his 1936 film *Lost Horizon,* sizzles in the summer, when temperatures routinely reach 90°F. The acres of orange and avocado groves here evoke postcard images of agricultural Southern California from decades ago. This is a lush, slow-moving place, where many artists and celebrities have sought refuge from life in the fast lane. The town can be easily explored on foot; you can also hop on the **Ojai Valley Trolley** (⊕ www.ojaitrolley.com ⊠ 25¢) which rides on an hour-long loop around town (between 7:40 and 5:40 on weekdays, 9 and 5 on weekends). If you tell the driver you're a visitor, you'll get an informal guided tour. Maps and tourist information are available at the **visitor center** (⊠ 150 W. Ojai Ave. ☎ 805/646–8126 ⊕ www.ojaichamber.org ⊙ Mon. and Wed.–Fri. 9:30–4:30, weekends 10–4).

The work of local artists is displayed in the Spanish-style shopping arcade along **Ojai Avenue** (Highway 150). Organic and specialty growers sell their produce on Sunday from 10 to 2 (9 to 1 in summer) at the farmers' market behind the arcade. The **Art Center** (⊠ 113 S. Montgomery St. ☎ 805/646–0117) exhibits artwork and presents theater and dance performances. The **Ojai Valley Museum** (⊠ 130 W. Ojai Ave. ☎ 805/640–1390) has exhibits on the valley's history and many Native American artifacts. The 18-mi **Ojai Valley Trail** (⊠ Parallel to Hwy. 33, from Soule Park in Ojai to the ocean in Ventura ☎ 805/654–3951 ⊕ www.

ojaichamber.org) is open to pedestrians, bikers, joggers, equestrians, and nonmotorized vehicles. You can access it anywhere along its route.

Where to Stay & Eat

★ $$–$$$ ✕ **The Ranch House.** The town's best eatery serves rich pâté appetizers; main dishes like tenderloin of venison in a red wine and juniper berry sauce, and grilled diver scallops with snow crab and bechamel sauce, are not to be missed. The verdant patio is a wonderful place to have Sunday brunch. ⊠ *S. Lomita Ave.* ☎ *805/646–2360* ⊟ *AE, D, DC, MC, V* ⊗ *Closed Mon. No lunch.*

$–$$$ ✕ **Suzanne's Cuisine.** Peppered filet mignon, linguine with steamed clams, and salmon with sauerkraut in a dill beurre blanc are among the offerings at this European-style restaurant. Game, seafood, and vegetarian dishes dominate the dinner menu, and salads and soups star at lunchtime. All the breads and desserts are made on the premises. ⊠ *502 W. Ojai Ave.* ☎ *805/640–1961* ⊟ *MC, V* ⊗ *Closed Tues. and 1st 2 wks in Jan.*

¢–$$ ✕ **Azu.** Delectable tapas, a full bar, slick furnishings, and piped jazz music lure diners to this popular European bistro. You can also order soups, salads, and traditional bistro fare such as veal shanks, roast duck, and cassoulet. Live music is sometimes performed after 9 PM, and breakfast is served on weekends. ⊠ *457 E. Ojai Ave.* ☎ *805/640–7987* ⊟ *MC, V.*

¢–$ ✕ **Ojai Café Emporium.** Best known for healthful, California-style salads such as the Topa Topa (greens with roasted chicken, kidney beans, corn chips, and taco seasoning), this casual downtown eatery across from the art center also offers make-your-own sandwiches, home-style fish cakes, California meat loaf, and fresh fish and pasta entrées. The cheery dining rooms and outdoor patio are open for breakfast, lunch, and dinner. ⊠ *108 S. Montgomery St.* ☎ *805/646–2723* ⊟ *AE, MC, V* ⊗ *No dinner Sun. and Mon.*

★ $$$$ 🏨 **Ojai Valley Inn & Spa.** This outdoorsy, golf-oriented resort and spa is set on beautifully landscaped grounds, with hillside views in nearly all directions. Nearby is the inn's 800-acre ranch, where you can take riding lessons and go on guided trail rides. In 2004 the resort underwent a huge, $65 million reconstruction. A restaurant, ballroom, and 100 guest rooms were added; all existing rooms and suites were refurbished to reflect the Spanish Colonial architecture of the original 1923 resort. All rooms have high-speed Internet, and wireless Internet is available throughout the property. If you're a history buff, ask for a room in the original 80-year-old adobe building. The three restaurants tout "Ojai regional cuisine," which incorporates locally grown produce and locally made foods. ⊠ *905 Country Club Rd., 93023* ☎ *805/646–5511 or 800/422–6524* ⊟ *805/646–7969* ⊕ *www.ojairesort.com* ⟲ *244 rooms, 61 suites* ⌂ *3 restaurants, in-room data ports, minibars, cable TV with movies, 18-hole golf course, 4 tennis courts, 3 pools, spa, hiking, horseback riding, bar, pub, children's programs (ages 3–12), Internet, convention center, some pets allowed (fee); no smoking* ⊟ *AE, D, DC, MC, V.*

$$ 🏨 **Oaks at Ojai.** Rejuvenation is the name of the game at this comfortable spa resort. The fitness package includes lodging, use of the spa facilities, a choice of 18 daily exercise classes, hikes, and fitness activities, and three nutritionally balanced, low-calorie meals a day, plus snacks and beverages. Nonguests can eat here, too, but it's mainly for the fitness-

conscious. Cell phone use is not allowed in public areas. Guests under age 16 are not recommended. ✉ *122 E. Ojai Ave., 93023* ☎ *805/646–5573 or 800/753–6257* 📠 *805/640–1504* 🌐 *www.oaksspa.com* *46 rooms* *Dining room, pool, gym, hair salon, hot tub, massage, sauna, spa; no smoking* 💳 *AE, D, MC, V* 🍽 *FAP* ☞ *2-night minimum stay.*

$–$$ **The Blue Iguana Inn & Cottages.** Artists run this Southwestern-style hotel, and their work (which is for sale) decorates the rooms. The small, cozy main inn is about 2 mi west of downtown. Its sister property, the Emerald Iguana Inn, consists of eight more art nouveau cottages closer to downtown Ojai. Suites and cottages all have kitchenettes. ✉ *11794 N. Ventura Ave. (Hwy. 33), 93023* ☎ *805/646–5277* 🌐 *www.blueiguanainn.com* *4 rooms, 7 suites, 8 cottages* *Some microwaves, refrigerators, some kitchenettes, cable TV, some in-room VCRs, pool, hot tub, massage, some pets allowed (fee); no smoking* 💳 *AE, D, DC, MC, V* 🍽 *CP weekends.*

The Arts

On Wednesday evenings in summer, all-American music played by the Ojai Band draws crowds to **Libbey Park** (✉ Ojai Ave. ☎ 805/640–2560 Free) in downtown Ojai. For more than five decades, the **Ojai Music Festival** (☎ 805/646–2094 🌐 www.ojaifestival.org) has attracted internationally known progressive and traditional musicians for outdoor concerts in Libbey Park on the weekend after late May.

en route

About 15 mi west of Ojai and 12 mi east of Santa Barbara is sheltered, sunny, often crowded **Carpinteria State Beach** (☎ 805/684–2811). From the mile-long strand you can sometimes see seals, sea lions, and gray whales in winter and spring. The historic section of quaint, beachside Carpinteria, is filled with antiques shops, restaurants, and galleries. Stop at the **Carpinteria Valley Museum of History** (✉ 956 Maple Ave. ☎ 805/684–3112) to view excellent exhibits on the area's Chumash Indian, Spanish–Mexican, and American heritage.

SANTA BARBARA

27 mi northwest of Ventura and 29 mi west of Ojai on U.S. 101.

Santa Barbara has long been an oasis for Los Angelenos seeking respite from hectic big-city life. The attractions begin at the ocean and end in the foothills of the Santa Ynez Mountains. A few miles up the coast—but still very much a part of Santa Barbara—is the exclusive residential district of Hope Ranch. Santa Barbara is on a jog in the coastline, so the ocean is actually to the south, instead of the west; for this reason, directions can be confusing. "Up" the coast toward San Francisco is west, "down" toward Los Angeles is east, and the mountains are north. A car is handy but not essential if you're planning to stay in town. The beaches and downtown are easily explored by bicycle or on foot, or you can take the local buses. A motorized San Francisco–style cable car operated by **Santa Barbara Trolley Co.** (☎ 805/965–0353 🌐 www.sbtrolley.com) makes 90-minute runs from 10 to 4 past major hotels, shopping

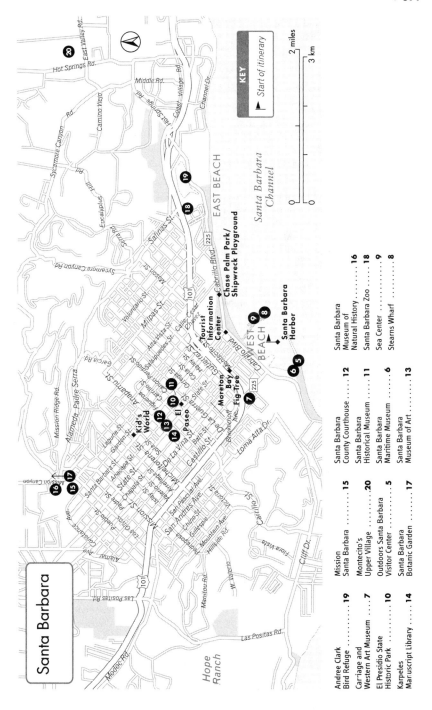

Santa Barbara

Andree Clark
Bird Refuge **19**

Carriage and
Western Art Museum **7**

El Presidio State
Historic Park **10**

Karpeles
Manuscript Library **14**

Mission
Santa Barbara **15**

Montecito's
Upper Village **20**

Outdoors Santa Barbara
Visitor Center **5**

Santa Barbara
Botanic Garden **17**

Santa Barbara
County Courthouse **12**

Santa Barbara
Historical Museum **11**

Santa Barbara
Maritime Museum **6**

Santa Barbara
Museum of Art **13**

Santa Barbara
Museum of
Natural History **16**

Santa Barbara Zoo **18**

Sea Center **9**

Stearns Wharf **8**

KEY

▲ Start of itinerary

areas, and attractions. Get off whenever you like, and pick up another trolley when you're ready to move on (they come every 45 minutes). The trolley departs from and returns to Stearns Wharf. The fare is $14 for the day.

From the Ocean to the Mountains

Santa Barbara's waterfront is beautiful, with palm-studded promenades and plenty of sand. In the few miles between the beaches and the hills are downtown, the old mission, and the botanical gardens. For maps and visitor information, drop by the **Santa Barbara Chamber of Commerce Visitor Information Center** (⊠ 1 Garden St., at Cabrillo Blvd. ☎ 805/965–3021 ⊕ www.sbchamber.org).

a good tour

Start your tour at the west end of Cabrillo Boulevard, with a stroll around ➤ **Santa Barbara Harbor.** You can take a ½-mi walk along the breakwater that protects the harbor, check out the tackle and bait shops, or hire a boat. At the base of the breakwater stop in at the **Outdoors Santa Barbara Visitor Center ❺** and the **Santa Barbara Maritime Museum ❻**; they're in the same building. For a cultural interlude walk three blocks up Castillo Street from the harbor to the **Carriage and Western Art Museum ❼**. Return to Cabrillo Boulevard, the main drag fronting the harbor, and stroll east along **West Beach** to **Stearns Wharf ❽**, where the **Sea Center ❾** is a major attraction.

To explore downtown, walk up **State Street** (it starts at Stearns Wharf) from the harbor and turn left on Montecito Street, then walk one block to the corner of Chapala Street for a look at the **Moreton Bay Fig Tree.** Planted in 1874 and transplanted to its present location in 1877, this tree is so huge it reputedly can provide shade for 1,000 people. Return to State Street and continue northwest (away from the harbor) past **El Paseo,** a handsome shopping arcade built around an old adobe home. Make a right at East Canon Perdido Street to reach **El Presidio State Historic Park ❿**. From here turn right on Santa Barbara Street and right onto De La Guerra Street to reach the entrance of the **Santa Barbara Historical Museum ⓫**. Now make a right onto Anacapa Street and walk three blocks to the **Santa Barbara County Courthouse ⓬**, at Anapamu Street. On the next block of Anapamu Street (at State Street) stands the **Santa Barbara Museum of Art ⓭**, and one block farther is the **Karpeles Manuscript Library ⓮**.

To see the sights of the foothills, hop into your car and take State Street northwest (away from the water) to Los Olivos Street. Turn right, and you'll soon see **Mission Santa Barbara ⓯**. From the mission you can walk the block north to the **Santa Barbara Museum of Natural History ⓰**. You'll probably want to drive the 1½ mi north (via Mission Canyon Road) to the **Santa Barbara Botanic Garden ⓱**. Once you've seen the flora, check out the fauna by heading back toward the ocean via Alameda Padre Serra, Montecito Street, and then Milpas Street to the **Santa Barbara Zoo ⓲**. More creatures await at the **Andree Clark Bird Refuge ⓳**, which is adjacent to the zoo. For a drive through a lush enclave of estates, head up into the hills to the Upper Village of **Montecito ⓴**.

TIMING You could spend an entire day on the harbor front, or devote only two or three hours to it if you drive and only stop briefly at the various attractions. Set aside an hour each for the art and natural history museums and for the botanic gardens. A spin through the zoo takes about an hour. Add plenty of time if you're a shopper—the stores and galleries around State Street may sidetrack you for hours.

What to See

⑲ Andree Clark Bird Refuge. This peaceful lagoon and gardens sits north of East Beach. Bike trails and footpaths, punctuated by signs identifying native and migratory birds, skirt the lagoon. ⊠ *1400 E. Cabrillo Blvd.* ✆ *Free.*

⑦ Carriage and Western Art Museum. The country's largest collection of old horse-drawn vehicles—painstakingly restored—is exhibited here. Everything from polished hearses to police buggies to old stagecoaches and circus vehicles is on display. In August the Old Spanish Days Fiesta borrows many of the vehicles for a jaunt about town. This is one of the city's true hidden gems, a wonderful place to help history come alive—especially for children. ⊠ *129 Castillo St.* ☎ *805/962–2353* ⊕ *www. carriagemuseum.org* ✆ *Free* ⊗ *Weekdays 8–3, Sun. 1–4.*

★ **⑩ El Presidio State Historic Park.** Founded in 1782, El Presidio was one of four military strongholds established by the Spanish along the coast of California. El Cuartel, the adobe guardhouse, is the oldest building in Santa Barbara and the second oldest in California. ⊠ *123 E. Canon Perdido St.* ☎ *805/965–0093* ⊕ *www.sbthp.org* ✆ *Free, donation suggested* ⊗ *Daily 10:30–4:30.*

⑭ Karpeles Manuscript Library. Ancient political tracts and old Disney cartoons are among the holdings at this facility, which also houses one of the world's largest privately owned collections of rare manuscripts. Fifty display cases contain a sampling of the archive's million-plus documents. ⊠ *21 W. Anapamu St.* ☎ *805/962–5322* ⊕ *www.karpeles. com* ✆ *Free* ⊗ *Daily 10–4.*

⑮ Mission Santa Barbara. Widely referred to as the "Queen of Missions," this is one of the most beautiful and frequently photographed buildings in coastal California. The architecture, which was originally built in 1786, evolved from adobe-brick buildings with thatch roofs to more permanent edifices as its population burgeoned. An earthquake in 1812 destroyed the third church built on the site. Its replacement, the present structure, is still a functioning Catholic church. The building is surrounded by cacti, palms, and other succulents. ⊠ *2201 Laguna St.* ☎ *805/682–4149* ⊕ *www.sbmission.org* ✆ *$4* ⊗ *Daily 9–5.*

FodorśChoice
★

⑳ Montecito. Since the late 1800s the tree-studded hills and valleys of this town have attracted the rich and famous (Hollywood icons, business tycoons, "Dot-commers" who divested before the crash, and "old money" families who installed themselves here years ago). Shady roads wind through the community, which consists mostly of gated estates. Swank boutiques line Coast Village Road, where well-heeled residents such as Oprah Winfrey and John Cleese sometimes browse for truffle oil, picture frames, and designer sweats. Residents also hang out in the

Upper Village, a chic shopping area with restaurants and cafés at the intersection of San Ysidro and East Valley roads. Montecito is just about 3 mi east of Santa Barbara. The 37-acre Montecito estate called

Fodor'sChoice
★ **Lotusland** (☎ 805/969–9990 ⊕ www.lotusland.org ☞ $15) once belonged to Polish opera singer Ganna Walska. Many of the exotic trees and other subtropical flora were planted in 1882 by horticulturist R. Kinton Stevens. On the two-hour guided tour (the only option for visiting), you'll see an outdoor theater, a topiary garden, a huge collection of rare cycads (an unusual plant genus that has been around since the time of the dinosaurs), and a lotus pond. Tours are conducted mid-February through mid-November, Wednesday through Saturday at 10 and 1:30. Reservations are required; call as early as possible, as tours fill up quickly. Children under 10 are not allowed, except on family tours, offered on Thursday and the second Saturday of each month.

❺ Outdoors Santa Barbara Visitor Center. The small office provides maps and other information about Channel Islands National Park, Channel Islands National Marine Sanctuary, and Los Padres National Forest. The same building houses the Santa Barbara Maritime Museum. ⊠ *113 Harbor Way* ☎ *805/884–1475* ☞ *Free* ⊙ *Daily 11–5; open in summer on Sat. 'til 7.*

⑰ Santa Barbara Botanic Garden. Scenic trails meander through the garden's 78 acres of native plants. The Mission Dam, built in 1806, stands just beyond the redwood grove and above the restored aqueduct that once carried water to Mission Santa Barbara. An ethnobotanical display demonstrates how Native Americans used plants to create baskets, clothing, and structures. ⊠ *1212 Mission Canyon Rd.* ☎ *805/682–4726* ⊕ *www.sbbg.org* ☞ *$6* ⊙ *Mar.–Oct., weekdays 9–5, weekends 9–6; Nov.–Feb., weekdays 9–4, weekends 9–5. Guided tours daily at 2; additional tour on weekends at 11.*

★ ⑫ Santa Barbara County Courthouse. Hand-painted tiles and a spiral staircase infuse the courthouse with the grandeur of a Moorish palace. This magnificent building was completed in 1929, part of a rebuilding process after a 1925 earthquake destroyed many downtown structures. At the time Santa Barbara was also in the midst of a cultural awakening, and the trend was toward an architecture appropriate to the area's climate and history. The result is the harmonious Mediterranean-Spanish look of much of the downtown area, especially the municipal buildings. An elevator rises to an arched observation area in the courthouse tower that provides a panoramic view of the city. The murals in the ceremonial chambers on the courthouse's second floor were painted by an artist who did backdrops for some of Cecil B. DeMille's films. ⊠ *1100 block of Anacapa St.* ☎ *805/962–6464* ⊕ *www.santabarbaracourthouse.org* ⊙ *Weekdays 8:30–4:45, weekends 10–4:45. Free guided tours Mon., Tues., and Fri. at 10:30, Mon.–Sat. at 2.*

need a break? Both children and adults can enjoy themselves at **Kids' World** (⊠ Garden St. at Micheltorena St.), a public playground with a complex, castle-shaped maze of fanciful climbing structures, slides, and tunnels built by Santa Barbara parents.

⑪ Santa Barbara Historical Museum. The historical society's museum exhibits decorative and fine arts, furniture, costumes, and documents from the town's past. Adjacent to it is the Gledhill Library, a collection of books, photographs, maps, and manuscripts. ⊠ *136 E. De La Guerra St.* ☎ *805/966–1601* ⊠ *Museum by donation; library $2–$5 per hr for research* ۞ *Museum Tues.–Sat. 10–5, Sun. noon–5; library Tues.–Fri. 10–4, 1st Sat. of month 10–1:30. Free guided tours Wed. and weekends at 1:30.*

۞ ⑥ Santa Barbara Maritime Museum. California's seafaring history is the focus at this museum. High-tech, hands-on exhibits, such as a sportfishing activity that lets you catch a "big one," make this a fun stop for families. ⊠ *113 Harbor Way* ☎ *805/962–8404* ⊕ *www.sbmm.org* ⊠ *$5* ۞ *June–Aug., Thurs.–Tues. 11–6; Sept.–May, Thurs.–Mon. 11–5.*

⑬ Santa Barbara Museum of Art. The highlights of this museum's permanent collection include ancient sculpture, Asian art, impressionist paintings, contemporary Latin American art, and American works in several media. ⊠ *1130 State St.* ☎ *805/963–4364* ⊕ *www.sbmuseart.org* ⊠ *$7; free on Sunday* ۞ *Tues.–Sun. 11–5. Free guided tours Tues.–Sun. at noon and 1.*

۞ ⑯ Santa Barbara Museum of Natural History. The gigantic skeleton of a blue whale greets you at the entrance of this complex. The major draws include the planetarium, space lab, and a gem and mineral display. A room of dioramas illustrates Chumash Indian history and culture. Startlingly alive-looking stuffed specimens, complete with nests and eggs, roost in the bird diversity room. Many exhibits have interactive components. Outdoors you can stroll on nature trails that wind through the serene oak-studded grounds. ⊠ *2559 Puesta del Sol Rd.* ☎ *805/682–4711* ⊕ *www.sbnature.org* ⊠ *$7* ۞ *Daily 10–5.*

۞ ⑱ Santa Barbara Zoo. The natural settings of the zoo shelter elephants, gorillas, exotic birds, and big cats such as the rare amur leopard, a thick-furred, high-altitude dweller from Asia. For small children, there's a scenic railroad and barnyard petting zoo. ⊠ *500 Niños Dr.* ☎ *805/962–5339* ⊕ *www.santabarbarazoo.org* ⊠ *$9; parking $3* ۞ *Daily 10–5.*

۞ ⑨ Sea Center. A branch of the Santa Barbara Museum of Natural History, the Sea Center specializes in Santa Barbara Channel marine life and conservation. In 2002 it closed temporarily to begin construction of a new, $6.5 million facility slated to open in early 2005. When completed, the new Sea Center seems destined to be a fascinating, hands-on marine science laboratory that lets you participate in experiments, projects, and exhibits, including touch tanks. ⊠ *211 Stearns Wharf* ☎ *805/962–0885 or 805/682–4711* ⊕ *www.sbnature.org* ☞ *Call for information on reopening date, hrs, and admission.*

> **need a break?**
>
> The antique carousel, large playground with a nautical theme, picnic areas, and snack bar make the scenic waterfront **Chase Palm Park and Shipwreck Playground** (⊠ Cabrillo Blvd. between Garden St. and Calle Cesar Chavez) a favorite destination for kids and parents.

⑧ **Stearns Wharf.** Built in 1872, historic Stearns Wharf is Santa Barbara's most visited landmark. Expansive views of the mountains, cityscape, and harbor unfold from every vantage point on the three-block-long pier. Although it's a nice walk from the Cabrillo Boulevard parking areas, you can also park on the pier and then wander through the shops or stop for a meal at one of the wharf's restaurants. ⊠ *Cabrillo Blvd. at the foot of State St.* ☎ *805/897–2683 or 805/564–5531.*

Where to Stay & Eat

$$$–$$$$ ✕ **Bouchon.** This upscale restaurant showcases fine local wines, produce, and regional specialties like ahi tuna and organic veal chops. The mood is intimate and the wine selection huge. ⊠ *9 W. Victoria St.* ☎ *805/730–1160* ▭ *AE, DC, MC, V* ☉ *No lunch.*

$$$–$$$$ ✕ **The Stonehouse.** Part of the San Ysidro Ranch resort, this elegantly rustic restaurant is housed in a century-old granite farmhouse. The menu includes prime fillet of beef with a Gorgonzola-mushroom-cabernet sauce, couscous-crusted salmon with creamy lentils and a pineapple curry sauce, and many vegetarian options. You can have breakfast or lunch—salads, pastas, and sandwiches—on the tree house–like outdoor patio; at night, the candlelit dining room is very romantic. ⊠ *900 San Ysidro La., Montecito* ☎ *805/969–4100* ⚲ *Reservations essential* ▭ *AE, DC, MC, V.*

$$$–$$$$ ✕ **Wine Cask.** Seared peppercorn ahi tuna and braised oxtail are among
Fodor's Choice the most popular entrées at this slick restaurant, which has a beautiful
★ wooden interior and Santa Barbara's most extensive wine list. In fine weather, couples seek out the romantic outdoor patio. ⊠ *813 Anacapa St.* ☎ *805/966–9463* ⚲ *Reservations essential* ▭ *AE, DC, MC, V.*

$$–$$$ ✕ **Olio e Limone.** Sophisticated Italian cuisine (with an emphasis on Sicily) is served up at this restaurant near the Arlington Center for the Performing Arts. Surprises abound here; be sure to try unusual dishes like ribbon pasta with quail and sausage in a mushroom ragout, duck ravioli, or swordfish with Sicilian ratatouille. ⊠ *17 W. Victoria St.* ☎ *805/899–2699* ▭ *AE, D, DC, MC, V.*

$$–$$$ ✕ **Palace Grill.** Acclaimed for its Cajun and creole dishes such as blackened redfish and jambalaya with dirty rice, the Palace also serves Caribbean fare, including a delicious coconut shrimp dish. If you're spicephobic, you can choose pasta, soft-shell crab, or filet mignon. Be prepared to wait as long as 45 minutes for a table on Friday and Saturday nights, when reservations are taken for a 5:30 seating only. ⊠ *8 E. Cota St.* ☎ *805/963–5000* ▭ *AE, MC, V.*

$–$$$ ✕ **Arigato Sushi.** Fans of authentic Japanese food will appreciate the freshness of the seafood at this restaurant and sushi bar. As well as traditional dishes, the menu also includes innovative creations like sushi pizza on seaweed and Hawaiian sashimi salad. ⊠ *1225 State St.* ☎ *805/965–6074* ⚲ *Reservations not accepted* ▭ *AE, MC, V* ☉ *No lunch.*

$–$$ ✕ **Brophy Bros.** The outdoor tables at this casual harborside restaurant have perfect views of the marina and mountains. The staff serves up enormous, exceptionally fresh fish dishes—don't miss the seafood salad—and provides you with a pager if there's a long wait for a table. You can stroll along the waterfront until the beep lets you know your table's ready. ⊠ *119 Harbor Way* ☎ *805/966–4418* ▭ *AE, MC, V.*

$–$$ ✕ **Roy.** Owner-chef Leroy Gandy serves a $20 fixed-price dinner—a real bargain—that includes a small salad, fresh soup, homemade organic bread, and a selection from a rotating list of contemporary American main courses. If you're lucky, the entrée choices might include grilled wild king salmon with a chardonnay beurre blanc, or chicken breast sautéed in tequila and lime. You can also choose from an à la carte menu of inexpensive appetizers and entrées, plus local wines. Half a block from State Street in the heart of downtown, Roy is a favorite spot for late-night dining (it's open until midnight and has a full bar). ⊠ *7 W. Carrillo St.* ☎ *805/966–5636* ⊟ *AE, D, DC, MC, V* ⊗ *No lunch.*

¢–$ ✕ **The Taj Cafe.** Traditional village-style Indian cooking and exotic decor—fabrics, curtains, and artwork are all imported from the East— make for a deliciously different dining experience here. The chef uses organic spices to create a host of lean, healthful dishes, like tandoori entrées, curries, masalas, vegetarian dishes, and Frankies (Bombay-style burritos). Can't decide? Try the Taj Special, with samples of various tandoori dishes, or one of the many combination plates. ⊠ *905 State St.* ☎ *805/564–8280* ⊟ *AE, D, MC, V.*

¢–$ ✕ **Your Place.** Tasty seafood (try the sea scallops garnished with crispy basil), curries, and vegetarian dishes keep this small restaurant packed for lunch and dinner. Locals consistently rate it the best Thai restaurant in town. ⊠ *22 N. Milpas St.* ☎ *805/966–5151* ⊟ *AE, MC, V* ⊗ *Closed Mon.*

¢ ✕ **Go Fish and Chips.** This tiny café—the brainchild of one of Santa Barbara's most successful restaurateurs—cooks up melt-in-your-mouth fish: grilled, battered, or crumbed. Noted Louisiana chef Paul Prudhomme reputedly came up with the seasoning recipe for the sweet-potato fries. You can also order homemade clam chowder and crab cakes, coconut shrimp, corn dogs, or fried clams, calamari, or scallops. Order to go if you can't stay. ⊠ *505 State St.* ☎ *805/962–7090* ⊟ *MC, V.*

★ **¢** ✕ **La Super-Rica.** Praised by Julia Child, this food stand with a patio on the east side of town serves some of the spiciest Mexican dishes between Los Angeles and San Francisco. Fans drive for miles to fill up on the soft tacos served with yummy spicy or mild sauces and legendary beans. Three daily specials are offered each day. ⊠ *622 N. Milpas St., at Alphonse St.* ☎ *805/963–4940* ⊟ *No credit cards.*

★ **$$$$** ✕🏨 **Four Seasons Biltmore Santa Barbara.** Surrounded by lush, perfectly manicured gardens, Santa Barbara's grande dame has long been a favorite for quiet, California-style luxury. The sumptuous 10,000-square-foot spa, which includes 10 treatment rooms, a pool, and gardens, is an oasis for rejuvenation. Dining is formal at the indoor La Marina Restaurant ($$$–$$$$), where the California-Continental menu changes monthly; The Patio ($$–$$$) is outdoors and more casual. ⊠ *1260 Channel Dr., 93108* ☎ *805/969–2261 or 800/332–3442* 🖷 *805/565–8323* ⊕ *www.fourseasons.com* ⤵ *196 rooms, 17 suites* ⌂ *2 restaurants, room service, in-room data ports, minibars, cable TV, in-room VCRs, putting green, 3 tennis courts, pool, health club, hot tub, spa, croquet, bar, babysitting, children's programs (ages 5–12), concierge, Internet, business services, meeting rooms, some pets allowed; no smoking.* ⊟ *AE, D, DC, MC, V.*

$$$$ 🏨 **Inn of the Spanish Garden.** A half-block from the Presidio in the heart of downtown, this elegant Spanish-Mediterranean retreat celebrates

Santa Barbara style, from tile floors, wrought-iron balconies and exotic plants to original art by famed local plein air artists. The luxury rooms have private balconies or patios, fireplaces, Frette linens, deep soaking tubs, and high-speed Internet. In the evening, you can order a glass of wine and relax in the candlelit courtyard. This inn is a good choice if you want to park your car for most of your stay and walk to theaters, restaurants, and shuttle buses. ⊠ *915 Garden St., 93101* ☎ *805/564–4700 or 866/564–4700* 🖷 *805/564–4701* ⊕ *www.spanishgardeninn.com* 🖘 *23 rooms* ⅋ *Fans, in-room data ports, minibars, cable TV with movies, in-room VCRs, pool, gym, hot tub, massage, lounge, wine bar, laundry service, concierge, Internet, business services, meeting rooms, free parking; no smoking* ⊟ *AE, D, MC, V* ⍔ *CP.*

★ **$$$$** 🏨 **San Ysidro Ranch.** At this romantic hideaway, where John and Jackie Kennedy spent their honeymoon, guest cottages are scattered among 14 acres of orange trees and flower beds. All have down comforters and wood-burning stoves or fireplaces; many have private outdoor spas, and one has its own pool. Seventeen miles of hiking trails crisscross 500 acres of open space surrounding the property. The Stonehouse Restaurant and Plow & Angel Bistro are Santa Barbara institutions. ⊠ *900 San Ysidro La., Montecito 93108* ☎ *805/969–5046 or 800/368–6788* 🖷 *805/565–1995* ⊕ *www.sanysidroranch.com* 🖘 *38 units* ⅋ *2 restaurants, room service, in-room data ports, refrigerators, cable TV, in-room VCRs, 2 tennis courts, pool, gym, massage, billiards, boccie, horseshoes, bar, playground, Internet, some pets allowed (fee); no smoking* ⊟ *AE, DC, MC, V* ⍔ *2-day minimum stay on weekends, 3 days on holiday weekends.*

★ **$$$$** 🏨 **Simpson House Inn.** If you're a fan of traditional B&Bs, this property, with its beautifully appointed Victorian main house and acre of lush gardens, is for you. If privacy and luxury are your priority, choose one of the elegant cottages or a room in the century-old barn; each has a wood-burning fireplace, luxurious bedding, and state-of-the-art electronics (several even have whirlpool baths). In-room massages and other spa services are available. ⊠ *121 E. Arrellaga St., 93101* ☎ *805/963–7067 or 800/676–1280* 🖷 *805/564–4811* ⊕ *www.simpsonhouseinn.com* 🖘 *11 rooms, 4 cottages* ⅋ *Some in-room hot tubs, some refrigerators, cable TV, in-room VCRs, bicycles, croquet; no smoking* ⊟ *AE, D, MC, V* ⍔ *2-night minimum stay on weekends* ⍾ *BP.*

$$$$ 🏨 **Montecito Inn.** Every room at this late-1920s marble palace is adorned with original posters from the films of Charlie Chaplin. The glass doors to the conference room are etched with the great man's image, and the video library contains his entire oeuvre. The rooms on the second floor open onto a cloisterlike arched colonnade. Most rooms have basic bathrooms, although some of the suites have large marble whirlpool tubs. Suites also have vast Romanesque-style marble fireplaces. ⊠ *1295 Coast Village Rd., Montecito 93108* ☎ *805/969–7854 or 800/843–2017* 🖷 *805/969–0623* ⊕ *www.montecitoinn.com* 🖘 *53 rooms, 8 suites* ⅋ *Restaurant, some refrigerators, cable TV with movies, in-room VCRs, pool, gym, hot tub, bicycles, bar, meeting room, no-smoking rooms; no a/c in some rooms* ⊟ *AE, D, DC, MC, V* ⍾ *CP.*

$$$–$$$$ 🏨 **The Upham.** Built in 1871 this downtown Victorian has been restored as a hotel surrounded by an acre of gardens. Period furnishings and antiques adorn the rooms, some of which have fireplaces and private patios. Guest rooms vary from small to spacious. The sister property across the street, the 1898 Country House, is a true B&B with seven upscale rooms ($$$–$$$$). ⊠ *1404 De la Vina St., 93101* ☎ *805/ 962–0058 or 800/727–0876* 🖷 *805/963–2825* ⊕ *www.uphamhotel.com* ⥲ *46 rooms, 4 suites* ♨ *Restaurant, cable TV, Internet, meeting rooms; no a/c in some rooms, no smoking* ⊟ *AE, DC, MC, V* ⥱ *2-night minimum stay on weekends* ⑩ *CP.*

¢–$ 🏨 **Motel 6 Santa Barbara Beach.** A half block from East Beach amid fancier hotels sits this basic but comfortable motel, which was the first Motel 6 in existence. It's an incredible bargain for the location and fills quickly; book months in advance if possible. Kids 17 and under stay free. Two sister properties in Carpinteria, 12 mi south of Santa Barbara and 1 mi from the beach, offer equally comfortable rooms at even lower rates. ⊠ *443 Corona Del Mar Dr., 93103* ☎ *805/564–1392 or 800/466–8356* 🖷 *805/963–4687* ⊕ *www.motel6.com* ⥲ *51 rooms* ♨ *In-room data ports, some microwaves, some refrigerators, cable TV with movies, pool, some pets allowed, no-smoking rooms* ⊟ *AE, D, DC, MC, V.*

Nightlife & the Arts

Most major hotels present entertainment nightly during the summer season and on weekends all year. Much of the town's bar, club, and live music scene centers around lower State Street (between the 300 and 800 blocks). The thriving arts district, with theaters, restaurants, and cafés, starts around the 900 block of State Street and continues north to the Arlington Center for the Performing Arts, in the 1300 block. Santa Barbara supports a professional symphony and a chamber orchestra. The proximity to the University of California at Santa Barbara assures an endless stream of visiting artists and performers. To see what's scheduled around town, pick up a copy of the free weekly *Santa Barbara Independent* newspaper.

NIGHTLIFE Rich leather couches, a crackling fire in chilly weather, a cigar balcony, and pool tables draw a fancy Gen-X crowd to **Blue Agave** (⊠ 20 E. Cota St. ☎ 805/899–4694) for good food and designer martinis. All types of people hang out at **Darghan's** (⊠ 18 E. Ortega St. ☎ 805/568–0702), a lively pub with four pool tables, a great selection of draft beer and Irish whiskeys, and a full menu of traditional Irish dishes. A chic after-theater crowd heads to **Epiphany** (⊠ 21 W. Victoria St. ☎ 805/564–7100) to hang out at the sleek wine bar and order from the sophisticated bar menu. The **James Joyce** (⊠ 513 State St. ☎ 805/962–2688), which sometimes hosts folk and rock performers, is a good place to have a few beers and while away an evening.

Call ahead to reserve an outdoor table at **Indochine** (⊠ 434 State St. ☎ 805/ 962–0154), a sleek Thai-style nightclub filled with Southeast Asian furniture and art, open only Thursday, Friday, and Saturday nights. **Joe's Cafe** (⊠ 536 State St. ☎ 805/966–4638), where steins of beer accompany hearty bar food, is a fun, if occasionally rowdy, collegiate scene. The bartenders at **Left at Albuquerque** (⊠ 803 State St. ☎ 805/564– 5040) pour 141 types of tequila, making the Southwestern-style bar one of Santa Barbara's less sedate nightspots. Smooth martinis, and balconies overlooking State Street, attract a crowd of varying ages to **Rocks** (⊠ 801

State St. ☎ 805/884–1190). **SOhO** (✉ 1221 State St. ☎ 805/962–7776), a hip restaurant and bar, presents weeknight jazz; on weekends, the mood livens with good blues and rock.

The **Plow & Angel** (✉ San Ysidro Ranch, 900 San Ysidro La., Montecito ☎ 805/969–5046) books mellow jazz performers. The bar is perfect for those seeking quiet conversation. A slick sports bar attached to an upscale steakhouse owned by the maker of Lucky Brand Dungarees, **Lucky's** (✉ 1279 Coast Village Rd., Montecito ☎ 805/565–7540) attracts a flock of hip, fashionably dressed patrons hoping to see and be seen.

THE ARTS **Arlington Center for the Performing Arts** (✉ 1317 State St. ☎ 805/963–4408), a Moorish-style auditorium, is the home of the Santa Barbara Symphony. **Center Stage Theatre** (✉ 700 block of State St., 2nd fl. of Paseo Nuevo ☎ 805/963–0408) presents plays, music, dance, and readings. **Ensemble Theatre Company** (✉ 914 Santa Barbara St. ☎ 805/962–8606) stages plays by authors ranging from J. B. Priestley to David Mamet. The **Lobero Theatre** (✉ 33 E. Canon Perdido St. ☎ 805/963–0761), a state landmark, hosts community theater groups and touring professionals. In Montecito, the **Music Academy of the West** (✉ 1070 Fairway Rd. ☎ 805/969–4726) showcases orchestral, chamber, and operatic works.

Sports & the Outdoors

BEACHES Santa Barbara's beaches don't have the big surf of the shoreline farther south, but they also don't have the crowds. You can usually find a solitary spot to swim or sunbathe. In June and July, fog often hugs the coast until about noon. The wide swath of sand at the east end of Cabrillo Boulevard on the harbor front is a great spot for people-watching. **East Beach** (✉ 1118 Cabrillo Blvd. ☎ 805/897–2680) has sand volleyball courts, summertime lifeguard and sports competitions, and arts-and-crafts shows on Sunday and holidays. You can use showers, a weight room, and lockers (bring your own towel) and rent umbrellas and boogie boards at the Cabrillo Bathhouse. Next door, there's an elaborate jungle-gym play area for kids. The usually gentle surf at **Arroyo Burro County Beach** (✉ Cliff Dr. at Las Positas Rd.) makes it ideal for families with young children.

BICYCLING The level, two-lane, 3-mi **Cabrillo Bike Lane** passes the Santa Barbara Zoo, the Andree Clark Bird Refuge, beaches, and the harbor. There are restaurants along the way, and you can stop for a picnic along the palm-lined path looking out on the Pacific. **Wheel Fun Rentals** (✉ 22 State St. ☎ 805/966–6733) has bikes, quadricycles, and skates.

BOATS & **Adventours Outdoor Excursions** (☎ 805/899–2929) arranges everything from
CHARTERS kayak to mountain-bike excursions. **Santa Barbara Sailing Center** (✉ Santa Barbara Harbor launching ramp ☎ 805/962–2826 or 800/350–9090) offers sailing instruction, rents and charters sailboats, and organizes dinner and sunset champagne cruises, island excursions, and whale-watching trips. **Sea Landing** (✉ Cabrillo Blvd. at Bath St. and the breakwater ☎ 805/963–3564) operates surface and deep-sea fishing charters year-round. From Sea Landing, the **Condor Express** (☎ 805/963–3564), a 75-

foot high-speed catamaran, whisks up to 149 passengers toward the Channel Islands on dinner cruises, whale-watching excursions, and pelagic bird trips. **Truth Aquatics** (☎ 805/962–1127) departs from the Santa Barbara Harbor to ferry passengers to Channel Islands National Park. Their three dive boats also take scuba divers on single- and multiday trips.

GOLF Robert Trent Jones Jr. designed the stunning par-71 **Rancho San Marcos Golf Course** (⊠ 12½ mi north of Santa Barbara on Hwy. 154 ☎ 805/683–6334). Greens fees range from $125 to $145 and include a golf cart and driving range time. **Santa Barbara Golf Club** (⊠ Las Positas Rd. and McCaw Ave. ☎805/687–7087) has an 18-hole, par-70 course. The greens fees are $30–$40; an optional cart costs $12 per person.

TENNIS Many hotels in Santa Barbara have courts. The **City of Santa Barbara Parks and Recreation Department** (☎ 805/564–5418) operates public courts with lighted play until 9 PM weekdays. You can purchase day permits ($5) at the courts, or call the department. **Las Positas Municipal Courts** (⊠ 1002 Las Positas Rd.) has six lighted hard courts open daily. The 12 hard courts at the **Municipal Tennis Center** (⊠ 1414 Park Pl., near Salinas St. and U.S. 101) include an enclosed stadium court and three lighted courts open daily. **Pershing Park** (⊠ 100 Castillo St., near Cabrillo Blvd.) has eight lighted courts available for public play after 5 PM weekdays and all day on weekends and Santa Barbara City College holidays.

Shopping

SHOPPING AREAS **State Street,** roughly between Cabrillo Boulevard and Sola Street, is the commercial hub of Santa Barbara and a shopper's paradise. Chic malls, quirky storefronts, antiques emporia, elegant boutiques, and funky thrift shops abound here. **Paseo Nuevo** (⊠ 700 and 800 blocks of State St.), an open-air mall anchored by chains such as Nordstrom and Macy's, also contains a few local institutions like the children's clothier This Little Piggy. You can do your shopping on foot or by a battery-powered trolley (25¢) that runs between the waterfront and the 1300 block.

Shops, art galleries, and studios share the courtyard and gardens of **El Paseo** (⊠ Canon Perdido St. between State and Anacapa Sts.), a historic arcade. Antiques and gift shops are clustered in restored Victorian buildings on **Brinkerhoff Avenue** (⊠ 2 blocks west of State St. at West Cota St.). Serious antiques hunters can head a few miles south of Santa Barbara to the beach town of **Summerland,** which is full of shops and markets.

CLOTHING The complete line of **Big Dog Sportswear** (⊠ 6 E. Yanonali St. ☎ 805/963–8728) is sold at the Santa Barbara–based company's flagship store. **Channel Islands Surfboards** (⊠ 29 State St. ☎ 805/966–7213) stocks the latest in California beachwear, sandals, and accessories. **Territory Ahead** (⊠ Main store: 515 State St. ☒ Outlet store: 400 State St. ☎ 805/962–5558), a high-quality outdoorsy catalog company, sells fashionably rugged clothing for men and women. **Pierre Lafond–Wendy Foster** (⊠ 833 State St. ☎ 805/966–2276) is a casual-chic clothing store for women.

en route | If you choose to drive north via U.S. 101 without detouring to the Solvang/Santa Ynez area, you will drive right past some good beaches. In succession from east to west, **El Capitan, Gaviota, and Refugio state beaches** all have campsites, picnic tables, and fire rings. If you'd like to encounter nature without roughing it, you can try "comfort camping" at **El Capitan Canyon** (✉ 11560 Calle Real, north side of El Capitan State Beach exit ☎ 866/352–2729). The safari tents and cedar cabins here have fresh linens and creature comforts.

SANTA BARBARA COUNTY
INCLUDING SOLVANG

Residents refer to the glorious 30-mi stretch of coastline from Carpinteria to Gaviota as the South Coast. The Santa Ynez Mountains divide the county geographically; U.S. 101 passes through a mountain tunnel leading inland. Northern Santa Barbara County used to be known for its sprawling ranches and strawberry and broccoli fields. Today its 60-plus wineries and 18,000 acres of vineyards dominate the landscape from the Santa Ynez Valley, in the south, to Santa Maria in the north.

Santa Ynez

㉑ *31 mi north of Goleta via Hwy. 154.*

Founded in 1882, the tiny town of Santa Ynez still has many of its original frontier buildings. You can walk through the three-block downtown area in just a few minutes, shop for antiques, and hang around the old-time saloon. At some of the eponymous valley's best restaurants, you just might bump into one of the many celebrities who own nearby ranches. Just south of Santa Ynez on the Chumash Indian reservation lies the sprawling, Las Vegas–style **Chumash Casino Resort** (✉ 3400 E. Hwy. 246 ☎ 877/248–6274). The casino has 2,000 slot machines, and the property includes three restaurants, a spa, and upscale hotel ($$–$$$$) that was completed in 2004.

off the beaten path | **SAN MARCOS PASS** – A former stagecoach route, Highway 154 winds its spectacular way southeast from Santa Ynez through the Los Padres National Forest. Eight miles from Santa Ynez, **Cachuma Lake Recreation Area** (✉ Hwy. 154 ☎ 805/686–5054 ⊕ www.sbparks.com) centers around a jewel of an artificial lake. Hiking, fishing, and boating are popular here, and there are eagle- and wildlife-watching excursions aboard the *Osprey,* a 48-foot cruiser. The lively, one-of-a-kind **Cold Spring Tavern** (✉ 5995 Stagecoach Rd., off Hwy. 154 ☎ 805/967–0066), near Cachuma Lake, has been serving travelers since stagecoach days. Part biker hangout and part romantic country hideaway, the tavern specializes in game dishes, like rabbit and venison, along with such American standards as ribs, steak, and great chili. The tavern serves lunch and dinner daily, plus breakfast on weekends.

★ ¢–$$ ✕ **Trattoria Grappolo.** Authentic Italian fare, an open kitchen, and festive, family-style seating make this trattoria equally popular with celebrities from Hollywood and ranchers from the Santa Ynez Valley. Italian favorites on the extensive menu range from thin-crust pizza to homemade ravioli, risottos, and seafood linguine to grilled lamb chops in red wine sauce. The noise level tends to rise in the evening, so this isn't exactly the spot for a romantic getaway. ✉ *3687-C Sagunto St.* ☎ *805/688–6899* ▤ *MC, V* ⊘ *No lunch Mon.*

$$$$ 🏨 **Santa Ynez Inn.** It looks like a historic B&B, but this posh two-story Victorian inn in downtown Santa Ynez was built from scratch in 2002. The owners have furnished all the rooms with authentic historical pieces. The inn caters to a discerning crowd with the finest amenities—Frette linens, thermostatically controlled heat and air-conditioning, DVD/CD entertainment systems, and custom-made bathrobes. Most rooms have gas fireplaces, double steam showers, and whirlpool tubs. Rates include a phenomenal evening wine and hors d'oeuvres hour and a full breakfast. The Santa Ynez Inn Wine Cellar, about 50 yards from the main building, is open to the public for wine tasting 10–4 Thursday–Monday. ✉ *3627 Sagunto St., 93460* ☎ *805/688–5588 or 800/643–5774* ☒ *805/686–4294* ⊕ *www.santaynezinn.com* ⇦ *14 rooms* ⬓ *In-room data ports, some in-room hot tubs, gym, hot tub, massage, library, laundry service, concierge, meeting rooms; no smoking* ▤ *AE, D, MC, V.*

Sports & the Outdoors

The scenic rides operated by **Windhaven Glider** (✉ Santa Ynez Airport, Hwy. 246 ☎ 805/688–2517) cost between $85 and $155 and last up to 30 minutes.

Los Olivos

㉒ *4 mi north of Santa Ynez on Hwy. 154.*

This pretty village in the Santa Ynez Valley was once on the Spanish-built El Camino Real (Royal Highway) and later a stop on major stagecoach and rail routes. It's so sleepy today, though, that TV's *Return to Mayberry* was filmed here. A row of tasting rooms, art galleries, antiques stores, and country markets lines Grand Avenue. At **Los Olivos Tasting Room & Wine Shop** (✉ 2905 Grand Ave. ☎ 805/688–7406 ⊕ www.losolivoswines.com), you can sample locally produced wines and pick up winery maps. **Los Olivos Wine & Spirits Emporium** (✉ 2531 Grand Ave. ☎ 805/688–4409 or 888/729–4637 ⊕ www.sbwines.com) is a 1920s cabin sct in a field about ½-mi south of the Los Olivos flagpole. It serves as the main tasting room for a number of small but well-known wineries, such as Lane Tanner, Qupé, and Fiddlehead.

Firestone Vineyard (✉ 5000 Zaca Station Rd. ☎ 805/688–3940 ⊕ www.firestonewine.com) has been around since 1972. It has daily tours, grassy picnic areas, and hiking trails in the hills overlooking the valley; the views are fantastic.

Where to Stay & Eat

$$–$$$$ ✕ **Brothers Restaurant at Mattei's Tavern.** In the stagecoach days, Mattei's
Fodor's Choice Tavern provided wayfarers with hearty meals and warm beds. In early
★ 2000, chef-owners and brothers Matt and Jeff Nichols renovated the
1886 building, and while retaining the original character, transformed
it into one of the best restaurants in the valley. The casual, unpreten-
tious dining rooms with their red velvet wallpaper and historic photos
reflect the rich history of the tavern. The menu changes every few weeks
but often includes house favorites such as foie gras with spiced apples,
prime rib, grilled veal chops and salmon, and the loally famous jalapeño
cornbread. There's also a full bar, and an array of vintages from the cus-
tom-built cedar wine cellar. ⊠ *2350 Railway Ave.* ☎ *805/688–4820*
⌕ *Reservations essential* ⊟ *AE, MC, V* ⊘ *No lunch.*

$$$–$$$$ ✕▨ **The Ballard Inn.** Set among orchards and vineyards in the tiny town
of Ballard, 2 mi south of Los Olivos, this inn makes an elegant wine-
country escape. Rooms are furnished with antiques and original art. Seven
rooms have wood-burning fireplaces; the inn provides room phones and
TVs upon request. At the Ballard Inn Restaurant ($$–$$$), which serves
dinner Wednesday through Sunday, owner-chef Budi Kazali creates sump-
tuous French-Asian dishes in one of the area's most romantic dining rooms.
⊠ *2436 Baseline Ave., Ballard 93463* ☎ *805/688–7770 or 800/638–2466*
🖷 *805/688–9560* ⊕ *www.ballardinn.com* ⇌ *15 rooms* ⌕ *Restaurant,*
in-room data ports, bicycles; no room phones ⊟ *AE, MC, V* ❘O❘ *BP.*

$$$–$$$$ ▨ **Fess Parker's Wine Country Inn and Spa.** This luxury inn includes an
elegant, tree-shaded French Country main building and an equally at-
tractive annex across the street with a pool and a hot tub. The spacious
accommodations have fireplaces, seating areas, and wet bars; three also
have private hot tubs. ⊠ *2860 Grand Ave., 93441* ☎ *805/688–7788*
or 800/446–2455 🖷 *805/688–1942* ⊕ *www.fessparker.com* ⇌ *20*
rooms, 1 suite ⌕ *Restaurant, cable TV, pool, hot tub, spa, Internet, meet-*
ing rooms, some pets allowed; no smoking ⊟ *AE, DC, MC, V* ❘O❘ *CP.*

Solvang

☾ ㉓ *5 mi south of Los Olivos on Alamo Pintado Rd.; Hwy. 246, 3 mi east*
of U.S. 101.

You'll know you've reached the town of Solvang when the architecture
suddenly changes to half-timber buildings and windmills. This town was
settled in 1911 by a group of Danish educators (the flatlands and rolling
green hills reminded them of home), and even today, more than two-
thirds of the residents are of Danish descent. Although it's attracted tourists
for decades, in recent years it has become more sophisticated with gal-
leries, upscale restaurants, and wine-tasting rooms. A good way to get
your bearings is to park your car in one of the many public lots and
stroll around town. Stop in at the visitor center, at 2nd Street and
Copenhagen Drive, for maps and helpful advice on what to see and do.
Don't forget to stock up on Danish pastries from the town's excellent
bakeries before you leave.

Housed in an 1884 adobe, the **Rideau Vineyard** (⊠ 1562 Alamo Pintado
Rd. ☎ 805/688–0717 ⊕ www.rideauvineyard.com) tasting room pro-

vides simultaneous blasts from the area's ranching past and from its hand-harvested, Rhone-varietal winemaking present.

Just outside Solvang is the **Sanford Winery** (⊠ 7250 Santa Rosa Rd. ☎ 805/688–3300 ⊕ www.sanfordwinery.com), which helped put Santa Barbara County on the international wine map with a 1989 pinot noir. Today Sanford has one of the most environmentally sensitive tasting rooms and picnic areas in the valley. All their vineyards are certified organic, and the pinot noirs and chardonnays are exceptional.

Where to Stay & Eat

$$–$$$$ ✕ **The Hitching Post.** You'll find everything from grilled artichokes to ostrich at this casual eatery just outside of Solvang, but most people come for what is said to be the best Santa Maria–style barbecue in the state. The oak used in the barbecue imparts a wonderful smoky taste. ⊠ *406 E. Hwy. 246* ☎ *805/688–0676* ▭ *AE, MC, V* ⊙ *No lunch.*

$–$$ ✕ **Bit O' Denmark.** Perhaps the most authentic Danish eatery in Solvang, this restaurant occupies an old beamed building that was a church until 1929. Two specialties of the house are the *Frikadeller* (meatballs with pickled red cabbage, potatoes, and thick brown gravy) and the *Medisterpølse* (Danish beef and pork sausage with cabbage). ⊠ *473 Alisal Rd.* ☎ *805/688–5426* ▭ *AE, D, MC, V.*

★ $$$$ ⊞ **Alisal Guest Ranch and Resort.** Since 1946, this 10,000-acre ranch has been popular with celebrities and plain folk alike. There are lots of activities to choose from here: horseback riding, golf, fishing, sailing in the 100-acre spring-fed lake—although you can also just lounge by the pool. The ranch-style rooms and suites come with garden views, covered porches, high-beam ceilings, and wood-burning fireplaces, with touches of Spanish tile and fine Western art. A jacket is required at the nightly dinners (which are included in your room rate). ⊠ *1054 Alisal Rd., 93463* ☎ *805/688–6411 or 800/425–4725* 🖷 *805/688–2510* ⊕ *www.alisal.com* ⇨ *36 rooms, 37 suites* ⚷ *Restaurant, room service, refrigerators, 2 18-hole golf courses, 7 tennis courts, pool, bicycles, billiards, croquet, hiking, horseback riding, Ping-Pong, shuffleboard, volleyball, bar, babysitting, children's programs (ages 6 and up); no a/c, no room TVs* ▭ *AE, DC, MC, V* ¶◯¶ *MAP.*

$$$–$$$$ ⊞ **Petersen Village Inn.** Like most of Solvang's buildings, this upscale B&B wouldn't seem out of place in a small European village. The canopy beds here are plush, the bathrooms small but sparkling. Rates include a complete dinner for two in the guests-only Cafe Provence—prepared by Swiss chef Erminio Dal-Fuoco—and a European buffet breakfast. ⊠ *1576 Mission Dr., 93463* ☎ *805/688–3121 or 800/321–8985* 🖷 *805/688–5732* ⊕ *www.peterseninn.com* ⇨ *39 rooms, 1 suite* ⚷ *Dining room, in-room data ports, cable TV, Internet, meeting rooms; no smoking* ▭ *AE, MC, V* ¶◯¶ *MAP.*

$–$$ ⊞ **Royal Scandinavian Inn.** A half block from the outlet mall and across the street from Solvang's main drag, this tasteful, country-theme motel has lots of family-friendly amenities. ⊠ *400 Alisal Rd., 93463* ☎ *805/688–8000 or 800/624–5572* 🖷 *805/688–0761* ⊕ *www.royalscandinavianinn.com* ⇨ *126 rooms, 7 suites* ⚷ *Restaurant, in-room data ports, cable TV with movies, pool, gym, hot tub, lounge, no-smoking rooms* ▭ *AE, D, DC, MC, V.*

¢–$$ ☒ **Best Western King Fredric Inn.** Rooms at this comfortable and central motel are fairly spacious. If you want to stay right in Solvang and don't want to spend a fortune, this is a good bet. ☒ *1617 Copenhagen Dr., 93463* ☎ *805/688–5515 or 800/549–9955* 🖷 *805/688–1600* ☞ *44 rooms* ⚬ *Cable TV with movies, pool, hot tub, no-smoking rooms* 🖃 *AE, D, MC, V.*

The Arts

PCPA Theaterfest (☎ 805/922–8313 ⊕ www.pcpa.org), the Pacific Conservatory of the Performing Arts, presents contemporary and classic plays as well as musicals in theaters in Solvang and Santa Maria. Summer events in Solvang are held in the open-air Festival Theatre, on 2nd Street off Copenhagen Drive.

Lompoc

㉔ *20 mi west of Solvang on Hwy. 246.*

Known as the flower-seed capital of the world, Lompoc is blanketed with vast fields of brightly colored flowers that bloom from May through August. For five days around the last weekend of June, the **Lompoc Valley Flower Festival** (☎ 805/735–8511 ⊕ www.flowerfestival.org) brings a parade, carnival, and crafts show to town.

At ☪ **La Purisima Mission State Historic Park** you can see Mission La Purisima Concepción, the most fully restored mission in the state. Founded in 1787, it stands in a stark and still remote location and powerfully evokes the lives of California's Spanish settlers. Docents lead tours every afternoon, and displays illustrate the secular and religious activities that were part of mission life. From March through October the mission hosts special events, including crafts demonstrations by costumed docents. ☒ *2295 Purisima Rd., off Hwy. 246* ☎ *805/733–3713* ⊕ *www. lapurisimamission.org* ☞ *$4 per vehicle* ☉ *Daily 9–5; tour at 2 Tues.–Sun., additional tour weekends at 10.*

SAN LUIS OBISPO COUNTY
FROM PISMO BEACH TO SAN SIMEON

San Luis Obispo County's pristine landscapes and abundant wildlife areas, especially those around Morro Bay and Montaña de Oro State Park, have long attracted nature lovers. In the south, Pismo Beach and other coastal towns have great sand and surf; inland, an up-and-coming wine region stretches from the Edna and Arroyo Grande Valleys in the south to Paso Robles in the north. With historic attractions, a booming cultural scene, and eclectic restaurants, the college town of San Luis Obispo is at the heart of the county.

Pismo Beach

㉕ *Hwy. 1, about 40 mi north of Lompoc.*

About 20 mi of sandy shoreline begins at the town of Pismo Beach, optimistically nicknamed the "Bakersfield Riviera." The southern end of

town runs along sand dunes, some of which are open to cars and other vehicles. The northern section sits perched above chalky cliffs.

For a town with a population of less than 10,000, Pismo Beach has a slew of hotels and restaurants. Despite the neon signs announcing all accommodations and dining spots, the area doesn't feel overly touristy. Most of the best hotels and restaurants provide great views of the Pacific Ocean. Good beachfront walks, top-quality clam chowder, and a popular Dixieland jazz festival in February are prime attractions.

An ecofriendly winery built from straw bales, **Claiborne & Churchill** (✉ 2649 Carpenter Canyon Rd., San Luis Obispo ☎ 805/544–4066 ⊕ www.claibornechurchill.com) makes small lots of specialty wines like dry riesling and Gewürztraminer.

en route

★ ☾

The spectacular **Guadalupe-Nipomo Dunes Preserve** stretches 18 mi along the coast south of Pismo Beach to Guadalupe. It's the largest and most ecologically diverse dune system in the state, and a habitat for more than 200 species of birds as well as sea otters, black bears, bobcats, coyotes, and deer. The 1,500-foot Mussel Rock is the highest beach dune in the western states. At least six major movies were filmed here, including Cecil B. DeMille's *The Ten*

Commandments. There are several entrances to the dunes; the main ones are at Oso Flaco Lake (about 13 mi south of Pismo Beach on Highway 1, then 3 mi west on Oso Flaco Road) and at the far west end of Highway 166 (Main Street) in Guadalupe. At the **Dunes Center** (✉ 1055 Guadalupe St., 1 mi north of Hwy. 166 ☎ 805/343–2455 ⊕ www.dunescenter.org ⊗ Tues.–Sun. 10–4), you can get all sorts of dune and wildlife information and view an exhibit about *The Ten Commandments* movie set, which is buried near Guadalupe Beach. Parking at Oso Flaco Lake is $4 per vehicle.

Where to Stay & Eat

$$–$$$$ ✗ **Cracked Crab.** This traditional Eastern Seaboard–style crab shack imports fresh seafood daily from Australia, Alaska, and the East Coast. Fish is local and line-caught, much of the produce is organic, and everything is made from scratch. For a real treat, don a bib and chow through a bucket of steamed shellfish, along with Cajun sausage, potatoes, and corn on the cob. The menu changes daily. ✉ *751 Price St.* ☎ *805/773–2722* ⟨ *Reservations not accepted* ☰ *AE, D, MC, V.*

$–$$ ✗ **Giuseppe's.** The classic flavors of southern Italy are highlighted at this cheery, rustic downtown spot. Most recipes originate from Bari, a seaport on the Adriatic; the menu includes breads and pizzas baked in the wood-burning oven, hearty dishes like osso buco and lamb, and homemade pastas. The restaurant grows its own organic tomatoes, basil, peppers, and herbs. ✉ *891 Price St.* ☎ *805/773–2870* ⟨ *Reservations not accepted* ☰ *AE, D, MC, V* ⊗ *No lunch weekends.*

¢   ✗ **Splash Café.** Folks line up all the way down the block for clam chowder served in a sourdough bread bowl at this wildly popular seafood stand. You can also order fresh steamed clams, burgers, hot dogs, calamari, and more—and nearly everything on the menu is $5.75 or less. The cheap storefront, a favorite with locals and savvy visitors, is open daily for lunch and dinner, but closes early in the evening weekdays during low-season. ✉ *197 Pomeroy St.* ☎ *805/773–4653* ☰ *MC, V.*

$$$–$$$$ ✗▦ **Sea Venture Resort.** The bright, homey rooms at this hotel all have fireplaces and featherbeds; most have balconies with private hot tubs, and some have beautiful ocean views. A breakfast basket is delivered to your room in the morning, and the elegant Sea Venture Restaurant ($$–$$$)—with sweeping ocean vistas on the third floor—features fresh seafood and local wines. ✉ *100 Ocean View Ave., 93449* ☎ *805/773–4994 or 800/662–5545* ⎙ *805/773–0924* ⊕ *www.seaventure.com* ⇨ *50 rooms* ⟨ *Restaurant, fans, in-room data ports, minibars, refrigerators, in-room VCRs, hot tubs, spa, bicycles, meeting rooms; no a/c, no smoking* ☰ *AE, D, DC, MC, V* ⎮◯⎮ *CP.*

$$$$ ▦ **Pismo Lighthouse Suites.** This oceanfront resort, which was bought and overhauled in 2003, includes 70 deluxe two-room, two-bath suites. Some are suitable for couples, others for families—but all have nautical-style furnishings, private balconies or patios, and high-speed Internet. Ask for a corner oceanfront suite for the best views. There's a pool and a central sport court, where you can play chess on a life-size board. ✉ *2411 Price St., 93449* ☎ *805/773–2411 or 800/245–2411* ⎙ *805/773–1508* ⊕ *www.pismolighthousesuites.com* ⇨ *70 suites* ⟨ *In-room data ports, microwaves, refrigerators, cable TV with movies and video* *games, putting green, pool, gym, badminton, Ping-Pong, laundry facilities; no smoking ⊟ AE, D, DC, MC, V ❑ CP.*

$$$-$$$$ ❑ **The Cliffs at Shell Beach.** Perched dramatically on an oceanfront cliff, this resort is surrounded by lawns and palm trees. The rooms are modern, with Spanish marble bathrooms (some have hot tubs), and the ones facing the beach have wonderful views. This resort is extremely pet-friendly—all visiting dogs receive a bed, two dishes, and bottled water, and the concierge can arrange dog-walking services. ⊠ *2757 Shell Beach Rd., 93449* ☎ *805/773–5000 or 800/826–7827* ☐ *805/773–0764* ⊕ *www.cliffsresort.com* ⇗ *142 rooms, 23 suites* ♨ *Restaurant, room service, cable TV with movies, pool, gym, indoor hot tub, outdoor hot tub, sauna, spa, badminton, volleyball, bar, dry cleaning, laundry facilities, concierge, Internet, business services, meeting rooms, some pets allowed; no smoking ⊟ AE, D, DC, MC, V.*

$$-$$$ ❑ **Sycamore Mineral Springs Resort.** This modern resort's hot mineral springs, which bubble up amid stands of oak and sycamore, have rejuvenated thousands of spa guests since 1897. Each room and suite has its own private balcony with a hot tub; about half have mineral water piped in. Suites also include cozy fireplaces. The West Meadow suites, across Avila Beach Drive, offer exceptional privacy in a pristine setting. If you can't stay at the resort, you can still soak in one of its outdoor wooden hot tubs for an hour or two. ⊠ *1215 Avila Beach Dr., San Luis Obispo 93405* ☎ *805/595–7302 or 800/234–5831* ⊕ *www.sycamoresprings.com* ⇗ *26 rooms, 50 suites* ♨ *Restaurant, room service, in-room hot tubs, some microwaves, some refrigerators, cable TV, some in-room VCRs, pool, outdoor hot tubs, massage; no smoking ⊟ AE, D, MC, V.*

$-$$ ❑ **Shell Beach Motel.** Just 2½ blocks from the beach, this basic but cozy lodge is a great bargain for the area. You can choose from king, queen, or double-queen rooms; all have English country-style furnishings and floral details painted on the walls and ceilings. ⊠ *653 Shell Beach Rd., 93449* ☎ *805/773–4373 or 800/549–4727* ☐ *805/773–6208* ⊕ *www.shellbeachmotel.com* ⇗ *9 rooms* ♨ *In-room data ports, microwaves, refrigerators, cable TV with movies, pool; no a/c ⊟ MC, V.*

en route From Pismo Beach take U.S. 101 about 4 mi north to **Avila Beach and Port San Luis.** Both are old fishing villages that face south onto a cove, thus missing out on the fog that rolls in off the ocean. In the 1990s Avila Beach was basically torn down to clean up extensive oil seepage. The promenade has been fully restored; it's a fantastic spot for beachfront strolls and views of the hilly coastline and port. The new town is slowly but surely emerging, with hotels and shops that harken back to the funky character of the old village. Port San Luis is still functioning, with a vibrant fish market on the pier.

San Luis Obispo

❷⓺ *Hwy. 1, 15 mi north of Pismo Beach.*

About halfway between San Francisco and Los Angeles, San Luis Obispo is an appealing urban center set among gentle hills and extinct volcanoes. California Polytechnic State University, known as Cal Poly, gives the town collegiate energy. San Luis Obispo has restored its old railroad depot as well as several Victorian-era homes. On Thursday from 6 PM to 9 PM a four-block-long farmers' market lines Higuera Street.

San Luis Obispo is the commercial center of Edna Valley/Arroyo Grande Valley wine country, whose appellations stretch east–west from San Luis Obispo and Arroyo Grande near the coast toward Lake Lopez in the inland mountains. Many of the wineries line Highway 227 and connecting inland roads. The region is best known for chardonnay and pinot noir, although many wineries experiment with other varietals and blends. Wine-touring maps are readily available at attractions and lodgings throughout San Luis Obispo County.

★ **Mission San Luis Obispo de Tolosa,** established in 1772, overlooks San Luis Obispo Creek. A museum exhibits artifacts of the Chumash Indians and early Spanish settlers. ⊠ *751 Palm St.* ☎ *805/543–6850* ⊕ *www.missionsanluisobispo.org* ⊠ *$2 suggested donation* ⊘ *Apr.–Oct., daily 9–5; late Oct.–Mar., daily 9–4.*

♻ **San Luis Obispo County Museum and History Center** presents revolving exhibits on various aspects of county history—such as Native American life, California ranchos, and how railroads affected the region. A separate children's room has themed activities where kids can earn prizes. ⊠ *696 Monterey St.* ☎ *805/543–0638* ⊕ *www.slochs.org* ⊠ *Free* ⊘ *Wed.–Sun. 10–4.*

For sweeping views of the Edna Valley and the unusual volcanic *morros* (small volcanic peaks) that pop up from the valley floor, go to the upscale tasting bar at **Edna Valley Vineyard** (⊠ 2585 Biddle Ranch Rd. ☎ 805/544–5855 ⊕ www.ednavalley.com). A refurbished century-old schoolhouse serves as tasting room for **Baileyana Winery** (⊠ 5828 Orcutt Rd. ☎ 805/269–8200 ⊕ www.baileyana.com).

♻ **San Luis Obispo Children's Museum.** This delightful museum encourages education through exploration in a cheery, interactive, hands-on environment. Kids can race to a fire on a fire engine, report the news, slide down a dinosaur, or head into "outer space." Bring along a picnic; there are outdoor tables in a shady patio area near a creek. ⊠ *1010 Nipomo St.* ☎ *805/ 544–5437* ⊕ *www.slokids.org* ⊠ *$5* ⊘ *Tues.–Sat. 11–5, Sun. noon–4.*

Where to Stay & Eat

$–$$$ ✕ **Buona Tavola.** Homemade pasta with scampi in a creamy saffron sauce and porcini mushroom risotto are among the northern Italian dishes served at this local favorite. Daily fresh fish and salad specials and an impressive wine list attract a steady stream of regulars. In good weather you can dine on the flower-filled patio. ⊠ *1037 Monterey St.* ☎ *805/ 545–8000* ▭ *AE, D, MC, V* ⊘ *No lunch weekends.*

$–$$$ ✕ **Cafe Roma.** Authentic northern Italian cuisine is the specialty at this Railroad Square restaurant. Beneath a large mural of Tuscany, you can sit and dine on squash-filled ravioli with a sage-and-butter sauce or filet mignon glistening with port and Gorgonzola. ⊠ *1020 Railroad Ave.* ☎ *805/541–6800* ▭ *AE, D, DC, MC, V* ⊘ *Closed Sun.*

$–$$ ✕ **Le Fandango Bistro.** Spicy Basque flavors take French cuisine to new heights at this intimate restaurant with an open kitchen. In the evening dine on traditional rabbit stew, escargot, foie gras, duck, seafood, and lamb dishes, or choose from eight daily specials. Casual bistro-style dishes dominate the lunch menu. ⊠ *717 Higuera St.* ☎ *805/544–5515* ⊟ *AE, D, MC, V* ☙ *No lunch Sun. and Mon.*

$–$$ ✕ **Novo Restaurant and Bakery.** You can take a culinary world tour at this sleek, casual downtown eatery in the heart of downtown; the salads, soups, tapas (smaller plates for sharing with friends) and larger traditional dishes come from nearly every continent. The wine and beer list also covers the globe (and includes local favorites). Many of the decadent desserts are baked at the restaurant's sister property in Cambria, the French Corner Bakery. ⊠ *726 Higuera St.* ☎ *805/543–3986* ⊟ *MC, V.*

★ **¢–$** ✕ **Big Sky Café.** A hip gathering spot for breakfast, lunch, and dinner, Big Sky has a wide-ranging menu—it includes dishes from the Mediterranean, North Africa, and the Southwest. Most of the ingredients, however, are local and organically grown. ⊠ *1121 Broad St.* ☎ *805/545–5401* ⚫ *Reservations not accepted* ⊟ *AE, MC, V.*

$–$$$ ⊡ **Morgan's Mansions.** You can choose to stay in one of three "mansions" here (actually just enhanced hotel buildings), each of which celebrates a distinct style and era: Londonderry (English Tudor/Elizabethan), California Craftsman, and Plantation (Georgia/South Florida). The oversize rooms have elegant furnishings, widescreen TVs and DVD players, and original art by California artists; some rooms have rocking chairs, fireplaces, and jetted tubs. A European breakfast is served in the Gate House or delivered to your room. Ask for an art tour if you like what you see on the walls. ⊠ *1941 Monterey St., 93401* ☎ *805/541–1122 or 800/593–0333* ⊞ *805/541–2475* ⊕ *www.morgansmansions.com* ⇨ *25 rooms* ⚭ *Room service, in-room data ports, refrigerators, cable TV, Internet, business services, meeting room, some pets allowed; no smoking* ⊟ *AE, D, MC, V* ⦿⚬ *CP.*

$$–$$$ ⊡ **Madonna Inn.** From its rococo bathrooms to its pink-on-pink froufrou steak house, the Madonna Inn is the ultimate in kitsch. Each room is unique, to say the least: Rock Bottom is all stone; the Safari Room is decked out in animal skins. Comic relief aside, the Madonna is pretty much a gussied-up motel, so don't expect much in the way of luxury. ⊠ *100 Madonna Rd., 93405* ☎ *805/543–3000 or 800/543–9666* ⊞ *805/543–1800* ⊕ *www.madonnainn.com* ⇨ *86 rooms, 22 suites* ⚭ *Restaurant, café, cable TV with movies, massage, bar, meeting rooms; no a/c in some rooms, no smoking* ⊟ *AE, D, MC, V.*

$$–$$$ ⊡ **Petit Soleil.** A cobblestone courtyard, lavender water sprinkled in the rooms, and French music piped in the halls all help create a sense of Provençal village life at this cheery north side inn. The individually themed rooms have whimsical art, custom furnishings, CD players and candles. Rates include French and local wines paired with appetizers in the late afternoon–evening and a full homemade breakfast in the sun-filled patio or dining room. ⊠ *1473 Monterey St., 93401* ☎ *805/549–0321 or 800/676–1588* ⊞ *805/549–0383* ⊕ *www.petitsoleilslo.com* ⇨ *15 rooms* ⚭ *Fans, cable TV, Internet, business services, meeting room; no a/c, no smoking* ⊟ *AE, MC, V* ⦿⚬ *BP.*

$$ ⊡ **Garden Street Inn.** You can walk to most downtown restaurants and attractions from this fully restored, two-story Italianate–Queen Anne, built in 1887. The individually themed rooms, each with private bath, are filled with antiques; some have stained-glass windows, fireplaces, and hot tubs. Wine and appetizers are served in the cozy dining room in the evening; there's also a lavish homemade breakfast when you rise. ⊠ *1212 Garden St., 93401* ☏ *805/545–9802 or 800/488–2045* 🖷 *805/545–9403* ⊕ *www.gardenstreetinn.com* 🖙 *9 rooms, 4 suites* ♿ *In-room data ports; no TV in some rooms, no smoking* ⊟ *AE, D, MC, V* ◉ *BP.*

¢ 🖾 **Peach Tree Inn.** Extra touches like rose gardens, free video checkout, and flower-filled vases turn this modest, family-run motel into a relaxing creek-side haven. Four rooms have king and sofa beds with private patios overlooking the creek. The sunny breakfast room has a refrigerator and microwave for guest use, and snacks are available all day and evening. ⊠ *2001 Monterey St., 93401* ☏ *805/543–3170 or 800/227–6396* 🖷 *805/543–7673* ⊕ *www.peachtreeinn.com* 🖙 *37 rooms* ♿ *In-room VCRs, Internet; no smoking* ⊟ *AE, D, DC, MC, V* ◉ *CP.*

Nightlife & the Arts

NIGHTLIFE   The club scene in this college town is centered on Higuera Street off Monterey Street. The **Frog and Peach** (⊠ 728 Higuera St. ☏ 805/595–3764) is a decent spot to nurse a beer and listen to music. **Linnaea's Cafe** (⊠ 1110 Garden St. ☏ 805/541–5888), a mellow java joint, sometimes hosts poetry readings, as well as blues, jazz, and folk music performances. Chicago-style **Mother's Tavern** (⊠ 725 Higuera St. ☏ 805/541–8733), often voted "best bar" in local polls, draws crowds with good pub food, a full bar, eclectic wine list, and live entertainment in a historic turn-of-the-century setting (complete with antique U.S. flags and a wall-mounted moose head).

THE ARTS   The **Performing Arts Center** (⊠ 1 Grand Ave. ☏ 805/756–7222 for information, 805/756–2787 for tickets outside CA, 888/233–2787 for tickets in CA) at Cal Poly hosts concerts and recitals. The **San Luis Obispo Mozart Festival** (☏ 805/781–3008) takes place in late July and early August. Not all the music is Mozart; you'll also hear Haydn and other composers. **San Luis Obispo Art Center** (⊠ 101 Broad St., at Mission Plaza ☏ 805/543–8562) displays and sells a diverse mix of traditional work and cutting-edge arts and crafts by Central Coast artists (closed Tuesday).

Sports & the Outdoors

A hilly greenbelt with vast amounts of open space and hiking trails surrounds the city of San Luis Obispo. For information on trailheads, call the city Parks and Recreation Department (805/781–7300) or visit www.slocity.org/parksandrecreation to download an open space trail map.

en route   From San Luis Obispo you can reach Morro Bay by continuing north on Highway 1 or by following the coastline along South Bay Boulevard 10 mi to the quaint residential villages of **Los Osos and Baywood Park.** Check out the tide pools, watch the waves roll into the bluffs, and picnic in the eucalyptus groves at **Montaña de Oro State Park** (⊠ 7 mi south of Los Osos on Pecho Rd. ☏ 805/528–0513 or 805/772–7434 ⊕ www.parks.ca.gov). The park has miles of nature trails along rocky shoreline, sandy beaches, and hills overlooking some of California's most spectacular scenery.

Morro Bay

㉗ *14 mi north of San Luis Obispo on Hwy. 1.*

Commercial fishermen in the town of Morro Bay slog around the harbor in galoshes, and old-style ships teeter in its protected waters. Locals are proud of the 576-foot-high **Morro Rock** (⊠ At the northern end of the Embarcadero), one of nine such small volcanic peaks, or morros, in the area. A short walk leads to a breakwater, with the harbor on one side and the crashing waves of the Pacific on the other. Morro Bay is a wildlife preserve where endangered falcons and other birds nest. You can't climb on Morro Rock, but even from its base you can see that the peak is alive with birds. The center of the action on land is the **Embarcadero** (⊠ On the waterfront from Beach St. to Tidelands Park), which is lined with lodgings and stylish restaurants. The town's well-designed aquarium is here, as is the outdoor Giant Chessboard, made up of nearly life-size, hand-carved pieces.

★ ☺ The **Morro Bay State Park Museum of Natural History** reopened in 2002 following a $3.5 million renovation. The 26 hands-on exhibits and interactive activities here teach kids and adults about the natural environment—both in the Morro Bay estuary and the rest of the planet. ⊠ *State Park Rd.* ☏ *805/772–2694* ⊕ *www.morrobaymuseum.org* ✉ *$2* ⊙ *Daily 10–5.*

Where to Stay & Eat

$$–$$$ ✕ **Dorn's.** This seafood café, which overlooks the harbor, resembles a Cape Cod cottage. It's open for breakfast, lunch, and dinner; the excellent fish and calamari steaks are on the evening menu. ⊠ *801 Market Ave.* ☏ *805/772–4415* ▭ *D, MC, V.*

$$–$$$ ✕ **Windows on the Water.** Every table at Morro Bay's most elegant and popular restaurant has great views of the water. The menu changes with the season but always focuses on fresh fish and quality local ingredients. Brunch is served on high-season weekends. ⊠ *699 Embarcadero* ☏ *805/772–0677* ▭ *AE, D, DC, MC, V* ⊙ *No lunch.*

¢ ✕ **Taco Temple.** This tiny, family-run café serves some of the freshest California-style Mexican food in the region; the fish tacos with mango salsa, in particular, are superb. Make an effort to find this tucked-away gem— it's in the corner of a supermarket parking lot in North Morro Bay, on the frontage road parallel to Highway 1, just north of the Highway 41 junction. ⊠ *2680 N. Main St., at Elena* ☏ *805/772–4965* ▭ *No credit cards* ⊙ *Closed Tues.*

$$–$$$$ ▦ **The Inn at Morro Bay.** This beautifully situated complex has romantic, contemporary-style rooms with CD players and featherbeds. Many have fireplaces, private decks with spa tubs, and bay views; others look out at extensive gardens. There's an on-site wellness center with spa and massage treatments, a golf course across the road, and a heron rookery nearby (although even bird-lovers should think twice about booking a room near the nesting grounds—the morning din can be overwhelming). ⊠ *60 State Park Rd., 93442* ☏ *805/772–5651 or 800/321–9566* ▤ *805/772–4779* ⊕ *www.innatmorrobay.com* ⮑ *97 rooms, 1 cottage*

⛄ *2 restaurants, room service, cable TV with movies, pool, spa, mountain bikes, bar, meeting room; no smoking* ▤ *AE, D, DC, MC, V.*

$–$$ ⊞ **Embarcadero Inn.** Despite its boxy gray exterior, rooms at this waterfront hotel are cheery and welcoming. All are decorated with old maritime photographs and have balconies facing the sea. ⊠ *456 Embarcadero, 93442* ☎ *805/772–2700 or 800/292–7625* 🖷 *805/772–1060* ⊕ *www. embarcaderoinn.com* ⇱ *29 rooms, 3 suites* ⛄ *Microwaves, refrigerators, cable TV with movies, in-room VCRs, 2 hot tubs, Internet, nosmoking rooms* ▤ *AE, D, DC, MC, V* ⊚I *CP.*

¢–$ ⊞ **Adventure Inn.** Nautical murals decorate this small motel facing Morro Rock. Rooms are plain but comfortable. Amenities include coffeemakers and free HBO. ⊠ *1150 Embarcadero, 93442* ☎ *805/772–5607 or 800/799–5607* ⊕ *www.adventureinn.net* ⇱ *16 rooms* ⛄ *Restaurant, fans, refrigerators, cable TV with movies, pool, hot tub, no-smoking rooms* ▤ *AE, D, MC, V* ⊚I *CP.*

Sports & the Outdoors

Kayak Horizons (⊠ 551 Embarcadero ☎ 805/772–6444) rents kayaks and gives lessons and guided tours. **Sub-Sea Tours** (⊠ 699 Embarcadero ☎ 805/772–9463) operates glass-bottom boats and has kayak and canoe rentals and lessons. **Virg's Sport Fishing** (⊠ 1215 Embarcadero ☎ 805/772–1222) conducts deep-sea fishing and whale-watching trips.

Paso Robles

㉘ *30 mi north of San Luis Obispo on U.S. 101.*

Spanish explorers originally named this area El Paso de Robles, or "pass of oaks," presumably for the trees that dominated the countryside. The Salinan Indians and Franciscan fathers also called it Agua Caliente for its underground mineral hot springs. In the 1860s tourists began flocking to Paso Robles to "take the cure" in hot springs and mud baths; others settled in the area to farm and raise cattle. Today, the wine industry dominates the region; there are more than 60 wineries and 250 vineyards here. (You can pick up a regional wine-touring map at most hotels, wineries, and attractions in the area.) Area wineries are primarily known for robust red wines—particularly zinfandels, cabernets, merlots, and Rhône varietals.

Paso Robles maintains its dual identities—cowboy town and esoteric wine region—surprisingly well. Small-town friendliness prevails at the fanciest restaurants, and wineries tend to treat visitors like neighbors. Seated at a tasting room bar, you can easily find yourself chatting with a rancher about trail rides in the hills while the owner-winemaker points out the merits of his latest vintages.

Much of Paso Robles community life centers around **City Park** (⊠ Spring St. between 11th and 12th Sts.), the historic square in the heart of downtown. Folks tend to gather around the fountain, gazebo, and horseshoe pits while kids romp on the playground. Restaurants, wine bars, antiques stores, and boutiques line the perimeter. Although a 2003 earthquake demolished several buildings around the main square—including the venerable clock tower—and damaged several others, the city is rebuilding them as quickly as possible. Most businesses in the area continue to operate as usual; those that are still being restored plan to reopen by early 2005.

The lakeside **Paso Robles Hot Springs & Spa,** a day spa on 240 hilly acres near the intersection of U.S. 101 and Highway 46E, is a great place to relax before and after wine tasting. Soak in a private indoor or outdoor hot tub fed by natural mineral springs, or indulge in a massage or facial (book treatments in advance). ⊠ *3725 Buena Vista Dr.* ☎ *805/238–4600* ⊕ *www.pasohotsprings.com* ☒ *Hot tubs $10 per person per hr* ☉ *Daily.*

Water-ski, fish for bass, trout, and bluegill, or lounge on the vast expanse of shoreline at **Lake Nacimiento Resort,** 16 mi northwest of downtown Paso Robles. There are campsites, family lodges, a full-service marina with boat and equipment rentals, a restaurant (open late May through early September), a general store, horseshoe pits, volleyball, and basketball. In the summer you can swim in the pool for a fee. ⊠ *10625 Nacimiento Lake Dr., Bradley 93426* ☎ *805/238–3256 or 800/323–3839* ⊕ *www.nacimientoresort.com* ☒ *$10 day use, for up to 2 people; $3 for each additional person* ☉ *Daily.*

Even if you don't drink wine, stop at **Eberle Winery** (⊠ North side of Hwy. 46E, 3½ mi east of U.S. 101 ☎805/238–9607 ⊕www.eberlewinery. com) for a fascinating tour of the 16,000-square-foot underground wine caves. The winery is known for premium handcrafted wines produced in limited quantities. Named for the wild mustangs that roam the Carrizo Plains east of the area, **Wild Horse Winery & Vineyards** (⊠ 1437 Wild Horse Winery Ct., Templeton ☎ 805/434–2541 ⊕ www. wildhorsewinery.com) helped establish the Central Coast as a significant winegrowing region. It's best known for classy pinot noir, chardonnay, and merlot; the owners also grow wonderful heirloom tomatoes. Small but swank **Justin Vineyards & Winery** (⊠ 11680 Chimney Rock Rd. ☎ 805/238–6932 or 800/726–0049 ⊕ www.justinwine.com) lies at the western end of Paso Robles wine country. It's well worth the 15-mi drive along quiet country roads through the hills: the property is widely acclaimed for its Bordeaux-style blends, and you can tour its 12,000 square feet of underground caves. There's also a tiny restaurant and a three-room luxury inn. Also tucked in the far-west hills of Paso Robles, **Tablas Creek Vineyard** (⊠ 9339 Adelaida Rd. ☎ 805/237–1231 ⊕ www. tablascreek.com) produces limited quantities of Châteauneuf-du-Pape style wines, using vines imported from Beaucastel, France, and organic farming techniques. Tours include a chance to graft your own grapevine.

Where to Stay & Eat

$$–$$$$ ✕ **McPhee's Grill.** The grain silos across the street and the floral oil-cloths on the tables belie the sophisticated cuisine at this casual eatery. Housed in an 1860s building in the tiny town of Templeton (just south of Paso Robles), the restaurant serves up creative, contemporary versions of traditional Western fare—such as steaks and chops with ancho-chile apricot glaze. ⊠ *416 Main St., Templeton* ☎ *805/ 434–3204* ▭ *AE, D, MC, V.*

$–$$$ ✕ **Bistro Laurent.** Owner-chef Laurent Grangien has devised a winning menu for his authentic, unpretentious French bistro, set in an 1890s brick building across from City Park. Traditional dishes like osso buco, cassoulet, rack of lamb, vichyssoise, and onion soup are featured, but there are also contemporary specials and wines from around the world. With advance notice, Grangien will prepare you a picnic basket; if you'd rather lunch indoors, you can try Le Petit Marcel, a tiny nook next door to the main restaurant that's open just for lunch Monday–Saturday ⊠ *1202 Pine St., at 12th St.* ☎ *805/226–8191* ▤ *MC, V* ☉ *Closed Sun.*

¢ ✕ **Joe's Place.** You might have to wait for a seat at this downtown greasy spoon with its long counter and few tables, but locals swear it serves the best breakfast in town. Joe's is famous for its biscuits, sausage gravy, and spicy sauces; try the spicy chilaquiles. The lunch menu includes hefty burritos, sandwiches, burgers, salads, and chili. ⊠ *608 12th St.* ☎ *805/238–5637* ▤ *MC, V* ☉ *No dinner.*

$$$$ ▦ **Villa Toscana.** The Weyrich family of Martin & Weyrich Winery created this Tuscan-style village smack in the middle of their vineyard. The eight comfy, ultraposh suites are differently decorated, but all have huge baths with oversized whirlpool tubs, spacious sitting areas, and balconies overlooking the vineyard—brilliant at sunrise. Spa treatments can be arranged in your suite. The private, guests-only Bistro Restaurant serves elaborate breakfasts, as well as afternoon wine and hors d'oeuvres. For the ultimate getaway, stay in the Winemaker's Residence, a 3,500-square-foot apartment with a full kitchen and a private balcony with hot tub. ⊠ *4230 Buena Vista Rd., 93446* ☎ *805/238–5600* 🖷 *805/238–5605* ⊕ *www.myvillatoscana.com* ⇨ *8 suites, 1 apartment* ⌂ *Restaurant, in-room data ports, in-room hot tubs, microwaves, refrigerators, cable TV with movies, in-room VCRs, pool, massage, lounge, Internet; no smoking* ▤ *AE, D, MC, V* ❙❙❙ *BP.*

$$$–$$$$ ▦ **Summerwood Inn.** Rooms at this elegant B&B, set next to the Summerwood Winery, have different wine themes. The Merlot and Bordeaux rooms have king-size cherrywood sleigh beds and are decorated in jewel tones. For ultimate self-indulgence, stay in the Cabernet Suite (actually more of an extra-large room) with private deck and luxurious bath. All units have gas fireplaces and balconies overlooking the vineyards, and include a cooked-to-order breakfast. ⊠ *2130 Arbor Rd., 1 mi west of U.S. 101 at Hwy. 46 W and Arbor Rd., 93446* ☎ *805/227–1111* 🖷 *805/227–1112* ⊕ *www.summerwoodwine.com* ⇨ *9 rooms* ⌂ *Cable TV; no smoking* ❙❙❙ *BP* ▤ *AE, MC, V.*

$–$$ ▦ **Paso Robles Inn.** In the 1890s, the Paso Robles Inn was a luxurious destination for visitors seeking rejuvenation in the town's hot springs. In 1940 a fire destroyed all but the west wing of the original hotel; the restored wing is now this inn's centerpiece. Pipes bring hot spring water into private spa tubs here, and the oversize rooms also have fireplaces. In the newer wings, many units also have fireplaces and hot tubs, and some overlook oak-studded gardens, streams, and waterfalls. ⊠ *1103 Spring St., 93446* ☎ *805/238–2660 or 800/676–1713* 🖷 *805/238–4707* ⊕ *www. pasoroblesinn.com* ⇨ *98 rooms* ⌂ *Restaurant, coffee shop, some in-room hot tubs, some microwaves, refrigerators, cable TV, pool, gym, hot tub, lounge, meeting rooms, no-smoking rooms* ▤ *AE, D, DC, MC, V.*

¢ ▦ **Adelaide Inn.** Family-owned and -managed, the Adelaide Inn provides hotel-style amenities at motel prices. It's a clean, friendly oasis behind a conglomerate of gas stations and fast-food outlets just west of the U.S.

101 and Highway 46E interchange. ✉ *1215 Ysabel Ave., 93446* ☎ *805/ 238–2770 or 800/549–7276* 🖷 *805/238–3497* ⊕ *www.adelaideinn.com* ⚏ *In-room data ports, refrigerators, cable TV with movies, miniature golf, putting green, pool, hot tub, laundry facilities, laundry service, business services, no-smoking rooms* 🍴 *CP* ⊟ *AE, D, DC, MC, V.*

Cambria

㉙ *28 mi west of Paso Robles on Hwy. 46; 20 mi north of Morro Bay on Hwy. 1.*

Cambria, an artists' colony with many late-Victorian homes, is divided into the newer West Village and the original East Village. Each section has B&Bs, restaurants, art galleries, and shops. The local architecture and street names—as well the name of the town—reflect the legacy of the Welsh miners who settled here in the 1890s. Motels line Moonstone Beach Drive, which runs along the coast. **Leffingwell's Landing** (✉ North end of Moonstone Beach Dr. ☎ 805/927–2070), a state picnic ground, is a good place for examining tidal pools and watching otters as they frolic in the surf. Footpaths wind along the beach side of the drive.

Nit Wit Ridge. Arthur Beal (aka Captain Nit Wit, Der Tinkerpaw) spent 51 years building a home and terraced rock garden out of collected materials: rocks, wood, abalone shells, car parts, TV antennas—you name it. The site, just above Cambria's West Village, is now a State Historical Landmark. You can join a 45-minute guided tour of the house and grounds and hear all about Beal's colorful life. Reservations are required. ✉ *881 Hillcrest Dr.* ☎ *805/927–2690* 🖃 *Free* ☉ *Daily by appointment; tours usually every hr 10–4.*

Where to Stay & Eat

$$$–$$$$ ╳ **The Sea Chest.** By far the best seafood restaurant in town, this clifftop inn serves all kinds of fish from local waters and around the world. The oyster bar is highly recommended, both by those who live here and those who visit. If you can, come early to catch the sunset through the windows. ✉ *6216 Moonstone Beach Dr.* ☎ *805/927–4514* ⚏ *Reservations not accepted* ⊟ *No credit cards* ☉ *Closed Tues. Sept.–May. No lunch.*

$$–$$$ ╳ **The Black Cat.** At this swank, intimate French-American bistro, you can sink into the leopard-print cushions, order tapas, and choose from an eclectic list of local and imported wines. Chef Brett Albrecht's menu changes daily, but typically includes creative fusion dishes such as sea bass with homemade chorizo or duck with cherry sauce and couscous. Next door, the Black Market sells specialty foods. ✉ *1602 Main St.* ☎ *805/ 927–1600* ⚏ *Reservations essential* ⊟ *AE, D, DC, MC, V* ☉ *Closed Tues. and Wed. No lunch.*

$–$$$ ╳ **Hamlet Restaurant at Moonstone Gardens.** Set amid 3 acres of luxuriant gardens, the Hamlet has an enchanting patio, and stunning ocean views from the upstairs dining room and bar. Entrées range from calamari and hamburgers to rack of lamb. Be sure to save room for the homemade lemon ice cream. ✉ *Exotic Gardens Rd., Hwy. 1 at Moonstone Beach Dr.* ☎ *805/927–3535* ⊟ *AE, MC, V.*

$–$$ ✕ **Robin's.** A truly multiethnic dining experience awaits you at this antiques-filled restaurant, where you can choose from tandoori prawns, quesadillas, Thai red curry, numerous salads (more for lunch than dinner), vegetarian entrées, hamburgers, and some truly fine desserts. The eclectic menu emphasizes fresh fish and produce from local markets. ⊠ *4095 Burton Dr.* ☎ *805/927–5007* ▭ *MC, V.*

¢–$$$ ✕▥ **Cambria Pines Lodge.** With lots of recreational facilities and a range of accommodations—from rustic cabin rooms to elegant fireplace suites—this 26-acre retreat just steps from downtown is an especially good choice for families. The gorgeous gardens—dedicated to roses, succulents, organic vegetables, and many other themes—also attract garden-lovers and wedding parties. Local seafood, wines, and organic produce, along with filet mignon and prime rib, lure diners from throughout the area to the in-house lodge restaurant ($$). Bands play light rock, folk, and other music in the lounge. ⊠ *2905 Burton Dr.* ☎ *805/927–4200* 🖷 *805/927–4016* ⊕ *www.cambriapineslodge.com* 🗭 *52 rooms, 19 cabins, 55 suites* ⟂ *Restaurant, some microwaves, some refrigerators, cable TV, some in-room VCRs, indoor pool, exercise equipment, hair salon, hot tub, sauna, spa, volleyball, bar, lounge, meeting rooms, some pets allowed; no smoking* ▭ *AE, D, DC, MC, V.*

$$$–$$$$ ▥ **Fog Catcher Inn.** The landscaped gardens and 10 thatch-roofed buildings here evoke an English country village. Most rooms have ocean views. All have fireplaces and are decorated in floral chintz with light-color wood furniture. ⊠ *6400 Moonstone Beach Dr., 93428* ☎ *805/927–1400 or 800/425–4121* 🖷 *805/927–0204* ⊕ *www.fogcatcherinn.com* 🗭 *51 rooms, 9 suites* ⟂ *Minibars, refrigerators, cable TV, pool, hot tub, some pets allowed; no smoking* ▭ *AE, D, DC, MC, V* ⦿ *CP.*

$$$ ▥ **J. Patrick House.** Monterey pines and flower gardens surround this Irish-theme country inn, which sits on a hilltop near Cambria's East Village. All rooms—one in the main log house, along with a sunny dining room and parlor, and seven in a separate carriage house—have traditional country furnishings, wood-burning fireplaces, private baths, and window seats. The full vegetarian breakfast always includes a hot entrée such as eggs Florentine or French toast. ⊠ *2990 Burton Dr., 93428* ☎ *805/927–3812 or 800/341–5258* ⊕ *www.jpatrickhouse.com* 🗭 *8 rooms* ⟂ *Concierge; no room phones, no room TVs, no smoking* ▭ *MC, V* ⦿ *BP.*

$–$$ ▥ **Moonstone Landing.** Friendly staff, lots of amenities and reasonable rates make this new motel a good choice if you want to stay right on Moonstone Beach. All rooms have Mission-style furnishings, DVD players, fireplaces, and Internet access. A few of the deluxe rooms, which have marble whirlpool tubs and showers, offer some of the best views in Cambria. ⊠ *6240 Moonstone Beach Dr., 93428* ☎ *805/927–0012 or 800/830–4540* 🖷 *805/927–0014* ⊕ *www.moonstonelanding. com* 🗭 *29 rooms* ⟂ *Microwaves, refrigerators, cable TV with movies, in-room VCRs, hot tub, Internet; no smoking* ▭ *AE, MC, D, V* ⦿ *CP.*

$–$$ ▥ **San Simeon Pines Seaside Resort.** Amid 9 acres of pines and cypress, this motel-style resort has its own golf course and is directly across from Leffingwell's Landing. The accommodations include cottages with landscaped backyards. Parts of the complex are for adults only; others are reserved for families. ⊠ *7200 Moonstone Beach Dr., San Simeon 93452*

☎ *805/927–4648* ∰ *www.sspines.com* ↪ *58 rooms* ⚲ *Cable TV, 9-hole golf course, pool, croquet, shuffleboard, playground, meeting rooms; no smoking* ▤ *AE, MC, V.*

¢–$ ⊞ **Bluebird Inn.** Rooms at this garden motel near Cambria's East Village include simply furnished doubles and nicer creek-side suites with patios, fireplaces, refrigerators, and TVs with VCRs. The Bluebird isn't the fanciest place, but if you don't require beachside accommodations, it's a bargain. The wooded gardens are beautiful. ✉ *1880 Main St., 93428* ☎ *805/927–4634 or 800/552–5434* 🖷 *805/927–5215* ∰ *www.bluebirdmotel.com* ↪ *37 rooms* ⚲ *Some refrigerators, cable TV, some in-room VCRs, no-smoking rooms* ▤ *AE, D, MC, V.*

San Simeon

㉚ *Hwy. 1, 9 mi north of Cambria and 65 mi south of Big Sur.*

Whalers founded San Simeon in the 1850s but had virtually abandoned the town by the time Senator George Hearst reestablished it 20 years later. Hearst bought up most of the surrounding ranch land, built a 1,000-foot wharf, and turned San Simeon into a bustling port. His son, William Randolph Hearst, further developed the area during the construction of Hearst Castle. Today the town, which is 3 mi east of the castle estate, is basically a row of gift shops, restaurants, and motels along Highway 1.

A large and growing colony (at last count 5,000–7,000 members) of elephant seals gathers every year at ♡ **Piedras Blancas Elephant Seal Rook,** on the beaches near Piedras Blancas Lighthouse. The huge males with their pendulous, trunklike noses typically start appearing on shore in late November, and the females begin to arrive in December to give birth—most babies are born in the last two weeks of January. The newborn pups spend about four weeks nursing before their mothers head out to sea, leaving them on their own. The seals return once or twice in the spring and summer months to molt or rest, but not en masse as in winter. You can watch them from the bluffs just a few feet above the beach. Park at the vista point just south of Piedras Blancas Lighthouse (4½ mi north of Hearst San Simeon State Historical Monument) and follow the signs. Docents are often on hand to give background information and statistics. ✉ *Friends of the Elephant Seals, 250 San Simeon Ave., Suite 3, 93452* ☎ *805/924–1628* ∰ *www.elephantseal.org* ✇ *Free* ☉ *Daily.*

★ At **Hearst San Simeon State Historical Monument,** Hearst Castle sits in solitary splendor atop La Cuesta Encantada (the Enchanted Hill). Its buildings and gardens are spread over the 127 acres that were the heart of newspaper magnate William Randolph Hearst's 250,000-acre ranch. Hearst devoted nearly 30 years and about $10 million to building this elaborate estate. He commissioned renowned architect Julia Morgan—who was also responsible for buildings at the University of California at Berkeley—but he was very much involved with the final product, a hodgepodge of Italian, Spanish, Moorish, and French styles. The 115-room main building and three huge "cottages" are connected by terraces and staircases and surrounded by pools, gardens, and statuary. In its heyday the castle was a playground for Hearst and his guests, many of whom were Hollywood celebrities. Construction began in 1919 and was never officially completed. Work was halted in 1947 when Hearst had to leave San Simeon due to failing health. The Hearst family presented the property to the state of California in 1958.

Buses from the visitor center zigzag up the hillside to the neoclassical extravaganza above. Guides conduct four different daytime tours and (part of the year) one evening tour of various parts of the main house and grounds. Tour No. 1, the most basic, is recommended for newcomers. Daytime tours take about two hours. Docents in period costume portray Hearst's guests and staff for the slightly longer evening tour, which begins at sunset. All tours include a half-mile walk and between 150 and 400 stairs. A 40-minute film shown at a giant-screen theater gives a sanitized version of Hearst's life and of the construction of the castle. Reservations for the tours, which can be made up to eight weeks in advance, are necessary. ⊠ *San Simeon State Park, 750 Hearst Castle Rd.* ☎ *805/927–2020 or 800/444–4445* ⊕ *www.hearstcastle.com* ✉ *Daytime tours $24, evening tours $30* ⊙ *Tours daily 8:20–3:20, later in summer; additional tours take place most Fri. and Sat. evenings Mar.–May and Sept.–Dec.* ⊟ *AE, D, MC, V.*

Fodor'sChoice
★
On one of California's most spectacular drives, **Highway 1** snakes north along the coast from San Simeon toward Big Sur. Even more rugged than the coastline north of Big Sur, this stretch of oceanfront is a rocky world of mountains, cliffs, and beaches. On some of the beaches, huge elephant seals lounge nonchalantly, seemingly oblivious to the attentions of rubberneckers. But it's best not to get too close to them—although they may look lethargic, they're still wild animals. ⊠ *Hwy. 1 from San Simeon to Big Sur.*

Where to Stay & Eat

$–$$ ✕☒ **Best Western Cavalier Oceanfront Resort.** Reasonable rates, an oceanfront location, evening bonfires, and well-equipped rooms—some with wood-burning fireplaces and private patios—make this motel a good choice. If you've just finished a tour of Hearst San Simeon State Historical Monument and want to eat lunch or dinner right away, stop at the Cavalier Restaurant (¢–$$$; 805/927–3276) for grilled steak or seafood. ⊠ *9415 Hearst Dr., 93452* ☎ *805/927–4688 or 800/826–8168* ☎ *805/927–6472* ⊕ *www.cavalierresort.com* ⌨ *90 rooms* ₫ *2 restaurants, in-room data ports, refrigerators, cable TV, in-room VCRs, 2 pools, gym, hot tub, laundry facilities, meeting rooms, some pets allowed; no smoking* ⊟ *AE, D, DC, MC, V.*

BIG SUR COASTLINE

Long a retreat of artists and writers, the Big Sur area contains ancient forests and a rugged coastline that residents have protected from overdevelopment. Much of the region lies within several state parks and the more than 165,000-acre Ventana Wilderness, itself part of the Los Padres National Forest.

Julia Pfeiffer Burns State Park

㉛ *52 mi north of San Simeon on Hwy. 1.*

Julia Pfeiffer Burns State Park offers some fine hiking, from an easy half-mile stroll with marvelous coastal views to a strenuous 6-mi trek through the redwoods. The big attraction here, an 80-foot waterfall that drops into the ocean, gets crowded in the summer; still, it's clear why Julia Pfeiffer Burns, the daughter of one of the area's first white settlers, liked to sit here and contemplate nature. Migrating whales, as well as harbor seals and sea lions, can sometimes be spotted not far from shore. ✉ *Big Sur Station #1, 93920* ☎ *831/667–2315* ⊕ *www.parks.ca.gov* 🔳 *$5* ⊘ *Daily sunrise–sunset.*

Where to Eat

$$–$$$ ✕ **Ragged Point Inn.** A good place to brunch or lunch near the area's parks, this restaurant, perched on the cliffs near the southernmost end of Big Sur, is not as fancy as the places farther north. But neither are the prices, and the food—sandwiches, salads, pastas, and fish and meat dishes—is tasty. ✉ *Hwy. 1, about 35 mi south of Julia Pfeiffer Burns State Park* ☎ *805/927–5708* ▭ *AE, D, MC, V.*

Big Sur

㉝ *Hwy. 1, 8½ mi north of Pfeiffer Big Sur State Park; 26 mi south of Carmel.*

The countercultural spirit of Big Sur—which is not so much a town as it is a string of coast-hugging properties along Highway 1—is alive and well today. It is largely influenced by the presence of the Esalen Institute, a center for alternative education and East–West philosophical study that first became wildly popular in the 1960s. Back then, people flocked to Esalen to explore the idea of higher consciousness, and to take the waters at the property's hot springs. Today, there are many posh resorts hidden among the redwoods of Big Sur, where well-heeled urbanites can seek body-and-soul invigoration and gaze at some of the country's most spectacular views.

★ The graceful arc of **Bixby Creek Bridge** (✉ Hwy. 1, 13 mi south of Carmel) is a photographer's dream. Built in 1932, it spans a deep canyon, more than 100 feet wide at the bottom. From the parking area on the north side you can admire the view or walk across the 550-foot span. **Point Sur State Historic Park,** a century-old lighthouse, still stands watch from atop a large volcanic rock. Four lighthouse keepers lived here with their families until 1974, when the light station became automated. Their homes and working spaces are open to the public on 2½- to 3-hour ranger-led tours. Considerable walking, including up two stairways, is involved. Strollers are not allowed; you'll have to carry small children in a backpack. ✉ *Hwy. 1, 19 mi south of Carmel* ☎ *831/625–4419* ⊕ *www.cal-parks.ca.gov* 🔳 *$5* ⊘ *Tours generally Nov.–Mar., Sat. 10 and 2, Sun. 10; Apr.–Oct., Wed. 10 and 2, Sat. 10 and 2, Sun. 10; call to confirm.*

Pfeiffer Big Sur State Park

32 *11 mi north of Julia Pfeiffer Burns State Park on Hwy. 1.*

A short hiking trail at Pfeiffer Big Sur State Park ($5 per vehicle for day use) leads through a redwood-filled valley to a waterfall. You can double back or continue on the more difficult trail along the valley wall for views of the treetops. You can stop in at the Big Sur Station visitor center, off Highway 1, less than ½ mi south of the park entrance, for information about the entire area. ⊠ *47225 Hwy. 1* ☎ *831/667–2315* ⊕ *www.parks.ca.gov* ⊘ *Daily 8–4:30.*

Through a hole in one of the big rocks at secluded **Pfeiffer Beach,** you can watch the waves break first on the sea side and then on the beach side. The 2-mi road from the highway to the beach descends sharply. ⊠ *Off Hwy. 1, ½ mi south of Big Sur Station* 🖼 *$5 per vehicle, day use.*

Where to Stay & Eat

$–$$$ ✕ **Nepenthe.** This property, once owned by Orson Welles and Rita Hayworth, has what may be the best coastal view between San Francisco and Los Angeles. The food is overpriced but good; there are burgers, sandwiches, and salads for lunch, and fresh fish and hormone-free steaks for dinner. For real drama, though, settle on the terraced deck in the late afternoon, order a glass from the extensive wine list, and watch the sun slip into the Pacific Ocean. The adjacent outdoor Café Kevah serves breakfast and lunch. ⊠ *Hwy. 1, 2½ mi south of Big Sur Station* ☎ *831/667–2345* ▤ *AE, MC, V.*

$$$$ ✕🖼 **Post Ranch Inn.** This luxurious retreat, designed exclusively for
Fodor'sChoice adult getaways, has remarkably environmentally conscious architecture.
★ The redwood guesthouses, all of which have views of the sea or the mountains, blend almost invisibly into a wooded cliff 1,200 feet above the ocean. Each unit has its own fireplace, stereo, private deck, and massage table. On-site activities include everything from yoga to star-gazing. The inn's restaurant, Sierra Mar ($$$$), serves cutting-edge American food at lunch and dinner, including a stellar four-course prix-fixe menu. ⊠ *Hwy. 1, 1½ mi south of the Pfeiffer Big Sur State Park entrance, 93920* ☎ *831/667–2200 or 800/527–2200* 🖷 *831/667–2824* ⊕ *www. postranchinn.com* ↩ *30 units* ⟡ *Restaurant, in-room hot tubs, refrigerators, 2 pools, gym, spa, bar, library, Internet; no room TVs, no smoking* ▤ *AE, MC, V* ⦿ *BP.*

$$$$ ✕🖼 **Ventana Inn & Spa.** Hundreds of celebrities, from Oprah Winfrey
Fodor'sChoice to Sir Anthony Hopkins, have escaped to Ventana, a romantic resort
★ on 243 tranquil acres 1,200 foot above the Pacific. The activities here are purposely limited. You can sunbathe (there is a clothing-optional deck and pool), walk or ride horses in the nearby hills, or pamper yourself with mind-and-body treatments at the Allegria Spa or in your own private quarters. All rooms have walls of natural wood and cool tile floors; some have private hot tubs on their patios. The inn's Cielo restaurant ($$$$) showcases fine California cuisine and wine. ⊠ *Hwy. 1, ⅕ mi south of Pfeiffer Big Sur State Park, 93920* ☎ *831/667–2331 or 800/628–6500* 🖷 *831/667–2419* ⊕ *www.ventanainn.com* ↩ *29 rooms, 31 suites, 3*

houses ⚑ *Restaurant, in-room VCRs, 2 pools, gym, 2 Japanese baths, sauna, spa, bar, library; no TVs in some rooms, no smoking* ☰ *AE, D, DC, MC, V* ✆ *2-night minimum stay on weekends and holidays; children allowed only in houses* ❍ *BP.*

$–$$$ ✕☲ **Deetjen's Big Sur Inn.** This historic 1930s Norwegian-style property is endearingly rustic and charming, especially if you're not too attached to creature comforts. The room doors lock only from the inside, and your neighbors can often be heard through the walls. Still, Deetjen's is a special place. Its buildings are nestled in the redwoods, and many have their own fireplaces. The restaurant ($$–$$$) in the main house serves roast duck, steak, and rack of lamb for dinner and wonderfully light and flavorful pancakes for breakfast. ✉ *Hwy. 1, 3½ mi south of the Pfeiffer Big Sur State Park entrance, 93920* ☎ *831/667–2377 inn, 831/667– 2378 restaurant* 🖷 *831/667–0466* ⊕ *www.deetjens.com* ✆ *20 rooms* ⚑ *Restaurant; no room phones, no room TVs, no smoking* ☰ *MC, V.*

$$–$$$ ☲ **Big Sur Lodge.** The motel-style cottages here, which sit in a meadow surrounded by trees in Pfeiffer Big Sur State Park, make it a good choice for families. Some rooms have fireplaces, and some have kitchens. ✉ *47225 Hwy. 1 (Pfeiffer Big Sur State Park entrance), 93920* ☎ *831/ 667–3100 or 800/424–4787* 🖷 *831/667–3110* ⊕ *www.bigsurlodge. com* ✆ *61 rooms* ⚑ *Restaurant, grocery, some kitchenettes, seasonal pool, meeting rooms; no room phones, no room TVs, no smoking* ☰ *AE, MC, V.*

$–$$ ☲ **Big Sur River Inn.** The Big Sur River flows past the forested grounds of this property. In summer you can sip afternoon drinks on the riverbanks in summer, or lounge around the swimming pool. Some rooms are merely functional, but others are very pretty; ask for one of the upper-floor rooms that's paneled in gnarled redwood. ✉ *Hwy. 1, 2 mi north of the Pfeiffer Big Sur State Park entrance, 93920* ☎ *831/667–2700* 🖷 *831/667–2743* ⊕ *www.bigsurriverinn.com* ✆ *14 rooms, 6 suites* ⚑ *Restaurant, pool, bar; no room phones, no room TVs, no smoking* ☰ *AE, MC, V.*

¢–$ ☲ **Glen Oaks Motel.** At this simple, adobe brick-and-redwood building in the heart of Big Sur, you can choose between comfortable motel-style rooms and frontier-style cottages in the woods. All are decorated with photos of Big Sur land and seascapes; the cottages have gas fireplaces. ✉ *Hwy. 1, 1 mi north of the Pfeiffer Big Sur State Park entrance, 93920* ☎ *831/667–2105* 🖷 *831/667–1105* ⊕ *www.glenoaksbigsur.com* ✆ *15 rooms, 2 cottages* ⚑ *Restaurant; no room phones, no room TVs, no smoking* ☰ *No credit cards.*

⚠ **Pfeiffer Big Sur State Park.** Redwood trees tower over this large campground. It's often crowded in summer, so reserve a site as far ahead as possible. There are no hookups. ⚑ *Flush toilets, dump station, drinking water, guest laundry, showers, fire grates, fire pits, picnic tables, food service, public telephone, general store, ranger station* ✆ *218 sites* ✉ *Hwy. 1, 8½ mi south of Point Sur State Historic Park* ☎ *800/444– 7275 for reservations* ⊕ *www.parks.ca.gov* ▣ *$15–$20.*

THE CENTRAL COAST A TO Z

To research prices, get advice from other travelers, and book travel arrangements, visit ⊕ *www.fodors.com*

AIRPORTS & TRANSFERS

America West Express, American Eagle, Delta/Delta Connection, Horizon Air, and United Express fly to Santa Barbara Municipal Airport, 12 mi from downtown. American Eagle, Mesa/America West, and Skywest/United Express provide service to San Luis Obispo County Regional Airport, 3 mi from downtown San Luis Obispo. *See* Air Travel *in* Smart Travel Tips A to Z for airline phone numbers.

Santa Barbara Airbus shuttles travelers between Santa Barbara and Los Angeles for $40 one-way and $75 round-trip (slight discount with 24-hour notice, larger discount for groups of six or more). The Santa Barbara Metropolitan Transit District Bus 11 runs every 30 minutes from the airport to the downtown transit center. A taxi between the airport and the hotel district runs $15 to $20.

🛈 **Santa Barbara Municipal Airport** ⊠ 500 Fowler Rd., Santa Barbara ☎ 805/683-4011 ⊕ www.flysba.com. **Santa Barbara Airbus** ☎ 805/964-7759, 800/733-6354, 800/423-1618 in CA ⊕ www.sbairbus.com. **Santa Barbara Metropolitan Transit District** ☎ 805/683-3702 ⊕ www.sbmtd.gov. **San Luis Obispo County Regional Airport** ⊠ 903-5 Airport Dr., San Luis Obispo ☎ 805/781-5205 ⊕ www.sloairport.com.

BUS TRAVEL

Greyhound provides service from San Francisco and Los Angeles to San Luis Obispo, Ventura, and Santa Barbara. From Monterey and Carmel, Monterey-Salinas Transit operates buses to Big Sur between May and mid-October. From San Luis Obispo, Central Coast Transit runs buses around Santa Maria and out to the coast. Santa Barbara Metropolitan Transit District provides local service. The State Street and Waterfront shuttles cover their respective sections of Santa Barbara during the day. South Coast Area Transit buses serve the entire Ventura County region.

🛈 **Central Coast Transit** ☎ 805/541-2228 ⊕ www.slorta.org. **Greyhound** ☎ 800/231-2222 ⊕ www.greyhound.com. **Monterey-Salinas Transit** ☎ 831/899-2555 ⊕ www.mst.org. **San Luis Obispo Transit** ☎ 805/541-2877 ⊕ www.slorta.org. **Santa Barbara Metropolitan Transit District** ☎ 805/683-3702 or 805/963-3364 ⊕ www.sbmtd.gov. **South Coast Area Transit** ☎ 805/643-3158 for Oxnard and Ventura ⊕ www.scat.org.

CAR RENTAL

Most major car-rental companies have offices in San Luis Obispo, Santa Barbara, and Ventura. *See* Car Rental *in* Smart Travel Tips A to Z for national rental agency phone numbers.

CAR TRAVEL

Highway 1 and U.S. 101 run north–south and more or less parallel along the Central Coast, with Highway 1 hugging the coast and U.S. 101 running inland. The best way to see the most dramatic section of the Central Coast, the 70 mi between Big Sur and San Simeon, is by heading south on Highway 1—you'll be on the ocean side of the road and will get the best views. Don't expect to make good time along here: the road is narrow and twisting with a single lane in each direction, making it difficult to pass the many lumbering RVs. In fog or rain the drive can be downright nerve-racking. Once you start south from Carmel, there is no route east from Highway 1 until Highway 46 heads inland from Cambria to connect with U.S. 101. Along some stretches farther south, Highway 1 and U.S. 101 join and run together for a while. At Morro Bay, Highway 1 moves inland for 13 mi and connects with U.S. 101 at San Luis Obispo. From here south to Pismo Beach the two highways run concurrently. South of Pismo Beach to Las Cruces the roads separate, then run together all the way to Oxnard. Along any stretch where they are separate, U.S. 101 is the quicker route.

U.S. 101 and Highway 1 will get you to the Central Coast from Los Angeles and San Francisco. If you are coming from the east, you can take Highway 46 west from I–5 in the Central Valley (near Bakersfield) to U.S. 101 at Paso Robles, where it becomes narrower as it continues to the coast, intersecting Highway 1 a few miles south of Cambria. Highway 33 heads south from I–5 at Bakersfield to Ojai. About 60 mi north of Ojai, Highway 166 leaves Highway 33, traveling due west through the Sierra Madre to Santa Maria at U.S. 101 and continuing west to Highway 1 at Guadalupe. South of Carpinteria, Highway 150 winds from Highway 1/U.S. 101 through sparsely populated hills to Ojai. From Highway 1/U.S. 101 at Ventura, Highway 33 leads to Ojai and the Los Padres National Forest. South of Ventura, Highway 126 runs east from Highway 1/U.S. 101 to I–5.

🚗 Road Conditions **Caltrans** ☎ 800/427-7623 ⊕ www.dot.ca.gov/hq/roadinfo.

EMERGENCIES
In case of emergency dial 911.

🚗 Hospitals **Big Sur Health Center** ⊠ Hwy. 1¼ mi south of River Inn, Big Sur ☎ 831/667-2580 is open weekdays 10–5. **Cottage Hospital** ⊠ Pueblo and Bath Sts., Santa Barbara ☎ 805/682-7111, 805/569-7210 for emergency. **Sierra Vista Regional Medical Center** ⊠ 1010 Murray Ave., San Luis Obispo ☎ 805/546-7600.

TOURS
Cloud Climbers Jeep and Wine Tours offers four types of daily tours: wine tasting, mountain, sunset, and a discovery tour for families. These trips to the Santa Barbara/Santa Ynez mountains and wine country are conducted in open-air, six-passenger jeeps. Fares range from $69 to $95 per adult. The company also arranges biking, horseback riding, and trap-shooting tours by appointment. Breakaway Tours and Event Planning can take you on a customized tour to wineries, Hearst Castle, and other attractions in San Luis Obispo County and as far south as the Santa Ynez Valley. Vehicles range from a 14-passenger van to full-size motor coaches; fares vary. Wine Adventures operates customized Santa Barbara County tours and narrated North County wine country tours in 25-passenger mini-coaches. Fares for the wine tours are $79 per person.

Spencer's Limousine & Tours offers customized tours of the city of Santa Barbara and wine country via sedan, limousine, van, or minibus. A four-hour basic tour with at least four participants costs about $50 per person. Sultan's Limousine Service has a fleet of super stretches; each can take up to eight passengers on Paso Robles and Edna Valley–Arroyo Grande wine tours and tours of the San Luis Obispo County coast. Hiring a limo for a four-hour wine country tour typically costs $360–$410 with tip. The Wine Affair runs daily 5½-hour bus tours through Paso Robles wine country. Fees are $39 per person.

🚌 **Cloud Climbers Jeep and Wine Tours** ☎ 805/965-6654 ⊕ www.ccjeeps.com. **Breakaway Tours and Event Planning** ☎ 805/783-2929 or 800/799-7657 ⊕ www. breakaway-tours.com. **Spencer's Limousine & Tours** ✉ Santa Barbara ☎ 805/884-9700 ⊕ www.spencerslimo.com. **Sultan's Limousine Service** ✉ Paso Robles ☎ 805/466-3167 ⊕ www.sultanslimo.com. **Wine Adventures** ✉ 3463 State St., #228, Santa Barbara ☎ 805/965-1074 ⊕ www.welovewines.com. **The Wine Affair** ✉ Cypress Cove Inn 6348 Moonstone Beach Dr., Cambria ☎ 805/927-2600 or 800/568-8517 ⊕ www. moonstonehotels.com.

TRAIN TRAVEL

The Amtrak *Coast Starlight,* which runs between Los Angeles and Seattle via Oakland, stops in Paso Robles, San Luis Obispo, Santa Barbara, and Oxnard. Amtrak runs several *Pacific Surfliner* trains daily between San Luis Obispo, Santa Barbara, Los Angeles, and San Diego. Metrolink Regional Rail Service trains connect Ventura and Oxnard with Los Angeles and points between.

🚆 **Amtrak** ☎ 800/872-7245, 805/963-1015 in Santa Barbara, 805/541-0505 in San Luis Obispo ⊕ www.amtrakcalifornia.com. **Metrolink** ☎ 800/371-5465 [within service area], 213/347-2800 ⊕ www.metrolinktrains.com.

VISITOR INFORMATION

🛈 **Cambria Chamber of Commerce** ☎ 805/927-3624 ⊕ www.cambriachamber.org. **Central Coast Tourism Council** ✉ Box 14011, San Luis Obispo 93406 ☎ 805/934-2129 ⊕ www.centralcoast-tourism.com. **Ojai Valley Chamber of Commerce** ☎ 805/646-8126 ⊕ www.ojaichamber.org. **Oxnard Visitors Bureau** ✉ 200 W. 7th St. ☎ 805/385-7545 or 800/269-6273 ⊕ www.oxnardtourism.com. **Paso Robles Visitors and Conference Bureau** ✉ 1225 Park St. ☎ 805/238-0506 or 800/406-4040 ⊕ www.visitpasoroblesca. com. **Paso Robles Vintners and Growers Association** ✉ 1940 Spring St. ☎ 805/239-8463 ⊕ www.pasowine.com. **San Luis Obispo Chamber of Commerce** ✉ 1039 Chorro St. ☎ 805/781-2777 ⊕ www.visitslo.com. **San Luis Obispo Vintners and Growers Association** ☎ 805/541-5868 ⊕ www.slowine.com. **San Luis Obispo County Visitors and Conference Bureau** ✉ 1037 Mill St. ☎ 805/541-8000 or 800/634-1414 ⊕ www. sanluisobispocounty.com. **Santa Barbara Conference and Visitors Bureau** ✉ 12 E. Carrillo St. ☎ 805/966-9222 or 800/927-4688 ⊕ www.santabarbaraca.com. **Santa Barbara County Vintners' Association** ☎ 805/688-0881 or 800/218-0881 ⊕ www.sbcountywines. com. **Santa Ynez Valley Visitors Association** ☎ 800/269-6273 ⊕ www.syvva.com. **Solvang Conference & Visitors Bureau** ✉ 1511 Mission Dr. ☎ 805/688-6144 or 800/468-6765 ⊕ www.solvangusa.com. **Ventura Visitors and Convention Bureau** ✉ 89 S. California St., #C ☎ 805/648-2075 or 800/333-2989 ⊕ www.ventura-usa.com.

MONTEREY BAY

FROM CARMEL TO SANTA CRUZ

10

Updated by
Lisa M.
Hamilton

FAMOUS FOR ITS SCENIC BEAUTY, the Monterey Peninsula is also steeped in history. The town of Monterey was California's first capital, and the Carmel Mission was headquarters for California's mission system. John Steinbeck immortalized the area in *Cannery Row,* and Robert Louis Stevenson strolled its streets, gathering inspiration for *Treasure Island.*

Blessed with abundant and diverse life both above and below its waters, present-day Monterey Bay includes both resplendent marine habitats and luxurious resorts. The towns that make up the area, and which are set along the 90-mi crescent of coastline like jewels in a tiara, combine the funky beachcomber elements of California culture with refined elegance.

About 2,500 years ago the Ohlone Indians recognized the region's potential and became its first settlers. Europeans followed in 1542, when the white-sand beaches, pine forests, and rugged coastline captivated explorer Juan Rodríguez Cabrillo, who claimed the Monterey Peninsula for Spain. Spanish missionaries, Mexican rulers, and land developers have come and gone throughout the centuries since then, yet the area's natural assets and historic sites remain remarkably untarnished.

In 1770 Monterey became the capital of the Spanish territory of Alta California. Commander Don Gaspar de Portola established the first of California's four Spanish presidios here, and Father Junípero Serra founded the second of 21 Franciscan missions (he later moved it to Carmel). Mexico revolted against Spain in 1810; a decade later, a treaty was signed and the newly independent Mexico claimed Alta California as its own. By the mid-1840s Monterey had grown into a lively seaport that attracted Yankee sea traders, and land from California to Texas was coveted by the United States. On July 7, 1846, Commodore John Sloat raised the flag of the United States over the Custom House. For Anglos, being governed by the United States proved far more profitable than being aligned with Mexico. But for the Ohlone Indians, the transition to American rule was disastrous: state and federal laws passed in the late 1800s took away rights and property that had been granted them by Spain and Mexico.

California's constitution was framed in Monterey's Colton Hall, but the town was nearly forgotten once gold was discovered at Sutter's Mill on the American River. After the gold rush, the state capital moved to Sacramento, while in Monterey the whaling industry boomed until the early 1900s. Tourists began to arrive at the turn of the 20th century with the opening of the Del Monte Hotel, the most palatial resort the West Coast had ever seen. Writers and artists such as John Steinbeck, Henry Miller, Robinson Jeffers, and Ansel Adams also discovered Monterey Bay, adding their legacy to the region while capturing its magic on canvas, paper, and film. In the 1920s and 1930s Cannery Row's sardine industry took off, but by the late 1940s and early 1950s the fish had disappeared. The causes are still in dispute, though overfishing, water contamination, and a change in ocean currents were the likely culprits.

Today the Monterey Peninsula's diverse cultural and maritime heritage is evident in the town's 19th-century buildings and busy harbor. Can-

Although it's compact, the Monterey Peninsula is chock-full of diversions. In Carmel you can shop 'til you drop, and when summer and weekend hordes overwhelm the town's clothing boutiques, art galleries, housewares outlets, and gift shops, you can slip off to enjoy the coast. Fans of Victorian architecture will want to search out the many fine examples in Pacific Grove. If you have an interest in California history and historic preservation, the place to start is Monterey, with its adobe buildings along the downtown Path of History.

10

Numbers in the text correspond to numbers in the margin and on the Monterey Bay and Monterey maps.

If you have
3 days

Start in ► 🖼 **Carmel** ❶ to visit Carmel Mission and Tor House if it's open. Leave yourself plenty of time to browse the shops of Ocean Avenue, then stroll over to Scenic Road and spend time on Carmel Beach before dinner. On the following day, motor up **17-Mile Drive** ❸ in the morning, stopping at Point Lobos State Reserve to take in the views. That afternoon visit a few of the buildings in 🖼 **Monterey** ❺–⓴. Spend your final day along Cannery Row and **Fisherman's Wharf** ⓱. Don't miss the **Monterey Bay Aquarium** ⓳. Catch the sunset from the bustling wharf or slip into the serene bar at the Monterey Plaza Hotel and Spa.

If you have
5 days

Spend your first day and second morning following the itinerary above, but instead of continuing to Monterey on your second afternoon, explore the shoreline and Victorian houses of 🖼 **Pacific Grove** ❹. Start Day 3 at the **Monterey Bay Aquarium** ⓳ and enjoy the afternoon either relaxing on the waterfront in 🖼 **Monterey** ❺–⓳ or getting a glimpse of the city's fascinating past at Monterey State Historic Park. The next morning, get up-close and personal with Monterey Bay marine life by boarding a whale-watching or other cruise vessel at **Fisherman's Wharf** ⓱. Spend the afternoon on the wharf and along Cannery Row. On your last day, head up the Monterey–Salinas Highway and stop for a taste of wine at Ventana Vineyards, then visit **San Juan Bautista** ㉑, a classic mission village.

nery Row has been reborn as a tourist attraction with shops, restaurants, hotels, and the Monterey Bay Aquarium. The bay itself is protected by the Monterey Bay National Marine Sanctuary, the nation's largest undersea canyon—which is bigger and deeper than the Grand Canyon. The preserve supports a rich brew of marine life, from fat, barking sea lions to tiny plantlike anemones. Indeed, nature is still at its best around Monterey Bay, as the view from almost anywhere along Highway 1 will show you.

Exploring Monterey Bay

The individual charms of its towns complement Monterey Bay's natural beauty. Santa Cruz sits at the northern tip of the crescent formed by

Monterey Bay; the Monterey Peninsula, including Monterey, Pacific Grove, and Carmel, occupies the southern end. In between, Highway 1 (sometimes also called the Pacific Coast Highway) cruises along the coastline, passing windswept beaches piled high with sand dunes. Along the route are artichoke fields and the towns of Watsonville and Castroville.

About the Restaurants

Between San Francisco and Los Angeles, some of the finest dining to be found is around Monterey Bay. The surrounding waters are full of fish, wild game roams the foothills, and the inland valleys are the vegetable basket of California; nearby Castroville dubs itself the "artichoke capital of the world." Except at beachside stands and inexpensive eateries, where anything goes, casual but neat resort wear is the norm. The few places where more formal attire is required are noted.

About the Hotels

Monterey-area accommodations range from no-frills motels to luxurious resorts. Many of the area's small inns and B&Bs pamper the traveler in grand style, serving not only full breakfasts but afternoon or early evening wine and hors d'oeuvres. Pacific Grove has quietly turned itself into the region's B&B capital; Carmel also has fine B&Bs. Truly lavish resorts, with everything from featherbeds to heated floors, cluster in exclusive Pebble Beach and pastoral Carmel Valley. Many of these accommodations are not suitable for children, so if you're traveling with kids, be sure to ask before you book.

Around Monterey Bay high season runs April through October. Rates during winter, especially at the larger hotels, may drop by 50% or more, and B&Bs often offer midweek specials in the off-season. However, even the simplest of the area's lodgings are expensive, and most properties require a two-night stay on weekends.

WHAT IT COSTS					
	$$$$	$$$	$$	$	¢
RESTAURANTS	over $30	$23–$30	$16–$22	$10–$15	under $10
HOTELS	over $250	$176–$250	$121–$175	$90–$120	under $90

Restaurant prices are for a main course at dinner, excluding sales tax of 7½%–8¼% (depending on location). Hotel prices are for two people in a standard double room in high season, excluding service charges and 10%–10½% tax.

Timing

Summer is peak season, with crowds everywhere and generally mild weather. A sweater or windbreaker is nearly always necessary along the coast, where a cool breeze usually blows and fog is on the way in or out. Inland, temperatures in Salinas or Carmel Valley can be 15 or 20 degrees warmer than those in Carmel and Monterey. Off-season, from November through April, fewer people visit and the mood is mellower. Rainfall is heaviest in January and February.

10

Fine Dining In California you can eat well, and around Monterey Bay you can eat very, very well. Monterey and Carmel fairly burst at the seams with exceptional restaurants, with Monterey's Montrio Bistro—a temple of California cuisine—leading the pack. In Monterey you can also find excellent Mediterranean (Stokes Restaurant & Bar) and French (Fresh Cream) cooking. For more great French food head to Carmel, where Casanova presents southern French and northern Italian cuisine, and Robert's Bistro offers classic French fare. Even in Santa Cruz, a town not famed for its restaurants, you can please your palate at the Mediterranean-inspired Bittersweet Bistro, and at Theo's, which specializes in seasonal American dishes.

Great Golf Since the opening of the Del Monte Golf Course in 1897, golf has been an integral part of the Monterey Peninsula's social and recreational scene. Pebble Beach's championship courses host prestigious tournaments, and though the greens fees at these courses can run well over $200, elsewhere on the peninsula you'll find less expensive—but still challenging and scenic—options. Many hotels will help with golf reservations or have golf packages; inquire when you book your room.

Whale-Watching On their annual migration between the Bering Sea and Baja California, thousands of gray whales pass close by the Monterey coast. They are sometimes visible through binoculars from shore, but a whale-watching cruise is the best way to get a close look at these magnificent mammals. The migration south takes place from December through March. January is prime viewing time. The migration north occurs from March through June. In addition, some 2,000 blue whales and 600 humpbacks pass the coast and are easily spotted in late summer and early fall. Smaller numbers of minke whales, orcas, sperm whales, and fin whales have been sighted in mid-August. Even if no whales surface, bay cruises almost always encounter other enchanting sea creatures, such as sea otters, sea lions, and porpoises.

MONTEREY PENINSULA

If you want to see small towns and spectacular vistas, be sure to visit the stretch of coast between Big Sur and Monterey. Each of the communities here is distinct, and you'll see everything from thatch-roofed cottages to palatial estates, rolling hills to craggy cliffs.

Carmel

▶ ❶ *26 mi north of Big Sur on Hwy. 1.*

Although the community has grown quickly through the years and its population quadruples with tourists on weekends and in summer, Carmel retains its identity as a quaint village. Self-consciously charming, the town is populated by many celebrities, major and minor, and has more than its share of quirky ordinances. For instance, women wearing high heels do not have the right to pursue legal action if they trip and fall on the cobblestone streets; drivers who hit a tree and leave the scene are charged with hit-and-run; live music is banned in local watering holes; and ice-cream parlors are not allowed to sell cones—only cups—because children might drop them, leaving unsightly puddles on the pretty streets. Buildings still have no street numbers—and consequently no mail delivery (if you really want to see the locals, go to the post office). Artists started this community, and their legacy is evident in the numerous galleries. Wandering the side streets off Ocean Avenue, where you can poke into hidden courtyards and stop at cafés for tea and crumpets, is a pleasure.

Downtown Carmel's chief lure is shopping, especially along its main street, **Ocean Avenue,** between Junipero Avenue and Camino Real; the architecture here is a mishmash of ersatz Tudor, Mediterranean, and other styles. **Carmel Plaza** (⊠ Ocean and Junipero Aves. ☎ 831/624–0138), in the east end of the village proper, holds more than 50 shops and restaurants.

Long before it became a shopping and browsing destination, Carmel was an important religious center during the establishment of Spanish California. That heritage is preserved in the Mission San Carlos Borroméo del Rio Carmelo, more commonly known as the **Carmel Mission.** Founded in 1771, it served as headquarters for the mission system in California under Father Junípero Serra. Adjoining the stone church is a tranquil garden planted with California poppies. Museum rooms at the mission include an early kitchen, Serra's spartan sleeping quarters, and the first college library in California. ⊠ *3080 Rio Rd., at Lasuen Dr.* ☎ *831/624–3600* ⊕ *www.carmelmission.org* 🖾 *$4* ☉ *Weekdays 9:30–4:30, weekends 10:30–4:30.*

Scattered throughout the pines in Carmel are houses and cottages originally built for the writers, artists, and photographers who discovered the area decades ago. Among the most impressive dwellings is **Tor House,** a stone cottage built in 1919 by poet Robinson Jeffers on a craggy knoll overlooking the sea. Portraits, books, and unusual art objects fill the low-ceiling rooms. The highlight of the small estate is Hawk Tower, a detached edifice set with stones from the Carmel coastline—as well as one from the Great Wall of China. The docents who lead tours (six persons maximum) are well informed about the poet's work and life. Reservations for tours are recommended. ⊠ *26304 Ocean View Ave.* ☎ *831/ 624–1813* ⊕ *www.torhouse.org* 🖾 *$7* ☞ *No children under 12* ☉ *Tours on the hr Fri.–Sat. 10–3.*

Carmel's greatest beauty is its rugged coastline, with pine and cypress forests and countless inlets. **Carmel Beach** (⊠ End of Ocean Ave.), an easy walk from downtown shops, has sparkling white sands and magnificent sunsets. **Carmel River State Beach** stretches for 106 acres along Carmel Bay. On sunny days the waters appear nearly as turquoise as those of the Caribbean. The sugar-white beach is adjacent to a bird sanctuary, where you might spot pelicans, kingfishers, hawks, and sandpipers. ⊠ *Off Scenic Rd. south of Carmel Beach* ☎ *831/624–4909 or 831/649– 2836* ⊕ *www.cal-parks.ca.gov* 🖾 *Free* ☉ *Daily 9* AM*–sunset.*

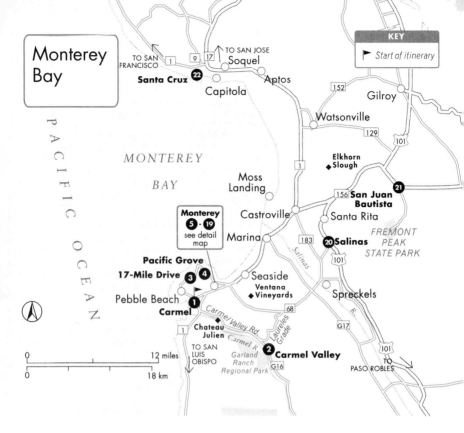

★ **Point Lobos State Reserve,** a 350-acre headland harboring a wealth of marine life, lies a few miles south of Carmel. The best way to explore the reserve is to walk along one of its many trails. The Cypress Grove Trail leads through a forest of Monterey cypress (one of only two natural groves remaining), which clings to the rocks above an emerald-green cove. Sea Lion Point Trail is a good place to view sea lions. From those and other trails you may also spot otters, harbor seals, and (during winter and spring) migrating whales. An additional 750 acres of the reserve is an undersea marine park open to qualified scuba divers. Arrive early (or in late afternoon) to avoid crowds; the parking lots fill up. No pets are allowed. ✉ *Hwy. 1* ☎ *831/624–4909, 831/624–8413 for scuba-diving reservations* ⊕ *www.pointlobos.org* ✍ *$5 per vehicle* ⊙ *Apr.–Oct., daily 9–7; Nov.–Mar., daily 9–5.*

Where to Stay & Eat

★ **$$$–$$$$** ✕ **Casanova.** Southern French and northern Italian cuisine come together at Casanova, one of the most romantic restaurants in Carmel. A heated outdoor garden and more than 1,800 domestic and imported vintages from the hand-dug wine cellar enhance the dining experience. A highlight of the seasonal menu is the grilled veal chop with sautéed morel mushrooms, but all entrées come with an antipasto plate and choice of appetizers. Private dining and a special menu are offered at Van Gogh's

Table, a very special table imported from France's Auberge Ravoux. ⊠ *5th Ave. between San Carlos and Mission Sts.* ☎ *831/625–0501* ⌕ *Reservations essential* ▭ *AE, MC, V.*

$$–$$$$ ✕ **L'Escargot.** Chef-owner Kericos Loutas personally cares for each plate of food served at this romantic and thankfully unpretentious French restaurant. Take his recommendation and order the duck confit in puff pastry or the bone-in steak in truffle butter; or, if you can't decide, choose the three-course prix fixe dinner. Service is warm and attentive. ⊠ *Mission St. between 4th and 5th Aves.* ☎ *831/620–1942* ⌕ *Reservations essential* ▭ *AE, DC, MC, V* ☯ *Closed Tues. No lunch.*

$$–$$$$ ✕ **Kurt's Carmel Chop House.** USDA-prime steaks and chops are cooked over almond and oak woods at this stylish steak house. There are also many seafood dishes and inventive appetizers, but few vegetarian choices. ⊠ *5th Ave. and San Carlos* ☎ *831/625–1199* ⌕ *Reservations essential* ▭ *AE, MC, V* ☯ *No lunch.*

$$–$$$ ✕ **Anton and Michel.** Expect superb European cuisine at this elegant restaurant in Carmel's shopping district. The rack of lamb and chateaubriand are especially good; both are carved at the table. The ultimate treats, however, are the flaming desserts. You can dine in the outdoor courtyard in summer. ⊠ *Mission St. and 7th Ave.* ☎ *831/624–2406* ⌕ *Reservations essential* ▭ *AE, D, DC, MC, V.*

$$–$$$ ✕ **Flying Fish.** Simple in appearance yet bold with its flavors, this Japanese–California seafood restaurant has quickly established itself as one of Carmel's most inventive eateries. Among the best entrées is the almond-crusted sea bass served with Chinese cabbage and rock shrimp stir-fry. ⊠ *Mission St. between Ocean and 7th Aves.* ☎ *831/625–1962* ▭ *AE, D, MC, V* ☯ *Closed Tues. No lunch.*

$$–$$$ ✕ **Grasing's Coastal Cuisine.** Chef Kurt Grasing's contemporary adaptations of European provincial and American cooking include a roast rack of lamb marinated in pomegranate juice, and medallions of pork with shiitake mushrooms, bacon, peas, and polenta. A casually elegant dining room, gracious service, and an extensive wine list make this one of Carmel's top restaurants. ⊠ *6th Ave. and Mission St.* ☎ *831/624–6562* ⌕ *Reservations essential* ▭ *AE, D, DC, MC, V.*

$–$$$ ✕ **Bahama Billy's.** The energy is electric at this always-bustling Caribbean bar and restaurant. An excellent and diverse menu combined with a lively crowd make this a prime spot for fun and good eating in Carmel. Particularly good is the ahi tuna, which is rolled in Jamaican jerk seasoning, seared, and served with aioli. Because it's outside the area covered by the town's strict zoning laws, there is often live music in the bar. ⊠ *Barnyard Shopping Center, Hwy. 1 and Carmel Valley Rd.* ☎ *831/626–0430* ⌕ *Reservations essential* ▭ *AE, D, MC, V.*

$–$$$ ✕ **Caffè Napoli.** Redolent of garlic and olive oil, this small, atmospheric Italian restaurant is a favorite of locals, who come for the crisp-crusted pizzas, house-made pastas, and fresh seafood. The grilled artichokes and fresh salmon are specialties of the house, but it's hard to go wrong with anything on the menu. There's also a good Italian wine list. ⊠ *Ocean Ave. and Lincoln St.* ☎ *831/625–4033* ⌕ *Reservations essential* ▭ *MC, V.*

$–$$$ ✕ **Lugano Swiss Bistro.** Fondue is the centerpiece here. The house specialty is a version made with Gruyère, Emmentaler, and Appenzeller. Rotisserie-broiled meats are also popular here, and include rosemary chicken, plum-basted duck, and fennel pork loin. Ask for a table in the back room, which contains a hand-painted street scene of Lugano. ⊠ *The Barnyard, Hwy. 1 and Carmel Valley Rd.* ☎ *831/626–3779* ☷ *AE, DC, MC, V* ⊘ *Closed Mon.*

¢–$$$ ✕ **Jack London's.** If anyone's awake after dinner in Carmel, he's at Jack London's. This publike local hangout is the only Carmel restaurant to serve food until midnight. The menu includes everything from snacks like nachos to steaks. ⊠ *Su Vecino Court on Dolores St. between 5th and 6th Aves.* ☎ *831/624–2336* ☷ *AE, D, DC, MC, V.*

¢–$$ ✕ **The Cottage Restaurant.** If you're looking for the best breakfast in Carmel, this is the place: the menu offers six different preparations of eggs Benedict, and all kinds of sweet and savory crepes. Sandwiches and homemade soups are served at lunch, and there are dinner specials on weekends, but you'll have the best meals here in the morning. ⊠ *Lincoln St. between Ocean and 7th Aves.* ☎ *831/625–6260* ☷ *MC, V* ⊘ *No dinner Sun.–Wed.*

$$$–$$$$ ✕🏨 **Park Hyatt Carmel Highlands Inn.** High on a hill overlooking the Pacific, this place has superb views. Accommodations include king rooms with fireplaces, suites with personal Jacuzzis, and full town houses with all the perks. The excellent prix fixe menus at the inn's Pacific's Edge restaurant ($$$$; jackets recommended) blend French and California cuisine; the sommelier helps choose the perfect wines. ⊠ *120 Highlands Dr., 93921* ☎ *831/620–1234, 800/682–4811, 831/622–5445 for restaurant* 🖷 *831/626–1574* ⊕ *highlandsinn.hyatt.com* ⤳ *37 rooms, 105 suites* ♨ *2 restaurants, room service, in-room data ports, in-room safes, some in-room hot tubs, some kitchenettes, refrigerators, cable TV with movies, some in-room VCRs, golf privileges, tennis privileges, pool, gym, 3 hot tubs, bicycles, 2 lounges, piano, babysitting, laundry service, concierge, Internet, business services, meeting rooms, some pets allowed (fee); no a/c, no smoking* ☷ *AE, D, DC, MC, V.*

$$$$ 🏨 **Tradewinds Inn.** This hotel has been around long enough to have been a favorite of Bing Crosby's, but it has never looked like this before. The 1950s-era motel reopened in fall of 2003 with a new glamorous decor inspired by the South Seas. Each room has a tabletop fountain and orchids, and the courtyard houses waterfalls and a meditation garden. Amazingly, this chic boutique hotel has been owned by the same family since it opened in 1959. It's one of the few of its kind in downtown Carmel. ⊠ *Mission St. at 3rd Ave., 93921* ☎ *831/624–2776 or 800/624–6665* 🖷 *831/624–0634* ⊕ *www.carmeltradewinds.com* ⤳ *26 rooms, 2 suites* ♨ *In-room data ports, some in-room hot tubs, minibars, cable TV, outdoor hot tub, massage, concierge, business services, meeting room, some pets allowed (fee); no a/c, no smoking* ☷ *AE, MC, V* ⊚ *CP.*

$$$–$$$$ 🏨 **Tickle Pink Inn.** Atop a towering cliff, this inn has views of the Big Sur coastline, which you can contemplate from your private balcony. After falling asleep to the sound of surf crashing below, you'll wake to a continental breakfast and the morning paper in bed. If you prefer the company of fellow travelers, breakfast is also served buffet-style in the lounge, as is complimentary wine and cheese in the afternoon. Many rooms have wood-burning fireplaces, and there are six luxurious spa suites. ⊠ *155 Highlands Dr., 93923* ☎ *831/624–1244 or 800/635–4774*

🖨 831/626–9516 ⊕ *www.ticklepink.com* 📳 *24 rooms, 11 suites* 🛇 *Fans, in-room data ports, some in-room hot tubs, refrigerators, cable TV, in-room VCRs, outdoor hot tub, concierge; no a/c, no smoking* ⊟ *AE, DC, MC, V* ▮◉▮ *CP.*

$$$–$$$$ 🖫 **La Playa Hotel.** Norwegian artist Christopher Jorgensen built this property's original structure in 1902 for his bride, a member of the Ghirardelli chocolate clan. The property has since undergone many additions and now resembles a Mediterranean estate. Though some rooms are small and could use a few modern amenities, the location more than compensates. You can also opt for a cottage; most have full kitchens and wood-burning fireplaces, and all have patios or terraces. ✉ *Camino Real at 8th Ave., 93921* ☎ *831/624–6476 or 800/582–8900* 🖨 *831/624–7966* ⊕ *www.laplayahotel.com* 📳 *75 rooms, 5 cottages* 🛇 *Restaurant, refrigerators, cable TV, pool, massage, bar, laundry service, business services, meeting rooms; no a/c, no smoking* ⊟ *AE, DC, MC, V.*

★ $$–$$$$ 🖫 **Cobblestone Inn.** Stones from the Carmel River cover the exterior walls of this English-style country inn; inside, the work of local painters is on display. Guest rooms have stone fireplaces, as well as thick quilts on the beds. Antiques in the cozy sitting room, and afternoon wine and hors d'oeuvres, contribute to the homey feel. ✉ *Junipero Ave. between 7th and 8th Aves., 93921* ☎ *831/625–5222 or 800/833–8836* 🖨 *831/625–0478* ⊕ *www.foursisters.com* 📳 *22 rooms, 2 suites* 🛇 *In-room data ports, refrigerators, cable TV, bicycles; no a/c, no smoking* ⊟ *AE, DC, MC, V* ▮◉▮*BP.*

$$–$$$$ 🖫 **Cypress Inn.** The decorating style here is luxurious but refreshingly simple. Rather than chintz and antiques, there are wrought-iron bed frames, wooden armoires, and rattan armchairs. Some rooms have fireplaces, some hot tubs, and one (room 215) even has its own sunny veranda that looks out on the ocean. The in-town location makes walking to area attractions easy, and pet owners will be pleased to hear that dog-loving owner (and movie star) Doris Day welcomes animal companions. ✉ *Lincoln St. and 7th Ave., Box Y, 93921* ☎ *831/624–3871 or 800/443–7443* 🖨 *831/624–8216* ⊕ *www.cypress-inn.com* 📳 *33 rooms, 1 suite* 🛇 *Fans, in-room data ports, some in-room hot tubs, cable TV, bar, laundry service, concierge, some pets allowed (fee); no a/c in some rooms, no smoking* ⊟ *AE, MC, V* ▮◉▮ *CP.*

$$–$$$$ 🖫 **Pine Inn.** A favorite with generations of Carmel visitors, the Pine Inn has Victorian-style furnishings, complete with grandfather clock, padded fabric wall panels, antique tapestries, and marble tabletops. Only four blocks from the beach, the property includes a brick courtyard of specialty shops and a modern Italian restaurant. ✉ *Ocean Ave. and Monte Verde St., 93921* ☎ *831/624–3851 or 800/228–3851* 🖨 *831/624–3030* ⊕ *www.pine-inn.com* 📳 *43 rooms, 6 suites* 🛇 *Restaurant, fans, some in-room data ports, some refrigerators, cable TV, bar, laundry service, meeting room; no a/c, no smoking* ⊟ *AE, D, DC, MC, V.*

$–$$$$ 🖫 **Carmel River Inn.** Besides attracting those looking for a relative bargain in pricey Carmel, this half-century-old inn appeals to travelers who enjoy a bit of distance from the madding crowd. There are 10 acres of gardens on the property, but area beaches are only 1½ mi away. The blue-and-white motel at the front of the property contains units with cable TV, small refrigerators, and coffeemakers. Cabins out back sleep up to six; some have fireplaces and kitchens. ✉ *Hwy. 1 at Carmel River*

Bridge, 93922 ☎ *831/624–1575 or 800/882–8142* 🖷 *831/624–0290* ⊕ *www.carmelriverinn.com* ➹ *19 rooms, 24 cabins* ♢ *Some microwaves, refrigerators, cable TV, pool, Internet, some pets allowed (fee), no-smoking rooms; no a/c* ☰ *MC, V.*

$–$$$$ ⊡ **Mission Ranch.** The property at Mission Ranch is gorgeous and includes a sprawling sheep pasture, bird-filled wetlands, and a sweeping view of the ocean. The ranch is nicely decorated but low-key, with a 19th-century farmhouse as the central building. Other accommodations include rooms in a converted barn, and several cottages, many with fireplaces. Though the ranch belongs to movie star Clint Eastwood, relaxation, not celebrity, is the focus here. ⊠ *26270 Dolores St., 93923* ☎ *831/624–6436 or 800/538–8221* 🖷 *831/626–4163* ➹ *31 rooms* ♢ *Restaurant, fans, in-room data ports, some in-room hot tubs, some refrigerators, cable TV, 6 tennis courts, pro shop, gym, piano bar; no a/c, no smoking* ☰ *AE, MC, V* ⦿**l** *CP.*

$–$$ ⊡ **Lobos Lodge.** The white-stucco motel units here are set amid cypress, oaks, and pines on the edge of the business district. All accommodations have fireplaces and some have private patios. ⊠ *Monte Verde St. and Ocean Ave., 93921* ☎ *831/624–3874* 🖷 *831/624–0135* ⊕ *www.loboslodge.com* ➹ *28 rooms, 2 suites* ♢ *Fans, in-room data ports, refrigerators, cable TV, no-smoking rooms; no a/c* ☰ *AE, MC, V* ⦿**l** *CP.*

$–$$ ⊡ **Sea View Inn.** In a residential area a few hundred feet from the beach, this restored 1905 home has a double parlor with two fireplaces, Oriental rugs, canopy beds, and a spacious front porch. Afternoon tea and evening wine and cheese are offered daily. Because of the fragile furnishings and quiet atmosphere, families with kids will likely be more comfortable elsewhere. ⊠ *Camino Real between 11th and 12th Aves., 93921* ☎ *831/624–8778* 🖷 *831/625–5901* ⊕ *www.seaviewinncarmel.com* ➹ *8 rooms, 6 with private bath* ♢ *No a/c, no room phones, no room TVs, no smoking* ☰ *AE, MC, V* ⦿**l** *CP.*

$–$$ ⊡ **Tally Ho Inn.** Boasting an English garden courtyard, this is one of the few small hotels in Carmel's center with good views of the ocean. Penthouse units have fireplaces. ⊠ *Monte Verde St. and 6th Ave., 93921* ☎ *831/624–2232 or 877/482–5594* 🖷 *831/624–2661* ⊕ *www.tallyho-inn.com* ➹ *12 rooms, 2 suites* ♢ *Some fans, some in-room data ports, cable TV, laundry service; no a/c, no smoking* ☰ *AE, D, DC, MC, V* ⦿**l** *CP.*

The Arts

Carmel Bach Festival (☎ 831/624–2046 ⊕ www.bachfestival.org) has presented the works of Johann Sebastian Bach and his contemporaries in concerts and recitals since 1935. The festival runs for three weeks, starting mid-July. **Monterey County Symphony** (☎ 831/624–8511 ⊕ www.montereysymphony.org) performs classical concerts from October through May at the Sunset Community Cultural Center.

The **Pacific Repertory Theater** (☎ 831/622–0700 ⊕ www.pacrep.org) puts on the Carmel Shakespeare Festival from August through October and performs contemporary dramas and comedies at several area venues from February through July. **Sunset Community Cultural Center** (⊠ San Carlos St. between 8th and 10th Aves. ☎ 831/624–3996), which presents concerts, lectures, and headline performers, is the Monterey Bay area's top venue for the performing arts.

Shopping

ART GALLERIES **Carmel Art Association** (⊠ Dolores St. between 5th and 6th Aves. ☎ 831/624–6176 ⊕ www.carmelart.org) exhibits the paintings, sculptures, and prints of local artists. **Galerie Pleine Aire** (⊠ Dolores St. between 5th and 6th Aves. ☎ 831/625–5686) showcases oil paintings by a group of seven local artists. **Highlands Sculpture Gallery** (⊠ Dolores St. between 5th and 6th Aves. ☎ 831/624–0535) is devoted to contemporary indoor and outdoor sculpture, primarily works in stone, bronze, wood, metal, and glass. **Masterpiece Gallery** (⊠ Dolores St. and 6th Ave. ☎ 831/624–2163) shows early California impressionist art. **Photography West Gallery** (⊠ Ocean Ave. and Dolores St. ☎ 831/625–1587) exhibits photography by Ansel Adams and other 20th-century artists.

SPECIALTY SHOPS **Madrigal** (⊠ Carmel Plaza and Mission St. ☎ 831/624–3477) carries sportswear, sweaters, and accessories for women. **Mischievous Rabbit** (⊠ Lincoln Ave. between 7th and Ocean Aves. ☎ 831/624–6854) sells toys, nursery accessories, books, music boxes, china, and children's clothing, and specializes in Beatrix Potter items. **Pat Areias Sterling** (⊠ Ocean Ave. between Lincoln Ave. and Delores St. ☎ 831/626–8668) puts a respectfully modern spin on the Mexican tradition of silversmithing with its line of sterling silver belt buckles, jewelry, and accessories. **Shop in the Garden** (⊠ Lincoln Ave. between Ocean and 7th Aves. ☎ 831/624–6047) is an indoor-outdoor sculpture garden where you can buy fountains and other garden accoutrements. You'll hear the tinkle of its wind chimes before you see the courtyard establishment.

Carmel Valley

❷ *10 mi east of Carmel, Hwy. 1 to Carmel Valley Rd.*

Carmel Valley Road, which heads inland from Highway 1 south of Carmel, is the main thoroughfare through the town of Carmel Valley, a secluded enclave of horse ranchers and other well-heeled residents who prefer the area's sunny climate to the fog and wind on the coast. Tiny Carmel Valley Village, about 13 mi southeast of Carmel via Carmel Valley Road, has several crafts shops and art galleries. The Village is also home to the **Bernardus Tasting Room,** where you can sample many of the wines—including older vintages and reserves—from the nearby Bernardus Winery and Vineyard. ⊠ *5 W. Carmel Valley Rd.* ☎ *800/223–2533* ⊗ *Daily 11–5.*

Garland Ranch Regional Park (⊠ Carmel Valley Rd., 9 mi east of Carmel ☎ 831/659–4488 ⊕ www.mprpd.org/parks/garland.html) has hiking trails across nearly 4,500 acres of property. The beautiful **Château Julien** winery, recognized internationally for its chardonnays and merlots, gives tours on weekdays at 10:30 and 2:30 and weekends at 12:30 and 2:30, all by appointment. The tasting room is open daily. ⊠ *8940 Carmel Valley Rd.* ☎ *831/624–2600* ⊕ *www.chateaujulien.com* ⊗ *Weekdays 8–5, weekends 11–5.*

Where to Stay & Eat

$–$$ ✕ **Café Rustica.** Italian-inspired country cooking is the focus at this lively roadhouse. Specialties include roasted meats, pastas, and pizzas from the wood-fired oven. Because of the tile floors, it can get quite noisy inside; opt for a table outside if you want a quieter meal. ☒ *10 Delfino Pl.* ☎ *831/659–4444* ⚐ *Reservations essential* ☐ *MC, V* ☒ *Closed Wed.*

¢ ✕ **Wagon Wheel Coffee Shop.** This local hangout decorated with wagon wheels, cowboy hats, and lassos serves up terrific hearty breakfasts; *huevos rancheros* (Mexican-style fried eggs on corn tortillas, covered in a mild chile sauce), Italian sausage, trout and eggs, and biscuits and gravy all hit the spot. The lunch menu includes a dozen different burgers and other sandwiches. ☒ *Valley Hill Center, Carmel Valley Rd. next to Quail Lodge* ☎ *831/624–8878* ☐ *No credit cards* ☒ *No dinner.*

★ $$$$ ✕☐ **Bernardus Lodge.** Oenophiles and gourmands will appreciate the first-rate spa and outstanding cuisine at this luxury resort. Spacious guest rooms have vaulted ceilings, featherbeds, fireplaces, patios, and double-size bathtubs. Marinus, the intimate, formal dining room ($$$$; jacket recommended), emphasizes modern French cuisine. Chef Cal Stamenov is one of the area's masters; he changes the menu daily to reflect availability of local game and produce. ☒ *415 Carmel Valley Rd., 93924* ☎ *831/659–3131 or 888/648–9463* ⊟ *831/659–3529* ⊕ *www.bernardus. com* ⟿ *57 rooms* ⚐ *2 restaurants, room service, in-room data ports, minibars, refrigerators, cable TV with movies, some in-room VCRs, tennis court, pool, gym, hair salon, hot tub, sauna, spa, steam room, croquet, hiking, lawn bowling, bar, lobby lounge, laundry service, concierge, Internet, meeting room; no smoking* ☐ *AE, D, DC, MC, V.*

★ $$$$ ✕☐ **Quail Lodge.** On the grounds of a private country club, this resort gives you access to an 850-acre wildlife preserve frequented by deer and migratory fowl. Modern rooms with European styling are clustered in several low-rise buildings. Each room has a private deck or patio overlooking the golf course, gardens, or lake. The Covey at Quail Lodge ($$–$$$$; jacket recommended) serves continental cuisine in a romantic lakeside dining room. Standout dishes include rack of lamb, mustard-crusted salmon, and mousseline of sole. ☒ *8205 Valley Greens Dr., 93923* ☎ *831/624–1581 or 800/538–9516* ⊟ *831/624–3726* ⊕ *www. quaillodge.com* ⟿ *83 rooms, 14 suites* ⚐ *2 restaurants, room service, some fans, in-room data ports, some in-room faxes, some in-room safes, some in-room hot tubs, minibars, refrigerators, cable TV with movies and video games, 18-hole golf course, putting green, 4 tennis courts, pro shop, 2 pools, gym, hot tub, sauna, spa, steam room, bicycles, croquet, hiking, 2 bars, babysitting, laundry service, concierge, Internet, business services, meeting rooms, some pets allowed (fee), no-smoking rooms; no a/c in some rooms* ☐ *AE, DC, MC, V.*

$$$$ ☐ **Stonepine Estate Resort.** Set on 330 pastoral acres, this former estate
Fodor'sChoice of the Crocker banking family has been converted to an ultra-luxuri-
★ ous inn. The oak-paneled main château holds eight elegantly furnished rooms and suites, and a dining room for guests (although with advance reservations, it is also possible for nonguests to dine here). The property's "cottages" are equally opulent, each with its own luxurious identity (the Hermes House has four fireplaces and a 27-foot-high living room ceiling). Fresh flowers, afternoon tea, and evening champagne are offered daily. This is a quiet property, best suited to couples traveling without children. ☒ *150 E. Carmel Valley Rd., 93924* ☎ *831/659 2245* ⊟ *831/659–5160* ⊕ *www.stonepinecalifornia.com* ⟿ *8 rooms, 4 suites,*

3 cottages ⚘ Dining room, room service, fans, in-room data ports, some in-room safes, some in-room hot tubs, minibars, cable TV, in-room VCRs, 5-hole golf course, 2 tennis courts, 2 pools, gym, massage, mountain bikes, archery, hiking, horseback riding, library, piano, recreation room, laundry service, concierge, Internet; no a/c, no smoking ⊟ AE, MC, V ✺ BP.

$$–$$$ 🏨 **Carmel Valley Lodge.** This small inn has rooms surrounding a garden patio, and separate one- and two-bedroom cottages with fireplaces and full kitchens. ⊠ *8 Ford Rd., at Carmel Valley Rd. 93924* ☎ *831/659–2261 or 800/641–4646* 🖷 *831/659–4558* ⊕ *www.valleylodge.com* 🛏 *19 rooms, 4 suites, 8 cottages ⚘ Kitchenettes, refrigerators, cable TV, in-room VCRs, pool, exercise equipment, hot tub, sauna, horseshoes, Ping-Pong, Internet, some pets allowed (fee), no-smoking rooms; no a/c* ⊟ *AE, MC, V* ✺ *CP.*

Sports & the Outdoors

The **Golf Club at Quail Lodge** (⊠ 8000 Valley Greens Dr. ☎ 831/624–2770) incorporates several lakes into its course. Depending on the season and day of the week, greens fees range from $115 to $140 for guests and $125 to $175 for nonguests, including cart rental. **Rancho Cañada Golf Club** (⊠ 4860 Carmel Valley Rd., 1 mi east of Hwy. 1 ☎ 831/624–0111) is a public course with 36 holes, some of them overlooking the Carmel River. Fees range from $35 to $80, plus $34 for cart rental, depending on course and tee time.

17-Mile Drive

③ *Off North San Antonio Rd. in Carmel or off Sunset Dr. in Pacific*
Fodor'sChoice *Grove.*
★

Primordial nature resides in quiet harmony with palatial late 20th-century estates along 17-Mile Drive, which winds through an 8,400-acre microcosm of the Monterey coastal landscape. Dotting the drive are rare Monterey cypress, trees so gnarled and twisted that Robert Louis Stevenson described them as "ghosts fleeing before the wind." Some sightseers balk at the $8-per-car fee collected at the gates—this is the only private toll road west of the Mississippi—but most find the drive well worth the price. An alternative is to grab a bike: cyclists tour for free, as do those with confirmed lunch or dinner reservations at one of the hotels.

You can take in views of the impeccable greens at **Pebble Beach Golf Links** (⊠ 17-Mile Dr. near the Lodge at Pebble Beach ☎ 800/654–9300 ⊕ www.pebblebeach.com) over a drink or lunch at the Lodge at Pebble Beach. The ocean plays a major role in the 18th hole of the famed golf course. Each winter the course is the main site of the AT&T Pebble Beach Pro-Am (formerly the Bing Crosby Pro-Am), where show business celebrities and golf pros team up for one of the nation's most glamorous tournaments.

Many of the stately homes along 17-Mile Drive reflect the classic Monterey or Spanish mission style typical of the region. A standout is the **Crocker Marble Palace,** about a mile south of the Lone Cypress (see below). It's a private waterfront estate inspired by a Byzantine castle, easily identifiable by its dozens of marble arches.

Bird Rock, the largest of several islands at the southern end of the Monterey Country Club's golf course, teems with harbor seals, sea lions, cormorants, and pelicans. Sea creatures and birds—as well as some very friendly ground squirrels—also make use of **Seal Rock,** the largest of a group of islands south of Bird Rock. The most-photographed tree along 17-Mile Drive is the weather-sculpted **Lone Cypress,** which grows out of a precipitous outcropping above the waves about 2 mi south of Seal Rock. You can stop for a view of the Lone Cypress at a parking area, but you can't walk out to the tree.

Where to Stay & Eat

$$$$ ✕⊡ **Inn at Spanish Bay.** This resort sprawls across a breathtaking stretch of shoreline, and has lush, 600-square-foot rooms. Peppoli's restaurant ($–$$$), which serves Tuscan cuisine, overlooks the coast and the golf links; Roy's Restaurant ($–$$$) serves more casual and innovative Euro–Asian fare. When you stay here, you're also allowed privileges at the Lodge at Pebble Beach, which is under the same management. ⊠ *2700 17-Mile Dr., Pebble Beach 93953* ☎ *831/647–7500 or 800/ 654–9300* 🖷 *831/644–7960* ⊕ *www.pebblebeach.com* 🖙 *252 rooms, 17 suites* ♢ *3 restaurants, room service, in-room data ports, minibars, refrigerators, cable TV with movies and video games, in-room VCRs, 18-hole golf course, 8 tennis courts, pro shop, pool, fitness classes, health club, sauna, steam room, beach, bicycles, hiking, bar, lobby lounge, laundry service, concierge, Internet, business services, meeting rooms; no a/c, no smoking* ▤ *AE, D, DC, MC, V.*

★ $$$$ ✕⊡ **Lodge at Pebble Beach.** All rooms have fireplaces and many have wonderful ocean views at this circa 1919 resort. The golf course, tennis club, and equestrian center are posh. Overlooking the 18th green, the intimate Club XIX restaurant ($$$$; jackets recommended) serves expertly prepared French cuisine. When staying here, you also have privileges at the Inn at Spanish Bay. ⊠ *1700 17-Mile Dr., Pebble Beach 93953* ☎ *831/624–3811 or 800/654–9300* 🖷 *831/644–7960* ⊕ *www. pebblebeach.com* 🖙 *142 rooms, 19 suites* ♢ *3 restaurants, coffee shop, in-room data ports, some in-room hot tubs, minibars, refrigerators, cable TV with movies and video games, in-room VCRs, 18-hole golf course, 12 tennis courts, pro shop, pool, gym, health club, sauna, spa, beach, bicycles, horseback riding, 2 bars, lobby lounge, laundry service, concierge, Internet, business services, meeting rooms, some pets allowed; no a/c, no smoking* ▤ *AE, D, DC, MC, V.*

★ $$$$ ⊡ **Casa Palmero.** This exclusive spa resort evokes a stately Mediterranean villa. Rooms are decorated with sumptuous fabrics and fine art; each has a wood-burning fireplace and heated floor, and some have private outdoor patios with in-ground Jacuzzis. Complimentary cocktail service is offered each evening in the main hall and library. The spa is state-of-the-art, and you have use of all facilities at the Lodge at Pebble Beach and the Inn at Spanish Bay. ⊠ *1518 Cypress Dr., Pebble Beach 93953* ☎ *831/622–6650 or 800/654–9300* 🖷 *831/622–6655* ⊕ *www. pebblebeach.com* 🖙 *21 rooms, 3 suites* ♢ *Room service, in-room data ports, some in-room hot tubs, minibars, refrigerators, cable TV with* *movies and video games, in-room VCRs, golf privileges, pool, health club, spa, bicycles, billiards, lounge, library, laundry service, concierge, meeting rooms; no a/c, no smoking* ⊟ *AE, D, DC, MC, V.*

Sports & the Outdoors

GOLF The **Links at Spanish Bay** (⊠ 17-Mile Dr., north end ☎ 831/624–3811, 831/624–6611, or 800/654–9300), which hugs a choice stretch of shoreline, is designed in the rugged manner of a traditional Scottish course, with sand dunes and coastal marshes interspersed among the greens. Greens fees are $210, plus $25 for cart rental (cart included for resort guests); nonguests can reserve tee times up to two months in advance.

Pebble Beach Golf Links (⊠ 17-Mile Dr. near the Lodge at Pebble Beach ☎ 831/624–3811, 831/624–6611, or 800/654–9300) attracts golfers from around the world, despite greens fees of $350, plus $25 for an optional cart (complimentary cart for guests of the Pebble Beach and Spanish Bay resorts). Nonguests can reserve a tee time only one day in advance on a space-available basis (up to a year for groups); resort guests can reserve up to 18 months in advance.

Peter Hay (⊠ 17-Mile Dr. ☎ 831/625–8518 or 831/624–6611), a 9-hole, par-3 course, charges $20 per person, no reservations necessary. **Poppy Hills** (⊠ 3200 Lopez Rd., at 17-Mile Dr. ☎ 831/625–2035), a splendid 18-hole course designed in 1986 by Robert Trent Jones Jr., has greens fees of $125–$150; an optional cart costs $30. Individuals may reserve up to one month in advance, groups up to a year.

Spyglass Hill (⊠ Stevenson Dr. and Spyglass Hill Rd. ☎ 831/624–3811, 831/624–6611, or 800/654–9300) is among the most challenging Pebble Beach courses. With the first 5 holes bordering on the Pacific and the other 18 reaching deep into the Del Monte Forest, the views offer some consolation. Greens fees are $250; an optional cart costs $25 (the cart is complimentary for resort guests). Reservations are essential and may be made up to one month in advance (18 months for guests).

HORSEBACK
RIDING
The **Pebble Beach Equestrian Center** (⊠ Portola Rd. and Alva La. ☎ 831/624–2756) offers guided trail rides along the beach and through 26 mi of bridle trails in the Del Monte Forest.

Pacific Grove

❹ *3 mi north of Carmel on Hwy. 68.*

If not for the dramatic strip of coastline in its backyard, Pacific Grove could easily pass for a typical small town in the heartland. The town, which began as a summer retreat for church groups more than a century ago, recalls its prim and proper Victorian heritage in its host of tiny board-and-batten cottages and stately mansions.

Even before the church groups flocked here, Pacific Grove had been receiving thousands of annual pilgrims in the form of bright orange-and-black monarch butterflies. Known as Butterfly Town USA, Pacific Grove is the winter home of monarchs that migrate south from Canada and the Pacific Northwest to take residence in pine and eucalyptus groves from October through March. The sight of a mass of butterflies hanging from the branches like a long, fluttering veil is unforgettable.

A prime way to enjoy Pacific Grove is to walk or bicycle along its 3 mi of city-owned shoreline, a cliff-top area following Ocean View Boulevard that is landscaped with native plants and has benches on which to sit and gaze at the sea. You can spot many types of birds here, including colonies of web-foot cormorants crowding the massive rocks rising out of the surf.

Among the Victorians of note is the **Pryor House** (⊠ 429 Ocean View Blvd.), a massive, shingled, private residence with a leaded- and beveled-glass doorway. **Green Gables** (⊠ 5th St. and Ocean View Blvd. ☎ 831/375–2095), a romantic Swiss Gothic–style mansion with peaked gables and stained-glass windows, is a B&B.

🕲 The view of the coast is gorgeous from **Lovers Point Park** (☎ 831/648–5730), on Ocean View Boulevard midway along the waterfront. The park's sheltered beach has a children's pool and picnic area. Glass-bottom boat rides, which provide views of the plant and sea life below, are offered
🕲 in summer. At the 1855-vintage **Point Pinos Lighthouse,** the oldest continuously operating lighthouse on the West Coast, you can learn about the lighting and foghorn operations and wander through a small museum containing U.S. Coast Guard memorabilia. ⊠ *Lighthouse Ave. off Asilomar Blvd.* ☎ *831/648–5716* ⊕ *www.pgmuseum.org* 🎟 *$2* ⊙ *Thurs.–Mon. 1–4.*

Monarchs sometimes vary their nesting sites from year to year, but the **Monarch Grove Sanctuary** (⊠ 1073 Lighthouse Ave., at Ridge Rd. ⊕ www. pgmuseum.org) is a fairly reliable spot for viewing the butterflies between October and February. If you are in Pacific Grove when the monarch butterflies aren't, you can view the well-crafted butterfly tree
🕲 exhibit at the **Pacific Grove Museum of Natural History.** The museum also displays 400 mounted birds and has a touch gallery for children. ⊠ *165 Forest Ave.* ☎ *831/648–3116* ⊕ *www.pgmuseum.org* 🎟 *Free* ⊙ *Tues.–Sun. 10–5.*

Asilomar State Beach (☎ 831/372–4076), a beautiful coastal area, is on Sunset Drive between Point Pinos and the Del Monte Forest in Pacific Grove. The 100 acres of dunes, tidal pools, and pocket-size beaches form one of the region's richest areas for marine life—including surfers, who migrate here most winter mornings.

Where to Stay & Eat

$$–$$$$ ✕ **Old Bath House.** This romantic converted bathhouse overlooks the water at Lovers Point. The menu makes the most of local produce and seafood (such as Monterey Bay shrimp) and specializes in game meats. There is also a less expensive menu for late-afternoon diners. ⊠ *620 Ocean View Blvd.* ☎ *831/375–5195* ▤ *AE, D, DC, MC, V* ⊙ *No lunch.*

$–$$$ ✕ **Fandango.** With its stone walls and country furniture, Fandango has the earthy feel of a southern European farmhouse. The menu follows suit: calf liver and onions, and paella served in a skillet, are popular choices. For those who prefer more decadent fare, there's caviar and an impressive selection of vintage champagnes. ⊠ *223 17th St.* ☎ *831/372–3456* ☐ *AE, D, DC, MC, V.*

$–$$$ ✕ **Passion Fish.** South American artwork and artifacts decorate the room, but both Latin and Asian flavors infuse the dishes here. Chef Ted Wolters shops at local farmers' markets several times a week to find the best produce available. He pairs it with fresh local fish and creative sauces; try the crispy squid with spicy orange-cilantro vinaigrette. ⊠ *701 Lighthouse Ave.* ☎ *831/655–3311* ☐ *AE, D, MC, V* ⊘ *Closed Tues. No lunch.*

$$ ✕ **Joe Rombi's.** Pastas, fish, and veal are the specialties at this modern trattoria, which is the best in town for Italian food. The sautéed veal with red-wine reduction, mozzarella, and herbs is especially good. The staff here is convivial and welcoming. ⊠ *208 17th St.* ☎ *831/373–2416* ☐ *AE, MC, V* ⊘ *Closed Mon. and Tues.*

$–$$ ✕ **Fishwife.** Fresh fish with a Latin accent makes this a favorite of locals for lunch or a casual dinner. Good bets are the green-lipped mussels (steamed and served with velouté sauce and salsa) and—for large appetites—any of the fisherman's bowls, which feature fresh fish served with rice, beans, spicy cabbage, salsa, vegetables, and a tortilla. ⊠ *1996½ Sunset Dr., at Asilomar Blvd.* ☎ *831/375–7107* ☐ *AE, D, MC, V.*

$–$$ ✕ **Peppers Mexicali Cafe.** This cheerful white-walled restaurant serves fresh seafood and traditional dishes from Mexico and Latin America. The entrées are complemented by excellent red and green salsas (made fresh throughout the day) and the large selection of beers. ⊠ *170 Forest Ave.* ☎ *831/373–6892* ☐ *AE, D, DC, MC, V* ⊘ *Closed Tues. No lunch Sun.*

$–$$ ✕ **Taste Café and Bistro.** A favorite of locals, Taste serves hearty European-inspired California cuisine in a casual, airy room with high ceilings and an open kitchen. Meats are excellent here, particularly the marinated lamb fillets and the filet mignon. ⊠ *1199 Forest Ave.* ☎ *831/655–0324* ☐ *AE, MC, V* ⊘ *Closed Mon.*

★ $$$–$$$$ ▣ **Martine Inn.** The glassed-in parlor and many guest rooms at this Mediterranean-style villa have stunning ocean views. The inn is furnished with exquisite antiques, including an 1860 Chippendale Revival four-poster bed, movie costume designer Edith Head's entire bedroom suite, and the owner's collection of classic racecars on display in the patio area. Lavish breakfasts—and elaborate dinners of up to 12 courses—are served on lace-clad tables set with china, crystal, and silver. Because of the fragility of the antiques, the inn is not suitable for children. ⊠ *255 Ocean View Blvd., 93950* ☎ *831/373–3388 or 800/852–5588* 🖷 *831/ 373–3896* ⊕ *www.martineinn.com* ⇗ *24 rooms* ♿ *Some fans, in-room data ports, refrigerators, hot tub, Internet, meeting rooms, no-smoking rooms; no a/c, no room TVs* ☐ *AE, D, MC, V* ⏧ *BP.*

$–$$$$ ▣ **The Inn at 213 Seventeen Mile Drive.** Set in a residential area just past town, this carefully restored 1920s craftsman-style home and cottage has spacious, well-appointed rooms. The affable innkeepers offer complimentary wine and hors d'oeuvres in the evening and tea and snacks throughout the day. Redwood, cypress, and eucalyptus trees tower over the garden and outdoor hot tub. ⊠ *213 17-Mile Dr., 93950* ☎ *831/ 642–9514 or 800/526–5666* 🖷 *831/642–9546* ⊕ *www.innat17.com* ⇗ *14 rooms* ♿ *Some fans, some in-room fireplaces, in-room data ports, cable TV, hot tub; no a/c, no smoking* ☐ *AE, MC, V* ⏧ *BP.*

★ **$$–$$$** 🏨 **Green Gables Inn.** Stained-glass windows and ornate interior details compete with spectacular ocean views at this Queen Anne–style mansion, built by a businessman for his mistress in 1888. Rooms in a carriage house perched on a hill out back are larger, have more modern amenities, and afford more privacy, but rooms in the main house have more charm. ⊠ *301 Ocean View Blvd., 93950* ☎ *831/375–2095 or 800/722–1774* 🖷 *831/375–5437* ⊕ *www.foursisters.com* 📱 *10 rooms, 6 with bath; 1 suite* 🛁 *Some fans, some in-room data ports, some in-room hot tubs, some cable TV, some in-room VCRs, bicycles; no a/c, no smoking* 🖃 *AE, MC, V* ⭗ *BP.*

$$–$$$ 🏨 **Lighthouse Lodge and Suites.** Near the tip of the peninsula, this complex straddles Lighthouse Avenue—the lodge is on one side, the all-suites facility on the other. With daily afternoon barbecues, it's a woodsy alternative to downtown Pacific Grove's B&B scene. Suites have fireplaces and whirlpool tubs. Standard rooms are simple, but they're decently sized and much less expensive. ⊠ *1150 and 1249 Lighthouse Ave., 93950* ☎ *831/655–2111 or 800/858–1249* 🖷 *831/655–4922* ⊕ *www.lhls. com* 📱 *64 rooms, 31 suites* 🛁 *Fans, in-room data ports, some kitchenettes, microwaves, minibars, refrigerators, cable TV with movies, pool, hot tub, meeting rooms, some pets allowed (fee); no a/c, no smoking* 🖃 *AE, D, DC, MC, V* ⭗ *BP.*

$–$$ 🏨 **Asilomar Conference Center.** This former YWCA retreat, set in a woodsy, 105-acre oceanfront state park, may bring back fond memories of summer camp. There's Ping-Pong in the lodge, volleyball and campfires outside—but thankfully, no bunk beds. The rooms are tasteful and modern, if simple, and spread among different buildings separated by woods and sandy paths. Rooms are available to the general public only when not booked for conferences. ⊠ *800 Asilomar Blvd., 93950* ☎ *831/372–8016* 🖷 *831/372–7227* ⊕ *www.visitasilomar.com* 📱 *313 rooms* 🛁 *Dining room, some refrigerators, pool, beach, bicycles, billiards, business services, meeting rooms; no a/c, no room phones, no room TVs, no smoking* 🖃 *AE, MC, V* ⭗ *BP.*

Sports & the Outdoors

GOLF Greens fees at the 18-hole **Pacific Grove Municipal Golf Links** (⊠ 77 Asilomar Blvd. ☎ 831/648–5777) run between $32 and $38 (you can play 9 holes for between $18 and $20), with an 18-hole twilight rate of $20. Optional carts cost $28. The course has spectacular ocean views on its back nine. Tee times may be reserved up to seven days in advance.

TENNIS The **Pacific Grove Municipal Courts** (⊠ 515 Junipero St. ☎ 831/648–5729) are available for public play for a small hourly fee. The pro shop here rents racquets and offers lessons.

MONTEREY

Early in the 20th century Carmel Martin, the first mayor of the city of Monterey, saw a bright future for his town: "Monterey Bay is the one place where people can live without being disturbed by manufacturing and big factories. I am certain that the day is coming when this will be the most desirable place in the whole state of California." It seems that Mayor Martin was not far off the mark.

Historic Monterey

2 mi southeast of Pacific Grove via Lighthouse Ave.; 2 mi north of Carmel via Hwy. 1.

a good tour

You can glimpse Monterey's early history in the well-preserved adobe buildings at **Monterey State Historic Park.** Far from being a hermetic period museum, the park facilities are an integral part of the day-to-day business life of the town—within some of the buildings are a store, a theater, and government offices. Some of the historic houses are graced with gardens that are worthy sights themselves. Free guided tours of Casa Soberanes, Larkin House, Cooper-Molera Adobe, and Stevenson House are given on an erratic schedule, but when the buildings are open you're welcome to wander through on your own. Spend the first day of your Monterey visit exploring the historic park, starting at **Stanton Center ❺**, which also houses the **Maritime Museum of Monterey ❻**. Take the guided 90-minute tour of the park (call for times), after which you can tour some or all of the following historic adobes and their gardens. Start next door to the Maritime Museum at **Pacific House ❼** and cross the plaza to the **Custom House ❽**. It's a short walk up Scott Street to **California's First Theatre ❾**, then one block down Pacific to **Casa Soberanes ❿**. Afterward, see the **Stevenson House ⓫**, **Cooper-Molera Adobe ⓬**, **Larkin House ⓭**, and **Colton Hall ⓮**. Stop in at the **Monterey Museum of Art ⓯**, and finish the day at **La Mirada ⓰**.

Start day two on **Fisherman's Wharf ⓱**, then head for the **Presidio of Monterey Museum ⓲**. Spend the rest of the day on **Cannery Row,** which has undergone several transformations since it was immortalized in John Steinbeck's 1945 novel of the same name. The street that Steinbeck described was crowded with sardine canneries processing, at their peak, nearly 200,000 tons of the smelly silver fish a year. During the mid-1940s, however, the sardines disappeared from the bay, causing the canneries to close. Through the years the old tin-roof canneries have been converted into restaurants, art galleries, and malls with shops selling T-shirts, fudge, and plastic sea otters. Recent tourist development along the row has been more tasteful, however, and includes several stylish inns and hotels. The **Monterey Plaza Hotel and Spa,** on the site of a historic estate at 400 Cannery Row, is a great place to relax over a drink and watch for sea otters. Wisps of the neighborhood's colorful past appear at **651 Cannery Row,** whose tile Chinese dragon roof dates to 1929.

Next, head to 800 Cannery Row, a weathered wooden building that was the site of **Pacific Biological Laboratories.** Edward F. Ricketts, the inspiration for Doc in *Cannery Row,* did much of his marine research here. The **Wing Chong Building,** at 835 Cannery Row, is the former Wing Chong Market that Steinbeck called Lee Chong's Heavenly Flower Grocery in *Cannery Row.* Step back into the present at the spectacular **Monterey Bay Aquarium ⓳** and commune with the marine life.

TIMING   Depending on how quickly you tour (it's easy to spend a couple of hours at both the maritime museum and the art museum), Day 1 will be a long one, but all of the historic park sites are in a small area. Monterey Museum of Art and La Mirada are a short drive or taxi ride from the his-

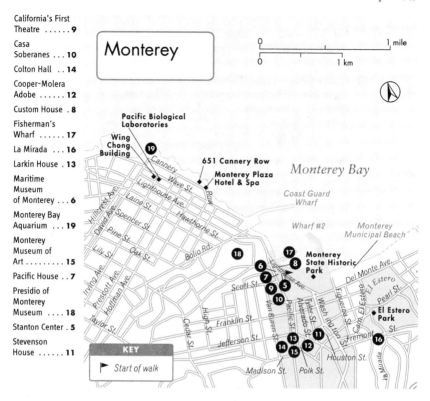

toric park. Day 2 will also be full; it's easy to linger for hours at Fisherman's Wharf and the aquarium.

What to See

9 California's First Theatre. This building began its life in 1846 as a saloon and lodging house for sailors. Four years later stage curtains were fashioned from army blankets and some U.S. officers staged plays to the light of whale oil lamps. The adobe building has been used as a theater off and on in the years since, and is open on a limited basis as it undergoes renovation. ☒ *Monterey State Historic Park, Scott and Pacific Sts.* ☎ *831/375–4916* ☞ *Free* ☉ *Call for hrs.*

10 Casa Soberanes. A classic low-ceiling adobe structure built in 1842, this was once a Custom House guard's residence. Exhibits at the house survey life in Monterey from the era of Mexican rule to the present. There's a peaceful garden in back. ☒ *Monterey State Historic Park, 336 Pacific St.* ☎ *831/649–7118* ☞ *Free* ☉ *Daily 8–5; 30-min tours Tues. 1 PM, Fri. 11:30 AM.*

14 Colton Hall. A convention of delegates met in 1849 to draft the first state constitution at California's equivalent of Independence Hall. The stone building, which has served as a school, a courthouse, and the county seat, is a museum furnished as it was during the constitutional convention. The extensive grounds outside the hall surround the Old Monterey Jail. The museum closes each day from noon to 1. ⊠ *Monterey State Historic Park, 500 block of Pacific St., between Madison and Jefferson Sts.* ☎ *831/646–5640* ⊡ *Free* ⊘ *Daily 10–4.*

⑫ **Cooper-Molera Adobe.** The restored 2-acre complex includes a house dating from the 1820s, a visitor center, a bookstore, and a large garden enclosed by a high adobe wall. The mostly Victorian-era antiques and memorabilia that fill the house provide a glimpse into the life of a prosperous early sea merchant's family. ⊠ *Monterey State Historic Park, Polk and Munras Sts.* ☎ *831/649–7118* ⊡ *Free* ⊘ *Call for hrs; 45-min tours Wed. and weekends 1 PM.*

❽ **Custom House.** This adobe structure built by the Mexican government in 1827—now California's oldest standing public building—was the first stop for sea traders whose goods were subject to duties. At the beginning of the Mexican-American War, in 1846, Commodore John Sloat raised the American flag over the building and claimed California for the United States. The house's lower floor displays cargo from a 19th-century trading ship. ⊠ *Monterey State Historic Park, 1 Custom House Plaza, across from Fisherman's Wharf* ☎ *831/649–2909* ⊡ *Free* ⊘ *Thurs.–Mon. 10–3.*

☺ ⑰ **Fisherman's Wharf.** The mournful barking of sea lions provides a steady soundtrack all along Monterey's waterfront, but the best way to actually view the whiskered marine mammals is to walk along this aging pier across from Custom House Plaza. Most of the commercial fishermen that once used the pier have moved to Wharf No. 2, a five-minute walk away, and now Fisherman's Wharf is lined with souvenir shops, fish markets, seafood restaurants, and popcorn stands. It's undeniably touristy, but still a lively and entertaining place to bring children. The wharf is also the departure point for many fishing, diving, and whale-watching trips. ⊠ *At the end of Calle Principal* ☎ *831/373–0600* ⊕ *www.montereywharf.com.*

⑯ **La Mirada.** Asian and European antiques fill this 19th-century adobe house. A newer 10,000-square-foot gallery space, designed by Charles Moore, houses Asian and California regional art. Outdoors are magnificent rose and rhododendron gardens. The entrance fee for La Mirada includes admission to the Monterey Museum of Art. ⊠ *720 Via Mirada, at Fremont St.* ☎ *831/372–3689* ⊡ *$5* ⊘ *Wed.–Sat. 11–5, Sun. 1–4.*

need a break?	El Estero Park's **Dennis the Menace Playground** (⊠ Pearl St. and Camino El Estero ☎ 831/646–3866) is an imaginative play area designed by the late Hank Ketcham, the well-known cartoonist. The equipment is on a grand scale and made for daredevils; there's a roller slide, a clanking suspension bridge, and a real Southern Pacific steam locomotive. You can rent a rowboat or a paddleboat for cruising around U-shape Lake El Estero, populated with an assortment of ducks, mud hens, and geese. The park is open 10–dusk and closed Monday except for holidays.

For a little down time, kick off your shoes at **Del Monte Beach** (E North of Del Monte Ave., east of Wharf No. 2), where the shallow waters are usually warm and calm enough for wading. It's a favorite spot for beginning divers, who come to see the sandy-bottom ecosystem, which is unusual for the area. Depending on the tides, this can be a great place for finding sand dollars.

⓭ Larkin House. A veranda encircles the second floor of this architecturally significant two-story adobe built in 1835, whose design bears witness to the Mexican and New England influences on the Monterey style. The rooms are furnished with period antiques, many of them brought from New Hampshire by the building's namesake, Thomas O. Larkin, an early California statesman. ⊠ *Monterey State Historic Park, 510 Calle Principal, between Jefferson and Pacific Sts.* ☎ *831/649–7118* ☑ *Free* ⊙ *Call for hrs; 45-min tours Wed. and weekends 2 PM.*

❻ Maritime Museum of Monterey. This collection of maritime artifacts belonged to Allen Knight, who was Carmel's mayor from 1950 to 1952. The highlight—set among the ship models, scrimshaw items, and nautical prints—is the enormous, multifaceted Fresnel lens from the lighthouse at Point Sur Light Station. ⊠ *Monterey State Historic Park, 5 Custom House Plaza* ☎ *831/372–2608* ☑ *$10* ⊙ *Daily 10–5.*

⊙ ⓳ Monterey Bay Aquarium. The minute you hand over your ticket at this
FodorśChoice   extraordinary aquarium you are surrounded by sea creatures; right at
★   the entrance, you can see dozens of them swimming in a three-story-tall, sunlit kelp forest tank. The beauty of the exhibits here is that they are all designed to give a sense of what it's like to be in the water with the animals—sardines swim around your head in a circular tank, jellyfish drift in and out of view in dramatically lighted spaces that suggest the ocean depths. A petting pool gives you a hands-on experience with bat rays, and the million-gallon "Outer Bay" tank shows the vast variety of creatures (from sharks to placid-looking turtles) that live in the Eastern Pacific. The only drawback to the experience is that it must be shared with the throngs of people that crowd the place daily; most think it's worth it. ⊠ *886 Cannery Row* ☎ *831/648–4888, 800/756–3737 in CA for advance tickets* ⊕ *www.montereybayaquarium.org* ☑ *$17.95* ⊙ *Late May–early Sept., daily 9:30–6; early Sept.–late May, daily 10–6.*

⓯ Monterey Museum of Art. Photographs by Ansel Adams and Edward Weston, as well as works by other artists who have spent time on the Peninsula, are on display here. There is also a colorful collection of international folk art; the pieces range from Kentucky hearth brooms to Tibetan prayer wheels. The entrance fee for the Monterey Museum of Art includes admission to La Mirada. ⊠ *559 Pacific St., across from Colton Hall* ☎ *831/372–5477* ⊕ *www.montereyart.org* ☑ *$5* ⊙ *Wed.–Sat. 11–5, Sun. 1–4.*

❼ Pacific House. Once a hotel and saloon, this visitor center and museum now commemorates early-California life with gold-rush relics and photographs of old Monterey. The upper floor displays Native American artifacts, including gorgeous baskets and pottery. ⊠ *Monterey State Historic Park, 10 Custom House Plaza* ☎ *831/649–7118* ☑ *Free* ⊙ *Tues., Wed., and Fri.–Sun. 10–3.*

CloseUp

THE UNDERWATER KINGDOM

W HILE MONTEREY'S COASTAL LANDSCAPES ARE STUNNING, their beauty is more than equaled by the wonders that lie offshore. The huge Monterey Bay National Marine Sanctuary—which stretches 276 mi, from north of San Francisco almost all the way down to Santa Barbara—teems with abundant life, and has a topography as diverse as that above ground.

The preserve's 5,322 square mi include vast submarine canyons, which reach down 10,663 feet at their deepest point. They also encompass dense forests of giant kelp—a kind of seaweed that can grow more than a hundred feet from its roots on the ocean floor. These kelp forests are especially robust off Monterey.

The sanctuary was established in 1992, to protect the habitat in which these species thrive. Some animals can be seen quite easily from land. In summer and winter you might glimpse the offshore spray of gray whales as they migrate between their summer feeding grounds in Alaska and their breeding grounds in Baja. Clouds of marine birds—including white-faced ibis, three types of albatross, and more than 15 types of gull—skim above the waves, or roost in the rock islands along 17-Mile Drive. Sea otters dart and gambol in the calmer waters of the Bay; and of course, you can watch the sea lions—and hear their round-the-clock barking—on the wharves in Santa Cruz and Monterey.

There are many other creatures that the sanctuary supports, however, which remain unseen by most on-land visitors. Some of these are enormous, like the giant blue whales that arrive to feed on plankton during the summer months; others, like the more than 22 species of red algae in these waters, are microscopic. So whether you choose to visit the Monterey Bay Aquarium, take a whale-watch trip, or look out to sea with your binoculars, remember—you are seeing just a small part of a vibrant underwater kingdom.

---

18 **Presidio of Monterey Museum.** This spot has been significant for centuries as a town, a fort, and the site of several battles, including the skirmish in which the pirate Hipoleto Bruchard conquered the Spanish garrison that stood here. Its first incarnation was as a Native American village for the Rumsien tribe; then it became known as the landing site for explorer Sebastien Vizcaíno in 1602, and father of the California missions, Father Serra, in 1770. The indoor museum tells the stories; the outdoor sites are marked with plaques. ⊠ *Corporal Ewing Rd., lower Presidio Park, Monterey Presidio* ☎ *831/646–3456* ⊕ *www.monterey.org/ museum/pom* ⊠ *Free* ⊘ *Mon. 10–1, Thurs.–Sat. 10–4, Sun. 1–4.*

➤ **5** **Stanton Center.** This is the place to go to load up on maps and area information. You can also view a free 20-minute film about Monterey State Historic Park, and take a 90-minute walking tour along the 2-mi Path of History, marked by round gold tiles set into the sidewalk. The tour passes several landmark buildings and details their history and significance. Admission to most sites along the walk is free, and most are open daily. ⊠ *Monterey State Historic Park, 5 Custom House Plaza* ☎ *831/*

649–7118 ⊕ *www.mbay.net/~mshp* 🖼 *Free; park tours $5* ⊙ *Thurs.–Sat.
10–4, Sun. 1–4.*

⓫ Stevenson House. This house was named in honor of author Robert
Louis Stevenson, who boarded here briefly in a tiny upstairs room.
Items from his family's estate furnish Stevenson's room; period-decorated chambers elsewhere in the house include a gallery of the author's
memorabilia and a children's nursery stocked with Victorian toys and
games. At this writing, Stevenson house was closed for renovations, but
you can still wander around the grounds. ⊠ *Monterey State Historic
Park, 530 Houston St.* ☎ *831/649–7118* 🖼 *Free.*

**off the
beaten
path**

VENTANA VINEYARDS – A short drive from downtown Monterey
leads to this winery, which is known for its chardonnays and
rieslings. Ventana's knowledgeable and hospitable owners, Doug and
LuAnn Meador, invite you to bring a lunch to eat while tasting wines
on the patio. ⊠ *2999 Monterey–Salinas Hwy. #10, Hwy. 68* ☎ *831/
372–7415* ⊕ *www.ventanavineyards.com* ⊙ *Daily 11–5.*

Where to Stay & Eat

★ **$$$–$$$$** ✕ **Fresh Cream.** Both the views of the bay and the imaginative French
cuisine are superb at this restaurant on Heritage Harbor. The menu, which
changes weekly, might include rack of lamb Dijonnaise, roast duck in
black-currant sauce, or sautéed scallops with dill fettucini and arti-
chokes. Service is formal, and though there is no requirement for dress,
men will feel more comfortable in a jacket. ⊠ *99 Pacific St., Suite 100C*
☎ *831/375–9798* ✍ *Reservations essential* ▤ *AE, D, DC, MC, V*
⊙ *No lunch.*

$$–$$$ ✕ **Duck Club.** This elegant and romantic dining room of the Monterey
Plaza Hotel and Spa is built over the waterfront on Cannery Row. The
inventive dinner menu includes seared scallops with artichoke-potato
mash, wood-roasted duck, and homemade pastas. Breakfast is served
as well. ⊠ *400 Cannery Row* ☎ *831/646–1706* ▤ *AE, D, DC, MC,
V* ⊙ *Closed Mon. No lunch.*

$$–$$$ ✕ **Monterey's Fish House.** Casual yet stylish, and removed from the hub-
bub of the wharf, this always-packed seafood restaurant attracts locals
and frequent visitors to the city. If the dining room is full, you can wait
at the bar and savor deliciously plump oysters on the half shell. The bar-
tenders and waitstaff will gladly advise you on the perfect wine to go
with your poached, blackened, or oak-grilled seafood. ⊠ *2114 Del
Monte Ave.* ☎ *831/373–4647* ✍ *Reservations essential* ▤ *AE, D, DC,
MC, V* ⊙ *No lunch weekends.*

★ **$$–$$$** ✕ **Stokes Restaurant & Bar.** This 1833 adobe building has housed, in the
past, the first wood-fired oven in California; the printer that cranked
out the state's first newspaper; and a ballroom, bakery, and private res-
idence. Now, in its latest incarnation as a restaurant, it serves tasty Cal-
ifornia-style cuisine along with comfort-food standbys (such as calzones
and pork chops). ⊠ *500 Hartnell St.* ☎ *831/373–1110* ✍ *Reservations
essential* ▤ *AE, D, DC, MC, V* ⊙ *No lunch Sun.*

$–$$$ ✕ **Montrio Bistro.** This quirky, converted historic firehouse, with its rawhide
Fodor'sChoice walls and iron indoor trellises, has a wonderfully sophisticated menu. Chef
★ Tony Baker uses organic produce and meats to create imaginative dishes
that reflect the local agriculture, such as baby artichoke risotto and whole
stuffed quail with savory French toast and apple-blackberry reduction.
Likewise, the wine list draws primarily on California, and many come from
the Monterey area. ☒ *414 Calle Principal* ☎ *831/648–8880* ⌕ *Reservations essential* ▭ *AE, D, DC, MC, V* ⊘ *No lunch.*

$–$$$ ✕ **Tarpy's Roadhouse.** Fun, dressed-down roadhouse lunches and dinners
are served in this renovated farmhouse from the early 1900s. The kitchen
serves up all the favorites Mom used to make—ribs, meat loaf, steak—
only better. Eat indoors by a fireplace or outdoors in the courtyard.
☒ *2999 Monterey–Salinas Hwy., Hwy. 68 at Canyon Del Rey Rd.*
☎ *831/647–1444* ⌕ *Reservations essential* ▭ *AE, D, MC, V.*

¢–$$ ✕ **Thai Bistro.** This cheery mom-and-pop restaurant serves excellent,
authentic Thai cuisine from family recipes. Though technically just over
the city line in Pacific Grove, it is within walking distance of Cannery
Row and the Monterey Aquarium. ☒ *159 Central Ave., Pacific Grove*
☎ *831/372–8700* ▭ *AE, D, MC, V.*

¢ ✕ **Old Monterey Cafe.** Breakfast here, which is served until closing time
(2:30 PM), includes fresh-baked muffins and eggs Benedict. You can also
order good soups, salads, and sandwiches from the lunch menu. This
is a great place to relax with a cappuccino after touring Monterey's historic adobes. ☒ *489 Alvarado St.* ☎ *831/646–1021* ⌕ *Reservations not
accepted* ▭ *D, MC, V* ⊘ *No dinner.*

★ $$$$ ▥ **Monterey Plaza Hotel and Spa.** This full-service hotel commands a waterfront location on Cannery Row, where frolicking sea otters can be
observed from the wide outdoor patio and many room balconies. The
architecture blends early California and Mediterranean styles, and also
echoes elements of the old cannery design. The property is meticulously
maintained and offers both simple and luxurious accommodations.
There is also a full-service spa for pampering, and fine dining on-site at
the Duck Club. ☒ *400 Cannery Row, 93940* ☎ *831/646–1700 or 800/
368–2468* ⎙ *831/646–0285* ⊕ *www.montereyplazahotel.com* ⟿ *280
rooms, 10 suites* ⌂ *2 restaurants, room service, fans, in-room data
ports, minibars, cable TV with movies, health club, spa, laundry service, concierge, Internet, business services, meeting rooms; no a/c, no
smoking* ▭ *AE, D, DC, MC, V.*

$$$–$$$$ ▥ **Hotel Pacific.** All the rooms at this modern adobe-style hotel are junior suites, handsomely appointed with featherbeds, hardwood floors,
fireplaces, and balconies or patios. The rates include afternoon tea, and
wine and cheese. ☒ *300 Pacific St., 93940* ☎ *831/373–5700 or 800/554–
5542* ⎙ *831/373–6921* ⊕ *www.hotelpacific.com* ⟿ *104 rooms, 1 suite*
⌂ *Fans, in-room data ports, refrigerators, cable TV, in-room VCRs, 2
hot tubs, meeting rooms; no a/c, no smoking* ▭ *AE, D, DC, MC, V* ⎊ *CP.*

$$$–$$$$ ▥ **Old Monterey Inn.** One of just two residential-area B&Bs in Monterey,
Fodor'sChoice this Tudor-style country manor, completed in 1929, is replete with hand-
★ carved window frames, balustrades, and Gothic archways. The landscaping includes a rose garden, which is surrounded by giant holly
trees, gnarled oaks, and majestic redwoods. The inn has featherbeds,
truffles and champagne delivery, sumptuous breakfasts—which you

can have brought to your bedside—and impeccable service. Because of the expensive and fragile furnishings, this is not a suitable place to bring children of any age. ✉ *500 Martin St., 93940* ☎ *831/375–8284 or 800/ 350–2344* 🖷 *831/375–6730* ⊕ *www.oldmontereyinn.com* ⇨ *7 rooms, 2 suites, 1 cottage* ☌ *In-room data ports, cable TV, in-room VCRs, hot tub, concierge; no a/c, no smoking* ▤ *MC, V* ❙○❙ *BP.*

$$$–$$$$ 🖳 **Spindrift Inn.** This boutique hotel on Cannery Row, under the same management as the Hotel Pacific and the Monterey Bay Inn, has beach access and a rooftop garden that overlooks the water. Spacious rooms with sitting areas, hardwood floors, fireplaces, and down comforters are among the indoor pleasures. This is an adults-only property. ✉ *652 Cannery Row, 93940* ☎ *831/646–8900 or 800/841–1879* 🖷 *831/646– 5342* ⊕ *www.spindriftinn.com* ⇨ *42 rooms* ☌ *In-room data ports, refrigerators, cable TV, in-room VCRs, minibars, concierge; no a/c, no smoking* ▤ *AE, D, DC, MC, V* ❙○❙ *CP.*

$–$$$$ 🖳 **The Beach Resort.** The rooms here may be nondescript, but this Best Western hotel has a great waterfront location about 2 mi north of town that affords views of the bay and the city skyline. The grounds are pleasantly landscaped, and there's a large pool with a sunbathing area. ✉ *2600 Sand Dunes Dr., 93940* ☎ *831/394–3321 or 800/242–8627* 🖷 *831/393–1912* ⊕ *www.montereybeachresort.com* ⇨ *196 rooms* ☌ *Restaurant, some fans, in-room data ports, refrigerators, cable TV with movies, pool, exercise equipment, hot tub, spa, beach, lounge, laundry facilities, business services, meeting rooms, some pets allowed (fee); no smoking* ▤ *AE, D, DC, MC, V.*

$–$$ 🖳 **Cypress Tree Inn.** Spacious and immaculate rooms here (about 2 mi from downtown) cost much less than in hotels adjacent to the wharf area. Many rooms have hot tubs; some have their own fireplaces. ✉ *2227 N. Fremont St., 93940* ☎ *831/372–7586 or 800/446–8303* 🖷 *831/372–2940* ⊕ *www.cypresstreeinn.com* ⇨ *55 rooms* ☌ *In-room data ports, some in-room hot tubs, some kitchenettes, microwaves, refrigerators, cable TV, hot tub, sauna, laundry facilities; no a/c, no smoking* ▤ *AE, D, DC, MC, V.*

☪ **$–$$** 🖳 **Monterey Bay Lodge.** Location (on the edge of Monterey's El Estero Park) and superior amenities give this motel an edge over others along the busy Munras Avenue motel row. Indoor plants and a secluded courtyard with a heated pool are other pluses at this cheerful facility. ✉ *55 Camino Aguajito, 93940* ☎ *831/372–8057 or 800/558–1900* 🖷 *831/ 655–2933* ⊕ *www.montereybaylodge.com* ⇨ *43 rooms* ☌ *Restaurant, in-room data ports, refrigerators, cable TV, in-room VCRs, pool, hot tub, some pets allowed (fee), no-smoking rooms* ▤ *AE, D, DC, MC, V.*

¢–$ 🖳 **Quality Inn Monterey.** This attractive motel has a friendly, country-inn feeling. Rooms are light and airy, some have fireplaces—and the price is right. ✉ *1058 Munras Ave., 93940* ☎ *831/372–3381* 🖷 *831/372– 4687* ⊕ *www.qualityinnmonterey.com* ⇨ *55 rooms* ☌ *In-room data ports, microwaves, refrigerators, cable TV, in-room VCRs, indoor pool, hot tub; no smoking* ▤ *AE, D, DC, MC, V* ❙○❙ *CP.*

Nightlife & the Arts

NIGHTLIFE **Bluefin** (✉ 685 Cannery Row ☎ 831/375–7000) offers live music, dancing, and 19 pool tables, and welcomes all ages until 8 PM nightly. **Planet**

Gemini (✉ 625 Cannery Row ☎ 831/373–1449) presents comedy shows on weekends and dancing to a DJ or live music most nights. **Sly McFly's** (✉ 700-A Cannery Row ☎ 831/372–3225) has live jazz and blues every night.

THE ARTS **Dixieland Monterey** (☎ 831/633–5053 or 888/349–6879 ⊕ www. dixieland-monterey.com), held on the first full weekend of March, presents trad-jazz bands in cabarets, restaurants, and hotel lounges on the Monterey waterfront. The **Monterey Bay Blues Festival** (☎ 831/394–2652 ⊕ www.montereyblues.com) draws blues fans to the Monterey Fairgrounds the last weekend in June. The **Monterey Jazz Festival** (☎ 831/373–3366 ⊕ www.montereyjazzfestival.org), the world's oldest, attracts jazz and blues greats from around the world to the Monterey Fairgrounds on the third full weekend of September.

Near Cannery Row, **Barbary Coast Theater** (✉ 324 Hoffman ☎ 831/655–4992) performs vaudeville acts and spoofy comedy-melodramas. Audience participation is encouraged. **Monterey Bay Theatrefest** (☎ 831/622–0700) presents free outdoor performances at Custom House Plaza on weekend afternoons and evenings from late June to mid-July. The **Wharf Theater** (✉ Fisherman's Wharf ☎ 831/649–2332) focuses on American musicals past and present.

Sports & the Outdoors
Throughout most of the year, the Monterey Bay area is a haven for those who love the outdoors. Residents are an active bunch; tennis, golf, surfing, fishing, biking, hiking, scuba diving and kayaking are popular activities. Golf and tennis are less popular, however, in the rainy winter months—when the waves grow larger and adventurous surfers flock to the water.

BICYCLING For bicycle rentals, visit **Bay Bikes** (✉ 640 Wave St. ☎ 831/646–9090). **Adventures by the Sea, Inc.** (✉ 299 Cannery Row ☎ 831/372–1807) rents tandem and standard bicycles.

FISHING **Randy's Fishing Trips** (✉ 66 Fisherman's Wharf ☎ 831/372–7440 or 800/251–7440) has been operating under the same skippers since 1958. **Sam's Fishing Fleet** (✉ 84 Fisherman's Wharf ☎ 831/372–0577 or 800/427–2675) has been fishing the Monterey Bay since 1914. **Monterey Sport Fishing** (✉ 96 Fisherman's Wharf ☎ 831/372–2203 or 800/200–2203) has one of the largest boats in the area and can accommodate up to 100 people for half- or full-day fishing trips.

GOLF Greens fees at the 18-hole **Del Monte Golf Course** (✉ 1300 Sylvan Rd. ☎ 831/373–2700) are $95, plus $20 per person for an optional cart. The $25 twilight special (plus cart rental) begins two hours before sunset.

KAYAKING **Monterey Bay Kayaks** (✉ 693 Del Monte Ave. ☎ 831/373–5357, 800/649–5357 in CA ✉ 2390 Hwy. 1, Moss Landing ☎ 800/649–5357 ⊕ www.montereybaykayaks.com) rents equipment and conducts classes and natural-history tours. Their Moss Landing store, about 20 mi north of Monterey, offers the same services and is a good departure point for exploration of the Elkhorn Slough.

SCUBA DIVING   Monterey Bay waters never warm to the temperatures of their southern California counterparts (the warmest they get is low 60s), but that's
one reason why the marine life here is so extraordinary. All but the faintest
of heart will want to throw on a wetsuit and explore this underwater
ecosystem, one of the world's most diverse. The Monterey Bay National
Marine Sanctuary, home to mammals, seabirds, fishes, invertebrates, and
plants, encompasses a 276-mi shoreline and 5,322 square mi of ocean.
The staff at **Aquarius Dive Shop** (☒ 2040 Del Monte Ave. ☏ 831/375–
1933) gives diving lessons and tours and rents equipment. Their **scuba-
diving conditions information line** (☏ 831/657–1020) is updated daily.

SKATING   **Del Monte Gardens** (☒ 2020 Del Monte Ave. ☏ 831/375–3202) is an old-
fashioned rink for roller-skating and in-line skating. **Monterey Skate
Park** (☒ Next to Lake El Estero behind Sollecito Ballpark ☏ 831/646–
3866) is an unsupervised park open daily from 9 AM to dusk.

WALKING   From Custom House Plaza, you can walk along the coast in either direction on the 29-mi long **Monterey Bay Coastal Trail** (☏ 831/372–3196
⊕ www.mprpd.org/parks/coastaltrail.html) for spectacular views of the
sea. It runs all the way from north of Monterey to Pacific Grove, with
sections continuing around Pebble Beach.

WHALE-   Though trips are not as frequent as with commercial groups, the **Amer-
WATCHING   ican Cetacean Society** (☏ 831/625–2120 or 831/372–6919) leads the best
(and least expensive) whale watches in the bay, and all proceeds go to
marine mammal research. **Monterey Bay Whale Watch**, which operates
out of Sam's Fishing at Fisherman's Wharf (☏ 831/375–4658), also offers tours guided by marine biologists.

Shopping

Antiques and reproductions of merchandise popular in Monterey in the
1850s are available at **The Boston Store** (☒ Monterey State Historic Park,
1 Custom House Plaza, across from Fisherman's Wharf ☏ 831/649–3364).
The Cooper Store (☒ Polk and Munras Sts., in the Cooper-Molera Adobe
☏ 831/649–7111) is an 1800s-themed shop that is dedicated to the
preservation of antiquities in the Monterey State Historic Park. Bargain
hunters can sometimes find little treasures at the **Cannery Row Antique
Mall** (☒ 471 Wave St. ☏ 831/655–0264), which houses 150 local vendors under one roof. **Old Monterey Book Co.** (☒ 136 Bonifacio Pl., off Alvarado St. ☏ 831/372–3111) specializes in antiquarian books and prints.
Historical Society–operated, **The Pickett Fence** (☒ Monterey State Historic
Park, 1 Custom House Plaza, across from Fisherman's Wharf ☏ 831/
649–3364) sells high-end garden accessories and furnishings.

SANTA CRUZ COUNTY

Less manicured than its upscale Monterey Peninsula neighbors to the
south, Santa Cruz is the big city on this stretch of the California coast.
A haven for people opting out of the rat race and a bastion of 1960s-
style counterculture, Santa Cruz has been at the forefront of such
quintessential "left coast" trends as organic food, medicinal marijuana,
and environmentalism. Between Santa Cruz and the Monterey Penin-

sula, the quieter towns of Capitola, Soquel, and Aptos have their own quality restaurants, small inns, resorts, and antiques shops.

Salinas

⓴ *17 mi east of Monterey via Hwy. 68.*

Salinas is the locus of a rich agricultural valley where fertile soil, an ideal climate, and a good water supply produce optimum growing conditions for crops such as lettuce, broccoli, tomatoes, strawberries, flowers, and wine grapes. This unpretentious town may lack the sophistication and scenic splendors of the coast, but it will interest literary and architectural buffs. Turn-of-the-20th-century buildings have been the focus of ongoing renovation, much of it centered on the original downtown area of South Main Street, with its handsome stone storefronts. The memory and literary legacy of Salinas native (and winner of Pulitzer and Nobel prizes) John Steinbeck are honored here.

The **National Steinbeck Center** is a museum and archive dedicated to the life and works of John Steinbeck. Many exhibits are interactive, bringing to life Steinbeck worlds such as Cannery Row, Hooverville (from *The Grapes of Wrath*), and the Mexican Plaza (from *The Pearl*). The library and archives contain Steinbeck first editions, notebooks, photographs, and audiotapes. Access to the archives is by appointment only. The center has information about Salinas's annual Steinbeck Festival, in August, and about tours of area landmarks mentioned in his novels. ✉ *1 Main St.* ☎ *831/796–3833* ⊕ *www.steinbeck.org* 🎟 *$11* ⊙ *Daily 10–5.*

The **Jose Eusebio Boronda Adobe,** former home of a high-profile Juan Bautista consort, has been impeccably maintained. The furniture and decorations inside—some of them original—depict the California lifestyle of the 1840s. ✉ *333 Boronda Rd.* ☎ *831/757–8085* 🎟 *Free; donation requested* ⊙ *Weekdays 10–2; weekends by appointment.*

A Taste of Monterey Wine Tasting Visitors Center holds regular wine tastings from 35 local vintners. Those who want to visit the wineries themselves can get a map here (and at the center's other location, in Monterey's Fisherman's Wharf) for the self-guided driving tour of 20 wineries between Monterey and King City. ✉ *700 Cannery Row* ☎ *831/646–5446* ⊙ *Daily 11–6.*

Where to Eat

$–$$$ ✕ **Hullabaloo.** There's elegant lighting and white tablecloths, but this local hangout still feels relaxed and fun. The prices are noticeably lower than in more touristy nearby towns. You can get great lunchtime burgers here, and dinner specials include sand dabs over lobster-whipped potatoes and a surf-and-turf of hangar steak and shrimp scampi. ✉ *228 S. Main St.* ☎ *831/757–3663* 🖃 *AE, D, DC, MC, V* ⊙ *No lunch weekends.*

$ ✕ **Steinbeck House.** John Steinbeck's birthplace, a Victorian frame house, has been converted into a lunch-only (11:30–2) eatery run by the volunteer Valley Guild. The restaurant displays some Steinbeck memorabilia. There's no à la carte service; the set menu includes soup or salad, vegetable, main dish, and nonalcoholic beverage. Dishes such as zucchini lasagna and spinach crepes are created using locally grown produce. ⊠ *132 Central Ave.* ☎ *831/424–2735* ☰ *MC, V* ⊘ *Closed Sun. and 3 wks in late Dec. and early Jan.*

¢–$ ✕ **One Main Street Café.** Inside the Steinbeck Center, this bright café is a good pick for lunch in Salinas. The menu is based on ingredients grown in the surrounding valley, and portions are huge and hearty. The house specialty is artichokes, which you can order fire-roasted, deep-fried, or served with a jalapeño spread. ⊠ *1 Main St.* ☎ *831/775–4738* ☰ *AE, MC, V* ⊘ *No dinner.*

San Juan Bautista

㉑ *U.S. 101, 20 mi north of Salinas.*

Sleepy San Juan Bautista has been protected from development since 1933, when much of the town became a state park. This is about as close to early-19th-century California as you can get. Small antiques shops and art galleries line the side streets, and throughout the year the town hosts weekend events—including a Victorian Ball, an American Indian festival, and the Peddler's Faire, an open-air bazaar of crafts and antiques.

The centerpiece of **San Juan Bautista State Historic Park** is a wide green plaza ringed by historic buildings: a restored blacksmith shop, a stable, a pioneer cabin, and a jailhouse. The **Castro-Breen Adobe,** furnished with Spanish colonial antiques, gives a glimpse of mid-19th-century domestic life in the village. Running along one side of the town square is **Mission San Juan Bautista** (⊠ 408 S. 2nd St. ☎ 831/623–2127 ⊘ Cemetery daily 9:30–5 ▣ Cemetery $2), founded by Father Fermin de Lasuen in 1797. Adjoining the long, low, colonnaded structure is the mission cemetery, where more than 4,300 Native Americans who converted to Christianity are buried in unmarked graves.

★ ☽ After the mission era, San Juan Bautista became an important crossroads for stagecoach travel. The principal stop in town was the **Plaza Hotel,** a collection of adobe buildings with furnishings from the 1860s. On **Living History Day,** which takes place on the first Saturday of each month, costumed volunteers engage in quilting bees, tortilla making, butter churning, and other frontier activities. ⊠ *2nd and Franklin Sts., off Hwy. 156* ☎ *831/623–4881 or 831/623–4526* ⊕ *www.cal-parks.ca.gov* ▣ *$2* ⊘ *Daily 10–4:30.*

Fremont Peak Observatory is located at 3,000 feet—which means that even when the fog rolls into Monterey Bay, the sky here is usually dark and clear. From late-April through October the observatory holds public stargazing events through its 30-inch telescope every Saturday night (except when there's a full moon); on the first Saturday afternoon of each month, you can also observe the sun through a special solar telescope. ⊠ *Fremont State Park, Hwy. 156, 11 mi south of San Juan Bautista* ☎ *831/623–2465* ▣ *Free.*

en route

★

About halfway between Monterey and Santa Cruz, east of the tiny harbor town of Moss Landing, is one of only two federal research reserves in California, the **Elkhorn Slough at the National Estuarine Research Reserve** (✉ 1700 Elkhorn Rd., Watsonville ☎ 831/ 728–2822 ⊕ www.elkhornslough.org 🏷 $2.50 ☉ Wed.–Sun. 9–5). Its 1,400 acres of tidal flats and salt marshes form a complex environment that supports some 300 species of birds. A walk along the meandering waterways and wetlands can reveal hawks, white-tailed kites, owls, herons, and egrets. On weekends guided walks to the heron rookery are offered at 10 and 1.

Santa Cruz

㉒ *34 mi northwest of Salinas; 48 mi north of Monterey on Hwy. 1.*

The surrounding mountains shelter the beach town of Santa Cruz from the coastal fog and from the smoggy skies of the San Francisco Bay area and Silicon Valley. The climate here is mild, and it is usually sunnier than other northerly coastal areas.

The heart of downtown Santa Cruz is along Pacific Avenue south of Water Street, where you'll find shops, restaurants, and other establishments in the outdoor **Pacific Garden Mall.**

Santa Cruz gets some of its youthful spirit from the nearby **University of California at Santa Cruz.** The school's redwood buildings are perched on the forested hills above town; with its sylvan setting and sweeping ocean vistas, the campus is tailor-made for the contemplative life. ✉ *Bay and High Sts.* ☎ *831/459–0111* ⊕ *www.ucsc.edu.*

☽ Santa Cruz has been a seaside resort since the mid-19th century. The Looff carousel and classic wooden Giant Dipper roller coaster at the **Santa Cruz Beach Boardwalk** date from the early 1900s. Elsewhere along the boardwalk, the Casino Fun Center has its share of video-game technology. But this is still primarily a place for good old-fashioned family fun: rides, games, corn dogs, and chowder fries. ✉ *Along Beach St. west from San Lorenzo River* ☎ *831/423–5590 or 831/426–7433* ⊕ *www. beachboardwalk.com* 🏷 *$23.95, day pass for unlimited rides* ☉ *Late May–early Sept., daily; early Sept.–late May, weekends only, weather permitting, call for hrs.*

The **Santa Cruz Municipal Wharf** (☎ 831/420–6025 ⊕ www. santacruzwharf.com), just up the beach from the boardwalk, is lined with restaurants, shops, and seafood takeout windows. The barking sea lions that lounge in heaps under the wharf's pilings enliven the area.

Drive southwest from the municipal wharf on West Cliff Drive about ¾ mi to the promontory at **Seal Rock,** where you can watch pinnipeds hang out, sunbathe, and occasionally frolic. The **Mark Abbott Memorial Lighthouse,** adjacent to the promontory, was built in 1868. Aside from being the site of a fabulous view, it's worth a stop for the **Santa Cruz Surfing Museum** located on its ground floor. The historical photographs are fun, and the display of boards from over the years includes a heavy redwood plank (from before the days of fiberglass) and the remains of a modern board that was munched by a great white shark. ⊠ *701 W. Cliff Dr.* ☎ *831/420–6289* ⊕ *www.santacruzmuseums.org* ✆ *Free* ☉ *Late May–early Sept., Wed.–Mon. noon–4; early Sept.–late May, Thurs.–Mon. noon–4.*

About 1¼ mi west of the lighthouse is secluded **Natural Bridges State Beach,** a stretch of soft sand with tidal pools and a natural rock bridge nearby. From October to early March a colony of monarch butterflies resides here. ⊠ *2531 W. Cliff Dr.* ☎ *831/423–4609* ⊕ *www.parks.ca.gov* ✆ *Parking $3* ☉ *Park daily 8 AM–sunset. Visitor center Oct.–Feb., daily 10–4; Mar.–Sept., weekends 10–4.*

Where to Stay & Eat

★ **$$$–$$$$** ✕ **Theo's.** On a quiet side street in a residential neighborhood, Theo's serves mainly three- and five-course prix fixe dinners. Seasonal standouts include duck with garden vegetables and currants, as well as rack of lamb with ratatouille. Much of the produce comes from the ¾-acre organic garden behind the restaurant, where you can stroll between courses. Service is gracious and attentive, and the wine list is outstanding. ⊠ *3101 N. Main St., Soquel* ☎ *831/462–3657* ⚑ *Reservations essential* ☰ *AE, MC, V* ☉ *Closed Sun. and Mon. No lunch.*

★ **$$–$$$** ✕ **Bittersweet Bistro.** A large old tavern with cathedral ceilings houses this popular bistro, where chef-owner Thomas Vinolus draws culinary inspiration from the Mediterranean. The menu changes seasonally, but regular highlights include the outstandingly fresh fish specials, grilled vegetable platter, seafood *puttanesca* (pasta with a spicy sauce of garlic, tomatoes, anchovies, and olives), and grilled lamb tenderloin. The decadent chocolate desserts are not to be missed. ⊠ *787 Rio Del Mar Blvd., off Hwy. 1, Aptos* ☎ *831/662–9799* ☰ *AE, MC, V* ☉ *No lunch.*

$$–$$$ ✕ **Oswald's.** Intimate and stylish, this tiny courtyard bistro serves sophisticated yet unpretentious European-inspired California cooking. The menu changes seasonally, but might include such items as perfectly prepared sherry-steamed mussels or sautéed veal livers. ⊠ *1547-E Pacific Ave.* ☎ *831/423–7427* ⚑ *Reservations essential* ☰ *AE, D, DC, MC, V* ☉ *Closed Mon. No lunch.*

$–$$$ ✕ **Shadowbrook.** To get to this romantic spot overlooking Soquel Creek, you can take a cable car or walk the stairs down a steep, fern-lined bank beside a running waterfall. Dining room options include the rooftop Redwood Room, the wood-paneled Wine Cellar, and the airy, glass-enclosed Garden Room. Prime rib and grilled seafood are the stars of the simple menu. A cheaper menu of light entrées is available in the lounge. Champagne brunch is served on Sunday. ⊠ *1750 Wharf Rd., Capitola* ☎ *831/475–1571* ☰ *AE, D, DC, MC, V* ☉ *No lunch weekends.*

$$ ✕ **Gabriella Café.** This tiny, intimate café displays the work of local artists, and the seasonal Italian menu features organic produce from area farms. Highlights include the steamed mussels, braised lamb shank, and grilled portobello mushrooms. ⊠ *910 Cedar St.* ☎ *831/457–1677* ☰ *AE, MC, V.*

¢–$ ✕ **Seabright Brewery.** Great burgers, seafood, and stellar house-made microbrews make this a favorite local hangout. Sit outside on the large patio or inside at one of the comfortable, spacious booths. ⊠ *519 Seabright Ave.* ☎ *831/426–2739* ☰ *AE, MC, V.*

¢ ✕ **Zachary's.** With its mostly young clientele, this noisy café defines the funky essence of Santa Cruz. It also dishes up great breakfasts: omelets, sourdough pancakes, artichoke frittatas, and "Mike's Mess"—eggs scrambled with bacon, mushrooms, and home fries, then topped with sour cream, melted cheese, and fresh tomatoes. ⊠ *819 Pacific Ave.* ☎ *831/427–0646* ⌖ *Reservations not accepted* ▭ *MC, V* ☉ *Closed Mon. No dinner.*

♻ **$$$$** ⊞ **Seascape Resort.** On a bluff overlooking Monterey Bay, Seascape is a perfect place to unwind. The spacious suites sleep from two to six people; each has a kitchenette and fireplace, and most have ocean-view patios with barbecue grills. The resort is about 9 mi south of Santa Cruz. ⊠ *1 Seascape Resort Dr., Aptos 95003* ☎ *831/688–6800 or 800/929–7727* ⌖ *831/685–0615* ⊕ *www.seascaperesort.com* ⤳ *285 suites* ⌂ *Restaurant, room service, in-room data ports, some kitchens, some kitchenettes, cable TV with movies and video games, golf privileges, 3 pools, health club, 3 hot tubs, spa, beach, children's programs (ages 5–10), laundry service, Internet, business services, convention center, meeting room; no a/c, no smoking* ▭ *AE, D, DC, MC, V.*

$$$–$$$$ ⊞ **Inn at Depot Hill.** This inventively designed B&B in a former rail depot sees itself as a link to the era of luxury train travel. Each double room or suite, complete with fireplace and feather beds, is inspired by a different destination—Italy's Portofino, France's Côte d'Azur, Japan's Kyoto. One suite is decorated like a Pullman car for a railroad baron. Some accommodations have private patios with hot tubs. This is a great place for an adults-only weekend. ⊠ *250 Monterey Ave., Capitola 95010* ☎ *831/462–3376 or 800/572–2632* ⌖ *831/462–3697* ⊕ *www.innatdepothill.com* ⤳ *8 rooms, 4 suites* ⌂ *Fans, in-room data ports, cable TV, in-room VCRs, hot tub; no a/c, no smoking* ▭ *AE, D, MC, V* ⟡ *BP.*

$$$–$$$$ ⊞ **Pleasure Point Inn.** Tucked in a residential neighborhood at the east end of town, this modern Mediterranean-style B&B sits right across the street from the ocean and a popular surfing beach (where surfing lessons are available). The rooms are handsomely furnished and include such deluxe amenities as wireless Internet access and dimmer switches; some rooms have fireplaces. You have use of the large rooftop sun deck and hot tub, which overlook the Pacific. Since this is a popular romantic getaway spot, it's best not to bring kids. ⊠ *2-3665 E. Cliff Dr., 95062* ☎ *831/469–6161 or 877/557–2567* ⌖ *831/479–1347* ⊕ *www.pleasurepointinn.com* ⤳ *4 rooms* ⌂ *Fans, in-room data ports, in-room safes, some in-room hot tubs, minibars, refrigerators, cable TV, hot tub, beach; no a/c, no smoking* ▭ *MC, V* ⟡ *CP.*

★ **$$$** ⊞ **Historic Sand Rock Farm.** On the site of a former winery, this century-old Arts and Crafts–inspired farmhouse, surrounded by 10 acres of forest and meadow, has been beautifully restored and modernized. There are comfortable, spacious rooms here, and sumptuous breakfasts are served. Most rooms have their own Jacuzzi tubs; if yours doesn't, there's also a large outdoor hot tub. ⊠ *6901 Freedom Blvd., Aptos 95003* ☎ *831/688–8005* ⌖ *831/688–8025* ⊕ *www.sandrockfarm.com* ⤳ *3 rooms, 2 suites* ⌂ *Fans, in-room data ports, some in-room hot tubs, cable TV, in-room VCRs, outdoor hot tub, Internet; no a/c, no smoking* ▭ *AE, MC, V* ⟡ *BP.*

$$–$$$ ▦ **Babbling Brook Inn.** Though it's smack in the middle of Santa Cruz, this B&B has lush gardens, a running stream, and tall trees that make you feel like you're in a secluded wood. All rooms have fireplaces (though a few are electric) and feather beds; most have private patios. Complimentary wine, cheese, and fresh-baked cookies are available in the afternoon. ✉ *1025 Laurel St., 95060* ☎ *831/427–2456 or 800/866–1131* 📠 *831/427–2457* ⊕ *www.babblingbrookinn.com* ⤳ *13 rooms* ⚐ *In-room hot tubs, cable TV, in-room VCRs; no a/c, no smoking* ▱ *AE, D, DC, MC, V* ⦿| *BP.*

$$–$$$ ▦ **Coast Santa Cruz Hotel.** Just a short stroll from the boardwalk and wharf, this resort opens right onto Cowell Beach. Though the hotel is a concrete monolith, all rooms have private balconies or patios overlooking the Pacific. If it's too cold to swim in the ocean, you can head for the heated swimming pool and hot tub. ✉ *175 W. Cliff Dr., 95060* ☎ *831/426–4330 or 800/663–1144* 📠 *831/427–2025* ⤳ *147 rooms, 16 suites* ⚐ *Restaurant, room service, in-room safes, refrigerators, cable TV with movies and video games, pool, 2 hot tubs, bar, laundry service, business services, Internet, no-smoking rooms* ▱ *AE, D, DC, MC, V.*

The Arts

Shakespeare Santa Cruz (✉ Performing Arts Complex, University of California at Santa Cruz ☎ 831/459–2121 ⊕ www.shakespearesantacruz. org) stages a six-week Shakespeare festival in July and August that may also include the occasional modern dramatic performance. Most performances are outdoors in the striking Redwood Glen. A holiday program is also performed in December.

Sports & the Outdoors

BICYCLING To go local you can park the car and rent a beach cruiser at **Bike Shop Santa Cruz** (✉ 1325 Mission St. ☎ 831/454–0909). Mountain bikers should head to **Another Bike Shop** (✉ 2361 Mission St. ☎ 831/427–2232) for tips on the best trails around and a look at cutting-edge gear made and tested locally.

BOATS & **Chardonnay Sailing Charters** (☎ 831/423–1213) accommodates 49 pas-
CHARTERS sengers for year-round cruises on Monterey Bay. The 70-foot *Chardonnay II* leaves from the yacht harbor in Santa Cruz. Food and wine are served on many of their cruises, and appearances by guest chefs and local astronomers are common. Reservations are essential. **Original Stagnaro Fishing Trips** (✉ Center of Santa Cruz Municipal Wharf ☎ 831/427–2334) operates salmon-, albacore-, and rock-cod-fishing expeditions; the fees ($45–$55) include bait. The company also runs whale-watching cruises ($30) between December and April.

SURFING **Manresa State Beach** (✉ Manresa Dr., La Selva Beach ☎ 831/761–1795), south of Santa Cruz, has premium surfing conditions, but the currents can be treacherous; campsites are available if you're brave enough to stay. The surf at **New Brighton State Beach** (✉ 1500 State Park Dr., Capitola ☎ 831/464–6330) has challenging surf and campsites. Surfers gather for spectacular waves and sunsets at **Pleasure Point** (✉ E. Cliff and Pleasure Point Drs.). **Steamer's Lane,** near the lighthouse on West Cliff Drive, has a decent break. The area plays host to several competitions in summer.

The most welcoming place in town for surf gear is **Paradise Surf Shop** (⊠ 3961 Portola Dr. ☎ 831/462–3880). The shop is owned by local amateur longboarder Sally Smith and run by women who aim to help everyone feel comfortable on the water. Boards, suits, and other gear can be bought and rented here. **Cowell's Beach 'n' Bikini Surf Shop** (⊠ 30 Front St. ☎ 831/427–2355) rents surfboards and wet suits and offers lessons.

MONTEREY BAY A TO Z

To research prices, get advice from other travelers, and book travel arrangements, visit ⊕ www.fodors.com.

AIRPORTS & TRANSFERS

Monterey Peninsula Airport is 3 mi east of downtown Monterey (take Olmstead Road off Highway 68). It is served by American, American Eagle, America West, United, and United Express. *See* Air Travel *in* Smart Travel Tips A to Z *for airline phone numbers.* Taxi service is available for about $9–$10, and Monterey–Salinas Transit has buses to and from the airport Monday through Saturday.

🛈 **Monterey Peninsula Airport** ⊠ 200 Fred Kane Dr., Monterey ☎ 831/648–7000 ⊕ www.montereyairport.com. **Carmel Taxi** ☎ 831/624–3885. **Monterey Airport Taxi** ☎ 831/626–3385. **Monterey-Salinas Transit** ☎ 831/899–2555. **Yellow Checker Cabs** ☎ 831/646–1234.

BUS TRAVEL

Greyhound serves Santa Cruz and Monterey from San Francisco three or four times daily. The trips take about 3 or 4½ hours, respectively. Monterey-Salinas Transit provides frequent service between the peninsula's towns and many major sightseeing spots and shopping areas. The base fare is $1.75, with an additional $1.75 for each zone you travel into. A day pass costs $3.50–$7, depending on how many zones you'll be traveling through. Monterey-Salinas Transit also runs the WAVE shuttle, which links major attractions on the Monterey waterfront. The free shuttle operates late May through early September, daily from 9 to 6:30.

🛈 **Greyhound** ☎ 800/231–2222 ⊕ www.greyhound.com. **Monterey-Salinas Transit** ☎ 831/424–7695 ⊕ www.mst.org.

CAR RENTAL

Most of the major agencies have locations in downtown Santa Cruz and at the Monterey Airport. *See* Car Rental *in* Smart Travel Tips A to Z *for national car-rental agency phone numbers.*

CAR TRAVEL

Parking is especially difficult in Carmel and in the heavily touristed areas of Monterey.

Two-lane Highway 1 runs north–south along the coast, linking the towns of Santa Cruz, Monterey, and Carmel. Highway 68 runs east from Pacific Grove toward Salinas at U.S. 101. North of Salinas, the freeway (U.S. 101) links up with Highway 156 to San Juan Bautista. The drive south from San Francisco to Monterey can be made comfortably in three hours or less. The most scenic way is to follow Highway 1 down the coast past flower, pumpkin, and artichoke fields and the seaside communities of Pacifica, Half Moon Bay, and Santa Cruz. Unless you drive on sunny weekends when locals are heading for the beach, the two-lane coast highway may take no longer than the freeway.

A sometimes faster route is I–280 south from San Francisco to Highway 17, north of San Jose. Highway 17 crosses the redwood-filled Santa Cruz Mountains between San Jose and Santa Cruz, where it intersects with Highway 1. The traffic can crawl to a standstill, however, heading into Santa Cruz. Another option is to follow U.S. 101 south through San Jose to Prunedale and then take Highway 156 west to Highway 1 south into Monterey.

From Los Angeles the drive to Monterey can be made in 5–6 hours by heading north on U.S. 101 to Salinas and then west on Highway 68. The spectacular but slow alternative is to take U.S. 101 to San Luis Obispo and then follow the hairpin turns of Highway 1 up the coast. Allow about three extra hours if you take this route.

EMERGENCIES

In the event of an emergency, dial 911. Monterey Bay Dental Society provides dentist referrals and Monterey County Medical Society can refer you to a doctor. The Surf 'n' Sand pharmacy in Carmel is open on weekdays from 9 to 6, Saturday from 9 to 1. There is a 24-hour Walgreen's pharmacy in Seaside, about 4 mi northeast of Monterey via Highway 1.

🏥 Hospitals **Community Hospital of Monterey Peninsula** ✉ 23625 Holman Hwy., Monterey ☎ 831/624–5311. **Dominican Hospital** ✉ 1555 Soquel Dr., Santa Cruz ☎ 831/462–7700.

🏥 Pharmacies **Surf 'n' Sand** ✉ 6th and Junipero Aves., Carmel ☎ 831/624–1543. **Walgreen's** ✉ 1055 Fremont Blvd., Seaside ☎ 831/393–9231.

🏥 Referrals **Monterey Bay Dental Society** ☎ 831/658–0168. **Monterey County Medical Society** ☎ 831/655–1019.

LODGING

Bed and Breakfast Innkeepers of Santa Cruz County is an association of innkeepers that can help you find a B&B. Monterey County Conventions and Visitors Bureau Visitor Services operates a lodging referral line and publishes an informational brochure with discount coupons that are good at restaurants, attractions, and shops. Monterey Peninsula Reservations will assist you in booking lodgings.

🛏 **Bed and Breakfast Innkeepers of Santa Cruz County** ☎ 831/688–0444 ⊕ www.santacruzbnb.com. **Monterey County Conventions and Visitors Bureau Visitor Services** ☎ 800/555–9283 ⊕ www.gomonterey.org. **Monterey Peninsula Reservations** ☎ 888/655–3424 ⊕ www.monterey-reservations.com.

TOURS

California Parlor Car Tours operates motor-coach tours from San Francisco that include one or two days in the Monterey Peninsula. Ag Venture Tours runs wine-tasting, sightseeing, and agricultural tours in the Monterey, Salinas, Carmel Valley, and Santa Cruz areas.

🚌 **California Parlor Car Tours** ☎ 415/474–7500 or 800/227–4250 ⊕ www.calpartours.com. **Ag Venture Tours** ☎ 831/384–7686 ⊕ www.agventuretours.com.

TRAIN TRAVEL

Amtrak's *Coast Starlight,* which runs between Los Angeles, Oakland, and Seattle, stops in Salinas. Connecting Amtrak Thruway buses serve Monterey and Carmel.

🚹 **Amtrak** ✉ 11 Station Pl., Salinas ☎ 800/872-7245 ⊕ www.amtrakcalifornia.com.

VISITOR INFORMATION

🚹 **Monterey County Vintners and Growers Association** ☎ 831/375-9400 ⊕ www. montereywines.org. **Monterey County Convention & Visitors Bureau** ☎ 800/555-9283 ⊕ www.gomonterey.org **Monterey Peninsula Visitors and Convention Bureau** ✉ 380 Alvarado St., Monterey 93942 ☎ 831/649-1770 ⊕ www.monterey.com. **Salinas Valley Chamber of Commerce** ✉ 119 E. Alisal St., Salinas 93901 ☎ 831/424-7611 ⊕ www. salinaschamber.com. **Santa Cruz County Conference and Visitors Council** ✉ 1211 Ocean St., Santa Cruz 95060 ☎ 831/425-1234 or 800/833-3494 ⊕ www.scccvc.org. **Santa Cruz Mountain Winegrowers' Association** ✉ 7605-A Old Dominion Ct., Aptos 95003 ☎ 831/479-9463 ⊕ www.scmwa.com.

THE PENINSULA & SOUTH BAY
SOUTH OF SAN FRANCISCO

11

FIND YOUR INNER GEEK
at San Jose's Tech Museum of Innovation ⇨*p.486*

SEE SPLENDOR IN THE GRASS
The Rodin sculpture garden at the Iris and B.
Gerald Cantor Center for Visual Arts ⇨*p.475*

MARVEL AT MUMMIES
The Rosicrucian Egyptian Museum ⇨*p.485*

GET SPOOKED
at the Winchester Mystery House ⇨*p.486*

PRETEND YOU'RE IN MOROCCO
seated on floor cushions at Cafe Gibraltar ⇨*p.473*

Updated by
Lisa M.
Hamilton

TWO PARALLEL WORLDS LIE SOUTH OF SAN FRANCISCO. On the fog-shrouded San Mateo County coast, rural towns perch between undeveloped hills and rugged coastline. Most of the hamlets that dot the coast are no more than a few blocks long, with just enough room for a couple of B&Bs, restaurants, and boutiques or galleries. As you wind your way from one to the other, past Christmas tree farms, pumpkin patches, and stunning beaches, you'll find that the pace of life is slower here than in the rest of the Bay Area.

Over the Santa Cruz Mountains from the coast, the Inland Peninsula pulses with prosperity and creative energy. Many visitors to the Bay Area associate the Peninsula with traffic congestion and suburban sprawl, and indeed, much of the region from Santa Clara County to San Francisco is clogged with office complexes and strip-mall shopping centers. But a closer look at the Peninsula reveals redwood forests, and vast stretches of tawny hills where hawks soar overhead. Stanford University's bucolic campus is wonderful to visit, as are the wooded former country estates built by 19th-century mining and transportation "bonanza kings"—early adopters who realized the area's potential long before the "dot.com" boom.

Farther south is the heart of Silicon Valley, the birthplace of the tiny electronic chips and circuits that support the information superhighway. Beyond what seems to be an endless sprawl of office parks, intertwined highways, shopping centers, and high-rises, the South Bay contains old-fashioned neighborhoods and abundant green hills. There are diverse towns such as Santa Clara, with its 200-year-old mission; Saratoga, with its fine antiques stores and French restaurants; and San Jose—the third-largest city on the West Coast—with its flourishing downtown center, its many micro-neighborhoods, and a growing ribbon of urban green connecting the city from north to south.

Exploring the Peninsula & South Bay

You'll need a car to get around. The stretch of Highway 1 that leads north from the Monterey Bay area passes through a sparsely populated landscape punctuated by only a few small towns. By contrast, the Inland Peninsula and South Bay is a tangle of freeways, especially in the area around San Jose—so it's best to avoid driving during rush hour.

About the Restaurants
Gone are the days when Peninsula and South Bay food lovers had to drive to San Francisco for an exceptional meal. Today some of the country's greatest chefs have recognized the area's appeal, opening trendy bistros and eateries, especially in San Jose's revitalized downtown. Dining in the South Bay might be a little less formal than in San Francisco—and a little less expensive—but that doesn't mean you won't need reservations. Along the coast, however, restaurants are strictly casual, and unless otherwise noted, you can generally walk in without waiting for a table.

About the Hotels
Along the coastal peninsula, accommodations tend to have some character and cater to weekend tourists and San Franciscans; distinctive inns

Numbers in the text correspond to numbers in the margin and on the Peninsula & South Bay and Downtown San Jose maps.

11

If you have
1 day

Spend your morning in ➤ **Palo Alto ⑥**, taking a look around town and a tour of Stanford University. In the afternoon head for ⊞ **San Jose ⑨**–**⑳** and the **Tech Museum of Innovation ⑬**, the **Rosicrucian Egyptian Museum ⑰**, and the **Winchester Mystery House ⑲**. Depending on your taste, have a raucous evening at Big Lil's Barbary Coast Dinner Theater or an evening of symphony, ballet, or theater at San Jose's Center for Performing Arts.

If you have
3 days

Spend your first day on the coast, noodling around ➤ **Año Nuevo State Reserve ①**, **Pescadero State Beach ②**, **Half Moon Bay ③**, and **Moss Beach ④**. After overnighting in a Half Moon Bay B&B, drive Route 92 through the countryside to I–280 and head south to **Woodside ⑤**, where you can tour Filoli (except Monday November–January). Drive south on I–280 to the Sand Hill Road exit and take that route to the central campus of Stanford University. Take an afternoon tour of the university and its Iris and B. Gerald Cantor Center for Visual Arts, then have dinner in ⊞ **Palo Alto ⑥**. On your third day stop in **Santa Clara ⑦** to see Mission Santa Clara de Asis, or if you have kids in tow, you might want to treat them to a morning at Paramount's Great America. Devote your afternoon to ⊞ **San Jose ⑨**–**⑳** and its attractions, then take a sunset drive to **Saratoga ⑧**.

and B&Bs are the norm. Because of the weekend demand on the coast you'd be wise to make reservations as far in advance as possible. Inland Peninsula and South Bay lodgings generally attract business travelers—most are chain motels and hotels, though a number of B&Bs have popped up in recent years. During the week, when business conventions are in full swing, many of these hotels are booked up to two weeks in advance. However, some are nearly empty on weekends—and this is when rates plummet and package deals abound.

WHAT IT COSTS					
	$$$$	$$$	$$	$	¢
RESTAURANTS	over $30	$23–$30	$16–$22	$10–$15	under $10
HOTELS	over $250	$176–$250	$121–$175	$90–$120	under $90

Restaurant prices are for a main course at dinner, excluding sales tax of 8¼% (depending on location). Hotel prices are for two people in a standard double room in high season, excluding service charges and 10% tax.

Timing

The hills that separate the Santa Clara Valley from the coast keep summertime fog from blowing into the Inland Peninsula and South Bay. This means that there are usually drastic variations in temperature between the coast and the inland area from April through October. In July you can expect foggy weather and temperatures in the mid-60s along the coastline, while just inland the days are sunny, with temperatures in the mid-80s. The rainy season runs from about November through March, and temperatures are generally constant across the region; daytime highs are ordinarily in the 50s and 60s.

THE COASTAL PENINSULA
UP HIGHWAY 1 FROM AÑO NUEVO
TO MOSS BEACH

The coastal towns between Santa Cruz and San Francisco were founded in the late 18th century by Spanish explorer Gaspar de Portola. After Mexico won its independence from Spain in 1822, the peninsula was used by its new residents to raise food for the Mission Dolores in San Francisco. The agriculture industry began with simple cattle ranching, but the following century saw the advent of vegetable farms and fruit orchards. As food production grew, so did the building of lighthouses and ships, to ease the transport of goods to San Francisco. You can still visit the short, squat, Point Montara Lighthouse, in Montara, 1 mi north of Moss Beach. Drive north from Santa Cruz (Chapter 10) to San Francisco along scenic Highway 1, hugging the twists and turns of the coast, or venture 11 mi inland at Half Moon Bay, over hilly Route 92 to San Mateo.

Año Nuevo State Reserve

▶ ❶ *21 mi north of Santa Cruz on Hwy. 1.*

At the most southerly point of the San Mateo County Coast, Año Nuevo is the world's only approachable mainland rookery for elephant seals. If you know you'll be in the area between mid-December and March, make reservations early for a 2½-hour guided walking tour to view the huge (up to 2 ½ tons), furry elephant seals mating or birthing, depending on the time of year. Tours stay on schedule even in bad weather, so bring a raincoat just in case. From April through November the seals are less active, but you can still see them lounging on the beach. The area's visitor center has natural history exhibits and a fascinating film about the seals. There are also plenty of hiking trails in the area. ✉ *Hwy. 1, 13 mi south of Pescadero* ☎ *650/879–0227, 800/444–4445 for tour reservations* 💲 *$4, parking $5* ⊙ *Tours leave every 15 min, daily 8:45–3.*

en route About 6 mi north of Año Nuevo State Reserve stands the 115-foot **Pigeon Point Lighthouse,** one of the tallest on the West Coast. Built in 1872, it has been used as a backdrop in numerous TV shows and commercials. The light from the 8,000-pound Fresnel lens can be seen from 20 mi out at sea. The former coast guard quarters have now been converted to a youth hostel. You can still visit the park, but the lighthouse itself is closed indefinitely for repairs. ✉ *Pigeon Point Rd. and Hwy. 1* ☎ *650/879–2120* 💲 *$2* ⊙ *Daily 8–sunset, tours late May–early Sept. and weather permitting rest of yr, Fri.–Sun. 10:30–4.*

Beaches The main draw of coastal San Mateo County is its beaches. From Montara to Pescadero the strands accessible from Highway 1 are surprisingly uncrowded. Fog and cool weather may keep many people out of the water for large portions of the year, but the unspoiled beauty and wildlife make these beaches a treasure of the Bay Area. Some standouts are San Gregorio and Pomponio for strolling and sunbathing; windy Waddell Creek for windsurfing and kite-surfing; and Fitzgerald Marine Preserve for tidepooling. Then again, since nearly three-quarters of the county (70%) is open space, there's enough beach that you can usually find a good one by simply pulling over wherever you see a patch of sand.

11

Historic Homesteads The communities of the Peninsula and South Bay have worked hard to preserve their parklands and turn-of-the-20th-century homesteads. In Woodside, Filoli stands as one of the great California country houses that remain intact. The Winchester Mystery House, in San Jose, may be the best-known site, but look beyond the tales of ghosts to see the sprawling farmhouse it once was. You can also visit former vineyards and historic homes in the Santa Cruz Mountains, notably Villa Montalvo and the Mountain Winery in Saratoga.

Pescadero

❷ *12 mi north of Año Nuevo State Reserve on Hwy. 1.*

As you walk down Stage Road, Pescadero's main street, it's hard to believe you're only 30 minutes from Silicon Valley. The few short blocks of the downtown area could almost serve as the backdrop for a western movie, with Duarte's Tavern serving as the centerpiece. In fact, Pescadero was larger in the late 19th century than it is today. This is a good place to stop for a bite or to browse for antiques. The town's real attractions, though, are spectacular beaches and hiking.

If a quarantine is not in effect (watch for signs), from November through April you can look for mussels at **Pescadero State Beach** amid tidal pools and rocky outcroppings. Barbecue pits and picnic tables make this the perfect spot for a family beach picnic. Across U.S. 101, the **Pescadero Marsh Natural Preserve** has hiking trails that cover 600 acres of marshland. Early spring and fall are the best times to come, when there are lots of migrating birds and other wildlife to see. ⊠ *14 ½ miles south of Half Moon Bay on Hwy. 1* ☎ *650/879–2170* 🎫 *Free, parking $5* ☉ *Daily 8AM–sunset.*

If you prefer mountain trails to sand dunes, head for **Pescadero Creek County Park,** an 8-acre expanse of shady, old-growth redwood forests, grasslands, and mountain streams. The park is actually composed of three smaller ones: Heritage Grove Redwood Preserve, Sam McDonald Park, and San Mateo Memorial County Park. The Old Haul Road Trail, 6½ mi long,

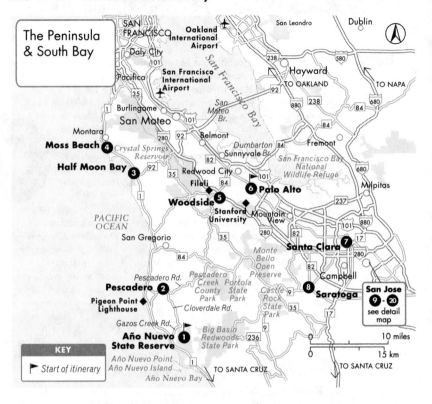

The Peninsula & South Bay

KEY

▶ Start of itinerary

runs the length of the park. Campsites cost $18 per night. ✉ *Pescadero Road off Hwy. 1* ☎ *650/879–0238* ⏰ *Daily 8AM–sunset.*

Where to Eat

¢–$$$　✕ **Duarte's Tavern.** This 19th-century roadhouse serves simple American fare, with a menu based on locally grown vegetables and fresh fish. The house specialty is the abalone ($40), but other terrific choices include artichoke soup and old-fashioned berry pie à la mode. The restaurant's bar dates back to 1894, and is a great place to sip a whiskey; since it's also the local liquor store, however, don't be surprised if some locals ask for their orders to go. ✉ *202 Stage Rd.* ☎ *650/879–0464* 🖃 *AE, MC, V.*

en route　In addition to beautiful scenery and expansive state beaches, one thing you'll pass on your way from Pescadero to Half Moon Bay is the town of San Gregorio and its idiosyncratic **San Gregorio General Store** (✉ Rte. 84 at Stage Rd., 1 mi east of Hwy. 1 ☎ 650/726–0565). Part old-time saloon, part hardware store, part grocery, the place has been a fixture in town since the late 1800s. The current Spanish-style structure replaced the original wooden building when it burned down in 1930. Come to browse through the hodgepodge items—camp stoves, books, and boots, to name just a few—or to listen to Irish music and bluegrass on weekend afternoons.

Half Moon Bay

❸ *16 mi north of Pescadero on Hwy. 1.*

The largest and most visited of the South Bay communities, Half Moon Bay is nevertheless a tiny town with a population of fewer than 10,000. Although the town doesn't look like much from the highway, once you turn onto Main Street, you'll find five blocks of vibrant galleries, shops, and cafés, many of which occupy renovated 19th-century buildings. The town comes to life on the third weekend in October, when 250,000 people gather for the **Half Moon Bay Art and Pumpkin Festival** (☎650/726–9652).

The 4-mi stretch of **Half Moon Bay State Beach** (✉ Hwy. 1, west of Main St. ☎ 650/726–8819) is perfect for long walks, kite flying, and picnic lunches, though the 50°F water and dangerous currents make swimming inadvisable. There are three access points, one in Half Moon Bay and two south of town off the highway. To find them, look for road signs that have a picture of footsteps.

Where to Stay & Eat

$$–$$$$ ✕ **Cetrella.** This is the coast at its most dressed up. The restaurant is all polished wood and pressed tablecloths, and hits every gourmet mark— adventurous wine list, sumptuous cheese course, and live jazz and salsa music Thursday through Saturday. The menu—which features local organic ingredients—is largely Provençal, with some yummy Spanish surprises, such as a variety of *tapas* (small plates of different hors d'oeuvres). Seafood lovers, however, may want to order oysters directly from the raw bar. ✉ *845 Main St.* ☎ 650/726–4090 ▤ *AE, MC, V.*

$$–$$$ ✕ **Pasta Moon.** The wood-burning oven tips you off to the thin-crust pizzas that are served in this small restaurant. The rest of the menu highlights seasonal dishes made from local organic produce, as well as handmade pastas, a wonderfully crispy roast chicken, and grilled quail. ✉ *315 Main St.* ☎ 650/726–5126 ▤ *AE, D, DC, MC, V.*

$$ ✕ **San Benito House.** Tucked inside a historic inn in the heart of Half Moon Bay, this ground-floor restaurant serves a limited dinner menu that changes weekly and often includes bouillabaisse, roasted quail, sea bass or wild sturgeon, and house-made ravioli or other pastas. By day the kitchen prepares memorable sandwiches with bread baked in the restaurant's oven and sells them, deli style, for picnics by the sea. ✉ *356 Main St.* ☎ 650/726–3425 ▤ *AE, DC, MC, V* ⊗ *No dinner Mon.–Wed.*

¢–$ ✕ **Two Fools.** Big organic salads and burritos are the draw at this place, but some of the more unusual menu choices—like the homemade nut loaf, and meat loaf topped with caramelized onions in a fresh-baked bun— are equally good. ✉ *408 Main St.* ☎ 650/712–1222 ▤ *AE, D, MC, V* ⊗ *No dinner Mon.*

$$$$ ▥ **The Ritz-Carlton.** With its enormous but elegantly decorated rooms, secluded oceanfront property, and a staff that waits on guests hand and foot, this golf and spa resort defines opulence. Attention to detail is considered right down to the silver service, china, and 300 thread-count Egyptian cotton sheets. During cocktail hour, view the ocean from the plush conservatory bar, or tucked under a heavy blanket on an Adirondack chair on the lawn. ✉ *1 Miramontes Point Rd., 94019* ☎ 650/

712–7000 or 800/241–3333 ⊟ 650/712–7070 ⊕ www.ritzcarlton. com ⟲ 261 rooms, 22 suites ⚭ Restaurant, room service, in-room data ports, in-room safes, 18-hole golf course, 6 tennis courts, hot tub, sauna, spa, steam room, bar, babysitting, laundry service, concierge, business services, meeting rooms, airport shuttle, no-smoking rooms ⊟ AE, D, DC, MC, V.

$$–$$$$ ⌂ **Mill Rose Inn.** Luxurious extras at this B&B include fireplaces, brass beds stacked high with down comforters, coffee, cocoa, and fruit baskets in the guest rooms, as well as decanters of sherry and brandy in the parlor. The gardens are full of roses and climbing sweet peas. Room rates include champagne breakfast and afternoon snacks. ⊠ 615 Mill St., 94019 ☎ 650/726–8750 or 800/900–7673 ⊟ 650/726–3031 ⊕ www. millroseinn.com ⟲ 4 rooms, 2 suites ⚭ Some in-room hot tubs, refrigerators, cable TV, in-room VCRs, Internet, meeting room; no smoking, no a/c ⊟ AE, D, DC, MC, V ⧖ BP.

$$–$$$$ ⌂ **Old Thyme Inn.** The owners of this 1898 Princess Anne Victorian love herbs and flowers, and if you have a green thumb of your own, this is the place for you. The gardens alongside the house burst with blossoms year-round, guest rooms are filled with fragrant bouquets, and each room is named after an herb and decorated in its colors. Antiques, homemade breakfasts, complimentary sherry, and afternoon snacks enhance the sense of homeyness. ⊠ 779 Main St., 94019 ☎ 650/726–1616 or 800/720–4277 ⊟ 650/726–6394 ⊕ www.oldthymeinn.com ⟲ 7 rooms ⚭ In-room data ports, some in-room hot tubs, cable TV, in-room VCRs, concierge; no smoking, no a/c ⊟ AE, D, MC, V ⧖ BP.

Sports

The **Bicyclery** (⊠ 101 Main St. ☎ 650/726–6000) rents bikes and can provide information on organized rides up and down the coast. If you prefer to go it alone, try the 3-mi bike trail that leads from Kelly Avenue in Half Moon Bay to Mirada Road in Miramar.

Moss Beach

❹ 7 mi north of Half Moon Bay on Hwy. 1; 20 mi south of San Francisco on Hwy. 1.

Moss Beach was a busy outpost during Prohibition, when regular shipments of liquid contraband from Canada were unloaded at the secluded beach and hauled off to San Francisco. The town stayed under the radar out of necessity, with only one local hotel and bar where Bay Area politicians and gangsters could go for a drink while waiting for their shipments. Today, although it has grown into a cheerful surfing town with charming shops and restaurants, it is still all but invisible from the highway—a good hideaway for those allergic to crowds.

The biggest Moss Beach attraction is the **Fitzgerald Marine Reserve** (⊠ California and North Lake Sts. ☎ 650/728–3584), a 3-mi stretch of bluffs and tidepools. Since the reserve was protected in 1969, scientists have discovered 25 new aquatic species here; depending on the tide, you'll most likely find shells, anemones, or starfish.

Just off the coast at Moss Beach is **Mavericks;** when there's a big swell, it's one of the biggest surfing breaks in the world. Waves here have reportedly reached 60 feet in height, and surfers get towed out to them by Jet Skis. The break is a mile offshore, so seeing it from the coast can be tough and requires a demanding hike; the intrepid can get photocopied directions at the Distillery restaurant, then drive 3 mi south for the trail out of **Pillar Point Harbor.** Even if you're not hunting for waves, the harbor is a nice place to wander, with its laid back restaurants and waters full of fishing boats and sea lions.

Built in 1928 after two horrible shipwrecks on the point, the **Point Montara Lighthouse** still has its original light keeper's quarters from the late 1800s. Gray whales pass this point during their migration from November through April, so bring your binoculars. Visiting hours coincide with morning and afternoon check-in and check-out times at the adjoining youth hostel ($18–$22 dorm beds, $57 private room). ⊠ *16th St. at Hwy. 1, Montara* ☎ *650/728–7177* ☯ *Daily 8AM–sunset.*

Where to Stay & Eat

$$–$$$ ✕ **The Distillery.** During Prohibition this two-tier restaurant perched on a cliff was the first stop for the Canadian liquor unloaded on the beach below. Now, the only reminder of the spot's outlaw history is a resident ghost who visits from time to time—allegedly the soul of a 1930s adulteress. Upstairs, the dinner restaurant is candlelit and has a good surf-and-turf menu. Things are more casual (and less expensive) at the self-service lunch spot and bar downstairs, where the deck can get downright rowdy on sunny weekends. On chilly afternoons couples can cuddle under heavy woolen blankets on swinging benches and sip wine while watching the fog roll in. ⊠ *140 Beach Way* ☎ *650/728–5595* ⊕ *www.mossbeachdistillery.com* ⊟ *D, DC, MC, V.*

★ $$ ✕ **Cafe Gibraltar.** One meal at this restaurant can make you feel like you've been on a whirlwind tour of the Mediterranean. Chef-owner Jose Luiz Ugalde is a master of creative dishes, particularly the sweet and spicy (many sauces contain fruits such as apricots and currants). The flavors are unexpected—calamari baked with cinnamon, lavender crème brûlée—and the atmosphere is sensual, with peach walls lit by flickering candles and four booths draped with curtains and lined with pillows (no chairs). Located 2 mi south of Moss Beach on the east side of the highway, it's a bit hard to find, but well worth the hunt. At signs for Pillar Point Harbor, turn inland onto Capistrano, and then right onto Alhambra. ⊠ *425 Avenue Alhambra, at Palma Ave., El Granada* ☎ *650/560–9039* ⊕ *www.cafegibraltar.com* ⊟ *AE, MC, V* ☯ *Closed Mon. No lunch.*

★ ¢ ✕ **Three–Zero Cafe.** This busy restaurant at the tiny Half Moon Bay Airport is a local favorite, especially for weekend breakfasts. The food is standard—eggs and pancakes for breakfast, burgers for lunch—but reliably good. Get a window table, and as you eat watch two-seater planes take off and land on the runway 20 feet away. ⊠ *Hwy. 1, 2 mi south of Moss Beach, El Granada* ☎ *650/573–3701* ⊟ *MC, V* ☯ *No dinner.*

$$$–$$$$ ▣ **Seal Cove Inn.** Travel writer Karen Brown has written guidebooks to inns all over the world, and this is what she has created at home. Her inn is modern but charming and warm, with all windows looking onto flower gardens and toward cypress trees that border the marine reserve. Rooms have antique bed frames and writing desks, plush mattresses, lounge chairs, and fireplaces. Upstairs rooms have cathedral ceilings and balconies. Full breakfast and evening wine and hors d'oeuvres are served in the parlor and dining room. ☒ *221 Cypress Ave., 94038* ☎ *650/728–4114 or 800/995–9987* ☒ *650/728–4116* ⊕ *www.sealcoveinn.com* ⬏ *8 rooms, 2 suites* ⚥ *Minibars, refrigerators, in-room VCRs; no a/c* ⊺⊙⎮ *BP* ⊟ *AE, D, MC, V.*

$–$$ ⊡ **The Goose and Turrets.** Artifacts from the international travels of innkeepers Raymond and Emily Hoche-Mong fill the shelves of this inn 8 mi north of Half Moon Bay. A full home-cooked breakfast, afternoon goodies, and homemade chocolate truffles are sure to make anyone feel at home. Some rooms have fireplaces. ☒ *835 George St., Montara 94037* ☎ *650/728–5451* ☒ *650/728–0141* ⊕ *goose.montara.com* ⬏ *5 rooms* ⚥ *Boccie, piano; no-smoking, no a/c* ⊟ *AE, D, DC, MC, V* ⊺⊙⎮ *BP.*

THE INLAND PENINSULA

Much of your first impression of the Inland Peninsula will depend on where and when you enter. Take the 30-mi stretch of U.S. 101 from San Francisco along the eastern side of the Peninsula, and you'll see office complex after shopping center after corporate tower—and you'll likely get caught in horrific morning and evening commuter traffic. On the west side, however, the less crowded I–280 takes you past soul-soothing hills, lakes, and reservoirs.

Woodside

⑤ *31 mi south of San Francisco via I–280.*

West of Palo Alto, Woodside is a tiny rustic town where weekend warriors stock up on espresso and picnic fare before charging off on their mountain bikes. Blink once, and you're past the town center. The main draw here is the wealth of surrounding lush parks and preserves.

★ One of the few great country houses in California that remains intact is **Filoli.** Built 1915–17 for wealthy San Franciscan William B. Bourn II, it was designed by Willis Polk in a Georgian-revival style, with redbrick walls and a tile roof. The name is Bourn's acronym for "fight, love, live." As interesting as the house are the 16 acres of formal gardens, which include a sunken garden and a teahouse in the Italian Renaissance style. From June through September Filoli hosts a series of Sunday afternoon jazz concerts. Bring a picnic or buy a box lunch; Filoli provides tables, sodas, wine, fruit, and popcorn. In December the mansion is festively decorated for a series of holiday events: brunches, afternoon teas, Christmas concerts, and more. ☒ *Cañada Rd. near Edgewood Rd.* ☎ *650/364–8300* ⊕ *www.filoli.org* ⊠ *$10* ⊙ *Mid-Feb.–Oct., Tues.–Sat. 10–3:30* ☞ *Reservations are essential for guided tours.*

Where to Eat

$–$$$ ✕ **Bucks in Woodside.** This casual restaurant typifies Silicon Valley's unusual approach to corporate culture. The walls may be decorated with giant plastic alligators and Elvis paintings, but the guy in bike shorts at the next table may well be a high-power tech executive. The menu is a grab bag of crowd pleasers: soups, sandwiches, burgers, and salads. For breakfast there's a "U-do-it" omelet in addition to standard choices. ⊠ *3062 Woodside Rd.* ☎ *650/851–8010* ⊟ *AE, D, MC, V.*

¢–$$$ ✕ **Woodside Bakery and Café.** The bakery section of this bustling spot is perfect for a cup of hot cocoa and a fresh-baked pastry; the café area in the courtyard is equally pleasant for a glass of wine and a meal. Although the café menu focuses mostly on light pastas and salads, there are also a few more substantial entrées like oven-braised lamb shank and baked Dijon chicken. ⊠ *3052 Woodside Rd.* ☎ *650/851–0812* ⊟ *AE, MC, V.*

Palo Alto

► ❻ *34 mi south of San Francisco via I–280 or U.S. 101.*

Palo Alto's main attraction is the pastoral campus of Stanford University, which encompasses 8,200 acres of grassy hills. Downtown Palo Alto is full of restaurants, shops, and diversions catering to high-income Peninsula residents as well as the university crowd. A wander up and down University Avenue and its surrounding side streets will reveal such attractions as the Stanford Theatre (a 1920s-style movie palace)—and the always-popular Barbie Hall of Fame.

Stanford University was former California governor Leland Stanford's horse-breeding farm, and the land is still known as the Farm. Founded in 1885 and opened in 1891, the university occupies a campus designed by Frederick Law Olmsted. Its unique California mission—Romanesque sandstone buildings, joined by arcades and topped by red-tile roofs—are mixed with newer buildings in variations on Olmstead's style. The 285-foot Hoover Tower is a landmark and a tourist attraction; an elevator ($2) leads to an observation deck that provides sweeping views. Free one-hour **walking tours** (⊠ Serra St., opposite Hoover Tower ☎ 650/723–2560) of the Stanford campus leave daily at 11 and 3:15 from the visitor center in the front hall of Memorial Auditorium. ⊠ *Galvez St. at Serra St.* ☎ *650/723–2300* ⊕ *www.stanford.edu.*

★ **The Iris and B. Gerald Cantor Center for Visual Arts,** one of the most comprehensive and varied art collections in the Bay Area, includes works from pre-Columbian periods through the modern. Included is the world's largest collection—180 pieces—of Rodin sculptures outside Paris, many of them displayed in the outdoor garden (for a spectacular sight, visit these at night during a full moon). Other highlights include a bronze Buddha from the Ming dynasty, wooden masks and carved figurines from 18th- and 19th-century Africa, paintings by Georgia O'Keeffe, and sculpture by Willem de Kooning and Bay Area artist Robert Arneson. The exceptional café has a menu—all organic—and clientele that's savvy but unpretentious. You can sit in the airy dining room or on the sunny terrace overlooking the Rodin garden. ⊠ *328 Lomita Dr. and Museum Way, off Palm Dr. at Stanford University* ☎ *650/723–4177* ⊕ *ccva.stanford.edu* ⊠ *Free* ☉ *Wed., Fri.–Sun. 11–5, Thurs. 11–8. Rodin Sculpture Garden tours Sat. at 11, Sun. at 3.*

Tucked into a small, heavily wooded plot is the **Papua New Guinea Sculpture Garden,** filled with tall, ornately carved poles, drums, and stones—all created in the 1990s by 10 artists from Papua New Guinea. Complementing them are plants from Melanesia, including a huge, gorgeous Silk Oak tree. Detailed plaques explain the concept and the works. ⊠ *Santa Teresa St. and Lomita Dr., at Stanford University* 🎟 *Free.*

Two-hour tours of the **Stanford Linear Accelerator Center (SLAC)** reveal the workings of the 2-mi-long electron accelerator, which is used by Stanford University scientists for research into elementary particles. Call for times and reservations. ⊠ *Sand Hill Rd., 3 mi west of the central campus* 🕾 *650/926–2204.*

off the beaten path

PALO ALTO BAYLANDS NATURE PRESERVE – East of downtown Palo Alto is a wetlands area of creeks, sloughs, mudflats, and freshwater and saltwater marshland, where you can find some of the best bird-watching in the area. The area supports more than 150 bird species, and is an important stopover on the Pacific Flyway. You can walk the Bay Trail through the middle of the preserve and visit the Lucy Evans Nature Interpretive Center, or bring a canoe and explore by water. ⊠ *East end of Embarcadero Rd.* 🕾 *650/329–2506* 🎟 *Free* ⊙ *Daily 8AM–sunset.*

Where to Stay & Eat

★ **$$–$$$$** ╳ **Evvia.** This Greek restaurant is no shish-kebab joint. The dining rooms are decorated in the fashion of a (superbly tasteful) Greek country house, with copper pots and garlic wreaths lining the mantles. The menu is rustic yet elegant, and ranges from the familiar—roast chicken, Greek salad—to the adventurous—boar confit in phyllo with dried apricots and slow-cooked cabbage. ⊠ *420 Emerson St.* 🕾 *650/326–0983* ⌂ *Reservations essential* ⊟ *AE, D, DC, MC, V* ⊙ *No lunch weekends.*

$$–$$$ ╳ **L'Amie Donia.** Chef-owner Donia Bijan, who made a name for herself at San Francisco's Sherman House and Brasserie Savoy, has decorated her utterly charming French bistro in sunny yellow and soothing blue. Her seasonal menus focus on flavorful fare that one might find in the French countryside: roast beets with warm goat cheese and walnuts, rabbit with mustard sauce, pan-roasted veal chop with an almond crust. ⊠ *530 Bryant St.* 🕾 *650/323–7614* ⌂ *Reservations essential* ⊟ *AE, D, MC, V* ⊙ *Closed Sun. and Mon. and late Dec.–mid-Jan. No lunch.*

★ **$$–$$$** ╳ **Flea Street Café.** The staff at this romantic, friendly restaurant has been on board for decades and takes great care in preparing and serving food. Ingredients are selected from farmers that owner Jesse Cool knows personally, and the dishes are fresh and inventive: the winter *fritto misto* (batter-fried vegetables) includes Meyer lemon slices; spring oysters are served with avocado and smoked trout. ⊠ *3607 Alameda de las Pulgas* 🕾 *650/854–1226* ⊟ *AE, MC, V* ⊙ *Closed Mon. No lunch.*

$$–$$$ ╳ **Spago.** Silicon Valley's best and brightest have made a hit out of Wolfgang Puck's splashy, dashing Spago. The fare is inventive Californian, the service flawless. Flat breads, bread sticks, and specialty loaves will tide you over until the real food arrives. Dinner might include roast chicken breast with ricotta gnocchi or grilled quail with a white-bean cassoulet.

The tasty desserts are artistically presented; don't miss the satsuma parfait. ☒ *265 Lytton Ave.* ☎ *650/833–1000* ⌂ *Reservations essential* ⊟ *AE, D, DC, MC, V* ⊗ *No lunch weekends.*

$–$$$ ✕ **Zibibbo.** The menu changes seasonally at this two-story Victorian establishment, where you can sit in a garden, a glassed-in atrium, or a dining room. Even the pickiest diner is likely to find something appealing on the unusually long menu, which includes such creative dishes as crispy saffron rice balls with chorizo, and pork loin with a pomegranate-molasses glaze. Vegetarians will be happy here, too; there are many tempting meat-free choices. ☒ *430 Kipling St.* ☎ *650/328–6722* ⊟ *AE, DC, MC, V.*

$ ✕ **JZ Cool Eatery.** Comfort food favoring local organic ingredients—such as homemade meat loaf topped with caramelized onions—is the focus at this spot in downtown Menlo Park. Touches such as butcher-block tables and potato salad disguise the health-conscious bent; you might just forget the food here is supposed to be good for you. ☒ *827 Santa Cruz Ave., Menlo Park* ☎ *650/325–3665* ⊟ *AE, MC, V.*

¢ ✕ **Pasta?** The most expensive pasta dish here—and there are many on the menu—is $9. This is good food, plain and simple, made with fresh seasonal ingredients and presented with care. In addition to such standard pasta dishes as salmon fettuccine, there are always a few lighter selections made without heavy oils, cheese, or salt. A handful of meat and fish entrées, such as pork medallions with Chianti sauce, are priced well below $10. Naturally, the place does a brisk business with students. ☒ *326 University Ave.* ☎ *650/328–4585* ⊟ *MC, V.*

¢ ✕ **Pluto's.** This loud and lively restaurant is known for fresh, custom-made salads, sandwiches, and buffet-style hot meals. By visiting different serving stations, you can have a salad made with toppings like grilled fennel and roasted peppers, or build your own sandwich with choices like marinated flank steak and grilled eggplant. ☒ *482 University Ave.* ☎ *650/853–1556* ⊟ *MC, V.*

★ $$$$ ⌂ **Garden Court Hotel.** The outside of this boutique hotel looks like an Italian villa, with columns and arches, a dormer roof, and bougainvillea-draped balconies. The tastefully furnished, sunlit interior is equally appealing. Some rooms overlook a lush central courtyard, others have fireplaces or four-poster beds; all suites have private terraces. Ground-floor shops and restaurants include Il Fornaio. ☒ *520 Cowper St., 94301* ☎ *650/322–9000 or 800/824–9028* 🖷 *650/324–3609* ⊕ *www. gardencourt.com* ⇘ *50 rooms, 12 suites* ⌂ *Restaurant, room service, in-room data ports, some in-room hot-tubs, room TVs with movies, gym, bar, laundry service, concierge, Internet, business services, meeting rooms, no-smoking rooms* ⊟ *AE, D, DC, MC, V.*

$$$$ ⌂ **Sheraton Hotel Palo Alto.** This hotel caters to business travelers, yet manages to evoke a tranquil haven; the koi pond winding from the pool area through landscaped gardens is a vision of serenity (request an even-numbered room for a better view of the pond). The hotel is amazingly quiet considering its site on a busy intersection one block from the Stanford Shopping Center. Rooms are standard-issue business style, with typical amenities. ☒ *625 El Camino Real, 94301* ☎ *650/328–2800 or 800/874–3516* 🖷 *650/327–7362* ⇘ *350 rooms* ⌂ *Restaurant, room* *service, in-room data ports, pool, gym, lounge, laundry facilities, laundry service, concierge, business services, meeting room, no-smoking floor* ⊟ *AE, D, DC, MC, V.*

$$$$ ▦ **Stanford Park Hotel.** The original oil paintings, antiques, tapestries, and forest-green color scheme make this stately hotel feel more like an English hunt club than a hotel in Silicon Valley. Rooms are welcoming, with fireplaces, vaulted ceilings, English yew-wood armoires, and framed hunting scenes. The Duck Club Restaurant continues the hunting motif with a menu that includes quite a few game meats. ⊠ *100 El Camino Real, 94025* ☎ *650/322–1234 or 800/368–2468* 🖷 *650/322–0975* ⊕ *www.woodsidehotels.com* 🛏 *163 rooms* ♿ *Restaurant, in-room data ports, minibars, pool, gym, bar, lobby lounge, laundry service, concierge, business services, meeting room; no smoking* ⊟ *AE, DC, MC, V.*

$$$–$$$$ ▦ **The Victorian on Lytton.** Only a block from downtown Palo Alto, this inn attracts business travelers who want comfort and amenities without too many frills. Innkeepers Susan and Maxwell Hall gutted the building—a former apartment complex—and completely configured the interior to accommodate spacious rooms, some with canopy beds. Complimentary breakfast is ordered the night before and brought to your room in the morning. ⊠ *555 Lytton Ave., 94301* ☎ *650/322–8555* 🖷 *650/322–7141* ⊕ *www.victorianonlytton.com* 🛏 *10 rooms* ♿ *No-smoking rooms; no a/c* ⊟ *AE, MC, V* ⦿ *BP.*

¢–$$ ▦ **Cowper Inn.** This former Victorian home in a quiet residential neighborhood is one of the least expensive lodging options around, and it's charming to boot. The cozy parlor has a brick fireplace, a piano, and a big window looking out on tree-lined Cowper Street. Breakfast includes homemade muffins and granola and fresh-squeezed orange juice. ⊠ *705 Cowper St., 94301* ☎ *650/327–4475* 🖷 *650/329–1703* ⊕ *www. cowperinn.com* 🛏 *14 rooms, 12 with bath* ♿ *Cable TV, piano; no a/c, no smoking* ⊟ *AE, MC, V* ⦿ *CP.*

SOUTH BAY
WEST OF SAN JOSE

To many the South Bay is synonymous with Silicon Valley, the center of high-tech research and the corporate headquarters of such giants as Apple, Sun Microsystems, Oracle, and Hewlett-Packard. But Silicon Valley is more a state of mind than a place—it's an attitude held by the legions of software engineers, programmers, and computerphiles who call the area home. That home is becoming increasingly visitor-friendly; within the sprawl are appealing towns whose history stretches back centuries, a thriving arts scene, and shops and restaurants to satisfy the most discerning tastes.

Santa Clara

❼ *40 mi south of San Francisco on Hwy. 101.*

Santa Clara has two major attractions at opposite ends of the sightseeing spectrum: Mission Santa Clara de Asis, founded in 1777, and

Paramount's Great America, northern California's answer to Disneyland. Although many visitors head straight to the amusement park, Santa Clara has plenty of history and is worthy of a visit—despite its ubiquitous shopping malls and sterile business parks.

Santa Clara University, founded in 1851 by Jesuits, was California's first college. The campus's **de Saisset Art Gallery and Museum** shows a permanent collection that includes California mission artifacts and gold-rush-era pieces, California-theme artwork, and contemporary Bay Area art, especially prints. ⊠ *500 El Camino Real* ☎ *408/554–4528* ⊕ *www. scu.edu/desaisset* ✉ *Free* ⊙ *Tues.–Sun. 11–4.*

In the center of Santa Clara University's campus is the **Mission Santa Clara de Asis**, the first of California's original missions to honor a female saint. In 1926 the mission chapel was destroyed by fire. Roof tiles of the current building, a replica of the original, were salvaged from earlier structures, which dated from the 1790s and 1820s. Early adobe walls and a spectacular rose garden with 4,500 roses—many of the varieties classified as antique—remain intact as well. Part of the wooden Memorial Cross, from 1777, is set in front of the church. ⊠ *500 El Camino Real* ☎ *408/554–4023* ⊕ *www.scu.edu/visitors/mission* ✉ *Free* ⊙ *Self-guided tours daily 1–sundown.*

☺ At the gigantic theme park **Paramount's Great America,** each section recalls a familiar part of North America: Hometown Square, Yukon Territory, Yankee Harbor, or County Fair. Popular attractions include the Drop Zone Stunt Tower, the tallest free-fall ride in North America; a *Top Gun* movie-theme roller coaster, whose cars travel along the outside of a 360-degree loop track; and Nickelodeon Splat City, 3 acres of obstacle courses apparently designed for kids who love to get wet and dirty. You can get to the park via Valley Transit Authority, Caltrain, and BART. ⊠ *Great America Pkwy. between U.S. 101 and Rte. 237, 6 mi north of San Jose* ☎ *408/988–1776* ⊕ *www.pgathrills.com* ✉ *$47.99, parking $10* ⊙ *Apr., May, Sept. and Oct. weekends; June–Aug., daily; opens 10 AM, closing times vary* ⊟ *AE, D, MC, V.*

The **Carmelite Monastery** is a fine example of Spanish ecclesiastical architecture. Built in 1917, it's on the grounds of a mission-era ranch crossed by shady walkways and dotted with benches perfect for quiet contemplation. ⊠ *1000 Lincoln St.* ☎ *408/296–8412* ⊕ *members.aol.com/ santaclaracarmel* ✉ *Free* ⊙ *Grounds: daily 6:30–4:15.*

Skylights cast natural light for viewing the exhibitions in the **Triton Museum of Art.** A permanent collection of 19th- and 20th-century sculpture by Bay Area artists is displayed in the garden, which you can see through a curved-glass wall at the rear of the building. Indoor galleries present excellent, eclectic shows of contemporary Native American work. ⊠ *1505 Warburton Ave.* ☎ *408/247–3754* ⊕ *www.tritonmuseum. org* ✉ *$2 suggested donation* ⊙ *Fri.–Wed. 11–5, Thurs. 11–9.*

The **Harris-Lass Historic Museum** is built on Santa Clara's last farmstead. A restored house, summer kitchen, and barn convey what life was like on the farm from the early 1900s through the 1930s. Guided tours take place every half hour until 3:30. ⊠ *1889 Market St.* ☎ *408/249–7905* ⊠ *$3* ⊙ *Weekends noon–4.*

Where to Stay & Eat

$$–$$$$ ✕ **Birk's.** Silicon Valley's businesspeople come to this sophisticated American grill to unwind. High-tech sensibilities will appreciate the modern open kitchen and streamlined, multilevel dining area—yet the menu is traditional, strong on steaks and chops. An oyster bar adds a lighter element, as do the simply prepared but high-quality organic vegetable dishes such as garlic mashed potatoes and creamed spinach. ⊠ *3955 Freedom Cir., at Hwy. 101 and Great America Pkwy.* ☎ *408/980–6400* ⊟ *AE, D, DC, MC, V* ⊙ *No lunch weekends.*

$–$$ ✕ **Mio Vicino.** Mio's is a small, bare-bones, checkered-tablecloth Italian bistro in Old Santa Clara. The menu includes a long list of classic and contemporary pastas—and if you don't see it on the menu, just ask. The house specialties are shellfish pasta and chicken cannelloni. ⊠ *1290 Benton St.* ☎ *408/241–9414* ⊠ *384 E. Campbell Ave., Campbell* ☎ *408/ 378–0335* ⊟ *MC, V* ⊙ *No lunch weekends.*

¢ ✕ **Chez Sovan.** This Cambodian jewel is a departure from the average South Bay restaurant—and a reliable one. The noodle dishes, grilled meats, and curries are all excellently flavored. Specialties of the house are the spring rolls and the rice noodles in tamarind sauce. ⊠ *2425 S. Bascom Ave.* ☎ *408/371–7711* ⊟ *AE, MC, V.*

$$$ ⊞ **Embassy Suites.** This upper-end chain hotel attracts Silicon Valley business travelers—but since the rates plummet on the weekends, it's even better suited to families bound for Paramount's Great America. All lodgings are two-room suites, and rates include cooked-to-order breakfasts and evening beverages. ⊠ *2885 Lakeside Dr., 95054* ☎ *408/496– 6400 or 800/362–2779* ⊠ *408/988–7529* ⊕ *www.embassy-suites.com* ⊷ *257 suites* ⍩ *Restaurant, room service, in-room data ports, refrigerators, cable TV with movies, pool, gym, hot tub, sauna, lounge, Internet, business services, meeting room, airport shuttle, free parking, no-smoking rooms* ⊟ *AE, D, DC, MC, V* ⍉ *BP.*

$ ⊞ **Madison Street Inn.** At this Queen Anne Victorian, complimentary afternoon refreshments and a full breakfast are served on a brick garden patio with a bougainvillea-draped trellis. The inn feels like a private home, with its green-and-red-trimmed facade and individually styled rooms that range from homey to fancy. ⊠ *1390 Madison St., 95050* ☎ *408/249– 5541 or 800/491–5541* ⊠ *408/249–6676* ⊕ *www.madisonstreetinn.com* ⊷ *6 rooms, 4 with bath* ⍩ *Some fans, in-room data ports, some microwaves, some refrigerators, cable TV, pool, hot tub, bicycles, laundry service, Internet, meeting room, some pets allowed; no a/c in some rooms, no TV in some rooms, no smoking* ⊟ *AE, D, DC, MC, V* ⍉ *BP.*

Saratoga

❽ *12 mi southwest of Santa Clara on Hwy. 85.*

A 10-mi detour southwest of San Jose's urban core puts you in the heart of Saratoga, at the foot of the Santa Cruz Mountains. Once an artists' colony, the town is now home to many Silicon Valley CEOs, whose mansions dot the hillsides. Spend a slow-paced afternoon exploring Big Basin Way, the ⅓-mi main drag of the Village, as the downtown area is locally known. Here you'll find antiques stores, galleries, spas, and a handful of worthwhile restaurants.

★ Built in 1912 by former governor James Phelan, **Villa Montalvo** is a striking white mansion presiding over an expansive lawn. You can picnic and lounge on the lawn amidst sculptures or stroll through the art gallery, whose changing exhibits feature work by local artists and artists-in-residence. Additional draws are a gift shop and 175-acre park with several hiking trails, as well as a first-rate summer concert series and year-round literary events. ⊠ *15400 Montalvo Rd.* ☎ *408/961–5800* ⊕ *www.villamontalvo.org* ⊠ *Free* ⊙ *Park weekdays 8–5, weekends 9–5; gallery Wed.–Sun. 1–4.*

For a quick driving tour of the hills with their sweeping valley views, ★ drive south out of Saratoga on Big Basin Way, which is **Scenic Highway 9.** The road leads into the Santa Cruz Mountains, all the way to the coast at the city of Santa Cruz. But you can take in some great views about 1½ mi out of town by taking a right on Pierce Road and driving out to the **Mountain Winery.** Built by Paul Masson in 1905 and now listed on the National Register of Historic Places, it is constructed of masonry and oak to resemble a French country chateau. Although it no longer serves its original purpose, Mountain Winery now hosts winemaker dinners and a summer concert series. Walking tours are available for free if you call in advance.

Where to Stay & Eat

★ $$$–$$$$ ✕ **Sent Sovi.** At this small, flower-filled restaurant, housed in a quaint cottage on Saratoga's quiet main street, chef and co-owner David Kinch creates a changing menu of elegant French-inspired fare. Two excellent entrées are the marinated hanger steak with cheddar mashed potatoes, and the pork tenderloin with dried cherries and smoked pecans; desserts are equally tantalizing. A five-course tasting menu will let you sample more widely from Kinch's formidable repertoire. ⊠ *14583 Big Basin Way* ☎ *408/867–3110* ⌕ *Reservations essential* ⊟ *AE, MC, V* ⊙ *Closed Mon. No lunch.*

¢–$ ✕ **Willow Street Wood-Fired Pizza.** What began as a quaint "secret" pizzeria in the Willow Glen neighborhood just south of downtown has become one of the best and trendiest spots in the South Bay. Individual cheese pizzas are wood-fire baked to perfection, and so are more adventurous choices such as pizzas with chicken and Brie, or artichoke and goat cheese. During lunch you can order from a quick and downsize version of the dinner menu. Reservations are accepted only for parties of eight or more, but smaller parties can call ahead to secure a spot on the waiting list. ⊠ *1072 Willow St.* ☎ *408/971–7080* ⌕ *Reservations not accepted* ⊟ *AE, MC, V.*

$$$–$$$$ ▥ **Inn at Saratoga.** This European-style inn is only 20 minutes from San Jose, but its aura of calm makes it feel far from the Silicon Valley buzz. Rooms are decorated in soft earth tones and include sitting alcoves that overlook a peaceful stream. In the evening wine and hors d'oeuvres are set out in the cozy lobby and, although modern business conveniences

are available, they are discreetly hidden. ✉ *20645 4th St., 95070* ☎ *408/867–5020 or 800/543–5020* 🖷 *408/741–0981* ⊕ *www.innatsaratoga.com* ⇥ *42 rooms, 3 suites* ⚒ *In-room data ports, refrigerators, cable TV, in-room VCRs, exercise equipment, laundry service, Internet, business services, meeting room; no smoking* ▭ *AE, DC, MC, V* ❘⊙❘ *CP.*

$–$$$ ▥ **Saratoga Oaks Lodge.** This small and cozy place occupies a site that once housed the tollgate to a private road heading over the Santa Cruz Mountains. Several rooms have fireplaces and steam baths. Town is a short stroll away, so the location is quiet but convenient. ✉ *14626 Big Basin Way, 95070* ☎ *408/867–3307 or 888/867–3588* 🖷 *408/867–6765* ⊕ *www.saratogaoakslodge.com* ⇥ *15 rooms, 5 suites* ⚒ *In-room data ports, microwaves, refrigerators, cable TV; no smoking* ▭ *AE, D, MC, V* ❘⊙❘ *CP.*

SAN JOSE

San Jose has its own ballet, symphony, repertory theater, nationally recognized museums, downtown nightlife, and exclusive hotels. Downtown can be easily explored by foot, and Guadalupe River Park, a 3-mi belt of trees and gardens, connects downtown with the Children's Discovery Museum to the south. The chain of parks and playgrounds extends north to San Jose International Airport. A 21-mi light-rail system links downtown to the business district and Paramount's Great America to the north, and to several suburbs and malls to the south. You will still need a car to get to outlying communities and such sights as the Egyptian Museum and the Winchester Mystery House.

A walking tour of downtown San Jose is detailed in a brochure available from the Convention and Visitors Bureau. The self-guided walk leads you past the 14 historic buildings described in the brochure. Vintage trolleys operate in downtown San Jose from 10:30 to 5:30 in summer and on some holidays throughout the year. You can buy trolley tickets at vending machines in any transit station.

Downtown San Jose & Vicinity

4 mi east of Santa Clara on Hwy. 82; 55 mi south of San Francisco on Hwy. 101 or I–280.

a good tour

Much of downtown San Jose can be toured easily on foot. Start at the ▶ **Children's Discovery Museum** ⑨ and be sure to wander around the outside of this outrageously purple building. Crossing through the surrounding park, take a stroll through the "herd" of larger-than-life animal sculptures facing San Carlos Street. The nearby steps lead down to Guadalupe Creek and a parallel walking path; a good detour heads north to the San Jose Arena and the **Guadalupe River Park** ⑩, with a carousel and children's playground.

Back at the sculpture park, continue east on San Carlos Street into the heart of downtown San Jose. Immediately on the left is the Center for the Performing Arts, home to the city's ballet and symphony. San Jose's McEnery Convention Center and the visitor center are diagonally across

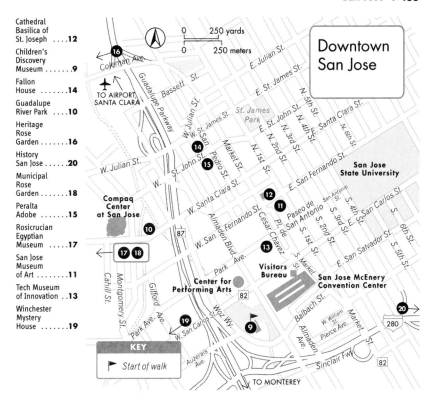

the road. In front of the center an outdoor skating rink (open daily) is set up from mid-November to mid-January.

Continue down San Carlos Street and turn left on Market Street; ahead is Plaza de Cesar Chavez. On the square's northeast corner are the must-see **San Jose Museum of Art** ⑪ and adjacent **Cathedral Basilica of St. Joseph** ⑫. On the square's western edge at Park Avenue is the **Tech Museum of Innovation** ⑬, with its children-friendly hands-on exhibits.

Follow Market Street north from the plaza and turn left on Santa Clara Street. For a glimpse of the historic Hotel De Anza, walk four blocks ahead to the corner of North Almaden Boulevard. Otherwise, walk one block, turn right on San Pedro Street, and continue two blocks—past the sidewalk cafés and restaurants—to St. John Street and turn left. The **Fallon House** ⑭ will be on your right, the **Peralta Adobe** ⑮ on your left. At this point you can turn around and go east three blocks on St. John Street and board the light-rail to return to your starting point.

Pick up your car and drive northwest from the center of town on Coleman Avenue. At Taylor Street take a right to reach **Heritage Rose Garden** ⑯. After you've strolled the grounds, head southwest on Taylor Street, which turns into Naglee Avenue at Alameda. Naglee will take you to the **Rosicrucian Egyptian Museum** ⑰ and, across the street, the **Municipal Rose Garden** ⑱. When you're done there, continue southwest on Naglee until it turns into Forest Avenue, which intersects Winchester Boulevard. Turn left onto Winchester Boulevard to reach **Winchester Mystery House** ⑲. Finally, take I–280 east to Highway 82 (Monterey Road) south and turn left on Phelan Avenue. At Kelley Park you can visit **History San Jose** ⑳. To return to downtown, backtrack to Monterey Road and turn right to drive north.

TIMING   The walking portion of this tour can easily be completed in about two hours. However, if you decide to spend time in the museums or at a café along San Pedro Street, give yourself at least four hours. The length of the driving tour depends on how long you spend at each sight. Plan on anywhere from three to six hours.

What to See

⑫ **Cathedral Basilica of St. Joseph.** This Renaissance-style cathedral embodies the idea of resurrection: it is the fifth church of St. Joseph built in San Jose (the fourth on this site). All its predecessors have perished in earthquakes and other natural disasters. The original adobe church began serving the residents of the pueblo of San Jose in 1803. The current and longest-standing incarnation, built in 1877, is a grand cathedral with stained-glass windows and murals. ✉ *80 S. Market St.* ☎ *408/283–8100* ⊕ *www.stjosephcathedral.org.*

☙ ▶ ⑨ **Children's Discovery Museum of San Jose.** You can't miss this angular purple building that seems to rise from the creek across from the convention center. Exhibits here explore the world of how things work, from why water gushes to why springs go boing. Everything is hands-on, so kids can blow gigantic bubbles, dress up in old-timey clothes, or climb on the oversize animal sculptures outside while tired parents picnic on the lawn. The gallery shows art by children from all over the world. ✉ *180 Woz Way, at Auzerais St.* ☎ *408/298–5437* ⊕ *www.cdm.org* ✉ *$7* ☉ *Tues.–Sat. 10–5, Sun. noon–5.*

⑭ **Fallon House.** San Jose's seventh mayor, Thomas Fallon, built this Victorian mansion in 1855. The house's period-decorated rooms can be viewed on a 90-minute tour that includes the Peralta Adobe and a screening of a video about the two houses. ✉ *175 W. St. John St.* ☎ *408/993–8182* ⊕ *www.historysanjose.org* ✉ *$6, includes admission to Peralta Adobe* ☉ *Guided tours weekends noon–5.*

☙ ⑩ **Guadalupe River Park.** This downtown park includes the Arena Green, next to the sports arena, with a carousel, children's playground, and artwork honoring five champion figure skaters from the area. The River Park path, which stretches for 3 mi, starts at the Children's Discovery Museum and runs north, ending at the Arena Green. ✉ *345 W. Santa Clara St.* ☎ *408/277–5904* ⊕ *www.grpg.org* ✉ *Free.*

⑯ **Heritage Rose Garden.** The newer of the city's two rose gardens has won national acclaim for its 5,000 rosebushes and trees. This quiet, 4-acre retreat has benches perfect for a break or a picnic and is alongside the still-developing Historic Orchard, which has fruit trees indigenous to the Santa Clara Valley. The garden is northwest of downtown, near the airport. ⊠ *Taylor and Spring Sts.* ☎ *408/298–7657* 🖾 *Free* ☉ *Daily dawn–dusk.*

⑳ History San Jose. Southeast of the city center, occupying 25 acres of Kelley Park, this outdoor "museum" highlights the history of San Jose and the Santa Clara Valley. You can see 28 historic and reconstructed buildings, hop an antique trolley, observe letterpress printing, and grab a snack at O'Brien's Ice Cream Parlor and Candy Store. On weekdays admission is free, but the buildings are closed except for the galleries, Pacific Hotel, and the candy store. ⊠ *1650 Senter Rd., at Phelan Ave.* ☎ *408/287–2290* ⊕ *www.historysanjose.org* 🖾 *$6* ☉ *Tues.–Sun. noon–5; call for weekend tour times.*

⑱ Municipal Rose Garden. Installed in 1931, the Municipal Rose Garden is one of several outstanding green spaces in the city's urban core—and certainly the most fragrant. West of downtown San Jose you'll find 5½ acres of roses here, with 4,000 shrubs and trees in 189 well-labeled beds, as well as walkways, fountains, and trellises. Some of the neighboring homes in the Rose Garden district date to the time of the city's founding. ⊠ *Naglee and Dana Aves.* ☎ *408/277–4191* 🖾 *Free* ☉ *Daily 8* AM*–sunset.*

⑮ Peralta Adobe. California pepper trees shade the last remaining structure (circa 1797) from the Pueblo de Guadalupe, the original settlement from which the modern city of San Jose was born. This whitewashed, two-room house has been furnished to show what home life was like during the Spanish occupation and the Mexican rancho era. ⊠ *184 W. St. John St.* ☎ *408/993–8182* ⊕ *www.historysanjose. org* 🖾 *$6, includes admission to Fallon House* ☉ *Guided tours weekends noon–5.*

★ **⑰ Rosicrucian Egyptian Museum.** Owned by the Rosicrucian Order (a modern-day group devoted to the study of metaphysics for self-improvement), this museum exhibits the West Coast's largest collection of Egyptian and Babylonian antiquities, including mummies, and an underground replica of a rock tomb. The museum's entrance is a reproduction of the Avenue of Ram Sphinxes from the Temple at Karnak in Egypt. The complex, 3 mi from downtown, is surrounded by a garden filled with palms, papyrus, and other plants recalling ancient Egypt. ⊠ *1342 Naglee Ave., at Park Ave.* ☎ *408/947–3635* ⊕ *www. egyptianmuseum.org* 🖾 *$9* ☉ *Tues.–Fri. 10–5, weekends 11–6.*

⑪ San Jose Museum of Art. Housed in a former post office building, this museum doesn't attempt to compete with the larger, swankier art museums in San Francisco. Instead, it does its own thing. The permanent collection of paintings, sculpture, photography, and large-scale multimedia installations is solid, with an emphasis on cutting-edge California and Latino artists. The massive Dale Chihuly glass sculpture hanging above the lobby hints at the appreciation for futuristic, high-tech pieces. ⊠ *110 S. Market St.* ☎ *408/294–2787 or 408/271–6840* ⊕ *www. sjmusart.org* 🖾 *Free* ☉ *Tues.–Sun. 11–5.*

😊 ⑬ **Tech Museum of Innovation.** Designed by renowned architect Ricardo
Fodor'sChoice Legorreta of Mexico City, this museum of technology is both high-tech
★ and hands-on. Exhibits allow you to create an action movie in a video
editing booth, solve the story behind a crime scene using real forensic
techniques, and talk with a roaming robot named Zaza. Another highlight is the 299-seat Hackworth IMAX Dome Theater. ✉ *201 S. Market St., at Park Ave.* ☎ *408/294–8324* ⊕ *www.thetech.org* 🔖 *Museum
$9, IMAX $9, combination ticket $16* ⊙ *Daily 10–5.*

😊 ⑲ **Winchester Mystery House.** Convinced that spirits would harm her if construction ever stopped, firearms heiress and house owner Sarah Winchester
constantly added to her house. For 38 years, beginning in 1884, she kept
a revolving crew of carpenters at work creating a bizarre 160-room
labyrinth with stairs going nowhere and doors that open into walls. Today
the house (which is on the National Register of Historic Places) is a favorite family attraction, and though the grounds are no longer overgrown,
the place retains an air of mystery. You can explore the house on the 65-
minute estate tour or the 50-minute behind-the-scenes tour (these usually depart every 20–30 minutes); every Friday the 13th there's also a
special evening flashlight tour. ✉ *525 S. Winchester Blvd., between
Stevens Creek Blvd. and I–280* ☎ *408/247–2101* ⊕ *www.
winchestermysteryhouse.com* 🔖 *Mansion tour $19.95, behind-the-scenes
tour $16.95, combination ticket $24.95* ⊙ *June–Sept., daily 9–7; May
and Oct., Sun.–Thurs. 9–5, Fri. and Sat. 9–7; Nov.–Apr., daily 9–5.*

Free art abounds in the storefronts of downtown San Jose courtesy of
a program called **Phantom Galleries** (☎ 408/271–5151). Exhibits rotate
bi-monthly in empty storefronts beginning at the corner of San Fernando
Street and South 1st Street, down to Santa Clara Street. Call to find out
about the latest installations.

Where to Stay & Eat

$$$–$$$$ ✕ **A. P. Stump's.** With its tin ceilings, dramatic lighting, and gold- and
copper-tone walls, this restaurant's extravagant interior is well-matched
to the food. Chef-partner Jim Stump offers creative dishes on his fre-
quently changing menu, which may include sesame ahi with bok choy
and soba noodle cake, molasses-glazed pork chop with huckleberry
sauce, or one of his signature dishes like lobster corn pudding. If you
plan to come in spring or summer, ask about the program of outdoor
live-music performances. ✉ *163 W. Santa Clara St.* ☎ *408/292–9928*
🍽 *AE, D, DC, MC, V* ⊙ *No lunch weekends.*

★ **$$–$$$$** ✕ **Emile's Restaurant.** In a city that's gone through numerous changes,
Emile's has remained a solidly popular downtown dining spot for
decades. The menu, which focuses on European-influenced California
cuisine, is given a slightly decadent edge by Swiss chef-owner Emile
Mooser: duck a l'orange is flavored with Grand Marnier; beef tournedo
is wrapped in bacon and served with Béarnaise sauce; sorbets are topped
with vodka. ✉ *545 S. 2nd St.* ☎ *408/289–1960* 🍽 *AE, D, DC, MC,
V* ⊙ *Closed Sun. and Mon.*

$$–$$$$ ✕ **Paolo's.** This local favorite is now run by the fourth generation of a
family of Italian restaurateurs who arrived in California in 1917. The
menu is 100% Italian, mainly classics. There are a few surprises, though,

A FRUITFUL PAST

THERE WAS A TIME—not so long ago, in fact—when the Silicon Valley was known by a very different name: "The Valley of Heart's Delight."

The name came from the Valley's rich and fertile soil, which proved perfect for growing sweet, "delightful" fruit of all kinds. Fruit growers first began settling in the area in the 1860s, but it wasn't until the transcontinental railroad arrived in 1869 that the industry blossomed, giving the Valley its "fruit basket" identity that would remain in place for almost a century.

At the height of the industry in the 1940s and 1950s, there were 5 million fruit trees in the Valley—so many, it's said, that in the springtime, the area between Mt. Hamilton and the Santa Cruz Mountains looked like a snow drift for all the white blossoms there.

Today no commercial orchards remain; however, the tradition is still upheld in a few public places around the South Bay. In 1998 the town of Sunnyvale broke ground on **Orchard Heritage Park** (⊠ 550 East Remington Dr. ☎ 408/749–0220), a working apricot orchard open to the public. In San Jose, Guadalupe Gardens includes **The Historic Orchard** (⊠ 715 Spring St. ☎ 408/298–7657). The 3.3 acres commemorate the diversity of the Valley's agricultural past, with 250 trees growing apples, apricots, pomegranates, persimmons, and other kinds of fruit. You may also catch glimpses of the Valley's fruitful past in neighborhood backyards— where flowering lemon and plum trees still delight at least a few hearts.

like buckwheat pasta stuffed with potato, cheese, and caramelized savoy cabbage. Italophiles will love the wine list, which has more than 450 vintages—most of them, naturally, from the mother country. ⊠ 333 W. San Carlos St. ☎ 408/294–2558 ⊟ AE, D, DC, MC, V ⊘ Closed Sun. No lunch Sat.

$$–$$$ ✕ **Menara Moroccan Restaurant.** The delicious cumin- and coriander-spiced cuisine is only part of what makes dining here an exotic experience. Arched entryways, lazily spinning ceiling fans, and a tile fountain all evoke a glamorous Moroccan palace. If sitting on jewel-tone cushions and feasting on lamb with honey, delicately spiced chicken kebabs, or hare with paprika doesn't make you feel like you've traveled to a distant land, then just wait 'til the belly dancers arrive for their nightly performance. ⊠ 41 E. Gish Rd. ☎ 408/453–1983 ⊟ AE, D, MC, V ⊘ No lunch.

★ **$–$$** ✕ **71 Saint Peter.** The selection at this downtown restaurant is somewhat small, but each dish is prepared with care by chef-owner Mark Tabak (you can watch him at work in the glass-walled kitchen). Two menu highlights are the seafood linguine—a mix of clams, shrimp, and scallops in a basil-tomato broth—and the roasted duck in a raspberry–black pepper demi-glace. The ceramic-tile floors and wood-beam ceiling add rustic touches to the warm elegant atmosphere. ⊠ *71 N. San Pedro St.* ☎ *408/971–8523* ▭ *AE, D, DC, MC, V* ⊘ *Closed Sun. No lunch Sat.*

¢–$ ✕ **Lou's Living Donut Museum.** If you want a real taste of San Jose, do like the locals and stop for a sweet breakfast or afternoon snack at Lou's, two blocks from the Children's Discovery Museum. Lou's serves a variety of handmade doughnuts—from pumpkin to old-fashioned chocolate—and lets you watch the bakers in action. This family-run shop has been around since 1955; the owners are glad to talk to you about the history of the shop and of San Jose. ⊠ *387 Delmas Ave.* ☎ *408/295–5887* ▭ *No credit cards* ⊘ *Closed Sun. No dinner.*

¢ ✕ **Tofoo Com Chay.** This bare-bones vegetarian restaurant is a favorite of college students and local hipsters. There's no table service—order from the counter from a selection of sandwiches and simple entrées—but the food is reliably good, as well as super cheap. ⊠ *388 E. Santa Clara St.* ☎ *408/286–6335* ▭ *No credit cards* ⊘ *Closed Sun.*

¢ ✕ **White Lotus.** The Southeast Asian–influenced meatless dishes at this slightly worn restaurant are deliciously prepared using fresh ingredients. Choose from an extensive menu of vegetable and meat-substitute entrées, like soft, chewy, pan-fried rice noodles with tofu and crisp vegetables; curry "chicken"; or spicy garlic eggplant. Start your meal with an order of crunchy imperial rolls or Thai sweet-and-sour soup. ⊠ *80 N. Market St.* ☎ *408/977–0540* ▭ *MC, V* ⊘ *Closed Sun.*

$$$–$$$$ ▦ **The Fairmont.** This downtown gem is as opulent as its sister property in San Francisco. Get lost in the lavish lobby sofas under dazzling chandeliers, or dip your feet in the fourth-floor pool, which is surrounded by exotic palms. Rooms have every imaginable comfort, from down pillows and custom-designed comforters to oversize bath towels changed twice a day. ⊠ *170 S. Market St., 95113* ☎ *408/998–1900 or 800/866–5577* 🖷 *408/287–1648* ⊕ *www.fairmont.com* ⊷ *731 rooms, 74 suites* ⌕ *3 restaurants, room service, in-room data ports, some in-room faxes, in-room safes, some in-room hot tubs, minibars, refrigerators, cable TV with movies and video games, pool, health club, massage, steam room, lobby lounge, laundry service, concierge, Internet, business services, meeting rooms, no-smoking rooms, no-smoking floor* ▭ *AE, D, DC, MC, V.*

★ $$–$$$$ ▦ **Hotel De Anza.** This lushly appointed art deco hotel has hand-painted ceilings, a warm coral-and-green color scheme, and an enclosed terrace with towering palms and dramatic fountains. Business travelers will appreciate the many amenities, including a full-service business center and personal voice-mail services—not to mention the fireside lounge, where jazz bands often play. ⊠ *233 W. Santa Clara St., 95113* ☎ *408/286–1000 or 800/843–3700* 🖷 *408/286–0500* ⊕ *www.hoteldeanza.com* ⊷ *90 rooms, 10 suites* ⌕ *Restaurant, in-room data ports, some in-room hot tubs, minibars, refrigerators, cable TV with movies, in-room VCRs, gym, bar, laundry service, concierge, Internet, business services, no-smoking rooms* ▭ *AE, D, DC, MC, V.*

Nightlife & the Arts

NIGHTLIFE Try **Big Lil's Barbary Coast Dinner Theater** (⊠ 157 W. San Fernando St. ☎ 408/295–7469) for an evening of turn-of-the-20th-century melodrama, vaudeville, and audience participation (lots of popcorn throwing) on Friday and Saturday evenings. Just west of downtown, the **Garden City Lounge** (✉ 360 S. Saratoga Ave. ☎ 408/244–3333) has jazz nightly with no cover charge. **Agenda** (✉ 399 S. 1st St. ☎ 408/380–3042) is one of the most popular nightspots downtown, with a restaurant on the main floor, a bar upstairs, and a nightclub on the bottom floor. Pick up a pool cue at trendy **South First Billiards** (✉ 420 S. 1st St. ☎ 408/294–7800), amid the burgeoning cluster of small clubs in an area called SoFA—South of First Area—along 1st and 2nd streets south of San Carlos Avenue.

THE ARTS The **Center for Performing Arts** (✉ 255 Almaden Blvd. ☎ 408/277–3900) is the city's main performance venue. **American Musical Theatre of San Jose** (☎ 408/453–7108) presents a half dozen musicals per year. **San Jose Symphony** (☎ 408/288–2828) performs in fall, winter, and spring. **Ballet San Jose Silicon Valley** (☎ 408/288–2800) performs from October through May. **San Jose Repertory Theatre** (✉ 101 Paseo de San Antonio ☎ 408/367–7255) occupies a contemporary four-story, 528-seat theater, dubbed the Blue Box because of its angular blue exterior. **City Lights Theater Co.** (✉ 529 S. 2nd St. ☎ 408/295–4200) presents progressive and traditional programs in an intimate 99-seat theater.

Sports & the Outdoors

GOLF **San Jose Municipal Golf Course** (✉ 1560 Oakland Rd. ☎ 408/441–4653) is an 18-hole course. Greens fees are $32 on weekdays and $46 on weekends. Cart rental is $25 extra. **Cinnabar Hills Golf Club** (✉ 23600 McKean Rd. ☎ 408/323–5200) is a 27-hole course. Greens fees are $80 on weekdays and $100 on weekends until 2 PM; late afternoon fees are considerably lower.

SPECTATOR SPORTS The 17,496-seat **HP Pavilion at San Jose** (✉ Santa Clara St. at Autumn St. ☎ 408/287–9200, 408/998–3497 for tickets), known locally as the Shark Tank (even just "the Tank"), is home to the National Hockey League's **San Jose Sharks.** The building looks like a giant hothouse, with its glass entrance, shining metal armor, and skylight ceiling. Inside, hockey alternates with other sporting events and concerts. **Spartan Stadium** (✉ 7th St. between E. Alma Ave. and E. Humboldt St. ☎ 877/757–8849) hosts the **San Jose Earthquakes** major league soccer team (formerly the San Jose Clash), as well as qualifying games for international competitions. The **Hellyer Velodrome** (✉ 985 Hellyer Ave. ☎ 408/226–9716) attracts national-class cyclists and Olympians in training to races from May through August.

THE PENINSULA & SOUTH BAY A TO Z

To research prices, get advice from other travelers, and book travel arrangements, visit ⊕ www.fodors.com.

AIRPORTS & TRANSFERS

All the major airlines serve San Francisco International Airport, and most of them fly to San Jose International Airport. South & East Bay Airport Shuttle can transport you between the airport and Saratoga, Palo

Alto, and other destinations. *See* Air Travel *in* Smart Travel Tips A to Z for airline phone numbers.

🛪 **San Francisco International Airport** ✉ Off U.S. 101, 15 mi south of downtown, San Francisco ☎ 650/761-0800. **San Jose International Airport** ✉ 1661 Airport Blvd., off Hwy. 87, San Jose ☎ 408/277-4759 ⊕ www.sjc.org. **South & East Bay Airport Shuttle** ☎ 408/225-4444 or 800/548-4664.

BUS TRAVEL

SamTrans buses travel to Moss Beach and Half Moon Bay from the Daly City BART station. Another bus connects Half Moon Bay with Pescadero. Each trip takes approximately one hour. Call for schedules, because departures are infrequent. The Valley Transportation Authority (VTA) shuttle links downtown San Jose to the CalTrain station, across from the Arena, every 20 minutes during morning and evening commute hours.

🛪 **SamTrans** ☎ 800/660-4287. **VTA Shuttle** ☎ 408/321-2300 ⊕ www.vta.org.

CAR RENTAL

You can rent a car at the San Jose airport from any of the many major agencies. Specialty Rentals offers standard cars and luxury vehicles; it has an office in Palo Alto and will deliver a car to you anywhere on the Peninsula or at the airport. *See* Car Rental *in* Smart Travel Tips A to Z for national rental agency phone numbers.

🛪 **Local Agencies Specialty Rentals** ☎ 650/856-9100 or 800/400-8412.

CAR TRAVEL

Public transportation to coastal areas is limited, so it's best to drive. To get to Moss Beach or Half Moon Bay, take Highway 1, also known as the Coast Highway, south along the length of the San Mateo coast. When coastal traffic is heavy, especially on summer weekends, you can also reach Half Moon Bay via I–280, the Junipero Serra Freeway; follow it south as far as Route 92, where you can turn west toward the coast. To get to Pescadero, drive south 16 mi on Highway 1 from Half Moon Bay. For Año Nuevo continue south on Highway 1 another 12 mi.

By car the most pleasant route down the Inland Peninsula to Palo Alto, Woodside, Santa Clara, and San Jose is I–280, which passes along Crystal Springs Reservoir. U.S. 101, also known as the Bayshore Freeway, is more direct but also more congested. To avoid the often-heavy commuter traffic on Highway 101, use I–280 during rush hours.

To reach Saratoga, take I–280 south to Highway 85 and follow Highway 85 south toward Gilroy. Exit on Saratoga–Sunnyvale Road, go south, and follow the signs to the Village—about 2½ mi. Signs will also direct you to Hakone Gardens, Villa Montalvo, and on concert nights, the Mountain Winery.

EMERGENCIES

In an emergency dial 911.

🛪 **Hospitals San Jose Medical Center** ✉ 675 E. Santa Clara St., San Jose ☎ 408/998-3212. **Stanford Hospital** ✉ 300 Pasteur Dr., Palo Alto ☎ 650/723-4000.

TRAIN TRAVEL

CalTrain runs from 4th and Townsend streets in San Francisco to Palo Alto ($4.50 each way); from there take the free Marguerite shuttle bus to the Stanford campus and the Palo Alto area. Buses run about every 15 minutes from 6 AM–7:45 PM and are timed to connect with trains and public transit buses.

CalTrain service continues south of Palo Alto to Santa Clara's Railroad and Franklin streets stop, near Santa Clara University ($5.25 one-way), and to San Jose's Rod Diridon station ($6 one-way). The trip to Santa Clara takes approximately 1¼ hours; to San Jose, it's about 1½ hours.

Valley Transportation Authority buses run efficiently throughout the Santa Clara Valley, although not as frequently as you might like. Operators can help you plan routes.

In San Jose, light-rail trains run 24 hours a day and serve most major attractions, shopping malls, historic sites, and downtown. Trains run every 10 minutes weekdays from 6 AM to 8 PM and vary during weekends and late-night hours from every 15 minutes to once an hour. Tickets are valid for two hours; they cost $1.40 one-way or $4 for a day pass. Buy tickets at vending machines in any transit station. For more information call or visit the Downtown Customer Service Center.

🚊 **CalTrain** ☎ 800/660-4287. **Downtown Customer Service Center** Light Rail ⊠ 2 N. 1st St., San Jose ☎ 408/321-2300. **Marguerite Shuttle** ☎ 650/723-9362. **Valley Transportation Authority** ☎ 408/321-2300 or 800/894-9908.

VISITOR INFORMATION

🚊 **California State Parks Bay Area District Office** ⊠ 250 Executive Park Blvd., Suite 4900, San Francisco 94134 ☎ 415/330-6300. **Half Moon Bay Chamber of Commerce** ⊠ 520 Kelly Ave., Half Moon Bay 94019 ☎ 650/726-8380 ⊕ www.halfmoonbaychamber. org. **Palo Alto Chamber of Commerce** ⊠ 325 Forest Ave., Palo Alto 94301 ☎ 650/324-3121. **San Jose Convention and Visitors Bureau** ⊠ 125 South Market St., 3rd fl., San Jose 95113 ☎ 800/726-5673, 408/295-2265, or 408/295-9600 ⊕ www.sanjose.org. **Santa Clara Chamber of Commerce and Convention and Visitors Bureau** ⊠ 1850 Warburton Ave., Santa Clara 95052 ☎ 408/244-8244 ⊕ www.santaclarachamber.org. **Saratoga Chamber of Commerce** ⊠ 14485 Big Basin Way, Saratoga 95070 ☎ 408/867-0753 ⊕ www.saratogachamber.org. **Woodside Town Hall** ⊠ 2955 Woodside Rd., Woodside 94062 ☎ 650/851-6790.

SAN FRANCISCO

WITH SAUSALITO & BERKELEY

12

IN ITS FIRST LIFE San Francisco was little more than a small, well-situated settlement. Founded by Spaniards in 1776, it was prized for its natural harbor, so commodious that "all the navies of the world might fit inside it," as one visitor wrote. Around 1849 the discovery of gold at John Sutter's sawmill in the nearby Sierra foothills transformed the sleepy little settlement into a city of 30,000. Millions of dollars' worth of gold was panned and blasted out of the hills, the impetus for the development of a western Wall Street. Fueled by the 1859 discovery of a fabulously rich vein of silver in Virginia City, Nevada, San Francisco became the West Coast's cultural fulcrum and major transportation hub, and its population soared to 342,000. In 1869 the transcontinental railway was completed, linking the once-isolated western capital to the East. San Francisco had become a major city of the United States.

"Loose," "tolerant," and even "licentious" are words used to describe San Francisco. Bohemian communities thrive here. As early as the 1860s the Barbary Coast—a collection of taverns, whorehouses, and gambling joints along Pacific Avenue close to the waterfront—was famous, or infamous. North Beach, the city's Little Italy, became the home of the Beat movement in the 1950s (Herb Caen, the city's best-known columnist, coined the term "beatnik"). Lawrence Ferlinghetti's City Lights, a bookstore and publishing house that still stands on Columbus Avenue, brought out, among other titles, Allen Ginsberg's *Howl* and *Kaddish*. In the 1960s the Free Speech movement began at the University of California Berkeley, and Stanford's David Harris, who went to prison for defying the draft, numbered among the nation's most famous student leaders. The Haight-Ashbury district became synonymous with hippiedom, giving rise to such legendary bands as Jefferson Airplane and the Grateful Dead. Southwest of the Haight is the onetime Irish neighborhood known as the Castro, which during the 1970s became identified with gay and lesbian liberation.

Technically speaking, it's only California's fourth-largest city, behind Los Angeles, San Diego, and nearby San Jose. But that statistic is misleading: the Bay Area, extending from the bedroom communities north of Oakland and Berkeley south through the peninsula and the San Jose area, is really one continuous megacity, with San Francisco as its heart.

EXPLORING SAN FRANCISCO

Updated by
Denise M. Lelu

"You could live in San Francisco a month and ask no greater entertainment than walking through it," wrote Inez Hayes Irwin, author of *The Californiacs,* an effusive 1921 homage to the state of California and the City by the Bay. Her claim remains true today: as in the 1920s, touring on foot is the best way to experience this diverse metropolis.

San Francisco is a relatively small city. About 800,000 residents live on a 46½-square-mi tip of land between San Francisco Bay and the Pacific Ocean. San Franciscans cherish the city's colorful past; many older buildings have been spared from demolition and nostalgically converted into modern offices and shops, and longtime locals rue the sites that got away. The neighborhoods of San Francisco retain strong cultural, political, and ethnic identities. Locals know this pluralism is the real life of the city. Experiencing San Francisco means visiting the neighborhoods: the colorful Mission District, the gay Castro, countercultural Haight Street, swank Pacific Heights, lively Chinatown, ever bohemian North Beach, and arts- and news media–oriented SoMa, among others.

Numbers in the text correspond to numbers in the margin and on the neighborhood maps.

Union Square Area

Much of San Francisco may feel like a collection of small towns strung together, but the Union Square area bristles with big-city bravado. The city's finest department stores do business here, along with such exclusive emporiums as Tiffany & Co. and Prada and such big-name franchises as Niketown and Virgin Megastore. There are several dozen hotels within a three-block walk of the square, and the downtown theater district and many fine arts galleries are nearby.

a good
walk

Begin three blocks south of Union Square at the **San Francisco Visitor Information Center ①** ▶, on the lower level of Hallidie Plaza at Powell and Market streets. Up the escalators on the east side of the plaza, where Powell dead-ends into Market, lies the **cable-car terminus ②** for two of the city's three lines. Head north on Powell from the terminus to Geary Street, make a left, and walk west 1½ blocks into the theater district for a peek at the **Geary Theater ③**. Backtrack on the north side of Geary Street, where the sturdy and stately **Westin St. Francis Hotel ④** dominates Powell between Geary and Post streets. **Union Square ⑤** is across Powell from the hotel's main entrance.

Maiden Lane ⑥ is a two-block alley directly across Stockton Street from Union Square that runs east parallel to Geary. When the lane ends at Kearny Street, turn left, walk 1½ blocks to Sutter Street, make a right, and walk a half block to the **Hallidie Building ⑦**. After viewing this historic building, reverse direction and head west 1½ blocks up Sutter to the fanciful beaux-arts–style **Hammersmith Building ⑧**, on the southwest corner of Sutter Street and Grant Avenue. In the middle of the next block, at 450 Sutter, stands a glorious 1928 art-deco skyscraper, a masterpiece of terra-cotta and other detailing; handsome Maya-inspired designs adorn its exterior and interior surfaces. From here, backtrack a half block east to Stockton Street and take a right. In front of the Grand Hyatt hotel sits **Ruth Asawa's Fantasy Fountain ⑨**. Union Square is a half block south on Stockton.

TIMING Allow two hours to see everything around Union Square. If you're a shopper, give yourself extra time.

What to See

🕐 **②** **Cable-car terminus.** San Francisco's signature red cable cars were declared National Landmarks—the only ones that move—in 1964. Two of the three operating lines begin and end their runs at Powell and Market streets. The more dramatic Powell–Mason line climbs up Nob Hill, then winds through North Beach to Fisherman's Wharf. The Powell–Hyde line

If you have
3 days

Spend your first morning day checking out Fisherman's Wharf and Pier 39. Jump a cable car (the Powell-Hyde line is the most dramatic) at the wharf and take in sweeping views of the bay as you rattle your way to Union Square. Charming Maiden Lane is worth a look. On the second day, begin with a walk on the Golden Gate Bridge, then explore North Beach, the Italian quarter, filled with tempting food, beat-era landmarks, and reminders of the city's bawdy past. Move on to labyrinthine Chinatown. Begin your third day by taking a ferry from Pier 41 to the infamous Alcatraz prison. Spend the rest of the day in whichever neighborhood most appeals to you: the Haight, the epicenter of 1960s counterculture, whose streets are lined with excellent music and book shops and cool vintage-clothing stores; colorful, gay-friendly Castro, brimming with shops and cafés; or the mural-filled Mission District, a neighborhood of twentysomething hipsters and working-class Latino families. Simple Mission Dolores, built in 1776, is San Francisco's oldest standing structure.

12

If you have
5 days

Follow the three-day itinerary above, and on the morning of your fourth day walk up Telegraph Hill to Coit Tower; you'll be rewarded with breathtaking views of the bay and the city's tightly stacked homes. Head for the Marina neighborhood, and if you love chocolate, stop at Ghirardelli Square, which includes a shopping center and the tempting Ghirardelli Chocolate Factory. Make a beeline for the end of the Marina and the stunning Palace of Fine Arts. Don't miss the Palace's hands-on science museum, the Exploratorium. In the afternoon join in-line skaters, joggers, and walkers in picnic-perfect Golden Gate Park—more than 1,000 acres of greenery stretching from the Haight to the Pacific. On Day 5, explore one of the neighborhoods you missed on Day 3, and in the afternoon take the ferry to Sausalito or head to the East Bay to explore formerly radical, still-offbeat Berkeley.

---

also crosses Nob Hill but then continues up Russian Hill and down Hyde Street to Victorian Park, across from the Buena Vista Café and near Ghirardelli Square. Buy your ticket ($3 one-way) on board or at the police information booth near the turnaround. If it's just the experience of riding a cable car you're after, board the less-busy California line at Van Ness Avenue and ride it down to the Hyatt Regency hotel. ⊠ *Powell and Market Sts., Union Sq.*

❸ **Geary Theater.** The American Conservatory Theater (ACT), one of North America's leading repertory companies, uses the 1,035-seat Geary as its main venue. Built in 1910, the theater has a serious neoclassic design lightened by colorful carved terra-cotta columns depicting a cornucopia of fruits. Damaged heavily in the 1989 earthquake, the Geary has been completely restored to gilded splendor. ⊠ *415 Geary St., box office at 405 Geary St., Union Sq.* ☏ *415/749–2228.*

❼ **Hallidie Building.** Named for cable-car inventor Andrew S. Hallidie, this 1918 structure is best viewed from across the street. Willis Polk's revolutionary glass-curtain wall—believed to be the world's first such fa-cade—hangs a foot beyond the reinforced concrete of the frame. The reflecting glass, decorative exterior fire escapes that appear to be metal balconies, and Venetian Gothic cornice are worth noting. Ornamental bands of birds at feeders stretch across the building on several stories. ⊠ *130 Sutter St., between Kearny and Montgomery Sts., Union Sq.*

❽ Hammersmith Building. Glass walls and a colorful design distinguish this four-story beaux-arts–style structure, built in 1907. The Foundation for Architectural Heritage once described the building as a "commercial jewel box." Appropriately, it was designed for use as a jewelry store. ⊠ *301 Sutter St., at Grant Ave., Union Sq.*

❻ Maiden Lane. Known as Morton Street in the raffish Barbary Coast era, this former red-light district reported at least one murder a week dur-ing the late 19th century. After the 1906 fire destroyed the brothels, the street emerged as Maiden Lane, and it has since become a chic pedes-trian mall stretching two blocks, between Stockton and Kearny streets.

With its circular interior ramp and skylights, the handsome brick 1948 structure at **140 Maiden Lane**, the only Frank Lloyd Wright building in San Francisco, is said to have been his model for the Guggenheim Mu-seum in New York. ⊠ *Between Stockton and Kearny Sts., Union Sq.*

❾ Ruth Asawa's Fantasy Fountain. Local artist Ruth Asawa's sculpture, a wonderland of real and mythical creatures, honors the city's hills, bridges, and architecture. Children and friends helped Asawa shape the hundreds of tiny figures from baker's clay; these were assembled on 41 large panels from which molds were made for the bronze casting. ⊠ *In front of Grand Hyatt at 345 Stockton St., Union Sq.*

▶ ❶ San Francisco Visitor Information Center. A multilingual staff operates this facility below the cable-car terminus. Staffers answer questions and provide maps and pamphlets. You can also pick up discount coupons and hotel brochures here. ⊠ *Hallidie Plaza, lower level, Powell and Mar-ket Sts., Union Sq.* ☎ *415/391–2000 or 415/283–0177* ⊕ *www.sfvisitor. org* ☽ *Weekdays 9–5, Saturday 9–3; also Sun. 9–3 May–Sept.*

❺ Union Square. The heart of San Francisco's downtown since 1850, the 2½-acre square takes its name from the violent pro-union demonstra-tions staged here before the Civil War. At center stage, the *Victory Mon-ument,* by Robert Ingersoll Aitken, commemorates Commodore George Dewey's victory over the Spanish fleet at Manila in 1898. The 97-foot Corinthian column, topped by a bronze figure symbolizing naval con-quest, was dedicated by Theodore Roosevelt in 1903 and withstood the 1906 earthquake. An open-air stage and central plaza, a café, gardens, a visitor information booth, and four sculptures by the artist R. M. Fis-cher draw strollers to the square. ⊠ *Bordered by Powell, Stockton, Post, and Geary Sts., Union Sq.*

❹ Westin St. Francis Hotel. The second-oldest hotel in the city, established in 1904, was conceived by railroad baron and financier Charles Crocker and his associates as a hostelry for their millionaire friends. After the hotel was ravaged by the 1906 fire, a larger, more luxurious Italian Re-

12

The Bay & Its Bridges

The sight of a suit-clad stockbroker unloading a Windsurfer from his Land Rover is not uncommon in San Francisco, where the bay beckons to pleasure seekers of every stripe. On sunny weekends the bay teems with sailboats, and when the surf's up, daredevils in wet suits line the beaches. Those not inclined to get wet opt to board one of the various ferries, tour boats, and dinner cruises to get a view of all three bridges—the Golden Gate, the Richmond, and the Bay—as well as Angel and Treasure islands and the legendary Alcatraz.

Hidden Lanes & Stairways

Although it has its share of major boulevards, San Francisco is a city of small side streets—many one-way-only lanes and out-of-the-way stairways. Whether you're in Chinatown, Nob Hill, North Beach, Pacific Heights, Potrero Hill, or Russian Hill, there's always a quiet lane or stairway nearby. A few of the most scenic hidden corners are in Nob Hill, Russian Hill, and North Beach.

The Hills

Anyone who's afraid of heights would do well to stay away from San Francisco, where almost everything worth getting to lies at the top of or just beyond a steep hill. Driving the city feels like riding a roller coaster. But for all the challenges they present to drivers and walkers, the hills are what give San Francisco its distinct look and its dazzling bay views. It's a city of hills—Nob Hill, Russian Hill, Telegraph Hill, Potrero Hill, and others—that look out at larger hills across the bay.

Patches of Green

With its hills and fresh air, its myriad parks and waterfront promenades, San Francisco is an outdoor-person's dream. Golden Gate Park, with more than 1,000 acres of trails and fields, is deservedly popular, but there are other choices. The Presidio, a former military base, encompasses almost 1,500 acres of hilly, wooded trails interspersed with old army barracks. The Marina, which stretches from the Presidio to the northern waterfront, is the turf of choice for a stylishly outfitted crowd of runners and skaters. Along the western shore you find the 275-acre Lincoln Park; the 6-mi loop around Lake Merced; and the Great Highway, a 3-mi ocean-side stretch with a paved jogging path.

Wining & Dining

Europhiles who bemoan the lack of a sophisticated food and wine culture in America have nothing to complain about in San Francisco. As the birthplace of California cuisine—cooking that combines fresh, locally grown ingredients in visually stunning ways—and as the neighbor of Napa Valley, the metro area has been attracting notable chefs for years. They include Traci Des Jardinière, Gary Danko, and Mark Franz.

---

naissance–style residence was opened in 1907. The hotel's checkered past includes the ill-fated 1921 bash in the suite of the silent-film comedian Fatty Arbuckle, at which a woman became ill and later died. Arbuckle endured three sensational trials for rape and murder before being acquitted, by which time his career was kaput. In 1975 Sara Jane Moore,

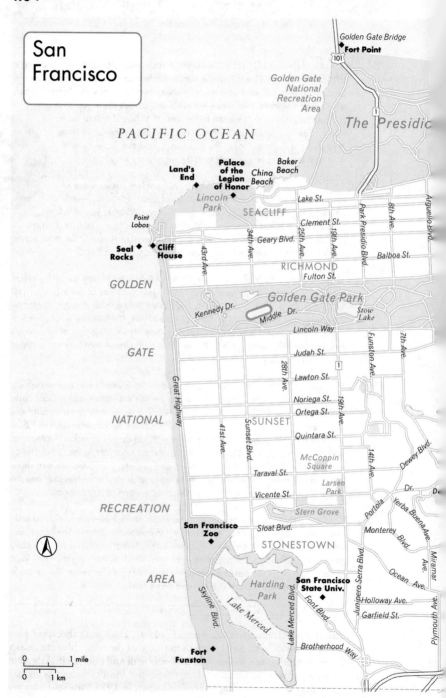

San Francisco

PACIFIC OCEAN

Golden Gate Bridge
Fort Point
101

Golden Gate
National
Recreation
Area

The Presidio

Land's
End

Palace
of the
Legion
of Honor

China
Beach

Baker
Beach

Lincoln
Park

Lake St.

SEACLIFF

Clement St.

34th Ave.

Geary Blvd.

25th Ave.

19th Ave.

Park Presidio Blvd.

8th Ave.

Arguello Blvd.

Point
Lobos

Seal
Rocks

Cliff
House

43rd Ave.

RICHMOND

Balboa St.

Fulton St.

GOLDEN

Golden Gate Park

Kennedy Dr.

Middle Dr.

Stow
Lake

Lincoln Way

GATE

Judah St.

28th Ave.

Funston Ave.

7th Ave.

Great Highway

Lawton St.

19th Ave.

Noriega St.

NATIONAL

41st Ave.

Sunset Blvd.

Ortega St.

SUNSET

Quintara St.

14th Ave.

Dewey Blvd.

McCoppin
Square

Taraval St.

Larsen
Park

Dr.

D

Vicente St.

RECREATION

Stern Grove

San Francisco
Zoo

Sloat Blvd.

STONESTOWN

Monterey

Portola

Yerba Buena Ave.

Miramar
Ave.

Junípero Serra Blvd.

Ocean Ave.

Plymouth Ave.

AREA

Harding
Park

San Francisco
State Univ.

Font Blvd.

Holloway Ave.

Garfield St.

Skyline Blvd.

Lake Merced

Lake Merced Blvd.

Fort
Funston

Brotherhood Way

0   1 mile
0   1 km

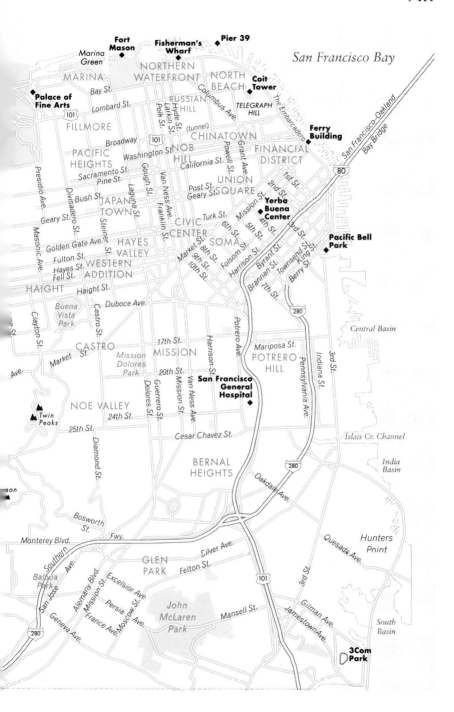

In & Around Downtown San Francisco

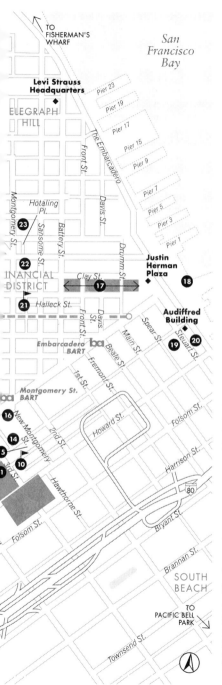

standing among a crowd outside the hotel, attempted to shoot then-president Gerald Ford. ⊠ *335 Powell St., at Geary St., Union Sq.* ☎ *415/397–7000* ⊕ *www.westin.com.*

SoMa & the Embarcadero

SoMa was once known as South of the Slot, in reference to the cable-car slot that ran up Market Street. Industry took over most of the area when the 1906 earthquake collapsed most of the homes into their quicksand bases. Huge sections of the industrial neighborhood were razed to make way for an ambitious multiuse redevelopment project in the 1960s and '70s, and SoMa emerged as a focal point of San Francisco's cultural life. Alternative artists set up shop, and key players in San Francisco's arts scene migrated to the area in the 1990s. Today glitzy projects such as the Four Seasons Hotel and residential complex are juxtaposed with still-gritty stretches of Mission and Market streets, creating a friction that keeps the neighborhood interesting. At the heart of the action in this area are the San Francisco Museum of Modern Art and the Center for the Arts at Yerba Buena Gardens. Along the waterfront from south of Market to North Beach stretches the Embarcadero.

a good walk

The **San Francisco Museum of Modern Art** ⑩ ⏵ dominates a half block of 3rd Street between Howard and Mission streets. Use the crosswalk near SFMOMA's entrance to head across 3rd Street into Yerba Buena Gardens. To your right after you've walked a few steps, a sidewalk leads to the main entrance of the **Yerba Buena Center for the Arts** ⑪. Straight ahead is the East Garden of Yerba Buena Gardens and beyond that, on the 4th Street side of the block, is the **Metreon** ⑫ entertainment, retail, and restaurant complex. A second-level walkway in the southern portion of the East Garden, above the Martin Luther King Jr. waterfall, arches over Howard Street, leading to the main (south) entrance to Moscone Convention Center and the **Rooftop@Yerba Buena Gardens** ⑬ facilities.

Exit the rooftop, head north up 4th Street to Mission Street, and walk east on Mission (toward SFMOMA) past the monolithic San Francisco Marriott, also known as the "jukebox" Marriott because of its exterior design. Just before St. Patrick's Catholic Church, turn left onto the pedestrian walkway Yerba Buena Lane past a water course, shops, and restaurants to the plaza on Market Street at the foot of Grant Avenue. The Mexican Museum and the Contemporary Jewish Museum were to open on this block in 2005, but problems with funding are delaying the projects. Head east on Market Street past historic Lotta's Fountain, and then walk south on 3rd Street to Mission Street; a half block east on Mission is the headquarters of the **California Historical Society** ⑭. Across the street and a few steps farther east is the **Cartoon Art Museum** ⑮.

Continue east on Mission Street, turn left onto New Montgomery Street, and continue to Market Street and the **Palace Hotel** ⑯. Enter via the Market Street entrance, checking out the Pied Piper Bar, Garden Court restaurant, and main lobby. Exit via the lobby onto New Montgomery Street and make a left, which will bring you back to Market Street. Turn right and head toward the waterfront. Toward the end of Market a three-tier pedestrian mall connects the five buildings of the **Embarcadero Center** ⑰ office-retail complex. Across the busy Embarcadero roadway from the plaza stands the port's trademark, the **Ferry Building** ⑱.

The ground floor of the ornate 1889 Audiffred Building, on the southwest corner of the Embarcadero and Mission Street, houses Boulevard restaurant. Head west on Mission Street along the side of Boulevard and cross Steuart Street. In the middle of the block is the entrance to the historic sections of **Rincon Center** ⑲, worth seeing for the famous murals and the old Rincon Annex Post Office. Continue south within the center to its newer portions and make a left as you exit through the doors near Chalkers Billiards. Across Steuart Street is the Jewish Community Federation Building, which is housing the **Contemporary Jewish Museum** ⑳ for now.

TIMING The walk above takes a good two hours, more if you visit the museums and galleries. SFMOMA merits about two hours; the Center for the Arts and the Cartoon Art Museum, 45 minutes each.

What to See

⑭ **California Historical Society.** The society, founded in 1871, administers a vast repository of Californiana—500,000 photographs, 150,000 manuscripts, thousands of books, periodicals, and paintings, as well as gold-rush paraphernalia. ⊠ *678 Mission St., SoMa* ☎ *415/357–1848* ⊕ *www.californiahistoricalsociety.org* ✉ *$3, free 1st Tues. of month* ⊙ *Wed.–Sat. noon–4.30; galleries close between exhibitions.*

⑮ **Cartoon Art Museum.** Krazy Kat, Zippy the Pinhead, Batman, and other colorful cartoon icons greet you at the Cartoon Art Museum. In addition to a 12,000-piece permanent collection, a 3,000-volume library, and a CD-ROM gallery, changing exhibits examine everything from the influence of underground comics to the output of women and African-American cartoonists. ⊠ *655 Mission St., SoMa* ☎ *415/227–8666* ⊕ *www.cartoonart.org* ✉ *$6, pay what you wish 1st Tues. of month* ⊙ *Tues.–Sun. 11–5.*

⑳ **Contemporary Jewish Museum.** Exhibits at this small museum survey Jewish art, history, and culture. Call ahead before visiting; the museum sometimes closes between exhibits. In the next few years the museum plans to move into state-of-the-art, Daniel Libeskind–designed quarters south of Market, on Mission Street between 3rd and 4th streets. ⊠ *121 Steuart St., Embarcadero* ☎ *415/788–9990* ⊕ *www.jmsf.org* ✉ *$5, free 1st Mon. of month* ⊙ *Sun.–Fri. noon–6.*

⑰ **Embarcadero Center.** John Portman designed this five-block complex built during the 1970s and early 1980s. Shops and restaurants abound on the first three levels; there's ample office space on the floors above. Louise Nevelson's 54-foot-tall black-steel sculpture, *Sky Tree,* stands guard over Building 3 and is among 20-plus artworks throughout the center. ⊠ *Clay St., between Battery St. and the Embarcadero* ☎ *415/772–0734* ⊕ *www.embarcaderocenter.com.*

★ ⑱ **Ferry Building.** The beacon of the port area, erected in 1896, has a 230-foot clock tower modeled after the campanile of the cathedral in Seville,

Spain. On the morning of April 18, 1906, the four great clock faces on the tower, powered by the swinging of a 14-foot pendulum, stopped at 5:17—the moment the great earthquake struck—and stayed still for 12 months. Today the building houses local favorites such as Acme Bread, Scharffen Berger Chocolate, Cowgirl Creamery, and Slanted Door (San Francisco's beloved Vietnamese restaurant), which share space with the street-level gourmet Market Hall. The waterfront promenade extends from the piers on the north side of the building south to the Bay Bridge, and ferries behind the building sail to Sausalito, Larkspur, Tiburon, and the East Bay. ⊠ *The Embarcadero at foot of Market St., Embarcadero.*

🄲 ⓬ **Metreon.** Child's play meets the 21st century at this Sony entertainment center. An interactive play area is based on Maurice Sendak's *Where the Wild Things Are*. Portal 1, a high-tech interactive arcade, includes an Extreme Sports Adventure Room. A 15-screen multiplex, an IMAX theater, retail shops, and outposts of some of the city's favorite restaurants are all part of the complex. ⊠ *101 4th St., between Mission and Howard Sts., SoMa* 🕾 *800/638–7366* ⊕ *www.metreon.com.*

⓰ **Palace Hotel.** The city's oldest hotel, a Sheraton property, opened in 1875. Fire destroyed the original Palace after the 1906 earthquake, despite the hotel's 28,000-gallon reservoir fed by four artesian wells; the current building dates from 1909. President Warren Harding died at the Palace while still in office in 1923, and the body of King Kalakaua of Hawaii spent a night here after he died in San Francisco in 1891. The managers play up this ghoulish past with talk of a haunted guest room. ⊠ *2 New Montgomery St., SoMa* 🕾 *415/512–1111* ⊕ *www.sfpalace.com.*

⓳ **Rincon Center.** A sheer five-story column of water resembling a mini-rainstorm is the centerpiece of the indoor arcade at this mostly modern office-retail complex. The lobby of the streamline moderne–style former post office on the Mission Street side contains a Works Project Administration mural by Anton Refregier. The 27 panels depict California life from the days when Native Americans were the state's sole inhabitants through World War I. A permanent exhibit below the murals contains photographs and artifacts of life in the Rincon area in the 1800s. ⊠ *Bordered by Steuart, Spear, Mission, and Howard Sts., SoMa.*

🄲 ⓭ **Rooftop@Yerba Buena Gardens.** Fun is the order of the day among these brightly colored concrete and corrugated-metal buildings atop Moscone Convention Center South. The historic **Looff carousel** ($2 for two rides) twirls daily 11–6. South of the carousel is **Zeum** (🕾 415/777–2800 ⊕ www.zeum.org), a high-tech, interactive arts-and-technology center ($7) geared to children ages eight and over. Kids can make Claymation videos, work in a computer lab, and view exhibits and performances. Zeum is open 11–5 Tuesday through Sunday in summer and Wednesday through Sunday in winter. Also part of the rooftop complex are gardens, an ice-skating rink, and a bowling alley. ⊠ *4th St. between Howard and Folsom Sts., SoMa.*

▶ ⓾ **San Francisco Museum of Modern Art** (SFMOMA). Mario Botta designed
FodorśChoice the striking SFMOMA facility, completed in early 1995, which consists
★ of a sienna brick facade and a central tower of alternating bands of black

and white stone. Inside, natural light from the tower floods the central atrium and some of the museum's galleries. Works by Henri Matisse, Pablo Picasso, Georgia O'Keeffe, Frida Kahlo, Jackson Pollock, and Andy Warhol form the heart of the diverse permanent collection. The photography holdings are also strong. ⊠ *151 3rd St., SoMa* ☎ *415/357–4000* ⊕ *www.sfmoma.org* ⌨ *$10, free 1st Tues. of month, ½-price Thurs. 6–9* ☉ *Late May–early Sept., Fri.–Tues. 10–6, Thurs. 10–9; early Sept.–late May, Fri.–Tues. 11–6, Thurs. 11–9; call for hrs for special exhibits.*

⓫ **Yerba Buena Center for the Arts.** The dance, music, theater, visual arts, films, and videos presented at this facility in Yerba Buena Gardens range from the community-based to the international and lean toward the cutting edge. ⊠ *701 Mission St., SoMa* ☎ *415/978–2787* ⊕ *www. yerbabuenaarts.org* ⌨ *Galleries $6, free 1st Tues. of month* ☉ *Galleries Tues.–Sun. 11–5, 1st Thurs. of month 11–8; box office Tues.–Sun. 11–6.*

Heart of the Barbary Coast

It was on Montgomery Street, in the Financial District, that Sam Brannan proclaimed the historic gold discovery that took place at Sutter's Mill on January 24, 1848. The gold rush brought streams of people from across America and Europe, and the population of San Francisco jumped from a mere 800 in 1848 to more than 25,000 in 1850 and to about 135,000 in 1870. Other fortune seekers, including saloon keepers, gamblers, and prostitutes, all flocked to the so-called Barbary Coast (now Jackson Square and the Financial District). Along with the quick money came a wave of violence. In 1852 the city suffered an average of two murders and one major fire each day. Since then the red-light establishments have edged upward to the Broadway strip of North Beach, and Jackson Square evolved into a sedate district of refurbished brick buildings decades ago.

a good walk

Bronze sidewalk plaques mark the street corners along the 50-sight, approximately 3¾-mi Barbary Coast Trail. The trail begins at the Old Mint, at 5th and Mission streets, and runs north through downtown, Chinatown, Jackson Square, North Beach, and Fisherman's Wharf, ending at Aquatic Park. For information about the sites on the trail, pick up a brochure at the San Francisco Visitor Information Center (⇨ Union Square Area).

To catch the highlights of the Barbary Coast Trail and a glimpse of a few important Financial District structures, start on Montgomery Street, between California and Sacramento streets, at the **Wells Fargo Bank History Museum** ㉑ ▶.

Two blocks north on Montgomery from the Wells Fargo museum stands the **Transamerica Pyramid** ㉒, between Clay and Washington streets. Walk through the tranquil redwood grove on the pyramid's east side, and you'll exit on Washington Street, across which you can see Hotaling Place to your left. Walk west (left) to the corner, cross Washington Street, and walk back to Hotaling. This historic alley is your entrance to **Jackson Square** ㉓, the heart of the Barbary Coast. Of particular note here are the former A. P. Hotaling whiskey distillery, on the corner of Hotaling Place, and the 1850s structures around the corner in the 700 block of Montgomery Street. To see these buildings, walk west on Jackson from the distillery and make a left on Montgomery. Then head south on Montgomery to Washington Street, make a right, and cross Columbus Avenue. Head north (to the right) up Columbus to the **San Francisco Brewing Company** ㉔, the last standing saloon of the Barbary Coast era and a place overflowing with freshly brewed beers and history.

TIMING Two hours should be enough time to see everything on this tour. The Wells Fargo museum (open only on weekdays) deserves a half hour.

What to See

㉓ **Jackson Square.** Here was the heart of the Barbary Coast of the Gay '90s. Although most of the red-light district was destroyed in the 1906 fire, old redbrick buildings and narrow alleys recall the romance and rowdiness of the early days. Some of the city's earliest business buildings, survivors of the 1906 quake, still stand in Jackson Square, between Montgomery and Sansome streets. Restored 19th-century brick buildings line Hotaling Place, which connects Washington and Jackson streets. The lane is named for the head of the **A. P. Hotaling Company whiskey distillery** (⌧ 451 Jackson St., at Hotaling Pl.), which was the largest liquor repository on the West Coast in its day. The Italianate Hotaling building reveals little of its infamous past, but a plaque on the side of the structure repeats a famous query about its surviving the quake: IF, AS THEY SAY, GOD SPANKED THE TOWN FOR BEING OVER FRISKY, WHY DID HE BURN THE CHURCHES DOWN AND SAVE HOTALING'S WHISKEY?

In the 700 block of **Montgomery Street,** Bret Harte wrote his novel *The Luck of Roaring Camp* at No. 730. He toiled as a typesetter for the spunky *golden-era* newspaper, which occupied No. 732 (now part of the building at No. 744). ⌧ *Jackson Sq. district bordered by Broadway and Washington, Montgomery, and Sansome Sts., Financial District.*

㉔ **San Francisco Brewing Company.** Built in 1907, this pub looks like a museum piece from the Barbary Coast days. An old upright piano sits in the corner under the original stained-glass windows. Take a seat at the mahogany bar, where you can look down at the white-tile spittoon. An adjacent room holds the handmade copper brewing kettle used to produce a dozen beers by means of old-fashioned gravity-flow methods. ⌧ *155 Columbus Ave., North Beach* ☎ *415/434–3344* ⊕ *www. sfbrewing.com* ☉ *Mon.–Sat. 11:30–2 AM, Sun. noon–2 AM.*

㉒ **Transamerica Pyramid.** The city's most photographed high-rise is this 853-foot-tall structure. Designed by William Pereira and Associates in 1972, the initially controversial icon has become more acceptable to most locals over time. A fragrant redwood grove along the east side of the building, replete with benches and a cheerful fountain, is a placid patch in which to unwind. ⌧ *600 Montgomery St., Financial District* ⊕ *www. tapyramid.com.*

▶ ㉑ **Wells Fargo Bank History Museum.** There were no formal banks in San Francisco during the early years of the gold rush, and miners often entrusted their gold dust to saloon keepers. In 1852 Wells Fargo opened its first bank in the city, and the company soon established banking offices in the mother-lode camps throughout California. Stagecoaches and pony-express riders connected points around the burgeoning state. The museum displays samples of nuggets and gold dust from mines, a mural-size map of the Mother Lode, original art by western artists Charles M. Russell and Maynard Dixon, mementos of the poet bandit Black Bart, and an old telegraph machine on which you can practice sending codes. The showpiece is the red Concord stagecoach, the likes of which carried passengers from St. Joseph, Missouri, to San Francisco in three weeks during the 1850s. ✉ *420 Montgomery St., Financial District* ☎ *415/396–2619* ⌨ *Free* ⊙ *Weekdays 9–5.*

Chinatown

Prepare to have your senses assaulted in Chinatown, bordered roughly by Bush, Kearny, and Powell streets and Broadway. Pungent smells waft out of restaurants, fish markets, and produce stands. Good-luck banners of crimson and gold hang beside dragon-entwined lampposts, pagoda roofs, and street signs with Chinese calligraphy. Honking cars chime in with shoppers bargaining loudly in Cantonese or Mandarin. Add to this the sight of millions of Chinese-theme goods spilling out of the shops along Grant Avenue, and you get an idea of what Chinatown is all about.

a good
walk

While wandering through Chinatown's streets and alleys, don't forget to look up. Above street level, many older structures—mostly brick buildings that replaced rickety wooden ones destroyed during the 1906 earthquake—have ornate balconies and cornices. The architecture on the 900 block of Grant Avenue (at Washington Street) and Waverly Place (west of and parallel to Grant Avenue between Sacramento and Washington streets) is particularly noteworthy.

Enter Chinatown through the green-tile **Chinatown Gate** ㉕ ⌐, on Grant Avenue at Bush Street. Shops selling souvenirs, jewelry, and home furnishings line Grant north past the gate. Continue on Grant to Clay Street and turn right. A half block down on your left is **Portsmouth Square** ㉖. A walkway on the eastern edge of the park leads over Kearny Street to the 3rd fl. of the Holiday Inn, where you find the **Chinese Culture Center** ㉗.

Backtrack on the walkway to Portsmouth Square and head west up Washington Street a half block to the **Old Chinese Telephone Exchange** ㉘ (now the Bank of Canton), and then continue west on Washington Street. Cross Grant Avenue and look for Waverly Place a half block up on the left. One of the best examples of this alley's traditional architecture is the **Tin How Temple** ㉙. After visiting Waverly Place and Tin How, walk back to Washington Street. Several herb shops do business in this area. Two worth checking out are Superior Trading Company, at No. 839, and the Great China Herb Co., at No. 857.

Across Washington Street from Superior is Ross Alley. Head north on Ross toward Jackson Street, stopping along the way to watch the bakers at the **Golden Gate Fortune Cookies Co.** ㉚ Turn right on Jackson. When you get to Grant Avenue, don't cross it. For some of Chinatown's best pastries, turn left and stop by No. 1029, the Golden Gate Bakery. The markets in the 1100 block of Grant Avenue carry intriguing delicacies, such as braised pig noses and ears, eels, and all manner of live game birds and fish.

Head west on Pacific Avenue to Stockton Street, turn left, and walk south past Stockton Street's markets. At Clay Street make a right and head halfway up the hill to the **Chinese-American National Museum and Learning Center** ③. Return to Stockton Street and make a right; a few doors down is the **Kong Chow Temple** ㉜, and next door is the elaborate Chinese Six Companies building.

TIMING Allow at least two hours to see Chinatown. Brief stops will suffice at the cultural center and temples.

What to See

▶ ㉕ **Chinatown Gate.** Stone lions flank the base of a pagoda-topped gate, the official entrance to Chinatown. The lions and the glazed clay dragons atop the largest of the gate's three pagodas symbolize, among other things, wealth and prosperity. The fish whose mouths wrap tightly around the crest of this pagoda also symbolize prosperity. The four Chinese characters immediately beneath the pagoda represent the philosophy of Sun Yat-sen (1866–1925), the leader who unified China in the early 20th century. The vertical characters under the left pagoda read "peace" and "trust," the ones under the right pagoda "respect" and "love." ⊠ *Grant Ave. at Bush St., Chinatown.*

㉛ **Chinese-American National Museum and Learning Center.** This airy, light-filled gallery has displays about the Chinese-American experience from 19th-century agriculture to 21st-century food and fashion trends. A separate room hosts rotating exhibits by contemporary Chinese-American artists; another describes the building's time as the Chinatown YWCA, which served as a meeting place and residence for Chinese women in need of social services. ⊠ *965 Clay St., Chinatown* ☎ *415/391–1188* ⊕ *www.chsa.org* ✉ *$3, free 1st Thurs. of month* ☉ *Tues.–Fri. 11–4, weekends noon–4.*

㉗ **Chinese Culture Center.** The San Francisco Redevelopment Commission agreed to let **Holiday Inn** build in Chinatown if the chain provided room for a Chinese culture center. Inside the center are the works of Chinese and Chinese-American artists as well as traveling exhibits relating to Chinese culture. Walking tours ($12; make reservations a week ahead) of historic points in Chinatown begin here most days at 10 AM. ⊠ *Holiday Inn, 750 Kearny St., 3rd fl., Chinatown* ☎ *415/986–1822* ⊕ *www.c-c-c.org* ✉ *Free* ☉ *Tues.–Sat. 10–4.*

☾ ㉚ **Golden Gate Fortune Cookies Co.** Walk down Ross Alley and you'll likely be invited into this small cookie factory. The workers sit at circular motorized griddles and wait for dollops of batter to drop onto a tiny metal plate, which rotates into an oven. A few moments later out comes a cookie that's pliable and ready for folding. A bagful of cookies costs $2 or $3; personalized fortunes are also available. ⊠ *56 Ross Alley, west of and* *parallel to Grant Ave. between Washington and Jackson Sts., Chinatown* ☎ *415/781–3956* ✉ *Free* ☉ *Daily 10–7.*

㉜ Kong Chow Temple. The god to whom the members of this temple pray represents honesty and trust. Take the elevator up to the fourth floor, where incense fills the air. Amid the statuary, flowers, and richly colored altars, a couple of plaques announce that MRS. HARRY S. TRUMAN CAME TO THIS TEMPLE IN JUNE 1948 FOR A PREDICTION ON THE OUTCOME OF THE ELECTION . . . THIS FORTUNE CAME TRUE. The temple's balcony has a good view of Chinatown. ✉ *855 Stockton St., Chinatown* ☎ *No phone* ✉ *Free* ☉ *Mon.–Sat. 9–4.*

㉘ Old Chinese Telephone Exchange. Most of Chinatown burned down after the 1906 earthquake, and this building—today the Bank of Canton—set the style for the new Chinatown. The intricate three-tier pagoda was built in 1909. The exchange's operators were renowned for their prodigious memories, about which the San Francisco Chamber of Commerce boasted in 1914: "These girls respond all day with hardly a mistake to calls that are given (in English or one of five Chinese dialects) by the name of the subscriber instead of by his number—a mental feat that would be practically impossible to most high-schooled American misses." ✉ *Bank of Canton, 743 Washington St., Chinatown.*

㉖ Portsmouth Square. Captain John B. Montgomery raised the American flag here in 1846, claiming the area from Mexico. The square—a former potato patch—was the plaza for Yerba Buena, the Mexican settlement that was renamed San Francisco. Robert Louis Stevenson, the author of *Treasure Island,* lived on the edge of Chinatown in the late 19th century and often visited the square. Bruce Porter designed the bronze galleon that sits atop a 9-foot-tall granite shaft in the square's northwestern corner in honor of the writer. With its pagoda-shape structures, Portsmouth Square is a favorite spot for morning tai chi and afternoon Chinese chess. ✉ *Bordered by Walter Lum Pl. and Kearny, Washington, and Clay Sts., Chinatown.*

★ ㉙ Tin How Temple. Day Ju, one of the first three Chinese to arrive in San Francisco, dedicated this temple to the Queen of the Heavens and the Goddess of the Seven Seas in 1852. In the temple's entryway, elderly ladies can often be seen preparing "money" to be burned as offerings to various Buddhist gods or as funds for ancestors to use in the afterlife. Red-and-gold lanterns adorn the ceiling and the smell of incense is usually thick. The gold-leaf wood carving suspended from the ceiling depicts the north and east sides of the sea, which Tin How and other gods protect. A statue of Tin How sits in the middle back of the temple. ✉ *125 Waverly Pl., Chinatown* ☎ *No phone* ✉ *Free, donations accepted* ☉ *Daily 9–4.*

North Beach & Telegraph Hill

Novelist and resident Herbert Gold calls North Beach "the longest-running, most glorious American bohemian operetta outside Greenwich Village." Indeed, to anyone who's spent some time in its eccentric old bars and cafés or wandered the neighborhood, North Beach evokes everything from the Barbary Coast days to the no-less-rowdy beatnik era. Italian bakeries appear frozen in time, homages to Jack Kerouac and Allen Ginsberg pop up everywhere, and the modern equivalent of the Barbary Coast's "houses of ill repute," strip joints, do business on Broadway. Less than a square mile, North Beach is the most densely populated district in the city—and among the most cosmopolitan.

a good walk

City Lights Bookstore ㉝ ▶, on Columbus Avenue, is a must-see landmark in North Beach. To the south, the triangular Sentinel Building, where Kearny Street and Columbus Avenue meet at an angle, grabs the eye with its unusual shape and mellow green patina. To the north of Broadway and Columbus is the heart of Italian North Beach.

Walk southeast across Columbus to City Lights Bookstore. Three of the most atmospheric bars in San Francisco are near here: Vesuvio, Specs, and Tosca. For joltingly caffeinated espresso drinks, also to the tune of opera, head north on Columbus a block and a half on the same side of the avenue as City Lights to Caffe Puccini, at No. 411.

Head up the east side of Columbus Avenue past Grant Avenue. On the northeast corner of Columbus and Vallejo Street is the Victorian-era **St. Francis of Assisi Church** ㉞. Go east on Vallejo Street to Grant Avenue and make another left. Check out the eclectic shops and old-time bars and cafés between Vallejo and Union streets.

Turn left at Union Street and head west to Washington Square, an oasis of green amid the tightly packed streets of North Beach. On the north side of the park, on Filbert, stands the double-turreted **Saints Peter and Paul Catholic Church** ㉟.

After you've had your fill of North Beach, head up **Telegraph Hill** ㊱ from Washington Square. Atop the hill is **Coit Tower** ㊲. Head east up Filbert Street at the park; turn left at Grant Avenue and go one block north, then right at Greenwich Street, and ascend the steps on your right. Cross the street at the top of the first set of stairs and continue up the curving stone steps to Coit Tower. The tower can also be reached by car (though parking is very tight) or public transportation.

TIMING It takes a little more than an hour to walk the tour, but the point in both North Beach and in Telegraph Hill is to linger—set aside at least a few hours.

What to See

★ ㉝ **City Lights Bookstore.** Designated a city landmark, the hangout of Beat-era writers—Allen Ginsberg and Lawrence Ferlinghetti among them—remains a vital part of San Francisco's literary scene. Still leftist at heart, the store has a replica of a revolutionary mural destroyed in Chiapas, Mexico, by military forces. ⊠ *261 Columbus Ave., North Beach* ☎ *415/362–8193* ⊕ *www.citylights.com* ⊘ *Daily 10 AM–11:30 PM.*

㊲ **Coit Tower.** Among San Francisco's most distinctive skyline sights, this 210-foot-tall tower stands as a monument to the city's volunteer firefighters.
Fodor'sChoice ★ During the early days of the gold rush, Lillie Hitchcock Coit was said to have deserted a wedding party and chased down the street after her fa-

vorite engine, Knickerbocker No. 5, while clad in her bridesmaid finery. She was soon made an honorary member of the Knickerbocker Company. Lillie died in 1929 at the age of 86, leaving the city $125,000 to "expend in an appropriate manner . . . to the beauty of San Francisco." Inside the tower, 19 depression-era murals depict economic and political life in California. ⊠ *Telegraph Hill Blvd. at Greenwich St. or Lombard St., North Beach* ☎ *415/362–0808* ☞ *$3.75* ☉ *Daily 10–6.*

③④ St. Francis of Assisi Church. The 1860 building stands on the site of the frame parish church that served the Catholic community during the gold rush. Its solid terra-cotta facade complements the many brightly colored restaurants and cafés nearby. ⊠ *610 Vallejo St., North Beach* ☎ *415/ 983–0405* ⊕ *www.shrinesf.org* ☉ *Daily 11–5.*

③⑤ Saints Peter and Paul Catholic Church. Camera-toting visitors focus their lenses on the Romanesque splendor of what's often called the Italian Cathedral. Completed in 1924, the church has Disneyesque stone-white towers that are local landmarks. ⊠ *666 Filbert St., at Washington Sq., North Beach* ☎ *415/421–0809* ⊕ *www.stspeterpaul.san-francisco.ca.us/church.*

③⑥ Telegraph Hill. The name came from one of the hill's earliest functions—in 1853 it became the location of the first Morse code signal station. Hill residents have some of the best views in the city, as well as the most difficult ascents to their aeries. The hill rises from the east end of Lombard Street to a height of 284 feet and is capped by Coit Tower. ⊠ *Bordered by Lombard, Filbert, Kearny, and Sansome Sts., North Beach.*

Nob Hill & Russian Hill

Once called the Hill of Golden Promise, Nob Hill was officially dubbed during the 1870s when "the Big Four"—Charles Crocker, Leland Stanford, Mark Hopkins, and Collis Huntington, who were involved in the construction of the transcontinental railroad—built their hilltop estates. The hill itself was called Snob Hill, a term that survives to this day. The 1906 earthquake and fire destroyed all the palatial mansions, except for portions of the Flood brownstone. The old San Francisco families of Russian Hill, a few blocks north of Nob Hill, were joined during the 1890s by bohemian artists and writers that included Charles Norris, George Sterling, and Maynard Dixon. Today, simple studios, spiffy pieds-à-terre, Victorian flats, Edwardian cottages, and boxlike condos rub elbows on the hill. The bay views here are some of the city's best.

a good walk

Begin on California and Taylor streets at the majestic **Grace Cathedral** ㊳ ☞. From the cathedral walk east (toward Mason Street and downtown) on California Street to the **Pacific Union Club** ㊴. Across Mason Street from the club is the lush **Fairmont San Francisco** ㊵, with its quirky Tonga Room tiki bar. Directly across California Street is the **Mark Hopkins Inter-Continental Hotel** ㊶, famed for panoramic views from its Top of the Mark lounge. Walk north on Mason Street to the **Cable Car Museum** ㊷.

From the Cable Car Museum continue four blocks north on Mason Street to Vallejo Street, turn west, and start climbing the steps that lead to the multilevel **Ina Coolbrith Park** ㊸. The Flag House, one of several brown-shingle prequake buildings in this area, is to your left at Taylor Street. Cross Taylor Street and ascend the Vallejo steps; the view east takes in downtown and the Bay Bridge. Continue west from the top of the Vallejo steps to two secluded Russian Hill alleys. Down and to your left is Florence Place, an enclave of 1920s stucco homes, and down a bit farther on your right is Russian Hill Place, with a row of 1915 Mediterranean town houses designed by Willis Polk. After reemerging on Vallejo Street from the alleys, walk north (right) on Jones Street one short block to Green Street. Head west (left) halfway down the block to the octagonal **Feusier House** ㊹. Backtrack to Jones Street, and head north to **Macondray Lane** ㊺. Walk west (to the left) on Macondray and follow it to Leavenworth Street. Head north (to the right) on Leavenworth to the bottom of **Lombard Street** ㊻, the "Crookedest Street in the World." Continue north one block on Leavenworth and then east one block on Chestnut Street to the **San Francisco Art Institute** ㊼.

TIMING   The tour covers a lot of ground, much of it steep. If you're in reasonably good shape, you can complete this walk in 3½ to 4 hours, including 30-minute stops at Grace Cathedral and the Cable Car Museum. Add time for gazing at the bay from Ina Coolbrith Park or enjoying tea or a cocktail at one of Nob Hill's grand hotels.

What to See

★ ☉ ㊷ **Cable Car Museum.** San Francisco once had more than a dozen cable-car barns and powerhouses. The only survivor, this 1907 redbrick structure, has photographs, old cable cars, signposts, ticketing machines, and other memorabilia dating from 1873. The massive powerhouse wheels that move the entire cable-car system steal the show; the design is so simple it seems almost unreal. You can also go downstairs to the sheave room and check out the innards of the system. A 15-minute video describes how it all works or you can opt to read the detailed placards. ✉ *1201 Mason St., at Washington St., Nob Hill* ☎ *415/474–1887* ⊕ *www.cablecarmuseum.com* ▨ *Free* ☉ *Oct.–Mar., daily 10–5; Apr.–Sept., daily 10–6.*

㊵ **Fairmont San Francisco.** The hotel's dazzling opening was delayed a year by the 1906 quake, but since then the marble palace has hosted presidents, royalty, and movie stars. Things have changed since its early days, however: on the eve of World War I you could get a room for as low as $2.50 per night, meals included. Nowadays, prices go as high as $8,000, which buys a night in the eight-room, Persian art–filled penthouse suite that was showcased regularly in the 1980s TV series *Hotel.* ✉ *950 Mason St., Nob Hill* ☎ *415/772–5000* ⊕ *www.fairmont.com.*

㊹ **Feusier House.** Octagonal houses were once thought to make the best use of space and enhance the physical and mental well-being of their occupants. A brief mid-19th-century craze inspired the construction of several in San Francisco. Only the Feusier House, built in 1857 and now a private residence amid lush gardens, and the Octagon House remain standing. ✉ *1067 Green St., Russian Hill.*

▶ ㊳ **Grace Cathedral.** The seat of the Episcopal Church in San Francisco, this soaring Gothic structure took 53 years to build. The gilded bronze doors at the east entrance were taken from casts of Lorenzo Ghiberti's Gates of Paradise, which are on the baptistery in Florence, Italy. A black-and-bronze stone sculpture of St. Francis by Beniamino Bufano greets you as you enter. The 35-foot-wide labyrinth, a large, purplish rug, is a replica of the 13th-century stone maze on the floor of the Chartres cathedral. ⊠ *1100 California St., at Taylor St., Nob Hill* ☎ *415/749–6300* ⊕ *www.gracecathedral.org* ☉ *Weekdays 7–5:45, weekends 7–5.*

❸ Ina Coolbrith Park. Beloved for its spectacular bay views and manicured gardens, this spot is unusual because it's vertical—that is, rather than being one open space, it's composed of a series of terraces up a very steep hill. A poet, Oakland librarian, and niece of Mormon prophet Joseph Smith, Ina Coolbrith (1842–1928) introduced Jack London and Isadora Duncan to the world of books. For years she entertained literary greats in her Macondray Lane home near the park. In 1915 she was named poet laureate of California. ⊠ *Vallejo St. between Mason and Taylor Sts., Russian Hill.*

❹ Lombard Street. The block-long "Crookedest Street in the World" makes
Fodor'sChoice eight switchbacks down the east face of Russian Hill between Hyde and
★ Leavenworth streets. Residents bemoan the traffic jam outside their front doors, and occasionally the city attempts to discourage drivers by posting a traffic cop near the top of the hill. If no one is standing guard, join the line of cars waiting to drive down the steep hill, or avoid the whole morass and walk down the steps on either side of Lombard. ⊠ *Lombard St. between Hyde and Leavenworth Sts., Russian Hill.*

❺ Macondray Lane. Enter this "secret garden" under a lovely wooden trellis and proceed down a quiet cobbled pedestrian street lined with Edwardian cottages and flowering plants and trees. A flight of steep wooden stairs at the end of the lane leads to Taylor Street—on the way down you can't miss the bay views. If you've read any of Armistead Maupin's *Tales of the City* or sequels, you may find the lane vaguely familiar. It's the thinly disguised setting for part of the series' action. ⊠ *Jones St. between Union and Green Sts., Russian Hill.*

❹ Mark Hopkins Inter-Continental Hotel. Built on the ashes of railroad tycoon Mark Hopkins's grand estate, this 19-story hotel went up in 1926. A combination of French château and Spanish Renaissance architecture, with noteworthy terra-cotta detailing, it has hosted statesmen, royalty, and Hollywood celebrities. The 11-room penthouse was turned into a glass-walled cocktail lounge in 1939: the **Top of the Mark** is remembered fondly by thousands of World War II veterans who jammed the lounge before leaving for overseas duty. With its 360-degree views, the lounge is a wonderful spot for a nighttime drink. ⊠ *999 California St., at Mason St., Nob Hill* ☎ *415/392–3434* ⊕ *www.markhopkins.net.*

❹ Pacific Union Club. The former home of silver baron James Flood cost a whopping $1.5 million in 1886, when even a stylish Victorian like the Haas-Lilienthal House cost less than $20,000. All that cash did buy some structural stability. The Flood residence was the only Nob Hill mansion to survive the 1906 earthquake and fire. The Pacific Union Club, a bastion of the wealthy and powerful, purchased the house in 1907 and commissioned Willis Polk to redesign it; the architect added the semicircular wings and 3rd floor. ⊠ *1000 California St., Nob Hill.*

47 **San Francisco Art Institute.** A Moorish-tile fountain in a tree-shaded courtyard draws the eye as soon as you enter the institute. The highlight of a visit is Mexican master Diego Rivera's *Making of a Fresco Showing the Building of a City* (1931), in the student gallery to your immediate left inside the entrance. Rivera himself is in the fresco—his back is to the viewer—and he's surrounded by his assistants. The older portions of the Art Institute were erected in 1926. Ansel Adams created the school's fine-arts photography department in 1946, and school directors established the country's first fine-arts film program. The **Walter & McBean Galleries** (☎ 415/749–4563 ☉ Mon.–Sat. 11–6) exhibit the often provocative works of established artists. ⊠ *800 Chestnut St., North Beach* ☎ *415/771–7020* ⊕ *www.sanfranciscoart.edu* ⊠ *Galleries free* ☉ *Student gallery daily 8–8.*

Pacific Heights & Japantown

Pacific Heights defines San Francisco's most expensive and dramatic real estate. Grand Victorians line the streets, mansions and town houses are often priced in the millions, and there are magnificent views from almost any point in the neighborhood. Japantown, or Nihonmachi, is centered on the southern slope of Pacific Heights, north of Geary Boulevard between Fillmore and Laguna streets. Around 1860 a wave of Japanese immigrants arrived in San Francisco, which they called Soko. By the 1930s they had opened shops, markets, meeting halls, and restaurants and established Shinto and Buddhist temples. Japantown is a relatively safe area, but the Western Addition, south of Geary Boulevard, can be dangerous at night; after dark also avoid straying too far west of Fillmore Street just north of Geary.

a good walk

Pacific Heights lies on an east–west ridge along the city's northern flank from Van Ness Avenue to the Presidio and from California Street to the Marina. Begin your tour by taking in the views from **Alta Plaza Park** **48** ▶, at the intersection of Steiner and Jackson streets. Walk east on Jackson Street several blocks to the **Whittier Mansion** **49**, on the corner of Jackson and Laguna streets. Make a right on Laguna and a left at the next block, Washington Street. The patch of green that spreads southeast from here is Lafayette Park. Walk on Washington along the edge of Lafayette Park past the formal French **Spreckels Mansion** **50**, at the corner of Octavia Street, and continue east two more blocks to Franklin Street. Turn left (north); halfway down the block stands the handsome **Haas-Lilienthal House** **51**. Head back south on Franklin Street, stopping to view several **Franklin Street buildings** **52**. At California Street, turn right (west) to see more **noteworthy Victorians** **53** on that street and Laguna Street.

Continue west on California Street to begin the Japantown segment of your tour. When you reach Buchanan Street, turn left (south). The open-air **Japan Center Mall** **54** is a short block of shoji-screened buildings on Buchanan Street between Post and Sutter streets. Cross Post Street and enter the three-block **Japan Center** **55**. A second-level bridge spans Webster Street, connecting the Kinokuniya and Kintetsu buildings. Make a right after you cross the bridge and then a left. There are usually several fine ikebana arrangements in the windows of the headquarters of the Ikenobo Ikebana Society of America. **Kabuki Springs & Spa** ⑤⑥ is on the northeast corner of Geary and Fillmore.

TIMING Set aside about two hours to see the sights mentioned here, not including the tours of the Haas-Lilienthal House. Although most of the attractions are walk-bys, you are covering a good bit of pavement. The Japantown tour, on the other hand, is very compact. Not including a visit to the Kabuki Springs, an hour will probably suffice.

What to See

❹❽ Alta Plaza Park. Landscape architect John McLaren, who also created Golden Gate Park, designed Alta Plaza in 1910, modeling its terracing on the Grand Casino in Monte Carlo, Monaco. From the top you can see Marin to the north, downtown to the east, Twin Peaks to the south, and Golden Gate Park to the west. ⊠ *Bordered by Clay, Steiner, Jackson, and Scott Sts., Pacific Heights.*

❺❷ Franklin Street buildings. What at first looks like a stone facade on the **Golden Gate Church** (⊠ 1901 Franklin St., Pacific Heights) is actually redwood painted white. A Georgian-style residence built in the early 1900s for a coffee merchant sits at 1735 Franklin. On the northeast corner of Franklin and California streets is a **Christian Science church**; built in the Tuscan Revival style, it's noteworthy for its terra-cotta detailing. The **Coleman House** (⊠ 1701 Franklin St., Pacific Heights) is an impressive twin-turreted Queen Anne mansion that was built for a gold-rush mining and lumber baron. Don't miss the large, brilliant-purple stained-glass window on the house's north side. ⊠ *Franklin St. between Washington and California Sts., Pacific Heights.*

❺❶ Haas-Lilienthal House. A small display of photographs on the bottom floor of this elaborate 1886 Queen Anne house, which cost a mere $18,500 to build, makes clear that it was modest compared with some of the giants that fell victim to the 1906 earthquake and fire. The Foundation for San Francisco's Architectural Heritage operates the home, whose carefully kept rooms provide an intriguing glimpse into late-19th-century life. Volunteers conduct one-hour house tours three days a week and an informative two-hour tour ($8) of the eastern portion of Pacific Heights on Sunday afternoon. ⊠ *2007 Franklin St., between Washington and Jackson Sts., Pacific Heights* ☎ *415/441–3004* ⊕ *www.sfheritage.org* ✉ *Entry $8* ☉ *1-hr tour Wed. and Sat. noon–4, last tour at 3, Sun. 11–5, last tour at 4; 2-hr tour Sun. at 12:30.*

❺❺ Japan Center. The noted American architect Minoru Yamasaki created this 5-acre complex, which opened in 1968. The development includes a hotel; a public garage with discounted validated parking; shops selling Japanese furnishings, clothing, cameras, music, porcelain, pearls, and paintings; an excellent spa; and a multiplex cinema. Between the Miyako Mall and Kintetsu Building are the five-tier, 100-foot-tall **Peace Pagoda** and the Peace Plaza. ⊠ *Bordered by Geary Blvd. and Fillmore, Post, and Laguna Sts., Japantown* ☎ *415/922–6776.*

54 Japan Center Mall. The buildings lining this open-air mall are of the shoji school of architecture. Seating in this area can be found on local artist Ruth Asawa's twin origami-style fountains, which sit in the middle of the mall; they're squat circular structures made of fieldstone, with three levels for sitting and a brick floor. ✉ *Buchanan St. between Post and Sutter Sts., Japantown* ☎ *No phone.*

★ **56 Kabuki Springs & Spa.** Japantown's house of tranquillity offers a treatment regimen that includes facials, salt scrubs, and mud and seaweed wraps. You can take your massage in a private room with a bath or in a curtained-off area. The communal baths ($16 before 5 PM, $20 after 5 and all weekend) contain hot and cold tubs, a large Japanese-style bath, a sauna, a steam room, and showers. ✉ *1750 Geary Blvd., Japantown* ☎ *415/922–6000* ⊕ *www.kabukisprings.com* ⊙ *Daily 10–9:45.*

53 Noteworthy Victorians. Two **Italianate Victorians** (✉ 1818 and 1834 California St., Pacific Heights) stand out on the 1800 block of California. A block farther is the Victorian-era **Atherton House** (✉ 1990 California St., Pacific Heights), whose mildly daffy design incorporates Queen Anne, Stick-Eastlake, and other architectural elements. The oft-photographed **Laguna Street Victorians,** on the west side of the 1800 block of Laguna Street, cost between $2,000 and $2,600 when they were built in the 1870s. ✉ *California St. between Franklin and Octavia Sts., and Laguna St. between Pine and Bush Sts., Pacific Heights.*

50 Spreckels Mansion. The estate was built for sugar heir Adolph Spreckels and his wife, Alma. Mrs. Spreckels was so pleased with her house that she commissioned George Applegarth to design another building in a similar vein: the California Palace of the Legion of Honor. One of the city's great iconoclasts, Alma Spreckels was the model for the bronze figure atop the Victory Monument in Union Square. ✉ *2080 Washington St., at Octavia St., Pacific Heights.*

49 Whittier Mansion. With a Spanish-tile roof and scrolled bay windows on all four sides, this was one of the most elegant 19th-century houses in the state. An anomaly in a town that lost most of its grand mansions to the 1906 quake, the Whittier Mansion was built so solidly that only a chimney toppled over during the disaster. ✉ *2090 Jackson St., Pacific Heights.*

Civic Center

The Civic Center—the Beaux-Arts complex between McAllister and Grove streets and Franklin and Hyde streets that includes City Hall, the War Memorial Opera House, the Veterans Building, and the old public library, now home of the Asian Art Museum and Cultural Center—is a product of the "City Beautiful" movement of the early 20th century. City Hall, completed in 1915 and renovated in 1999, is the centerpiece.

a good walk

Start at **United Nations Plaza** 57 ☞, set on an angle between Hyde and Market streets. Walk west across the plaza toward Fulton Street, which dead-ends at Hyde Street, and cross Hyde. Towering over the block of Fulton between Hyde and Larkin streets is the Pioneers Monument. The new main branch of the San Francisco Public Library is south of the monument. North of it is the **Asian Art Museum** 🔢, in the old library build-ing. The patch of green west of the museum is Civic Center Plaza, and beyond that is **City Hall** 🔢. If City Hall is open, walk through it, exiting on Van Ness Avenue and turning right. If the building's closed, walk around it to the north—to the right as you're facing it—and make a left at McAllister. Either way you end up at McAllister Street and Van Ness Avenue. Looking south (to the left) across the street on Van Ness, you see three grand edifices, each of which takes up most of its block. On the southwestern corner of McAllister and Van Ness Avenue is the Vet-erans Building. A horseshoe-shape carriage entrance on its south side separates the building from the **War Memorial Opera House** 🔢. In the next block of Van Ness Avenue, across Grove Street from the opera house, is Louise M. Davies Symphony Hall. From Davies, head west (to the right) on Grove Street to Franklin Street, turn left (south), walk one block to Hayes Street, and turn right (west). This takes you to Hayes Valley and the hip strip of galleries, shops, and restaurants between Franklin and Laguna streets. Like Japantown, the Civic Center borders the West-ern Addition; it's best not to stray west of Laguna at night.

TIMING Walking around the Civic Center should take about 45 minutes. The Asian Art Museum merits an hour; another half hour or more can be spent browsing in the shops along Hayes Street.

What to See

★ 🔢 **Asian Art Museum.** One of the largest collections of Asian art in the world is housed within this museum's monumental, imposing exterior. More than 15,000 sculptures, paintings, and ceramics from 40 countries, il-lustrating major periods of Asian art, are stored here, with about 2,500 pieces on display. Holdings highlight Buddhism in Southeast Asia and early China and include a large, jewel-encrusted, 19th-century Burmese Buddha seated on a throne. ⊠ *200 Larkin St., between McAllister and Fulton Sts., Civic Center* ☎ *415/668–8921 or 415/379–8801* ⊕ *www. asianart.org* ⊠ *$10, free 1st Tues. of month; tea demo $5* ⊙ *Tues., Wed., and Fri.–Sun. 10–5; Thurs. 10–9.*

🔢 **City Hall.** This masterpiece of granite and marble was modeled after St. Peter's cathedral in Rome. City Hall's bronze and gold-leaf dome dom-inates the area. The classical influences of Paris-trained architect Arthur Brown Jr., who also designed Coit Tower and the War Memorial Opera House, can be seen throughout the structure. The palatial interior, full of grand arches and with a sweeping central staircase, is impressive. Some noteworthy events that have taken place here include the hosing—down the central staircase—of civil-rights and freedom-of-speech protesters in 1960 and the murders of Mayor George Moscone and openly gay supervisor Harvey Milk in 1978. Inside City Hall you can view pieces from the currently homeless **Museum of the City of San Francisco** (⊕ www.sfmuseum.org), including historical items, maps, photographs, and the enormous head of the Goddess of Progress statue, which crowned the original City Hall building when it crumbled during the 1906 earth-quake. ⊠ *Bordered by Van Ness Ave. and Polk, Grove, and McAllis-ter Sts., Civic Center* ☎ *415/554–6023* ⊕ *www.ci.sf.ca.us/cityhall* ⊠ *Free* ⊙ *Weekdays 8–8, Saturday noon–4.*

▶ **⑤⑦ United Nations Plaza.** Brick pillars listing various nations and the dates of their admittance into the United Nations line the plaza, and its floor is inscribed with the goals and philosophy of the United Nations charter. ⊠ *Fulton St. between Hyde and Market Sts., Civic Center.*

⑥⓪ War Memorial Opera House. All the old opera houses were destroyed in the 1906 quake, but lusty support for opera continued. The San Francisco Opera didn't have a permanent home until the War Memorial Opera House was inaugurated in 1932 with a performance of *Tosca.* Modeled after its European counterparts, the building has a vaulted and coffered ceiling, marble foyer, two balconies, and a huge silver art-deco chandelier that resembles a sunburst. ⊠ *301 Van Ness Ave., Civic Center* ☎ *415/621–6600* ⊕ *www.sfwmpac.org.*

The Northern Waterfront

For the sights, sounds, and smells of the sea, hop the Powell–Hyde cable car from Union Square and take it to the end of the line. The views as you descend Hyde Street toward the bay are breathtaking—tiny sailboats bob in the whitecaps, Alcatraz hovers ominously in the distance, and the Marin Headlands form a rugged backdrop to the Golden Gate Bridge. Once you reach sea level at the cable-car turnaround, Aquatic Park and the National Maritime Museum are immediately to the west, and the commercial attractions of the Fisherman's Wharf area are to the east. Bring good walking shoes and a jacket or sweater for midafternoon breezes or foggy mists.

a good walk

Begin at Polk and Beach streets at the **National Maritime Museum ⑥①** ▶. Across Beach from the museum is Ghirardelli Square, a complex of shops, cafés, and galleries in an old chocolate factory. Continue east on Beach to Hyde Street and make a left. At the end of Hyde is the **Hyde Street Pier ⑥②.** South on Hyde a block and a half is the former Del Monte **Cannery ⑥③,** which holds more shops, cafés, and restaurants. Walk east from the Cannery on Jefferson Street to **Fisherman's Wharf ⑥④.** A few blocks farther east is **Pier 39 ⑥⑤.**

TIMING   For the entire Northern Waterfront circuit, set aside a couple of hours, not including boat tours, which take from one to three hours or more. All attractions here are open daily.

What to See

★ **Alcatraz Island.** The boat ride to the island is brief (15 minutes) but affords beautiful views of the city, Marin County, and the East Bay. The audio tour, highly recommended, includes observations of guards and prisoners about life in one of America's most notorious penal colonies. A separate ranger-led tour surveys the island's ecology. Plan your schedule to allow at least three hours for the visit and boat rides combined. Reservations, even in the off-season, are recommended. ⊠ *Pier 41, Fisherman's Wharf* ☎ *415/773–1188 boat schedules and information, 415/705–5555, 800/426–8687 credit-card ticket orders, 415/705–1042 park information* ☞ *$11.50; $16 with audio tour; $23.50 evening tour, including audio* ☉ *Ferry departures every 30–45 min Sept.–late May, daily 9:30–2:15, 4:20 for evening tour Thurs.–Sun. only; late May–Aug.,*

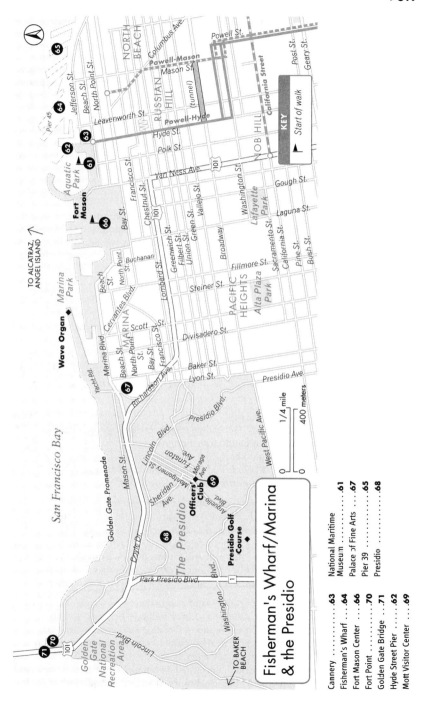

Fisherman's Wharf/Marina & the Presidio

daily 9:30–4:15, 6:30 and 7:30 for evening tour ⊕ *www.nps.gov/alca/index.htm.*

63 Cannery. The three-story structure was built in 1894 to house what became the Del Monte Fruit and Vegetable Cannery. Today it contains shops, art galleries, a comedy club (Cobb's), and some unusual restaurants. ✉ *2801 Leavenworth St., Fisherman's Wharf* ☎ *415/771–3112* ⊕ *www.thecannery.com.*

64 Fisherman's Wharf. Ships creak at their moorings; seagulls cry out for a handout. By midafternoon the fishing fleet is back to port. The chaotic streets of the wharf have numerous seafood restaurants, among them sidewalk stands where shrimp and crab cocktails are sold in disposable containers. T-shirts and sweats, gold chains galore, redwood furniture, acres of artwork, and generally amusing street artists also beckon visitors.

Most of the entertainment at the wharf is schlocky and overpriced, with one notable exception: the splendid **Musée Mécanique** (☎ 415/346–2000 ☉ late May–early Sept., daily 10–8; rest of yr, weekdays 11–7, weekends 10–8), a time-warped arcade with antique mechanical contrivances, including peep shows and nickelodeons. Some favorites are the giant and rather creepy "Laughing Sal," an arm-wrestling machine, and mechanical fortune-telling figures, which speak from their curtained boxes. Admission is free, but you may want to bring change to play the games.

The USS *Pampanito* (✉ Pier 45, Fisherman's Wharf ☎ 415/775–1943 ☉ Oct.–late May, Sun.–Thurs. 9–6, Fri. and Sat. 9–8; rest of yr, Thurs.–Tues. 9–8, Wed. 9–6) provides an intriguing if mildly claustrophobic glimpse into life on a submarine during World War II. Admission is $7. ✉ *Jefferson St. between Leavenworth St. and Pier 39, Fisherman's Wharf.*

62 Hyde Street Pier. One of the wharf area's best bargains, the pier always crackles with activity. Depending on the time of day, you might see boatbuilders at work or children manning a ship as though it were still the early 1900s. A highlight is the collection of historic vessels, all of which can be boarded. ✉ *Hyde and Jefferson Sts., Fisherman's Wharf* ☎ *415/561–7100* ⊕ *www.maritime.org* 🎫 *Ships $5* ☉ *Daily 9:30–5.*

▶ 61 National Maritime Museum. You'll feel as if you're out to sea when you step inside this sturdy, rounded structure. Part of the **San Francisco Maritime National Historical Park,** which includes Hyde Street Pier, the museum exhibits ship models, maps, and other artifacts chronicling the development of San Francisco and the West Coast through maritime history. ✉ *Aquatic Park at the foot of Polk St., Fisherman's Wharf* ☎ *415/561–7100* ⊕ *www.nps.gov* 🎫 *Donation suggested* ☉ *Daily 10–5.*

65 Pier 39. The most popular—and commercial—of San Francisco's waterfront attractions, the pier draws millions of visitors each year to browse through its dozens of shops. Ongoing free entertainment, accessible validated parking, and nearby public transportation ensure crowds most days. Brilliant colors enliven the double-decker **San Francisco Carousel** (🎫 $2 per ride), decorated with images of such city landmarks as the Golden Gate Bridge and Lombard Street. At **Aquarium of the Bay**

(☎ 415/623–5300 or 888/732–3483 ⊕ www.aquariumofthebay.com
💳 $12.95), moving walkways transport you through a space sur-
rounded on three sides by water filled with indigenous San Francisco
Bay marine life, from fish and plankton to sharks. The aquarium is open
June through September daily 9–8, otherwise weekdays 10–6, weekends
10–7. ✉ *Beach St. at the Embarcadero, Fisherman's Wharf* ⊕ *www.
pier39.com.*

The Marina & the Presidio

The Marina district was a coveted place to live until the 1989 earthquake, when the area's homes suffered the worst damage in the city—
largely because the Marina is built on landfill. Many homeowners and
renters fled in search of more-solid ground, but young professionals quickly
replaced them, changing the tenor of this formerly low-key neighborhood. The number of upscale coffee emporiums skyrocketed, a bank became a Williams-Sonoma, and the local grocer gave way to a Pottery
Barn. West of the Marina is the sprawling Presidio, a former military
base. The Presidio has superb views and the best hiking and biking areas
in San Francisco.

a good drive

Though you can visit the sights below using public transportation, this
is the place to use your car if you have one. You might even consider
renting one for a day to cover the area, as well as Lincoln Park, Golden
Gate Park, and the western shoreline.

Start at **Fort Mason Center** 🟢 ▶, whose entrance for automobiles is off
Marina Boulevard at Buchanan Street. If you're coming by bus, take Bus
30–Stockton heading north (and later west); get off at Chestnut and Laguna streets and walk north three blocks to the pedestrian entrance at
Marina Boulevard and Laguna. To get from Fort Mason to the **Palace
of Fine Arts** 🟢 by car, make a right on Marina Boulevard. The road curves
past a small marina and the Marina Green. Turn left at Divisadero Street,
right on North Point Street, left on Baker Street, and right on Bay Street,
which passes the palace's lagoon and dead-ends at the Lyon Street parking lot. Part of the palace complex is the **Exploratorium**, a hands-on science museum. (If you're walking from Fort Mason to the palace, the
directions are easier: Follow Marina Boulevard to Scott Street. Cross to
the south side of the street—away from the water—and continue past
Divisadero Street to Baker Street; turn left; the palace lagoon is on your
right. To take Muni, walk back to Chestnut and Laguna streets and take
Bus 30–Stockton continuing west; get off at North Point and Broder-
ick streets and walk west on North Point.)

The least confusing way to drive to the **Presidio** 🟢 from the palace is to
exit from the south end of the Lyon Street parking lot and head east
(left) on Bay Street. Turn right (south) onto Baker Street, and right
(west) on Francisco Street, taking it across Richardson Avenue to Lyon
Street. Turn south (left) on Lyon and right (west) on Lombard Street,
and go through the main gate to Presidio Boulevard. Turn right on Lincoln Boulevard and left on Funston Avenue to Moraga Avenue and the
Presidio's **Mott Visitor Center** 🟢 at the Officers' Club. (To take the bus

to the Presidio, walk north from the palace to Lombard Street and catch Bus 28 heading west; it stops on Lincoln near the visitor center.)

From the visitor center head back up Funston Avenue and turn left on Lincoln Boulevard. Lincoln winds through the Presidio past a large cemetery and some vista points. After a couple of miles is a parking lot marked FORT POINT on the right. Park and follow the signs leading to **Fort Point ⑩**, walking downhill through a lightly wooded area. To walk the short distance to the **Golden Gate Bridge ⑪**, follow the signs from the Fort Point parking lot; to drive across the bridge, continue on Lincoln Boulevard a bit and watch for the turnoff on the right. Bus 28 serves stops fairly near these last two attractions; ask the driver to call them out.

TIMING   The time it takes to see this area varies greatly, depending on whether you take public transportation or drive. If you drive, plan to spend at least three hours, not including a walk across the Golden Gate Bridge or hikes along the shoreline—each of which takes a few hours. With or without kids, you could easily pass two hours at the Exploratorium.

What to See

★ ☾ **Exploratorium.** The curious of all ages flock to this fascinating "museum of science, art, and human perception." The more than 650 exhibits focus on sea and insect life, computers, electricity, patterns and light, language, the weather, and much more. Reservations are required to crawl through the pitch-black, touchy-feely Tactile Dome, a 15-minute adventure. ⊠ *3601 Lyon St., at Marina Blvd., Marina* ☏ *415/561–0360 general information, 415/561–0362 Tactile Dome reservations* ⊕ *www. exploratorium.edu* ☑ *$12, free 1st Wed. of month; Tactile Dome $3 extra* ⊙ *Tues.–Sun. 10–5.*

▶ ㊅ **Fort Mason Center.** Originally a depot for the shipment of supplies to the Pacific during World War II, the fort was converted into a cultural center in 1977. Here you'll find the vegetarian restaurant Greens and shops, galleries, and performance spaces, most of which are closed Monday. There's also plentiful free parking—a rarity in the city.

The **Museo Italo-Americano** (⊠ Bldg. C ☏ 415/673–2200) mounts impressive exhibits of Italian and Italian-American paintings, sculpture, etchings, and photographs. Admission is $3. Exhibits in the **San Francisco African-American Historical and Cultural Society** (⊠ Bldg. C ☏ 415/441–0640) document past and contemporary black arts and culture. Admission is $2. Both museums are open Wednesday through Sunday noon–5.

The **San Francisco Craft and Folk Art Museum** (⊠ Bldg. A ☏ 415/775–0990) is an airy space with exhibits of American folk art, tribal art, and contemporary crafts. The museum is open Tuesday through Friday and Sunday 11–5, Saturday 10–5. Admission is $4. At the free **SFMOMA Artists Gallery** (⊠ Bldg. A ☏ 415/441–4777) you can rent or buy what you see. It's open Tuesday through Saturday 11:30–5:30. ⊠ *Buchanan St. and Marina Blvd., Marina* ☏ *415/979–3010 event information* ⊕ *www.fortmason.org.*

🌣 **⑦ Fort Point.** Designed to mount 126 cannons with a range of up to 2 mi, the fort was constructed between 1853 and 1861 to protect San Francisco from sea attack during the Civil War—but it was never used for that purpose. It was, however, used as a coastal-defense-fortification post during World War II, when soldiers stood watch here. This National Historic Site is a museum filled with military memorabilia. On days when Fort Point is staffed, guided group tours and cannon drills take place. ✉ *Marine Dr. off Lincoln Blvd., Presidio* ☎ *415/556–1693* ⊕ *www. nps.gov/fopo* ▧ *Free* ☉ *Fri.–Sun. 10–5.*

★ **⑦ Golden Gate Bridge.** The suspension bridge that connects San Francisco with Marin County has long wowed sightseers with its simple but powerful art-deco design. Completed in 1937 after four years of construction, the 2-mi span and its 750-foot towers were built to withstand winds of more than 100 mph. The east walkway yields a glimpse of the San Francisco skyline and the bay islands, while the view west takes in the wild hills of the Marin Headlands, the curving coast south to Land's End, and the majestic Pacific Ocean. A vista point on the Marin side affords a spectacular city panorama. ✉ *Lincoln Blvd. near Doyle Dr. and Fort Point, Presidio* ☎ *415/921–5858* ⊕ *www.goldengatebridge. org* ☉ *Pedestrians and bicyclists: daily sunrise–sunset.*

⑥⑨ Mott Visitor Center. Tucked away in the Presidio's mission-style Officers' Club, the William P. Mott Jr. Visitor Center dispenses maps, brochures, and schedules for guided walking and bicycle tours, along with information about the Presidio's past, present, and future. History boards tell the story of the Presidio, from military outpost to self-sustaining park. ✉ *50 Moraga Ave., Presidio* ☎ *415/561–4323* ☉ *Daily 9–5.*

⑥⑦ Palace of Fine Arts. The rosy rococo palace is the sole survivor of the many tinted-plaster structures built for the 1915 Panama-Pacific International Exposition, the world's fair that celebrated San Francisco's recovery from the 1906 earthquake and fire. Bernard Maybeck designed this faux Roman Classic beauty, which was reconstructed in concrete and reopened in 1967. The massive columns, great rotunda, and swan-filled lagoon have been used in countless fashion layouts and films. ✉ *Baker and Beach Sts., Marina* ☎ *415/561–0364 palace tours* ⊕ *www.exploratorium. edu/palace* ▧ *Free* ☉ *Daily 24 hrs.*

Fodor'sChoice ★

⑥⑧ Presidio. Part of the **Golden Gate National Recreation Area**, the Presidio was a military post for more than 200 years. Don Juan Bautista de Anza and a band of Spanish settlers first claimed the area in 1776. It became a Mexican garrison in 1822 when Mexico gained its independence from Spain; U.S. troops forcibly occupied the Presidio in 1846. The U.S. Sixth Army was stationed here until October 1994, when the coveted space was transferred into civilian hands. Today, after much controversy, the area is being transformed into a self-sustaining national park with a combination of public, commercial, and residential projects. The more than 1,400 acres of hills, majestic woods, and redbrick army barracks include two beaches, a golf course, a visitor center, and picnic sites. ✉ *Between the Marina and Lincoln Park, Presidio* ⊕ *www.nps.gov/prsf.*

Golden Gate Park

William Hammond Hall conceived one of the nation's great city parks and began in 1870 to put into action his plan for a natural reserve with no reminders of urban life. John McLaren finished Hall's work during his tenure as park superintendent, from 1890 to 1943, transforming 1,000 desolate brush- and sand-covered acres into a rolling, landscaped oasis. Urban reality now encroaches on all sides, but the park remains a great getaway. The fog can sweep into the park with amazing speed; always bring a sweatshirt or jacket.

Because the park is so large, a car comes in handy if you're going to tour it from one end to the other—though you'll still do a fair amount of walking. Muni serves the park. Buses 5–Fulton and 21–Hayes stop along its northern edge, and the N–Judah light-rail car stops a block south of the park between Stanyan Street and 9th Avenue, then two blocks south and the rest of the way west.

a good walk

The **Conservatory of Flowers** ⑫ ▶ is the first stop on this walk. Less than a block away at the intersection of Middle and Bowling Green drives is a sign for the National AIDS Memorial Grove. Before you enter the grove, follow the curve of Bowling Green Drive to the left, past the Bowling Green to the Children's Playground. If you have kids in tow, you'll probably be spending time here. If not, still take a peek at the vintage Herschell-Spillman Carousel.

Reverse direction on Bowling Green Drive and enter the **National AIDS Memorial Grove** ⑬, a sunken meadow that stretches west along Middle Drive East. At the end of the wheelchair-access ramp make a left to view the Circle of Friends; then continue west along the graded paths (ignore the staircase on the right halfway through the grove) to another circle with a poem by Thom Gunn. Exit north from this circle. As you're standing in the circle looking at the poem, the staircase to take is on your left. At the top of the staircase make a left and continue west on Middle Drive East. This brings you to the back entrance of the California Academy of Sciences, which is closed for renovations until 2008. (The temporary SoMa location is at 875 Howard Street in the ⇨ Union Square Area.)

A hundred feet shy of the 9th Avenue and Lincoln Way entrance to Golden Gate Park is the main entrance to **Strybing Arboretum & Botanical Gardens** ⑭. Take the first right after the bookstore. Follow the path as it winds north and west. Take the second right and look for signs for the Fragrance and Biblical gardens.

Backtrack from the gardens to the path you started on and make a right. As the path continues to wind north and west, you see a large fountain to the left. Just before you get to the fountain, make a right and head toward the duck pond. A wooden footbridge on the pond's left side crosses the water. Signs on the other side identify the fowl in the pond. Stay to the right on the path, heading toward the exit gate. Just before the gate, continue to the right to the Primitive Garden. Take the looped boardwalk past ferns, gingko, cycads, conifers, moss, and other plants. At the

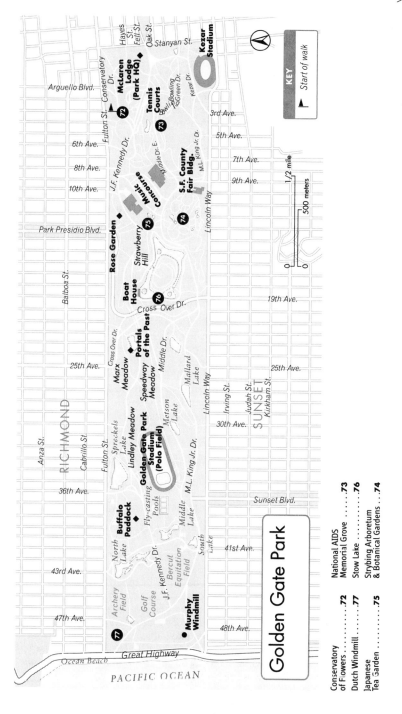

Golden Gate Park

end of the loop, make a left and then a right, exiting via the Eugene L. Friend gate. Go straight ahead on the crosswalk to the blacktop path on the other side. Make a right, walk about 100 feet, and make a left on Tea Garden Drive. A few hundred feet east of here is the entrance to the **Japanese Tea Garden** 🄬.

Tour the garden, exiting near the gate you entered. Make a left and continue past the former Asian Art Museum and the M. H. de Young Memorial Museum; both buildings are closed for construction. A crosswalk leads south to the Music Concourse, with its gnarled trees, century-old fountains and sculptures, and the Golden Gate Bandshell. Turn left at the closest of the fountains and head east toward the bronze sculpture of Francis Scott Key.

Turn left at the statue and proceed north through two underpasses. At the end of the second underpass, you'll have traveled about 2 mi. If you're ready to leave the park, take the short staircase to the left of the blue-and-green playground equipment. At the top of the staircase is the 10th Avenue and Fulton Street stop for Bus 5–Fulton heading back downtown. If you're game for walking ½ mi more, make an immediate left as you exit the second underpass, cross 10th Avenue, and make a right on John F. Kennedy Drive. After approximately ¼ mi the Rose Garden is on your right. Continue west to the first stop sign. To the left is a sign for **Stow Lake** 🄬. Follow the road past the log cabin to the boathouse.

From Stow Lake it's the equivalent of 30 long blocks on John F. Kennedy Drive to the western end of the park and the ocean. If you walk, you pass meadows, the Portals of the Past, the buffalo paddock, and a 9-hole golf course. You can skip most of this walk by proceeding west on John F. Kennedy Drive from the stop sign mentioned above, making the first right after you walk underneath Cross-Over Drive, and following the road as it winds left toward 25th Avenue and Fulton. On the northwest corner of Fulton Street and 25th Avenue, catch Bus 5–Fulton heading west, get off at 46th Avenue, walk one block west to 47th Avenue, and make a left. Make a right on John F. Kennedy Drive.

By foot or vehicle, your goal is the **Dutch Windmill** 🄬 and adjoining garden.

TIMING You can easily spend an entire day in Golden Gate Park, especially if you walk the whole distance. Even if you plan to explore just the eastern end of the park (up to Stow Lake), allot at least two hours.

What to See

► 🄬 **Conservatory of Flowers.** Built in the late 1870s, the oldest building in the park is the last remaining wood-frame Victorian conservatory in the country. It's also a copy of the conservatory in the Royal Botanical Gardens in Kew, England, with a spectacular, 14-ton glass dome atop its perch. The gardens in front of the conservatory are planted seasonally, with the flowers often fashioned like billboards depicting the Golden Gate Bridge or other city sights. ✉ *John F. Kennedy Dr. at Conservatory Dr., Golden Gate Park* 🖃 *$5* ☉ *Tues.–Sun. 9–4:30* ⊕ *www. conservatoryofflowers.org.*

77 Dutch Windmill. Two windmills anchor the western end of Golden Gate Park. The restored 1902 Dutch Windmill once pumped 20,000 gallons of well water per hour to the reservoir on Strawberry Hill. With its heavy concrete bottom and wood-shingled arms and upper section, the windmill cuts quite the sturdy figure. ⊠ *Between 47th Ave. and the Great Hwy., Golden Gate Park.*

★ **75 Japanese Tea Garden.** A peaceful 4-acre landscape of small ponds, streams, waterfalls, stone bridges, Japanese sculptures, *mumsai* (bonsai) trees, perfect miniature pagodas, and some nearly vertical wooden "humpback" bridges, the tea garden was created for the 1894 Mid-Winter Exposition. Go in the spring if you can (March is particularly beautiful), when the cherry blossoms are in bloom. ⊠ *Tea Garden Dr. off John F. Kennedy Dr., Golden Gate Park* ☏ *415/752–4227 or 415/752–1171* ⊠ *$3.50* ☉ *Mar.–Sept., daily 9–6; Oct.–Feb., daily 9–5.*

73 National AIDS Memorial Grove. San Francisco has lost many residents, gay and straight, to AIDS. This 15-acre grove, started in the early 1990s by people with AIDS and their families and friends, was conceived as a living memorial to those the disease has claimed. Coast live oaks, Monterey pines, coast redwoods, and other trees flank the grove, which is anchored at its east end by the stone Circle of Friends. ⊠ *Middle Dr. E, west of tennis courts, Golden Gate Park* ⊕ *www.aidsmemorial.org.*

☺ **76 Stow Lake.** One of the most picturesque spots in Golden Gate Park, this placid body of water surrounds Strawberry Hill. A couple of bridges allow you to cross over and ascend the hill. A waterfall cascades from the top of the hill, and panoramic views make it worth the short hike up here. Just to the left of the waterfall sits the elaborate Chinese Pavilion, a gift from the city of Taipei. It was shipped in 6,000 pieces and assembled on the shore of Strawberry Hill Island in 1981. ⊠ *Off John F. Kennedy Dr., ½ mi west of 10th Ave., Golden Gate Park* ☏ *415/752–0347.*

74 Strybing Arboretum & Botanical Gardens. The 55-acre arboretum specializes in plants from areas with climates similar to that of the Bay Area, such as the west coast of Australia, South Africa, and the Mediterranean; more than 8,000 plant and tree varieties bloom in gardens throughout the grounds. Maps are available at the main and Eugene L. Friend entrances. ⊠ *9th Ave. at Lincoln Way, Golden Gate Park* ☏ *415/661–1316* ⊕ *www.strybing.org* ⊠ *Free* ☉ *Weekdays 8–4:30, weekends 10–5* ☞ *Tours from bookstore weekdays at 1:30, weekends at 10:20 and 1:30; tours from Friend Gate Wed., Fri., and Sun. at 2.*

The Western Shoreline

Including Lincoln Park From Land's End in Lincoln Park you have some of the best views of the Golden Gate (the name was given to the opening of San Francisco Bay long before the bridge was built) and the Marin Headlands. From the historic Cliff House south to the sprawling San Francisco Zoo, the Great Highway and Ocean Beach run along the western edge of the city. The wind is often strong along the shoreline, summer fog can blanket the ocean beaches, and the water is cold and usually too rough for swimming. Carry a jacket and bring binoculars.

A car is useful out here. There are plenty of hiking trails, and buses travel to all the sights mentioned, but the sights are far apart. Start at **Lincoln Park** 78 . The park entrance is at 34th Avenue and Clement Street. Those without a car can take Bus 38–Geary—get off at 33rd Avenue and walk north (to the right) one block on 34th Avenue to the entrance. At the end of 34th Avenue (labeled on some maps as Legion of Honor Drive within Lincoln Park) is the **California Palace of the Legion of Honor** 79 , a splendid art museum. From the museum, head back out to Clement Street and follow it west. At 45th Avenue, Clement turns into Seal Rock Drive. When Seal Rock dead-ends at 48th Avenue, turn left on El Camino del Mar and right on Point Lobos Avenue. After a few hundred yards, you see parking lots for **Sutro Heights Park** 80 and the **Cliff House** 81 . (To get from the Legion of Honor to Point Lobos Avenue by public transit, take Bus 18 from the Legion of Honor parking lot west to the corner of 48th and Point Lobos avenues.) Two large concrete lions near the southeast corner of 48th and Point Lobos guard the entrance to Sutro Heights Park. After taking a quick spin through the park, exit past the lions, cross Point Lobos, make a left, and walk down to the Cliff House. From the Cliff House it's a short walk farther downhill to Ocean Beach.

The **San Francisco Zoo** 82 is a couple of miles south, at the intersection of the Great Highway and Sloat Boulevard. If you're driving, follow the Great Highway (heading south from the Cliff House, Point Lobos Avenue becomes the Great Highway), turn left on Sloat Boulevard, and park in the zoo's lot on Sloat. The hike along Ocean Beach from the Cliff House to the zoo is a flat but scenic 3 mi. To take public transportation from the Cliff House, reboard Bus 18, which continues south to the zoo.

TIMING   Set aside at least three hours for this tour—more if you don't have a car. You can easily spend an hour in the Palace of the Legion of Honor and 1½ hours at the zoo.

What to See

★ 79 **California Palace of the Legion of Honor.** Spectacularly situated on cliffs overlooking the ocean, the Golden Gate Bridge, and the Marin Headlands, this landmark building is a fine repository of European art. A pyramidal glass skylight in the entrance court illuminates the lower-level galleries, which exhibit prints and drawings, English and European porcelain, and ancient Assyrian, Greek, Roman, and Egyptian art. The 20-plus galleries on the upper level display the permanent collection of European art from the 14th century to the present day. The noteworthy Auguste Rodin collection includes two galleries devoted to the master and a third with works by Rodin and other 19th-century sculptors. ⊠ *34th Ave. at Clement St., Lincoln Park* ☎ *415/863–3330* ⊕ *www.thinker.org* ⊠ *$8, $2 off with Muni transfer, free Tues.* ☉ *Tues.–Sun. 9:30–5.*

81 **Cliff House.** The third incarnation of the Cliff House dates from 1909. The complex, which includes restaurants, a pub, and a gift shop, remains open while undergoing a gradual renovation to restore its early-20th-century look. Below the Cliff House is a fine observation deck. To the north of the Cliff House are the ruins of the glass-roof **Sutro Baths,** which

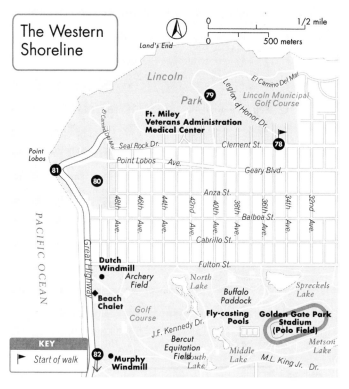

The Western
Shoreline

you can explore on your own. Six enormous baths (some freshwater and some seawater), more than 500 dressing rooms, and several restaurants covered 3 acres north of the Cliff House and accommodated 25,000 bathers. ⊠ *1090 Point Lobos Ave., Lincoln Park* ☎ *415/386–3330* ⊕ *www.cliffhouse.com* ⊡ *Free* ⊙ *Weekdays 9* AM–10:30 PM, *weekends 8:30* AM–11 PM.

▶ **78** **Lincoln Park.** Large Monterey cypresses line the fairways at Lincoln Park's 18-hole golf course, and there are scenic walks throughout the 275-acre park. The trail out to **Land's End** starts outside the Palace of the Legion of Honor, at the end of El Camino del Mar. ⊠ *Entrance at 34th Ave. at Clement St.*

🐾 **82** **San Francisco Zoo.** More than 1,000 birds and animals—220 species altogether—reside here. Among the more than 130 endangered species are the snow leopard, Sumatran tiger, jaguar, and Asian elephant. African Kikuyu grass carpets the circular outer area of **Gorilla World,** one of the largest and most natural gorilla habitats of any zoo in the world. Trees and shrubs create communal play areas. Fifteen species of rare monkeys—including colobus monkeys, white ruffed lemurs, and macaques—live and play at the two-tier **Primate Discovery Center,** which contains

23 interactive learning exhibits on the ground level. The **Feline Conservation Center**, a natural setting for rare cats, plays a key role in the zoo's efforts to encourage breeding among endangered felines. ⊠ *Sloat Blvd. and 45th Ave., Sunset, Muni L–Taraval streetcar from downtown* ☎*415/753–7080* ⊕*www.sfzoo.org* ✉*$10, $1 off with Muni transfer, free 1st Wed. of month* ☉ *Daily 10–5. Children's zoo late May–early Sept., daily 10:30–4:30; rest of yr, weekdays 11–4, weekends 10:30–4:30.*

⑳ Sutro Heights Park. Monterey cypresses and Canary Island palms dot this cliff-top park on what were the grounds of the home of eccentric mining engineer and former San Francisco mayor Adolph Sutro. Photos on placards depict what you would have seen before the house burned down in 1896. All that remains of the main house is its foundation. San Francisco City Guides (☎ 415/557–4266) runs a free Saturday tour of the park that starts at 2 (meet at the lion statue at 48th and Point Lobos avenues). ⊠ *Point Lobos and 48th Aves., Lincoln Park.*

Mission District

The sunny Mission District wins out in San Francisco's system of microclimates—it's always the last to succumb to fog. Italian and Irish in the early 20th century, the Mission became heavily Latino in the late 1960s, when immigrants from Mexico and Central America began arriving. Gentrification in the late 1990s led to skyrocketing rents, causing clashes between the longtime residents forced out and the wealthy yuppies moving in. Still a bit scruffy in patches, the Mission lacks some of the glamour of other neighborhoods, but a walk through it provides the opportunity to mix with a heady cross section of San Franciscans.

a good walk

The spiritual heart of the old Mission lies within the thick, white adobe walls of **Mission Dolores** ㉝ ▶, where Dolores Street intersects with 16th Street. From the Mission, cross Dolores Street and head east on 16th Street. Tattooed and pierced hipsters abound a block from Mission Dolores, but the eclectic area still has room for a place like Creativity Explored, where people with developmental disabilities work on art and other projects. At the intersection of 16th and Valencia streets, head south (to the right) and make a left on 24th Street. The atmosphere becomes distinctly Latin-American. A half block east of Folsom Street, mural-lined Balmy Alley runs south from 24th Street to 25th Street. A few steps farther east on 24th Street is the **Precita Eyes Mural Arts and Visitors Center** ㉞. From the center continue east past St. Peter's Church, where Isías Mata's mural *500 Years of Resistance*, on the exterior of the rectory, reflects on the struggles and survival of Latin-American cultures. At 24th and Bryant streets is the **Galería de la Raza/Studio 24** ㉟ art space.

Diagonally across from the Galería, on Bryant at the northeast corner near 24th Street, you can catch Bus 27–Bryant to downtown.

TIMING The above walk takes about two hours, including brief stops at the various sights listed. If you plan to go on a mural walk with Precita Eyes or if you're a browser who tends to linger, add at least another hour.

The Mission District/Noe Valley

What to See

⓼ Galería de la Raza/Studio 24. San Francisco's premier showcase for Latino art, the gallery exhibits the works of local and international artists. Next door is the nonprofit Studio 24, which sells prints and paintings by Chicano artists as well as folk art, mainly from Mexico. ⊠ *2857 24th St., at Bryant St., Mission* 🕾 *415/826–8009* ⊕ *www.galeriadelaraza. org* ⊙ *Gallery Tues.–Sun. noon–6, Studio 24 Wed.–Sun. noon–6.*

★ ⌐ **⓼ Mission Dolores.** Two churches stand side by side at this mission, including the small adobe **Mission San Francisco de Asís**, the oldest standing structure in San Francisco. Completed in 1791, it's the sixth of the 21 California missions founded by Father Junípero Serra in the 18th and early 19th centuries. Its ceiling depicts original Ohlone Indian basket designs, executed in vegetable dyes. The tiny chapel includes frescoes and a hand-painted wooden altar; some artifacts were brought from Mexico by mule in the late 18th century. ⊠ *Dolores and 16th Sts., Mission* 🕾 *415/621–8203* ⊕ *www.sfmuseum.org/hist5/misdolor.html* 🖭 *Free, donations welcome, audio tour $7* ⊙ *Daily 9–4.*

⓼ Precita Eyes Mural Arts and Visitors Center. The nonprofit arts organization sponsors guided walks of the Mission District's murals. Most tours start with a 45-minute slide presentation. The bike and walking trips, which take between one and three hours, pass several dozen murals. May is Mural Awareness Month, with visits to murals-in-progress and presentations by artists. You can pick up a map of 24th Street's murals at the center. ⊠ *2981 24th St., Mission* 🕾 *415/285–2287* ⊕ *www.precitaeyes. org* 🖭 *Center free, tours $10–$12* ⊙ *Center weekdays 10–5, Sat. 10–4, Sun. 11–4; walks weekends at 11 and 1:30 or by appointment.*

The Castro & the Haight

The Castro district—the social, cultural, and political center of the gay and lesbian community in San Francisco—is one of the liveliest and most welcoming neighborhoods in the city, especially on weekends. On Saturday and Sunday, the streets teem with folks out shopping, pushing political causes, heading to art films, and lingering in bars and cafés.

Young people looking for an affordable spot in which they could live according to new precepts began to move into the big old Victorians in the Haight in the late 1950s and early 1960s. By 1966 the Haight had become a hot spot for rock bands including the Grateful Dead and Jefferson Airplane.

a good walk

Begin at **Harvey Milk Plaza** ⓼ ⌐ on the southwest corner of 17th and Market streets; it's outside the south entrance to the Castro Street Muni station (K, L, and M streetcars stop here). Across Castro Street from the plaza is the neighborhood's landmark, the **Castro Theatre** ⓼. Many shops line Castro Street between 17th and 19th streets, 18th between Sanchez and Eureka streets, and Market Street heading east toward downtown. After exploring the shops, get ready for a strenuous walk. For an unforgettable vista, continue north on Castro Street two blocks to 16th Street, turn left, and head up the steep hill to Flint Street. Turn right on Flint and follow the trail on the left (just past the tennis courts) up the hill.

The beige buildings on the left contain the **Randall Museum** ⑱ for children. Turn right up the dirt path, which soon loops back up Corona Heights. At the top you're treated to an all-encompassing view of the city.

Now continue north to walk the Haight Street tour. Follow the trail down the other side of Corona Heights to a grassy field. The gate to the field is at the intersection of Roosevelt Way and Museum Way. Turn right on Roosevelt (head down the hill) and cross Roosevelt at Park Hill Terrace. Walk up Park Hill to Buena Vista Avenue, turn left, and follow the road as it loops west and south around Buena Vista Park to Central Avenue. Head down Central two blocks to Haight Street and make a left.

Continue west to the fabled **Haight-Ashbury intersection** ⑱. A motley contingent of folks attired in retro fashions and often sporting hippie-long hair hangs here. One block south of Haight and Ashbury (at 710 Ashbury) is the Grateful Dead house, the pad that Jerry Garcia and band inhabited in the 1960s. The stores along Haight Street up to Shrader Street are worth checking out.

TIMING   Allot 60 to 90 minutes to visit the Castro district. Set aside an extra hour to hike Corona Heights and visit the Randall Museum. The distance covered here is only several blocks, and although there are shops aplenty and other amusements, an hour or so should be enough.

What to See

★ ⑳ **Castro Theatre.** The neon marquee is the neighborhood's great landmark, and the 1,500-seat art-deco theater, which opened in 1922, is the grandest of San Francisco's few remaining movie palaces. Janet Gaynor, who in 1927 won the first Oscar for best actress, worked as an usher here. The Castro's elaborate Spanish baroque interior is fairly well preserved. The crowd can be enthusiastic and vocal, talking back to the screen as loudly as it talks to them. ⌧ *429 Castro St., Castro* ☎ *415/621–6120.*

⑱ **Haight-Ashbury intersection.** On October 6, 1967, hippies took over the intersection of Haight and Ashbury streets to proclaim the "Death of Hip." If they thought hip was dead then, they'd find absolute confirmation of it today, what with the Gap holding court on one quadrant of the famed corner. Among the folks who hung out in or near the Haight during the late 1960s were writers Richard Brautigan, Allen Ginsberg, Ken Kesey, and Gary Snyder; anarchist Abbie Hoffman; rock performers Marty Balin, Jerry Garcia, Janis Joplin, and Grace Slick; LSD champion Timothy Leary; and filmmaker Kenneth Anger.

⚑ ⑱ **Harvey Milk Plaza.** An 18-foot-long rainbow flag, a gay icon, flies above this plaza named for the man who electrified the city in 1977 by being elected to its Board of Supervisors as an openly gay candidate. The liberal Milk hadn't served a full year of his term before he and Mayor George Moscone, also a liberal, were shot in November 1978 at City Hall. Milk's assassination shocked the gay community, which became infuriated when the infamous "Twinkie defense"—that junk food had led to diminished mental capacity—resulted in a manslaughter verdict for White. During the so-called White Night Riot of May 21, 1979, gays and their

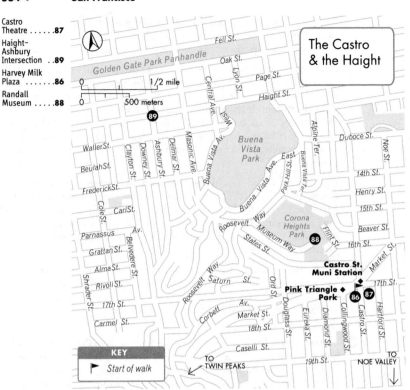

sympathizers stormed City Hall, torching its lobby and several police cars. ⊠ *Southwest corner of Castro and Market Sts., Castro.*

Randall Museum. In addition to a greenhouse, woodworking and ceramics studios, and a theater, the museum has an educational animal room with birds, lizards, snakes, spiders, and other creatures that cannot be released to the wild due to injury or other problems. Spread over 16 acres of public land, the museum sits beneath a hill variously known as Red Rock, Museum Hill, and, correctly, Corona Heights. ⊠ *199 Museum Way, off Roosevelt Way, Castro* ☎ *415/554–9600* ⊕ *www.randallmuseum.org* ☑ *Free* ☉ *Tues.–Sat. 10–5.*

WHERE TO EAT

Updated by
Sharon Silva

Since the city's earliest days, food lovers have flocked to San Francisco—a place where diversity rules and trends are set. Nearly every ethnic cuisine represented—from Afghan to Indian to Vietnamese. And although locals have long headed to the Mission District for Latin food, to Chinatown and the Richmond District for Asian food, and to North Beach for Italian food, they also know that every part of the city offers dining experiences beyond the neighborhood tradition.

	WHAT IT COSTS				
	$$$$	$$$	$$	$	¢
AT DINNER	over $30	$23–$30	$15–$22	$10–$14	under $10

Prices are per person for a main course. The final tab will include tax of 8.5%.

Union Square

Contemporary

★ $$$–$$$$ ✕ **Postrio.** There's always a chance of seeing a celebrity here, including the owner of this legendary eatery, superchef Wolfgang Puck, who periodically commutes here from Los Angeles. A stunning three-level bar and dining area is connected by copper handrails and accented with museum-quality contemporary paintings. The seasonal lunch and dinner menus are Californian with Mediterranean and Asian overtones, including the restaurant's signature Chinese roast duck. ⊠ *545 Post St., Union Sq.* ☎ *415/776–7825* ⚖ *Reservations essential* ⊟ *AE, D, DC, MC, V* ⊙ *No lunch Sun.*

French

★ $$$$ ✕ **Fleur de Lys.** The creative cooking of French chef–part owner Hubert Keller has brought every conceivable culinary award to this romantic spot. The interior's distinctive feature is its tented ceiling, 900 yards of draped and swathed fabric. The three-, four-, and five-course prix-fixe menus include dishes such as venison loin on salsify, filet mignon with braised endives and roast pears, and porcini-dusted skate wing. ⊠ *777 Sutter St., Union Sq.* ☎ *415/673–7779* ⚖ *Reservations essential* �🏠 *Jacket required* ⊟ *AE, D, DC, MC, V* ⊙ *Closed Sun. No lunch.*

Mediterranean

★ ¢–$$ ✕ **Cortez.** The restaurant, in the theater district's Hotel Adagio, serves beautifully presented small plates in a setting outfitted with eye-catching Calder-inspired mobile lights in bright red, yellow, blue, and green. The tapas-size dishes range from raw tuna on shaved fennel and fig-and-arugula salad with serrano ham and manchego cheese to mint-seasoned lamb rib chops and butternut-squash ravioli dressed with sage. ⊠ *Hotel Adagio, 550 Geary St., Union Sq.* ☎ *415/292–6360* ⊟ *AE, MC, V* ⊙ *No lunch.*

Seafood

$$$–$$$$ ✕ **Farallon.** Outfitted with sculpted jellyfish lamps, kelp-covered columns,
Fodor'sChoice and sea-urchin chandeliers, this swanky Pat Kuleto–designed restaurant
★ is loaded with style *and* customers. Chef Mark Franz changes the menu regularly, but fried squid with squid-ink risotto, artichoke soup with brioche croutons, and local petrale sole with linguine and sugar snap peas circulate in and out of the offerings. Nationally known pastry chef Emily Luchetti Meyer delivers wonderful finales. ⊠ *450 Post St., Union Sq.* ☎ *415/956–6969* ⊟ *AE, D, DC, MC, V* ⊙ *No lunch Sun. or Mon.*

Vietnamese

$$–$$$ ✕ **Le Colonial.** The stamped tin ceiling, period photographs, slow-moving fans, and tropical plants re-create a 1920s French-colonial setting

Where to Eat In & Around Downtown

for the upscale Vietnamese food. Local blue bloods come for the salt-and-pepper calamari with citrus dipping sauce; coconut-crusted crab cakes; soup of rice noodles, chicken, and Asian herbs; and wok-seared beef tenderloin. ⊠ *20 Cosmo Pl., Union Sq.* ☎ *415/931–3600* ⌲ *Reservations essential* 🖃 *AE, MC, V* ⊗ *No lunch.*

SoMa & the Embarcadero

American

$$–$$$ ✕ **Town Hall.** Chefs Mitchell and Steven Rosenthal, who have long headed the kitchen at Wolfgang Puck's popular Postrio, have also opened their own, more casual place. The fare is new American: warm frisée salad with Smithfield ham, poached egg, and cider vinegar; cornmeal-stuffed roast quail; San Francisco–inspired cioppino; cedar-planked salmon. The wines, many by the glass, complement the food. The space, with dark wood floors, exposed brick walls, white wainscoting, contemporary art, and an outdoor patio, comfortably blends old with new. ⊠ *342 Howard St., SoMa* ☎ *415/908–3900* 🖃 *AE, MC, V* ⊗ *No lunch weekends.*

Contemporary

$$$–$$$$ ✕ **Bacar.** An understated brick-and-glass exterior hides one of the city's most wine-savvy restaurants. The by-the-glass list runs pages; wines by the bottle require a hefty book. In other words, serious wine drinkers feel at home in this stylish place. The food menu is far smaller—and nicely unfussy—with a half dozen or so choices in each category. An aromatic seafood stew, seared duck breast, and roast rack of lamb with seasonal garnishes are among the satisfying main courses. ⊠ *448 Brannan St., SoMa* ☎ *415/904–4100* 🖃 *AE, DC, MC, V* ⊗ *No lunch.*

★ $$$–$$$$ ✕ **Boulevard.** Two of San Francisco's top restaurant talents—chef Nancy Oakes and designer Pat Kuleto—are responsible for this high-profile eatery in the magnificent 1889 Audiffred Building, a Parisian look-alike that was one of the few downtown structures to survive the 1906 earthquake. Oakes's menu, with its nod to the French kitchen, is seasonally in flux, but you can count on her signature juxtapositioning of classy fare, such as squab stuffed with chanterelles and foie gras, with comfort food, like wood-oven-roasted rack of lamb. Portions are generous; save room (and calories) for one of the dynamite—and pricey—desserts, such as tangerine custard tart with citrus sorbet. ⊠ *1 Mission St., Embarcadero* ☎ *415/543–6084* ⌲ *Reservations essential* 🖃 *AE, D, DC, MC, V* ⊗ *No lunch weekends.*

★ $$$–$$$$ ✕ **Fifth Floor.** Chef Laurent Gras, who has cooked alongside such notable French culinary stars as Alain Ducasse and Guy Savoy, puts together elegant, sophisticated, visually stunning plates that keep interested—and well-heeled—diners coming to this top-drawer restaurant. The 75-seat room, with dark wood and zebra-stripe carpeting, is where exquisite dishes such as duck breast with huckleberries or slow-cooked pork belly with truffles are served from a seasonal menu. ⊠ *Palomar Hotel, 12 4th St., SoMa* ☎ *415/348–1555* ⌲ *Reservations essential* 🖃 *AE, DC, MC, V* ⊗ *Closed Sun. No lunch.*

★ $$–$$$$ ✕ **Hawthorne Lane.** This big, handsome restaurant draws a crowd to a quiet alley not far from the Yerba Buena Center. The place is divided into two rooms: the first, with a beautiful oval cherrywood bar, comfy upholstered booths, and well-spaced tables, has a lively ambience, while the second is a more formal, light-flooded dining room. Truffled beef tartare, caviar-accented parsnip-and-scallop soup, and lamb with yogurt sauce and grilled flat bread are among the typical offerings on the menu, which is seasonal. The bread basket, full of house-made delights such as biscuits, bread sticks, and rolls, is the best in town. ⊠ *22 Hawthorne St., SoMa* ☎ *415/777–9779* ⊟ *D, DC, MC, V* ⊙ *No lunch weekends.*

$$–$$$ ✕ **One Market.** A giant among American chefs, Bradley Ogden gained fame at Campton Place and later at his Lark Creek Inn in Marin County. This huge, bustling brasserie across from the Ferry Building is his popular San Francisco outpost. The two-tier dining room, done in mustard tones, seats 170 and serves a seasonal—and surprisingly homey—menu that might include salmon fillet cloaked in wild mushrooms, pork shoulder with green-onion farro (a light brown grain), and fallen chocolate cake with blood-orange compote. The service is polished. The wine list includes the best California labels, and there's even a local boutique brandy to sip at meal's end. ⊠ *1 Market St., Embarcadero* ☎ *415/777–5577* ⌕ *Reservations essential* ⊟ *AE, DC, MC, V* ⊙ *Closed Sun. No lunch Sat.*

French

★ $$ ✕ **Piperade.** Longtime San Francisco chef Gerald Hirogoyen serves an appealing French Basque menu full of the rustic dishes—both small and large—of his childhood. Among them are *piquillo* peppers (pimientos) stuffed with salt cod, *pipérade* (cooked peppers and tomatoes served with serrano ham and a poached egg), lamb marinated in thyme and vinegar, and grilled cod with chorizo and potatoes. To stay with the theme, try a Basque wine from the impressive list and a wedge of the traditional almond-laced Basque cake. Hirogoyen has also opened a small café and take-out operation around the corner. ⊠ *1015 Battery St., Embarcadero* ☎ *415/391–2555* ⊟ *AE, MC, V* ⊙ *Closed Sun. No lunch Sat.*

Indian

★ ¢–$ ✕ **Chaat Café.** Indian snacks—*chaat*—are the specialty at this no-frills establishment (part of a small chain) adorned with big, bright-color paintings of Indian women. Thin, chewy naan accompanies curries—fish, lamb, chicken, and veggie versions—and is used for wraps, including one filled with tasty tandoori lamb, onions, and cilantro. Small, hollow bread puffs into which you spoon seasoned potatoes and chickpeas—a dish called *pani puri* here—and chicken and fish *pakora* (fritters) are also good choices. ⊠ *320 3rd St., SoMa* ☎ *415/979–9946* ⌕ *Reservations not accepted* ⊟ *MC, V.*

Mediterranean

★ $$–$$$ ✕ **LuLu.** The food is satisfyingly uncomplicated and delectable. Beneath a high, barrel-vaulted ceiling, you can feast on fritto misto of artichokes, fennel, and lemon slices; mussels roasted in an iron skillet; wood-oven-roasted poultry, meats, and shellfish; and a small selection of pizzas and pastas. There is a well-supplied raw bar, and main-course specials include a rotisserie-prepared main course that changes daily. ⊠ *816 Folsom St., SoMa* ☎ *415/495–5775* ⊟ *AE, D, DC, MC, V.*

Vietnamese

★ **$$–$$$** ✕ **Slanted Door.** In 2004 chef-owner Charles Phan, who has gained national fame with his upmarket, Western-accented Vietnamese fare, moved the Slanted Door into the busy Ferry Building, where it occupies a large space outfitted with sleek wooden tables and chairs, a cocktail lounge and bar, and a big bay view. (At this writing, he plans to expand the original Mission District location into a casual noodle restaurant, slated to open by 2005.) Phan's popular dishes—crispy sweet-and-sour whole fish, clay-pot chicken with chilies and ginger, shaking beef (tender beef cubes with garlic and onion), green papaya salad—made the move, too, to the cheers of his faithful customers. ⊠ *Ferry Bldg., Embarcadero at Market St., Embarcadero* 🕾 *415/861–8032* 🖃 *AE, MC, V.*

Financial District

Chinese

¢–$ ✕ **Yank Sing.** The city's oldest teahouse prepares 100 varieties of dim sum on a rotating basis, serving some 60 varieties daily. The Spear Street location, near one end of the Rincon Center atrium, is big and comfortable; the older, Stevenson Street site is smaller, a cozier refuge for neighborhood office workers who fuel up on steamed buns and parchment chicken at lunchtime. ⊠ *49 Stevenson St., Financial District* 🕾 *415/541–4949* ⚑ *Reservations essential* 🖃 *AE, DC, MC, V* ✆ *No dinner* ✉ *1 Rincon Center, 101 Spear St., Financial District* 🕾 *415/957–9300* ⚑ *Reservations essential* 🖃 *AE, DC, MC, V* ✆ *No dinner.*

French

★ **$–$$$** ✕ **Jeanty at Jack's.** Chef Philippe Jeanty, who made a name for himself in the wine country, oversees this brass-and-wood, three-story brasserie in the former Jack's restaurant, a San Francisco institution since 1864. The food is as French as the chef, with cassoulet, steak frites, rabbit terrine, bouillabaisse, and coq au vin among the traditional offerings. ⊠ *615 Sacramento St., Financial District* 🕾 *415/693–0941* 🖃 *AE, D, MC, V.*

Japanese

$$–$$$$ ✕ **Kyo-ya.** With extraordinary authenticity, this showplace in the Palace Hotel replicates the refined experience—rarely found outside Japan—of dining in a first-class Japanese restaurant. In Japan a *kyo-ya* is a nonspecialized restaurant that serves a wide range of food. Here, the range is spectacular, encompassing tempuras, one-pot dishes, deep-fried and grilled meats, and two dozen sushi selections. ⊠ *Palace Hotel, 2 New Montgomery St., at Market St., Financial District* 🕾 *415/546–5000* 🖃 *AE, D, DC, MC, V* ✆ *Closed Sun. and Mon. No lunch Sat.*

Seafood

★ **$$$–$$$$** ✕ **Aqua.** Quietly elegant, ultrafashionable, heavily mirrored, and populated by a society crowd, this spot is among the city's most lauded seafood restaurants—and among the most expensive. Chef Laurent Manrique, who is known for using exquisite ingredients and classic techniques, assembles beautiful preparations that are refined but not overly fussy: tuna tartare with Moroccan spices and lemon confit, hamachi (yellowfin tuna) with pickled daikon, and Atlantic cod with mixed seafood, serrano ham, and peppers. ⊠ *252 California St., Financial District* ☎ *415/956-9662* ⌕ *Reservations essential* ⌂ *Jacket and tie* ▭ *AE, DC, MC, V* ⊘ *No lunch weekends.*

$–$$ ✕ **Tadich Grill.** Owners and locations have changed many times since this old-timer opened during the gold-rush era, but the 19th-century atmosphere remains. Simple sautés are the best choices, or cioppino during crab season (October to May), Pacific halibut in season (January to May), and old-fashioned house-made tartar sauce anytime. Seating is at the counter as well as in private booths, but expect long lines for a table at lunchtime on weekdays. ⊠ *240 California St., Financial District* ☎ *415/391-2373* ⌕ *Reservations not accepted* ▭ *MC, V* ⊘ *Closed Sun.*

Spanish

★ **$$** ✕ **B44.** The cluster of wonderful European eateries on Belden Place includes this spare, modern Spanish restaurant, which draws locals with its menu of Catalan tapas and paellas. The open kitchen sends out small plates such as white anchovies with pears and Idiazábal cheese, sherry-scented fish cheeks, warm octopus with tiny potatoes, and blood sausage with white beans. The paellas, each serving presented in an iron skillet, bring together inviting combinations such as chicken, rabbit, and mushrooms. ⊠ *44 Belden Pl., Financial District* ☎ *415/986-6287* ▭ *AE, MC, V* ⊘ *Closed Sun. No lunch Sat.*

Chinatown

Chinese

¢–**$$$** ✕ **Great Eastern.** Cantonese chefs are known for their expertise with seafood, and the kitchen here continues that venerable tradition. Tanks filled with Dungeness crabs, black bass, abalone, catfish, shrimp, and other creatures of fresh- and saltwater occupy a corner of the main dining room, a handsome space with jade-green wainscoting and dark-wood accents. A wall-hung menu in both Chinese and English lists the costs of selecting what can be pricey indulgences. ⊠ *649 Jackson St., Chinatown* ☎ *415/986-2550* ▭ *AE, MC, V.*

¢–**$$$** ✕ **R&G Lounge.** The name conjures up an image of a dark bar with a cigarette-smoking piano player, but the restaurant is actually as bright as a new penny. Downstairs is a no-tablecloth dining room that's packed at lunch and dinner. The classier upstairs space is a favorite stop for Chinese businessmen on expense accounts. The street-level space on Kearny is a comfortable spot to wait for a table to open. A menu with photographs helps you pick from the many wonderful, sometimes pricey, always authentic dishes—such as salt-and-pepper Dungeness crab. ⊠ *631 Kearny St., Chinatown* ☎ *415/982-7877 or 415/982-3811* ▭ *AE, D, DC, MC, V.*

North Beach

Afghan

★ **$–$$** ✕ **Helmand.** Authentic Afghan cooking is served at amazingly low prices in elegant surroundings, amid white table linens and Afghan carpets. Highlights include *aushak* (leek-filled ravioli served with yogurt and ground beef), pumpkin with yogurt-and-garlic sauce, and any of the lamb dishes, in particular the kebab strewn with yellow split peas and served on Afghan flat bread. ⊠ *430 Broadway, North Beach* ☎ *415/362–0641* ⊟ *AE, MC, V* ⊗ *No lunch.*

Contemporary

$$–$$$$ ✕**Moose's.** Ed Moose and his wife, Mary Etta, are well known in San Francisco and beyond, so local and national politicians and media types typically turn up at their restaurant. The regularly changing menu, the work of chef-partner Jeffrey Amber, is sophisticated without being fancy, with dishes like sautéed chicken livers with huckleberries, lobster risotto, and rib eye with cauliflower-potato gratin. The surroundings are classic and comfortable, with views of Washington Square. ⊠ *1652 Stockton St., North Beach* ☎ *415/989–7800* ⚑ *Reservations essential* ⊟ *AE, D, DC, MC, V* ⊗ *No lunch Mon.–Wed.*

Italian

★ **$–$$** ✕**Tommaso's.** This place can claim San Francisco's first wood-fired pizza oven, installed in the 1930s when the restaurant opened. The oven is still here, and the restaurant, with its coat hooks, boothlike dining nooks, and communal table running the length of the basement dining room, has changed little since those early days. The pizzas' delightfully chewy crusts, creamy mozzarella, and full-bodied house-made sauce have kept legions of happy customers returning for years. ⊠ *1042 Kearny St.* ☎ *415/398–9696* ⊟ *MC, V* ⊗ *Closed Mon. No lunch.*

¢–$ ✕**L'Osteria del Forno.** An Italian-speaking staff, a small and unpreten-
Fodor'sChoice tious dining area, and irresistible aromas drifting from the open kitchen
★ make customers who pass through the door of this modest storefront operation feel as if they've stumbled into Italy. The kitchen produces small plates of simply cooked vegetables, a few baked pastas, a roast of the day, creamy polenta, and thin-crust pizzas—including a memorable "white" pie topped with porcini mushrooms and mozzarella. ⊠ *519 Columbus Ave., North Beach* ☎ *415/982–1124* ⚑ *Reservations not accepted* ⊟ *No credit cards* ⊗ *Closed Tues.*

Nob Hill & Russian Hill

French

$$$$ ✕**Masa's.** This restaurant, with its chocolate-brown walls, white fab-
Fodor'sChoice ric ceiling, and red-silk-shaded lanterns, is still one of the country's most
★ celebrated food temples. Chef Ron Siegel, famous for besting Japan's Iron Chef, is at the helm, and his efforts have pleased the fussiest restaurant critics. Dinners are prix fixe. Tastings menus come in 3, 6, and 9 courses. All menus are laced with fancy ingredients and priced accordingly ($65–$150). ⊠ *Hotel Vintage Court, 648 Bush St., Nob Hill* ☎ *415/989–7154* ⚑ *Reservations essential* ⌂ *Jacket required* ⊟ *AE, D, DC, MC, V* ⊗ *Closed Sun. and Mon. No lunch.*

Italian

★ **$–$$$** ✕**Antica Trattoria.** With pale walls, dark wood floors, cloth-draped tables, and a partial view of the kitchen, the dining room exudes a strong sense of restraint. A small, regularly shifting menu delivers archetypal

Italian dishes like fennel with blood oranges and red onions, gnocchi with scallops, and *bistecca* (steak) to rival what you find in Florence. The genial service by the largely Italian staff is polished but not stiff. ✉ *2400 Polk St., Russian Hill* ☎ *415/928–5797* ⌕ *Reservations essential* ▤ *DC, MC, V* ☉ *Closed Mon. No lunch.*

Van Ness/Polk

Italian

$$$–$$$$ ✕**Acquerello.** Pale yellow walls, a lofty beamed ceiling, white linens, fresh flowers, and exquisite china set an elegant scene at one of the most romantic spots in town. Both the service and the food are exemplary, and the menu covers the full range of Italian cuisine. Lobster *panzerotti* (raviolilike stuffed pasta); venison loin over polenta; seared duck breast with squash puree; and risotto with butternut squash, pancetta, rosemary, and 25-year-old balsamic vinegar are all memorable. ✉ *1722 Sacramento St., Van Ness/Polk* ☎ *415/567–5432* ▤ *AE, D, MC, V* ☉ *Closed Sun. and Mon. No lunch.*

Seafood

¢–$ ✕**Swan Oyster Depot.** Half fish market and half diner, this small, slim
Fodor's Choice seafood operation, open since 1912, has no tables, only a narrow mar-
★ ble counter with about a dozen and a half stools. Most people come in to buy perfectly fresh salmon, halibut, crabs, and the like to take home. Everyone else hops onto one of the rickety stools to enjoy a bowl of clam chowder——the only hot food served—a dozen oysters, or half a cracked crab. ✉ *1517 Polk St., Van Ness/Polk* ☎ *415/673–1101* ▤ *No credit cards* ☉ *Closed Sun. No dinner.*

Lower Pacific Heights & Japantown

Contemporary

★ **$$–$$$** ✕**Quince.** Photographs of quinces line the walls of this small, elegant eatery in one of San Francisco's most fashionable neighborhoods. The address draws a crowd that's mostly well heeled but not stuffy. Michael Tusk, who has cooked at the legendary Chez Panisse and Oliveto, oversees the kitchen. The menu, which changes daily, includes such inviting dishes as pappardelle with rabbit and olives, a salad of grilled fresh sardines, pasta with wild mushrooms, duck with parsnips and quince, roast squab, and more. ✉*1701 Octavia St., Lower Pacific Heights* ☎*415/ 775–8500* ⌕ *Reservations essential* ▤ *AE, MC, V* ☉ *No lunch.*

★ **¢–$$** ✕**Chez Nous.** The concept here is Spanish tapas, although the small dishes—duck-leg confit, baked goat cheese with oven-roasted tomatoes, french fries and aioli spiked with harissa sauce—cross borders into other cuisines. Grilled asparagus sprinkled with lemon zest and lamb rib chops seasoned with herbes de Provence are among the other choices. The stylish yet casual and noisy dining room has wood floors, zinc-topped tables, and blue walls. ✉ *1911 Fillmore St., Lower Pacific Heights* ☎ *415/441–8044* ⌕ *Reservations not accepted* ▤ *MC, V.*

Italian

$$–$$$ ✕**Vivande Porta Via.** Tucked in among the boutiques on upper Fillmore Street, this longtime Italian delicatessen-restaurant, operated by well-known chef and cookbook author Carlo Middione, draws a crowd at lunch and dinner for both its take-out and sit-down fare. Shelves are laden with wines, olives, and other gourmet goods. The regularly changing menu includes a half dozen pastas and risottos and as many meat and fish main dishes. ⊠ *2125 Fillmore St., Lower Pacific Heights* ☎ *415/346–4430* ▤ *AE, D, DC, MC, V.*

Japanese

$–$$ ✕ **Mifune.** Thin, brown soba and thick, white udon are the specialties at this North American outpost of an Osaka-based noodle empire. A line often snakes out the door, but the house-made noodles are worth the wait. Seating is at wooden tables, where diners can be heard slurping down big bowls of such traditional Japanese combinations as *nabeyaki udon* (wheat noodles topped with tempura, chicken, and fish cake) and *tenzaru* (cold noodles and hot tempura with gingery dipping sauce) served on lacquered trays. ⊠ *Japan Center, Kintetsu Bldg., 1737 Post St., Japantown* ☎ *415/922–0337* ⌔ *Reservations not accepted* ▤ *AE, D, DC, MC, V.*

¢–$$ ✕ **Maki.** *Wappa-meshi,* rice topped with meat or fish and steamed in a bamboo basket, is the specialty at this small, lovely restaurant with blond-wood tables and white walls. The sashimi; braised yams, daikon, and pork; and freshwater eel on rice in a lacquer box are also recommended. Everything is served on beautiful tableware. Maki stocks an impressive assortment of sakes. ⊠ *Japan Center, Kinokuniya Bldg., 1825 Post St., Japantown* ☎ *415/921–5215* ▤ *MC, V* ☉ *Closed Mon.*

Civic Center/Hayes Valley

Contemporary

$$$–$$$$ ✕ **Jardinière.** One of the city's most talked-about restaurants since its open-
FodorsChoice   ing in the late 1990s, Jardinière continues to be *the* place to dine before
★   a performance at the nearby Opera House or any time you have something to celebrate. The chef-owner is Traci Des Jardins, and the sophisticated interior, with its eye-catching oval atrium and curving staircase, is the work of designer Pat Kuleto. From velvety squash soup to roast lamb loin with flageolet beans to exquisite chocolate and fruit desserts, the menu is a match for the decor. ⊠ *300 Grove St., Hayes Valley* ☎ *415/861–5555* ⌔ *Reservations essential* ▤ *AE, DC, MC, V* ☉ *No lunch.*

German

$–$$ ✕ **Suppenküche.** Bratwurst and braised red cabbage and a long list of German beers rule at this lively, hip outpost of simple German cooking in the trendy Hayes Valley corridor. Strangers sit down together at unfinished pine tables. The food—potato pancakes with house-made applesauce, sauerbraten, cheese spaetzle, schnitzel, apple strudel—is tasty and easy on the pocketbook, and the brews are first-rate. ⊠ *601 Hayes St., Hayes Valley* ☎ *415/252–9289* ▤ *AE, MC, V* ☉ *No lunch.*

Mediterranean

$$–$$$ ✕ **Zuni Café.** The southern French–Italian menu, created by nationally
FodorsChoice   known chef Judy Rodgers, packs in an eclectic crowd until late in the
★   evening. A balcony dining area overlooks the long, copper bar, where

a first-rate oyster selection and drinks are dispensed. The menu changes daily, but the superb whole roast chicken and Tuscan bread salad for two are always on it. ⊠ *1658 Market St., Hayes Valley* ☎ *415/552–2522* ⌕ *Reservations essential* ▤ *AE, MC, V* ⊘ *Closed Mon.*

Fisherman's Wharf

French

$$$$ ✕ **Gary Danko.** Chef Gary Danko's daily-changing menu of highly so-
Fodor'sChoice phisticated plates has kept fans returning again and again. The cost of
★ a meal ($58–$78) is pegged to the number of courses, from three to five. Plates may include risotto with lobster, rock shrimp, and winter vegetables; roast quail stuffed with chanterelles and foie gras; and lamb loin with potato gratin. The wine list is the size of a small-town phone book, and the banquette-lined room is stunning. ⊠ *800 N. Point St., Fisherman's Wharf* ☎ *415/749–2060* ⌕ *Reservations essential* ▤ *AE, D, DC, MC, V* ⊘ *No lunch.*

Seafood

$–$$$ ✕ **McCormick & Kuleto's.** This seafood emporium in Ghirardelli Square is a visitor's dream come true: a fabulous view of the bay from every seat in the house, an Old San Francisco atmosphere, and dozens of varieties of fish and shellfish prepared in scores of international ways. The food has its ups and downs—stick with the simplest preparations, such as oysters on the half shell and grilled fish. ⊠ *Ghirardelli Sq. at Beach and Larkin Sts., Fisherman's Wharf* ☎ *415/929–1730* ▤ *AE, D, DC, MC, V.*

Cow Hollow/Marina

French

¢–$$ ✕ **Isa.** Young, talented chef Luke Sung and his wife, Kitty, run this tiny storefront restaurant, which has a heated, candlelit back patio. The menu is divided into small and large plates, all of them French-style tapas meant to be shared. The menu changes seasonally but might offer such exquisite dishes as sea bass wrapped in paper-thin potato slices, mussels in white-wine-and-shallot broth, and seared foie gras atop a bed of sautéed fruit. The wine list is smartly crafted. ⊠ *3324 Steiner St., Marina* ☎ *415/567–9588* ▤ *MC, V* ⊘ *Closed Sun. No lunch.*

Italian

$$$–$$$$ ✕ **Merenda.** The kitchen applies many French and contemporary California touches to the sophisticated Italian fare at this intimate restaurant, the domain of chef Keith Luce and his wife, Raney, who runs the front of the house. Featherlight house-made pastas, al dente risottos, and roast rabbit exemplify the dishes on the menu, which changes several times a year and is prix fixe. The wine list is well matched to the food. Service can be uneven at times, so bring a measure of patience. ⊠ *1809 Union St., Cow Hollow* ☎ *415/346–7373* ⌕ *Reservations essential* ▤ *MC, V* ⊘ *No lunch Sun.–Thurs.*

Mediterranean

$$–$$$ ✕ **PlumpJack Café.** This clubby dining room, with its smartly attired clientele of bankers and brokers, socialites and society scions, takes its name from an opera composed by oil tycoon and music lover Gordon Getty, whose son is a partner here. The seasonal menu, the creation of chef James Ormsby, spans the Mediterranean. Dishes might include pan-roasted duck breast with caramelized apples, lamb osso buco with saffron-potato puree, or yellowtail with ginger-lime sweet potatoes. ✉ *3127 Fillmore St., Cow Hollow* ☎ *415/463–4755* ▤ *AE, DC, MC, V* ☺ *No lunch weekends.*

The Mission

Contemporary

$$–$$$ ✕ **Foreign Cinema.** The Bay Area is home to many of the country's most respected independent filmmakers, so it's no surprise that this innovative spot is a hit. In the hip, loftlike space not only can you sit down to oysters on the half shell or carpaccio with french fries and horseradish sauce, but you also can watch film classics such as Zhang Yimou's *Raise the Red Lantern* and Jacques Demy's *The Umbrellas of Cherbourg* projected on the wall in the large inner courtyard. ✉ *2534 Mission St., Mission* ☎ *415/648–7600* ▤ *AE, MC, V* ☺ *Closed Mon. No lunch Tues.–Fri.*

★ **¢–$** ✕ **Andalu.** The menu includes some 30 globe-circling small plates, including tuna-tartare-filled miniature tacos, curly polenta fries, and flat-iron steak with green-peppercorn sauce. The wine list is equally global. The hip, bi-level dining room has tables outfitted in aquamarine and black. Don't overlook the dessert of doughnut holes and thick, hot cocoa topped with whipped cream. ✉ *3198 16th St., Mission* ☎ *415/ 621–2211* ▤ *AE, MC, V* ☺ *No lunch.*

French

★ **$$–$$$** ✕ **Chez Papa.** This small, simply outfitted corner restaurant has brought France to Potrero Hill. Small plates include mussels in wine, lamb chops on ratatouille, and deep-fried smelt with lemon. Typically Parisian desserts include crème brûlée, tarte tatin, and cherry clafouti. ✉ *1401 18th St., Potrero Hill* ☎ *415/824–8210* ⌕ *Reservations essential* ▤ *AE, DC, MC, V* ☺ *No lunch Sun.*

Italian

$–$$ ✕ **Delfina.** The loyal clientele keeps coming for Craig Stoll's simple yet
Fodor's Choice exquisite Italian fare at this hopping spot. The interior is simple, with
★ hardwood floors, aluminum-topped tables, a tiled bar, and a casual but sophisticated ambience. The menu changes daily, but among the usual offerings are grilled squid on a bed of tiny white beans; orecchiette with broccoli rabe and chickpeas; and halibut atop olives and braised fennel. ✉ *3621 18th St., Mission* ☎ *415/552–4055* ⌕ *Reservations essential* ▤ *MC, V* ☺ *No lunch.*

Latin

★ **$–$$** ✕ **Alma.** Chef Johnny Alamilla creates a mix of Nuevo Latino flavors in this small, comfortably urban space of blue walls and wood floors. Crispy red-onion rings accompany hanger steak, Peruvian quinoa and garlic-scallion potatoes complement grilled pork chop, and sweet-potato flan partners with seared duck breast. Even the wine list carries a Latino stamp, with wines from Argentina, Chile, and Uruguay. ✉ *1101 Valencia St., Mission* ☎ *415/401–8959* ▭ *MC, V* ⊘ *Closed Sun. No lunch.*

The Castro & the Haight

American-Casual

★ ¢–$$ ✕ **Chow.** Wildly popular and unpretentious, this spot serves honest fare—pizzas from the wood-fired oven, thick burgers of grass-fed beef, spaghetti with meatballs—made with the best local ingredients and priced for diners watching their wallets. The savvy try to leave room for an order of the superb cannoli, made according to a family recipe of chef-owner Tony Gulisano. ✉ *215 Church St., Castro* ☎ *415/552–2469* ⌑ *Reservations not accepted* ▭ *MC, V.*

Pan-Asian

¢ ✕ **Zao Noodle Bar.** Good prices, fresh ingredients, and generous portions have made this minichain a success. The menu items span Asia, from Vietnamese rice noodles with seared pork to Thai green-curry-coconut prawns with ramen. Among the beverages are topflight sakes served in martini glasses and Zao-ginger-orange cooler. The black and red decor, with plenty of wood, is as hip as the food and the diners. ✉ *3583 16th St., Castro* ☎ *415/864–2888* ⌑ *Reservations not accepted* ▭ *MC, V.*

Indian

¢–$$ ✕ **Indian Oven.** The tandoori specialties—chicken, lamb, breads—make this cozy Victorian storefront one of the Lower Haight's most popular restaurants. *Sag paneer* (spinach with Indian cheese) and *aloo gobhi* (potatoes and cauliflower with black mustard seeds and other spices) are also excellent. This is not a place to linger over *lassi* (a cold yogurt drink) on Friday and Saturday nights, when the mostly twenty- and thirtysomething clientele waiting for tables overflows onto the sidewalk. ✉ *233 Fillmore St., Lower Haight* ☎ *415/626–1628* ▭ *AE, D, DC, MC, V* ⊘ *No lunch.*

Thai

★ ¢–$$ ✕ **Thep Phanom.** The fine fare and the lovely interior at this Lower Haight institution keep local food critics and restaurant goers singing Thep Phanom's praises. Duck is deliciously prepared in several ways—in a fragrant curry, minced for salad, atop a mound of spinach. Seafood (in various guises) is another specialty. ✉ *400 Waller St., Lower Haight* ☎ *415/431–2526* ▭ *AE, D, DC, MC, V* ⊘ *No lunch.*

Richmond District

Chinese

★ ¢–$$$ ✕ **Parc Hong Kong Restaurant.** This tablecloth Cantonese restaurant has long been known as a place to enjoy such classy plates as smoked black cod and Peking duck. The kitchen is especially celebrated for its seafood, which is plucked straight from tanks. Chefs here keep up with whatever is hot in Hong Kong eateries, so check on what's new with the generally genial waiters. ✉ *5322 Geary Blvd., Richmond* ☎ *415/668–8998* ▭ *AE, D, DC, MC, V.*

Japanese

★ ¢–$$ ✕ **Kabuto A&S.** Master chef Sachio Kojima flashes his knives before an admiring crowd, which can't get enough of his buttery yellowfin tuna or golden sea urchin on pads of pearly rice. In addition to serving fine sushi and sashimi, the restaurant also offers small, cooked plates, in its cozy, 20-seat dining room and at the dozen-seat sushi bar. Don't overlook the excellent selection of sakes, each one rated for dryness and labeled with its place of origin. ⊠ *5121 Geary Blvd., Richmond* ☎ *415/752–5652* ▤ *MC, V* ☉ *Closed Wed.*

Vietnamese

★ ¢–$$ ✕ **Le Soleil.** The kitchen at this light-filled, pastel restaurant prepares traditional Vietnamese dishes from every part of the country. Try the excellent raw-beef salad; shaking beef (tender beef cubes in a vinegary sauce); or large prawns simmered in a clay pot. A large aquarium of tropical fish adds to the tranquil mood. ⊠ *133 Clement St., Inner Richmond* ☎ *415/668–4848* ▤ *MC, V.*

Sunset District

American-Casual

$$–$$$ ✕ **Beach Chalet.** In a historic colonnaded building with handsome Works Project Administration–produced murals depicting San Francisco in the mid-1930s, the Beach Chalet is the place to watch the waves break on the shore and the sun set over the Pacific Ocean. The fine microbrewery beers run the gamut from a light pilsner to a pale ale, but the dinner menu seldom produces more-than-okay food. At midday, the prices are lower, the food simpler, and the view better. ⊠ *1000 Great Hwy., Sunset* ☎ *415/386–8439* ▤ *MC, V.*

WHERE TO STAY

Updated by
Andy Moore

Few U.S. cities can rival San Francisco's variety in lodging. Its plush hotels rank among the world's finest; its renovated buildings house small hostelries with European flair; its grand Victorian-era homes serve as bed-and-breakfasts; and its private residences rent rooms, apartments, and cottages. You can even find accommodations in boats bobbing on the bay, but the popular chain hotels and motels found in most American cities are here, too. The city's hilly topography and diversity of neighborhoods contribute to each property's unique sense of place, and you may feel like a kid in a candy store as you go about choosing which of the approximately 32,000 rooms here will be your home-away-from-home.

WHAT IT COSTS				
$$$$	**$$$**	**$$**	**$**	**¢**
FOR 2 PEOPLE over $250	$200–$250	$150–$199	$90–$149	under $90

Prices are for two people in a standard double room in high season, excluding 14% tax.

Union Square/Downtown

★ **$$$$** ⊞ **Campton Place.** Highly attentive service is the hallmark of this small, top-tier hotel behind a simple brownstone facade. Many rooms are smallish, but all are elegant in a contemporary Italian style, with light earth tones and handsome pearwood paneling and cabinetry. Bathrooms have deep soaking tubs, and double-paned windows keep city noises out. ⊠ *340 Stockton St., Union Sq., 94108* ☎ *415/781–5555 or 800/235–4300* 🖷 *415/955–5536* ⊕ *www.camptonplace.com* ↴ *101 rooms, 9 suites* ⚊ *Restaurant, room service, in-room data ports, in-room safes, minibars, some microwaves, cable TV with movies and video games, exercise equipment, gym, bar, lobby lounge, dry cleaning, laundry service, concierge, Internet, business services, meeting room, parking (fee), some pets allowed (fee), no kids under 17, no-smoking floors* ⊟ *AE, DC, MC, V.*

$$$$ ⊞ **Clift.** Behind a stately, beige brick facade lies this "hotel as art" showplace, as conceived by entrepreneur Ian Schrager and artist-designer Philippe Starck. The cavernous lobby contains groupings of whimsical art objects meant to encourage a surreal mood. Spacious rooms, in shades of ivory, gray, and lavender, have blond-wood and see-through orange acrylic furniture, plus two huge mirrors on otherwise empty walls. ⊠ *495 Geary St., Union Sq., 94102* ☎ *415/775–4700 or 800/652–5438* 🖷 *415/441–4621* ⊕ *www.clifthotel.com* ↴ *337 rooms, 26 suites* ⚊ *Restaurant, room service, in-room data ports, in-room safes, minibars, cable TV with movies, in-room VCRs, gym, bar, lobby lounge, babysitting, dry cleaning, laundry service, concierge, Internet, business services, meeting rooms, parking (fee), some pets allowed (fee), no-smoking floors* ⊟ *AE, D, DC, MC, V.*

★ **$$$$** ⊞ **Hotel Nikko.** The vast marble lobby of this Japan Airlines–owned hotel is airy and serene, and its rooms are among the most handsome in the city. Look for gold drapes; wheat-color wall coverings; furniture with clean, elegant lines; and ingenious window shades that screen the sun while allowing views of the city. The excellent, complimentary fifth-floor fitness facility has traditional *ofuros* (Japanese soaking tubs), a *kamaburo* (Japanese sauna), and a glass-enclosed rooftop pool and whirlpool. A multilingual staff provides attentive service. ⊠ *222 Mason St., Union Sq., 94102* ☎ *415/394–1111 or 800/645–5687* 🖷 *415/421–0455* ⊕ *www. hotelnikkosf.com* ↴ *510 rooms, 22 suites* ⚊ *Restaurant, room service, in-room data ports, in-room fax, some in-room safes, some in-room hot tubs, some kitchenettes, minibars, cable TV with movies and video games, indoor pool, gym, hair salon, Japanese baths, massage, sauna, bar, babysitting, dry cleaning, laundry service, concierge, concierge floor, Internet, business services, meeting rooms, car rental, parking (fee), some pets allowed, no-smoking floors* ⊟ *AE, D, DC, MC, V.*

$$$–$$$$ ⊞ **Hotel Monaco.** A cheery 1910 beaux-arts facade and snappily dressed
Fodor'sChoice doormen welcome you into the plush lobby, with its grand marble stair-
★ case, French inglenook fireplace, and vaulted ceiling with murals of World War I–era planes and hot-air balloons. Rooms are full of flair, with vivid stripes and colors, Chinese-inspired armoires, canopy beds, and high-back upholstered chairs. Outer rooms have bay-window seats overlooking

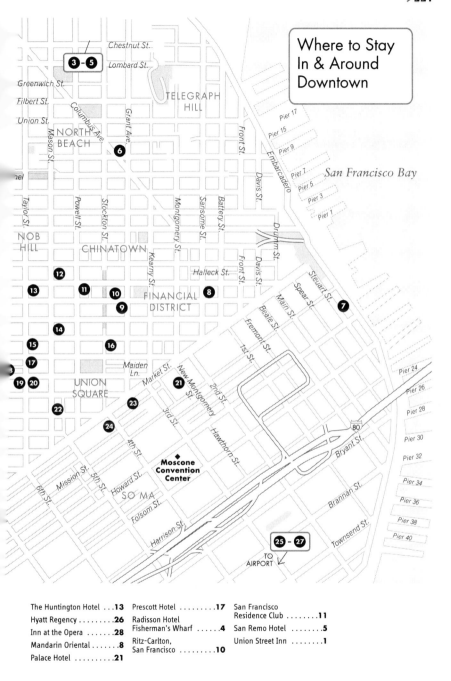

Where to Stay In & Around Downtown

Chestnut St.

3 - 5

Lombard St.

Greenwich St.

Filbert St.

Union St.

TELEGRAPH HILL

Pier 17

Pier 15

Pier 9

NORTH BEACH

6

San Francisco Bay

Pier 7

Pier 5

Pier 3

Pier 1

NOB HILL

CHINATOWN

Halleck St.

12

13 **11** **10**

8

9

FINANCIAL DISTRICT

7

14

15

16

17

Maiden Ln.

21

19 **20**

UNION SQUARE

Pier 24

Pier 26

Pier 28

22

23

24

Pier 30

80

Pier 32

Moscone Convention Center

SO MA

Pier 34

Pier 36

Pier 38

25 - 27

TO AIRPORT

Pier 40

the bustling theater district. If you didn't bring a pet, request a "companion goldfish." ⊠ *501 Geary St., Union Sq., 94102* ☎ *415/292–0100* 🖷 *415/292–0111* ⊕ *www.monaco-sf.com* ⇨ *181 rooms, 20 suites* ⌂ *Restaurant, café, room service, in-room data ports, in-room fax, in-room safes, some in-room hot tubs, minibars, cable TV with movies and video games, some in-room VCRs, gym, hot tub, massage, sauna, spa, steam room, bar, babysitting, dry cleaning, laundry service, concierge, Internet, business services, convention center, meeting rooms, parking (fee), some pets allowed, no-smoking floors* ▭ *AE, D, DC, MC, V.*

$$–$$$$ 🏨 **Prescott Hotel.** Although not as famous as many other hotels in the area, this relatively small establishment provides extremely personalized service, as well as preferred reservations at Postrio, the Wolfgang Puck restaurant attached to its lobby. Rooms, which are filled with cherry-wood furniture, are handsomely decorated in dark autumn colors and have bathrooms with marble-top sinks. Complimentary coffee and evening wine are offered by a flickering fireplace in the living room. ⊠ *545 Post St., Union Sq., 94102* ☎ *415/563–0303* 🖷 *415/563–6831* ⊕ *www. prescotthotel.com* ⇨ *155 rooms, 9 suites* ⌂ *Restaurant, room service, in-room data ports, in-room fax, minibars, cable TV with movies and video games, some in-room VCRs, gym, bar, concierge, concierge floor, Internet, business services, meeting rooms, parking (fee), some pets allowed, no-smoking floors* ▭ *AE, D, DC, MC, V.*

$$$ 🏨 **Hotel Rex.** Literary and artistic creativity are celebrated at this stylish
Fodor's Choice place named after writer Kenneth Rexroth. Shelves of antiquarian books
★ line the 1920s-style lobby lounge, where the proprietors often host book readings and roundtable discussions. Although the spacious rooms evoke the spirit of 1920s salon society with muted checkered bedspreads, striped carpets, and restored period furnishings, they also have modern touches such as CD players, and complimentary Aveda hair and skin products. ⊠ *562 Sutter St., Union Sq., 94102* ☎ *415/433–4434 or 800/433–4434* 🖷 *415/433–3695* ⊕ *www.thehotelrex.com* ⇨ *92 rooms, 2 suites* ⌂ *Café, room service, in-room data ports, minibars, refrigerators, cable TV with movies, bar, lobby lounge, babysitting, dry cleaning, laundry service, concierge, Internet, business services, meeting rooms, parking (fee), no-smoking floors* ▭ *AE, D, DC, MC, V.*

★ **$–$$** 🏨 **Hotel Adagio.** The gracious, Spanish-colonial facade of this 16-story, theater-row hotel complements its chic, modern interior. Walnut furniture, bronze light fixtures, and brown and deep orange hues dominate the spacious rooms, half of which have city views—and two penthouse suites have terraces looking out on the neighborhood. ⊠ *550 Geary St., Union Sq., 94102* ☎ *415/775–5000 or 800/228–8830* 🖷 *415/775–9388* ⊕ *www.thehoteladagio.com* ⇨ *169 rooms, 2 suites* ⌂ *Restaurant, room service, fans, in-room data ports, in-room safes, minibars, refrigerators, room TVs with movies and video games, gym, bar, lounge, babysitting, dry cleaning, laundry service, Internet, meeting rooms, parking (fee), no-smoking floors; no a/c* ▭ *AE, D, DC, MC, V.*

★ **$** 🏨 **Hotel Beresford Arms.** Surrounded by fancy molding and 10-foot-tall windows, the red-carpeted lobby of this ornate brick Victorian shows why the building is on the National Register of Historic Places. Rooms with dark-wood antique-reproduction furniture vary in size and setup:

junior suites have sitting areas and either a wet bar or kitchenette, while full suites have two queen beds, a Murphy bed, and a kitchen. All suites have a bidet in the bathroom. ⊠ *701 Post St., Union Sq., 94109* ☎ *415/673–2600 or 800/533–6533* 📠 *415/929–1535 or 800/533–5349* ⊕ *www.beresford.com* 🛏 *83 rooms, 12 suites* ⟁ *Fans, in-room data ports, some in-room hot tubs, some kitchens, some kitchenettes, minibars, some microwaves, refrigerators, cable TV, in-room VCRs, dry cleaning, laundry service, concierge, Internet, business services, parking (fee), some pets allowed, no-smoking floors; no a/c* ▭ *AE, D, DC, MC, V* ⦿ *CP.*

★ ¢–$ ⊞ **Grant Plaza Hotel.** Amazingly low room rates make this hotel a find for budget travelers wanting views of the striking architecture and fascinating street life of Chinatown. Small, modern rooms are sparkly clean, with newer, slightly more expensive digs on the top floor and quieter quarters in the back. Take the elevator up to view two large, beautiful stained-glass windows. ⊠ *465 Grant Ave., Chinatown, 94108* ☎ *415/434–3883 or 800/472–6899* 📠 *415/434–3886* ⊕ *www.grantplaza.com* 🛏 *71 rooms, 1 suite* ⟁ *Some fans, some in-room data ports, some in-room VCRs, Internet, business services, parking (fee), no-smoking rooms; no a/c* ▭ *AE, D, DC, MC, V.*

Financial District

$$$$ ⊞ **Mandarin Oriental.** Two towers connected by glass-enclosed sky bridges compose the top 11 floors of San Francisco's third-tallest building. There are spectacular panoramas from every room (each has binoculars), and windows open so you can hear the "ding ding" of the cable cars some 40 floors below. Mandarin Rooms have extra-deep tubs next to picture windows. All rooms have 260-thread-count Egyptian-cotton sheets, three phones, two kinds of robes, and terry slippers. ⊠ *222 Sansome St., Financial District, 94104* ☎ *415/276–9888* 📠 *415/433–0289* ⊕ *www.mandarinoriental.com* 🛏 *154 rooms, 4 suites* ⟁ *Restaurant, room service, in-room data ports, in-room safes, some in-room hot tubs, some kitchenettes, minibars, cable TV with movies and video games, some in-room VCRs, gym, massage, lobby lounge, piano, babysitting, dry cleaning, laundry service, concierge, Internet, business services, convention center, meeting rooms, parking (fee), some pets allowed (fee), no-smoking rooms* ▭ *AE, D, DC, MC, V.*

FodorsChoice
★

★ $$$–$$$$ ⊞ **Harbor Court.** The exemplary service of the friendly staff earns high marks for this cozy hotel overlooking the Embarcadero and within shouting distance of the Bay Bridge. Guest rooms are smallish but have double sets of soundproof windows and include fancy touches such as partially canopied upholstered beds, tasteful faux-textured walls, and Roman shades and tapestries. Some rooms have bay (and bridge) views. The hotel provides discounts for the adjacent YMCA and free weekday limo service within the Financial District. ⊠ *165 Steuart St., SoMa, 94105* ☎ *415/882–1300* 📠 *415/882–1313* ⊕ *www.harborcourthotel.com* 🛏 *130 rooms, 1 suite* ⟁ *In-room data ports, in-room fax, minibars, room TVs with movies and video games, dry cleaning, laundry service, concierge, Internet, business services, meeting rooms, parking (fee), some pets allowed, no-smoking rooms* ▭ *AE, D, DC, MC, V.*

★ **$–$$$$** 🏨 **Hyatt Regency.** The 20-story gray concrete structure, at the foot of Market Street, is the focal point of the Embarcadero Center. The spectacular 17-story atrium lobby is a marvel, with sprawling trees, a shimmering stream, and a huge fountain. Rooms—all with city or bay views, and some with bay-view balconies—have an attractive, contemporary look, with light-color walls and carpets, handsome cherry furniture, and ergonomic desk chairs. ⊠ *5 Embarcadero Center, Embarcadero, 94111* ☎ *415/788–1234 or 800/233–1234* 🖷 *415/398–2567* ⊕ *sanfranciscoregency.hyatt. com* 🛏 *760 rooms, 45 suites ⚒ 2 restaurants, café, dining room, room service, in-room data ports, in-room safes, minibars, cable TV with movies, gym, 2 bars, lobby lounge, dry cleaning, laundry service, concierge, business services, convention center, meeting rooms, car rental, parking (fee), no-smoking floors* 🖃 *AE, D, DC, MC, V.*

SoMa

$$$$ 🏨 **Four Seasons Hotel San Francisco.** On floors 5–17 of a skyscraper, this
Fodor'sChoice luxurious hotel is sandwiched between multimillion-dollar condos, elite
★ shops, and a premier sports-and-fitness complex—and while you're here, you can indulge in a little surreptitious celebrity-hunting. Elegant rooms with contemporary artwork and fine linens have floor-to-ceiling windows overlooking Yerba Buena Gardens, the bay, or the city. All have deep soaking tubs and glass-enclosed showers. Guests have free use of the junior Olympic pool, full-size indoor basketball court, and the rest of the magnificent facilities at Sports Club/LA. ⊠ *757 Market St., SoMa, 94103* ☎ *415/633–3000* 🖷 *415/633–3009* ⊕ *www.fourseasons. com* 🛏 *231 rooms, 46 suites ⚒ Restaurant, room service, in-room data ports, in-room safes, minibars, cable TV with movies and video games, some in-room VCRs, indoor pool, health club, sauna, spa, steam room, basketball, volleyball, bar, dry cleaning, laundry service, concierge, Internet, business services, meeting rooms, parking (fee), some pets allowed, no-smoking floors* 🖃 *AE, D, DC, MC, V.*

★ **$$$–$$$$** 🏨 **Hotel Palomar.** The top five floors of this green-tiled and turreted 1908 Pacific Place Building provide an urbane and luxurious oasis above the busiest part of town. Rooms have muted leopard-pattern carpeting, drapes with bold navy-and-cream stripes, and sleek furniture echoing a 1930s moderne sensibility. Sparkling bathrooms provide a "tub menu" with various herbal and botanical infusions to tempt adventurous bathers. In-room spa services are arranged through Spa Equilibrium. ⊠ *12 4th St., SoMa, 94103* ☎ *415/348–1111* 🖷 *415/348–0302* ⊕ *www. hotelpalomar.com* 🛏 *182 rooms, 16 suites ⚒ Restaurant, room service, in-room data ports, in-room fax, in-room safes, some in-room hot tubs, minibars, cable TV with movies and video games, some in-room VCRs, gym, massage, bar, lounge, babysitting, dry cleaning, laundry service, concierge, Internet, business services, meeting rooms, parking (fee), some pets allowed (fee), no-smoking floors* 🖃 *AE, D, DC, MC, V.*

★ **$$–$$$$** 🏨 **Palace Hotel.** This landmark hotel was the world's largest and most luxurious when it opened in 1875. Completely rebuilt after the earthquake and fire of 1906, it now has a stunning entryway and the fabulous belle-epoque Garden Court restaurant, with its graceful chandeliers and stained-glass domed ceiling. Rooms, with twice-daily maid service and nightly turndown, have high ceilings, reproduction-antique furnishings, and marble bathrooms. ⊠ *2 New Montgomery St., SoMa, 94105* ☎ *415/512–1111* 🖷 *415/543–0671* ⊕ *www.sfpalace.com* ➥ *517 rooms, 34 suites* ♿ *3 restaurants, room service, in-room data ports, in-room safes, some in-room hot tubs, refrigerators, cable TV with movies and video games, indoor pool, gym, indoor hot tub, sauna, spa, steam room, bar, dry cleaning, laundry service, concierge, business services, meeting rooms, parking (fee), no-smoking floors* ⊟ *AE, D, DC, MC, V.*

Nob Hill

★ **$$$$** 🏨 **The Huntington Hotel.** This redbrick, ivy-covered hotel has provided stately and gracious personal service to Humphrey Bogart, Lauren Bacall, Pablo Picasso, and Luciano Pavarotti. Rooms and suites, many of which have great views of Grace Cathedral, the bay, or the city skyline, are large because they used to be apartments; all have large antique desks. The Nob Hill Spa has a sunny indoor-outdoor area with panoramic city views, as well as an indoor pool with a fireplace lounge and 10 rooms for massages, facials, and body wraps. ⊠ *1075 California St., Nob Hill, 94108* ☎ *415/474–5400 or 800/227–4683* 🖷 *415/474–6227* ⊕ *www. huntingtonhotel.com* ➥ *100 rooms, 35 suites* ♿ *Restaurant, room service, in-room data ports, in-room fax, in-room safes, some in-room hot tubs, some kitchenettes, minibars, some refrigerators, cable TV with movies, indoor pool, gym, massage, sauna, spa, steam room, bar, piano, dry cleaning, laundry service, concierge, business services, meeting rooms, parking (fee), no-smoking floors* ⊟ *AE, D, DC, MC, V.*

$$$$ 🏨 **Ritz-Carlton, San Francisco.** This world-class hotel is a stunning trib-
Fodor'sChoice ute to beauty and attentive, professional service. Beyond the 17 Ionic
★ columns of the neoclassic facade, crystal chandeliers illuminate Georgian antiques and museum-quality 18th- and 19th-century paintings in the lobby. All rooms have featherbeds with 300-thread-count Egyptian cotton Frette sheets and down comforters. Afternoon tea in the Lobby Lounge—overlooking the beautifully landscaped garden courtyard—is a San Francisco institution. ⊠ *600 Stockton St., at California St., Nob Hill, 94108* ☎ *415/296–7465* 🖷 *415/291–0288* ⊕ *www.ritzcarlton.com* ➥ *294 rooms, 42 suites* ♿ *2 restaurants, room service, in-room data ports, in-room safes, minibars, refrigerators, cable TV with movies and video games, some in-room VCRs, indoor pool, exercise equipment, gym, indoor hot tub, massage, steam room, 3 bars, lobby lounge, piano bar, shop, babysitting, dry cleaning, laundry service, concierge, concierge floor, Internet, business services, meeting rooms, parking (fee), some pets allowed, no-smoking floors* ⊟ *AE, D, DC, MC, V.*

★ **$$–$$$$** 🏨 **Fairmont San Francisco.** The history of this hotel, which commands the top of Nob Hill like a European palace, includes triumph over the 1906 earthquake and the creation of the United Nations Charter here in 1945. Architect Julia Morgan's 1907 lobby design includes alabaster walls and gilt-embellished ceilings supported by Corinthian columns. Gracious rooms, done in pale color schemes, have high ceilings, fine darkwood furniture, colorful Chinese porcelain lamps, and marble bathrooms. Rooms in the Tower are generally larger and have better views. An array of amenities and services (including free chicken soup if you're under the weather) keeps loyal guests coming back. ⊠ *950 Mason St., Nob Hill, 94108* ☎ *415/772–5000* 🖷 *415/772–5086* ⊕ *www.fairmont.com* ⤺ *526 rooms, 65 suites* 🖎 *2 restaurants, room service, in-room data ports, in-room fax, in-room safes, minibars, cable TV with movies and video games, health club, hair salon, spa, steam room, 3 bars, lobby lounge, lounge, nightclub, shops, babysitting, dry cleaning, laundry service, concierge, Internet, business services, convention center, meeting rooms, car rental, parking (fee), some pets allowed (fee), no-smoking floors* ▭ *AE, D, DC, MC, V.*

¢–$ 🏠 **San Francisco Residence Club.** In contrast to the neighboring showplace hotels, this humble guesthouse has million-dollar views, a money-saving meal plan, and a pleasant garden patio. Most of the rooms in this rambling and somewhat timeworn Victorian share baths, although some have sweeping bay vistas. The international clientele ranges from leisure travelers and business professionals to longer-term residents who take advantage of the full American breakfast *and* dinner. An advance deposit via check is required. ⊠ *851 California St., Nob Hill, 94108* ☎ *415/421–2220* 🖷 *415/ 421–2335* ⊕ ⤺ *84 rooms, 71 with shared bath* 🖎 *Dining room, some refrigerators, piano, laundry facilities, no-smoking rooms; no a/c, no room phones, no TV in some rooms* ▭ *No credit cards* ⍾⍾ *MAP.*

Fisherman's Wharf/North Beach

$$–$$$$ 🏠 **Argonaut Hotel.** When this four-story brick building was part of the
Fodor's Choice world's largest fruit and vegetable canning complex in 1907, there was
★ no Jefferson Street—boats docked right up against the walls. Today it's part of San Francisco's Maritime National Historical Park, as well as a luxury hotel that's a tribute to nautical chic. Anchors, ropes, compasses, and a row of cruise-ship deck chairs find their way into the lively lobby decor. Spacious rooms, many of which have a sitting area with a sofa bed, have exposed-brick walls, wood-beamed ceilings, and white-washed wooden furniture that evokes a beach mood. Windows are open to the sea air, the sounds of the waterfront, and unimpeded views of the bay. Suites come with extra-deep whirlpool tubs and telescopes for close-up views of passing ships. ⊠ *495 Jefferson St., at Hyde St., Fisherman's Wharf, 94109* ☎ *415/563–0800* 🖷 *415/563–2800* ⊕ *www. argonauthotel.com* ⤺ *239 rooms, 13 suites* 🖎 *Restaurant, room service, in-room data ports, in-room safes, some in-room hot tubs, minibars, refrigerators, cable TV with movies and video games, in-room VCRs, gym, bar, lounge, babysitting, dry cleaning, laundry service, concierge, Internet, convention center, meeting rooms, parking (fee), some pets allowed, no-smoking rooms* ▭ *AE, D, DC, MC, V.*

★ $$–$$$ 🏠 **Radisson Hotel Fisherman's Wharf.** Directly facing Alcatraz, this city block–size hotel and shopping area at Fisherman's Wharf has vast, clear views of the bay. Contemporary rooms, most of which have water vistas, are decorated with cherrywood furniture and black-and-tan-stripe drapes. A landscaped courtyard and heated pool are in the center of the hotel complex. ⊠ *250 Beach St., Fisherman's Wharf, 94133* ☎ *415/ 392–6700* 🖷 *415/986–7853* ⊕ *www.radisson.com* ⤺ *355 rooms* 🖎 *In-room data ports, in-room safes, some refrigerators, cable TV with movies and video games, pool, gym, dry cleaning, laundry service, con-*

cierge, business services, meeting rooms, parking (fee), no-smoking rooms ▤ AE, D, DC, MC, V.

$$ ▦ **Hotel Bohème.** This small hotel in historic North Beach takes you back in time with cast-iron beds, large mirrored armoires, and memorabilia recalling the Beat generation. Screenwriters from Francis Ford Coppola's nearby American Zoetrope studio stay here often, as do poets and other artists. Rooms have a bistro table, two chairs, and tropical-style mosquito netting over the bed; bathrooms have cheerful yellow tiles and tiny showers. Rooms in the rear are quieter, especially on weekends. ✉ *444 Columbus Ave., North Beach, 94133* ☎ *415/433–9111* 🖷 *415/362– 6292* ⊕*www.hotelboheme.com* ⤴*15 rooms* ♢ *Fans, in-room data ports, cable TV, concierge; no a/c, no smoking* ▤ *AE, D, DC, MC, V.*

¢ ▦ **San Remo Hotel.** A few blocks from Fisherman's Wharf, this three-story 1906 Italianate Victorian was once home to longshoremen and Beats. A narrow stairway from the street leads to the front desk and labyrinthine hallways. Rooms are small but charming, with antique furnishings. About a third of the rooms have sinks, and all rooms share scrupulously clean black-and-white-tile shower and toilet facilities with pull-chain toilets. ✉ *2237 Mason St., North Beach, 94133* ☎ *415/776–8688 or 800/ 352–7366* 🖷*415/776–2811* ⊕*www.sanremohotel.com* ⤴*64 rooms with shared baths* ♢ *Fans, laundry facilities, Internet, parking (fee); no a/c, no room phones, no room TVs, no smoking* ▤ *AE, MC, V.*

Fodor'sChoice
★

Cow Hollow

★ $$–$$$$ ▦ **Union Street Inn.** With the help of precious family antiques and unique artwork, innkeepers Jane Bertorelli and David Coyle turned this green-and-cream 1902 Edwardian into a delightful B&B. Equipped with candles, fresh flowers, wine glasses, and fine linens, rooms are popular with honeymooners and romantics. The Carriage House, with its whirlpool tub, is set off from the main house by an old-fashioned English garden with lemon trees. ✉ *2229 Union St., Cow Hollow, 94123* ☎ *415/346– 0424* 🖷*415/922–8046* ⊕*www.unionstreetinn.com* ⤴*6 rooms* ♢ *Cable TV, parking (fee); no a/c in some rooms, no smoking* ▤*AE, MC, V* ⦿*BP.*

★ $–$$ ▦ **Hotel Del Sol.** Once a typical 1950s-style motor court, the Del Sol is now an atypical artistic statement. The sunny yellow-and-blue, three-story building and courtyard are a riot of stripes and bold colors. Rooms open onto the courtyard's heated pool and hammock under towering palm trees and evoke a beach-house mood with plantation shutters, tropical-stripe bedspreads, and rattan chairs. Bathrooms are small. Family suites have child-friendly furnishings and games. ✉ *3100 Webster St., Cow Hollow, 94123* ☎ *415/921–5520 or 877/433–5765* 🖷 *415/931– 4137* ⊕ *www.thehoteldelsol.com* ⤴ *46 rooms, 11 suites* ♢ *In-room data ports, in-room safes, some kitchenettes, some microwaves, some refrigerators, cable TV, some in-room VCRs, pool, bicycles, dry cleaning, laundry service, concierge, free parking, no-smoking rooms; no a/c in some rooms* ▤ *AE, D, DC, MC, V* ⦿ *CP.*

Civic Center/Van Ness

★ $–$$$ ▦ **Alamo Square Inn.** A large, 1895 Queen Anne home, an 1896 Tudor Revival mansion, and a small apartment building combine to form this extravagantly romantic B&B overlooking the terraced, grassy hilltop park for which it is named. The sky-blue house is a bit of Victoriana, with elaborate wainscoting and wonderful period antiques decorating the interior. One suite has peaked ceilings and a sunken whirlpool tub; another has bookcases with hundreds of old volumes and a fireplace. Oriental carpets cover lustrous hardwood floors, and the apartments have fully equipped kitchens. ⊠ *719 Scott St., at Fulton St., Western Addition, 94117* ☎ *415/922–2055 or 800/345–9888* 🖷 *415/931–1304* ⊕ *www.alamoinn.com* 🛏 *9 rooms, 3 suites, 2 apartments* ⟡ *Dining room, some in-room hot tubs, some kitchens, some refrigerators, babysitting, dry cleaning, laundry facilities, Internet, business services, meeting room, free parking, no-smoking rooms; no a/c, no TV in some rooms* ⊟ *AE, MC, V* ⟡l *BP.*

★ $ 🏨 **The Archbishop's Mansion.** Everything here is extravagantly romantic, starting with the cavernous common areas, where a chandelier used in the movie *Gone with the Wind* hangs above a 1904 Bechstein grand piano once owned by Noël Coward. Rooms are individually decorated with intricately carved antiques; many have whirlpool tubs or fireplaces. Although the B&B isn't within easy walking distance of many restaurants or attractions, its perch on the corner of Alamo Square near the Painted Ladies—San Francisco's famous Victorian homes—makes for a scenic, relaxed stay. ⊠ *1000 Fulton St., Western Addition/Alamo Sq., 94117* ☎ *415/563–7872 or 800/543–5820* 🖷 *415/885–3193* ⊕ *www.thearchbishopsmansion.com* 🛏 *10 rooms, 5 suites* ⟡ *Dining room, some fans, in-room data ports, some in-room hot tubs, cable TV, in-room VCRs, piano, dry cleaning, concierge, meeting room, some free parking; no a/c, no smoking* ⊟ *AE, D, MC, V* ⟡l *CP.*

$ 🏨 **Inn at the Opera.** Within a block or so of Davies Symphony Hall and the War Memorial Opera House, this hotel has hosted Luciano Pavarotti and Mikhail Baryshnikov. Beyond the marble-floor lobby, compact standard rooms have dark-wood furnishings, queen-size beds, coffeemakers, terry robes, and attractive touches like sheet music lining the bureau drawers. ⊠ *333 Fulton St., Van Ness/Civic Center, 94102* ☎ *415/863–8400 or 800/325–2708* 🖷 *415/861–0821* ⊕ *www.innattheopera.com* 🛏 *30 rooms, 18 suites* ⟡ *Restaurant, room service, fans, in-room data ports, some kitchenettes, some microwaves, some refrigerators, cable TV, some in-room VCRs, bar, babysitting, dry cleaning, concierge, business services, parking (fee); no a/c, no smoking* ⊟ *AE, DC, MC, V* ⟡l *CP.*

The Airport

★ $$$–$$$$ 🏨 **Hotel Sofitel–San Francisco Bay.** Set on a lagoon in a business park with several big-name corporate headquarters nearby, this hotel is a warm, inviting haven within this somewhat sterile area. Parisian lampposts, a métro sign, and a poster-covered kiosk bring an unexpected French theme to the public spaces. Done in pale earth tones, accommodations include fine linens and bath products, complimentary turndown service, Evian water, and fresh orchids. Many staff members speak both French and English. ⊠ *223 Twin Dolphin Dr., Redwood City, 94065* ☎ *650/598–9000* 🖷 *650/598–0459* ⊕ *www.hotelsofitelsfbay.com* 🛏 *379 rooms, 42 suites* ⟡ *Restaurant, coffee shop, patisserie, picnic area, room ser-*

vice, in-room data ports, in-room fax, minibars, cable TV with movies and video games, pool, gym, bar, lobby lounge, piano bar, shop, dry cleaning, laundry service, concierge, Internet, business services, meeting rooms, airport shuttle, free parking, some pets allowed (fee), no-smoking rooms ☰ *AE, DC, MC, V.*

★ $$ ▨ **Embassy Suites San Francisco Airport, Burlingame.** This California Mission–style hostelry is set on the bay, with clear views of airplanes flying above distant San Francisco. It centers on a nine-story atrium and tropical garden replete with towering palms, bamboo and banana plants, a koi-filled stream, and a waterfall. Two-room suites have a work area, sleeper sofa, wet bar, microwave, and refrigerator. Rates include a full breakfast and unlimited evening cocktails. ⊠ *150 Anza Blvd., Burlingame, 94010* ☎ *650/342–4600 or 800/362–2779* 🖨 *650/343–8137* ⊕ *www. embassyburlingame.com* ↪ *340 suites* ⚖ *Restaurant, in-room data ports, kitchenettes, microwaves, refrigerators, cable TV with movies and video games, indoor pool, gym, hot tub, sauna, bar, dry cleaning, laundry service, concierge, Internet, business services, meeting rooms, airport shuttle, free parking, some pets allowed (fee), no-smoking floors; no kids under 18* ☰ *AE, DC, MC, V* ⦿ *BP.*

NIGHTLIFE & THE ARTS

Updated by Sharron Wood From ultrasophisticated piano bars to come-as-you-are dives that reflect the city's gold-rush past, San Francisco has a tremendous variety of evening entertainment. Enjoy a night out at the opera in the Civic Center area or hit the hip SoMa neighborhood for straight-up rock or retro jazz. Except at a few skyline lounges, you're not expected to dress up. Nevertheless, jeans are the exception and stylish dress the norm at most nightspots.

The Arts

The best guide to arts and entertainment events in San Francisco is the "Datebook" section, printed on pink paper, in the *San Francisco Sunday Chronicle.* Also consult any of the free alternative weeklies.

City Box Office (⊠ 180 Redwood St., Suite 100, off Van Ness Ave. between Golden Gate Ave. and McAllister St., Civic Center ☎ 415/392–4400 ⊕ www.cityboxoffice.com), has a charge-by-phone service for many concerts and lectures. You can charge tickets for everything from jazz concerts to Giants games by phone or online through **Tickets.com** (☎ 415/776–1999, 510/762–2277, or 800/955–5566 ⊕ tickets.com). Half-price, same-day tickets for many local and touring stage shows go on sale (cash only) at 11 AM Tuesday through Saturday at the **TIX Bay Area** (⊠ Powell St. between Geary and Post Sts., Union Sq. ☎ 415/433–7827 ⊕ www.theatrebayarea.org/tix/tix.shtml) booth on Union Square.

Dance

★ **San Francisco Ballet.** Under artistic director Helgi Tomasson, both classical and contemporary works have won admiring reviews. Tickets and information are available at the **War Memorial Opera House.** ⊠ *War Memorial Opera House, 301 Van Ness Ave., Civic Center* ☎ *415/865–2000* ⊕ *www.sfballet.org.*

Music

★ **San Francisco Opera.** Founded in 1923, this world-renowned company has resided in the Civic Center's War Memorial Opera House since the building's completion, in 1932. Over its split season—September through January and June through July—the opera presents about 70 performances of 10 to 12 operas. Translations are projected above the stage during almost all non-English operas. Long considered a major international company and the most important operatic organization in the United States outside New York, the opera frequently embarks on productions with European opera companies. Ticket prices are about $25–$195. The full-time box office is at 199 Grove Street, at Van Ness Avenue. ⊠ *War Memorial Opera House, 301 Van Ness Ave., at Grove St., Civic Center* ☎ *415/864–3330 tickets* ⊕ *www.sfopera.com.*

San Francisco Symphony. The symphony performs from September through May, with additional summer performances of light classical music and show tunes. Michael Tilson Thomas, who is known for his innovative programming of 20th-century American works, is the music director, and he and his orchestra often perform with soloists of the caliber of Andre Watts, Gil Shaham, and Renée Fleming. Tickets run about $15–$100. ⊠ *Davies Symphony Hall, 201 Van Ness Ave., at Grove St., Civic Center* ☎ *415/864–6000* ⊕ *www.sfsymphony.org.*

Theater

★ **American Conservatory Theater.** Not long after its founding in the mid-1960s, the city's major nonprofit theater company became one of the nation's leading regional theaters. During its season, which runs from early fall to late spring, ACT presents approximately eight plays, from classics to contemporary works, often in rotating repertory. In December ACT stages a much-loved version of Charles Dickens's *A Christmas Carol.* The **ACT ticket office** (⊠ 405 Geary St., Union Sq. ☎ 415/749–2228) is next door to Geary Theater, the company's home. ⊠ *Geary Theater, 425 Geary St., Union Sq.* ⊕ *www.act-sfbay.org.*

Magic Theatre. Once Sam Shepard's favorite showcase, the Magic presents works by rising American playwrights, such as Matthew Wells, Karen Hartman, and Claire Chafee. ⊠ *Fort Mason, Bldg. D, Laguna St. at Marina Blvd.* ☎ *415/441–8822* ⊕ *www.magictheatre.org.*

Nightlife

For information on who's performing where, check out the "Datebook" insert of the *San Francisco Chronicle,* or consult the free *San Francisco Bay Guardian,* which lists neighborhood, avant-garde, and budget-priced events. The *SF Weekly* is also free and packed with information on arts events around town. Another handy reference is the weekly *Where* magazine, offered free in most major hotel lobbies and at Hallidie Plaza (Market and Powell streets).

Bars

★ **Beach Chalet.** This restaurant-microbrewery, in a historic building filled with Works Project Administration murals from the 1930s, has a stunning view overlooking the Pacific Ocean. ⊠ *1000 Great Hwy., near Martin Luther King Jr. Dr., Golden Gate Park* ☎ *415/386–8439.*

Big 4 Bar. On the ground floor of the Huntington Hotel is this quietly opulent spot for piano music (daily from about 5 PM to 11:30). ⊠ *The Huntington Hotel, 1075 California St., Nob Hill* ☎ *415/474–5400.*

Buena Vista Café. The wharf area's most popular bar introduced Irish coffee to the New World—or so it says. ⊠ *2765 Hyde St., at Beach St., Fisherman's Wharf* ☎ *415/474–5044.*

Carnelian Room. On the 52nd floor of the Bank of America Building, this restaurant-lounge has what is perhaps the loftiest view of San Francisco's magnificent skyline. ⊠ *555 California St., at Kearny St., Financial District* ☎ *415/433–7500.*

★ **Eos Restaurant and Wine Bar.** A narrow and dimly lighted space with more than 400 wines by the bottle and 40-plus by the glass offers two different wine flights, one red and one white, every month. ⊠ *901 Cole St., at Carl St., Haight* ☎ *415/566–3063.*

★ **Harry Denton's Starlight Room.** Velvet booths and romantic lighting help re-create the 1950s high life on the 21st floor of the Sir Francis Drake Hotel. ⊠ *Sir Francis Drake Hotel, 450 Powell St., between Post and Sutter Sts., Union Sq.* ☎ *415/395–8595.*

Jade Bar. This narrow tri-level space with floor-to-ceiling windows, a 15-foot waterfall, and stylish sofas and banquettes attracts a near-capacity crowd even midweek. ⊠ *650 Gough St., between McAllister and Fulton Sts., Hayes Valley* ☎ *415/869–1900.*

Laszlo. At this nightspot attached to the Foreign Cinema restaurant, a bi-level design, dim lighting, and candles on each table set the scene for a romantic tête-à-tête over a classy cocktail or single-malt whiskey. ⊠ *2532 Mission St., between 21st and 22nd Sts., Mission* ☎ *415/401–0810.*

Ovation. On weekends a pianist plays and the fireplace crackles at this romantic restaurant-lounge at the Inn at the Opera. ⊠ *Inn at the Opera, 333 Fulton St., near Franklin St., Hayes Valley* ☎ *415/553–8100.*

★ **Redwood Room.** Bizarre video installations, sleek seating, a lush monochromatic look, and arts-and-entertainment patrons contribute to the glamorous feel of this trendy place. You usually have to be on the guest list to get in Thursday through Saturday. ⊠ *495 Geary St., at Taylor St., Union Sq.* ☎ *415/929–2372.*

Ritz-Carlton Lobby Lounge. In the tastefully appointed lobby lounge, a harpist plays during high tea (about 1–5:15) and a jazz pianist performs Friday and Saturday nights. ⊠ *600 Stockton St., at California St., Nob Hill* ☎ *415/296–7465.*

★ **Seasons Bar.** Discreet staff members in dark suits serve cocktails and salty nibbles while a piano player entertains, usually Tuesday through Saturday evenings. ⊠ *Four Seasons Hotel San Francisco, 757 Market St., between 3rd and 4th Sts., SoMa* ☎ *415/633–3000.*

Specs'. This old-fashioned watering hole conveys a sense of the North Beach of days gone by and is a hidden hangout for artists, poets, and other heavy drinkers. ⊠ *12 Saroyan Pl., off Columbus Ave., North Beach* ☎ *415/421–4112.*

Top of the Mark. A famous magazine photograph immortalized this place, on the 19th floor of the Mark Hopkins Inter-Continental, as a hot spot for World War II servicemen on leave or about to ship out. ⊠ *Mark Hopkins Inter-Continental, 999 California St., at Mason St., Nob Hill* ☎ *415/616–6916.*

Tosca Café. This place has an Italian flavor, with opera, big-band, and Italian standards on the jukebox, plus an antique espresso machine that's nothing less than a work of art. ☒ *242 Columbus Ave., near Broadway, North Beach* ☏ *415/391–1244.*

★ **Vesuvio Café.** The second-floor balcony of this bohemian hangout, little altered since its 1960s heyday, is a fine vantage point for watching the colorful Broadway-Columbus intersection. ☒ *255 Columbus Ave., at Broadway, North Beach* ☏ *415/362–3370.*

Cabaret

asiaSF. The entertainment here, as well as gracious food service, is provided by "gender illusionists." These gorgeous men don daring dresses and strut in impossibly high heels on top of the bar, which serves as a catwalk. ☒ *201 9th St., at Howard St., SoMa* ☏ *415/255–2742.*

★ **Club Fugazi.** Its claim to fame is *Beach Blanket Babylon*, a wacky musical send-up of San Francisco moods and mores that has run since 1974 and become the longest-running show of its genre. Order tickets as far ahead as possible. ☒ *678 Green St., at Powell St., North Beach* ☏ *415/ 421–4222.*

Dance Clubs

DNA Lounge. The sounds change nightly at this venerable dance club, with psychedelic-trance (aka psytrance), deep house, and gothic music well represented. ☒ *375 11th St., between Harrison and Folsom Sts., SoMa* ☏ *415/626–1409.*

★ **El Rio.** Acts at this casual spot range from funk and soul DJs on Monday to Arab dance music on Thursday and a packed world-music dance party on Friday; bands play on Saturday. No matter what day you attend, expect to find a diverse crowd. ☒ *3158 Mission St., between Cesar Chavez and Valencia Sts., Mission* ☏ *415/282–3325.*

★ **111 Minna Gallery.** A gallery by day and bar and dance club by night, this unpretentious warehouse space is often full of artsy young San Franciscans who prefer it to some of the glitzier dance clubs. Call for details. ☒ *111 Minna St., between Mission and Howard and 2nd and New Montgomery Sts., SoMa* ☏ *415/974–1719.*

Roccapulco. With live music and salsa dancing on Friday and Saturday, this cavernous dance hall and restaurant knows how to bring 'em in. ☒ *3140 Mission St., between Precita and Cesar Chavez Sts., Mission* ☏ *415/648–6611.*

Gay & Lesbian Nightlife

MEN **Café Flore.** More of a daytime destination, this café attracts a mixed crowd, including poets, students, and fashionistas. ☒ *2298 Market St., at Noe St., Castro* ☏ *415/621–8579.*

The Cinch. The Wild West–theme neighborhood bar has pinball machines, pool tables, and a smoking patio, and it's not the least bit trendy. ☒ *1723 Polk St., between Washington and Clay Sts., Van Ness/Polk* ☏ *415/776–4162.*

Divas. In the rough-and-tumble Tenderloin, around the corner from the Polk Street bars, this is *the* place for transvestites, transsexuals, and their admirers. ☒ *1081 Post St., at Larkin St., Tenderloin* ☏ *415/928–6006.*

Eagle Tavern. Bikers are courted with endless drink specials and, increasingly, live rock music at this spot, one of the few SoMa bars remaining from the days before AIDS and gentrification. ⊠ *398 12th St., at Harrison St., SoMa* ☏ *415/626–0880.*

★ **Martuni's.** A mixed crowd enjoys cocktails in the refined environment of this elegant bar at the intersection of the Castro, the Mission, and Hayes Valley. Variations on the martini are a specialty. ⊠ *4 Valencia St., at Market St., Mission* ☏ *415/241–0205.*

Midnight Sun. One of the Castro's longest-standing and most popular bars has giant video screens playing episodes of *Will and Grace, The Simpsons, Queer Eye for the Straight Guy,* and other TV shows. ⊠ *4067 18th St., at Castro St., Castro* ☏ *415/861–4186.*

The Stud. Nearly four decades after its opening in 1966, this bar is still going strong seven days a week. Each night's music is different—from funk, soul, and hip-hop to 1980s tunes and disco favorites. ⊠ *399 9th St., at Harrison St., SoMa* ☏ *415/252–7883.*

WOMEN **Lexington Club.** According to its slogan, "every night is ladies' night" at
★ this all-girl club geared toward lesbians in their twenties and thirties. ⊠ *3464 19th St., at Lexington St., Mission* ☏ *415/863–2052.*

Jazz

★ **Bruno's.** The long bar and plush red booths are comfortable places to indulge in a swanky cocktail while listening to local jazz bands. ⊠ *2389 Mission St., at 20th St., Mission* ☏ *415/648–7701.*

Cafe du Nord. Strictly top-notch local talent plays some of the coolest jazz, blues, rock, and alternative sounds in town at this basement bar. ⊠ *2170 Market St., between Church and Sanchez Sts., Castro* ☏ *415/ 861–5016.*

★ **Jazz at Pearl's.** Dim lighting; a plush, 1930s supper-club style; and great straight-ahead jazz make this an ideal spot for a romantic evening. Cover is $5–$10. ⊠ *256 Columbus Ave., at Broadway, North Beach* ☏ *415/291–8255.*

Rock, Pop, Folk & Blues

Bimbo's 365 Club. The plush main room and adjacent lounge of this club, here since 1951, retain a retro vibe perfect for the "Cocktail Nation" programming that keeps the crowds entertained. ⊠ *1025 Columbus Ave., at Chestnut St., North Beach* ☏ *415/474–0365.*

★ **Boom Boom Room.** Top-notch blues acts attract old-timers and hipsters alike. ⊠ *1601 Fillmore St., at Geary Blvd., Japantown* ☏ *415/673–8000.*

Fillmore. San Francisco's most famous rock-music hall serves up a varied menu of national and local acts: rock, reggae, grunge, jazz, folk, acid house, and more. ⊠ *1805 Geary Blvd., at Fillmore St., Western Addition* ☏ *415/346–6000.*

★ **Great American Music Hall.** Top-drawer entertainment at this great, eclectic nightclub runs the gamut from the best in blues, folk, and jazz to alternative rock and American roots music. ⊠ *859 O'Farrell St., between Polk and Larkin Sts., Tenderloin* ☏ *415/885–0750.*

Last Day Saloon. Rising local bands as well as major acts perform blues, hip-hop, rock, funk, country, or jazz at this club. ⊠ *406 Clement St., between 5th and 6th Aves., Richmond* ☏ *415/387–6343.*

The Saloon. North Beach locals in the know favor this usually raucous blues and rock spot. ✉ *1232 Grant Ave., near Columbus Ave., North Beach* ☎ *415/989–7666.*

Slim's. National touring acts—mostly classic rock, blues, jazz, and world music—are the main event at this venue, one of SoMa's most popular nightclubs. ✉ *333 11th St., between Harrison and Folsom Sts., SoMa* ☎ *415/522–0333.*

SPORTS & THE OUTDOORS

Updated by
John A.
Vlahides

Temperatures rarely drop below 50°F here, so it's no surprise that visitors and residents alike are drawn outdoors. The captivating views are a major part of the appeal, as are the city's 3,500 acres of parks and open spaces. On the best days, even longtime city dwellers marvel at the sun sparkling on the bay and the cool, crisp air, which couldn't seem much cleaner.

Beaches

Nestled in a quiet cove between the lush hills adjoining Fort Mason, Ghirardelli Square, and Fisherman's Wharf, **Aquatic Park** (⊕ www.nps.gov/safr) has a tiny, ¼-mi-long sandy beach with gentle water. Facilities include restrooms and showers. **Baker Beach** (✉ Gibson Rd. off Bowley St., southwest corner of Presidio), with gorgeous views of the Golden Gate Bridge and the Marin Headlands, is a local favorite. The pounding surf and strong currents make swimming a dangerous prospect. **China Beach,** one of the city's safest swimming beaches, is a 600-foot strip of sand, south of the Presidio and Baker Beach. It has gentle waters as well as changing rooms, bathrooms, showers, grills, drinking water, and picnic tables. Although **Ocean Beach** isn't the city's cleanest shore, this wide, sandy expanse stretches for more than 3 mi along the Great Highway, south of the Cliff House, making it ideal for long walks and runs. Because of extremely dangerous currents, swimming isn't recommended.

Baseball

★ Home field for the National League's **San Francisco Giants** (✉ SBC Park, 24 Willie Mays Plaza, between 2nd and 3rd Sts., China Basin ☎ 415/972–2000 or 800/734–4268 ⊕ sanfrancisco.giants.mlb.com) is downtown's **SBC Park. Tickets.com** (☎ 510/762–2255 Baseball Line, 415/478–2277, 800/225–2277 ⊕ www.tickets.com) sells game tickets. Its Baseball Line charges a per-ticket fee of up to $5, plus a per-call processing fee of $3.50.

Football

The **San Francisco 49ers** (✉ 3Com Park, Jamestown Ave. and Harney Way, Bayview Heights ☎ 415/656–4900 ⊕ www.sf49ers.com) play at **3Com Park,** near the San Mateo County border. Single-game tickets, available via **Ticketmaster** (☎ 415/421–8497 ⊕ www.ticketmaster.com), almost always sell out far in advance.

SHOPPING

Shopping Neighborhoods

Updated by
Sharron Wood

The Castro/Noe Valley. Often called the gay capital of the world, it's also a major shopping destination for nongay travelers, filled with men's clothing boutiques, home-accessories stores, and various specialty shops.

Chinatown. The intersection of Grant Avenue and Bush Street marks the gateway to 24 blocks of shops, restaurants, and markets. Dominating the exotic cityscape are the sights and smells of food. Racks of Chinese silks, toy trinkets, colorful pottery, baskets, and carved figurines are displayed chockablock on the sidewalks.

Fisherman's Wharf. Sightseers crowds this area and with good reason: Pier 39, the Anchorage, Ghirardelli Square, and the Cannery. Each has shops and restaurants, as well as outdoor entertainment—musicians, mimes, and magicians. Best of all are the wharf's view of the bay and its proximity to cable-car lines.

The Haight. Haight Street is a perennial attraction for visitors, if only to see the sign at Haight and Ashbury streets. These days chain stores such as Gap and Ben & Jerry's have taken over large storefronts near the famous intersection, but it's still possible to find high-quality vintage clothing, funky shoes, and folk art from around the world in this always-busy neighborhood.

Jackson Square. A dozen or so of San Francisco's finest retail antiques dealers, many of which occupy Victorian-era buildings, are here on the northeastern edge of the Financial District.

North Beach. Although it's sometimes compared to New York City's Greenwich Village, North Beach is only a fraction of the size, clustered tightly around Washington Square and Columbus Avenue. Most of its businesses are small eateries, cafés, and shops selling clothing, antiques, and vintage wares.

Pacific Heights. Pacific Heights residents seeking fine items for their luxurious homes head straight for Fillmore Street between Post Street and Pacific Avenue, and Sacramento Street between Lyon and Maple streets, where private residences alternate with fine clothing and gift shops and housewares stores.

SoMa. High San Francisco rents mean there aren't many discount outlets in the city, but a few do exist in the semi-industrial zone south of Market Street (SoMa). At the other end of the spectrum is the gift shop of the San Francisco Museum of Modern Art, which sells books, handmade ceramics, art-related games, and other great gift items.

Union Square. Serious shoppers head straight to San Francisco's main shopping area and the site of most department stores, as well as the Virgin Megastore, the Disney Store, Borders Books and Music, and Frette. Nearby are the pricey international boutiques of Alfred Dunhill, Cartier, Emporio Armani, Gucci, Hermès of Paris, Louis Vuitton, and Versace.

Malls & Department Stores

Crocker Galleria. Forty or so mostly upscale shops and restaurants a few blocks east of Union Square are housed in this complex beneath a glass dome. ⊠ *50 Post St., at Kearny St., Financial District* ☎ *415/ 393–1505.*

Embarcadero Center. Shops, restaurants, offices, and a popular art movie theater—plus the Hyatt Regency hotel—make up the Embarcadero Center, downtown at the end of Market Street. Most of the stores are branches of upscale national chains, such as Ann Taylor, Banana Republic, and Pottery Barn. It's one of the few major shopping centers with an underground parking garage. ⊠ *Clay and Sacramento Sts. between Battery and Drumm Sts.* ☎ *415/772–0734.*

Japan Center. The three-block complex includes an 800-car public garage and three shop-filled buildings. Especially worthwhile are the Kintetsu and Kinokuniya buildings, where shops and showrooms sell bonsai trees, antique kimonos, *tansu* (Japanese chests), and colorful glazed dinnerware and teapots. ⊠ *Bordered by Laguna, Fillmore, and Post Sts. and Geary Blvd.* ☎ *No phone.*

★ **Gump's.** Stocked with large decorative vases, ornate Asian-inspired furniture, and extravagant jewelry, this airy store exudes a museumlike aura. Luxurious bed linens are tucked away upstairs. ⊠ *135 Post St., between Grant Ave. and Kearny St., Union Sq.* ☎ *415/982–1616.*

Macy's. Downtown has two behemoth branches of this retailer. One— with entrances on Geary, Stockton, and O'Farrell streets—houses the women's, children's, furniture, and housewares departments. The men's department occupies its own building, across Stockton Street. ⊠ *170 O'Farrell St., at Stockton St., Union Sq.* ☎ *415/397–3333* ⊠ *Men's branch:* ⊠ *50 O'Farrell St. (entrance on Stockton St.), Union Sq.* ☎ *415/ 397–3333.*

Neiman Marcus. The surroundings, which include a Philip Johnson–designed checkerboard facade, gilded atrium, and stained-glass skylight, are as high class as the goods showcased in them. The mix includes designer men's and women's clothing and accessories as well as posh household wares. ⊠ *150 Stockton St., at Geary Blvd., Union Sq.* ☎ *415/362–3900.*

★ **Nordstrom.** This service-oriented store specializes in designer fashions, accessories, cosmetics, and, most notably, shoes. The space, with spiral escalators circling a four-story atrium, is stunning. ⊠ *San Francisco Shopping Centre, 865 Market St., between 4th and 5th Sts., Union Sq.* ☎ *415/243–8500.*

San Francisco Shopping Centre. The center, across from the cable-car turnaround at Powell and Market streets, has spiral escalators that wind up through the sunlit atrium. Inside are 65 retailers, including Nordstrom and Godiva. ⊠ *865 Market St., between 4th and 5th Sts.* ☎ *415/ 495–5656.*

Saks Fifth Avenue. A central escalator ascends past a series of designer boutiques, which give Saks the feel of an exclusive multilevel mall. ⊠ *384 Post St., at Powell St., Union Sq.* ☎ *415/986–4300.*

SIDE TRIPS FROM SAN FRANCISCO

Updated by
Lisa M.
Hamilton &
Denise M. Leto

One of San Francisco's best assets is its surroundings. To the north is Marin County, where the lively waterfront town of Sausalito has bougainvillea-covered hillsides, an expansive yacht harbor, and an artists' colony. To the east is Berkeley, a colorful university town. Explore a bit beyond the city limits and you're bound to discover what makes the Bay Area such a coveted place to live.

Sausalito

Like much of San Francisco, Sausalito had a raffish reputation before it went upscale. The town served as a port for whaling ships during the 19th century. By the mid-1800s wealthy San Franciscans were making Sausalito their getaway across the bay. They built lavish Victorian summer homes in the hills, many of which still stand. In 1875 the railroad from the north connected with ferryboats to San Francisco, bringing the merchant and working classes with it. This influx of hardworking, fun-loving folk polarized the town into "wharf rats" and "hill snobs," and the waterfront area grew thick with saloons, gambling dens, and bordellos.

Sausalito developed its bohemian flair in the 1950s and '60s, when a group of artists established a houseboat community here. Today more than 450 houseboats are docked in Sausalito, which has since also become a major yachting center. The ferry is the best way to get to Sausalito from San Francisco; you get more romance (and less traffic) and disembark in the heart of downtown.

The U.S. Army Corps of Engineers uses the **Bay Model** to reproduce the rise and fall of tides, the flow of currents, and the other physical forces at work on the bay. ⊠ *2100 Bridgeway, at Marinship Way* 🕿 *415/332–3870* ⊕ *www.spn.usace.army.mil/bmvc* ⊠ *Free* ☉ *late May–early Sept., Tues.–Fri. 9–4, weekends 10–5; rest of yr, Tues.–Sat. 9–4.*

ⓒ The **Bay Area Discovery Museum** fills five former military buildings with entertaining and enlightening hands-on exhibits related to science and the arts. Kids and their families can fish from a boat at the indoor wharf, explore the skeleton of a house, and make multitrack recordings. From San Francisco take the Alexander Avenue exit from U.S. 101 and follow signs to East Fort Baker. ⊠ *557 McReynolds Rd., at East Fort Baker* 🕿 *415/339–3900* ⊕ *www.badm.org* ⊠ *$7* ☉ *Tues.–Fri. 9–4, weekends 10–5.*

Where to Stay & Eat

$-$$$ ✕ **Poggio.** One of the few restaurants in Sausalito to attract both food-savvy locals and tourists, Poggio serves modern Tuscan cuisine in a handsome, open-walled space that spills onto the street in the style of restaurants on the Italian Riviera. Expect dishes such as grilled lamb chops with roasted eggplant, braised artichokes with polenta, and feather-light gnocchi. ⊠ *777 Bridgeway* 🕿 *415/332–7771* ⌔ *Reservations essential* ⊟ *AE, D, MC, V.*

★ **$-$$** ✕ **Fish.** For fresh seafood, you can't beat this gleaming dockside fish house, 1 mi north of downtown and owned by one of the Bay Area's top chefs (formerly of Masa's in San Francisco). Order at the counter, and then grab a seat by the floor-to-ceiling windows or at a picnic table on the pier, overlooking the yachts and fishing boats. Most of the fish is caught locally and hauled in from boats right on the dock. ⊠ *350 Harbor Dr.* 🕿 *415/331–3474* ⌔ *Reservations not accepted* ⊟ *No credit cards* ☉ *Closed Mon. and Tues.*

$$$$ ⌂ **Casa Madrona.** What began as a small inn with a handful of historic accommodations in a 19th-century landmark house has expanded over the decades to incorporate a variety of lodgings and a top-notch spa, all tiered down the hill in the center of town. The design in the original rooms and suites ranges from the cutesiness of what's called the Artist's Loft to elegant Mediterranean and Asia-inspired motifs. ⊠ *801 Bridgeway, 94965* ☎ *415/332–0502 or 800/567–9524* 🖷 *415/332–2537* ⊕ *www.casamadrona.com* ⤳ *63 rooms, 14 suites* ♨ *Restaurant, in-room data ports, minibars, cable TV, in-room VCRs, hot tub, spa, concierge, dry cleaning, laundry service, meeting rooms; no a/c, no smoking* ⊟ *AE, D, DC, MC, V* ⏣ *CP.*

$–$$ ⌂ **Hotel Sausalito.** Soft yellow, green, and orange tones create a warm Mediterranean feel at this well-run inn with handmade furniture and tasteful original art and reproductions. The rooms, some of which have harbor or park views, range from small quarters good for budget-minded travelers to commodious suites. ⊠ *16 El Portal, 94965* ☎ *415/332–0700 or 888/442–0700* 🖷 *415/332–8788* ⊕ *www.hotelsausalito.com* ⤳ *14 rooms, 2 suites* ♨ *In-room data ports, cable TV, concierge, no-smoking rooms; no a/c* ⊟ *AE, DC, MC, V* ⏣ *CP.*

Berkeley

Although Berkeley has grown alongside the University of California, which dominates its history and contemporary life, the university and the town are not synonymous. The city of 100,000 facing San Francisco across the bay has other interesting attributes. It's culturally diverse and politically adventurous, a breeding ground for social trends, a bastion of the counterculture, and an important center for Bay Area writers, artists, and musicians.

The **Berkeley Visitor Information Center** (⊠ University Hall, Room 101, 2200 University Ave., at Oxford St. ☎ 510/642–5215) is the starting point for the free, student-guided tours of the campus, which last 1½ hours and start at 10 on weekdays.

The **University of California Berkeley Art Museum** has an interesting collection of works that spans five centuries, with an emphasis on contemporary art. Changing exhibits line the spiral ramps and balcony galleries. Don't miss the museum's series of vibrant paintings by abstract expressionist Hans Hofmann. ⊠ *2626 Bancroft Way* ☎ *510/642–0808, 510/642–1124 film-program information* ⊕ *www.bampfa.berkeley.edu* ⊠ *$8* ⊙ *Wed. and Fri.–Sun. 11–5, Thurs. 11–7.*

About 13,500 species of plants from all over the world flourish in the 34-acre **University of California Botanical Garden.** Free garden tours are given Thursday, Saturday, and Sunday at 1:30. Benches and shady picnic tables make this a relaxing alternative to the busy main campus. ⊠ *200 Centennial Dr.* ☎ *510/643–2755* ⊕ *botanicalgarden.berkeley.edu* ⊠ *$3, free Thurs.* ⊙ *late May–early Sept., Mon. and Tues. 9–5, Wed.–Sun. 9–8; rest of yr, daily 9–5. Closed 1st Tues. of month.*

⟳ At the fortresslike **Lawrence Hall of Science,** a dazzling hands-on science center, kids can look at insects under microscopes, solve crimes using chemical forensics, and explore the physics of baseball. ⊠ *Centennial Dr. near Grizzly Peak Blvd.* ☎ *510/642–5132* ⊕ *www.lawrencehallofscience. org* ⌑ *$8.50* ⊙ *Daily 10–5.*

Where to Stay & Eat

$$–$$$$ ╳ **Chez Panisse Café & Restaurant.** The downstairs portion of Alice Wa-
Fodor'sChoice ters's legendary eatery is noted for its formality and personal service.
★ Here, the daily-changing multicourse dinners are prix fixe and pricey. Upstairs, in the informal café, the crowd is livelier, the prices are lower, and the ever-changing menu is à la carte. The food is simpler, too: try the penne with new potatoes, arugula, and sheep's-milk cheese or the fresh figs with Parmigiano-Reggiano cheese and arugula. ⊠ *1517 Shattuck Ave., north of University Ave.* ☎ *510/548–5525 restaurant, 510/ 548–5049 café* ⌑ *Reservations essential* ▤*AE, D, DC, MC, V* ⊙ *Closed Sun. No lunch in restaurant.*

$$–$$$ ╳ **Café Rouge.** You can recover from 4th Street shopping in this spacious two-story bistro, complete with zinc bar, skylights, and festive lanterns. The short, seasonal menu ranges from the sophisticated rack of lamb and juniper-berry-cured pork chops to homey spit-roasted chicken or pork loin. ⊠ *1782 4th St.* ☎ *510/525–1440* ▤ *MC, V* ⊙ *No dinner Mon.*

$$ ╳ **Rivoli.** Italian-inspired dishes using fresh, mostly organic California ingredients star on a menu that changes every three weeks. Typical meals include fresh line-caught fish, pastas, and inventive offerings such as its trademark portobello fritters with aioli. ⊠ *1539 Solano Ave.* ☎ *510/526–2542* ⌑ *Reservations essential* ▤ *AE, D, DC, MC, V* ⊙ *No lunch.*

¢–$ ╳ **Bette's Oceanview Diner.** Buttermilk pancakes are just one of the specialties at this 1930s-inspired diner, complete with checkered floors and burgundy booths. The wait for a seat can be long. ⊠ *1807 4th St.* ☎ *510/ 644–3230* ⌑ *Reservations not accepted* ▤ *MC, V* ⊙ *No dinner.*

$$$$ ▥ **Claremont Resort and Spa.** This hotel beckons like a gleaming white
Fodor'sChoice castle in the hills. Traveling executives come for the business amenities,
★ including rooms outfitted with computer terminals, T-1 Internet connections, guest e-mail addresses, and oversize desks. The Claremont also shines for leisure travelers, drawing honeymooners and families alike with its luxurious suites, therapeutic massages, and personalized yoga workouts at the on-site spa. ⊠ *41 Tunnel Rd., at Ashby and Domingo Aves., 94705* ☎ *510/843–3000 or 800/323–7500* ▤ *510/843–6629* ⊕ *www.claremontresort.com* ⌫ *262 rooms, 17 suites* ⌕ *2 restaurants, café, in-room data ports, in-room safes, some in-room hot tubs, some minibars, some refrigerators, cable TV, in-room VCRs, 10 tennis courts, 2 pools, health club, hair salon, hot tub, sauna, spa, steam room, 2 bars, children's programs (ages 6 wks–10 yrs), dry cleaning, laundry service, concierge, Internet, business services, meeting rooms, parking (fee), no-smoking floor* ▤ *AE, D, DC, MC, V.*

$$ ▥ **Hotel Durant.** Long the mainstay of parents visiting their children at U.C. Berkeley, the hotel is a good option for those who want to be a short walk from campus and from the restaurants and shops of Telegraph Avenue. Rooms, accented with dark wood set against deep jewel tones, are small without feeling cramped. ⊠ *2600 Durant Ave., 94704* ☎ *510/845–8981* ▤ *510/486–8336* ⊕ *www.hoteldurant.com* ⌫ *135*

rooms, 5 suites ☼ Restaurant, room service, in-room data ports, some refrigerators, cable TV with movies, sports bar, dry cleaning, laundry service, concierge, business services, meeting room, parking (fee), no-smoking floors; no a/c ⊟ AE, D, DC, MC, V.

$ 🔲 **French Hotel.** The only hotel in north Berkeley, this three-level brick structure has a certain *pensione* feel. Rooms have pastel or brick walls and modern touches such as white wire baskets in lieu of dressers. Balconies make the rooms seem larger than their modest dimensions. ⊠ 1538 Shattuck Ave., 94709 ☎ 510/548–9930 🖷 510/548–9930 🖙 18 rooms ☼ Café, room service, cable TV with movies, dry cleaning, laundry service, concierge, business services, free parking; no a/c ⊟ AE, D, DC, MC, V.

SAN FRANCISCO A TO Z

To research prices, get advice from other travelers, and book travel arrangements, visit ⊕ www.fodors.com

AIR TRAVEL

Heavy fog is infamous for causing chronic delays into and out of San Francisco. If you're heading to the East Bay, make every effort to fly into Oakland International Airport, which is easy to navigate and accessible by public transit. Of the major carriers, Alaska, America West, American, Continental, Delta, Southwest, United, and US Airways fly into both Oakland and San Francisco. JetBlue Airways services Oakland. Northwest flies into San Francisco only. Midwest Express and Frontier Airlines, two smaller carriers, both fly into San Francisco. *See* Air Travel *in* Smart Travel Tips A to Z for airline phone numbers.

AIRPORTS & TRANSFERS

The major gateway to San Francisco is San Francisco International Airport (SFO), off U.S. 101 15 mi south of the city. Oakland International Airport (OAK) is across the bay, not much farther away from downtown San Francisco (via I–880 and I–80), but rush-hour traffic on the Bay Bridge may lengthen travel times considerably.

🚺 San Francisco International Airport (SFO) ☎ 650/761-0800 ⊕ www.flysfo.com. Oakland International Airport (OAK) ☎ 510/577-4000 ⊕ www.flyoakland.com.

TRANSFERS **From San Francisco International Airport:** A taxi ride to downtown costs $35–$40. Airport shuttles are inexpensive and generally efficient. The SFO Airporter ($13) picks up passengers at baggage claim (lower level) and serves selected downtown hotels. Lorrie's Airport Shuttle and SuperShuttle both stop at the upper-level traffic islands and take you anywhere within the city limits of San Francisco. They charge $14–$17, depending on your destination. Shuttles to the East Bay, such as Bay-Porter Express, also depart from the upper-level traffic islands; expect to pay around $35. Another inexpensive way to get to San Francisco is via SamTrans Bus 292 (55 minutes, $1.25–$2.50) and KX (35 minutes, $3.50; only one small carry-on bag permitted). Board the SamTrans buses at the north end of the lower level. You can take BART directly to downtown San Francisco; the trip takes about 30 minutes and costs less than

$5. Trains leave from the international terminal every 15 minutes on weekdays and every 20 minutes on weekends.

From Oakland International Airport: A taxi to downtown San Francisco costs $35–$40. BayPorter Express and other shuttles serve major hotels and provide door-to-door service to the East Bay and San Francisco. Marin Door to Door serves Marin County for a flat $50 fee. The best way to get to San Francisco via public transit is to take the AIR BART bus ($2) to the Coliseum/Oakland International Airport BART station (BART fares vary depending on where you're going; the ride to downtown San Francisco costs $3.15).

🚩 **American Airporter** ☎ 415/202-0733 ⊕ americanairporter.com. **BayPorter Express** ☎ 415/467-1800 ⊕ www.bayporter.com. **East Bay Express Airporter** ☎ 510/547-0404. **Lorrie's Airport Shuttle** ☎ 415/334-9000 ⊕ www.sfovan.com. **Marin Door to Door** ☎ 415/457-2717 ⊕ www.marindoortodoor.com. **SamTrans** ☎ 800/660-4287 ⊕ www.samtrans.com. **SFO Airporter** ☎ 877/877-8819 or 650/624-0500 ⊕ www.sfoairporter.com. **South & East Bay Airport Shuttle** ☎ 408/559-9477. **SuperShuttle** ☎ 415/558-8500 or 800/258-3826 ⊕ www.supershuttle.com. **VIP Airport Shuttle** ☎ 408/885-1800 or 800/235-8847 ⊕ www.yourairportride.com.

BOAT & FERRY TRAVEL

Tickets for Blue & Gold Fleet ferries to Sausalito are sold at Pier 41 (next to Fisherman's Wharf). Golden Gate Ferry runs daily to and from Sausalito, leaving from Pier 1, behind the San Francisco Ferry Building, which is at the foot of Market Street on the Embarcadero.

🚩 **Blue & Gold Fleet** ☎ 415/705-5555 ⊕ www.blueandgoldfleet.com. **Golden Gate Ferry** ☎ 415/923-2000 ⊕ www.goldengateferry.org.

BUS TRAVEL TO & FROM SAN FRANCISCO

Greyhound, the only long-distance bus company serving San Francisco, operates buses to and from most major cities in the country.

🚩 **Greyhound** ✉ 425 Mission St., SoMa ☎ 800/231-2222 or 415/495-1569 ⊕ www.greyhound.com.

BUS & TRAIN TRAVEL WITHIN SAN FRANCISCO

BART: Bay Area Rapid Transit (BART) trains, which run until midnight, connect San Francisco with Oakland, Berkeley, Pittsburgh/Bay Point, Richmond, Fremont, and Dublin/Pleasanton. Trains also travel south from San Francisco as far as Milbrae. The BART-SFO Extension Project connects downtown San Francisco to San Francisco International Airport; a ride is $4.95. Intra-city San Francisco fares are $1.25; inter-city fares are $2.15–$7.45.

Bus: Outside the city, AC Transit serves the East Bay, and Golden Gate Transit serves Marin County.

Caltrain: Caltrain connects San Francisco to Palo Alto, San Jose, Santa Clara, and many smaller cities en route. In San Francisco, trains leave from the main depot, at 4th and King streets, and a rail-side stop at 22nd and Pennsylvania streets. One-way fares are $1.75–$8, depending on the number of zones through which you travel. Trips last 1 to 1½ hours.

Muni: The San Francisco Municipal Railway, or Muni, operates light-rail vehicles, the historic streetcar line along Fisherman's Wharf and Market Street, trolley buses, and the world-famous cable cars. On buses and streetcars, the fare is $1.25. Exact change is required, and dollar bills are accepted in the fare boxes. For all Muni vehicles other than cable cars, 90-minute transfers are issued free upon request at the time the fare is paid. Transfers are valid for two additional transfers in any direction. Cable cars cost $3 and include no transfers.

AC Transit 510/839-2882 www.actransit.org. **Bay Area Rapid Transit** (BART) 650/992-2278 www.bart.gov. **Caltrain** 800/660-4287 www.caltrain.com. **Golden Gate Transit** 415/923-2000 www.goldengate.org. **San Francisco Caltrain Station** 700 4th St., at King St. 800/660-4287.

San Francisco Municipal Railway System (Muni) 415/673-6864 www.sfmuni.com.

CAR RENTAL

All of the national car-rental companies have offices at the San Francisco and Oakland airports. *See* Car Rental *in* Smart Travel Tips A to Z for national rental agency phone numbers.

CAR TRAVEL

Driving in San Francisco can be a challenge because of the hills, one-way streets, and traffic. Although rush "hour" is 6–10 AM and 3–7 PM, you can hit gridlock on any day at any time, especially over the Bay Bridge and leaving and/or entering the city from the south. Sunday-afternoon traffic can be heavy as well, especially over the bridges.

PARKING   Remember to curb your wheels when parking on hills—turn wheels away from the curb when facing uphill, toward the curb when facing downhill. On certain streets, parking is forbidden during rush hours. Look for the warning signs; illegally parked cars are towed immediately. Downtown parking lots are often full, and most are expensive. Large hotels often have parking available, but it doesn't come cheap; many charge as much as $40 a day for the privilege.

LODGING

The San Francisco Convention and Visitors Bureau publishes a free lodging guide with a map and listings of San Francisco and Bay Area hotels. You can also reserve a room, by phone or via the Internet, at more than 60 bureau-recommended hotels. San Francisco Reservations, in business since 1986, can arrange reservations at more than 200 Bay Area hotels, often at special discounted rates. Hotellocators.com also offers online and phone-in reservations at special rates.

Hotellocators.com 9 Sumner St., San Francisco 94103 800/576-0003 858/581-1730 www.hotellocators.com. **San Francisco Convention and Visitors Bureau** 415/391-2000 general information, 415/283-0177, 888/782-9673 lodging service www.sfvisitor.org. **San Francisco Reservations** 800/677-1500 www.hotelres.com.

TAXIS

Taxi service is notoriously bad in San Francisco, and hailing a cab can be frustratingly difficult in some parts of the city, especially on weekends. In a pinch, hotel taxi stands are an option, as is calling for a pickup. But be forewarned: taxi companies frequently don't answer the phone in peak periods. Taxis in San Francisco charge $2.85 for the first ⅓ mi,

45¢ for each additional ⅓ mi, and 45¢ per minute in stalled traffic. There is no charge for additional passengers; there is no surcharge for luggage. **City Wide Cab** ☎ 415/920-0700. **DeSoto Cab** ☎ 415/970-1300. **Luxor Cab** ☎ 415/282-4141. **Veteran's Taxicab** ☎ 415/552-1300. **Yellow Cab** ☎ 415/626-2345.

SIGHTSEEING TOURS

BUS & VAN TOURS In addition to bus and van tours of the city, most tour companies run excursions to various Bay Area and Northern California destinations, such as Marin County. City tours generally last 3½ hours and cost $37–$40. Great Pacific Tours conducts city tours in passenger vans (starting at $40). San Francisco Sightseeing (Gray Line), a much larger, corporately owned outfit, operates 42-passenger motor coaches and motorized cable cars ($16–$52). For about $15 more, either tour operator can supplement a city tour with a bay cruise.

Great Pacific Tour ☎ 415/626-4499 ⊕ www.greatpacifictour.com. **San Francisco Sightseeing** ☎ 415/558-9400 ⊕ www.graylinesanfrancisco.com.

WALKING TOURS The best way to see San Francisco is to hit the streets. Tours of various San Francisco neighborhoods generally cost $15–$40. Some tours explore culinary themes, such as Chinese food or coffeehouses: lunch and snacks are often included. Others focus on architecture or history.

Architecture Tours **"Victorian Home Walk"** ☎ 415/252-9485 ⊕ www.victorianwalk.com. **Culinary Tours** **"Chinatown with the Wok Wiz"** ☎ 415/981-8989 ⊕ www.wokwiz.com. **"Javawalk"** ☎ 415/673-9255 ⊕ www.javawalk.com. **General Interest Tours** **City Guides** ☎ 415/557-4266 ⊕ www.sfcityguides.org. **San Francisco Convention and Visitors Bureau** ☎ 415/391-2000 ⊕ www.sfcvb.org. **San Francisco Visitor Information Center** ⊠ Hallidie Plaza, lower level, Powell and Market Sts., Union Sq. ☎ 415/391-2000, 415/392-0328 TDD ⊕ www.sfvisitor.org. **Historic Tours** **Chinese Culture Center** ☎ 415/986-1822 ⊕ www.c-c-c.org. **Trevor Hailey** ☎ 415/550-8110 ⊕ www.webcastro.com/castrotour.

TRAIN TRAVEL TO & FROM SAN FRANCISCO

Amtrak trains travel to the Bay Area from some cities in California and the United States. The *Coast Starlight* travels north from Los Angeles to Seattle, passing the Bay Area along the way. Amtrak also has several inland routes between San Jose, Oakland, and Sacramento. The *California Zephyr* route travels from Chicago to the Bay Area. San Francisco doesn't have an Amtrak station, but there is one in Emeryville, just over the Bay Bridge, as well as in Oakland. A free shuttle operates between these two stations and the Ferry Building, the CalTrain station, and several other points in downtown San Francisco.

Amtrak ☎ 800/872-7245 ⊕ www.amtrak.com.

VISITOR INFORMATION

Berkeley Convention and Visitors Bureau ⊠ 2015 Center St., 1st fl., Berkeley 94704 ☎ 800/847-4823 or 510/549-7040 ⊕ www.berkeleycvb.com. **San Francisco Convention and Visitors Bureau** ⌂ 201 3rd St., Suite 900, 94103 ☎ 415/391-2000, 415/392-0328 TDD ⊕ www.sfvisitor.org. **San Francisco Visitor Information Center** ⊠ Hallidie Plaza, lower level, Powell and Market Sts., Union Sq. ☎ 415/391-2000, 415/392-0328 TDD ⊕ www.sfvisitor.org.

THE WINE COUNTRY

13

Updated by
Sharron Wood

IN 1862, AFTER AN EXTENSIVE TOUR of the wine-producing areas of Europe, Count Agoston Haraszthy de Mokcsa reported a promising prognosis about his adopted California: "Of all the countries through which I passed, not one possessed the same advantages that are to be found in California. . . . California can produce as noble and generous a wine as any in Europe; more in quantity to the acre, and without repeated failures through frosts, summer rains, hailstorms, or other causes."

The "dormant resources" that the father of California's viticulture saw in the balmy days and cool nights of the temperate Napa and Sonoma valleys have come to fruition today. The wines produced here are praised and savored by connoisseurs throughout the world. The area also continues to be a proving ground for the latest techniques of grape growing and wine making.

Ever more competitive, vintners constantly hone their skills, aided by the scientific expertise of graduates of the nearby University of California at Davis and by the practical knowledge of the grape growers. They experiment with high-density vineyard planting, canopy management (to control the amount of sunlight that reaches the grapes), and filtration of the wine.

For many, wine making is a second career. Any would-be wine maker can rent the cumbersome, costly machinery needed to stem and press the grapes. Many say making wine is a good way to turn a large fortune into a small one, but that hasn't deterred the doctors, former college professors, publishing tycoons, art dealers, and others who come here to try their hand at it.

In 1975 Napa Valley had no more than 20 wineries; today there are more than 240. In Sonoma County, where the web of vineyards is looser, there are well over 150 wineries, and development is now claiming the cool Carneros region, at the head of the San Francisco Bay, deemed ideal for growing the chardonnay grape. Nowadays many individual grape growers produce their own wines instead of selling their grapes to larger wineries. As a result, smaller "boutique" wineries harvest excellent, reasonably priced wines that have caught the attention of connoisseurs and critics, while the larger wineries consolidate land and expand their varietals.

This state-of-the-art viticulture has also given rise to a gastronomic renaissance. Inspired by the creative spirit that produces the region's great wines, esteemed chefs are opening restaurants in record numbers, making culinary history in the process.

In addition to great food and wine, you'll find a wealth of California history in the Wine Country. The town of Sonoma is filled with remnants of Mexican California and the solid, ivy-covered, brick wineries built by Haraszthy and his followers. Calistoga is a virtual museum of Steamboat Gothic architecture, replete with the fretwork and clapboard beloved of gold-rush prospectors and late-19th-century spa goers. A later architectural fantasy, the beautiful art nouveau mansion of the Beringer brothers, is in St. Helena, and the postmodern extravaganza of Clos Pegase is in Calistoga.

The area's natural beauty draws a continuous flow of tourists—from the late winter, when the vineyards bloom yellow with wild mustard, to the fall, when the grapes are ripe. Haraszthy was right: this is a chosen place.

Exploring the Wine Country

The Wine Country is composed of two main areas—the Napa Valley and the Sonoma Valley—but also includes the Carneros district, which straddles southern Sonoma and Napa counties. Five major paths cut through both valleys: U.S. 101 and Routes 12 and 121 through Sonoma County, and Route 29 north from Napa. The 25-mi Silverado Trail, which runs parallel to Route 29 north from Napa to Calistoga, is a more scenic, less crowded route with a number of distinguished wineries.

One of the most important viticultural areas in the Wine Country spreads across southern Sonoma and Napa counties. The Carneros region has a long, cool growing season tempered by maritime breezes and lingering fogs off the San Pablo Bay—optimum slow-growing conditions for pinot noir and chardonnay grapes. So exotic-looking are the misty Carneros marshlands that Francis Ford Coppola chose them as the location for scenes of the Mekong Delta in his 1979 movie *Apocalypse Now*. When the sun is shining, however, Carneros looks like a sprawling and scenic expanse of quintessential Wine Country, where wildflower meadows and vineyards stretch toward the horizon.

About the Restaurants

Many star chefs from urban areas throughout the United States have migrated to the Wine Country, drawn by the area's renowned produce and world-class wines—the products of fertile soil and near-perpetual sun during the growing season. As a result of this marriage of imported talent and indigenous bounty, food now rivals wine as the principal attraction of the region. Although excellent cuisine is available throughout the region, the little town of Yountville has become something of an epicurean crossroads. If you don't succeed at getting a much-coveted reservation at Thomas Keller's French Laundry, often described as one of the best restaurants in the country, then the more casual Bistro Jeanty and Bouchon, as well as a host of other restaurants in and around Yountville, are excellent choices.

Such high quality often means high prices, but you can also find appealing, inexpensive eateries. High-end delis serve superb picnic fare, and brunch is a cost-effective strategy at pricey restaurants.

With few exceptions (which are noted in individual restaurant listings), dress is informal. Where reservations are indicated as essential, you may need to make them a week or more ahead. In summer and early fall you may need to book several months ahead.

About the Hotels

Ranging from quaint to utterly luxurious, the area's many inns and hotels are usually exquisitely appointed. Most of the bed-and-breakfasts have historic Victorian and Spanish architecture and include a full

Numbers in the text correspond to numbers in the margin and on the Napa Valley and Sonoma Valley maps.

13

If you have 2 days

Start at the circa-1857 **Buena Vista Carneros Winery** 45 ➤ just outside Sonoma. From there, take Route 12 north to the Trinity Road/Oakville Grade. Drive east over the Mayacamas Mountains, then take Route 29 north into historic 🖾 **St. Helena** for lunch. After lunch in St. Helena, take the 30-minute tour of **Beringer Vineyards** 27. The next day continue north on Route 29 to **Calistoga** for an early-morning balloon ride, an afternoon trip to the mud baths, and a visit to **Clos Pegase** 34 before heading back to St. Helena for dinner at Greystone—the highly acclaimed restaurant of the **Culinary Institute of America** 28.

If you have 4 days

Concentrate on the Napa Valley north of Yountville. Make your first stop in **Oakville** ➤, where the circa-1880s **Oakville Grocery** 13 is the most popular place for picnic supplies and an espresso. Enjoy the picnic grounds at **Robert Mondavi** 15 before touring the winery and tasting the wine. If time permits, spend the night in the town of 🖾 **Rutherford** and visit either **Rutherford Hill Winery** 23 or the **Niebaum-Coppola Estate** 17, or continue north to 🖾 **St. Helena.** Take a look at the nearby Silverado Museum and visit the shopping complex surrounding the **Freemark Abbey Winery** 29. On your third day drive to 🖾 **Calistoga** for a balloon ride before heading north to **Old Faithful Geyser of California** 36; then continue on to **Robert Louis Stevenson State Park** 38, which encompasses the summit of Mount St. Helena. On the fourth day take Route 29 just north of Calistoga proper, head west on Petrified Forest Road, and then go south on Calistoga Road, which runs into Route 12. Follow Route 12 southeast to rustic **Glen Ellen,** then visit **Jack London State Historic Park** 47, and loop back north on Bennett Valley Road to beautiful **Matanzas Creek Winery** 53 in Santa Rosa.

If you have 7 days

Begin in the town of **Sonoma** ➤, whose colorful plaza and mission evoke early California's Spanish past. Afterward, head north to 🖾 **Glen Ellen** and the Valley of the Moon. Picnic and explore the grounds at **Jack London State Historic Park** 47. The next morning visit **Kenwood Vineyards** 51 before heading north to 🖾 **Healdsburg** in Dry Creek Valley via Santa Rosa and U.S. 101, where a host of "hidden" wineries—including **Ferrari-Carano Winery** 64—lie nestled in the woods along the roads. Spend the night in Healdsburg; then, on the third day, cross over into Napa Valley—take Mark Springs Road east off U.S. 101's River Road exit and follow the signs on Porter Creek Road to Petrified Forest Road to Route 29. Spend the day (and the night) in the Western-style town of 🖾 **Calistoga,** noted for its mud baths and mineral springs. Wake up early on the fourth day for a balloon ride. If you're feeling energetic, take to the Silverado Trail for a bike ride with stops at **Cuvaison** 32, **Stag's Leap Wine Cellars** 11, and **Clos du Val** 6. On Day 5, visit the galleries, shops, and eateries of **St. Helena** before heading to the **Oakville Grocery** 13, a must-see (and must-taste) landmark. Spend the night and visit the wineries in 🖾 **Rutherford.** On Day 6, explore nearby **Yountville,** stopping for lunch at one of its many acclaimed restaurants before heading up the hill to the **Hess Collection Winery and Vineyards** ⑧, on Mt. Veeder. Splurge on dinner at **Domaine Chandon** ⑩. On your last day, return to the town of Sonoma via the Carneros Highway, moving on to the landmark **Buena Vista Carneros Winery** ㊺ or **Gloria Ferrer Champagne Caves** ㊶.

---

breakfast highlighting local produce. The newer hotels tend to have a more modern, streamlined aesthetic, and many have state-of-the-art spas with massage treatments or spring-water pools. Numerous hotels and B&Bs have top-quality restaurants on their grounds, and all that don't still have spots providing gastronomic bliss just a short car ride away.

However, all of this comes with a hefty price tag. As the cost of vineyards and grapes has risen, so have lodging rates. Santa Rosa, the largest population center in the area, has the widest selection of moderately priced rooms. Try there if you've failed to reserve in advance or have a limited budget. In general, all accommodations in the area often have considerably lower rates on weeknights, and prices are about 20% lower in winter.

On weekends, two- or even three-night minimum stays are commonly required, especially at smaller inns and B&Bs. If you'd prefer to stay a single night, though, innkeepers are usually more flexible during winter. Many B&Bs book up long in advance of the summer and fall seasons, and they're often not suitable for children.

WHAT IT COSTS				
$$$$	**$$$**	**$$**	**$**	**¢**
RESTAURANTS over $30	$23–$30	$15–$22	$10–$14	under $10
HOTELS over $250	$200–$250	$150–$199	$90–$149	under $90

Restaurant prices are per person for a main course at dinner. Hotel prices are for two people in a standard double room in high season.

Timing

"Crush," the term used to indicate the season when grapes are picked and crushed, usually takes place in September or October, depending on the weather. From September until December the entire Wine Country celebrates its bounty with street fairs and festivals. The Sonoma County Harvest Fair, with its famous grape stomp, is held the first weekend in October. Golf tournaments, wine auctions, and art and food fairs occur throughout the fall.

In season (April through October), Napa Valley draws crowds of tourists, and traffic along Route 29 from St. Helena to Calistoga is often backed up on weekends. The Sonoma Valley, Santa Rosa, and Healdsburg are less crowded. In season and over holiday weekends it's best to book lodging, restaurant, and winery reservations well in advance. Many wineries give tours at specified times and require appointments.

To avoid crowds, visit the Wine Country during the week and get an early start (most wineries open around 10). Summer is usually hot and dry and autumn can be even hotter, so pack a sun hat if you go during these times.

THE NAPA VALLEY

With more than 240 wineries, the Napa Valley is the undisputed capital of American wine production. Famed for its unrivaled climate and neat rows of vineyards, the area is made up of small, quirky towns whose Victorian Gothic architecture—narrow, gingerbread facades and pointed arches—is reminiscent of a distant world. Yountville, in the lower Napa Valley, is compact and redolent of American history yet fast becoming a culinary hub. St. Helena, in the middle of the valley, is posh, with tony shops and elegant restaurants. Calistoga, near the north border of Napa County, feels like an Old West frontier town, with wooden-plank storefronts and people in cowboy hats.

Napa

46 mi from San Francisco via I–80 east and north, Rte. 37 west, and Rte. 29 north.

Established in 1848 and with a population of about 120,000, Napa is the oldest town as well as the largest city in the valley. It has been undergoing a cultural rebirth, especially since the 2001 opening of Copia: The American Center for Wine, Food & the Arts, which coincided with the sprucing up of the downtown area and the opening of many new restaurants. In 2003 the glamorous 1880 Napa Valley Opera House finally had its grand reopening after years of renovations.

The commercial hub for one of the richest wine-producing regions in the world, the city itself is urban and busy. But it's surrounded by some of California's prettiest agricultural lands. Most destinations in both the Napa and Sonoma valleys are easily accessible from here. For those seeking an affordable alternative to the hotels and B&Bs in the heart of the Wine Country, Napa is a good option. But choose lodgings right downtown or on the north side of town near Yountville, as parts of Napa are downright seedy.

★ ❶ **Domaine Carneros** occupies a 138-acre estate dominated by a classic château inspired by Champagne Taittinger's historic Château de la Marquetterie in France. Carved into the hillside beneath the winery, Domaine Carneros's cellars produce sparkling wines reminiscent of the Taittinger style and using only Carneros grapes. (It's in the Carneros wine district.) At night the château is a glowing beacon rising above the dark vineyards. Flights of wines and accompanying cheese plates and caviar can be ordered from tables inside or on the terrace overlooking the vineyards. ✉ *1240 Duhig Rd.* ☎ *707/257–0101* ⊕ *www.domainecarneros.com* ▣ *Tastings $5.75–$13.50, 45-min tour free* ☉ *Daily 10–6; tours daily at 10:15, 11, noon, 1, 2, 3, and 4.*

❷ **Artesa Vineyards & Winery,** formerly called Codorniu Napa, is bunkered into a Carneros hilltop. The Spanish owners now produce primarily still wines under the talented wine maker Don Van Staaveren (previously of Chateau St. Jean). With a modern, minimalist look in the tasting room and contemporary sculptures and fountains on the property, this place is a far cry from the many faux French châteaux and rustic Italian-style villas in the region. ⊠ *1345 Henry Rd., north off Old Sonoma Rd. and Dealy La.* ☎ *707/224–1668* 🖷 *707/224–1672* ⊕ *www.artesawinery. com* 🍷 *Tastings $2 and up, ½-hr tour free* ☉ *Daily 10–5; tours daily at 11 and 2.*

❸ Instead of tasting wine, you have the opportunity to try five types of sake at **Hakusan.** One of the more appealing choices is a plum-flavored dessert sake. Outside, a few placards near a Japanese garden explain the sake-making process. ⊠ *1 Executive Way* ☎ *707/258–6160* ⊕ *www. hakusan.com* 🍷 *Tasting $3* ☉ *Daily 10–5.*

❹ **Copia: The American Center for Wine, Food & the Arts** is a shrine to Amer-
Fodor'sChoice ican food and wine. An enormous variety of food-related art exhibits,
★ video screenings, food and wine tastings, and tours are scheduled daily (pick up a list from the information desk near the front door). The entry fee (halved on Wednesday) allows access to the exhibitions, informative tours, gift shop, and some introductory tastings and lectures. One-hour tours of the ever-changing gardens are very popular. Special programs, such as a luncheon exploration of wine and cheese pairings, are fantastic (additional fee required). ⊠ *500 1st St.* ☎ *707/259–1600* ⊕ *www.copia.org* 🍷 *$12.50* ☉ *Wed.–Mon. 10–5.*

❺ **Luna Vineyards,** the southernmost winery on the Silverado Trail, was established in 1995 by veterans of the Napa wine industry intent on making less-conventional wines, particularly Italian varieties. They've planted pinot grigio on the historic property and also produce sangiovese and merlot. ⊠ *2921 Silverado Trail* ☎ *707/255–2474* ⊕ *www.lunavineyards. com* 🍷 *Tasting and tour $5* ☉ *Daily 10–5; tours by appointment.*

❻ **Clos du Val,** founded by French owner Bernard Portet, produces a celebrated reserve cabernet. It also makes zinfandel, pinot noir, and chardonnay. Although the winery itself is austere, the French-style wines age beautifully. Anyone is welcome to try a hand at the boccie-style game of pétanque. ⊠ *5330 Silverado Trail* ☎ *707/259–2200* ⊕ *www.closduval. com* 🍷 *Tasting and tour $5* ☉ *Daily 10–5; tours by appointment.*

❼ Small **Pine Ridge Winery,** in the Stags Leap district, makes estate-bottled wines, including chardonnay, chenin blanc, and merlot, as well as a first-rate cabernet. Tours (by appointment) include barrel tastings in the winery's caves. ⊠ *5901 Silverado Trail* ☎ *707/252–9777* ⊕ *www. pineridgewinery.com* 🍷 *Tastings $10–$20, tour $20* ☉ *Daily 10:30–4:30; tours at 10, noon, and 2.*

❽ The **Hess Collection Winery and Vineyards** is a delightful discovery on a
Fodor'sChoice hilltop 9 mi northwest of the city of Napa. (Don't give up; the road lead-
★ ing to the winery is long and winding.) The simple, rustic limestone structure, circa 1903, contains Swiss owner Donald Hess's personal art collection, including mostly large-scale works by such contemporary European and American artists as Robert Motherwell, Francis Bacon, and

13

Galleries & Museums
Internationally famous artists, as well as local ones, exhibit their work in Napa and Sonoma Valley galleries. There are artistic styles to suit every taste, as more art dealers and collectors are discovering. Shows at most galleries are scheduled throughout the year.

Hot-Air Ballooning
Day after day, colorful balloons fill the morning sky high above the Wine Country's valleys. Balloon flights usually take place soon after sunrise, when the calmest, coolest conditions offer maximum lift and soft landings. Prices depend on the duration of the flight, number of passengers, and services. Some companies provide such extras as pickup at your lodging or champagne brunch after the flight. Expect to spend at least $185 per person.

Spas & Mud Baths
Mineral-water soaks, mud baths, and massage are rejuvenating local traditions. Calistoga, known worldwide as the Hot Springs of the West, is famous for its warm, springwater-fed mineral tubs and mud baths full of volcanic ash. Sonoma, St. Helena, and other towns also have full-service spas.

Wonderful World of Wine
Wine tasting can be an educational, fascinating, and even mysterious ritual. The sight of polished glasses and uniquely labeled bottles lined up in a row, the tour guide's commentary on the character of each wine, the decadent mood of the vineyards with their full-to-bursting grapes—all combine to create an anticipation that's gratified with the first sip of wine. Learning about the origin of the grapes, the terraces on which they're grown, the weather that nurtured them, and the methods by which they're transformed into wine will give you a new appreciation of wine—and a great afternoon (or all-day) diversion. For those new to the wine-tasting game, Robert Mondavi and Korbel Champagne Cellars give general tours geared toward teaching novices the basics on how wine and champagne are made and what to look for when tasting.

There are more than 400 wineries in Sonoma and Napa, so it pays to be selective when planning your visit. Better to mix up the wineries with other sights and diversions—a picnic, trips to local museums, a ride in a hot-air balloon—than attempt to visit too many in one day. Unless otherwise noted, the wineries in this chapter are open daily year-round and charge no fee for admission, tours, or tastings. In general, fees tend to be low or nonexistent in the Sonoma and Russian River valleys and from $3 to $10 in the Napa Valley. Sometimes tasting fees are refundable with the purchase of a bottle of wine.

Frank Stella. Cabernet sauvignon is the real strength here, though Hess also produces some fine chardonnays. The winery and the art collection are open for self-guided tours (free). ⊠ *4411 Redwood Rd., west of Rte. 29* ☎ *707/255–1144* ⊕ *www.hesscollection.com* ⊑ *Tasting $3* ⊙ *Daily 10–4.*

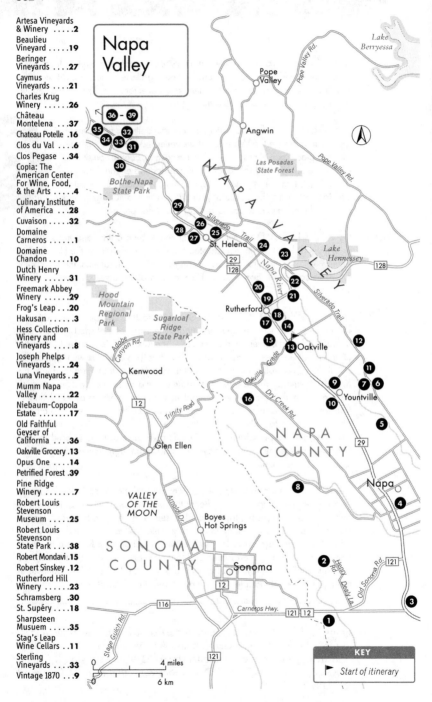

Napa Valley

KEY

► Start of itinerary

Where to Stay & Eat

★ **$-$$$** ✕ **Angèle.** Vaulted wood-beam ceilings, dim lights, and candles on every table set a romantic mood at this congenial and cozy French bistro. Classic dishes like French onion soup and coquilles St-Jacques (French scallops), served with cauliflower puree and roasted sun chokes, are well executed and served by an attentive staff. The charmingly rustic restaurant is housed in the Hatt Building, part of a complex of historic riverside structures in downtown Napa. ⊠ *540 Main St.* ☎ *707/252–8115* ▭ *AE, D, DC, MC, V.*

★ **$-$$$** ✕ **Bistro Don Giovanni.** Terra-cotta tile floors and high ceilings surround this lively, festive bistro. Here Italian food is served with French accents that are simultaneously inventive and comforting: risotto with squab and radicchio, pizza with pear and caramelized onions, and rabbit braised in pinot noir. Whole, wood-oven-roasted fish is an unusual specialty. Seats on the covered patio are coveted in fair weather. ⊠ *4110 Howard La., at Rte. 29* ☎ *707/224–3300* ▭ *AE, D, DC, MC, V.*

$-$$$ ✕ **Celadon.** Venture into downtown Napa for chef-owner Greg Cole's creative and enticing "global comfort food." Dishes such as flash-fried calamari with a chipotle-ginger glaze, and tasting plates such as crab cake laced with grainy mustard sauce, make this an ideal place to sample contemporary cuisine accompanied by any of the dozen wines available by the glass. ⊠ *500 Main St.* ☎ *707/254–9690* ▭ *AE, D, DC, MC, V* ⊘ *No lunch weekends.*

$-$$$ ✕ **Julia's Kitchen.** Named for Julia Child, the restaurant at Copia serves French-California cuisine that relies on the freshest regional ingredients. Salad greens and many other vegetables come from Copia's 3½ acres of organic gardens, just outside the door. Breast of free-range chicken might come with truffle mashed potatoes; calamari salad is sometimes garnished with freshly picked cucumbers. Diners can watch the chefs at work in the open kitchen. ⊠ *500 1st St.* ☎ *707/265–5700* ▭ *AE, MC, V* ⊘ *No lunch Tues. No dinner Mon.–Wed.*

¢-$$$ ✕ **ZuZu.** Spanish glass lamps, a carved-wood Latin-American goddess, and hammered-tin ceiling panels set the tone for a menu composed almost entirely of tapas. These little dishes so common in Spain are a rarity in the Wine Country, which may be why the in-crowd immediately adopted this lively place. White anchovies with endive, ratatouille, sea-scallop ceviche, and paella are typical fare. ⊠ *829 Main St.* ☎ *707/224–8555* ▭ *AE, MC, V* ⊘ *No lunch weekends.*

$-$$ ✕ **Foothill Cafe.** On the less glamorous side of Route 29, this low-key, whimsically decorated restaurant is a big favorite with locals, which is a high recommendation in such a food-savvy area. Typical dishes include peppercorn-crusted salmon and pork loin with mustard cream. Desserts tend toward the classic, like crème brûlée and apple crisp. ⊠ *2766 Old Sonoma Rd.* ☎ *707/252–6178* ▭ *AE, MC, V* ⊘ *Closed Mon. and Tues. No lunch.*

$$$$ ▤ **Carneros Inn.** A short drive from Napa in the rolling hills of the FodorsChoice Carneros district, this luxury resort attracts sybarites to its simple, so-
★ phisticated freestanding cottages. Inside, ethereal beds are piled high with fluffy pillows and covered with Frette linens and pristine white down comforters. High-tech amenities include DVD players, flat-panel TVs,

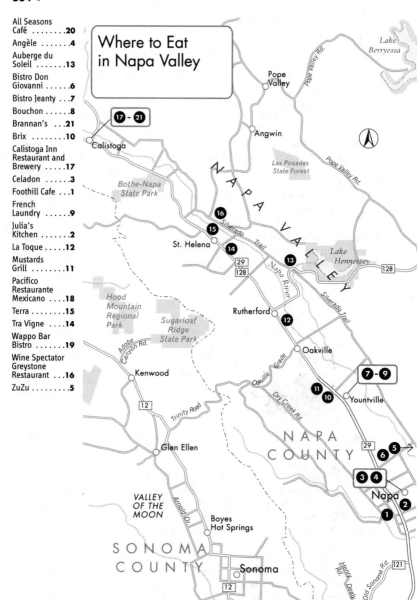

Where to Eat
in Napa Valley

and heated slate bathroom floors. Each cottage also has French doors opening onto a private courtyard with a gas-fired heater. The infinity pool invites impromptu dips day and night, and the hilltop dining room serves cocktails and dinner (guests only) overlooking the vineyards. ⊠ *4048 Sonoma Hwy., 94559* ☎ *707/299–4900* 🖷 *707/299–4950* ⊕ *www.thecarnerosinn.com* ⤳ *76 rooms, 10 suites* ⟁ *Restaurant, dining room, room service, in-room data ports, refrigerators, cable TV, in-room VCRs, pool, gym, hot tub, spa, bar, concierge, dry cleaning, laundry service, meeting rooms* ⊟ *AE, D, DC, MC, V.*

★ **$$$$** 🖸 **Milliken Creek Inn.** Views of the property's lavish landscaping and the Napa River enhance the already beautiful rooms at this inn, which replicates the style of British-colonial Asia. Khaki- and cream-color walls in the rooms surround rattan furniture, hydrotherapy spa tubs, and gauzy canopy beds with luscious linens. Outside you'll find Adirondack chairs, a fountain, and a pavilion for al fresco massages. ⊠ *1815 Silverado Trail, 94558* ☎ *707/255–1197 or 888/622–5775* ⊕ *www.millikencreekinn.com* ⤳ *12 rooms, 7 suites* ⟁ *In-room data ports, minibars, refrigerators, cable TV, in-room VCRs, hot tub, massage, wine bar, dry cleaning, concierge; no kids, no smoking* ⊟ *AE, D, DC, MC, V* ¶ⵙ *CP.*

$$$$ 🖸 **Oak Knoll Inn.** Uncommonly spacious guest rooms with Napa fieldstone walls and high beamed ceilings give this small inn an expansive feel. Seating areas with plush chairs and couches are perfect for enjoying the fireplace in each room. The views take in the pool and the hundreds of acres of vineyard beyond. The bathrooms aren't as lavish as those at similarly priced B&Bs, but the food, beautifully presented at the wine hour every evening and at a decadent breakfast, is reason enough to visit. Service is top-notch, and the innkeepers are happy to arrange winery visits and other activities. ⊠ *2200 E. Oak Knoll Ave., 4 mi south of Yountville* ☎ *707/255–2200* 🖷 *707/255–2296* ⊕ *www.oakknollinn.com* ⤳ *4 rooms* ⟁ *In-room data ports, refrigerators, pool, hot tub; no room TVs, no smoking* ⊟ *MC, V* ¶ⵙ *BP.*

$$$–$$$$ 🖸 **La Résidence.** Most of these deluxe accommodations, romantic and secluded amid extensive landscaping, are in two buildings: the French Barn and the Mansion, a renovated 1870s Gothic revival manor house built by a riverboat captain from New Orleans. Towering oaks bathe the entire property in shade. The spacious rooms have floral bedspreads and curtains, period antiques, and fireplaces, and most have double French doors that open onto verandas or patios. ⊠ *4066 Howard La., 94558* ☎ *707/253–0337* 🖷 *707/253–0382* ⊕ *www.laresidence.com* ⤳ *22 rooms, 1 suite* ⟁ *Some refrigerators, some cable TV, pool, hot tub; no TV in some rooms, no smoking* ⊟ *AE, D, DC, MC, V* ¶ⵙ *BP.*

$$–$$$$ 🖸 **Napa River Inn.** A 2½-acre complex includes restaurants, shops, a spa, and this waterfront inn. Accommodations in the 1884 Hatt Building maintain original architectural details, including maple hardwood floors; some rooms have canopy beds, fireplaces, and artwork depicting an 1880s river town. Brighter colors dominate in the adjacent Embarcadero building, where some rooms have small balconies and the decor has an understated nautical theme. ⊠ *500 Main St., 94559* ☎ *707/251–8500 or 877/251–8500* 🖷 *707/251–8504* ⊕ *www.napariverinn.com* ⤳ *65*

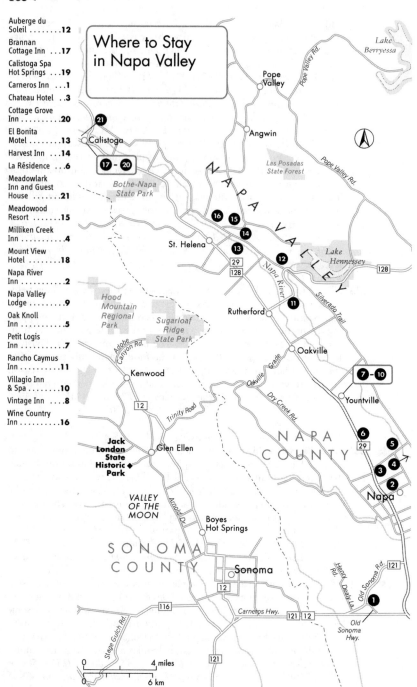

Where to Stay in Napa Valley

rooms, 1 suite ⚬ 2 restaurants, café, patisserie, in-room data ports, refrigerators, cable TV with video games, in-room VCRs, spa, bicycles, wine bar, shops, dry cleaning, laundry service, concierge, Internet, business services, meeting rooms, some pets allowed (fee); no smoking ⊟ AE, D, DC, MC, V ⦿ CP.

$–$$ 🏨 **Chateau Hotel.** Despite the name, this is a fairly simple motel with only the barest nod to France. Clean rooms, its location at the entrance to the Napa Valley, the adjacent restaurant, and free stays for children under age 12 are conveniences that make up for its lack of charm. ⊠ 4195 Solano Ave., west of Rte. 29 (exit at Trower Ave.), 94558 ☎ 707/253–9300, 800/253–6272 in CA 🖷 707/253–0906 ⊕ www. napavalleychateauhotel.com ⤶ 109 rooms, 6 suites ⚬ Some refrigerators, cable TV, pool, hot tub ⊟ AE, D, DC, MC, V ⦿ CP.

The Arts

In 1995 former telecommunications tycoon and vintner William Jarvis and his wife transformed a historic stone winery building in downtown Napa into the **Jarvis Conservatory,** an excellent venue for baroque French ballet and Spanish operetta known as *zarzuela.* Performances open to the public are held in conjunction with workshops and festivals centered on these two art forms. The conservatory presents opera nights featuring local talent the first Saturday of each month. ⊠ 1711 Main St. ☎ 707/ 255–5445 ⊕ www.jarvisconservatory.com.

Sports & the Outdoors

BIKING Thanks to the long country roads that wind through the region, bicycling is a popular pastime. The Silverado Trail, with its very gently rolling hills, is more scenic than Route 29, which nevertheless tempts some bikers with its pancake-flat aspect. **Napa Valley Bike Tours and Rentals** (⊠ 4080 Byway E, Napa ☎ 707/255–3377) rents bikes for $6–$10 per hour or $25–$40 per day. One-day winery tours are $105–$145, including lunch and van support.

GOLF The 18-hole course at the **Chardonnay Golf Club** (⊠ 2555 Jameson Canyon Rd. ☎ 707/257–8950) is a favorite among Bay Area golfers. Greens fees, $70 weekdays and $90 weekends in high season, include a cart. Within the vicinity of the Silverado Trail, the **Silverado Country Club** (⊠ 1600 Atlas Peak Rd. ☎ 707/257–0200) has two challenging 18-hole courses with a beautiful view at every hole. Greens fees for guests at the resort is $140, including a cart; the reciprocal rate for members of other clubs is $155.

Yountville

13 mi north of the town of Napa on Rte. 29.

Yountville has become the valley's boomtown. No other small town in the Wine Country has as many inns, shops, or world-class restaurants. ❾ Particularly popular is **Vintage 1870** (⊠ 6525 Washington St. ☎ 707/ 944–2451), a 26-acre complex of boutiques, restaurants, and fancy-food stores. The vine-cover brick shops, built in 1870, once housed a winery, livery stable, and distillery. The property's original mansion is now the Mexican-style Compadres Bar and Grill. Nearby, the Pacific Blues

Café is set in the 1868 train depot built by Samuel Brannan for his privately owned Napa Valley Railroad.

At the intersection of Madison and Washington streets is **Washington Square,** a complex of boutiques and restaurants. **Pioneer Cemetery,** the final resting place of town founder George Yount, is on the far side of Washington Street.

⑩ French-owned **Domaine Chandon** claims one of Yountville's prime pieces of real estate, on a knoll west of downtown. Tours of the sleek, modern facilities on the beautifully maintained property include sample flutes of the méthode champenoise sparkling wine. Champagne is $4–$12 per glass, hors d'oeuvres are available, and an elegant restaurant beckons. ⊠ *1 California Dr., west of Rte. 29* ☎ *707/944–2280* ⊕ *www.chandon.com* ✉ *Tours free* ⊙ *May–Oct., daily 10–6; Nov.–Apr., Sun.–Fri. 11–5, Sat. 10–6. Call for tour times.*

⑪ It was the 1973 cabernet sauvignon produced by **Stag's Leap Wine Cellars** that put the winery—and the California wine industry—on the map by placing first in the famous Paris tasting of 1976. Today, Stag's Leap makes cabernet, as well as chardonnay, sauvignon blanc, white riesling, merlot, and a petite sirah. ⊠ *5766 Silverado Trail* ☎ *707/265–2441* ⊕ *www.cask23.com* ✉ *Tastings $10–$30; tour $10* ⊙ *Daily 10–4:30; tours by appointment.*

⑫ **Robert Sinskey** makes estate-bottled wines, including chardonnay, cabernet, and merlot, but is best known for its pinot noir. ⊠ *6320 Silverado Trail* ☎ *707/944–9090* 🖷 *707/994–9092* ⊕ *www.robertsinskey.com* ✉ *Tasting $10; tour free* ⊙ *Daily 10–4:30; 1-hr tours by appointment.*

Where to Stay & Eat

$$$$
Fodor'sChoice
★

✕ **French Laundry.** An old stone building houses the most acclaimed restaurant in Napa Valley—and, indeed, one of the most highly regarded in the country. The prix-fixe menus ($115–$135), one of which is vegetarian, include five or nine courses and usually have two or three additional surprises, such as a tiny cone filled with salmon tartare. A full three hours will likely pass before you reach dessert. Chef Thomas Keller, with two James Beard awards, doesn't lack for admirers. Reservations are hard won and not accepted more than two months in advance (call two months ahead to the day). Didn't get a reservation? Try stopping by on the day you'd like to dine here to be considered if there's a cancellation. ⊠ *6640 Washington St.* ☎ *707/944–2380* ♒ *Reservations essential* ▤ *AE, MC, V* ⊙ *Closed 1st 2 wks in Jan. No lunch Mon.–Thurs.*

$$–$$$$

✕ **Brix.** The spacious dining room here has artisan glass, fine woods, and an entire wall of west-facing windows that overlooks vineyards. Many of the herbs used in the kitchen are grown in the adjacent garden. Mains might include fresh fettuccine with sugar snap peas or grilled Atlantic salmon with chanterelles and vanilla beurre blanc. Pizzas are cooked in a wood-burning oven. Fruit is a main ingredient in many of the desserts. ⊠ *7377 St. Helena Hwy. at Rte. 29* ☎ *707/944–2749* ▤ *AE, D, DC, MC, V.*

★ $$–$$$

✕ **Bouchon.** The team that brought French Laundry to its current pinnacle is behind this place, where everything from the snazzy zinc bar to the black vests on the waiters to the traditional warm-goat-cheese salad could have come straight from a Parisian bistro. *Boudin blanc* (white sausage) with potato puree and leg of lamb with white beans are among the hearty dishes served in the high-ceiling room. Late-night meals are served from a limited menu until 12:30. ⊠ *6534 Washington St.* ☎ *707/ 944–8037* ⊟ *AE, MC, V.*

$$–$$$ ✕ **Mustards Grill.** There's not an ounce of pretension at the first restau-
Fodor'sChoice rant of owner-chef Cindy Pawlcyn, despite the fact that it's booked solid
★ almost nightly with fans of her hearty cuisine. The menu mixes updated renditions of traditional American dishes like grilled fish, steak, and lemon meringue pie with innovative choices like seared ahi tuna on homemade sesame crackers with wasabi crème fraîche. A black-and-white marble tile floor, dark-wood wainscoting, and upbeat artwork set a scene that's casual but refined. Pawlcyn is also responsible for San Francisco's Fog City Diner and two other restaurants. ⊠ *7399 St. Helena Hwy., at Rte. 29, 1 mi north of town* ☎ *707/944–2424* ⌖ *Reservations essential* ⊟ *D, DC, MC, V.*

$–$$$ ✕ **Bistro Jeanty.** Philippe Jeanty's menu draws its inspiration from the cooking of his French childhood. His classic cassoulet will warm those nostalgic for bistro cooking, and classic coq au vin rises above the ordinary with the infusion of a spicy red-wine sauce. The scene here is Gallic through and through, with a small bar and a handful of tables in two crowded rooms. The best seats are in the back room, near the fireplace. ⊠ *6510 Washington St.* ☎ *707/944–0103* ⌖ *Reservations essential* ⊟ *MC, V.*

$$$$ ▥ **Napa Valley Lodge.** The balconies, covered walkways, and red-tile roof are reminiscent of a hacienda, and many of the rooms have fireplaces. Some second-floor accommodations, which are spacious, have vineyard views. A large pool area is landscaped with lots of greenery, and the Yountville Golf Course is across the street. ⊠ *2230 Madison St., at Rte. 29, 94599* ☎ *707/944–2468 or 800/368–2468* ☐ *707/944–9362* ⊕ *www.woodsidehotels.com/napa* ↷ *50 rooms, 5 suites* ⌂ *Room service, in-room data ports, minibars, refrigerators, cable TV with movies, pool, gym, hot tub, sauna, dry cleaning, laundry service, concierge, Internet, business services, meeting rooms; no smoking* ⊟ *AE, D, DC, MC, V* ⋈ *CP.*

★ **$$$–$$$$** ▥ **Villagio Inn & Spa.** Clusters of villa-like buildings make up this plush inn in the heart of Yountville. A linear fountain, like a canal, runs through the lushly landscaped property, just off Route 29, and steps from some of the country's top restaurants. Streamlined furnishings, subdued color schemes, and high ceilings enhance the sense of spaciousness in the guest rooms. Each room has a fireplace and, beyond louvered doors, a balcony or patio. A youthful vibe infuses the pool area, where the stereo is often blasting high-energy tunes and automated misters cool sunbathers on double-wide loungers. The full-service spa has its own pool and whirlpool. Rates include afternoon tea, a bottle of wine, and a generous champagne buffet breakfast. ⊠ *6481 Washington St., 94599* ☎ *707/944–8877 or 800/351–1133* ☐ *707/944–8855* ⊕ *www.villagio.com* ↷ *86 rooms, 26 suites* ⌂ *Room service, in-room hot tubs, cable TV, in-room VCRs, 2 tennis courts, pool, outdoor hot tub, spa, bicycles, lobby lounge, shops,* *dry cleaning, laundry service, concierge, business services, meeting rooms* ▭ *AE, DC, MC, V* 🍽 *CP.*

$$$–$$$$ **Vintage Inn.** Rooms in this luxurious inn are housed in two-story villas scattered around a lush, landscaped 3½-acre property. French fabrics and 19th-century antiques outfit spacious, airy guest rooms, all of which have a private patio or balcony, a fireplace, and a whirlpool tub in the bathroom. Some private patios have vineyard views. You're treated to a bottle of wine, champagne at breakfast, and afternoon tea. ✉ *6541 Washington St., 94599* ☎ *707/944–1112 or 800/351–1133* 📠 *707/944–1617* 🌐 *www.vintageinn.com* *68 rooms, 12 suites* *Dining room, room service, in-room hot tubs, refrigerators, cable TV, in-room VCRs, tennis court, pool, outdoor hot tub, bicycles, lobby lounge, shops, dry cleaning, laundry service, concierge, business services, meeting rooms, some pets allowed (fee), no-smoking rooms* ▭ *AE, DC, MC, V* 🍽 *CP.*

$$–$$$ **Petit Logis Inn.** Murals and 11-foot-high ceilings infuse a European elegance into the rooms of this small, charming, one-story inn, which was formerly a row of shops. Breakfast, included in the room rate, is provided by one of two nearby restaurants. The inn's proximity to many of Yountville's best restaurants (within walking distance) is another plus. ✉ *6527 Yount St., 94599* ☎ *707/944–2332 or 877/944–2332* 📠 *707/944–2388* 🌐 *www.petitlogis.com* *5 rooms* *In-room data ports, refrigerators, cable TV; no smoking* ▭ *AE, MC, V* 🍽 *BP.*

Oakville

2 mi west of Yountville on Rte. 29.

There are three reasons to visit the town of Oakville: its grocery store, its scenic mountain road, and its magnificent, highly exclusive winery. 13 The **Oakville Grocery** (✉ 7856 St. Helena Hwy., at Rte. 29 ☎ 707/944–8802), built in 1881 as a general store, carries high-end fare and difficult-to-find wines; custom-packed picnic baskets are a specialty. It's a pleasant place to sit on a bench out front and sip an espresso. Along the mountain range that divides Napa and Sonoma, the **Oakville Grade** (✉ West of Rte. 29) is a twisting half-hour route with breathtaking views of both valleys. Although the surface of the road is good, it can be difficult to negotiate at night, and trucks are advised not to attempt it at any time.

14 **Opus One,** the combined venture of California wine maker Robert Mondavi and the late French baron Philippe de Rothschild, is famed for its vast (1,000 barrels side by side on a single floor), semicircular cellar modeled on the Château Mouton Rothschild winery in France. The futuristic building is the work of the architects responsible for San Francisco's Transamerica Pyramid. The state-of-the-art facilities produce about 20,000 cases of ultrapremium Bordeaux-style red wine from grapes grown in the estate's vineyards and in the surrounding area. ✉ *7900 St. Helena Hwy., at Rte. 29* ☎ *707/963–1979* 📠 *707/944–1753* 🌐 *www.opusonewines.com* *Tasting $25; tour free* ⏲ *Daily 10–4; tasting and tours by appointment.*

⑮ At **Robert Mondavi,** perhaps the best-known winery in the United States, you're encouraged to take the 75- to 90-minute vineyard and winery tour followed by an appetizer and wine tasting. In-depth two- to four-hour tours and lunch tours are also popular. Afterward, visit the art gallery, or, in summer, stick around for a concert (from jazz to pop and world music). ⊠ *7801 St. Helena Hwy., at Rte. 29* ☎ *707/259–9463* ⊕ *www.robertmondaviwinery.com* 🖃 *Tasting fees $5–$30, tour $10* ☉ *Daily 9–5; tours by appointment.*

★ **⑯** **Chateau Potelle,** an out-of-the-way spot at nearly 2,000 feet on the slopes of Mt. Veeder, produces acclaimed estate zinfandel, chardonnay, and cabernet sauvignon. Jean-Noël and Marketta Fourmeaux were official tasters for the French government before establishing this winery in 1988, which they named for the château in the Champagne region belonging to Jean-Noël's family. The friendly, casual atmosphere and location away from the crowds in the valley below make it an ideal spot for a picnic. ⊠ *3875 Mt. Veeder Rd., 5 mi west of Rte. 29 off the Oakville Grade* ☎ *707/255–9440* ⊕ *www.chateaupotelle.com* 🖃 *$5; tasting free* ☉ *Nov.–mid-Apr., Thurs.–Mon. 11–5; mid-Apr.–Oct., daily 11–6.*

Rutherford

1 mi northwest of Oakville on Rte. 29.

From a fast-moving car, Rutherford is a quick blur of dark forest, a rustic barn or two, and maybe a country store. But don't speed by this tiny hamlet. With its singular microclimate and soil, this is an important viticultural center.

⑰
Fodor's Choice
★
In the 1970s, filmmaker Francis Ford Coppola bought the old Niebaum property, a part of the world-famous Inglenook estate. He resurrected an early Inglenook-like quality red with his first bottle of Rubicon, released in 1985. Since then, the **Niebaum-Coppola Estate** has consistently received high ratings, and in 1995 Coppola purchased the other half of the Inglenook estate; the ancient, ivy-covered château; and an additional 95 acres. A small museum in the château has displays documenting the history of the Inglenook estates as well as Coppola movie memorabilia, which include Don Corleone's desk and chair from *The Godfather* and costumes from *Bram Stoker's Dracula.* ⊠ *1991 St. Helena Hwy., at Rte. 29* ☎ *707/963–9099* ⊕ *www.niebaum-coppola.com* 🖃 *Tasting $10; tour $20* ☉ *Daily 10–5; château tours daily at 10:30, 12:30, and 2:30; vineyard tours daily at 11, weather permitting.*

⑱ Fine sauvignon blancs, semillons, and cabernet sauvignons are among the wines at which **St. Supéry** excels. This winery's unique discovery center allows you to inhale distinct wine aromas and match them with actual black pepper, cherry, citrus, and the like. A restored 1880 Victorian house is part of the excellent winery tour. Self-guided tours are free. ⊠ *8440 St. Helena Hwy. S, at Rte. 29* ☎ *707/963–4507* ⊕ *www.stsupery.com* 🖃 *Tastings $5–$10; tours free–$12* ☉ *May–Sept., daily 10–5:30; Oct.–Apr., daily 10–5; tours at 1 and 3.*

⑲ **Beaulieu Vineyard** still uses the same wine-making process, from crush to bottle, as it did the day it opened in 1900. The winery's cabernet is a benchmark of the Napa Valley. The Georges de Latour Private Reserve cabernet sauvignon consistently garners high marks from major wine publications. ⊠ *1960 St. Helena Hwy., at Rte. 29* ☎ *707/967–5200* ⊕ *www.bvwines.com* ⊠ *Tastings $5–$25* ⊙ *Daily 10–5, tours daily on the hr 11–4.*

㉐ **Frog's Leap** is the perfect place for wine novices to begin their education. Owners John and Julie Williams maintain a sense of humor and a humble attitude that translates into an informative and satisfying experience. They also happen to produce some of the finest zinfandel, cabernet sauvignon, and sauvignon blanc in the Wine Country. ⊠ *8815 Conn Creek Rd.* ☎ *707/963–4704* ⊕ *www.frogsleap.com* ⊠ *Tasting and tour free* ⊙ *Mon.–Sat. 10–4; tours and tastings by appointment.*

Fodor'sChoice
★

㉑ **Caymus Vineyards** is run by wine master Chuck Wagner, who started making wine on the property in 1972. His family, however, had been farming in the valley since 1906. Today a 100% cabernet sauvignon special selection is the winery's claim to fame. Caymus also turns out a superior white, the Conundrum, made of an unusual blend of grapes—sauvignon blanc, semillon, chardonnay, and viognier. Reserve to taste. ⊠ *8700 Conn Creek Rd.* ☎ *707/963–4204* ⊕ *www.caymus.com* ⊠ *Tasting free* ⊙ *Sales daily 10–4; tastings by appointment.*

A joint venture of Mumm—the French champagne house—and Seagram, **㉒** **Mumm Napa Valley** is considered one of California's premier sparkling-wine producers. Its Napa Brut Prestige and ultrapremium Vintage Reserve are the best known. The excellent tour and comfortable tasting room are two more reasons to visit. An art gallery contains a permanent exhibit of Ansel Adams photographs that record the wine-making process. ⊠ *8445 Silverado Trail* ☎ *707/967–7700* ⊕ *www. mummnapavalley.com* ⊠ *Tastings $5–$12; tour free* ⊙ *Daily 10–5; tours daily on the hr 10–3.*

㉓ The wine at **Rutherford Hill Winery** is aged in French oak barrels stacked in more than 44,000 square feet of caves—one of the largest winery cave systems in the United States. Tours of the caves can be followed by a picnic in oak, olive, or madrone orchards. ⊠ *200 Rutherford Hill Rd., east of Silverado Trail* ☎ *707/963–7194* ⊕ *www.rutherfordhill.com* ⊠ *Tastings $5–$10; tour $5* ⊙ *Daily 10–5; tours daily at 11:30, 1:30, and 3:30.*

Where to Stay & Eat

$$$$
Fodor'sChoice
★

✕▥ **Auberge du Soleil.** Every room at this elegant hotel has at least a small terrace, from which you can take in the views of the stunning property and its steep, olive tree–studded slopes. Guest rooms are dressed in cool tile and soothing earth tones, with a nod to the spare side of Southwestern style. Bathrooms are truly grand (as expected at this price level), many of them equipped with whirlpool tubs. The renowned Auberge du Soleil restaurant has a world-class wine list and serves dishes such as raw yellowfin tuna with baby beets and Florida red snapper with pureed cauliflower. The bar serves moderately priced fare like goat-cheese salads and mussels until 11 PM. ⊠ *180 Rutherford Hill Rd., off Silverado Trail north of Rte. 128, 94573* ☎ *707/963–1211 or 800/348–5406*

🖷 707/963–8764 ⊕ *www.aubergedusoleil.com* ⫣ *18 rooms, 32 suites*
⚘ *2 restaurants, in-room data ports, kitchenettes, refrigerators, cable
TV, in-room VCRs, 3 tennis courts, pool, gym, hot tub, massage, sauna,
spa, bar, concierge, business services, meeting rooms* 🖃 *AE, D, DC, MC,
V* ⏀ *EP.*

★ **$$$–$$$$** ✕⊡ **Rancho Caymus Inn and La Toque.** California-Spanish in style, this cozy
inn has well-maintained gardens and large suites with kitchens and whirl-
pool baths. Well-chosen details include wrought-iron lamps, tile murals,
stoneware basins, and window seats. But even if you don't stay here, come
for dinner at the understated La Toque, which gives Yountville's French
Laundry its toughest competition for Wine Country diners' haute-cui-
sine dollars. Reservations are essential, and jackets are preferred for
men. Chef-owner Ken Frank's changing prix-fixe menu ($$$$) is loaded
with intense flavors; dishes might include seared Sonoma foie gras with
dates and beef marrow on toasted brioche. Nature willing, a special truf-
fle menu is added in January and February. ✉ *1140 Rutherford Rd., east
of Rte. 29, 94573* 🕾 *707/963–1777, 800/845–1777 inn, 707/963–9770
restaurant* 🖷 *707/963–5387* ⊕ *www.ranchocaymus.com* ⫣ *27 suites*
⚘ *Restaurant, dining room, in-room data ports, minibars, refrigerators,
cable TV, wine bar; no smoking* 🖃 *AE, DC, MC, V* ☉ *Restaurant closed
Mon., Tues., and 1st 2 wks in Jan. No lunch* ⏀ *CP.*

St. Helena

2 mi northwest of Oakville on Rte. 29.

By the time pioneer wine maker Charles Krug planted grapes in St. He-
lena around 1860, quite a few vineyards already existed in the area. Today
the town greets you with its abundant selection of wineries, many of
which lie along the route from Yountville to St. Helena, and its won-
derful restaurants, including Greystone, on the West Coast campus of
the Culinary Institute of America. Many Victorian and false-front build-
ings dating from the late 19th and early 20th centuries distinguish the
downtown area. Arching sycamore trees bow across Main Street (Route
29) to create a pleasant, shady drive.

㉔ Bordeaux blends, Rhône varietals, and a cabernet sauvignon are the house
specialties at **Joseph Phelps Vineyards.** One of Napa's top wineries, it first
hit the mark with Johannisberg Riesling. ✉ *200 Taplin Rd.* 🕾 *707/963–
2745* ⊕ *www.jpvwines.com* ▭ *Tastings $5–$10* ☉ *Weekdays 8–5, Sat.
10–5, Sun. 10–4.*

㉕ For some nonalcoholic sightseeing, visit the **Robert Louis Stevenson Mu-
seum** (✉ 1490 Library La. 🕾 707/963–3757 ☉ Tues.–Sun. noon–4), next
door to the public library. Its eponymous memorabilia consists of more
than 8,000 artifacts, including first editions, manuscripts, and pho-
tographs. The museum is free (donation suggested). Grape-seed mud wraps
and ayurveda-inspired massages performed by two attendants are among
the trademarks of the **Health Spa Napa Valley** (✉ 1030 Main St. 🕾 707/
967–8800), which has a pool, steam room, and fitness facilities. Don't
worry if your treatments leave you too limp to operate your car: Tra
Vigne and other St. Helena restaurants are within walking distance.

㉖ The first winery founded in the Napa Valley, **Charles Krug Winery** opened in 1861 when Count Haraszthy lent Krug a small cider press. Today the Peter Mondavi family runs it. At this writing, tours have been suspended indefinitely because a major earthquake retrofit project is in the works, but you can still come for tastings. ⊠ *2800 N. Main St.* ☎ *707/963–5057* ⊕ *www.charleskrug.com* 🖼 *Tastings $5–$8* ☉ *Daily 10:30–5.*

㉘ The West Coast headquarters of the **Culinary Institute of America,** the country's leading school for chefs, are in the **Greystone Winery,** the former site of the Christian Brothers Winery and a national historic landmark. The campus consists of 30 acres of herb and vegetable gardens, a 15-acre merlot vineyard, and a Mediterranean-inspired restaurant, which is open to the public. Also on the property are a well-stocked culinary store, a quirky corkscrew-and-winepress museum, and a culinary library. Daily one-hour cooking demonstrations begin at 1:30 and 3:30, with an extra class at 10:30 on weekend mornings. ⊠ *2555 Main St.* ☎ *800/333–9242* ⊕ *www.ciachef.edu* 🖼 *Free, demonstrations $12.50* ☉ *Restaurant Sun.–Thurs. 11:30–9, Fri. and Sat. 11:30–10; store and museum daily 10–6.*

★ ㉗ Arguably the most beautiful winery in Napa Valley, the 1876 **Beringer Vineyards** is also the oldest continuously operating property. In 1883 Frederick and Jacob Beringer built the Rhine House Mansion, where tastings are held among pieces of Belgian art-nouveau hand-carved oak and walnut furniture and stained-glass windows. The introductory tour departs every hour. Longer tours and seminars on special topics such as wine-and-cheese pairings occur occasionally. ⊠ *2000 Main St., at Rte. 29* ☎ *707/963–4812* ⊕ *www.beringer.com* 🖼 *Tasting and tour $5–$30* ☉ *May 24–Oct. 26, daily 10–6; Oct. 27–May 23, daily 10–5; tours daily every hr 10–4.*

㉙ **Freemark Abbey Winery** was originally called the Tychson Winery, after Josephine Tychson, the first woman to establish a winery in California. It has long been known for its cabernets, whose grapes come from the fertile Rutherford Bench. All other wines are estate grown, including a much-touted late-harvest riesling. ⊠ *3022 St. Helena Hwy. N, at Rte. 29* ☎ *707/963–9694* ⊕ *www.freemarkabbey.com* 🖼 *Tasting $5* ☉ *Daily 10–5; tours by appointment.*

Where to Stay & Eat

★ $$–$$$ ✕ **Terra.** A romantic, candlelit restaurant housed in an 1888 stone foundry, Terra is especially known for its exquisite Mediterranean-inspired dishes, many with Asian touches. The duck rillettes with Belgian endive, grilled lobster with saffron risotto, and spaghettini with tripe are memorable. Desserts might include a huckleberry *crostata* (tart) with vanilla-bean ice cream. ⊠ *1345 Railroad Ave.* ☎ *707/963–8931* ⚜ *Reservations essential* ▤ *DC, MC, V* ☉ *Closed Tues. No lunch.*

★ $$–$$$ ✕ **Tra Vigne.** A fieldstone building has been transformed into a striking trattoria with a huge wood bar, 30-foot ceilings, and plush banquettes. Homemade mozzarella, dressed with olive oil and vinegar, and house-cured pancetta and prosciutto are preludes to rustic Tuscan specialties such as oak-grilled rabbit with fava beans. The outdoor courtyard in summer and fall is a sun-splashed Mediterranean vision of striped umbrellas and awnings, crowded café tables, and rustic pots overflowing with flowers. ⊠ *1050 Charter Oak Ave., east of Rte. 29* ☎ *707/963–4444* ⌕ *Reservations essential* ⊟ *D, DC, MC, V.*

$$–$$$ ✕ **Wine Spectator Greystone Restaurant.** The Culinary Institute of America runs this place in the handsome old Christian Brothers Winery. Century-old stone walls house a large and bustling restaurant, with cooking, baking, and grilling stations in full view. The menu has a Mediterranean spirit and emphasizes locally grown produce. Typical main courses include crispy striped bass with braised leeks and winter-vegetable potpie. ⊠ *2555 Main St.* ☎ *707/967–1010* ⊟ *AE, D, DC, MC, V.*

$$$$ ⊞ **Meadowood Resort.** Secluded at the end of a semiprivate road, this 256-acre resort has accommodations in a rambling country lodge and several bungalows. You need never leave the luxurious confines of the resort, where you can indulge in golf, tennis, hiking, fitness classes, and other sporty activities as well as an array of spa treatments. The elegant dining room ($$$$), open at dinner only, specializes in California Wine Country cooking. Seating is also available outdoors on a terrace overlooking the golf course. The Grill ($–$$), a less formal restaurant, serves a lighter menu of pizzas and spa food. ⊠ *900 Meadowood La., 94574* ☎ *707/963–3646 or 800/458–8080* 🖷 *707/963–5863* ⊕ *www.meadowood.com* ⌕ *40 rooms, 45 suites* ⌕ *2 restaurants, room service, in-room data ports, refrigerators, cable TV, 9-hole golf course, 7 tennis courts, 2 pools, health club, hot tub, massage, sauna, steam room, croquet, hiking, bar, concierge, business services, meeting rooms; no smoking* ⊟ *AE, D, DC, MC, V.*

$$$–$$$$ ⊞ **Harvest Inn.** Most rooms in this Tudor-esque inn on lushly landscaped grounds have wet bars, antique furnishings, and fireplaces. Some of the rooms are housed in cottages scattered around 8 acres. Pets are allowed in two rooms for a $75 fee. Complimentary breakfast is served in the breakfast room and on the patio overlooking the vineyards. ⊠ *1 Main St., 94574* ☎ *707/963–9463 or 800/950–8466* 🖷 *707/963–4402* ⊕ *www.harvestinn.com* ⌕ *51 rooms, 3 suites* ⌕ *Room service, in-room data ports, refrigerators, cable TV, in-room VCRs, 2 pools, 2 hot tubs, wine bar, concierge, meeting rooms, some pets allowed (fee)* ⊟ *AE, D, DC, MC, V* ⌕ *CP.*

$$$–$$$$ ⊞ **Wine Country Inn.** A pastoral landscape of hills surrounds this peaceful New England–style retreat. Rooms are filled with comfortable country-style furniture, and many have a wood-burning fireplace, a private hot tub, or a patio or deck overlooking the vineyards. A hearty country breakfast is served buffet-style in the sun-splashed common room. Wine tastings are scheduled in the afternoon. ⊠ *1152 Lodi La., east of Rte. 29, 94574* ☎ *707/963–7077* 🖷 *707/963–9018* ⊕ *www.winecountryinn.com* ⌕ *24 rooms, 5 suites* ⌕ *Refrigerators, pool, hot tub, business services; no room TVs, no smoking* ⊟ *MC, V* ⌕ *BP.*

$–$$$$ ⊞ **El Bonita Motel.** Window boxes and landscaped grounds are some of the pleasant touches at this motel with relatively elegant furnishings. Walls are dressed in muted pastels, and upholstery is floral. Family-friendly pluses include roll-away beds and cribs for a modest extra charge. ⊠ *195 Main St., at Rte. 29, 94574* ☎ *707/963–3216 or 800/541–3284*

🖺 707/963–8838 ⊕ *www.elbonita.com* 🗩 *37 rooms, 4 suites* ⚲ *In-room data ports, kitchenettes, microwaves, refrigerators, cable TV, pool, hot tub, sauna, Internet, business services, some pets allowed (fee); no smoking* ▤ *AE, D, DC, MC, V* ❑ *CP.*

Shopping

Art on Main (✉ 1359 Main St. ☎ 707/963–3350), one of the oldest galleries in the region, sells oils, watercolors, ceramics, and etchings by Northern California artists. The **Campus Store** (✉ Culinary Institute of America, 2555 Main St. ☎ 888/424–2433) is the place to shop for all things related to preparing and cooking food, from chef's pants to fish stock to cutlery. **Dean & Deluca** (✉ 607 St. Helena Hwy. S, at Rte. 29 ☎ 707/967–9980), a branch of the famous Manhattan store, is crammed with everything you need in the kitchen—including terrific produce and deli items—as well as a huge wine selection. Many of the cheeses sold here are produced locally. **I. Wolk Gallery** (✉ 1354 Main St. ☎ 707/963–8800) has works by established and emerging American artists—everything from abstract and contemporary realist paintings to high-quality works on paper and sculpture. **On the Vine** (✉ 1234 Main St. ☎ 707/963–2209) sells wearable art and unique jewelry with food and wine themes. Italian ceramics, tabletop decor, and other high-quality home accessories fill **Vanderbilt & Company** (✉ 1429 Main St. ☎ 707/963–1010), the prettiest store in town. Bargain hunters delight in designer labels like Escada and Donna Karan at the **St. Helena Premier Outlets** (✉ 3111 St. Helena Hwy. N, at Rte. 29 ☎ 707/963–7282) complex, across the street from Freemark Abbey Winery.

Calistoga

3 mi northwest of St. Helena on Rte. 29.

In addition to its wineries, Calistoga is noted for its mineral water, hot mineral springs, mud baths, steam baths, and massages. The Calistoga Hot Springs Resort was founded in 1859 by maverick entrepreneur Sam Brannan, whose ambition was to found "the Saratoga of California." He reputedly tripped up the pronunciation of the phrase at a formal banquet—it came out "Calistoga"—and the name stuck.

㉚ Schramsberg, perched on a wooded knoll on the southeast side of Route 29, is one of Napa's most historic wineries, with caves that were dug by Chinese laborers in 1880. Sparkling wines come in several styles and price ranges. If you want to taste, you must tour first. ✉ *1400 Schramsberg Rd.* ☎ *707/942–4558* ⊕ *www.schramsberg.com* 🍷 *Tasting and tour $20* ☉ *Daily 10–4; tours by appointment.*

It's worth taking a slight detour off the main artery to find the small **㉛ Dutch Henry Winery,** where wines are available only on-site or through mail order. Tastings are held in a working winery, where wine makers explain the process. This is a good place to try cabernet sauvignon and merlot. ✉ *4300 Silverado Trail* ☎ *707/942–5771* ⊕ *www.dutchhenry. com* 🍷 *Tasting $5* ☉ *Daily 10–5.*

㉜ Of the wines produced by **Cuvaison,** 65% are chardonnays, with pinot noir, cabernet sauvignon, and merlot rounding out the choices. Picnic grounds with a view of the valley are shaded by 350-year-old oak trees. ✉ *4550 Silverado Trail* ☎ *707/942–6266* ⊕ *www.cuvaison.com* ✍ *Tasting $8; tour free* ⊗ *Daily 10–5; tours Mon.–Sat. at 10:30.*

❸❸ Sterling Vineyards sits on a hilltop 1 mi south of Calistoga, its pristine white Mediterranean-style buildings reached by an aerial tramway from the valley floor. The view from the tasting room is superb, and the gift shop is one of the best in the valley. ✉ *1111 Dunaweal La., east off Rte. 29* ☎ *707/942–3300* ⊕ *www.sterlingvineyards.com* ✍ *$10, including tramway, self-guided tour, and tasting* ⊗ *Daily 10:30–4:30.*

❸❹ Designed by postmodern architect Michael Graves, the **Clos Pegase** winery is a one-of-a-kind structure packed with unusual art objects from the collection of art-book publisher and owner Jan Shrem. Works of art even appear in the underground wine tunnels. Cheese and other foods are for sale in the visitor center, ready to take to the shady picnic area. ✉ *1060 Dunaweal La., east off Rte. 29* ☎ *707/942–4981* ⊕ *www.clospegase. com* ✍ *Tastings $5–$10* ⊗ *Daily 10:30–5; tours daily at 11 and 2.*

Fodor's Choice
★

❸❺ The **Sharpsteen Museum,** in the center of town, has a magnificent diorama of the Calistoga Hot Springs Resort in its heyday. Other exhibits document the history of the Wappo, the original inhabitants of the area, and the career of Ben Sharpsteen, an animator at the Walt Disney studio. ✉ *1311 Washington St.* ☎ *707/942–5911* ⊕ *www.sharpsteen-museum.org* ✍ *$3 donation* ⊗ *Daily 11–4.*

Indian Springs, an old-time spa, has been pumping out 212°F water from its three geysers since the late 1800s. The place offers some of the best bargains on mud bathing and short massages and has an Olympic-size mineral-water pool. The 16 bungalows ($$$$) range from a studio duplex to a three-bedroom house. Reservations are recommended for spa treatments. ✉ *1712 Lincoln Ave., at Rte. 29* ☎ *707/942–4913* ⊕ *www. indianspringscalistoga.com* ⊗ *Daily 9–8.*

☙ ❸❻ Many families bring children to Calistoga to see **Old Faithful Geyser of California** blast its 60-foot tower of steam and vapor about every 30 minutes. (The frequency is affected by the moon, barometric pressure, tectonic activity, and recent rainfall.) One of just three regularly erupting geysers in the world, it's fed by an underground river that heats to 350°F. The spout usually lasts three minutes. Picnic facilities are available. ✉ *1299 Tubbs La., 1 mi north of Calistoga* ☎ *707/942–6463* ⊕ *www.oldfaithfulgeyser.com* ✍ *$8* ⊗ *Apr.–Sept., daily 9–6; Oct.–Mar., daily 9–5:30.*

❸❼ Château Montelena is a vine-covered stone French château constructed circa 1882 and set amid Chinese-inspired gardens, complete with a man-made lake with gliding swans and islands crowned by Chinese pavilions. Its wines include chardonnays, cabernet sauvignons, and a limited-production riesling. ✉ *1429 Tubbs La.* ☎ *707/942–5105* ⊕ *www. montelena.com* ✍ *Tasting $10* ⊗ *Daily 9:30–4; Mar.–Oct., tours at 9:30, 1:30, and by appointment; Nov.–Feb., call for tour times.*

☙ ❸❽ Robert Louis Stevenson State Park encompasses the summit of **Mount St. Helena.** It was here, in the summer of 1880, in an abandoned bunkhouse of the Silverado Mine, that Stevenson and his bride, Fanny Osbourne, spent their honeymoon. The stay inspired Stevenson's "The Silverado Squatters," and Spyglass Hill in *Treasure Island* is thought to be a portrait of Mount St. Helena. The park's approximately 3,600 acres are mostly undeveloped except for a fire trail leading to the site of the bunkhouse—which is marked with a marble tablet—and to the summit beyond. ⊠ *Rte. 29, 7 mi north of Calistoga* ☎ *707/942–4575* ⊕ *www. parks.ca.gov* 🖃 *Free* ☉ *Daily 8–sunset.*

🐾 ㊴ The **Petrified Forest** contains the remains of the volcanic eruptions of Mount St. Helena 3.4 million years ago. The force of the explosion uprooted the gigantic redwoods, covered them with volcanic ash, and infiltrated the trees with silica and minerals, causing petrifaction. Explore the museum, and then picnic on the grounds. ⊠ *4100 Petrified Forest Rd., 5 mi west of Calistoga* ☎ *707/942–6667* ⊕ *www.petrifiedforest.org* 🖃 *$5* ☉ *Late Apr.–early Sept., daily 9–6; early Sept.–late Apr., daily 9–5.*

Where to Stay & Eat

$$–$$$ ✕ **All Seasons Café.** Bistro cuisine takes a California spin in this sun-filled space, where tables topped with candles and flowers sit upon a black-and-white checkerboard floor. The seasonal menu, which includes homemade breads and dessert, might include organic greens, hand-rolled tagliatelle, pan-seared salmon, or braised lamb shank. Attentive service contributes to the welcoming atmosphere. ⊠ *1400 Lincoln Ave.* ☎ *707/ 942–9111* ▤ *D, MC, V* ☉ *No lunch most Mon.–Wed.; call for additional lunch dates in summer and fall.*

$$–$$$ ✕ **Calistoga Inn Restaurant and Brewery.** A tree-shaded patio on the banks of the Napa River draws diners to a lovely setting where meals are prepared with flair. Lunches are light, focusing on soups, salads, and sandwiches, while hearty main courses include grilled hanger steak with cabernet sauce and braised lamb shank with tapenade. ⊠ *1250 Lincoln Ave.* ☎ *707/942–4101* ▤ *AE, MC, V.*

$–$$$ ✕ **Brannan's.** Arts and Crafts–style lamps cast a warm glow over the booths and tables at Calistoga's best bet for hearty dishes. Look for beef tenderloin, served with garlic mashed potatoes, or roast chicken, served with butternut squash risotto. An attractive, well-stocked bar provides a congenial setting for cocktails or for desserts like chèvre cheesecake with pears and pecans. ⊠ *1374 Lincoln Ave.* ☎ *707/942–2233* ▤ *AE, D, MC, V.*

$–$$$ ✕ **Wappo Bar Bistro.** This colorful restaurant is an adventure in international dining. The menus covers the world, with dishes ranging from tandoori chicken and Thai coconut curry with prawns and vegetables to chiles rellenos and Turkish meze. ⊠ *1226 S. Washington St.* ☎ *707/ 942–4712* ▤ *AE, MC, V* ☉ *Closed Tues. and 1st 2 wks in Dec.*

★ ¢–$$ ✕ **Pacifico Restaurante Mexicano.** At first glance it looks like a Mexican chain restaurant, but be assured, the quality and ingenuity of the food here exceed that of standard franchises. Many choices showcase the regional cuisines of Mexico, such as the sweet and spicy fare of Oaxaca. The chiles rellenos *pacificos* (grilled, cheese-drizzled poblano chilies filled with onions, mushrooms, spinach, and peanuts) make a delicious, inventive dish. Hefty margaritas come in several varieties. ⊠ *1237 Lincoln Ave.* ☎ *707/942–4400* ▤ *MC, V.*

★ **$$$–$$$$** 🏨 **Cottage Grove Inn.** Elm trees shade 16 contemporary, individually decorated cottages. Cozy, skylit rooms come with plush furnishings, as well as wood-burning fireplaces, CD players, extra-deep two-person hot tubs, and porches with wicker rocking chairs. Spas and restaurants are within walking distance. Rates include afternoon wine and cheese. ⊠ *1711 Lincoln Ave., 94515* ☎ *707/942–8400 or 800/799–2284* 🖷 *707/942–2653* ⊕ *www.cottagegrove.com* ➥ *16 rooms* ⚒ *In-room safes, minibars, refrigerators, cable TV, in-room VCRs; no smoking* ▭ *AE, D, DC, MC, V* ⦿ *CP.*

$$–$$$$ 🏨 **Meadowlark Inn and Meadow Guest House.** Twenty hillside acres just north of downtown Calistoga surround this decidedly laid-back and sophisticated inn. The Main House is encircled by a veranda with views of the mountains and meadows, and many rooms here and in the Guest Wing have two-person whirlpool tubs and French doors opening onto a separate deck. The individual guesthouse provides the most seclusion, as well as a high-tech kitchen and a private outdoor sauna and hot tub. The pool and sauna area is clothing-optional. ⊠ *601 Petrified Forest Rd., 94515* ☎ *707/942–5651 or 800/942–5651* 🖷 *707/942–5023* ⊕ *www.meadowlarkinn.com* ➥ *8 rooms* ⚒ *Some refrigerators, cable TV, in-room VCRs, pool, hot tub, sauna, Internet, some pets allowed; no smoking* ▭ *AE, MC, V* ⦿ *BP.*

$–$$$ 🏨 **Mount View Hotel.** A National Historic Landmark, the Mount View conjures up images of Calistoga's 19th-century heyday. A full-service European spa provides state-of-the-art pampering, and three cottages are each equipped with a private redwood deck, whirlpool tub, and wet bar. ⊠ *1457 Lincoln Ave., 94515* ☎ *707/942–6877* 🖷 *707/942–6904* ⊕ *www.mountviewhotel.com* ➥ *20 rooms, 12 suites* ⚒ *Restaurant, some refrigerators, cable TV, pool, hot tub, spa, bar, concierge, Internet; no smoking* ▭ *AE, D, MC, V* ⦿ *CP.*

$–$$ 🏨 **Brannan Cottage Inn.** The pristine Victorian cottage with lacy white fretwork, large windows, and a shady porch is the only one of Sam Brannan's 1860 resort cottages still standing on its original site. Rooms have private entrances, and elegant stenciled friezes of stylized wildflowers cover the walls. ⊠ *109 Wapoo Ave., 94515* ☎ *707/942–4200* ⊕ *www.brannancottageinn.com* ➥ *6 rooms* ⚒ *Refrigerators; no TV in some rooms, no smoking* ▭ *AE, MC, V* ⦿ *BP.*

$–$$ 🏨 **Calistoga Spa Hot Springs.** No-nonsense motel-style rooms have kitchenettes stocked with utensils and coffeemakers, which makes them popular with families and travelers on a budget. The on-site spa includes mineral baths, mud baths, swimming pools, and a hot tub. There's also a supermarket a block away. ⊠ *1006 Washington St., 94515* ☎ *707/942–6269* 🖷 *707/942–4214* ⊕ *www.calistogaspa.com* ➥ *51 rooms, 1 suite* ⚒ *Kitchenettes, cable TV, 2 pools, wading pool, gym, massage, outdoor hot tub, spa, laundry facilities, meeting room; no smoking* ▭ *MC, V.*

Sports & the Outdoors

Getaway Adventures, Inc. (⊠ 1522 Lincoln Dr. ☎ 800/499–2453 ⊕ www.getawayadventures.com) runs kayak and bike tours in Napa and Sonoma. A daily "Sip 'N Cycle" tour brings you to five different area wineries, and includes lunch, for $115.

Shopping

For connoisseurs seeking hard-to-find wines, the **All Seasons Wine Shop** (✉ 1400 Lincoln Ave. ☎ 707/942–6828) is the place to visit. The **Calistoga Wine Stop** (✉ 1458 Lincoln Ave., No. 2 ☎ 707/942–5556), inside California's second-oldest existing train depot, carries more than 1,000 wines. Handcrafted candles are for sale at **Hurd Beeswax Candles** (✉ 3020 St. Helena Hwy. N, at Rte. 29 ☎ 707/963–7211).

THE SONOMA VALLEY

Although the Sonoma Valley may not have quite the cachet of the neighboring Napa Valley, wineries here entice with their unpretentious attitude and smaller crowds. Its name is Miwok for "many moons," but writer Jack London's nickname for the region—Valley of the Moon—is more fitting. The scenic valley, bounded by the Mayacamas Mountains on the east and Sonoma Mountain on the west, extends north from San Pablo Bay nearly 20 mi to the eastern outskirts of Santa Rosa. The varied terrain, soils, and climate (cooler in the south because of the bay influence and hotter toward the north) allow grape growers to raise cool-weather varietals such as chardonnay and pinot noir as well as merlot, cabernet sauvignon, and other heat-seeking vines. The valley is home to dozens of wineries, many of them on or near Route 12, a California Scenic Highway that runs the length of the valley, which is near the Sonoma–Napa county border. In addition to wineries, you can find a few tasting rooms on the historic plaza in the town of Sonoma.

Sonoma

14 mi west of Napa on Rte. 12; 45 mi from San Francisco, north on U.S. 101, east on Rte. 37, and north on Rte. 121/12.

Sonoma is the oldest town in the Wine Country. Its historic town plaza is the site of the last and the northernmost of the 21 missions established by the Franciscan order of Father Junípero Serra. It also includes the largest group of old adobes north of Monterey.

On your way into town from the south, you pass through the Carneros wine district, which straddles the southern sections of Sonoma and Napa counties. Sam Sebastiani, of the famous Sebastiani family, and his

40 wife, Vicki, have established their own hilltop winery, **Viansa,** in the Carneros district. Reminiscent of a Tuscan villa, the winery's ocher-color building is surrounded by olive trees and overlooks the valley. The grapes grown here depart from the traditionally Californian and include Sangiovese, Dolcetto, and Tocai Friulano. The Italian Marketplace on the premises sells delicious specialty sandwiches and salads to complement Viansa's Italian-style wines. The adjacent Wine Country Visitor Center has brochures and information. ✉ *25200 Arnold Dr.* ☎ *707/935–4700* ⊕ *www.viansa.com* 🖃 *Tour free* ☉ *Daily 10–5; tours daily at 11 and 2.*

41 The sparkling and still wines at **Champagne Caves** originated with a 700-year-old stock of Ferrer grapes. The method here is to age the wines in a "cava," or cellar, where several feet of earth maintain a constant temperature—an increasingly popular alternative to temperature-controlled warehouses. Call the day of your visit to confirm that tours will be conducted as scheduled. ⊠ *23555 Carneros Hwy., at Rte. 121* ☎ *707/996–7256* ⊕ *www.gloriaferrer.com* ☒ *Tastings $2–$3, tour free* ☉ *Daily 10:30–5:30; tours daily at noon, 2, and 4.*

㊷ In town, the **Mission San Francisco Solano,** whose chapel and school were used to bring Christianity to the Native Americans, is now a museum with a fine collection of 19th-century watercolors. ⊠ *114 Spain St. E* ☎ *707/938–9560* ☒ *$2, including Sonoma Barracks on the central plaza and Lachryma Montis* ☉ *Daily 10–5.*

㊸ A tree-lined driveway leads to **Lachryma Montis,** which General Mariano G. Vallejo, the last Mexican governor of California, built for his large family in 1852; the state purchased the home in 1933. The Victorian Gothic house, insulated with adobe, represents a blend of Mexican and American cultures. Opulent furnishings, including white-marble fireplaces and a French rosewood piano, are particularly noteworthy. ⊠ *W. Spain St. near 3rd St. E* ☎ *707/938–9559* ☒ *$2; tour free* ☉ *Daily 10–5; tours Friday at 2, weekends at 1 and 2.*

㊹ Originally planted by Franciscans of the Sonoma Mission in 1825, the **Sebastiani Vineyards** were bought by Samuele Sebastiani in 1904. Red wine is king here. ⊠ *389 4th St. E* ☎ *707/938–5532* ⊕ *www.sebastiani. com* ☒ *Tour $5* ☉ *Daily 10–5; tours weekdays at 11 and 3, weekends at 11, 1, and 3.*

㊺ **Buena Vista Carneros Winery** is the oldest continually operating winery in California. It was here, in 1857, that Count Agoston Haraszthy de Mokcsa laid the basis for modern California wine making, bucking the conventional wisdom that vines should be planted on well-watered ground by instead planting on well-drained hillsides. Chinese laborers dug tunnels 100 feet into the hillside, and the limestone they extracted was used to build the main house. The winery, which is surrounded by redwood and eucalyptus trees, has a specialty-foods shop, an art gallery, and picnic areas. The guided tour, which includes a tasting of premium wines, is $15, but the self-guided tour is free. ⊠ *18000 Old Winery Rd., off Napa Rd., follow signs from plaza* ☎ *707/938–1266 or 800/678–8504* ⊕ *www.buenavistawinery.com* ☒ *Tasting fees $5–$10, tour $15* ☉ *Daily 10–5; tours daily at 11 and 2.*

㊻ **Ravenswood,** dug into the mountains like a bunker, is famous for its zinfandel. The merlot should be tasted as well. Tours include barrel tastings of wines in progress in the cellar. ⊠ *18701 Gehricke Rd., off E. Spain St.* ☎ *707/938–1960* ⊕ *www.ravenswood-wine.com* ☒ *Tasting and tour $4* ☉ *Daily 10–5; tours at 10:30 by appointment.*

Where to Stay & Eat

$$–$$$ ✕ **La Salette.** Chef-owner Manny Azevedo, born in the Azores and raised in Sonoma, found culinary inspiration in his travels. The flavors of his dishes, such as prawns with tomato-peanut sauce and coconut rice or salt cod baked with white onions, stand strong while complementing

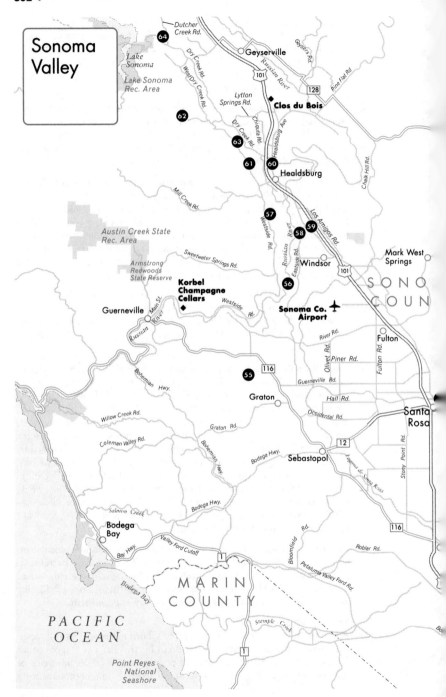

Sonoma
Valley

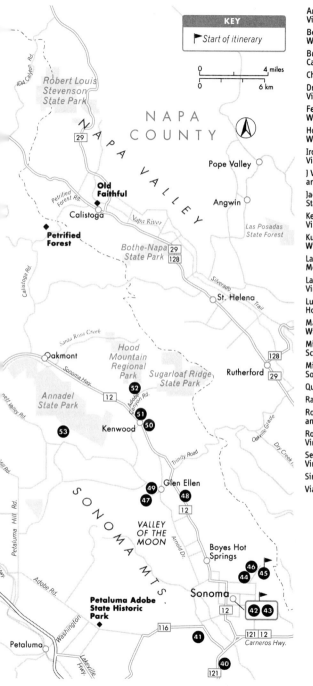

CloseUp

WINE COUNTRY SPAS

THE WINE COUNTRY WAS in the forefront of America's love affair with hot springs, mud baths, and spa treatments. Blessed with natural mineral ash from nearby volcanoes and mineral springs, areas around Calistoga and Sonoma were popular with Native Americans long before the stressed-out white man arrived. Today you can find spas of every stripe throughout the area.

Calistoga Spa Hot Springs is the best choice if you have several hours to lounge around. A house special is "The Works" ($120), a two-hour marathon of mud bath, mineral whirlpool, steam bath, blanket wrap, and massage. If you're booking any treatment, you can pay $5 and get all-day pool access as well. ⊠ 1006 Washington St., Calistoga ☎ 707/942–6269 ⊕ www.calistogaspa.com.

Dr. Wilkinson's is the oldest spa in Calistoga. Best known for its mud baths, it is perhaps the least chic of the bunch. ⊠ 1507 Lincoln Ave., Calistoga ☎ 707/942–4102 ⊕ www.drwilkinson.com.

The **Fairmont Sonoma Mission Inn & Spa** is the best-known sybaritic hot spot in the Wine Country. Arrive at least 45 minutes in advance of your appointment to spend some time in the bathing ritual room. ⊠ 18140 Sonoma Hwy. at Rte. 12, Sonoma ☎ 707/938–9000 ⊕ www.sonomamissioninn.com.

The **Garden Spa at MacArthur Place** has larger-than-life floral murals and the nicest, most expensive gift shop of all the Wine Country spas. The two-hour "Rose Garden" treatment ($199) includes a bath in rose petals, a rose-petal body polish, and an essential oil massage. ⊠ 29 E. MacArthur St., Sonoma ☎ 707/933–3193 ⊕ www.macarthurplace.com.

Health Spa Napa Valley is in a complex shared with an inn and a restaurant. The house specialty is ayurvedic treatments; for an unforgettable experience, book "The Abhyanga" ($180), which is performed by two practitioners. ⊠ 1030 Main St., St. Helena ☎ 707/967–8800 ⊕ www.napavalleyspa.com.

Facilities at **Kenwood Inn & Spa** claim the prettiest spa setting in the Wine Country, thanks to the vineyards across the road and the Mediterranean style of the inn. A specialty is "vinotherapie" treatments, which incorporate the use of grape-seed and grape-vine extracts. ⊠ 10400 Sonoma Hwy. at Rte. 12, Kenwood ☎ 707/833–1293 ⊕ www.kenwoodinn.com.

Lavender Hill Spa is in a country cottage on the edge of town. The nicest treatment rooms are in the rear, with views of the lavender garden. Freestanding bathhouses with two whirlpool tubs make this a particularly good spot for couples. ⊠ 1015 Foothill Blvd., Calistoga ☎ 707/942–4495 ⊕ www.lavenderhillspa.coms.

Lincoln Avenue Spa occupies a 19th-century bank building, a history suggested by elegant woodwork and a tiled steam room. House specialties include mint and green-tea wraps ($65). ⊠ 1339 Lincoln Ave., Calistoga ☎ 707/942–5296 ⊕ www.lincolnavenuespa.com.

The **Mount View Spa** is the most elegant in town; you won't find mud baths here, but it is one of the best places for facials. ⊠ 1457 Lincoln Ave., Calistoga ☎ 707/942–5789 ⊕ www.mountviewspa.com.

Nance's Hot Springs has mud baths, a mineral whirlpool bath, and mineral steam baths. You can find good bargains here if you arrive midweek; a hot mineral bath followed by a half-hour massage costs $55. ⊠ 1614 Lincoln Ave., Calistoga ☎ 707/942–6211.

each other. The variety of ports on the wine list emphasizes Azevedo's Portuguese heritage. Paintings and sculpture enliven the off-white walls in this eatery, which has patio seating for balmy evenings. ✉ *18625 Rte. 12, Boyes Hot Springs* ☎ *707/938–1927* ▭ *AE, MC, V* ⊙ *Closed Mon. and Tues. No lunch.*

$$–$$$ ✕ **Santé.** In the Fairmont Sonoma Mission Inn's formal restaurant, creative fare is served in a dining room that's both rustic (wrought-iron chandeliers) and elegant (Frette table linens). Chef Bruno Tison takes local seasonal ingredients and gives them a twist; foie gras, for instance, might be coupled with a savory flan. Main courses can include thick lamp chops, Muscovy duck breast, or even ostrich. ✉ *Fairmont Sonoma Mission Inn & Spa, 100 Boyes Blvd., 2 mi north of Sonoma, Boyes Hot Springs* ☎ *707/939–2415* ▭ *AE, DC, MC, V* ⊙ *No lunch.*

$–$$$ ✕ **The Girl & the Fig.** This popular restaurant was in Glen Ellen before migrating to the Sonoma Hotel, where it has revitalized the historic barroom with cozy banquettes and inventive French country cuisine. A seasonally changing menu may include something with figs, duck confit with green lentils, steak frites, or Provençale shellfish stew. The wine list is notable for its inclusion of Rhône and other less-common varietals. ✉ *Sonoma Hotel, Sonoma Plaza, 110 W. Spain St.* ☎ *707/938–3634* ▭ *AE, D, DC, MC, V.*

$–$$$ ✕ **Harmony Club.** This stylish, urbane spot has French doors thrown open to Sonoma's main plaza in fair weather and a large fireplace aglow in the evening. Dishes are unusual twists on California cuisine: brie fondue, duck confit with creamy lentils, or pan-roasted quail with grilled tomato polenta, pine nuts, and currants. The extensive wine list includes many choices from the Ledson Winery. Listen to nightly jazz and blues music played on the grand piano. ✉ *480 1st St. E* ☎ *707/996–9779* ▭ *AE, D, MC, V* ⊙ *Closed Tues.*

$$ ✕ **Meritage.** A fortuitous blend of southern French and northern Italian cuisine is the backbone of this restaurant, where chef Carlo Cavallo works wonders with house-made pastas. An oyster bar augments extensive seafood choices, and breakfast is available Wednesday through Sunday. Vegetarians can enjoy a special tasting menu, which can be adapted for vegans. The wine list includes blends from the major players in both Napa and Sonoma. ✉ *522 Broadway* ☎ *707/938–9430* ▭ *AE, MC, V* ⊙ *Closed Tues.*

$–$$ ✕ **The Big 3 Diner.** Overstuffed booths, ceiling fans, and an open kitchen give this corner bistro an informal feel. Country breakfasts, pizza from the wood-burning oven, and hearty American fare such as house-smoked meats are the specialties. The menu also includes several spa-cuisine items. ✉ *Fairmont Sonoma Mission Inn & Spa, 100 Boyes Blvd., at Rte. 12, Boyes Hot Springs* ☎ *707/938–9000* ▭ *AE, DC, MC, V* ⊙ *No dinner.*

$–$$ ✕ **Cafe La Haye.** In a postage-stamp-size kitchen, skillful chefs turn out half a dozen main courses that star on a small but worthwhile menu emphasizing local ingredients. Chicken, beef, pasta, fish, and risotto get deluxe treatment without fuss or fanfare. The offbeat dining room, hung with large, abstract paintings, turns out some of the best food for the price in the Wine Country. ✉ *140 E. Napa St.* ☎ *707/935–5994* ▭ *MC, V* ⊙ *Closed Mon. No dinner Sun., no lunch.*

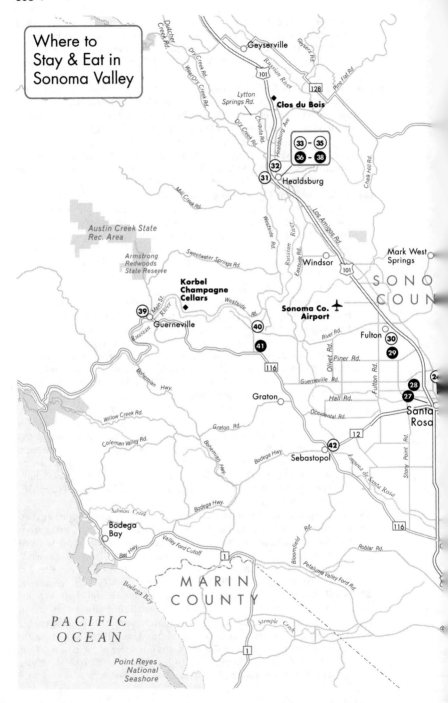

Where to
Stay & Eat in
Sonoma Valley

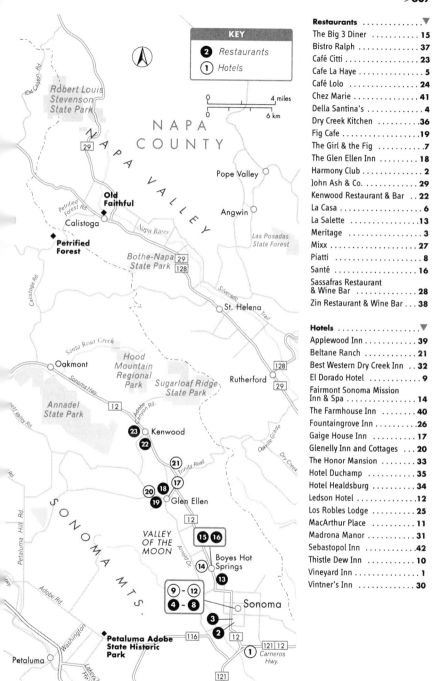

$-$$ ✕ **Della Santina's.** A longtime favorite with a charming, enclosed brick patio out back serves the most authentic Italian food in town. Daily fish and veal specials provide an alternative to other classic northern Italian pastas like linguine with pesto and lasagna Bolognese. Of special note are the gnocchi and, when available, petrale sole and sand dabs. ⊠ *133 E. Napa St.* ☎ *707/935–0576* ⊟ *AE, D, MC, V.*

$-$$ ✕ **Piatti.** A beautiful room opens onto one of the finest patios in the valley at this restaurant, the first in a minichain of trattorias. Pizza from the wood-burning oven and northern Italian specials (spit-roasted chicken, ravioli with spinach-ricotta filling) are served on the terrace or in a rustic space with an open kitchen and pastel images of vegetables on the walls. ⊠ *El Dorado Hotel, 405 1st St. W* ☎ *707/996–2351* ⊟ *AE, MC, V.*

¢-$$ ✕ **La Casa.** Whitewashed stucco and red tiles evoke Old Mexico at this spot around the corner from Sonoma's plaza. There's bar seating, a patio, and an extensive menu of traditional Mexican food: chimichangas and snapper Veracruz (with tomatoes, peppers, onions, and olives) for entrées, sangria for drink, and flan for dessert. The food isn't really the draw here; locals love the casual atmosphere and the margaritas. ⊠ *121 E. Spain St.* ☎ *707/996–3406* ⊟ *AE, D, DC, MC, V* ☉ *Closed Tues. Nov.–Mar.*

$$$$ ⊞ **Ledson Hotel.** This hotel's brickwork and wrought-iron balconies recall an opulent 19th-century home, and its six rooms are lavish in every way. King-size beds, piled high with pillows and silk bedding, sit on beautifully inlaid wooden floors. All rooms have enormous Jacuzzi tubs and balconies; three front rooms overlook Sonoma's main plaza. The only drawback is a somewhat awkward layout, which takes you through the first-floor Harmony Club restaurant on the way to your room. ⊠ *480 1st St. E, 95476* ☎ *707/996–9779* 🖶 *707/996–9776* ⊕ *www.ledsonhotel. com* ⇦ *6 rooms* ⌂ *Restaurant, wine bar, in-room data ports, refrigerators, cable TV, dry cleaning, laundry service; no smoking* ⊟ *AE, D, MC, V* ⎚ *BP.*

$$$$ ⊞ **MacArthur Place.** Chic country colors such as olive and lemon distinguish the accommodations at this sprawling complex. Rooms are in a remodeled historic mansion as well as in contemporary two-story structures tucked into the back of the property. Beyond the extensively landscaped grounds is a full-service spa, adjacent to the pool. ⊠ *29 E. MacArthur St., 95476* ☎ *707/938–2929 or 800/722–1866* 🖶 *707/933–9833* ⊕ *www. macarthurplace.com* ⇦ *35 rooms, 29 suites* ⌂ *Restaurant, room service, in-room data ports, some refrigerators, cable TV, in-room VCRs, pool, gym, hot tub, sauna, spa, croquet, bar, shop, dry cleaning, laundry service, concierge, Internet, business services; no smoking* ⊟ *AE, D, MC, V* ⎚ *CP.*

$$$-$$$$ ⊞ **The Fairmont Sonoma Mission Inn & Spa.** California Mission–style architecture combines with the elegance of a European luxury spa at this beautifully landscaped estate. Though not large, standard rooms are supremely comfortable; some have fireplaces and patios or balconies. The real draw is the 43,000-square-foot spa, where you can enjoy a vast array of treatments. Warm mineral water is pumped from beneath the property to feed the inn's pools. ⊠ *100 Boyes Blvd., at Rte 12, 2 mi north of Sonoma, Boyes Hot Springs 95476* ☎ *707/938–9000* 🖶 *707/*

938–4250 ⊕ *www.sonomamissioninn.com* ⤳ *168 rooms, 60 suites* ⟿ *2 restaurants, room service, in-room data ports, in-room safes, minibars, refrigerators, cable TV, 18-hole golf course, pro shop, 2 pools, fitness classes, gym, hair salon, hot tub, sauna, spa, bicycles, hiking, 2 bars, shops, babysitting, dry cleaning, laundry service, concierge, business services, meeting rooms; no smoking* ⊟ *AE, DC, MC, V.*

\$\$–\$\$\$
Fodor'sChoice
★

🖭 **Thistle Dew Inn.** The public rooms of this turn-of-the-20th-century Victorian home half a block from Sonoma Plaza are filled with collector's-quality Arts and Crafts furnishings. Four have private entrances and decks, and all have queen-size beds with antique quilts and private baths. Some rooms have fireplaces; some have whirlpools. Welcome bonuses include a hot tub and free use of the inn's bicycles. ⊠ *171 W. Spain St., 95476* ☎ *707/938–2909, 800/382–7895 in CA* 🖷 *707/938–2129* ⊕ *www.thistledew.com* ⤳ *5 rooms, 1 suite* ⟿ *In-room data ports, hot tub, bicycles, some pets allowed (fee); no room TVs, no smoking* ⊟ *AE, D, MC, V* ⏀ *BP.*

\$\$
🖭 **El Dorado Hotel.** A modern hotel in a remodeled 1843 building, this place has spare and simply elegant accommodations. Rooms reflect Sonoma's Mission era, with Mexican-tile floors and white walls. The best rooms are Nos. 3 and 4, which have larger balconies that overlook Sonoma Plaza. ⊠ *405 1st St. W, 95476* ☎ *707/996–3030 or 800/289–3031* 🖷 *707/996–3148* ⊕ *www.hoteleldorado.com* ⤳ *26 rooms* ⟿ *Restaurant, room service, in-room data ports, refrigerators, cable TV, in-room VCRs, pool, bar, laundry service, shops; no smoking* ⊟ *AE, MC, V* ⏀ *CP.*

\$–\$\$
🖭 **Vineyard Inn.** Built as a roadside motor court in 1941, this B&B inn with red-tile roofs brings a touch of Mexican village charm to an otherwise lackluster and somewhat noisy location at the junction of two main highways. It's across from two vineyards and is the closest lodging to Sears Point Raceway. Rooms have queen-size beds, and continental breakfast is included. ⊠ *23000 Arnold Dr., at junction of Rtes. 116 and 121, 95476* ☎ *707/938–2350 or 800/359–4667* 🖷 *707/938–2353* ⊕ *www.sonomavineyardinn.com* ⤳ *19 rooms, 3 suites* ⟿ *In-room data ports, cable TV, pool; no smoking* ⊟ *AE, MC, V* ⏀ *CP.*

Nightlife & the Arts

The **Sebastiani Theatre** (⊠ 476 1st St. E ☎ 707/996–2020), on historic Sonoma Square, schedules first-run movies.

Shopping

Sonoma Saveurs (⊠ Sonoma Plaza, 487 1st St. W ☎ 707/996–7007) specializes in foie gras and other local artisanal foods, such as duck rillettes, pancetta, and various pâtés. **Half-Pint** (⊠ Sonoma Plaza, 450 1st St. E ☎ 707/938–1722) carries fashionable clothing and accessories for infants and children. Several shops in the four-block **Sonoma Plaza** (⊠ Between E. Napa and E. Spain Sts. and 1st St. W and 1st St. E) attract food lovers from miles around. The **Sonoma Cheese Factory and Deli** (⊠ Sonoma Plaza, 2 Spain St. ☎ 707/996–1931), run by the same family for four generations, makes Sonoma Jack cheese and the tangy Sonoma Teleme. It has everything you could possibly need for a picnic. **Shushu Fufu** (⊠ Sonoma Plaza, 452 1st St. E ☎ 707/938–3876) is a chic shoe boutique with labels including Cole-Haan and Arche, makers of fine French walking shoes. Glitzy it's not, but the **Total Living Company** (⌂ 5 E. Napa St. ☎ 707/939–3900) is great for full-spectrum lightbulbs, well-designed household utensils, and clever items that make daily life easier.

Glen Ellen

7 mi north of Sonoma on Rte. 12.

Jack London lived in Sonoma Valley for many years. The craggy, quirky, and creek-bisected town of Glen Ellen commemorates him with place-names and nostalgic establishments. In the Jack London Village complex, the **Olive Press** (⌂ 14801 Arnold Dr. ☎ 707/939–8900) not only carries many local olive oils, serving bowls, books, and dining accessories but also presses fruit for a number of local growers, usually in the late fall. You can taste a selection of olive oils that have surprisingly different flavors. Also in the Jack London Village complex, **Jack London Bookstore** (⌂ 14300 Arnold Dr. ☎ 707/996–2888) carries books and memorabilia regarding the namesake author, as well as a quirky selection of used materials. It's closed Tuesday and Wednesday. Built in 1905, the **Jack London Saloon** (⌂ 13740 Arnold Dr. ☎ 707/996–3100 ⊕ www.jacklondonlodge.com) is decorated with London memorabilia.

In the hills above Glen Ellen—known as the Valley of the Moon—lies

47 **Jack London State Historic Park.** The author's South Seas artifacts and other personal effects are on view at the House of Happy Walls museum. The ruins of Wolf House, which London designed and which mysteriously burned down just before he was to move in, are close to the House of Happy Walls. Also restored and open to the public are a few farm outbuildings and the cottage where he lived and wrote. London is buried on the property. ⌂ 2400 London Ranch Rd. ☎ 707/938–5216 ⌂ Parking $5 ⊙ Park Nov.–Mar., daily 9:30–5; Apr.–Oct., daily 9:30–7. Museum daily 10–5.

48 **Arrowood Vineyards** is neither as old nor as famous as some of its neighbors, but wine makers and critics are quite familiar with the excellent, handcrafted wines produced here. The winery's harmonious architecture overlooking the Valley of the Moon earned it an award from the Sonoma Historic Preservation League, and the wine-making equipment is state-of-the-art. A stone fireplace in the tasting rooms makes this an especially enticing destination in winter. The winery has been owned by Robert Mondavi since 2000, but wine maker Richard Arrowood has stayed on. ⌂ 14347 Sonoma Hwy., at Rte. 12 ☎ 707/935–2600 ⊕ www. arrowoodvineyards.com ⌂ Tastings $5–$10, tour $10, includes tasting ⊙ Daily 10–4:30; tours daily at noon.

As you drive along Route 12, you see orchards and rows of vineyards flanked by oak-covered mountain ranges. One of the best-known local

★ **49** wineries is **Benziger Family Winery**, situated on a sprawling estate in a bowl with 360-degree sun exposure. Among the first wineries to identify certain vineyard blocks for particularly desirable flavors, Benziger is noted for its merlot, pinot blanc, chardonnay, and fumé blanc. Tram tours through the vineyards cover everything from regional microclimates and geography to a glimpse of the extensive cave system. Tours depart several times a day, weather permitting. ⊠ *1883 London Ranch Rd.* ☎ *707/935–3000, 888/490–2739 tram-tour schedule* ⊕ *www.benziger. com* ⊠ *Tastings $5–$10; tour $10* ⊗ *Daily 10–4:30.*

Where to Stay & Eat

$$–$$$ ✕ **Glen Ellen Inn Restaurant.** Recommended for romantic evenings, this restaurant adjusts its seafood and pasta offerings according to seasonal availability. Look for braised lamb shank with homemade pasta and seafood risotto. Desserts such as cinnamon-brandy bread pudding are large enough to share. Seats on the covered patio are more attractive than those inside. ⊠ *13670 Arnold Dr.* ☎ *707/996–6409* ▭ *AE, MC, V* ⊗ *No lunch Wed. or Thurs.*

$–$$ ✕ **The Fig Cafe.** Celadon booths, yellow tablecloths, and flowers on each table mean that the latest in the string of Sondra Bernstein's popular Napa Valley restaurants seems summery and airy even in the middle of winter. Artisanal cheeses and charcuterie plates are popular appetizers, while entrées like braised pot roast and grilled hanger steak tend to be hearty. Don't forget to look on the chalkboard for frequently changing desserts, like butterscotch pot de crème. ⊠ *13690 Arnold Dr.* ☎ *707/938–2130* ▭ *AE, D, MC, V* ⊗ *Closed Tues. and Wed. No lunch.*

$$$$
★ **Gaige House Inn.** The comfort of a 19th-century residence blends with contemporary, uncluttered furnishings accented with Asian details at this elegant country inn. Some of the largest accommodations—and the most private—are cottages behind the house, overlooking the pool or Calabazas Creek. Rooms in the main house have their own charm; some have fireplaces, and one opens onto the pool. Another has one of the most glamorous bathrooms in the Wine Country, bigger than many hotel rooms, and with a whirlpool tub and separate shower area more than large enough for two. The green lawn, striped awnings, white umbrellas, and magnolias around the large pool conjure up a manicured Hamptons-like glamour in the midst of rustic Glen Ellen. ⊠ *13540 Arnold Dr., 95442* ☎ *707/935–0237 or 800/935–0237* 🖷 *707/935–6411* ⊕ *www.gaige.com* ⟿ *12 rooms, 3 suites* ⚱ *In-room data ports, some in-room safes, refrigerators, cable TV, pool, hot tub; no smoking* ▭ *AE, D, DC, MC, V* ⍟ *BP.*

$$–$$$$ **Glenelly Inn and Cottages.** On the outskirts of Glen Ellen, this sunny little establishment, built as an inn in 1916, offers all the comforts of home—plus a hot tub in the garden. Rooms, each individually decorated, tend toward a simple country style; many have four-poster beds and floral fabrics. Breakfast is served in front of the common room's cobblestone fireplace, as are local delicacies in the afternoon. Innkeeper Kristi Hallamore Jeppesen has two children of her own, so this is an unusually kid-friendly inn. ⊠ *5131 Warm Springs Rd., 95442* ☎ *707/996–6720* 🖷 *707/996–5227* ⊕ *www.glenelly.com* ⟿ *8 rooms, 2 suites* ⚱ *Some refrigerators, some in-room VCRs, outdoor hot tub, laundry facilities; no a/c in some rooms, no TVs in some rooms, no smoking* ▭ *AE, D, MC, V* ⍟ *BP.*

$–$$$ **Beltane Ranch.** On a slope of the Mayacamas range on the eastern side of the Sonoma Valley lies this 1892 ranch house, which is thought to have been built by Mary Ellen Pleasant, a shrewd San Francisco businesswoman who was the daughter of slaves. The Wood family, who have lived on the premises since 1936, have stocked the comfortable living room with dozens of books about the area. The rooms, furnished with antiques, open onto the building's wraparound porch. The cottage apartment, created out of the gardener's quarters, has a sitting room. ⊠ *11775 Sonoma Hwy., at Rte. 12, 95442* ☎ *707/996–6501* ⊕ *www. beltaneranch.com* ↪ *3 rooms, 3 suites* ♿ *Tennis court, hiking; no a/c, no room TVs* ▭ *No credit cards* ⏐◉⏐ *BP.*

Kenwood

3 mi north of Glen Ellen on Rte. 12.

Kenwood has a historic train depot and several restaurants and shops that specialize in locally produced goods. Its inns, restaurants, and winding roads nestle in soothing bucolic landscapes.

50 **Kunde Estate Winery** lies on 2,000 acres and is managed by the fourth generation of Kunde-family grape growers and wine makers. The standard tour of the grounds includes its extensive caves. A tasting and dining room lies 175 feet below a chardonnay vineyard. Tastings usually include viognier, chardonnay, cabernet sauvignon, and zinfandel. ⊠ *10155 Sonoma Hwy., at Rte. 12,* ☎ *707/833–5501* ⊕ *www.kunde.com* ⊠ *Tastings $5–$10; tour free* ⊙ *Daily 10:30–4:30, tours Fri.–Sun. 11–3.*

51 The beautifully rustic grounds at **Kenwood Vineyards** complement the tasting room and artistic bottle labels. Although Kenwood produces all premium varietals, the winery is best known for its Jack London Vineyard reds—pinot noir, zinfandel, merlot, and a unique Artist Series cabernet. Most weekends the winery offers a free food-and-wine pairing, but there are no tours. ⊠ *9592 Sonoma Hwy., at Rte. 12* ☎ *707/833–5891* ⊕ *www.kenwoodvineyards.com* ⊠ *Tasting free* ⊙ *Daily 10–4:30.*

52 The landscaping and design of **Landmark Vineyards,** established by the heirs of John Deere, are as classical as the winery's wine-making methods. Those methods include two fermentations in French oak barrels and the use of the yeasts present in the skins of the grapes rather than the addition of manufactured yeasts to create the wine. Landmark's chardonnays have been particularly well received, as has the winery's pinot noir. ⊠ *101 Adobe Canyon Rd., off Sonoma Hwy.* ☎ *707/833–1144 or 800/452–6365* ⊕ *www.landmarkwine.com* ⊠ *Tasting free–$10; tour free* ⊙ *Daily 10–4:30; horse-drawn-wagon vineyard tours Apr.–Sept., Sat. 11:30–3:30.*

Where to Eat

$–$$$ ✕ **Kenwood Restaurant & Bar.** One of the enduring favorites in an area known for fine dining, this is where Napa and Sonoma chefs eat on their nights off. You can indulge in California country cuisine in the sunny, South of France–style dining room or head through the French doors to the patio for a memorable view of the vineyards. Dishes might include prawns simmered in a saffron Pernod sauce or beef bourguignon with mashed potatoes. ⊠ *9900 Sonoma Hwy., at Rte. 12* ☎ *707/833–6326* ▭ *MC, V* ⊙ *Closed Mon. and Tues.*

★ ¢–$$ ✕ **Café Citti.** The aroma of garlic envelops the neighborhood whenever the Italian chef-owner is roasting chickens at this homey roadside café. Deli items, hot pastas, and soups make this an excellent budget stop. ⊠ *9049 Sonoma Hwy., at Rte. 12* ☎ *707/833–2690* ▭ *MC, V.*

ELSEWHERE IN SONOMA COUNTY

At nearly 1,598 square mi, Sonoma is far too large a county to cover in one or two days. The landmass extends from San Pablo Bay south to Mendocino County and from the Mayacamas Mountains on the Napa side west to the Pacific Ocean. One of the fastest-growing counties in Northern California, Sonoma is still rather sparsely populated; even the county seat, Santa Rosa, has fewer than 120,000 residents.

Within this varied terrain are hills and valleys, rivers, creeks, lakes, and tidal plains that beg to be explored. Wineries can be found from the cool flatlands of the south to the hot interior valleys to the foggy coastal regions. To be sure, Sonoma offers much more than wine, though the county, with 60,000 acres of vineyards, contributes to the north coast's $4 billion–a–year wine industry. And Sonoma, though less famous than Napa, in fact has more award-winning wines.

In addition to the Sonoma Valley, the major grape-growing appellations include the Alexander and Dry Creek valleys, close to Healdsburg, along with the Russian River Valley to the west of U.S. 101. The last has been gaining an international reputation for its pinot noir, which thrives in the valley climate cooled by the presence of morning and evening fog.

Guerneville, a popular summer destination for gays and lesbians, and neighboring Forestville are in the heart of the Russian River Valley. Dozens of small, winding roads and myriad wineries make this region a delight to explore, as do small towns such as Occidental.

After meandering westward for miles, the Russian River arrives at its destination at Jenner, one of several towns on Sonoma's 62 mi of coastline. A number of state beaches offer tide-pooling and fishing. Although less dramatic than the beaches on the far north coast, those along Sonoma's coast offer cooling summer winds and plenty of restaurants serving ocean-fresh seafood.

Santa Rosa

8 mi northwest of Kenwood on Rte. 12.

Santa Rosa is the Wine Country's largest city and a good bet for moderately priced hotel rooms, especially for those who have not reserved in advance.

★ ⑤ **Matanzas Creek Winery** specializes in three varietals—sauvignon blanc, merlot, and chardonnay—and makes a hard-to-find sparkling wine. All three varietals have won glowing reviews from various magazines. Huge windows in the visitor center overlook a field of 3,100 tiered and fragrant lavender plants. Acres and acres of gardens planted with unusual grasses and plants from all over the world have caught the attention of horticulturists. After you taste the wines, ask for the self-guided garden-tour book before taking a stroll. ✉ *6097 Bennett Valley Rd.* ☎ *707/ 528–6464 or 800/590–6464* ⊕ *www.matanzascreek.com* 🍷 *Tasting $5; tour free* ⊙ *Daily 10–4:30; tours weekdays at 10:30 and 3, weekends at 10:30, by appointment.*

❺❹ The **Luther Burbank Home and Gardens** commemorates the great botanist who lived and worked on these grounds for 50 years, single-handedly developing the modern techniques of hybridization. Arriving as a young man from New England, he wrote: "I firmly believe . . . that this is the chosen spot of all the earth, as far as nature is concerned." The Santa Rosa plum, Shasta daisy, and lily of the Nile agapanthus are among the 800 or so plants he developed or improved. In the music room of his house, a Webster's dictionary of 1946 lies open to a page on which the verb "burbank" is defined as "to modify and improve plant life." ✉ *Santa Rosa and Sonoma Aves.* ☎ *707/524–5445* ⊕ *www.lutherburbank.org* 🍷 *Gardens free, guided tour of house and greenhouse $4, audio garden tour $3* ⊙ *Gardens daily 8–dusk; tours Apr.–Oct., Tues.–Sun. 10–3:30.*

Where to Stay & Eat

$$–$$$ ✕ **John Ash & Co.** Patio seating, views out over vineyards, and a cozy indoor fireplace make this slightly formal restaurant a draw on both summer and winter evenings. The California cuisine incorporates a bit of France, Italy, and even Asia, but the ingredients are largely local: Hog Island oysters come from Tomales Bay, and the goat cheese in the ravioli comes from Laura Chenel, local cheese maker extraordinaire. Entrées may include Dungeness crab cakes or pan-seared ahi tuna. The wine list is impressive even by Wine Country standards. A café menu offers bites between meals. ✉ *4330 Barnes Rd., River Rd. exit west from U.S. 101* ☎ *707/527–7687* ▭ *AE, D, DC, MC, V* ⊙ *No lunch Sat.*

$$–$$$ ✕ **Mixx.** Great service and an eclectic mix of dishes made with locally grown ingredients define this small restaurant with large windows, high ceilings, and Italian blown-glass chandeliers. House-made ravioli, grilled Cajun prawns, and grilled leg of lamb are among the favorites of the many regulars, and the kids' menu makes it a favorite with families. The frequently changing wine list includes more than a dozen choices by the glass. ✉ *135 4th St., at Davis St., behind mall on Railroad Sq.* ☎ *707/ 573–1344* ▭ *AE, D, MC, V* ⊙ *Closed Sun.*

★ $–$$$ ✕ **Café Lolo.** This small, sophisticated spot is the territory of chef and co-owner Michael Quigley, who has single-handedly made downtown Santa Rosa a culinary destination. His dishes stress fresh ingredients and an eye for presentation. Popular choices include seared scallops with butternut-squash risotto and penne with sausage and pecorino. ✉ *620 5th St.* ☎ *707/576–7822* ▭ *AE, MC, V* ⊙ *Closed Sun. No lunch Sat.*

$–$$ ✕ **Sassafras Restaurant & Wine Bar.** Chef Jack Mitchell changes the modern American menu here frequently to reflect what's fresh at the market. The wine list is heavy on California vintages but also includes Canadian and East Coast labels. Dishes that sound familiar get a contemporary twist: pizza is topped with spicy shrimp and cilantro pesto, and quail is served with pinto beans and mole. ✉ *1229 N. Dutton Ave.* ☎ *707/578–7600* ▭ *AE, D, DC, MC, V* ⊙ *No lunch weekends.*

$$$-$$$$ 🖼 **Vintner's Inn.** Set on 50 acres of vineyards, this French provincial inn has large rooms, many with wood-burning fireplaces, and a trellised sundeck. Breakfast is complimentary, and the nearby John Ash & Co. restaurant is tempting for other meals. Discount passes to an affiliated health club are available. ⊠ *4350 Barnes Rd., River Rd. exit west from U.S. 101, 95403* ☎ *707/575–7350 or 800/421–2584* 🖶 *707/575–1426* ⊕ *www.vintnersinn.com* ⤵ *38 rooms, 6 suites* ⚐ *Restaurant, room service, in-room data ports, in-room safes, minibars, refrigerators, cable TV, hot tub, lounge, dry cleaning, laundry service, concierge, business services, meeting room; no smoking* ▭ *AE, D, DC, MC, V* ⧘⧘ *BP.*

★ **$-$$** 🖼 **Fountaingrove Inn.** A redwood sculpture and a wall of cascading water distinguish the lobby at this elegant, comfortable hotel and conference center. A refined restaurant and bar has piano music and a stellar menu. For an additional fee you have access to a nearby 18-hole golf course, a tennis court, and a health club. ⊠ *101 Fountaingrove Pkwy., near U.S. 101, 95403* ☎ *707/578–6101 or 800/222–6101* 🖶 *707/544–3126* ⊕ *www.fountaingroveinn.com* ⤵ *88 rooms, 36 suites* ⚐ *Restaurant, room service, in-room data ports, refrigerators, cable TV, golf privileges, pool, hot tub, piano bar, dry cleaning, laundry service, Internet, business services, meeting rooms, some pets allowed (fee), no-smoking rooms* ▭ *AE, D, DC, MC, V* ⧘⧘ *CP.*

¢–$ 🖼 **Los Robles Lodge.** The pleasant, relaxed motel overlooks a pool that's set into a grassy landscape. Some rooms have whirlpools, while others allow pets. ⊠ *1985 Cleveland Ave., Steele La. exit west from U.S. 101, 95401* ☎ *707/545–6330 or 800/255–6330* 🖶 *707/575–5826* ⊕ *www.losrobleslodge.com* ⤵ *104 rooms* ⚐ *Restaurant, coffee shop, in-room data ports, in-room safes, some microwaves, refrigerators, cable TV with movies, pool, wading pool, hot tub, gym, sauna, bar, laundry facilities, business services, some pets allowed (fee), no-smoking rooms* ▭ *AE, D, DC, MC, V.*

Nightlife & the Arts

The **Luther Burbank Center for the Arts** (⊠ 50 Mark West Springs Rd. ☎ 707/546–3600) presents concerts, plays, and other performances by locally and internationally known artists. For symphony, ballet, and other live theater performances throughout the year, call the **Spreckels Performing Arts Center** (⊠ 5409 Snyder La. ☎ 707/588–3434) in Rohnert Park.

Russian River Valley

5 mi northwest of Santa Rosa.

The Russian River flows all the way from Mendocino to the Pacific Ocean, but in terms of wine making, the Russian River Valley is centered on a triangle with points at Healdsburg, Guerneville, and Sebastopol. Tall redwoods shade many of the two-lane roads that access this scenic area, where, thanks to the cooling marine influence, pinot noir and chardonnay are the king and queen of grapes. For a free map of the area, contact **Russian River Wine Road** (📮 Box 46, Healdsburg 95448 ☎ 800/723–6336 ⊕ www.wineroad.com).

58 Of the 225 acres of Russian River Vineyards belonging to **J Vineyards and Winery,** 150 are planted with pinot noir grapes. Since the wine makers here believe that wine should be experienced with food, your tasting fee brings you a flight of four wines, each matched with two bites of hors d'oeuvres. Dry sparkling wines are a specialty. ⊠ *11447 Old Redwood Hwy.* ☎ *707/431–3646* 🍷 *Tasting $10* ⊕ *www.jwine.com* ☉ *Daily 11–5.*

55 Tucked into Green Valley, **Iron Horse Vineyards** is equally successful at making still wine as it is the sparkling type. Three hundred acres of rolling, vine-covered hills seem a world away from the much more developed Napa Valley. Tours are available by appointment on weekdays. ⊠ *9786 Ross Station Rd., near Sebastopol* ☎ *707/887–1507* ⊕ *www. ironhorsevineyards.com* 🍷 *Tours $5* ☉ *Daily 10:30–3:30.*

56 **Rochioli Vineyards and Winery** claims one of the prettiest picnic sites in the area, with tables overlooking vineyards. The winery makes one of the county's best chardonnays but is especially known for its pinot noir and sauvignon blanc. ⊠ *6192 Westside Rd.* ☎ *707/433–2305* ☉ *Feb.–Oct., daily 10–5; Nov.–Jan., daily 11–4.*

★ **57** At **Hop Kiln Winery,** you can easily spot the triple towers of the old hop kiln, a California state historical landmark. One of the friendliest wineries in the Russian River area, Hop Kiln has a vast tasting room steps away from a duck pond where you can picnic. This is a good place to try light wines such as riesling or A Thousand Flowers (a fruity gewürztraminer blend), but be sure to try some of the big-bodied reds as well. ⊠ *6050 Westside Rd., Healdsburg* ☎ *707/433–6491* ⊕ *www. hopkilnwinery.com* 🍷 *Tasting free* ☉ *Daily 10–5.*

59 Old Vine zinfandel, along with chardonnay and pinot noir, is top of the line at **Rodney Strong Vineyards.** A walkway around the tasting room provides views of the tanks and barrels below, and placards explain the history of the winery and the art of making casks. Picnic areas overlook the vineyards. ⊠ *11455 Old Redwood Hwy.* ☎ *707/433–6511* ⊕ *www. rodneystrong.com* 🍷 *Tasting and tour free* ☉ *Daily 10–5; tours daily at 11 and 3.*

off the beaten path

KORBEL CHAMPAGNE CELLARS – To be called champagne, a wine must be made in the French region of Champagne or it's just sparkling wine. But despite the objections of the French, champagne has entered the lexicon of California wine makers, and many refer to their sparkling wines as champagne. Whatever you call it, Korbel produces a tasty, reasonably priced wine as well as its own beer, which is available at a brewpub on the premises. The wine tour, one of the best in Sonoma County, clearly explains the process of making sparkling wine. The winery's 19th-century buildings and gorgeous rose gardens are a delight in their own right. ⊠ *13250 River Rd., Guerneville* ☎ *707/824–7000* ⊕ *www.korbel.com* 🍷 *Tasting and tour free* ☉ *Oct.–Apr., daily 9–4:30; May–Sept., daily 9–5; tours on the hr 10–3.*

Where to Stay & Eat

$–$$ ✕**Chez Marie.** It took a New Orleans chef to turn this tiny restaurant into a California auberge. Forestville is light on places to eat, so Chez Marie fills up with locals familiar with the rustic French specialties, such as cassoulet and *ris de veau* (veal sweetbreads). Desserts tend to reflect the chef's New Orleans heritage; look for pecan pie in addition to crème brûlée. ⊠ *6675 Front St., Forestville* ☎ *707/887–7503* ☾ *Closed Mon. and Tues. No lunch.*

★ **$$–$$$$** ▣ **Applewood Inn.** On a knoll in the shelter of towering redwoods, this hybrid inn has two distinct types of accommodations. Those in the original Belden House are comfortable but modest in scale. Most of the 10 accommodations in the newer buildings are larger and airier. The buildings cluster around a Mediterranean-style courtyard complete with gurgling fountains. Cooking classes are available at an on-site cooking school, La Buona Forchetta. ⊠ *13555 Rte. 116, Guerneville 95421* ☎ *707/869–9093 or 800/555–8509* ⊟ *707/869–9170* ⊕ *www. applewoodinn.com* ⤴ *19 rooms* ⟆ *Restaurant, in-room data ports, cable TV, pool, outdoor hot tub; no a/c in some rooms, no smoking* ▱ *AE, MC, V* ⦿*❙ BP.*

$$–$$$ ▣ **The Farmhouse Inn.** Deluxe accommodations in an 1873 farmhouse have featherbeds, wood-burning fireplaces, and private saunas. The restaurant ($$$), open for dinner Thursday through Sunday, relies largely on seasonal local products and fresh seafood. A meeting room and efficient staff make it a good place to mix business and pleasure. ⊠ *7871 River Rd., Forestville 95436* ☎ *707/887–3300 or 800/464–6642* ⊟ *707/887–3311* ⊕ *www.farmhouseinn.com* ⤴ *6 rooms, 2 suites* ⟆ *Restaurant, refrigerators, pool, massage, sauna, boccie, croquet, concierge, meeting rooms; no room TVs, no smoking* ▱ *AE, D, DC, MC, V* ⦿*❙ BP.*

$–$$ ▣ **Sebastopol Inn.** Simple but stylish rooms in a California country style are tucked behind a historic train station; some have views over a wetlands preserve. The offbeat coffeehouse Coffee Catz, on the property, is convenient for light meals. ⊠ *6751 Sebastopol Ave., Sebastopol 95472* ☎ *707/829–2500* ⊟ *707/823–1535* ⊕ *www.sebastopolinn.com* ⤴ *29 rooms, 2 suites* ⟆ *Coffee shop, in-room data ports, microwaves, refrigerators, cable TV, pool, hot tub, spa, dry cleaning, laundry facilities, laundry service; no smoking* ▱ *AE, D, DC, MC, V.*

Healdsburg

17 mi north of Santa Rosa on U.S. 101.

The countryside around Dry Creek Valley and Healdsburg is a fantasy of pastoral bliss—beautifully overgrown and in constant repose. Alongside the relatively untrafficked roads, country stores offer just-plucked fruits and vine-ripened tomatoes. Wineries here are barely visible, tucked behind groves of eucalyptus or hidden high on fog-shrouded hills.

Healdsburg itself is centered on a fragrant plaza surrounded by shady trees, upscale antiques shops, spas, and restaurants. A whitewashed bandstand is the venue for free summer concerts, where the music ranges from jazz to bluegrass.

Where to Stay & Eat

$$–$$$ ✕ **Zin Restaurant and Wine Bar.** Concrete walls and floors, large canvases on the walls, and servers in jeans and white shirts give the restaurant a casual, industrial, and slightly artsy feel. The American cuisine—such as grilled hanger steak with Gruyère-potato gnocchi and wild mushrooms, or the red beans and rice with andouille sausage—is hearty and highly seasoned. True to the restaurant's name, the wine list includes dozens of zinfandels, including half a dozen by the glass. ⊠ *344 Center St.* ☎ *707/ 473–0946* ▱ *AE, MC, V.*

$–$$$ ✕ **Bistro Ralph.** Ralph Tingle has discovered a formula for success with his California home-style cuisine, serving up a small menu that changes weekly. Typical dishes include peppered filet mignon with a brandy reduction and sautéed salmon with fava beans. The stark industrial space includes a stunning wine rack of graceful curves fashioned in metal and wood. Take a seat at the bar and chat with the locals, who love this place just as much as out-of-towners do. ⊠ *109 Plaza St., off Healdsburg Ave.* ☎ *707/433–1380* ▱ *MC, V* ☉ *Closed Sun.*

★ $$$$ ✕▥ **Hotel Healdsburg.** The green facade of this three-story luxury hotel blends nicely with Healdburg's elegant town plaza, across the street. The attention to detail is striking, from the sleek, modern decor to the six-foot-long bathtubs, the Frette bathrobes, and the wide, uncarpeted hallways. The attached restaurant, Dry Creek Kitchen, serves celebrity chef Charlie Palmer's cuisine in an elegant and subdued setting. ⊠ *25 Matheson St., 95448* ☎ *707/431–2800 or 800/889–7188* ⊕ *707/431–0414* ⊕ *www.hotelhealdsburg.com* ⥽ *49 rooms, 6 suites* △ *Restaurant, room service, in-room data ports, refrigerators, cable TV, in-room VCRs, pool, gym, hot tub, spa, bar, dry cleaning, laundry service, concierge, Internet, meeting rooms, no-smoking rooms* ▱ *AE, D, DC, MC, V* ⊚ *CP.*

$$$–$$$$ ▥ **The Honor Mansion.** Each room is unique at this photogenic 1883 Italianate Victorian. Rooms in the main house preserve a sense of the building's Victorian heritage, whereas the larger suites out back are comparatively understated. Luxurious touches such as lovely antiques and featherbeds are found in every room, and suites have the added advantage of private outdoor hot tubs and a deck. ⊠ *14891 Grove St., 95448* ☎ *707/433–4277 or 800/554–4667* ⊕ *707/431–7173* ⊕ *www. honormansion.com* ⥽ *5 rooms, 8 suites* △ *In-room data ports, refrigerators, cable TV, some in-room VCRs, putting green, tennis court, pool, hot tub, basketball, boccie, shop* ▱ *AE, MC, V* ☉ *Closed 1 wk around Christmas* ⊚ *BP.*

★ $$$–$$$$ ▥ **Hotel Duchamp.** Six identical, freestanding villas are archetypes of spare design, with concrete floors, white walls, and furniture composed strictly of right angles. Luxe lily-white bedding keeps the rooms from feeling spartan, as do CD players loaded with groovy global dance music. Bathrooms decked out in stainless steel and white tile have showers that could fit four and have just as many showerheads. The four cottages named after artists are larger and less minimalist, with mostly mid-century furniture and quirky, artsy touches. ⊠ *421 Foss St.* ☎ *707/431– 1300 or 800/431–9341* ⊕ *707/431–1333* ⊕ *www.duchamphotel.com* ⥽ *8 rooms, 2 suites* △ *In-room data ports, in-room safes, minibars, refrigerators, cable TV, in-room VCRs, pool, hot tub, wine bar, some pets allowed (fee); no smoking* ▱ *AE, MC, V* ⊚ *CP.*

$$$–$$$$ 🛏 **Madrona Manor.** The oldest continuously operating inn in the area, this 1881 Victorian mansion, surrounded by 8 acres of wooded and landscaped grounds, is straight out of a storybook. Sleep in the splendid three-story mansion, the carriage house, or one of two separate cottages. Romantic candlelight dinners are served in the dining room Wednesday through Sunday, and there's jazz on the veranda on Saturday evenings from May through July, plus on Friday from August through October. ⊠ *1001 Westside Rd., central Healdsburg exit off U.S. 101 and then left on Mill St., 95448* ☎ *707/433–4231 or 800/258–4003* 🖷 *707/433–0703* ⊕ *www.madronamanor.com* 🛏 *17 rooms, 6 suites* ⚘ *Restaurant, in-room data ports, pool, bar, meeting rooms; no room TVs, no smoking* ⊟ *MC, V* ❅ *BP.*

Shopping

Oakville Grocery (⊠ 124 Matheson St. ☎ 707/433–3200) has a bustling Healdsburg branch filled with wine, condiments, and deli items. A terrace with ample seating makes a good place for an impromptu picnic. For a good novel, children's literature, and books on interior design and gardening, head to **Levin & Company** (⊠ 306 Center St. ☎ 707/433–1118), which also stocks a lot of CDs and tapes and has a small art gallery upstairs. **Tip Top Liquor Warehouse** (⊠ 90 Dry Creek Rd. ☎ 707/431–0841) has a large selection of local wines, including some hard-to-find labels.

Every Saturday morning from early May through November, Healdsburg locals gather at the open-air **Farmers' Market** (⊠ North Plaza parking lot, North and Vine Sts. ☎ 707/431–1956) to pick up supplies from local producers of vegetables, fruits, flowers, cheeses, and olive oils. An additional market takes place Tuesday 4–6:30 PM from June through October.

Dry Creek & Alexander Valleys

On the west side of U.S. 101, Dry Creek Valley remains one of the least-developed appellations in Sonoma. Zinfandel grapes flourish on the benchlands, whereas the gravelly, well-drained soil of the valley floor is better known for chardonnay and, in the north, sauvignon blanc. The wineries in this region tend to be smaller and clustered in bunches.

The Alexander Valley, which lies east of Healdsburg, has a number of family-owned wineries. Most can be found right on Highway 28, which runs through this scenic, diverse region where zinfandel and chardonnay grow particularly well.

Giuseppe and Pietro Simi, two brothers from Italy, began growing ⑥⓪ grapes in Sonoma in 1876. Though the operations at **Simi Winery**, in the Alexander Valley, are strictly high-tech these days, the winery's tree-studded entrance area and stone buildings recall a more genteel era. The tour highlights the winery's rich history. ⊠ *16275 Healdsburg Ave., Dry Creek Rd. exit off U.S. 101* ☎ *707/433–6981* ⊕ *www.simiwinery.com* 🍷 *Tastings $5–$10; tour $3* ⊙ *Daily 10–5. Tours Feb.–Nov., daily at 11, 1, and 3; Dec.–Jan., daily at 11 and 2.*

⑥① **Dry Creek Vineyard,** whose fumé blanc is an industry benchmark, is also earning notice for its reds, especially zinfandels and cabernets. Picnic beneath the flowering magnolias and soaring redwoods. ⊠ *3770 Lam-*

bert Bridge Rd. ☎ 707/433–1000 ⊕ *www.drycreekvineyard.com* ☜ *Tastings free–$5* ☉ *Daily 10:30–4:30; tours by appointment.*

62 Housed in a California Mission–style complex off the main drag, **Michel-Schlumberger** produces ultrapremium wines including chardonnay, merlot, and pinot blanc, but its reputation is based on the exquisite cabernet sauvignon. ⊠ *4155 Wine Creek Rd.* ☎ 707/433–7427 or 800/447–3060 ⊕ *www.michelschlumberger.com* ☜ *Tasting and tour free* ☉ *Tastings and tours at 11 and 2, by appointment.*

63 An unassuming winery in a wood–and–cinder block barn, **Quivira** produces some of the most interesting wines in Dry Creek Valley. Though it is known for its exquisitely balanced and fruity zinfandel, it also makes a superb blend of red varietals called Dry Creek Cuvée. Redwood and olive trees shade the picnic area. ⊠ *4900 W. Dry Creek Rd.* ☎ 707/431–8333 ⊕ *www.quivirawine.com* ☜ *Tasting and tour free* ☉ *Daily 11–5; tours by appointment.*

Noted for its beautiful Italian villa–style winery and visitor center (the breezy courtyard is covered with just about every kind of flower imag-
64 inable), **Ferrari-Carano Winery** produces chardonnays, fumé blancs, and merlots. Tours take you between the rows of grapevines right into the vineyards themselves. ⊠ *8761 Dry Creek Rd., Dry Creek Valley* ☎ 707/433–6700 ⊕ *www.ferrari-carano.com* ☜ *Tasting $3; tour free* ☉ *Daily 10–5; tours Mon.–Sat. at 10 AM, by appointment.*

> **off the beaten path**
>
> **CLOS DU BOIS** – Some of the best wines from Clos du Bois, 5 mi north of Healdsburg on Route 116, are made from the relatively unusual purple-black Malbec grapes. Aged in oak barrels for 20 months, the wine goes well with rich meat dishes. Other standout wines include the reserve cabernet sauvignons and merlots. ⊠ *19410 Geyserville Ave., Geyserville* ☎ 707/857–3100 or 800/222–3189 ⊕ *www.closdubois.com* ☜ *Tasting $5* ☉ *Daily 10–4:30. No tours.*

Where to Stay

$–$$ ☷ **Best Western Dry Creek Inn.** Continental breakfast and a bottle of wine are complimentary at this three-story Spanish Mission–style motel. Midweek discounts are available. A casual family restaurant is next door. Deluxe rooms are slightly more spacious and muted in color than the standard rooms. ⊠ *198 Dry Creek Rd., 95448* ☎ 707/433–0300 or 800/222–5784 ☎ 707/433–1129 ⊕ *www.drycreekinn.com* ⇲ *103 rooms* ☖ *Restaurant, in-room data ports, refrigerators, cable TV, pool, hot tub, laundry facilities, some pets allowed (fee), no-smoking rooms* ⊟ *AE, D, DC, MC, V* ⏀ *CP.*

WINE COUNTRY A TO Z

To research prices, get advice from other travelers, and book travel arrangements, visit www.fodors.com.

BUS TRAVEL

Greyhound runs buses from the Transbay Terminal at 1st and Mission streets in San Francisco to Sonoma, Napa, Santa Rosa, and Healdsburg.

Sonoma County Area Transit offers daily bus service to points all over the county. VINE (Valley Intracity Neighborhood Express) provides bus service within the city of Napa and between other Napa Valley towns. **🔁 Greyhound** 🕿 800/231-2222. **Sonoma County Area Transit** 🕿 707/576-7433 or 800/345-7433. **VINE** (Valley Intracity Neighborhood Express) 🕿 707/255-7631.

CAR TRAVEL

Although traffic on the two-lane country roads can be heavy, the best way to get around the sprawling Wine Country is by private car.

From San Francisco, cross the Golden Gate Bridge, and then go north on U.S. 101, east on Route 37, and north and east on Route 121. For Sonoma wineries, head north at Route 12; for Napa, turn left (to the northwest) when Route 121 runs into Route 29.

From Berkeley and other East Bay towns, take Interstate 80 north to Route 37 west to Route 29 north, which will take you directly up the middle of the Napa Valley. To reach Sonoma County, take Route 121 west off Route 29 south of Napa (the city). From points north of the Wine Country, take U.S. 101 south to Geyserville and take Route 128 southeast to Calistoga and Route 29. Most Sonoma County wine regions are clearly marked and accessible off U.S. 101; to reach the Sonoma Valley, take Route 12 east from Santa Rosa.

LODGING

🔁 Bed & Breakfast Association of Sonoma Valley ✉ 3250 Trinity Rd., Glen Ellen 95442 🕿 707/938-9513 or 800/969-4667 ⊕ www.sonomabb.com. **The Wine Country Inns of Sonoma County** 🕿 800/946-3268 ⊕ www.winecountryinns.com.

TOURS

Full-day guided tours of the Wine Country usually include lunch and cost about $55–$72 per person. The guides, some of whom are winery owners themselves, know the area well and may show you some lesser-known cellars. Reservations are usually required.

Gray Line (✉ 350 8th St., San Francisco 94103 🕿 415/558–9400) has buses that tour the Wine Country. **Great Pacific Tour Co.** (✉ 518 Octavia St., Civic Center, San Francisco 94102 🕿 415/626–4499 ⊕ www.greatpacifictour.com) operates full-day tours of Napa and Sonoma, including a restaurant or picnic lunch, in passenger vans that seat 14. **HMS Travels Food and Wine Trail** (✉ 707-A 4th St., Santa Rosa 95404 🕿 707/526–2922 or 800/367–5348) runs customized tours of the Wine Country for six or more people, by appointment only. The **Napa Valley Wine Train** (✉ 1275 McKinstry St., Napa 94559 🕿 707/253–2111 or 800/427–4124 ⊕ www.winetrain.com) allows you to enjoy lunch, dinner, or weekend brunch on one of several restored 1915–17 Pullman railroad cars that run between Napa and St. Helena. Prices range from $69.50 for brunch and $75 for lunch to $85 for dinner. Special gourmet events and murder-mystery packages are more expensive. In winter service is sometimes limited to Thursday through Sunday; call ahead.

HOT-AIR BALLOONING For views of the ocean coast, the Russian River, and San Francisco on a clear day, Above the Wine Country operates out of Santa Rosa, although many flights actually originate outside Healdsburg. The cost is $195 per person, including a champagne brunch. Balloons Above the Valley is a reliable organization; rides are $185 per person, including a champagne brunch after the flight. Bonaventura Balloon Company schedules early-morning flights (exact times vary) out of Calistoga or, depending on weather conditions, St. Helena, Oakville, or Rutherford. The company's deluxe balloon flight ($198–$220 per person, depending on optional activities) may include a picnic or a breakfast at the Meadowood Resort. Pilots are well versed in Napa Valley lore. Napa Valley Balloons charges $185 per person, including a picnic brunch.

Above the Wine Country 707/829-9850 or 888/238-6359 www.balloontours.com. **Balloons Above the Valley** Box 3838, Napa 94558 707/253-2222, 800/464-6824 in CA www.balloonrides.com. **Bonaventura Balloon Company** 707/944-2822 www.bonaventuraballoons.com. **Napa Valley Balloons** Box 2860, Yountville 94599 707/944-0228, 800/253-2224 in CA www.napavalleyballoons.com.

VISITOR INFORMATION

Napa Valley Conference and Visitors Bureau 1310 Napa Town Center, Napa 94559 707/226-7459 www.napavalley.com. **Sonoma County Tourism Program** 520 Mendocino Ave., Suite 210, Santa Rosa 95401 707/565-5383 or 800/576-6662 www.sonomacounty.com. **Sonoma Valley Visitors Bureau** 453 1st St. E, Sonoma 95476 707/996-1090 www.sonomavalley.com.

THE NORTH COAST

FROM MUIR BEACH TO CRESCENT CITY

(14)

Updated by
Denise M.
Leto, Lisa
Trottier & John
A. Vlahides

THE 386 MILES between San Francisco Bay and the Oregon state line is a land of spectacular scenery, secret beaches, and uncrowded national, state, and local parks. Migrating whales and other sea mammals swim within sight of the dramatic bluffs that make the shoreline north of San Francisco one of the most photographed landscapes in the country. The area is also historically rich, having been the home of the Native American Miwok and Pomo tribes, Russian fur traders, Hispanic settlers, and more contemporary fishing folk and loggers. All have left visible legacies.

In between lonely stretches of cypress- and redwood-studded highway, it's a pleasant surprise to find small, funky towns—many of which contain art galleries, small inns, and imaginative restaurants whose menus highlight locally grown produce. Only a handful of towns in this sparsely populated region have more than 1,000 inhabitants.

About the Restaurants

Despite its small population, the North Coast lays claim to several well-regarded restaurants. Seafood is abundant, as are locally grown vegetables and herbs. In general, dining options are more varied near the coast than inland. Dress is usually informal, though dressy casual is the norm at some of the pricier establishments listed.

About the Hotels

Restored Victorians, rustic lodges, country inns, and chic hotels are among the accommodations available along the North Coast. Hardly any have air-conditioning (the ocean breezes make it unnecessary), and many have no phones or TVs. In several towns there are only one or two places to spend the night; some of these lodgings are destinations in themselves. Make summer and weekend B&B reservations as far ahead as possible—rooms at the best inns often sell out months in advance. In winter you're likely to find reduced rates and nearly empty inns and bed-and-breakfasts. For some of the area's most noteworthy lodging options, check out ⊕ www.uniquenorthwestinns.com.

WHAT IT COSTS				
$$$$	**$$$**	**$$**	**$**	**¢**
RESTAURANTS over $30	$23–$30	$16–$22	$10–$15	under $10
HOTELS over $250	$176–$250	$121–$175	$90–$120	under $90

Restaurant prices are for a main course at dinner, excluding sales tax of 7¼% (depending on location). Hotel prices are for two people in a standard double room in high season, excluding service charges and 8%–10% tax.

Exploring the North Coast

Exploring the Northern California coast is easiest by car. Highway 1 is a beautiful if sometimes slow and nerve-racking drive. You should stop frequently to appreciate the views, and there are many portions of the highway along which you can't drive faster than 20–40 mph. You can still have a fine trip even if you don't have much time, but be realistic and don't plan to drive too far in one day. The itineraries below proceed north from Marin County, just north of San Francisco.

Numbers in the text correspond to numbers on the North Coast maps.

If you have
3 days

Some of the finest redwoods in California are found less than 20 mi north of San Francisco in **Muir Woods National Monument** ❶ ▶. After walking through the woods, stop for an early lunch in Inverness (on Sir Francis Drake Boulevard, northwest from Highway 1) or continue on Highway 1 to **Fort Ross State Historic Park** ❼. Catch the sunset and stay the night in ⌕ **Gualala** ❿. On Day 2 drive to ⌕ **Mendocino** ⓮. Spend the next day and a half browsing in the many galleries and shops and visiting the historic sites, beaches, and parks of this cliff-side enclave. Return to San Francisco via Highway 1, or the quicker (3½ hours, versus up to 5) and less winding route of Highway 128 east (off Highway 1 at the Navarro River, 10 mi south of Mendocino) to U.S. 101 south.

14

If you have
7 days

Early on your first day, walk through **Muir Woods National Monument** ❶ ▶. Then visit **Stinson Beach** ❷ for a walk on the shore and lunch. In springtime and early summer head north on Highway 1 to Bolinas Lagoon, where you can see birds nesting at Audubon Canyon Ranch. At other times of the year (or after you've visited the ranch) continue north on Highway 1. One-third of a mile beyond Olema, look for a sign marking the turnoff for the Bear Valley Visitor Center, the gateway to the **Point Reyes National Seashore** ❸. Tour the reconstructed Miwok village near the visitor center. Spend the night in nearby Inverness or one of the other coastal Marin County towns. The next day stop at Goat Rock State Beach and **Fort Ross State Historic Park** ❼ on the way to ⌕ **Mendocino** ⓮. On your third morning head toward **Fort Bragg** ⓯ for a visit to the Mendocino Coast Botanical Gardens. If you're in the mood to splurge, drive inland on Highway 1 to U.S. 101 north and spend the night at the Benbow Inn in ⌕ **Garberville** ⓰. Otherwise, linger in the Mendocino area and drive inland the next morning. On Day 4 continue north through parts of **Humboldt Redwoods State Park** ⓱, including the Avenue of the Giants. Stop for the night in the Victorian village of ⌕ **Ferndale** ⓲ and visit the cemetery and the Ferndale Museum. On Day 5 drive to ⌕ **Eureka** ⓳. Have lunch in Old Town, visit the shops, and get a feel for local marine life on a Humboldt Bay cruise. Begin Day 6 by driving to **Patrick's Point State Park** ㉒ to enjoy stunning views of the Pacific from a point high above the surf. Have a late lunch overlooking the harbor in **Trinidad** ㉑ before returning to Eureka for the night. Return to San Francisco on Day 7. The drive back takes six hours on U.S. 101; it's nearly twice as long if you take Highway 1.

Timing
The North Coast is a year-round destination, though when you go determines what you will see. The migration of the Pacific gray whales is a wintertime phenomenon, which lasts roughly from mid-December to early April. In July and August views are often obscured by fog. The coastal climate is quite similar to San Francisco's, although winter nights are colder than in the city.

MARIN COUNTY

Much of the beautiful Marin County coastline is less than an hour from San Francisco, but its pristine landscapes can make you feel far from urban life. You can easily visit most of the sights here, especially those in the southern coastal area, by taking day trips from the city.

Muir Woods National Monument

★ ❶ *12 mi northwest of the Golden Gate Bridge.*

The 550 acres of Muir Woods National Monument contain some of the most majestic redwoods in the world—some nearly 250 feet tall and 1,000 years old. The stand of old-growth *Sequoia sempervirens* became one of the country's first national monuments in 1905; environmental naturalist John Muir, for whom the site was named, declared it "the best tree lover's monument that could be found in all of the forests of the world."

The hiking trails here vary in difficulty and distance. One of the easiest is the 2-mi, wheelchair-accessible **loop trail,** which crosses streams and passes ferns and azaleas, as well as magnificent redwood groves. The most popular are **Bohemian Grove** and the circular formation called **Cathedral Grove,** where crowds of tourists can often be heard oohing and aahing in several languages. If you prefer a little more serenity, consider the challenging **Dipsea Trail,** which climbs west from the forest floor to soothing views of the ocean and the Golden Gate Bridge.

The weather in Muir Woods is usually cool and often wet, so wear warm clothes and shoes appropriate for damp trails. Picnicking and camping aren't allowed, and pets aren't permitted. Parking can be difficult here—the lots are small and the crowds are large—so try to come early in the morning or late in the afternoon. The **Muir Woods Visitor Center** has a wide selection of books and exhibits on redwood trees and the history of Muir Woods.

To get here from San Francisco, take U.S. 101 north across the Golden Gate Bridge to the Mill Valley–Stinson Beach exit and then follow signs to Highway 1 north. ⊠ *Panoramic Hwy. off Hwy. 1* ☎ *415/388–2595* ⊕ *www.nps.gov/muwo* ✉ *$3* ☉ *Daily 8 AM–sunset.*

off the beaten path

Small but scenic, **Muir Beach,** a rocky patch of shoreline off Route 1 in the northern headlands, is a good place to stretch your legs and gaze out at the Pacific. Locals often walk their dogs here, and anglers and boogie boarders share the gentle surf. At one end of the strand is a cluster of waterfront homes, and at the other are the bluffs of Golden Gate National Recreation Area.

Where to Stay & Eat

$$$ 🍽 **Pelican Inn.** With a fireplace nearly wherever you look, the Pelican is the coziest place in southern Marin. Although the building was erected in the 1980s, it feels like a centuries-old farmhouse transplanted from

Beaches The waters of the Pacific Ocean along the North Coast are fine for seals, but most humans find the temperatures downright arctic. When it comes to spectacular cliffs and seascapes, though, the North Coast beaches are second to none. You can explore tidal pools, watch sea birds and sea lions, or dive for abalone—and you'll often have the beach all to yourself. South to north, Stinson Beach, Limantour Beach (at Point Reyes National Seashore), the beaches in Manchester and Van Damme state parks, and the 10-mi strand in MacKerricher State Park are among the most notable.

14

Fishing Depending on the season, you can fish for rockfish, salmon, and steelhead in rivers such as Gualala and Smith, and in lakes such as those in MacKerricher State Park. Deep-sea charters leave from Fort Bragg, Eureka, and elsewhere for ocean fishing. There's particularly good abalone diving around Jenner, Fort Ross, Point Arena, Westport, and Trinidad.

Whale-Watching From any number of excellent observation points along the coast, you can watch gray whales during their annual winter migration season (mid-December to early April). In summer and fall, you can see blue or humpback whales. Point Reyes Lighthouse, Gualala Point Regional Park, Point Arena Lighthouse, and Patrick's Point State Park are just a few of the places where you stand a good chance of spotting one of the giant sea creatures. Whale-watching cruises also operate out of several towns, including Bodega Bay and Fort Bragg.

---

the English countryside. Rooms are romantic and plush, many with canopy beds and pretty views. The downstairs lounge is a lovely place to read or sip tea. The restaurant is equally quaint—especially the dining room, housed in a conservatory—but the food is heavy, hit-or-miss English fare. A better bet is chocolate cake, Guinness, and a game of darts in the small pub. ⊠ *10 Pacific Way, off Rte. 1, Muir Beach 94965* ☎ *415/383–6000* 🖨 *415/383–3424* ⊕ *www.pelicaninn.com* ☞ *7 rooms* ⚐ *Restaurant, pub; no a/c, no room phones, no room TVs* ⊟ *MC, V* ⏀ *BP.*

Stinson Beach

❷ *20 mi northwest of Golden Gate Bridge.*

Stinson Beach is the most expansive strand of sand in Marin County. It's as close (when the fog hasn't rolled in) as you'll get to the stereotypical feel of a Southern California beach. On any hot summer weekend every road to Stinson Beach is jam-packed, so factor this into your plans.

Where to Stay & Eat

$–$$ ✕ **Parkside Cafe.** Most people know the Parkside for its beachfront snack bar, but inside is the best restaurant in Stinson Beach. The food is classic Cal cuisine, with lots of goat cheese and seasonal ingredients.

Breakfast—a more traditional spread of pancakes, omelets, and the like—is a favorite among locals. The sunny patio, less of a "scene" than elsewhere in town, is sheltered by vines to keep down the wind. (If you can't stop for a full meal, consider an ultrathick milk shake from the snack bar.) ⊠ *43 Arenal Ave.* ☎ *415/868–1272* ▭ *D, MC, V.*

¢–$$ ✕ **Sand Dollar.** The oldest restaurant in town still attracts all the old salts from Muir Beach to Bolinas, but these days they sip whiskey over an up-to-date bar or on the spiffy deck. The food is good—mainly familiar ingredients combined imaginatively, such as salmon crusted with anchos—but the real draw is the lively atmosphere. Musicians play here every once in a while, and sunny afternoons find the deck so full that people sip beer while sitting on the railings. ⊠ *3458 Rte. 1* ☎ *415/868–0434* ▭ *AE, MC, V.*

¢–$$$ ▥ **Stinson Beach Motel.** Built in the 1930s, this motel is meticulously maintained. Everything is immaculate: freshly painted walls, good mattresses, and lovely gardens. The motel is on the main drag, so it's convenient to everything in town, but it can get loud on busy summer weekend days. Weekday room rates ($85–$125) are a bargain for the north coast. ⊠ *3416 Hwy. 1, 94970* ☎ *415/868–1712* 🖶 *415/868–1790* ⊕ *www.stinsonbeachmotel.com* ⇆ *7 rooms* ⌂ *Some kitchenettes, cable TV; no a/c, no room phones* ▭ *D, MC, V.*

---

en route | Audubon Canyon Ranch, a 1,000-acre wildlife sanctuary along the Bolinas Lagoon, gets the most traffic during late spring, when great blue herons and egrets nest in the trees covering the hillside. It's a spectacular sight, these large birds in white and gray dotting the tops of the evergreens. Quiet trails through the rest of the preserve offer tremendous vistas of the Bolinas Lagoon and Stinson Beach and fabulous birding. Access to these areas is available only on guided nature walks, well worth it if you can get a space. A small museum, open all year, surveys the region's geology and natural history. ⊠ *4900 Rte. 1, between Stinson Beach and Bolinas* ☎ *415/868–9244* ⊕ *www.egret.org* 🎟 *$10 suggested donation* ⊙ *Mid-Mar.–mid-July, weekends 10–4; and by appointment.*

Point Reyes National Seashore

❸ *Approximately 35 mi north of the Golden Gate Bridge.*

Fodor's Choice
★

One of the Bay Area's most spectacular treasures and the only national seashore on the West Coast, the 66,500-acre **Point Reyes National Seashore** (⊕ www.nps.gov/pore) encompasses hiking trails, secluded beaches, and rugged grasslands as well as **Point Reyes**, a triangular peninsula that juts into the Pacific.

When explorer Sir Francis Drake sailed along the California coast in 1579, he missed the Golden Gate and San Francisco Bay, but he did land at what he described as a convenient harbor, now thought to be Drake's Bay, which flanks the point on the east. Today Point Reyes's hills and dramatic cliffs attract other kinds of explorers: hikers, whale-watchers, and solitude seekers.

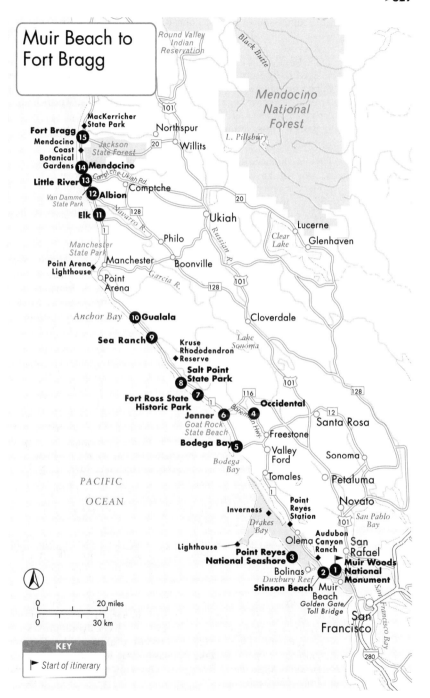

Muir Beach to Fort Bragg

Fort Bragg ⑮
MacKerricher State Park
Northspur
Mendocino Coast Botanical Gardens ⑭ **Mendocino**
Jackson State Forest
101
20
Willits
L. Pillsbury
Mendocino National Forest
Round Valley Indian Reservation
Black Butte

Little River ⑬
Comptche-Ukiah Rd.
Comptche
Albion ⑫
Van Damme State Park
Elk ⑪
Navarro R.
128
Ukiah
20
Lucerne
Glenhaven
Clear Lake

Philo
Russian R.

Manchester State Park
Manchester
Boonville
Garcia R.
101
128
Point Arena Lighthouse
Point Arena

Anchor Bay ⑩ **Gualala**
Cloverdale
Lake Sonoma

Sea Ranch ⑨
Kruse Rhododendron Reserve
Salt Point State Park
⑧
⑦ **Fort Ross State Historic Park**
Jenner ⑥
116
Occidental
Goat Rock State Beach
④
12
Santa Rosa
128

Bodega Bay ⑤
Bohemian Hwy
Freestone
Valley Ford
Sonoma

Bodega Bay
Tomales
Petaluma

PACIFIC OCEAN

Point Reyes Station
Inverness
Drakes Bay
Novato
San Pablo Bay
101

Audubon Canyon Ranch
Olema
San Rafael
Lighthouse
Point Reyes National Seashore ③
Muir Woods National Monument
Bolinas
② ①
Duxbury Reef
Stinson Beach
Muir Beach
Golden Gate Toll Bridge
San Francisco Bay
San Francisco
280

0   20 miles
0   30 km

KEY
▶ *Start of itinerary*

In the southernmost part of Point Reyes National Seashore, accessed through Bolinas, is the free **Point Reyes Bird Observatory** (PRBO; ✉ Mesa Rd. ☎ 415/868–0655 ⊕ www.prbo.org). Those not interested in birds might find it ho-hum, but birders adore it. The visitor center, open daily sunrise–5 PM, is small yet has excellent interpretive exhibits, including a comparative display of real birds' talons. What really warrants a visit, though, are the surrounding woods, which harbor nearly 225 bird species. As you hike the quiet trails through forest and along ocean cliffs, you're likely to see biologists banding birds to aid in the study of their life cycles.

Mile-long **Duxbury Reef** is the largest shale intertidal reef in North America. Look for starfish, barnacles, sea anemones, purple urchins, limpets, sea mussels, and the occasional abalone. But check a tide table (⊕ www.wrh.noaa.gov/Monterey/marine.html) if you plan to explore the reef—it's accessible only at low tide. To get here, take Mesa Road and turn left onto Overlook Drive and then right on Elm Avenue.

The **Bear Valley Visitor Center** (✉ Bear Valley Rd. west of Rte. 1 ☎ 415/464–5100), open weekdays 9–5 and weekends 8–5, has informative exhibits about the park wildlife. Rangers here dispense information about beaches, whale-watching, hiking trails, and camping. A ½-mi path from the visitor center leads to **Kule Loklo,** a brilliantly reconstructed Miwok village that sheds light on the daily lives of the region's first inhabitants. From here, trails also lead to the park's free campgrounds (camping permits are required).

The **Point Reyes Lighthouse** (✉ Western end of Sir Francis Drake Blvd. ☎ 415/669–1534 ☉ Thurs.–Mon. 10–4:30, except in very windy weather), in operation since December 1, 1870, is one of the premier attractions of the Point Reyes National Seashore. It occupies the tip of Point Reyes, 22 mi from the Bear Valley Visitor Center, a scenic 45-minute drive over hills scattered with old cattle ranches. On busy whale-watching weekends (late December through March), parking at the forged-iron-plate lighthouse may be restricted by park staff; on these days buses shuttle visitors to the top of the stairs leading down to the lighthouse (bus $5, admission free). Once there, consider whether you have it in you to walk down—and up—the 308 steps to the lighthouse. The view from the bottom is worth the effort, but the whales are visible from the cliffs above the lighthouse.

In late winter and spring, wildlife enthusiasts should make a stop at **Chimney Rock,** just before the lighthouse, and take the short walk to the Elephant Seal Overlook. Even from up on the cliff, the males look enormous as they spar for the resident females.

You can experience the diversity of Point Reyes's ecosystems on the scenic **Coast Trail,** which starts at the Palomarin Trailhead, just outside Bolinas. From here it's a 3-mi trek through eucalyptus groves and pine forests and along seaside cliffs to beautiful Bass Lake. To reach the Palomarin Trailhead, take Bolinas–Olema Road toward Bolinas, follow signs to the Point Reyes Bird Observatory, and then continue until the road dead-ends.

Where to Stay & Eat

$–$$ ✕ **Station House Cafe.** In good weather hikers fresh from the park fill the adjoining garden to enjoy alfresco dining. The focus is on traditional American food—fresh popovers hit the table as soon as you arrive— and local ingredients dominate the menu. Steamed mussels, grilled salmon, and barbecued oysters are all predictable hits. The place is also open for breakfast. ⊠ *11180 Rte. 1, Point Reyes Station* ☎ *415/663– 1515* ⊟ *D, MC, V.*

¢–$ ✕ **Tomales Bay Foods and Indian Peach Food.** A renovated hay barn off the main drag houses this mecca for gourmands (open until 6 PM). There are three separate businesses here: a stand showcasing local or- ganic fruits and vegetables; a shop selling artisanal cheeses from around the world (including some made in the building, at the famed Cowgirl Creamery); and a kitchen drawing on both of its neighbors' products to create exquisite sandwiches, salads, and soups. You can eat at a café table or on the lawn, but most people take their picnics out to more- scenic spots. ⊠ *80 4th St., Point Reyes Station* ☎ *415/663–9335 cheese shop, 415/663–8478 deli* ⊟ *MC, V* ⊗ *Closed Mon. and Tues.*

¢   ✕ **Café Reyes.** In a triangular, semi-industrial room with glazed concrete floors and ceilings high enough to accommodate several full-size mar- ket umbrellas, you can choose from a variety of Californian, Mexican, and Thai dishes. Baked eggplant-and-goat-cheese torte; baby-back ribs; and burritos with baby-shrimp-and-vegetable stir-fry, ginger sauce, and chutney are dished out with efficiency. A spacious patio accommodates diners on nice days. ⊠ *11101 Rte. 1, Point Reyes Station* ☎ *415/663– 9493* ⊟ *No credit cards.*

¢   ✕ **Priscilla's Café.** This casual eatery in Inverness, a few miles northwest of Point Reyes Station, is a good stop for a quick bite: pizza, sandwiches, salad, pastries, and espresso. ⊠ *12781 Sir Francis Drake Blvd., Inver- ness* ☎ *415/669–1244* ⊟ *AE, MC, V.*

$$$–$$$$ ✕⊡ **Manka's.** Rooms in this 1917 hunting lodge and its cluster of build-
Fodor's Choice   ings are rustic in nature but entirely indulgent, each with some combi-
★   nation of sturdy leather and overstuffed armchairs, mica-cloched lamps, and fireplaces. The Fishing Cabin and Manka's Cabin both have a pri- vate outdoor hot tub and shower. The bayside Boathouse, a short drive away, has a sitting room, kitchen, library, and two bathrooms. The food ($$$$) is spectacular, commonly regarded as among the best in North- ern California. Nearly all ingredients come from within 15 mi of the lodge, so the dinner menu changes daily according to what local farm- ers, fishermen, and foragers offer chef-owner Margaret Grade. Vegetarians, beware: the prix-fixe menus are heavy on the meat. Lunch isn't served, and the restaurant is closed Tuesday and Wednesday (January through March it's open only Friday and Saturday). ⊠ *30 Callendar Way, at Ar- gyll Way, Inverness 94937* ☎ *415/669–1034* ⊕ *www.mankas.com* ⇆ *8 rooms, 1 suite, 4 cabins* ⚿ *Restaurant, some in-room hot tubs; no a/c, no phones in some rooms, no room TVs, no smoking* ⊟ *MC, V* ⊙| *BP.*

$$$–$$$$ ⊡ **Blackthorne Inn.** There's no other inn quite like the Blackthorne, a com- bination of whimsy and sophistication in the woods. The giant tree-house- like structure has spiral staircases, a 3,500-square-foot deck, and a fireman's pole. The solarium was made with timbers from San Francisco wharves, and the outer walls are salvaged doors from a railway station. The best room is aptly named the Eagle's Nest, perched as it is in the glass-sheathed octagonal tower that crowns the inn. ☒ *266 Vallejo Ave., Inverness 94937* ☎ *415/663–8621* ⊕ *www.blackthorneinn. com* ⇆ *3 rooms, 1 suite* ⚐ *Dining room, hot tub; no a/c, no room phones, no room TVs* ⊟ *MC, V* ⦶ *BP.*

$$–$$$ ⊡ **Ten Inverness Way.** This is the kind of place where you sit around after breakfast and share tips for hiking in nearby Point Reyes National Seashore. The living room of this low-key inn has a stone fireplace and library. Some rooms have dormer ceilings with skylights; patchwork quilts, folksy murals, and well-worn antiques are among the homespun touches. Wine and cheese and fresh-baked cookies are nice extras. ☒ *10 Inverness Way, 94937* ☎ *415/669–1648* ⊟ *415/669–7403* ⊕ *www. teninvernessway.com* ⇆ *4 rooms, 1 suite* ⚐ *Dining room, hot tub; no a/c, no room phones, no room TVs* ⊟ *D, MC, V* ⦶ *BP.*

¢ ⊡ **Point Reyes Hostel.** This dorm-style lodging (separate quarters for men and women) in an old clapboard ranch house is a good deal, and it's the only lodge within the Point Reyes National Seashore. A family-size guest room is limited to those with children five and under and must be reserved well in advance. ☒ *Off Limantour Rd., 94956* ☎ *415/663–8811* ⊕ *www.norcalhostels.org* ⇆ *44 beds* ⚐ *Kitchen; no a/c, no room TVs* ⊟ *MC, V.*

CAMPING Within the Point Reyes National Seashore are four hike-in campgrounds in isolated wilderness areas (no dogs allowed) for $12 per night for up to six people. Reservations are essential and can be booked up to three months in advance; to reserve call ☎ 415/663–8054 weekdays between 9 and 2 PM or inquire in person at the Bear Valley Visitor Center. For detailed information about camping, contact the park at ☎ 415/464–5100 or visit www.nps.gov/pore. All sites have barbecue pits, picnic tables, pit toilets, and food-storage lockers; the water isn't potable.

An 8-mi hike from the Bear Valley Visitor Center leads to **Coast Camp,** with 14 oceanfront campsites. **Glenn Camp,** a 5-mi trek from the nearest road, has 12 campsites in a quiet valley. The most popular place for campers to sleep is **Sky Camp,** a 2½-mi hike from the visitor center. It has two group sites and a dozen individual sites. **Wildcat Camp** has seven sites on a bluff that is a rugged 6½-mi trek from the nearest road and a short walk from the ocean.

Sports & the Outdoors

Blue Waters Kayaking (☒ 12938 Sir Francis Drake Blvd., Inverness ☎ 415/669–2600 ⊕ www.bwkayak.com) rents kayaks and offers tours and lessons. **Five Brooks Stables** (☒ 8001 Hwy. 1, Olema ☎ 415/663–1570 ⊕ www.fivebrooks.com) rents horses and equipment. Trails from the stables wind through Point Reyes National Seashore and along the beaches. Rides run from one to six hours and cost $35–$165.

COASTAL SONOMA COUNTY

The gently rolling countryside of coastal Marin gives way to more dramatic sceneray north of Bodega Bay. Cows seem to cling for their lives on the steep inclines surrounding Highway 1—which now curves and winds right along the coast. The stunning vistas and car-commercial hairpin turns make this one of the most exhilarating drives north of San Francisco.

Occidental

❹ *Approximately 67 mi north of San Francisco on Rte. 1*

A village surrounded by the redwood forests, orchards, and vineyards of western Sonoma County, Occidental is so small that you might drive right through the town and barely take notice. A 19th-century logging hub with a present-day bohemian feel, Occidental has a top-notch B&B, good eats, and a handful of art galleries and crafts and clothing boutiques, all of which make the town an ideal base for day trips to Sonoma Coast beaches, Bodega Bay, Armstrong Redwoods Reserve, and Point Reyes National Seashore.

off the
beaten
path

OSMOSIS ENZYME BATH & MASSAGE – The tiny town of Freestone, 3 mi south of Occidental and 7½ mi east of Bodega Bay off Route 12 (Bodega Highway), is famous regionally as the home of the unique Osmosis Enzyme Baths. This spa, in a two-story clapboard house on extensive grounds, specializes in several treatments, including a detoxifying "dry" bath in a blend of enzymes and fragrant wood shavings (which give the entire spa an odd but not unpleasant odor). After 20 minutes in the tub, opt for a 75-minute massage in one of the freestanding Japanese-style pagodas near the creek that runs through the property. ⊠ *209 Bohemian Hwy., Freestone* ☎ *707/823–8231* ✇ *Free with purchase of service* ⊘ *Daily 9–8.*

Where to Stay & Eat

¢–$$ ✕ **Willow Wood Market Café.** About 5 mi east of Occidental in the village of Graton is one of the best-kept secrets in the Wine Country. Tucked among the market merchandise are a number of tables and a counter where casually dressed locals sit down to order freshly made soups and salads or heartier American fare such as a roasted half chicken served with mashed potatoes. ⊠ *9020 Graton Rd., Graton* ☎ *707/522–8372* ⊛ *Reservations not accepted* ☐ *MC, V.*

$$$–$$$$ ▦ **The Inn at Occidental.** Antiques, quilts, original artwork, and folk pieces
Fodor'sChoice fill this colorful and friendly inn. Most guest rooms are spacious and
★ have private patios. Themed rooms—such as the Cirque du Sonoma Room, with a bright yellow-and-red color scheme—brim with personality; others are more sedate but just as comfortable and pleasant. A fireplace and fine Asian rugs create a dignified but laid-back mood in the ground-floor living room of the original house, where guests gather for evening hors d'oeuvres and wine. The two-bedroom Sonoma Cottage, which allows pets for an additional fee, goes for $600 a night. ⊠ *3657 Church St., 95465* ☎ *707/874–1047 or 800/522–6324* ☐ *707/874–1078* ⊕ *www.innatoccidental.com* ↘ *13 rooms, 3 suites* ⚒ *Dining room, in-room data ports, some in-room hot tubs, some refrigerators, Internet, some pets allowed (fee); no room TVs, no smoking* ☐ *AE, D, DC, MC, V* ⍥ *BP.*

Bodega Bay

5 *65 mi north of San Francisco via U.S. 101 and Rte. 1.*

Bodega Bay (where Alfred Hitchcock's *The Birds* takes place) is one of the busiest harbors on the Sonoma County coast. Commercial boats pursue fish as well as the famed Dungeness crabs. T-shirt shops and galleries line both sides of Route 1; a short drive around the harbor leads to the Pacific. This is the last stop, town-wise, before Gualala and is a good spot for stretching your legs and taking in the salt air. For a closer look at Bodega Bay, visit the **Bodega Marine Laboratory** (☎707/875–2211), a 326-acre reserve on nearby Bodega Head. Open Friday from 2 to 4 PM, the lab gives free tours and peeks at intertidal invertebrates, such as sea stars and sea anemones (suggested donation of $2).

Where to Stay & Eat

$$–$$$ ✕⌂ **Inn at the Tides.** The condominium-style buildings at this complex have spacious rooms with high ceilings and an uncluttered look. All rooms have views of the harbor, and some have fireplaces. The inn's two restaurants ($$–$$$$) serve both old-style and more adventurous seafood dishes. Scenes from Alfred Hitchcock's *The Birds* were filmed in one of the inn's restaurants and the adjacent parking lot. ✉ *800 Rte. 1, 94923* ✇ *Box 640* ☎ *707/875–2751 or 800/541–7788* 🖨 *707/875–2669* ⊕ *www.innatthetides.com* ➫ *86 rooms* ⌂ *2 restaurants, room service, cable TV, refrigerators, pool, hot tub, sauna, bar, laundry facilities, meeting rooms; no a/c, no smoking* ▤ *AE, D, MC, V* ◉ *CP.*

$$$–$$$$ ⌂ **Sonoma Coast Villa Inn and Spa.** This secluded oasis in the coastal hills near Bodega Bay is a most unusual inn. Founded as an Arabian-horse ranch in 1976, the 60-acre property has a single-story row of accommodations beside a swimming pool. Red-tile roofs, a stucco exterior, and two courtyards create a European feel. Rooms have slate floors, French doors, beamed ceilings, and wood-burning fireplaces. ✉ *16702 Rte. 1, Bodega 94922* ☎ *707/876–9818 or 888/404–2255* 🖨 *707/876–9856* ⊕ *www.scvilla.com* ➫ *16 rooms* ⌂ *Refrigerators, cable TV, in-room VCRs, putting green, pool, hot tub, spa, billiards, Ping-Pong, meeting rooms; no a/c, no smoking* ▤ *AE, MC, V* ◉ *CP.*

Sports & the Outdoors

Bodega Bay Sportfishing (✉Bay Flat Rd. ☎707/875–3344) charters ocean-fishing boats and rents equipment. The operators of the 400-acre **Chanslor Guest Ranch** (✉2660 Rte. 1 ☎707/875–3333) lead guided horseback rides, some along the beach.

Shopping

The **Ren Brown Collection** (✉ 1781 Rte. 1 ☎ 707/875–2922) at the north end of town is renowned for its selection of Asian arts, crafts, furnishings, and design books. Contemporary Japanese prints are a specialty.

Jenner

6 *10 mi north of Bodega Bay on Rte. 1.*

The Russian River empties into the Pacific Ocean at Jenner. The town has a couple of good restaurants and some shops. South of the Russian

River is windy **Goat Rock State Beach,** where a colony of sea lions (walk north from the parking lot) resides most of the year. The beach, just west of Route 1 about 1 mi south of Jenner, is open daily from 8 AM to sunset; there's no day-use fee.

Where to Eat

★ **$–$$$** ✕ **River's End.** The feeling is rustic rather than refined at this romantic restaurant, where at the right time of year you can view sea lions lazing on the beach below. The creative and sometimes elaborately presented fare, however, belies the cabinlike ambience. Eclectic dishes run the gamut from continental to Indonesian, with seafood dishes a specialty. Open hours sometimes vary, so call to confirm. The owner also rents four rustic cabins and several rooms ($–$$) overlooking the ocean. ⊠ *Rte. 1, north end of Jenner* ☎ *707/865–2484* ▭ *MC, V* ☉ *Closed Tues. and Wed. Apr.–Oct. and Mon.–Thurs. Nov.–Mar.*

Fort Ross State Historic Park

❼ *11 mi north of Jenner on Rte. 1.*

Fort Ross, completed in 1821, became Russia's major fur-trading outpost in California. The Russians brought Aleut sea-otter hunters down from Alaska. By 1841 the area was depleted of seals and otters, and the Russians sold their post to John Sutter, later of gold-rush fame. After a local Anglo rebellion against the Mexicans, the land fell under U.S. domain, becoming part of California in 1850. The state park service has reconstructed Fort Ross, including its Russian Orthodox chapel, a redwood stockade, the officers' barracks, and a blockhouse. The excellent museum here documents the history of the fort and some of the north coast. ⊠ *Rte. 1* ☎ *707/847–3286* ▦ *$4 per vehicle, day use* ☉ *Daily 10–4:30* ☞ *No dogs allowed past parking lot and picnic area.*

Where to Stay

¢–**$$$** ▦ **Fort Ross Lodge.** About 1½ mi north of its namesake fort, this lodge has a wind-bitten feel to it. Some of the rooms have views of the shoreline; others have private hot tubs. Six hill units have saunas, hot tubs, and fireplaces. ⊠ *20705 Rte. 1, 95450* ☎ *707/847–3333 or 800/968–4537* ▧ *707/847–3330* ⊕ *www.fortrosslodge.com* ⊅ *22 rooms* ⚭ *Refrigerators, cable TV, in-room VCRs, hot tub, sauna; no a/c* ▭ *AE, MC, V.*

Sports & the Outdoors

Burke's Canoe Trips (⊠ Mirabel Rd. at River Rd., Forestville ☎ 707/887–1222 ⊕ www.burkescanoetrips.com) rents canoes for cruising down the Russian River; the best time to go is from May through October. Return shuttle service is provided.

Salt Point State Park

★ ❽ *2 mi north of Fort Ross on Hwy. 1.*

Any noise made by other visitors to this 6,000-acre park is washed away by the sound of the surf pounding on the rocky shore. Seals sun themselves at Gerstle Cove, and the surrounding meadows of wild brush host more birds than humans. This is a good place to picnic or let off steam on a long drive. Don't miss the unusual *tafonis*—caverns in the sandstone caused by centuries of erosion by wind and rain—near the park's entrance at Fisk Mill Cove. A five-minute walk uphill from the parking lot leads to a dramatic view of Sentinel Rock, an excellent spot for sunsets. ⊠ *Hwy. 1* ☎ *707/847–3221* ☜ *$4 per vehicle* ☉ *Daily sunrise–sunset.*

Kruse Rhododendron Reserve, a peaceful 317-acre forested park, has thousands of rhododendrons that bloom in light shade in the late spring. ⊠ *Hwy. 1, north of Fisk Mill Cove* ☜ *Free.*

Where to Stay

¢ ⌂ **Stillwater Cove Ranch.** Six miles north of Jenner, this former boys' school overlooking Stillwater Cove has been transformed into a family-oriented lodge. Group accommodations are also available in a bunkhouse and a dairy barn. The grounds are pleasant, with 50 acres of forests and wide lawns traversed by resident peacocks. ⊠ *22555 Hwy. 1, 95450* ☎ *707/847–3227* ⮑ *6 rooms* ▤ *No credit cards.*

⚠ **Salt Point State Park Campgrounds.** There are two excellent campsites in the park. Gerstle Cove campground, on the west side of Highway 1, is set on a wooded hill with some sites overlooking the ocean. Woodside campground offers more trees and protection from the wind; it is on the east side of Highway 1. Woodside is closed December–March 15. Reservations are accepted March–October. ⚕ *Flush toilets, drinking water, fire grates, picnic tables; no pets* ⮑ *Gerstle Cove, 29 sites; Woodside, 79 sites* ⊠ *20705 Hwy. 1, 95450* ☎ *800/444–7275* ☜ *$12.*

Sea Ranch

⑨ *18 mi northwest of Fort Ross on Hwy. 1.*

Sea Ranch is a dramatically positioned development of stylish homes on 5,000 acres overlooking the Pacific. To appease critics, the developers provided public beach-access trails off Highway 1 south of Gualala. Even some militant environmentalists deem the structures designed by William Turnbull and Charles Moore to be reasonably congruent with the surroundings; some folks find the weathered wooden buildings beautiful.

Where to Stay & Eat

$$$–$$$$ ╳⌂ **Sea Ranch Lodge.** High on a bluff with ocean views, the lodge is close to beaches, trails, and golf. Some rooms have fireplaces, while others have hot tubs. Handcrafted wood furnishings and quilts create an earthy yet contemporary look. The restaurant ($$–$$$), which overlooks the Pacific, serves good seafood and homemade desserts. Try the five-course chef's dinner for a special treat. ⊠ *60 Sea Walk Dr., 95497* ☎ *707/785–2371 or 800/732–7262* ⊟ *707/785–2917* ⊕ *www.searanchlodge.com* ⮑ *20 rooms, 2 suites* ⚕ *Restaurant, some in-room TVs, massage, shop, babysitting, concierge, meeting rooms; no smoking* ▤ *AE, MC, V* ¹⊙¹ *BP.*

MENDOCINO COUNTY

The timber industry gave birth to most of the small towns strung along this stretch of the California coastline. Although tourism now drives the economy, the region has retained much of its old-fashioned charm. And the beauty of the coastal landscapes has not changed.

Gualala

⑩ *11 mi north of Sea Ranch on Hwy. 1.*

This former lumber port remains a sleepy drive-through except for the several ocean-view motels, which make serviceable headquarters for exploring the coast. The town lies north of the Gualala River—a good place for fishing. On the Gualala River's Sonoma side, **Gualala Point Regional Park** (⊠ 1 mi south of Gualala on Hwy. 1 ☎ 707/785–2377), open daily from 8 AM until sunset, is an excellent whale-watching spot. The park has picnicking ($3 day-use fee) and camping.

Where to Stay & Eat

$$–$$$ ✕ **Pangaea.** The area's best dinners are found in Pangaea's artsy jewel-colored rooms, where the well-traveled chef serves imaginative seasonal food, such as lavender duck breast, hangar steak, and local-caught salmon. ⊠ *39165 Hwy. 1* ☎ *707/884–9669* ▤ *MC, V* ☉ *No lunch.*

¢–$ ✕ **The Food Company.** "Home-style gourmet" fare is the focus of this café; you can get it to go or served in the sunroom or at picnic tables on the lawn. Picnic-ready prepared foods such as asparagus salad, barbecued pork, and stuffed squash are big sellers. You can also pick up staples like wine, cheese, fresh-baked bread, and the locally famous gingersnap cookies. ⊠ *38411 Hwy. 1, ½ mi north of Gualala* ☎ *707/884–1800* ⊕ *www.thefoodcompanyonline.com* ▤ *MC, V.*

¢–$$$ ✕▥ **St. Orres.** The unexpected sight of two wooden, Russian-style onion domes rising alongside Highway 1 makes this one of the North Coast's most eye-catching inns. Two rooms in the main building have private baths and balconies that overlook the ocean. The other smaller, darker rooms have shared baths and garden views. Cottages, which are set in the tranquil woods behind the inn, feel both rustic and opulent, and have in-room hot tubs and wood-burning stoves. (The newest, best, and priciest is the Black Chanterelle cottage.) You can enjoy a fixed-price dinner ($$$$) served under one of the soaring domes. ⊠ *36601 Hwy. 1, 2 mi north of Gualala, 95445* ☎ *707/884–3303* ▤ *707/ 884–1840* ⊕ *www.saintorres.com* ↬ *8 rooms, 6 with shared bath, 13 cottages* ᕕ *Restaurant, some in-room hot tubs, some kitchenettes, hot tub, sauna, beach; no room phones, no room TVs, no smoking* ▤ *MC, V* ❏ *BP.*

$$–$$$ ▥ **Mar Vista Cottages.** The dozen 1930s cottages at Mar Vista have been beautifully restored over the last few years. Intentionally slim on modern amenities (think no TV, no phone, no radio—not even a clock), the thoughtfully appointed and sparkling clean cottages are big on retro charm: windows are hung with embroidered drapes, coffee percolates on a white enamel stove in the full, if diminutive, kitchen, and straw sun hats hang from hooks, ready for your walk down to Fish Rock Beach. Some have wood-burning or gas stoves. Outside, where benches frame the blustery coastline, you can snip fresh greens from the organic garden for your supper. ⊠ *35101 S. Hwy 1, 5 mi north of Gualala, 95445* ☎ *707/884–3522 or 877/855–3522* ▤ *707/884–4861* ⊕ *www.*

marvistamendocino.com ⤴ *8 1-bedroom cottages, 4 2-bedroom cottages* ⚫ *Kitchens, outdoor hot tub, beach; no room phones, no room TVs* ▤ *AE, MC, V.*

$$–$$$ ⊡ **Old Milano Hotel.** This not-so-old hotel—the original 1905 mansion on the property burned a few years back—is one of the most beautiful sunset spots on the coast. You can stay in one of five modern cottages or a train caboose. Some cottages have spa tubs; four have gas fireplaces. The caboose has a wood-burning stove and brakeman's seats. ✉ *38300 Hwy. 1, 95445* ☎ *707/884–3256* 🖷 *707/884–4249* ⊕ *www.oldmilanohotel.com* ⤴ *5 cottages, 1 caboose* ⚫ *Hot tub; no room TVs* ▤ *MC, V* ⦿*BP.*

¢–$$ ⊡ **Gualala Hotel.** Gualala's oldest hotel, which once housed timber-mill workers, has small, no-nonsense rooms furnished with well-worn antiques. Most rooms share baths, but new owners are talking about a renovation that would change that—call ahead. Rooms in the front have ocean views (and some street noise). The rustic first-floor saloon was a haunt of Jack London's. ✉ *39301 Hwy. 1* ☎ *707/884–1054* 🖷 *707/884–3908* ⊕ *www.gualalahotel.com* ⤴ *19 rooms, 5 with bath* ⚫ *Restaurant, bar; no room TVs* ▤ *AE, D, MC, V.*

⛺ **Gualala Point Regional Park Campground.** Right on the Gualala River, this campground offers both riverfront campsites and others nestled in the giant redwood forest. None have hookups. ⚫ *Flush toilets, drinking water, showers, fire pits* ⤴ *19 drive-in sites, 6 walk-in sites* ✉ *Hwy. 1, 1 mi south of Gualala* ☎ *707/565–2267* ⊕ *www.sonoma-county.org/camping* ⊘ *Year-round* ▱ *$16.*

en route For a dramatic view of the surf and, in winter, migrating whales, take the marked road off Highway 1 north of the fishing village of Point Arena to the **Point Arena Lighthouse** (☎ 707/882–2777). First constructed in 1870, the lighthouse was damaged by the 1906 earthquake that devastated San Francisco. Rebuilt in 1907, it towers 115 feet from its perch above the sea. The lighthouse is open for tours daily from 10 until 3:30, until 4:30 in summer; admission is $5. As you continue north on Highway 1 toward Mendocino, there are several beaches, most notably the one at **Manchester State Park,** 3 mi north of Point Arena.

Elk

⓫ *39 mi north of Gualala on Hwy. 1.*

There's not much happening on the streets of this former timber town, but that's exactly why people love it. The beautiful, rocky coastline is the perfect place for romance or quiet escape.

Where to Stay & Eat

★ **$$$$** ✕ **Inn at Victorian Gardens** Perhaps the most coveted tables on the coast are at this Manchester inn, 13 mi south of Elk, where Tuesday through Sunday Luciano and Pauline Zamboni serve an elaborate multicourse dinner ($150 per couple, including wines) that feels more like an intimate party than a restaurant meal. There are four inn rooms upstairs, which are lovely, but nearly impossible to book; it's a better idea to call a month in advance for a dinner reservation, and stay somewhere else. ⊠ *14409 S. Hwy. 1* ☎ *707/882–3606* ⊕ *www.innatvictoriangardens. com* ☐ *MC, V* ☺ *Closed Mon. No lunch.*

$$$$ ╳⊞ **Harbor House.** Constructed in 1916, this redwood Craftsman-style house is as elegant as its location is rugged. Rooms in the main house are decorated with antiques and have gas fireplaces. The newer cottages are luxurious; each has a fireplace and deck. Your room rate includes breakfast and a four-course dinner (except on weeknights during January and February, when the rates drop drastically). The ocean-view restaurant ($$$$; reservations essential), which serves California cuisine on a prix-fixe menu, is highly recommended; there's limited seating for nonguests. ⊠ *5600 S. Hwy. 1, 95432* ☎ *707/877–3203 or 800/720–7474* ⊕ *www.theharborhouseinn.com* ⊰ *6 rooms, 4 cottages* ♿ *Restaurant; no room TVs, no room phones* ☐ *AE, MC, V* � *MAP.*

★ $$–$$$$ ╳⊞ **Elk Cove Inn.** Perched on a bluff above pounding surf and a driftwood-strewn beach, this property has stunning views from most rooms. A stone-and-cedar-shingle Arts-and-Crafts–style building houses plush spa suites with cathedral ceilings. Spread among four cottages and a grand main house, the older accommodations are each unique and decorated in soothing tones. Suites have stereos and fireplaces; most have wood-burning stoves. The full bar is open daily, and a newly opened restaurant, the Cove, serves dinner. ⊠ *6300 S. Hwy. 1, 95432* ☎ *707/877–3321 or 800/275–2967* ☐ *707/877–1808* ⊕ *www.elkcoveinn.com* ⊰ *7 rooms, 4 suites, 4 cottages* ♿ *Some refrigerators, some in-room hot tubs, spa, beach, bar; no room TVs* ☐ *AE, D, MC, V* 101 *BP.*

Albion

12 *9 mi north of Elk on Hwy. 1.*

A hamlet nestled next to its namesake river, Albion has played host to many visitors—from the original settlers, the Pomo Indians, to Sir Francis Drake in the late 16th century, to Russian fur traders three centuries later. Over the years fires have destroyed most of the town's historical buildings, so the town today is defined by its most recent settlers, many of whom are staunch environmentalists. It is quieter and less touristy than the neighboring towns to the north.

Where to Stay & Eat

$$–$$$ ╳ **Ledford House.** The only thing separating this bluff-top wood-and-glass restaurant from the Pacific Ocean is a great view. Entrées include hearty bistro dishes—stews, cassoulets, and pastas—and large portions of grilled meats and freshly caught fish. ⊠ *3000 N. Hwy. 1* ☎ *707/937–0282* ⊕ *www.ledfordhouse.com* ☐ *AE, DC, MC, V* ☺ *Closed Mon. and Tues. No lunch.*

$$–$$$$ ╳⊞ **Albion River Inn.** Contemporary New England–style cottages at this inn overlook the dramatic bridge and seascape where the Albion River empties into the Pacific. All but two have decks facing the ocean. Six have spa tubs with ocean views; all have fireplaces. The traditional, homey rooms are filled with antiques; at the glassed-in restaurant ($$–$$$), the grilled meats and fresh seafood are as captivating as the views. ⊠ *3790*

N. Hwy. 1, 95410 ☎ *707/937–1919 or 800/479–7944* 🖷 *707/937–2604* ⊕ *www.albionriverinn.com* ➲ *20 rooms* ♿ *Restaurant, some in-room hot tubs, concierge; no smoking* ▤ *AE, D, DC, MC, V* ⎜○⎜ *BP.*

Little River

⑬   *3 mi north of Albion on Hwy. 1.*

Van Damme State Park is best known for its beach and for being a prime abalone diving spot. Upland trails lead through lush riparian habitat and the bizarre Pygmy Forest, where acidic soil and poor drainage have produced mature cypress and pine trees that are no taller than a person. The visitor center has displays on ocean life and Native American history. There's a $4 day-use fee. ⊠ *Hwy. 1* ☎ *707/937–5804 for park, 707/937–4016 for visitor center* ⊕ *www.parks.ca.gov.*

Where to Stay & Eat

$$–$$$$ ✕ **Little River Inn Restaurant.** There are fewer than a dozen entrées on this inn's menu, but they're all very good; if you're lucky, the choices might include loin of lamb, locally caught salmon, or grilled polenta with vegetables. Main courses come with soup or salad. Less expensive appetizers, salads, and sandwiches are served in the ocean-view Ole's Whale Watch Bar. The adjoining inn is more like a laid-back resort, and has some relatively inexpensive rooms. ⊠ *7901 N. Hwy. 1* ☎ *707/937–5942* ▤ *AE, MC, V.*

$$–$$$$ ✕▥ **Heritage House.** Every part of this rambling ocean-side resort has a stunning view. The decor ranges from frilly to tastefully spare. The real draw is the amenities—many units have private decks, fireplaces, and whirlpool tubs. The restaurant ($$–$$$) is more formal than most on the coast and has a superb wine list. Salmon, quail, sirloin, and elegant desserts are the standouts on the evening menu. The restaurant is closed from early December through mid-February. ⊠ *5200 N. Hwy. 1, 95456* ☎ *707/937–5885 or 800/235–5885* 🖷 *707/937–0318* ⊕ *www.heritagehouseinn.com* ➲ *58 rooms, 10 suites* ♿ *Restaurant, some in-room hot tubs, massage, beach, lounge, concierge; no room phones, no room TVs* ▤ *AE, MC, V.*

★ $$–$$$ ▥ **Glendeven Inn.** If Mendocino is the New England village of the West Coast, then Glendeven is the local country manor. The main house was built in 1867 and is surrounded by acres of gardens. Inside are five rooms, three with fireplaces. A converted barn holds an art gallery. The 1986 Stevenscroft building, with its high gabled roof, contains four rooms with fireplaces. The carriage-house suite makes for a romantic retreat. ⊠ *8205 N. Hwy. 1, 95456* ☎ *707/937–0083 or 800/822–4536* 🖷 *707/937–6108* ⊕ *www.glendeven.com* ➲ *6 rooms, 4 suites* ♿ *No room TVs* ▤ *AE, MC, D, V* ⎜○⎜ *BP.*

Mendocino

★ ⑭   *2 mi north of Little River on Hwy. 1; 153 mi from San Francisco, north on U.S. 101, west on Hwy. 128, and north on Hwy. 1.*

Logging created the first boom in the windswept town of Mendocino, which flourished for most of the second half of the 19th century. As the timber industry declined, many residents left, but the town's setting was too beautiful for it to remain neglected. Artists and craftspeople began flocking here in the 1950s, and in their wake came entrepreneurial types who opened restaurants, cafés, and inns. By the 1970s a full-scale revival was underway. A bit of the old town can be seen in such dives as Dick's Place, a bar near the Mendocino Hotel, but the rest of the small downtown area is devoted almost exclusively to contemporary restaurants and shops.

Mendocino may look familiar to fans of *Murder, She Wrote*; the town played the role of Cabot Cove, Maine, on the television show. The subterfuge worked because so many of the town's original settlers had come here from the Northeast and built houses in the New England style. The Blair House, at 45110 Little Lake Street, was the home of Jessica Fletcher (Angela Lansbury's character) in the series. Mendocino was also the backdrop for the Elia Kazan film adaptation of John Steinbeck's *East of Eden*. The building on Main Street (at Kasten Street) that houses the astronomy-oriented Out of This World store was the Bay City Bank in the 1955 movie, which starred James Dean.

An 1861 structure holds the **Kelley House Museum,** whose artifacts include Victorian-era furniture and historical photographs of Mendocino's logging days. ⊠ *45007 Albion St.* ☎ *707/937–5791* ✉ *$2* ☺ *June–Aug., Thurs.–Tues. 1–4; Sept.–May, Fri.–Mon. 1–4.*

The **Mendocino Art Center** (⊠ 45200 Little Lake St. ☎ 707/937–5818 or 800/653–3328), which hosts exhibits and art classes and contains a gallery and a theater, is the nexus of Mendocino's flourishing art scene.

The tiny green-and-red **Temple Kwan Tai** (⊠ Albion St., west of Kasten St. ☎ 707/937–5123) was built in 1854, making it the oldest Chinese temple on the North Coast. It's open only by appointment, but by peering in the window you can see just about everything there is to see.

The restored **Ford House,** built in 1854, serves as the visitor center for Mendocino Headlands State Park. The house has a scale model of Mendocino as it looked in 1890, when the town had 34 water towers and a 12-seat public outhouse. From the museum, you can head out on a 3-mi trail across the spectacular seaside cliffs that border the town. ⊠ *Main St. west of Lansing St.* ☎ *707/937–5397* ✉ *Free, $2 donation suggested* ☺ *Daily 11–4.*

★ The **Mendocino Coast Botanical Gardens** offer something for nature lovers in every season. Even in winter, heather and Japanese tulips bloom. Along 2 mi of trails with ocean views and observation points for whale-watching is a splendid profusion of flowers. The rhododendrons are at their peak from April through June, and the dahlias are spectacular in August. ⊠ *18220 N. Hwy. 1,1 mi south of Fort Bragg* ☎ *707/964–4352* ⊕ *www.gardenbythesea.org* ✉ *$7.50* ☺ *Mar.–Oct., daily 9–5; Nov.–Feb., daily 9–4.*

Mendocino's ocean breezes might seem too chilly for grape growing, but summer days can be quite warm just over the hills in the **Anderson Valley,** where the cool nights permit a longer ripening period.

Chardonnays and pinot noirs find the valley's climate particularly hospitable. Tasting here is a decidedly more laid-back affair than in the Napa and Sonoma valleys. Most tasting rooms are open from 11 to 5 daily and charge a nominal sampling fee (usually deducted if you purchase any wine).

Husch (✉ 4400 Hwy. 128, Philo ☎ 707/895–3216 or 800/554–8724), one of the valley's oldest wineries, sells renowned chardonnays and a superb gewürztraminer. At the elegant tasting room at **Roederer Estate** (✉ 4501 Hwy. 128, Philo ☎ 707/895–2288), you can taste (for $3) sparkling wines produced by the American affiliate of the famous French champagne maker. **Pacific Echo** (✉ 8501 Hwy. 128, Philo ☎ 800/824–7754) was the first Anderson Valley winery to produce critically acclaimed sparkling wines. **Fetzer Vineyards** (✉ 45070 Main St., between Lansing and Kasten Sts., Mendocino ☎ 707/937–6190 or 800/860–3347) has a tasting room next to the Mendocino Hotel & Garden Suites. *To get to the Anderson Valley from Mendocino, take Hwy. 1 south to Hwy. 128 east. The valley begins about 10 mi in from the coast and continues all the way to U.S. 101.*

Where to Stay & Eat

$$–$$$$
Fodor'sChoice
★
✗ **Cafe Beaujolais.** The Victorian cottage that houses this popular dinner-only restaurant is surrounded by a garden of heirloom and exotic plantings. A commitment to the freshest possible organic, local, and hormone-free ingredients guides the chef here. The menu is eclectic and ever-evolving, but often includes free-range duck, line-caught fish, and Yucatecan-Thai crab cakes. An adjacent bakery turns out nine delicious varieties of bread from a wood-fired oven. The restaurant typically closes for a month or more in winter. ✉ *961 Ukiah St.* ☎ *707/937–5614* ⊕ *www.cafebeaujolais.com* ▭ *D, MC, V.*

$–$$$
✗ **955 Ukiah Street Restaurant.** A homey, woodsy interior and creative California cuisine make this spot a perennial favorite. Specialties of the house include fresh fish, duck cannelloni, peppercorn New York steak, and spinach and red chard ravioli. ✉ *955 Ukiah St.* ☎ *707/937–1955* ⊕ *www.955restaurant.com* ▭ *MC, V* ☉ *Closed Mon. and Tues. No lunch.*

$$$$
✗▢ **Stanford Inn by the Sea.** This family-run, dog-friendly property feels like the Northern California version of an old-time summer resort. Several long buildings house guest rooms that range from cozy to chic, many with ocean views, fireplaces, and paintings by local artists. On the spacious grounds you'll find organic gardens, llamas, and a sandy river beach where you can rent a kayak or canoe and head 8 mi upstream. The spa, in-room massage, and yoga classes are complemented by the hearty vegetarian cuisine at The Ravens restaurant ($–$$$). ✉ *South of Mendocino, east on Comptche-Ukiah Rd. (off Hwy. 1), 95460* ☎ *707/937–5615 or 800/331–8884* 🖶 *707/937–0305* ⊕ *www.stanfordinn.com* ⮂ *31 rooms, 10 suites* ⚫ *Refrigerators, cable TV with movies, in-room VCRs, indoor pool, hot tub, sauna, bicycles, some pets allowed (fee); no smoking* ▭ *AE, D, DC, MC, V* ⁙ *BP.*

$–$$$$ ✕🔲 **MacCallum House.** This inn makes the most of its 2 acres in the mid-
Fodor'sChoice dle of town. Each room has its own character: the main house feels like
★ the mansion of a wealthy friend, the cottages are bright and honeymoon-
y, and the renovated barn and water tower contain lavish, cedar-walled
suites. The property is dotted with rose bushes, some planted by the orig-
inal owner in the the late 1800s. At the excellent restaurant ($$–$$$$;
reservations essential), the dishes highlight local ingredients and are pre-
pared daily from scratch (including the ice cream and mozzarella cheese).
Rates include a sumptuous breakfast. The restaurant is closed early January through mid-February. ✉ *45020 Albion St., 95460* ☎ *707/937–
0289 or 800/609–0492* ⊕ *www.maccallumhouse.com* ➴ *11 rooms, 9
cottages, 11 suites* ♤ *Restaurant, in-room data ports, cable TV, in-
room VCRs, bar* ▭ *AE, D, MC, V* ¶Ol *BP.*

$–$$$$ ✕🔲 **Mendocino Hotel & Garden Suites.** From the outside, this hotel's pe-
riod facade and wide balcony make it look like something out of the
Wild West. Inside, though, the stained-glass lamps, polished wood, and
Persian rugs are undeniably posh. Most rooms have private baths;
deluxe garden rooms have fireplaces and TVs. The wood-paneled restau-
rant ($–$$$), fronted by a solarium, serves fine fish entrées and the best
ollalieberry (common to the Northern California coast) deep-dish pie
in California. ✉ *45080 Main St., 95460* ☎ *707/937–0511 or 800/
548–0513* 🖷 *707/937–0513* ⊕ *www.mendocinohotel.com* ➴ *51 rooms,
14 with shared bath* ♤ *Restaurant, room service, bar; no TV in some
rooms* ▭ *AE, MC, V.*

★ **$$$–$$$$** 🔲 **Whitegate Inn.** With its white picket fence, latticework gazebo, and
romantic garden, the Whitegate is a picture-book Victorian. High ceil-
ings, floral fabrics, and pastel walls define the public spaces and the lux-
urious rooms, all of which have fireplaces. Best of all, you can watch
the ocean breakers from the deck out back. ✉ *499 Howard St., 95460*
☎ *707/937–4892 or 800/531–7282* 🖷 *707/937–1131* ⊕ *www.
whitegateinn.com* ➴ *6 rooms, 1 cottage* ♤ *Cable TV, Internet, some
refrigerators, some VCRs, some pets allowed; no kids under 9, no smok-
ing* ▭ *AE, MC, V* ¶Ol *BP.*

$$–$$$$ 🔲 **Agate Cove Inn.** Facing the Mendocino Headlands across a rocky
cove, this inn is ideally situated for winter whale-watching. Adiron-
dack chairs are set on a small deck for just that purpose; you can borrow the inn's binoculars for a closer look. There are four single and
four duplex cottages; two more rooms are in the 1860s farmhouse,
where country breakfasts are served in a dining room with an ocean
view. ✉ *11201 N. Lansing St., 95460* ☎ *707/937–0551 or 800/527–
3111* 🖷 *707/937–0550* ⊕ *www.agatecove.com* ➴ *10 rooms* ♤ *In-
room VCRs, massage, shop, concierge; no room phones, no smoking*
▭ *MC, V* ¶Ol *BP.*

$$–$$$$ 🔲 **Alegria.** A pathway from the back porch to Big River Beach makes
this the only oceanfront lodging in Mendocino. Each room has some-
thing special and unique: beautiful bamboo floors; a woodstove; sun-
set views from a perfectly positioned window seat. Despite its central
location, the property is more private than others in town; it feels like
a quiet retreat. The hot tub, surrounded by jasmine vines, is wonderful
at night. ✉ *44781 Main St., 95460* ☎ *707/937–5150 or 800/780–*

7905 ⊕ *www.oceanfrontmagic.com* ⇨ *6 rooms, 1 suite* △ *Some kitchenettes, some microwaves, refrigerators, in-room VCRs, hot tub, concierge* ▭ *AE, MC, V* ⏐◉⏐ *BP.*

★ **$$–$$$$** ▣ **Brewery Gulch Inn.** This tasteful inn gives a modern twist to the elegance of Mendocino. Furnishings are redwood and leather, beds are plush, and all rooms but two have whirlpool tubs with views. The luxury is in tune with the surrounding nature: large windows frame views of the 10-acre property, bird-filled trees, and winding paths that lead through native plant gardens. An organic farm that's on-site (but out of earshot) provides ingredients for the sumptuous breakfast menu. ⊠ *9401 Hwy. 1, 1 mi south of Mendocino, 95460* ☎ *707/937–4752 or 800/578–4454* ⎙ *707/937–1279* ⊕ *www.brewerygulchinn.com* ⇨ *10 rooms* △ *In-room data ports, some in-room hot tubs, cable TV, in-room VCRs, massage, shop, concierge, meeting room; no smoking* ⏐◉⏐ *BP* ▭ *AE, MC, V.*

$$–$$$$ ▣ **Packard House.** One of four landmark homes on Executive Row, this Carpenter Gothic Victorian is being renovated by its owners to incorporate a more modern aesthetic. Combining traditional romantic touches like soaking tubs for two and pillow-top beds with 21st century touches like wireless and Internet access throughout the building, the remade Packer House stands out in a traditional town. ⊠ *45170 Little Lake St., 95460* ☎ *707/937–2677 or 888/453–2677* ⊕ *www.packardhouse. com* ⇨ *4 rooms, 1 suite* △ *Cable TV, in-room VCRs, in-room data ports, massage, concierge; no smoking* ▭ *MC, V* ⏐◉⏐ *BP.*

$$–$$$ ▣ **Blackberry Inn.** Each single-story unit here has a false front, creating the image of a frontier town. There is a bank, a saloon, Belle's Place (of hospitality), and "offices" for doctors and sheriffs, as well as other themed accommodations. Rooms are cheery and spacious. Most have wood-burning stoves or fireplaces and at least partial ocean views. The inn is a short drive east of town down a quiet side street. ⊠ *44951 Larkin Rd., 95460* ☎ *707/937–5281 or 800/950–7806* ⊕ *www. blackberryinn.biz* ⇨ *17 rooms* △ *In-room data ports, cable TV, some in-room hot tubs, some kitchenettes, some pets allowed; no smoking* ▭ *MC, V* ⏐◉⏐ *CP.*

$$–$$$ ▣ **Joshua Grindle Inn.** The original farmhouse of this B&B, which sits on a 2-acre hilltop, contains five guest rooms, a parlor, and a dining room. Two other buildings, the Watertower (an upper room has windows on all four sides) and the Cottage, hold five additional rooms. Furnishings throughout are simple but comfortable American antiques: Salem rockers, wing chairs, steamer-trunk tables, painted pine beds. ⊠ *44800 Little Lake Rd., 95460* ☎ *707/937–4143 or 800/474–6353* ⊕ *www. joshgrin.com* ⇨ *10 rooms* △ *In-room hot tubs, some cable TV, massage, concierge; no room phones, no kids under 12, no smoking* ▭ *MC, V* ⏐◉⏐ *BP.*

Nightlife & the Arts

Mendocino Theatre Company (⊠ Mendocino Art Center, 42500 Little Lake St. ☎ 707/937–4477) has been around for more than two decades. The community theater's repertoire ranges all over the contemporary map, including works by David Mamet, Neil Simon, and local playwrights.

Patterson's Pub (✉ 10485 Lansing St. ☎ 707/937–4782), an Irish-style watering hole, is a friendly gathering place day or night, though it becomes boisterous as the evening wears on. Bands entertain on Friday night.

Sports & the Outdoors

Catch-A-Canoe and Bicycles Too (✉ Stanford Inn by the Sea, Comptche-Ukiah Rd., off Hwy. 1 ☎ 707/937–0273) rents kayaks and regular and outrigger canoes as well as mountain and suspension bicycles.

Shopping

Many artists exhibit their work in Mendocino, and the streets of this compact town are so easily walkable that you're sure to find a gallery with something that strikes your fancy. Start your gallery tour at the **Mendocino Art Center** (✉ 45200 Little Lake St. ☎ 707/937–5818 or 800/653–3328). **Old Gold** (✉ 6 Albion St. ☎ 707/937–5005) is a good place to look for locally crafted jewelry.

Fort Bragg

⓯ *10 mi north of Mendocino on Hwy. 1.*

This basically blue-collar town is the commercial center of Mendocino County. Fort Bragg has undergone quite a few changes in the past several years—largely because the declining timber industry has been steadily replaced by a boom in tourism (especially charter-boat excursions). The city has also attracted many artists, some who've left Mendocino seeking coastal serenity at a lower price.

The **Skunk Train,** a remnant of the region's logging days, dates from 1885 and travels a round-trip route—through redwood forests inaccessible to automobiles—between Fort Bragg and the town of Northspur, 21 mi inland. Back in the 1920s, a fume-spewing gas-powered train car used to shuttle passengers along the same route; it earned the nickname Skunk Train, and the entire line has been called that ever since. Luckily, the replica of the Skunk Train car that now runs on the historic route smells a lot better than the original. ✉ *Foot of Laurel St.* ☎ *707/964–6371 or 800/866–1690* ⊕ *www.skunktrain.com* 🎫 *Round-trip $17–$35* ☉ *Departs Fort Bragg 10 AM and 2:15 PM.*

★ **MacKerricher State Park** includes 9 mi of sandy beach and several square miles of dunes. Fishing (at a freshwater lake stocked with trout), canoeing, hiking, jogging, bicycling, beachcombing, camping, and harbor-seal watching at Laguna Point are among the popular activities, many of which are accessible to travelers with disabilities. Whales can often be spotted from December to mid-April from the nearby headland. Rangers lead nature hikes in the summer. ✉ *Hwy. 1, 3 mi north of Fort Bragg* ☎ *707/937–5804* 🎫 *Free.*

Where to Stay & Eat

$$–$$$ ✕ **The Restaurant.** The name may be generic, but this place, which has operated under the same ownership since 1973, isn't. California cuisine, like lemon chicken over panfried noodles and seafood stew, is served in a dining room that doubles as an art gallery. ✉ *418 N. Main St.* ☎ *707/964–9800* 🖃 *MC, V* ☉ *Closed Tues. and Wed. No lunch.*

¢–$$ ✕ **Mendo Bistro.** Fort Bragg's most happening, buzzing restaurant can be found on the second floor of the Company Store complex downtown. Pasta is made fresh on the premises here; a house specialties are rigatoni with Italian sausage, capers, and roasted peppers and linguine with rock shrimp, garlic, and lemon butter. The crab cakes are also excellent. ⊠ *301 N. Main St.* ☎ *707/964–4974* ▤ *AE, D, DC, MC, V* ☽ *No lunch.*

¢–$$ ✕ **Sharon's by the Sea.** Beautiful Noyo Harbor is just outside the windows at this unpretentious restaurant at the end of the Noyo Harbor pier. The menu's excellent seafood—all of which comes from local waters—is complemented by house-made breads and desserts, and a good selection of Mendocino County wines. ⊠ *32096 N. Harbor Dr., at south end of Fort Bragg* ☎ *707/962–0680* ⊕ *www.sharonsbythesea.com* ▤ *AE, MC, V.*

¢ ✕ **Headlands Coffeehouse.** The coffeehouse acts as a cultural center and local gathering place. Musicians perform every night, and crowds are kept sated with enchiladas, quiche, and barbecued tofu. ⊠ *120 E. Laurel St.* ☎ *707/964–1987* ▤ *D, MC, V.*

$–$$ ▥ **Weller House Inn.** Rooms in this 1886 mansion are decorated with Victorian-style wallpaper and furnishings; the baths have hand-painted tiles. The third-floor breakfast room, which is 900 square feet and paneled in California redwood, was once a ballroom. Newer accommodations are in a water tower on the property—at 51 feet the tallest building in town—topped by a hot tub with spectacular ocean views. Guest rooms have jacks but no phones; request one if you need a lifeline. ⊠ *524 Stewart St., 95437* ☎ *707/964–4415 or 877/893–5537* ☎ *707/961–1281* ⊕ *www.wellerhouse.com* ⇲ *10 rooms* ♻ *Some in-room hot tubs, some microwaves, some refrigerators; no room phones, no TV in some rooms, no smoking* ▤ *AE, D, DC, MC, V* ꒐ *BP.*

¢–$$ ▥ **Surf and Sand Lodge.** As its name implies, this hotel sits practically right on the beach; pathways lead from the property down to the rock-strewn shore. All rooms are bright and clean, although the six cheapest don't have views. The nicest of the second-story rooms have hot tubs and fireplaces. ⊠ *1131 N. Main St., 95437* ☎ *707/964–9383 or 800/964–0184* ☎ *707/964–0314* ⊕ *www.surfsandlodge.com* ⇲ *30 rooms* ♻ *In-room VCRs, refrigerators, some in-room hot tubs, beach; no smoking* ▤ *AE, D, MC, V.*

△ **MacKerricher State Park.** The campsites here are in woodsy spots about a quarter mile from the ocean. There are no hookups. Make reservations for summer weekends as early as possible (reservations are taken April–mid-October), unless you want to try your luck getting one of the 25 sites that are available on a first-come, first-served basis each day. ♻ *Flush toilets, drinking water, showers, fire pits, picnic tables* ⇲ *150 sites* ⊠ *Hwy. 1, 3 mi north of Fort Bragg* ☎ *800/444–7275 for reservations* ▤ *$20.*

Nightlife

Caspar Inn (⊠ 14957 Caspar Rd. ☎ 707/964–5565) presents blues, rock, hip-hop, and alternative rock every day but Monday. If you feel like staying over after a show, there are simple, inexpensive rooms upstairs.

Sports & the Outdoors

All Aboard Adventures (✉ 32400 N. Harbor Dr. ☎ 707/964–2079) operates whale-watching trips from December through mid-April, as well as fishing excursions all year. **Ricochet Ridge Ranch** (✉ 24201 N. Hwy. 1 ☎ 707/964–7669) guides groups on horseback to MacKerricher State Park.

| en route | North of Fort Bragg on Highway 1, just past the mill town of Westport, the road cuts inland around the **King Range,** a mountain stretch so rugged it was impossible to build Highway 1 through it. **Richardson Grove State Park**, north of Leggett along U.S. 101, marks your first encounter with the truly giant redwoods, but there are even more magnificent stands farther north, in Humboldt and Del Norte counties. Before heading into the wilderness, stop for an espresso or a beer at the **Lost Coast Inn** (✉ 38921 Hwy. 1, Westport ☎ 707/964–5584), a B&B whose bar–coffeehouse has a chess set and friendly resident dog. |

REDWOOD COUNTRY

FROM GARBERVILLE TO CRESCENT CITY

The majestic redwoods that grace California's coast become more plentiful as you head north. Their towering ancient presence defines the landscape.

Garberville

🔟 *70 mi from Fort Bragg, north and east on Hwy. 1 and north on U.S. 101; 204 mi north of San Francisco on U.S. 101.*

Although it's the largest town in the vicinity of Humboldt Redwoods State Park, Garberville hasn't changed much since timber was king. The town is a pleasant place to stop for lunch, pick up picnic provisions, or poke through arts-and-crafts stores. A few miles below Garberville is an elegant Tudor resort, the Benbow Inn. Even if you are not staying there, stop in for a drink or a meal; the architecture and gardens are lovely.

Where to Stay & Eat

¢ ✕ **Woodrose Cafe.** This modest eatery serves basic breakfast items until 1 PM on the weekends and breakfast and healthful lunches every weekday. Dishes include chicken, big salads, burritos, and vegetarian specials. ✉ *911 Redwood Dr.* ☎ *707/923–3191* ▭ *No credit cards* ☾ *No dinner.*

★ $$–$$$$ ✕▦ **Benbow Inn.** South of Garberville alongside the Eel River, this Tudor-style manor resort is the equal of any in the region. The most luxurious of the antiques-filled rooms are on the terrace, with fine river views; some rooms have fireplaces. Guests have canoeing, tennis, golf, and pool privileges at an adjacent property. The wood-paneled restaurant ($$–$$$) serves American cuisine, and specializes in locally caught salmon and

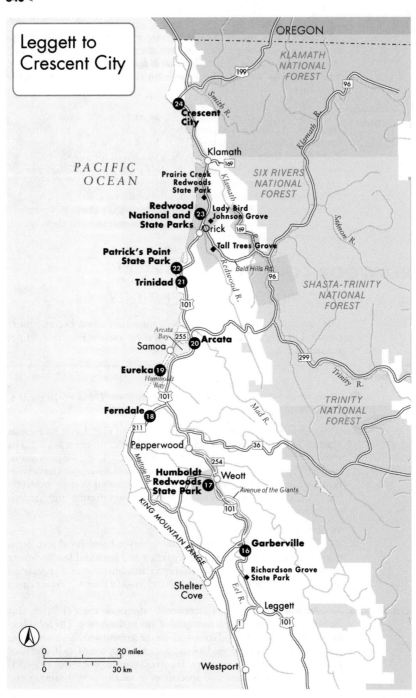

Leggett to
Crescent City

trout. ⊠ *445 Lake Benbow Dr., 95542* ☎ *707/923–2124 or 800/355–3301* 🖨 *707/923–2897* ⊕ *www.benbowinn.com* ⇥ *43 rooms, 1 cottage* ⚲ *Restaurant, some refrigerators, some cable TV, some in-room VCRs, massage, golf privileges, lake, lobby lounge* ⊟ *AE, D, MC, V* ⊘ *Closed early Jan.–early Apr.*

Humboldt Redwoods State Park

🕲 ⑰ *15 mi north of Garberville on U.S. 101.*

At the **Humboldt Redwoods State Park Visitor Center** you can pick up information about the redwoods, waterways, and recreational activities in the 53,000-acre park. One helpful brochure describes a self-guided auto tour of the park, with short and long hikes into redwood groves. ⊠ *Ave. of the Giants, 2 mi south of Weott* ☎ *707/946–2409 park, 707/946–2263 visitor center* 🖭 *Free; $2 day-use fee for parking and facilities in Williams Grove and Women's Federation Grove* ⊘ *Park daily; visitor center Mar.–Oct., daily 9–5; Nov.–Feb., daily 10–4.*

The **Avenue of the Giants** (Highway 254) begins about 7 mi north of Garberville and winds north, more or less parallel to U.S. 101, toward Pepperwood. Some of the tallest trees on the planet tower over this stretch of two-lane blacktop. The road follows the south fork of the Eel River and cuts through part of Humboldt Redwoods State Park. Reached via a ½-mi trail off Avenue of the Giants is **Founders Grove** (⊠ Hwy. 254, 4 mi north of Humboldt Redwoods State Park Visitor Center). One of the most impressive trees here—the 362-foot-long Dyerville Giant—fell to the ground in 1991; its root base points skyward 35 feet. **Rockefeller Forest** (⊠ Mattole Rd., 6 mi north of Humboldt Redwoods State Park Visitor Center) is the largest remaining coastal redwood forest. It contains 40 of the 100 tallest trees in the world.

Ferndale

⑱ *30 mi from Weott, north on U.S. 101 to Hwy. 211 west.*

The residents of this stately town maintain some of the most sumptuous Victorian homes in California. Many of them were built by 19th-century Scandinavian, Swiss, and Portuguese dairy farmers who were drawn to the area's mild climate; the queen of them all is the Gingerbread Mansion, built in 1899. An old graveyard slopes down Ocean Avenue west of Main Street. Many shops carry a self-guided tour map that shows the town's most interesting historical buildings.

The main building of the **Ferndale Museum** hosts changing exhibitions of Victoriana and has a display of an old-style barbershop and another of Wiyot Indian baskets. In the annex are a horse-drawn buggy, a re-created blacksmith's shop, and antique farming, fishing, and dairy equipment. ⊠ *515 Shaw Ave.* ☎ *707/786–4466* 🖭 *$1 donation* ⊘ *June–Sept., Tues.–Sat. 11–4, Sun. 1–4; Oct.–Dec. and Feb.–May, Wed.–Sat. 11–4, Sun. 1–4.*

Eel River Delta Tours (✉ 285 Morgan Slough Rd. ☎ 707/786–4187) conducts two-hour boat trips that examine the wildlife and history of the Eel River's estuary and salt marsh.

Where to Stay

$$–$$$ 🏠 **Gingerbread Mansion.** This beautifully restored Victorian B&B is dazzling enough to rival San Francisco's "painted ladies." The exterior has detailed spindlework, turrets, and gables; inside, the guest rooms are decorated in plush, flowery period splendor. Some rooms have views of the mansion's English garden; one has side-by-side bathtubs. One particularly posh suite is the Veneto, which has hand-painted scenes of Venice on the walls and ceiling as well as marble floors. ✉ *400 Berding St., off Brown St., 95536* ☎ *707/786–4000 or 800/952–4136* ⊕ *www. gingerbread-mansion.com* 🛏 *11 rooms, 4 suites* 🛆 *No room TVs, no smoking* 🝗 *AE, MC, V* ⊚ *BP.*

Shopping

Among the shops along Main Street, **Golden Gait Mercantile** (✉ 421 Main St. ☎ 707/786–4891) seems to have been left back in time; it sells Burma Shave products and old-fashioned long johns as well as penny candy.

Eureka

⑲ *10 mi north of Ferndale and 269 mi north of San Francisco on U.S. 101.*

With a population of 28,500, Eureka is the North Coast's largest city. Over the past century, it has gone through several cycles of boom and bust—first with mining and later with timber and fishing—but these days, tourism is becoming a healthy industry. This is largely due to the nearly 100 Victorian buildings here (which have caused some to refer to the town as "the Williamsburg of the West"), and a newly renovated downtown area with smart shops and a walking pier that looks onto the harbor. The splendid **Carson Mansion** (✉ M and 2nd Sts.) was built in 1885 for timber baron William Carson. A private men's club now occupies the house. Right across the road is another stunning Victorian—also built by the Carson family—known as the **Pink Lady** (✉ M and 2nd Sts.). For proof that contemporary architects still have the skills to build Victoriana, check out the **Carter House B&B** (✉ 3rd and L Sts.), a replica of a San Francisco building that burned in the 1906 earthquake.

At the **Eureka Chamber of Commerce** you can pick up maps with self-guided driving tours of Eureka's architecture, and also learn about organized tours. ✉ *2112 Broadway* ☎ *707/442–3738 or 800/356–6381* ⊘ *Weekdays 8:30–5, Sat. 10–4.*

The **Clarke Memorial Museum** contains a beautiful collection of northwestern California Native American basketry, as well as artifacts from Eureka's Victorian, logging, and maritime eras. ✉ *240 E St.* ☎ *707/ 443–1947* 🖾 *Donations suggested* ⊘ *Tues.–Sat. 11–4.*

The structure that gave **Fort Humboldt State Historic Park** its name once protected white settlers from Native Americans. Ulysses S. Grant was posted here in 1854. The old fort is no longer around, but on its grounds are a museum, ancient steam engines (operators rev them up on the third

Saturday of every month), and a logger's cabin. The park is a good place for a picnic. ✉ *3431 Fort Ave.* ☎ *707/445–6567 or 707/445–6547* 🖃 *Free* ⊙ *Daily 8–5:30.*

To explore the waters and see the buildings around Eureka, take a 75-minute, narrated **Humboldt Bay Harbor Cruise.** ✉ *Pier at C St.* ☎ *707/ 445–1910 or 707/444–9440* 🖃 *Harbor cruise $12.50; cocktail cruise $8.50* ⊙ *Harbor cruise departs May–Oct., daily at 1 and 2:30. Cocktail cruise departs Wed.–Sat. at 5:30.*

Where to Stay & Eat

★ **$$–$$$** ✕ **Restaurant 301.** The wine list at Eureka's most elegant restaurant is so extensive that several rooms in the hotel upstairs have been converted into "cellars." The cuisine is no less exquisite; ingredients are hand-selected from the farmers' market, local cheesemakers and ranchers, and the on-site gardens. Dishes are prepared with a delicate hand and a sensuous imagination—try the roasted rainbow trout stuffed with caramelized onion and served with a nut-brown lemon butter or the rib eye with chèvremashed potatoes and asparagus. The narrow, L-shape dining room makes each table feel private. ✉ *301 L St.* ☎ *707/444–8062* 🖃 *AE, D, DC, MC, V* ⊙ *No lunch.*

¢–$$ ✕ **Cafe Waterfront.** This airy local landmark serves a solid basic menu of burgers and steaks, but the real standouts are the daily seafood specials—lingcod, shrimp, and other treats fresh from the bay across the street. The building, listed on the National Register of Historic Places, was a saloon and brothel until the 1950s. Two rooms, named after former ladies of the house, are available as "rooms to let." ✉ *102 F St.* ☎ *707/443–9190* 🖃 *MC, V.*

★ **¢–$** ✕ **Samoa Cookhouse.** A longtime logger's hangout, this eatery serves up family-style meals at its long wooden tables. Meat dishes like fried chicken, baked ham, and chicken Marsala predominate. Save room (if you can) for the homemade apple pie or strawberry shortcake. ✉ *Cookhouse Rd.; from U.S. 101 cross Samoa Bridge, turn left onto Samoa Rd., then left 1 block later onto Cookhouse Rd.* ☎ *707/442–1659* 🖃 *AE, D, MC, V.*

¢ ✕ **Ramone's.** A casual bakery café, Ramone's serves light sandwiches from dawn to 6 PM. ✉ *209 E. St.* ☎ *707/442–6082* 🖃 *MC, V* ⊙ *No dinner.*

$$–$$$$ ⊞ **Carter House.** According to owner Mark Carter, his staff has been trained always to say "Yes." Whether it's breakfast in bed or an in-room massage, someone here will make sure you get what you want. Rooms—in two main buildings and several cottages—have varying floor plans and are individually decorated. The luscious honeymoon suite (nicknamed "The Loveshack") comes with a professional-grade kitchen, where you can have the restaurant's chef cook you a private dinner. ✉ *301 L St., 95501* ☎ *707/444–8062 or 800/404–1390* 🖷 *707/444–8067* ⊕ *www. carterhouse.com* 🛏 *32 rooms, 15 suites* ⚐ *Restaurant, cable TV, some in-room hot tubs, some kitchens, some minibars, massage, shop, concierge, meeting rooms; no smoking* 🖃 *AE, D, DC, MC, V* ⦿ *BP.*

★ **$–$$$** ⊞ **Abigail's Elegant Victorian Mansion.** This meticulously restored Eastlake mansion in a residential neighborhood lives up to its name. Each room is completely decked out in period furnishings, down to the carved-wood beds, fringed lamp shades, and pull-chain commodes. You can rent from a library of 1920s, '30s, and '40s movies, or play croquet on the rosebush-encircled lawn. You can also arrange for a guided tour of local Victoriana in an antique automobile. ✉ *1406 C St., 95501* ☎ *707/444-3144* 🖨 *707/442-3295* ⊕ *www.eureka-california.com* ☞ *4 rooms* ☼ *Sauna, croquet, laundry service* ☰ *MC, V* ⦿⎮ *BP.*

Nightlife
Lost Coast Brewery & Cafe (✉ 617 4th St. ☎ 707/445-4480), a bustling microbrewery, is the best place in town to relax with a pint of ale or porter. Soups, salads, and light meals are served for lunch and dinner (about $15).

Sports & the Outdoors
Hum-Boats (✉ A Dock, Woodley Island Marina ☎ 707/443-5157) provides sailing rides, sailboat rentals, guided kayak tours, and sea kayak rentals and lessons (year-round; by appointment only in winter). The company also runs a water-taxi service on Humboldt Bay.

Shopping
Eureka has several art galleries in the district running from C to I streets between 2nd and 3rd streets. Specialty shops in Eureka's Old Town include **Gepetto's** toy shop (✉ 416 2nd St. ☎ 707/443-6255), a stash of folk art at **Flying Tiki Trading** (✉ 630 2nd St. ☎ 707/441-1234), and the original **Restoration Hardware** (✉ 417 2nd St. ☎ 707/443-3152), a good place to find stylish yet functional home and garden accessories and clever polishing and cleaning products.

Arcata

⓴ *9 mi north of Eureka on U.S. 101.*

The home of Humboldt State University is one of the few California burgs to retain a town square. A farmers' market takes place in the square on Saturday morning from April through November. For a self-guided tour of Arcata that includes some of its restored Victorian buildings, pick up a map from the **chamber of commerce** (✉ 1635 Heindon Rd. ☎ 707/822-3619 ⊕ www.arcatachamber.com), open daily 9–5.

Where to Stay & Eat

$-$$$ ✕ **Abruzzi.** Salads and hearty pasta dishes take up most of the menu at this upscale Italian restaurant, in the lower level of Jacoby's Storehouse on the town square. Don't miss the linguine *pescara*, with a spicy seafood-and-tomato sauce. ✉ *H and 8th Sts.* ☎ *707/826-2345* ☰ *AE, D, MC, V* ⦿ *No lunch.*

¢ ✕ **Crosswinds.** Tasty breakfast and lunch fare at reasonable prices make this place popular with university students. Hit the sunny Victorian dining room shortly after the 7:30 AM opening, though, and you'll have the place to yourself. ✉ *10th and I Sts.* ☎ *707/826-2133* ☰ *D, MC, V* ⦿ *Closed Mon. and Tues. No dinner.*

¢-$ 🏨 **Hotel Arcata.** Rooms at this historic landmark overlooking the town square are clean and modest, but flowered bedspreads and claw-foot bathtubs lend them a bit of character. You get free access to a nearby gym with an indoor pool, hot tub, and yoga classes when you stay here. Tomo ($), the restaurant on the ground floor, serves sushi as well as other Japanese dishes. ⊠ *708 9th St., 95521* ☎ *707/826–0217 or 800/344–1221* 🖷 *707/826–1737* 🌐 *www.hotelarcata.com* ❑ *32 rooms* ☖ *Restaurant, meeting room* ▤ *AE, D, DC, MC, V* ⦿ *CP.*

Shopping

Plaza Design (⊠ 808 G St. ☎ 707/822–7732), one of Arcata's impressive selection of book, housewares, clothing, fabric, and other shops, specializes in gifts, paper products, and innovative furnishings.

Trinidad

㉑ *14 mi north of Arcata on U.S. 101.*

Trinidad got its name from the Spanish mariners who entered the bay on Trinity Sunday, June 9, 1775. The town became a principal trading post for the mining camps along the Klamath and Trinity rivers. As mining, and then whaling, faded, so did the luster of this former boomtown. The one family that owns nearly all the commercial real estate here has strived to keep Trinidad from becoming solely a tourist town. Consequently, Trinidad Bay and the surrounding village have enough sights and activities to accommodate visitors but remain quiet, inexpensive, and genuinely charming.

Where to Stay & Eat

★ **$$–$$$** ✕ **Larrupin' Cafe.** Locals consider this restaurant one of the best places to eat on the North Coast. Set in a two-story house on a quiet country road north of town, it's often thronged with people enjoying mesquite-grilled ribs, fresh seafood, Cornish game hen, and spanikopita. ⊠ *1658 Patrick's Point Dr.* ☎ *707/677–0230* ☖ *Reservations essential* ▤ *No credit cards* ⊙ *Closed Tues. and Wed. in winter, Tues. in summer. No lunch.*

$–$$$ ✕ **Seascape.** With its glassed-in main room and patio for outdoor dining, this casual spot takes full advantage of its location on Trinidad Bay. Dinners showcase local seafood, particularly Dungeness crab in winter, but are a bit pricey; lunches and breakfasts are a good bet, with hearty helpings of hotcakes and waffles in the morning, and crab cocktail, fish-and-chips, and a sole sandwich midday. ⊠ *1 Bay St.* ☎ *707/677–3762* ▤ *D, MC, V.*

¢–$ ✕ **Katy's Smokehouse.** This tiny smokehouse has been doing things the same way since the 1940s, curing day-boat, line caught fish with its original smokers. The fare is traditional (and chemical-free) but still imaginative; a popular choice is the smoked salmon cured with brown sugar, alongside albacore jerky and smoked scallops. The shopkeepers are great talkers and have loads of information about fishing. There's no seating or restaurant service, but if you buy bread and drinks in town, you can make a picnic with the fixings here and walk to the waterside for lunch (or an early dinner—the restaurant closes at 6 PM). ⊠ *740 Edwards St.* ☎ *707/677–0151* 🌐 *www.katyssmokehouse.com* ▤ *MC, V.*

$$$ 🏠 **Trinidad Bay Bed & Breakfast.** This Cape Cod–style shingled house overlooks the harbor and the coastline to the south. The innkeepers can provide a wealth of information about the nearby wilderness, beach, and top fishing spots. A crackling fire warms the living room in chilly weather; one room has its own fireplace. ⊠ *560 Edwards St., Box 849, 95570* ☎ *707/677–0840* 🖷 *707/677–9245* ⊕ *www.trinidadbaybnb. com* ⊄ *2 rooms* ⚲ *Some microwaves, some refrigerators; no room TVs, no room phones* ⊟ *MC, V* ☉ *Closed mid-Nov.–mid-Feb.* ⁑ *BP.*

$$$ 🖭 **Turtle Rocks Oceanfront Inn.** This comfortable inn has the best view in Trinidad, and the builders have made the most of it. Each room's private, glassed-in deck overlooks the ocean and rocks where sea lions lay sunning. The surrounding landscape has been left wild and natural; tucked among the low bushes are sundecks for winter whale-watching and summer catnaps. Patrick's Point State Park is a short walk away. ⊠ *3392 Patrick's Point Dr., 95570* ☎ *707/677–3707* ⊕ *www.turtlerocksinn.com* ⊄ *6 rooms, 1 suite* ⚲ *Cable TV* ⊟ *AE, D, MC, V* ⁑ *BP.*

Patrick's Point State Park

★ ㉒ *5 mi north of Trinidad and 25 mi north of Eureka on U.S. 101.*

On a forested plateau almost 200 feet above the surf, Patrick's Point has stunning views of the Pacific, great whale- and sea-lion watching in season, picnic areas, bike paths, and hiking trails through old-growth spruce forest. There are also tidal pools at Agate Beach and a small museum with natural-history exhibits. Because the park is far from major tourist hubs, there are few visitors (most are local surfers), which leaves the land sublimely quiet. ☎ *707/677–3570* ▱ *$6 per vehicle.*

Where to Stay

⚠ **Patrick's Point State Park Campground.** In a spruce and alder forest above the ocean (just a handful of sites have sea views), Patrick's Point campground has all amenities except RV hookups. In summer, it's best to reserve in advance. ⚲ *Flush toilets, drinking water, showers, bear boxes, fire pits* ⊄ *124 sites* ⊠ *U.S. 101, 4150 Patrick's Point Dr.* ☎ *800/444–7275 for reservations* ⊕ *www.reserveamerica.com* ☉ *Year-round* ▱ *$19.*

Redwood National and State Parks

㉓ *22 mi north (Orick entrance) of Trinidad on U.S. 101.*

After 115 years of intensive logging, this 106,000-acre parcel of towering trees came under government protection in 1968, marking the California environmentalists' greatest victory over the timber industry. Redwood National and State Parks encompasses one national and three state parks (Prairie Creek Redwoods, Del Norte Coast Redwoods, and Jedediah Smith Redwoods) and is more than 40 mi long. There is no admission fee to the national park, but the state parks charge a $4 fee for use of the picnicking areas.

At the **Redwood Information Center** you can get brochures, advice, and a free permit to drive up the steep, 17-mi road (the last 6 mi are gravel) to reach the Tall Trees Grove. Whale-watchers will find the deck of the visitor center an excellent observation point, and bird-watchers will enjoy the nearby Freshwater Lagoon, a popular layover for migrating water-fowl. ⊠ *Off U.S. 101, Orick* ☎ *707/464–6101 Ext. 5265.*

At **Tall Trees Grove** a 3-mi round-trip hiking trail leads to the world's tallest redwood, as well as its third- and fifth-tallest ones.

Within **Lady Bird Johnson Grove,** off Bald Hills Road, is a short circular trail leading through splendid redwoods. This section of the park was dedicated by and named for the former first lady. For additional views take Davison Road to Fern Canyon. This gravel road winds through 4 mi of second-growth redwoods, then hugs a bluff 100 feet above the pounding Pacific surf for another 4 mi.

To reach the entrance to **Prairie Creek Redwoods State Park** (☎ *707/464–6101 Ext. 5300*), take the Prairie Parkway exit off the Route 101 bypass. Extra space has been paved alongside the parklands, providing fine vantage points from which to observe an imposing herd of Roosevelt elk grazing in the adjoining meadow. Prairie Creek's Revelation Trail is fully accessible to those with disabilities. ⊠ *Park Headquarters: 1111 2nd St., Crescent City* ☎ *707/464–6101 Ext. 5064.*

Where to Stay

¢ 🏨 **Hostelling International–Redwood National Park.** This century-old inn is a stone's throw from the ocean; hiking begins just beyond its doors. Lodging is dormitory-style. Reserve well in advance for the hostel's one private room. ⊠ *14480 U.S. 101, at Wilson Creek Rd., 20 mi north of Orick, Klamath 95548* ☎🏨 *707/482–8265* ⊕ *www.norcalhostels.org* ☼ *Closed Dec.–Feb.* ⚷ *Kitchen, laundry facilities* ☱ *MC, V.*

Crescent City

🎯 *40 mi north of Orick on U.S. 101.*

Del Norte County's largest town (population just under 5,000) is named for the shape of its harbor; during the 1800s this was an important steamship stop. At the bottom of B Street at **Popeye's Landing** you can rent a crab pot, buy some bait, and try your luck at crabbing. At low tide from April through October, you can walk from the pier across the ocean floor to the **Battery Point Lighthouse** (☎ *707/464–3089*). Tours ($3) of the 1856 structure are given at low tide April through October, Wednesday through Sunday between 10 and 4, and by appointment the rest of the year.

Where to Stay & Eat

$–$$$ ✕ **Harbor View Grotto.** This glassed-in dining hall overlooking the Pacific is known for its fresh fish entrées. The white, two-story building is marked only by a neon sign that reads RESTAURANT, but inside things are clean, friendly, and low-key. ⊠ *150 Starfish Way* ☎ *707/464–3815* ☱ *D, MC, V.*

¢ 🏨 **Curly Redwood Lodge.** A single redwood tree produced the 57,000 board feet of lumber used to build this lodge. The rooms make the most of that tree, with paneling, platform beds, and dressers built into the walls. ⊠ *701 U.S. 101 S, 95531* ☎ *707/464–2137* 🖶 *707/464 1655* ⊕ *www. curlyredwoodlodge.com* ⤙ *36 rooms* ⚷ *Cable TV* ☱ *AE, DC, MC, V.*

en route

Travelers continuing north to the **Smith River** near the Oregon state line will find fine trout and salmon fishing as well as a profusion of flowers. Ninety percent of America's lily bulbs are grown in this area.

THE NORTH COAST A TO Z

To research prices, get advice from other travelers, and book travel arrangements, visit ⊕ www.fodors.com

AIRPORTS & TRANSFERS

Arcata/Eureka Airport receives United Express and Alaska Airlines flights from San Francisco. The airport is in McKinleyville, which is 16 mi from Eureka. *See* Air Travel *in* Smart Travel Tips A to Z for airline phone numbers. A taxi costs about $40 and takes roughly 20 minutes. Door to Door Airport Shuttle costs $17 to Arcata and Trinidad, $20 to Eureka, and $45 to Ferndale for two people, $50 for three. Buses on Redwood Transit run to Arcata (33 min) and Eureka (51 min), both trips for $1.70. Note, however, that weekday buses operate only between 6 AM and 6 PM and Saturday buses are even more restricted. There is no Sunday bus service.

🚩 **Arcata/Eureka Airport** ✉ 3561 Boeing Ave., McKinleyville ☎ 707/839-5401. **Door to Door Airport Shuttle** ☎ 707/442-9266 or 888/338-5497 ⊕ www.doortodoorairporter. com. Buses on **Redwood Transit** ☎ 707/443-0826 ⊕ www.hta.org.

BUS TRAVEL

Greyhound buses travel along U.S. 101 from San Francisco to Seattle, with regular stops in Eureka and Crescent City. Bus drivers will stop in other towns along the route if you specify your destination when you board. Humboldt Transit Authority connects Eureka, Arcata, Scotia, Fortuna, and Trinidad.

🚩 **Greyhound** ☎ 800/231-2222 ⊕ www.greyhound.com. **Humboldt Transit Authority** ☎ 707/443-0826 ⊕ www.hta.org.

CAR RENTAL

Hertz rents cars at the Arcata/Eureka Airport, but call the reservation desk in advance if your flight will arrive late in the evening—the staff sometimes goes home early. *See* Car Rental *in* Smart Travel Tips A to Z for national rental agency phone numbers.

CAR TRAVEL

Although there are excellent services along Highway 1 and U.S. 101, the main north–south coastal routes, gas stations, and mechanics are few and far between on the smaller roads. If you're running low on fuel and see a gas station, stop for a refill. Driving directly to Mendocino from San Francisco is quicker if, instead of driving up the coast on Highway 1, you take U.S. 101 north to Highway 128 west (from Cloverdale) to Highway 1 north. For information on the condition of roads in northern California, call the Caltrans Highway Information Network's voice-activated system.

🚩 Road Conditions **Caltrans Highway Information Network** ☎ 800/427-7623 ⊕ http://www.dot.ca.gov.

EMERGENCIES

In an emergency dial 911. In state and national parks, park rangers serve as police officers and will help you in any emergency. Bigger towns along the coast have hospitals, but for major medical emergencies you will need to go to San Francisco.

🚩 **General Hospital** ✉ 2200 Harrison St., Eureka, ☎ 707/445-5111. **Sutter Coast Hospital** ✉ 800 E. Washington Blvd., Crescent City ☎ 707/464-8511. **Eureka Police Department** ✉ 604 C St., Eureka ☎ 707/441-4060. **Mendocino Coast District Hospital** ✉ 700 River Dr., Fort Bragg ☎ 707/961-1234. **Mendocino County Sheriff** ✉ 951 Low Gap Rd., Ukiah ☎ 707/463-4411.

VISITOR INFORMATION

🚩 **Eureka/Humboldt County Convention and Visitors Bureau** ✉ 1034 2nd St., Eureka 95501 ☎ 707/443-5097 or 800/346-3482 ⊕ www.redwoodvisitor.org. **Fort Bragg-Mendocino Coast Chamber of Commerce** ✉ 332 N. Main St., Fort Bragg 95437 ☎ 707/961-6300 or 800/726-2780 ⊕ www.mendocinocoast.com. **Mendocino County Alliance** ✉ 525 S. Main St., Ukiah 95482 ☎ 707/462-7417 or 866/466-3636 ⊕ www.gomendo.com. **Redwood Empire Association** ✉ Pier 39, San Francisco 94133 ☎ 415/956-3491 ⊕ www.redwoodempire.com. **Sonoma County Tourism Program** ✉ 520 Mendocino Ave., Suite 210, Santa Rosa 95401 ☎ 707/565-5383 ⊕ www.sonomacounty.com. **West Marin Chamber of Commerce** ☎ 415/663-9232 ⊕ www.pointreyes.org.

THE GOLD COUNTRY

WITH SACRAMENTO

ALL ABOARD
the California State Railroad Museum ⇨*p.664*

HEY, ARNOLD!
Tour the halls of power in the
California State Capitol ⇨*p.665*

LIVE IN THE PAST
at historic B&Bs like the Imperial Hotel, Foxes,
and Dunbar House ⇨*p.675, 676, 680*

GO FOR THE GOLD RUSH
at Columbia State Historic Park ⇨*p.680*

TASTE A PASTY
Cousin Jack Pasties ⇨*p.687*

Updated by
Reed Parsell

A NEW ERA DAWNED FOR CALIFORNIA when James Marshall turned up a gold nugget in the tailrace of a sawmill he was constructing along the American River. Before January 24, 1848, Mexico and the United States were still wrestling for ownership of what would become the Golden State. With Marshall's discovery the United States tightened its grip on the region, and prospectors from all over the world came to seek their fortunes in the Mother Lode.

As gold fever seized the nation, California's population of 15,000 swelled to 265,000 within three years. The mostly young, mostly male adventurers who arrived in search of gold—the '49ers—became part of a culture that discarded many of the conventions of the eastern states. It was also a violent time. Yankee prospectors chased Mexican miners off their claims, and California's leaders initiated a plan to exterminate the local Native American population. Bounties were paid and private militias were hired to wipe out the Native Americans or sell them into slavery. California was now to be dominated by the Anglo.

The boom brought on by the gold rush lasted scarcely 20 years, but it changed California forever. It produced 546 mining towns, of which fewer than 250 remain. The hills of the Gold Country were alive, not only with prospecting and mining but also with business, the arts, gambling, and a fair share of crime. Opera houses went up alongside brothels, and the California state capitol, in Sacramento, was built with the gold dug out of the hills. A lot of important history was made in Sacramento, the center of commerce during this period. Pony Express riders ended their nearly 2,000-mi journeys in the city in the 1860s. The transcontinental railroad, completed in 1869, was conceived here.

By the 1960s the scars that mining had inflicted on the landscape had largely healed. To promote tourism, locals began restoring vintage structures, historians developed museums, and the state established parks and recreation areas to preserve the memory of this extraordinary episode in American history.

One of California's least expensive—and least sophisticated—destinations, the gold-mining region of the Sierra Nevada foothills is not without its pleasures, natural and cultural. Today you can come to Nevada City, Auburn, Coloma, Sutter Creek, and Columbia not only to relive the past but also to explore art galleries and to stay at inns full of character. Spring brings wildflowers, and in fall the hills are colored by bright red berries and changing leaves. Because it offers a mix of indoor and outdoor activities, the Gold Country is a great place to take the kids.

Exploring the Gold Country

Visiting Old Sacramento's museums is a good way to immerse yourself in history, but the Gold Country's heart lies along Highway 49, which winds the 325-mi north–south length of the historic mining area. The highway, often a twisting, hilly, two-lane road, begs for a convertible with the top down.

About the Restaurants

American, Italian, and Mexican fare are common in the Gold Country, but chefs also prepare ambitious continental, French, and California cuisine. Grass Valley's meat- and vegetable-stuffed *pasties,* introduced by 19th-century gold miners from Cornwall, are one of the region's more unusual treats.

About the Hotels

Full-service hotels, budget motels, small inns, and even a fine hostel can all be found in Sacramento. The main accommodations in the larger towns along Highway 49—among them Placerville, Nevada City, Auburn, and Mariposa—are chain motels and inns. Many Gold Country B&Bs occupy former mansions, miners' cabins, and other historic buildings.

WHAT IT COSTS				
$$$$	**$$$**	**$$**	**$**	**¢**
RESTAURANTS over $30	$22–$30	$15–$21	$8–$14	under $8
HOTELS over $225	$170–$225	$120–$169	$70–$119	under $70

Restaurant prices are for a main course at dinner, excluding sales tax of 7%–8% (depending on location). Hotel prices are for two people in a standard double room in high season, excluding service charges and 7%–8% tax.

Timing

The Gold Country is most pleasant in spring, when the wildflowers are in bloom, and in fall. Summers are beautiful but hot: temperatures of 100°F are common. Sacramento winters tend to be cool with occasionally foggy and/or rainy days. Throughout the year Gold Country towns stage community and ethnic celebrations. In December many towns deck themselves out for Christmas. Sacramento hosts the annual Jazz Jubilee over Memorial Day weekend and the California State Fair in August and early September. East of the town of Sutter Creek, flowers bloom on Daffodil Hill in March.

SACRAMENTO & VICINITY

The gateway to the Gold Country, the seat of state government (headed by Governor Arnold Schwarzenegger, at this writing), and an agricultural hub, the city of Sacramento plays many important contemporary roles. Nearly 2 million people live in the metropolitan area. The continuing influx of newcomers seeking opportunity, sunshine, and lower housing costs than in coastal California has made it one of the nation's fastest growing regions. The central "midtown" area contains most of the city's culture and much of its charm, though pedestrians-only K Street Mall has a persistent panhandling problem. An infusion of upscale, popular restaurants, nightclubs, and breweries is nevertheless energizing the downtown scene. Ten miles west is the college town of Davis, which, like nearby Woodland, is beginning to feel more suburban than agricultural because many Sacramento workers are settling there.

Numbers in the text correspond to numbers in the margin and on the Sacramento and the Gold Country maps.

If you have 1 day

Increasing traffic makes a drive from Sacramento to and along Highway 49 potentially long and frustrating. Instead, if you have only one day to spend in the area, stick to ► **Sacramento** ❶–⓯. Begin at **Sutter's Fort** ⓮, and then walk down J Street or take a bus to the **Capitol** ❿ for a free tour. Its huge park is pleasant for picnics. Next, head to Old Sacramento, perhaps detouring through the vibrant Downtown Plaza mall for a drink in its River City Brewing Co. Explore the **California State Railroad Museum** ❶, and, time permitting, take a one-hour river cruise before dining at one of Old Sacramento's many good restaurants.

If you have 5 days

Start your trip in ► ⚐ **Sacramento** ❶–⓯, where you can visit the **California State Railroad Museum** ❶ and **Sutter's Fort** ⓮ and take a riverboat cruise. On the second day, drive to **Placerville** ⓲ to see Hangtown's Gold Bug Mine and continue to ⚐ **Sutter Creek** ㉑. Day 3 starts with a visit to the Amador County Museum, in **Jackson** ㉒, after which you can head south on Highway 49 and northeast on Highway 4 for lunch in **Murphys** ㉔. Return to Highway 49 and continue south to Columbia State Historic Park, in ⚐ **Columbia** ㉕. You can relive the 1800s by dining and spending the night at the City Hotel. If you've been itching to pan for gold, do that on the morning of Day 4. Drive back north on Highway 49 to **Coloma** ㉙ and Marshall Gold Discovery State Historic Park, and head to ⚐ **Auburn** ㉚ to spend the night. On your last day, stop at Empire Mine State Historic Park in **Grass Valley** ㉛ and pay a visit to **Nevada City** ㉜.

Sacramento contains more than 2,000 acres of natural and developed parkland. Grand old evergreens, deciduous and fruit-bearing trees (many lawns and even parks are littered with oranges in springtime), and giant palms give it a shady, lush quality. Genteel Victorian edifices sit side by side with art deco and postmodern skyscrapers, though cheap-looking apartment buildings abound in midtown, and stuccoed suburbs are obliterating a lot of the greater metro area's rural charm.

Exploring Sacramento

Driving 87 mi northeast of San Francisco (I–80 to Hwy. 99 or I–5) not only brings you to the Golden State's seat of government, but also can take you back in time to the gold rush days. Wooden sidewalks and horse-drawn carriages on cobblestone streets lend a 19th-century feel to Old Sacramento, a 28-acre district along the Sacramento River waterfront. The museums at the north end hold artifacts of state and national significance, and historic buildings house shops and restaurants. River cruises and train rides are fun family diversions for an hour or two. Call the **Old Sacramento Events Hotline** (☎ 916/558–3912) for information about living-history re-creations and merchant hours.

a good tour

Old Sacramento, the capitol and park surrounding it, and Sutter's Fort lie on an east–west axis that begins in the west at the Sacramento River. The walk from Old Sacramento to the state's capitol is easy, and brings you through the Downtown Plaza shopping mall and down K Street. This area becomes quite festive during the Thursday evening outdoor market. A DASH (Downtown Area Shuttle) bus and the No. 30 city bus both link Old Sacramento, the K Street Mall, the convention center, downtown, midtown, and Sutter's Fort in a loop that goes eastward on J Street and westward on L Street. The fare is 50¢ within this area, and buses run every 15 minutes weekdays, every 20 minutes Saturday, and every 30 minutes Sunday.

Park your car in the municipal garage under I–5 at 2nd Street (enter on I Street between 2nd and 3rd streets), and head to the superb ▶ **California State Railroad Museum ❶**; then browse the hardware and household items at the **Huntington, Hopkins & Co. Store ❷**. Next door are the hands-on exhibits of the **Discovery Museum History Center ❸**.

To learn more about Sacramento's role in rail history, walk a few paces south to the **Central Pacific Passenger Depot ❹**. The Central Pacific Freight Depot, next to the passenger depot, houses a public market (closed Monday) where merchants sell food and gifts. The foot of K Street (at Front Street) is a great spot for viewing the Sacramento River wharf and the restored stern-wheeler the *Delta King*. The **Old Sacramento Schoolhouse Museum ❺**, near the *Delta King,* is a popular low-tech attraction.

On 2nd Street the **Old Sacramento Visitor Information Center ❻** is in the same block as the **California Military Museum ❼**. A must-see a few blocks south of Old Sacramento is the **Crocker Art Museum ❽**, the oldest art museum in the American West. From here walk south on Front Street to the **Towe Auto Museum ❾**. If you'd rather skip the automotive museum, walk up 3rd Street to the Capitol Mall, which leads to the **capitol ❿**. Still going strong? Explore the **California State History Museum ⓫** at O and 10th streets, one block south of the capitol, and examine the facade of the handsome **Leland Stanford Mansion ⓬**, a block west of that. Or walk north to H Street and then east to the **Governor's Mansion ⓭**. Otherwise, walk back to your car via J Street.

A bit more than a mile to the east is **Sutter's Fort ⓮**, Sacramento's earliest Euro-American settlement. (Take the DASH or No. 30 city bus, or, if you feel like checking out funky shops and eateries, walk up J Street at least one way.) North of the fort is the **California State Indian Museum ⓯**.

TIMING   This tour makes for a leisurely day. Most of the attractions are open daily, except for the military, state history, and art museums, which are closed Monday, and the Huntington, Hopkins & Co. Store.

What to See

❼ **California Military Museum.** A storefront entrance leads to three floors containing more than 30,000 artifacts—uniforms, weapons, photographs, documents, medals, and flags of all kinds—that trace Californians' roles in the military throughout U.S. history. Recent exhibits have included

Historic Hotels & Inns

The Gold Country abounds in well-preserved examples of gold-rush-era architecture, so why not experience the history up-close by staying at an inn or hotel that dates back to those colorful years? Plenty of old mansions have been converted to inns and B&Bs, and several hotels have been in operation since the gold rush. The very Victorian Imperial Hotel in Amador City opened in 1879, while the stone Murphys Historic Hotel & Lodge in Murphys has served guests such as Mark Twain and Black Bart since 1855. Columbia has the 1856 City Hotel and the 1857 Fallon Hotel, the latter of which was restored by the state of California. In Jamestown, the National Hotel offers an authentic 1859 experience.

15

Shopping

Shoppers visit the Gold Country in search of antiques, collectibles, fine art, quilts, toys, tools, decorative items, and furnishings. Handmade quilts and crafts can be found in Sutter Creek, Jackson, and Amador City. Auburn and Nevada City support many gift boutiques. Sacramento's commuter communities, such as Elk Grove (south), Folsom (east), and Roseville (northeast), are exploding with subdivisions and with them inevitably come the standard suburban assortment of chain stores and strip malls.

Theater

For weary miners in search of diversion, theater was a popular form of entertainment in the Gold Country. It still is, and you can take in a show at several venues dating from the era. The Woodland Opera House, opened in 1885, mounts musical theater productions September through July. Nevada City's Nevada Theatre, built in 1865, is the home of the Foothill Theater Company. In Columbia State Historic Park, the Historic Fallon House Theater presents dramas, comedies, and musicals.

---

a study of Native Americans in the U.S. Armed Forces and displays on the post–September 11 wars in Afghanistan and Iraq. ⊠ *1119 2nd St.* ☎ *916/442–2883* ✉ *$3* ☉ *Tues.–Sun. 10–4.*

need a break? The **River City Brewing Co.** (⊠ Downtown Plaza ☎ 916/447–2739) is the best of several breweries that have cropped up in the capital city. The brewery is at the west end of the K Street Mall, between the capitol and Old Sacramento.

☝ ⓫ **California State History Museum.** Drawing from the vast collections of the California State Archives, this state-of-the-art museum vividly portrays the story of California's land, people, and politics. Though many exhibits utilize modern technology, there are also scores of archival drawers that you can pull out to see the real artifacts of history and culture—from the California State Constitution to surfing magazines. Board a 1949 cross-country bus to view a video on immigration, visit a Chinese herb shop maintained by a holographic proprietor, or stand on a gubernatorial balcony overlooking a sea of cameras and banners.

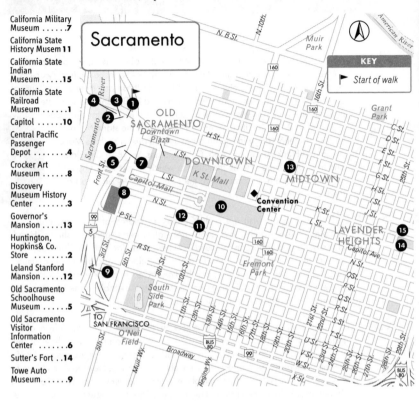

There's also a café. ✉ *1020 O St.* ☎ *916/653-7524* ⊕ *www.
goldenstatemuseum.org* 🎟 *$5* ⊗ *Tues.–Sat. 10–5, Sun. noon–5.*

🖑 ⓯ **California State Indian Museum.** Among the interesting displays at this well-
organized museum is one devoted to Ishi, the last Yahi Indian to emerge
from the mountains, in 1911. Ishi provided scientists with insight into
the traditions and culture of this group of Native Americans. Arts-and-
crafts exhibits, a demonstration village, and an evocative 10-minute video
bring to life the multifaceted past and present of California's native peo-
ples. ✉ *2618 K St.* ☎ *916/324–0971* ⊕ *www.parks.ca.gov* 🎟 *$2*
⊗ *Daily 10–5.*

🖑 ▶ ❶ **California State Railroad Museum.** Near what was once the terminus of
Fodor's Choice the transcontinental and Sacramento Valley railroads (the actual terminus
★ was at Front and K streets), this 100,000-square-foot museum has 21
locomotives and railroad cars on display and 46 exhibits. You can walk
through a post office car and peer into cubbyholes and canvas mailbags,
enter a sleeping car that simulates the swaying on the roadbed and the
flashing lights of a passing town at night, or glimpse the inside of the
first-class dining car. Allow at least two hours to enjoy the museum. ✉*125
I St.* ☎ *916/445–6645* ⊕ *www.csrmf.org* 🎟 *$4* ⊗ *Daily 10–5.*

★ ❿ **Capitol.** The Golden State's capitol was built in 1869. The lacy plasterwork of the 120-foot-high rotunda has the complexity and colors of a Fabergé egg. Underneath the gilded dome are marble floors, glittering chandeliers, monumental staircases, replicas of 19th-century state offices, and legislative chambers decorated in the style of the 1890s. Guides conduct tours of the building and the 40-acre Capitol Park, which contains a rose garden, an impressive display of camellias (Sacramento's city flower), and the California Vietnam Veterans Memorial. ✉ *Capitol Mall and 10th St.* ☎ *916/324–0333* ✉ *Free* ☉ *Daily 9–5; tours hourly 9–4.*

☾ ❹ **Central Pacific Passenger Depot.** At this reconstructed 1876 station there's rolling stock to admire, a typical waiting room, and a small restaurant. A steam-powered train departs hourly (April through September) from the freight depot, south of the passenger depot, making a 40-minute loop along the Sacramento riverfront. ✉ *930 Front St.* ☎ *916/445–6645* ✉ *$3, free with same-day ticket from California State Railroad Museum; train ride $6 additional* ☉ *Depot daily 10–5. Train Apr.–Sept. weekends; Oct.–Dec., 1st weekend of month.*

❽ **Crocker Art Museum.** The oldest art museum in the American West has a collection of art from Europe, Asia, and California, including *Sunday Morning in the Mines* (1872), a large canvas by Charles Christian Nahl depicting aspects of the original mining industry, and the magnificent *The Great Canyon of the Sierra, Yosemite* (1871), by Thomas Hill. The museum's lobby and ballroom retain the original 19th-century woodwork, plaster moldings, and English tiles. ✉ *216 O St.* ☎ *916/264–5423* ⊕ *www.crockerartmuseum.org* ✉ *$6* ☉ *Tues., Wed., and Fri.–Sun. 10–5, Thurs. 10–9.*

☾ ❸ **Discovery Museum History Center.** The building that holds this child-oriented museum is a replica of the 1854 city hall and waterworks. Interactive history, science, and technology exhibits examine the evolution of everyday life in the Sacramento area. You can pan for gold, examine a Native American thatch hut, or experience the goings-on in the former print shop of the *Sacramento Bee.* The Gold Gallery displays nuggets and veins. ✉ *101 I St.* ☎ *916/264–7057* ✉ *$5* ☉ *June–Aug., daily 10–5; Sept.–May, Tues.–Sun. 10–5.*

❽ **Governor's Mansion.** This 15-room house was built in 1877 and used by the state's chief executives from the early 1900s until 1967, when Ronald Reagan vacated it in favor of a newly built home in the more upscale suburbs. Many of the Italianate mansion's interior decorations were ordered from the Huntington, Hopkins & Co. hardware store, one of whose partners, Albert Gallatin, was the original occupant. Each of the seven marble fireplaces has a petticoat mirror that ladies strolled past to see if their slips were showing. The mansion is said to have been one of the first homes in California with an indoor bathroom. ✉ *1526 H St.* ☎ *916/323–3047* ✉ *$2* ☉ *Daily 10–4; tours hourly.*

❷ **Huntington, Hopkins & Co. Store.** This museum is a replica of the 1855 hardware store opened by Collis Huntington and Mark Hopkins, two of the Big Four businessmen who established the Central Pacific Railroad. Picks, shovels, gold pans, and other paraphernalia used by miners during the gold rush are on display, along with household hardware and appliances from the 1880s. Some items, such as blue enamelware, wooden toys, gold pans, and oil lamps, are for sale. ⊠ *113 I St.* ☎ *916/ 323-7234* 🖾 *Free* ☉ *Hrs vary.*

⑫ Leland Stanford Mansion. The home of Leland Stanford, a railroad baron, California governor, and U.S. senator, was built in 1856, with additions in 1862 and the early 1870s. Years have passed since it closed for repairs, and several more may go by before public tours are resumed. In the meantime it's interesting to view the transformation of the exterior. ⊠ *802 N St.* ☎ *916/324-0575.*

☾ ⑤ Old Sacramento Schoolhouse Museum. Sacramento's first school welcomed students in August 1849 and closed permanently four months later due to muddy streets. Five years passed before another public school opened. Today it's a kid-friendly attraction that shows what one-room schoolhouses were like in the California Central Valley and foothills in the late 1800s. ⊠ *Front and L Sts.* ☎ *No phone* 🖾 *Free* ☉ *Mon.–Sat. 10–4, Sun. noon–4.*

⑥ Old Sacramento Visitor Information Center. Obtain brochures about nearby attractions, check local restaurant menus, and get advice from the helpful staff here. ⊠ *1101 2nd St., at K St.* ☎ *916/442-7644* ⊕ *www. oldsacramento.com* ☉ *Daily 10–5.*

★ ☾ ⑭ Sutter's Fort. Sacramento's earliest Euro-American settlement was founded by German-born Swiss immigrant John Augustus Sutter in 1839. Audio speakers give information at each stop along a self-guided tour that includes a blacksmith's shop, bakery, prison, living quarters, and livestock areas. Costumed docents sometimes reenact fort life, demonstrating crafts, food preparation, and firearms maintenance. ⊠ *2701 L St.* ☎ *916/445-4422* ⊕ *www.parks.ca.gov* 🖾 *$2* ☉ *Daily 10–5.*

☾ ⑨ Towe Auto Museum. With more than 150 vintage automobiles on display, and exhibits ranging from the Hall of Technology to Dreams of Speed and Dreams of Cool, this museum explores automotive history and car culture. A 1920s roadside café and garage exhibit re-creates the early days of motoring. The gift shop sells vintage-car magazines, model kits, and other car-related items. ⊠ *2200 Front St., 1 block off Broadway* ☎ *916/442-6802* ⊕ *www.toweautomuseum.org* 🖾 *$7* ☉ *Daily 10–5.*

Where to Stay & Eat

$$–$$$$ ✕ **The Firehouse.** Consistently rated by local publications as among the city's top 10 restaurants, the Firehouse has a full bar, courtyard seating (its signature attraction), and creative American cookery, such as antelope topped with a blueberry and walnut chutney. Visitors who can afford to treat themselves to a fine and leisurely meal can do no better in Old Sacramento. ⊠ *1112 2nd St.* ☎ *916/442-4772* ⊟ *AE, MC, V* ☉ *Closed Sun. No lunch Sat.*

★ $$–$$$ ✕ **Biba.** Owner Biba Caggiano is an authority on Italian cuisine, author of several cookbooks, and the star of a national TV show on cooking.

The capitol crowd flocks here for homemade ravioli, osso buco, grilled pork loin, and veal and rabbit specials. A pianist adds to the upscale ambience nightly. ⊠ *2801 Capitol Ave.* ☎ *916/455–2422* ⚑ *Reservations essential* ▤ *AE, DC, MC, V* ☉ *Closed Sun. No lunch Sat.*

$$–$$$ ✕ **Rio City Café.** Contemporary and seasonal Mediterranean and Californian cuisine and huge floor-to-ceiling windows with views of an Old Sacramento wharf are the dual attractions of this bright restaurant. ⊠ *1110 Front St.* ☎ *916/442–8226* ▤ *AE, D, DC, MC, V.*

★ **$–$$$** ✕ **The Waterboy.** Rural French cooking and California cuisine are the culinary treasures at this popular midtown restaurant, featuring such distinct dishes as chicken potpie, veal sweetbreads, and beet salad. This is where top local restaurateurs go when they want a good meal. ⊠ *2000 Capitol Ave.* ☎ *916/498–9891* ▤ *AE, D, DC, MC, V* ☉ *Closed Mon. No lunch weekends.*

$–$$ ✕ **Centro.** The motorcycle with a skeleton rider in the front window denotes the vibrant wackiness that spices up this popular midtown Mexican eatery. Bright yellow booths and salsa music add to the ambience, but the tasty food—well outside the taco-burrito realm—is the real attraction. Centro's bar attracts the beautiful people. ⊠ *2730 J St.* ☎ *916/442–2552* ▤ *AE, DC, MC, V* ☉ *No lunch weekends.*

$–$$ ✕ **Joe's Crab Shack.** This nationwide chain restaurant has a special place in Old Sacramento—hanging over the Sacramento River. A few strides south of the *Delta King,* this shabby-chic, seaside-funky restaurant has been a smash hit since opening in 2003. Go around sundown, and watch the yellow paint on nearby Tower Bridge, one of Sacramento's landmarks, subtly change. ⊠ *1210 Front St.* ☎ *916/553–4249* ⊕ *www.joescrabshack.com* ▤ *AE, DC, MC, V.*

¢–$$ ✕ **Tapa the World.** As defined at this midtown bar and restaurant, tapas are bite-size portions of meats, seafood, chicken, and veggies shared at the table. One of Sacramento's liveliest night spots (it's open 'til midnight), Tapa often presents Flamenco and Spanish classical music performers. ⊠ *2125 J St.* ☎ *916/442–4353* ▤ *AE, D, DC, MC, V.*

¢–$ ✕ **Ernesto's Mexican Food.** Customers wait up to an hour for a table on Friday and Saturday evenings at this popular midtown dinner restaurant. Fresh ingredients are stressed in the wide selection of entrées, and the margaritas are especially refreshing. A lively bar helps kill time before tables become available. Request an outdoor table if you're more interested in conversation than too-loud, canned Mexican music. ⊠ *16th and S Sts.* ☎ *916/441–5850* ▤ *AE, D, DC, MC, V.*

$$$ ✕▣ **Sterling Hotel.** This gleaming-white Victorian mansion three blocks from the capitol has rose-color guest rooms with handsome furniture, including four-poster or canopy beds. Bathrooms are tiled in Italian marble and have Jacuzzi tubs. Restaurant Chanterelle ($$) serves contemporary continental cuisine in its candlelit dining room and pleasant patio area. ⊠ *1300 H St., 95814* ☎ *916/448–1300 or 800/365–7660* ⊠ *916/448–8066* ⊕ *www.sterlinghotel.com* ⊷ *17 rooms, 2 suites* ⚘ *Restaurant, room service, in-room data ports, bar, dry cleaning, business services, meeting room, parking (fee), no-smoking rooms* ▤ *AE, D, DC, MC, V.*

★ **$$–$$$$** ⊞ **Amber House Bed & Breakfast Inn.** This B&B near the capitol encompasses three homes. The original house, the Poet's Refuge, is a craftsman-style home with five bedrooms named for famous writers. The 1913 Mediterranean-style Artist's Retreat has a French Impressionist motif. The third, an 1897 Dutch colonial–revival home named Musician's Manor, has gardens that occasionally host weddings. Baths are tiled in Italian marble; some have skylights and two-person spa tubs. The Emily Dickenson Room's double-sided fireplace warms both the bathroom and bedroom. ⊠ *1315 22nd St., 95816* ☎ *916/444–8085 or 800/755–6526* ⓕ *916/552–6529* ⊕ *www.amberhouse.com* ⟿ *14 rooms* ⚭ *In-room data ports, cable TV, in-room VCRs, concierge; no smoking* ⊟ *AE, D, DC, MC, V* ⏏❙ *BP.*

★ **$–$$$$** ⊞ **Hyatt Regency Sacramento.** With a marble-and-glass lobby and luxurious rooms, this hotel across from the capitol and adjacent to the convention center is arguably Sacramento's finest. The multitiered, glass-dominated hotel has a striking Mediterranean design. The best rooms have Capitol Park views. The service and attention to detail are outstanding. Governor Schwarzenegger, whose family still resides in Southern California, camps out here several nights a week. ⊠ *1209 L St., 95814* ☎ *916/443–1234 or 800/633–7313* ⓕ *916/321–3799* ⊕ *www.hyatt. com* ⟿ *500 rooms, 24 suites* ⚭ *2 restaurants, pool, gym, hot tub, bar, dry cleaning, laundry service, concierge, business services, meeting room, car rental, parking (fee)* ⊟ *AE, D, DC, MC, V.*

$$–$$$ ⊞ **Delta King.** This grand old riverboat, now permanently moored on Old Sacramento's waterfront, once transported passengers between Sacramento and San Francisco. Among many notable design elements are its main staircase, mahogany paneling, and brass fittings. The best of the 43 staterooms are on the river side toward the back of the boat. The boat's theater gains more critical acclaim every year, though patrons must sometimes tune out the creaking floorboards above. ⊠ *1000 Front St., 95814* ☎ *916/444–5464 or 800/825–5464* ⓕ *916/447–5959* ⊕ *www.deltaking.com* ⟿ *44 rooms* ⚭ *Restaurant, lounge, theater, meeting room, parking (fee)* ⊟ *AE, D, DC, MC, V* ⏏❙ *CP.*

$–$$ ⊞ **Holiday Inn Capitol Plaza.** Despite its decided lack of charm, this high-rise hotel has modern rooms and the best location for visiting Old Sacramento and the Downtown Plaza. It's also within walking distance of the capitol. ⊠ *300 J St., 95814* ☎ *916/446–0100 or 800/465–4329* ⓕ *916/446–7371* ⊕ *www.holiday-inn.com* ⟿ *362 rooms, 4 suites* ⚭ *Restaurant, minibars, cable TV, pool, gym, bar, shop, concierge floor, convention center, no-smoking rooms* ⊟ *AE, DC, MC, V.*

$ ⊞ **Best Western Sutter House.** Many of the pleasant, modern rooms in this downtown hotel open onto a courtyard surrounding a pool. The stylish restaurant, Grape's, serves contemporary cuisine. A complimentary full breakfast is offered. ⊠ *1100 H St., 95814* ☎ *916/441–1314 or 800/830–1314* ⓕ *916/441–5961* ⊕ *www.thesutterhouse.com* ⟿ *97 rooms, 1 suite* ⚭ *Restaurant, pool, lounge, laundry service, free parking, no-smoking floor* ⊟ *AE, D, DC, MC, V* ⏏❙ *BP.*

$ ⊞ **Radisson Hotel Sacramento.** Mediterranean-style two-story buildings cluster around a large artificial lake on an 18-acre landscaped site a few miles northeast of downtown. Rooms are enlivened with art deco appointments and furnishings; many have a patio or balcony. More resort-like than other Sacramento-area hotels, the Radisson presents summer jazz concerts in a lakeside amphitheater and holds barbecues on warm evenings. ✉ *500 Leisure La., 95815* ☎ *916/922–2020 or 800/333–3333* 🖷 *916/649–9463* ⊕ *www.radisson.com/sacramentoca* ⮐ *307 rooms, 22 suites* ♨ *2 restaurants, room service, pool, lake, gym, outdoor hot tub, boating, bicycles, bar, convention center* ▭ *AE, D, DC, MC, V.*

¢ ▦ **Sacramento International Hostel.** This 1885 Victorian mansion has a grand mahogany staircase, a stained-glass atrium, frescoed ceilings, and carved and tiled fireplaces. Dormitory rooms and bedrooms suitable for singles, couples, and families are available, as is a communal kitchen. In 2002 the building was moved across the street and spruced up considerably. Its access to downtown remains superb. ✉ *925 H St., 95814* ☎ *916/443–1691 or 800/909–4776 Ext. 40* 🖷 *916/443–4763* ⊕ *www.norcalhostels.org* ⮐ *70 beds* ♨ *Kitchen; no room TVs* ▭ *MC, V.*

Nightlife & the Arts

Downtown Events Line (☎ 916/442–2500) has recorded information about seasonal events in the downtown area.

Nightlife

The **Blue Cue** (✉ 1004 28th St. ☎ 916/442–7208), upstairs from Centro restaurant, is an eclectic billiard lounge known for its large selection of single-malt scotches. The **Fox and Goose** (✉ 1001 R St. ☎ 916/443–8825) is a casual pub with live music (including open-mike Monday). Traditional pub food (fish-and-chips, Cornish pasties) is served on weekday evenings from 5:30 to 9:30. **Harlow's** (✉ 2708 J St. ☎ 916/441–4693) draws a young crowd to its art deco bar-nightclub for live music after 9. **Streets of London Pub** (✉ 1804 J St. ☎ 916/498–1388) is popular among Anglophiles and stays open until 2 AM every night except Sunday, when it closes an hour earlier.

The Arts

Sacramento Community Center Theater (✉ 13th and L Sts. ☎ 916/264–5181) hosts concerts, opera, and ballet. The **Sacramento Light Opera Association** (✉ 1419 H St. ☎ 916/557–1999) presents Broadway shows at the Sacramento Community Center Theater and in the huge Music Circus tent in summer. If you want the really *big* picture, the **Esquire Theater** (✉ 13th St. on the K St. Mall ☎ 916/446–2333), screens IMAX movies. For art films, visit the funky **Tower Theater** (✉ 2508 Land Park Dr. ☎ 916/442 1700), a few minutes southeast of downtown. The **Crest Theatre** is another place to see art films.

Shopping

Top local artists and craftspeople exhibit their works at **Artists' Collaborative Gallery** (✉ 1007 2nd St. ☎ 916/444–3764). The **Elder Craftsman** (✉ 130 J St. ☎ 916/264–7762) specializes in items made by local senior citizens. **Gallery of the American West** (✉ 121 K St. ☎ 916/446–6662) has a large selection of Native American arts and crafts. **Arden Fair Mall** (✉ Off I-80, northeast of downtown) is Sacramento's largest shopping center. **Downtown Plaza,** comprising the K Street Mall along with many neighboring shops and restaurants, has shopping and entertainment. There's a Thursday-night market in the summer and an outdoor ice-skating rink in winter. Side Trips from Sacramento

Woodland

16 *20 mi northwest of Sacramento on I–5.*

Woodland's downtown lies frozen in a quaint and genteel past. In its heyday it was one of the wealthiest cities in California, established in 1861 by gold seekers and entrepreneurs. Once the boom was over, attention turned to the rich surrounding land, and the area became an agricultural gold mine. The legacy of the old land barons lives on in the Victorian homes that line Woodland's wide streets. Many of the houses have been restored and are surrounded by lavish gardens.

More than 300 touring companies, including John Philip Sousa's marching band, and Frank Kirk, the Acrobatic Tramp, appeared at the **Woodland Opera House,** built in 1885 (and rebuilt after it burned in 1892). Now restored, the building hosts concerts and, September through July, a season of musical theater. Free weekly guided tours reveal old-fashioned stage technology. ⊠ *Main and 2nd Sts.* ☎ *530/666–9617* ⊕ *www. wohtheatre.org* ☉ *Daily 10–5, tours Tues. 1–4.*

This 10-room classical revival home of settler William Byas Gibson was purchased by volunteers and restored as the **Yolo County Historical Museum.** You can see collections of furnishings and artifacts from the 1850s to 1930s. Old trees and an impressive lawn cover the 2-acre site off Highway 113. ⊠ *512 Gibson Rd.* ☎ *530/666–1045* 🖃 *$2* ☉ *Daily 9–5; tours Mon. and Tues. 10–4, weekends noon–4.*

Old trucks and farm machinery seem to rumble to life within the shed-like **Heidrick Ag History Center,** where you can see the world's largest collection of antique agricultural equipment. Also here are interactive exhibits, a food court, gift shop, and kids' play area. ⊠ *1962 Hays La.* ☎ *530/666–9700* 🖷 *530/666–9712* ⊕ *www.aghistory.org* 🖃 *$6* ☉ *Weekdays 10–5, Sat. 10–6, Sun. 10–4.*

Where to Stay & Eat

$–$$$ ✕ **Ludy's Main Street BBQ.** This big, casual restaurant next door to the Opera House looks like something out of the *Beverly Hillbillies.* You can tuck into huge portions of ribs, beef, chicken, or fish-and-chips, or have a half-pound burger slathered in red sauce. On the patio, water misters cool you in summer, and heaters keep you toasty in winter. There is a kids' menu. ⊠ *667 Main St.* ☎ *530/666–4400* 🖃 *AE, MC, V.*

$–$$$ ✕ **Morrison's Upstairs.** The Victorian building that houses this restaurant is registered as a State Historic Landmark. Downstairs is a bar, deli, and patio. The top floor, once the attic, is full of nooks and alcoves where you can have your meal. Furnished throughout with polished wood tables that suit the style of the house, Morrison's serves burgers and sandwiches, scampi, Chinese chicken salad, pasta, prime rib, and vegetarian selections. ⊠ *428½ 1st St.* ☎ *530/666–6176* 🖃 *AE, D, DC, MC, V.*

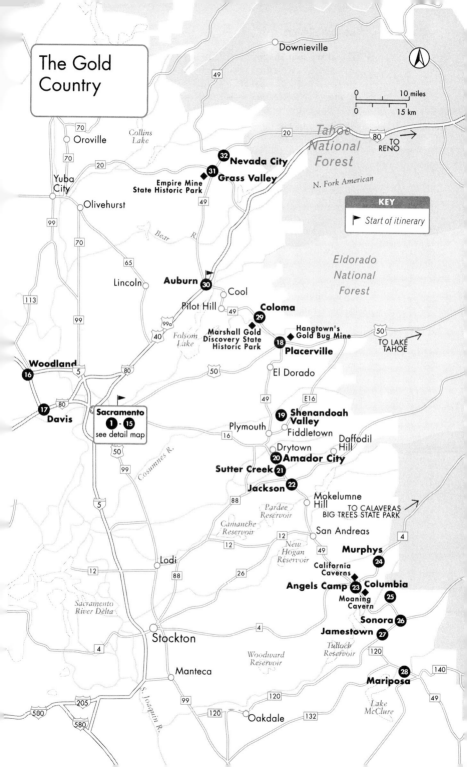

The Gold Country

KEY

▶ *Start of itinerary*

0 ——— 10 miles
0 ——— 15 km

Downieville

Oroville

Collins Lake

Tahoe National Forest

80 TO RENO

Yuba City

Olivehurst

32 Nevada City
31 Grass Valley
Empire Mine State Historic Park

N. Fork American

Lincoln

Auburn 30
Cool
Pilot Hill

Eldorado National Forest

Coloma
29
Marshall Gold Discovery State Historic Park
Hangtown's Gold Bug Mine
18 Placerville

TO LAKE TAHOE

Woodland 16

Folsom Lake

El Dorado

Davis 17

Sacramento
1 - 15
see detail map

19 Shenandoah Valley
Plymouth
Fiddletown
Daffodil Hill

Drytown
20 Amador City
Sutter Creek 21
Jackson 22

Mokelumne Hill
TO CALAVERAS BIG TREES STATE PARK

Lodi

Pardee Reservoir

Camanche Reservoir

New Hogan Reservoir

San Andreas

Murphys 24

California Caverns
Angels Camp 23 **Columbia**
Moaning Cavern
25
Sonora 26
Jamestown 27

Stockton

Manteca

Woodward Reservoir

Tulloch Reservoir

Mariposa 28

Lake McClure

Oakdale

$ ⊞ Best Western Shadow Inn. Palm trees wave over the landscaped pool area at this two-story hotel. Some rooms have wet bars and kitchenettes. ⊠ *584 N. East St., 95776* ☎ *530/666–1251* 🖷 *530/662–2804* ⊕ *www.bestwestern.com* ⇆ *120 rooms* ⚬ *Some kitchenettes, cable TV, pool, hot tub, laundry facilities, business services* ⊟ *AE, D, DC, MC, V* ⌾ *CP.*

$ ⊞ Valley Oaks Inn. Rooms in this two-story motel have basic furnishings and amenities. ⊠ *600 N. East St., 95695* ☎ *530/666–5511* ⇆ *62 rooms* ⚬ *Refrigerators, cable TV, pool* ⊟ *AE, D, DC, MC, V.*

¢ ⊞ Cinderella Motel Woodland. Rooms here are clean and basic, which makes this a good choice in a town without many lodging options. ⊠ *99 W. Main St.* ☎ *530/662–1091* 🖷 *530/662–2804* ⇆ *30 rooms* ⚬ *Refrigerators, cable TV with movies, in-room VCRs, pool, hot tub, some pets allowed (fee); no smoking* ⊟ *AE, D, DC, MC, V.*

Davis

⑰ *10 mi west of Sacramento on I–80.*

Though it began as—and still is—a rich agricultural area, Davis doesn't feel like a cow town. It's home to the University of California at Davis, whose students hang at the cafés and bookstores in the central business district, making the city feel a little more cosmopolitan. The city has long enjoyed a progressive, liberal reputation (it's been called "the People's Republic of Davis"), but a rash of new yuppie-stocked subdivisions reflect how Davis is becoming more of a mainstream commuter community, whether residents admit it or not. The university is a leader in viticulture education and has one of the West Coast's top veterinary programs.

The center of action in town is the **Davis Campus of the University of California,** which ranks among the top 25 research universities in the United States. You can take tours of the campus, which depart from Buehler Alumni and Visitors Center. The **Mondavi Center for the Performing Arts,** a strikingly modern glass structure off I–80 offers a busy and varied schedule of performances. ⊠ *1 Shields Ave.* ☎ *530/752–8111* ⊕ *www.ucdavis.edu* ⊙ *Tours weekends 11:30 and 1:30, weekdays by appointment.*

The work by northern California craftspeople displayed at the **Artery,** an artists' cooperative, includes decorative and functional ceramics, glass, wood, jewelry, fiber arts, painting, sculpture, drawing, and photography. ⊠ *207 G St.* ☎ *530/758–8330* ⊕ *www.arteryart.com* ⊙ *Mon.–Thurs. and Sat. 10–6, Fri. 10–9, Sun. noon–5.*

WHERE TO STAY & EAT

$–$$$ ✕ **Café California.** The locals who gather at this downtown Davis eatery favor such dishes as a salad of prawns and baby greens with avocado-tarragon vinaigrette, Cajun-style prime rib with chili onion rings, and roast chicken with garlic mashed potatoes. The contemporary dining room is set with white linens. ⊠ *808 2nd St.* ☎ *530/757–2766* 🖷 *530/758–5236* ⊟ *AE, MC, V.*

$–$$$ ✕ **Soga's.** Watercolors by local artists hang on the walls of this elegant restaurant. The California-style menu features various presentations of salmon filet, swordfish, and veal and also offers vegetable plates. You can eat on the long, covered patio in good weather. ⊠ *217 E St.* ☎ *530/757–1733* ⚓ *Reservations essential* ⊟ *AE, D, MC, V* ⊗ *No lunch weekends.*

$–$$ ⌂ **Hallmark Inn.** Two buildings with clean, modern rooms make up this inn, which is five blocks from the University of California campus and is next door to a restaurant. ⊠ *110 F St., 95616* ☎ *530/758–8623 or 800/753–0035* ⊕ *www.hallmarkinn.com* ⤲ *135 rooms* ⚐ *Restaurant, some refrigerators, pool, free parking* ⊟ *AE, D, DC, MC, V.*

$ ⌂ **Aggie Inn.** This hotel, less than a block from the campus, is named for the University of California at Davis "Aggies," the school's team name. Rooms are clean and basic; convenience is what this place is about. ⊠ *245 1st St., 95616* ☎ *530/756–0352* 🖷 *530/753–5738* ⊕ *www. stayanight.com* ⤲ *25 rooms, 9 suites* ⚐ *Some in-room hot tubs, some kitchenettes, outdoor hot tub, sauna, laundry service* ⊟ *AE, D, DC, MC, V* ⦿ *CP.*

$ ⌂ **Best Western University Lodge.** This three-story hotel is a good place to stop if you have business at the university, which is one block away. ⊠ *123 B St., 95616* ☎ *530/756–7890* 🖷 *530/756–0245* ⊕ *www. bestwestern.com* ⤲ *53 rooms* ⚐ *Some kitchenettes, microwaves, refrigerators, cable TV, exercise equipment, spa, some pets allowed* ⊟ *AE, D, DC, MC, V* ⦿ *CP.*

THE GOLD COUNTRY—SOUTH
HIGHWAY 49 FROM PLACERVILLE TO MARIPOSA

South of its junction with U.S. 50, Highway 49 traces in asphalt the famed Mother Lode. The sleepy former gold-rush towns strung along the road have for the most part been restored and made presentable to visitors with an interest in one of the most frenzied episodes of American history.

Placerville

⑱ *10 mi south of Coloma on Hwy. 49; 44 mi east of Sacramento on U.S. 50.*

It's hard to imagine now, but in 1849 about 4,000 miners staked out every gully and hillside in Placerville, turning the town into a rip-roaring camp of log cabins, tents, and clapboard houses. The area was then known as Hangtown, a graphic allusion to the nature of frontier justice. It took on the name Placerville in 1854 and became an important supply center for the miners. Mark Hopkins, Philip Armour, and John Studebaker were among the industrialists who got their starts here.

★ ☾ **Hangtown's Gold Bug Mine,** owned by the City of Placerville, centers on a fully lighted mine shaft open for self-guided touring. A shaded stream runs through the park, and there are picnic facilities. ⊠ *North on Bedford Ave., 1 mi off U.S. 50* ☎ *530/642–5207* ⊕ *www.goldbugpark.org* 🖃 *$3* ⊗ *Tours mid-Apr.–Oct., daily 10–4; Nov.–mid-Apr., weekends noon–4. Gift shop Mar.–Nov., daily 10–4.*

| off the beaten path | **APPLE HILL** – Roadside stands sell fresh produce from more than 50 family farms in this area. During the fall harvest season (from September through December), members of the Apple Hill Growers Association open their orchards and vineyards for apple and berry picking, picnicking, and wine and cider tasting. Many sell baked items and picnic food. ⊠ *About 5 mi east of Hwy. 49; take Camino exit from U.S. 50* ☎ *530/644–7692.* |

Where to Stay & Eat

★ **$$–$$$$** ✕ **Zachary Jacques.** It's not easy to locate (call for directions), but finding this country-French restaurant is worth the effort. Appetizers on the seasonal menu might include escargots or mushrooms prepared in several ways, roasted garlic with olive oil served on toast, or spicy lamb sausage. Standard entrées include roast rack of lamb, beef stew, and scallops and shrimp in lime butter. The attached wine bar opens at 4:30. ⊠ *1821 Pleasant Valley Rd., 3 mi east of Diamond Springs* ☎ *530/626–8045* ▤ *AE, MC, V* ☾ *Closed Mon. and Tues. No lunch.*

$$–$$$ ✕ **Café Luna.** Tucked into the back of the Creekside Place shopping complex is a small restaurant with about 30 seats inside, plus outdoor tables overlooking a creek. The menu, which changes weekly, encompasses many cuisines, including Indian, Russian, and Thai. ⊠ *451 Main St.* ☎ *530/642–8669* ▤ *AE, D, MC, V* ☾ *Closed Sun. No dinner Mon. and Tues.*

$–$$ ✕ **Lil' Mama D. Carlo's Italian Kitchen.** This comfortable Italian restaurant with a pleasant staff serves large portions of homemade pasta and chicken; the vegetarian dishes are heavy on the garlic. A wine bar highlights local varieties. ⊠ *482 Main St.* ☎ *530/626–1612* ▤ *AE, MC, V* ☾ *Closed Mon. and Tues. No lunch.*

$$–$$$ ⌸ **Seasons Bed & Breakfast.** A 10-minute walk from downtown, one of Placerville's oldest homes has been transformed into a lovely and relaxing oasis. The main house, cottages, and gardens are filled with paintings and sculptures. Privacy is treasured here. A suite with a sitting room and stained-glass windows occupies the main house's top floor. One cottage has a little white picket fence around its own minigarden; another has a two-person shower. ⊠ *2934 Bedford Ave., 95667* ☎ *530/626–4420* ⊕ *www.theseasons.net* ⇌ *3 rooms, 1 suite* ⌕ *No-smoking rooms* ▤ *MC, V* ⃝ *BP.*

$ ⌸ **Best Western Placerville Inn.** This motel's serviceable rooms are decorated in the chain's trademark pastels. The pool comes in handy during hot summer months. ⊠ *6850 Greenleaf Dr., near Missouri Flats exit of U.S. 50, 95667* ☎ *530/622–9100 or 800/854–9100* ⎙ *530/622–9376* ⊕ *www.bestwestern.com* ⇌ *105 rooms* ⌕ *Cable TV, pool, free parking* ▤ *AE, D, DC, MC, V.*

Shenandoah Valley

⑲ *20 mi south of Placerville on Shenandoah Rd., east of Hwy. 49.*

The most concentrated Gold Country wine-touring area lies in the hills of the Shenandoah Valley, east of Plymouth. Robust Zinfandel is the primary grape grown here, but vineyards also produce cabernet sauvignon,

sauvignon blanc, and other varietals. Most wineries are open on weekend afternoons; several have shaded picnic areas, gift shops, and galleries or museums; all have tasting rooms.

Sobon Estate (✉ 14430 Shenandoah Rd. ☎ 209/245–6554) operates the Shenandoah Valley Museum, illustrating pioneer life and wine making in the valley. It's open daily from 9:30 to 5. At **Charles Spinetta Winery** (✉ 12557 Steiner Rd. ☎ 209/245–3384 ⊕ www.charlesspinettawinery. com), you can see a wildlife art gallery in addition to tasting the wine. It's open weekdays from 8 to 4 and weekends from 9:30 to 4:30. The gallery at **Shenandoah Vineyards** (✉ 12300 Steiner Rd. ☎ 209/245–4455), open daily from 10 to 5, displays contemporary art.

Where to Stay

$$ 🏠 **Amador Harvest Inn.** This B&B adjacent to Deaver Vineyards occupies a bucolic lakeside spot in the Shenandoah Valley. A contemporary Cape Cod–style structure has homey guest rooms with private baths. Public areas include a living room with fireplace and a music room with a view of the lake. ✉ *12455 Steiner Rd., 95669* ☎ *209/245–5512 or 800/217–2304* 🖨 *209/245–5250* ⊕ *www.amadorharvestinn.com* 🛏 *4 rooms* ⚹ *No room TVs* 🖃 *AE, MC, V* ⦿ *BP.*

Amador City

㉑ *6 mi south of Plymouth on Hwy. 49.*

The history of tiny Amador City mirrors the boom-bust-boom cycle of many Gold Country towns. With an output of $42 million in gold, its Keystone Mine was one of the most productive in the Mother Lode. After all the gold was extracted, the miners cleared out, and the area suffered. Amador City now derives its wealth from tourists, who come to browse through its antiques and specialty shops, many of them on or off Highway 49.

Where to Stay & Eat

★ $-$$ ✕🏠 **Imperial Hotel.** The whimsically decorated mock-Victorian rooms at this 1879 hotel give a modern twist to the excesses of the era. Antique furnishings include iron-and-brass beds, gingerbread flourishes, and, in one room, art deco appointments. The two front rooms, which can be noisy, have balconies. The menu at the hotel's fine restaurant ($–$$$) changes quarterly and ranges from vegetarian to country hearty to contemporary eclectic. You can eat in the bright dining room or on the patio but only for dinner and not on Monday or Tuesday. The hotel has a two-night minimum stay on weekends. ✉ *Hwy. 49, 95601* ☎ *209/267–9172* 🖨 *209/267–9249* ⊕ *www.imperialamador.com* 🛏 *6 rooms* ⚹ *Restaurant, bar* 🖃 *AE, D, DC, MC, V* ⦿ *BP.*

Sutter Creek

★ ㉒ *2 mi south of Amador City on Hwy. 49.*

Sutter Creek is a charming conglomeration of balconied buildings, Victorian homes, and neo–New England structures. The stores along Highway 49 (called Main Street in the town proper) are worth visiting for works by the many local artists and craftspeople. Seek out the **J. Monteverde General Store** (⊠ 3 Randolph St.), a typical turn-of-the-20th-century emporium with vintage goods on display (but not for sale), an elaborate antique scale, and a chair-encircled potbellied stove in the corner. Only open weekends 10–3, it closes in January. You can also stop by the **Sutter Creek Visitor Center** (⊠ 11A Randolph St. ☎ 209/267–1344 or 800/400–0305) also open weekends 10–3, for information.

off the
beaten
path

DAFFODIL HILL – Each spring a 4-acre hillside east of Sutter Creek erupts in a riot of yellow and gold as 300,000 daffodils burst into bloom. The garden is the work of members of the McLaughlin family, which has owned this site since 1887. Daffodil plantings began in the 1930s. The display usually takes place between mid-March and mid-April. ⊠ *From Main St. (Hwy. 49) in Sutter Creek, take Shake Ridge Rd. east 13 mi* ☎ *209/223–0350* ⊕ *www.amadorcountychamber.com* ⌨ *Free* ⊙ *Mid-Mar.–mid-Apr., daily 9–5.*

Where to Stay & Eat

$–$$$ ✗ **Zinfandel's.** Black-bean chili in an edible bread tureen, and smoked mussels and bay shrimp with roasted garlic cloves are among the appetizers at this casual restaurant. On the adventurous menu are such entrées as rack of lamb marinated in red wine, garlic, and rosemary on garlic smashed potatoes with mushroom port sauce. ⊠ *51 Hanford St.* ☎ *209/267–5008* ⊟ *AE, D, MC, V* ⊙ *Closed Mon.–Wed. No lunch.*

¢–$ ✗ **Back Roads Coffee House.** Airy and spacious, Back Roads is roughly in the middle of a frenzied four-block stretch of Highway 49 where traffic crawls and sidewalks bulge. Muffins, pastries, and coffee seem to be the biggest draws here, though hot, simple breakfasts are available. The lunch menu includes soups and salads. All the tables have a small stack of Trivial Pursuit cards, which should amuse baby boomers and trivia buffs. ⊠ *74 Main St.* ☎ *209/267–0440* ⊟ *D, MC, V* ⊙ *No dinner.*

¢–$ ✗ **Chatterbox Café.** This classic 1940s luncheonette has only five tables and 14 counter stools. Read a vintage newspaper or examine the jazz instruments and Disney memorabilia on the shelves while you wait for your chicken-fried steak, burger, homemade pie, or hot-fudge sundae. The menu is as big as the Chatterbox is small. Beer and wine are available. ⊠ *39 Main St.* ☎ *209/267–5935* ⊟ *AE, D, MC, V* ⊙ *No dinner Wed.–Mon.*

★ $$–$$$ ⬜ **Foxes Bed & Breakfast.** The rooms in this 1857 white-clapboard house are handsome, with high ceilings, antique beds, and armoires. All have queen-size beds; five have gas fireplaces. Breakfast is cooked to order and delivered on a silver service to your room or to the gazebo in the garden. ⊠ *77 Main St., 95685* ☎ *209/267–5882 or 800/987–3344* 🖨 *209/267–0712* ⊕ *www.foxesinn.com* ⮠ *5 rooms, 2 suites* ⚭ *Some cable TV, some in-room VCRs, no-smoking rooms* ⊟ *D, MC, V* ⦿❙ *BP.*

$–$$ ⬜ **Eureka Street Inn.** Original redwood paneling, wainscoting, beams, and cabinets as well as lead- and stained-glass windows lend the Eureka Street Inn—formerly the Picture Rock Inn—a certain coziness. The craftsman-style bungalow was built in 1914 as a family home. Most rooms have gas-log fireplaces, and wireless Internet is available.

✉ *55 Eureka St., 95685* ☎ *209/267–5500 or 800/399–2389* ⊕ *www. eurekastreetinn.com* ⌨ *4 rooms* ⚴ *No room TVs* ▭ *AE, D, MC, V* ⭐ *BP.*

$ 🏨 **Historian Inn.** If you're touring the Gold Country on a budget, this hotel is a good choice. The rooms contain coffeemakers and two queen-size beds; three rooms are wheelchair accessible. ✉ *271 Hanford St., 95685* ☎ *209/267–9177* 🖷 *209/267–5303* ⌨ *52 rooms* ⚴ *Cable TV* ▭ *D, MC, V* ⭐ *CP.*

Jackson

❷❷ *8 mi south of Sutter Creek on Hwy. 49.*

Jackson wasn't the Gold Country's rowdiest town, but the party lasted longer here than most anywhere else: "girls' dormitories" (brothels) and nickel slot machines flourished until the mid-1950s. Jackson also had the world's deepest and richest gold mines, the Kennedy and the Argonaut, which together produced $70 million in gold. These were deep-rock mines with tunnels extending as much as a mile underground. Most of the miners who worked the lode were of Serbian or Italian origin, and they gave the town a European character that persists to this day. Jackson has pioneer cemeteries whose headstones tell the stories of local Serbian and Italian families. The terraced cemetery on the grounds of the handsome **St. Sava Serbian Orthodox Church** (✉ 724 N. Main St.) is the most impressive of the town's burial grounds.

The heart of Jackson's historic section is the **National Hotel** (✉ 2 Water St. ☎ 209/233–0500), which operates an old-time saloon in the lobby. The hotel is especially active on weekends, when people come from miles around to participate in Saturday-night sing-alongs.

The **Amador County Museum,** built in the late 1850s as a private home, provides a colorful take on gold-rush life. Displays include a kitchen with a woodstove, the Amador County bicentennial quilt, and a classroom. A time line recounts the county's checkered past. The museum conducts hourly tours of large-scale working models of the nearby Kennedy Mine. ✉ *225 Church St.* ☎ *209/223–6386* 🏷 *Museum free; mine tours $1* 🕑 *Wed.–Sun. 10–4.*

Where to Stay & Eat

$$–$$$$ ✕ **Upstairs Restaurant.** Chef Layne McCollum takes a creative approach to contemporary American cuisine with a menu that changes weekly. The baked-Brie and roast-garlic appetizer and the soups are specialties. Local wines are reasonably priced. Downstairs from the 12-table restaurant there's a street-side bistro and wine bar. ✉ *164 Main St.* ☎ *209/ 223–3342* ▭ *AE, D, MC, V* 🕑 *Closed Mon. and Tues.*

¢–$ ✕ **Rosebud's Classic Café.** Art deco accents and music from the 1930s and 1940s set the mood at this homey café. Among the classic American dishes served are hot roast beef, turkey, and meat loaf with mashed potatoes smothered in gravy. Charbroiled burgers, freshly baked pies, and espresso coffees round out the lunch menu. Omelets, hotcakes, and many other items are served for breakfast. ✉ *26 Main St.* ☎ *209/223– 1035* ▭ *MC, V* 🕑 *No dinner.*

$$–$$$ ⚏ **Court Street Inn.** This Victorian has tin ceilings and a redwood staircase. The cozy first-floor Burgundy Court Room has a fireplace; the Champagne Court Room has a large whirlpool bathtub and a fireplace. The Indian House, a two-bedroom cottage, has a large bathroom, a 61-inch TV with VCR, and a stereo. A third building, Vintage Court, contains a suite with a deck, TV, and VCR. ✉ *215 Court St., 95642* ☎ *209/223–0416 or 800/200–0416* 🖶 *209/223–5429* ⊕ *www.courtstreetinn.com* ⇗ *3 rooms, 3 suites* ⚘ *Outdoor hot tub* ☰ *AE, D, MC, V* ⏐◎⏐ *BP.*

$ ⚏ **Best Western Amador Inn.** Convenience and price are the main attractions of this two-story motel just off the highway. Many rooms have gas fireplaces. If you want an in-room refrigerator and microwave, you'll need to pay $5 extra. ✉ *200 S. Hwy. 49, 95642* ☎ *209/223–0211 or 800/543–5221* 🖶 *209/223–4836* ⊕ *www.bestwestern.com* ⇗ *118 rooms* ⚘ *Restaurant, pool, laundry service* ☰ *AE, D, DC, MC, V.*

Angels Camp

㉓ *20 mi south of Jackson on Hwy. 49.*

Angels Camp is famed chiefly for its May jumping-frog contest, based on Mark Twain's short story "The Celebrated Jumping Frog of Calaveras County." The writer reputedly heard the story of the jumping frog from Ross Coon, proprietor of Angels Hotel, which has been in operation since 1856.

Angels Camp Museum has gold-rush relics—photos, rocks, petrified wood, old blacksmith and mining equipment, and a horse-drawn hearse. The carriage house out back holds 31 carriages and an impressive display of mineral specimens. ✉ *753 S. Main St.* ☎ *209/736–2963* 🎫 *$2* ☉ *Jan. and Feb., weekends 10–3; Mar.–Dec., daily 10–3.*

⎧ off the
  beaten
  path ⎫

CALIFORNIA CAVERNS – A ½-mi subterranean trail winds through large chambers and past underground streams and lakes. There aren't many steps to climb, but it's a strenuous walk with some narrow passageways and steep spots. The caverns, at a constant 53°F, contain crystalline formations not found elsewhere, and the 80-minute guided tour explains local history and geology. ✉ *9 mi east of San Andreas on Mountain Ranch Rd., then about 3 mi on Cave City Rd., follow signs* ☎ *209/736–2708* 🎫 *$12* ☉ *Usually May–Dec., but call ahead.*

MOANING CAVERN – A 235-step spiral staircase leads into this vast cavern. More adventurous sorts can rappel into the chamber—ropes and instruction are provided. Otherwise, the only way inside is via the 45-minute tour, during which you'll see giant (and still growing) stalactites and stalagmites and an archaeological site that holds some of the oldest human remains yet found in America (an unlucky person has fallen into the cavern about once every 130 years for the last 13,000 years). ✉ *Parrots Ferry Rd., 2 mi south of Vallecito, off Hwy. 4 east of Angels Camp* ☎ *209/736–2708* ⊕ *www.caverntours.com* 🎫 *$12* ☉ *May–Oct., daily 9–6; Nov.–Apr., weekdays 10–5, weekends 9–5.*

MARK TWAIN AND HIS JUMPING FROG

I N DECEMBER 2003 NEAR ANGELS CAMP in Calaveras County, a cattle rancher's children happened upon some red-legged frogs—the type Mark Twain had described in his breakthrough story, "Jim Smiley and His Jumping Frog." The story, reprinted in The Celebrated Jumping Frog of Calaveras County and Other Sketches (1867), made the man born Samuel Langhorne Clemens famous. It also made the springtime frog-jumping contest an offbeat attraction for Gold Country visitors. So it wasn't surprising that the famous frogs' appearance made big news. They hadn't been seen in the area since 1969.

Twain's short but influential affiliation with California began in 1864, after a two-year newspaper-reporting stint in Virginia City, Nevada. After landing a similar job for San Francisco's Morning Call, he was soon unemployed and for three months shared a one-room cabin on Jackass Hill, 8 mi from Angels Camp. He heard about the jumping frogs in a local bar and wrote his story in the cabin. Today a short detour off Highway 49 brings you to a replica of the original cabin, which burned down and was reconstructed twice, most recently in 2003–04. The jumping-frog story first appeared in the New York Saturday Gazette on November 18, 1865. Years later, Twain recounted that though the man featured in the tale was named Greeley, his name was changed to Smiley because the Gazette's print shop didn't possess enough G's.

In 1866 Twain was commissioned by the Sacramento Union to write about his adventures in the Hawaiian islands, acquainting mainland Americans with what would become our 50th state. But later that year, Twain relocated to Buffalo, New York, leaving California and the newspaper business—never having been anything but a reporter—apparently without regrets. He told Galaxy magazine in 1870: "I am not the editor of a newspaper and shall always try to do right and be good so that God will not make me one."

Murphys

 10 mi northeast of Angels Camp on Hwy. 4.

Murphys is a well-preserved town of white picket fences, Victorian houses, and interesting shops. Horatio Alger and Ulysses S. Grant came through here, staying at Murphys Historic Hotel & Lodge when they, along with many other 19th-century visitors, came to see the giant sequoia groves in nearby Calaveras Big Trees State Park.

The **Kautz Ironstone Winery and Caverns** is worth a visit even if you don't drink wine. Tours take you into underground tunnels cooled by a waterfall from a natural spring and include a performance on a massive automated pipe organ. The winery schedules concerts during spring and summer in its huge outdoor amphitheater, plus art shows and other events on weekends. On display is a 44-pound specimen of crystalline gold. Visit the deli for lunch. ⊠ *1894 6 Mile Rd.* ☎ *209/728–1251* ☉ *Daily 10–5.*

off the beaten path

CALAVERAS BIG TREES STATE PARK – This state park protects hundreds of the largest and rarest living things on the planet—magnificent giant sequoia redwood trees. Some are nearly 3,000 years old, 90 feet around at the base, and 250 feet tall. The park's self-guided walks range from a 200-yard trail to 1-mi and 5-mi (closed in winter) loops through the groves. There are campgrounds and picnic areas; swimming, wading, fishing, and sunbathing on the Stanislaus River are popular in summer. ⊠ *Off Hwy. 4, 15 mi northeast of Murphys, 4 mi northeast of Arnold* ☎ *209/795–2334* 🔁 *$4 per vehicle, day use; campsites $16* ⊙ *Park daily sunrise–sunset, day use; visitor center May–Oct., daily 10–4; Nov.–Apr., weekends 11–3.*

Where to Stay & Eat

$–$$ ✕ **Grounds.** Light Italian entrées, grilled vegetables, chicken, seafood, and steak are the specialties at this bistro and coffee shop. Sandwiches, salads, and homemade soups are served for lunch. The crowd is friendly and the service attentive. ⊠ *402 Main St.* ☎ *209/728–8663* 🗀 *MC, V* ⊙ *No dinner Mon. and Tues.*

★ $$$–$$$$ ▦ **Dunbar House 1880.** The oversize rooms in this elaborate Italianate-style home have brass beds, down comforters, gas-burning stoves, and claw-foot tubs. Broad wraparound verandas encourage lounging, as do the colorful gardens and large elm trees. The Cedar Room's sunporch has a two-person whirlpool tub, and the Sequoia Room has a two-person whirlpool spa and shower. In the afternoon you are treated to trays of appetizers and wine in your room. ⊠ *271 Jones St., 95247* ☎ *209/728–2897 or 800/692–6006* 🗎 *209/728–1451* ⊕ *www.dunbarhouse.com* 🛏 *3 rooms, 2 suites* ♦ *Refrigerators, in-room VCRs* 🗀 *AE, MC, V* ¡◯¡ *BP.*

$ ▦ **Murphys Historic Hotel & Lodge.** This 1855 stone hotel, whose register has seen the signatures of Mark Twain and the bandit Black Bart, figured in Bret Harte's short story "A Night at Wingdam." Accommodations are in the hotel and a modern motel-style addition. The older rooms are furnished with antiques, many of them large and hand-carved. The hotel has a convivial old-time saloon, which can be noisy into the wee hours. ⊠ *457 Main St., 95247* ☎ *209/728–3444 or 800/532–7684* 🗎 *209/728–1590* ⊕ *www.murphyshotel.com* 🛏 *29 rooms, 20 with bath* ♦ *Restaurant, bar, meeting room* 🗀 *AE, D, DC, MC, V.*

Columbia

㉕ *14 mi south of Angels Camp via Hwy. 49 to Parrots Ferry Rd.*

Columbia is the gateway for Columbia State Historic Park, which is one of the Gold Country's most visited sites.

Ⓒ **Columbia State Historic Park,** known as the Gem of the Southern Mines,
Fodor'sChoice comes as close to a gold-rush town in its heyday as any site in the Gold
★ Country. You can ride a stagecoach, pan for gold, and watch a black-smith working at an anvil. Street musicians perform in summer. Restored or reconstructed buildings include a Wells Fargo Express office, a Masonic temple, stores, saloons, two hotels, a firehouse, churches, a school,

and a newspaper office. All are staffed to simulate a working 1850s town. The park also includes the **Historic Fallon House Theater,** where a full schedule of entertainment is presented. ⊠ *11175 Washington St.* ☎ *209/ 532–0150* ⊕ *www.parks.ca.gov* ⌑ *Free* ☉ *Daily 9–5.*

Where to Stay & Eat

$–$$ ✕⊡ **City Hotel.** The rooms in this restored 1856 hostelry are furnished with period antiques. Two have balconies overlooking Main Street, and six rooms open onto a second-floor parlor. All the accommodations have private half-baths, with showers nearby; robes and slippers are provided. The restaurant ($$–$$$; closed Monday), one of the Gold Country's best, serves French-accented California cuisine complemented by a large selection of the state's respected wines. The What Cheer Saloon is right out of a western movie. Combined lodging, dinner, and theater packages are available. ⊠ *22768 Main St., 95310* ☎ *209/532–1479 or 800/ 532–1479* 📠 *209/532–7027* ⊕ *www.cityhotel.com* ➦ *10 rooms* △ *Restaurant, bar* ⊟ *AE, D, MC, V* ⊚ *CP.*

¢–$$ ⊡ **Fallon Hotel.** Restored by the state of California, this 1857 hotel features rooms with antiques and private half-baths. (There are separate men's and women's showers.) If you occupy one of the five balcony rooms, you can sit outside with your morning coffee and watch the town wake up. ⊠ *11175 Washington St., 95310* ☎ *209/532–1470* 📠 *209/532–7027* ⊕ *www.cityhotel.com* ➦ *14 rooms* △ *No room TVs* ⊟ *AE, D, MC, V* ⊚ *CP.*

The Arts

Sierra Repertory Theater Company (☎ 209/532–4644) presents a full season of dramas, comedies, and musicals at the Historic Fallon House Theater and another venue in East Sonora.

Sonora

㉖ *4 mi south of Columbia via Parrots Ferry Rd. to Hwy. 49.*

Miners from Mexico founded Sonora and made it the biggest town in the Mother Lode. Following a period of racial and ethnic strife, the Mexican settlers moved on, and Yankees built the commercial city that is visible today. Sonora's historic downtown section sits atop the Big Bonanza Mine, one of the richest in the state. Another mine, on the site of nearby Sonora High School, yielded 990 pounds of gold in a single week in 1879. Reminders of the gold rush are everywhere in Sonora, in prim Victorian houses, typical Sierra-stone storefronts, and awning-shaded sidewalks. Reality intrudes beyond the town's historic heart, with strip malls, shopping centers, and modern motels. If the countryside surrounding Sonora seems familiar, that's because it has been the backdrop for many movies over the years. Scenes from *High Noon, For Whom the Bell Tolls, The Virginian, Back to the Future III,* and *Unforgiven* were filmed here.

The **Tuolumne County Museum and History Center** occupies a building that served as a jail until 1951. Restored to an earlier period, it houses a jail museum, vintage firearms and paraphernalia, a case with gold nuggets, a cute exhibit on soapbox derby racing in hilly Sonora, and the libraries of a historical society and a genealogical society. ⊠ *158 W. Bradford St.* ☎ *209/532–1317* 🖼 *Free* ☉ *Daily 10–4.*

Where to Stay & Eat

$–$$ ✕ **Banny's Cafe.** Its pleasant environment and hearty yet refined dishes make Banny's a quiet alternative to Sonora's noisier eateries. Try the grilled salmon fillet with scallion rice and ginger-wasabi-soy aioli. ⊠ *83 S. Stewart St.* ☎ *209/533–4709* ▭ *D, MC, V* ☉ *No lunch Sun.*

¢–$ ✕ **Garcia's Taqueria.** This casual, inexpensive eatery serves Mexican and southwestern fare with an emphasis on seafood. However, vegetarians and vegans are also well-served here. ⊠ *145 S. Washington St.* ☎ *209/ 588–1915* ▭ *No credit cards* ☉ *Closed Sun.*

$$–$$$$ 🏠 **Barretta Gardens Bed and Breakfast Inn.** This inn is perfect for a romantic getaway or a special business meeting. Its elegant Victorian rooms vary in size, but all are furnished with period pieces. The three antiques-filled parlors carry on the Victorian theme. A French bakery on the property provides the fresh pastries at breakfast. ⊠ *700 S. Barretta St., 95370* ☎ *209/532–6039 or 800/206–3333* 🖨 *209/ 532–8257* ⊕ *www.barrettagardens.com* 🛏 *5 rooms* ♨ *Hot tub* ▭ *AE, MC, V* ⧖ *CP.*

$–$$ 🏠 **Best Western Sonora Oaks Motor Hotel.** The standard motel-issue rooms at this East Sonora establishment are clean and roomy; the larger ones have outdoor sitting areas. Suites have fireplaces, whirlpool tubs, and tranquil hillside views. Because the motel is right off Highway 108, the front rooms can be noisy. ⊠ *19551 Hess Ave., 95370* ☎ *209/533– 4400 or 800/532–1944* 🖨 *209/532–1964* ⊕ *www.bestwestern.com* 🛏 *96 rooms, 4 suites* ♨ *Restaurant, pool, outdoor hot tub, lounge, meeting room* ▭ *AE, D, DC, MC, V.*

Jamestown

㉗ *4 mi south of Sonora on Hwy. 49.*

Compact Jamestown supplies a touristy, superficial view of gold-rush-era life. Shops in brightly colored buildings along Main Street sell antiques and gift items.

The California State Railroad Museum operates **Railtown 1897** at what were the headquarters and general shops of the Sierra Railway from 1897 to 1955. The railroad has appeared in more than 200 movies and television productions, including *Petticoat Junction, The Virginian, High Noon,* and *Unforgiven.* You can view the roundhouse, an air-operated 60-foot turntable, shop rooms, and old locomotives and coaches. Six-mile, 40-minute steam train rides through the countryside operate on weekends during part of the year. ⊠ *5th Ave. and Reservoir Rd., off Hwy. 49* ☎ *209/984–3953* ⊕ *www.csrmf.org* 🖼 *Roundhouse tour $2; train ride $6* ☉ *Daily 9:30–4:30. Train rides Apr.–Oct., weekends 11–3; Nov., Sat. 11–3.*

Where to Stay & Eat

$–$$ ✕🏠 **National Hotel.** The National has been in business since 1859, and the furnishings—brass beds, patchwork quilts, and lace curtains—are authentic but not overly embellished. The saloon, which still has its original redwood bar, is a great place to linger. The popular restaurant ($–$$$) serves big lunches: hamburgers and fries, salads, and Italian entrées. More upscale continental cuisine is prepared for dinner (reservations essential). ⊠ *18183 Main St., 95327* ☎ *209/984–3446, 800/894–3446 in CA* 🖷 *209/984–5620* ⊕ *www.national-hotel.com* 🛏 *9 rooms* ⚐ *Restaurant, in-room data ports, in-room VCRs, bar* ▤ *AE, D, DC, MC, V* ⍥ *CP.*

Mariposa

28 *50 mi south of Jamestown on Hwy. 49.*

Mariposa marks the southern end of the Mother Lode. Much of the land in this area was part of a 44,000-acre land grant Colonel John C. Fremont acquired from Mexico before gold was discovered and California became a state.

At the **California State Mining and Mineral Museum,** a glittering 13-pound chunk of crystallized gold makes it clear what the rush was about. Displays include a replica of a typical tunnel dug by hard-rock miners, a miniature stamp mill, and a panning and sluicing exhibit. ⊠ *Mariposa County Fairgrounds, Hwy. 49* ☎ *209/742–7625* ⊡ *$2* ⍥ *May–Sept., daily 10–6; Oct.–Apr., Wed.–Mon. 10–4.*

Where to Stay & Eat

$–$$$ ✕ **Charles Street Dinner House.** Ever since Ed Uebner moved here from Chicago to become the owner-chef in 1980, Charles Street has been firmly established as the classiest dinner joint in town—plus, it's centrally located. The extensive menu, which won't appeal to vegetarians, includes beef, chicken, pork, lamb, duck, and lobster. ⊠ *Hwy. 140 at 7th St.* ☎ *209/966–2366* ▤ *D, MC, V* ⍥ *Closed Mon. and Tues. No lunch.*

$ ✕ **Castillo's Mexican Food.** Tasty tacos, enchiladas, *chiles rellenos* (stuffed, batter-fried, mild chili peppers), and burrito combinations plus chimichangas, fajitas, steak, and seafood are served in a casual storefront. ⊠ *4995 5th St.* ☎ *209/742–4413* ▤ *MC, V.*

$–$$ ⊡ **Little Valley Inn.** Pine paneling, historical photos, and old mining tools recall Mariposa's heritage at this modern B&B with six bungalows. A suite that sleeps five people includes a full kitchen. All rooms have private entrances, baths, and decks. The large grounds include a creek where you can pan for gold. ⊠ *3483 Brooks Rd., off Hwy. 49, 95338* ☎ *209/742–6204 or 800/889–5444* 🖷 *209/742–5099* ⊕ *www.littlevalley.com* 🛏 *4 rooms, 1 suite, 1 cabin* ⚐ *Refrigerators, horseshoes* ▤ *AE, MC, V* ⍥ *BP.*

$ ⊡ **Mariposa Lodge.** Thoroughly modern and somewhat without character, the Mariposa nevertheless is a solid option for those who want to stay warm and within 30 mi of Yosemite National Park without spending a fortune. ⊠ *5052 Hwy. 140, 95338* ☎ *209/966–3607* 🖷 *209/742–7038* 🛏 *45 rooms* ⚐ *Pool, outdoor hot tub, no-smoking rooms* ▤ *AE, MC, V.*

THE GOLD COUNTRY—NORTH
HIGHWAY 49 FROM COLOMA TO NEVADA CITY

Highway 49 north of Placerville links the towns of Coloma, Auburn, Grass Valley, and Nevada City. Most are gentrified versions of once-rowdy mining camps, vestiges of which remain in roadside museums, old mining structures, and restored homes now serving as inns.

Coloma

㉙ *8 mi northwest of Placerville on Hwy. 49.*

The California gold rush started in Coloma. "My eye was caught with the glimpse of something shining in the bottom of the ditch," James Marshall recalled. Marshall himself never found any more "color," as gold came to be called.

★ Most of Coloma lies within **Marshall Gold Discovery State Historic Park.** Though crowded with tourists in summer, Coloma hardly resembles the mob scene it was in 1849, when 2,000 prospectors staked out claims along the streambed. The town's population grew to 4,000, supporting seven hotels, three banks, and many stores and businesses. But when reserves of the precious metal dwindled, prospectors left as quickly as they had come. A working replica of an 1840s mill lies near the spot where James Marshall first saw gold. A trail leads to a monument marking Marshall's discovery. The museum is not as interesting as the outdoor exhibits. ⊠ *Hwy. 49* ☎ *530/622–3470* ⊕ *www.parks. ca.gov* ⊠ *$4 per vehicle, day use* ☉ *Park daily 8 AM–sunset. Museum daily 10–4:30.*

Where to Stay

$–$$$ 🏠 **Coloma Country Inn.** Five of the rooms at this B&B on 5 acres in the state historic park are inside a restored 1852 Victorian. Two suites, one with a kitchenette, are in the carriage house. Appointments include antique double and queen-size beds, handmade quilts, stenciled friezes, and fresh flowers. The owners can direct you to tour operators offering rafting trips on the American River. ⊠ *345 High St., 95613* ☎ *530/622–6919* 🖨 *530/622–1795* ⊕ *www.colomacountryinn.com* ⊅ *5 rooms, 3 with bath; 2 suites* ⌂ *Kitchenette* ☰ *No credit cards* ⦿ *BP.*

Auburn

▶ **㉚** *18 mi northwest of Coloma on Hwy. 49; 34 mi northeast of Sacramento on I–80.*

Auburn is the Gold Country town most accessible to travelers on Interstate 80. An important transportation center during the gold rush, Auburn has a small Old Town district with narrow climbing streets, cobblestone lanes, wooden sidewalks, and many original buildings. Fresh produce, flowers, baked goods, and gifts are for sale at the farmers' market, held Saturday morning year-round.

Auburn's standout structure is the **Placer County Courthouse.** The classic gold-dome building houses the Placer County Museum, which documents the area's history—Native American, railroad, agricultural, and mining—from the early 1700s to 1900. ⊠ *101 Maple St.* ☏ *530/889–6500* ⊠ *Free* ☉ *Tues.–Sun. 11–4.*

The **Bernhard Museum Complex,** whose centerpiece is the former Traveler's Rest Hotel, was built in 1851. A residence and adjacent winery buildings reflect family life in the late Victorian era. The carriage house contains period conveyances. ⊠ *291 Auburn–Folsom Rd.* ☏ *530/889–6500* ⊠ *Free* ☉ *Tues.–Fri. 10:30–3, weekends noon–4.*

The **Gold Country Museum** surveys life in the mines. Exhibits include a walk-through mine tunnel, a gold-panning stream, and a replica saloon. ⊠ *1273 High St., off Auburn–Folsom Rd.* ☏ *530/889–6500* ⊠ *Free* ☉ *Tues.–Fri. 10–3:30, weekends 11–4.*

Where to Stay & Eat

\$\$–\$\$\$ ✕ **Le Bilig French Café.** Simple and elegant cuisine is the goal of the chefs at this country-French café on the outskirts of Auburn. Escargots, coq au vin, and quiche are standard offerings; specials might include salmon in parchment paper. ⊠ *11750 Atwood Rd., off Hwy. 49 near the Bel Air Mall* ☏ *530/888–1491* ☐ *MC, V* ☉ *Closed Mon. and Tues. No lunch.*

★ **\$–\$\$\$** ✕ **Latitudes.** Delicious multicultural cuisine is served up in an 1870 Victorian. The menu (with monthly specials from diverse geographical regions) includes seafood, chicken, beef, and turkey entrées prepared with the appropriate Mexican spices, curries, cheeses, or teriyaki sauce. Vegetarians and vegans have several inventive choices, too. Sunday brunch is deservedly popular. ⊠ *130 Maple St.* ☏ *530/885–9535* ☐ *AE, D, MC, V* ☉ *Closed Mon. and Tues.*

¢–\$ ✕ **Awful Annie's.** Big patio umbrellas (and outdoor heaters when necessary) allow patrons to take in the view of the Old Town from this popular spot for breakfast—one specialty is a chili omelet—or lunch. ⊠ *160 Sacramento St.* ☏ *530/888–9857* ☐ *AE, MC, V* ☉ *No dinner.*

\$–\$\$ ▥ **Comfort Inn.** The contemporary-style rooms at this well-maintained property are softened with teal and pastel colors. Though it's close to the freeway, the hotel is fairly quiet. The expanded continental breakfast includes many choices of baked goods, cereals, fruits, and juices. ⊠ *1875 Auburn Ravine Rd., north of Forest Hill exit of I–80, 95603* ☏ *530/885–1800 or 800/626–1900* ☐ *530/888–6424* ⇘ *77 rooms, 2 suites* ♿ *In-room data ports, pool, gym, spa, laundry facilities, meeting room, no-smoking floor* ☐ *AE, D, DC, MC, V* ⏀ *CP.*

\$–\$\$ ▥ **Holiday Inn.** On a hill above the freeway across from Old Town, this hotel has an imposing columned entrance but a welcoming lobby. Rooms are chain-standard but attractively furnished. All have work areas and coffeemakers. Those nearest the parking lot can be noisy. ⊠ *120 Grass Valley Hwy., 95603* ☏ *530/887–8787 or 800/814–8787* ☐ *530/887–9824* ⊕ *www.6c.com* ⇘ *96 rooms, 6 suites* ♿ *Restaurant, room service, in-room data ports, pool, gym, spa, bar, business services, convention center* ☐ *AE, D, DC, MC, V.*

\$–\$\$ ▥ **Power's Mansion Inn.** This inn hints at the lavish lifestyle enjoyed by the gold-rush gentry. Two light-filled parlors have gleaming oak floors, Asian antiques, and ornate Victorian chairs and settees. A second-floor maze of narrow corridors leads to the guest rooms, which have brass and pencil-post beds. The honeymoon suite has a fireplace and heart-shape hot tub. ⊠ *164 Cleveland Ave., 95603* ☎ *530/885–1166* 🖷 *530/885–1386* ⊕ *www.vfr.net/~powerinn* ➳ *10 rooms, 3 suites* ♨ *In-room fax, some in-room hot tubs, fax, business services* ▤ *AE, MC, V* ⦿ *BP.*

Grass Valley

㉛ *24 mi north of Auburn on Hwy. 49.*

More than half of California's total gold production was extracted from mines around Grass Valley, including the Empire Mine, which, along with the North Star Mining Museum, is among the Gold Country's most fascinating attractions. Unlike neighboring Nevada City, urban sprawl surrounds Grass Valley's historic downtown.

In the center of town, on the site of the original, stands a reproduction of the **Lola Montez House** (⊠ 248 Mill St. ☎ 530/273–4667 or 800/655–4667), home of the notorious dancer. Montez, who arrived in Grass Valley in the early 1850s, was no great talent—her popularity among miners derived from her suggestive "spider dance"—but her loves, who reportedly included composer Franz Liszt, were legendary. According to one account, she arrived in California after having been "permanently retired from her job as Bavarian king Ludwig's mistress," literary muse, and political adviser. She apparently pushed too hard for democracy, which contributed to his overthrow and her banishment as a witch—or so the story goes. The memory of licentious Lola lingers in Grass Valley, as does her bathtub (on the front porch of the house). The Grass Valley/Nevada County Chamber of Commerce is headquartered here.

The landmark **Holbrooke Hotel** (⊠ 212 W. Main St. ☎ 530/273–1353 or 800/933–7077), built in 1851, hosted Lola Montez and Mark Twain as well as Ulysses S. Grant and a stream of other U.S. presidents. Its restaurant-saloon is one of the oldest operating west of the Mississippi.

★ The hard-rock gold mine at **Empire Mine State Historic Park** was one of California's richest. An estimated 5.8 million ounces were extracted from its 367 mi of underground passages between 1850 and 1956. On the 50-minute tours you can walk into a mine shaft, peer into the mine's deeper recesses, and view the owner's "cottage," which has exquisite woodwork. The visitor center has mining exhibits, and a picnic area is nearby. ⊠ *10791 E. Empire St., south of Empire St. exit of Hwy. 49* ☎ *530/273–8522* ⊕ *www.parks.ca.gov* ➲ *$1* ⊙ *May–Aug., daily 9–6; Sept.–Apr., daily 10–5. Tours May–Aug., daily on the hr 11–4; Sept.–Apr., weekends at 1 (cottage only) and 2 (mine yard only), weather permitting.*

☙ Housed in the former North Star powerhouse, the **North Star Mining Museum** displays the 32-foot-high enclosed Pelton Water Wheel, said to be the largest ever built. It was used to power mining operations and was a forerunner of the modern turbines that generate hydroelectricity.

Hands-on displays are geared to children. There's a picnic area nearby. ✉ *Empire and McCourtney Sts., north of Empire St. exit of Hwy. 49* ☎ *530/273–4255* 🖼 *Donation requested* ⊙ *May–mid-Oct., daily 10–5.*

Where to Stay & Eat

¢ ✕ **Cousin Jack Pasties.** Meat- and vegetable-stuffed pasties are a taste of the region's history, having come across the Atlantic with Cornish miners and their families in the mid-19th century. The flaky crusts practically melt in your mouth. A simple food stand, which sometimes closes early on dreary winter days, Jack's is nonetheless a local landmark and dear to its loyal clientele. ✉ *Auburn and Main Sts.* ☎ *530/272–9230* ⊟ *No credit cards.*

$ ⌂ **Holiday Lodge.** This modest hotel is close to many of the town's main attractions, and its staff can help point you toward—or arrange—gold-panning excursions and historical tours of the Gold Country. ✉ *1221 E. Main St., 95945* ☎ *530/273–4406 or 800/742–7125* ↳ *35 rooms* ♨ *Pool, sauna* ⊟ *AE, MC, V* ⦿ *CP.*

Nevada City

32 *4 mi north of Grass Valley on Hwy. 49.*

Nevada City, once known as the Queen City of the Northern Mines, is the most appealing of the northern Mother Lode towns. The iron-shutter brick buildings that line the narrow downtown streets contain antiques shops, galleries, bookstores, boutiques, B&Bs, restaurants, and a winery. Horse-drawn carriage tours add to the romance, as do gas streetlamps. At one point in the 1850s Nevada City had a population of nearly 10,000, enough to support much cultural activity.

With its gingerbread-trim bell tower, **Firehouse No. 1** is one of the Gold Country's most photographed buildings. A museum, it houses gold-rush artifacts and a Chinese joss house (temple). Also on display are relics of the ill-fated Donner Party, a group of 19th-century travelers who, trapped in the Sierra Nevada by winter snows, were forced to cannibalize their dead in order to survive. ✉ *214 Main St.* ☎ *530/ 265–5468* 🖼 *Donation requested* ⊙ *Apr.–Nov., daily 11–4; Dec.–Mar., Thurs.–Sun. 11:30–4.*

The redbrick **Nevada Theatre,** constructed in 1865, is California's oldest theater building in continuous use. Mark Twain, Emma Nevada, and many other notable persons appeared on its stage. Housed in the theater, the **Foothill Theater Company** (☎ *530/265–8587 or 888/ 730–8587*) hosts theatrical and musical events. Old films are screened here, too. ✉ *401 Broad St.* ☎ *530/265–6161, 530/274–3456 for film show times.*

The **Miners Foundry,** erected in 1856, produced machines for gold mining and logging. The Pelton Water Wheel, a source of power for the mines (the wheel also jump-started the hydroelectric power industry), was invented here. A cavernous building, the foundry hosts plays, concerts, an antiques show, weddings, receptions, and other events; call for a schedule. ✉ *325 Spring St.* ☎ *530/265–5040* ⊙ *Mon.–Fri. 10–4.*

You can watch wine being created while you sip at the **Nevada City Winery,** where the tasting room overlooks the production area. ⊠ *Miners Foundry Garage, 321 Spring St.* ☎ *530/265–9463 or 800/203–9463* ⊕ *www.ncwinery.com* ✉ *Free* ☉ *Tastings daily noon–5.*

THE GOLD COUNTRY A TO Z

To research prices, get advice from other travelers, and book travel arrangements, visit ⊕ *www.fodors.com.*

AIRPORTS & TRANSFERS

Sacramento International Airport is served by Alaska, American, America West, Delta, Frontier, Horizon Air, Northwest, Southwest, TWA, United, and US Airways. *See* Air Travel *in* Smart Travel Tips A to Z *for airline phone numbers.* A private taxi from the airport to downtown Sacramento is about $20. The cost of the Super Shuttle from the airport to downtown Sacramento is $11. Call in advance to arrange transportation from your hotel to the airport.

🛈 **Sacramento International Airport** ⊠ 6900 Airport Blvd., 12 mi northwest of downtown off I-5, Sacramento ☎ 916/874-0700 ⊕ www.sacairports.org. **Super Shuttle** ☎ 800/258-3826.

BOAT TRAVEL

Sacramento's riverfront location enables you to sightsee while getting around by boat. A water taxi run by River Otter Taxi Co. serves the Old Sacramento waterfront during spring and summer, stopping at points near restaurants and other sights. Channel Star Excursions operates the *Spirit of Sacramento,* a riverboat that takes passengers on happy-hour, dinner, lunch, and champagne-brunch cruises in addition to one-hour narrated tours.

🛈 **Channel Star Excursions** ⊠ 110 L St. ☎ 916/552-2933 or 800/433-0263. **River Otter Taxi Co.** ☎ 916/446-7704.

BUS TRAVEL

Getting to and from SIA can be accomplished via taxi, the Super Shuttle, or by Yolo County Public Bus 42, which operates a circular service around SIA, downtown Sacramento, West Sacramento, Davis, and Woodland. Other Gold Country destinations are best reached by private car.

Greyhound serves Sacramento, Davis, Auburn, and Placerville. It's a two-hour trip from San Francisco's Transbay Terminal, at 1st and Mission streets, to the Sacramento station, at 7th and L streets.

Sacramento Regional Transit buses and light-rail vehicles transport passengers in Sacramento. Most buses run from 6 AM to 10 PM, most trains from 5 AM to midnight. A DASH (Downtown Area Shuttle) bus and the No. 30 city bus both link Old Sacramento, midtown, and Sutter's Fort. The fare is 50¢ within this area.

🛈 **Greyhound** ☎ 800/231-2222 ⊕ www.greyhound.com. **Sacramento Regional Transit** ☎ 916/321-2877 ⊕ www.sacrt.com. **Yolo County Bus** ☎ 530/666-2837 ⊕ www.yolobus.com.

CAR RENTAL

You can rent a car from any of the major national chains at Sacramento International Airport. *See* Car Rental *in* Smart Travel Tips A to Z *for national car-rental agency phone numbers.*

CAR TRAVEL

Traveling by car is the most convenient way to see the Gold Country. From Sacramento, three highways fan out toward the east, all intersecting with Highway 49: I–80 heads 34 mi northeast to Auburn; U.S. 50 goes east 40 mi to Placerville; and Highway 16 angles southeast 45 mi to Plymouth. Highway 49 is an excellent two-lane road that winds and climbs through the foothills and valleys, linking the principal Gold Country towns.

Sacramento lies at the junction of I–5 and I–80, not quite 90 mi northeast of San Francisco. The 406-mi drive north on I–5 from Los Angeles takes seven to eight hours. I–80 continues northeast through the Gold Country toward Reno, about 136 mi (three hours or so) from Sacramento.

EMERGENCIES

In an emergency dial 911. Each of the following medical facilities has an emergency room open 24 hours a day.

🚩 Hospitals **Mercy Hospital of Sacramento** ⊠ 4001 J St., Sacramento ☎ 916/453-4424. **Sutter General Hospital** ⊠ 2801 L St., Sacramento ☎ 916/733-8900. **Sutter Memorial Hospital** ⊠ 52nd and F Sts., Sacramento ☎ 916/733-1000.

LODGING

A number of organizations can supply information about Gold Country B&Bs and other accommodations.

🚩 **Amador County Innkeepers Association** ☎ 209/267-1710 or 800/726-4667. **Gold Country Inns of Tuolumne County** ☎ 209/533-1845. **Historic Bed & Breakfast Inns of Grass Valley & Nevada City** ☎ 530/477-6634 or 800/250-5808.

TOURS

Gold Prospecting Adventures, LLC, based in Jamestown, arranges gold-panning trips.

🚩 **Gold Prospecting Adventures, LLC** ☎ 209/984-4653 or 800/596-0009 ⊕ www.goldprospecting.com.

TRAIN TRAVEL

Several trains operated by Amtrak stop in Sacramento and Davis. Trains making the 2½-hour trip from Jack London Square, in Oakland, stop in Emeryville (across the bay from San Francisco), Richmond, Martinez, and Davis before reaching Sacramento; some stop in Berkeley and Suisun-Fairfield as well.

🚩 **Amtrak** ☎ 800/872-7245 ⊕ www.amtrakcalifornia.com.

VISITOR INFORMATION

🚩 **Amador County Chamber of Commerce** ⊠ 125 Peek St., Jackson 95642 ☎ 209/223-0350 ⊕ www.amadorcountychamber.com. **Davis Chamber of Commerce** ⊠ 130 G St., Davis 95616 ☎ 530/756-5160 ⊕ www.davischamber.com. **El Dorado County Chamber of Commerce** ⊠ 542 Main St., Placerville 95667 ☎ 530/621-5885 or 800/457-6279 ⊕ www.eldoradocounty.org. **Grass Valley/Nevada County Chamber of Com-**

merce ⊠ 248 Mill St., Grass Valley 95945 ☎ 530/273-4667 or 800/655-4667 ⊕ www. ncgold.com/chamber. **Mariposa County Visitors Bureau** ⊠ 5158 Hwy. 140, Mariposa 95338 ☎ 209/966-7081 or 800/208-2434 ⊕ mariposa.yosemite.net/visitor. **Nevada City Chamber of Commerce** ⊠ 132 Main St., Nevada City 95945 ☎ 530/265-2692. **Sacramento Convention and Visitors Bureau** ⊠ 1303 J St., Suite 600, Sacramento 95814 ☎ 916/264-7777 ⊕ www.sacramentocvb.org. **San Joaquin Convention & Visitors Bureau** ⊠ 46 W. Freemont St., Stockton 95202 ☎ 209/943-1987 or 800/350-1987 ⊕ www. ssjcvb.org. **Tuolumne County Visitors Bureau** ⊠ 542 Stockton St., Sonora 95370 ☎ 209/533-4420 or 800/446-1333 ⊕ www.thegreatunfenced.com. **Woodland Chamber of Commerce** ⊠ 307 1st St., Woodland 95695 ☎ 530/662-7327 or 888/843-2636 ⊕ www.woodlandchamber.org.

LAKE TAHOE

WITH RENO, NEVADA

16

Updated by
John A.
Vlahides

LAKE TAHOE IS THE LARGEST ALPINE LAKE IN NORTH AMERICA, famous for its clarity, deep blue water, and surrounding snowcapped peaks. Straddling the state line between California and Nevada, it lies 6,225 feet above sea level in the Sierra Nevada. The border gives this popular resort region a split personality. About half its visitors are intent on low-key sightseeing, hiking, fishing, camping, and boating. The rest head directly for the Nevada side, where bargain dining, big-name entertainment, and the lure of a jackpot draw them into the glittering casinos.

The first white explorer to gaze upon this spectacular region was Captain John C. Fremont, in 1844, guided by the famous scout Kit Carson. Not long afterward, silver was discovered in Nevada's Comstock Lode, at Virginia City. As the mines grew larger and deeper, the Tahoe Basin's forests were leveled to provide lumber for subterranean support (had the forests been left untouched, Lake Tahoe might well have become a national park). By the early 1900s wealthy Californians were building lakeside estates here, some of which still stand. Improved roads brought the less affluent in the 1920s and 1930s, when modest bungalows began to appear. The first casinos opened in the 1940s. Ski resorts inspired another development boom in the 1950s and 1960s, turning the lake into a year-round destination.

Though Lake Tahoe possesses abundant natural beauty and accessible wilderness, nearby towns are highly developed, and roads around the lake are often congested with traffic. Those who prefer solitude can escape to the many state parks, national forests, and protected tracts of wilderness that ring the 22-mi-long, 12-mi-wide lake. At a vantage point overlooking Emerald Bay, on a trail in the national forests that ring the basin, or on a sunset cruise on the lake itself, you can forget the hordes and the commercial development. You can even pretend that you're Mark Twain, who found "not fifteen other human beings throughout its wide circumference" when he visited the lake in 1861 and wrote that "the eye never tired of gazing, night or day, calm or storm."

Exploring Lake Tahoe

The typical way to explore the Lake Tahoe area is to drive the 72-mi road that follows the shore through wooded flatlands and past beaches, climbing to vistas on the rugged southwest side of the lake and passing through busy commercial developments and casinos on its northeastern and southeastern edges. Undeveloped Lake Tahoe–Nevada State Park occupies more than half of the Nevada side of Lake Tahoe, stretching along the shore from just north of Zephyr Cove to just south of the upscale community of Incline Village. The California side is more developed, particularly South Lake Tahoe, but there are no garish casino towers, and much wilderness remains immediately outside developed towns.

About the Restaurants

On weekends and in high season, expect a long wait in the more popular restaurants. Always try to reserve a table in advance. During slower periods, some places may close temporarily or limit their hours, so call to make sure your choice is open. Casinos use their restaurants to at-

It takes only one day to "see" Lake Tahoe—to drive around the lake, stretch your legs at a few overlooks, take a nature walk, and wander among the casinos at Stateline. But if you have more time, you can laze on a beach and swim, venture onto the lake or into the mountains, and sample Tahoe's finer restaurants. If you have five days, you may become so attached to Tahoe that you begin visiting real-estate agents.

Numbers in the text correspond to numbers in the margin and on the Lake Tahoe map.

16

If you have 3 days

On your first day stop in **South Lake Tahoe** ❶ ➤ and pick up provisions for a picnic lunch. Start in **Pope-Baldwin Recreation Area** ❷ and check out Tallac Historic Site. Head west on Highway 89, stopping at the Lake Tahoe Visitor Center and the **Emerald Bay State Park** ❸ lookout. Have a tailgate picnic at the lookout, or hike down to Vikingsholm, a Viking castle replica. In the late afternoon explore the trails and mansions at **Sugar Pine Point State Park** ❺; then backtrack on Highway 89 and U.S. 50 for dinner in **Stateline** ❸ or in South Lake Tahoe. On Day 2 cruise on the *Tahoe Queen* out of South Lake Tahoe or the MS *Dixie II* out of **Zephyr Cove** ❷ and then ride the Heavenly Gondola at Heavenly Mountain Resort in South Lake Tahoe. Carry a picnic for lunch high above the lake, and (except in snow season) take a walk on one of Heavenly's nature trails. You can try your luck at the Stateline casinos before dinner. Start your third day by heading north on U.S. 50, stopping at Cave Rock and (after turning north on Highway 28) at Sand Harbor Beach. If there's no snow on the ground, tour the Thunderbird Lodge (reservations essential) for a glimpse of life at an old-Tahoe estate just south of **Incline Village** ⓫, or else continue on to **Crystal Bay** ❾. If you have time, drive to **Tahoe City** ❼ to see the Gatekeeper's Cabin Museum, or make the 45-minute drive down to **Reno** ⓮ for dinner and some nightlife.

If you have 5 days

Spend your first morning at **Pope-Baldwin Recreation Area** ❷ ➤. After a picnic lunch head to the Lake Tahoe Visitor Center and the **Emerald Bay State Park** ❸ lookout. Hike to Vikingsholm or move on to **Sugar Pine Point State Park** ❺. Have dinner in **South Lake Tahoe** ❶. On your second day cruise on the *Tahoe Queen* or MS *Dixie II*; then pack a picnic, ride the Heavenly Gondola, and possibly take a hike. Spend the late afternoon or early evening sampling the worldly pleasures of the **Stateline** ❸ casinos. On Day 3 visit Cave Rock, and the Thunderbird Lodge (reservations essential), just south of **Incline Village** ⓫, where you can have a late lunch before heading to **Crystal Bay** ❿ and playing the slots, or to nearby Kings Beach State Recreation Area, where you can spend the late afternoon on the beach. That evening, drive down to **Reno** ⓮ for dinner and entertainment. On your fourth day hang out at Sand Harbor Beach. If the high-mountain desert appeals, spend Day 5 in the Great Basin, touring Carson City and Virginia City and the vast expanse of the eastern Sierra. Alternatively, head to **D. L. Bliss State Park** ❹ for a hike; then drive to **Tahoe City** ❼ for lunch and a tour of the Gatekeeper's Cabin Museum. Afterward, visit **Olympic Valley** ❽ and ride the cable car to High Camp at Squaw Valley for a sunset cocktail.

tract gaming customers. Marquees often tout "$8.99 prime rib dinners" or "99¢ breakfast specials." Some of these meal deals, usually found in the coffee shops and buffets, may not be top quality, but at those prices, it's hard to complain. The finer restaurants in casinos, however, deliver pricier food, as well as reasonable service and a bit of atmosphere. Unless otherwise noted, even the most expensive area restaurants welcome customers in casual clothes—not surprising in this year-round vacation spot—but don't expect to be served in most places if you're barefoot, shirtless, or wearing a skimpy bathing suit.

About the Hotels

Quiet inns on the water, motels near the casino area, rooms at the casinos themselves, lodges close to ski runs, and home and condo rentals everywhere else are among your Tahoe lodging options. During summer and ski season the lake is crowded; reserve space as far in advance as possible. Spring and fall give you a little more leeway and lower—sometimes significantly lower—rates.

WHAT IT COSTS					
	$$$$	**$$$**	**$$**	**$**	**¢**
RESTAURANTS	over $30	$23–$30	$16–$22	$10–$15	under $10
HOTELS	over $250	$176–$250	$121–$175	$90–$120	under $90

Restaurant prices are for a main course at dinner, excluding sales tax of 7%–7¼% (depending on location). Hotel prices are for two people in a standard double room in high season, excluding service charges and 9%–12% tax.

Timing

Most Lake Tahoe accommodations, restaurants, and even a handful of parks are open year-round, but many visitor centers, mansions, state parks, and beaches are closed from November through May. During those months, multitudes of skiers and other winter-sports enthusiasts are attracted to Tahoe's downhill resorts and cross-country centers, North America's largest concentration of skiing facilities. Ski resorts try to open by Thanksgiving, if only with machine-made snow, and can operate through May or later. During the ski season, Tahoe's population swells on the weekends. If you're able to come midweek, you'll have the resorts and neighboring towns almost to yourself. Bear in mind, though, that Tahoe is a popular wedding and honeymoon destination: on Valentine's Day the chapels become veritable assembly lines.

Unless you want to ski, you'll find that Tahoe is most fun in summer, when it's cooler here than in the scorched Sierra Nevada foothills, the clean mountain air is bracingly crisp, and the surface temperature of Lake Tahoe is an invigorating 65–70°F (compared to 40–50°F in winter—brrr!). This is also the time, however, when it may seem as if every tourist at the lake—100,000 on peak weekends—is in a car on the main road circling the 72-mi shoreline. Weekdays are busy as well. The crowds and congestion increase as the day wears on, so the best strategy for avoiding the crush is to do as much as you can early in the day. The parking lots of the Lake Tahoe Visitor Center, Vikingsholm, and Gatekeeper's

16

Camping

Campgrounds abound in the Tahoe area, operated by the California and Nevada state park departments, the U.S. Forest Service, city utility districts, and private operators. Sites range from primitive and rustic to upscale and luxurious. Make reservations far ahead for summer, when sites are in high demand.

Gambling

Six casinos are clustered on a strip of U.S. 50 in Stateline, and five casinos operate on the north shore. And, of course, in Reno there are more than a dozen major and a dozen minor casinos. Open 24 hours a day, 365 days a year, these gambling halls have table games, race and sports books, and thousands of slot and video-poker machines. There is no charge to enter, and there is no dress code; as long as you're wearing money, you'll be welcome.

Great Golf

The Tahoe area is nearly as popular with golfers as it is with skiers. More than a dozen superb courses dot the mountains around the lake, with magnificent views, thick pines, fresh cool air, and lush fairways and greens. Encountering wildlife is not uncommon if you have to search for your ball out-of-bounds.

Hiking

There are five national forests in the Tahoe Basin and a half-dozen state parks. The main areas for hiking include the Tahoe Rim Trail, a 165-mi path along the ridgelines that now completely rings the lake; Desolation Wilderness, a vast 63,473-acre preserve of granite peaks, glacial valleys, subalpine forests, the Rubicon River, and more than 50 lakes; and the trail systems in D. L. Bliss, Emerald Bay, Sugar Pine Point, and Lake Tahoe–Nevada state parks and near Lake Tahoe Visitor Center. The Pacific Crest Trail, a high-mountain foot trail connecting Mexico to Canada, runs along the Sierra Crest just west of the lake. To the south of Lake Tahoe sits the Mokelumne Wilderness, a whopping 100,848-acre preserve, one of several undeveloped tracts that extend toward Yosemite, which is accessible via the Tahoe-Yosemite Trail, a 186-mi trek.

Skiing & Snowboarding

The mountains around Lake Tahoe are bombarded by blizzards throughout most winters and sometimes in fall and spring; 10- to 12-foot bases are not uncommon. The Sierra often boasts the deepest snowpack on the continent, but because of the relatively mild temperatures over the Pacific, falling snow can be very heavy and wet—it's nicknamed "Sierra Cement" for a reason. The upside is that you can sometimes ski and board as late as July, you probably won't get frostbite, and you'll likely get a tan. The profusion of downhill resorts guarantees an ample selection of terrains, conditions, and challenges, including backcountry access at several resorts, most notably at Alpine Meadows, Sugar Bowl, and Sierra-at-Tahoe. Snowboarding is permitted at all Tahoe ski areas.

The Lake Tahoe area is also a great destination for Nordic skiers. You can even cross-country ski on fresh snow right on the lakeshore beaches. "Skinny" (i.e., cross-country) skiing at the resorts can be costly, but you get the benefits of machine grooming and trail preparation. If it's bargain Nordic you're after, take advantage of thousands of acres of public forest and parkland trails.

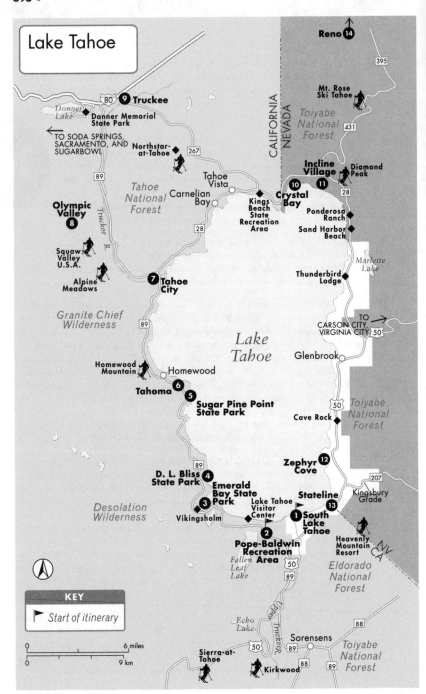

Lake Tahoe

Reno **14**

395

Mt. Rose
Ski Tahoe

Toiyabe
National
Forest

431

CALIFORNIA
NEVADA

80 **9** Truckee

*Donner
Lake*
Donner Memorial
State Park

TO SODA SPRINGS,
SACRAMENTO, AND
SUGARBOWL

Northstar-
at-Tahoe
267

89

*Tahoe
National
Forest*

Tahoe
Vista

Carnelian
Bay

Incline
Village
10 **11**

Diamond
Peak

28

Crystal
Bay

Kings
Beach
State
Recreation
Area

Ponderosa
Ranch

**Olympic
Valley
8**

28

Sand Harbor
Beach

*Marlette
Lake*

Squaw
Valley
U.S.A.

Truckee R.

Thunderbird
Lodge

Alpine
Meadows

7 Tahoe
City

*Lake
Tahoe*

TO
CARSON CITY,
VIRGINIA CITY 50

*Granite Chief
Wilderness*

89

Glenbrook

Homewood
Mountain

Homewood

Tahoma **6**
5

50 *Toiyabe
National
Forest*

**Sugar Pine Point
State Park**

Cave Rock

Zephyr
Cove **12**

207

D. L. Bliss
State Park **4**

**Emerald
Bay State
Park**

3

Lake Tahoe
Visitor
Center

Stateline
13

Kingsbury
Grade

*Desolation
Wilderness*

Vikingsholm

1 South
Lake
Tahoe

**Pope-Baldwin
Recreation
2** **Area**

Heavenly
Mountain
Resort

NV
CA

*Fallen
Leaf
Lake*

50

89

*Eldorado
National
Forest*

KEY

▶ *Start of itinerary*

*Echo
Lake*

Upper Truckee R.

50

89

Sorensens

88

*Toiyabe
National
Forest*

0   6 miles
0   9 km

Sierra-at-
Tahoe

50

88

Kirkwood

89

Cabin Museum can be jammed at any time, and the lake's beaches can be packed. September and October, when the throngs have dispersed but the weather is still pleasant, are among the most satisfying—and cheapest—months to visit Lake Tahoe.

CALIFORNIA SIDE

With the exception of Stateline, Nevada—which, aside from its casino-hotel towers, seems almost indistinguishable from South Lake Tahoe, California—the California side is more developed than the Nevada side. Here you'll find both commercial enterprises—restaurants, motels, lodges, resorts, residential subdivisions—and public-access facilities, such as historic sites, parks, campgrounds, marinas, and beaches.

South Lake Tahoe

▶ ❶ *50 mi south of Reno on U.S. 395 and U.S. 50; 198 mi northeast of San Francisco on I–80 and U.S. 50.*

South Lake Tahoe's raison d'être is tourism: the casinos of nearby Stateline, Nevada; the ski slopes at Heavenly Mountain; the beaches, docks, bike trails, and campgrounds all around the south shore; and the backcountry of Eldorado National Forest and Desolation Wilderness. Motels, lodges, and restaurants line U.S. 50 near town.

Whether you ski or not, you'll appreciate the impressive view of Lake Tahoe from the **Heavenly Gondola.** Its 138 eight-passenger cars travel from the middle of town 2½ mi up the mountain in 13 minutes. When the weather's fine, you can take one of three hikes around the mountaintop and then have lunch at Adventure Peak Grill. Heavenly also offers day care for children. ⊠ *Downtown* ☎ *775/586–7000 or 800/432–8365* ⊕ *www. skiheavenly.com* ⊠ *$22* ☉ *Summer, daily 9–9; winter, daily 9–4.*

Fodor's Choice
★

Where to Stay & Eat

★ $$–$$$ ✕ **Evan's.** The sophisticated, contemporary California menu includes such specialties as seared foie gras with curried ice cream and roast pineapple, and venison in a raspberry demi-glace. The 40-seat dining room is intimate, with tables a little close together, but the service and food are excellent. ⊠ *536 Emerald Bay Rd.* ☎ *530/542–1990* ⚌ *Reservations essential* ▤ *MC, V* ☉ *No lunch.*

★ $–$$$ ✕ **Café Fiore.** This northern Italian restaurant may be the most romantic spot in town, with only seven candlelit tables. The menu lists a variety of pastas and meat dishes and several daily fish specials. Sautéed veal dishes are the house specialty. Leave room for the homemade white-chocolate ice cream. ⊠ *1169 Ski Run Blvd.* ☎ *530/541–2908* ⚌ *Reservations essential* ▤ *AE, MC, V* ☉ *No lunch.*

¢–$$ ✕ **Freshies.** When you've had your fill of junk food, come here for delicious, healthful meals. Specialties include seafood and vegetarian dishes, but there are always good grilled meats available, like Hawaiian spare ribs and free-range rib-eye steaks. Though it's in a minimall and you may have to wait for a table, it's worth it. ⊠ *3300 Lake Tahoe Blvd.* ☎ *530/542–3630* ⚌ *Reservations not accepted* ▤ *MC, V.*

¢–$$ ✕ **Scusa!** The kitchen here turns out big plates of linguine with clam sauce, veal Marsala, and chicken piccata. There's nothing fancy or esoteric about the menu, just straightforward Italian-American food. Try the exceptionally good bread pudding for dessert. ☒ *1142 Ski Run Blvd.* ☎ *530/ 542–0100* ⊟ *AE, MC, V* ⊘ *No lunch.*

¢–$ ✕ **Orchid's Thai.** If you're hungry for Thai, Orchid's serves good food at reasonable prices in an attractive, dining room with pumpkin-color walls. When every place in town is booked, this is a great backup. They even take reservations. ☒ *2180 Lake Tahoe Blvd.* ☎ *530/544–5541* ⊟ *AE, D, DC, MC, V* ⊘ *No Sunday lunch.*

¢ ✕ **Red Hut Café.** A vintage-1959 Tahoe diner, all chrome and red plastic, the Red Hut is a tiny place with a dozen counter stools and a dozen booths. It's a traditional breakfast spot for those in the know, who come for the huge omelets; the banana, pecan, and coconut waffles; and other tasty vittles. There's another branch in Stateline, too. ☒ *2749 U.S. 50* ☎ *530/ 541–9024* ⌖ *Reservations not accepted* ⊟ *No credit cards* ⊘ *No dinner* ☒ *227 Kingsbury Grade Stateline, NV* ☎ *775/588–7488.*

★ $$–$$$$ ✕▣ **Embassy Suites and Echo Restaurant.** All rooms are suites at this large, full-service hotel just over the state line in California, where there are no casinos to disturb the quiet. The extra-spacious accommodations are perfect for families, as every unit contains a pull-out sofa. Rates include full breakfast and evening cocktails. The excellent in-house restaurant, Echo ($$–$$$), serves an eclectic mix of modern and traditional dishes: expect everything from mac and cheese to pan-seared foie gras. ☒ *4130 Lake Tahoe Blvd., 96150* ☎ *530/544–5400 or 800/362–2779* 🖷 *530/ 544–4900* ⊕ *www.embassysuites.com* ⇌ *400 suites* ⌂ *Restaurant, in-room data ports, microwaves, refrigerators, cable TV with movies and video games, indoor pool, exercise equipment, indoor hot tub, sauna, ski storage, bar, lounge, laundry facilities, meeting rooms, parking (fee)* ⊟ *AE, D, DC, MC, V* ☗ *BP.*

$$$–$$$$ **FodorśChoice** ★ ▣ **Black Bear Inn Bed and Breakfast.** South Lake Tahoe's most luxurious inn feels like one of the great old lodges of the Adirondacks. Its living room has rough-hewn beams, plank floors, cathedral ceilings, Persian rugs, and even an elk's head over the giant river-rock fireplace. Built in the 1990s with meticulous attention to detail, the five inn rooms and three cabins feature 19th-century American antiques, fine art, and fireplaces; cabins also have kitchenettes. Never intrusive, the affable innkeepers provide a sumptuous breakfast in the morning and wine and cheese in the afternoon. ☒ *1202 Ski Run Blvd., 96150* ☎ *530/544–4451 or 877/232–7466* ⊕ *www.tahoeblackbear.com* ⇌ *5 rooms, 3 cabins* ⌂ *Dining room, in-room data ports, some in-room hot tubs, some kitchenettes, cable TV with movies, in-room VCRs, outdoor hot tub, ski storage, lounge; no kids under 16, no smoking* ⊟ *MC, V* ☗ *BP.*

★ $$$–$$$$ ▣ **Marriott's Grand Residence and Timber Lodge.** At the base of Heavenly Gondola, right in the center of town, stand these two giant, modern condominium properties operated by Marriott. Though both are extremely comfortable, Timber Lodge feels more like a family vacation resort; Grand Residence is geared toward luxury travelers. Units vary in size from studios to three bedrooms, and some have amenities like stereos, fireplaces, daily maid service, and full kitchens. Ask about vacation packages.

✉ *1001 Park Ave., 96150* ☎ *530/542–8400 or 800/627–7468* 🖷 *530/524–8410* ⊕ *www.marriott.com* ⤷ *431 condos* ♻ *In-room data ports, some in-room hot tubs, some kitchens, cable TV, outdoor pool, gym, 2 indoor hot tubs, ice-skating, ski shop, ski storage, laundry facilities, laundry service, concierge; no smoking* ▭ *AE, D, DC, MC, V.*

$$$ ▦ **Tahoe Seasons Resort.** It's a 150-yard walk to California Lodge of Heavenly Mountain Resort from this all-suites hotel, where every room has a two-person sunken hot tub. Most units have gas fireplaces, and some can sleep up to six people. The lobby is decorated in early-'80s style, but the rooms are very comfortable, and the service is good. ✉ *3901 Saddle Rd., 96157* ☎ *530/541–6700 or 800/540–4874* 🖷 *530/541–0653* ⊕ *www.tahoeseasons.com* ⤷ *183 suites* ♻ *Restaurant, room service, in-room hot tubs, kitchenettes, minibars, microwaves, refrigerators, cable TV, in-room VCRs, 2 tennis courts, outdoor pool, outdoor hot tub, billiards, volleyball, downhill skiing, ski shop, ski storage, lounge, video game room, concierge, meeting rooms; no smoking* ▭ *AE, DC, MC, V.*

★ $–$$$ ▦ **Inn by the Lake.** Across the road from a beach, this luxury motel has spacious, spotless rooms and suites decorated in soft autumn colors. All have balconies; some have lake views, wet bars, and kitchens. In the afternoon the staff sets out cookies and cider. ✉ *3300 Lake Tahoe Blvd., 96150* ☎ *530/542–0330 or 800/877–1466* 🖷 *530/541–6596* ⊕ *www.innbythelake.com* ⤷ *87 rooms, 13 suites* ♻ *Room service, in-room data ports, some in-room hot tubs, some kitchens, some minibars, cable TV with movies and video games, outdoor pool, sauna, bicycles, ski storage, dry cleaning, laundry facilities, meeting rooms* ▭ *AE, D, DC, MC, V* ❡⊙❚ *CP.*

$–$$ ▦ **Camp Richardson.** A 1920s lodge, a few dozen cabins, and a small inn comprise this resort, nestled beneath giant pine trees on 80 acres of land on the southwest shore of Lake Tahoe. The rustic log cabin–style lodge has simple, attractive accommodations. The cabins (one-week minimum in summer) have lots of space, fireplaces or wood stoves, and kitchenettes; some can sleep eight. The Beachside Inn has more modern amenities and sits right on the lake, but its rooms feel like those in an ordinary motel. A glass-bottom trimaran makes trips to Emerald Bay directly from the resort. Rates drop significantly after Labor Day, making it a bargain for skiers and off-season travelers. ✉ *1900 Jameson Beach, 96150* ☎ *530/542–6550 or 800/544–1801* 🖷 *530/541–1802* ⊕ *www.camprichardson.com* ⤷ *28 lodge rooms, 47 cabins, 7 inn rooms, 300 campsites* ♻ *Restaurant, some microwaves, some refrigerators, beach, boating, marina, waterskiing, fishing, bicycles, cross-country skiing, sleigh rides, general store; no phones in some rooms, no a/c, no TV in some rooms, no smoking* ▭ *AE, D, MC, V.*

★ ¢–$$$ ▦ **Sorensen's Resort.** Escape from civilization by staying in Eldorado National Forest, 20 minutes south of town. In a log cabin at this woodsy 165-acre resort, you can lie on a hammock beneath the aspens or sit in a rocker on your own front porch. All but three of the cabins have a kitchen and wood-burning stove or fireplace. There are also three modern homes that sleep six. Request a room away from the road. ✉ *14255 Hwy. 88, Hope Valley 96120* ☎ *530/694–2203 or 800/423–9949* ⊕ *www.sorensensresort.com* ⤷ *28 cabins with bath, 2 rooms* *with shared bath, 4 houses ⚴ Restaurant, some fans, some kitchens, some kitchenettes, pond, sauna, boating, fishing, bicycles, croquet, hiking, cross-country skiing, ski shop, ski storage, tobogganing, library, babysitting, children's programs (ages 3–18), playground, some pets allowed; no a/c, no room phones, no room TVs, no smoking.*

¢–$$ 🖭 **Best Western Station House Inn.** It's a short walk to the beach, the Heavenly Gondola, or the casinos from this modern, well-kept, two-story motel off the main drag. The beds are comfortable, and the entire property is immaculate. ⊠ *901 Park Ave., 96150* ☎ *530/542–1101 or 800/822–5953* 🖷 *530/542–1714* ⊕ *www.stationhouseinn.com* ⤳ *100 rooms, 2 suites ⚴ Restaurant, cable TV, pool, outdoor hot tub, ski storage, bar, dry cleaning, Internet* ⊟ *AE, D, DC, MC, V* ⏐⊙⏐ *BP.*

Sports & the Outdoors

FISHING   **Tahoe Sports Fishing** (⊠ Ski Run Marina ☎ 530/541–5448, 800/696–7797 in CA) is one of the largest and oldest fishing-charter services on the lake. Trips include all necessary gear and bait, and the crew cleans and packages your catch.

GOLF   The 18-hole, par-71 **Lake Tahoe Golf Course** (⊠ U.S. 50, between Lake Tahoe Airport and Meyers ☎ 530/577–0788) has a driving range. Greens fees start at $51; a cart (mandatory Friday to Sunday) costs $21.

HIKING   The south shore is a great jumping-off point for day treks into nearby Eldorado National Forest and Desolation Wilderness. Hike a couple of miles on the **Pacific Crest Trail** (⊠ Echo Summit, about 12 mi southwest of South Lake Tahoe off U.S. 50 ☎ 916/349–2109 or 888/728–7245 ⊕ www.pcta.org). The Pacific Crest Trail leads into **Desolation Wilderness** (⊠ El Dorado National Forest Information Center ☎ 530/644–6048 ⊕ www.fs.fed.us/r5/eldorado), where you can pick up trails to gorgeous backcountry lakes and mountain peaks (bring a map). Late May through early September, the easiest way to access Desolation Wilderness is via boat taxi ($14 round-trip) across Echo Lake from **Echo Chalet** (⊠ Echo Lakes Rd., off U.S. 50 near Echo Summit ☎ 530/659–7207 ⊕ www.echochalet.com).

KAYAKING   **Kayak Tahoe** (⊠ Timber Cove Marina at Tahoe Paradise ☎ 530/544–2011) has long been teaching people to kayak on Lake Tahoe and the Truckee River. Lessons and excursions (Emerald Bay, Cave Rock, Zephyr Cove) are offered June through September. You can also rent a kayak and paddle solo.

MOUNTAIN   With so much national forest land surrounding Lake Tahoe, you may
BIKING   want to try mountain biking. You can rent both road and mountain bikes and get tips on where to ride them from the friendly staff at **Tahoe Mountain Sports Ltd.** (⊠ 4008 Lake Tahoe Blvd. ☎ 530/542–4000).

SCUBA DIVING   **Sun Sports** (⊠ 3564 Lake Tahoe Blvd. ☎ 530/541–6000) is a full-service PADI dive center with rentals and instruction.

SKIING   Straddling two states, vast **Heavenly Mountain Resort**—composed of nine
★   peaks, two valleys, and four base-lodge areas, and boasting the largest snowmaking system in the western United States—has something for every skier. Beginners can choose wide, well-groomed trails—accessed

via the tram from the California Lodge or the gondola from downtown South Lake Tahoe—or short and gentle runs in the Enchanted Forest area. The Sky Express high-speed quad chair whisks intermediate and advanced skiers to the summit for wide cruisers or steep tree skiing. Mott and Killebrew canyons draw expert skiers to the Nevada side for the steep chutes and thick-timber slopes. For snowboarders there's High Roller Terrain Park, near the Olympic lift. The ski school, like everything else at Heavenly, is large and offers everything from learn-to-ski packages to canyon-adventure tours. Skiing lessons are available for children age four and up; there's day care for infants older than six weeks. ⊠ *Ski Run Blvd. off Hwy. 89/U.S. 50, Stateline, NV* ☎ *775/586–7000 or 800/432–8365* ⊕ *www.skiheavenly.com* ⚲ *86 trails on 4,800 acres, rated 20% beginner, 45% intermediate, 35% expert. Longest run 5½ mi, base 6,540', summit 10,067'. Lifts: 30, including 1 aerial tram, 1 gondola, 2 high-speed 6-passenger lifts, and 5 high-speed quads.*

Thirty-six miles south of Lake Tahoe, **Kirkwood Ski Resort** is a destination resort with 135 condominiums, shops and restaurants, and a spa. But with 500 annual inches of snowfall, Kirkwood draws crowds with outstanding skiing. The rocky chutes off the very top are rated expert-only, but intermediate and beginner skiers can enjoy vast bowls, where they can ski through trees or on wide, open trails. There are three freestyle terrain parks with varying degrees of difficulty; one is so technically challenging that it requires a separate ticket. Nonskiers can snowshoe, snowskate, snowmobile, or go on a dog-sled ride. There's also an ice-skating rink. The children's ski school has programs for ages 4–12, and there's day care for children two to six years old. If it's cross-country you're interested in, the resort has 58 mi of superb groomed-track skiing, with skating lanes, instruction, and rentals. ⊠ *Hwy. 88, 14 mi west of Hwy. 89* ☎ *209/258–6000 downhill, 209/258–7248 cross-country, 209/258–7000 lodging information, 209/258–3000 snow phone* ⚲ *72 trails on 2,300 acres, rated 15% beginner, 50% intermediate, 20% advanced, 15% expert. Longest run 2½ mi, base 7,800', summit 9,800'. Lifts: 14.*

Often overlooked by skiers and boarders rushing to Heavenly or Kirkwood, **Sierra-at-Tahoe** has meticulously groomed intermediate slopes, some of the best tree skiing in California, and guided backcountry access. Extremely popular with boarders, Sierra also has two terrain parks, including a superpipe with 17-foot walls. For nonskiers there's a snow-tubing hill. Sierra has a low-key atmosphere that's great for families. ⊠ *12 mi from South Lake Tahoe off of U.S. 50, near Echo Summit* ☎ *530/659–7453* ⊕ *www.sierraattahoe.com* ⚲ *46 trails on 2,000 acres, rated 24% beginner, 50% intermediate, 25% advanced. Longest run 2½ mi, base 6,640', summit 8,852'. Lifts: 11, including 3 high-speed quads.*

At Sorensen's Resort, **Hope Valley Cross Country** (⊠ 14255 Hwy. 88, just east of Hwy. 89, Hope Valley ☎ 530/694–2266) provides instruction and equipment rentals to prepare you for striding and telemarking. The outfit has 36 mi of trails through Eldorado National Forest, 6 of which are groomed.

If you don't want to pay the high cost of rental equipment at the resorts, you'll find reasonable prices and expert advice at **Tahoe Mountain Sports Ltd.** (⊠ Downhill: 4008 Lake Tahoe Blvd. ☎ 530/542–4000 ⊠ Cross-Country: South Y Center, Hwy. 89 and U.S. 50 ☎ 530/544–2284). Downhill enthusiasts can get regular and demo-package downhill skis and snowboards, while cross-country skiers can get information on local trails.

Pope-Baldwin Recreation Area

▶ ❷ *5 mi west of South Lake Tahoe on Hwy. 89.*

To the west of South Lake Tahoe, U.S. 50 and Highway 89 come together, forming an intersection nicknamed "the Y." If you head northwest on Highway 89 and follow the lakefront, commercial development gives way to national forests and state parks. One of these is Pope-Baldwin Recreation Area.

The lakeside **Tallac Historic Site** is a pleasant place to take a stroll or have a picnic. Among its attractions are **Pope House,** the magnificently restored 1894 mansion of George S. Pope, who made his money in shipping and lumber and hosted the business and cultural elite of 1920s America. There are two other estates here. One belonged to entrepreneur "Lucky" Baldwin; today it houses the **Baldwin Museum,** a collection of family memorabilia and Washoe Indian artifacts. The other, called the Valhalla, belonged to Walter Heller and is now used for community events. The site hosts summertime cultural activities including a Renaissance festival. Docents conduct tours of the Pope House in summer. In winter, you can cross-country ski around the site (bring your own equipment). ⊠ *Hwy. 89* ☎ *530/541–5227* ⊕ *www.tahoeheritage.org* ⊠ *Free; Pope House tour $3* ☉ *Grounds daily sunrise–sunset; Pope House and Baldwin Museum late May–mid-June, weekends 10–4; mid-June–early Sept., daily 10–4.*

The U.S. Forest Service operates the **Lake Tahoe Visitor Center,** on Taylor Creek. You can visit the site of a Washoe Indian settlement; walk self-guided trails through meadow, marsh, and forest; and inspect the Stream Profile Chamber, an underground underwater display with windows that afford views right into Taylor Creek (in fall you may see spawning kokanee salmon digging their nests). In summer U.S. Forest Service naturalists organize discovery walks and nighttime campfires with singing and marshmallow roasts. ⊠ *Hwy. 89, 3 mi north of junction with U.S. 50* ☎ *530/543–2674 June–Oct., 530/525–7277 year-round* ⊕ *www.fs.fed.us/r5/ltbmu* ⊠ *Free* ☉ *June–Sept., daily 8–5:30; Oct., weekends 8–5:30.*

Emerald Bay State Park

❸ *4 mi west of Pope-Baldwin Recreation Area on Hwy. 89.*

Fodor'sChoice
★

Emerald Bay, a 3-mi-long and 1-mi-wide fjordlike inlet on Lake Tahoe's shore, was carved by a massive glacier millions of years ago. Famed for its jewel-like shape and colors, it surrounds Fannette, Tahoe's only island. Highway 89 curves high above the lake through Emerald Bay State Park; from the Emerald Bay lookout, the centerpiece of the park, you can survey the whole scene.

A steep 1-mi-long trail from the lookout leads down to **Vikingsholm,** a 38-room estate completed in 1929. The original owner, Lora Knight, had this precise replica of a 1,200-year-old Viking castle built out of materials native to the area. She furnished it with Scandinavian antiques and hired artisans to build period reproductions. The sod roof sprouts wildflowers each spring. There are picnic tables nearby and a gray-sand beach for strolling. The hike back up is hard (especially if you're not yet acclimated to the elevation), but there are benches and stone culverts to rest on. At the 150-foot peak of Fannette Island are the remnants of a stone structure known as the Tea House, built in 1928 so that guests of Lora Knight could have a place to enjoy afternoon refreshments after a motorboat ride. The island is off-limits from February through June to protect nesting Canada geese. The rest of the year it's open for day use. ⊠ *Hwy. 89* ☎ *530/ 541–3030 summer, 530/525–7277 year-round* 💲 *$5* ⊙ *Late May–mid-June, weekends call for hrs; mid-June–Sept., daily 10–4.*

Sports & the Outdoors

HIKING Leave your car in the parking lot for Eagle Falls picnic area (near Vikingsholm; arrive early for a good spot), and head to **Eagle Falls,** a short but fairly steep walk-up canyon. You'll have a brilliant panorama of Emerald Bay from this spot, near the boundary of Desolation Wilderness. If you want a full-day's hike and you're in good shape, continue 5 mi, past Eagle Lake, to Upper and Middle Velma Lakes (bring a map).

SWIMMING Hike past Eagle Falls (about 1 mi from the parking lot) to **Eagle Lake,** where you can shed your clothes (bring a suit weekends) and dive into cold water.

D. L. Bliss State Park

❹ *3 mi north of Emerald Bay State Park on Hwy. 89.*

D. L. Bliss State Park takes its name from Duane LeRoy Bliss, a 19th-century lumber magnate. At one time Bliss owned nearly 75% of Tahoe's lakefront, along with local steamboats, railroads, and banks. The Bliss family donated these 1,200 acres to the state in the 1930s. The park now shares 6 mi of shoreline with Emerald Bay State Park. At the north end of Bliss is Rubicon Point, which overlooks one of the lake's deepest spots. Short trails lead to an old lighthouse and Balancing Rock, which weighs 250,000 pounds and balances on a fist of granite. A 4¼-mi trail leads to Vikingsholm and provides stunning lake views. Two white-sand beaches front some of Tahoe's warmest water. ⊠ *Hwy. 89* ☎ *530/525–7277* 💲 *$6 per vehicle, day use* ⊙ *Late May–Sept., daily sunrise–sunset.*

Camping

¢ ⌂ **D. L. Bliss State Park Campground.** In one of California's most beautiful spots, quiet, wooded hills make for blissful family camping near the lake. The campground is open June to September, and reservations are accepted up to seven months in advance. ⊠ *Off Hwy. 89, 17 mi south* *of Tahoe City on lake side* ☎ *800/444–7275* ⊕ *www.reserveamerica.com* ⇨ *168 sites* ⚭ *Flush toilets, drinking water, showers, bear boxes, fire pits, grills, picnic tables, public telephone, swimming.*

Sugar Pine Point State Park

★ ⑤ *8 mi north of D. L. Bliss State Park on Hwy. 89.*

The main attraction at Sugar Pine Point State Park is **Ehrman Mansion,** a 1903 stone-and-shingle summer home furnished in period style. In its day it was the height of modernity, with a refrigerator, an elevator, and an electric stove. Also in the park are a trapper's log cabin from the mid-19th century, a nature preserve with wildlife exhibits, a lighthouse, the start of the 10-mi-long biking trail to Tahoe City, and an extensive system of hiking and cross-country skiing trails. ⊠ *Hwy. 89* ☎ *530/525–7982 mansion (in season), 530/525–7232 year-round* ⊠ *$6 per vehicle, day use* ☉ *Mansion July–early Sept., daily 11–4.*

Camping

¢ ⚲ **Sugar Pine Point State Park Campground/General Creek Campground.** This beautiful and homey campground on the mountain side of Highway 89 is one of the few public ones to remain open in winter, when it is popular with cross-country skiers. There are no hookups here, and the showers operate from late May to early September only. ⊠ *Hwy. 89, 1 mi south of Tahoma* ☎ *916/638–5883 or 800/444–7275* ⊕ *www.reserveamerica.com* ⇨ *175 sites* ⚭ *Flush toilets, drinking water, showers, bear boxes, fire pits, grills, public telephone, swimming.*

Tahoma

⑥ *1 mi north of Sugar Pine Point State Park on Hwy. 89; 23 mi south of Truckee on Hwy. 89.*

The quiet west shore offers a glimpse back in time to "Old Tahoe." Tahoma exemplifies life on the lake in its early days, with rustic, lakeside vacation cottages that are far from the blinking lights of the South Shore's casinos. In 1960 Tahoma hosted the Olympic nordic skiing competitions. Today there's little to do here except stroll by the lake and listen to the wind in the trees.

Where to Stay

★ $–$$$ ▥ **Tahoma Meadows B&B Cottages.** Rooms in these freestanding vacation cabins are individually decorated, and some have claw-foot tubs and fireplaces. Lovingly maintained by charming on-site owners, the cabins make a great retreat for families and couples. Tariffs for cabins without kitchens include a delicious family-style breakfast. ⊠ *6821 W. Lake Blvd.,* ⬧ *Box 810, 96142* ☎ *530/525–1553 or 866/525–1553* ⊕ *www.tahomameadows.com* ⇨ *15 cabins* ⚭ *Restaurant, some kitchens, cable TV, outdoor hot tub, some pets allowed (fee); no a/c, no room phones, no smoking* ▭ *AE, D, MC, V* ⦿ *Some BP.*

Sports & the Outdoors

You'll feel as though you're going to ski into the lake when you schuss down the face of **Homewood Mountain Resort**—and you could if you really wanted to, since the mountain rises right off the shoreline. This is the favorite area of locals on a fresh-snow day, since you can find lots of untracked powder. It's also the most protected and least windy Tahoe ski area during a storm. There aren't any high-speed lifts, but there are rarely any lines and the ticket prices are some of the cheapest around. It may look small as you drive by, but most of the resort is not visible from the road. ⊠ *Hwy. 89* ☎ *530/525–2992* ⊕ *www.skihomewood. com* ☞ *56 trails on 1,260 acres, rated 15% beginner, 50% intermediate, and 35% advanced. Longest run 2 mi, base 6,240', summit 7,880'. Lifts: 4 chair lifts, 4 surface lifts.*

Tahoe City

❼ *10 mi north of Sugar Pine Point State Park on Hwy. 89; 14 mi south of Truckee on Hwy. 89.*

Tahoe City has a compact area of stores and restaurants, all within walking distance of the Outlet Gates, where water is spilled into the Truckee River to control the surface level of the lake. Giant trout are commonly seen in the river from Fanny Bridge, so-called for the views of the backsides of sightseers leaning over the railing. Here, Highway 89 bears northwest, away from the lake, and parallels the river toward Squaw Valley, Donner Lake, and Truckee. Highway 28 continues northeast around the lake toward Kings Beach and Nevada.

★ The **Gatekeeper's Cabin Museum** preserves a little-known part of the region's history. Between 1910 and 1968 the gatekeeper who lived on this site was responsible for monitoring the level of the lake, using a hand-turned winch system to keep the water at the correct level. That winch system is still used today. A Native American basket museum is in an adjacent wing. ⊠ *130 W. Lake Blvd.* ☎ *530/583–1762* ✉ *$2* ⊙ *May–mid-June and Sept., Wed.–Sun. 11–5; mid-June–late Aug., daily 11–5.*

In the middle of town, the **Watson Cabin Living Museum,** a 1909 log cabin built by Robert M. Watson and his son, is filled with some century-old furnishings and many reproductions. Docents are available to answer questions and will lead tours with advance arrangements. ⊠ *560 N. Lake Blvd.* ☎ *530/583–8717 or 530/583–1762* ✉ *Donation suggested* ⊙ *Late May–June, weekends noon–4; July–early Sept., Wed.–Mon. noon–4.*

Where to Stay & Eat

$$–$$$$ ✕ **Christy Hill.** Sit near the fireplace in the sparsely decorated, whitewashed dining room or outside on the deck. While you take in great views of the lake, you can dine on California cuisine, including fresh seafood, beef, Australian lamb loin, and pasta. The service is professional, and desserts are especially delicious (try the pecan ice cream or fruit cobbler). Come early to see the sunset—and you'll understand why the entrée prices are so high. ⊠ *Lakehouse Mall, 115 Grove St.* ☎ *530/583– 8551* ⌔ *Reservations essential* ▤ *AE, MC, V* ⊙ *Closed Mon. early Sept.–Thanksgiving and Apr. and May. No lunch.*

$$–$$$ ✕ **Jake's on the Lake.** Overlooking the water, large, handsome rooms of oak and glass are the backdrop for steaks and an extensive selection of seafood. The lounge gets crowded with bar-hopping boaters, who pull up to the big pier outside. ⊠ *Boatworks Mall, 780 N. Lake Blvd.* ☏ *530/583–0188* ▭ *AE, MC, V* ⊘ *No lunch weekdays.*

★ **$$–$$$** ✕ **Wolfdale's.** Wolfdale's brought California cuisine to Lake Tahoe in 1984, and these days the weekly menu continues to include imaginative entrées, merging Asian and European cooking. Among the examples are sea bass tempura, Asian braised duck leg and breast, and coconut crepe stuffed with stir-fried vegetables. Tables in the comfortable dining room are well-spaced. ⊠ *640 N. Lake Blvd.* ☏ *530/583–5700* ⚱ *Reservations essential* ▭ *MC, V* ⊘ *Closed Tues. No lunch.*

★ **$–$$$** ✕ **Fiamma.** Everything from soup stock to gelato is made from scratch at this modern mom-and-pop northern Italian trattoria. Settle into one of the comfy, romantic booths, where hot focaccia hits the table as soon as you arrive, or sit at the always-bustling wine bar with wine aficionados and hip, young singles. The menu includes roasted and grilled meats, homemade pastas, and pizzas from the wood-fired oven. ⊠ *521 N. Lake Blvd.* ☏ *530/581–1416* ⚱ *Reservations essential* ▭ *AE, MC, V* ⊘ *No lunch.*

¢–$ ✕ **Fire Sign Café.** There's often a wait at the west shore's best spot for breakfast and lunch, but it's worth it. The pastries are made from scratch, the salmon is smoked in-house, and there's real maple syrup for the many flavors of pancakes and waffles. The eggs Benedict are delicious. ⊠ *1785 W. Lake Blvd.* ☏ *530/583–0871* ▭ *AE, MC, V* ⊘ *No dinner.*

★ **$–$$$** ✕▥ **Sunnyside Restaurant and Lodge.** The views are superb at this pretty little lodge, right on the lake, just 3 mi south of Tahoe City. All but four rooms have balconies and locally crafted furnishings; some have river-rock fireplaces and wet bars, and some have pull-out sofas. The lodge is great for couples, but it's not geared to families. The restaurant ($–$$$) serves standard preparations of seafood, steaks, and pasta. The dockside bar gets packed with boaters and Bacchanalian revelers. Be forewarned: this is not a quiet place on weekends in summer. ⊠ *1850 W. Lake Blvd.,* ⏚ *Box 5969, 96145* ☏ *530/583–7200 or 800/822–2754* ▤ *530/583–2551* ⊕ *www.sunnysidetahoe.com* ⇲ *18 rooms, 5 suites* ⚱ *Restaurant, room service, fans, in-room data ports, cable TV, in-room VCRs, beach, bar; no a/c, no smoking* ▭ *AE, MC, V* ⦿⊙ *CP.*

$$$–$$$$ ▥ **Chinquapin Resort.** A deluxe development built in the 1970s on 95 acres of forested land and a mile of lakefront lies 3 mi northeast of Tahoe City. Within are one- to four-bedroom town houses and condos with great views of the lake and the mountains. Each unit has a fireplace, a fully equipped kitchen, and a washer and dryer. A one-week minimum stay is required in summer and late December; two- and three-night minimums apply the rest of the year. ⊠ *3600 N. Lake Blvd., 96145* ☏ *530/583–6991 or 800/732–6721* ▤ *530/583–0937* ⊕ *www.chinquapin.com* ⇲ *172 town houses and condos* ⚱ *Kitchens, cable TV, 7 tennis courts, pool, 2 saunas, 2 beaches, hiking, horseshoes; no a/c* ▭ *AE, D, MC, V.*

$$–$$$$ ▥ **Cottage Inn.** Avoid the crowds by staying just south of town in one of these tidy, circa-1938 log cottages under the towering pines on the west shore of the lake. Cute as a button, with knotty-pine paneling and a gas-flame stone fireplace, each unit typifies old-Tahoe style while embracing you with up-to-date comfort. There's also a private beach. ⊠ *1690 W. Lake Blvd.* ⌂ *Box 66, 96145* ☎ *530/581–4073 or 800/ 581–4073* 🖷 *530/581–0226* ⊕ *www.thecottageinn.com* ⇥ *20 rooms, 12 suites* ⌂ *Some in-room hot tubs, cable TV, in-room VCRs, lake, sauna, beach; no a/c, no kids under 12, no smoking* ⊟ *MC, V* ⫼◯⫼ *BP.*

$–$$ 🖥 **Tahoe City Travelodge.** As motels go, this one is excellent. Its rooms are well-maintained and larger than average, and have either double or king-size beds, big bathrooms with massage showers and hair dryers, and coffeemakers. There's also a great lake-view deck with a hot tub and a sauna. ⊠ *455 N. Lake Blvd., Box 84, 96145* ☎ *530/583– 3766 or 800/578–7878* 🖷 *530/583–8045* ⊕ *www.travelodge.com* ⇥ *47 rooms* ⌂ *In-room data ports, microwaves, refrigerators, cable TV, some in-room VCRs, outdoor pool, hot tub, sauna* ⫼◯⫼ *CP* ⊟ *AE, D, DC, MC, V.*

Sports & the Outdoors

GOLF Golfers use pull carts or caddies at the 9-hole **Tahoe City Golf Course** (⊠ Hwy. 28 ☎ 530/583–1516), which opened in 1917. Though rates vary by season, the maximum greens fees are $30 for 9 holes, $50 for 18; a power cart costs $16 to $24.

MOUNTAIN **Cyclepaths Mountain Bike Adventures** (⊠ 1785 W. Lake Blvd. ☎ 530/581–
BIKING 1171 or 800/780–2453) is a combination full-service bike shop and bike-adventure outfitter. It offers instruction in mountain biking, guided tours (from half-day to weeklong excursions), tips for self-guided bike touring, bike repairs, and books and maps on the area.

RIVER RAFTING In summer you can take a self-guided raft trip down a gentle, 5-mi stretch of the Truckee River through **Truckee River Rafting** (☎ 530/583–7238 or 888/584–7238). They will shuttle you back to your car at the end of your two- to four-hour trip.

SKIING The locals' favorite place to ski, **Alpine Meadows Ski Area** is also the
★ unofficial telemarking hub of the Sierra. With 495 inches of snow annually, Alpine has some of Tahoe's most reliable conditions. It's usually one of the first areas to open in November and one of the last to close in May or June. Alpine isn't the place for arrogant show-offs; instead, you'll find down-to-earth alpine fetishists. The two peaks here are well suited to intermediate skiers, but for experts there's also an open boundary to the backcountry (take "High Traverse" from the summit). Snowboarders and hot-dog skiers will find a terrain park with a half-pipe, superpipe, rails, and tabletops, as well as a boardercross course. Alpine is a great place to learn to ski, and the Tahoe Adaptive Ski School here teaches and coaches those with physical and mental disabilities. There's also an area for overnight RV parking. ⊠ *Off Hwy. 89, 6 mi northwest of Tahoe City and 13 mi south of I–80* ☎ *530/ 583–4232 or 800/441–4423, 530/581–8374 snow phone* ⊕ *www. skialpine.com* ☞ *100 trails on 2,000 acres, rated 25% beginner, 40% intermediate, 35% advanced. Longest run 2½ mi, base 6,835′, summit 8,637′. Lifts: 12, including 1 high-speed 6-passenger lift and 1 high-speed quad.*

CloseUp

SKI-PATROL POOCHES

All around Tahoe, from bars to ski shops, you'll spot posters of dogs wearing ski-patrol vests riding a chairlift. Stars in their own right, these pooches are the search-and-rescue dogs of Alpine Meadows.

In 1982 an avalanche inundated Alpine's base lodge, destroying a building and a ski lift and killing six people. Search-and-rescue teams brought in a German shepherd named Bridget to help recover the missing from beneath the snow. Though she was unable to help save any victims, she inspired the idea for trained "staff dogs" to be on hand in case of another catastrophe.

Now an integral part of Alpine's safety preparedness, these golden retrievers and chocolate Labradors are the personal pets of ski-patrol employees. Each dog meets exacting standards of obedience and conduct and must undergo two years of rigorous training. They must be able to get

on and off a ski lift, ride a snowmobile, and keep up with patrollers anywhere on the mountain, including icy cornices, craggy chutes, and steep slopes. Goldens and labs have the right temperament, the right size, and the right fur—long enough to keep them warm but short enough not to get covered in chunky snowballs that weigh them down. They're also able to smell human beings through heavy snow.

Currently there are 12 dogs on staff, including three puppies in training. You can visit them at the ski patrol hut at the top of the Summit Six, Sherwood, or Lakeview chairlift. And if you've become a fan, you can pick up the poster or patrol-puppy trading cards, with an image of a dog on the front and obscure facts and figures on the back. To obtain the free cards, call the resort at 530/583–4232 or e-mail info@skialpine.com.

You can rent skis, boards, and snowshoes at **Tahoe Dave's Skis and Boards** (⊠ 620 N. Lake Blvd. ☎ 530/583–0400), which has the area's best selection of downhill rental equipment. If you plan to ski or board the backcountry, you'll find everything from crampons to tranceivers at **The Backcountry** (⊠ 690 N. Lake Blvd. ☎ 530/581–5861).

Olympic Valley

🔞 7 mi north of Tahoe City via Hwy. 89 to Squaw Valley Rd.; 8½ mi south of Truckee via Hwy. 89 to Squaw Valley Rd.

Olympic Valley got its name in 1960, when Squaw Valley USA, the ski resort here, hosted the winter Olympics. Snow sports remain the primary activity, but once summer comes, you can hike into the adjacent Granite Chief Wilderness, ride horseback through alpine meadows, or lie by a swimming pool in one of the Sierra's prettiest valleys.

The centerpiece of Olympic Valley is the **Village at Squaw Valley** (☎ 530/584–6268 ⊕ www.villageatsquaw.com), a pedestrian mall beneath several four-story stone-and-timber buildings, where you'll find restaurants, boutiques, and cafés. The village often hosts events and festivals.

🐾 Make it a point to visit **Waxen Moon** (☎ 530/584–6006), a shop where you can make your own candles—a godsend for parents traveling with kids when the weather isn't cooperating. Call or stop by to make reservations, especially during high season.

You can ride the Squaw Valley Cable Car up to **High Camp,** which at 8,200 feet commands superb views of Lake Tahoe and the surrounding mountains. In summer you can go for a hike, sit by the pool at the High Camp Bath and Tennis Club, or have a cocktail and watch the sunset. In winter you can ski, ice-skate, or snow tube. There's also a restaurant, lounge, and small Olympic museum. ☒ *Cable Car Bldg., Squaw Valley* ☎ *530/583–6985 cable car, 530/581–7278 restaurant reservations* ⊕ *www.squaw.com* ☒ *Cable car $19; special packages include swimming or skating* ☉ *Open daily; call for hrs.*

Where to Stay & Eat

$$$ ✕ **Graham's of Squaw Valley.** Sit by a floor-to-ceiling river-rock hearth under a knotty-pine peaked ceiling in the intimate dining room in the Christy Inn Lodge. The mostly southern European menu changes often, but expect dishes like cassoulet seafood paella, pheasant ragout with pasta, or a simple grilled rib eye with sautéed onions. You can also stop in at the bar for wine and appetizers by the fire. ☒ *1650 Squaw Valley Rd.* ☎ *530/581–0454* ▭ *MC, V* ⚐ *Reservations essential* ☉ *Closed Mon. No lunch.*

$$–$$$ ✕ **Balboa Café** The top choice for lunch at Squaw is also a cushy, romantic spot for dinner. Aside from having the best burger in the valley, Balboa serves a varied menu of contemporary California cuisine, including steak frites and Cobb salad at lunch, and ahi tuna tartare, Muscovy duck breast, and grilled lamb chops at dinner. ☒ *Village at Squaw Valley, 1995 Squaw Valley Rd.* ☎ *530/583–5850* ⚐ *Reservations essential* ▭ *AE, MC, V.*

$$–$$$ ✕ **PlumpJack.** The best restaurant at Olympic Valley is also one of the
Fodor'sChoice finest anywhere at the lake. In the luxurious, beautifully lighted din-
★ ing room, there is little adornment on the walls to distract you from the exquisite haute-contemporary cuisine. Expect seafood, game, and meats, most garnished with reductions of natural juices that maximize the food's flavors. If you have a dietary restriction, the chef will make something special—and delicious—for you. The wine list is exceptional for its variety and surprisingly low prices. ☒ *1920 Squaw Valley Rd.* ☎ *530/583–1576 or 800/323–7666* ⚐ *Reservations essential* ▭ *AE, MC, V.*

$$–$$$ ✕ **Mamsake.** The hip and happening spot for sushi at Squaw serves stylized presentations of nigiri and maki in an industrial chic room. Sit at the bar and watch extreme ski movies, many of which were filmed right outside the window. ☒ *The Village at Squaw Valley* ☎ *530/584–0110* ▭ *AE, MC, V.*

$$$ ✕☒ **Resort at Squaw Creek.** This vast, 650-acre resort-within-a-resort offers all the amenities and services you could possibly want. The glass-and-concrete buildings aren't quite typical mountain lodges, but the resort's extensive facilities make it good for large groups and families. Some units have fireplaces and full kitchens. Montagna ($$$–$$$$) serves contemporary northern Italian cuisine (dinner only). In winter the resort oper-

ates its own chairlift to the mountain. ☒ *400 Squaw Creek Rd., 96146* ☎*530/583–6300 or 800/327–3353* 🖷*530/581–5407* ⊕*www.squawcreek. com* ⇌*203 rooms, 200 suites* ♨ *3 restaurants, coffee shop, some kitchens, minibars, cable TV with movies and video games, 18-hole golf course, 2 tennis courts, 3 outdoor pools, health club, hair salon, 4 hot tubs, sauna, spa, cross-country skiing, downhill skiing, ice-skating, ski shop, ski storage, sleigh rides, sports bar, shops, children's programs (ages 4–12), dry cleaning, laundry service, concierge, Internet, business services, meeting rooms, free parking* ⊟ *AE, D, DC, MC, V.*

$$$–$$$$
Fodor'sChoice
★
🏨 **PlumpJack Squaw Valley Inn.** If style and luxury are a must, Plump-Jack should be your first choice. Right next to the Village at Squaw Valley, the inn building originally housed visiting dignitaries during the 1960 Olympics. Every room comes equipped with down comforters, luxurious linens, and hooded terrycloth robes to wear on your way to the outdoor hot tubs. The bar is a happening après-ski destination, and the restaurant (*above*) is superb. PlumpJack may not have an on-site spa or fitness center, but the service—personable and attentive—can't be beat. Not all of the rooms have bathtubs, so if it matters, request one when you book. ☒ *1920 Squaw Valley Rd., 96146* ☎ *530/583–1576 or 800/323–7666* 🖷 *530/583–1734* ⊕ *www.plumpjack.com* ⇌ *56 rooms, 5 suites* ♨ *Restaurant, some in-room hot tubs, minibars, cable TV, in-room VCRs, 2 outdoor hot tubs, massage, cross-country skiing, downhill skiing, ski storage, bar, shop, dry cleaning, laundry service, concierge, meeting rooms, free parking; no a/c* ⊟ *AE, MC, V* ♚ *BP.*

$$–$$$$
🏨 **Squaw Valley Lodge.** You can ski right to the doors of this all-suites condo complex, which offers many of the amenities of a full-service hotel. The units are individually owned and styled, so there's no uniformity to the decor, but all of them come with down comforters, daily maid service, oversize soaking tubs, and well-stocked kitchens or kitchenettes. There's also an excellent fitness center with plenty of sports-conditioning equipment. The only drawback is thin walls, so request a quiet room when you book. ☒ *201 Squaw Peak Rd., 96146* ☎ *530/583–5500 or 800/922–9970* 🖷 *530/583–0326* ⊕ *www.squawvalleylodge.com* ⇌ *142 units* ♨ *Some kitchens, some kitchenettes, cable TV, outdoor pool, exercise equipment, 4 indoor hot tubs, 3 outdoor hot tubs, sauna, steam room, downhill skiing, laundry facilities, concierge, Internet, meeting rooms, free parking* ⊟ *AE, DC, MC, V.*

Sports & the Outdoors

GOLF   The **Resort at Squaw Creek Golf Course** (☒ 400 Squaw Creek Rd. ☎ 530/583–6300), an 18-hole championship course, was designed by Robert Trent Jones, Jr. The $55–$115 greens fees include the use of a cart.

HIKING   The Granite Chief Wilderness and the high peaks surrounding Olympic Valley are accessible by foot, but save yourself a 2,000-foot elevation gain by riding the Squaw Valley Cable Car to **High Camp** (☎ 530/583–6985), where you can begin a trek to Shirley Lake and then head back down-canyon to the valley for a beautiful 4-mi, half-day hike. In late summer, there are full-moon night hikes from High Camp.

HORSEBACK RIDING You can rent a horse or a pony from **Squaw Valley Stables** (✉ 1525 Squaw Valley Rd. ☎ 530/583–7433), which offers instruction as well as group and private rides.

ICE-SKATING You can ice-skate year-round at the **Olympic Ice Pavillion** (✉ High Camp, Squaw Valley ☎ 530/583–6985). You can buy a ride up the mountain and a pass to skate for $22, including skate rental. In summer you can pay $5 extra to swim or sit in the hot tub after you skate. Prices drop after 5 PM.

ROCK CLIMBING Before you rappel down a granite monolith, you can hone your skills at the **Headwall Climbing Wall** (✉ Near Village at Squaw Valley ☎ 530/583–7673), at the base of the cable car.

Next to the Olympic Village Lodge, on the far side of the creek, the **Squaw Valley Adventure Center** (☎ 530/583–7673) has a ropes course, a 50-foot tower, and a giant swing.

SKIING ★ Known for some of the toughest skiing in the Tahoe area, **Squaw Valley USA** was the centerpiece of the 1960 winter Olympics. Although the immense resort has changed significantly since then, Squaw remains the definitive North Tahoe resort. The skiing is world-class, with steep chutes and cornices on six peaks. Expert skiers often head directly to the untamed terrain of the infamous KT-22 face, which has bumps, cliffs, and gulp-and-go chutes. For beginners, there are plenty of wide, groomed trails near the High Camp lift and around the more challenging Snow King Peak. Snowboarders and hot-dog skiers can tear up the two fantastic terrain parks, which include a giant superpipe. Lift prices include night skiing until 9 PM, and tickets for skiers under 12 are only $5. ✉ *Hwy. 89, 5 mi northwest of Tahoe City ☎ 530/583–6985, 800/545–4350 reservations, 530/583–6955 snow phone ✆ 100 trails on 4,300 acres, rated 25% beginner, 45% intermediate, 30% advanced. Longest run 3 mi, base 6,200′, summit 9,050′. Lifts: 31, including a gondola-style funitel, a cable car, 7 high-speed chairs, and 18 fixed-grip chairs, which together can move 49,000 skiers an hr.*

If you don't want to pay resort prices, you can rent and tune downhill skis and snowboards at **Tahoe Dave's Skis and Boards** (✉ Squaw Valley Rd. at Hwy. 89 ☎ 530/583–5665).

Cross-country skiers will enjoy looping through the valley's giant alpine meadow. The **Resort at Squaw Creek** (✉ 400 Squaw Creek Rd. ☎ 530/583–6300) rents cross-country equipment and provides trail maps.

SWIMMING There are dramatic views from the pool deck at the **High Camp Bath and Tennis Club** (☎ 530/581–7255), where you can swim laps or soak in the 25-person hot tub for $24, which includes the cable car ride; for $3 more you can ice-skate, too, year-round. Prices drop after 5. The **Resort at Squaw Creek** (✉ 400 Squaw Creek Rd. ☎ 530/583–6300) has a giant swimming pool and a miniature water park; nonguests pay $25 for day use.

TENNIS You'll find two tennis courts at the **Resort at Squaw Creek** (✉ 400 Squaw Creek Rd. ☎ 530/583–6300). **High Camp Bath and Tennis Club** (☎ 530/583–6985) has six courts. Call for reservations and information on lessons and clinics.

Truckee

❾ *13 mi northwest of Kings Beach on Hwy. 267; 14 mi north of Tahoe City on Hwy. 89.*

Old West facades line the main street of Truckee, a favorite stopover for people traveling from the San Francisco Bay area to the north shore of Lake Tahoe. Around 1863, the town was officially established, and by 1868, it had gone from a stagecoach station to a major stopover for trains bound for the Pacific via the new transcontinental railroad. Freight and passenger trains still stop every day at the depot right in the middle of town. There are many galleries, tchotchke shops, and boutiques, but you will also find low-key diners, discount skiwear, and an old-fashioned five-and-dime store. Stop by the **information booth** (⊠ Railroad St. at Commercial Rd.) in the Amtrak depot for a walking-tour map of historic Truckee.

Donner Memorial State Park and Emigrant Trail Museum commemorates the Donner Party, a group of 89 westward-bound pioneers who were trapped in the Sierra in the winter of 1846–47 in snow 22 feet deep. Only 47 survived, some by resorting to cannibalism and others by eating animal hides. The museum's hourly slide show details the Donner Party's plight. Other displays and dioramas relate the history of other settlers and of railroad development through the Sierra. In the park, you can picnic, hike, camp, and go boating, fishing, and water-skiing in summer; winter brings cross-country skiing and snowshoeing on groomed trails. ⊠ *Donner Pass Rd., off I–80, 2 mi west of Truckee* ☎ *530/582–7892 museum, 800/444–7275 camping reservations* ⊕ *www.parks.ca.gov* ▧ *Museum $2* ☉ *Museum daily 9–4.*

off the beaten path

TAHOE NATIONAL FOREST – Draped along the Sierra Nevada Crest above Lake Tahoe, the national forest offers abundant outdoor recreation: picnicking and camping in summer, and in winter, snowshoeing, skiing, and sledding over some of the deepest snowpack in the West. The **Big Bend Visitor Center** occupies a state historic landmark within the forest, 10 mi west of Donner Summit. This area has been on major cross-country routes for centuries, ever since Native Americans passed through trading acorns and salt for pelts, obsidian, and other materials. Between 1844 and 1860, more than 200,000 emigrants traveled to California along the Emigrant Trail, which passed nearby; you can see rut marks left by wagon wheels scraping the famously hard granite. Later the nation's first transcontinental railroad ran through here (and still does), as do U.S. 40 (the old National Road), and its successor, I–80. Exhibits in the visitor center explore the area's transportation history. There are also occasional exhibits focusing on natural history. Take the Rainbow–Big Bend exit off I–80. ⊠ *U.S. 40, Soda Springs* ☎ *530/426–3609 or 530/265–4531* ⊕ *www.fs.fed.us/r5/tahoe/recreation* ▧ *Free* ☉ *Hrs vary.*

Where to Stay & Eat

$$–$$$ ✕ **Cottonwood.** Perched above town on the site of North America's first chairlift, the Cottonwood restaurant is a veritable institution. The bar is decked out with old wooden skis, sleds, skates, and photos of Truckee's early days. In the dining area, an ambitious menu—everything from grilled New York strip steak to vegetarian risotto—is served on white linen beneath an open-truss ceiling. On weekends there's live music. ⊠ *Old Brockway Rd., off Hwy. 267, ¼ mi south of downtown* ☎ *530/587–5711* ⚐ *Reservations essential* ▤ *AE, DC, MC, V* ⊘ *No lunch.*

★ **$$–$$$** ✗ **Moody's.** The closest thing to a supper club this side of San Francisco, Moody's serves contemporary California cuisine in a stylish dining room, with pumpkin-color walls, burgundy velvet banquettes, and art deco fixtures. Half of the offerings change daily and often include organically grown ingredients. Look for the ahi tuna "four ways," seared foie gras, braised short ribs, and roasted or stewed free-range chicken. In summer you can dine outside on a large brick patio surrounded by potted flowers. The restaurant serves a limited afternoon menu, and on weekends there's live jazz in the always-busy bar. ⊠ *1007 Bridge St.* ☎ *530/587–8831* ▤ *AE, D, DC, MC, V* ⚐ *Reservations essential.*

$$ ✗ **Dragonfly.** Flavors are bold at this old-town restaurant, where every dish is artfully prepared and stylishly presented. The eclectic Southeast Asian–inspired menu changes twice monthly and is served in a bright, contemporary second-floor dining room, unless you choose to eat on the terrace (in warm weather), overlooking Main Street and the train depot. Lunch is a bargain, and there are always lots of choices for vegetarians. ⊠ *10118 Donner Pass Rd.* ☎ *530/587–0557* ▤ *D, MC, V* ⊘ *Closed Tues.*

$–$$ ✗ **Pianeta.** Right on the main drag of old-town Truckee, this northern Italian trattoria makes delicious pasta dishes—including homemade ravioli and lasagna Bolognese—and entrées like double-cut marinated lamb chops with mint pesto, and jumbo-shrimp scampi. For a lighter meal, sit at the bar and order from the extensive list of appetizers. The exposed stone walls may make you feel as if you're eating inside a Tuscan farmhouse. ⊠ *10069 Donner Pass Rd.* ☎ *530/587–4694* ▤ *AE, MC, V* ⚐ *Reservations essential* ⊘ *No lunch.*

$$$–$$$$ ✗▣ **Northstar-at-Tahoe Resort.** The area's most complete destination resort is especially popular with families, thanks to its many sports activities—from golf and tennis to skiing and snowshoeing—and its concentration of restaurants, shops, recreation facilities, and accommodations (the Village Mall). Lodgings range from hotel rooms to condos to private houses, some with ski-in, ski-out access. Guests receive free lift tickets and on-site shuttle transportation and have complimentary access to the Swim and Racquet Club's swimming pools, outdoor hot tubs, fitness center, and teen center. True North ($–$$$; reservations essential) serves contemporary American cooking prepared with organically grown produce and all-natural meats. ⊠ *Hwy. 267, 6 mi southeast of Truckee* ✉ *Box 129, 96160* ☎ *530/562–1010 or 800/466–6784* ⊜ *530/562–2215* ⊕ *www.northstarattahoe.com* ⇥ *270 units* ⚐ *6 restaurants, some kitchens, some kitchenettes, some microwaves, cable TV, in-room VCRs, 18-hole golf course, 12 tennis courts, bicycles, horseback riding, cross-country skiing, downhill skiing, ski shop, ski storage, recreation room, video game room, shops, babysitting, children's programs (ages 2–6), laundry facilities, meeting rooms; no a/c in some rooms, no smoking* ▤ *AE, D, MC, V.*

$–$$ 🏨 **River Street Inn.** This 1885 wood-and-stone inn was at times a boardinghouse and a brothel. Now completely modernized, the uncluttered, comfortable rooms are simply decorated, with attractive, country-style wooden furniture. The sumptuous beds have top-quality mattresses, down comforters, and high-thread-count sheets. Bathrooms have claw-foot tubs. The affable proprietors are there when you need them, then disappear when you want privacy. ⊠ *10009 E. River St., 96161* ☎ *530/550–9290* 🖷 *530/582–2391* ⊕ *www.riverstreetinntruckee.com* ⤺ *11 rooms* ♿ *Cable TV, in-room VCRs; no a/c, no room phones, no smoking* ▭ *MC, V* ⊙ *CP.*

¢–$$ 🏨 **Truckee Hotel.** Constructed in 1873, this four-story hotel is one of the town's oldest buildings. Antiques fill the Victorian-style rooms; several have private bathrooms with claw-foot tubs. All rooms are clean and comfortable, if a bit small. Request a quiet room, if it matters. ⊠ *10007 Bridge St., 96161* ☎ *530/587–4444 or 800/659–6921* 🖷 *916/ 587–1599* ⊕ *www.truckeehotel.com* ⤺ *37 rooms, 29 with shared bath.* ♿ *Restaurant, bar; no a/c, no TV in some rooms, no smoking* ▭ *AE, MC, V* ⊙ *CP.*

Sports & the Outdoors

GOLF   The **Coyote Moon Golf Course** (⊠ 10685 Northwoods Blvd. ☎ 530/ 587–0886) is both challenging and beautiful, with no houses to spoil the view; fees range from $95 to $155, including cart. **Northstar** (⊠ Hwy. 267 ☎ 530/562–1010) has open links–style play and tight, tree-lined fairways, including water hazards; fees range from $40 to $110, including cart. The water hazards at **Old Greenwood** (⊠ off the Prosser Village Rd. exit—Exit 190—from I-80; call for specific directions ☎ 530/550– 0844), north Lake Tahoe's only Jack Nicklaus signature course, are trout streams, and you can even fish them; the $100–$170 fee includes a cart.

HORSEBACK   **Northstar Stables** (⊠ Hwy. 267 at Northstar Dr. ☎ 530/562–2480) of-
RIDING   fers guided 45-minute, half-day, and full-day (for experienced riders only) rides. Instruction is provided, ponies are available for tots, and you can even board your own horse here.

MOUNTAIN   In summer you can rent a bike and ride the lifts up the mountain at **North-**
BIKING   **star-at-Tahoe** (⊠ Hwy. 267 ☎ 530/562–2268) for 100 mi of challenging terrain.

SKIING   There are several smaller resorts around Truckee, which give you access to the Sierra's slopes at more reasonable prices. Though you'll sacrifice vertical rise and high-speed lifts, you can ski or board and still have money left over for room and board. Check out **Boreal** (⊠ Boreal/Castle Peak exit of I–80 ☎ 530/426–3666 ⊕ www.borealski.com), **Donner Ski Ranch** (⊠ 19320 Donner Pass Rd., Norden ☎ 530/426–3635), **Soda Springs** (⊠ Soda Springs exit of 1–80, Soda Springs ☎ 530/426–1010), and **Tahoe Donner** (⊠ 11603 Slalom Way ☎ 530/587–9444 ⊕ www. tahoedonner.com).

Northstar-at-Tahoe may be the best all-around family ski resort at Tahoe. With two tree-lined, northeast-facing, wind-protected bowls, it's the ideal place to ski in a storm. The meticulous grooming and long cruisers make it an intermediate skier's paradise. Boarders are especially welcome, with an awesome terrain park, including a 400-foot-long superpipe, a half pipe, rails and boxes, and lots of kickers. Experts can ski the steeps and bumps off Lookout Mountain, where there's never a line for the high-speed quad. Northstar-at-Tahoe has 28 mi of groomed trails, including double-set tracks and skating lanes. The school has programs for skiers ages four and up, and day care is available for toilet-trained tots. ⊠ *Hwy. 267, 6 mi southeast of Truckee* ☎ *530/562–1010, 530/562–1330 snow phone* 🖷 *530/562–2215* ⊕ *www.skinorthstar.com* ☞ *72 trails on 2,420 acres, rated 25% beginner, 50% intermediate, 25% advanced. Longest run 2.9 mi, base 6,400′, summit 8,600′. Lifts: 17, including a gondola and 5 high-speed quads.*

Opened in 1939 by Walt Disney, **Sugar Bowl** is the oldest—and one of the best—resorts at Tahoe. Atop Donner Summit, it receives an incredible 500 inches of snowfall annually. Four peaks are connected by 1,500 acres of skiable terrain, with everything from gentle groomed corduroy to wide-open bowls to vertical rocky chutes and outstanding tree-skiing. Snowboarders can hit two terrain parks and an 18½-foot superpipe. Because it's more compact than some of the area's mega-resorts, there's a certain gentility here that distinguishes Sugar Bowl from its competitors, making this a great place for families and a low-pressure, low-key place to learn to ski. There's limited lodging at the base area. ⊠ *Donner Pass Rd., 3 mi east of Soda Springs/Norden exit of I–80, 10 mi west of Truckee* ☎ *530/426–9000 information and lodging reservations, 530/426–1111 snowphone, 866/843–2695 lodging referral* ⊕ *www.sugarbowl.com* ☞ *84 trails on 1,500 acres, rated 17% beginner, 45% intermediate, 38% advanced. Longest run 3 mi, base 6,883′, summit 8,383′. Lifts: 12, including 4 high-speed quads.*

For the ultimate in groomed conditions, head to the nation's largest cross-country ski resort, **Royal Gorge** (⊠ Soda Springs–Norden exit of I–80, Soda Springs ☎ 530/426–3871 ⊕ www.royalgorge.com). It has 197 mi of 18-foot-wide track for all abilities, 88 trails on 9,172 acres, 2 ski schools, and 10 warming huts. Four cafés, two hotels, and a hot tub and sauna are among the facilities.

You can save money by renting skis and boards at **Tahoe Dave's** (⊠ 10200 Donner Pass Rd. ☎ 530/582–0900), which has the area's best selection and also repairs and tunes equipment.

Carnelian Bay to Kings Beach

5–10 mi northeast of Tahoe City on Hwy. 28.

The small lakeside commercial districts of Carnelian Bay and Tahoe Vista service the thousand or so locals who live in the area year-round and the thousands more who have summer residences or launch their boats here. Kings Beach, the last town heading east on Highway 28 before the Nevada border, is to Crystal Bay what South Lake Tahoe is to Stateline: a bustling California village full of motels and rental condos, restaurants and shops, used by the hordes of hopefuls who pass through on their way to the casinos.

🔄 The 28-acre **Kings Beach State Recreation Area,** one of the largest such areas on the lake, is open year-round. The 700-foot-long beach becomes crowded with people swimming, sunbathing, jet-skiing, riding in paddleboats, spiking volleyballs, and tossing Frisbees. There's a good playground and picnic area here. ⊠ *N. Lake Blvd., Kings Beach* ☎ *530/546-7248* 🔁 *Free* ☉ *Daily 24 hrs.*

Where Stay & Eat

★ **$$–$$$$** ✕ **Wild Goose.** Soft leather banquettes and polished mahogany tables complement the gorgeous lake views in this casually elegant 100-seat dining room. Sliding glass doors open up to a lakeside deck beneath towering pines. Come early to see the sunset. The menu features fine European-inspired contemporary California cuisine. ⊠ *7320 N. Lake Blvd., Tahoe Vista* ☎ *530/546-3640* ⚓ *Reservations essential* ▤ *AE, D, MC, V* ☉ *Closed Mon. No lunch Oct.–May.*

$$–$$$ ✕ **Gar Woods Grill and Pier.** Here you can take in terrific views through the dining room's plate glass windows and from the heated outdoor deck. There are salads and sandwiches at lunch, and steaks and grilled fish at dinner, but the best meal here is Sunday brunch. At all hours in season, the bar gets packed with boaters who pull up to the restaurant's pier. ⊠ *5000 N. Lake Blvd., Carnelian Bay* ☎ *530/546-3366* ▤ *AE, MC, V.*

$$–$$$ ✕ **Spindleshanks.** This handsome road house, decorated with floor-to-ceiling knotty pine, serves a variety of fresh seafood, grilled meats, and house-made pastas. At peak periods, the convivial atmosphere can be a bit loud, but after a glass of wine, you won't notice. In the morning the bar area becomes an espresso and breakfast café. ⊠ *6873 N. Lake Blvd.* ☎ *530/546-2191 or 530/546-8684* ⚓ *Reservations essential* ▤ *AE, MC, V* ☉ *No lunch.*

$–$$$ ✕ **Jason's Beachside Grille.** If the kids want burgers but you want bourbon, Jason's has a full bar as well as steaks, 17 different kinds of burgers, tasty teriyaki chicken, and a big salad bar. The whole place is wood, from floor to ceiling, giving it a cozy feel. Expect to wait for a table by the fireplace; you can't reserve unless there are more than seven in your group. In summer dine outside on a deck overlooking the lake. ⊠ *8338 N. Lake Blvd.* ☎ *530/546-3315* ⚓ *Reservations not accepted* ▤ *AE, D, DC, MC, V.*

$–$$ ✕ **Lanza's.** Lanza's serves good old-fashioned Italian-American food on red-and-white–checked tablecloths in a pine-paneled dining room. There's lasagna, manicotti, veal piccata, and eggplant Parmesan, but you can also order your own pasta-and-sauce combination. Leave room for the homemade spumoni. ⊠ *7739 N. Lake Blvd., next to Safeway, Kings Beach* ☎ *530/546-2434* ⚓ *Reservations not accepted* ▤ *MC, V* ☉ *No lunch.*

¢ ✕ **Log Cabin Caffe.** Almost always hopping, this Kings Beach eatery specializes in hearty breakfast and lunch entrées—five kinds of eggs Benedict, Mexican and smoked salmon scrambles, omelets, pancakes, and waffles. They also serve sandwiches and freshly baked pastries. Get here early on weekends for the popular brunch. ⊠ *8692 N. Lake Blvd., Kings Beach* ☎ *530/546-7109* ▤ *MC, V* ☉ *No dinner.*

$$$–$$$$ 🛏 **Shore House.** Every room has a gas fireplace and featherbed at this lakefront B&B in Tahoe Vista. The comfortable guest rooms all have private entrances and extra touches like bathrobes and rubber duckies in the bathtubs; many have great views of the water. There's also a private beach. ✉ *7170 N. Lake Blvd., Tahoe Vista 96148* ☎ *530/546–7270 or 800/207–5160* ⊕ *www.shorehouselaketahoe.com* ⏎ *8 rooms, 1 cottage* ⟁ *Refrigerators, outdoor hot tub, beach; no a/c, no room phones, no room TVs, no smoking* ▭ *D, MC, V* ⦿ *BP.*

¢–$$ ▦ **Ferrari's Crown Resort.** One of the few remaining family-owned and -operated motels in Kings Beach, Ferrari's has straightforward motel rooms in a resort setting, great for families with kids. It sits right on the lake, and some rooms have awesome views. Kids love the pool; adults enjoy the hot tub. There's also kayak rental on-site. ✉ *8200 N. Lake Blvd., Kings Beach 96143* ☎ *530/546–3388 or 800/645–2260* ⎙ *530/546–3851* ⊕ *www.tahoecrown.com* ⏎ *45 rooms* ⟁ *Some kitchenettes, some refrigerators, cable TV, pool, lake, indoor hot tub, beach, Ping-Pong; no a/c in some rooms, no smoking* ▭ *AE, D, MC, V.*

¢–$$ ▦ **Rustic Cottages.** These charming clapboard cottages sit clustered beneath tall pine trees across the road from Lake Tahoe. Cozy, simple, and well cared for, they offer an inexpensive alternative to a motel. All have patios, and some have fireplaces and kitchens. If the cottages are booked, ask about the well-run sister property, Tahoe Vista Lodge and Cabins, just up the road. ✉ *7449 N. Lake Blvd.,* ⌂ *Box 18, Tahoe Vista 96148* ☎ *530/546–3523 or 888/778–7842* ⎙ *530/546–0146* ⊕ *www.rusticcottages.com* ⏎ *20 cottages* ⟁ *Some kitchens, microwaves, refrigerators, cable TV, in-room VCRs, some pets allowed (fee); no a/c, no room phones, no smoking* ▭ *AE, D, MC, V* ⦿ *CP.*

Sports & the Outdoors

SNOWMOBILING **Snowmobiling Unlimited** (✉ Hwy. 267, 3 mi north of Hwy. 28, Kings Beach ☎ 530/583–7192) conducts 1½-, 2-, and 3-hour guided cross-country tours, mostly along the trails in nearby Tahoe National Forest. They provide open-face helmets and mittens, but bring your own goggles or sunglasses.

WINDSURFING   Learn to skitter across the icy blue waters of the lake with one of Tahoe's kindest instructors at **Windsurf North Tahoe** (✉ 7276 N. Lake Blvd., Tahoe Vista ☎ 530/546–5857 or 800/294–6378).

NEVADA SIDE

You don't need a highway sign to know when you've crossed from California into Nevada: the flashing lights and elaborate marquees of casinos announce legal gambling in garish hues.

Crystal Bay

🔟 *1 mi east of Kings Beach on Hwy. 28; 30 mi north of South Lake Tahoe via U.S. 50 to Hwy. 28.*

Right at the Nevada border, Crystal Bay has a cluster of casinos. The **Cal-Neva Lodge** (✉ 2 Stateline Rd. ☎ 775/832–4000) is bisected by the state line. Opened in 1927, this joint has weathered many scandals, the largest involving former owner Frank Sinatra (he lost his gaming license in the 1960s for alleged mob connections). The **Tahoe Biltmore** (✉ Hwy.

28 at Stateline Rd. ☎ 775/831–0660) serves its popular $1.99 break-fast special 24 hours a day and on weekends has dancing to a DJ. **Jim Kelley's Nugget** (✉ Hwy. 28 at Stateline Rd. ☎ 775/831–0455) serves 101 kinds of beers. The **Crystal Bay Club** (✉ Hwy. 28 at Stateline Rd. ☎ 775/831–0512) has a restaurant with a towering open-truss ceiling that looks like a wooden ship's hull.

Where to Stay & Eat

★ **$$–$$$** ✕ **Soule Domain.** Some of Lake Tahoe's more creative and delicious din-ners are served in this 1927 pine-log cabin across from the Tahoe Bilt-more. Chef-owner Charles Edward Soule IV's specialties include curried cashew chicken, smoked-rabbit ravioli, rock shrimp with sea scallops, and a vegan sauté. ✉ *Cove St., ½ block up Stateline Rd. from Hwy. 28* ☎ *530/546–7529* ⌕ *Reservations essential* ▭ *AE, DC, MC, V* ☉ *No lunch.*

$–$$$$ ▥ **Cal-Neva Lodge.** All the rooms in this hotel-casino have views of Lake Tahoe and the mountains. The hotel also rents seven two-bedroom chalets and 12 cabins with living rooms. There is an arcade for children and cabaret entertainment for grown-ups. Though some of the public areas look a bit shabby, the rooms are generally well maintained. Ask about the tours of the secret tunnel that Frank Sinatra built so that he could steal away unnoticed to Marilyn Monroe's cabin. ✉ *2 Stateline Rd.* ⌂ *Box 368, 89402* ☎ *775/832–4000 or 800/225–6382* 🖷 *775/831–9007* ⊕ *www.calnevaresort.com* ⇅ *220 rooms, 20 suites, 12 cab-ins* ⌂ *Restaurant, coffee shop, room service, cable TV with movies, in-room VCRs, tennis court, pool, gym, indoor hot tub, massage, sauna, spa, bar, cabaret, casino, video game room, dry cleaning, concierge, air-port shuttle, some pets allowed* ▭ *AE, D, DC, MC, V.*

Incline Village

⓫ *3 mi east of Crystal Bay on Hwy. 28.*

Incline Village, Nevada's only privately owned town, dates to the early 1960s, when an Oklahoma developer bought 10,000 acres north of Lake Tahoe. His idea was to sketch out a plan for a town without a central commercial district, hoping to prevent congestion and to preserve the area's natural beauty. One-acre lakeshore lots originally fetched $12,000 to $15,000; today you couldn't buy even the land for less than several million. Check out **Lakeshore Drive,** along which you'll see some of the most expensive real estate in Nevada.

George Whittell, a San Francisco socialite who once owned 50,000 acres of property along the lake, built the **Thunderbird Lodge** in 1936. You can tour the mansion and the grounds by reservation only, and though it's pricey, it offers a rare glimpse back to a time when only the very wealthy had homes at Tahoe. You can take a bus tour from the Incline Village Visitors Bureau, a 45-passenger catamaran tour from Incline Vil-lage, or a 1950, 21-passenger wooden cruiser from Zephyr Cove (which includes lunch). ✉ *5000 Hwy. 28* ☎ *775/832–8750 or 800/468–2463,*

775/832–1606 bus, 775/588–3000 or 888/867–6394 Zephyr Cove boat, 775/832–1234 or 800/553–3288 Incline Village boat ✆ *$25 bus tour, $65–$90 boat tour* ⊙ *May–Oct., call for tour times.*

off the
beaten
path

LAKE TAHOE–NEVADA STATE PARK – Protecting much of the lake's eastern shore from development, Lake Tahoe–Nevada State Park comprises several units that stretch from Incline Village to Zephyr Cove. Beaches and trails provide access to a wilder side of the lake, whether you are into cross-country skiing, hiking, or just relaxing at a picnic. One of the most popular units is **Sand Harbor Beach** (✉ Hwy. 28, 4 mi south of Incline Village ☎ 775/831–0494), so popular that it is sometimes filled to capacity by 11 AM on summer weekends. Stroll the boardwalk and read the information signs to get a good lesson in the local ecology.

Where to Stay & Eat

$$–$$$ ✕ **Frederick's.** Sit at one of the 15 copper-covered tables at this intimate bistro, which serves a mishmash of European and Asian cooking. Try the braised lamb shank, Parmesan gnocchi, or the deliciously fresh sushi rolls. Ask for a table by the fire. ✉ *907 Tahoe Blvd.* ☎ *775/832–3007* ⌕ *Reservations essential* ▤ *AE, MC, V* ⊙ *Closed Mon. and Tues. No lunch.*

★ $$ ✕ **Le Bistro.** Incline Village's hidden gem, Le Bistro serves expertly prepared French-country cuisine in a relaxed, cozy, romantic dining room. The chef-owner makes everything himself, using only organically grown ingredients, and changes the menu almost daily. Try the five-course prix-fixe menu ($38), which can also be paired with wines. Service is gracious and attentive. The restaurant is hard to find; be sure to ask directions when you book. ✉ *120 Country Club Dr., #29* ☎ *775/831–0800* ⌕ *Reservations essential* ▤ *AE, D, DC, MC, V* ⊙ *Closed Sun. and Mon. No lunch.*

$–$$ ✕ **Azzara's.** An Italian family restaurant with a light, inviting dining room, Azzara's serves a dozen pasta dishes and many pizzas, as well as chicken, veal, shrimp, and beef. Dinners include soup or salad, a vegetable, and olive-oil garlic bread. ✉ *Incline Center Mall, 930 Tahoe Blvd.* ☎ *775/831–0346* ▤ *MC, V* ⊙ *Closed Mon. No lunch.*

★ $$$–$$$$ ✕▥ **Hyatt Regency Lake Tahoe.** Once a dowdy casino hotel, the Hyatt underwent a $60 million renovation between 2001 and 2003 and is now a sophisticated full-service destination resort. Located on 26 acres of prime lakefront property, the resort has a range of luxurious accommodations, from tower-hotel rooms to cozy lakeside cottages. The Lone Eagle Grille ($$–$$$$) serves steaks and seafood in one of the north shore's most handsome lake-view dining rooms. There's also a state-of-the-art, 20,000-square-foot spa. Standard rates are high, but look for midweek or off-season discounts. ✉ *Lakeshore and Country Club Drs., 89450*

☏ 775/831–1111 or 888/899–5019 ⊟775/831–7508 ⊕www.laketahoe. hyatt.com ⇔ 432 rooms, 28 suites ⅄ 4 restaurants, café, room service, in-room data ports, in-room safes, some kitchenettes, minibars, cable TV with movies and video games, golf privileges, outdoor pool, lake, exercise equipment, hair salon, outdoor hot tub, 2 saunas, spa, beach, dock, boating, jet skiing, waterskiing, mountain bikes, volleyball, ski shop, ski storage, 3 bars, lobby lounge, casino, video game room, shop, children's programs (ages 3–12), dry cleaning, laundry service, concierge, concierge floor, Internet, business services, meeting rooms, no-smoking floor ⊟ AE, D, DC, MC, V.

The Arts

Sand Harbor Beach hosts a **pop-music festival** (☏ 775/832–1606 or 800/ 468–2463) each July. Also at Sand Harbor Beach, the **Lake Tahoe Shakespeare Festival** (☏775/832–1616 or 800/747–4697) is held outdoors with the lake as a backdrop, from mid-July through August.

Sports & the Outdoors

Incline Village's **recreation center** (✉ 980 Incline Way ☏775/832–1300) has an eight-lane swimming pool and a fitness area, basketball court, game room, and snack bar.

GOLF **Incline Championship** (✉ 955 Fairway Blvd. ☏ 775/325–8801) is an 18-hole, par-72 course with a driving range. Greens fees are $125. **Incline Mountain** (✉ 690 Wilson Way ☏ 775/325–8801) is an easy 18-holer; par is 58. Greens fees start at $50; optional power carts at both courses cost $15.

MOUNTAIN BIKING You can rent bikes and get helpful tips from **Flume Trail Bikes** (✉ Spooner Summit, Hwy. 28, ½ mi north of U.S. 50, Glenbrook ☏ 775/887–8844 or 775/749–5349 ⊕ www.theflumetrail.com), which also operates a bike shuttle to popular trailheads. Ask about the secluded rental cabins for overnight rides.

SKIING A fun family mood prevails at **Diamond Peak,** which has many special programs and affordable rates. Snowmaking covers 75% of the mountain, and runs are groomed nightly. The ride up the 1-mi Crystal chair rewards you with some of the best views of the lake from any ski area. Diamond Peak is less crowded than the larger areas and provides free shuttles to nearby lodging. It's a great place for beginners and intermediates, and it's appropriately priced for families. There are a half-pipe and superpipe for snowboarders. **Diamond Peak Cross-Country** (✉ Off Hwy. 431 ☏ 775/832–1177) has 22 mi of groomed track with skating lanes. The trail system rises from 7,400 feet to 9,100 feet, with endless wilderness to explore. *✉ 1210 Ski Way, off Hwy. 28 to Country Club Dr. ☏ 775/832–1177 or 800/468–2463 ⇔ 29 trails on 655 acres, rated 18% beginner, 46% intermediate, 36% advanced. Longest run 2½ mi, base 6,700′, summit 8,540′. Lifts: 6, including 2 high-speed quads.*

Ski some of the highest slopes at Tahoe, and take in bird's-eye views of Reno and the Carson Valley at **Mt. Rose Ski Tahoe.** Though more compact than the bigger Tahoe resorts, Mt. Rose has the area's highest base elevation and consequently the driest snow. The mountain has a wide variety of terrain. The most challenging is the Chutes, 200 acres of gulp-and-go advanced-to-expert vertical, opened in the 2004–2005 season. Intermediates can choose steep groomers or mellow, wide-open boulevards. Beginners have their own corner of the mountain, with gentle, non-threatening, wide slopes. Boarders and tricksters have three terrain parks to choose from, on opposite sides of the mountain, allowing them to follow the sun as it tracks across the resort. Because of its elevation, the mountain gets hit hard in storms; check conditions before heading up during inclement weather. ⊠ *Hwy. 431, 11 mi north of Incline Village* ☎ *775/849–0704 or 800/754–7673* ⊕ *www.skirose.com* ⌕ *61 trails on 1,200 acres, rated 20% beginner, 30% intermediate, 40% advanced, 10% expert. Longest run 2½ mi, base 8,260', summit 9,700'. Lifts: 6, including 1 high-speed 6-passenger lift.*

On the way to Mt. Rose from Incline Village, **Tahoe Meadows** (⊠ Hwy. 431) is the most popular area near the north shore for noncommercial cross-country skiing, sledding, tubing, snowshoeing, and snowmobiling.

You'll find superbly groomed tracks and fabulous views of Lake Tahoe at **Spooner Lake Cross-Country** (⊠ Spooner Summit, Hwy. 28, ½ mi north of U.S. 50, Glenbrook ☎ 775/887–8844 ski phone, 775/749–5349 reservations ⊕ www.spoonerlake.com). It has more than 50 mi of trails on more than 9,000 acres, and two charming, secluded cabins are available for rent for overnight treks.

| en route | As you head south on Highway 28 toward the south shore, you can take a detour away from the lake (east) on U.S. 50 to reach two interesting towns. After about 10 mi on U.S. 50, take U.S. 395 north for 1 mi to Nevada's capital, **Carson City.** Most of its historic buildings and other attractions, including the Nevada State Museum and the Nevada Railroad Museum, are along U.S. 395, the main street through town. About a 30-minute drive up Highway 342 northeast of Carson City is the fabled mining town of **Virginia City,** one of the largest and most authentic historical mining towns in the West. It's chock-full of mansions, museums, saloons, and, of course, dozens of shops selling everything from amethysts to yucca. |

Zephyr Cove

⑫ *22 mi south of Incline Village via Hwy. 28 to U.S. 50.*

The largest settlement between Incline Village and Stateline is Zephyr Cove, a tiny resort. It has a beach, marina, campground, picnic area, coffee shop in a historic log lodge, rustic cabins, and nearby riding stables.

★ Nearby **Cave Rock** (⊠ U.S. 50, 4 mi north of Zephyr Cove ☎ 775/831–0494), 75 feet of solid stone at the southern end of Lake Tahoe–Nevada State Park, is the throat of an extinct volcano. Tahoe Tessie, the lake's version of the Loch Ness monster, is reputed to live in a cavern below the impressive outcropping. For the Washoe Indians, this area is a sacred burial site. Cave Rock towers over a parking lot, a lakefront picnic ground, and a boat launch.

<table>
<tr><td>

off the
beaten
path

</td><td>

KINGSBURY GRADE – This road, also known as Highway 207, is one
of three that access Tahoe from the east. Originally a toll road used
by wagon trains to get over the crest of the Sierra, it has sweeping
views of the Carson Valley. Off Highway 206, which intersects
Highway 207, is Genoa, the oldest settlement in Nevada. Along Main
Street are a museum in Nevada's oldest courthouse, a small state
park, and the state's longest-standing saloon.

</td></tr>
</table>

Stateline

⑬ *5 mi south of Zephyr Cove on U.S. 50.*

Stateline is a great border town in the Nevada tradition. Its four high-
rise casinos are as vertical and contained as the commercial district of
South Lake Tahoe, on the California side, is horizontal and sprawling.
And Stateline is as relentlessly indoors-oriented as the rest of the lake
is focused on the outdoors. This strip is where you'll find the most concentrated action at Lake Tahoe: restaurants (including typical casino buf-
fets), showrooms with famous headliners and razzle-dazzle revues,
tower-hotel rooms and suites, and 24-hour casinos.

Where to Stay & Eat

★ **$$–$$$** ✕ **Mirabelle.** The French-Alsatian–born chef-owner prepares everything
on the menu himself, from puff pastry to chocolate cake to homemade
bread. Specialties include an Alsatian onion tart, escargots, and rack of
lamb. Leave room for the dessert soufflés. On Monday from April
through June, the chef holds cooking classes that culminate with a
grand repast in the casual, airy dining room. ⊠ *290 Kingsbury Grade*
☎ *775/586–1007* 🍴 *AE, MC, V* ⊘ *Closed Mon. No lunch.*

$$–$$$$ ✕▣ **Harveys Resort Hotel/Casino.** This resort, which started as a cabin
in 1944, is now Tahoe's largest. Premium rooms have custom furnish-
ings, oversize marble baths, and minibars. Although it was acquired by
Harrah's and has lost some of its cachet, Harveys remains a fine prop-
erty. Llewelyn's ($$$–$$$$), atop the hotel, has drop-dead views and ex-
cellent continental food in an elegant dining room, and the Emerald Theater
is the Harveys showroom. ⊠ *U.S. 50 at Stateline Ave., 89449* ☎ *775/
588–2411 or 800/648–3361* 🖨 *775/782–4889* ⊕ *www.harrahs.com/
our_casinos/hlt* 🛏 *705 rooms, 38 suites* ⚤ *8 restaurants, minibars, cable
TV with movies, pool, health club, hair salon, hot tub, spa, casino,
showroom, concierge, car rental, meeting rooms* 🚭 *AE, D, DC, MC, V.*

$–$$$$ ✕▣ **Harrah's Tahoe Hotel/Casino.** Luxurious guest rooms here have two
full bathrooms, each with a television and telephone. Upper-floor rooms
have views of the lake or mountains. Top-name entertainment is pre-
sented in the South Shore Room. Among the restaurants, the romantic
16th-floor Summit ($$$$) is a standout, but bring a credit card; there's
also a buffet on the 16th floor. A tunnel runs under U.S. 50 to Harveys,
which Harrah's now owns. ⊠ *U.S. 50 at Stateline Ave., 89449* ☎ *775/
588–6611 or 800/427–7247* 🖨 *775/588–6607* ⊕ *www.harrahstahoe.
com* 🛏 *470 rooms, 62 suites* ⚤ *7 restaurants, room service, in-room
data ports, cable TV with movies, indoor pool, health club, hair salon,
hot tub, casino, showrooms, laundry service, car rental, meeting rooms,
kennel* 🚭 *AE, D, DC, MC, V.*

$–$$$ ⊞ **Caesars Tahoe.** Most of the luxury-kitsch rooms and suites at Caesars have oversize tubs, king-size beds, two telephones, and a view of Lake Tahoe or the encircling mountains (some overlook the parking lot). Famous entertainers perform in the 1,600-seat Circus Maximus. Planet Hollywood is also here. ⊠ *55 U.S. 50* ⬠ *Box 5800, 89449* ☎ *775/588–3515 or 800/648–3353* 📠 *775/586–2068* ⊕ *www.caesars.com* 🛏 *328 rooms, 112 suites ⚄ 5 restaurants, coffee shop, in-room data ports, cable TV with movies, 4 tennis courts, indoor pool, health club, hot tub, sauna, spa, showroom, car rental, meeting rooms* ⊟ *AE, D, DC, MC, V.*

¢–$ ⊞ **Lakeside Inn and Casino.** With the smallest of the Stateline casinos, the Lakeside has good promotional room rates and simple, attractive accommodations in two-story motel-style buildings away from the casino. ⊠ *U.S. 50 at Kingsbury Grade, Box 5640, 89449* ☎ *775/588–7777 or 800/624–7980* 📠 *775/588–4092* ⊕ *www.lakesideinn.com* 🛏 *115 rooms, 9 suites ⚄ Restaurant, in-room data ports, pool, casino* ⊟ *AE, D, DC, MC, V.*

Nightlife

Each of the major casinos has its own showroom, including Harrah's **South Shore Room** (☎ 775/588–6611). They feature everything from comedy to magic acts to floor shows to Broadway musicals. If you want to dance, check out the racy scene at Caesar's **Club Nero** (⊠ 55 U.S. 50 ☎ 775/588–3515).

Sports & the Outdoors

Right on the lake, **Edgewood Tahoe** (⊠ U.S. 50 and Lake Pkwy., behind Horizon Casino ☎ 775/588–3566) is an 18-hole, par-72 course with a driving range. The $200 greens fees include a cart (though you can walk if you wish).

Side Trip to Reno

⓮ *32 mi east of Truckee on I–80; 38 mi northeast of Incline Village via Hwy. 431 and U.S. 395.*

Established in 1859 as a trading station at a bridge over the Truckee River, Reno grew along with the silver mines of nearby Virginia City (starting in 1860), the railroad (railroad officials named the town in 1868), and gambling (legalized in 1931). Once the gaming and divorce capital of the United States, the city built itself a monument: The famous Reno Arch, a sign over the upper end of Virginia Street, proclaims it THE BIGGEST LITTLE CITY IN THE WORLD. Reno is still a gambling town, with most of the casinos crowded into five square blocks downtown. Besides the casino-hotels, Reno has a number of cultural and family-friendly attractions. Temperatures year-round in this high-mountain-desert climate are warmer than at Tahoe, though it rarely gets as hot here as in Sacramento and the Central Valley, making strolling around town a pleasure. In recent years, a few excellent restaurants have shown up outside the hotels, but aside from a few notable exceptions, lodging continues to be nothing special.

☾ **Circus Circus** (⊠ 500 N. Sierra St. ☎ 775/329–0711 or 800/648–5010 ⊕ www.circusreno.com), marked by a neon clown sucking a lollipop, is the best stop for families with children. A midway above the casino floor has clowns, games, fun-house mirrors, and circus acts. **Eldorado** (⊠ 345 N. Virginia St. ☏ 775/786–5700 or 800/648–5966 ⊕ www. eldoradoreno.com) is action packed, with tons of slots, good bar-top video poker, and great coffee-shop and food-court fare. **Harrah's** (⊠ 219 N. Center St. ☏ 775/786–3232 or 800/648–3773 ⊕ www.harrahs. com) occupies two city blocks, with a sprawling casino and an outdoor promenade; it also has a 29-story Hampton Inn annex. Minimums are low, and service is friendly. **Silver Legacy** (⊠ 407 N. Virginia St. ☏ 775/ 329–4777 or 800/687–8733 ⊕ www.silverlegacyresort.com) has a Victorian-theme casino with a 120-foot-tall mining rig that mints silver-dollar tokens. The **Downtown River Walk** (⊠ S. Virginia St. and the Truckee River ⊕ www.renoriver.org) often hosts special events featuring street performers, musicians, dancers, food, art exhibits, and games. At one end, a 2,600-foot-long white-water kayaking course, which runs right through the city, has become quite an attraction.

☺ On the University of Nevada campus, the sleekly designed **Fleischmann Planetarium** has films and astronomy shows. ⊠ 1600 N. Virginia St. ☏ 775/784–4811 ⊕ www.planetarium.unr.nevada.edu ◻ Exhibits free, films and star shows $7 ☉ Weekdays 8–8, weekends 11–8.

★ The **Nevada Museum of Art**, the state's largest museum and only accredited art museum, has changing exhibits in a dramatic modern building. ⊠ 160 W. Liberty St. ☏ 775/329–3333 ⊕ www.nevadaart.org ◻ $7 ☉ Tues., Wed., and Fri.–Sun. 11–6, Thurs. 11–8.

More than 220 antique and classic automobiles, including an Elvis
☺ Presley Cadillac, are on display at the **National Automobile Museum.** ⊠ Mill and Lake Sts. ☏ 775/333–9300 ⊕ www.automuseum.org ◻ $8 ☉ Mon.–Sat. 9:30–5:30, Sun. 10–4.

off the beaten path

VICTORIAN SQUARE – In Reno's sister city to the east, this square is fringed by restored turn-of-the-20th-century houses and Victorian-dressed casinos and storefronts. Its bandstand is the focal point of many festivals. ⊠ Victorian Ave. between Rock Blvd. and Pyramid Way, Sparks.

Where to Stay & Eat

★ $$$–$$$$ ✕**LuLou's.** Modern art adorns the exposed brick walls of the small dining room at this innovative restaurant. Drawing influences from Europe and Asia, the chef has imported contemporary urban cooking to the Great Basin. The menu changes often, and you can expect to see anything from foie gras and duck confit to pot stickers and chicken curry. ⊠ 1470 S. Virginia St. ☏ 775/329–9979 ⌂ Reservations essential ⊟ AE, D, DC, MC, V ☉ Closed Sun. and Mon. No lunch.

★ $$–$$$ ✕**Fourth St. Bistro.** You'll find deliciously simple, perfectly prepared cooking at this charming bistro, where the chef-owner uses organic produce and meats whenever possible. The casual white-tablecloth dining room, with its sponge-painted walls, is comfortable and inviting. ⊠ 3065 W. 4th St. ☏ 775/323–3200 ⌂ Reservations essential ⊟ AE, D, DC, MC, V ☉ Closed Mon. and Tues. No lunch.

$–$$ ✕ **Beaujolais Bistro.** Modern adaptations of classic French dishes are served in a comfortable, airy dining room with exposed brick walls and parquet floor. Everything here is French—the waiters, the wine, and even the music—but service is warm and friendly. On the menu, expect beef Bourguignon, roast duck, coq au vin, seafood sausage, and steak frites, adeptly prepared by the chef-owner. ⊠ *130 West St.* ☎ *775/323–2227* ⌕ *Reservations essential* ▤ *AE, D, MC, V* ⊘ *Closed Sun. and Mon. No lunch Sat.*

¢–$ ✕ **Bangkok.** If you want to eat well in a pretty dining room but don't want to break the bank, come to this charming Thai restaurant, where delicious soups, salads, stir-fries, and curries are prepared by a Thai national. On Friday and Saturday nights, from 11 to 3, the restaurant becomes the Hooka Lounge, with belly dancing and Dionysian revelry. ⊠ *55 Mt. Rose St.* ☎ *775/322–0299* ▤ *AE, D, DC, MC, V* ⊘ *Closed Sun.*

¢–$$$ ✕▨ **Harrah's.** This is one of the nicer hotels in downtown Reno. Large guest rooms decorated in blues and mauves overlook downtown and the entire mountain-ringed valley. The dark and romantic dining room at Harrah's Steak House ($$–$$$$) serves excellent prime steaks and seafood. ⊠ *219 N. Center St., 89501* ☎ *775/786–3232 or 800/648–3773* ⊕ *www.harrahs.com* ⋈ *565 rooms* ♨ *6 restaurants, room service, in-room safes, some in-room hot tubs, some refrigerators, cable TV with movies and video games, pool, health club, casino, showroom, video game room, dry cleaning* ▤ *AE, D, DC, MC, V.*

$–$$ ✕▨ **Siena Hotel Spa Casino.** Reno's most luxurious hotel has attractive rooms and deliciously comfortable beds, courtesy of pillow-top mattresses and down comforters. At check-in, you won't have to navigate past miles of slot machines to find the front desk, since the casino is in a self-contained room off the elegant lobby. Lexie's ($$–$$$) serves organic steaks and fresh seafood in a sleek and elegant modern dining room overlooking the river. There's also a small full-service spa. ⊠ *1 S. Lake St., 89501* ☎ *775/337–6260 or 877/743–6233* ⊜ *775/321–5870* ⊕ *www.sienareno.com* ⋈ *193 rooms, 21 suites* ♨ *Restaurant, coffee shop, room service, in-room data ports, minibars, refrigerators, cable TV, pool, health club, spa, lounge, wine bar, casino, dry cleaning, laundry service, concierge, Internet, business services, meeting rooms, airport shuttle* ▤ *AE, D, DC, MC, V.*

¢–$$ ✕▨ **Eldorado.** Smack dab in the middle of glittering downtown sits the Eldorado, an all-suites tower whose rooms overlook the mountains or the lights of the city. La Strada ($–$$) serves great northern Italian cooking in a romantic room; the Roxy ($$–$$$$) serves roasted meats in an over-the-top, faux-European courtyard. Both restaurants have excellent wine lists. ⊠ *345 N. Virginia St., 89501* ☎ *775/786–5700 or 800/648–5966* ⊜ *702/322–7124* ⊕ *www.eldoradoreno.com* ⋈ *836 suites* ♨ *8 restaurants, room service, in-room data ports, some in-room hot tubs, cable TV with movies, pool, hot tub, casino, video game room, meeting rooms* ▤ *AE, D, DC, MC, V.*

¢ ✕▨ **Truckee River Lodge.** If you're on a budget or traveling with kids and don't want to sleep in a casino, try this hotel, which feels more like a motel. It has clean rooms with kitchenettes and a good, cheap vegetarian restaurant, the Pneumatic Diner (¢), on the second floor. The hotel is within walking distance of downtown sights. ⊠ *501 W. 1st St., 89503* ☎ *775/786–8888 or 800/635–8950* 🖷 *775/348–4769* ⊕ *www. truckeeriverlodge.com* ➮ *203 rooms, 7 suites* ⚭ *Restaurant, kitchenettes, cable TV, some in-room VCRs, exercise equipment, shop, laundry facilities, Internet, some pets allowed (fee); no smoking* ⊟ *AE, D, DC, MC, V.*

$$ 🏠 **Plumas House.** Escape from the madding crowds and blinking lights at this charming B&B in a residential area south of downtown. The owners, who have backgrounds in the antiques and decorating industries, have attended to every detail in the individually styled rooms. ⊠ *1000 Plumas St., 89509* ☎ *775/786–1164* ⊕ *www.plumashouse.com* ➮ *3 rooms, 1 cottage* ⚭ *Some kitchenettes, some pets allowed; no TV in some rooms, no smoking* ⊟ *MC, V* ⊙ *BP.*

Sports & the Outdoors
If you want to kayak the white-water course through downtown, try **Sierra Adventures** (⊠ 2204 Dickerson Rd. ☎ 775/323–8928 ⊕ www. wildsierra.com). In addition to rentals and instruction, they also operate full-day rafting trips down the Truckee River.

LAKE TAHOE A TO Z

To research prices, get advice from other travelers, and book travel arrangements, visit ⊕ *www.fodors.com*

AIR TRAVEL
Reno–Tahoe International Airport, in Reno, 35 mi northeast of the closest point on the lake, is served by Alaska, American, America West, Continental, Delta, Northwest, Skywest, Southwest, and United airlines. (*See* Air Travel *in* Smart Travel Tips *for airline phone numbers*

🛈 **Reno–Tahoe International Airport** ⊠ U.S. 395, exit 65B, Reno, NV ☎ 775/328–6400 ⊕ www.renoairport.com.

BUS TRAVEL
Greyhound stops in Sacramento, Truckee, South Lake Tahoe, and Reno, Nevada. Blue Go runs along U.S. 50 and through the neighborhoods of South Lake Tahoe daily from 6 AM to 12:15 AM; it also operates a 24-hour door-to-door van service to most addresses in South Lake Tahoe and Stateline for $3 per person. Tahoe Area Regional Transit (TART) operates buses along Lake Tahoe's northern and western shores between Tahoma (from Meeks Bay in summer) and Incline Village daily from 6:30 to 6:30. Free shuttle buses run among the casinos, major ski resorts, and motels of South Lake Tahoe. Tahoe Casino Express runs 14 daily buses between Reno–Tahoe Airport and hotels in Stateline.

🛈 **Greyhound** ☎ 800/231–2222. **Blue Go** ☎ 530/542–6077. **Tahoe Area Regional Transit (TART)** ☎ 530/550–1212 or 800/736–6365. **Tahoe Casino Express** ☎ 775/785–2424 or 800/446–6128.

CAR RENTAL
The major car-rental agencies—Hertz, Avis, Budget, National, Thrifty, Enterprise, and Dollar—all have counters at Reno–Tahoe International Airport. Enterprise has an outlet at the Lake Tahoe Airport (in South

Lake Tahoe); Avis has one at Harrah's Stateline; Hertz has one at Harveys, in Stateline; and Dollar has counters at the Reno Hilton, Reno's Circus Circus, and Caesars Tahoe. *See* Car Rental *in* Smart Travel Tips A to Z *for national car-rental agency phone numbers.*

CAR TRAVEL

Lake Tahoe is 198 mi northeast of San Francisco, a drive of less than four hours in good weather. Avoid the heavy traffic leaving the San Francisco area for Tahoe on Friday afternoon and returning on Sunday afternoon. The major route is I–80, which cuts through the Sierra Nevada about 14 mi north of the lake. From there Highway 89 and Highway 267 reach the west and north shores, respectively. U.S. 50 is the more direct route to the south shore, taking about two hours from Sacramento. From Reno you can get to the north shore by heading south on U.S. 395 for 10 mi, then west on Highway 431 for 25 mi. For the south shore, head south on U.S. 395 through Carson City, and then turn west on U.S. 50 (50 mi total).

The scenic 72-mi highway around the lake is marked Highway 89 on the southwest and west shores, Highway 28 on the north and northeast shores, and U.S. 50 on the east and southeast. Sections of Highway 89 sometimes close in winter, making it impossible to complete the circular drive. Interstate 80, U.S. 50, and U.S. 395 are all-weather highways, but there may be delays as snow is cleared during major storms. Carry tire chains from October through May, or rent a four-wheel-drive vehicle (rental agencies do not offer tire chains for rent).

🚗 **California Highway Patrol** ☎ 530/587–3510. **Cal-Trans Highway Information Line** ☎ 800/427–7023. **Nevada Department of Transportation Road Information** ☎ 877/687–6237. **Nevada Highway Patrol** ☎ 775/687–5300.

EMERGENCIES

In an emergency dial 911.

🚑 Hospitals **Barton Memorial Hospital** ✉ 2170 South Ave., South Lake Tahoe ☎ 530/541–3420. **St. Mary's Regional Medical Center** ✉ 235 W. 6th St., Reno NV ☎ 775/770–3188. **Tahoe Forest Hospital** ✉ 10121 Pine Ave., Truckee ☎ 530/587–6011.

LODGING

The Lake Tahoe Visitors Authority provides information on southshore lodging. North Lake Tahoe Resort Association can give you information about accommodations on the north shore and in Truckee. Contact the Reno-Sparks Convention and Visitors Authority for lodging reservations in the Reno metropolitan area.

🏨 **Lake Tahoe Visitors Authority** ☎ 800/288–2463 ⊕ www.virtualtahoe.com. **North Lake Tahoe Resort Association** ☎ 800/824–6348 ⊕ www.tahoefun.org. **Reno-Sparks Convention and Visitors Authority** ☎ 775/827–7647 or 888/448–7366 ⊕ www.renolaketahoe.com.

SPORTS & THE OUTDOORS

If you are planning to spend any time outdoors around Lake Tahoe, whether hiking, climbing, or camping, be aware that weather conditions can change quickly in the Sierra: to avoid a life-threatening case of hypothermia, always bring a pocket-size, fold-up rain poncho (available in all sporting goods stores) to keep you dry. Wear long pants and a hat. Carry plenty of water. Because you'll likely be walking on granite, wear sturdy, closed-toe hiking boots, with soles that grip rock. If you're going into the backcountry, bring a signaling device (such as a mirror), energy bars, emergency whistle, compass, map, and water purifier. When heading out alone, tell someone where you're going and when you're coming back.

If you plan to ski, be aware of resort elevations. In the event of a winter storm, determine the snow level before you choose the resort you'll ski. Often the level can be as high as 7,000 feet, which means rain at some resorts but snow at others. For storm information, check the National Weather Service's Web page. To save money on lift tickets, look for packages offered by lodges and resorts. It's usually cheaper to ski midweek, and some resorts offer family discounts. Free shuttle-bus service is available between most ski resorts and nearby lodgings. If you plan to do any backcountry skiing, check with the U.S. Forest Service for conditions.

If you plan to camp in the backcountry, you'll likely need a wilderness permit, which you can pick up at the Lake Tahoe Visitor Center or at a ranger station at the entrance to any of the national forests. For reservations at campgrounds in California state parks, contact Park.net.

🚩 **Lake Tahoe Visitor Center** ✉ Hwy. 89 ☎ 530/573-2674 in season only ⊕ www. fs.fed.us/r5/ltbmu. **National Weather Service** ⊕ www.wrh.noaa.gov/reno. **Park.net** ☎ 800/444-7275 ⊕ www.reserveamerica.com. **U.S. Forest Service** ☎ 530/587-2158 backcountry recording ⊕ www.fs.fed.us/r5.

TOURS

Several boats tour Lake Tahoe. The 500-passenger *Tahoe Queen,* a glass-bottom paddle-wheeler, makes 2¼-hour sightseeing cruises year-round and three-hour dinner-dance cruises April–October from South Lake Tahoe. Fares range from $22 to $49. In winter the boat becomes the only waterborne ski shuttle in the world: $89 covers hotel transfers, breakfast, transportation across the lake to Squaw Valley, and dinner; $129 includes a lift ticket. The *Sierra Cloud,* a large trimaran, cruises the north shore area morning and afternoon, May through October. The fare is $45. The 550-passenger MS *Dixie II,* a stern-wheeler, sails year-round from Zephyr Cove to Emerald Bay on lunch and dinner cruises. Fares range from $25 to $51. Also in Zephyr Cove, the *Woodwind II,* a 50-passenger catamaran, sails on regular and champagne cruises April–October. Fares range from $26 to $32.

Gray Line/Frontier Tours runs daily tours to South Lake Tahoe, Carson City, and Virginia City. Lake Tahoe Balloons conducts excursions year-round over the lake or over the Carson Valley for $129 per person for half-hour flights and $195 for hour-long flights (champagne brunch included). Soar Minden offers glider rides and instruction over the lake and the Great Basin. Flights cost $95 to $210 and depart from Minden-Tahoe Airport, a municipal facility in Minden, Nevada.

🚩 *Tahoe Queen* ✉ Ski Run Marina, off U.S. 50, South Lake Tahoe ☎ 530/541-3364 or 800/238-2463. *Sierra Cloud* ✉ Hyatt Regency Lake Tahoe, Incline Village ☎ 775/

831-1111. **MS** *Dixie II* ✉ Zephyr Cove Marina, Zephyr Cove ☎ 775/588-3508. *Woodwind II* ✉ Zephyr Cove Resort, U.S. 50, Zephyr Cove ☎ 775/588-3000. **Gray Line/Frontier Tours** ☎ 775/331-8687 or 800/831-2877. **Lake Tahoe Balloons** ☎ 530/544-1221 or 800/872-9294. **Soar Minden** ☎ 775/782-7627 or 800/345-7627.

TRAIN TRAVEL

Amtrak's cross-country rail service makes stops in Truckee and Reno. The *California Zephyr* stops in both towns once daily eastbound (Salt Lake, Denver, and Chicago) and once daily westbound (Sacramento and Oakland), blocking traffic for 5 to 10 minutes. Amtrak also operates several buses daily between Reno and Sacramento to connect with the *Coast Starlight,* which runs south to southern California and north to Oregon and Washington.

🚩 **Amtrak** ☎ 775/329-8638 or 800/872-7245 ⊕ www.amtrakcalifornia.com.

VISITOR INFORMATION

🚩 **Carson City Chamber of Commerce** ✉ 1900 S. Carson St., Carson City, NV 87901 ☎ 775/882-1565 ⊕ www.carsoncitychamber.com. **Lake Tahoe Visitors Authority** ✉ 1156 Ski Run Blvd., South Lake Tahoe 96150 ☎ 530/544-5050 or 800/288-2463 ⊕ www.virtualtahoe.com. **North Lake Tahoe Resort Association** ⌂ Box 5578, Tahoe City 96145 ☎ 530/583-3494 or 800/824-6348 🖶 530/581-4081 ⊕ www.tahoefun.org. **Reno-Sparks Convention and Visitors Authority** ✉ 4590 S. Virginia St., Reno, NV 89502 ☎ 775/827-7600 or 800/367-7366 ⊕ www.renolaketahoe.com. **U.S. Forest Service** ☎ 530/587-2158 backcountry recording ⊕ www.fs.fed.us/r5.

THE FAR NORTH
WITH LAKE SHASTA, MT. SHASTA & LASSEN VOLCANIC NATIONAL PARK

Updated by
Christine
Vovakes

THE WONDROUS LANDSCAPE of California's northeastern corner, relatively unmarred by development, congestion, and traffic, is the product of volcanic activity. At the southern end of the Cascade Range, Lassen Volcanic National Park is the best place to witness the far north's fascinating geology. Beyond the sulfur vents and bubbling mud pots, the park owes much of its beauty to 10,457-foot Mt. Lassen and 50 wilderness lakes. The most enduring image of the region, though, is Mt. Shasta, whose 14,162-foot snowcapped peak beckons outdoor adventurers of all kinds. There are many versions of Shasta to enjoy—the mountain, the lake, the river, the town, the dam, and the forest—all named after the Native Americans known as the Shatasla, or Sastise, who once inhabited the region.

Its soaring mountain peaks, wild rivers teeming with trout, and almost unlimited recreational possibilities make the far north the perfect destination for sports lovers. You won't find many hot nightspots or cultural enclaves, but you will find some of the best hiking and fishing in the state. The region offers a glimpse of old California—natural, rugged, and inspiring.

Exploring the Far North

The far north encompasses all of four vast counties—Tehama, Shasta, Siskiyou, and Trinity—as well as parts of Butte, Modoc, and Plumas counties. The area stretches from the valleys east of the Coast Range to the Nevada border and from the almond and olive orchards north of Sacramento to the Oregon border. A car is essential for touring the area unless you arrive by public transportation and plan to stay put in one town or resort.

About the Restaurants

Redding, the urban center of the far north, has the greatest selection of restaurants. In the smaller towns, cafés and simple eateries are the rule, though trendy innovative restaurants have been popping up. Dress is always informal.

About the Hotels

Aside from the large chain hotels and motels in the Redding area, most accommodations in the far north blend rusticity, simplicity, and coziness. That's just fine with most of the folks who visit, as they spend much of their time outdoors. Wilderness resorts close in fall and reopen after the snow season ends in May.

The far north—especially the mountainous backcountry—is gaining popularity as a tourist destination. For summer holiday weekends make lodging reservations well in advance. The Web site of the **California Association of Bed & Breakfast Inns** (⊕ www.cabbi.com) lists numerous B&Bs in the far north region.

WHAT IT COSTS				
$$$$	**$$$**	**$$**	**$**	**¢**
RESTAURANTS over $30	$23–$30	$16–$22	$10–$15	under $10
HOTELS over $250	$176–$250	$121–$175	$90–$120	under $90

Restaurant prices are for a main course at dinner, excluding sales tax of 7¾% (depending on location). Hotel prices are for two people in a standard double room in high season, excluding service charges and 7¼% tax.

Timing

This region attracts more tourists in summer than at any other time of year. Residents of the Sacramento Valley, which is usually dry and scorching during the dog days of summer, tend to flee to the milder climes of the mountains to the north and east. The valley around Redding is mild in winter, while snow falls at higher elevations. In winter Mt. Shasta is a great place for downhill and cross-country skiing—and even ice fishing at the area's many high-elevation lakes. Snow closes the roads to some of the region's most awesome sights, including much of Lassen Volcanic National Park, from October until late May. During the off-season many restaurants and museums here have limited hours, sometimes closing for extended periods.

FROM CHICO TO MT. SHASTA
ALONG I–5

The far north is bisected, south to north, by Interstate 5 (I–5), which winds through historic towns, museums, and state parks. Halfway to the Oregon border is Lake Shasta, a favorite recreation destination, and farther north stands the spectacular snowy peak of Mt. Shasta.

Chico

❶ *180 mi from San Francisco, east on I–80, north on I–505 to I–5, and east on Hwy. 32; 86 mi north of Sacramento on Hwy. 99.*

Chico (which is Spanish for "small") sits just west of Paradise in the Sacramento Valley and offers a welcome break from the monotony of I–5. The Chico campus of California State University, the scores of local artisans, and the area's agriculture (primarily almond orchards) all influence the culture here. Chico's true claim to fame, however, is the popular Sierra Nevada Brewery, which keeps locals and beer drinkers across the country happy with its distinctive microbrews.

★ The sprawling 3,670-acre **Bidwell Park** (✉ River Rd. south of Sacramento St. ☎ 530/895–4972), is a community green space straddling Big Chico Creek, where scenes from *Gone with the Wind* and the 1938 version of *Robin Hood* (starring Errol Flynn) were filmed. It provides the region with a recreational hub, and includes a golf course, swimming areas, and paved biking, hiking, and in-line skating trails. The third-largest city-

Numbers in the text correspond to numbers in the margin and on the Far North map.

If you have 3 days

From I-5 north of Redding, head northeast on Highways 299 and 89 to ► **McArthur–Burney Falls Memorial State Park** ❽. To appreciate the falls, take a short stroll to the overlook or hike down for a closer view. Continue north on Highway 89. Long before you arrive in the town of 🖼 **Mt. Shasta** ❼, you will spy the conical peak for which it is named. The central Mt. Shasta exit east leads out of town along Everitt Memorial Highway. Take this scenic drive, which climbs to almost 8,000 feet. The views of the mountain and the valley below are extraordinary. Stay overnight in town. On the second day head south on I-5 toward **Lake Shasta** ❺, visible on both sides of the highway. Have a look at Lake Shasta Caverns and the Shasta Dam before heading west on Highway 299 to spend the night in 🖼 **Weaverville** ❹ or south on I-5 to overnight in 🖼 **Redding** ❸, where you can stroll across the translucent span of the Sundial Bridge at Turtle Bay Exploration Park. The next day visit Shasta State Historic Park and Weaverville Joss House, on Highway 299.

If you have 5 or 6 days

Get a glimpse of the far north's heritage in ► **Red Bluff** ❷ before heading north on I-5 to the town of 🖼 **Mt. Shasta** ❼. On Day 2, drop by the Forest Service ranger station to check on trail conditions on the mountain and to pick up maps. Pack a picnic lunch before taking Everitt Memorial Highway up the mountain. After exploring it, head south on I-5 and spend the night in 🖼 **Dunsmuir** ❻ at the Railroad Park Resort, where all the accommodations are old cabooses. On your third day take an early morning hike in nearby Castle Crags State Park. Continue south on I-5 to **Lake Shasta** ❺ and tour Shasta Dam Visitor's Center. Spend the night camping in the area or in 🖼 **Redding** ❸. On your fourth morning head west on Highway 299, stopping at Shasta State Historic Park on your way to 🖼 **Weaverville** ❹. Spend the night there or back in Redding. If you will be leaving the area on your fifth day but have a little time, zip north and visit Lake Shasta Caverns. If you're spending the night in Redding and it's between late May and early October, spend the next day and a half exploring **Lassen Volcanic National Park** ⓫. Highway 44 heads east from Redding into the park.

---

run park in the country, Bidwell starts as a slender strip downtown and expands eastward toward the Sierra foothills.

★ The renowned **Sierra Nevada Brewing Company,** one of the pioneers of the microbrewery movement, still has a hands-on approach to beer making. You can tour the brew house, and see how the beer is produced—from the sorting of hops through fermentation and bottling. You can also visit the gift shop and enjoy a hearty lunch or dinner in the brewpub (it's closed Monday). ✉ *1075 E. 20th St.* ☎ *530/345–2739* 🖷 *530/893–9358* ⊕ *www.sierranevada.com* ✉ *Free* ☺ *Tours Sun.–Fri. 2:30, Sat. noon–3 on the ½ hr.*

★ In **Bidwell Mansion State Historic Park** you can take a one-hour tour of approximately 20 of the mansion's rooms. Built between 1865 and 1868 by General John Bidwell, the founder of Chico, the 26-room home was designed by Henry W. Cleaveland, a San Francisco architect. Bidwell and his wife welcomed many distinguished guests to the distinctive pink Italianate mansion, including President Rutherford B. Hayes, naturalist John Muir, suffragist Susan B. Anthony, and General William T. Sherman. ⊠ *525 The Esplanade* ☎ *530/895–6144* ☞ *$2* ☉ *Wed.–Fri. noon–5, weekends 10–5, last tour at 4.*

Where to Stay & Eat

$–$$ ✕ **Red Tavern.** With its warm butter-yellow walls and mellow lighting, this is one of Chico's most refined restaurants. The menu, inspired by fresh local produce, changes seasonally. If you're lucky, it might include lamb chops with a lemon–pine nut crust or stuffed Atlantic salmon with Swiss chard, bacon, and sage butter. There's a great California wine list, and also a full bar. ⊠ *1250 The Esplanade* ☎ *530/894–3463* ▤ *AE, MC, V* ☉ *Closed Sun. No lunch.*

¢–$ ✕ **Kramore Inn.** Crepes—from ham and avocado to crab cannelloni—are this inn's specialty, along with Hungarian mushroom soup. The menu also includes salads, stir-fries, Asian dishes, and pastas. Brunch is available on Sunday from 9 to 2. ⊠ *1903 Park Ave.* ☎ *530/343–3701* ▤ *AE, D, MC, V.*

¢ ✕ **Madison Bear Garden.** This downtown favorite two blocks south of the Chico State campus is a great spot for checking out the vibrant college scene while enjoying a delicious burger and a vast selection of brews. ⊠ *316 W. 2nd St.* ☎ *530/891–1639* ▤ *MC, V.*

$–$$ ▥ **Johnson's Country Inn.** Nestled in an almond orchard five minutes from downtown, this Victorian-style farmhouse with a wraparound veranda is a welcome change from motel row. It is full of antique furnishings and modern conveniences. ⊠ *3935 Morehead Ave., 95928* ☎▤ *530/ 345–7829 or 866/872–7780* ⊕ *www.chico.com/johnsonsinn* ☞ *4 rooms* ♤ *Internet, fax; no in-room TV, no smoking* ▤ *AE, MC, V* ⦿ *BP.*

Shopping

Made in Chico (⊠232 Main St. ☎530/894–7009) sells locally made goods, including pottery, olives, almonds, and Woof and Poof creations—whimsical home decor items, such as stuffed Santas, elves, animals, and pillows. Beautiful custom-made etched, stained, and beveled glass is created at **Needham Studios** (⊠ 237 Broadway ☎ 530/345–4718). Shop and watch demonstrations of glass blowing at the **Satava Art Glass Studio** (⊠ 819 Wall St. ☎ 530/345–7985).

Red Bluff

▶ ❷ *41 mi north of Chico on Hwy 99.*

Historic Red Bluff is a gateway to Mount Lassen National Park. Established in the mid-19th century as a shipping center and named for the color of its soil, the town is filled with dozens of restored Victorians. It's a great home base for outdoor adventures in the area.

Camping   In the vast expanses of the far north, pristine campgrounds make overnighting in the great outdoors a singular pleasure. There are hundreds of campgrounds here: some small and remote with few facilities; others with nearly all the conveniences of home; and still others somewhere in between.

Fishing   Cascading rivers, lakes of many shapes and sizes, and bountiful streams draw anglers to the far north. The Trinity River below the Lewiston Dam and the upper Sacramento River near Dunsmuir are excellent fly-fishing spots. Anglers say the large trout of Eagle Lake are especially feisty quarry. Lake Shasta holds 21 types of fish, including rainbow trout and salmon.

Hiking   With so much wilderness, it's no wonder the far north has some of California's finest—and least crowded—hiking areas. In the shadow of Mt. Shasta, Castle Crags State Park has 28 mi of hiking trails, including rewarding routes at lower altitudes. Plumas National Forest, a protected area of 1.2 million acres, is laced with trails. Hikers in Lassen Volcanic National Park can explore wondrous landscapes formed by centuries of volcano activity.

The **Kelly-Griggs House Museum,** a beautifully restored 1880s home, holds an impressive collection of antique furniture, housewares, and clothing arranged as though a refined Victorian-era family were still in residence. A Venetian glass punch bowl sits on the dining room table; in the upstairs parlor costumed mannequins seem eerily frozen in time. *Persephone,* the painting over the fireplace, is by Sarah Brown, daughter of abolitionist John Brown, whose family settled in Red Bluff. ⊠ *311 Washington St.* ☎ *530/527–1129* 🖃 *Donation suggested* ☉ *Thurs.–Sun. 1–3.*

William B. Ide Adobe State Historic Park is named for the first and only president of the short-lived California Republic of 1846. The Bear Flag Party proclaimed California a sovereign nation, separate from Mexican rule, and the republic existed for 25 days before it was taken over by the United States. The republic's flag has survived, with only minor refinements, as California's state flag. The park's main attraction is an adobe home built in the 1850s and outfitted with period furnishings. There's also a carriage shed, a blacksmith shop, and a small visitor center. Home tours are available on request. ⊠ *21659 Adobe Rd.* ☎ *530/ 529–8599* ⊕ *www.ideadobe.tehama.k12.ca.us* 🖃 *$4 per vehicle* ☉ *Park and picnic facilities daily 8 AM–sunset.*

Where to Stay & Eat

¢–$$ ✕ **Crystal Steak & Seafood Co.** Along with meat and seafood dishes, a Cajun combo of shrimp, chicken, and spicy sausages in bourbon sauce over rice is the house specialty. ⊠ *343 S. Main St.* ☎ *530/527–0880* ▭ *AE, D, MC, V* ☉ *No lunch weekends.*

¢–$ ✕ **Snack Box.** Unabashedly corny pictures and knickknacks decorate this renovated Victorian cottage, which serves hearty soups, omelets, burg-

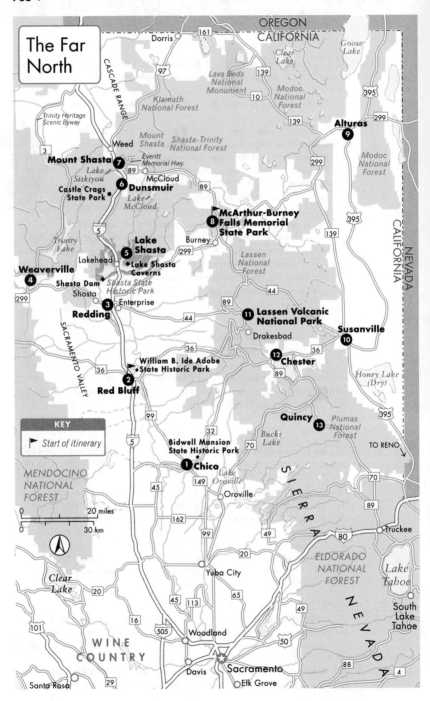

The Far North

OREGON
CALIFORNIA

Dorris

CASCADE RANGE

Trinity Heritage
Scenic Byway

Klamath
National Forest

Lava Beds
National
Monument

Clear
Lake

Goose
Lake

Modoc
National
Forest

Weed

Mount
Shasta

Shasta-Trinity
National Forest

Alturas
9

Mount Shasta 7
Everitt
Memorial Hwy.

Lake
Siskiyou

McCloud

Modoc
National
Forest

Dunsmuir 6

Castle Crags
State Park

Lake
McCloud

McArthur-Burney
Falls Memorial
State Park 8

Burney

Lake
Shasta 5

Lakehead

Lake Shasta
Caverns

Lassen
National
Forest

Weaverville
4

Shasta Dam
Shasta State
Historic Park

Shasta

Enterprise

Redding 3

Lassen Volcanic
National Park 11

Susanville
10

Drakesbad

William B. Ide Adobe
State Historic Park

Red Bluff 2

Chester 12

Honey Lake
(Dry)

Bidwell Mansion
State Historic Park

Quincy 13

Plumas
National
Forest

Chico 1

Bucks
Lake

TO RENO

KEY

Start of itinerary

MENDOCINO
NATIONAL
FOREST

Lake
Oroville

Oroville

0   20 miles
0   30 km

Yuba City

Clear
Lake

ELDORADO
NATIONAL
FOREST

Lake
Tahoe

South
Lake
Tahoe

Truckee

WINE
COUNTRY

Woodland

Santa Rosa

Davis

Sacramento

Elk Grove

NEVADA

SACRAMENTO VALLEY

SIERRA NEVADA

CALIFORNIA
NEVADA

ers, and sandwiches. ✉ *257 Main St., 1 block from Kelly-Griggs House Museum* ☎ *530/529–0227* ▭ *AE, MC, V* ⊘ *No dinner.*

¢ ✕ **Countryside Deli.** Heaping platters of country-fried steak and meat loaf with mashed potatoes and gravy are the draw at this deli. Its old-fashion soda fountain, lined with red-topped swivel seats, is the perfect place to enjoy a hot fudge sundae or banana split. ✉ *1007 Main St.* ☎ *530/529–3869* ▭ *MC, V* ⊘ *Closed weekends.*

¢–$$ ▣ **The Jeter Victorian Inn.** On sunny days, breakfast is served in the garden pavilion outside this 1881 Victorian home. The four guest rooms are elegantly decorated with antiques and period furnishings; two have private baths, and the Imperial Room has a Jacuzzi. A separate cottage is also available. ✉ *1107 Jefferson St., 96080* ☎ *530/527–7574* ⊕ *www.jetervictorianinn.com* ⤝ *4 rooms, 2 with bath; 1 cottage* △ *No phones, no TV in some rooms, no smoking* ▭ *MC, V* ⵏ⦾ⵏ *BP.*

¢ ▣ **Lamplighter Lodge.** Although its name may evoke log cabins, this property is actually a motel on the town's main street. Simple rooms are equipped with mini-refrigerators and microwaves. The pool area is a great place to relax on sweltering summer days, and the Red Rock Cafe next door is open for meals and snacks. ✉ *210 S. Main St., 96080* ☎ *530/527–1150* ⤝ *50 rooms, 2 suites* △ *Microwaves, refrigerators, pool* ▭ *AE, D, MC, V* ⵏ⦾ⵏ *CP.*

Redding

❸ *32 mi north of Red Bluff on I–5.*

As the largest city in the far north, Redding is an ideal headquarters for exploring the surrounding countryside. Curving along the Sacramento River, **Turtle Bay Exploration Park** has a museum, an arboretum with walking trails, and lots of interactive exhibits for children, including a miniature dam, a gold-panning area, and a Butterfly House where monarchs emerge from their cocoons. The main draw at the park, however, is the stunning, newly unveiled **Sundial Bridge,** a modernist pedestrian footbridge designed by world-renowned Spanish architect Santiago Calatrava. The bridge's architecture consists of a translucent, illuminated span that stretches across the river, and—most strikingly—a soaring white 217-foot needle that casts a slender moving shadow, like a sundial's, over the water and surrounding trees. Watching the sun set over the river from this bridge is a magical experience. Children 4–16 pay about half the adult admission to the park, and there's no charge for kids under 3. ✉ *800 Auditorium Dr.* ☎ *530/243–8850* ⊕ *www.turtlebay.org* ⬚ *$11* ⊘ *Closed Mon. Sept.–May.*

Where to Stay & Eat

$–$$$ ✕ **Hatch Cover.** Dark-wood paneling and views of the adjacent Sacramento River create the illusion of dining aboard a ship, especially on the outside deck with its views of Mt. Shasta. The menu emphasizes seafood, but you can also get steaks, chicken, pasta, and combination plates. The appetizer menu is extensive. ✉ *202 Hemsted Dr., from Cypress Ave. exit off I–5, turn left, then right on Hemsted Dr.* ☎ *530/223–5606* ▭ *AE, D, MC, V* ⊘ *No lunch weekends.*

$–$$$ ✕ **Jack's Grill.** Famous for its 16-ounce steaks, this popular bar and steak house also serves shrimp and chicken. A town favorite, the place is usually jam-packed and noisy. ✉ *1743 California St.* ☎ *530/241–9705* ▤ *AE, D, MC, V* ☺ *Closed Sun. No lunch.*

¢–$ ✕ **Klassique Kafe.** Two sisters run this small bustling restaurant that caters to locals looking for simple but hearty breakfast and lunch fare. The hot luncheon specials served daily might include butter beans and ham with corn bread, or chicken and dumplings. ✉ *2427 Athens Ave.* ☎ *530/244–4939* ▤ *AE, D, MC, V* ☺ *Closed Sat. No dinner.*

★ ¢–$$ ✕▥ **The Red Lion.** Adjacent to I–5, and close to Redding's convention center and regional recreation sites, this hotel is a top choice for both business and vacation travelers. Rooms are spacious and comfortable; a large patio surrounded by landscaped grounds is a relaxing spot to enjoy an outdoor meal or snack. There are irons, ironing boards, and hair dryers in the rooms, and video games in the public areas. The hotel's restaurant, Waters Seafood Grill, is a popular place for locals. ✉ *1830 Hilltop Dr., Hwy. 44/299 exit from I–5, 96002* ☎ *530/221–8700 or 800/733–5466* 🖷 *530/221–0324* ⊕ *www.redlion.com* ⮐ *192 rooms, 2 suites* ⚘ *Restaurant, coffee shop, room service, pool, wading pool, gym, hot tub, bar, airport shuttle* ▤ *AE, D, DC, MC, V.*

$$$–$$$$ ▥ **Brigadoon Castle Bed & Breakfast.** Fifteen winding miles from I–5 is this Elizabethan-style castle, nestled atop an 86-acre estate. Guest rooms have marble baths, antique furnishings, and luxurious upholstery; in the common room are a fireplace, a satellite TV, and a wall of videos to choose from. A separate 1,250-square-foot cottage is also available. Evening snacks are included in the rates. ✉ *9036 Zogg Mine Rd., Igo 96047* ☎ *530/396–2785 or 888/343–2836* 🖷 *530/396–2784* ⊕ *www.brigadooncastle.com* ⮐ *4 rooms* ⚘ *Hot tub; no room phones, no room TVs* ▤ *AE, MC, V* ⦿ *BP.*

Sports & the Outdoors
The **Fly Shop** (✉ 4140 Churn Creek Rd. ☎ 530/222–3555) sells fishing licenses and has information about guides, conditions, and fishing packages.

en route   Six miles west of Redding on Highway 299, **Shasta State Historic Park** (☎ 530/243–8194 🎫 $2) stands where Shasta City thrived in the mid- to late 1800s. Its 19 acres of half-ruined brick buildings and overgrown graveyards, accessed via trails, are a reminder of the glory days of the California gold rush. The former county courthouse building, jail, and gallows have been restored to their 1860s appearance. The Courthouse Museum (Wed.–Sun. 10–5) houses a visitor center, information desk, art gallery, and interactive exhibits, including a storytelling hologram "ghost" locked in the jail. The Litsch General Store, in operation from 1850 to 1950, is now a museum, with displays of many items that were sold here.

Weaverville

➍ *46 mi west of Redding on Hwy. 299 (called Main St. in town).*

Weaverville is an enjoyable amalgam of gold-rush history and tourist kitsch. Named after John Weaver, one of three men who built the first cabin here in 1850, the town has an impressive downtown historic district. Weaverville is a popular headquarters for family vacations and biking, hiking, fishing, and gold-panning excursions.

★ Weaverville's main attraction is the **Weaverville Joss House,** a Taoist temple built in 1874 and called Won Lim Miao ("the temple of the forest beneath the clouds") by Chinese miners. The oldest continuously used Chinese temple in California, it attracts worshipers from around the world. With its golden altar, antique weaponry, and carved wooden canopies, the Joss House is a piece of California history that can best be appreciated on a guided 30-minute tour. The original temple building and many of its furnishings—some of which came from China—were lost to fire in 1873, but members of the local Chinese community soon rebuilt it. ⊠ *Oregon and Main Sts.* ☎ *530/623–5284* ✉ *Museum free; guided tour $2* ☉ *Wed.–Sun. 10–5.*

Trinity County Courthouse (⊠ Court and Main Sts.), built in 1856 as a store, office building, and hotel, was converted to county use in 1865. The Apollo Saloon, in the basement, became the county jail. It is the oldest courthouse still in use in California.

Trinity County Historical Park houses the **Jake Jackson Memorial Museum,** which has a blacksmith shop, a stamp mill (where ore is crushed) from the 1890s that is still in use, and the original jail cells of the Trinity County Courthouse. ⊠ *508 Main St.* ☎ *530/623–5211* ☉ *May–Oct., daily 10–5; Nov.–Apr., Tues. and Sat. noon–4.*

off the beaten path

TRINITY HERITAGE SCENIC BYWAY – This road, shown on many maps as Highway 3, runs north from Weaverville for 120 mi up to its intersection with I–5, south of Yreka. The Trinity Alps and Lewiston Lake, formed by the Trinity Dam, are visible all along this beautiful, forest-lined road, which is often closed in winter. As it climbs from 2,000 feet to 6,500 feet, most of the route follows a path established by early miners and settlers.

Where to Stay & Eat

¢–$$ ✕ **La Grange Café.** In two brick buildings dating from the 1850s (they're among the oldest edifices in town), this eatery serves buffalo and other game meats, pasta, fresh fish, and farmers' market vegetables when they're available. There's a full premium bar, and the wine list has 135 vintages. ⊠ *226 Main St.* ☎ *530/623–5325* ▬ *AE, D, MC, V* ☉ *Closed Sun. in Nov.–Mar.*

¢ ✕ **La Casita.** A traditional selection of Mexican food is on the menu here, including quesadillas (try the version with roasted chili peppers), tostadas, enchiladas, tacos, and tamales. Many dishes are available without meat. Open from late morning through early evening, this casual spot is great for a mid-afternoon snack. ⊠ *254 Main St.* ☎ *530/623–5797* ▬ *No credit cards.*

¢ ▥ **Red Hill Motel.** This 1940s-era property is popular with anglers, who appreciate the outdoor fish-cleaning area on the premises. The separate wooden lodgings, painted red and surrounded by pine trees, encircle a grassy knoll. One cozy cabin with full kitchen is good for families; two others have kitchenettes, and the rest have mini-refrigerators and microwaves. ⊠ *Red Hill Rd., 96093* ☎ *530/623–4331* ⊕ *www. redhillresorts.com* ⇨ *4 rooms, 6 cabins, 2 duplexes* ⚭ *Some kitchens, some microwaves, some refrigerators, cable TV* ⊟ *AE, D, MC, V.*

Sports & the Outdoors

Below the Lewiston Dam, east of Weaverville on Highway 299, is the **Fly Stretch** of the Trinity River, a world-class fly-fishing area. The **Pine Cove Boat Ramp,** on Lewiston Lake, provides fishing access for those with disabilities—decks here are built over prime trout-fishing waters. Contact the **Weaverville Ranger Station** (⊠ 210 Main St. ☎ 530/623–2121) for maps and information about hiking trails in the Trinity Alps Wilderness.

Shopping

Hays Bookstore (⊠ 106 Main St. ☎ 530/623–2516) is a general bookstore that includes books on the natural history, attractions, and sights of the far north.

Lake Shasta Area

★ ❺ *12 mi north of Redding on I–5.*

Twenty-one types of fish inhabit **Lake Shasta,** including rainbow trout and salmon. The lake region also has the largest nesting population of bald eagles in California. You can rent fishing boats, ski boats, sailboats, canoes, paddleboats, Jet Skis, and windsurfing boards at one of the many marinas and resorts along the 370-mi shoreline.

Stalagmites, stalactites, flowstone deposits, and crystals entice people of all ages to the **Lake Shasta Caverns.** To see this impressive spectacle, you must take the two-hour tour, which includes a catamaran ride across the McCloud arm of Lake Shasta and a bus ride up Grey Rock Mountain to the cavern entrance. The caverns are 58°F year-round, making them a cool retreat on a hot summer day. The most awe-inspiring of the limestone rock formations is the glistening Cathedral Room, which appears to be gilded. During peak summer months (June–August), tours depart every half hour; in April, May, and September it's every hour. A gift shop is open from 8 to 4:30. ⊠ *Shasta Caverns Rd. exit off I–5* ☎ *530/238–2341 or 800/795–2283* ⊕ *www.lakeshastacaverns. com* 🎫 *$18 adults, $9 children 4–12* ☽ *June–Aug., daily 9–4 with departures every ½ hr; Apr., May, and Sept., daily 9–3 with departures every hr; Oct.–Mar., daily 10–2 with departures every 2 hrs.*

Shasta Dam is the second-largest concrete dam in the United States (only Grand Coulee in Washington is bigger). At dusk, the sight of Mt. Shasta gleaming above the not-quite-dark water of its namesake lake is magical. The worthwhile visitor center has computerized photographic tours of the dam construction, video presentations, fact sheets, and historic displays. Tours of the dam have resumed, with some restrictions. Call for an update. ⊠ *16349 Shasta Dam Blvd.* ☎ *530/275–4463* ⊕ *www. usbr.gov/mp/ncao* ☽ *Visitor center weekdays 8:30–4:30, weekends 8–5.*

Where to Stay & Eat

$–$$$ ✕ **Tail o' the Whale.** As its name suggests, this restaurant has a nautical theme. You can enjoy a panoramic view of Lake Shasta here while you indulge in spicy Cajun pepper shrimp, charbroiled salmon, seafood fettuccine in a garlic cream sauce, and prime rib with scampi. ✉ *10300 Bridge Bay Rd., Bridge Bay exit off I–5* ☎ *530/275–3021* 🍴 *D, MC, V.*

🔺 **Antlers Campground.** On a level bluff above the Sacramento River arm of Lake Shasta, this campground is surrounded by oak and pine forest. Open year-round, the campground is adjacent to Antlers Boat Ramp, and a nearby marina resort has watercraft rentals, on-water fueling, and a small store. Some campsites are near the lakeshore, but direct access to the water is difficult. Reservations are taken mid-May through early September only. ⛴ *Flush toilets, pit toilets, drinking water, fire pits, picnic tables* ⇥ *59 sites, no hookups* ✉ *Antlers Rd., 1 mi east of I–5* ☎ *530/ 275–8113* 🖨 *530/275–8344* 🌐 *www.reserveusa.com* 💳 *$18–$30* 🍴 *AE, D, MC, V.*

Sports & the Outdoors

FISHING **The Fishin' Hole** (✉ 3844 Shasta Dam Blvd., Shasta Lake City ☎ 530/ 275–4123) is a bait-and-tackle shop a couple of miles from the lake. It sells fishing licenses and provides information about conditions.

HOUSEBOATING Houseboats here come in all sizes except small. As a rule, rentals are outfitted with cooking utensils, dishes, and most of the equipment you'll need—all you supply are the food and the linens. When you rent a houseboat, you will receive a short course in how to maneuver your launch before you set out. You can fish, swim, sunbathe on the flat roof, or sit on the deck and watch the world go by. The shoreline of Lake Shasta is beautifully ragged, with countless inlets; it's not hard to find privacy. Expect to spend a minimum of $350 a day for a craft that sleeps six. A three-day, two-night minimum is customary. Prices are often lower during the off-season (Sept.–May). The **Shasta Cascade Wonderland Association** (✉ 1699 Hwy. 273, Anderson 96007 ☎ 530/365–7500 or 800/ 474–2782 🌐 www.shastacascade.com) provides names of rental companies and prices for Lake Shasta houseboating. **Bridge Bay Resort** (✉ 10300 Bridge Bay Rd., Redding ☎ 800/752–9669) rents houseboats, Jet Skis, fishing boats, and patio boats.

Dunsmuir

❻ *10 mi south of Mt. Shasta on I–5.*

Castle Crags State Park surrounds the town of Dunsmuir, which was named for a 19th-century Scottish coal baron who offered to build a fountain if the town was renamed in his honor. The town's other major attraction is the Railroad Park Resort, where you can spend the night in restored railcars.

★ Named for its 6,000-foot glacier-polished crags, which tower over the Sacramento River, **Castle Crags State Park** offers fishing in Castle Creek, hiking in the backcountry, and a view of Mt. Shasta. The crags draw climbers and hikers from around the world. The 4,350-acre park has 28 mi of hiking trails, including a 2¾-mi access trail to **Castle Crags Wilderness,** part of the **Shasta-Trinity National Forest.** There are excellent trails at lower altitudes, along with picnic areas, restrooms, showers, and campsites. ⊠ *Castle Crags exit off I–5; follow for ¼ mi* ☎ *530/235–2684* ⚑ *$4 per vehicle, day use.*

Where to Stay

👐 **$** 🏨 **Railroad Park Resort.** The antique cabooses here were collected over more than three decades and have been converted into cozy motel rooms in honor of Dunsmuir's railroad legacy. The resort has a vaguely *Orient Express*–style dining room and a lounge fashioned from vintage railcars. The landscaped grounds contain a huge steam engine and a restored water tower. There's also an RV park and campground. ⊠ *100 Railroad Park Rd., 96025* ☎ *530/235–4440 or 800/974–7245* 🖷 *530/235–4470* ⊕ *www.rrpark.com* ⚑ *23 cabooses, 4 cabins* ⚒ *Restaurant, some kitchenettes, refrigerators, cable TV with movies, pool, hot tub, some pets allowed (fee)* ▤ *AE, D, MC, V.*

⚠ **Castle Crags State Park Campground.** Craggy peaks tower above this campground surrounded by tall evergreens. It's a great base for hiking and rock climbing. The site can accommodate RVs up to 27 feet long. Six environmental sites—with pit toilets, and no parking or running water—in relatively undisturbed areas are for tents only. Reservations essential late May–early September ⚒ *Flush toilets, pit toilets, showers, picnic tables* ⚑ *76 sites, no hookups* ⊠ *15 mi south of Mt. Shasta, Castella exit off I–5* ☎ *530/235–2684* ⊕ *www.parks.ca.gov* ⚑ *$14–$17* ▤ *D, MC, V* ☉ *Year-round.*

Mt. Shasta

❼ *34 mi north of Lake Shasta on I–5.*

The crown jewel of the 2.5-million-acre Shasta-Trinity National Forest, Mt. Shasta, a 16-million-year-old dormant volcano, is a mecca for day hikers. It's especially enticing in spring, when fragrant Shasta lilies and other flowers adorn the rocky slopes. The paved road reaches only as far as the timberline; the final 6,000 feet are a tough climb of rubble, ice, and snow (the summit is perpetually ice-packed). Only a hardy few are qualified to make the trek to the top.

The town of Mt. Shasta has real character and some fine restaurants. Lovers of the outdoors and backcountry skiers abound, and they are more than willing to offer advice on the most beautiful spots in the region, which include out-of-the-way swimming holes, dozens of high mountain lakes, and a challenging 18-hole golf course with 360 degrees of spectacular views.

Where to Stay & Eat

$–$$$ ✗ **Michael's Restaurant.** Wood paneling, candlelight, and wildlife prints by local artists create an unpretentious backdrop for favorites like prime rib and filet mignon, and Italian specialties such as stuffed calamari, scallopini, and linguine with pesto. ⊠ *313 N. Mt. Shasta Blvd.* ☎ *530/926–5288* ▤ *AE, D, MC, V* ☉ *Closed Sun. and Mon.*

★ **$–$$$** ✗ **Trinity Café.** Once a small home, this cozy restaurant has a bistro feel and a frequently changing dinner menu inspired by seasonal ingredients. The nightly specials might include a garlicky, vegetarian portobello mushroom with linguine, locally caught salmon or trout, or cabernet-braised lamb with toasted couscous. Chef-owner Bill Truby trained in Napa Valley, and brings an extensive knowledge of wine pairings to the menu. ⊠ *622 N. Mt. Shasta Blvd.* ☎ *530/926–6200* ⊟ *MC, V* ☺ *Closed Sun. and Mon. No lunch.*

$–$$ ✕ **Lily's.** This restaurant in a white-clapboard home, framed by a picket fence and arched trellis, serves everything from steaks and pastas to Mexican and vegetarian dishes. One of the tastiest choices is the Jalisco–marinated rib-eye steak with greens, tomatoes, and Asiago cheese. The *huevos rancheros* (sunny-side-up eggs on tortillas in a mildly spicy sauce) or the scrambled eggs with salsa are delicious choices for brunch. ⊠ *1013 S. Mt. Shasta Blvd.* ☎ *530/926–3372* ⊟ *AE, D, MC, V.*

¢ ✕ **Has Beans.** The aroma of fresh-roasted coffee beans wafts from this small coffee shop, a favorite gathering spot for locals. Pastries, made daily, include muffins and scones, and blackberry fruit bars in season. ⊠ *1011 S. Mt. Shasta Blvd.* ☎ *530/926–3602* ⊟ *MC, V.*

★ $–$$$ ✕⌂ **Mount Shasta Resort.** Private chalets are nestled among tall pine trees along the shore of Lake Siskiyou, all with gas-log fireplaces and full kitchens. The resort's Highland House Restaurant, above the clubhouse of a spectacular 18-hole golf course, has uninterrupted views of Mt. Shasta. Large steaks and herb-crusted calamari are menu highlights. Take the Central Mount Shasta exit west from I–5, then go south on Old Stage Road. ⊠ *1000 Siskiyou Lake Blvd., 96067* ☎ *530/926–3030 or 800/ 958–3363* 🖨 *530/926–0333* ⊕ *www.mountshastaresort.com* ⇥ *65 units* ⚘ *Restaurant, some kitchenettes, some microwaves, some refrigerators, 18-hole golf course, spa, sports bar, meeting room* ⊟ *AE, D, DC, MC, V.*

$ ⌂ **Best Western Tree House Motor Inn.** The clean, standard rooms at this motel less than a mile from downtown Mt. Shasta are decorated with natural-wood furnishings. Some of the nicer ones have vaulted ceilings and mountain views. ⊠ *111 Morgan Way, at I–5 and Lake St., 96067* ☎ *530/926–3101 or 800/545–7164* 🖨 *530/926–3542* ⊕ *www. bestwestern.com* ⇥ *98 rooms, 5 suites* ⚘ *Restaurant, refrigerators, indoor pool, hot tub* ⊟ *AE, D, DC, MC, V* ⊌ *BP.*

⚠ **Lake Siskiyou Camp Resort.** On the west side of Lake Siskiyou, the sites on this 250-acre resort sit beneath tall pine trees that filter the light. Group sites, evening movies, and power boat and kayak rentals make it a great spot for families; there's also a marina, a free boat-launch ramp, and a fishing dock. ⚘ *Flush toilets, full hookups, showers, general store, swimming (lake)* ⇥ *200 tent sites, 150 RV sites* ⊠ *4239 W. A. Barr Rd., 3 mi southwest of city of Mt. Shasta* ☎ *530/926–2618 or 888/ 926–2618* ⊕ *www.lakesis.com* 🖹 *$18–$25* ⚘ *Reservations essential* ⊟ *D, MC, V* ☺ *Apr.–Oct.*

Sports & the Outdoors

GOLF At 6,100 yards, the **Mount Shasta Resort** golf course isn't long, but it's beautiful and challenging, with narrow, tree-lined fairways and several lakes and other waterways. Greens fees range from $35 to $50, depending on the day of the week and the season; carts rent for another $12–$18, and clubs can be rented, too. ⊠ *1000 Siskiyou Lake Blvd.* ☎ *530/ 926–3052* ⊕ *www.mountshastaresort.com/golfing.htm.*

THE PACIFIC FLYWAY

You don't need wings to catch the Pacific Flyway. All it takes is a car, a good map, and high-powered binoculars to follow the flight path of more than 250 bird species that migrate through far northern California and stop at wildlife refuges on their way.

Eagles and hawks make their visits in winter; more than a million waterfowl pass through in fall. Returning migrants such as pelicans, cranes, and songbirds like the marsh wren and ruby-crowned kinglet arrive in March, just in time to herald the spring; goslings, ducklings, and other newly-hatched waterfowl paddle through the wetlands in summer.

February and March are especially good viewing times, when people are scarce but wildlife thrives in the cold climate. Many birds enter their breeding season during these months, and you can hear their unusual mating calls and witness aerial ballets as vividly plumed males pursue females.

One of the most impressive Pacific Flyway stopovers is on the California-Oregon border: the 46,900-acre Lower Klamath National Wildlife Refuge, established by President Theodore Roosevelt in 1908 as the country's first waterfowl refuge. The area has the largest winter concentration of bald eagles in the lower 48 states. For $3 you can take a 10-mi auto tour through parts of the refuge, where the eagles feed from December through mid-March. (From I–5 north of Mt. Shasta, take the Highway 97 turnoff to Highway 161, and follow the signs.) Even if you're not already an avid bird-watcher, you likely will be after a visit to this special place.

HIKING The **Forest Service Ranger Station** (☎ 530/926–4511 or 530/926–9613) keeps tabs on trail conditions and gives avalanche reports.

MOUNTAIN CLIMBING **Fifth Season Mountaineering Shop** (✉ 300 N. Mt. Shasta Blvd. ☎ 530/926–3606 or 530/926–5555) rents skiing and climbing equipment and operates a recorded 24-hour climber-skier report. **Shasta Mountain Guides** (☎ 530/926–3117 ⊕ www.shastaguides.com) leads hiking, climbing, and ski-touring groups to the summit of Mt. Shasta.

SKIING On the southeast flank of Mt. Shasta, **Mt. Shasta Board & Ski Park** has three lifts on 425 skiable acres. It's a great place for novices because three-quarters of the trails are for beginning or intermediate skiers. The area's vertical drop is 1,390 feet, with a top elevation of 6,600 feet. The longest of the 31 trails is 1¾ mi. A package for beginners, available through the ski school, includes a lift ticket, ski rental, and a lesson. The school also runs ski and snowboard programs for children. There's night skiing for those who want to see the moon rise as they schuss. The base lodge has a simple café, a ski shop, and a ski–snowboard rental shop. The park's Cross-Country Ski and Snowshoe Center, with 18 mi of trails, is on the same road. ✉ Hwy. 89 exit east from I–5, south of Mt. Shasta ☎ 530/926–8610 or 800/754–7427 ⊕ www.skipark.com ☺ Sun.–Tues. 9–4; Wed.–Sat. 9 AM–10 PM.

THE BACKCOUNTRY
INCLUDING LASSEN VOLCANIC NATIONAL PARK

East of I–5, the far north's main corridor, dozens of scenic two-lane roads crisscross the wilderness, leading to dramatic mountain peaks and fascinating natural wonders. Small towns settled in the second half of the 19th century seem frozen in time, except that they are well equipped with tourist amenities.

McArthur–Burney Falls Memorial State Park

★ ☾ ⌐ **❽** *Hwy. 89, 52 mi southeast of Mt. Shasta and 41 mi north of Lassen Volcanic National Park.*

Just inside the park's southern boundary, Burney Creek wells up from the ground and divides into two falls that cascade over a 129-foot cliff into a pool below. Countless ribbonlike streams pour from hidden moss-covered crevices; resident bald eagles are frequently seen soaring overhead. You can walk a self-guided nature trail that descends to the foot of the falls, which Theodore Roosevelt—according to legend—called "the eighth wonder of the world." You can also swim at Lake Britton; lounge on the beach; rent motorboats, paddleboats, and canoes; or relax at one of the camp sites or picnic areas. The camp store is open from early May to the end of October. ✉ *24898 Hwy. 89, Burney 96013* ☎ *530/335–2777* 💲 *$6 per vehicle for day use.*

Where to Stay

⚠ **McArthur–Burney Falls Memorial State Park.** Campsites here in the evergreen forests abut Burney Falls, several springs, a half dozen hiking trails, and Lake Britton. Boating and fishing are popular pursuits. Some sites can accommodate 35-foot RVs. Reservations are essential from Memorial Day to Labor Day. ♿ *Flush toilets, dump station, showers, picnic tables, general store, swimming (lake)* ⌁ *98 RV sites, no hookups, 24 tent sites* ✉ *McArthur–Burney Falls Memorial State Park, Hwy. 89* ☎ *530/335–2777* ⊕ *www.parks.ca.gov* 💲 *$15–$20* ▭ *D, MC, V* ☼ *Year-round.*

Alturas

❾ *86 mi northeast of McArthur–Burney Falls Memorial State Park on Hwy. 299.*

Alturas is the county seat and largest town in northeastern California's Modoc County. The Dorris family arrived in the area in 1874, built Dorris Bridge over the Pit River, and later opened a small wayside stop for travelers. Today the Alturas area is a land of few people but much rugged natural beauty. Travelers come to see eagles and other wildlife, the Modoc National Forest, and active geothermal areas.

Modoc County Museum exhibits—which include Native American artifacts, firearms, and a steam engine—explore the development of the area from the 15th century through World War II. ✉ *600 S. Main St.* ☎ *530/233–6328* 💲 *Donations accepted* ☼ *May–Oct., Tues.–Sat. 10–4.*

Modoc National Forest encompasses 1.6 million acres and protects 300 species of wildlife, including Rocky Mountain elk, wild horses, mule deer, and pronghorn antelope. In spring and fall, watch for migratory waterfowl as they make their way along the Pacific Flyway above the forest. Hiking trails lead to Petroglyph Point, one of the largest panels of rock art in the United States. ⊠ *800 W. 12th St.* ☎ *530/233–5811* 🖶 *530/233–8709* ⊕ *www.fs.fed.us/r5/modoc.*

Established to protect migratory waterfowl, the 6,280-acre **Modoc National Wildlife Refuge** gives refuge to Canada geese, Sand Hill cranes, mallards, teal, wigeon, pintail, white pelicans, cormorants, and snowy egrets. The refuge is open for hiking, bird-watching, and photography, but one area is set aside for hunters. Regulations vary according to season. ⊠ *1½ mi south of Alturas on Hwy. 395* ☎ *530/233–3572* 🎫 *Free* ⊙ *Daily dawn–dusk.*

off the
beaten
path

LAVA BEDS NATIONAL MONUMENT – Thousands of years of volcanic activity created this rugged landscape, which is distinguished by cinder cones, lava flows, spatter cones, pit craters, and more than 400 underground lava tube caves. During the Modoc War (1872–73), Modoc Indians under the leadership of their chief "Captain Jack" Kientopoos took refuge in a natural lava fortress now known as Captain Jack's Stronghold. They managed to hold off U.S. army forces, which outnumbered them 20 to 1, for five months. When exploring this area, be sure to wear hard-soled boots; other safety gear like lights and hard hats are available for rent and sale at the Indian Well Visitor Center, at the park's south end. This is where summer activities like guided walks, cave tours, and campfire programs depart from. ⊠ *Forest Service Rte. 10, 72 mi northwest of Alturas (Hwy. 299 west from Alturas to Hwy. 139, northwest to Forest Service Rte. 97, to Forest Service Rte. 10)* ☎ *530/667–2282* ⊕ *www. nps.gov/labe* 🎫 *$10 per vehicle; $5 on foot, bicycle, or motorcycle* ⊙ *Visitor center late May–early Sept., daily 8–6; early Sept.–late May, daily 8–5.*

Where to Stay & Eat

$–$$　✕ **Brass Rail.** This authentic Basque restaurant offers hearty dinners at fixed prices that include wine, homemade bread, soup, salad, side dishes, coffee, and ice cream. Steak, lamb chops, fried chicken, shrimp and scallops are among the best entrée selections. A full bar and lounge adjoin the dining area. ⊠ *395 Lakeview Hwy.* ☎ *530/233–2906* 🍴 *MC, V* ⊙ *Closed Mon.*

¢　🏨 **Best Western Trailside Inn.** The only hotel in town with a swimming pool, this property is just 2 mi north of Rachael Dorris Park, 3 mi south of Devils Garden, and 5 mi north of Modoc Wildlife Reserve. It's also five blocks south of the Modoc County Museum. A fax machine is available in the lobby, and each room has a coffeemaker. ⊠ *343 N. Main St., 96101* ☎ *530/233–4111* 🖶 *530/233–3180* 🛏 *38 rooms* ⚴ *Some kitchenettes, some microwaves, cable TV, pool, Internet, some pets allowed* 🍴 *AE, DC, MC, V.*

¢ ⊞ **Hacienda.** In the heart of farm country, this motel is marked with a large 19th-century wagon wheel out front. The spacious, spotless rooms have bright bedspreads and ample natural light from large windows. A gas station, fast-food restaurants, and a supermarket are all within five blocks. ⊠ *201 E. 12th St., 96101* ☎ *530/233–3459* ⟿ *20 rooms* ⟳ *Some kitchenettes, some microwaves, refrigerators, cable TV, some pets allowed, no-smoking rooms* ⊟ *AE, D, DC, MC, V.*

⚠ **Medicine Lake Campground.** One of several small campgrounds on the shores of Medicine Lake, this spot lies at 6,700 feet above sea level, near the western border of Modoc National Forest. Sites can accommodate vehicles up to 22 feet. The lake, 14 mi south of Lava Beds National Monument, is a popular vacation spot with fishing, boating, and waterskiing. ⟳ *Pit toilets, drinking water, fire pits, picnic tables, swimming (lake)* ⟿ *22 sites, no hookups* ⊠ *Off Forest Service Rd. 44N38, Hwy. 139 to County Rd. 97 west to Forest Service Rd. 44N38, follow signs* ☎ *530/667–2246* ⊕ *www.r5.fs.fed.us/modoc* ▢ *$7* ⟋ *Reservations not accepted* ⊟ *No credit cards* ☾ *July–Oct.*

Susanville

❿ *104 mi south of Alturas via Rte. 395; 65 mi east of Lassen Volcanic National Park via Hwy. 36.*

Susanville wears its history on its walls, telling the tale of its rich history through murals painted on buildings in the historic uptown area. Established as a trading post in 1854, it is the second-oldest town in the western Great Basin. You can take a self-guided tour around the original buildings, and stop for a bite at one of the restaurants now housed within them; or, if you'd rather work up a sweat, you can hit the Bizz Johnson Trail and Eagle Lake recreation areas just outside of town.

Bizz Johnson Trail follows a defunct line of the Southern Pacific Railroad for 25 mi. Known to locals as the Bizz, the trail is open for hikers, walkers, mountain bikers, and horseback riders. It follows the Susan River through a scenic landscape of canyons, bridges, and forests abundant with wildlife. ⊠ *Trailhead: 601 Richmond Rd.* ☎ *530/257–0456* ⊕ *www.ca.blm.gov/eaglelake/bizztrail.html* ▢ *Free.*

Anglers travel great distances to fish the waters of **Eagle Lake,** California's second largest, which is surrounded by high desert to the north and alpine forests to the south. The Eagle Lake trout is prized for its size and fighting ability. The lake is also popular for picnicking, hiking, boating, waterskiing and windsurfing, and bird-watching—ospreys, pelicans, western grebes, and many other waterfowl visit the lake. On land you might see mule deer, small mammals, and even pronghorn antelope. ⊠ *20 mi north of Susanville on Eagle Lake Rd.* ☎ *530/257–0456 for Eagle Lake Recreation Area, 530/825–3454 for Eagle Lake Marina* ⊕ *www.reserveusa.com.*

Where to Stay & Eat

★ **$–$$$** ✕ **St. Francis Champion Steakhouse.** It's all about meat at this Old West–theme restaurant, which occupies the ground floor of the historic St. Francis Hotel. Those who succeed in finishing the "grand champion"

64-ounce steak dinner within an hour get their meal on the house; otherwise, it'll cost you $54.95. ⊠ *830 Main St.* ☎ *530/257–4820* ⊟ *AE, MC, V* ☉ *Closed Sun.*

¢–$$ ✕ **Josefina's.** Popular with the locals, Josefina's makes its own salsas and tamales. The interior's Aztec accents are a perfect accompaniment to the menu's traditional Mexican fare of *chile rellenos* (mild, batter-fried chile peppers stuffed with cheese or a cheese-meat mixture), enchiladas, tacos, and fajitas. ⊠ *1960 Main St.* ☎ *530/257–9262* ⊟ *MC, V.*

★ ¢ ✕ **Grand Cafe.** Walking into this downtown coffee shop, which has been owned and operated by the same family since the 1920s, is like stepping back in time. At the old-fashioned counter, the swiveling seats have hat clips on the back; the booths have their own nickel jukeboxes. Wooden refrigerators are still used here, and if the homemade chili and fruit cobblers are any indication, they work just fine. ⊠ *730 Main St.* ☎ *530/257–4713* ⊟ *No credit cards* ☉ *Closed Sun. No dinner.*

¢–$ ⊡ **Best Western Trailside Inn.** This large, modern, business-friendly motel is in the heart of Susanville but only a quick drive from the area's recreational sites. Some rooms have wet bars, and you can enjoy homestyle cooking next door at the Black Bear Diner. ⊠ *2785 Main St., 96130* ☎ *530/257–4123* ⧉ *530/257–2665* ⊕ *www.bestwesterncalifornia.com* ⊷ *85 rooms* ♨ *In-room data ports, some refrigerators, cable TV, pool, meeting room, no-smoking rooms* ⊟ *AE, D, MC, V* ⦿ *CP.*

¢ ⊡ **High Country Inn.** Rooms are spacious in this two-story, colonial-style motel on the east edge of town. Complimentary continental breakfast is provided; more extensive dining is available next door at Country Chicken, a local outlet of the chain. All rooms have hair dryers and coffeepots; business suites have in-room data ports. ⊠ *3015 Riverside Dr., 96130* ☎ *530/257–3450* ⧉ *530/257–2460* ⊷ *66 rooms* ♨ *Some in-room data ports, microwaves, refrigerators, cable TV with movies, pool, outdoor hot tub; no smoking* ⊟ *AE, D, DC, MC, V* ⦿ *CP.*

△ **Eagle Campground.** One of 11 campgrounds surrounding Eagle Lake, this site is nestled among pine trees has a boat ramp. ♨ *Flush toilets, dump station, drinking water, showers, picnic tables* ⊷ *35 tent/RV sites, no hookups, 14 tent-only sites* ⊠ *County Rd. A-1, 14 mi north of Hwy. 36* ☎ *530/825–3212* ⊕ *www.reserveusa.com* ▨ *$15* ⊴ *Reservations essential* ⊟ *AE, D, MC, V* ☉ *Late May–mid-Oct.*

Lassen Volcanic National Park

⓫ *45 mi east of Redding on Hwy. 44; 48 mi east of Red Bluff on Hwy. 36.*

Fodor's Choice
★

Lassen Volcanic became a national park in 1916 because of its significance as a volcanic landscape. Several volcanoes—the largest of which is now Lassen Peak—have been active in the area for roughly 600,000 years, and have created an environment full of volcanic wonders including steam vents, mudpots, boiling pools, soaring peaks, and painted dunes. The Lassen Park Road (the continuation of Highway 89 within the park) provides access to these sights, and although it's closed to cars in winter, it's sometimes open to intrepid cross-country skiers and snowshoers. Maps and road guides are available at the Loomis Museum, and at the park headquarters, park entrance, and ranger stations. Also available is the park newspaper, *Peak Experiences,* which gives details on park attractions and facilities. *Park Headquarters* ☒ *38050 Hwy. 36E, Mineral 96063* ☎ *530/595–4444* ⊕ *www.nps.gov/lavo* ☒ *$10 per vehicle, $5 on foot or bicycle* ☉ *Park headquarters weekdays 8–4:30.*

In 1914 the 10,457-foot Lassen Peak came to life, in the first of 300 eruptions to occur over the next seven years. Molten rock overflowed the crater, and the mountain emitted clouds of smoke and hailstorms of rocks and volcanic cinders. Proof of the volcanic landscape's volatility becomes evident shortly after you enter the park at the **Sulphur Works Thermal Area.** Boardwalks take you over bubbling mud and boiling springs and through sulfur-emitting steam vents. ☒ *Lassen Park Rd., south end of park.*

The **Lassen Peak Hike** winds 2½ mi to the mountaintop. It's a tough climb—2,000 feet uphill on a steady, steep grade—but the reward is a spectacular view. At the peak you can see into the rim and view the entire park (and much farther, on a clear day). Be sure to bring sunscreen and water. ☒ *Off Lassen Park Rd., 7 mi north of southwest entrance.*

Along **Bumpass Hell Trail,** a scenic 3-mi round-trip hike to the park's most interesting thermal-spring area, you can view boiling springs, steam vents, and mud pots up close. You'll take a gradual climb of 500 feet to the highest point before you descend 250 feet toward the hissing steam of Bumpass Hell. Near the thermal areas it's important to stay on trails and boardwalks; what appears to be firm ground may be only a thin crust over scalding mud. ☒ *Off Lassen Park Rd., 6 mi north of southwest entrance.*

Hot Rock, a 400-ton boulder, tumbled down from the summit during an enormous volcanic surge on May 19, 1915. It was still hot to the touch when locals discovered it nearly two days later. Although cool now, it's still an impressive sight. ☒ *Lassen Park Rd., north end of park.*

Chaos Jumbles was created 300 years ago when an avalanche from the Chaos Crags lava domes spread hundreds of thousands of rocks, many of them 2–3 feet in diameter, over a couple of square miles. ☒ *Lassen Park Rd., north end of park.*

Where to Stay & Eat

¢ ✕⊡ **Lassen Mineral Lodge.** Rooms at this motel-style property, which is located at 5,000 feet, should be reserved as far ahead as possible. You can rent cross-country skis and snowshoes at the lodge's ski shop. There's also a general store. ☒ *Hwy. 36 E, Mineral 96063* ☎ *530/595–4422* ⊕ *www.minerallodge.com* ⤳ *20 rooms* ♭ *Restaurant, bar; no a/c, no room phones, no room TVs* ☰ *AE, D, MC, V.*

⚠ **Manzanita Lake Campground.** The largest of Lassen Volcanic National Park's eight campgrounds is near the northern entrance. It can accommodate vehicles up to 35 feet. A trail near the campground leads east to a crater that now holds Crags Lake. Summer reservations for group campgrounds can be made up to seven months in advance. There is no running water from the end of September until snow closes the campground. ♭ *Flush toilets, dump station, drinking water, showers,*

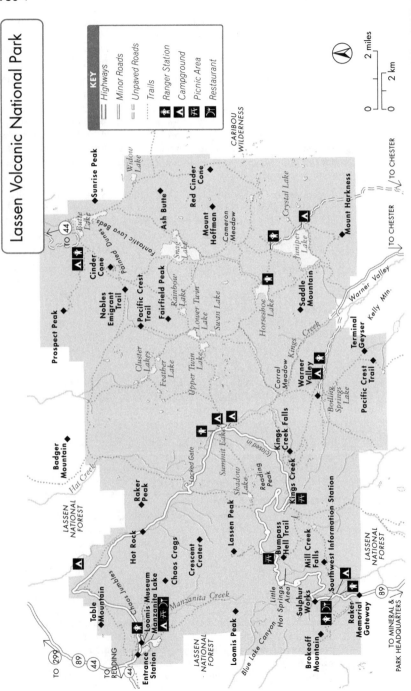

Lassen Volcanic National Park

KEY

▬▬	Highways
—	Minor Roads
==	Unpaved Roads
······	Trails
⛑	Ranger Station
◀	Campground
⛺	Picnic Area
🍴	Restaurant

0 ___ 2 miles
0 ___ 2 km

CARIBOU WILDERNESS

TO CHESTER

Widow Lake

Sunrise Peak

Red Cinder Cone

Ash Butte

Mount Hoffman

Crystal Lake

Mount Harkness

Butte Lake

Cinder Cone

Fantastic Lava Beds

Painted Dunes

Cameron Meadow

Juniper Lake

Prospect Peak

Nobles Emigrant Trail

Pacific Crest Trail

Fairfield Peak

Rainbow Lake

Snag Lake

Lower Twin Lake

Swan Lake

Horseshoe Lake

Saddle Mountain

Warner Valley

TO CHESTER

Cluster Lakes

Feather Lake

Upper Twin Lake

Kings Creek

Corral Meadow

Warner Valley

Boiling Springs Lake

Kelly Mtn.

Terminal Geyser

Pacific Crest Trail

Badger Mountain

Hat Creek

LASSEN NATIONAL FOREST

Raker Peak

Locked Gate

Summit Lake

Shadow Lake

Reading Peak

Kings Creek Falls

Kings Creek

(closed in)

Hot Rock

Lassen Peak

Crescent Crater

Chaos Crags

Bumpass Hell Trail

Mill Creek Falls

Southwest Information Station

LASSEN NATIONAL FOREST

Table Mountain

Chaos Jumbles

Loomis Museum
Manzanita Lake

Manzanita Creek

Little Hot Springs Area

Sulphur Works

Raker Memorial Gateway

TO REDDING

TO 299
89
44

Entrance Station

Loomis Peak

LASSEN NATIONAL FOREST

Blue Lake Canyon

Brokeoff Mountain

89

TO MINERAL &
PARK HEADQUARTERS

TO 44

fire pits, picnic tables ⤴ *148 tent/RV sites, no hookups, 31 tent sites* ⊠ *Off Lassen Park Rd., 2 mi east of junction of Hwys. 44 and 89* ☎ *530/595–4444* ⊕ *www.nps.gov/lavo/pphtml/camping.html* ☒ *$16* ⊟ *D, MC, V* ⊙ *June–late Oct., depending on snowfall.*

Chester

⑫ *36 mi west of Susanville on Hwy 36.*

The population of this small town on Lake Almanor swells from 2,500 to nearly 5,000 in summer as tourists come to visit. It serves as a gateway to Lassen Volcanic National Park.

Lake Almanor's 52 mi of shoreline lie in the shadow of Mt. Lassen, and are popular with campers, swimmers, waterskiers, and anglers. At an elevation of 4,500 feet, the lake warms to above 70°F for about eight weeks in summer. Information is available at the Almanor Ranger District headquarters. ⊠ *900 W. Hwy. 36* ☎ *530/258–2141* ⊙ *Open mid-May–mid-Oct.*

Lassen Scenic Byway is a 172-mi drive through the forested terrain, volcanic peaks, geothermal springs, and lava fields of Lassen National Forest and Lassen National Park. Along the way you'll pass through five rural communities where refreshments and basic services are available. Park information is available at Almanor Ranger District headquarters. ⊠ *900 W. Hwy. 36* ☎ *530/258–2141* ☒ *$10 per vehicle within Lassen National Park* ⊙ *Partially inaccessible in winter; call for road conditions.*

Where to Stay & Eat

$$–$$$ ✕ **Peninsula Station Bar and Grill.** Hungry outdoor recreationists throng the bar and patio dining area of this popular spot, to enjoy huge portions of steak, prime rib, and locally caught seafood. ⊠ *401 Peninsula Dr., on Lake Almanor Peninsula* ☎ *530/596–3538* ⊙ *Closed Mon. No lunch.* ⊟ *AE, DC, MC, V.*

★ **$–$$** ✕ **Benassi's.** Small and nondescript from the outside but homey inside, this restaurant and full bar on the north end of town specializes in northern Italian food. Everything served is homemade, including sauces, ravioli, and tortellini. Linguine with shrimp, and roasted chicken with rosemary potatoes are favorites, along with a prime rib dinner, which is served Friday and Saturday nights only. ⊠ *159 Main St.* ☎ *530/258–2600* ⊙ *Closed Mon. Oct.–Apr. No dinner Sun.* ⊟ *MC, V.*

¢–$$ ✕ **Cynthia's.** Bordering a brook near the center of town, Cynthia's serves California home-style cuisine with a French touch. Specialties include light meat dishes, pastas, and salads, all made with fresh seasonal ingredients. Its bakery is known for rustic pizzas and artisan breads. The bar offers wines and microbrews. Hours change frequently, so call to check. ⊠ *278 Main St.* ☎ *530/258–1966* ⊙ *Closed weekends. No dinner Tues.–Thurs. early Sept.–late May* ⊟ *MC, V.*

¢–$ ✕ **Kopper Kettle Cafe.** Locals return again and again to this tidy restaurant that serves savory home-cooked lunch and dinner, and breakfast whenever you've got a hankering for eggs with biscuits and gravy or other morning fare. A junior–senior menu, and beer and wine are avail-

able. The patio is open in summer. ⊠ *243 Main St.* ☎ *530/258–2698*
☰ *AE, D, MC, V* ☉ *No dinner Nov.–Mar.*

★ ¢–$$ ⊡ **Bidwell House.** This 1901 ranch house sits on 2 acres of cottonwood-studded lawns and gardens, and has views of Lake Almanor and Mt. Lassen. Chairs and swings make the front porch inviting, and there are plenty of puzzles and games in the sunroom. Some rooms have wood-burning stoves, claw-foot or Jacuzzi tubs, hardwood floors, and antiques. A separate cottage, which sleeps six, has a kitchen. The inn's special-ties—omelets and blueberry-walnut pancakes—are the stars of the daily full breakfast. ⊠ *1 Main St., 96020* ☎ *530/258–3338* ⊕ *www. bidwellhouse.com* ◁ *14 rooms, 2 with shared bath* ⚬ *Cable TV; no a/c, no room phones, no smoking* ☰ *MC, V* ⃝ *BP.*

¢ ⊡ **Chester Manor Motel.** Within easy walking distance of restaurants and stores, this remodeled 1950s-era one-story motel is clean and comfort-able. Six of the 18 rooms are two-bedroom suites; all rooms have hair dryers. ⊠ *306 Main St., 96020* ☎ *530/258–2441 or 888/571–4885* ⊞ *530/258–3523* ◁ *12 rooms, 6 suites* ⚬ *Microwaves, refrigerators, cable TV with movies, Internet; no a/c, no smoking* ☰ *AE, MC, V.*

Quincy

⑬ *67 mi southwest of Susanville via Hwys. 36 and 89.*

A center for mining and logging in the 1850s, Quincy is nestled against the western slope of the Sierra Nevada. The county seat and largest com-munity in Plumas County, the town is rich in historic buildings that have been the focus of preservation and restoration efforts. The four-story courthouse on Main Street, one of several stops on a self-guided tour, was built in 1921 with marble posts and staircases. The arts are thriv-ing in Quincy, too: catch one of the plays or bluegrass performances at the Town Hall Theatre.

The main recreational attraction in central Plumas County, **Bucks Lake Recreation Area** is located 17 mi southwest of Quincy at 5,200 feet. Dur-ing warm months the lake's 17-mi shoreline, two marinas, and eight camp-grounds attract anglers and water-sports enthusiasts. Trails through the tall pines beckon hikers and horseback riders. In winter, much of the area remains open for snowmobiling and cross-country skiing. ⊠ *Bucks Lake Rd.* ☎ *530/283–5465 or 800/326–2247* ⊕ *www.plumascounty.org.*

Plumas County is known for its wide-open spaces, and the 1.2-million-acre **Plumas National Forest,** with its high alpine lakes and crystal-clear woodland streams, is a beautiful example. Hundreds of campsites are maintained in the forest, and picnic areas and hiking trails abound. You can enter the forest from numerous sites along Highways 70 and 89. ⊠ *159 Lawrence St.* ☎ *530/283–2050* ⊞ *530/283–4156* ⊕ *www.r5. fs.fed.us/plumas* ☉ *U.S. Forest Service office weekdays 8–4:30.*

The cultural, home arts, and industrial history displays at the **Plumas County Museum** contain artifacts dating to the 1850s. Highlights include collections of Maidu Indian basketry, pioneer weapons, and rooms de-picting life in the early days of Plumas County. There's a blacksmith shop and gold-mining cabin, equipment from the early days of logging, a restored buggy, and railroad and mining exhibits. ⊠ *500 Jackson St.* ☎ *530/283–6320* 🖷 *530/283–6081* 💷 *$2* ◷ *Weekdays 8–5, year-round; call ahead for weekends.*

Where to Stay & Eat

¢–$$ ✕ **Sweet Lorraine's Good Food Good Feelings.** You can choose to eat upstairs by candlelight or in the more casual downstairs bar and dining area. Sweet Lorraine's serves hearty fare such as Cajun meat loaf with roasted-garlic mashed potatoes, as well as lighter items; it also has a great assortment of microbrews and wine. Reservations are recommended. ⊠ *384 Main St.* ☎ *530/283–5300* ▤ *MC, V* ◷ *Lunch Mon.–Fri. 11:30–2; dinner Mon.–Sat. 5–9. Closed Sun.*

$–$$ 🏠 **Feather Bed.** The quaint romanticism of an 1893 Queen Anne Victorian plus proximity to Quincy's town center are the draws here. Furnishings are antique, and the views of the Sierra Nevada spectacular. The five rooms in the main house have claw-foot tubs. Two private guest cottages have fireplaces and outside decks. Classical music plays softly in the morning, and breakfast begins with smoothies made with homegrown blackberries or raspberries. Fresh fruit or baked fruit crunch and home-baked bread or muffins accompany hot entrées. ⊠ *542 Jackson St., 95971* ☎ *530/ 283–0102 or 800/696–8624* ⊕ *www.featherbed-inn.com* 🛏 *5 rooms, 2 cottages* ⚬ *Cable TV in some rooms, bicycles, airport shuttle* ▤ *AE, D, DC, MC, V* ⎍⧉ *BP.*

THE FAR NORTH A TO Z

To research prices, get advice from other travelers, and book travel arrangements, visit ⊕ www.fodors.com.

AIRPORTS & TRANSFERS

Chico Municipal Airport and Redding Municipal Airport are served by United Express. Horizon Air also uses the airport in Redding. *See* Air Travel *in* Smart Travel Tips A to Z *for airline phone numbers.* There is no shuttle service from either airport, but taxis can be ordered. The approximate cost from the airport to downtown Redding is $20–$25, and it's $12–$15 from the Chico airport to downtown.

🛩 **Chico Municipal Airport** ⊠ 150 Airpark Blvd., off Cohasset Rd. ☎ 530/879–3910. **Redding Municipal Airport** ⊠ Airport Rd. ☎ 530/224–4320. **Taxi Service, Chico** ☎ 530/893–4444 or 530/342-2929. **Taxi Service, Redding** ☎ 530/246-0577 or 530/ 222-1234.

BUS TRAVEL

Greyhound buses travel I–5, serving Chico, Red Bluff, Redding, Dunsmuir, and Mt. Shasta. Butte County Transit serves Chico, Oroville, and elsewhere. Chico Area Transit System, which is affiliated with Butte County Transit, provides bus service within Chico. The vehicles of the Redding Area Bus Authority operate daily except Sunday within Redding, Anderson, and Shasta Lake. STAGE buses serve Siskiyou County, on weekdays only, from Yreka to Dunsmuir, stopping in Mt. Shasta and other towns, and provide service in Scott Valley, Happy Camp, Hornbrook, and the Klamath River area. Lassen Rural Bus serves the Susanville, northeast Lake Almanor, and south Lassen County areas, running weekdays except holidays. Lassen Rural Bus connects with Plumas County Transit, which serves the Quincy area, and with Modoc County Sage Stage, which serves the Alturas area.

🚊 **Butte County Transit/Chico Area Transit System** ☎ 530/342-0221 ⊕ www.bcag. org/transit.htm. **Greyhound** ☎ 800/229-9424 ⊕ www.greyhound.com. **Lassen Rural Bus** ☎ 530/252-7433. **Modoc County Sage Stage** ☎ 530/233-3883. **Plumas County Transit** ☎ 530/283-2538 ⊕ www.aworkforce.org/ptransit. **Redding Area Bus Authority** ☎ 530/241-2877 ⊕ www.ci.redding.ca.us. **STAGE** ☎ 530/842-8295 ⊕ www. co.siskiyou.ca.us.

CAMPING

Some campgrounds in California's far north get booked as much as a year in advance for the Fourth of July. Although that's not the norm, it's still a good idea to make summer reservations 2–3 months in advance. You can reserve a site at many of the region's campgrounds through ReserveAmerica and ReserveUSA.

🚊 Campground Reservations **ReserveAmerica** ☎ 877/444-6777 ⊕ www. reserveamerica.com. **ReserveUSA** ☎ 800/444-7275 ⊕ www.reserveusa.com.

CAR RENTAL

Avis and Hertz serve Redding Municipal Airport. Budget and Hertz serve Chico Municipal Airport. Enterprise has branches in Chico, Red Bluff and Redding. *See* Car Rental *in* Smart Travel Tips A to Z *for national rental agency phone numbers.*

CAR TRAVEL

An automobile is virtually essential for touring the far north unless you arrive by bus, plane, or train and plan to stay put in one town or resort. I–5, an excellent four-lane divided highway, runs up the center of California through Red Bluff and Redding and continues north to Oregon. The other main roads in the area are good two-lane highways that are, with few exceptions, open year-round. Chico is east of I–5 on Highway 32. Lassen Volcanic National Park can be reached by Highway 36 from Red Bluff or (except in winter) Highway 44 from Redding. Highway 299 connects Redding and Alturas. Highway 139 leads from Susanville to Lava Beds National Monument. Highway 89 will take you from Mt. Shasta to Quincy. Highway 36 links Chester and Susanville. If you are traveling through the far north in winter, always carry snow chains in your vehicle. For information on the condition of roads in northern California, call the Caltrans Highway Information Network's voice-activated system. At the prompt say the route number in which you are interested, and you'll hear a recorded message about current conditions.

🚊 **Caltrans Highway Information Network** ☎ 800/427-7623.

EMERGENCIES

In an emergency dial 911.

🚊 Hospitals **Enloe Medical Center** ✉ 1531 Esplanade, Chico ☎ 530/891-7300. **Banner-Lassen Medical Center** ✉ 1800 Spring Ridge Dr., Susanville ☎ 530/252-2000. **Mercy Medical Center** ✉ 2175 Rosaline Ave., Redding ☎ 530/225-6000.

TRAIN TRAVEL

Amtrak has stations in Chico, Redding, and Dunsmuir and operates buses that connect to Greyhound service through Redding, Red Bluff, and Chico. **Amtrak** ⊠ W. 5th and Orange Sts., Chico ⊠ 1620 Yuba St., Redding ⊠ 5750 Sacramento Ave., Dunsmuir ☎ 800/872-7245 ⊕ www.amtrakcalifornia.com.

VISITOR INFORMATION

Alturas Chamber of Commerce ⊠ 522 S. Main St., Alturas 96101 ☎ 530/233-4434 ⊕ www.alturaschamber.org. **Chester-Lake Almanor Chamber of Commerce** ⊠ 529 Main St., Chester 96020 ☎ 530/258-2426 or 800/350-4838 ⊕ www.chester-lakealmanor. com. **Chico Chamber of Commerce** ⊠ 300 Salem St., 95928 ☎ 530/891-5556 or 800/ 852-8570 ⊕ www.chicochamber.com. **Lassen County Chamber of Commerce** ⊠ 84 N. Lassen St., Susanville 96130 ☎ 530/257-4323 ⊕ lassencountychamber.org. **Plumas County Visitors Bureau** ⊠ Hwy. 70, ½ mi west of downtown, Quincy 95971 ☎ 530/ 283-6345 or 800/326-2247 ⊕ www.plumascounty.org. **Quincy Chamber of Commerce** ⊠ 464 Main St., Quincy 95971 ☎ 530/283-0188 ⊕ www.psln.com/qchamber. **Red Bluff-Tehama County Chamber of Commerce** ⊠ 100 Main St., Red Bluff 96080 ☎ 530/527-6220 or 800/655-6225 ⊞ 530/527-2908 ⊕ www. redbluffchamberofcommerce.com. **Shasta Cascade Wonderland Association** ⊠ 1699 Hwy. 273, Anderson 96007 ☎ 530/365-7500 or 800/474-2782 ⊕ www.shastacascade. org. **Siskiyou County Visitors Bureau** ⊠ 508 Chestnut St., Mt. Shasta 96067 ☎ 530/ 926-3850 or 877/747-5496 ⊞ 530/926-3680 ⊕ www.visitsiskiyou.org.

CALIFORNIA AT A GLANCE

Fast Facts

Nickname: The Golden State
Capital: Sacramento
Motto: Eureka! ("I have found it!")
State song: *I Love You, California*
State bird: Valley quail
State flower: Golden poppy
State tree: California redwood
Administrative divisions: 58 counties
Entered the Union: September 9, 1850 (the 31st state)
Population: 34.3 million
Population density: 216 people per square mi
Median age: 33.6

Infant mortality rate: 5.4 deaths per 1,000 births
Literacy: 24% have trouble with basic reading; 41% spoke a language other than English at home, usually Spanish. 47% do not speak English "very well."
Ethnic groups: White 45%; Latino 34%; Asian 12%; black 6%; other 3%
Religion: Unaffiliated 54%; Catholic 30%; Protestant 10%; Jewish 3%; other 2%; Muslim 1%

California is where you can't run any farther without getting wet.
Neil Morgan

Geography & Environment

Land area: 158,693 sq mi, the third largest state
Coastline: 1,200 mi, all on the Pacific Ocean
Terrain: The Coast Range divides the coastline from the fertile Central Valley, which has the massive Sierra Nevada to its east. Dry wastelands in the southern part of the state include the 15,000 square mi Mojave Desert. Highest point., Mt. Whitney, 14,491 feet
Islands: Catalina Island, Channel Islands, Farallon Islands
Natural resources: Arable soil, cement, gravel, lumber, natural gas, petroleum, sand
Natural hazards: Earthquakes, floods, wildfires

Environmental issues: Logging in northern California and its effect on erosion, river ecosystems; air quality remains a problem, especially in the Los Angeles basin; water shortages throughout the state, especially in the Imperial Valley; wastewater treatment in Mexico border towns

California is a place in which a boom mentality and a sense of Chekhovian loss meet in uneasy suspension; in which the mind is troubled by some buried but ineradicable suspicion that things had better work here, because here, beneath that immense bleached sky, is where we run out of continent.
Joan Didion

Economy

GSP: $1.4 trillion
Per capita income: $33,749
Unemployment: 6.5%
Work force: 17.5 million; trade, transportation, and utilities 19%; government 17%; professional and business services 15%; education and health services 11%; manufacturing 11%; other 11%; leisure and hospitality 10%; construction 6%
Major industries: Computers, electronics, farming, fishing, food processing, film/TV, machinery, metal products, tourism, transportation equipment, wine

Agricultural products: Almonds, broccoli, carrots, cotton, dairy products, flowers, grapes, lettuce, onions, oranges, strawberries, tomatoes
Exports: $109.8 billion
Major export products: Electronic and electric equipment, food products, industrial machinery and computers; scientific and measuring instruments, transportation equipment

California may have a very great sea-board, and a large city or two, yet that the agricultural products of the whole surface now are not, and never will be, equal to one half part of those of the State of Illinois; no, nor yet a fourth, or perhaps a tenth part.

Daniel Webster

Did You Know?

• The world's most prolific grape vine once lived in California: it yielded more than 9.9 tons of fruit during several of the years it lived, between 1842 and 1920.

• The lowest point in the United States is California's Death Valley, 282 feet below sea level. It's within 100 mi of Mt. Whitney (14,491 feet above sea level), the highest point in the lower 48 states.

• California's giant sequoias are the earth's most massive trees. Native to the west side of the Sierra Nevada, they can reach a girth of 30 feet, living 3,200 years. In 1925 a 300-foot sequoia in Kings Canyon National Park was named the nation's Christmas tree.

• As a nation, California's economy would be among the 10 largest in the world.

• California is rarely thought of for its winters, but the state holds the world record for most snowfall in one storm— 189 inches fell on the frigid Mount Shasta in 1959.

• Don't get caught bothering the state's monarch butterflies. In some cities, you may be fined $500 for doing so.

• California is the nation's most popu-lated state. One out of every nine Americans lives within its borders.

• There are an estimated 500,000 detectable earthquakes in California every year.

• Before she became famous, Marilyn Monroe was crowned the "Artichoke Queen" of Castroville, California, the self-proclaimed Artichoke Center of the World.

• The world's first McDonald's was opened in San Bernardino by Dick and Mac McDonald in 1948.

It used to be said that you had to know what was happening in America because it gave us a glimpse of our future. Today, the rest of America, and after that Europe, had better heed what happens in California, for it already reveals the type of civilization that is in store for all of us.

Alistair Cooke

INDEX